Tony Redmond's Microsoft® Exchange Server 2003 with SP1

Related Titles from Digital Press

Kieran McCorry, *Microsoft Exchange 2003 Deployment and Migration,*
ISBN 1-55558-316, 400pp, 2004

Pierre Bijaoui, *Scaling Microsoft Exchange Server,* ISBN 1-55558-239-7, 552pp, 2002

Sue Mosher, *Microsoft Outlook Programming: Jumpstart for Administrators, Developers,
and Power Users,* ISBN 1-55558-286-9, 620pp, 2002

Jerry Cochran, *Mission-Critical Microsoft® Exchange 2003: Designing and Building Reliable
Exchange Servers,* ISBN 1-55558-294-X, 480pp, 2003

Micky Balladelli and Jan DeClercq, *Mission-Critical Active Directory: Architecting a
Secure and Scalable Infrastructure,* ISBN 1-55558-240-0, 512pp, 2001

Mike Daugherty, *Monitoring and Managing Microsoft Exchange 2000 Server,*
ISBN 1-55558-232-X, 432pp, 2001

Mike Daugherty, *Monitoring and Managing Microsoft Exchange 2003 Server,*
ISBN 1-55558-302-4, 512pp, 2004

Kevin Laahs, Emer McKenna, and Don Vickers, *Microsoft SharePoint Portal Server: Building
Knowledge Sharing Applications,* ISBN 1-55558-244-3, 544pp, 2002

Kevin Laahs, Emer McKenna, and Veli-Matti Vanamo, *Microsoft SharePoint Portal Server V2.0:
Planning, Design, and Implementation,* ISBN 1-55558-301-6, 512pp, 2004

Jan DeClercq, *Windows 2003 Server Security Infrastructures,* ISBN 1-55558-283-4, 800pp, 2004

Alain Lissoir, *Understanding WMI: Exploiting Microsoft's Windows Management Instrumentation
in Mission-Critical Computing Infrastructures,* ISBN 1-55558-266-4, 580pp, 2003

Alain Lissoir, *Leveraging WMI: Using Windows Management Instrumentation to Solve
Windows Management Problems,* ISBN 1-55558-299-0, 924pp, 2003

**For more information or to order these and other Digital Press titles,
please visit our Web site at www.books.elsevier.com/digitalpress**

At www.books.elsevier.com/digitalpress you can:

- Join the Digital Press Email Service and have news about our books delivered right to your desktop
- Read the latest news on titles
- Sample chapters on featured titles for free
- Question our expert authors and editors
- Download free software to accompany select texts

Tony Redmond's Microsoft® Exchange Server 2003 with SP1

Tony Redmond

ELSEVIER
DIGITAL
PRESS

Amsterdam • Boston • Heidelberg • London • New York • Oxford
Paris • San Diego • San Francisco • Singapore • Sydney • Tokyo

Digital Press is an imprint of Elsevier.

Copyright © 2005, Hewlett-Packard Development Company, L.P. All rights reserved.

No part of this publication may be reproduced, stored in a retrieval system, or transmitted in any form or by any means, electronic, mechanical, photocopying, recording, or otherwise, without the prior written permission of the publisher.

 Recognizing the importance of preserving what has been written, Elsevier Science prints its books on acid-free paper whenever possible.

Library of Congress Cataloging-in-Publication Data

Application submitted.

British Library Cataloguing-in-Publication Data

A catalogue record for this book is available from the British Library.

ISBN 1-55558-330-X

The publisher offers special discounts on bulk orders of this book.
For information, please contact:

Manager of Special Sales
Elsevier Science
200 Wheeler Road
Burlington, MA 01803
Tel: 781-313-4700
Fax: 781-313-4882

For information on all Digital Press publications available, contact our World Wide Web home page at: http://www.digitalpress.com or http://www.books.elsevier.com/digitalpress

10 9 8 7 6 5 4 3 2 1

Printed in the United States of America

To Deirdre, who continues to cope with me despite my email addiction.

Contents

Foreword   xxi

Preface   xxiii

Acknowledgments   xxvii

1   A Brief History of Exchange   1

     1.1   Exchange first generation   1
     1.2   Exchange second generation   5
          1.2.1   Titanium   8
          1.2.2   Microsoft support policy   10
          1.2.3   Supporting Windows   12
     1.3   Exchange 2003 SP1   14
          1.3.1   Web releases and utilities   16
          1.3.2   More help to move from Exchange 5.5   16
     1.4   Exchange third generation   18
          1.4.1   The competition   20
     1.5   Simple steps to prepare for the move   22
     1.6   Deploying Exchange 2003   23
          1.6.1   Upgrade time   26
          1.6.2   Deployment tools   28
     1.7   Some things that Microsoft still has to do   30
          1.7.1   Administrative flexibility   31
          1.7.2   Collaboration   32
          1.7.3   Application development   33
          1.7.4   Too many servers   33
          1.7.5   Security   34
     1.8   Moving on   34

2 Exchange and the Active Directory — 35

2.1	The Active Directory	36
	2.1.1 Multiple forests or just one	37
	2.1.2 Components of the Active Directory	39
	2.1.3 Moving to a Windows namespace	40
	2.1.4 Forests, trees, and domains	41
	2.1.5 Domain renaming	44
	2.1.6 The Global Catalog	44
2.2	Preparing the Active Directory for Exchange	45
2.3	Active Directory replication	46
	2.3.1 Replication basics	46
	2.3.2 When Active Directory replication happens	49
	2.3.3 Active Directory naming contexts	50
	2.3.4 Transforming DCs to GCs	53
	2.3.5 USNs and replication	55
	2.3.6 Urgent replication	59
	2.3.7 Intra- and intersite replication	60
	2.3.8 High watermark vector tables and up-to-date vector tables	64
	2.3.9 AD replication changes in Windows 2003	65
2.4	The Active Directory Connector	67
	2.4.1 Connection agreements	70
	2.4.2 Handling multiple recipient containers	75
	2.4.3 How the ADC performs synchronization	76
	2.4.4 Scheduling a connection agreement	77
	2.4.5 Primary and nonprimary connection agreements	78
	2.4.6 Synchronizing multiple Exchange 5.5 organizations	79
	2.4.7 Site replication services	80
2.5	The LegacyExchangeDN attribute	82
2.6	DSAccess—Exchange's directory access component	84
	2.6.1 DSAccess tasks	87
	2.6.2 Selecting DCs and GCs for DSAccess	88
	2.6.3 Automatic topology detection	91
	2.6.4 Directory suitability tests	92
2.7	Interaction between Global Catalogs and clients	96
	2.7.1 How many GCs do I need?	98
	2.7.2 The GC logon cache	102
2.8	Exchange and the Active Directory schema	104
	2.8.1 The impact of updating the schema with new GC attributes	106

		2.8.2	Updating the schema with an installation	106
		2.8.3	Changing the schema	109
		2.8.4	Updating the schema for ambiguous name resolution	112
		2.8.5	Exchange-specific permissions	113
	2.9	Running Exchange in multiple forests		115
		2.9.1	Costs of multiple forests	116
		2.9.2	Directory synchronization	117
		2.9.3	Calendar interoperability	118
		2.9.4	Common platforms	120
		2.9.5	Moving users between different Exchange organizations	120
	2.10	Active Directory tools		124
		2.10.1	ADSIEDIT	124
		2.10.2	LDP and LDIFDE	130
		2.10.3	ADSI programming interface	131

3 Exchange Basics   133

	3.1	The organization		133
		3.1.1	Back to the past—Exchange sites	134
		3.1.2	Naming the organization	136
	3.2	Access control		136
		3.2.1	Administrative delegation	138
	3.3	Administrative and routing groups		145
		3.3.1	Defining an administrative group	146
		3.3.2	Moving from sites to administrative groups	148
		3.3.3	No way to change administrative group design	152
		3.3.4	Moving to native mode	153
		3.3.5	The move to LocalSystem	154
		3.3.6	Routing groups	156
		3.3.7	Routing group design	157
	3.4	Mailboxes and user accounts		160
		3.4.1	Accessing Exchange attributes for mail-enabled objects	163
		3.4.2	Moving mailboxes	168
	3.5	Distribution groups		172
		3.5.1	Forming Windows groups	174
		3.5.2	Expanding distribution lists	177
		3.5.3	How many objects can I have in a group?	178
		3.5.4	Managing distribution lists	179

		3.5.5	Protected groups	182
		3.5.6	Suppressing OOF	183
		3.5.7	Using public folder repositories for distribution lists	184
		3.5.8	Using groups for permissions	185
	3.6		Query-based distribution groups	185
		3.6.1	Creating new query-based groups	187
		3.6.2	Using custom attributes in query-based groups	191
		3.6.3	Using query-based distribution groups	192
	3.7		Summarizing Exchange basics	194
4	**Outlook—The Client**			**195**
	4.1		MAPI—Messaging Application Protocol	196
		4.1.1	Outlook	198
		4.1.2	Supporting MAPI clients	199
		4.1.3	Profile changes after moving between administrative groups	201
		4.1.4	Authentication	202
	4.2		Making Outlook a better network client for Exchange	203
		4.2.1	Why RPC latency is important to Exchange	204
		4.2.2	Networking improvements in Outlook 2003	206
		4.2.3	Cached Exchange mode	211
		4.2.4	Drizzle synchronization	213
		4.2.5	Download activity	214
		4.2.6	Incremental synchronization	219
		4.2.7	Deploying cached Exchange mode	220
		4.2.8	Compression and buffers	224
		4.2.9	Conflict resolution	226
		4.2.10	Is Outlook 2003 the best Exchange client?	228
	4.3		How many clients can I support at the end of a pipe?	230
	4.4		Blocking client access	232
		4.4.1	Blocking Outlook clients	235
		4.4.2	Blocking clients for Internet Protocol access	236
		4.4.3	Selective blocks	237
	4.5		New mail notifications	239
	4.6		Junk mail processing	239
		4.6.1	Detecting junk mail	240
		4.6.2	How Outlook's junk mail filter works	241
		4.6.3	More about rules	248
	4.7		The Offline Address Book (OAB)	249
		4.7.1	OAB generation process	257
		4.7.2	OAB name resolution	261

4.8	Free/busy information		262
	4.8.1	Other system folders	266
4.9	Personal folders and offline folder files		267
	4.9.1	Personal folders	267
	4.9.2	Mail delivery to personal folders	269
	4.9.3	Configuring PSTs	273
	4.9.4	PST archiving	275
4.10	Offline folder files		277
	4.10.1	OST synchronization	278
	4.10.2	Restricting synchronization traffic	282
	4.10.3	The local calendar	283
4.11	SCANPST—first aid for PSTs and OSTs		285
	4.11.1	The value of an OST	287
4.12	Working offline or online		288
4.13	Outlook command-line switches		289

5 Outlook Web Access   291

5.1	Second-generation OWA		293
	5.1.1	The strategic relationship between IIS and Exchange	294
	5.1.2	IIS changes in Exchange 2003	296
5.2	The OWA architecture		296
	5.2.1	HTTP-DAV extensions	298
5.3	Functionality: rich versus reach or premium and basic		301
	5.3.1	Updating slowly	310
	5.3.2	Limiting richness	311
	5.3.3	Spell checking	312
	5.3.4	Subscriptions	314
	5.3.5	Forms or cookie authentication	316
	5.3.6	Some missing features in OWA	319
	5.3.7	Password updates	321
5.4	Suppressing Web beacons and attachment handling		322
5.5	OWA administration		325
	5.5.1	OWA scalability	331
5.6	Exchange's URL namespace		333
	5.6.1	FreeDocs	336
5.7	Customizing OWA		337
	5.7.1	Branding	341
	5.7.2	Segmenting OWA functionality	342
5.8	OWA firewall access		344
	5.8.1	Securing OWA	346
	5.8.2	IPSec	347

		5.8.3	Leaving sensitive files around	349
		5.8.4	IE enhanced security	349
	5.9	OWA for all		350

6 Internet and Other Clients — 353

	6.1	IMAP4 clients		353
		6.1.1	IMAP virtual server settings	358
	6.2	POP3 clients		361
	6.3	LDAP directory access for IMAP4 and POP3 clients		361
	6.4	Supporting Apple Macintosh		364
	6.5	Supporting UNIX and Linux clients		366
	6.6	Exchange Mobile Services		367
		6.6.1	Exchange ActiveSync	371
		6.6.2	Outlook Mobile Access	373
	6.7	Pocket PC clients		375
		6.7.1	Connection options	376
		6.7.2	Accessing email with the Pocket PC	378
		6.7.3	Security and passwords	378
		6.7.4	Explaining Pocket PC synchronization	379
		6.7.5	Using the Pocket PC	382
	6.8	Palm Pilots		384
	6.9	Mobile BlackBerries		384
		6.9.1	BlackBerry Enterprise Server (BES)	386
		6.9.2	Using the BlackBerry	390
		6.9.3	The Good option	392
		6.9.4	Is a handheld better than a Pocket PC?	394
	6.10	Sending messages without clients		395
	6.11	Client licenses		398

7 The Store — 399

	7.1	Structure of the Store		399
	7.2	Exchange ACID		401
	7.3	EDB database structure		403
		7.3.1	EDB page structure	404
		7.3.2	Within the trees	404
		7.3.3	Database tables and fields	406
		7.3.4	Tables in a Mailbox Store	408
		7.3.5	Search Folders	410
		7.3.6	The checkpoint file	414
		7.3.7	Page checksum	416

7.4	The streaming file		417
7.5	Transaction logs		418
	7.5.1	Managing transaction logs	419
	7.5.2	Creating new generations of transaction logs	421
	7.5.3	Reserved logs	424
	7.5.4	Locating transaction logs	425
	7.5.5	Transactions, buffers, and commitment	426
	7.5.6	Examining a transaction log	428
	7.5.7	Dumping a transaction log	429
	7.5.8	Data records	431
	7.5.9	Transaction log I/O	432
	7.5.10	Protecting transaction logs	433
	7.5.11	Transaction log checksum	434
	7.5.12	Circular logging	435
	7.5.13	Database zeroing	436
7.6	Store partitioning		436
	7.6.1	The advantages of storage groups	437
	7.6.2	Planning storage groups	438
	7.6.3	Does single-instance storage matter anymore?	441
7.7	Managing storage groups		446
	7.7.1	Store status	448
	7.7.2	Planning storage groups	449
	7.7.3	Creating new storage groups	452
7.8	ESE database errors		456
	7.8.1	Hard and soft recoveries	458
7.9	Background maintenance		463
	7.9.1	Background tasks	465
	7.9.2	Some registry settings to control background maintenance	468
	7.9.3	Tracking background maintenance	470
7.10	Database utilities		473
	7.10.1	Running ESEUTIL	474
	7.10.2	ISINTEG	481
	7.10.3	ESEFILE	482
	7.10.4	Error Correcting Code—Exchange 2003 SP1	483
7.11	The epoxy layer		484
7.12	The Public Store		485
	7.12.1	The goals for public folders	485
7.13	Laying out a public folder design		488
	7.13.1	Top-level hierarchies	490
	7.13.2	Should you deploy dedicated public folder servers?	492

	7.13.3	Auditing public folders	494
	7.13.4	Mail-enabling a public folder	496
	7.13.5	Public folder favorites	498
	7.13.6	Public folder permissions	499
7.14	Public folder replication		502
	7.14.1	Creating new replicas	505
	7.14.2	Public folder referrals	507
	7.14.3	Scheduling replication	509
	7.14.4	When public folder replication happens	511
	7.14.5	How replication occurs	511
	7.14.6	Monitoring the flow of replication	513
	7.14.7	Backfilling public folders	516
	7.14.8	Replicating public folders with Exchange 5.5	517
	7.14.9	Erasing zombies	518
	7.14.10	Problems with public folder replication	519
	7.14.11	Long-term options for public folders	521
7.15	ExIFS—the Exchange Installable File System		522
	7.15.1	The role of ExIFS	525

8 Performance and Clusters 533

8.1	Aspects of Exchange performance		534
	8.1.1	Storage	535
	8.1.2	Multiple CPUs	537
	8.1.3	Memory	538
	8.1.4	Using more than 1 GB of memory	540
	8.1.5	Advanced performance	542
8.2	Measuring performance		543
	8.2.1	Performance measuring tools	544
	8.2.2	The difference between vendor testing and your testing	546
8.3	Cloning, snapshots, and lies		549
	8.3.1	Volume ShadowCopy Services	552
	8.3.2	Using VSS with Exchange 2003	554
8.4	Virtual Exchange servers		555
8.5	A brief history of clustering Exchange		556
8.6	Second-generation Exchange clusters		557
	8.6.1	The complexity of clusters	558
8.7	Microsoft cluster basics		560
	8.7.1	Resources	560
	8.7.2	Resource groups and other cluster terms	560
	8.7.3	Installing Exchange on a cluster	565

		8.7.4	What clusters do not support	566
		8.7.5	Dependencies	567
		8.7.6	Clusters and memory fragmentation	567
		8.7.7	Monitoring virtual memory use	571
		8.7.8	RPC client requests	573
		8.7.9	Upgrading a cluster with a service pack	574
		8.7.10	Stretched clusters and Exchange	574
		8.7.11	Deciding for or against a cluster	575
		8.7.12	Does Exchange 2003 make a difference to clusters?	577
		8.7.13	Clusters—in summary	579

9 Getting the Mail through—Routing and Message Delivery 581

	9.1	SMTP and X.400		582
	9.2	The evolution of SMTP		583
		9.2.1	SMTP extensions in Exchange	585
		9.2.2	SMTP virtual servers	592
		9.2.3	Relays	594
		9.2.4	Changing SMTP banners	595
		9.2.5	Installing Exchange servers in the DMZ	597
		9.2.6	The ongoing role of the X.400 MTA	598
	9.3	The transport core		599
		9.3.1	Domain and link queues	603
	9.4	Processing incoming messages		604
		9.4.1	SMTP messages	604
		9.4.2	MAPI messages	608
		9.4.3	HTTP messages	608
		9.4.4	X.400 messages	608
		9.4.5	Foreign connectors	609
	9.5	Categorization and routing		609
		9.5.1	Handling messages for protected groups	610
		9.5.2	Moving messages off queues	611
		9.5.3	Unreachable domains	619
		9.5.4	Exchange and MX records	622
	9.6	Routing groups		623
		9.6.1	Routing group master	625
		9.6.2	Creating new routing groups	627
		9.6.3	Routing groups and public folder referrals	631
	9.7	Link state routing		632
		9.7.1	Routing, retries, and updates	640
		9.7.2	Looking at routing information	642

9.8	Connecting routing groups		645
	9.8.1 Creating a routing group connector		646
9.9	Creating an SMTP connector		650
	9.9.1 Encrypted SMTP communications		654
	9.9.2 Delivery restrictions for SMTP-based connectors		654
9.10	Creating an X.400 connector		656
	9.10.1 Deciding when to use an X.400 connection		663
9.11	Understanding routing		664
	9.11.1 WinRoute		664
9.12	SMTP logging		667
9.13	SMTP archiving		671
9.14	Global messaging settings		675
	9.14.1 Internet message formats		676
	9.14.2 Global message delivery settings		680
9.15	Combating the menace of spam		681
	9.15.1 Blocking relays		684
	9.15.2 Defining message filters		687
	9.15.3 Connection filters and real-time blackhole lists		690
	9.15.4 Configuring a connection filter policy		692
	9.15.5 Return status codes		693
	9.15.6 Sender filters		695
	9.15.7 Recipient filters		697
9.16	Exchange Intelligent Message Filter (IMF)		699
	9.16.1 Where to deploy IMF		701
	9.16.2 Installing IMF		702
	9.16.3 Message Stores and SCL		706
	9.16.4 Applying IMF to SMTP virtual servers		707
	9.16.5 IMF licensing		708

10 Managing Exchange: Users 711

10.1	ESM and other consoles		711
	10.1.1 Other Exchange management snap-ins		716
	10.1.2 Finding out about server versions		718
	10.1.3 Running ESM on workstations		720
10.2	User access		721
	10.2.1 Creating accounts and mailboxes		724
	10.2.2 Maintaining mailbox details		728
	10.2.3 Restricting mailboxes		731
	10.2.4 Mailbox quotas		733
	10.2.5 Mailbox surrogacy		738

10.3	User authentication		741
10.4	Defining a document retention policy		744
10.5	The Exchange Mailbox Manager		746
	10.5.1	Email and discovery	747
	10.5.2	Email retention policies	750
	10.5.3	Defining a policy for mailbox management	750
	10.5.4	Running Mailbox Manager	752
	10.5.5	Mailbox Manager notification messages	754
	10.5.6	Mailbox Manager diagnostics	756
10.6	Archiving messages		757
	10.6.1	Internal snooping (but nicely)	761
10.7	Exploring the deleted items cache		764
	10.7.1	Recovering items	765
	10.7.2	Setting a deleted item retention period	767
	10.7.3	Cleaning the cache	770
	10.7.4	Sizing the cache	770
10.8	Decommissioning mailboxes		775
	10.8.1	Mailboxes and document retention	776
	10.8.2	Creating a blackhole for messages	777
	10.8.3	Redirecting messages	778
	10.8.4	Using Outlook rules to process messages	779
	10.8.5	User death	781
10.9	Helping users to do a better job		782
	10.9.1	Eliminating bad habits to reduce network and storage demands	782
	10.9.2	Abusing disclaimers	790
	10.9.3	Out of office notifications	791
	10.9.4	Some other bad email habits	792
10.10	Email and viruses		793
	10.10.1	A brief history of office viruses	794
	10.10.2	The Melissa virus, Outlook, and variants	794
	10.10.3	Luring users toward infection	796
	10.10.4	The dangers of HTML	797
	10.10.5	The damage caused by viruses	800
	10.10.6	Multistage protection	803
10.11	Exchange antivirus tools		807
	10.11.1	The problems with MAPI	807
	10.11.2	VSAPI—virus scanning API	808
	10.11.3	AV impact on multilingual clients	810
	10.11.4	Selecting the right AV product	811

11 Managing Exchange: Servers 815

- 11.1 System policies — 815
- 11.2 Recipient policies — 817
  - 11.2.1 Generating SMTP addresses — 822
  - 11.2.2 Changing display names — 822
- 11.3 Recipient update services — 825
  - 11.3.1 Mail-enabling objects — 828
  - 11.3.2 Processing server details — 831
- 11.4 Backups — 832
  - 11.4.1 Creating a backup strategy — 833
  - 11.4.2 Backups and storage groups — 836
  - 11.4.3 Backup operations — 837
  - 11.4.4 Backup patch file — 841
  - 11.4.5 Checkpoint file — 842
  - 11.4.6 Restoring a database — 843
  - 11.4.7 Third-party backup utilities — 847
  - 11.4.8 Backing up individual mailboxes — 852
  - 11.4.9 Restoring an Exchange server — 853
  - 11.4.10 Recovery servers — 856
  - 11.4.11 Recovering a Mailbox Store — 858
  - 11.4.12 Rapid online, phased recovery — 864
- 11.5 Recovering deleted mailboxes — 866
  - 11.5.1 MRC: Mailbox Recovery Center — 868
- 11.6 The Recovery Storage Group — 870
  - 11.6.1 Encountering database problems — 872
  - 11.6.2 Creating a temporary "dial-tone" database — 874
  - 11.6.3 Creating the RSG — 876
  - 11.6.4 Restoring the database — 879
  - 11.6.5 Using ExMerge to recover mailbox data — 881
  - 11.6.6 Cleaning up — 883
- 11.7 The ExMerge utility — 884
  - 11.7.1 Running ExMerge in batch mode — 891
  - 11.7.2 Other recovery utilities — 891
- 11.8 Risk management — 892
- 11.9 The message tracking center — 893
  - 11.9.1 Tracking messages — 895
  - 11.9.2 Changing tracking log location — 897
  - 11.9.3 Changes in Exchange 2003 — 899
  - 11.9.4 Starting to track messages — 899
  - 11.9.5 Tracking log format — 903

	11.9.6 Understanding message tracking log data	904
	11.9.7 Analyzing Message Tracking Data	908
11.10	ExchDump	909
	11.10.1 Running ExchDump	910
11.11	Monitoring Exchange	915
	11.11.1 Monitoring and notifications	919
11.12	Standard diagnostics	924
	11.12.1 Turning up logging	925
11.13	Management frameworks	927
11.14	Exchange and WMI	929

Appendix A: Recommended Books for Further Reading — 931

Appendix B: Message Tracking Log Codes — 933

Appendix C: TCP/IP Ports Used by Exchange — 937

Glossary — 941

Index — 951

Foreword

When I first started with the Exchange team and I wanted to get an outside view, it was an easy choice—Tony Redmond was the first person I talked to. Tony has more history with Exchange than anyone else that I know outside Microsoft. He didn't let me down. His 10-year love affair with Exchange and his straightforward style meant that I got the complete picture—the many great things about the product that he liked and the things that "he'd prefer to see improved" (my paraphrase).

As the world-wide technical leader for the Exchange community at Hewlett Packard (originally at Digital Equipment Corporation and then Compaq Computer), Tony sees an incredibly diverse set of enterprise customers with widely varying messaging needs. In this book, he brings all that knowledge and experience to you.

That knowledge is incredibly valuable. Today, all businesses recognize how vitally important their messaging systems are. The challenges of delivering mission-critical messaging service in a world of highly mobile workforces and a hostile environment of SPAM and virus attacks are, to say the least, daunting.

Exchange 2003 reflects the accumulated experience of five product versions, 15 years of development and literally thousands of person-years invested—experience directed at meeting those challenges, and at providing advanced messaging and scheduling services to businesses the world over. Exchange 2000 incorporated significant architectural changes, most notably the change from the internal directory of Exchange 5.5 to Active Directory, the distributed infrastructure for businesses. Active Directory is highly leveraged: User access and profile information can be managed uniformly across multiple applications, not just for Exchange. As well, Active Directory provides management infrastructure for business applications and services, and for desktop and server computing resources. It's an investment with payoff that steadily increases over time.

Exchange 2003 built on Exchange 2000, adding many customer driven features and improvements in administration, storage management, availability, and support for mobile devices. Exchange 2003 Service Pack 1, released in May 2004, continued the advances with the highest level of customer proven reliability, improved migration tools, ease of use enhancements, and the broad availability of the Intelligent Message Filter, a core tool in the SPAM-fighting arsenal of Exchange. The integrated innovation of Exchange 2003 and Outlook 2003 on the Windows Server 2003 platform provide a whole new experience for roaming users. Outlook Cached mode transparently manages and updates the offline message store and RPC over HTTPS provides secure VPN-less access across the Internet, easily and seamlessly transferring messages in the background with whatever link bandwidth is available.

The bottom line: With the experience built into Exchange 2003, and with Tony at your side, you've got the best on your team as you build and run the messaging infrastructure for your business—Enjoy!

Dave Thompson
Vice President
Exchange Business Unit

Preface

Covering Exchange

The Exchange product has steadily become more complex over the years. In 1996, the problems that system administrators and designers faced were simpler than today. Hardware was significantly less capable, and some of the early deployments rolled out on 100-MHz Pentiums equipped with 128 MB of memory and a whole 4 GB of disk. While these systems did not support the thousands of mailboxes that today's servers commonly take on, they were as difficult to manage because the management tools and utilities were not as developed as today. However, the overall environment was less demanding, which in turn meant that it was easier for people to write books about Exchange.

Given everything that has happened since 1996 and today, I am not so sure that Exchange is easy to write about anymore. Massive tomes have replaced the slim volumes that could credibly claim to contain all the best practices that you need to deploy Exchange. I have given up trying to cover everything, because I know I just cannot hope to discuss all possible topics, so I am afraid that this book represents a very personal view of the challenges of understanding the technology inside Exchange and how best to deploy it. I therefore seek your indulgence if I omit your favorite topic and can only suggest that you check out some of the other books about Exchange.

Exchange 2003 encore

My original Exchange 2003 book appeared soon after Microsoft shipped the product. When the time came to reprint, it was apparent that enough new material existed to warrant a new edition. The new material includes the updates introduced in Exchange 2003 Service Pack 1, the Intelligent Message Filter, the changes Microsoft has made in its future strategy for Exchange, and many different pieces of information that became available as we have used Exchange 2003 in daily production. Overall, there are over 100 separate updates in this edition, some small, but all, I think, useful. Best practice for successful deployments has not changed fundamentally, but, as always, the devil is in the detail.

Product names

I fully acknowledge all trademarks and registered names of products used throughout the book, especially when I have forgotten to do so in passing. For the sake of clarity, product names are shortened and version numbers are not used unless necessary to tie functionality to a specific version. For example, I refer to the Microsoft Exchange Server product as "Exchange," unless it is necessary to state a specific version such as "Exchange 2003," "Exchange 5.5," and so on. In the same manner, I use Windows as the generic term for Microsoft's enterprise server operating system and only spell out "Windows 2000," "Windows NT 4.0," or "Windows Server 2003 Enterprise Edition" when necessary to identify a specific release.

Omissions

In my previous books about Exchange, I attempted to cover technology that I omit here. Possibly the most notable omission is the advanced security subsystem, the part of Exchange that deals with digital signatures and message encryption. You now enable advanced security through a mixture of client and server components. The Key Management Server (KMS) disappears from Exchange 2003, since the Windows 2003 Certificate Server now takes its role. The rich version of the Outlook Web Access client now supports message signing and encryption, so there is change on the client side too. My decision to omit advanced security, which typically occupied a complete chapter in previous books, is simply a reflection that not many organizations actually deployed advanced security. Many system administrators looked at what Exchange had to offer and deployed the KMS to check things out, but the sheer amount of additional administrative overhead normally stopped things from going any further. This does not mean that advanced security is not valuable: It does mean that organizations have other priorities on which to spend their time. It might also indicate that the pace of change marked by the transition of X.509 V1 certificates to X.509 V3 certificates, the introduction and general support of S/MIME, the changing role of the KMS, and the different ways that clients support advanced security have combined to prevent organizations from deploying advanced security until things settle down in this area. In the meantime, if you are interested in advanced security, I suggest that you get some specialized consulting help, because you will need it to have a successful deployment.

I also made the decision to remove any mention of the Exchange Conferencing and Instant Messaging subsystems. These subsystems are optional components of Exchange 2000 that Microsoft removed in Exchange 2003. I think this is a result of some market pressures, because Conferencing was never successful enough to justify the engineering expense needed to maintain the subsystem, and the free versions of Instant Messaging have phased out the need for most organizations to deploy their own special version. If you need Instant Messaging, you can deploy MSN Messenger, AOL IM, Yahoo! Messenger, Jabber, or applications that allow you to communicate with users of many different messaging systems. Once again, the Exchange branded version did not succeed, so it lost its way inside the product. The nature of Microsoft is that it does not give up after just one attempt, so its Greenwich initiative (or, to give the product its real name, Microsoft Office Live Communication Server 2003), based on less proprietary protocols such as Session Initiation Protocol (SIP), is likely to be more successful. In the interim, you can continue to run the Exchange 2000 version of IM as long as you keep an Exchange 2000 server around to host the service.

I covered SharePoint Portal Server (SPS) in my Exchange 2000 book. It was early days for SPS, but the product demonstrated enormous potential. In fact, SPS was the first V1.0 product from Microsoft that I was truly able to deploy and use without worry. The fact that SPS used a modified version of the Exchange Store also made it a good candidate for discussion in any book about Exchange. Since then, Microsoft has taken SPS forward and moved its focus away from Exchange toward SQL. In addition, it integrated SharePoint Team Services (STS) into Windows 2003, so it becomes part of the basic Windows functionality. I still think the SharePoint product family is a very interesting and useful technology, but as it lost its connection to Exchange, I concluded that I did not have the luxury of page space to be able to continue coverage. There are, after all, so many topics to discuss about the basic Exchange 2003 server.

URLs

Where appropriate, I have provided URLs as pointers to additional sources of information, such as product sites. However, given the ever-changing nature of the Internet, it is entirely possible that the URL will have changed between the time of writing and the time you attempt to access the site. Please use the URL as a starting point for information, and, if it does not work, use your favorite search engine to find the correct site.

Acknowledgments

Clearly, I could not have brought all this information together without the help of many people. My colleagues at HP are a constant source of inspiration, not only with their ideas but also with the probing and questioning of the concepts we have about best practice for Windows and Exchange. Best practice evolves and does not remain static, because we have to base it on experience gained through deployment.

Among those I have to thank at HP are Stan Foster, Bert Quarfordt, Kathy Pollert, Pierre Bijaoui, Kevin Laahs, Kieran McCorry, Donald Livengood, Daragh Morrissey, Veli-Matti Vanamo, and all the other members of the HP messaging community.

I also received a lot of support from Microsoft from folks such as Mohsen Al-Ghosein (now replaced in his role as VP of Exchange by David Thompson), Terry Myerson, Ken Ewert, Marc Olsen, Aaron Hartwell, Glen Anderson, David Lemson, and many others I have bothered with questions and from whom I have been grateful to receive responses.

A book does not come together without a lot of work behind the scenes. I am grateful for the support of Theron Shreve, the publishing editor at Digital Press, and Pam Chester, both of whom have helped me whenever I needed to get past a knot in the publication process. I also acknowledge the help I received from Alan Rose and his team at Multiscience Press Inc., who copyedited, generated proofs, indexed, and generally humored me as the book came together. I especially need to thank Lauralee Reinke who formatted the book and coped admirably with a continuous stream of changes.

Perfect enough

There comes a time when the writing has to cease, when there is no more information to discuss on your selected topics, when you simply cannot write another word, or when your publisher tells you that the book is now so large it would qualify as a weapon in some people's hands. "Perfect enough" is a term used to describe the HP-Compaq merger: Not everything worked; not everything was as good as it could be; but enough people, technology, and processes came together on time and in enough detail to allow two huge companies to merge. I think this book qualifies to be "perfect enough" and hope that you agree.

A Brief History of Exchange

All applications have their own unique history, which has influenced their design and functionality, and Exchange is no different. The events that have shaped Exchange include Microsoft's corporate directions and strategy, hardware performance and capability, the needs of customers, the actions of competitors, and the evolution of the Internet. All of these inputs have helped to bring Exchange to the shape it is today. You can expect that similar events will drive future development.

Predicting the future is always difficult, especially when computer software or hardware is involved. Given what we know of Microsoft's strategic direction for Exchange, you can divide the history of Exchange—past and future—into three generations of product. Microsoft has delivered two product generations, and the third will not arrive in fully functional form until 2006 at the earliest.

1.1 Exchange first generation

Microsoft delivered the first generation of Exchange in March 1996 as Exchange 4.0, and it is still running on many servers as Exchange 5.5, suitably equipped with the latest service pack. You can characterize the first generation of servers through the use of proprietary technology and protocols. The Exchange 4.0 to 5.5 products were part of Microsoft's push into the enterprise application market. While SQL/Server showed signs of being a player in the database market, it still had not made the grade in 1996, and Exchange 4.0 was Microsoft's first enterprise application that truly achieved widespread deployment.

By one measure, Exchange 4.0 was extraordinarily late in shipping, as it debuted some 39 months after Microsoft's original date. Building an enterprise application is always difficult, but there were two special reasons that

Exchange was more difficult than the average enterprise application. First, Exchange was the first Microsoft application to make extensive demands on the operating system. Up to then, Windows NT essentially hosted stand-alone applications, where computers served single purposes such as database servers or file and print servers. Exchange upped the ante and demanded that system administrators and designers begin to think about their Windows NT deployments as a single integrated whole rather than islands of separate applications. The concept of a single Exchange organization that spanned the complete company caused many administrators to look at how they dealt with Windows NT. Exchange also exposed some weaknesses in Windows NT: The security model was not very good and forced the creation of resource domains to hold Exchange servers and restrict administrative access.

The second reason why Exchange was a difficult application to develop was Microsoft's desire to be all things to all people. The messaging world in 1993–1995 (the time when much of the design work for Exchange was completed) was a very fractured entity. It was a multiprotocol proprietary world, where most major corporations ran multiple messaging systems that could not communicate very well. In fact, getting simple text messages to travel from one system to another was often a matter for celebration. Corporations allowed departments to select different email systems for many reasons. Perhaps the department was running a specific operating system such as OpenVMS or UNIX and had to select an email system that supported that platform. Perhaps the department built an underground email system that the corporate managers didn't know of by installing PCs that ran Microsoft Mail, Banyan VINES, or Lotus cc:Mail to serve small user communities. Or perhaps a salesperson had simply done a good job of selling a specific email system to a department for some reason or another. In any case, it was usual to find global corporations struggling to cope with how to make 10 or even 20 different email systems interoperate together. X.400 was the only viable way to connect disparate email systems together, and while X.500 promised great things for unified corporate directories, it had largely failed to make an impact.

Microsoft's problem was that it had to sell Exchange to the people who ran different email systems. The Exchange team had to provide a way to interoperate with the existing system during the migration period; they had to provide tools to migrate user accounts and mailboxes; and they had to support the favorite features found in the various systems, because customers would not buy Exchange if they ended up with reduced functionality. It is enlightening to read some of the original Exchange design documents and to chart how the product features accumulated over time. The result was a highly functional email system, which could interoperate with many other email systems, but Exchange certainly took time to build and even longer to debug.

As it turned out, being so late enabled Microsoft to take advantage of greater maturity in both hardware and the Windows NT operating system. It is interesting to speculate what would have happened had an immature Exchange product been rushed out to meet an arbitrary date and had to cope with the type of hardware and software environments that were available in 1994–1995. Even with the delay, companies deployed the first Exchange servers on early Pentium-powered systems running at 50 or 66 MHz and equipped with 64 MB of memory and perhaps 3 to 4 GB of disk. Windows NT 3.51 provided the platform. The early servers supported user populations of up to 200 mailboxes and provided a way for Microsoft to begin the migration of its existing Microsoft Mail population over to a new architecture.

Migrating users off Microsoft Mail was an important influence on Exchange 4.0, largely because it provided a solid user base that could be trumpeted in the marketing war between Microsoft and Lotus, who rapidly became the big two candidates for enterprise messaging deployments. Lotus had the early advantage, because Lotus Notes had been in the market far earlier and had already built a substantial user base, so it was important for Exchange to gain traction and build a user community.

Exchange 5.0 followed in October 1996 and served as a patch-up release. The final rush to get Exchange 4.0 out the door had left some components with known defects and these had to be addressed. In addition, Microsoft had started to get serious about the Internet and had realized the impact that the Internet would have on messaging, so Exchange 5.0 marked the first real integration of SMTP into the product. For many experienced Microsoft observers, the release of Exchange 5.0 served notice that Exchange was ready to deploy—no one would ever deploy the first version of a Microsoft application unless it was necessary, so the number of installations began to creep up from what had been a slow start. While suspicion about the reliability and robustness of Exchange 4.0 had been a contributory factor in slowing down deployments, the need to pay some attention to the Windows NT structure, to build a migration strategy, and to get used to the new application were other reasons why Exchange had a slow start. Microsoft reached 1 million mailboxes after about eight months, and then things took off to a point where customers deployed a million new mailboxes every month from mid-1997 onward.

Exchange 5.0 continued to ship an improved version of the Capone client, which the development team had built and included in Exchange 4.0. This client was designed as a simple email processor—create, send, forward, reply, and print messages. The separate Schedule+ application delivered nonintegrated calendaring, and there was no evidence of other Personal Information Manager (PIM) features such as contacts, notes, and the journal. Outlook, part of the Microsoft Office personal application suite, first appeared in 1997 to take over as the basic client for Exchange and deliver the missing PIM features. The first version of Outlook did not perform as well as the Exchange client and suffered from the same type of feature bloat as the other Office applications, a trend that has continued to this day.

The first version of Outlook Web Access (OWA) also appeared with Exchange 5.0. As we will discuss later, the concept of a Web-based client is very attractive to anyone who has to deploy and support thousands of clients. The original architecture worked, but OWA was not very scalable and missed many features when compared with Outlook. Despite this, OWA has been popular with customers from day one and it continues to grow in popularity today.

Exchange 5.5 arrived in November 1997. Microsoft integrated a full suite of Internet protocols (POP3, IMAP4, HTTP, SMTP, and NNTP) along with connectors for Lotus Notes, IBM PROFS, and IBM SNADS to aid migration from these systems. The connectors were the result of the purchase of LinkAge, a Canadian company, in May 1997. Exchange 5.5 lifted the 16-GB restriction on the size of the Information Store database and was the first version to support Microsoft Cluster Services in an active-passive two-node configuration. Unfortunately, clustering was an expensive solution that did not really deliver the functionality and reliability that many companies required, so it never really took off. Indeed, the pace of development in hardware enabled Exchange to support thousands of mailboxes on multi-CPU servers, so companies were able to compare the costs of dividing user communities across a set of highly specified servers against clusters, and most chose to go with individual servers.

Exchange 5.5 marked the final play in the first generation. Microsoft steadily improved the software through service packs and Exchange 5.5 is able to run very nicely on Windows 2000, a fact that has caused many companies to delay their migration to the second generation of Exchange. The cost to upgrade an existing Windows NT infrastructure to Windows 2000 or Windows 2003 and do all the redesign and architecture work to build a new Windows infrastructure has slowed migration projects. Some analysts estimate that 70 percent of Exchange's installed base still ran Exchange 5.5 in early 2003, meaning that the vast majority of Exchange 2000 deployments were new implementations and that relatively few large organizations had migrated to Exchange 2000. As with any number-counting exercise, it is hard to know quite how accurate these estimations are. However, given the millions of Exchange seats in production, we can predicate that Exchange 5.5 servers will be running in production for a number of years yet, possibly well past the time when Microsoft ceases to provide formal support.

1.2 Exchange second generation

After four years, the original Exchange architecture was beginning to show some flaws. Design decisions reached in 1993–1995 did not match the world of 1997–1999, and the experience gained of running Exchange in production revealed the need to make a number of changes at the core. In addition, the work to develop the next generation of Windows NT was finally ending with the release of Windows 2000. Among the most important flaws that Microsoft had to address were:

- Implementing a single large database for mailboxes imposes a scalability limit. Few companies were willing to put more than 3,000 mailboxes on a server because of the impact on users if the database experienced any hardware or software problems.

- The Exchange 5.5 clustering solution is weak and expensive. Microsoft needed to move to active-active clustering, which allowed Exchange to use all of the hardware in the cluster as well as the ability to have more than two nodes in a cluster.

- The Message Transfer Agent (MTA) provides message routing functionality for the first-generation Exchange servers. Microsoft originally purchased the MTA code from a small U.K. company, and, although the Exchange developers extensively modified and enhanced the code over the years, its roots meant the code base was complex and difficult to update and maintain. The MTA uses the X.400 protocol, but the world of messaging now largely uses the SMTP Internet protocol. In addition, the MTA is relatively inflexible in the way that it makes routing decisions and is therefore not very resistant to changes that can occur in a dynamic environment.

- The Exchange 5.5 administrative model works superbly for small installations but is not flexible enough for large, distributed enterprises. The administration tools were developed with small servers in mind and do not work well for larger systems.

- The first-generation OWA architecture uses Active Server Pages and does not scale to take advantage of new hardware. In addition, the first-generation OWA client is very restricted in comparison to other clients.

- Exchange 5.5 has its own directory, an acceptable solution when the operating system does not incorporate a directory service. Windows 2000 and Windows 2003 leverage the Active Directory, and it makes sense for applications to exploit a common directory whenever possible.

Many companies used the same list of reasons to justify the migration to Exchange 2000, including:

- The reduction of cost that can be achieved by operating fewer servers: The experience of real-life migration projects such as HP's proves that you can consolidate Exchange 5.5 servers to a smaller set of Exchange 2000 servers, and then consolidate further when you introduce Exchange 2003.

- The availability of more comprehensive administrative tools such as Microsoft Operations Manager (MOM).

- A need to build more robustness into operational procedures by exploiting partitioned databases.

- The fact that Microsoft is pouring its development effort into the current and next generations of Exchange and therefore pays little attention to fixing anything for Exchange 5.5.

Although Exchange 5.5 is a very fine messaging system, which works well on Windows 2000, the overall feeling is that it was time to move on. Microsoft launched Exchange 2000, the first release in the second generation of Exchange, in September 2000. Microsoft certainly accomplished the jump from first to second generation but achieved mixed success: The new version of OWA proved to be hugely popular and delivered the necessary combination of features, robustness, and scalability to make browsers more than a viable client platform for large user communities. On the other hand, the Store had encountered many problems with memory fragmentation and other issues in active-active clustering, and Exchange clusters are not yet a compelling solution for companies that seek the highest possible level of reliability and availability. Jettisoning Exchange's own directory in favor of the Active Directory also posed problems, and the management tools were not as smooth as they could have been. Service packs delivered since have improved matters, especially around the interaction between

Exchange and the Active Directory, but companies that deployed Exchange 2000 early also had to cope with a large number of hot fixes, as Microsoft sometimes rushed to deal with the challenges posed by making so many fundamental changes in the underlying technology.

Looking back, we should not have been surprised at the problems that Microsoft had to solve. Exchange 4.0 was not perfect either, and it took two releases (to Exchange 5.5) before the first generation of Exchange really bedded in and became a solid enterprise-class messaging system. Exchange 2000 built on the achievements of Exchange 5.5, and there were many examples where companies successfully deployed Exchange 2000 well before the release of service pack 2. It can be argued that the people who encountered problems were those who attempted to probe the edge of the envelope by overstressing clusters; partitioning the Store to the utmost degree; or implementing on top of an unstable and underprepared Windows 2000 infrastructure; and there's no doubt that all of these situations occurred.

Microsoft Exchange Server 2003, codenamed "Titanium,"[1] is the most functional and powerful version of Exchange built to date, even if Microsoft has stripped out some of the collaboration and application development features found in Exchange 2000. Exchange 2003 enjoys all of the advantages of development based on customer feedback from actual Exchange 2000 deployments. The changes and improvements made to Windows have also assisted Exchange 2003 greatly—the world of Windows has not stayed static since Microsoft released Windows 2000 in 1999, and it is easier to build and deploy a stable infrastructure today. The personal touch cannot be overlooked either. Quite a number of system administrators were a little overwhelmed at the knowledge upgrade required to cope with Windows 2000, Exchange 2000, and new hardware advances that appeared around the same time. It is difficult for administrators to move seamlessly from a Windows NT 4.0/Exchange 5.5 environment to Windows 2000/Exchange 2000 while also focusing on domain redesign, potentially upgrading other applications, server consolidation, and the introduction of technologies such as Storage Area Networks and clusters. Early movers enjoy the benefits of new technology first, but it is a double-edged sword. Those who waited, maybe even to follow the well-aged adage of always waiting for the second version of a Microsoft product, can follow on now to move into the second generation on a solid platform of improved software, better hardware, and a vast amount of experience.

---

1. Titanium follows on from Platinum, the code name for Exchange 2000, and Osmium, the code name for Exchange 5.5.

1.2.1 Titanium

Exchange 2003 builds on Exchange 2000 and uses the same architectural underpinnings, so in many ways you can look at Exchange 2003 as an upgrade similar to the move from Exchange 5.0 to Exchange 5.5. It can coexist with both Exchange 5.5 and Exchange 2000 to allow customers to introduce Exchange 2003 easily into current organizations. However, you can only upgrade an Exchange 2000 server to Exchange 2003, so if you still run Exchange 5.5, you must go through an upgrade to Exchange 2000 first. In addition, the Exchange 2000 servers must be running SP3 (or later), and the operating system must be at Windows 2000 SP3 (or later) before you can perform an in-place upgrade from Exchange 2000 to Exchange 2003. You should also upgrade any servers that host the Active Directory Connector (ADC) to the version of the ADC provided with Exchange 2003 before beginning any in-place upgrades. Finally, you must upgrade any front-end servers to Exchange 2003 before you upgrade any back-end servers. As with all architectural upgrades, planning is critical and it is important to sequence change in the right order.

You can run Exchange 2003 on Windows 2000 (SP3 or greater) or Windows 2003 (but not the Web server edition of Windows 2003). The latter is preferred because of IIS 6.0, which is more robust and secure and has better memory management than its predecessor. You can run the Enterprise version of Exchange 2003 on the standard version of Windows 2003, selecting the Enterprise version of Windows 2003 if you are interested in large clusters. As with Exchange 2000, if you want to use the Enterprise version of Exchange, you need to deploy the Enterprise version of Windows. You can use the Datacenter version of Windows if you want to run four-way clusters on Exchange 2000, but you only need the Enterprise edition of Windows 2003 to support up to eight-way Exchange 2003 clusters, a change that may provoke renewed interest in clusters as server consolidation cranks up the number of mailboxes supported by servers. Aside from the sheer cost, relatively few companies deployed Windows Datacenter to support Exchange 2000 four-way clusters, because it is possible to achieve the necessary degree of uptime for email systems with either standard servers or smaller clusters, provided you manage the systems correctly and pay attention to detail. As is always the case, no amount of expensive hardware can compensate for inadequate management (systems or otherwise).

Differences still exist between the standard and enterprise editions of Exchange that deserve discussion. The enterprise edition is slightly more expensive, but it is the most suitable for enterprise deployments because it supports database partitioning, clustering, and includes the X.400 connector. These features are important when you want to support thousands of mailboxes on a server or want to build large datacenters, but they are less important when you only need to support a few hundred users and the standard edition suffices. In a change from Exchange 2000, you can use the standard edition in front-end/back-end configurations.

Exchange 2003 focuses on messaging above all, so Microsoft's incursions into the world of extended collaboration services comes to a grinding halt with the exclusion of Instant Messaging (IM), Chat, and Conferencing Services (think of a server-based version of NetMeeting), all extensions of Exchange 2000. You can upgrade an Exchange 2000 server that hosts the Chat and Conferencing components and they continue working, but you should consider how you want to use these components in the future and whether you should replace them now. However, you must remove IM (and KMS) from an Exchange 2000 server before you can upgrade it to Exchange 2003. Microsoft has replaced the Exchange 2000 version of IM with their Microsoft Office Live Communications Server, but does not now explicitly link instant messaging with Exchange.

You do not have to upgrade domain controllers and Global Catalog servers to Windows 2003 before you can begin to deploy Exchange 2003, providing that these servers run Windows 2000 SP3 or later. However, you can gain some advantages by upgrading the controllers used by Exchange 2003 to Windows 2003, including support for MAPI RPC transmission over HTTP (this feature requires Outlook 2003 clients) and improved replication of large distribution groups. The benefits of the upgrade include reductions in network traffic for Active Directory replication and a reduced load on Exchange servers.

Apart from IIS, Microsoft has integrated Exchange 2003 more tightly with other Microsoft server products. For example, the Exchange management pack for Microsoft Operations Manager, which used to be an optional extra, is now included in the base product. This may entice some extra customer interest in Microsoft's management framework over competing offerings such as NetIQ AppManager. Features such as RPC over HTTP can exploit the tighter integration between Exchange and Microsoft Internet Security and Acceleration Server[2] (ISA), where its Web Publishing wizard recognizes and supports the need to secure Exchange communications.

---

2. You need Feature Pack 1 (or later) for ISA. See www.microsoft.com/isaserver.

1.2.2 Microsoft support policy

Losing support is a terrifying prospect for any IT manager. It is also a prompt that maybe it is time to move forward and install a new version of software. Microsoft's support policy sets clear deadlines regarding when you can expect to have support for older versions of Exchange and Outlook and so helps set timelines for when you need to have work done to prepare for a migration.

The basic policy is as follows:

- Microsoft provides mainstream support for products during the first five years of their life.

- For two years after mainstream support ends, companies can buy extended support. This offer only applies for business and development software, which includes Exchange. You can also pay Microsoft PSS for individual support incidents if you prefer not to buy a contract.

- Online support (the Microsoft Knowledge Base) is available for at least eight years after a product's initial release.

To put this policy in context, Microsoft released Exchange 5.5 in November 1997. Therefore, if Microsoft implemented the policy as written, mainstream support for Exchange 5.5 would finish at the end of 2003 (five years and a month after first release). However, because the normal approach for a migration from Exchange 5.5 is to move first to Windows 2000 and implement the Active Directory, the process tends to be extended. Customers have been slow to move, and a 2003 deadline proved unacceptable to many. Microsoft, therefore, extended the deadline for regular support for Exchange 5.5 to December 31, 2004, with a year of extended support available (at an additional cost) to the end of 2005. At the same time, Microsoft improved the abilities of the migration toolset in SP1 and the Web-provided support tools to help customers move to Exchange 2003. See http://www.microsoft.com/exchange/support/lifecycle/Changes.asp for details of the formal Microsoft position covering Exchange 5.5 support. Extending the date to the end of 2004 aligned the end of support for Exchange 5.5 with that for Windows NT 4.0. You will have to pay Microsoft for support if you want to continue using Exchange 5.5 after 2004. The writing is now very much on the wall, and the lifetime of Exchange 5.5 has an endpoint, which is clearly visible; Microsoft is very unlikely to extend the support again. Mainstream support for Exchange 2000 lasts through 2006 and extended support through 2008.

1.2 Exchange second generation

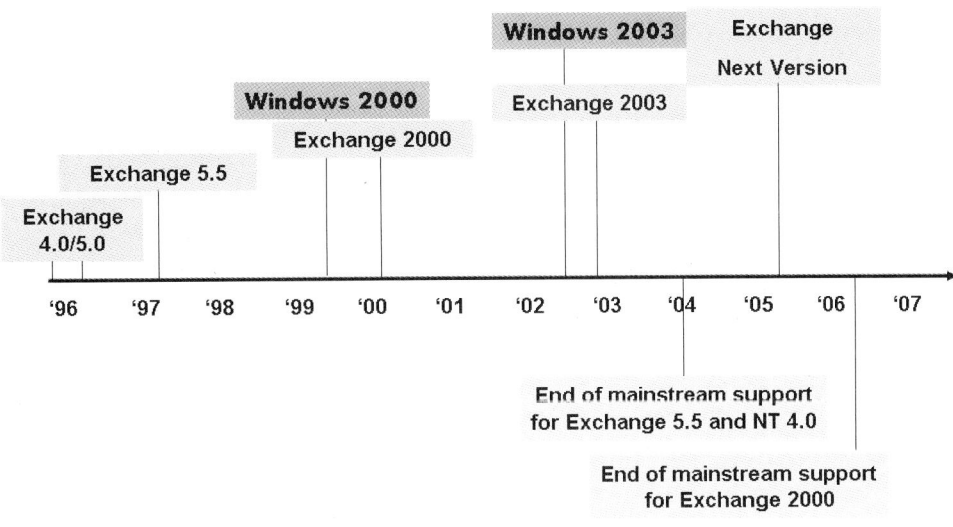

Figure 1.1 *Exchange and Windows timelines.*

Figure 1.1 illustrates the timeline from the launch of Exchange 4.0 through a finger-in-the-air prediction regarding when the next major revision of Exchange might appear.

There are several examples of companies that have not upgraded older Exchange servers to even Exchange 5.5. For example, some of the companies that tested beta releases of Exchange 2003 operated Exchange 4.0 SP2 and Exchange 5.0 SP1 servers. The good news is that everything works, because Exchange 2003 maintains backward compatibility through MAPI (for interserver communications in a mixed-mode site) and SMTP and X.400 (for general messaging). The caveat here is that Microsoft does not formally test the combination of Exchange 2003 with servers earlier than Exchange 5.5 SP3, so obtaining support may be an issue if you run into problems.

In addition to software upgrades, Microsoft asks customers to install the latest service pack for any product as soon as their deployment schedules allow and often provides "encouragement" by declining to address support issues unless you encounter the problem with the latest service pack. The formal statement is that Microsoft supports the current service pack and the preceding service pack. Sometimes a good Microsoft Technical Account Manager (TAM) can help get support for earlier service packs, but it is generally a good idea to deploy service packs as soon as you have tested them for compatibility with your production environment.

Of course, you need to consider more than just Exchange and look at the version of the operating system you run, third-party products, client software, and so on to build a complete matrix of your support exposure and requirements. For example, Outlook 2000 has mainstream support until June 30, 2004.

1.2.3 Supporting Windows

Some confusion exists as to the version of Windows you have to deploy to be able to run Exchange 2000 or Exchange 2003. The situation is simple even if the reasons are not:

- Exchange 2000 only runs on a Windows 2000 server (including Advanced Server and Datacenter Server).
- Exchange 2003 can run on either a Windows 2000 (SP3) or Windows 2003 server.
- Exchange 2003 supports native-mode Windows 2000 and Windows 2003 environments or mixed-mode environments that include both types of servers.
- Exchange 2003 requires domain controllers and Global Catalog servers to run Windows 2003 or Windows 2000 SP3 (or later). Note that Microsoft does not support Exchange 2003 running on a domain controller, but it does support Exchange 2003 running on a Global Catalog server. It is also important that if you run Exchange 2003 on a Global Catalog server, you do not change the server role and downgrade it to a normal server or domain controller, since this may influence some Exchange features. These restrictions should not affect enterprise deployments, since it is best practice to avoid running Exchange on a Global Catalog, but may be more important for smaller deployments where less hardware is available.

Table 1.1 lists the valid combinations of Windows and Exchange. See Microsoft Knowledge Base article 321648 for more information about the product support matrix and to obtain information about specific requirements. For example, because Exchange 2003 requires secure LDAP, you can only run Exchange 2003 on a Windows 2000 server that you upgrade to SP3 or better.

The reasons why you cannot run Exchange 2000 on Windows 2003 are complicated. Exchange and Windows have very close connections at many points, including the Active Directory, IIS, and DNS, as well as the protocols and virtual servers enabled by IIS, including SMTP, HTTP, and IMAP.

Table 1.1 *Exchange and Windows Support Matrix*

Exchange/OS	NT 4.0	Windows 2000	Windows 2000 in Windows 2003	Windows 2003
Exchange 5.5 SP3	Yes	Yes	Yes	No
Exchange 2000 SP1	No	Yes	Yes	No
Exchange 2000 SP2–SP3	No	Yes	Yes	No
Exchange 2003 (and service packs)	No	Yes	Yes	Yes

Microsoft could have done the work to make Exchange 2000 operate on Windows 2003, but many of the required changes would have been architectural in nature and not appropriate for a service pack, which is what it would have released (because Exchange 2003 is also available). For example, the Exchange 2003 installation procedure is able to lock down IIS 6.0 in a mode that still allows Exchange to serve dynamic data for Outlook Web Access. Because of the huge differences between IIS 5.0 and IIS 6.0, Microsoft would have had to do a lot of work to upgrade the Exchange 2000 installation procedure to handle IIS 6.0, and, even then, it would have only done half the work. Accordingly, Microsoft made the decision to restrict Exchange 2000 to Windows 2000. Perhaps it is also taking the opportunity of making the subliminal point that the best combination is now Exchange 2003 running on Windows 2003. This is probably true, but it will take people a little while to get there, since an operating system upgrade is not something that everyone eagerly anticipates.

However, while you cannot install Exchange 2000 on a Windows 2003 server, you can run Exchange 2000 in an environment where you have deployed Windows 2003. For example, you can upgrade domain controllers and Global Catalog servers to take advantage of the improvements in Active Directory and continue to run applications such as Exchange, SQL, and file and print services on Windows 2000 servers. In much the same way, you can continue to run Exchange 5.5 servers on either Windows 2000 or Windows NT 4.0 inside a Windows 2003 environment while you prepare for and then execute the migration. In all cases, if you decide to deploy Exchange on Windows 2000, make sure that you install the latest service pack first, along with any security patches or other hot fixes recommended by Microsoft. In addition, deploy the same base level of the operating system everywhere to make support easier.

1.3 Exchange 2003 SP1

Microsoft launched Service Pack 1 (SP1) for Exchange 2003 in May 2004, roughly eight months after Exchange 2003 appeared. With earlier versions of Exchange, service packs often appeared faster and more frequently, possibly indicating that Microsoft was building features into Exchange faster than it could test them, so more bugs appeared. Today's development pace is more measured, indicating that the product is more stable and that it is more feature rich, so Microsoft does not have to rush out service packs to make things work after customers find flaws. SP1 includes a mixture of bug fixes, updates to existing features, and some new UI to make it easier to deploy and manage features that first appeared in Exchange 2003. In addition, SP1 includes some new tools to help customers migrate from Exchange 5.5, which is rapidly approaching the end of its supported lifetime. As always, a service pack presents a challenge to administrators who need to decide how quickly to deploy the new software, the impact it might have on their production environment, and how to test it with third-party products.

You can break down the contents of SP1 into several categories:

- Bug fixes: As with all complex software products, engineers make literally hundreds of fixes in response to customer reports, and SP1 includes a collection of fixes from small adjustments to major patches. Microsoft has also updated the API used by third-party antivirus products to improve the scanning of S/MIME-encrypted and TNEF-format messages. SP1 also improves the level of error reporting in the OAB generation process. This is a welcome step, because the OAB is so important for Outlook 2003 clients who operate in cached Exchange mode. If errors occur in the OAB generation process, the Exchange server (if it runs SP1) that generates the OAB now signals more detailed and complete information to the event log to help administrators debug the problem.

- Updates to existing features: For example, SP1 includes spell-check dictionaries for Danish, Finnish, Hebrew, Norwegian, and Swedish for Outlook Web Access users. It also updates the list of cell phones supported by Outlook Mobile Access and improves the UI delivered to these devices. Another improvement is that you no longer need to use the ExMerge utility in a Recovery Storage Group mailbox recovery process, since the Recover Mailbox Data option that SP1 includes in Exchange System Manager (ESM) as part of the Exchange Task Wizard now handles everything. Exchange's journaling feature can now handle BCC recipients and expands distribution group recipients before it captures messages, a worthwhile advance but not one that eliminates the need to consider full-fledged document archiving and retrieval products if you need this functionality.

- New UI: According to its own rules, Microsoft cannot update the user interface of a product in a bug fix and must wait for a service pack in order to ensure that the new UI is fully tested and documented. The biggest example of new UI in SP1 is the configuration options to make it easier to set up RPC over HTTP connections. I have frequently whined at the Exchange developers that they create great functionality and then mask it with a semicomplete UI or by forcing administrators to use an arcane command-line utility to implement it. Thankfully, the developers seem to be paying more attention to this aspect of the product, and the provision of the new UI to help configure RPC over HTTP connections, as well as the OWAWA utility, is good to see (see section 5.5). Of course, Microsoft still has some work to do to eliminate vestiges such as ESEUTIL that still linger on in Exchange, but all progress is welcome.

- New functionality: Service packs can include a completely new utility (such as the "Pilgrim" move server utility in Exchange 5.5 SP3) or complete functionality that a previous version of Exchange introduced. Exchange 2003 supports "hot" snapshots, but customers have been slow to introduce these into production, because the hardware (storage) and software (backup utilities) providers have not supported Exchange 2003 as quickly as they might. SP1 includes support for incremental and differential snapshot backups, so maybe this will be the spur to encourage more administrators to use snapshots—assuming hardware support, of course.

The infamous −1018 errors have been a scourge of the Store since Exchange first appeared. SP1 introduces the ability for the Store to detect and fix single bit errors that previous versions signal as −1018 errors. The net result is a reduction in the −1018 errors that you will now encounter on a server. If you do see such an error, you can be sure that it is probably not due to a software glitch and that something far more fundamental has caused it, probably in the storage subsystem, that requires your urgent attention. See section 7.10.4 for more information on how the Store detects and fixes single bit errors.

Note that you do not need to deploy SP1 to use the new Intelligent Message Filter (IMF), Microsoft's new antispam weapon. See section 9.16 for more details on IMF.

1.3.1 Web releases and utilities

At the same time that SP1 appeared, Microsoft shipped a new Web release (WR04) that contains a set of new tools you can use to administer Exchange 2003 servers. In the past, Microsoft traditionally released tools for Exchange by including them on the server CD. Now, Microsoft is moving to a more dynamic approach by including tools into "Web releases," which it can update more frequently and make available for download from www.microsoft.com/exchange. Each Web release has a number, and WR04 is the collection of tools that aligns loosely with SP1. WR04 contains two major tools of interest—Outlook Web Access Web Admin (OWAWA) and an Auto Accept Agent—as well as the Domain Rename Fixup (called XDR-Fixup), which is still important, because it allows administrators to complete the process of renaming a Windows domain that supports an Exchange organization, but it is probably of interest to a smaller community.

The Auto Accept Agent cleans up a problem that Microsoft has long had with resource mailboxes, which are mailboxes that control access to items that people want to book, such as conference rooms. When Outlook first appeared, you had to leave a client logged on to the mailbox to be able to accept incoming meeting requests to book the resource. Gradually, administrators automated the process by writing client-side code or server-side events, but all were unsatisfactory in one form or another. The Auto Accept Agent uses Exchange store events to handle meeting requests as they arrive for a resource mailbox, including determining if a conflict exists, cancellations, and updates. It is good to have a Microsoft solution to the problem, especially one that has been running inside Microsoft for some time!

Other tools that Microsoft publishes include a script to manage the contents of a server's "Badmail" directory to automatically archive or delete files (bad SMTP messages) that accumulate in the directory and a "profile flipper" (see section 4.1.3), which updates Outlook profiles so that users can continue to use the same profile after mailbox moves between Exchange organizations or sites. All these tools are available from Microsoft's Web site.

1.3.2 More help to move from Exchange 5.5

Aside from the general collection of fixes, updates, and new bits that come in any service pack, Microsoft tends to take the opportunity to focus on a customer requirement each time it releases a service pack. In this case, the need is to help customers move from Exchange 5.5 to Exchange 2003 before the support deadline for Exchange 5.5 expires in December 2004. Support for Windows NT 4.0 expires at the same time, and Exchange 5.5

cannot run on Windows 2003 (but it can run on Windows 2000), so in many cases it is time for a fundamental technology refresh.

The biggest change in SP1 is the new ability for the Exchange Move Mailbox Wizard to migrate mailboxes from an Exchange 5.5 server to an Exchange 2003 SP1 server in a mixed-mode organization when the two servers are in different administrative groups. Previously, you could only move mailboxes when the two servers were in the same administrative group (or site, in Exchange 5.5 terminology), or after you had completed the migration and transformed the organization into native mode. The Move Mailbox Wizard preserves mailbox rules and updates folder ACLs during the move to ensure that it preserves a complete mailbox environment instead of merely moving the mailbox contents. This is important, because some users accumulate many rules to process incoming messages, usually to refile new mail into different folders. It is not good for users to move to a new server only to find that they have to recreate all their rules. Note that you have to update servers that host the Active Directory Connector (ADC) to run the version of the ADC included in SP1 before you can move mailboxes across sites between Exchange 5.5 and 2003 servers. This is because the updated version of the ADC includes new code to ensure that users can continue to use distribution groups and access public folders after their mailboxes move to Exchange 2003.

Being able to move mailboxes between administrative groups may seem unimportant, but many companies opt to deploy Exchange 2003 by installing brand new Exchange 2003 servers using the latest hardware instead of upgrading older servers. At the same time, it is common practice to restructure the Exchange organization, because the administrative model used for Exchange 5.5 is not necessarily the best for Exchange 2003, especially if you are interested in eliminating some servers by consolidating onto fewer higher-specification servers, often accompanied by the removal of servers in branch offices.

Some administrators firmly believe that they should wait for the first service pack of any Microsoft product before they will even consider deploying the software. Exchange 2003 SP1 meets the requirements of these people, because it builds on a solid platform established by the initial release by making some features easier to use, fixing some deficiencies in others, and applying a general cleanup around the product. For people already running Exchange 2003, the decision to upgrade should be straightforward. The upgrade is easy, fast, and, apart from an IIS hot fix that affects Outlook Web Access (see Microsoft Knowledge Base article 831464) that you should apply anyway, SP1 does not require any changes to the underlying Windows infrastructure, so you should schedule it for the earliest possible opportunity. As always, before you upgrade a server, be sure to take a full backup before you proceed with the upgrade—just in case!

1.4 Exchange third generation

The third generation of Exchange is still in the design phase, and the first functional beta releases will not appear until 2005 at the earliest. Microsoft originally called the development of the third generation of Exchange the "Kodiak" project. However, at Tech Ed 2004 in San Diego, Microsoft announced that it had canceled the Kodiak project and instead planned to ship the features that represented Kodiak at different times. This looks awfully like the way that the original Cairo project evolved into some features that have appeared in Windows 2000 and 2003, and some that have still not appeared but may show up in a future release of Windows. No one will know exactly until plans firm up and especially until we see the first beta versions of a third-generation product. Until Microsoft has the answers to allow it to chart how to move from second- to third-generation Exchange, it is entirely possible that Microsoft will ship one or more additional versions based on today's architecture, continuing to drive the alignment with Office and probably associated with its Information Worker initiative.

A change in its storage strategy was a major focus for the third generation of Exchange. Since its inception, Exchange has used its own storage engine. The current Store uses the ESE (Extensible Storage Engine) database engine, variants of which also appear in the Active Directory and SharePoint Portal Server 2001 Store. In turn, ESE builds on Joint Engine Technology (JET), a generalized database engine that Microsoft has used for many purposes from Access to the database used to synchronize directory information between Exchange and Microsoft Mail.

The logic to justify using a separate database engine for Exchange is that the needs of a messaging system are very different from those of general database applications. A typical database attempts to place known limits around transactions in terms of the size and data, whereas a messaging system has to be able to handle messages that vary in size and content. The range in message type goes from a single-line message sent to a single recipient up to messages such as those with several multimegabyte attachments (of various types) sent to a distribution list, which is, in turn, composed of multiple nested distribution lists. Microsoft designed ESE to handle the huge variance in message traffic, and it has been successful in meeting this challenge. Microsoft addressed the problems that have been encountered as Exchange evolved, including new attachment types (streaming audio and video); an ever-increasing average message size; and the tendency of users to retain far more email than they need to, by increasing the maximum size of a database, store partitioning, and the inclusion of the streaming file as part of the Store. Instead of the original 16-GB limit, you can grow a database now to fill available disk space. Exchange is able to deal with the largest Storage Area Network available today, a situation very different from the original fixed disk configurations seen in 1996. Indeed, given the size of the engineering team that works on ESE compared with the SQL development team, the amount of development achieved to build Store features is remarkable.

Even as ESE evolved, Microsoft still faced the fact that it has been developing two database engines with all the attendant costs involved in design, engineering, bug testing, support, and release. Microsoft's long-term goal—expressed many times, including as a feature of the Cairo project—has been to move to a unified storage model that handles all types of data, including files, so it did not make sense to continue with two databases. One or the other had to give, and while ESE was successful, it did not have the strategic influence carried by SQL, so Microsoft established the long-term strategic goal in mid-2001 to move Exchange over and to use SQL as its future database engine.

Setting a strategic goal is but one small step along a path. Figuring out how to bring a hugely successful product with millions of users forward to use a new database engine is quite another. Exchange cannot use the current generation of the SQL database engine, because the current SQL platform did not take the needs of Exchange into account when Microsoft built this version. After an enormous internal debate, Microsoft therefore took the decision in 2001 that Exchange will use the Yukon next-generation SQL engine, and the work began to engineer in the necessary hooks and features to allow Yukon to support Exchange. It is always difficult for an outsider to comment with definity as to just what Microsoft plans to do, but the decision to cancel the Kodiak project means that a move to use the Yukon platform is less of an absolute and more of a perhaps. It is entirely possible that this strategy will change as Microsoft progresses its plans to move to unify its various storage engines into a smaller set. For example, the evolution of the WinFS (Windows File System) project in the "Longhorn" version of Windows Server may well influence the future storage platform for Exchange.

The potential benefits to customers are far more uncertain. It is true that SQL offers some features that ESE does not deliver today, such as better transaction rollback and higher scalability, but perhaps not enough to justify waiting for a fully functional release of an Exchange server that uses a new storage engine to warrant the pain of migration. Every migration, even from one version of Exchange to another within the same generation, causes expense and pain for administrators and users alike. You cannot expect the migration to any new version to be much different.

Microsoft realizes the issues and understands that it has to do an excellent job of communicating the benefits of the migration to customers while also continuing to add features and functionality to the second generation of Exchange. It will certainly be interesting to watch and see how Microsoft approaches this task as the time comes to release new servers and begin the migration to the third generation of Exchange.

1.4.1 The competition

Microsoft's own figures put the total number of Exchange client licenses sold at around 115 million. This does not mean that 115 million people use Exchange. The true number is less than 70 million, because Microsoft tends to oversell many seats to large corporations under the terms of enterprise licenses (where everyone in the company receives an Exchange client license). However, to put these figures into context, Exchange is the accepted market leader for messaging deployments, with about 60 percent of the market, and enjoys a healthy growth in its installed base year after year. Interestingly, 40 percent of Microsoft's Exchange business comes from the small to medium business market (under 500 seats), so while the large deployments receive the publicity, smaller installations deliver a lot of the base.

Exchange's competition has fluctuated dramatically over its lifetime. Exchange 4.0 competed against mainframe-based systems such as IBM PROFS and LAN-based systems such as Lotus cc:Mail. These systems had largely faded into the background by the time Exchange 5.5 shipped and the major competitor was Lotus Notes (Domino), a trend that continued into Exchange 2000. Today, Domino is still a major competitor for Exchange in the corporate arena (and especially so in Japan, where Domino is approximately six times as popular as Exchange), but it has been joined by systems based on "pure" Internet protocols. Exchange supports all of the Internet protocols, such as SMTP, MIME, IMAP, POP, and so on, but it seems to make a difference to some people when these protocols are associated with an SMTP MTA running on a UNIX or Linux server. The competitive landscape is completed by companies that attempt to leverage the strength of Outlook in the market and the number of desktops it occupies by offering an alternative to Exchange that allows companies to retain Outlook as the client. The best example of this is Oracle's Collaboration Suite, which is available for UNIX or Linux.

The Exchange development group has always worried about its competition and tried to learn from its strengths and weaknesses. Paranoia (a trait shared by many Microsoft development groups) has helped the group stay ahead of the competition, sometimes by adding features, sometimes by improving areas where it needed to, such as manageability and scalability. Microsoft has also focused on great interoperability with other messaging systems through SMTP and X.400 and the provision of migration tools to allow companies to move more easily to Exchange than to any other platform. For example, Microsoft has a Lotus Notes connector for Exchange that allows the smooth transfer of message and directory data between the two servers. It even has an Outlook 2002 connector for Lotus Notes, so that you can transfer mailbox data using a client rather than going anywhere near the server (pushing the work to migrate data down to users is a great idea, if you can get away with it). The net result is that Microsoft has always been able to stay ahead and grow market share for Exchange.

The jump from one technology generation to another always creates opportunity for the competition. For example, the move to Exchange 2000 forced customers to completely revamp their Windows infrastructure to deploy the Active Directory; implement a new security model; establish new administrative and management routines; and probably install new software packages for antivirus, cloning user accounts, directory synchronization, and so on. It was a lot of work and the bigger the company, the larger the price tag.

Two things flowed from the complexity Microsoft introduced in the changeover to Exchange 2000. First, companies were slow to deploy Exchange 2000 and were happy to stay with Exchange 5.5 (which works very well on Windows 2000); second, competitors had the chance to demonstrate that it was easier to move platform than upgrade all the components necessary to deploy Exchange 2000. In my experience, not many companies actually took the chance to move platform, but certainly a lot of angst was generated as competitors took every chance to inform customers of the work required to deploy Windows 2000 and then Exchange 2000. All of the fuss resulted in a situation where Exchange 5.5 became the largest competitor to Exchange 2000, as the majority of installations stubbornly stayed loyal to Exchange 5.5 and resisted the temptation to move to Exchange 2000 during the 2001–2003 time frame.

If you run Exchange 2000, then it is much easier to move to Exchange 2003, since you did all the hard work to establish Active Directory when you deployed Exchange 2000. The rule is, therefore, that upgrades within a generation of Exchange are easy; upgrades between Exchange generations take more work.

With this rule in mind, we can predict that similar angst will exist when the next generation of Exchange appears. Microsoft will face the undoubted technical challenge of making the migration as easy as possible for all concerned, but it will also face the challenge of holding off the competitors who will gather again to take advantage of any Microsoft weakness. It will be interesting to watch.

1.5 Simple steps to prepare for the move

Microsoft's provision of the ExDeploy toolset is very welcome, but these tools and those from third-party vendors will not gloss over the problems caused by a mismanaged Exchange 5.5 infrastructure. There are a number of things you can do to ensure the general well-being of your Exchange 5.5 systems before you begin the migration to Exchange 2003.

- Remove anomalies from the Exchange 5.5 Directory. These include mailboxes that are not associated with a Windows account or mailboxes that are associated with multiple accounts. Exchange 2003 mailboxes are extensions of Active Directory accounts, and only one mailbox can be linked with one account, so you will have problems with migrating these mailboxes. Most consulting companies have tools to check the Exchange 5.5 Directory for problems.

- Clean up the Exchange 5.5 Directory by deleting obsolete mailboxes, custom recipients, and distribution lists.

- Clean up the public folder hierarchy by deleting obsolete public folders.

- Clean up the Windows NT SAM by deleting obsolete accounts.

- Perform server/site consolidation with the Move Server Wizard in order to have a smaller number of servers to migrate.

- Run the DS/IS Consistency Checker to ensure that the ACLs on public folders are correct and that all public folders are homed.

- Clean up user mailboxes so that you have less data to move around between systems during the migration. Of course, this is not important if you plan an in-place upgrade, but it is still good to ask users to clean up their mailboxes and behave a little less like human pack rats.

- Remove old connectors or any add-on software that is no longer required.
- Document the entire Exchange organization carefully so that you know its state before the migration begins. It is also a good idea to have an idea of the desired end state.

These steps generate a streamlined Exchange infrastructure before the migration and reduce the chance that you will hit problems during the migration.

After you migrate an Exchange 5.5 server, do not be in a hurry to decommission it immediately. There is always a temptation to remove the old from an environment, but you may have forgotten to move something across to Exchange 2003, such as a lingering public folder whose sole replica remains on the old server. It is better practice to inspect the server carefully, then turn it off for a few days to see if any problems occur within your organization, and only then deinstall Exchange and remove the server.

1.6 Deploying Exchange 2003

The basic system requirements to begin an Exchange 2003 deployment are straightforward. The server needs to run Windows 2000 SP3 or Windows 2003, and you can only upgrade an existing Exchange server if it runs Exchange 2000 SP3 or later. After you've done all the hard work to ensure that you're running the right version of Windows and Exchange, the actual upgrade to Exchange 2003 is easy, and you should be able to apply it on all but the largest servers in a couple of hours. Be sure to take a backup before and after the upgrade, just in case you need to roll back.

Because Exchange depends on the Active Directory to hold information about the organization, servers, connectors, and users, you need to prepare the AD infrastructure before you can upgrade to Exchange 2003. Because of the requirement for secure LDAP access to support services, such as the Recipient Update Service (RUS), Active Directory Connector (ADC), and Site Replication Services (SRS), domain controllers (DCs) and Global Catalog servers (GCs) must run Windows 2000 SP3 before Exchange 2003 servers will bind to their AD service. If you have not yet upgraded these servers to SP3, you should make plans to do so before deploying Exchange 2003. The Exchange 2003 setup procedure actually checks to see whether the DCs and GCs run the right software versions, so this is not something you can avoid. The alternate approach is to install Windows 2003 on the DCs and GCs. However, most administrators are loathe to deploy a new operating system until they have fully tested the software and understand how to deploy it within their production environment. Fortunately, Exchange 2003 is happy to run on a Windows 2000 (SP3 or later) or Windows 2003 server.

Microsoft supports neither Exchange 2000 nor Exchange 5.5 on Windows 2003, so if your company plans to deploy Windows 2003 soon, you should consider a plan to move to Exchange 2003 first, since a concurrent upgrade of operating system and email servers creates a level of unacceptable complexity for most administrators. Note that you cannot upgrade a server from Exchange 5.5 to Exchange 2003 without going through Exchange 2000 first, so a phased approach is required to move to a new infrastructure. For example, if you run Exchange 2000 now, you can follow this upgrade schedule:

- Upgrade to Windows 2000 SP3.
- Upgrade Exchange 2000 to Exchange 2003 (and then apply service packs and hot fixes).
- Upgrade Windows 2000 to Windows 2003.

Of course, you could take a server through all these steps in a single day, but I only recommend this approach in a laboratory environment and it is not something that you would do in production. Instead, it is likely that you will need a week or so between each major upgrade step to allow the overall environment to settle down, replication operations to complete, and be ready to execute the next step. Note too the general rule that you cannot restore databases from an Exchange server to a server running an earlier release. This means that you have to be sure that you include disaster recovery considerations in your deployment plans.

If you have used Exchange 5.5 for awhile and are considering an upgrade of your server hardware, you can adopt a "moving train" approach to the deployment. This means that you introduce new servers[3] into your infrastructure by installing Windows 2003 and then Exchange 2003. When you are happy that the servers are functioning correctly and you have all the necessary pieces to integrate the servers into daily operations, you can then start to move mailboxes over to the new Exchange servers. Usually, the new

---

3. To ensure support and achieve best reliability, the hardware for any new servers should be included in Microsoft's Hardware Compatibility List (HCL).

hardware can replace several older servers, so you gradually consolidate your environment as you move mailboxes. If you are still running Windows NT 4.0, you should also be able to consolidate domain controllers and other infrastructure servers by replacing them with Windows 2003 equivalents. Eventually, you will have moved all the mailboxes, and you can then decommission the last Exchange 5.5 server and turn your organization from mixed (Exchange 5.5/Exchange 2003) to native mode (only Exchange 2003). The moving train approach is recommended by Microsoft because it is far easier to move mailboxes around, especially with the new functionality in Exchange 2003, than to perform multiple software upgrades on servers.

Some differences exist between the installation procedure requirements for Exchange 2000 and Exchange 2003. The .NET framework and ASP.NET components must be present on all Exchange 2003 servers. The Exchange 2003 installation procedure installs these components automatically when you install Exchange 2003 on a Windows 2000 server, but you have to install the ASP.NET components manually before you install Exchange 2003 on Windows 2003. The reason for the difference is that under Microsoft's Trustworthy Computing initiative, the general approach for Windows 2003 is never to install a system component unless you know that it is necessary. For the same reason, you have to install the IIS, NNTP, SMTP, and WWW services on Windows 2003 before proceeding with Exchange 2003. With respect to IIS 6.0, the Exchange 2003 installation procedure makes sure that IIS switches into Worker Process Isolation Mode and enables the various Exchange ISAPI interfaces (such as Outlook Mobile Access and Outlook Web Access).

In front-end/back-end configurations, where you have Exchange front-end servers that proxy incoming communications to back-end mailbox servers, you have to upgrade all the front-end servers within an administrative group to Exchange 2003 before you upgrade the back-end servers. You have to complete the upgrade to both front- and back-end servers before you can use the new Outlook Web Access client interface. Forms authentication works if only the front-end servers run Exchange 2003, but session timeouts are more reliable when all of the servers run Exchange 2003.

Exchange 2003 removes support for the Exchange 2000 Instant Messaging (IM), Key Management Server (KMS), Chat, and Conferencing components. The Windows 2003 Certificate Server takes over the role of KMS in terms of generating new certificates to users, maintaining revocation lists, and so on. You can continue to keep these servers in place and run them alongside new Exchange 2003 servers until you are ready to phase them out. Contact Microsoft for the most up-to-date recommendations on replacement strategies, because there are development activities in these areas that you may benefit from.

Finally, despite the prominence of the Active Directory, WINS is still required to deploy Exchange 2003, because dependencies exist in the setup program, Exchange System Manager, and cluster administration. For example, the setup program can only deal with server names that are 15 characters or less. For further information, see Microsoft Knowledge Base articles 251933 and 275335.

1.6.1 Upgrade time

The first step to deploying Exchange 2003 is to run the ForestPrep and DomainPrep procedures, both part of Exchange's setup utility. This is necessary even if you have an existing Exchange organization, and, just like the first time you ran these procedures, you have to run ForestPrep once for the forest and then run DomainPrep for every domain that hosts servers or mail-enabled objects, including the root domain—even if it seems to be empty of any mail-enabled objects. ForestPrep extends the AD schema with an additional set of object definitions over those required by Exchange 2000.

The actual installation of Exchange 2003 is not onerous and normally completes within an hour. Certainly, assuming that a server runs the necessary version of Windows and that you have prepared the infrastructure, perhaps by installing Windows 2003 on DCs and GCs, it should not take more than a couple of hours to complete the installation. Once the server restarts, the Store performs a schema upgrade and rebuilds any store indexes used by Exchange's full-text indexing feature, so CPU demand is heavier until these tasks complete. The upgrade procedure allows you to defer the full text rebuild to a more suitable time, if you want.

The nature of clusters is that they are more complex than standard servers, so you have more work to do. After applying an upgrade in the normal manner, open the Cluster Administrator utility, select the Exchange System Attendant resource for each Exchange virtual server in the cluster, and take the "Upgrade Exchange Virtual Server" option. In addition, because Exchange 2003 replaces EXRES.DLL (the resource DLL to control Exchange resources), you have to reboot the server. In most cases, you do not have to reboot a standard server after you upgrade to Exchange 2003.

Do remember to take a full backup before beginning to upgrade a server and then take another backup after the installation completes. The full backup beforehand should include the system state and system and application files as well as the Exchange databases. Afterward, let Exchange start up and mount the databases so that the Store stamps the databases with the new version number. This completes the upgrade process and you can then take a full online backup to ensure that you can recover the server if a subsequent problem occurs.

Note that apart from the first server in the organization, you no longer need permission over the full organization to be able to install an Exchange server. Instead, Exchange 2003 requires that you only need Exchange Full Administrator permission for the target administrative group to be able to add a new server, install a service pack or hot fix, or remove a server. A small but important change is that the Exchange 2003 installation procedure no longer assumes that it has the permissions necessary to add a server to the local Exchange Domain Servers global security group (Figure 1.2). Instead, you have to arrange for someone (such as an enterprise Windows administrator) to add the account after you install Exchange.

Unlike the situation with Exchange 2000 installations and service pack updates, the Exchange 2003 installation procedure does not attempt to reset default permissions on the organizational object at each server install. This fixes an irritating bug that allowed users to create top-level public folders after administrators had limited access to this feature. Another small but important change is that the installation procedure can proceed without the need to communicate with the forest's schema master (FSMO role). Instead

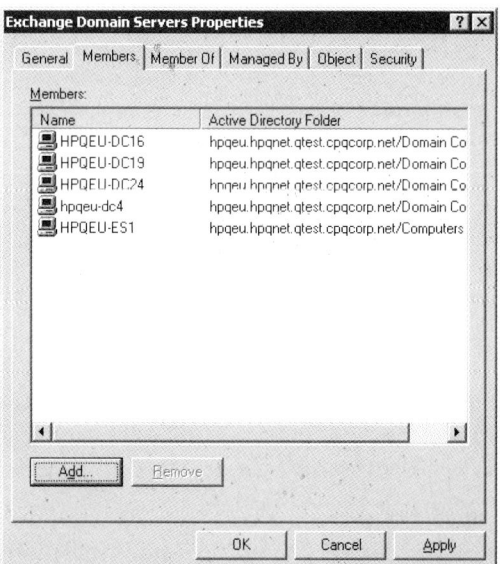

Figure 1.2
Membership of the Exchange Domain Servers group.

of insisting on connecting to the schema master to validate that the schema extensions for Exchange exist, the installation procedure now checks that the organization exists in the configuration naming context of the AD. The logic here is that the presence of the organization indicates that ForestPrep has updated the schema.

During installations, you can select the domain controller to communicate with by using the SETUP/ ChooseDC switch, which is useful when you know the most appropriate domain controller to use (ideally one that you know is fully up-to-date in terms of replication). It is also useful when you want to install many servers in a short period, since you can now spread the load across domain controllers or direct the installation procedure to use a powerful server reserved for the purpose. The final change is that the installation procedure no longer prompts you to enter the name of an organization until you install the first server in an organization. Instead, Exchange creates a placeholder GUID for the organization in the configuration container and you then populate the organization's visible name when you install the first server. These small but important changes make it much easier to deploy Exchange, especially inside large organizations.

1.6.2 Deployment tools

As Microsoft has had three years' hard experience of Exchange 2000 in production, it is not surprising that it has created a deployment kit to help you assess whether you need to take steps to prepare your infrastructure before you start. The tools and deployment guide are included in the \Support\ExDeploy folder in the server CD.

You can launch a wizard-like interface to the tools by invoking the compiled help file at \Support\ExDeploy\Exdeploy.chm. As you can see in Figure 1.3, ExDeploy offers tests that allow you to verify whether you are ready to deploy Exchange 2003 in specific circumstances, including upgrades and new server installations. Behind the scenes, ExDeploy calls the various executables as required and generates log files that you can find in the \Logs folder. Do not copy the ExDeploy files to a remote file share and execute ExDeploy from there, since you may see unpredictable results. Always execute ExDeploy from a local disk.

It is interesting to see that Microsoft provides many tools to assist administrators to migrate from Exchange 5.5 and reduce the number of support calls that Microsoft receives during migrations. This reflects the reality of a situation where installations have been slow to move because of the perceived difficulty of migration, so these tools exist to help people

1.6 Deploying Exchange 2003

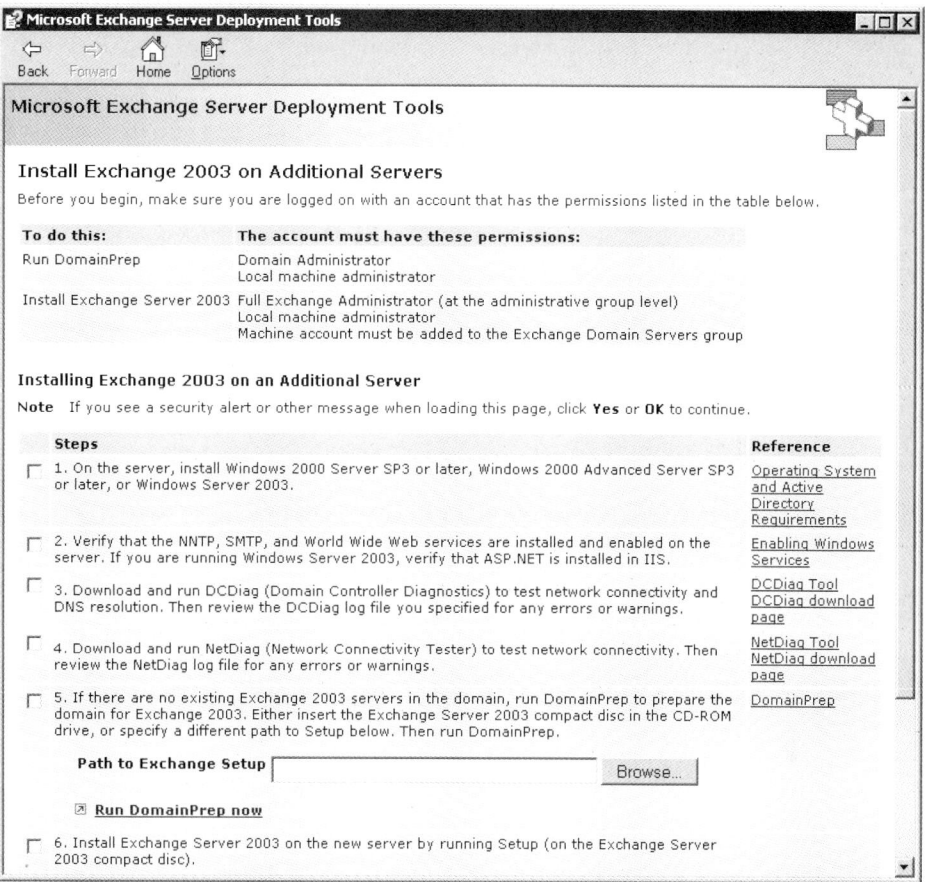

Figure 1.3 *ExDeploy.*

past the barrier. Among the more interesting items in the ExDeploy tool set are:

- OrgPrepCheck: Validates that the organizational requirements for Exchange 2003 exist before you install the first server. You run this tool after the ForestPrep and DomainPrep options in the installation procedure to ensure that Windows (AD and FRS) has correctly replicated security policies and groups to all necessary servers within the organization. OrgPrepCheck is actually a "tool group," because it calls several other tools to do its work, including OrgCheck, PolCheck, PubFoldCheck, and OrgNameCheck. The last tool checks for illegal characters in the organization name. Exchange organization, administrative group, routing group, and server names must comply with the character restrictions documented in RFC 821, which is a tighter restriction than that applied to Exchange 5.5. For example, you can no longer include brackets in any Exchange names.

- DCdiag: Tests the connectivity between an Exchange server and DCs.
- NetDiag: Tests the basic network configuration for a potential Exchange server. Separate versions exist for Windows 2000 and Windows 2003. See Microsoft Knowledge Base article 321708.
- SetupPrep: Checks that the infrastructure components that Exchange depends on (such as DNS) are available and functioning.
- ADCUserCheck: Scans an Exchange 5.5 directory store to create a recommended list of AD connection agreements to synchronize the Exchange 5.5 directory with the AD. This tool is used only to prepare an Exchange 5.5 server to migrate to Exchange 2000.
- DSScopeScan: Audits an Exchange 5.5 server and documents what it finds. Reports servers, stores, connectors, mailboxes, public folders, and so on—the essential data that you need to know to be able to scope the migration.

These are basic tools and may not include the same depth of functionality for functions such as directory management, which you can buy from ISVs such as NetIQ (www.netiq.com), Quest Software (www.quest.com), and BindView (www.bindview.com), but they exist for the specific purpose to help you to move smoothly to Exchange 2003. You could manually extract the same data that the tools analyze to figure things out for yourself, but it is much easier when you have automatic processing to provide a baseline. Anything that avoids work is welcome!

1.7 Some things that Microsoft still has to do

Exchange is a great messaging platform with lots of wonderful features. Its management infrastructure continues to improve, and you can connect Exchange to almost any other messaging system on the planet. On the face of it, it does not sound as if Microsoft has a lot more work to do with Exchange. Of course, we know that Microsoft wants to bring Exchange into a new generation and use a common storage engine, so there is plenty of engineering work on the horizon, but there are still a few things that Microsoft might have addressed in Exchange 2003.

1.7.1 Administrative flexibility

Most complaints center on administrative flexibility. Exchange began with a directory that forced administrative rigidity insofar as you could not easily change the shape of an organization after you installed servers, because server objects included organizational detail in their directory names. It was not until 1998 that Microsoft produced the Move Server Wizard to allow administrators to move a server from one site to another within an organization or to another organization. Even with the tool, the process was long and arduous and often as attractive as performing do-it-yourself brain surgery. Great hopes focused on Exchange 2000, when the Active Directory promised to liberate Exchange from the chains imposed by its own directory. Unhappily, while the situation is better, some gaps still exist. For example:

- Windows 2003 supports domain renaming, but you should not attempt to rename a domain (yet) if Exchange 2000 or 2003 servers are present. You can use Microsoft's domain fixup tool (XDR-Fixup) to complete the process of renaming a domain, but be sure that you have tested everything before you attempt to perform such a dramatic restructuring.

- You cannot move servers between domains within the same forest, so you have to decommission and then reinstall the server in the desired location.

- You cannot move servers between Exchange organizations. This implies a move between forests, because you can only have one Exchange organization per forest, which is in turn a further restriction on administrative flexibility.

- You cannot move servers between administrative groups.

Many of these restrictions exist because of the close dependency between Exchange and AD. For example, if you were able to drag and drop a server from one administrative group to another, the AD would then have to replicate the new organizational structure to every DC in the forest. If replication fails, then some servers will not have knowledge of the current organizational structure and may not be able to route email if a bridgehead server or a connector was involved in the move. If you have the right administrative permissions, you can drag and drop a server from one routing group to another, so it seems as if similar operations exist within Exchange.

Being able to drag and drop objects to change organizational structure is a nice user experience. However, you can imagine the possible replication complexity that results from a series of moves where an administrator first moves a server to one administrative group, realizes that was a mistake, and then moves the server to the place the administrator really wanted it to go. Scenarios such as this make Microsoft reluctant to implement any form of movement unless it is happy that it can perform the operations without affecting the overall stability of the messaging system. I could also complain —and do complain—about the way Microsoft introduces some functionality into Exchange that seems to be half-complete, naked in terms of user interface or reliant on registry hacks or command-line utilities. Of course, everyone wants Exchange to be functional, but I think we would also like to see it complete.

1.7.2 Collaboration

Microsoft has always wanted to make Exchange a platform for collaboration, but while it has been very willing, it has have also been terribly unsuccessful. The original play was on public folders, when Microsoft promised that you could accomplish great things by linking public folder storage with intelligent electronic forms. Public folders certainly store items, but the electronic forms never quite lived up to the promise of intelligence, and the original vision faded rapidly. Public folders have since become the great dumping ground for Exchange data. They can be useful, but do not expect to accomplish more than you can with a well-managed network file share. We return to the topic of public folders in Chapter 7.

Frustrated by the failure of public folders and driven by an intense need to be competitive with the Lotus Notes collaboration platform, Microsoft has launched many other collaboration initiatives around Exchange, including attempts to make Exchange a platform for workflow and intelligent document routing. It is fair to say that implementers greeted each initiative with less enthusiasm, leading us to a situation where the advent of the Instant Messaging and Conferencing Server add-on products for Exchange 2000 sank without trace very quickly.

Thankfully, Microsoft seems to have concluded that Exchange is great at messaging and awful at collaboration, so it should focus on maximizing the strengths and leave collaboration to other products, such as its SharePoint technologies, which it may integrate with Exchange in the future. Hopefully, we will see public folders fade away into history and Microsoft will replace them with something more functional, more flexible, and more powerful—perhaps in the next generation of Exchange. Given the focus on

SharePoint technology, it would not be a surprise to see Microsoft move in that direction as a replacement for public folders. Of course, focusing on messaging is a double-edged sword, because there are many alternative email servers available today. If Exchange is "just" an email server, why would you not move to another platform instead of upgrading to Exchange 2003 (or even more to the point, from Exchange 5.5 to Exchange 2000)? The answer is that it is still easier to move within technology generations than from one technology to another and the way that Outlook 2003 and Exchange 2003 now work more intelligently with each other makes the combination the best on the market.

1.7.3 Application development

How many APIs can a single product support? The answer is unclear, but Microsoft has certainly given Exchange every chance to lead in this category. Beginning with MAPI (several variants, including Simple MAPI and Common Messaging Calls), going on through interfaces such as Exchange Routing Objects, OLE/DB, several variations of CDO including CDOEXM (and not forgetting Outlook's programming model), and associations with Windows-driven APIs such as ADSI and ADO, life for an Exchange developer is a veritable alphabet soup. The problem here is simple. Given Microsoft's past record of introducing APIs and then moving on, what interface should a developer use to build code? MAPI is the only interface that has truly persisted from day one of Exchange.

Perhaps some relief is on the horizon. The advent of Microsoft .NET and the focus on XML and SOAP as the preferred mechanisms for general data interchange within the .NET framework mean that Exchange has to support XML and SOAP, especially with an eye on the future. The result is that we see the introduction of Exchange Server Objects (XSO) in Exchange 2003 to support SOAP access to Exchange functions.

1.7.4 Too many servers

Another issue that Microsoft has to address is the apparent support inside its development groups for the "one server, one application" approach to life. In the Windows NT 3.51 era, when hardware was much slower than today, this attitude was understandable, but it is hard to comprehend today. For example, in 1996 the first deployments of Exchange proceeded on 100-MHz servers equipped with 128 MB of memory and 4 GB of disk. These servers supported 250 to 400 mailboxes, and administrators did not rush to install anything else on the computer. Hardware improved over time, and so did the operating system, yet the almost subconscious idea lingered that you could only run one server application per physical computer. Microsoft has not helped by engineering server applications that cannot coexist, such as SharePoint Portal Server 2001 and Exchange 2000, but at least we now see initiatives such as server virtualization and partitioning becoming more common. The servers of today are far more powerful than the mainframes of even the recent past, so it is unacceptable to discover that you need multiple servers to run all the applications you need. The result is that everyone seems to deploy too many Windows servers, which drives up cost, administrative complexity, and even licensing fees when you deploy additional servers to manage and protect the extra servers. Microsoft needs to architect products to coexist together and then develop solid development and testing procedures to force this to happen. After all, if the world's biggest software development company cannot do this, who can?

1.7.5 Security

Securing Exchange is perhaps the area of biggest administrative change in the product's lifetime. Administrators used to worry only about file-level viruses that could infect their servers through floppy disks or network shares. Now, it is a constant battle against email viruses, hacker attacks, IIS meltdowns, spam, and all the other problems that seem to occur in an increasingly virulent world. Microsoft has improved Exchange 2003's capabilities so that the server can better filter incoming messages, protect distribution lists, and accommodate antivirus software (through the advent of the Intelligent Message Filter—see section 9.16), but this area is going to remain a challenge for both Microsoft and system administrators. The bad guys keep on getting smarter and the good guys have to run to keep up.

1.8 Moving on

Even with all its flaws and some maddening experiences, Exchange 2000 is still an extremely good email server. The only pity is that the need to roll out Windows 2000 and the AD has prevented so many people from finding this out. Exchange 2003 is even better. It is a solid, robust, scalable, and reliable email server that is packed full of functionality and supports a huge range of clients from smartphones to Web browsers. The biggest problem I have now is how to tell the story of Exchange 2003. Time to make a start.

2
Exchange and the Active Directory

Messaging systems depend on directories for a variety of needs. Fetching email addresses for users and knowing what server their mailboxes are located on is perhaps the most obvious, but directories also hold large amounts of configuration data, such as how servers connect together, permissions, and so on.

In the first generation of Exchange, the Directory Store (DS) held all of this data. The link between the DS and the other Exchange components, such as the Store and the MTA, that need to access directory data is simple, since all of the components reside on the same physical server. Thus, a network outage might prevent a first-generation Exchange server from contacting other servers to transfer email or stop users from connecting to mailboxes, but it will not stop the interaction between the different Exchange components. Because the DS is located on the same server, access to its data is also fast and reliable.

You cannot deny that having a local copy of the directory on every Exchange server has its advantages (such as always having a local directory available rather than having to depend on a network service), but it also implies a lot of replication traffic to keep all the copies of the directory synchronized. As the number of servers grows in an organization, the replication traffic expands dramatically. In addition, Microsoft designed the Exchange DS to be single purpose so other applications cannot use it. Exchange 2000 addressed these issues by supporting the AD and moving to a network-based directory model where servers do not maintain local copies of the directory. Instead, the AD comprises a set of Domain Controllers (DCs) and Global Catalog servers (GCs) distributed within the network to provide directory services to applications and the operating system. DCs hold a complete copy of all the objects belonging to a domain and a copy of objects replicated in the forest-wide configuration naming context (NC).

GCs hold a complete copy of all objects in their own domain plus partial copies of objects from all other domains within the forest.

Exchange accesses DCs and GCs for different purposes. DCs provide essential system configuration data, such as details of the servers and connectors installed within an organization. GCs provide information about user mailboxes and email addresses. The Routing Engine uses data taken from the GCs to route email, and MAPI clients, such as Outlook, use the same data as the Global Address List (GAL). Other clients use LDAP requests to search and retrieve information about recipients from the AD. Other examples of AD consumers include the Active Directory Connector, Recipient Update Service, and the Exchange System Manager (ESM) console.

2.1 The Active Directory

Messaging people know what a directory is because they have had to deal with many different versions of directories over the years. Exchange has had its own directory, Lotus Notes has its address book, and the Sun iPlanet mail server has an LDAP directory.

From a messaging standpoint, the ideal directory is:

- Available: If an application depends on a directory, it must be there all the time. If the application is distributed around an enterprise, often on a global level, then the directory must also be distributed and available wherever user populations or servers are found.

- Secure: Most access to a directory is in read operations, with a relatively small proportion of writes. Any access must be secure. Users must be able to see information they are authorized to access but nothing else. Only privileged users or applications should be able to update the directory.

- Scalable: Many Exchange servers support small communities, but some support very large corporate populations that span several hundred thousand mailboxes. As a directory gets larger, its responsiveness must be consistent.

- Accessible: The directory should be open to as many clients as possible through the provision of different client interfaces. Once they get in, all clients should be able to perform roughly equivalent operations against the directory at comparable speeds. In other words, no client should be favored or penalized in relation to another.

2.1 The Active Directory

The Internet has driven the definition of many standards to the benefit of everyone. LDAP and SMTP are obvious examples. During the debates to formulate standards, the question of how to define a directory has been considered many times. Here is a widely quoted description that comes from the "Introduction to Slapd and Slurpd," published by the University of Michigan:[1]

> "A directory is like a database but tends to contain more descriptive, attribute-based information. The information in a directory is generally read much more often than it is written. As a consequence, directories don't usually implement the complicated transaction or rollback schemes regular databases use for doing high-volume complex updates. Directory updates are typically simple all-or-nothing changes, if they are allowed at all. Directories are tuned to give quick response to high-volume lookup or search operations. They may have the ability to replicate information widely in order to increase availability and reliability while reducing response time. When directory information is replicated, temporary inconsistencies between the replicas may be OK, as long as they get in sync eventually."

It is good to compare this description of the characteristics of the ideal directory with Microsoft's implementation of the AD. In most cases, Microsoft has done a good job of matching up the AD against the definitions, at least on a feature-by-feature level. Implementation is the true test of any software, and there is no doubt that a bad implementation will ruin any product.

From Windows 2003, AD supports application partitioning to allow applications to create their own section of the directory and decide what data to hold and how and where it replicates. Some applications generate configuration and other data that is unsuited to the replication and control mechanisms used by a general-purpose directory such as AD, so it is good to have the ability to exercise more control. For example, if you install AD-integrated DNS in a new Windows 2003 deployment, DNS uses its own partition to avoid the need to replicate DNS information to GCs. However, neither Exchange 2000 nor 2003 use this feature.

2.1.1 Multiple forests or just one

When Microsoft initially released Exchange 2000, best practice for AD designs was very simple. Exchange supports a single organization per AD forest, so Microsoft and system integrators told customers that they should

---

1. Slapd is the standalone LDAP daemon, while Slurpd is the standalone LDAP update replication daemon. You can find the paper by using any of the common search engines. A good example is at http://www.aeinc.com/aeslapd/slapd-admin/1.html.

deploy a single AD forest and use that as the foundation of their deployment. Another major point of best practice was a focus on reducing the overall number of domains to simplify the infrastructure in response to the fact that most companies had deployed far too many Windows NT domains.

Some customers required multiple Exchange organizations, perhaps because they wanted to keep separate email systems for different operating units within the company—less often when they wanted to use different AD schemas. However, because no utilities existed to integrate the AD forests to create a single view of the Exchange organizations, not many companies took this route.

Over time, system designers realized that the restriction of one organization per forest limited the flexibility of Exchange in a period of great corporate volatility when mergers and acquisitions were the order of the day. Another influence was the realization that the forest is the only true security boundary for Windows—not the domain, as had been assumed. Since 2000, we have seen increasing interest in running multiple Exchange organizations and a corresponding requirement for utilities to bridge the gap between the organizations. Microsoft's normal answer to this need includes products such as Metadirectory Services (MMS), utilities to synchronize public folders between organizations, and documentation describing how to implement Exchange in a multiforest environment. Other companies have their own utilities. For example, HP's LDAP Directory Synchronization Utility[2] (LDSU) synchronizes entries from any LDAP-compliant directory, and you can use LDSU to synchronize entries between different instances of the AD.

If you start an AD design today, you may consider running two or more Exchange organizations and therefore two or more instances of AD. It is true that the larger the company, the more obvious the need to consider the multiforest option. If you are in this situation, you should take the time to read the latest opinions on the subject, including the white papers available from Microsoft. For now, we can summarize the situation as follows:

- The Exchange architecture assumes that servers run inside a single forest, so you attain full functionality immediately by deploying this model. Therefore, always commence a design by assuming that you will use a single instance of the AD and a single Exchange organization. This is always the best option when you operate a highly centralized management model where you can maintain

---

2. Search HP's Web site at www.hp.com for the latest information about LDSU.

tight control over security and access to sensitive systems such as domain controllers.

- Only consider a multiforest deployment when you have good need for such an implementation. For example, you may have an administrative model that gives great control to many units within the company, all of which want to manage their own servers and applications. Remember that multiple forests increase complexity and introduce the need for synchronization that does not exist in a single forest. In addition, you will probably need to deploy additional hardware (servers) to form the core of each forest. You may also need to deploy multiple instances of add-on applications to serve each forest. For example, a single instance of the BlackBerry Enterprise Server may be sufficient to serve users who have mailboxes on multiple servers in a small Exchange organization. With multiple organizations, you would need multiple BlackBerry Enterprise Servers. Management software may not be able to monitor and control servers in multiple organizations.

We can assume that the number of multiforest deployments will increase in the coming years and that Microsoft will respond with better tools and better flexibility in both Windows and Exchange. The basic building block remains the AD, so that is where we need to head next.

2.1.2 Components of the Active Directory

The AD is core to Windows and provides the repository for the operating system to store essential information required to run itself as well as dependent applications such as Exchange. As shown in Figure 2.1, many different objects can be stored in the AD, including:

- Users and groups
- Security credentials such as X.509 certificates
- Information about computers and applications
- Configuration data, including information about Windows sites
- DNS routing information

The schema defines the information held in the AD, including objects and their attributes. Applications can extend the schema to define their own objects or add additional properties to existing objects. Exchange relies on the AD for all user management, including the creation, modification, and deletion of mailboxes, and therefore extends the default schema to add

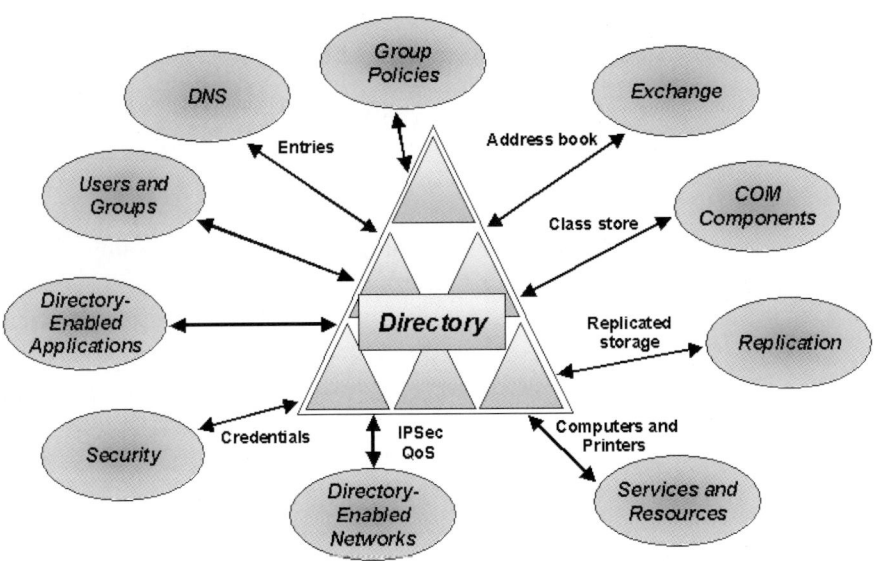

Figure 2.1   *The contents of the Active Directory.*

support for messaging properties, such as email addresses, the store where a user's mailbox is located, and so on. You can add messaging attributes to any object that can be mail enabled (users, contacts, public folders, and groups), although the same set of attributes is not available for each object type. A discussion about how you can change the schema begins is given in section 2.8.3.

2.1.3 Moving to a Windows namespace

The AD uses a hierarchical namespace. From Windows 2000 onward, DNS provides the default naming service for Windows, so Windows aligns the AD namespace with DNS. All objects in the directory have distinguished names based on the DNS namespace as implemented within a company. This is quite different from Windows NT, which uses a flat namespace.

Figure 2.2 illustrates the difference. The Windows NT namespace comes from a set of three master account domains (in this case, named dom1, dom2, and dom3). We also find that each master account domain has a set of resource domains beneath it. Each of the resource domains has a separate namespace, and one-way trust relationships form the link between each resource domain and its master account domain. Most large Exchange 5.5 deployments use this type of Windows NT domain structure to isolate

2.1 The Active Directory

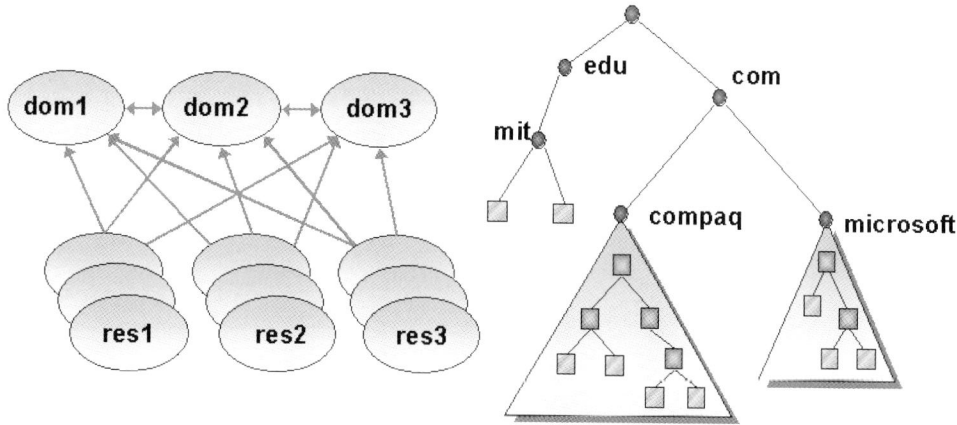

Figure 2.2 *Windows NT and AD namespaces.*

the Exchange servers from the master account domains and ensure that access to the servers is limited to accounts that hold the necessary permissions in the resource domain.

2.1.4 Forests, trees, and domains

DNS provides the foundation for the Windows namespace. A single Windows domain is a very simple namespace, but most organizations will have a namespace consisting of one or more trees of Windows domains. Windows defines a domain tree as a hierarchical organization of domains joined by trust relationships. Trees may be joined together to form a single forest, but in some cases the trees will be kept separate and may not be joined at all.

Figure 2.3 illustrates a design for an AD forest that spans three trees: one each for Compaq, Tandem, and Digital, the companies that merged in the 1996–1998 period to form Compaq Computer Corporation. Of course, Compaq merged with HP in 2002 and the AD designers had a chance to redo a Windows NT migration again, because HP still used Windows NT. After looking at various options, they made the decision to continue using the same AD forest and use their well-proven migration techniques to move users and other objects over into the forest. However, the details of how Compaq and HP came together in a technical sense around a common AD forest is enough material for a separate book, so for the moment we can use the original situation at Compaq to explore some of the design issues that you have to consider when you deploy AD.

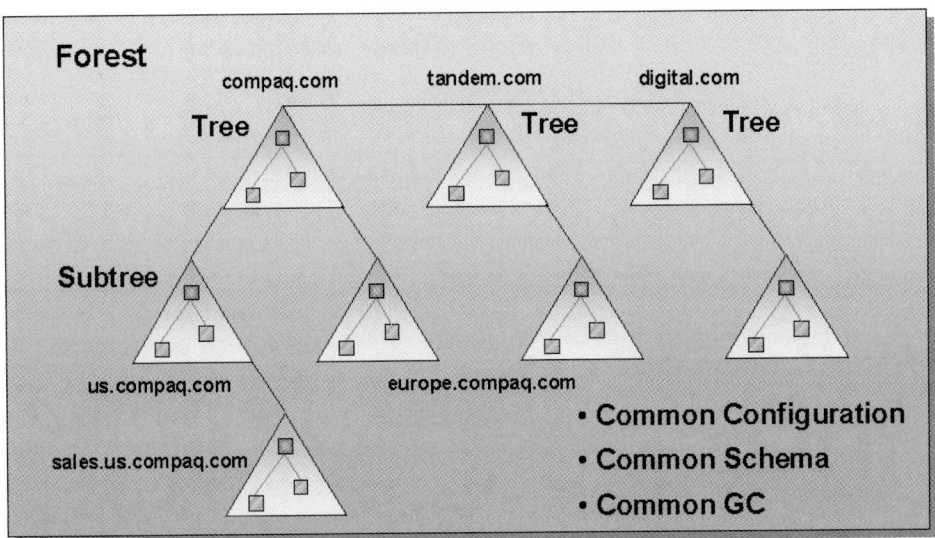

Figure 2.3 *AD forest and trees.*

The domains in each tree have a contiguous namespace, meaning that the namespace has a common root based on the name given to each domain at its level within the tree. Thus, the us.compaq.com domain shares a common namespace with compaq.com, as does the sales.us.compaq.com domain. Windows defines a forest as a collection of trees joined by Kerberos trust relationships. The three trees for Compaq, Tandem, and Digital form a forest, but each tree has its own namespace, which it does not share with the other trees. Thus, we say that a forest has a discontiguous namespace. Each of the trees maintains its own DNS database and namespace, but when you join the trees to form the forest, you can manage it as a single entity, providing you have the appropriate permissions. All the domains in a forest share a common configuration and schema, and the different domains replicate partial details of all of their objects to Global Catalog servers so that we can establish a single view of objects across the entire forest.

When the Compaq designers looked at the right AD structure for the organization, they could have decided to keep separate namespaces for each operating company and unify everything through the forest. However, the namespace was only one issue to consider when deciding what type of design to use. In other situations, such as when an ASP needs to host multiple companies within a single AD, you find that the opposite and multiple namespaces are used, one for each company. Other important factors included the need to unify the three companies with a common network built on the class "A" IP address space owned by Digital[3] and a desire to replace three different Windows NT designs with a common approach.

After considering all of the alternatives, Compaq decided to build a brand new Windows infrastructure instead of upgrading the three Windows NT implementations and attempting to unify objects in a forest of domains. Another factor that drove this decision is that a straight migration of many Windows NT infrastructures does not result in particularly good AD designs. This is understandable when you consider that many of the features exploited by administrators (such as resource domains) are workarounds to compensate for limitations in Windows NT, such as its limited security model. Other large companies took similar decisions when the time came for them to move to Windows 2000 and, in general, the approach of building a new Windows infrastructure and then cloning user accounts when they need to move is a good and valid method of implementing Windows. However, if you run a small company that has a single domain and just a few servers, a direct upgrade is the right path for you to take.

When finally deployed, Compaq's new Windows infrastructure used the cpqcorp.net namespace, retaining the existing compaq.com name for external communications. Servers received cpqcorp.net names as they joined the domain, and users started to use the new namespace as their accounts moved over.

It is worth emphasizing that the decision to use two separate namespaces for internal and external names has nothing whatsoever to do with Windows. Compaq made the decision for administrative convenience to avoid any confusion between internal and external systems and to make it easier to configure proxies for browsers. Thus, because I am located in Europe, I log on to the emea.cpqcorp.net domain. Anyone with experience in the DNS naming convention can scan a name like this and know that the domain is a child of cpqcorp.net, which is under the .net root of the overall DNS namespace. Note that the namespaces used by Windows and DNS can be different. At HP, we now have an hpqcorp.net DNS namespace running with the cpqcorp.net Windows namespace.

---

3. Digital was one of the original companies on the Internet, and as a result held a complete class "A" network. All IP addresses that begin with 16 now belong to Compaq. Network 15 was then added to the mix when HP and Compaq merged in 2002, and a network redesign is under way to decide how best to use these network addresses.

2.1.5 Domain renaming

According to the documentation, you can rename a domain after installation if you run a native-mode Windows 2003 forest. In other words, you can rename a domain in the midst of a deployment without having to reinstall the operating system on all of the controllers in a domain. However, without the XDR-Fixup utility, you cannot use this feature in any domain that supports an Exchange server. XDR-Fixup is available for download from the Microsoft Exchange Web site, and, as its name indicates, it "fixes things up" by adjusting the AD configuration data after a domain rename to allow Exchange to function properly afterward.

2.1.6 The Global Catalog

You can think of the Global Catalog (GC) as a special form of a DC that contains information replicated from every domain in a forest. The GC maintains a collection of every object in the AD, and the copy of the AD maintained on a GC is the closest comparison to the entries held in the "old" Exchange 5.5 Directory Store.

The GC contains full information about every object in its own domain plus partial information about the objects in other domains. You can update the objects from the GC's own domain, but the objects from other domains are read only. Windows defines the partial attribute set replicated by GCs by properties of the attributes set in the AD schema. You can modify attributes to include or exclude them in the replication set, always taking the impact on replication into account.

From a Windows perspective, you can perform updates to the AD schema only at the server that acts as the schema master for the forest. The default set of replicated attributes includes the information necessary to allow the GC to serve as a GAL for Exchange and its clients. The GC also holds information about the membership of universal groups, which can contain objects from any domain in the forest. During authentication, Windows performs a lookup against a GC to build a complete security ticket for a client. Of course, if you only operate a single domain, then all DCs are GCs and Windows can execute the lookup for universal group membership against the same controller. See section 2.6 for further information on how Exchange uses DCs and GCs.

The first DC in a domain is automatically a GC, and you can subsequently promote any other DC to become a GC by modifying the NTDS connection object of the server to mark it as a GC. This action forces the controller to publish a special "_gc" service record into DNS to advertise the fact that it now can act as a GC and begin the process of requesting information from other domains in the forest. At the same time, the server enables port 3268 for read-only access and starts a special "listener thread" in order to respond to replication messages sent to the GC from every other domain in the forest.

Typically, the GC satisfies queries that might be forest wide. For example, universal groups can contain users from any domain in a forest, so the membership of a universal group can only be resolved by consulting the GC, which you can browse to find objects that might not belong to a specific domain. You could find an object by drilling down through each domain in each tree, but it is obviously more convenient to consult the index provided by the GC.

Exchange clients depend on the GAL, so the role of the GC is tremendously important within an Exchange organization. Without easy access to a GC, clients will not be able to consult the GAL, but the dependency on the GC extends even deeper to the heart of Exchange. The Routing Engine validates mail addresses against the GC when it decides how to dispatch messages across available routes, so if replication is incomplete, you may find that you cannot send messages to some users whose mailboxes are located in domains that have problems replicating data to the GC.

2.2 Preparing the Active Directory for Exchange

The Exchange installation procedure includes two components to prepare the AD for Exchange. The ForestPrep component prepares a forest for Exchange by extending the schema and instantiates the Exchange organization in the configuration naming context, while the DomainPrep component prepares a domain to host mail-enabled objects, such as mailboxes, contacts, groups, and public folders, and, of course, Exchange servers.

You must run ForestPrep once, ideally in the root domain and on a server that is close (in network terms) to the schema master. You must run DomainPrep in every domain that hosts an Exchange server or mail-enabled objects, such as users, contacts, groups, or public folders. DomainPrep performs a number of functions, including creating the Exchange Domain Servers Global Security Group and the Exchange Enterprise Servers Local Security Group. As you install Exchange servers into a domain, the installation procedure adds the servers to these groups. Exchange subsequently uses the permissions gained through membership of these groups to read and modify user and configuration data.

DomainPrep also creates the Public Folder Proxy Container in each domain. The Public Folder Proxy object is an AD entry that allows Exchange to generate email addresses for mail-enabled public folders.

Initially, Microsoft did not make an explicit recommendation to run DomainPrep in the root domain of a forest if you did not plan to install any Exchange servers there. As it turns out, Exchange expects to find the public folder proxy object in all domains and if you do not run DomainPrep in the root domain, the Exchange Recipient Update Service may not create public folder proxy objects correctly. Therefore, best practice is to run DomainPrep in every domain that hosts any mail-enabled object plus the root domain.

Note that some minor inconsistencies exist between the AD schema and Exchange 2000 that force you to apply a patch to any forest that contains an Exchange 2000 server before you upgrade the forest to Windows 2003. See Microsoft Knowledge Base article 314649 for details.

2.3 Active Directory replication

As with the Exchange 5.5 Directory Store (DS), the AD replicates data concerning users, contacts, distribution lists (groups), and configuration between servers. Replication is the term that describes the propagation of data from an originating server to other connected servers, in this case within a Windows 2000/2003 domain or forest of domains. We could spend a lot of time delving into the details of how AD replication works, but this topic deserves its own book. Instead, we will look at the basics of AD replication between domain controllers and Global Catalog servers.

Understanding how AD replicates information is important for Windows and Exchange administrators alike. If replication cannot happen, Exchange or any other AD-enabled application will have problems. Successful Exchange projects invariably have a solid AD deployment in place before the installation of the first Exchange server.

2.3.1 Replication basics

The goal of any replication mechanism is to propagate data as quickly as possible so that all participants in replication receive updates and can build their own synchronized copy of the data. After replication has finished, all copies should be consistent. In a fast-moving networked environment, where users and computers update data all the time, it is difficult to achieve a state of perfect replication, so you can consider the AD partition hosted

2.3 Active Directory replication

on any individual DC to be in a state of loose consistency. In other words, while the vast majority of the data in the AD is consistent and synchronized with the server's replication partners, it is likely that outstanding replication operations are en route somewhere in the network. In a perfect world, we would have only one copy of the directory (unlikely a worldwide deployment) or be able to freeze changes for a time to allow all servers to perform any outstanding replication operations to achieve perfect synchronization throughout the network. Unfortunately, we do not live in a perfect world, so we have to be satisfied that the AD is loosely consistent at any point in time.

DCs are responsible for initiating and participating in replication operations. Each DC holds a complete read/write copy of the objects for its domain and acts since a replication partner for other DCs. Replication only occurs between DCs, since member servers do not hold a copy of the AD.

GCs hold a partial read-only copy of the objects for the other domains in the forest as well as the fully writable set of objects for its own domain. We say partial copy, because the GC replicates a subset of the full attribute set of objects from domains other than its own. You can change the AD schema to force replication of additional attributes.

When you compare the replication mechanisms used by Exchange 5.5 and the AD, you find many similarities, but there are important differences in the details of implementation. For example, the AD improves on the way the DS replicates information by implementing attribute-level replication, incorporating a multithreaded replication agent, and through the concept of high watermark vectors.

Attribute-level replication reduces the amount of data that a replication partner sends or receives after a change has occurred. The Exchange 5.5 DS replicates complete objects, even if only a single attribute is changed. This means that the DS must send between 4,000 and 6,000 bytes to each replication partner for every changed object. The AD only replicates the content of changed attributes, plus the GUID to identify the object and data to track replication. For example, if you change the display name for a user account, then the AD only sends that attribute to replication partners. The net effect is that the AD throttles back network traffic to only the size of the changed data and a buffer (perhaps 600 bytes in total, depending on the attribute that you update). In addition, the AD uses a multithreaded replication agent to be able to handle a high volume of replication requests.

To help monitor and control the flow of replication, the AD maintains a high watermark vector table on each DC. The table contains a row for every replication partner of the DC and includes the partner's highest known USN. A USN is a 64-bit number maintained by each controller to indicate how many changes have occurred on the domain controller. The AD also maintains USNs for every object in the directory and for every attribute in an object, so multiple USNs are involved in the replication process. Maintaining USNs at an attribute level allows the AD to control replication at that level rather than replicating complete objects.

As you can see in Figure 2.4, the AD tracks the changes made to an object; you can see both the USN value when the AD created the object (135,721) and the current USN (70,162,237). These USN values are specific to a DC; you will see other values if you connect to different DCs in the same domain. However, if we take the figures at face value, then this DC (part of HP's cpqcorp.net forest) processed over 70 million separate changes that it replicated to this domain controller in 33 months. Some of these changes originated on the DC, but given the size of HP's AD, the majority of changes are likely to have originated on other DCs. Another way of looking at this is that the domain controller processed nearly 71,000 changes in each of the 989 days since it originally created this object.

It is common to see such a heavy volume of changes in a large organization and this illustrates the replication traffic that the AD can handle, plus

Figure 2.4
Active Directory USNs.

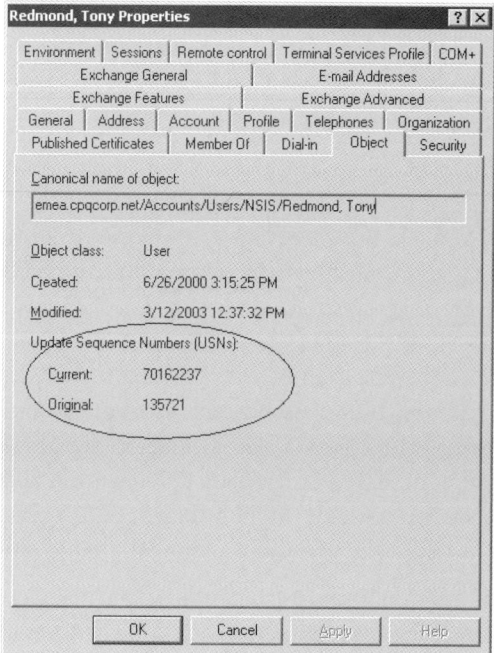

2.3 Active Directory replication

the wisdom of using a 64-bit number (a GUID) to hold USNs. Technically, when the number overflows because of the number of changes applied to a controller, the USN reverts to one and starts over again. This will provoke a huge amount of replication within a network, since the controller will ask its replication partners for "any change since USN 1," but you shouldn't worry too much about this situation, since it is extremely unlikely to occur in our lifetime (just like Y2K!).

2.3.2 When Active Directory replication happens

As with Exchange 5.5, the AD does not dispatch replication data immediately after changes occur. If this were to happen, updates might swamp the network if a program applied many changes over a short period. Consider what happens when you synchronize data from an external directory with the AD. Normally, synchronization processes update AD entries by applying instructions in an LDIF load file or through a direct LDAP connection to directory synchronization process using a tool such as MMS or HP's LDSU. The AD can process these instructions to add, change, or delete objects very quickly (programs have been written to add objects at well over 200 per second), and if replication were triggered after each individual update, everything would halt. Instead, the replication mechanism gathers changes together and sends out packages of replication data that its replication partners can apply. The exact method depends on whether the AD is replicating within a Windows site or between Windows sites, but in all cases the AD packages data instead of sending changes to individual objects.

Any change to the AD provokes some replication activity. The basic operations are:

- Object creation: for example, when you create a new user object, contact, or group.

- Object modification: for example, when you add a new SMTP address to a user, add a user or contact to a mail-enabled group, or if you move a user from one organizational unit to another.

- Object deletion: AD does not remove an object immediately. Instead, just as with Exchange 5.5, the AD creates a tombstone for the object and replicates this to other DCs to inform them that it has deleted the object. Tombstones have a default expiration time of 60 days, and, after this time, the AD permanently removes all trace of the object and completes the deletion by replicating the final state change.

The AD makes a distinction between two types of write operations. When you initiate an operation on a DC, the update that the AD applies to its local copy is an originating write. A replicated write is an operation that occurs as the result of incoming data that arrives from a replication partner for application to the local AD database. For example, if we increase the mailbox quota for a user on the HPDC1 DC and the AD then replicates the information to the HPDC2 DC, we refer to the update applied on HPDC2 as a replicated write.

The AD uses two internal GUIDs for each controller: one for the server itself and one for the database. The server GUID remains constant, even if the server name changes. The AD allocates a unique Server GUID to each DC and uses it to reference and identify specific DCs during replication operations.

The AD also creates a GUID to identify the copy of a database on a DC and sets it to be the same value as the server GUID. If you ever need to restore a database from a backup, the AD alters the database GUID to inform other DCs that you have restored the database and may therefore be in an inconsistent state and need to backfill and recover some previously replicated data.

2.3.3 Active Directory naming contexts

In Windows 2000, the AD organizes data into three separate naming contexts (NC). Windows 2003 introduces the application NC. A naming context is a tree of objects. In some definitions of directory terminology, a naming context represented the level of replication or referral within the directory, as follows:

- The configuration NC contains the objects that represent the structure of the directory (controllers, site topology, etc.). Because it uses the AD as its repository and stores information about its organization (connectors, servers, administrative groups, etc.) in the configuration NC, this part of the AD is very important to Exchange 2000/2003.

- The schema NC contains all the classes and attributes that define individual objects and their attributes.

- The domain NC defines all the other objects, such as users, groups, contacts, and computers. A separate domain NC exists for each domain in the forest.

Domains act as partitions within the AD. To some degree, domains also act as a replication boundary, but not for the schema, which the AD shares throughout the forest, or for the partial set of domain data that the AD replicates to GCs. Of course, if your deployment manages to use just one domain across a high-speed network, then the replication issue becomes very simple indeed and you will probably not have to worry about where you replicate data to and how long it takes to get there. On the other hand, even a single domain can run into replication issues if low-bandwidth links connect the sites and the topology is overly complex. Most corporate deployments will use multiple domains arranged into an AD forest. In these scenarios, the scope of replication becomes a very important issue, especially when you deploy an application that makes extensive use of the AD (such as Exchange) on top of the basic Windows infrastructure. For example, if AD replication does not work predictably across the forest, then the contents of the GAL will be inaccurate.

Naming contexts set boundaries for data replication. The configuration and schema are unique within a forest, which means that the AD must replicate these contexts to every DC in the forest, so they have a forest-wide scope. The AD only replicates domain objects to the controllers within a domain, so this naming context has a domain-wide scope. Besides storing the domain NC of its own domain, the AD includes a partial replica of all other domain NCs in the database held by a GC to build a complete picture across the forest. The partial replica of a domain NC contains roughly 30 percent of the data stored in the full replica of the NC, so each GC that you create incurs a replication penalty that grows with the number of domains in the forest.

Exchange exploits the fact that the GC provides a full view of the user objects in a forest to build address lists such as the GAL through LDAP filters that it applies to the copy of the AD hosted by a GC. The LDAP filter essentially "finds" every mail-enabled object known to the GC whose showInAddressBook flag is set to true. Because its content forms the basis of the GAL, the GC is extremely important to Exchange. For example, when Outlook clients want to look up an address in the GAL, behind the scenes Exchange fetches the information from the GC and responds to the client. The Exchange Routing Engine makes heavy use of GC data, because it needs to check email addresses in message headers to decide how best to route messages.

A typical AD forest that supports Exchange has one GAL, but you can create more with LDAP filters, a feature often used by service providers that supply Exchange to companies. In a Windows 2000 forest, the technical limit for the number of GALs or address lists in the forest is 800, and the limit comes from the number of values in an AD multivalued attribute.

With Windows 2003, the limit increases to 1,300. However, these are theoretical limits, and you would quickly lose yourself in a forest of GALs if you attempted to create so many address lists. The vast bulk of Exchange implementations are happy with just one GAL.

While Exchange makes heavy use of the GC for address validation and message routing, it also needs to access configuration data for management and other operational purposes. For example, you cannot navigate through a complete view of the organization if ESM cannot read it from the data held in the Microsoft Exchange container in the configuration NC. Figure 2.5 illustrates how Exchange stores information about connectors in the configuration NC. Exchange's DSAccess component manages the interaction between Exchange and the various DCs and GCs that are available to a server.

As you can see in Figure 2.5, the AD holds Exchange configuration data in a container called "Microsoft Exchange" under the "Services" container. A separate container holds the configuration data for the Active Directory Connector, if you install this component. The structure of the Exchange configuration data is similar to the structure you see when you view the organization through ESM. When you use ESM to manage Exchange,

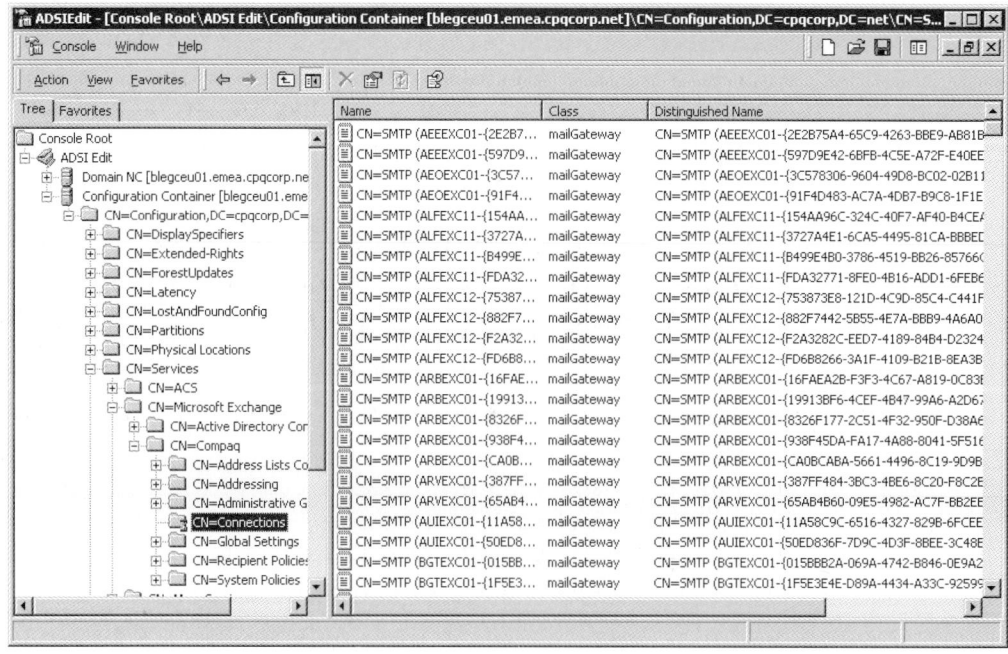

Figure 2.5 *Exchange routing information in the configuration NC.*

ESM reads the configuration data from the nearest DC. Generally, the larger the Exchange organization, the slower ESM performs, because of the amount of data it fetches from the AD.

You should only work with Exchange configuration data through ESM, mostly because its user interface will protect you from making mistakes, such as deleting an essential container. Sometimes, the need might arise to eradicate completely all traces of Exchange from an AD forest, perhaps because you have made a mistake (such as using the wrong organization name) when you first installed Exchange and you want to start over. You can use the ADSIEDIT utility (see section 2.10) to remove Exchange from an organization very quickly. Simply select the "Microsoft Exchange" container, right-click, and select "Delete" from the menu. Afterward, you need to wait for replication to occur to complete the removal of Exchange from the forest. This action will not roll back the schema changes that Exchange makes to the AD, but it does mean that you can restart the deployment of a brand new organization with ForestPrep. Note that removing Exchange in this way is a very drastic option, so be sure that you have good reason to remove the organization in this manner before you proceed. The best idea is to deinstall all Exchange servers from the organization, which should remove the organization when you remove the last server. Failing this, Knowledge Base article 312878 documents the approved Microsoft method to remove an Exchange organization from AD, while article 260378 provides some useful background information.

2.3.4 Transforming DCs to GCs

You turn DCs into GCs by changing the server's NTDS Settings property through the Active Directory Sites and Services console. Navigate to the site that holds the server, select the server, and view its NTDS Settings properties, as shown in Figure 2.6. Check the "Global Catalog" box to make the controller start to pull information from other domains. If you clear the checkbox, the server will revert to a DC and the AD will flush data from other domains from the local database. This process may not happen quickly, because it depends on the number of objects from other domains that exist in the local database. The KCC removes these objects every time it runs and spreads the load by deleting about 8,000 objects an hour. It is, therefore, obvious that it can take some days before a DC finally purges data for other domains from its database and, during this time, you cannot reverse the process and make the DC a GC again. In large forests, it may be faster to remove the DC, reinstall the server from scratch, and then reload the AD from media—but only if you run Windows 2003!

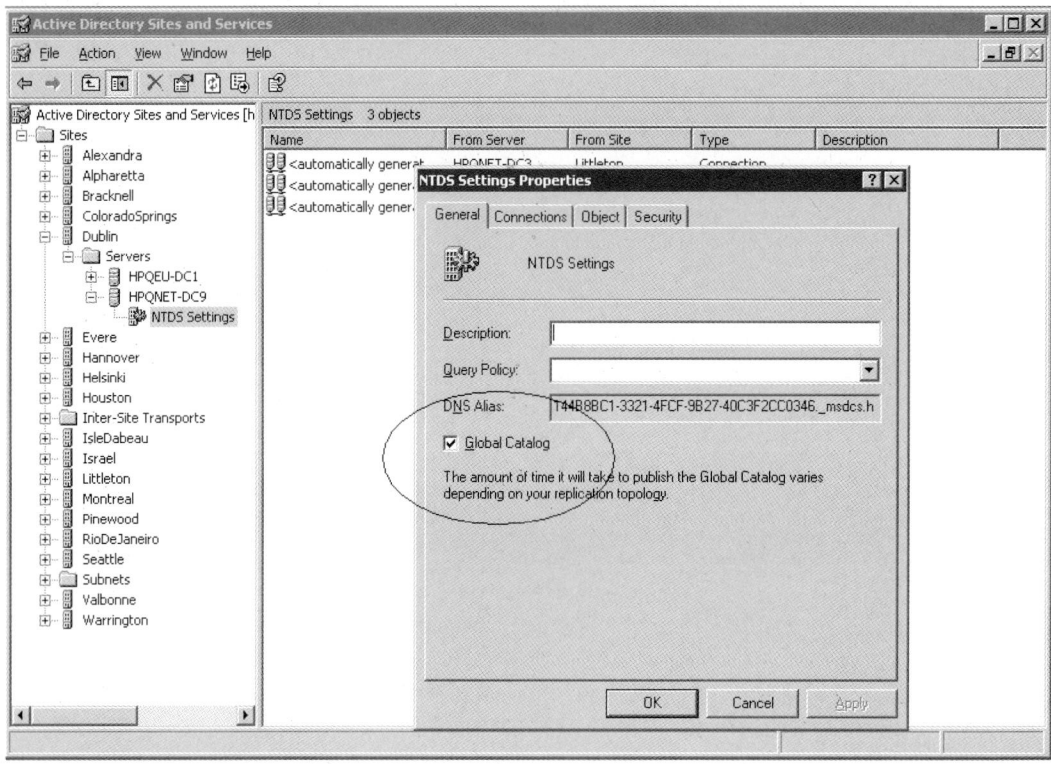

Figure 2.6   *Setting the Global Catalog property for a DC.*

As discussed earlier, changing a DC to a GC obviously generates replication activity. If you add a second GC to a site, the new GC always copies the partial replicas of other domain NCs from the existing GC. This avoids the need to broadcast replication requests outside the site boundary and thus potentially generate a flood of replication data within the forest. Otherwise, the exact impact on a network and Windows infrastructure depends on the complexity of the site topology, the number of domains in the forest, and the number of controllers involved in the replication process. Another point to consider is that changing a Windows 2000 controller to a GC updates the way that MAPI clients access the server through NSPI, and you have to reboot the server before clients can use it as a GC.

There is no good answer to how quickly the AD can replicate data from one part of a forest to another. Microsoft recommends using tools such as the Performance Monitor to review the performance of the NTDS Objects (such as DRA Outward Bytes Total and DRA Inward Bytes Total, or the total bytes consumed in outward and inward replication activity). However,

2.3 Active Directory replication

this is a rudimentary approach to the problem, and it is better to use the more sophisticated tools from companies such as NetIQ, Quest, or NetPro. In addition, to help gain an insight into potential problem areas for replication between sites and controllers, system integrators such as HP develop tools such as ADlatency and the OpenView Active Directory replication monitor to measure end-to-end replication latency and the overall effectiveness of replication inside a forest.

Exchange's dependency on GC availability and AD replication in general illustrates the point that unlike Windows NT domain designs, you cannot approach a design exercise for the AD in isolation from the applications that will use the infrastructure. This is a major and far-reaching change for any company that traditionally keeps infrastructure design teams separated from application design teams. It is common to find design teams that only focus on a specific part of the infrastructure and never consult anyone outside their immediate sphere of influence. The close and almost intimate dependency of Exchange 2000/2003 on the AD means that successful design teams treat the infrastructure as a whole rather than as separate parts. It is worth noting that while Exchange has a tremendous dependency on proper AD deployment and operation, you also have to manage other Windows and network components to bring everything together. For example, if you do not deploy DNS properly, DSAccess may not be able to locate DCs and GCs to fetch configuration and recipient information.

2.3.5 USNs and replication

As mentioned earlier, the AD uses USNs to track changes made to its objects. This is a variation of the mechanism used in Exchange 5.5 DS, which also uses USNs to track changes. The major difference between the two directories is that USNs are stored on a per-attribute basis to allow attribute-level replication to work. As with Exchange 5.5, there are two different USNs maintained for each object. The DC sets the value of the USNCreated attribute for a new object to the value of the server USN when it creates the object and then updates the USNChanged attribute each time it processes an update for the object. In this case, the AD sets the value of USNChanged to the current value of the server USN where the originating write occurs. You can see the value of a server USN by examining server properties, as shown in Figure 2.7. Now that we know the basics, we can track what happens during a simple set of replication operations.

This scenario uses two controllers in a domain called HPDC1 and HPDC2. The servers have been in operation for some time, so the values of the server USNs reflect the number of AD updates. For this example, we

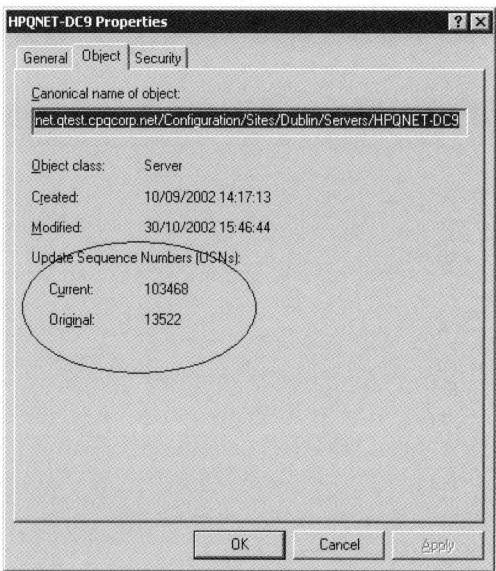

Figure 2.7
Server USN.

assume that HPDC1 begins with USN 10,925 and HPDC2 starts with 11,933.

We begin replication by creating a new user object on HPDC1. The AD automatically allocates the next USN in sequence based on the server USN, or 10,926. Note that the allocation of a USN is a one-time operation and the USN can never be reused, even if the create operation is interrupted and fails to complete. The next update on HPDC1 increases the USN by one. Table 2.1 lists a subset of the values maintained in the user object table in the database on HPDC1.

The following extract illustrates a number of important points:

- The DC automatically adds a number of values to each attribute to control replication.

- Each attribute populated as the AD creates the new user object receives the USN allocated to the object. The "Originating" USN is set to the same value, because the operation is initiated on the local server. This value will change as the AD updates attributes.

- The AD populates the "Originating DC GUID" with the GUID from the server where it creates the object. Again, this value can change if another DC updates an attribute.

- The version number is set to 1, because the DC has just created the object. This number is incremented as updates are applied. The AD

2.3 Active Directory replication

Table 2.1 *User Table in Active Directory (1)*

Attribute	Value	USN	Version	Timestamp	Originating DC GUID	Originating USN
First name	John	10,926	1	200208311245	HPDC1 GUID	10,926
Surname	Doe	10,926	1	200208311245	HPDC1 GUID	10,926
Mailbox server	HPDC1	10,926	1	200208311245	HPDC1 GUID	10,926
SMTP address	John.Doe@acme.com	10,926	1	200208311245	HPDC1 GUID	10,926

uses the version number to resolve replication conflicts that might occur if two or more controllers attempt to update the same attribute at roughly the same time. Conflicts are resolved by accepting the update with the highest version number. This is especially important when resolving conflicts for multivalued attributes (such as groups)—for example, if you make two changes to a group on one DC that overwrites a single change made to the same group on another DC later on.

- A timestamp (stored as a quadword) taken from the current date and time on the server is saved. The AD uses timestamps as a last resort to resolve replication conflicts that might occur if two or more controllers attempt to update the same attribute at roughly the same time and end up with a version number that is the same. Conflicts are resolved by accepting the last update according to the timestamps, using the timestamp from the originating write to arbitrate the conflict.

Note also that the AD assigns the new object the current value of the server USN (10,926) in its USNCreated and USNChanged attributes. We now replicate the information to HPDC2, which inserts the new information into its copy of the directory. Table 2.2 shows the values from HPDC2.

The AD changes the USN to reflect the server USN on HPDC2. The AD also assigns this value (11,934) to the USNChanged attribute, because this is the initial creation of the object on this controller. The timestamp now contains the date and time when HPDC2 applied the update. The originating DC GUID and the originating USN are still the values from HPDC1, because this is the controller where the update originated. We now see the difference between an originating write and a replicated write.

Table 2.3 demonstrates what happens after you update the user's title on HPDC2. We populate a previously blank attribute, which forces the USN

Table 2.2 User Table in Active Directory (2)

Attribute	Value	USN	Version	Timestamp	Originating DC GUID	Originating USN
First name	John	11,934	1	200208311247	HPDC1 GUID	10,926
Surname	Doe	11,934	1	200208311247	HPDC1 GUID	10,926
Mailbox server	HPDC1	11,934	1	200208311247	HPDC1 GUID	10,926
SMTP address	John.Doe@acme.com	11,934	1	200208311247	HPDC1 GUID	10,926

on HPDC2 to move to 11,935. The AD also updates the USNChanged value to 11,935. The AD then sets the originating DC GUID for this attribute to HPDC2, because the update originates from this controller, so the AD also updates the originating USN to the USN from HPDC2. Eventually, replication will occur back to HPDC1, which results in the values shown in Table 2.4. The timestamp is set to the value of the originating write.

The important things here are that the USN has been incremented according to the server USN for HPDC1, but because the write originated on HPDC2, the AD takes its server GUID and USN and uses them to update the database on HPDC1. The AD also updates the timestamp. However, the AD leaves the USNCreated value for the object unaltered at 10,926 but updates the USNChanged value to 10,927. Note that the AD leaves all the other attributes alone, since it only needs to update the value of the Title attribute.

While it may seem obvious to keep track of the controller that last updated an attribute by holding the server GUID, the role of the originat-

Table 2.3 User Table in Active Directory (3)

Attribute	Value	USN	Version	Timestamp	Originating DC GUID	Originating USN
First name	John	11,934	1	200208311245	HPDC1 GUID	10,926
Surname	Doe	11,934	1	200208311245	HPDC1 GUID	10,926
Mailbox server	HPDC1	11,934	1	200208311245	HPDC1 GUID	10,926
Title	Consultant	11,935	1	200208311255	HPDC2 GUID	11,935
SMTP address	John.Doe@acme.com	11,934	1	200208311245	HPDC1 GUID	10,926

2.3 Active Directory replication

Table 2.4 *User Table in Active Directory (4)*

Attribute	Value	USN	Version	Timestamp	Originating DC GUID	Originating USN
First name	John	10,926	1	200208311245	HPDC1 GUID	10,926
Surname	Doe	10,926	1	200208311245	HPDC1 GUID	10,926
Mailbox server	HPDC1	10,926	1	200208311245	HPDC1 GUID	10,926
Title	Consultant	10,927	1	200208311255	HPDC2 GUID	11,935
SMTP address	John.Doe@acme.com	10,926	1	200208311245	HPDC1 GUID	10,926

ing USN might be more obscure. The way that the AD uses the originating USN becomes more important as you increase the number of DCs that participate in replication. In fact, the AD uses the originating USN for propagation dampening, or the ability to stop replication operations from progressing if the AD has already updated the local database after an interchange of replication data with another controller. Propagation dampening is very important in large networks, since it eliminates unnecessary traffic and reduces the amount of system resources that are required to keep the directory in a consistent state.

2.3.6 Urgent replication

The normal replication process is sufficient to ensure that the AD replicates updates to attributes, such as telephone numbers, titles, or even email addresses between DCs, reasonably quickly. Two situations exist when fast replication is required. These are when a user account is locked out and when a new set of identifiers is issued by the RID master.

AD supports the concept of "forced" replication to get updates to domain controllers as quickly as possible after you lock out or disable accounts. This feature exists to prevent users from moving between domain controllers and logging in after an administrator has disabled or locked their accounts. If AD depended on normal replication in these instances, the danger exists that the newly locked out user could still authenticate against a controller that has not yet received the update and so continue to access resources. You should realize that this mechanism does not prevent users who previously logged on to the network from accessing the resources until their Kerberos ticket lifetime expires. In case of NTLM authentication, the users can continue to access resources until they log off.

Note that AD does not consider password updates as urgent. When you update your password, the controller that you make the change with replicates the new password to the PDC emulator master, which then replicates the updated password to other domain controllers in the next replication cycle. Note that the site topology might prevent a controller from communicating with the PDC emulator, but normal intersite replication will eventually get the change through.

Finally, if the RID master issues a new set of identifiers to a DC to allow it to generate unique identifiers for new accounts, the AD must send that information quickly to its destination. In all these cases, fast replication or rather a faster form of replication is performed by immediately sending out change notifications to replication partners, which then respond by pulling the update from the originating controller.

2.3.7 Intra- and intersite replication

Exchange 4.0 introduced the concept of a site to reflect locality in terms of network connectivity. The AD also uses the concept of a site but with some subtle differences. An Exchange site is a collection of servers that share good network connectivity, often because all the servers in the site are in a common location (office, city, country, or even continent). The definition of a Windows site is somewhat stricter. A Windows site is composed of a collection of one or more IP subnets, but, as with an Exchange site, a Windows site usually shares good bandwidth between the servers—preferably at least 256 KB.

In logical terms, as shown in Figure 2.8, a Windows infrastructure builds sites on top of the physical network, and sites map the physical network to create the AD site topology. Another way of thinking about this is to remember that sites are collections of servers in a location, whereas domains are collections of objects that may exist across multiple sites. In actuality, when you deploy your first Windows domain, it goes into the default site (called "default-first-site"). New DCs that join the domain also go into the same site unless you decide to create other sites to accommodate the requirements of the network. You introduce a domain into a site by creating a replica (DC) for the domain in the site. A domain may span many sites, and a site can host multiple domains as long as a DC for each domain is present in the site.

Windows limits domain NC replication to synchronous RPCs. This means that you can only include servers in a domain if they can establish

2.3 Active Directory replication

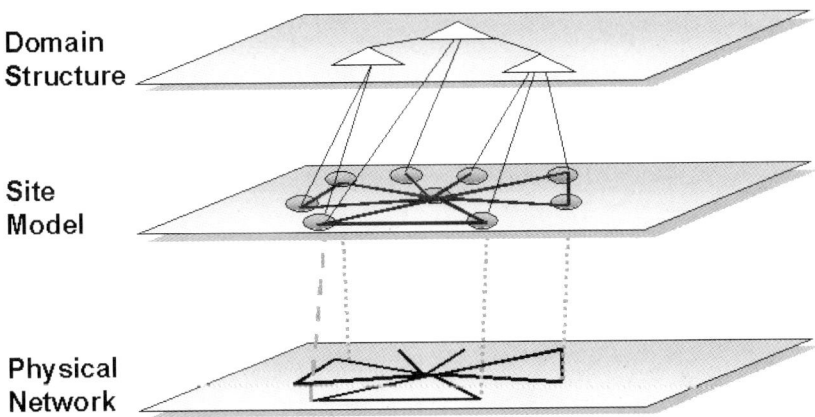

Figure 2.8
Windows domains, sites, and the network.

RPC connectivity with the other servers in the domain. The connection is not limited to a LAN, but within a WAN you find that RPCs are sensitive to latency and network availability and may time out or otherwise fail to complete. The requirement to support RPC connectivity means that some designs use domains to restrict replication and end up with more domains than strictly necessary. The AD can replicate the configuration and schema NCs through asynchronous SMTP messages, so replication can truly span the world. In this case, the AD uses the Windows SMTP service to send the messages containing replication data.

When you first create the forest, Windows creates a default site link. You cannot create a site without associating it with at least one site link, so you can either use the default link or create a new one. Site links connect together to allow replication to proceed. The existence of a site link indicates that network connectivity is available between the two sites. Unlike the automatic connection objects created by Windows to replicate data between two partners in a specific NC, you must create site links before intersite replication can proceed.

The Knowledge Consistency Checker (KCC) manages the creation of the intrasite topology and works with the Intersite Topology Generator (ISTG, a subprocess of the KCC) to ensure that Windows optimizes AD replication. The KCC is a service that runs on every DC to generate and optimize the AD replication topology by creating connection agreements between DCs. Costs range from 1 to 32,767, with 100 being the default. In general, the lower the cost, the better the network connectivity that exists between sites. Because they link sites, which are IP subnets, you can think of site links as WAN connections. Each site link has a cost, and the

ISTG uses the cost and site link schedule to determine which connection objects it must create to enable replication. The connection objects created by ISTG to link the different sites form a spanning tree, designed to avoid message looping, since updates flow between bridgehead servers in the sites. This is important with asynchronous replication, where messages that contain replication data may take some time to reach their final destination. Administrators can also create connection objects, but the usual approach is to let the ISTG create a default set and only interfere if necessary afterward.

Because good network connectivity is assumed, directory replication occurs automatically and frequently inside and between sites. Replication partners notify each other when they have updates, and the partners then pull the data from the originating server to update their directories. Even if no updates exist for replication, the DCs in a site exchange details of their latest USNs to update their vector tables and ensure that they miss no data. The AD uses the same pull mechanism for intersite replication. In this case, bridgehead servers hold data until their replication partners (bridgehead servers in other sites) request updates and then pull the data.

Because the AD assumes good connectivity exists between servers in a site, it never compresses replication data and uses RPCs to communicate between servers. By default, two DCs in a site replicate every five minutes. If more than three DCs exist in the same site, the KCC will set up the replication connections to ensure that changes from any DC within the site reach all other DCs within three hops. That is, any changes replicate to all DCs within 15 minutes. On the other hand, the AD always performs intersite replication according to a schedule, which allows administrators to distribute changes when they feel appropriate. If replication data is over 50 KB, the AD compresses it to between 10 percent to 15 percent of its original size before transmission, trading network consumption against the processing to compress and decompress the data.

The AD can replicate synchronously or asynchronously between sites. Synchronous replication occurs between two bridgehead servers within the same NC. The bridgehead server acknowledges receiving the data and then distributes it to other DCs in the site. Synchronous replication can only happen over a reliable and relatively high-speed connection. Asynchronous replication allows replication to occur over slow or unreliable links by sending SMTP messages using a component called Intersite Messaging (ISM-SMTP). ISM generates messages containing replication data and sends them through the basic SMTP service included in Windows. However, you cannot replicate the domain NC over SMTP, and the experience gained in

2.3 Active Directory replication

Table 2.5 *Characteristics of Active Directory Replication*

	Intrasite	Intersite
Transport	RPC	RPC or SMTP
Topology	Ring	Spanning tree
Replication Timing	Automatic when necessary (every five minutes by default)	According to schedule as defined by administrator
Replication Model	Notify and pull	Store and forward
Compression	None	Full (if over 50 KB)

enterprise deployments demonstrates that few if any large companies use SMTP replication with the AD. Because AD replication is so important, most large companies deploy DCs within the high-speed core parts of their networks to ensure that replication works predictably. The reduced cost of network seen since Microsoft introduced Windows 2000 has also reduced the attractiveness of asynchronous replication, so to some degree you can consider this a feature that may help in very specific circumstances (AD deployments over extended low-speed networks), but one that has hardly been proved in practice. Table 2.5 summarizes the differences between intra- and intersite replication for the AD.

Within a site, Windows sets the default schedule for DCs to send notifications of updates to their replication partners to 300 seconds (five minutes). You can change this interval for all members of a site, but there is little reason to do this normally unless you want to tune back the amount of replication traffic that the AD generates. One exception to the rule is when you want to send changes to the bridgehead server in the site so that it begins to replicate with its partner sites as soon as possible. This technique can propagate changes faster within a distributed AD, but you need to test and measure results before committing it to deployment.

Each site link and connection object has a schedule (Figure 2.9), which defines when the DCs associated with the connection object will replicate. Each time a replication slot occurs in the schedule, the DCs inside the site exchange information with each other to establish whether they need to replicate. The site link schedule takes precedence over the connection object schedule for intrasite replication. By default, site link schedules replicate every 180 minutes, so the bridgehead servers will "wake up" and attempt to replicate every three hours, which is usually enough to keep the directory up-to-date.

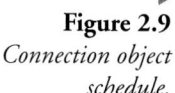

Figure 2.9
Connection object schedule.

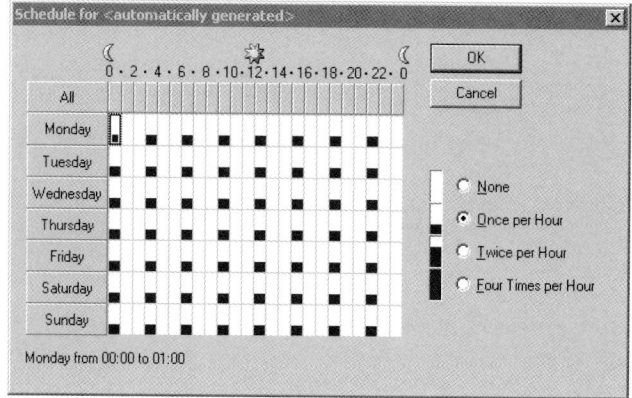

2.3.8 High watermark vector tables and up-to-date vector tables

The AD incorporates a number of propagation dampening mechanisms to control the amount of replication within the network. Propagation dampening means that a DC can suppress or ignore unnecessary replication under specific circumstances. In other words, if a DC receives information that it already knows, such as a request to create a new user object in its copy of the AD, the DC can discard the update. Elimination of unnecessary replication activities becomes more important as the number of controllers increases. Duplicating some work between two controllers is probably unimportant, but involving 100 or 200 controllers in a replication mechanism that generates "n" unnecessary activities per replication partner is a recipe for disaster.

Windows uses two tables to control propagation: the high watermark vector table and the up-to-date vector table (also sometimes called the state vector table) and maintains the two tables on every DC. The contents of the tables represent the current state of replication known to an individual DC.

The AD increments the controller USN as it performs each change, no matter whether it is to add, update, or delete an object. It then stores the USN with the object and any updated attributes. Increments also happen for unsuccessful operations, such as the failure to create a user account.

The high watermark vector table tracks the highest known USN from each replication partner. This information allows a DC to know whether it needs to request additional information from a replication partner to backfill data that may be missing, perhaps because of a failure to replicate properly in

2.3 Active Directory replication

the past. The AD uses the high watermark vector table to detect recent changes on a replication partner. If a DC has not received a recent update from a replication partner, it broadcasts its highest known USN to the partner. The receiving DC can then verify this data against its own high watermark vector table to discover whether any outstanding replication exists. If this is true, the DC can then request the information from a replication partner.

Knowing the USN from a replication partner also allows a controller to request precisely the data required to update its own directory without having to request "all changes." For example, if the highest known USN on controller DC20 is 17,754, and a replication notification arrives from DC20 saying that its current USN is 17,794, then the receiving controller knows that it still has to apply 40 updates to its copy of the directory and is able to issue a request to DC20 to provide the missing information.

The up-to-date vector table maintains a list of all replication partners and the highest originating write on each. When Windows has fully synchronized all of the controllers in a domain, the up-to-date vector table is the same everywhere. Each DC sends its up-to-date vector table to its replication partners as part of the replication cycle. The replication partner matches the USN in the up-to-date vector table with its high watermark vector table to identify any missing data. If the replication partner finds that some replication operations are outstanding, it will request updates. Otherwise, if the replication partner has already received the data—through replication with another DC—it makes no further attempt to replicate because of propagation dampening.

Within a small domain, these tables are not very important. However, their importance grows in line with the number of DCs. Each DC is likely to have a set of different replication partners, so replication data can flow along many different paths. If no mechanisms were in place to stop unnecessary replication, a DC might process updates multiple times after it contacts different replication partners, all of which want to provide the DC with the same information.

2.3.9 AD replication changes in Windows 2003

Windows 2003 introduces many AD upgrades, enhancements, and fixes. With respect to replication, the following are the most important changes:

- You can now promote a Windows 2003 server to become a domain controller using a copy of the AD on removable media. This makes it much easier to deploy controllers in a large network, because it removes the replication load necessary for the AD to populate a database on a new DC. For example, within HP's forest, network-based replication could take between three and five days to complete to promote a new controller. With load from media, a new controller is online within an hour.

- The AD is better at cleaning up "lingering" objects (ones that do not disappear completely in all controllers after the replication process completes) that remain in the database after deletion.

- Intersite replication is more efficient and consumes less bandwidth.

- The overall size of the AD database is usually smaller, because the database engine is more efficient and uses mechanisms such as single-instance storage of security descriptors. For example, when HP moved its Windows forest into native Windows 2003 mode, the DIT file shrank from 12 GB to 7.5 GB.

- GCs do not commence a full synchronization when you add new attributes to the partial attribute set in the AD schema. Large forests feel the effect of this change most, because of the number of controllers that participate in replication. Whereas changes to the partial attribute set in Windows 2000 might create a replication storm over five days before all of the GCs have a fully populated database, now you can assume that replication completes in under a day—assuming no network outages.

- Last logon timestamps are replicated.

- ITSG makes better decisions about the site connections that it creates.

- The AD now supports per-value replication for multivalue attributes. This is very important for groups (and Exchange makes extensive use of distribution groups) that hold group membership in a single multivalue attribute. Therefore, any change to group membership used to force the AD to replicate the complete membership now just replicates the changed value.

Administrators have gained a great deal of experience from managing directory replication for Exchange that they can apply to the AD. In particular, we know that it is easy to swamp a network with unnecessary and unwanted traffic if you allow directory information to replicate too frequently, and the same type of planning has to go into the AD. One immediate difference is that the AD replicates time-critical information, such as account disabling, as fast as reasonably possible.

While the AD is a critical component of successful Windows infrastructures, it is not the only component to manage. File Replication Services (FRS), which replicates SYSVOL and policies, are also a dependency for many applications. For example, if FRS replication is not working properly, the changes to server security policies applied by the Exchange installation program will not replicate from the server that you perform the installation on to other servers in the domain. One side effect of this failure is that you may be able to start the set of Exchange services on other servers, but you will not be able to mount the Store databases, because the services will not possess the necessary privileges!

2.4 The Active Directory Connector

The Active Directory Connector (ADC) supports unidirectional or bidirectional directory synchronization between the Exchange 5.5 DS and the AD. Synchronizing the two directories provides the following benefits:

- You can manage objects from the AD and the DS through a single interface, either the Exchange 5.5 administration program or the AD Users and Computers console. You can update attributes of objects and the ADC will replicate the changes to the other directory.

- You can deploy Exchange 2000/2003 servers alongside the existing Exchange 5.5 (SP3 or later) infrastructure in a reasonably graceful manner.

- You can use the information held in the DS to populate the AD to allow realistic testing of replication topologies before you commence final deployment of Exchange 2000/2003. Table 2.6 lists how the ADC creates DS objects in the AD.

Table 2.6 *Synchronization between Exchange and the Active Directory*

Exchange 5.5	Active Directory
Mailbox	User object (if the account can be mapped to a Windows 2000 domain)
	Disabled mail-enabled user object (if the account still resides in a Windows NT domain). You can also configure the CA to create a contact.
Custom recipient	Mail-enabled contact
Distribution list	Mail-enabled Universal Distribution Group

Bidirectional (two-way) synchronization is the most functional approach, and it achieves all the goals listed previously. Bidirectional synchronization means that you replicate information in both directions, so that the AD learns about mailboxes, custom recipients, and distribution lists held in the DS and vice versa. Bidirectional synchronization is likely to be the most common mode of operation unless you can move your Exchange 5.5 organization to Exchange 2000/2003 over a short period, such as a long weekend. This is certainly possible for small organizations but unlikely for large or distributed organizations.

Unidirectional (one-way) synchronization populates a directory on a one-off basis. For example, after you install the AD for the first time, the directory contains relatively little information. Unidirectional synchronization from a well-populated DS allows you to fill the AD with sufficient data to conduct realistic tests covering aspects such as intrasite and intersite replication. Because the information held in directories changes all the time, it is highly unlikely that you will use unidirectional synchronization for anything other than testing. In fact, Microsoft found that many administrators encountered problems when they attempted to deploy one-way replication, so this option is no longer supported in Exchange 2003.

Obviously, once you begin to migrate from Exchange 5.5 to Exchange 2000, users will depend on an accurate directory to be able to find their correspondents, including distribution lists. Without synchronization, the AD or the DS will only hold details of its own user communities. The ADC is not the only utility that you can use to synchronize DS data with the AD. Any LDAP-based synchronization utility (such as HP's LDSU) can read and write into the AD, so you can normally synchronize entries without recourse to intermediate load files. Load files are simple text files formatted in a particular manner to contain the information necessary to manipulate entries in a directory. Only Exchange 5.5 servers support the ADC, so if you have older servers, you must install at least one Exchange 5.5 server in every site to act as a bridgehead server between the site and the AD. The other servers in the site can continue running Exchange 4.0 or 5.0, but since you can only upgrade to Exchange 2000 from a server running Exchange 5.5, it is strongly recommended that you upgrade servers to Exchange 5.5 (with the latest service pack).

Figure 2.10 illustrates how DS objects from Exchange appear in the AD after replication. You can only map mailboxes to user objects if the ADC is able to resolve the name of the mailbox's primary Windows NT account against the AD. Two different versions of the ADC are available.

2.4 The Active Directory Connector

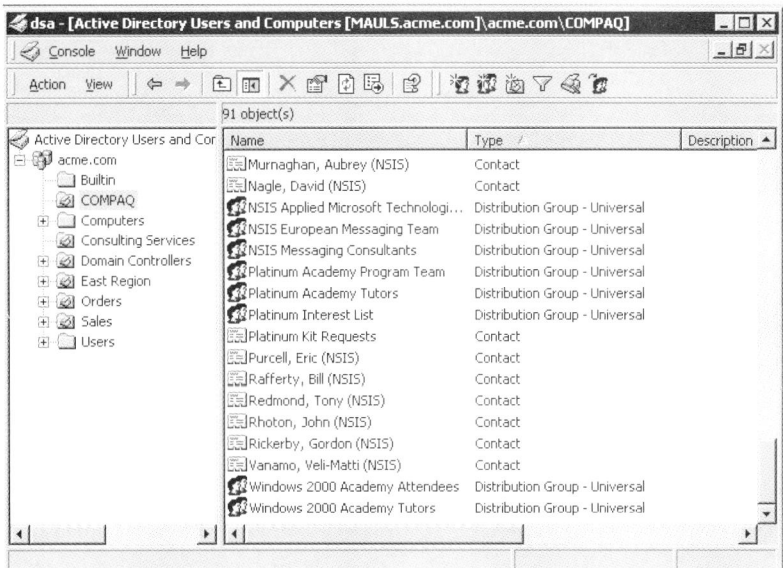

Figure 2.10
Exchange 5.5 data replicated to the Active Directory.

Windows 2000 comes with a basic version, while Exchange 2000 has an extended version. Because you want to replicate more than simple user, group, and contact objects between the two directories, you must use Exchange's version of the ADC. Some deployments start with the Windows version, just to get the AD populated, and then upgrade to the Exchange version before installing the first Exchange 2000/2003 server.

The version of the ADC provided with Exchange 2003 is smarter and contains additional functionality. First, the ADC console contains some tools to validate a target Exchange 5.5 organization to ensure that replication is possible. Second, you can run an ADC Connection Agreement wizard to automate setting up new connection agreements. The wizard does not overwrite existing agreements and it is a useful tool in straightforward situations where you do not need any special processing, such as replicating specific objects to different target containers. However, because these situations exist and it is always good to understand the basic technology, we should consider what a connection agreement is and the function that it serves. Before proceeding to create any connection agreements, make sure that your account is a member of the Local Administrators group on the server where the ADC runs; otherwise, you will be unable to save or modify an agreement. See Microsoft Knowledge Base articles 267373 and 249817 for details.

2.4.1 Connection agreements

You have to configure the ADC with one or more connection agreements before the ADC can replicate information between the DS and the AD. A connection agreement (CA) defines details of the objects to be replicated across a particular link, as well as the type of connection, how the servers will authenticate to each other (see Figure 2.11), and details of the servers that will participate in the link.

A single ADC can support multiple connection agreements, so it is possible to build a hub ADC to provide a single point of replication between all the sites in an Exchange organization and the AD. It is also possible to create multiple connection agreements on an ADC to handle a single Exchange site. In this case, each agreement is likely to control replication for a different recipient container in the site. Obviously, if an ADC has to manage a number of connection agreements, it consumes more system resources and the overall synchronization environment is more complex. According to Microsoft, no architectural restrictions exist on the number of agreements that a single ADC can support, but system resources become a practical constraint after 50 or so agreements. In situations where you need to run more than ten or so connection agreements, consider allocating a dedicated server for this work. Simplicity is better than complexity, and you

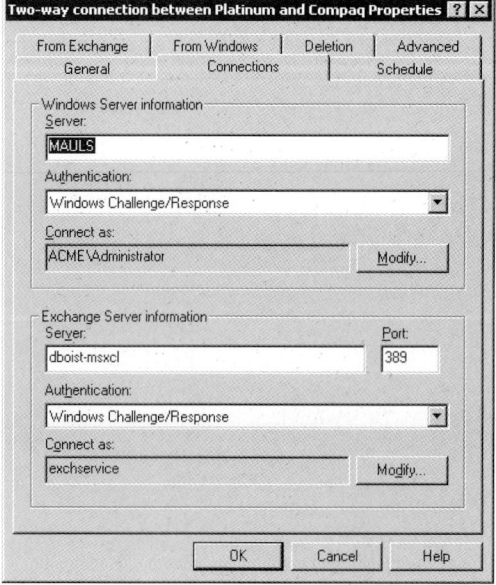

Figure 2.11
Configuring a connection agreement.

should, therefore, approach ADC deployments with the aim of restricting the number of agreements in place to the absolute minimum.

Distributed Exchange 5.5 organizations with many sites may require multiple ADC servers, with the connections spread between the servers. Organizations that already operate central Exchange routing sites (usually around a hub and spoke network) find that the central site is a good location for synchronization.

Direct IP connectivity is required between the servers at either side of a connection agreement. This requirement will influence how many ADC servers you need to deploy within a company. As with a Windows site, you can describe an Exchange 5.5 site to an island of high-capacity bandwidth. The initial design might start with an ADC for each Exchange site, and then reduce the number of ADCs by reviewing where sufficient IP connectivity is available to allow an ADC to handle multiple Exchange sites. There is no penalty except additional management overhead incurred to operate multiple ADCs. However, it is best to keep the number of ADC servers to one per Windows domain to reduce management effort, complexity, and replication traffic.

You make the decision to make a connection agreement uni- or bidirectional when you create the agreement, as shown in Figure 2.12. You can

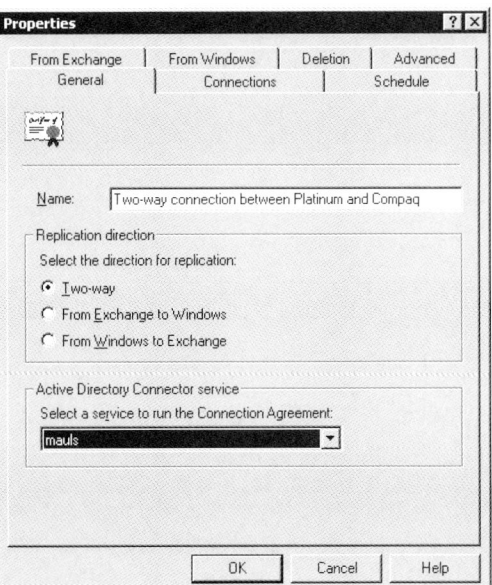

Figure 2.12
Determining the type of connection agreement.

change the agreement type afterward, so you can begin with a unidirectional load from the DS to the AD and then change the agreement to be bidirectional when you are ready to begin deploying Exchange 2000/2003 servers. However, as discussed earlier, Microsoft does not support one-way agreements, so it is best to configure all agreements as two way.

In the Exchange 5.5 architecture, each site exercises full control over its own set of mailbox, custom recipient, and distribution list objects. During Exchange 5.5 replication, each site pushes details of its objects to other sites, and the replication mechanism only permits a single path of replication between sites to avoid the possibility of duplicate replication. You can see this restriction in action if you attempt to create a directory replication connector between two Exchange sites when Exchange already replicates the objects from the sites via an intermediate site. Exchange will not create the new connector, because it will create duplicate entries in the DS. Connection agreements follow the same principle, and a connection agreement must exist between an ADC and every Exchange site before full bidirectional replication is possible. Because a Windows domain "owns" its objects, you also need a connection agreement for each Windows domain if you want to replicate DS information into the domain. Companies that run large, multisite Exchange organizations therefore require multiple connection agreements, even if they only want to synchronize with a single Windows domain.

Figure 2.13 shows how to add the recipient containers from a single Exchange 5.5 site to a connection agreement. The ADC will not allow you to select containers from multiple sites, since it retrieves information about available containers from the Exchange server specified in the Connections property page (Figure 2.11). In this case, the ADC connects via LDAP to port 389 on the DBOIST-MSXCL server, located in the "NSIS European Messaging Team" site, so we can only see the three containers in the site.

If you only want to populate the AD and do not care about subsequent updates, you can use unidirectional replication to populate the AD with data from many different Exchange sites. In this case, a single connection agreement is enough. Figure 2.14 shows how to add multiple recipient containers from different sites to a connection agreement for unidirectional replication.

The nature of replication presents all sorts of interesting challenges. Large distribution lists that incorporate members from multiple sites are a good example. A distribution list becomes a Windows universal distribution group after ADC replication. It is quite conceivable that not all members of

2.4 The Active Directory Connector

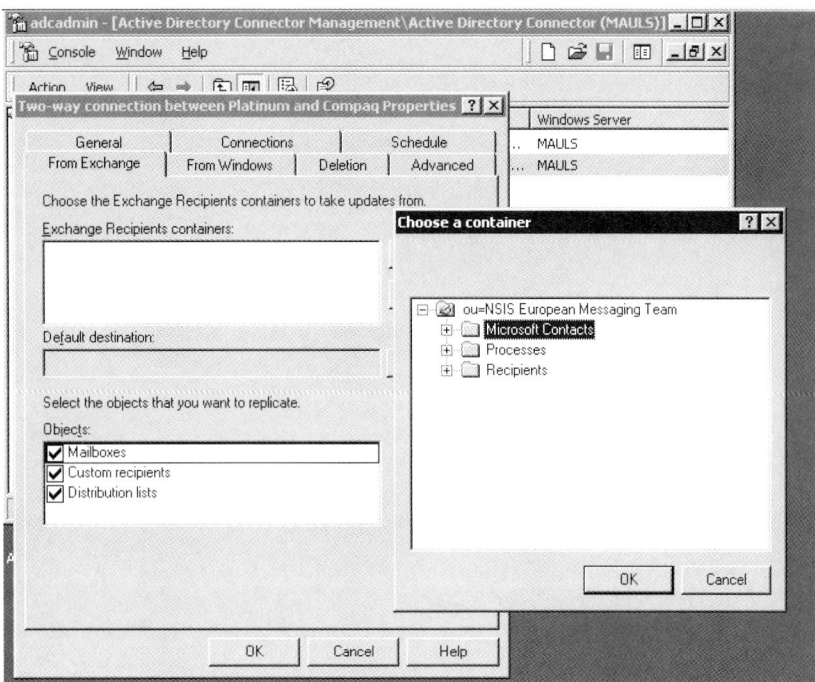

Figure 2.13
Specifying target containers for a bidirectional connection agreement.

the list exist as AD objects, because they are still awaiting replication. The AD cannot add invisible members to the new group, so an obvious problem exists if you replicate a half-empty group back to the DS. If the DS then removed the members who do not appear in the group, the affected users would lose any of the benefit of their list membership (access to public folders, etc.). Fortunately, the ADC solves the problem by writing details of members that it cannot find in the AD into an attribute for the group called "unmergedAtts." This allows Exchange 5.5 to maintain its membership, and the AD can merge in the missing members as they appear through replication.

Operating in a mixed-mode Windows domain also affects distribution groups. Universal security groups are not supported in a mixed-mode domain, so you can't use distribution groups to secure access to public folders on an Exchange 2000/2003 server in the same way that distribution lists are commonly used in Exchange 5.5. You will have to wait until you can move the domain to native mode before you can make the distribution groups into security groups. Alternatively, if it is going to be a long time before you can move a domain into native mode, you will probably end up creating separate universal security groups to protect public folders, and

Chapter 2

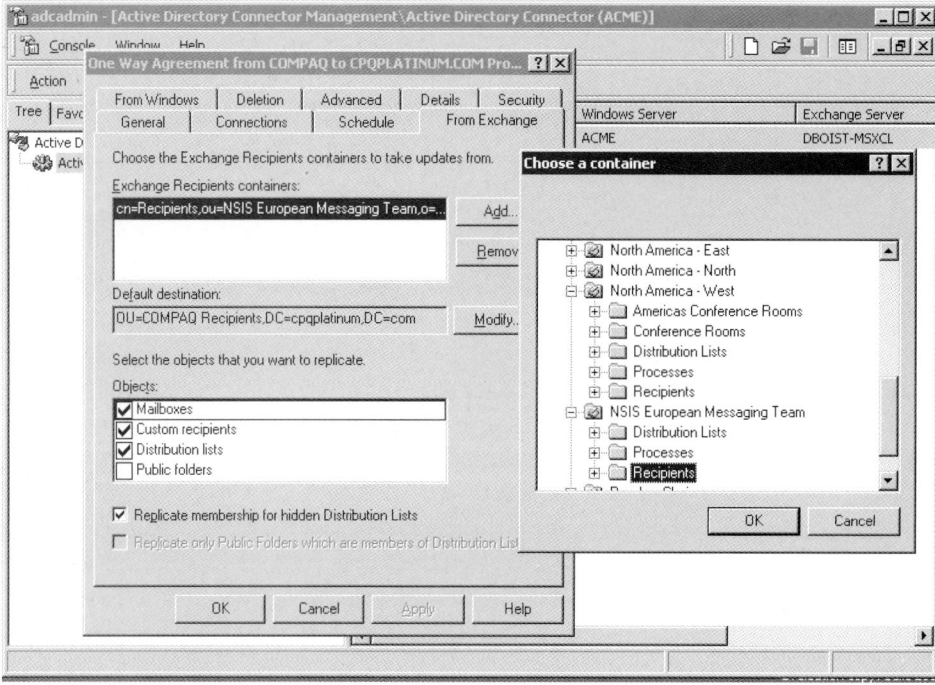

Figure 2.14   *Adding multiple Exchange sites to a connection agreement.*

include users who have Windows accounts in these groups. This is one reason why it is best practice to use a native-mode Windows domain to support Exchange.

One-way synchronization is straightforward; bidirectional synchronization is quite another matter. The major gain that you can achieve through bidirectional synchronization is the ability to make changes to objects in either the AD or the DS and have the change replicated back to the partner directory. There is a certain attraction in the concept of being able to use a single utility, such as AD Users and Computers, to manage users, contacts, and groups—even if the actual object "belongs" to Exchange 5.5.

However, you have to offset the attraction of being able to manage everything from one place by the potential difficulties of managing synchronization across a distributed network. Bidirectional synchronization works best with strong centralized management models but exposes some weakness when exposed to more distributed models. Once you have more than ten sites, multiple recipient containers that require complex connection agreements, and potentially multiple servers running the ADC, it becomes easier to set up all the connection agreements to be one way. This method forces you to manage Exchange 5.5 objects through Exchange and Windows objects through AD Users and Computers. While this might seem to be a retrograde step, it is not a problem in practice. As always, this technique makes sense in some situations but not in others. Consider both approaches and select the one that is most appropriate for the way that your company is organized.

2.4.2 Handling multiple recipient containers

By default, Exchange creates a container called "Recipients" in every site to be the default repository for mailboxes, custom recipients, and distribution lists. Companies that deployed Exchange 4.0 often created new recipient containers to divide address types or to allocate separate containers for all objects that belonged to a specific department or function. For example, they would have a container to hold all distribution lists or all custom recipients, or one specially created to hold all the recipients that belong to departments such as "Marketing" or "Finance." Less commonly, specific recipient containers sometimes act as the target for synchronization from other directories. For example, you could use a container called "Lotus Notes Recipients" to hold the custom recipient entries created for people in the Lotus Notes address book via the Lotus Notes Connector.

Microsoft introduced Address Book Views (Address Lists in Exchange 2000/2003) in Exchange 5.0 to allow administrators to create virtual views of recipients taken from different containers and eliminate the need to create recipient containers for departments or functions. Nevertheless, many Exchange deployments operate multiple recipient containers, and this has an impact on how you will deploy connection agreements.

Assume that you have a site with three separate containers: the standard "Recipients" container; one called "External Contacts," which holds custom recipients outside the company; and a container for VIP users. If the intention is to synchronize the entries from all these containers to a single organizational unit in the AD, the task is simple, because a single agreement is able to handle the requests. It is feasible to consider a plan where the ADC synchronizes all objects to a single organizational unit initially, followed by some refilling to different organizational units after you complete the migration to Exchange 2000 and you only deal with AD objects. However, if the need is to immediately direct the information from Exchange 5.5 into multiple organizational units, you then need a different connection agreement for each organizational unit.

2.4.3 How the ADC performs synchronization

The AD and DS both store a set of attributes or properties for each object. Replication ensures that the same set of objects exists in both directories and that the same values are present in the objects' attributes. Whenever you have multiple directories and are able to change objects in either directory and depend on scheduled synchronization to match everything up, you cannot achieve a state of absolute consistency across the two directories. The aim is to maintain the two directories in as close a state of consistency as possible. The nature of networked systems and the experience gained with the DS since 1996 mean that it is reasonably easy to attain a state of loose consistency (the directories are 99 percent synchronized). Driving toward tighter consistency requires frequent synchronization across reliable network links.

When replication occurs from the DS to the AD, an LDAP query is executed to discover outstanding changes in the DS (how many changes have taken place since the last known USN). The ADC then examines each returned object. Incoming objects from the DS are examined to retrieve values from the DN, NTGUID, and PrimaryNTAccount attributes. The NTGUID is a unique numeric value, which serves as the key for the object within the AD, while the PrimaryNTAccount attribute holds the SID for the account associated with the mailbox.

Since the GUID is the primary key for the AD, the ADC attempts to use it first to locate the object. If this search fails, we know that the object does not exist under this GUID, but it may be present using another GUID. To check, the ADC searches using the DN against the legacyExchangeDN attribute. The legacyExchangeDN attribute holds the DN for the object in the DS, so a successful search will turn up DS objects synchronized into the AD, perhaps through another CA. If we still cannot find the object, the ADC performs a final search using the SIDHistory attribute to see whether the object's SID can be found. Failure at this stage means that the object does not exist in the AD, so the ADC creates a brand new object according to the CA policy (user, contact, or disabled user). If the ADC can find the object at any stage, the ADC updates its values.

Note that whereas the AD supports attribute-level replication, the DS performs replication on an object level. In other words, even if you change just a single attribute on an object in the DS, it replicates the complete object. Replication happens at the lowest common denominator, so the ADC replicates data between the AD and DS at object level.

2.4 The Active Directory Connector

The process is a little simpler when coming from the AD to the DS. The AD can contain many different types of objects, most of which are not supported by the DS, so the query to locate outstanding updates applies a filter to ensure that synchronization is only attempted with mail-enabled objects.

When the ADC synchronizes AD objects into the DS, they receive a DN stored in the LegacyExchangeDN attribute. The ADC can subsequently use the DN as the key for lookups into the DS. If the ADC can find an object with its DN, and its NTGUID value matches an AD object, the ADC knows that it has already synchronized and can update its attributes; otherwise, the ADC creates a new object.

2.4.4 Scheduling a connection agreement

As with an Exchange 5.5 Directory Replication Connector, a schedule controls how often the ADC activates a connection agreement to check for updates to replicate. As discussed earlier, a replicated directory is normally in a state of loose consistency. Synchronization achieves a similar state of consistency between two directories, and the frequency that synchronization occurs determines the exact level of consistency. In other words, the more often you synchronize, the closer the two directories become. The options in an ADC schedule are "Always" (which forces a connection approximately every seven seconds[4]), "Never," or according to an exact schedule as set in the "Schedule" property page of the agreement (Figure 2.15).

Directories are often in a state of flux during migrations and their contents change more rapidly during periods when you move users from one environment to another. During migrations, you should schedule ADC connections to run very regularly, perhaps once per hour, and then tone back the schedule after the majority of users are moved to the new environment.

Determining a suitable schedule is, therefore, a balancing act between the need to replicate changes quickly and the desire to dedicate a reasonable amount of system resources to the job. Obviously, if you activate a connection agreement every ten minutes, the directories will stay in a higher state of consistency than a schedule that runs every two hours. However, the activation of each agreement generates some network traffic to allow the two directories to communicate to exchange updates. Operating a default schedule and allowing the ADC to check for updates at regular short intervals is not a problem when you have a few Exchange sites and recipient containers

---

4. The interval can be adjusted by setting the number of seconds in the Sync Sleep Delay value in the HKEY_LOCAL_MACHINE\System\CurrentControlSet\Services\MSADCParameters registry key.

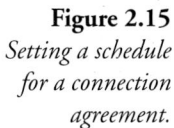

Figure 2.15
Setting a schedule for a connection agreement.

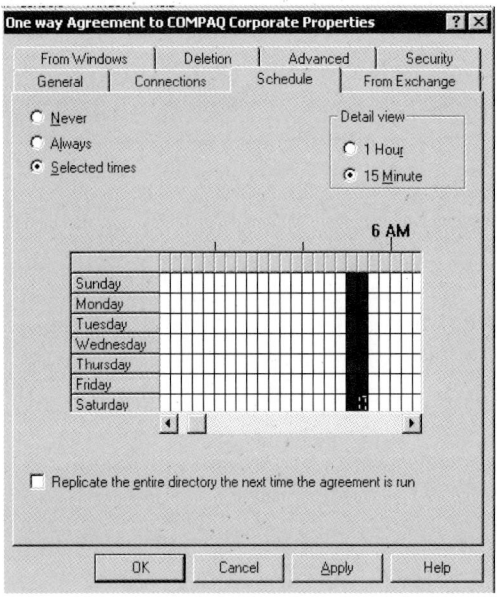

to process. However, in some of the larger and more complex deployments, which require bidirectional replication from 20 or 30 sites involving some degree of object remapping, you need to take care to ensure that the schedule for all the agreements managed by an ADC does not exhaust system resources. In these circumstances, you are more likely to end up with a situation where each agreement has its own phased schedule linked into an overall schedule that does not interfere with other agreements.

2.4.5 Primary and nonprimary connection agreements

You can set a connection agreement to be the primary agreement between an Exchange 5.5 organization and the AD or from the AD to an Exchange 5.5 organization. The default is for a connection agreement to be nonprimary. The difference is that a primary connection agreement is able to create new objects in its target directory, whereas a nonprimary agreement is only able to apply updates to existing objects. There should only be one primary agreement to any specific target within a directory, and, in this context, a target is defined as being from an Exchange 5.5 recipient container to an AD organizational unit or from an Exchange 5.5 site to an Exchange 2000 administrative group.

Two different options are available to control primacy. When the agreement has primacy "for the connected Exchange organization," it means that

2.4 The Active Directory Connector

the connection agreement can create new objects in the DS. When the agreement has primacy "for the connected Windows domain," the agreement is able to create new objects in the target domain in the AD. The first connection agreement established by the ADC is always a primary agreement, because you always need at least one primary agreement for the ADC to operate.

The concept of primacy for a connection agreement is present to prevent the ADC from creating duplicate objects, because administrators create multiple agreements that channel objects from the same source into a directory. There should only be a single prime agreement between each AD domain and an Exchange organization. The exception to this rule is when an agreement handles a particular set of objects (such as only custom recipients) not covered by any other agreement. If there are multiple AD domains that need to synchronize with an Exchange organization, multiple connection agreements will be necessary, and one agreement for each domain will be marked as primary.

Before you begin replication, you should create a plan to identify all the different sources (sites and recipient containers on the Exchange 5.5 side and organizational units in the AD) and decide how best to connect the dots together.

2.4.6 Synchronizing multiple Exchange 5.5 organizations

Some companies find themselves in a situation where they are running multiple Exchange 5.5 organizations, perhaps after a corporate merger. In this situation, they can merge the Exchange 5.5 organizations together using the Move Server Wizard utility before proceeding to migrate to Exchange 2000/2003, or they can use the ADC to combine the directory entries from the different organizations together into the AD and use the AD as the basis for creating one logical organization.

Connecting multiple Exchange 5.5 organizations via the ADC takes some planning. For example, you cannot begin by creating an interorganizational connection agreement as the first connection agreement for the ADC, since this will prevent you from deploying a production Exchange 2000/2003 environment. The correct approach is to:

- Select the Exchange 5.5 organization that will be the "prime" migration path to Exchange 2000/2003. This organization will synchronize with the AD via normal connection agreements. All of the other

Exchange 5.5 organizations will use interorganizational connection agreements.

- Use the version of the ADC provided with Exchange 2000 or 2003 and not the version shipped with Windows 2000, which does not support inter-organizational connections. Note that Microsoft provides an updated version of the ADC for Exchange 2003 and you have to update any existing ADCs that you established for Exchange 2000 by installing the new code from the Exchange 2003 CD. Apart from some bug fixes, the new version includes extra functionality in a set of ADC Tools that can automate the setup of connection agreements and the synchronization environment to a large degree. If you migrate from Exchange 5.5 to Exchange 2003 and use the ADC to synchronize information, the Exchange 2003 installation procedure expects you to run the ADC Tools before you can install an Exchange 2003 server into an Exchange 5.5 site.

- Configure the ADC with connection agreements to synchronize the primary Exchange 5.5 organization with the AD.

- When synchronization with the primary Exchange 5.5 organization is working properly, proceed to configure interorganizational connection agreements to incorporate the secondary Exchange 5.5 organizations. Figure 2.16 illustrates the creation of an interorganizational agreement.

Synchronizing multiple Exchange 5.5 organizations into the AD is not a simple task. You should practice by configuring agreements in a test environment and check that everything works as expected before proceeding to implement inside your production systems. You should also test alternative solutions, such as synchronizing all of the directories into a metadirectory or using a purpose-designed synchronization tool such as HP's LDSU.

2.4.7 Site replication services

Site replication services (SRS) allow an Exchange 2000/2003 server to share configuration data with downstream Exchange servers in a mixed-mode organization. Essentially, SRS mimics the DS Service Agent (DSA) so that a downstream Exchange server views an Exchange 2000 server as if it is running Exchange 5.5.

SRS is closely associated with the ADC, which you must configure on the Windows server before an Exchange 2000/2003 server can join a downstream site. It is important to make it clear that SRS has nothing to do with

2.4 The Active Directory Connector

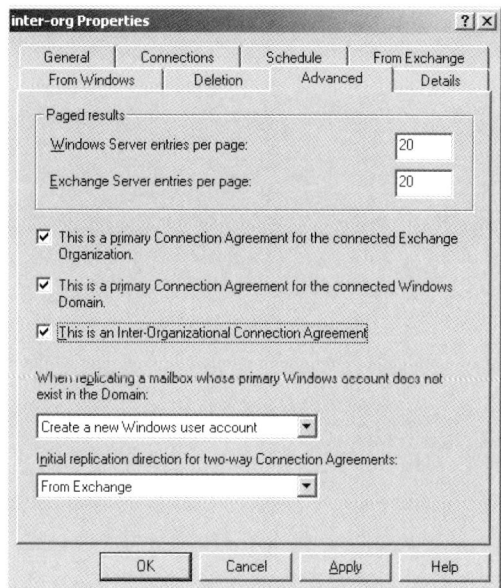

Figure 2.16
Configuring an interorganizational CA.

the exchange of data between servers, since this is entirely a function of the connection agreements managed by the ADC. Instead, the SRS provides a shadow Exchange 5.5 DS to allow other 5.5 servers to continue with Exchange directory replication in exactly the way that they did before a server moved to Exchange 2000/2003.

During the installation process, setup automatically configures the connection agreements necessary to replicate configuration data. SRS is configured and becomes operational under specific conditions:

- When the first Exchange 5.5 server is upgraded to Exchange 2000 in an existing site

- When the first Exchange 2000 or 2003 server is installed into an existing site

- When you upgrade a bridgehead server in an Exchange 5.5 site—often, the bridgehead server is a good candidate for the first server for upgrade.

Once configured, SRS is then able to share data about Exchange 2000/2003 servers, all of which are fetched from the configuration naming context in the AD with all the downstream servers in the site. SRS consists of the following three major components:

- A pseudo Exchange 5.5 DS with its replication engine

- The Exchange 5.5 Knowledge Consistency Checker (KCC), a component similar to the KCC used in AD replication, which validates the replication paths between Exchange 5.5 sites
- The Super Knowledge Consistency Checker (SKCC), new code that is able to act as an interface between the Exchange 2000/2003 configuration data held in the AD and the legacy site topology used by the Exchange 5.5 servers. The SKCC is, therefore, able to produce a complete picture of a mixed-mode organization.

SRS maintains a copy of the directory in a database called SRS.EDB to track the interchange of configuration data between Exchange 2000/2003 and the legacy servers. RPCs always carry replication data between SRS and the downstream servers. Remember that you need to take regular backups of the SRS database, ideally on the same schedule as the AD. If you lose the server that hosts SRS, you will have to restore the database from backup, and it is obviously much better if you use a recent backup. The alternative is to rebuild the SRS database by following the instructions contained in Microsoft Knowledge Base article 282061, but a restore is usually faster.

You manage Exchange 5.5 servers through the ADMIN program and have to possess administrator permission for a site before you can work with servers in that site. After you remove the last Exchange 5.5 server in a site, its entry still exists in the configuration data held in the AD. To remove the server, use the technique documented in Microsoft Knowledge Base article 284148 to connect to the Exchange 2000/2003 server that hosts the SRS and delete the entry.

SRS is one of the Exchange components not supported on a cluster. From a planning perspective, this means that you cannot use a cluster as the first Exchange 2000/2003 server in a mixed-mode site, because this server must run SRS to act as a bridgehead server for the site. The simple workaround is to install a nonclustered server to host the ADC and SRS first, then the cluster, and then remove the initial cluster after the organization moves into native mode.

2.5 The LegacyExchangeDN attribute

The original Exchange architecture allocated a fixed distinguished name to every object in the directory and used this value as the primary key for the object in the directory. Exchange composed distinguished names from the names of the containers along the path to an object in the directory. Primary keys are difficult to change and this implementation led to some problems in terms of flexibility. You could not change the name of an Exchange 5.5 site or move users between containers because these operations required the object to be deleted and then recreated with a new distinguished name that reflected the new location of the object within the directory.

Exchange now uses the AD as its directory, and, during the transition, the developers were careful to avoid the same issue. While the AD still uses distinguished names to reference objects, the distinguished name is no longer the primary key. Instead, when it creates a new object, the AD allocates a GUID (Global Unique Identifier) to it. You can move objects around the directory between containers as much as you want, which results in multiple changes to their distinguished names, but their GUIDs remain constant. Unlike previous versions of Exchange, no correlation exists between a user's distinguished name and a site or other administrative, security, or routing boundary.

You can view the distinguished name for an object using the ADSIEDIT utility. Select the object and then look at the value of the "distinguished name" attribute. The format is:

```
cn=Name, ou=Organizational Unit, dc=domain name,
dc=domain name
```

Therefore, the distinguished name for my Windows account might look like:

```
CN=Redmond\,
Tony,OU=Consulting,OU=Users,OU=Accounts,DC=emea,DC=cpqcorp,
DC=net
```

There is no correlation between distinguished names and email addresses. The change in distinguished name format occurs automatically as accounts are migrated, and Exchange hides the change from users in distinguished name format. However, many different pieces of the messaging puzzle store the old Exchange format distinguished name (such as the headers of old messages and MAPI profiles) to ensure backward compatibility.

Because two different formats are in use, some method is needed to ensure that the older addresses stored within the infrastructure are still valid. The AD accomplishes this goal by maintaining a separate attribute for every Exchange object, called the LegacyExchangeDN, which it populates via ADC synchronization with the distinguished name in the old format. You can think of LegacyExchangeDN as the "old" name for an Exchange object—something to ensure backward compatibility by always

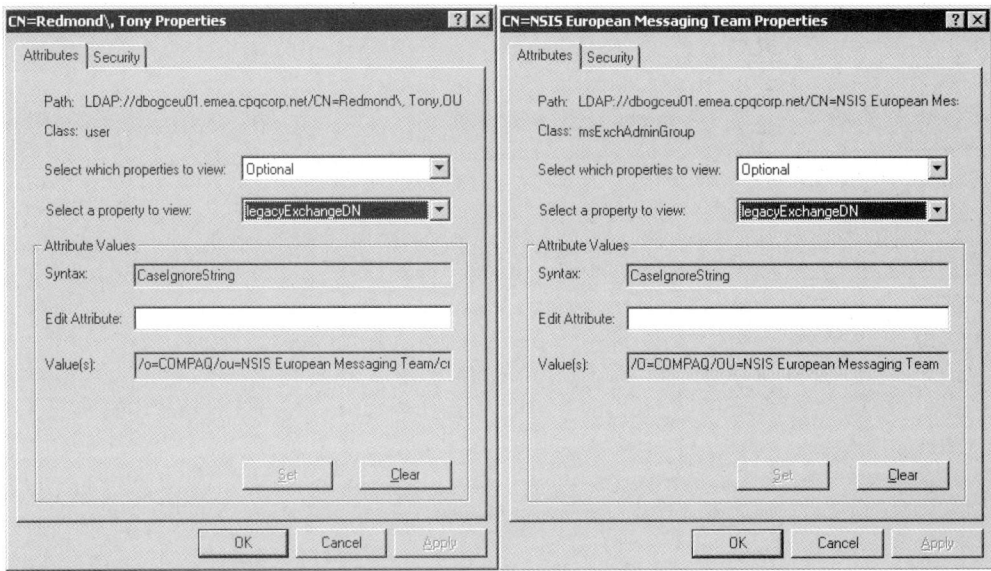

Figure 2.17 *LegacyExchangeDN values for a user and an administrative group.*

having something that an older version of Exchange or a utility built for an older version of Exchange can recognize and use. Figure 2.17 shows ADSIEDIT viewing the LegacyExchangeDN value for a user object (left) and an administrative group (right). The data for the administrative group comes from the Exchange container in the AD configuration naming context.

The AD indexes the LegacyExchangeDN attribute to enable fast lookup and automatically searches the index if a client attempts to search the AD using a distinguished name in the old format. Thus, MAPI profiles continue to work and clients can continue to reply to messages using old addresses, because the AD responds to the search executed by the SMTP Routing Engine when it attempts to resolve the address.

2.6 DSAccess—Exchange's directory access component

To reduce complexity in large applications it is common to create code for a specific purpose for use by other components. Microsoft designed DSAccess to manage the interaction between Exchange 2000/2003 and the AD by providing an API to components such as the Store to make queries to the AD without having to write their own access code. DSAccess also manages a cache of AD data—essentially recently accessed data—to improve query

2.6 DSAccess—Exchange's directory access component

performance by checking queries against the cache before searching the AD. The default size of the cache is 50 MB, divided into recipient data (essentially mail-enabled objects recently looked up in the AD) and configuration data about the Exchange organization. The shared cache reduces the load on the AD by eliminating queries that can be satisfied by cached data. Given the number of email addresses in message headers that it must validate and then use to decide what destination queue to place messages on, the Exchange Routing Engine is a major consumer of the DSAccess cache. The Routing Engine also needs to know about available messaging connectors, information that comes from the configuration data in the AD. In fact, without such a cache, the overall performance and message throughput of the Routing Engine would be very impaired, so you can see why this cache is so important to Exchange. Usually, you can leave DSAccess to manage its cache automatically, but a number of registry values are available to control how quickly items expire in the cache and how much memory Exchange allocates to the cache (Table 2.7). It is always better for system performance if an application can fetch data from memory instead of going to disk, so increasing the size of the DSAccess cache can be beneficial by reducing disk I/O and CPU usage. You should consider increasing the cache size for servers that operate inside large organizations (where it is less likely that any particular address is held in a standard size cache) or servers equipped with more than 1 GB of memory. Before changing anything, make sure that you evaluate how these values influence system performance for a test server. Make the changes at HKLM\System\CurrentControlSet\Services\MSExchangeDSAccess\Instance0.

Table 2.7 *Registry Values that Affect DSAccess*

Value	Meaning
CacheTTLUser (DWORD)	The expiration interval for the recipient cache set in seconds.
MaxEntriesUser (DWORD)	The maximum number of entries held in the cache. A value of 0 means the cache is only limited by its size.
MaxMemoryUser (DWORD)	The maximum amount of memory (in bytes) allocated to hold data about recipients. For example, a value of 58,720,256 means 50 MB. The maximum value is 0x000170A3 (equivalent to 94 MB).
CacheTTLConfig (DWORD)	The expiration interval for the configuration cache set in seconds.
MaxEntriesConfig (DWORD)	The maximum number of entries held in the configuration cache.
MaxMemoryConfig (DWORD)	The maximum amount of memory (in bytes) allocated to hold configuration data.

While you can adjust the overall size of the cache, you cannot adjust the maximum size of an object's attribute that the cache can hold (32 KB). In most circumstances, this size is perfectly adequate, but you can exceed the maximum if you deploy Exchange 2000 or 2003 in more than 100 domains in a forest. The number of domains is approximate and you can exceed this value, depending on the exact configuration. Microsoft Knowledge Base article 813814 provides background to the problem, which is due to the need to build ACLs for objects held in the cache. If an object's ACL grows past 32 KB, DSAccess cannot cache it and must then contact a DC or GC to retrieve the attributes of the affected objects whenever it needs to use one. As you can imagine, if the affected objects have anything to do with mail routing or are popular points for user access (such as a public folder), a server can consume a lot of bandwidth and processing to validate objects. This problem negates the value of the cache and normally affects the speed with which Exchange can process messages, thus leading to large queues. The good news is that this problem only appears in the largest Exchange deployments and only if you mail enable large numbers of domains. This problem underlines the need to follow best practice to simplify your AD structure as much as possible and to never mail enable a domain (by running DomainPrep) unless you need to host an Exchange server there. Note that the ACEs do not exist until you install the first Exchange server into the domain.

Microsoft Knowledge Base article 327378 explains another aspect of DSAccess in action. In this case, Exchange 2000 servers do not enforce mailbox quotas quickly. The default value of the user object cache (controlled by the CacheTTLUser registry value) causes the cache to be refreshed after ten minutes, which is acceptable for routing information. The cached data interacts with another cache in the Store that holds information (like quotas) about mailboxes. The Store refreshes its mailbox information cache every two hours. In some situations, it can be beneficial to follow the directions in the Knowledge Base article to adjust how the Store and DSAccess caches interact if you find that servers do not pick up updates to mailbox information quickly.

Although you might assume that they would gain a performance benefit, clients do not use the contents of the DSAccess recipient cache. In fact, this is logical, because clients use the most up-to-date recipient information or use a proxy (prior to Outlook 2000 SR2) or referral mechanism to locate a GC whenever access to recipient information is required.

Microsoft continues to learn from real-life deployments and to improve DSAccess performance. Their own figures reveal a 20 percent drop in

LDAP traffic between Exchange and GCs after organizations deployed SP3. Microsoft made further improvements in Exchange 2003, especially when you deploy Exchange in conjunction with Windows 2003 DCs and GCs to allow Exchange 2003 servers to take advantage of some performance improvements in the AD and a new feature called the GC logon cache.

2.6.1 DSAccess tasks

Apart from managing the contents of its cache, the major role of the DSAccess component is to find and control the set of DCs and GCs that Exchange uses when it needs to retrieve information from the directory. This role breaks down into a number of tasks:

- Perform suitability testing to determine that selected DCs and GCs function correctly before DSAccess uses them.

- Manage load balancing of LDAP requests within the local AD site if more than ten DCs and GCs are present.

- Perform graceful failovers to a new DC or GC to minimize the impact on clients and other Exchange components (such as the Routing Engine). DSAccess uses information about Windows site links and connection costs to determine the most appropriate controller to fail over to.

- In failover situations, DSAccess monitors for the local DC or GC to come back online. If this happens within five minutes, DSAccess automatically reconnects to that controller.

- Diagnostic logging to help troubleshoot problems.

We have already concluded that directory access is a fundamental need for a messaging system, so it is therefore obvious that DSAccess is one of the most critical parts of Exchange. If DSAccess fails or a network interruption occurs, other components cannot work; in particular, the Routing Engine will not be able to determine the list of DCs and GCs to work with so it will not be able to process messages, since the Routing Engine cannot validate email addresses. Other problem symptoms include the accumulation of large message queues (because the Routing Engine cannot move the messages off the queues), poor performance when expanding distribution groups, and clients that appear to "hang" when they attempt to access the directory.

Some messaging components can work without DSAccess. All Windows 2000 and 2003 servers are equipped with a basic SMTP service (part of IIS) and Routing Engine for use by applications that need to generate and send messages. For example, SharePoint Portal Server uses the SMTP service to send email subscription notifications when authors post new documents to folders in the SharePoint Store. The processing performed by the SMTP service to expand a Windows distribution group to determine the addresses for message delivery is another example. The Exchange installation program upgrades the standard SMTP components when it installs Exchange; afterward the Routing Engine and other components use DSAccess whenever possible.

2.6.2 Selecting DCs and GCs for DSAccess

When an Exchange server starts its services, DSAccess selects a single DC from the list of available DCs to use for configuration lookups, such as locating other Exchange servers in the organization and the connectors that link servers together. Exchange refers to this DC as the Configuration Domain Controller and it is a critical element, since this DC handles approximately 30 percent of all calls made to DSAccess. For this reason, all results of configuration lookups are held in a cache with a five-minute timeout so many subsequent calls can be handled from the cache rather than creating extra load on the DC. SP2 increases the default timeout value for this cache to 15 minutes—you can change the value through the registry (see the details in Table 2.7). This is a reasonable step to take, since configuration data is typically stable after the initial deployment/migration period. Microsoft made further performance improvements for DSAccess in Exchange 2000 SP3 by reducing the number of LDAP calls between servers and controllers.

ESM also uses the configuration DC to query the AD for information about the Exchange organization and make whatever changes it needs, such as updating server properties, applying policies to an administrative group, or adding new routing connectors. Remember, ESM only deals with the details of the Exchange configuration—administrative groups, routing groups, connectors, databases, and so on. The AD Users and Computers console processes users, contacts, and groups (including details of user mailboxes).

How can you determine what domain controllers an Exchange server uses? Up to Exchange 2000 SP2, the answer was DSADIAG, an unsupported command-line utility that lists some basic information about DSAccess. All Exchange servers now have a Directory Access property page that you can view through ESM to allow you to view and set the DCs and GCs used by DSAccess (Figure 2.18).

2.6 DSAccess—Exchange's directory access component

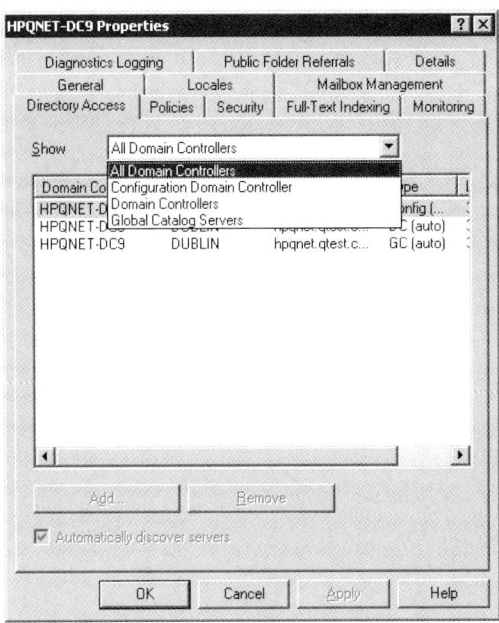

Figure 2.18
Directory access property page.

DSAccess builds the list of DCs through an automatic topology detection process, which searches for suitable DCs that are in the same Windows site as the Exchange server. Exchange can select any suitable DC as the configuration DC regardless of whether it is in the same domain as the Exchange server, since all DCs in a forest share the same configuration data. However, a DC will not be included in the list of suitable DCs if you have not run the DomainPrep procedure in its domain. If DSAccess cannot find a suitable DC in the same site, the selection process expands its search to look for any suitable DC in other sites. Alternatively, you can force DSAccess to use a specific DC through a registry setting (see Table 2.8) or by selecting a DC through the Directory Access property page for a server. However, be careful about making changes in the registry, since they tend to become permanent and may not necessarily be the best configuration, especially if new controllers join the network. If the chosen DC becomes unavailable later on, DSAccess attempts to locate another DC and connect to it using the same topology detection process.

Let us assume that you are brave and you want to tell DSAccess the DCs and GCs that you want it to use. In this example, we define one GC and one DC. You define in a set of values under a subkey. The subkey for the first GC is "UserGC1," or "UserDC1" for the first DC. If you want to define other controllers, you set up subkeys for UserDC2, UserDC3,

Table 2.8 *Registry Values to Allocate a Specific GC and DC for DSAccess*

Value	Data
For UserGC1:	
IsGC (DWORD)	1 (is a GC)
Hostname (REG_SZ)	FQDN of the GC (e.g., gc1.acme.com)
PortNumber (DWORD)	3268 decimal (the IP port to contact the GC)
For UserDC1:	
IsGC (DWORD)	0 (only a DC)
HostName (REG_SZ)	FQDN of the DC
PortNumber (DWORD)	389 decimal

UserDC4, and UserGC2, UserGC3, UserGC4, and so on. Define these values under HKLM\System\CurrentControlSet\MSExchangeDSAccess\Profiles\Default. Table 2.8 lists the set of values for the new GC and DC.

Other registry settings exist to allow you to implement a static mapping of the ports used by NSPI (Name Services Protocol Interface) and RFR (Referral Services). Outlook clients use NSPI and RFR to connect to the GAL, and sometimes you may wish to direct them to a specific port, especially if they access Exchange through a firewall. On an Exchange server, the registry values are set at: HKLM\System\CurrentControlSet\Services\MsExchangeSA\Parameters.

Set the port for NSPI in the DWORD value "TCP/IP NSPI Port" and for RFR in the DWORD value "TCP/IP Port." On a GC, you can also force a static mapping of the NSPI port by inserting a similar "TCP/IP Port" DWORD value at HKLM\System\CurrentControlSet\Services\NTDS\Parameters.

Some problems can occur with the maintenance of distribution groups when Outlook clients log on to one domain and the GC is in another, even when the AD connects everything into a single forest. Outlook allows users to update the contents of the group, but they have to be able to write the updated membership back into the group for the update to be effective. If everything belongs to the same domain, then the operation works, because Outlook passes the update to the GC, which applies it to the group. However, if the group belongs to another domain, then the GC is unable to update its contents, because the Partial Attribute Set that contains the membership data is read-only. For this reason, if you want to use Outlook to maintain distribution groups, make sure that the clients connect to GCs in the same domain. See Microsoft Knowledge Base articles 318074 and 281489 for more details.

2.6.3 Automatic topology detection

DSAccess usually exploits automatic topology detection to build a list of suitable GCs. Generally, we want to ensure fast access to recipient information to allow Exchange components such as the Routing Engine to resolve addresses, expand group membership, and route messages. Clients also need good response when they look for a recipient in the GAL or via an LDAP query. DSAccess prefers GCs in the same Windows site, and topology detection only goes outside the site if DSAccess cannot find a local GC. When this happens, the overall performance of an Exchange server may be slower, since it has to communicate across an extended network link each time it needs to retrieve information from a DC or GC. However, the overall impact on performance is mitigated, because Exchange always uses its local cache of directory information first and therefore only needs to make a network call to the directory when it cannot find information in the local cache. When the local controller comes back online, Exchange notices its presence and automatically switches back to use the local system without affecting server operations or clients, an area that Microsoft improved in Exchange 2003. Note that unlike DC selection, Windows domains play no role in identifying suitable GCs, since every GC in the forest holds the recipient data that Exchange needs.

DSAccess automatically rebuilds the GC list every ten hours (this value is based on the standard Kerberos timeout) or if a change occurs in the set of available GCs in the local site. Once it builds the list, DSAccess attempts to balance the load across all available GCs and uses a cache to hold the results of recipient lookups.

The Exchange 2003 installation program supports the /choosedc switch. Microsoft introduced this switch to avoid the problems that sometimes occurred in Exchange 2000 when the server selected a remote DC. While the installation still worked, selecting a remote DC slows things down. You can now use /choosedc to select the optimum DC for an installation, usually one that is near (in network terms) to the server where you are installing Exchange.

2.6.4 Directory suitability tests

The suitability tests provide some interesting background into how DSAccess goes about locating and selecting AD servers. Microsoft introduced the concept of "suitability" to determine whether an Exchange server should use a specific GC or DC server in Exchange 2000 SP2 and implemented the idea in a set of tests. Previously, DSAccess was quite happy to use a DC or GC if it responded to a query to port 389 or 3268—a simple test to see whether a server is offering an AD service. Unfortunately, deployment experience demonstrated that it is all too easy to end up with situations where Exchange connects to a heavily loaded GC, a DC in a remote site across a low-bandwidth connection, or a server that has not fully replicated the contents of the AD. All of these scenarios cause problems for Exchange—routing of messages slows, users experience timeouts when clients attempt to access the GAL, and users might even end up sending messages to outdated addresses.

The suitability tests verify that the server is contactable, responds to queries in a timely manner, and offers services that DSAccess can use. DSAccess divides the tests into three categories:

- Hard: determines whether it is possible for DSAccess to use a server. If a server fails these tests, DSAccess will not select it. For example, if the server is not reachable over port 389 (DC) or 3268 (GC), then it obviously is not an AD server. DSAccess also performs tests to determine whether the AD data on the server is synchronized and participating in normal replication activities, since it would be unwise for DSAccess to connect to an unsynchronized copy of the AD; Exchange would then conduct routing and other critical activities based on outdated information. Exchange also examines the DNS weights and priorities set through SRV records when it tests a server.

  Additionally, DSAccess uses Internet Control Message Protocol (ICMP) pings to determine whether GCs and DCs are "alive." In a front-end/back-end configuration, where the front-end servers are located in a DMZ and the back-end servers are inside the perimeter, it is common practice to disable ICMP traffic to avoid hacker attacks. When this happens, the pings fail, so DSAccess assumes that none of the DCs and GCs in its current topology map is available and therefore begins to examine the network again to discover new controllers to use. You can disable ICMP pings by setting a registry key, as described in Microsoft Knowledge Base article 320529.

2.6 DSAccess—Exchange's directory access component

- Soft: determines the optimum servers for DSAccess to use. For example, DSAccess always prefers to use a server that is in the same Windows 2000 site as the Exchange server. DSAccess also performs tests to determine the load on the server by measuring the speed with which the server responds to LDAP queries and the number of outstanding LDAP queries. DSAccess prefers not to connect to a server that is already heavily loaded, because slow responses from AD queries will slow processing of messages through the Routing Engine. For the same reason, DSAccess avoids a server that holds one of the operations or Flexible Single Master Operations (FSMO) roles for the domain or forest whenever possible, since these servers are also likely to be under load.

- Side: determines the role (DC or GC) that a server can fulfill. For example, is the server a GC?

If you turn diagnostic logging up to minimum (or greater) for the Topology component of the MSExchangeDSAccess service on a server (Figure 2.19), DSAccess reports the results of the suitability tests in the detail for event 2080 in the Application Event Log. As you can see in Figure 2.20, the results reported into the event log are not immediately obvious, but you can interpret the data as explained in the following text. Remember

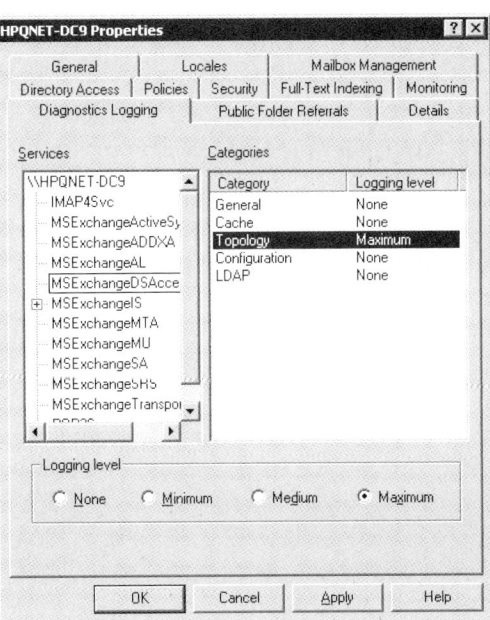

Figure 2.19
Setting diagnostics for DSAccess.

Chapter 2

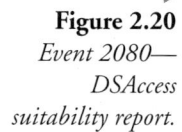

Figure 2.20
*Event 2080—
DSAccess
suitability report.*

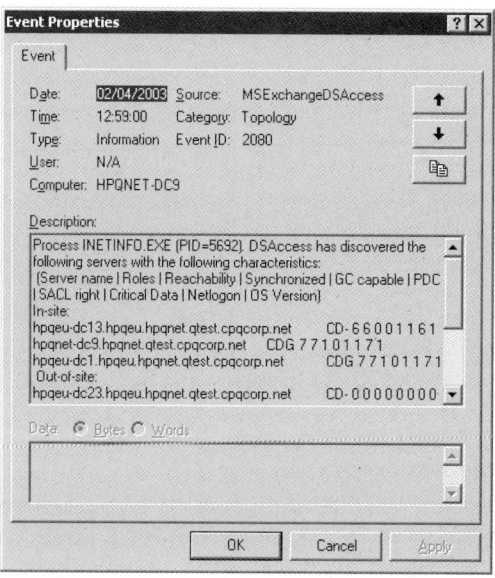

to tone down diagnostic logging after you recover as much data as you need; otherwise, the application event log quickly fills with DSAccess diagnostics.

Exchange divides the servers discovered by DSAccess into those that are in the same Windows site as the Exchange server and those that are outside the site. You will see the following data returned for each server that DSAccess examines:

- The name of the server: A list of the FQDNs of the controllers that are available inside and outside the Exchange server's Windows site—for example, dc1.europe.acme.net.

- The roles that this server can fulfill: D indicates that the server is a DC, G means GC, C means that the server is acting as the Configuration DC. In this case, CDG means that the selected server is able to act as the Configuration DC, DC, and GC.

- Whether or not the server is reachable: This value is a bit mask, where 1 means that the server is reachable as a GC through port 3268, 2 means that it is reachable as a DC through port 389, and 4 means that it can act as a configuration DC (also through port 389). A value of 7 indicates that the server is reachable through all ports and can act in any role. A value of 0 indicates that the server is completely unreachable and therefore DSAccess cannot use it.

2.6 DSAccess—Exchange's directory access component

- Whether or not the server is synchronized: The same bit mask values are used, so 1 means that the GC is synchronized, 2 that the DC is synchronized, and 4 that the configuration DC is synchronized. A value of 7 means that the server is completely synchronized.
- Whether the server is capable of acting as a GC: 1 indicates that it is.
- Whether or not the server is the PDC emulator for a domain: 0 indicates that it is not.
- Whether the server passes the SACL (System Access Control List) test: This test determines whether the server resides inside a domain that you have prepared for Exchange by running the DomainPrep part of the Exchange installation program. A value of 1 indicates that the SACL test passed.
- Whether the server hosts critical data: A value of 1 indicates that the Microsoft Exchange container exists in the configuration NC on this DC. The Exchange container stores critical data, such as server names, routing group information, connectors, and so on, that must be available for routing to work. DSAccess only selects a DC if it hosts this container.

On Windows 2003 servers with Exchange 2003, you see two additional figures. The first indicates whether the server responds to the Netlogon service, the second whether it is running Windows 2003.

You can gain additional information about the DSAccess component through the WMI ExchangeDSAccessProvider provider. Apart from the information reported through the normal UI, the WMI provider allows you to view other details, including:

- The number of asynchronous (nonblocking) connections that are currently open between Exchange and the DC
- The number of synchronous (blocking) connections that are currently open between Exchange and the DC
- How the DC was detected by DSAccess (manual or automatic)
- The type of directory (Active Directory or Exchange 5.5 DS) hosted by the DC
- Whether the DC responds to LDAP requests issued by Exchange in two seconds or less

DSAccess depends on DNS service (SRV) records to learn about available DCs and GCs. After they boot, controllers advertise their capabilities

Table 2.9 *DNS SRV Records Published by Windows Controllers*

Mnemonic	DNS SRV Record
LDAP	_ldap._tcp._<DnsDomainName>
DCByGUID	_ldap._tcp.<DomainGuid>.domains._msdcs.<DnsForestName>
KDC	_kerberos._tcp._dc._msdcs.<DnsDomainName>
DC	_ldap._tcp.dc._msdcs.<DnsDomainName>
GC	_ldap._tcp.gc._msdcs.<DnsForestName>
GenericGC	_gc._tcp.<DnsForestName>

by publishing SRV records in DNS. Table 2.9 lists the common SRV records published by GCs and DCs. You can influence the preference DSAccess has for a particular controller by changing its SRV weighting. Controllers with a low weighting are preferred to those with a high weighting. You can also configure GCs not to announce their availability in DNS. With Windows 2000 servers, you have to configure these settings in the registry, whereas you can use a Group Policy Object in Windows 2003, which makes life easier if you have to get down to this level of detail.

2.7 Interaction between Global Catalogs and clients

Global Catalog servers are tremendously important to Exchange clients. MAPI clients access the GAL through a GC, while Internet clients perform LDAP lookups against a GC to retrieve directory information. When compared with MAPI, the LDAP protocol is basic, so instead of depending on LDAP as a general-purpose access protocol for all Exchange clients, Microsoft uses NSPI, the Name Service Provider Interface. Only GCs support NSP, which means that MAPI clients cannot connect to a DC to retrieve the GAL.

For the purpose of GAL access, MAPI clients divide into two camps. Pre-Outlook 2000 clients base GAL access on the premise that every Exchange server has a dedicated directory service running on the same computer. Outlook 2000 and subsequent clients understand that the directory service can be located on another server elsewhere in the network. The Exchange DSProxy service handles incoming requests from clients for directory access and sends the requests on to a nearby GC for resolution.

2.7 Interaction between Global Catalogs and clients

During a session, DSProxy has to handle every directory access request from pre-Outlook 2000 clients and proxy them on to a GC. In other words, every time a pre-Outlook 2000 client connects to Exchange, DSProxy has to locate the most appropriate GC and pass on the requests to that GC.

Persistent referrals began with Outlook 2000 by being truly persistent. In this case, the lookup to locate the GC happens once, and after that Outlook 2000 always attempts to connect to the same GC without consulting DSProxy. The client holds the fully qualified domain name of the GC in its MAPI profile and uses it each time Outlook 2000 starts a session. If the GC is unavailable, the client then refers to Plan B and asks DSProxy for another referral, and the cycle starts again. This scheme works, but it is flawed since there is no way to implement load balancing or to select a more appropriate GC if one becomes available after Outlook 2000 has written details of the selected GC into its MAPI profile. Accordingly, from Outlook 2000 SP2 onward, the client ignores any information held in the MAPI profile and always consults DSProxy to determine what the best GC is at that point in time and then makes a connection to that GC. You can also control Outlook and point it to a specific GC by writing the fully qualified domain name of the GC into the following registry key:

```
HKEY_CURRENT_USER\Software\Microsoft\Exchange\Exchange Provider
Value Name: DS Server (REG_SZ)
Value Data: FQDN of preferred GC
```

While you can exercise a certain amount of control over client GC selection, you can do nothing to assure a smooth failover for a client if the GC goes offline. At worst, Outlook will freeze solid. At best, you see that you cannot contact the directory. In all cases, the easiest thing to do is to exit Outlook and restart the client to force DSProxy to select a new GC.

Outlook 2003 includes a neat feature to help you understand the connections that exist between client and server. To see the information, hold down the CTRL key when you click on the Outlook icon in the system tray and then select the "Connection Status" option to force Outlook to display the form shown in Figure 2.21. Outlook lists the connections it maintains to GCs and the mailbox server. The number of instances reported for each server attests to the multithreaded nature of communications between Outlook, Exchange (including any public folder replicas you are connected to), and AD. You are also able to see if any failures have occurred on a link and the average response time (in milliseconds). The "Avg Proc" column shows how many milliseconds the server spends compressing the RPC data for the client. For example, you can see that Outlook reports that the average

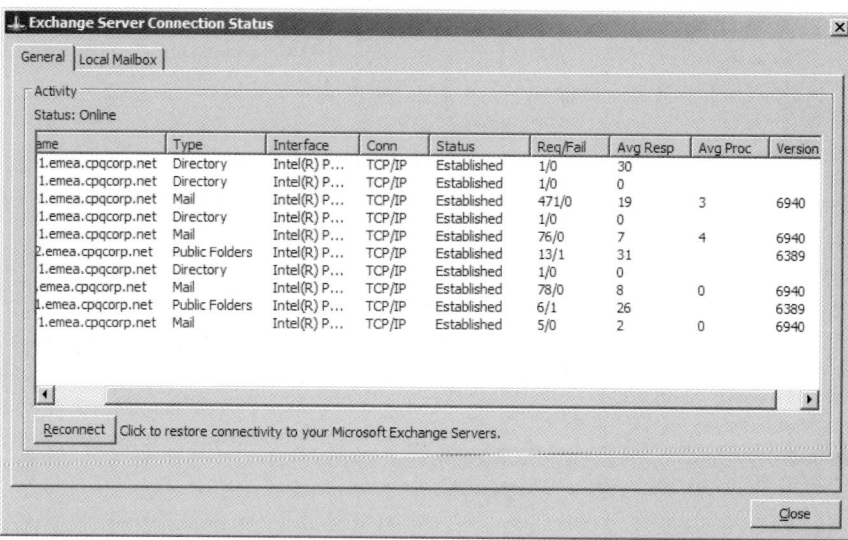

Figure 2.21   *Outlook connections to Exchange.*

response for the first "Mail" connection in Figure 2.21 is 19 milliseconds, and the server spends 3 milliseconds compressing the data. In effect, this means that the real round-trip time between server and client is 16 milliseconds. You can also see the version number of the Exchange server Outlook connects. In this instance, we can see that the servers hosting the mailbox and public folders run different builds of Exchange. The "Local Mailbox" tab on the Connection Status form allows you to monitor any replication activity that Outlook is currently processing. For example, if Outlook is downloading new messages into the Inbox, you will see this information listed here.

2.7.1 How many GCs do I need?

Determining just how many GCs are required to handle the load generated by Exchange is an interesting exercise. Among the factors that influence the decision are:

- AD design: If you are lucky enough to be able to deploy Exchange inside a single domain, by definition, all of the domain controllers are GCs and Exchange can use them for this purpose, since each controller holds a complete copy of all objects—configuration and user—for the entire forest. Through its suitability tests, DSAccess may select different controllers for different jobs, but every controller holds the same information. Contrast this to the situation in a multidomain forest, where GCs hold information significantly different from DCs. While the DSAccess suitability tests will locate the most suitable DC and GC for Exchange to use, DSAccess depends on the SRV records registered by DCs and GCs in the AD to know which computers offer these services. Therefore, it is essential that DNS operates reliably—this factor increases in importance with the number of controllers in the forest.

- Application load: Exchange depends on GCs for many purposes, including the expansion of distribution groups and validation of email addresses. Other applications may also use GCs and therefore contribute to the overall load that the environment generates on the GCs. Small deployments may consider using a single server to host both the GC and Exchange. It is best practice to avoid all-inclusive servers for corporate deployments, because their configuration is more complex, especially in the case of a failure and restore exercise, and because you can compromise AD security if many administrators have physical access to a domain controller.

- Available hardware: Clearly, a multi-CPU server equipped with 2 GB of memory is capable of supporting a heavier workload than a single-CPU server with 256-MB supports. As with most database applications, the AD is able to use memory to cache data and reference the data in memory instead of going to disk, so servers that have more memory usually help it to support a greater workload. Additional CPUs allow the server to partition the load generated by applications and avoid situations where a single application swamps the system with its demand. Some AD deployments may have commenced using older servers as DCs and GCs and find that the performance of these servers struggles as application load increases, perhaps because of a migration to Exchange. If you enhance the hardware for these servers, it will let them support more application demand. The alternative is to deploy additional servers, an unattractive option because it increases management workload.

- The number of mailboxes supported per server: Servers that support large mailbox populations generate higher loads on GCs than smaller servers do. For example, it is easy to appreciate that a server supporting 4,000 mailboxes generates a higher load than one supporting 500 mailboxes. Thus, as server numbers reduce through consolidation projects, it is important to focus on the overall number of mailboxes in the organization instead of concentrating purely on the number of servers.

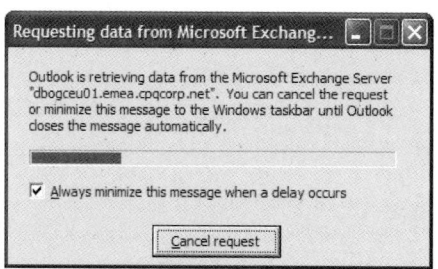

Figure 2.22
Outlook 2002 has problems talking with a GC.

With these points in mind, the usual starting points for any discussion about GC numbers and placement are:

- Make sure that every Exchange server is close to a GC and that every Windows site that hosts an Exchange server also has a GC. In this context, close means that the two servers are ideally on the same network segment or as near to this situation as you can achieve. Every network interruption causes problems for both the Exchange server and Outlook clients, so keeping a GC in close network proximity is a wise choice. The danger signal is when Outlook clients have problems retrieving information from a GC when users validate addresses in message headers, as shown in Figure 2.22. If you use Outlook 2003, you can reduce the user perception of the problem by running Outlook in cached Exchange mode and let "drizzle" background synchronization take care of communications. However, while cached Exchange mode helps, it cannot fix a fundamental problem caused by GC unavailability.

- In large Windows sites, make sure that you have at least one GC for every four Exchange processors. Originally, the recommendation was to have one GC for every four Exchange servers, but it has changed over time to reflect the fact that a large percentage of Exchange servers are multiprocessor systems. This is a rule of thumb and not a design principle that you need to follow always. In particular, if servers support large mailbox populations, monitor the workload generated on the GCs and add extra controllers once the GCs show any sign of stress. For example, inside HP, the design rule is: Begin with one GC everywhere we install an Exchange server and then add an extra GC for every 4,000 mailboxes.

- Consider creating a special AD site for Exchange servers and install GCs within the site for Exchange to use. The DSAccess suitability tests always prefer GCs that are within the same AD site as the Exchange server. This approach also keeps other demands (such as expanding distribution groups during the Windows logon process) away from the GCs that serve Exchange, which may be important in large deployments.

- To avoid possible performance problems, ensure that Exchange servers do not select the GC that Windows uses as the PDC emulator.[5] The PDC emulator usually experiences a heavy workload to handle account updates, and acting as a preferred GC for Exchange may introduce enough additional workload to affect the response to clients. For the same reason, you should avoid using GCs that handle intersite AD replication traffic as much as possible. In small AD deployments, this should not be a factor, since any server should be able to handle the replication traffic, but it can certainly cause concern inside large deployments.

- Always avoid a single point of failure. Because Exchange and Outlook depend so heavily on the GC, always make sure that a failure of one GC will not affect your users to a noticeable degree. You can configure Outlook 2002 (or later) clients to contact the "closest" GC or a preferred GC, which may be useful if you want to control exactly which GCs Outlook uses.[6]

While best practice is to separate Exchange from AD servers, you can certainly run Exchange 2003 on a server that also hosts the AD, and you may want to do so in small branch offices where hardware is limited. However, there are some points to bear in mind. First, you cannot run this configuration on a cluster, because Microsoft does not support Exchange and AD coexistence on a cluster. Second, the server must be a GC rather than a DC. Performance can be an issue, so Exchange and AD both like to absorb system resources, but in small branch offices, the server probably handles a limited user community, since any reasonably sized computer will be able to handle the load. When you run the two components on the same server, system shutdown is slower than normal, since DSAccess will time out several times before it shuts down, because the AD process (LSASS.EXE) shuts down before Exchange. You can avoid this issue by stopping the Information Store process manually before shutting down the system. Security is the biggest issue in coexistence. If Exchange administrators can log on at the server console, they can potentially elevate their permissions and gain access to restricted data. Obviously, you should trust your system administrators, but even so, it is best practice to avoid logons at the system console.

---

5. See Knowledge Base article 298879 for more information.
6. See Knowledge Base articles 319206, 317209, and 272290.

2.7.2 The GC logon cache

The GC logon cache is a new feature in Windows 2003 that can restrict the need to deploy additional GCs to resolve the membership of universal groups during the logon process. When a user authenticates by providing his or her credentials to a DC, Windows builds a security token that contains details of all the groups the user belongs to. For the DC to build the token, it has to resolve the membership of the groups, and the only way it can do this is by reference to a GC. Remember, only a GC contains details of the membership of universal groups, so given that Exchange is a major consumer of universal distribution groups, the accurate resolution of group membership is another reason why GCs are so important to Exchange. However, while it is good to contact a reliable source to resolve group membership, this can sometimes lead to situations where large organizations have to deploy more GCs than they want, especially inside Windows sites that serve small branch offices. The GC logon cache allows a Windows 2003 DC to maintain a local cache of group membership in its local AD database that it prefetches or periodically resolves against a GC. Thus, clients can authenticate themselves against a DC and have their group membership fully resolved if the details already exist in the cache. Note that a user must log on and successfully authenticate with a GC present before the local DC can cache his or her group membership. Group membership data exists in the local cache until it expires, normally after eight hours. You can change the expiration period by modifying the registry as follows (value in minutes):

```
Key:HKLM\System\CurrentControlSet\Services\NTDS\Parameters\
Value:Cached Membership Site Stickiness (DWORD)
```

Microsoft Knowledge Base article 241789 describes a workaround for Windows 2000 that instructs domain controllers to ignore GCs during user authentication.

Microsoft's idea is that you can reduce the number of GCs you deploy by only having the need to deploy DCs in each Windows site. In this scenario, the DCs need to connect to GCs to fetch group membership data, but you can keep these GCs at a central location and manage them there. Potentially, this gives you another advantage, because central sites often link together with high-speed ATM connections, so fast replication is seldom an issue. To enable the GC cache, you select the NTDS Site Settings object for the Windows site through the AD Sites and Services console and modify its properties, as shown in Figure 2.23. You can see that in this case, the Houston

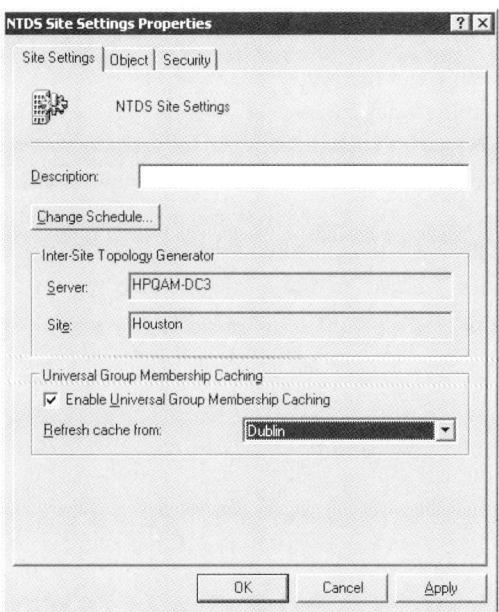

Figure 2.23
Enabling the GC cache.

site refreshes its GC cache from the Dublin site. The cache refreshing interval is based on the replication schedule for the site link.

As you deploy Windows 2003 DCs, you may decide to implement the GC logon cache. Before you do, be aware that this feature exposes a potential for someone to access information that is usually unavailable. For example, assume that you remove a user from a group that protects a public folder that holds sensitive information. The user's workstation is part of a Windows site that uses the GC logon cache. The problem occurs when the user has either not logged on recently (to pick up his or her new group membership) or the DC has not refreshed the local GC logon cache. In either case, it is conceivable that the user can continue to access the public folder, because the security token that the DC constructs during the logon process continues to include the credentials granted to the group.

All of this proves that the provision of a new feature that Microsoft intends to solve a particular problem (in this case, the deployment of too many GCs to serve small branch offices) can have an unfortunate side effect on an application, if you deploy it without thinking through the consequences. Best practice is, therefore, to keep existing GCs in place unless you are positive that they are no longer required.

2.8 Exchange and the Active Directory schema

Schemas define the structure of a database, including the object classes and the attributes held for each object. The AD schema is extensible by applications or enterprises to allow it to hold additional information. For example, you could extend the directory to add a new "Birthday" attribute for user objects, and then write an AD-enabled application that ran when a user logged on to check whether it was his or her birthday, generating an appropriate message on the day in question. First-generation Exchange includes 15 "custom" attributes for mailboxes that you can use for similar purposes, but you cannot extend the schema of the Exchange directory.

Exchange 2000 was the first application to extend the AD schema by adding new attributes that can then be associated with recipients (users, contacts, and groups) as well as configuration information about Exchange, such as administrative and routing groups. Exchange 2000 makes over 1,800 changes to the default schema, and Exchange 2003 follows up with a further set of over 140 changes and additions. For example, Exchange 2000 extends the user object with storage attributes to allow users to be associated with the Store where their mailboxes are located as well as any quotas placed on the mailboxes. Exchange also changes a number of index attributes so that they participate in address resolution. Among the changes made by Exchange 2003 are those necessary to support Outlook Mobile Access, the iNetOrgperson structure, and new features such as recipient filtering and protected distribution groups. Because Exchange 2003 extends the schema even more than Exchange 2000, you need to run the Exchange 2003 version of ForestPrep to ensure that the forest is properly prepared before you install the first Exchange 2003 server.

Depending on your configuration, you might apply two sets of schema changes during an Exchange deployment. The ADC applies the first set of changes to extend the schema to add a number of attributes used to synchronize between the DS and the AD. The Exchange 2000 installation program applies the second set of changes to round off the extensions required by Exchange when it installs the first server in the forest. However, if you deploy Exchange 2003 and you have not updated the schema, the schema changes for the ADC and Exchange are identical, so you only have to update the schema once. Applying schema updates is a CPU-intense activity, so be prepared for the server to be very occupied for a half hour or so during this phase of the installation.

The changes applied by the ADC include Exchange-specific attributes to be included in GC replication. The ADC is only required for deploy-

2.8 Exchange and the Active Directory schema

ments that must accommodate legacy servers; green field implementations that only deploy new Exchange servers do not use the ADC. The Exchange 2000 installation procedure is, therefore, able to apply a complete schema update or just updates that are a superset of those already implemented by the ADC. Exchange 2003 applies a single set of schema changes to the AD, so there is no differentiation between the ADC and Exchange.

Several phases occur during the schema update to allow the AD to commit changes to the database in a controlled manner. It is necessary to apply the changes in a staged manner to avoid any potential problems that might occur if a schema update is unable to reference a change applied earlier.

The Exchange installation procedure checks the current schema version for the forest when it begins and determines if it has to update anything. The check looks at the value of the ms-Exch-Schema-Version-Pt object, which holds the current schema number in its rangeUpper attribute. If the schema version is less than the required value, the installation procedure updates the schema. The ADC installation procedure checks the ms-Exch-Schema-Version-ADC to determine whether it has to update the schema. You can look into the SCHEMA9.LDF file on the server kit to check the schema version that the installation procedure will look for, and then use ADSIEDIT to

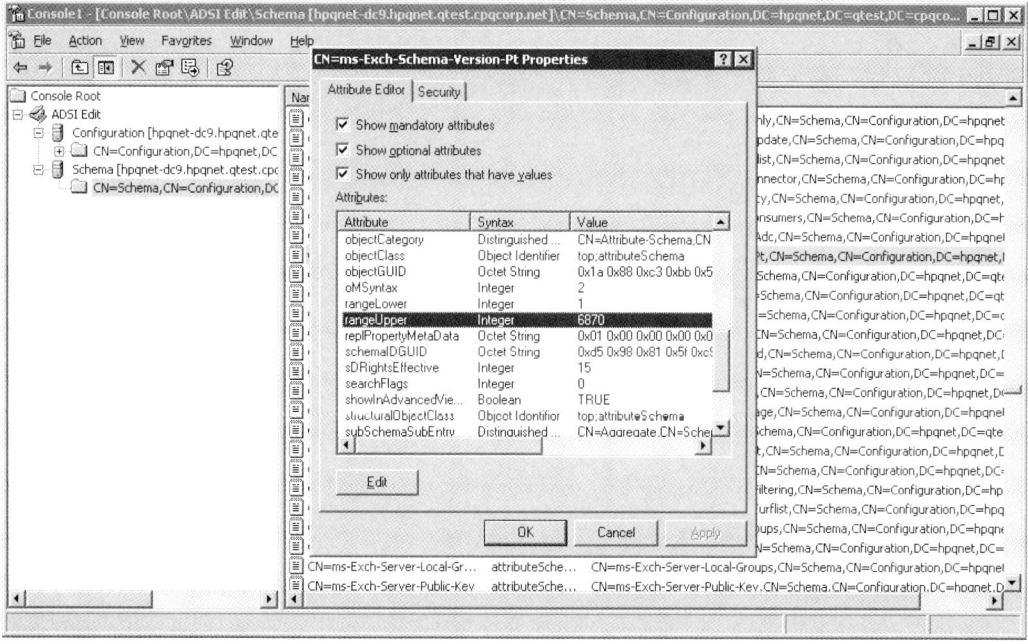

Figure 2.24   *Checking the schema version.*

connect to the schema and check the current value of the rangeUpper attribute for MS-Exch-Schema-Version-Pt to see if the two match. Figure 2.24 shows how ADSIEDIT reports the current schema version.

Future versions of Exchange service packs and hot fixes may include schema updates. The schema administrator (the person responsible for controlling changes made to the AD schema) may ask you to provide exact details of the updates before authorizing the update. This is a good example of how closely the base operating system administration team has to work with the messaging team.

2.8.1 The impact of updating the schema with new GC attributes

Whenever you update the schema with new attributes that you want to include in GC replication, the AD also modifies the isMemberOfPartial-AttributeSet attribute. In Windows 2000, such a change forces full synchronization across all GC servers in the forest, an operation that can generate a lot of replication traffic. According to Microsoft, the net bandwidth consumption for each GC is equivalent to that consumed when you promote a DC to become a GC. You should not notice the impact on small or high-bandwidth networks, but this can certainly be an issue if you need to update the schema for organizations that include many GC servers spread across different capacity network connections, when the subsequent replication activity may take a long time to complete.

Best practice is, therefore, to generate a schema update plan early in a project and make sure that you apply schema changes as early as possible in a deployment to minimize replication. Ideally, you should try to make the schema changes immediately after you create the forest, so that all new controllers pick up the new schema when you promote them from normal servers through the DCPROMO process. Better still, upgrade your forest to Windows 2003 and take advantage of the fact that its replication mechanism suppresses unnecessary activity like this and only replicates the changed information.

2.8.2 Updating the schema with an installation

The easiest way to update the schema is to just go ahead with the first Exchange server installation in a forest, but you can update the schema beforehand by utilizing two options that are included in the Exchange installation procedure. You execute SETUP with these options from an

2.8 Exchange and the Active Directory schema

administrator account that has full permission to modify the AD. Once the AD is prepared, you can perform subsequent installations of Exchange using accounts that have local administrative access, but are not privileged to change forest-wide settings such as updating the schema or adding the Exchange container to the configuration naming context.

The options are:

- SETUP /ForestPrep: This option runs in the root domain of the AD forest (or the domain that hosts the schema master—which is normally the root domain). /ForestPrep performs the set of changes to the schema, instantiates the Exchange organization, adds the Exchange container to the configuration naming context, and creates the Exchange Admins and All Exchange Servers universal groups. You cannot execute this command unless you are able to log on with Enterprise Admin and Schema Admin privileges. In addition, if you need to join an existing Exchange 5.5 organization, you must have at least read access to the DS. Note that if you plan to run a mixed-mode Exchange organization that includes both Exchange 2000/2003 and earlier servers, you should install the AD Connector (ADC) within the organization before you run the ForestPrep procedure. This is a mandatory step for Exchange 2000 (because of a dependency on a connection agreement to gather configuration data) and does no harm when you deploy Exchange 2003 servers. Organizations that run in native mode and therefore do not include legacy Exchange servers do not require an ADC. ForestPrep also creates a public folder proxy container in the root domain of the forest. Exchange uses the public folder proxy to hold the email addresses for mail-enabled public folders.

- SETUP /DomainPrep: You run this option in every domain where an Exchange 2000/2003 server is located. The option performs tasks such as creating the global groups used for Exchange administration. You must be a domain administrator to be able to run this option.

The ForestPrep option is a useful thing to execute if you want to replicate schema updates throughout the forest before you begin server installations. The sheer number of changes applied to the schema is a good reason to perform the installation (or schema update) of the first Exchange server close to the schema master (at least in network terms), since this will speed up processing of the schema changes. Windows makes schema changes to the configuration container of the AD on the target controller and then replicates them to the other controllers throughout the forest. Figure 2.25

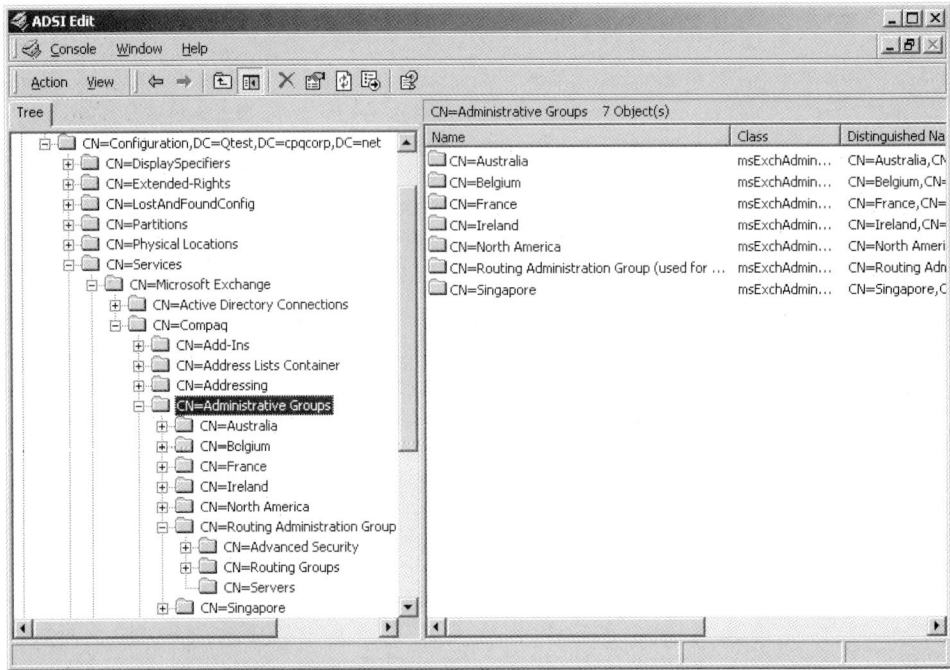

Figure 2.25 *The Exchange configuration container.*

shows the ADSIEDIT utility examining the properties of the AD container used to hold configuration details for Exchange. Every object in the AD has a distinguished name, so the container used to hold Exchange data is named <domain-name> /Configuration/ Services/ Microsoft Exchange, and it holds a number of other containers to store details of entities, such as routing and administrative groups, address lists, connectors, and so on. See section 2.6 for information about how Exchange connects to controllers to access the configuration data.

Because it offers you the ability to view just about every property of an AD object, ADSIEDIT is the most powerful and flexible utility to view Exchange data in the configuration container. However, if you simply want to look at the overall shape of the organization, you can use the AD Sites and Services snap-in, as shown in Figure 2.26. To do this, open the snap-in and select the "Show Services Node" option from the View menu. You can then see information about the services configured in the AD, including the ADC. Be careful when viewing information like this, since it is all too easy to make a mistake and delete something important.

2.8　Exchange and the Active Directory schema　　　　　　　　　　　　　　　　　　　　109

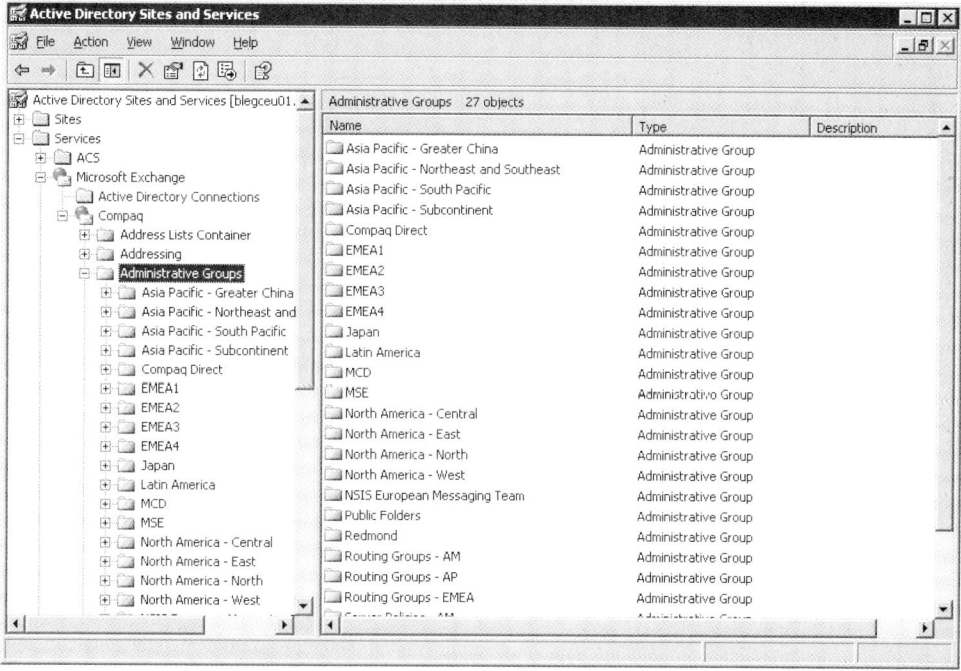

Figure 2.26　*Using AD Sites and Services to view configuration data.*

2.8.3　Changing the schema

The provision of an extendible schema is a major feature of the AD, but even though it is great to be able to customize the directory, the feature introduces some new issues for consideration. Updating the schema does not impose a performance penalty. The new attributes occupy no space in the database unless you populate the attributes with data. However, once you make a change to the schema, there is no way back (in Windows 2000). You cannot roll back the change, and the AD will replicate it throughout the forest. You can deactivate attributes by setting their isDefunct flag, but Microsoft does not support any way to remove them from the schema. In a fully functional Windows 2003 forest, you can reactivate a deactivated attribute.

Changing the schema is, therefore, something that you must treat very seriously and only perform when a change is justified and you fully understand the ramifications. For this reason, you should agree on any change up front with all of the domain administrators. Ideally, someone within the organization should take responsibility for arbitration of schema changes,

Chapter 2

and anyone who wishes to make a change should first consult that person. Schema anarchy is not a pretty sight! For this reason, some companies keep the membership of the Schema Admins group empty until they know they need to make a change, whereupon they add the necessary user to the group until after the change, when they revoke the membership.

It is also a good idea to apply as many schema changes as possible at the start of an implementation, since this means that every new DC will inherit the fully updated schema as part of the DCPROMO procedure. The alternative is to make schema changes as the need arises, but this means that you have to let the AD replicate each set of changes throughout the forest before you can proceed to deploy applications that depend on the schema update.

Attributes can be single valued (such as your home telephone number) or multivalued (such as the membership of a group). Before you change the schema to add a new attribute, you need the following information:

- The name of the new attribute and its purpose: In directory terminology, this is the common name. You can provide a separate description, although in many cases, for the standard AD attributes used by Windows or Exchange, the description is very similar to the name.

- Because the roots of AD are in X.500, each attribute and object has a unique X.500 object identifier, or OID. A national registration authority, such as the American National Standards Institute (ANSI),[7] issues OIDs. You can make up the value for an OID, and as long as the value does not clash with the OID of another attribute, you will not have a problem. However, if an application comes along in the future and attempts to add an attribute with an existing OID, then you will have a problem and the application will not be able to add the new attribute to the schema. One method that is sometimes used is to take the base OID for the DSA provider and append your company's international telephone number plus some sequence number to it to create the new OID. This method usually guarantees uniqueness.

- The type or syntax of the attribute and its maximum and minimum range: For example, an attribute held as string values will be stored as unicode strings and can range in size from one to whatever number of bytes is required to hold the maximum string length.

- Whether or not the AD should replicate the attribute to GCs: Clearly, the more attributes that are replicated, the more data that is transmitted across the network. Some attributes are not required

---

7. See http://www.ansi.org/public/services/reg_org.html.

2.8 Exchange and the Active Directory schema

enterprise-wide and can be restricted to an object's home domain. The AD has to replicate others, such as the attribute that holds details of an Exchange user's home mailbox server, throughout the forest to enable specific functionality, such as message routing. The impact of adding attributes to the Partial Attribute Set replicated to GCs is much less in Windows 2003.

- Whether the AD indexes the attribute and includes it in the Ambiguous Name Resolution (ANR) process: Exchange has supported ANR since Exchange 4.0.

Before we look at the details of how to change the schema, we need to update the system registry on the server where we want to apply the change. Ideally, you should apply all updates to the schema at the schema master. If not, the server that you use to make the change needs a fast connection to the schema master to make the change. Applications such as Exchange often include commands to update the schema in their installation procedures, but in this instance we update the schema via the AD Schema snap-in. By default, Windows does not activate the AD Schema snap-in, and you must register it before you can load the snap-in into an MMC console. Type the following command to register the snap-in:

```
C:> \WINNT\SYSTEM32\REGSVR32 SCHMMGMT.DLL
```

After the command successfully completes, you can start MMC with a blank console and load the Schema snap-in. You can then browse through the schema, as shown in Figure 2.27, which displays some of the additional attributes used for Exchange.

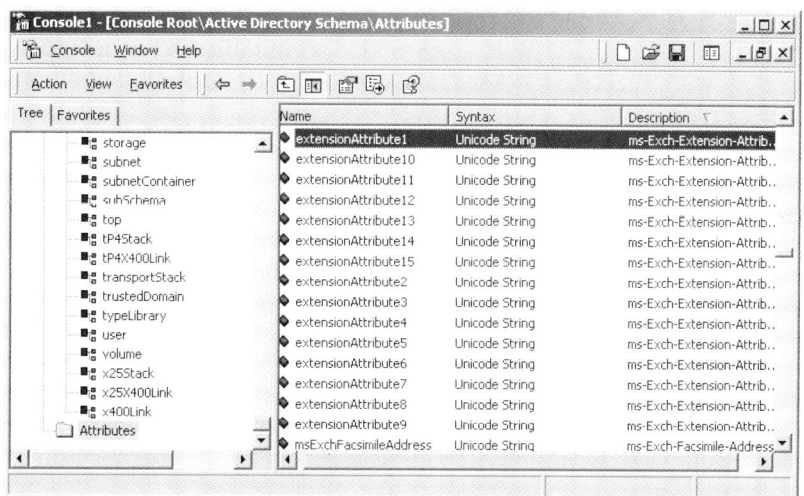

Figure 2.27
Viewing Exchange attributes in the AD schema.

Table 2.10 *Registry Values to Allow Schema Changes*

Value	Notes
Schema Update Allowed (DWORD)	Set to 1

To protect administrators against accidental changes, the Windows 2000 version of the schema console allows read-only access by default, so you need to update the registry to enable write access. To update the registry, go to the following key and insert the values shown in Table 2.10. You do not need to do this on a Windows 2003 server.

```
HKLM\System\CurrentControlSet\Services\NTDS\Parameters
```

The schema is loaded into memory on every DC in an area called the schema cache. To ensure that clients access changes promptly, the AD reloads the schema cache from disk every five minutes. If you change the schema, you can force the AD to reload the cache immediately from an option in the Schema snap-in. This ensures that all the changes are active before you attempt to use them.

2.8.4 Updating the schema for ambiguous name resolution

Ambiguous name resolution (sometimes called Automatic Name Resolution) is the process used by Exchange to search the AD to find addresses that match information provided by users. In other words, Exchange searches the AD against a number of different fields to find any matching addresses. If Exchange finds a number of matching addresses, we have an ambiguous name, and Exchange prompts the client to present the addresses to the users in a dialog for them to make the final selection.

Exchange checks attributes such as the first name, surname, display name, and mailbox alias during the ANR process. ANR is invoked whenever a user presses the CTRL/K sequence, or when an unresolved address is detected in the TO:, CC:, or BCC: fields of a message header. MAPI and Outlook Web Access (Figure 2.28) clients support ANR. Outlook Express also performs ANR, if you configure the client to check names against the AD before sending messages.

It may be advantageous to alter the schema to include a customized field in the ANR process. First-generation Exchange servers allocate 15 fields in the directory for site customization purposes. The AD provides a similar set, called extensionAttribute1 through extensionAttribute15. You could

2.8 Exchange and the Active Directory schema

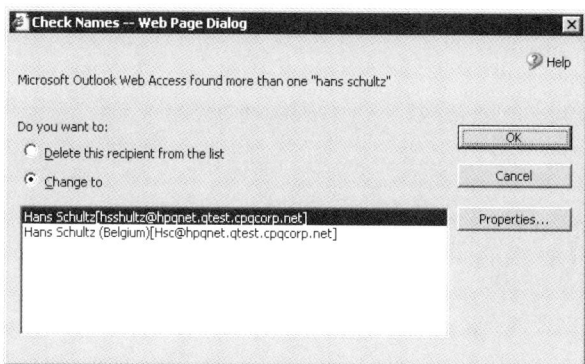

Figure 2.28
Ambiguous names detected by Outlook Web Access.

populate one of these fields with details such as a department code and add this attribute to the ANR process, if this makes sense within the company. Remember that changes to the schema are forest-wide, and you cannot reverse a change once made, so be sure to consider all aspects of making the change before implementation.

Three different properties govern whether Exchange can use an attribute for ANR. Figure 2.29 shows the properties of one of the custom attributes inherited from Exchange 5.5. Instead of "custom attribute 1" through "custom attribute 15," the attributes are ms-Exch-Extension-Attribute-1 through -15.

Looking at Figure 2.29, you might wonder why I say that three properties govern ANR when only one is marked as such. The reason is simple. The "Ambiguous Name Resolution" property determines whether the ANR process uses the attribute, but it is not very smart to mark an attribute for ANR if it is not indexed, and only slightly smarter to keep an attribute used by ANR out of the GC. After all, if the AD does not index the attribute, any attempt to check a name against the attribute will be very slow and frustrate users, and if the attribute is restricted to one domain, its value is useless anywhere else in the forest. For best effect, check all the properties.

2.8.5 Exchange-specific permissions

Along with an upgraded schema, Exchange also adds a set of permissions to AD to allow administrators to perform operations such as managing databases. The permissions, which Microsoft refers to as "extended rights," exist in the configuration container under "Extended-Rights," as shown in Figure 2.30. All of the rights that Exchange uses have an "ms-Exch" prefix, so they are easy to find.

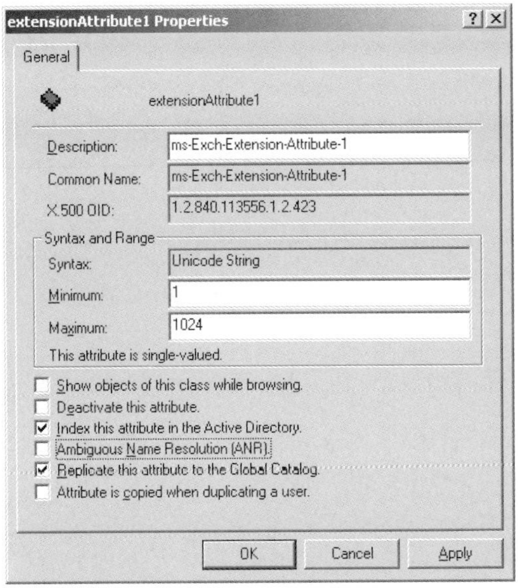

Figure 2.29 *Where to enable ANR resolution for a selected attribute.*

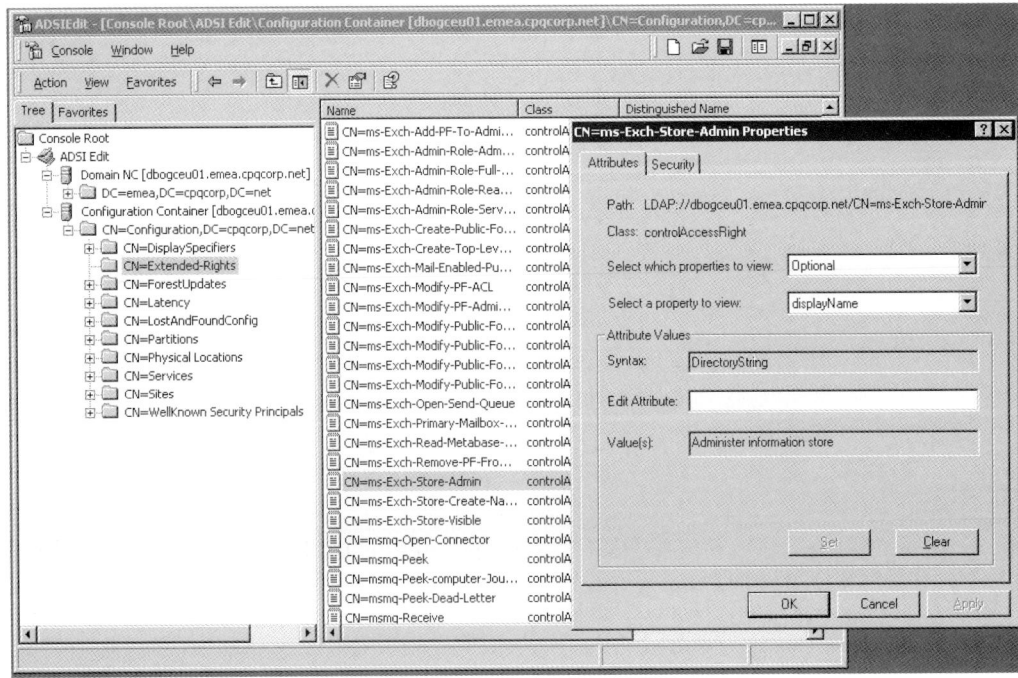

Figure 2.30 *Extended AD permissions used by Exchange.*

Property sets are a special type of extended right. A property set is a group of object properties that you can use to define access control on an object by manipulating multiple permissions in a single operation. For example, if you enable the Read Public Information (a property set) permission on a user object, you actually enable users to see the values in the object's email addresses, manager, and common name attributes. Exchange uses property sets extensively to simplify administrative operations. If it did not, we would be constantly updating permissions on AD objects to try to assign the necessary rights to get work done.

2.9 Running Exchange in multiple forests

When Microsoft launched Exchange 2000, its advice was simple: One AD forest was sufficient to support user accounts and directory-enabled applications such as Exchange. Microsoft underlined this approach by allowing only a single Exchange organization per AD forest. Indeed, in the early days of Windows 2000 it was a form of heresy to suggest that anyone might need to deploy multiple forests. However, times change and circumstances develop that require some companies to deploy multiple instances of Exchange, each in its own forest. Among the reasons to deploy multiple forests to support Exchange are:

- You need to support multiple Exchange organizations, each requiring a separate forest.

- You need to include Exchange organizations acquired through a company merger or acquisition.

- You need to isolate different parts of the business in separate Exchange organizations to make it easier for the company to divest operating entities.

- Operating units may have their own IT department, which makes its own decision on what email system to operate. If the IT department selects Exchange, it may not choose to join a corporate deployment and will run its own to maintain operational independence.

Perhaps the worst reason to deploy multiple forests is the situation when a unit within the company begins to deploy Exchange earlier than the official deployment and so establishes its own AD forest to support the deployment. You can migrate the users from this organization over to the corporate organization when it is ready or let the two organizations run together. In other situations, an operating unit of the company must operate a secure or isolated email system to comply with government regulations. For example, a financial services company may have to run one Exchange organization for its trading unit and another for its merchant banking division.

2.9.1 Costs of multiple forests

After you determine that the need exists to deploy multiple forests, you can proceed to assess the costs of deployment. Costs arise from:

- Software tools
- Complexity in administration
- The need to synchronize data between the forests
- The degree of fidelity required between the forests

The last point is possibly the most important, because synchronization of elements such as accounts is a simple task, while synchronization of data such as public folder contents is complex and requires more effort and

Table 2.11 *Costs to Exchange Data between Multiple Forests*

Outcome	Tools	Cost
Messaging connectivity	SMTP and X.400 connectors	None: part of basic Exchange functionality
Address book synchronization	LDAP synchronization utilities such as HP LDSU or Microsoft MMS 2003 (GALsync)	Effort required to map AD objects between multiple forests to achieve consistency in address book views
Cross-forest calendar scheduling	InterOrg Replication Utility for Free/Busy data	Basic scheduling works, the effort is needed to make free/busy data visible to users across the forests
Public folder content synchronization	InterOrg Public Folder Synchronization utility	Effort required to identify public folders that should be synchronized and then to establish synchronization schedules, plus ongoing monitoring
Shared infrastructure resources (DNS, DHCP, network, single sign-on)	Standard Windows tools	Design effort to establish various infrastructures, with most effort required for single sign-on architecture
Account and mailbox moves between forests	Microsoft ADMT (or third-party utilities) and Exchange Migration wizard	Planning and control of mailbox moves between forests

therefore cost. Table 2.11 lists the major cost elements in multiforest deployments.

You can use tools from Aelita, BindView, and other vendors to help move accounts and mailboxes between forests. These tools incur additional cost and the preferred approach is to use the free Microsoft tools (ADMT and the Exchange Migration wizard) whenever possible. However, you may have used other tools for other purposes, such as to migrate from Windows NT 4.0 to Windows 2000/2003 and can continue using them to aid cross-forest movement.

2.9.2 Directory synchronization

Exchange is an email server, so establishing messaging connectivity is the easiest part of multiforest operations. Given the SMTP-centric nature of Exchange 2000/2003, it is best to deploy SMTP connectors whenever possible. However, you may need to use X.400 connectors if the organizations share the same address space (such as two organizations that use hp.com as their address space). Assuming that messages can pass between Exchange servers in the different forests, the next issue is to build cross-forest address books by synchronizing details of mail-enabled objects so that each forest can build its own view of the complete environment. Generally, this means that you synchronize details of mail-enabled accounts, groups, and contacts from each source forest to the various target forests. You have the following choices:

- Deploy a full metadirectory solution, such as Microsoft Metadirectory Services (MMS).

- Deploy a simple LDAP directory synchronization solution, such as HP's LDSU or Microsoft's GALSync, a component of MMS.

- Write your own tool to exploit APIs such as ADSI and LDAP to work with the contents of the AD.

Microsoft bought the technology for MMS from a company called Zoomit some years ago and has since developed it to become a full metadirectory service. A metadirectory accepts feeds from sources such as the AD, normalizes the data, and then provides feeds to consumers. Note that MMS does not support LDAP access to data.

MMS is full of features, but it can be complex to deploy. In addition, you may not need a full metadirectory, especially if you only want to exchange information between directories that are very close in structure to each other—for example, to exchange information between two AD forests or between the AD and the Exchange 5.5 DS, or to synchronize user account information in the AD with an LDAP-compliant HR database such as PeopleSoft. Given the increasing number of multiforest deployments, Microsoft recognized that it had to make the directory synchronization process easier and the GALSync tool is the result.

GALsync is a special utility built on top of MMS to deal specifically with the challenge of multiple AD forests. As the name implies, GALsync generates a synchronized GAL, using some preconfigured management agents to gather data from the different forests. GALsync supports hub and spoke networks, where a central forest acts as the gathering point for information from multiple spoke forests, and fully meshed networks, where each forest synchronizes its data with the others. However, GALsync does not support daisy-chained synchronization, where forests provide their information to another forest, which then sends a collated set to a third forest, and so on.

While GALSync does a good job of combining user and contact information from multiple AD forests, sometimes you need to synchronize information from multiple LDAP-compliant sources or you need to exert more control over how information flows into a directory. For example, you might have to modify information from one directory before it can go into another directory. You might have to match attributes and transfer data held in an attribute in one directory and remap it to a different attribute in another directory. In these instances, it is best to deploy a utility such as LDSU (search www.hp.com to find the latest information), which is designed to work with any LDAP-based or flat file directory and perform anything from simple to complex processing on data during the synchronization process. As with a metadirectory, LDSU is also able to normalize data and generate feeds for different directories. LDSU synchronized the Exchange directories when Compaq and Digital merged in 1998 and again when HP and Compaq merged in 2002, so it is well versed in merger and acquistion scenarios.

2.9.3 Calendar interoperability

Many companies are satisfied when the different operating units can send messages to each other and share a common GAL. This represents the lowest acceptable degree of cross-organization integration within a company. Providing a way to share calendar and public folder data represents the next degree of integration and introduces another level of complexity.

Users can send calendar meeting requests as soon as you establish messaging connectivity, and the recipients are able to process the meeting requests and accept or reject the meeting and have its details inserted in their calendars. However, by default, meeting organizers cannot view the free and busy information for recipients outside their own Exchange organization, because Exchange holds free and busy data in a system public folder that Outlook searches when it needs to retrieve information about the schedule of potential meeting attendees. There are three approaches to the issue. You can:

- Ignore it and force users to send meeting requests between each other until all recipients can agree on a mutually acceptable time. This is a reasonable solution when you plan to merge users from multiple organizations into a common organization and do not want to expend the effort required to exchange free and busy information between the organizations.

- Ask users to publish their free and busy data to Microsoft's Internet Free/Busy Service. Essentially, this means that users sign on to a shared service maintained by Microsoft to publish free/busy data there. Other users can then consult your free/busy data by connecting to Microsoft's service. This approach is acceptable when you have only a small number of users that need to share free/busy data for a short time while you prepare a migration—for example, if you have a small number of senior executives in each organization who need to organize meetings with each other. The downside is that Microsoft plans to remove this service towards the end of 2004. See Microsoft Knowledge Base article 842166 for more information.

- Use Microsoft's InterOrg Replication Utility[8] to replicate free/busy data between the organizations. You can use the same tool to replicate data from other public folders as well. A copy of the latest InterOrg Replication Utility is in the /support directory on the Exchange 2003 server CD. The utility can replicate data between Exchange 5.5, Exchange 2000, and Exchange 2003 servers. This is the best option when you plan to operate multiple organizations alongside each other for sustained periods. Microsoft Knowledge Base article 238573 provides detailed instructions about how to deploy the InterOrg Replication Utility.

While all these solutions work, there is a clear requirement for user education and support. With the first option, users have to understand why

---

8. The original need for the InterOrg Replication Utility arose when Microsoft deployed two separate Exchange organizations—one for the Exchange team and the other for the rest of Microsoft. People wanted to be able to schedule common resources such as meeting rooms and so Microsoft developed a utility to exchange calendar data between Exchange organizations.

they can see free/busy data for one set of users and not for others. With the second option, they have to be instructed how to publish their free/busy data to Microsoft's Internet service and how to log on (with a Microsoft passport) to consult data for other users. The third option is the most transparent for users, but it is the most onerous for system administrators, who must install and operate the InterOrg Replication Utility and debug any problems that occur.

2.9.4 Common platforms

Organizations that come together because of mergers and acquisitions usually have separate Windows and network infrastructures to support users and applications—for example, separate Windows domains, physical networks, and so on down to client platforms and methods for remote access (RAS, VPN, etc.). Following a merger, you may decide to keep the separate infrastructures or consolidate. The former is the easiest but most expensive option, because of the almost inevitable duplication in servers and other infrastructure components. Consolidation is the most attractive financial option, because you can reduce the number of domains, eliminate redundant servers, merge networks together, and so on to make the infrastructure less complex and easier to manage. However, it takes a lot of time and effort to consolidate computer infrastructures, so this is not a project to jump into overnight.

2.9.5 Moving users between different Exchange organizations

You can use the standard Move Mailbox wizard to move mailboxes within the same organization, but moving from one organization to another poses a different challenge because of the requirement to create Windows accounts, preserve legacy email addresses, and so on. Microsoft provides the Exchange Migration wizard to move a user from one Exchange organization to another. Originally designed to migrate users from Exchange 5.5 to Exchange 2000, the wizard now accommodates movements between any Exchange organization (5.5, 2000, and 2003). As shown in Figure 2.31, you can also use the Migration wizard to move mailboxes from other messaging systems such as Lotus Notes and Novell GroupWise. The Migration wizard first appeared in Exchange 2000 SP1 and is now installed alongside other Exchange 2003 components as part of the standard kit, so you can access it like any other program in the Deployment Tools folder. The processing flow is as follows:

2.9 Running Exchange in multiple forests

- Select the migration type. In this case, we want to move one or more mailboxes from another Exchange server in a different organization, so select "Move from Microsoft Exchange."

- Select the target server and mailbox store for the mailboxes.

- Select the source server and provide login information for a permissioned account on that server. A trust relationship must exist between the source and target Windows domains. You must have Exchange administrator permission on both the source and target servers. If moving from a different email system, you must have the appropriate administrative permissions on the source server to allow the Migration wizard to extract messages and other items and transfer them to the target server. The source and target servers must share network connectivity and, due to the amount of data that some mailboxes hold, faster connections are obviously desirable.

- You then select the information to migrate. You can apply filters to move only messages within a specific date range (a year is the default option) or provide the wizard with a text file giving message subjects that you do not want to move. For example, you may decide not to move any messages that contain "Hi" as the subject, because these messages are unlikely to contain much business value.

- The wizard connects to the source server and displays a list of the mailboxes that it holds (left-hand screen in Figure 2.32). You select the mailboxes to move and then select the organizational unit in the

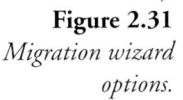

Figure 2.31
Migration wizard options.

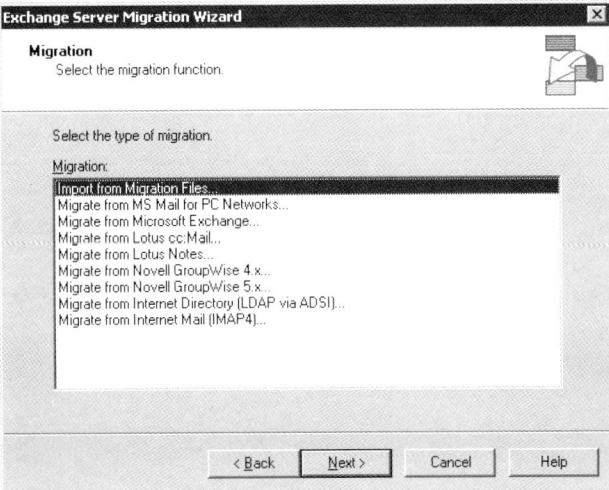

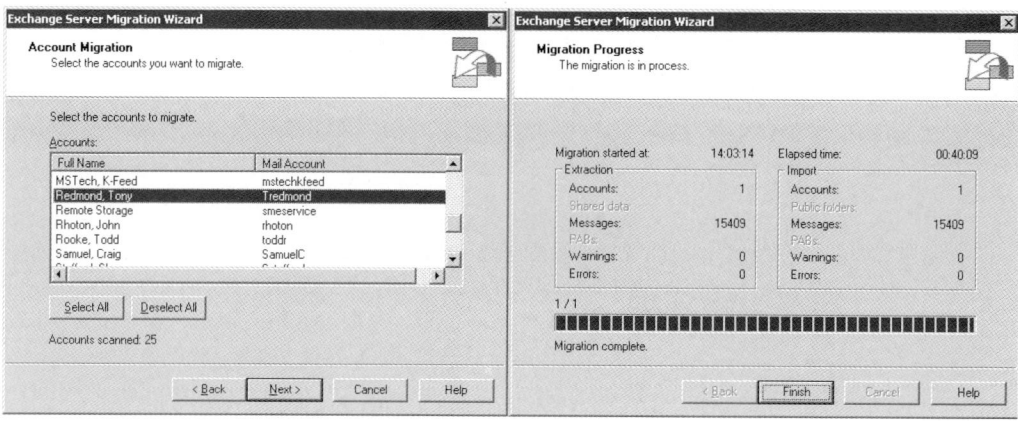

Figure 2.32 *The Exchange Migration wizard in action.*

AD to create new accounts for these users. The wizard then checks to see whether the accounts already exist, in which case you can opt to use the existing accounts, or it proposes new accounts. You can amend details of a new account by selecting it from the list, right-click, and taking the "Edit" option.

- The wizard then begins to process the mailboxes. It creates disabled Windows accounts using account information taken from the source system, creates the mailboxes in the target store, and then begins to transfer data, reporting information in a progress screen (right-hand screen in Figure 2.32). The wizard also writes information about its processing into the Application event log, as shown in Figure 2.33.

After the wizard finishes, you must enable the Windows account and create a new profile to allow the user to access his or her mailbox. The user must supply a new password when he or she logs on, or an administrator can reset the password and provide the new credentials to the user. Note that the contents of the source mailbox are not affected and you must remove mailboxes and accounts from the source system manually, but only after you are certain that the migration is successful.

Migrating mailboxes can take a long time to process. For example, the wizard required 40 minutes to move a mailbox with 15,409 items occupying 540,197 KB in the Store between two servers connected on the same LAN. During this period, Exchange generated 172 transaction logs (860 MB). As with all mailbox moves, it is best to perform these operations at system quiet times and ensure that you have sufficient capacity within the Store (to accept the new mailboxes) and on the disk that holds the transac-

2.9 Running Exchange in multiple forests

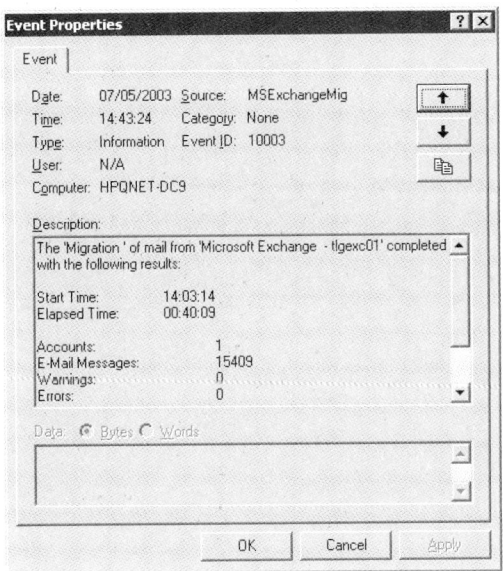

Figure 2.33
A successful migration.

tion logs. The migration wizard connects to mailboxes with MAPI and appears to be a normal logon. Users can remain logged on during the move, but this is a bad idea.

The Migration wizard preserves old email addresses to allow Exchange to deliver messages users send to old addresses. The wizard writes old email addresses into user records in the AD as SMTP, X.400, and X.500 proxy addresses, and the Exchange Routing Engine searches these addresses before it fails to route a message if it cannot find another match. Microsoft first used the technique of using X.500 proxy addresses to preserve old email addresses in the Exchange 5.5 Move Server Wizard, so it works. Figure 2.34 shows details of a user who has been through several corporate acquisitions, so the Migration wizard has preserved the old "digital.com," "compaq.com." and "hp.com" SMTP addresses, while the Recipient Update Service allocates a new primary SMTP proxy for the current Exchange organization (hpqnet.qtcst.cpqcorp.net). Similar processing has occurred for the X.400 addresses, and the set of X.500 addresses preserves the set of legacy Exchange first-generation internal addresses.

Aside from all the processing it already performs, the Exchange 2003 version of the Migration wizard ensures that users do not have to recreate their offline store file (OST), which is an important step given the prominence of cached Exchange mode introduced in Outlook 2003. Rebuilding an OST is always a pain, especially across a slow connection, so the

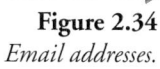

Figure 2.34
Email addresses.

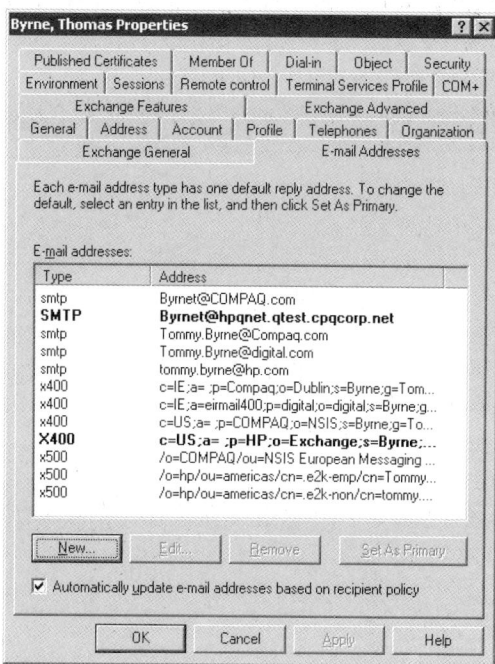

Exchange 2003 version of the wizard supports a new clone mode (invoked by running mailmig.exe with the /M switch). Clone mode transfers the value of the MapiEntryID attribute for the source mailbox to the target store to preserve the connection between the token held in the OST and the mailbox.

2.10 Active Directory tools

The AD is a complex place and sometimes you need additional tools to understand exactly what is happening. In this section, we look at two tools that are useful to Exchange administrators: ADSIEDIT and LDP. If you have the good fortune to use LDSU, the tool set includes the www.ldap-test utility to examine AD information.

2.10.1 ADSIEDIT

ADSIEDIT allows administrators to browse and manipulate raw AD data. ADSIEDIT is a double-edged sword: It certainly allows you to interrogate and view details of any of the AD naming contexts, but it is also very possible to change something best left untouched. First-generation Exchange

2.10 Active Directory tools

servers offered similar facilities by running the administration program in "raw mode"; some mistakes were made, such as deleting a complete recipient's container or altering the configuration of an organization, and sometimes a complete restore was necessary to fix the problem. The same is true of ADSIEDIT, and an inadvertent slip of the finger can stop Exchange from working if you make a mistake in the wrong place. However, generally administrators practice safe directory access by never changing an object unless they know the exact consequences.

Normally, you access the AD through the AD Users and Computers snap-in, which enforces rules and restrictions through its user interface. Another way of putting this is to say that AD Users and Computers stops administrators from making mistakes by changing or deleting important AD data. Windows does not include ADSIEDIT, and you must install it as part of the Windows Resource Kit, which you can find in the SUPPORT\TOOLS directory of the server kit. On either version, you can install the utility by copying adsiedit.dll from the Support Tools kit to the systemroot\system32 folder, then registering adsiedit.dll, and then loading the adsiedit.msc console into MMC. To register adsiedit.dll, type the following at a command prompt:

```
C:> cd systemroot\system32
C:> regsrv32 adsiedit.dll
```

To load the ADSIEDIT snap-in to MMC, start MMC and then click on the Add/Remove Snap-in option on the File menu. Then click on the "Add" button to view the snap-ins that are available on the server, and then select the ADSIEDIT snap-in from the list (Figure 2.35). Click Add, Close, and then OK to make the snap-in active in the console.

After you have loaded ADSIEDIT into MMC, you need to connect to an AD naming context before you can work with data. Right-click on the ADSIEDIT root and select the "Connect to" option to force ADSIEDIT to display the Connection Settings dialog shown in Figure 2.36. If you want to work with account and contact information, you connect to the Domain NC; if you want to work with configuration information, such as the Exchange organizational data, then you connect to the configuration NC. By default, ADSIEDIT attempts to connect to a GC in the local Windows site. You can click on the "ADSI Edit" root and connect to another controller elsewhere in the forest by typing the full name of the server. Note that the default connection is to the domain naming context for the selected server and that ADSIEDIT maintains any existing connections, including to the schema and configuration naming contexts, unless you use the "Remove" option to release the connection. Once connected, you can

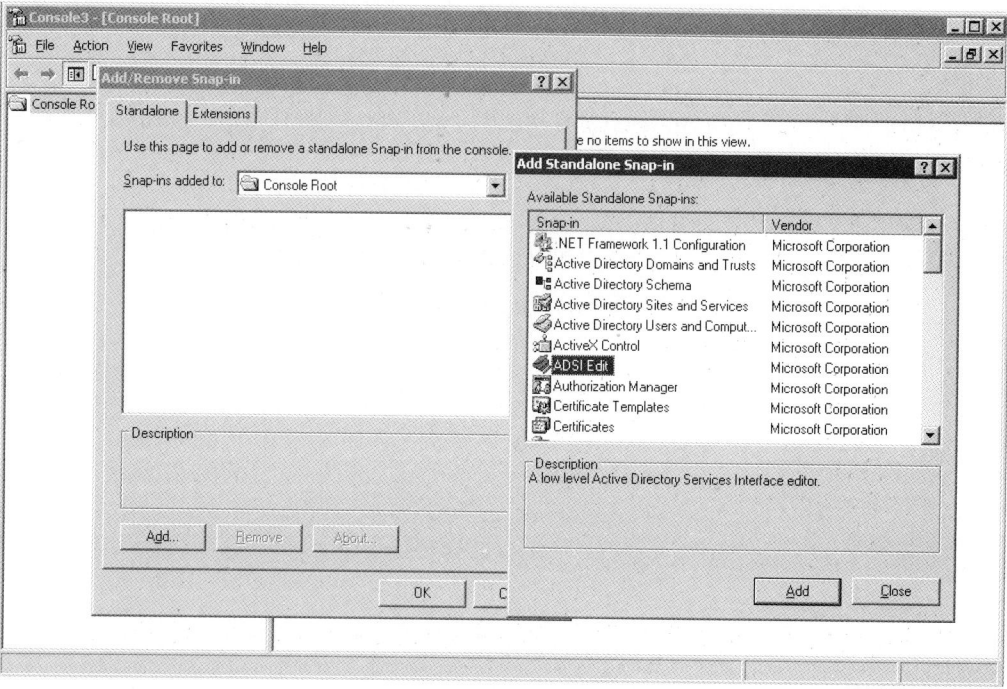

Figure 2.35   *Adding the ADSIEDIT snap-in to a console.*

browse the contents of each of the naming contexts in the same way as any other MMC console.

Figure 2.37 shows ADSIEDIT in action loaded into an MMC console. By default, ADSIEDIT connects to a GC in the local Windows site. You can click on the "ADSI Edit" root and connect to another controller elsewhere in the forest by typing the full name of the server, as shown in Figure 2.36. Note that the connection is made to the domain naming context on the selected server and that ADSIEDIT maintains any existing connections, including to the schema and configuration naming contexts, unless you use the "Remove" option to release the connection. Once connected, you can browse the contents of each of the naming contexts in the same way as any other MMC console. Figure 2.37 shows the contents of the domain naming context, so objects such as user accounts are listed. Note the query-based distribution group object shown here. Figure 2.38 shows samples of the schema naming context (left) and configuration naming context (right). In most cases, administrators use ADSIEDIT only to browse the schema and configuration and almost never make changes to these containers. There are two known exceptions to this statement. First, you may want to change an

2.10 Active Directory tools

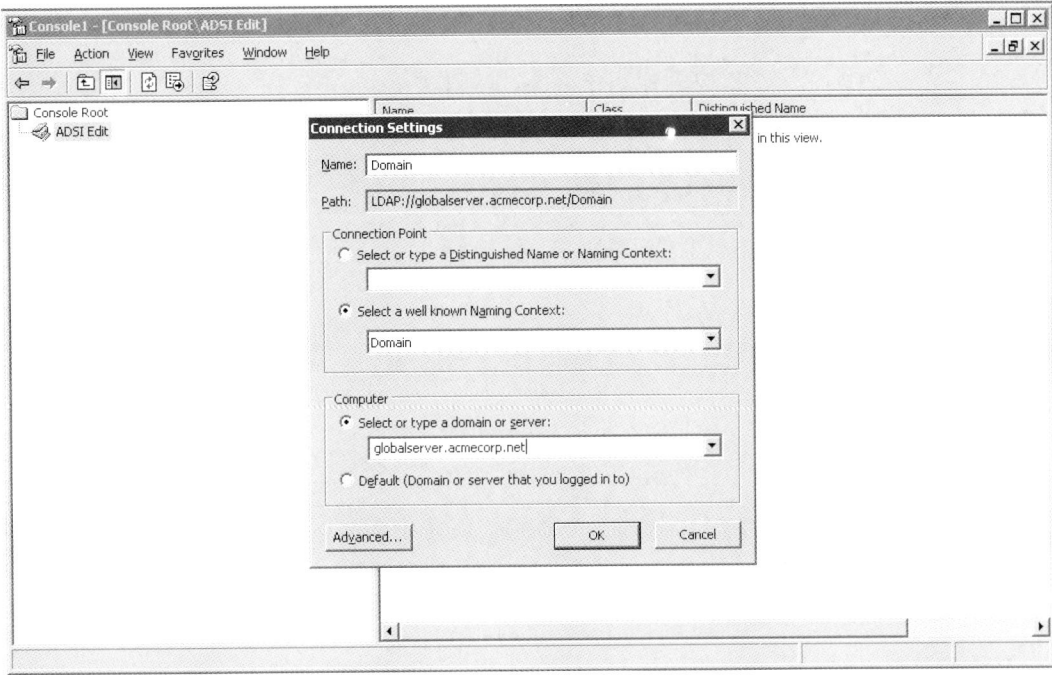

Figure 2.36   *Connecting ADSIEDIT to a naming context.*

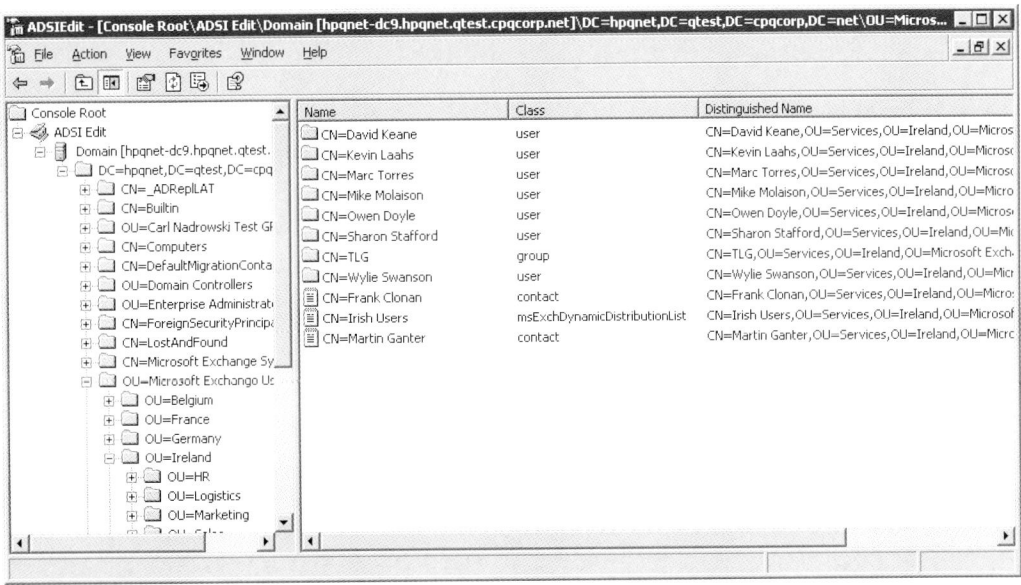

Figure 2.37   *The ADSIEDIT utility.*

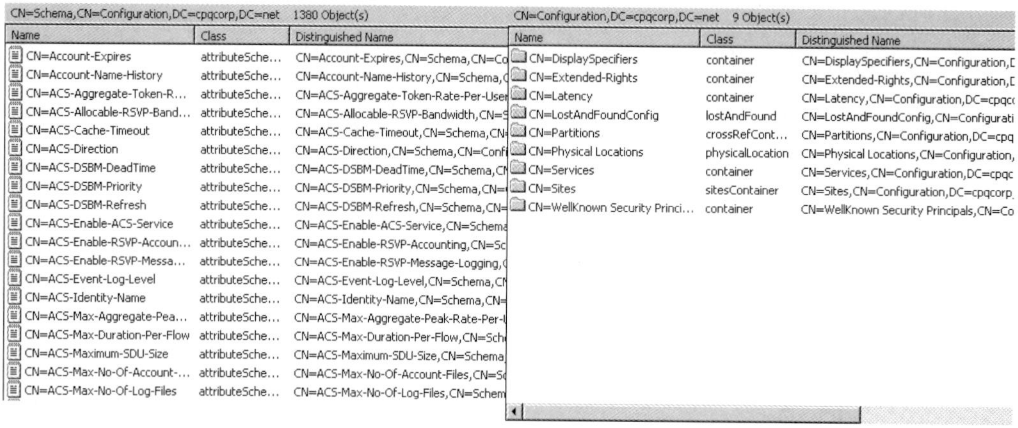

Figure 2.38 *Schema and configuration naming contexts.*

attribute so that Exchange uses it as part of the ambiguous name resolution process. Second, you must update server properties in the Microsoft Exchange container in the configuration naming context to change the location of the message tracking logs. A registry change is also required to update a network share before Exchange fully relocates the message tracking logs.

Administrators most commonly use ADSIEDIT to examine the properties of objects and verify that the right values exist in the various attributes. There are many and varied reasons why you should use ADSIEDIT for this purpose. Even the Advanced View of AD Users and Computers only reveals a limited selection of the attributes of an object, so you have to use a different tool (and ADSIEDIT is very convenient) if you want to examine the hidden attributes. Many of these attributes are very important in migration and directory synchronization projects. For example, you may want to verify that the ADC is writing the correct value into the legacyExchangeDN attribute after it synchronizes mailbox details from a legacy Exchange organization. On the other hand, if you are using your own procedures to synchronize the AD with a metadirectory, you may want to check that the synchronization process is writing values from the metadirectory into the correct attributes.

As an example, let us assume that the metadirectory holds information about business units and we have implemented code to transfer this data to the extensionAttribute15 attribute in the AD. To check that the synchronization code works correctly, we use ADSIEDIT to select any user object and then view its properties, selecting the appropriate attribute, as shown in Figure 2.39. As you can see, the string "TLG" exists in

2.10 Active Directory tools 129

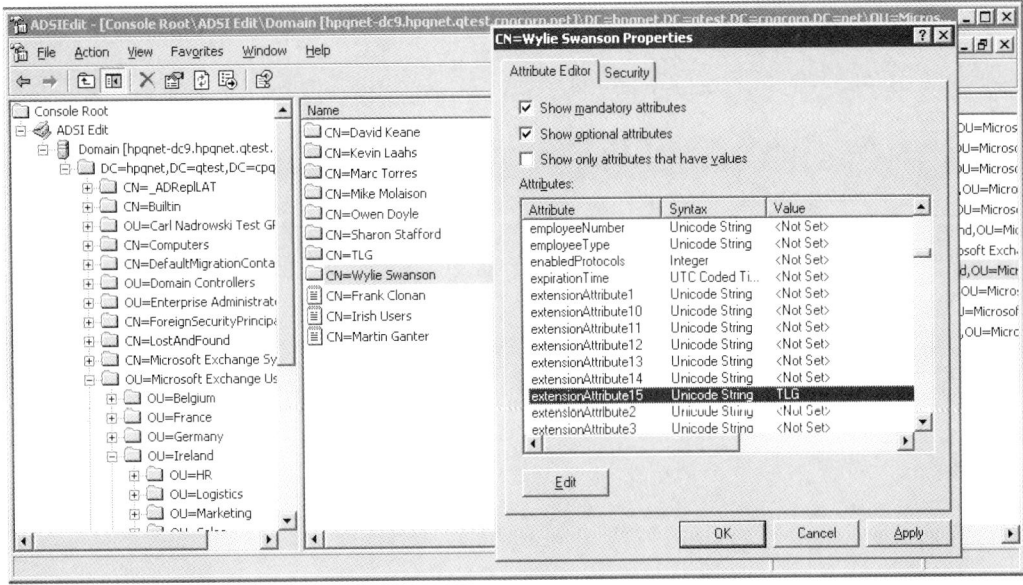

Figure 2.39 *Using ADSIEDIT to view properties of a user object.*

extensionAttribute15. If this is the value in the metadirectory, we know that the synchronization code works. Of course, if the wrong value is present we have another problem to solve! In passing, ADSIEDIT is much better in Windows 2003 than Windows 2000, because you can see a range of attribute values at one time rather than having to examine each individually. You can also suppress extraneous attributes and focus on a set such as the mandatory attributes or only look at attributes that have a value set. These are small but important points.

It is possible to use ADSIEDIT to edit the value of properties, but I cannot think of a good reason why anyone would do so. The sheer fact that the capability exists is enough for someone to try it, and it is technically possible to change something like one of the CN parts of a distinguished name to either alter the display name of the object or move the object to another container. No guarantee exists that the change will be valid or that other processing will be required to effect the desired change. Making changes via ADSIEDIT is an activity to attempt on a test system in order to verify the long-term effect before attempting to alter anything on a production system.

Windows administrators also use ADSIEDIT for many purposes. For example, assume that a domain controller suffers a catastrophic hardware

Chapter 2

failure and you do not want to reinstall the server. Because an administrator has not run the DCPROMO process to demote the server, it still exists in the AD as a domain controller with all of the associated roles and responsibilities, such as acting as a replication partner. In this case, you could use ADSIEDIT to remove all references of the server from the AD. Later on, if you wanted to reintroduce the controller, you can rebuild the server and then run DCPROMO to make it a domain controller.

2.10.2 LDP and LDIFDE

If you want to get even closer to raw data, the LDP utility is available. While ADSIEDIT is quite capable of performing brain surgery on the AD, LDP is able to examine individual nerves. LDP is a good example of a utility that works brilliantly in the hands of a software engineer or someone who knows his or her way around LDAP and needs to retrieve diagnostic information. If you just want to poke around the innards of the AD for a casual browse, use ADSIEDIT. LDP is just too dangerous, because the GUI does not protect you, so a simple slip or mistype of one character can have enormous consequences. The big difference between the two utilities is that you cannot examine many attributes together for an object with ADSIEDIT, whereas you can look at many together with LDP. In addition, even though the Windows 2003 version of LDP is improved, its user interface is very basic and it is easy to make a mistake. For example, you have to type in the name of an attribute when you modify it, whereas ADSIEDIT allows you to select the attribute from lists. Knowledge Base article 224543 is a good introduction to LDP and explains many of its functions.

Figure 2.40 shows the LDP utility connected to a DC. In this case, I began searching in the OU that holds some user accounts, selected one, and then began to modify an attribute. The Browse menu allows you to add, delete, or modify attributes for selected objects, but in most cases, you simply want to interrogate the AD to discover information about objects. You can see the contents of the OU in the tree view in the left-hand pane and some of the attributes and their values in the right-hand pane.

When you examine a user object, you can see a large amount of data, including the links to the distribution groups that the user belongs to and any organizational data that exists (the manager and direct reports). You can also look at security descriptors, while the replication option allows you to see replication metadata. This information is very valuable if you need to provide it to Microsoft PSS to help solve a complex problem, but it is not usually very valuable in day-to-day administration. After you have investi-

2.10 Active Directory tools

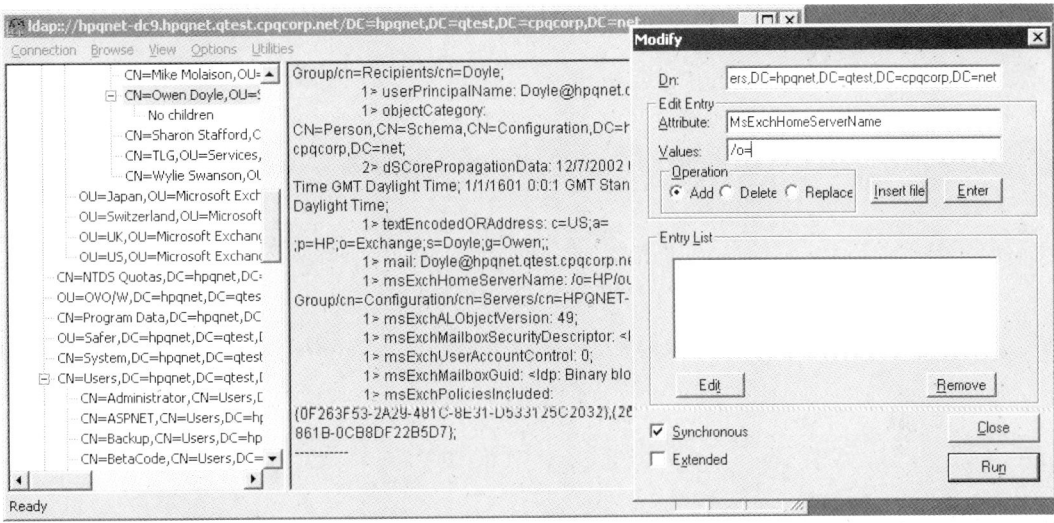

Figure 2.40 *LDP utility.*

gated the AD with LDP, you may want to change the values of some attributes. You can certainly do this with ADSIEDIT, but again you have to operate on one object at a time.

LDIFDE is a utility that exports or imports LDAP-compliant data into the AD. Knowledge Base article 237677 gives you a good overview of the process, but you will also need to become conversant with LDAP syntax and the set of attributes supported by the AD to process anything other than simple exports and imports. RFC 2254 is the authoritative source for information about LDAP search strings, while you can discover the names of the attributes that you want to work with by examining the properties of a selected object with ADSIEDIT or LDP.

LDIFDE works on very basic principles. You create a file that contains the operations you want to perform against the AD and then feed it to LDIFDE for execution. In most cases, the easiest way to accomplish the goal is to export data about the objects you want to process first, use a text editor to make whatever changes you want, and then run LDIFDE again to import the file and make the changes.

2.10.3 ADSI programming interface

The AD supports ADSI as its COM-compatible programmable interface, so there is nothing to stop programmers from performing whatever operations they need against the database. The same caveats apply as for ADS-IEDIT. Always perform multiple tests and understand the results and consequences of the changes before working with production data.

ADSI has been mentioned a couple of times in passing. Many of the tools that work with the Active Directory are based on ADSI, a standard set of COM interfaces that supports any directory for which a suitable ADSI provider is available. A provider is an interface to a specific directory. Active Directory is only one of the directories that currently support ADSI; the others include:

- IIS: For access to the Internet Information Server metabase
- NDS: For access to Novell Directory Services. Two variants are available: NDS for NetWare 4 and above and NWCompat for NetWare 3.
- WinNT: For access to information about Windows NT computers

The ADSI provider for the AD is LDAP, but this does not mean that ADSI is built on top of LDAP. Instead, it means that AD is the default LDAP-compliant directory that you find on Windows 2000 computers. If you are programming ADSI, you need to reference the LDAP provider, but you are still going through ADSI to get to the AD. Think of LDAP as the way to retrieve information from the AD and ADSI as the preferred programming interface.

3

Exchange Basics

3.1 The organization

Some messaging systems come together as a loose federation of servers. In such an arrangement, servers do not necessarily know about the other servers and must connect through central routers, perhaps by reference to a directory. Other systems, such as Exchange, use a far tighter arrangement. Exchange organizes servers into a single hierarchy called the organization and then divides the organization into administrative groups, all of which exist at the same level within the hierarchy. The concept and overall structure of the organization has not changed much since Microsoft introduced it in Exchange 4.0, except that the major organizational subunit is now administrative groups rather than sites.

Because all configuration data is in a single AD container, there can only be one Exchange organization per AD forest. The administrative group is core to Exchange and provides the foundation for management through permissions and policies.

As explained in Chapter 2, the AD holds details of the Exchange organization in the "Microsoft Exchange" container in the configuration NC (Figure 3.1), which the AD replicates to every domain controller in the forest. Therefore, every domain controller contains knowledge of every Exchange server in the forest, including the routing topology that connects all the servers.

You can have up to 1,000 Exchange servers in an organization. The limit is not hard coded as such but results from the fact that the default page size for results returned by the AD for directory queries can hold 1,000 entries. The limit exists for Exchange 2000 and Exchange 2003. You can argue that this limit restricts the usefulness of Exchange, but then you might struggle

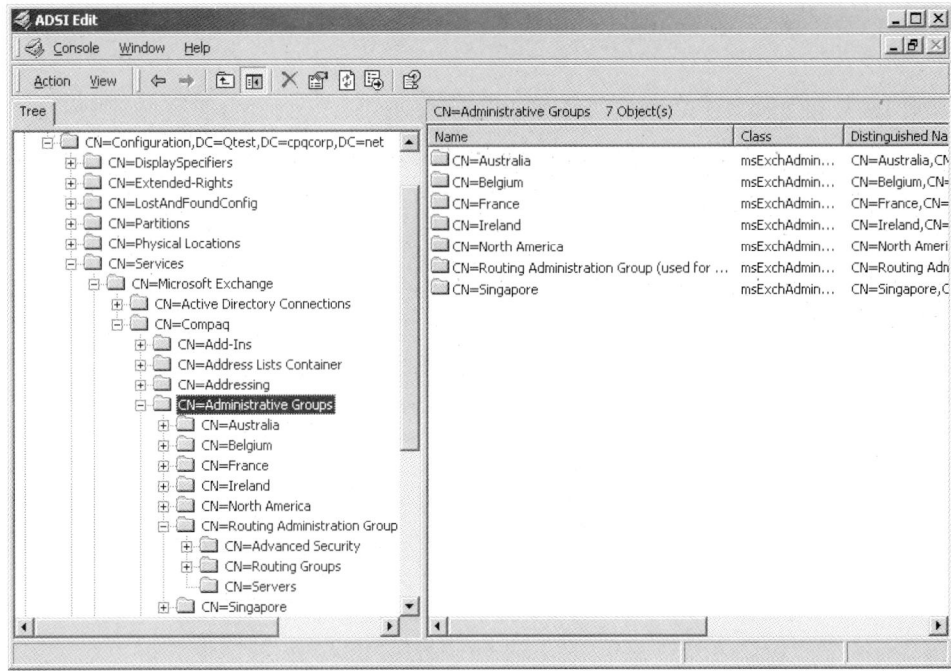

Figure 3.1 *Contents of the Microsoft Exchange AD container.*

to define exactly where the restriction is important. The vast majority of deployments cover 200 servers or less, and there is growing focus on reducing the number of servers in use through aggressive consolidation projects that take advantage of increased server and storage capabilities. Thus, while a small minority of projects might consider deploying more than 1,000 servers, the limit does not affect the majority.

3.1.1 Back to the past—Exchange sites

Best practice has long been for system designers to seek LAN-quality connectivity before attempting to combine Exchange servers. Early deployments (1996–1997) often struggled with the bandwidth requirement and resulted in organizations built from many sites, each of which had a small number of servers. Designers often centered sites on cities or countries to follow network connections. Generally, the more management units that exist in an organization, the harder it is for administrators to manage the organization. More messaging connectors are required to link the sites together and message routing is more complex. Each site increases the amount of directory replication traffic and it is easier for replication problems to occur. In addition, it is not easy to move mailboxes between sites, so larger sites allow greater flexibility in balancing mailboxes across servers.

As these lessons became better known and network costs started to decrease, companies consolidated and deployed larger sites. The Move Server Wizard is available from Exchange 5.5 SP3 onward to move servers from one site to another and you can use this tool to restructure an organization into a smaller number of sites. Moving to a smaller number of sites reduces replication and routing complexity and generally eases the strain on the network. However, while administration is generally easier and message routing is more consistent in large sites, the lack of granularity for management operations is a problem. Essentially, once you grant an account the necessary permissions to perform administrative tasks within a site, the account can manage all of the servers, connectors, and mailboxes within the site. This is not a problem with small sites, since a small number of administrators usually manage these sites, all of whom know the environment well, but it is an issue in the largest implementations, where sites might span entire continents. For instance, in a site that includes servers from every country in Europe, an administrator in France might take an action that affects the ability of a server in Norway to route messages. The French administrator might not even realize that a problem has occurred unless he or she monitors the operation of the Norwegian server. A greater degree of granularity would restrict the French administrator to operations affecting the local server.

Even though the site concept delivers a low degree of administrative granularity, it has proven effective in practice. There is no doubt that the site model served the first generation of Exchange well. It is easy to forget that Microsoft designed Exchange 4.0 when most NT servers had decidedly modest hardware configurations, and an initial goal of the Exchange 4.0 release was to move users off Microsoft Mail post offices, most of which served very small user communities. With small systems, it makes eminent sense to keep administration as easy and straightforward as possible, and the site model does this very well. Nevertheless, as corporate deployments of Exchange increased in size and scope, it became obvious that the site model had run out of steam, and Microsoft needed to make fundamental architectural changes to create a management model suitable for both large and small enterprises. Its solution moves away from the fixed nature of the site model to a more flexible model of administrative groups and routing groups. Some more flexibility is still needed, because neither Exchange 2000 nor 2003 has yet delivered the full promise originally anticipated, but the current administrative model is still better than Exchange 5.5.

3.1.2 Naming the organization

When Exchange first appeared, giving the organization an appropriate name seemed to be a very important item, largely because of the connection between the organization name and the internal X.400 addresses used for message routing. In addition, it was impossible to change the organization name after installation. Over time, administrators realized that users do not see the organization name and that email addresses do not have to relate to the organization name, so the fear of choosing an inappropriate name disappeared. Exchange 5.5 and Exchange 2000 still demand that you enter the final name for an organization when you install the first server (Exchange 5.5) or run ForestPrep (Exchange 2000). Exchange 2003 is more flexible, and you do not have to state the organization name when you run ForestPrep. If you do not know the final name, Exchange uses a dummy placeholder name instead (a GUID) so that you can instantiate the organization and not have to decide on the final name until the time comes to deploy the first server.

Given that we are in an era of rebranding, acquisitions, and mergers, it makes sense to avoid using the company's current name for the organization. In fact, some Exchange designers go so far as to use a generic name such as "Exchange," "Messaging," or "Email" instead. A generic name avoids problems when the company decides to change its name, or when another company acquires it. In any case, the salient fact is that only administrators see the organization name, so they are the only people who worry about it.

3.2 Access control

In its first-generation servers, Exchange implemented its own access control model through permissions placed on objects and held in the directory store. Now, Exchange 2000 and 2003 use the Windows access control model, and every object—databases, mailboxes, public folders, and so on—has an Access Control List (ACL) composed of Access Control Entries (ACEs) that link Security Identifiers (SIDs) to access rights. Table 3.1 lists some of the major differences between the current Exchange access control model and the model used by the first generation.

Increased granularity is the most important difference between the two models. Exchange is now more capable of controlling how objects inherit access control lists from parent containers. For example, in Exchange 5.5, if you set permissions at the organization level, all sites inherit the same

3.2 Access control

Table 3.1 *Exchange Access Control Models*

Access Control Model	Exchange 2000/03 and Windows 2000/03	Exchange 5.5
Objects controlled	Everything used by Exchange, including Store objects; has a Windows ACL.	Exchange maintains its own permissions for objects in its DS.
Granularity	Object	Container
ACE types	Grant and deny	Grant only
Valid holders	Any Windows security principal	Only Exchange objects can hold Exchange permissions.

permissions. Now, you can decide whether permissions flow from one container to the next and both grant and deny permissions rather than just granting permissions. For example, you can allow an administrator to manage everything on a server except a specific mailbox store that holds confidential mailboxes. This type of granularity is not possible in Exchange 5.5.

As an example of how ACLs work in practice, when you look at the Mailbox Rights for a mailbox (Figure 3.2), you view a human-friendly ver-

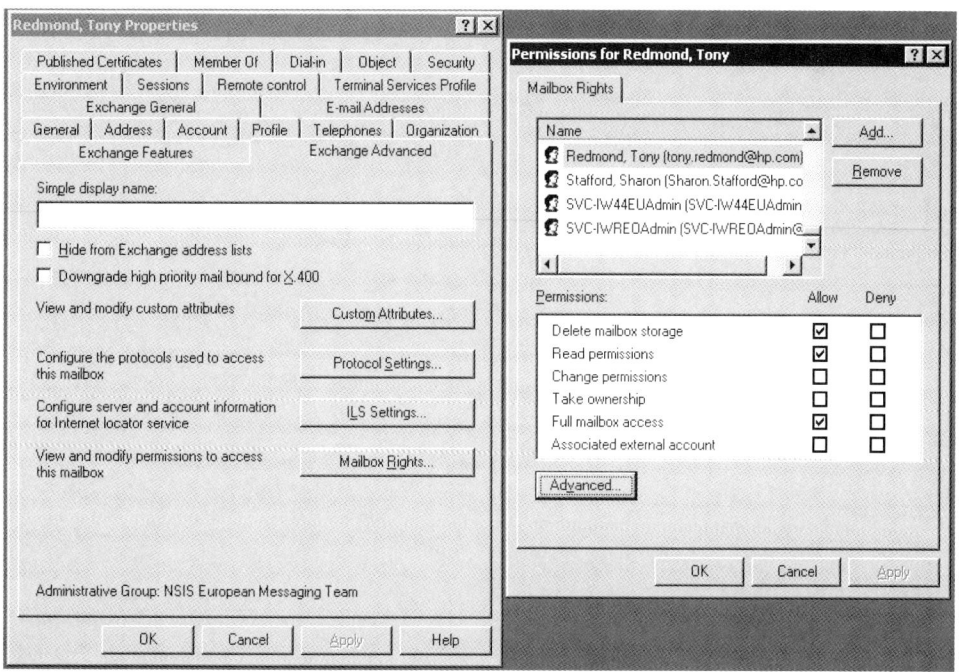

Figure 3.2 *Mailbox permissions.*

sion of the ACL that displays the accounts and the permissions that the accounts hold for the mailbox. In this case, you can see the account of the mailbox owner plus anyone who can connect to the mailbox for other reasons, such as an administrator who looks after someone's calendar or a service account.

By default, Exchange does not display the Security property page for the organization or administrative groups. To force the page to display, edit the registry at:

```
Key: HKCU\Software\Microsoft\Exchange\ExAdmin
Value: ShowSecurityPage (DWORD)
```

Set the value to 1 and restart ESM and you will be able to see the security information.

3.2.1 Administrative delegation

Exchange is a complex application that interacts with many other Windows components at different levels. Exchange also depends on the Windows security model to implement access control to different data, such as mailboxes, configuration data, and public folders.

To protect data properly, you need to use an account that holds extensive Windows administrative permissions to prepare the forest and its domains and then install the first Exchange 2003 server (Figure 3.3). The level of permissions required to perform various actions reduces in a controlled manner. Table 3.2 provides an overview of some important actions in the lifetime of an Exchange organization and the permissions you require to execute these actions, while Figure 3.4 illustrates the group membership that a "highly permissioned" account holds to prepare a forest for Exchange and then install the first server.

During the ForestPrep portion of the installation procedure, you are asked to nominate an account (that should already exist) to become the first holder of Exchange Full Administrator permission. You can then use this account to delegate administrative control over the organization or specific administrative groups to other accounts.

As we have seen, Exchange uses a hierarchical structure for its organization. The organization is the top level for permissions, followed by the administrative group and then an individual server. Permissions flow from top to bottom, so if you have rights over the organization, you can pretty well do what you want to any server. Behind the scenes, rights are instantiated as

3.2 Access control

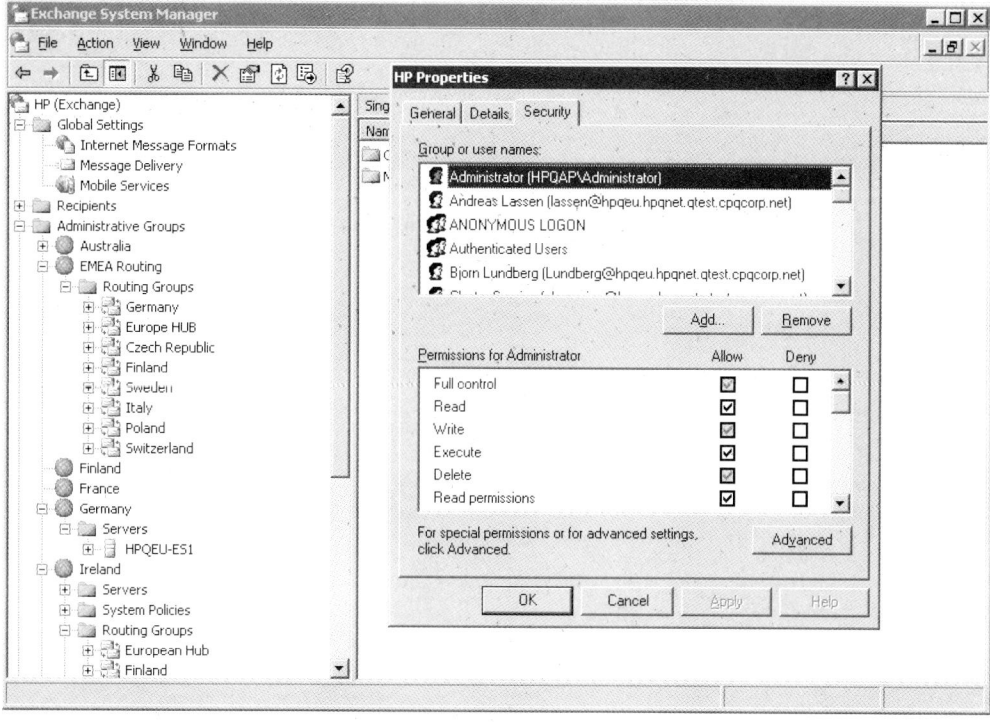

Figure 3.3 *Permissions on an Exchange organization.*

Table 3.2 *Permissions Required for Various Tasks*

Action	Required Permissions
Run ForestPrep within the forest for the first time	Member of the Enterprise Admins group and Schema Admins group
Run ForestPrep subsequently	Hold Exchange Full Administrator permission for the organization
Run DomainPrep in a domain	Member of Domain Admins group
Install or upgrade first Exchange 2003 server in the organization	Hold Exchange Full Administrator permission for the organization
Install or upgrade first Exchange 2003 server in a domain	Hold Exchange Full Administrator permission for the organization
Install or upgrade first Exchange 2003 server in an administrative group	Hold Exchange Full Administrator permission for the organization

Table 3.2 *Permissions Required for Various Tasks (continued)*

Action	Required Permissions
Install subsequent Exchange 2003 servers in a domain or administrative group	Hold Exchange Full Administrator permission for the target administrative group. Note that the machine account for the new server must be added to the Exchange Domain Servers security group by an administrator who can update this group's membership.
Upgrade an Exchange 2000 server that acts as a bridgehead server for a Directory Replication Connector	Hold Exchange Full Administrator permission for the organization
Install or remove Exchange 2003 server with SRS	Hold Exchange Full Administrator permission for the organization
Install Exchange virtual server in a cluster (after first installation)	Hold Exchange Full Administrator for the administrative group. Note that the installation program will allow you to select any administrative group, even if you do not hold the appropriate permission to install the virtual server into that group. If you select a wrong administrative group, the installation program displays an "Access Denied" error message.

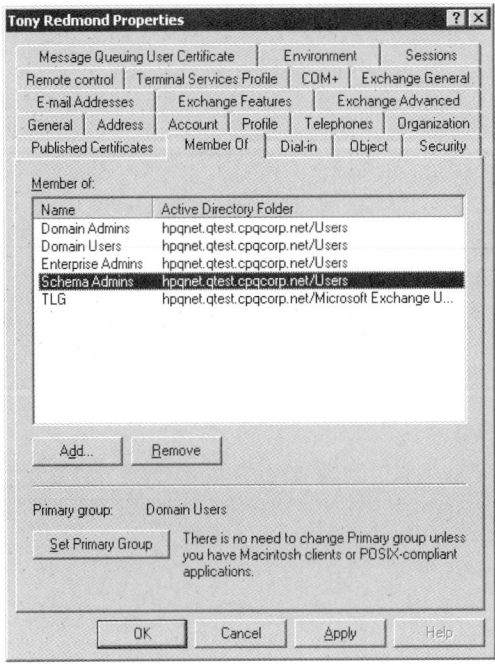

Figure 3.4 *A highly permissioned account.*

3.2 Access control

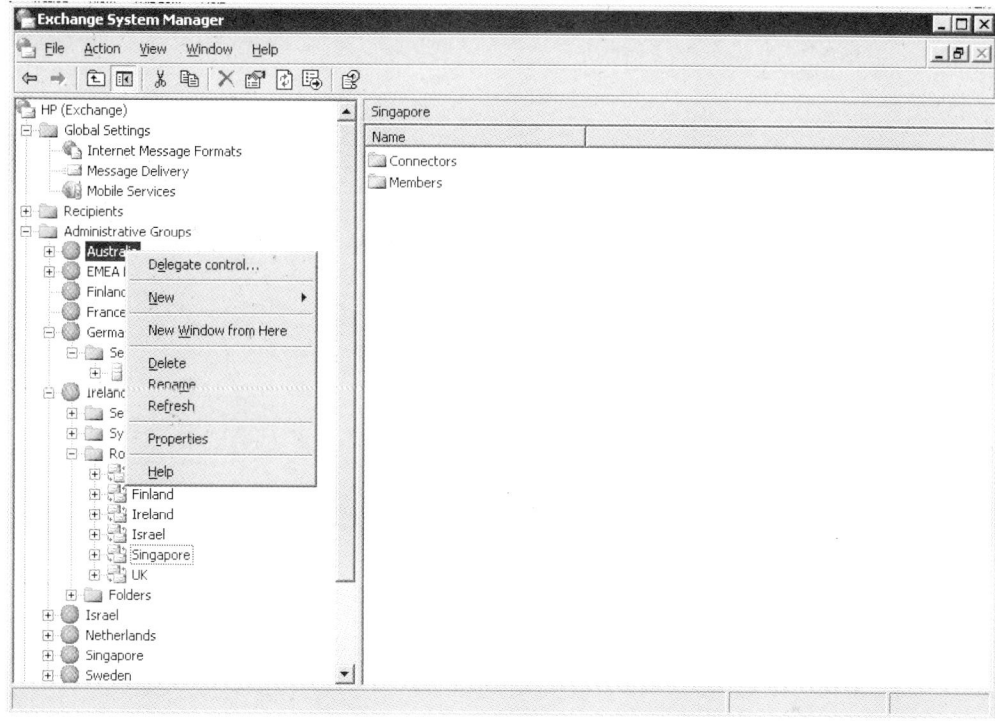

Figure 3.5 *Delegating control over an administrative group.*

entries in Windows Access Control Lists placed on various objects. Windows allows a fine degree of granularity within its security model, so Exchange uses a role-based model to delegate permissions within the organization. In this respect, a role is a collection of rights necessary to perform actions on Exchange data. You delegate roles to users with the Exchange Administration Delegation wizard.

You begin the delegation process by deciding on the level at which to delegate access, selecting either the organization or an administrative group. Figure 3.5 shows the menu revealed when you right-click on an administrative group. Selecting the "Delegate Control" option invokes the Administration Delegation wizard.

When the wizard starts, it displays a list of the users who already hold administrative permission for the selected object. Some of the users inherit their permissions from the organization, while others have already been delegated permissions for this level. If you look at the top left-hand screen in Figure 3.6, you can see the Windows accounts, the roles they currently hold, and whether they inherited the role.

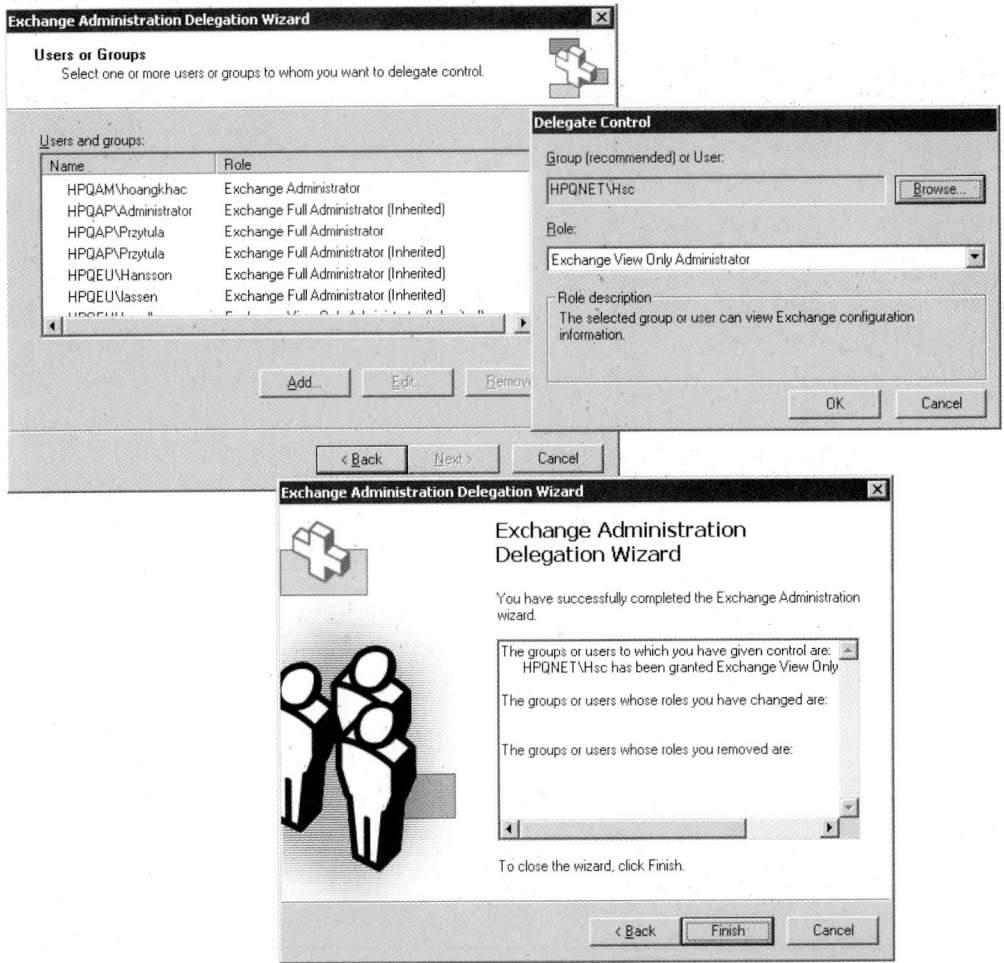

Figure 3.6 *Running the Delegation wizard.*

You can now select one of the existing holders or add a new account or group to delegate control over the object. Best practice is to use groups whenever possible, because it is easier to maintain permissions when they are group based. In this case, we select a user account (top right-hand screen) and then select the role we want to delegate. You have three options:

- Exchange Full Administrator means that the account or group has full permissions over the object, including the right to delegate access to other accounts or groups. You should restrict this role to as few people as possible, especially at the organization level. You need

Exchange Full Administrator permission to install the first Exchange server in an organization, and you need this permission to be able to remove a server that hosts SRS.

- Exchange Administrator means that the account or group holds the permissions necessary to perform all of the administrative operations for the selected object. For example, it can mount or dismount stores, stop and start Exchange services, and so on. This role is best for people who perform day-to-day management of Exchange servers. To administer an Exchange server, your account must also be a member of the computer's local Administrators group. You also need Exchange Administrator permission to be able to install or remove an Exchange server in an administrative group or to install a service pack on a server.

- Exchange View Administrator means that the group or object can examine all aspects of Exchange data for the object through ESM, but it cannot modify settings or add new data. This role is generally appropriate for people who need to monitor Exchange servers.

After selecting the object to delegate control to and the role to delegate, click on OK and then on Next to have the wizard execute the option.

If you examine the properties of the object after delegation and then click on the Security tab, you can see the effect of delegation in terms of the permissions that the user or group now holds. If you then click on the "Advanced" button, you can gain a better insight, because ESM then reveals the set of Exchange-related permissions that are most important in administrative terms. Figure 3.7 shows a selection of the permissions. As you can see, because we delegated the Exchange View Administrator role, the account does not hold many rights to work with Exchange data. Table 3.3 details the permissions held by each role. Note that even if you are an Exchange Full Administrator, you still do not have the right to access a user's mailbox and send email on his or her behalf; Exchange denies these rights explicitly by default. Of course, you can grant yourself these rights later on.

Generally, the Administration Delegation wizard does a good job and you should not have to alter rights afterward. In fact, it is best practice never to change permission on an object unless you have a good reason, and you should document all changes, just in case. Note that there is currently no way to "undelegate" Exchange permissions using the wizard or other utility. If you need to remove administrative access for an account, you must manually edit the access control lists on the Exchange objects. This is one reason

Figure 3.7
Examining permissions after delegation.

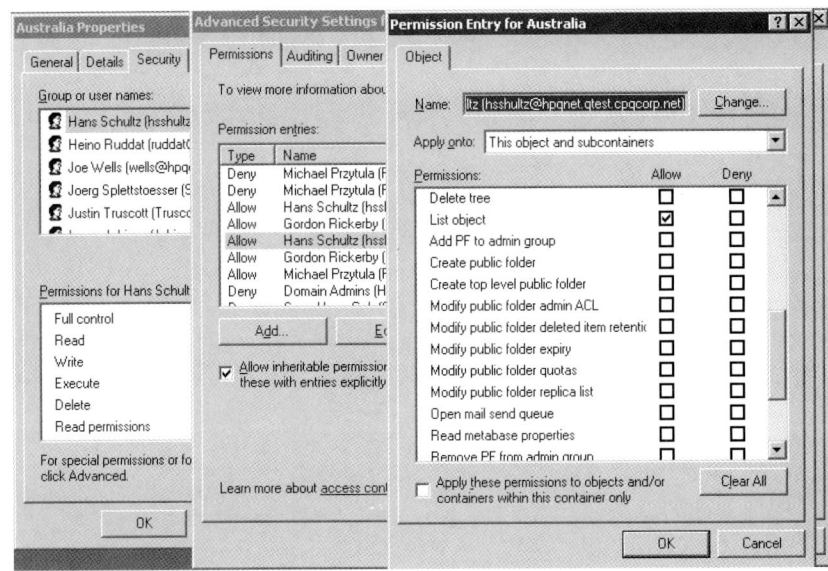

why it is best to delegate access to groups, because you can then simply remove the user account from the group. In addition, an account that holds the Full Exchange Administrator role is required to reinstall an Exchange 2000 server if this is necessary in a disaster recovery scenario.

Table 3.3 *Exchange Administrative Permissions*

Permission	Exchange View Administrator	Exchange Administrator	Exchange Full Administrator
Read properties	X	X	X
Write properties	—	X	X
List object	X	X	X
Add public folder to admin group	—	X	X
Create public folder	—	X	X
Create top-level public folder	—	X	X
Modify public folder admin ACL	—	X	X
Modify public folder deleted items retention period	—	X	X
Modify public folder expiration period	—	X	X

Table 3.3 *Exchange Administrative Permissions (continued)*

Permission	Exchange View Administrator	Exchange Administrator	Exchange Full Administrator
Modify public folder quotas	—	X	X
Modify public folder replica list	—	X	X
Open mail send queue	—	X	X
Read metabase properties	—	X	X
Remove public folder from admin group	—	X	X
Administer Store	—	X	X
Create named properties in Store	—	X	X
View Store status	—	X	X
Receive as	—	Deny	Deny
Send as	—	Deny	Deny
Change permission	—	—	X
Take ownership	—	—	X

Note that Outlook clients appear to allow you to give someone else the ability to send mail on your behalf through the "delegates" option. In this case, you grant the user editor permission (the highest level of permission) on your Inbox, which allows the user to create and edit items. Unfortunately, editor permission does not include "Send As," and if you want that person to be able to send messages on your behalf, you will have to make the change through AD Users and Computers. Microsoft Knowledge Base article 328927 explains why the bug exists.

3.3 Administrative and routing groups

We have already discussed some of the limitations of the Exchange 5.5 administrative model. Microsoft's response in Exchange 2000 and 2003 divides the management and routing responsibility previously held by sites into containers called "administrative groups" and "routing groups." It is still possible to have one person or group perform all administrative tasks for an Exchange server, but it is now feasible to devolve responsibility for different tasks at a far more granular level. The concept of "roles," essentially prepacked selections of permissions needed to perform certain tasks, makes it easy to assign permissions. Exchange 2000 and 2003 define "Exchange Full Administrator," "Exchange Administrator," and "Exchange View Only Administrator" roles.

For brand new organizations, the Exchange installation procedure creates default Administrative Groups and Routing Groups when you install the first Exchange 2000/2003 server. All Exchange servers join these groups until you create new administrative and routing groups. In mixed-mode organizations, Site Replication Services (SRS) are responsible for sharing configuration data about administrative and routing groups with Exchange 5.5 servers, and one server hosts the SRS function in each Exchange 5.5 site.

3.3.1 Defining an administrative group

An administrative group is a collection of Exchange objects that share a common set of permissions. An administrative group usually contains one or more mailbox servers, the policies that apply to the servers, routing groups, public folders, and other objects. If you have a mailbox store in an administrative group, you must also have a public store, and all of the front-end and back-end servers that work together must be in the same administrative group.

As you add objects to an administrative group, they inherit the permissions held by the group. This simplifies management, since you can be sure that the same permissions apply to all objects immediately after they are set on an administrative group. In Exchange 5.5 terms, servers in an administrative group share common settings in much the same way as servers in a site share settings, such as the site addressing defaults.

While administration groups usually hold at least one server, many large organizations deploy special administrative groups to hold a set of Exchange objects and isolate specific management responsibilities. For example, you can define an administrative group to hold all the routing groups in the organization so that only a special set of administrators can work with the routing topology. Another example is to create a special administrative group to hold all the server policies for the organization, which means that you can apply system policies at the level of the organization to make administrators manage the servers in a particular way rather than letting local administrators have full control over the servers. Figure 3.8 shows how you can assemble a set of system policies into a special administrative group that is under the control of central administrators. These policies are then

3.3 Administrative and routing groups   147

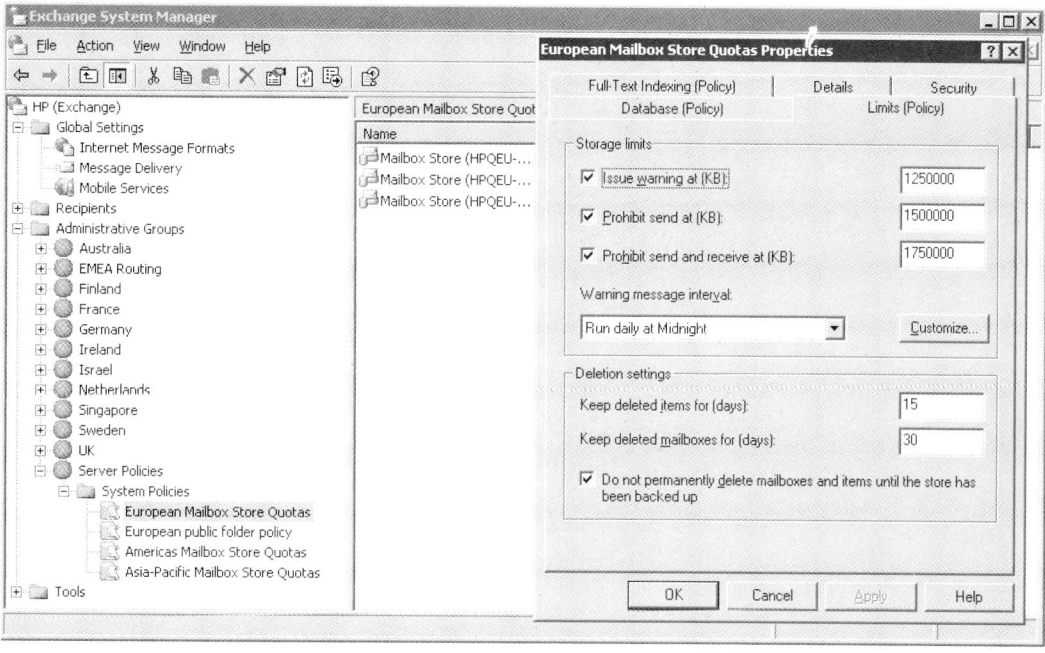

Figure 3.8   *A system policy applied to multiple stores.*

applied to servers (in this case, on a geographical basis) to ensure that all of the servers share common settings.

In this example, the policy defines that message tracking is enabled on servers that you apply the policy to, that message tracking logs include subject information, and that message tracking logs are kept for seven days. It is clearly easier to build a policy and have it applied centrally than rely on multiple administrators to apply the required policy on every server.

It is reasonably common to find situations where a department wants to control its own computers and is unwilling to permit management by a central IT department. With Exchange 5.5 we can handle this situation by placing the servers belonging to the department into a separate site, and probably a separate Windows NT resource domain. This is an effective technique to protect data for mailboxes belonging to sensitive departments or users such as HR or senior management, but it is easy to create multiple Exchange sites in a single physical location, which results in an increase in the overall complexity of the messaging environment. Remember, every additional site increases the overhead imposed by directory replication and the likelihood that something will go wrong in message routing. The Exchange approach is to create separate administrative groups for special departments or groups of users and place the servers that host the associated mailboxes within the new administrative groups. Access to perform administrative operations on the servers is then delegated to security groups or individual accounts.

Administrative groups exist as containers under the Microsoft Exchange container in the AD configuration NC, and administrators can create empty administrative groups immediately after you install the first server in the organization. This is a useful feature, since it allows you to sketch out the management model for the organization through a set of empty administrative and routing groups that you subsequently populate with server installations. By comparison, while you can plan the shape of an Exchange 5.5 organization, it is more common to build it server by server, because an Exchange 5.5 site cannot exist without any servers.

3.3.2 Moving from sites to administrative groups

When Exchange 2000/2003 operate in mixed mode and some Exchange 5.5 sites still exist in the organization, an administrative group is treated exactly like an Exchange 5.5 site to ensure backward compatibility. Exchange 5.5 has no knowledge of administrative groups, so Exchange 2000/2003 disguise their existence by representing each administrative group back to the Exchange 5.5 servers as a site. When operating in mixed mode, you can only have a single administrative group and a single routing group in each site, whereas when you move to native mode an administrative group can host multiple routing groups. Figure 3.9 illustrates this concept in action. The "NSIS European Messaging Team" site has two servers represented in the organization by an administrative group that includes a routing group with the same name.

Apart from checking the properties of an organization, you always know when an organization is operating in mixed mode because ESM provides some graphical clues. First, the folder icon for the site is white if no Exchange 2000/2003 server is present and tan otherwise. Second, the server icon is white for a legacy Exchange server and tan for Exchange 2000 or 2003.

Figure 3.9
A site is an administrative group and a routing group.

3.3 Administrative and routing groups

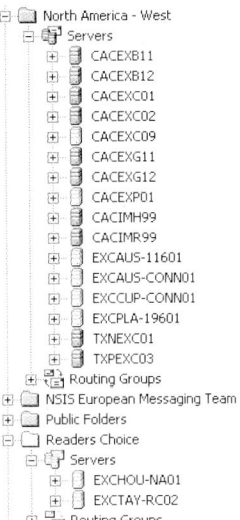

Figure 3.10
Mixed-mode exchange.

Figure 3.10 illustrates these points. The "North America – West" administrative group contains Exchange 2000/2003 and legacy servers. The icon for the administrative group is tan, while the icons for the servers are either tan (Exchange 2000/2003) or white (legacy). The "Readers Choice" administrative group is composed entirely of legacy servers, so its icon is white, as are the icons for the individual servers. ESM includes the version of Exchange running on a server as one of the server properties displayed when you expand the set of servers in an administrative group (you can also view the server version by selecting a specific server and looking at its properties).

An organization remains in mixed mode as long as it contains Exchange 5.5 servers. The first step to start moving away from the fixed structure mandated by mixed mode is to move the organization into native mode. You perform this step by changing the properties of the organization to switch it into native mode, but you cannot proceed until all of the servers are migrated to Exchange 2000 and then to Exchange 2003. Figure 3.11 illustrates the properties of the "Compaq" organization, and the "Change Mode" button is grayed out because the organization is still in mixed mode. Switching to native mode is a one-way operation. You cannot reverse a change to native mode unless you stop operations and restore the Active Directory and every Exchange server to a state prior to the change, something that is not feasible in most situations outside a laboratory.

Figure 3.11
Properties of an organization.

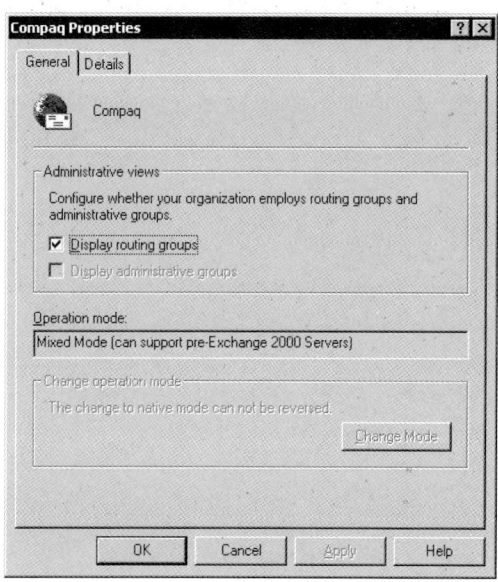

Creating a new administrative group is very straightforward. Open ESM and click on the Administrative Groups node, then select "New…" from the context-sensitive menu. Figure 3.12 illustrates the properties for a new administrative group during creation, while Figure 3.13 shows how ESM lists the current administrative groups.

Figure 3.12
Adding a new administrative group.

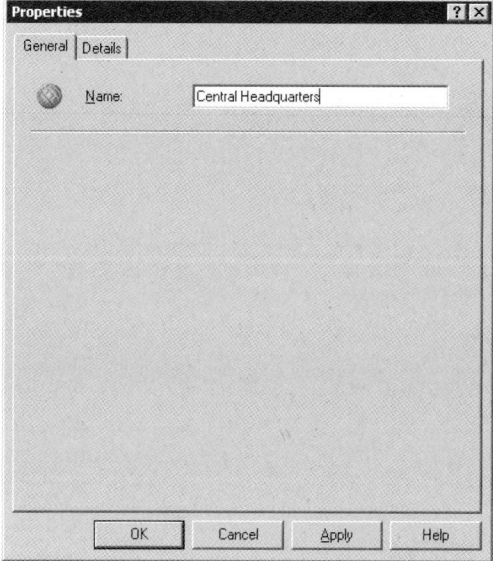

3.3 Administrative and routing groups

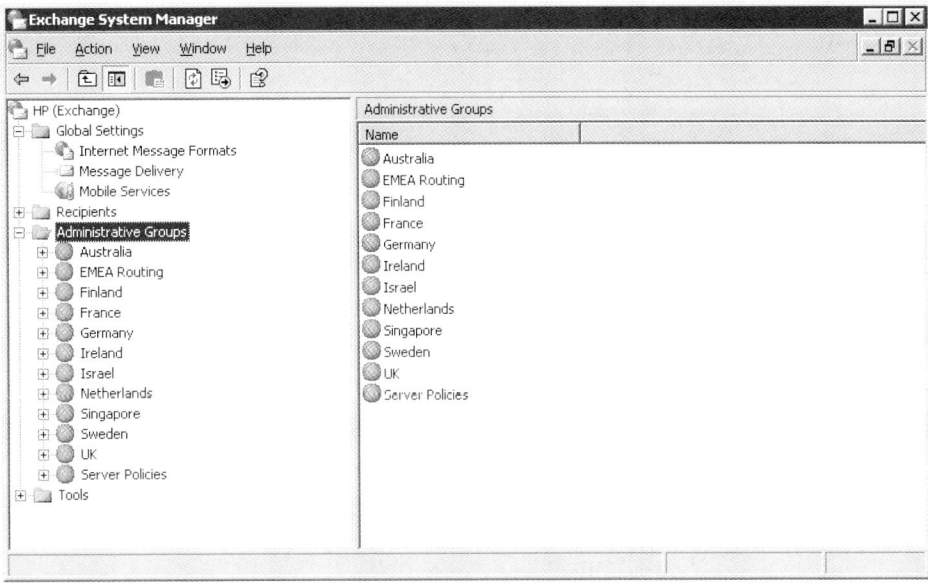

Figure 3.13   *Displaying administrative groups.*

Administrators may have to make some behavioral changes as organizations migrate to the new administrative model. Sites control the set of objects (servers, mailboxes, and so on) that form the site, so an administrator of a site is the only person who can modify objects belonging to the site. The AD uses a multimaster model, which does not tie objects to a site. Instead, the owning domain marks the initial administrative boundary, and enterprise administrators (those who have rights across an entire forest) have even greater scope. An Exchange administrator is, therefore, able to make changes to either configuration or user attributes according to his or her Windows permissions rather than any Exchange-specific rights, as is the case with Exchange 5.5.

As an illustration, let us assume that you have two Exchange 5.5 sites in New York and London. Each site has a separate set of administrators, and each operates in a separate Windows NT domain. After upgrading the servers to Exchange 2000/2003, we have two Exchange administration groups in the organization within a common Windows forest. Because the AD makes all objects available for modification, New York administrators are now able to change attributes for users in London. For instance, they could set new mailbox quotas or impose restrictions on the connectors people can now use. Suddenly, you can implement totally distributed management, possibly without administrators being aware of the effects and their new capabilities. I do not view this as a problem, but administrators need to be coached and agree upon a protocol for making changes to objects belonging to other administrative groups. If this does not happen, then problems may arise the first time that a remote administrator changes an object (and a local administrator notices).

3.3.3 No way to change administrative group design

The beta versions of Exchange 2000 included the ability to move servers by a simple drag-and-drop movement between administrative groups. However, while the feature worked, there were some problems behind the scenes and Microsoft removed the option to move servers before Exchange 2000 shipped. At the same time, Microsoft also removed the ability to rename administrative groups. In both cases, Microsoft was worried that replication latency might cause problems if the changes were not replicated quickly to all of the servers in an organization and cause potential problems within the organization. For example, consider the case when an administrator drags a server from one administrative group to another only to change his or her mind and reverse the action. The administrator then decides to move the server to a different administrative group, so we have three movements in quick succession with clear potential for confusion if these operations do not replicate quickly and precisely throughout the organization.

Another possible reason for mixed-mode organizations is that the site name (or administrative group name) forms part of the LegacyExchangeDN attribute that Exchange maintains for its AD objects to track their heritage prior to Exchange 2000. If you change the administrative group name, then you affect the value of the LegacyExchangeDN, and therefore conceivably lead to a situation where servers and other objects cannot make the necessary links within the organization. Taking away the ability to move and rename simplified Microsoft's design headaches and ensured backward compatibility, but it made the overall Exchange architecture very static and posed a new set of difficulties for system administrators.

The bottom line is that Exchange currently includes no method to move servers between administrative groups. If you make a mistake in placing servers in administrative groups, the only thing you can do is to create a new server and install it into the correct administrative group, and then move all the mailboxes across to the new server. You can then "clean up" by removing the server that caused the problem. This process is manual, network intensive, and time consuming and demonstrates the need to be as accurate as possible in the administrative group design first time round. Given the potential impact on the AD, it is highly unlikely that Microsoft will deliver the equivalent of the Exchange 5.5 "Move Server Wizard" tool in the near future.

3.3.4 Moving to native mode

Organizations commonly spend extended periods operating in mixed mode. It takes time to coordinate server upgrades across extended enterprises, especially when you depend on what might be a separate effort to deploy Windows and establish the necessary infrastructure for Exchange. As an example, Compaq began to deploy Exchange 2000 in the middle of 2000 and only managed to move into native mode in September 2002. At that point, Compaq was the world's largest Exchange 2000 organization with over 110,000 mailboxes, so you can expect to move from mixed to native mode sooner, but it does illustrate how slowly some migrations move. Of course, because HP had acquired Compaq, a new challenge emerged, as the Compaq Exchange 2000 organization started to cooperate and integrate with HP's Exchange 5.5 organization, and then to upgrade to Exchange 2003.

If you have a distributed organization with multiple administrative groups, you probably have multiple ADCs and connection agreements. Ensuring that you can move to native mode takes a certain amount of planning. Here are the basic steps.

- Gradually shut down and remove legacy Exchange 5.5 servers, taking care to remove any special components (public folder replicas, connectors, and roles such as OAB generation) from the server before removing it from the organization.
- Stop ADC replication.
- Remove any obsolete connectors.
- Remove SRS databases.
- Remove ADC services on any server that hosts an ADC.
- Check that no Exchange 5.5 servers exist in the organization and then switch to native mode.

Check for any problems after each stage. For example, ensure that messages route successfully, that directory synchronization proceeds normally, that you can add and remove users, that no server disappears from the Exchange organization, and so on. When you are happy that everything is ready, switch to native mode—but remember that this is a one-way trip and a massive restore exercise is required to move back, so perhaps wait one more day just to be sure before switching.

After you have moved into native mode, you may have further opportunities to clean up parts of your infrastructure, including:

- Removing any NT resource domains previously used to host Exchange servers
- Removing old Exchange administrative accounts and groups, including the service account that you used to run Exchange services
- Decommissioning and removing older versions of Exchange add-on software such as fax connectors, if you have replaced this software with newer versions

The aim is always to reduce complexity in your infrastructure by consolidating services onto a smaller number of servers. No migration to a new version of Exchange should result in an increase in servers unless the increase is temporary, such as the case when you acquire a set of servers from another company through a merger or acquisition. You can usefully deploy older servers released through consolidation as test servers or to take on less demanding tasks. For example, you can use old mailbox servers to host connectors or to test Exchange 2003.

3.3.5 The move to LocalSystem

The password of the site service account caused all manner of problems for Exchange 5.5 (and earlier) deployments. Because Exchange 5.5 uses its own directory, it needs a method to authenticate its own services to Windows when those services start. Windows runs the set of Exchange services (MTA, Information Store, and on so) under the security context of the service account. The password of the account is held in two places—the Windows SAM (or Active Directory) and the Exchange directory—and an option is available to update the password so that it is changed in both places. Unfortunately, if an administrator changes the password through Windows, synchronization does not occur and Windows detects the mismatch the next time it attempts to start Exchange. Exchange now avoids this problem by running its services under the security context of the LocalSystem account.

Most administrators understand the potential problems with the Exchange 5.5 service account and respond appropriately to avoid those problems. They have encountered all the common problems such as password mismatches, and solutions exist to help rescue the unwary. So, why did Microsoft elect to make changes in this area for Exchange 2000?

3.3 Administrative and routing groups

Microsoft decided to move from the service account to LocalSystem for three major reasons. First, Microsoft wanted to make Exchange easier to install and manage. Removing the requirement to select an account eliminated an opportunity to make a mistake. You cannot trust some administrators to set up or select a service account correctly, and some administrators use accounts in such a way that compromises system security.

Second, using LocalSystem to log on to Exchange services (Figure 3.14) creates a more secure Exchange server. Microsoft designed the LocalSystem account for system activities and protected it against interactive access. By contrast, the service account is a regular Windows account that anyone can log on to if he or she knows the password and then uses the elevated permissions held by the account to work with restricted data. Remember that if you can log on to the service account, you can access anyone's mailbox on a server. If you can access mailboxes, you can read anyone's mail or even send messages using other people's mailboxes. The use of LocalSystem has removed this opportunity for administrators to access mailboxes. Administrators can still break into someone's mailbox if they really want to, but it takes more work in an Exchange 2000/2003 environment.

Third, LocalSystem has no password to manage. Windows automatically changes the password for the LocalSystem account every seven days. The resulting password is more secure than the values administrators typically generate, because Windows selects random passwords.

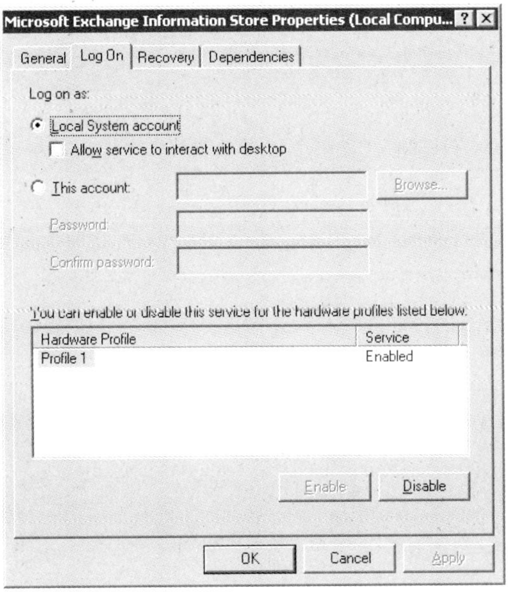

Figure 3.14
Information Store service logs on as LocalSystem.

The problems of synchronizing passwords between the SAM and the DS have now disappeared. The Exchange engineers might have chosen to continue using a dedicated service account, but using LocalSystem reduces the number of things you need to manage to operate Exchange successfully. With LocalSystem, the account is part of Windows, which manages the account automatically. Therefore, an Exchange administrator only needs to know that the set of Exchange services runs under the LocalSystem account.

The change to LocalSystem makes installation easier, too. With LocalSystem in place, administrators only have to think about a service account when Exchange runs in mixed-mode organizations that include legacy (pre-Exchange 2000) servers. Here, SRS has to know about the service account before it can successfully mimic the Exchange 5.5 DS to newer Exchange server.

3.3.6 Routing groups

By definition, a routing group is a collection of well-connected Exchange servers that are able to make point-to-point connections to each other. In many respects, this is very similar to the definition commonly used for Exchange 5.5 sites. Routing groups define the message topology—how messages are going to move between Exchange servers and out of the organization—if required. Routing groups are subservient to administrative groups, since Exchange arranges every routing group in the organizational hierarchy under an administrative group. This is a logical arrangement. servers belong to administrative groups and routing is a function performed by servers. Note that Exchange is flexible enough to permit a server to exist in a routing group different from its administrative group, again because the management model separates responsibility for server management and the routing topology. Routing groups are merely a convenient way to collect servers together into a message routing topology so that they can perform common routing operations, as we will see shortly.

Before we discuss administrative groups in detail and review how routing groups fit into the picture, it may be worthwhile to set down some simple definitions:

- Administrative groups manage objects, including servers.
- Routing groups manage the routing topology.
- Neither is exactly equivalent to an Exchange 5.5 site.
- Routing groups are subordinate to administrative groups and are always created inside administrative groups.

- A single administrative group can hold all the routing groups in an organization, with other administrative groups used to manage server components and operations.

- Routing groups connect together in the routing topology with a variety of connectors, including the routing group connector, SMTP connector, and X.400 connector.

Now that we have set down some principles, let us see what they might mean in practice.

3.3.7 Routing group design

The default approach for a brand new Exchange organization is to simplify administration, so ESM does not display routing groups. Hiding the presence of routing groups is by design. There are many Exchange 5.5 servers deployed in single-site or even single-server organizations (the version provided with BackOffice Small Business Server is an obvious example), and the administrators of these systems have no need to plumb the depths of routing group complexity. Routing groups are a great way for corporate administrators to decide how to route messages across a distributed enterprise, but that is a business problem entirely different from the one that faces small companies that have one or two servers.

The division of functions between administrative and routing groups is much more flexible and powerful than the equivalent scenario in Exchange 5.5. Routing groups operate under the context or within administrative groups, so you can use a single administrative group to manage multiple routing groups. This allows routing groups to span multiple administrative groups and provides another level of flexibility in terms of management granularity. As an example, Figure 3.15 shows multiple routing groups operating within the single "Routing Administrative Group." Only the administrators who have permission over the special routing administrative group can make changes that might affect routing. This is a convenient way to isolate the management and control of the routing topology from the day-to-day operations otherwise required for servers.

Companies that have different teams assigned to manage mailbox servers and connector servers in an Exchange 5.5 organization often place the connector servers in their own site to create a security and administrative boundary. Creating a specific administrative group that only holds routing groups creates a similar management context for Exchange 2000/2003.

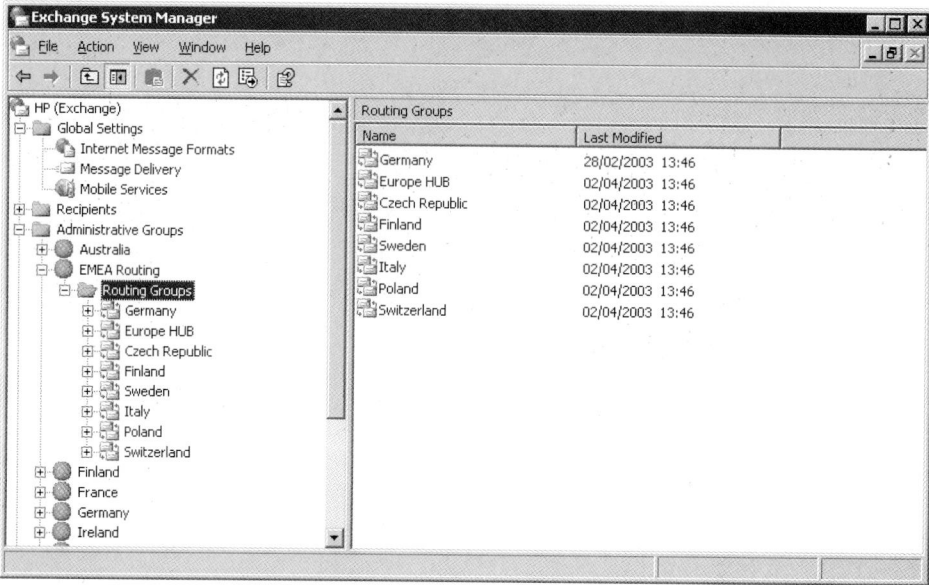

Figure 3.15 *Multiple routing groups operating within an administrative group.*

As an example of this concept in operation, look at the organization illustrated in Figure 3.16. Each country has a separate local administration team to take care of its Exchange servers, so we create an administrative group for each country and install servers according to their location. The "France" administrative group contains seven servers and the "Ireland" administrative group has just one. However, servers from both the France and Ireland administrative groups also appear in the "Routing Administrative Group," where they are members of routing groups based on the network links that connect the servers together.

In this case, a hub and spoke design network is in place and enough bandwidth is available to support the necessary point-to-point connectivity within a routing group, so we can place the Irish server (QEMEA-ES1) in the "Europe (HUB)" routing group. If we install other servers in the Ireland administrative group, we can create a separate Ireland routing group and connect it into the hub with a routing group connector, using QEMEA-ES1 as the bridgehead server. Of course, the extra servers in the Ireland administrative group could also join the hub routing group, but the point of having a hub routing group is for it to act as a hub for the messaging network—not to create a convenient dumping ground for lots of servers. In Exchange 5.5 terms, such a design is often referred to as a "strong hub" and is created by placing a server from each physical location into a hub site. It

3.3 Administrative and routing groups   159

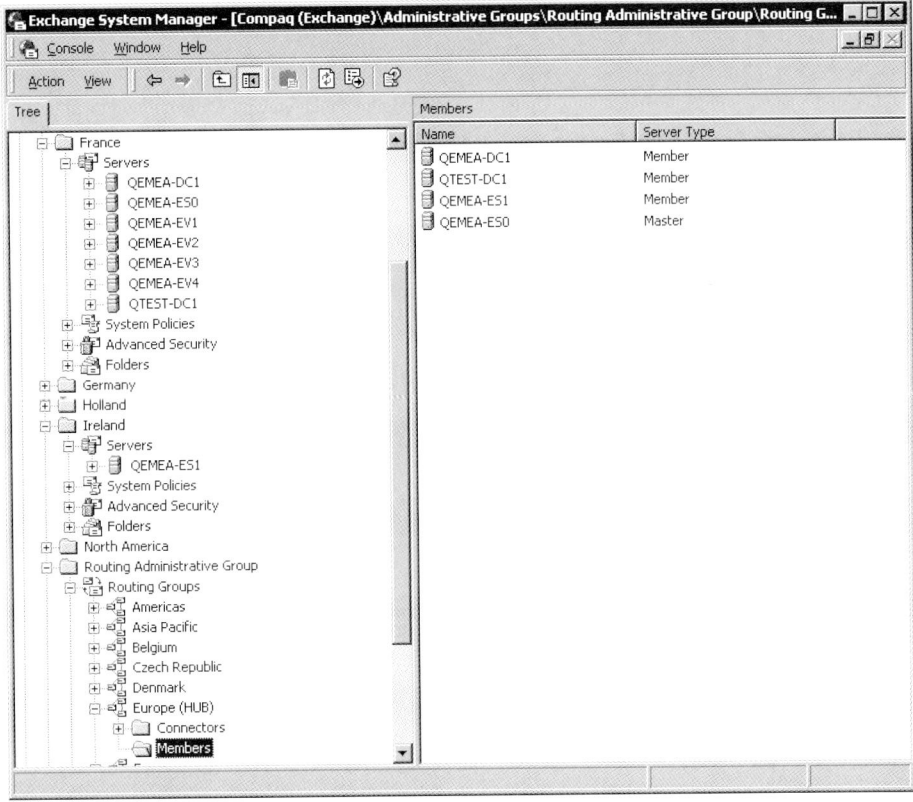

Figure 3.16   *Separating routing into a specific administrative group.*

is also interesting to note that the hub design so favored by Exchange 5.5 eliminates some of the benefits of the current Link State Routing model.

An alternative, and equally appropriate, design in many cases would be to create a separate Ireland routing group (similar to those for other countries, such as Germany and the United Kingdom), and use a routing group connector between Ireland and the Europe HUB routing group. In either case, appropriate delegations allow local administrators to perform mailbox operations and maintenance, with a separate central or corporate set of administrators to handle routing operations. This technique enforces a clear separation between server administration and the routing topology and illustrates the flexibility that is now available to system designers.

While the scenario that we have just discussed will be common in large deployments, at the other end of the spectrum it is entirely possible to have every Exchange server in an organization placed into a single routing and

Chapter 3

administrative group, which would be equivalent to installing all servers into a single Exchange 5.5 site. Outside small enterprises, this is an unlikely scenario, and it is much more common that medium to large enterprises will opt for multiple routing and administrative groups. Best practice is to seek to reduce the number of routing groups when you upgrade an organization to Exchange 2000/2003, because the more flexible and powerful Routing Engine now available enables simpler but more resilient routing topologies.

Microsoft recommends that you deploy no more than 250 routing groups inside an Exchange organization. Every routing group, server, and connector increases the amount of data that servers send to each other to update the link state table. Sending large amounts of updated information between servers will not affect you if network links are fast, but may influence matters across low-bandwidth connections.

3.4 Mailboxes and user accounts

You must mail enable an AD account before you can use it to access an Exchange mailbox. The process of mail enabling means that you complete the set of optional attributes to let the AD know that the account now owns a mailbox in a store on an Exchange server and can receive email, including the name of the server that hosts the mailbox and the store that the mailbox is in. Other important attributes include:

- The set of email addresses used to send and receive email (SMTP, X.400, and so on), including the primary address of each type

- The LegacyExchangeDN attribute for backward compatibility with older versions of Exchange

- The showInAddressBook attribute to ensure that other users can see the new mailbox in the GAL and other address lists. The Recipient Update Services updates this attribute.

- The MailNickname (alias) attribute used to identify the mailbox by IMAP and POP clients among others

- The msExchMailboxSecurityDescriptor attribute that controls access to the mailbox

We will meet these attributes in different situations throughout the book. Chapter 10 discusses many of the issues you will meet to design and apply consistent naming standards for attributes such as email addresses, display names, and so on.

3.4 Mailboxes and user accounts

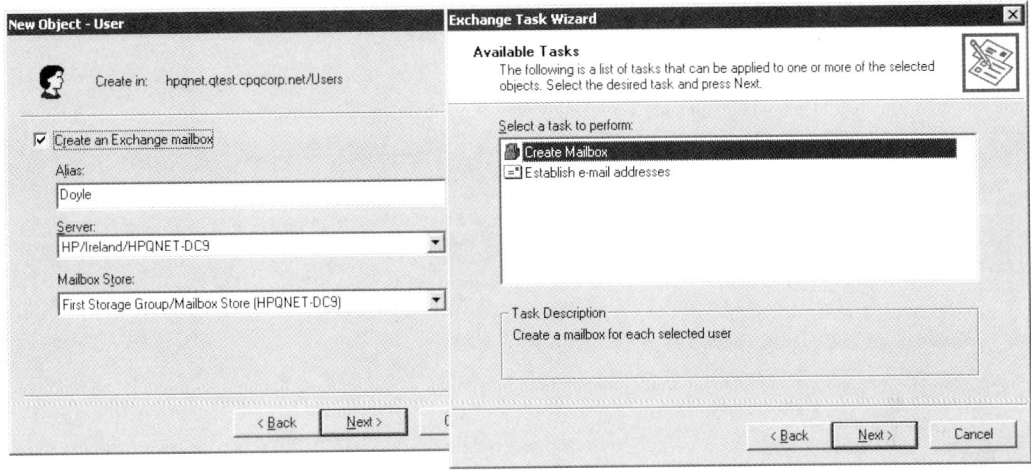

Figure 3.17   *Creating a new mailbox.*

Creating a mailbox (Figure 3.17) is a multiphase process, which flows like this:

- The administrator creates a new AD account and creates the mailbox at the same time, or he or she selects an existing account and invokes the Exchange Tasks wizard to create the mailbox. The left-hand screen in Figure 3.17 shows the dialog that Windows displays when you set up a mailbox as part of the account creation process, while the right-hand screen is the Exchange Tasks wizard.[1] If you select the wizard option to create a mailbox, you end up back to the left-hand screen to answer the fundamental question: Which server and storage group will hold the new mailbox? Note that you can create mailboxes programmatically using ADSI to set up the basic account structure and then populate the mailbox attributes through the IMailboxStore interface of CDOEXM.

- At this point, the AD account contains a subset of the full set of mailbox attributes and the user cannot yet use the account to send or receive email. The Recipient Update Service (RUS) runs on a scheduled basis and completes the population of mailbox attributes by adding information such as the email proxy attributes (SMTP, X.400, and so on) to the account. At least one RUS job runs for each domain that supports Exchange servers.

---

1. The Exchange setup program installs the Task wizard when it installs ESM. If you want to manage Exchange on another server or workstation, you need to install ESM there. The version of ESM provided with Exchange 2000 does not run on Windows XP workstations, but the version supplied with Exchange 2003 does.

- After RUS completes processing, the mailbox can receive new email, because the Exchange Routing Service is able to take incoming messages addressed to the mailbox and deliver them to the correct place. Up to this point, Exchange will reject any attempt to deliver a message to the mailbox, because it cannot resolve the address against the directory.

- The RUS is also responsible for including the new mailbox in the GAL by setting the ShowInAddressBook attribute to add the mailbox to the set of default address lists (unless you have set the attribute to hide the mailbox from the GAL). Users will not see new mailboxes in the GAL until the RUS successfully completes processing, which should take less than 15 minutes after you create the account. If you do not see a mailbox appear in the GAL after an hour or so, consider invoking a manual run of the RUS for the domain where you create the account. See Microsoft Knowledge Base articles 253828 and 327347 for more information.

- In terms of data structures in the mailbox store, Exchange does not fully instantiate the mailbox until the first user access to the mailbox or the first time that Exchange delivers a message to the mailbox. At this point, Exchange sets the mailbox rights (based on the access control entries in the msExchMailboxSecurityDescriptor attribute) on the mailbox's security descriptor in the Store. You will not be able to see the mailbox through ESM or ExIFS until the Store instantiates it as a response to a user logon or the delivery of new mail.

To force the pace, some administrators send an automatic message to the account soon after they create it to force Exchange to create the mailbox in the Store. While you might not be able to send a message by selecting the mailbox from the GAL, you can certainly send the message to the mailbox's SMTP address, since the Routing Engine is able to resolve the address by looking up the account immediately after the RUS has processed the account. You can consider using command-line utilities such as BLAT to create and send simple one-line messages as part of an automated mailbox creation process. Because of the mismatch between client and server MAPI components, do not install Outlook on an Exchange server just to test user mailboxes after you create them. If you want to connect to a user mailbox, use Outlook Web Access or Outlook Express instead.

Note that the first connection influences the names of the default folders that Exchange creates in the new mailbox. For example, if an English-language client connects, Exchange creates folders such as Inbox, Calendar, Sent Items, and so on, whereas if a Danish client connects, Exchange creates folders called Indbakke, Kalendar, and Sendt post. Many international companies have procedures to ensure that they create folders in the correct language immediately after they set up a mailbox or have Visual BASIC or other utilities to change folder names to another language afterward.[2] To complete the process, the AD replicates the attributes of the new mailbox, such as its set of email addresses, to all Global Catalog servers in the forest.

3.4.1 Accessing Exchange attributes for mail-enabled objects

You work with Exchange-specific attributes through a set of property pages that Windows dynamically loads from code distributed with Exchange whenever you create or edit a mail-enabled object using AD Users and Computers. Exchange 2003 extends ESM so that you can move or delete a mailbox or configure it for the Exchange options. However, to change other attributes, such as updating mailbox quotas, you have to access the set of Exchange-specific property pages through AD Users and Computers. The pages are:

- Exchange General: This property includes the mailbox alias, the store where the mailbox is located (equivalent to the Home-MDB attribute in Exchange 5.5), delivery restrictions and options, and storage limits. Exchange 2000 introduced the concept of system policies, a way to create and apply a consistent set of policies to multiple objects. For example, you can create a system policy to control storage quotas for mailboxes and deleted item retention periods. Afterward, you can apply the policy to as many mailbox stores as you wish—all in a single operation. If you want, you can then override the effect of the system policy by selecting individual accounts to give them different limits. For example, you can update your boss's account so that he or she has a much larger limit than the norm!

- Email Addresses: These properties include all of the email addresses held by a mail-enabled object, including the proxy addresses used by SMTP and other connectors. As with Exchange 5.5, an object can hold multiple addresses of a specific type (such as Lotus Notes, X.400, or Exchange's own X.500 address type), but only one address of each type will be "primary" and used by the Routing Engine to direct messages across a connector. The other addresses of each type allow Exchange to accept and deliver messages sent to addresses that a

---

2. Although the original Exchange client included this feature, Outlook, Outlook Web Access, and Outlook Express do not allow you to change the names of the default folders.

user may have used in the past (otherwise known as "grandfathered" addresses). Do not delete any of these addresses without understanding the consequences, since you can easily disable a mailbox in this way. For example, if you have used the Move Server Wizard to move an Exchange 5.5 server to another site or organization in the past, you will find X.500 addresses. The Routing Engine uses X.500 addresses to process messages sent to old addresses, such as when it creates a reply to a message that someone originally generated when a server was in its old site or organization. The Routing Engine is able to check the address on these messages against the X.500 addresses in the directory and reroute the message to its new destination.

- Exchange Features: This property page is only available for Exchange 2000 servers running on Windows 2000. The properties allow the administrator to control which of the advanced features (e.g., the Exchange integrated version of Instant Messaging) a user is able to access. You must enable each one of the features before someone can use it. The default is to disable access to everything. Not many companies deployed the Exchange 2000 versions of Instant Messaging and Conferencing, so it is unlikely that you will do much work with this page. However, for Exchange 2003, Microsoft has moved the protocol settings from the Advanced Property page to the Exchange Features (Figure 3.18) page. In addition, this page allows you to control the new wireless functionality for a user, so the Exchange Features page is now far more useful.

- Exchange Advanced: These properties are only visible if you select the "Advanced Features" option from the view menu in the AD Users and Computers console. The properties include a flag to hide an object from address lists, custom attributes, protocol settings, and mailbox rights (Figure 3.19).

You can find many of the other properties that you can set for Exchange 5.5 mailboxes, such as telephone numbers and organizational information, on other property pages (General, Telephone, Address, and so on). These properties are generic and can be set on any user or contact stored in the AD, even if they are not mail enabled. In mixed-mode environments, it is a best practice to use the Exchange 5.5 administrator program to work with Exchange 5.5 mail-enabled objects and ESM and AD Users and Computers to work with Exchange 2000/2003 equivalents.

Along with the property page extensions, Windows adds an entry for "Exchange Tasks" to the context-sensitive menu that is available when you work with user, contact, and group objects in AD Users and Computers

3.4 Mailboxes and user accounts

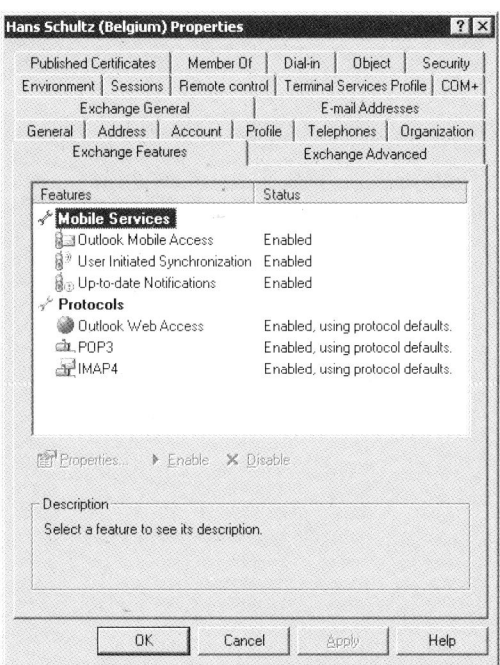

Figure 3.18
Exchange 2003 Features Property page.

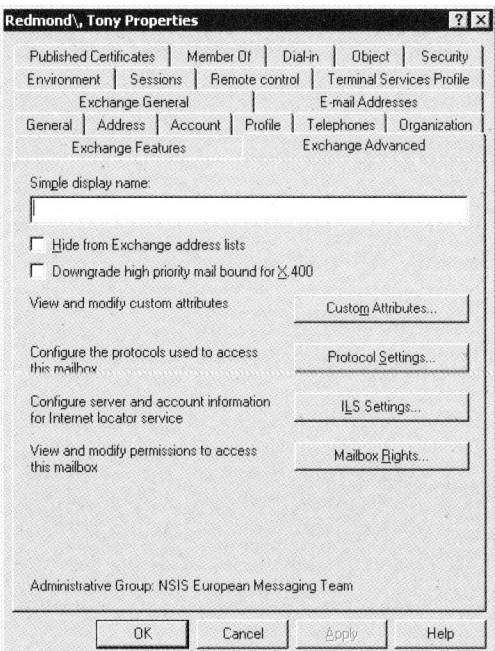

Figure 3.19
Exchange 2000 Advanced Properties.

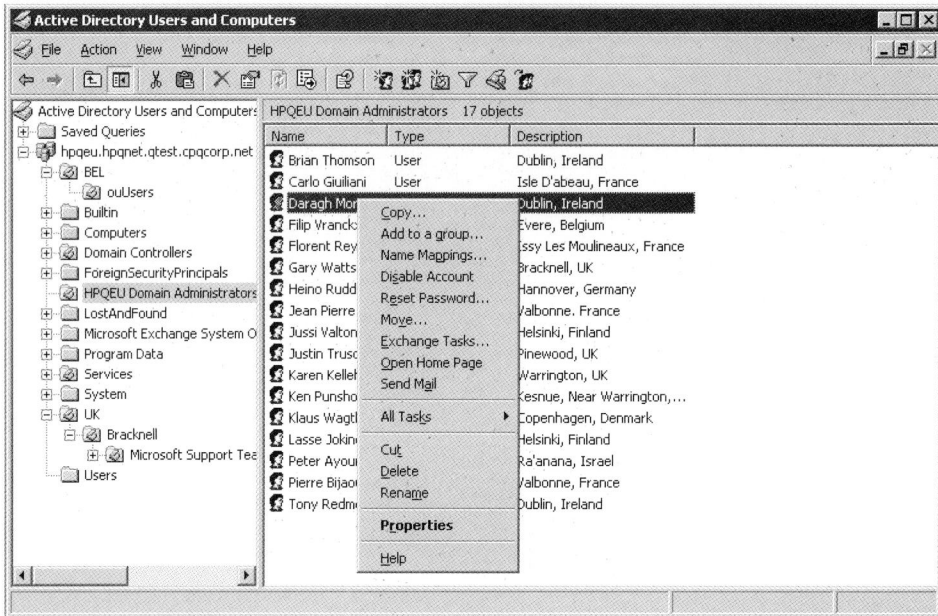

Figure 3.20 *Exchange Tasks added to the AD context-sensitive menu.*

(Figure 3.20). You can also work with mail-enabled accounts through the Exchange 2003 version of ESM.

You can select multiple objects to work with, or just select one. When chosen, the "Exchange Tasks" option activates a wizard to present a set of tasks that you can execute. The tasks displayed depend on the type of mail-enabled object you select. If you select multiple objects of different types, the wizard will present you with a complete set of tasks that you could potentially execute against the type of objects you have selected, but you might select an inappropriate option for a certain object that the wizard cannot perform. Figure 3.21 shows the result of selecting a group, user, and contact together and then invoking the wizard. As you can see, some of the options presented here do not make much sense. For example, you cannot enable Instant Messaging for a mail-enabled contact or hide membership for a user.

Common tasks for a user include:

- Moving a mailbox to another store, including a store on a different server in the same or different administrative group

- Deleting a mailbox, which turns the user object into a non-mail-enabled user

3.4 Mailboxes and user accounts

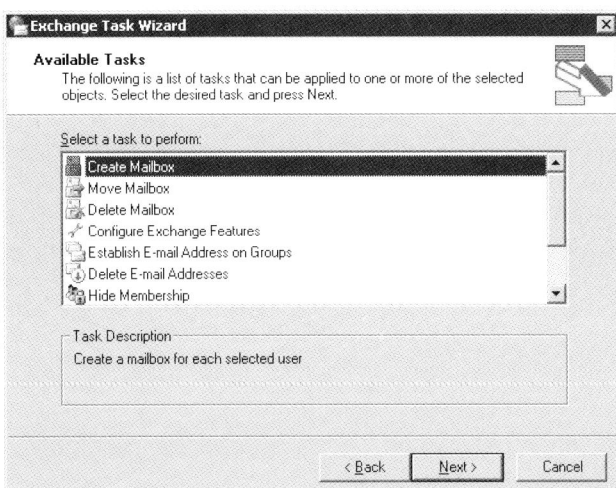

Figure 3.21
The Exchange Tasks wizard.

- Enabling or disabling Exchange features, such as Instant Messaging (Exchange 2000) or Exchange Mobile Services (Exchange 2003)

Common tasks for a group include:

- Hiding or revealing group membership. This means that Exchange alters the security descriptors on the group to prevent users from seeing who is a member of the group. From an Outlook perspective, it prevents users from selecting the group from the GAL and seeing members listed when Outlook views the properties of the group, as shown in Figure 3.22.

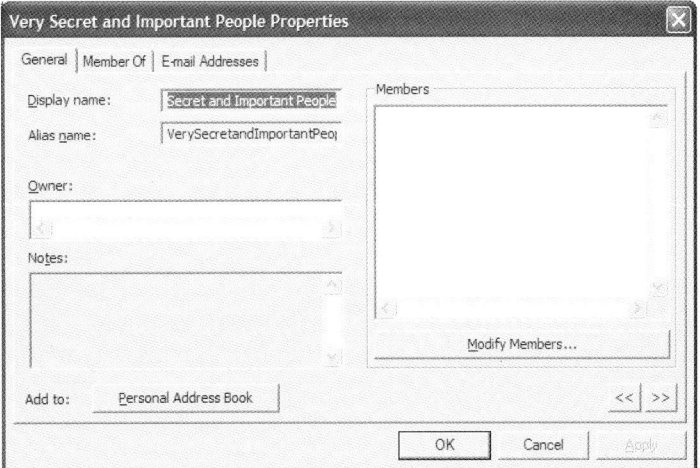

Figure 3.22
Hidden group membership.

- Deleting email addresses or designating a distribution list. The first option removes any existing email addresses that are set for the group, effectively stopping people from using the group to distribute messages. The second option adds an alias for the group, but you may need to add some specific address proxies for the group (such as an appropriate SMTP address) after you designate it as a distribution list before the list is fully effective.

Common tasks for a contact include:

- Deleting or enabling email addresses. Deleting email addresses removes contacts from the GAL, while enabling addresses will allow you to specify the types of address (X.400, SMTP, and so on) and their values for the contact.

3.4.2 Moving mailboxes

The Task Wizard usually performs actions instantaneously, assuming a fast connection between your workstation and the server. Moving a mailbox is the obvious exception, since it requires Exchange to transfer messages to another mailbox store, which might not be on the same server as the source. Depending on system load, moving large mailboxes (>100 MB) will take between five and ten minutes to perform if the two servers share the same LAN, up to approximately 500 MB an hour. Moving a mailbox is a binary operation—it either works or it does not. If a failure occurs somewhere along the process, you have to start again. Note that you need Exchange administrator permission for the administrative group for both the source and target server to be able to perform the move.

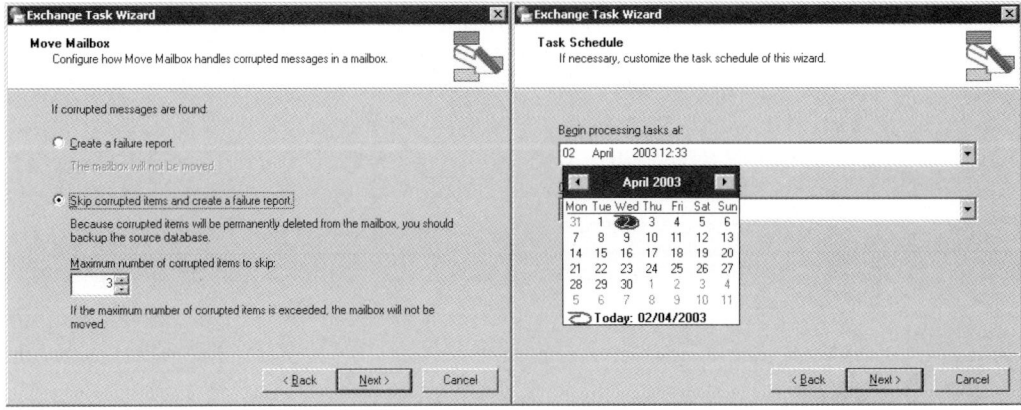

Figure 3.23   *The Exchange 2003 Move Mailbox wizard.*

Always make sure that you ask the mailbox owner to log off before commencing the move, and ensure that enough disk space is available to accommodate all the transaction logs that the move operation generates. Each transferred message is a transaction for both the source and target databases, so the disk that holds the transaction logs will handle a substantial I/O load during the transfer. Exchange 2003 improves move mailbox operations (Figure 3.23) as follows:

- You can now move mailboxes from both the ESM and AD Users and Computers consoles, whereas previously you could not move mailboxes from ESM. Because you can now run ESM on Windows XP workstations, you do not need to use servers to drive the migration process.

- The wizard can continue processing and move the mailbox even if it encounters some corrupt messages in the mailbox—the administrator is able to decide how many corrupt messages the wizard should skip, up to a hard-coded limit of 100. Clearly, if you meet a mailbox that has many corrupt messages, it is a sign that the underlying mailbox store is probably suffering from some sort of corruption that deserves your attention. Note that if the wizard skips any corrupt messages, it generates a report to show you what those messages are.

- You can move multiple mailboxes concurrently by selecting multiple mailboxes and then taking the "Move Mailbox" option. Exchange uses up to four threads per session to move mailbox content. As a guideline, expect to take approximately an hour to move a 500-MB mailbox, depending on system load and server capabilities.

- The Exchange 2003 version of Move Mailbox is much faster than Exchange 2000. According to Microsoft, because operations use up to four separate threads, things move about four times faster, but the actual results you achieve will vary according to environment. You can see the multithreaded nature of operations by selecting multiple mailboxes and moving them together (Figure 3.24). Of course, you can achieve further acceleration by using multiple workstations to move mailboxes.

- You can schedule moves to occur at a particular time. The System Attendant tracks and performs scheduled jobs at the requesting time, allowing you to ensure that mailboxes move when users are asleep!

- If users run Outlook 2003 and have a cached-mode mailbox, it is possible to continue working while Exchange moves their mailboxes. Exchange will not deliver new messages to the mailbox and queues

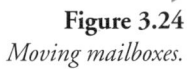

Figure 3.24
Moving mailboxes.

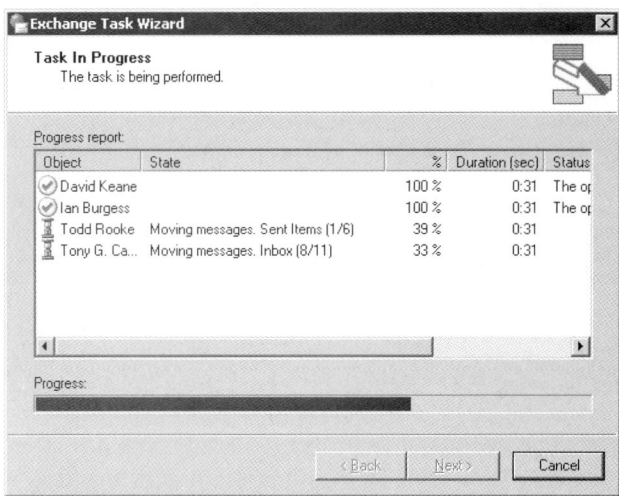

them on the source server while the move proceeds. When it has moved the mailbox, Exchange releases the messages and delivers them from the queue. Exchange notifies Outlook when the moved mailbox is ready to use, and Outlook then switches across (transparently) to access the new server and then transmits any messages that the user sent during the mailbox move. While it is possible to move Outlook 2003 users who work in cached Exchange mode, it might be tempting fate. Therefore, it is still a good idea to have users disconnect before the move starts and, if they use Outlook 2003, to have them set their connection status to "Work Offline." In addition, if a user attempts to log on during a mailbox move (as opposed to continue working during the move), the Store detects the connection attempt and logs event 9660, identifying the user name and distinguished name. The Store also flags an error to tell the user that a mailbox move is under way.

After a mailbox move, Exchange informs Outlook clients of the new server name to allow these clients to update their MAPI profile. Exchange redirects Outlook Web Access connects to the new server at the next connect, but you have to update settings manually for IMAP4 and POP3 clients.

In some cases, administrators report that newly moved mailboxes use larger quotas than the original. This is anecdotal evidence that is not consistent from server to server, but it is a good idea to check mailbox quotas before and after the move to ensure that users can keep working. Overall, the net impact of the changes to the move mailbox feature is that it is easier

3.4 Mailboxes and user accounts

to move mailboxes between servers, but it is an activity that you have to plan carefully.

The Exchange Task wizard captures details of its processing in log files, which it saves automatically in the \My Documents\Exchange Task Wizard Logs folder for the account that you use to run the wizard. The log files are in XML format, which is fantastic for everyone who can read and visualize XML format but remains a challenge for most people. Fortunately, you can apply style sheets to interpret the XML content and display it in a more

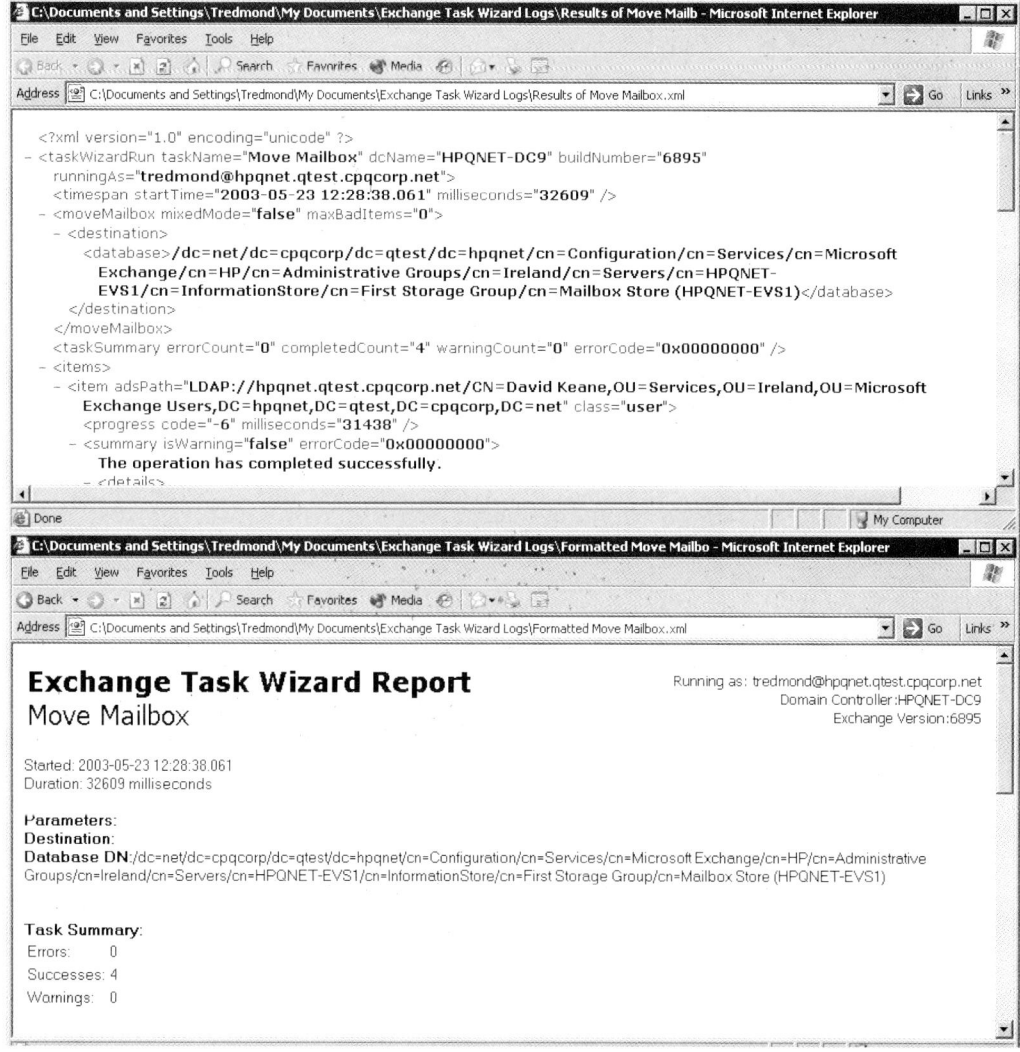

Figure 3.25   *Viewing Task wizard reports.*

understandable format. You can do the work yourself or ask your local Microsoft contact to help. In either case, after you have the style sheet, you can edit the XML report and insert the reference to the style sheet immediately after the first line in the file. For example:

```
<?xml version="1.0" encoding="unicode"?>
<?xml-stylesheet type="text/xsl" href="c:/exchsrvr/
TaskWizardReport.xslt"?>
```

In this case, we reference a style sheet called TaskWizardReport.xslt style in the indicated directory. You can see the effect of such a transformation by comparing the top and bottom screens in Figure 3.25. The top figure is the raw XML content generated by the Task wizard, while the bottom is the formatted result.

Microsoft made some very good changes in the move mailbox functionality in Exchange 2003, but a lingering problem persists (including SP1). Sometimes, at the end of the process when ESM displays the message "Updating the directory," the connection between ESM and the domain controller that ESM uses to update AD attributes times out. ESM cannot reestablish a connection to the domain controller and the move process goes into limbo and must eventually be terminated (the mailbox move is unsuccessful). After terminating the process, you will have to wait for a few minutes before you can reattempt to move the mailbox, since the AD has to sort out the problems caused by the abrupt termination. The workaround is to use AD Users and Computers to move mailboxes so you will not experience the same problem. Microsoft knows about the problem and is working on a fix. You can expect to see updated code in SP2 or a hot fix provided before that.

3.5 Distribution groups

There are three types of Windows groups:

- Universal groups
- Global groups
- Domain local groups

Universal groups are available anywhere within a forest. In other words, you can use a universal group to control access to any resource in the forest. Windows publishes details of universal groups in the GC, and clients resolve membership of universal groups when they log on by reference to a GC. This step ensures that clients receive a full set of credentials and are

3.5 Distribution groups   173

able to access resources through membership of any universal group they may hold.

Confusingly, Windows does not publish details of global groups in the GC. Similar to the definition of global groups used in Windows NT, global groups can be present in the ACL of any object in the forest, but they can only contain members from the domain that "owns" the group.

Domain local groups are the most restricted, since they only apply within the domain in which they are created. Again, Windows does not publish details of domain local groups in the GC. Domain local groups can contain universal or global groups along with individual users.

As you can see in Figure 3.26, Windows also defines groups by type. If a group is a "security" type, it means that the group holds a security principal and you can use it to control access to resources. A group that is a "distribution" type does not have a security principal, but you can use it with Exchange as a way to distribute messages, which is very close in style to the original definition of an Exchange distribution list. Figure 3.26 also shows that a security group can be mail enabled (the group has a published email address). A mail-enabled universal group that holds a security principal is the most powerful group. It is available anywhere in the forest, can be used to secure resources, and you can use the group as a traditional email distribution list.

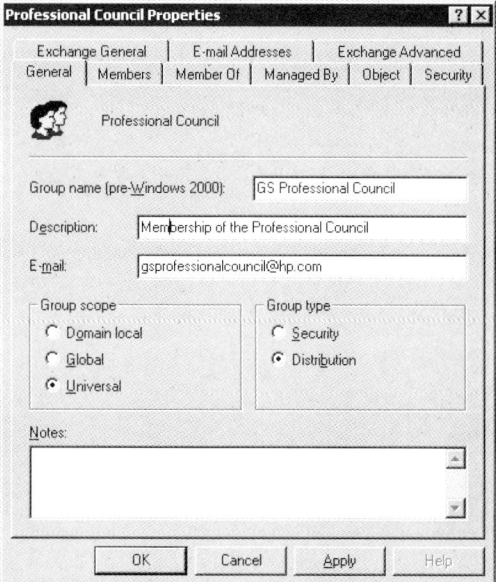

Figure 3.26
General properties of a Windows group.

Exchange is a messaging system, so it is extraneous to talk about distribution groups, even if this is accurate in terms of Windows. When you mail enable groups, they become functionally equivalent to distribution lists, so from this point on, I will only refer to groups when required by a feature or requirement of Windows and distribution groups in reference to Exchange.

3.5.1 Forming Windows groups

As with Exchange 5.5 distribution lists, Windows groups are composed of a set of backward pointers to individual directory objects (other groups, users, and contacts) that form the group. The left-hand screen in Figure 3.27 shows group membership as viewed through AD Users and Computers. The right-hand screen shows the membership of the same group, this time viewed through the ADSIEDIT utility. Here we see that the AD holds the membership of a group in a single, multivalued attribute called "Member" and that the attribute is formed by the distinguished name of each of the members. The AD uses the distinguished name as the pointer to the records for the individual members when it has to resolve or expand group membership. Because Windows builds a group through a set of pointers to AD objects, you have to be careful if you need to perform an authoritative restore of the AD to recover from a database failure, since you may affect

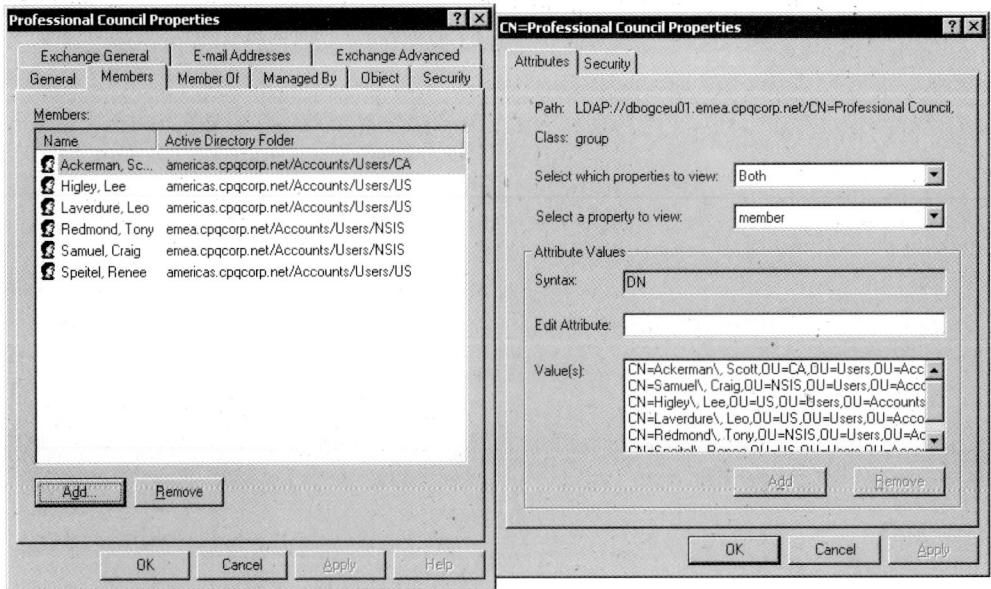

Figure 3.27 *Viewing group membership.*

group membership if the restore removes some of the pointers. For this reason, you should take great care to check important group membership after completing any AD restore.

The AD features attribute-level replication, but any change made to the membership of a group results in essentially the complete object being replicated, because the membership is held in a single attribute. This is true for Windows 2000, but the situation is a little different in Windows 2003, which includes a new mechanism called linked value replication (LVR). LVR addresses some of the problems associated with large distribution groups that span more than a few hundred members. People tend to leave and join groups on a regular basis, so the "churn" in membership generates an obvious issue in excessive network traffic to handle replication of the membership attribute. In addition, because the AD is a multimaster directory where any replica (DC) can originate an update, the danger exists that the AD will ignore updates when users make changes to group membership in multiple places at approximately the same time.

In this situation, the AD must reconcile changes coming in from multiple places without the benefit of human intelligence, and it does not always make the right decision. In Windows 2000, the AD is handicapped, because it updates only one attribute—the membership—for each of the changes it must reconcile. Thus, the change originating from the New York DC looks the same as the change from London. Which change should win? The AD uses its normal conflict resolution techniques to decide the "winner" (the update that is finally made). Timestamps eventually help to resolve the conflict, and the AD uses the last timed update to the group membership and applies that update to the group. Administrators may only know about a reconciliation snafu when a user complains that he or she is not able to access a public folder or that he or she does not receive email sent to a list. LVR helps to solve the conflict issue, because the AD is now able to resolve changes at the level of individual members rather than handling the complete group as one entity.

At this point, it is also worth noting that restoring the AD in a multi-domain environment may lose some updates applied to any data that the AD holds in a multivalue attribute. Windows 2003 is better than Windows 2000 in this respect, and an authoritative restore will recover any links associated with the domain that you perform the restore for, so the problem only arises for links that tie objects together across multiple domains. Group membership is the obvious example, but Exchange uses multivalue attributes for data such as organizational structures. When you restore data, you essentially roll back to the point in time when the backup occurred.

Many changes may take place between that time and the current time and there is no guarantee that the AD replication mechanism will be able to reconcile everything accurately, because (unlike public folders) there is no concept of a backfill request to allow one replica of the directory to request a complete refresh from another replica. There is also no way that you can know whether the AD is in an inconsistent state. For these reasons, it is a good idea to practice AD restores and to have a plan to take frequent backups of the system state of a DC in every domain in the forest, since you will rely on this data during restores. You may also want to check with companies that build AD utilities to see if they have a program to help with this problem.

The fact that multiple changes to a group can overwrite each other is a flaw in the directory that the AD multimaster model exposed in Windows 2000. The problem also exists in the Exchange 5.5 DS, the ancestor of the AD, but its effect is less obvious, because sites own distribution lists (the DS equivalent of distribution groups) and only administrators from the owning sites can modify list membership. Thus, you have a reduced potential that multiple administrators modify a list at any time. Going back even further, this issue did not exist in Windows NT 4.0, because you had to make changes to group membership at the PDC, which acted as an arbiter.

The last issue is that AD uses more memory (in a component called the version store) than it really needs to when it processes membership in one large chunk rather than being able to focus only on the members who change. The problem becomes more severe as groups grow in size. Adding two members to a group that contains ten objects clearly imposes less stress on the system than when you add the 3,001st object to a group that already holds 3,000. In fact, because the version store is a limited size, it may be exhausted if the AD attempts to make an excessive number of changes in a single operation. The exact point when exhaustion occurs is dependent on the group, members, and forest, but Microsoft knows that problems usually occur around the 5,000 mark. The solution introduced by LVR allows the AD to track changes to individual entries in multivalued attributes and specifically group membership. However, LVR is only available when the Windows 2003 forest runs in interim or full functional modes, and the AD downgrades the feature when it replicates between controllers of mixed vintage.

Considering this information, we can see that it makes sense from a pure AD perspective to limit the amount of updates applied to groups whenever possible, especially for universal groups, since the AD replicates them to every GC in the forest. However, universal groups are very important to

Exchange, since they are the only way to implement secure access to public folders and email distribution lists within multidomain implementations.

You can reduce the replication load by building the membership of universal groups from a set of global groups. This means that the effects of changes to group membership are restricted to the host domain of the users or contacts in the group, and the only replication to the GC occurs if a global group is added or removed from the universal group. Seeking to reduce replication in this way is a great example of how the needs of the base operating system do not match the needs of applications. If you include nested global groups in a universal distribution group, only Exchange servers in the same domain will be fully able to resolve group membership. This leads to a situation where you can send email to the same group from accounts in different domains and have messages delivered to different sets of people! Even worse, neither users nor administrators will be aware of the problem, because no problem exists in purely technical terms and Exchange signals no error messages. For this reason, it is a best practice only to use universal groups with Exchange.

3.5.2 Expanding distribution lists

The Exchange Routing Engine expands the membership of any distribution lists that a user includes in a message header and looks up the AD to find the preferred email address of each object in the lists. DSAccess handles the lookup process and may return email addresses from its local cache or after it looks up the AD. The Routing Engine uses the email addresses to help determine the optimum routing path for the message to reach the recipient and then to place the message on the right queue for transmission. All of this work happens in memory, and the Routing Engine does not expand the group membership to insert individual user names and email addresses in the header of the message. You can always view the membership of a group by selecting its name in the addressee list and then look at its properties. If the Routing Engine did expand group membership, Exchange would have to carry around unwanted and unnecessary information in message headers. By comparison, if you use a personal distribution list to address a message, Outlook (or another client) must expand the contents of the distribution list and add all of the recipients to the header before it can submit the message to Exchange. You can see the impact of distribution list expansion on the size of a message by comparing similar messages addressed and sent to a group and a list, each containing 20 members. The message sent to the group is always far smaller.

Large distribution lists (more than 100 members), or those that contain nested groups, can impose a considerable demand on system resources during expansion. The expansion load does not usually affect servers equipped with multiple CPUs, since one of the CPUs can handle the work. Users can notice the delay in sending a message to a large list (if they are a member of the list), since Exchange can take up to a minute or so to deliver a copy of the message back to the originator. The current version of Exchange may seem slower than Exchange 5.5 in distribution list expansion, but this is a cosmetic change due to the way that the Routing Engine works. The Exchange 5.5 MTA expands distribution lists and immediately begins delivery to local recipients, so they receive their copies first. Now, the Routing Engine goes through a complex categorization process to ensure that it handles all copies of the message in an optimal manner. Local recipients see their copies at approximately the same time as the Routing Engine places copies to remote recipients on its destination queues. Delivery may seem slower, but it happens in a very efficient manner.

3.5.3 How many objects can I have in a group?

Exchange 5.5 distribution lists support a maximum of 5,000 objects, a limit set by the user interface in the administration program and respected by clients such as Outlook. It is possible to add more than 5,000 objects to a list, but only programmatically, using an interface such as ADSI. The AD imposes the same limit for membership of its groups, although, once again, you can manipulate a group through ADSI to add more entries. However, because of some technical issues involved in replicating group membership, Microsoft recommends that you avoid building groups with 5,000 entries. My own opinion is a little stronger on this topic—the limit is technical, not realistic, and you create the potential for problems if you insist on using very large groups. Best practice is to keep group membership under 1,000 to make everything (membership, replication, update collisions, traffic) a lot easier to control. This is particularly true in large, multidomain implementations.

Note the use of the word "objects" when referring to group membership. An object can be a user account or contact, but it can also be another group, so you can build groups from a collection of nested groups and build very large logical groups in this manner. Nested groups greatly expand the total possible user population that you can address through a single directory entry. However, while it is nice to know that it is technically possible to create a megadistribution list to address thousands of users at a single key-

3.5 Distribution groups

stroke, once a list contains more than 200 users or so, it is also a weapon for people to use as a form of internal spam.

Windows does not impose a hard-coded limit to the number of groups that can exist in a forest, but you can run into a situation called "token bloat" that can prevent users from logging on. Token bloat occurs when the number of groups that a user belongs to is so large that Windows cannot fit all the groups into the security token. Because they are so useful for email, an Exchange environment is likely to use far more groups than a simple Windows deployment, and you may run into token bloat when you migrate from an earlier version of Exchange and Windows upgrades the distribution lists to groups. This is a good reason to review group membership and remove users from groups that they do not need to belong to.

3.5.4 Managing distribution lists

It is easy to set up new distribution lists, but some forget the hard work to maintain membership. In theory, updates should be automatic and the AD adjusts group membership as it deletes accounts and contacts. The normal problems include:

- Adding new members: Whom should someone contact if he or she wants to join the list? An easy way to inform people is to include instructions in the "Notes" section of the list's properties, since this text is visible to Outlook when you look at its properties through the GAL (Figure 3.28). Note that a user is only able to manage groups

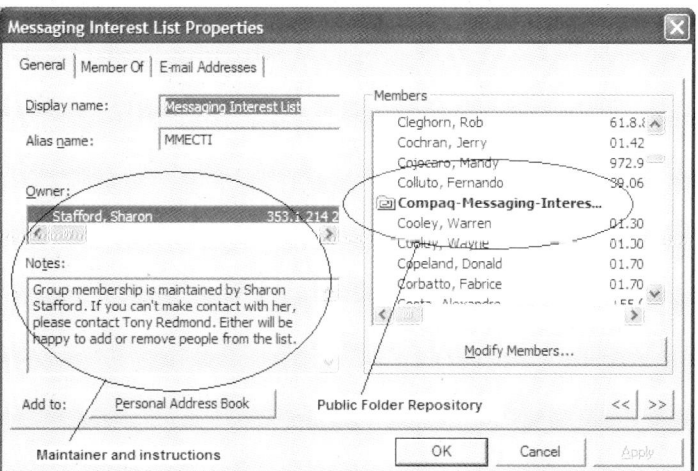

Figure 3.28
Details of a list maintainer and its PF repository.

that are part of the user's own domain and that you can control the ability for a manager to update the membership list by an attribute of the list. You cannot manage groups from other domains, because you are using an incomplete copy of the group replicated to a local GC rather than the full copy maintained by DCs in the owning domain. In addition, the group maintainer must have the correct Windows permissions (Allow Read Members and Allow Write Members) to be able to change the membership. You can grant these permissions at either the organizational unit (if the same maintainer takes care of multiple groups) or individual group level.

- The informational text can state whether the potential member should email a request to the maintainer or take another action to join the list. Some companies have sophisticated Web-based applications to allow users to maintain their own group membership, using ADSI to communicate with AD behind the scenes. You can use tools such as the AUTODL utility, which is part of the Exchange Resource Kit, to help users create, manage, and delete distribution lists.

- You know you have a problem when the list begins to receive "please let me in" messages from people who want to join, since this is a good indication that your procedures are not well known or do not work.

- You need to know who the members of the list are. This is easy for small lists, but it becomes increasingly difficult as the numbers grow, because the standard tools for list maintenance (through Outlook or AD Users and Computers) have no way to generate membership reports. The ONDL utility, part of the old BackOffice Resource Kit (you may need to ask Microsoft for a copy of the program, because it is not available for download), is a very simple way of generating a membership list that you can then manipulate with Excel or Access. Figure 3.29 shows some sample output from ONDL. The input is the group's alias and the output is a list of each member's alias and display name. Alternatively, you can write your own program and use ADSI to interrogate the AD and retrieve all the necessary information.

Figure 3.29
Sample ONDL output.

```
C:> ONDL MWIZ
Found alias "MWIZ" (Messaging Wizards):

abiven, Abiven, Pat
OchoaC, Alano, Cindie
…..
ZhangPi, Zhang, Pierre
hozihe, Zimmermann, Helga
** 574 Members **
```

3.5 Distribution groups

- Removing obsolete members: If your practice is to disable AD accounts and keep mailboxes for a period after their owners leave the company, you should remove them from all groups to prevent the mailboxes from receiving unwanted copies of email. It is a best practice for group owners to review the list regularly to remove recipients who no longer work for the company. Apart from filling Store databases with messages that no one will ever read, this step prevents the other group members from becoming annoyed when they send messages to the group only to receive multiple nondelivery notifications back. The most common reason for NDRs is that Exchange cannot deliver messages to the mailboxes of the disabled accounts (perhaps because the mailboxes have exceeded their quotas with all the messages that have arrived since the owner left the company).

You can block most nondelivery notifications by setting the "Exchange Advanced" properties (Figure 3.30) of the distribution group to:

- Suppress notifications completely.
- Send notifications back to the message originator.
- Send notifications to the owner of the group as defined in the "Managed by" property page.

The easiest option is to suppress nondelivery notifications for distribution lists, but this means that you never see any indication that someone

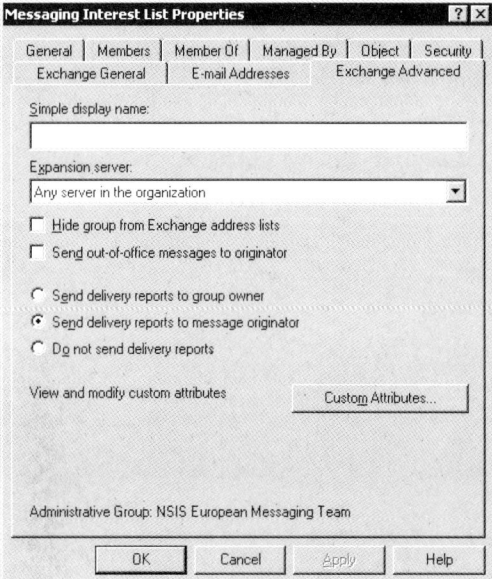

Figure 3.30
Properties of a distribution group.

has a problem—his or her mailbox quota is exceeded or Exchange makes an attempt to deliver to a mailbox that no longer exists, which could mean that directory replication is not working. Sending notifications back to the owner is acceptable if that person can take appropriate action. For example, if you allocate ownership to an administrative assistant, and he or she does not have the correct Windows permissions to modify group membership, then you will end up doing the work to maintain the group. Note that these properties are only valid for a single forest and single Exchange organization. If you operate in an environment where you use multiple Exchange organizations, the settings you make in one organization do not replicate to the others and you will still see notifications unless you turn them off everywhere.

3.5.5 Protected groups

Sometimes, the SMTP address of a distribution group gets outside a company. Apart from the obvious irritation if spam (otherwise called unsolicited commercial email) starts arriving for everyone on the list, there is a danger that unauthorized users could exploit the list to identify personnel within the company—for example, by a recruiter looking for specific talent. Exchange 2000 implements delivery restrictions for groups by checking that it could resolve the sender's address against the directory, but spammers

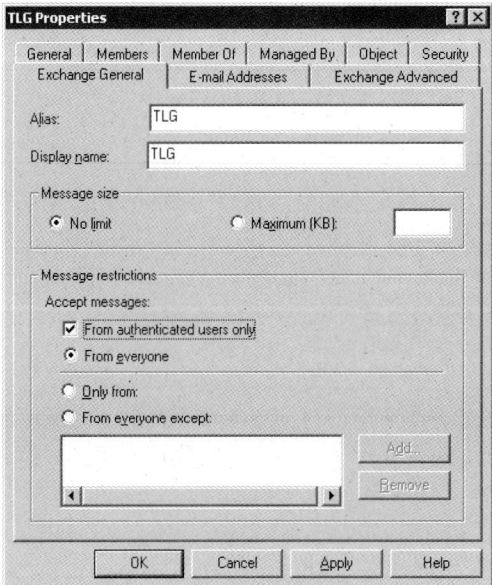

Figure 3.31
Limiting a group to authenticated users only.

can work around this check by spoofing their identity by inserting a perfectly valid email address in a message's "From:" field. For example, you might restrict a group so that only senior executives can send messages to it, only to be embarrassed when a spammer uses your chief executive's email address (which is often published or known externally) to address the troops.

With Exchange 2003, you can block such access by only allowing authenticated users (those who possess recognized NT credentials) to send messages to the list. In AD Users and Computers, select the list you want to protect and set the "From authenticated users only" checkbox on the Exchange General property page (Figure 3.31). This feature depends on a new attribute that Exchange 2003 introduces for user and distribution group objects (ms-Exch-Authenticated-Only), so you can only set authenticated restrictions on a group when working on a server that has the Exchange 2003 management components installed.

3.5.6 Suppressing OOF

People use out of office notifications, or OOFs,[3] to inform correspondents when they are unable to process messages immediately, such as when they are on vacation. This is a worthy feature, but its side effect is that OOF messages often contain confidential information that you would prefer not go outside the organization. For example, it is common for users to tell correspondents to contact someone else in their department if they need quick action and to give telephone numbers and other information. This information is very useful inside the company, but it can be even more valuable to someone who is trying to learn about company structure. Recruiters can use this information to identify people who do various jobs inside a company and, at the other end of the scale, those who create distribution lists to sell to spammers are delighted to add anyone's email address to their databases.

You can stop Exchange from sending OOF messages across a connector. This step certainly achieves the goal of blocking information going to external recipients, but it is radical surgery because it removes a useful feature from users. When you analyze the problem, the vast majority of problems come from OOF messages that go back to list servers or distribution lists

---

3. At first glance, it does not make sense to use OOF as the shortened version for "Out of Office." Microsoft's original Xenix (UNIX-based) email system called this feature "Out of Facility" (many U.S. companies refer to offices as facilities) and the tag stuck through the initial development of Exchange and remains to this day.

and not from OOF messages sent to friends. Therefore, it makes sense to apply a selective block and stop Exchange from generating OOF messages for incoming messages when you are not on the TO: or CC: list. For example, let us assume that you get a message from your mother, but you will not be able to reply for a few days because you are at an off-site meeting. In this case, you would certainly like Exchange to generate an OOF message to tell your mother that you will reply then. On the other hand, you probably do not want to send OOF messages in reply to every message that you receive because you belong to a very active Internet mailing list that discusses the finer points of wine appreciation or a similar subject.

On Exchange 2003 servers, you can force Exchange to check the set of message recipients to see whether a user explicitly appears in the recipient list rather than receiving a copy because he or she is a member of a distribution group. In this situation, Exchange can suppress OOF messages sent to the group and send them to individual recipients. To do this, you must create a new registry value as follows:

```
Key: HKLM\MSExchangeIS\ParametersSystem
Value: SuppressOOFsToDistributionLists (DWORD)
Set to: 1 (suppress); 0 (ignore)
```

Note that if you make this registry change, it will override the properties of distribution groups that otherwise control notifications.

3.5.7 Using public folder repositories for distribution lists

Popular email lists can attract a lot of traffic. Some of the messages that people send to the list will be very interesting and worthwhile and some will not, but in general the traffic represents a certain core of knowledge that you may want to keep. In this situation, you can add the address of a public folder to a list, which means that Exchange will automatically copy anything sent to the list to the public folder. This is an excellent way of building a record of the communication between the members of the list. An added advantage is that new people who join the list have a way to review previous discussions. At HP, many distribution lists have public folder repositories, some containing nearly 20,000 contributions gathered over the years. Once you start to collect items in the repository, you can then speed up searching for items by indexing the public folder using either Exchange full-text indexing or SharePoint Portal Server.

To add a public folder to a list, make sure that it is visible to the GAL and add it in the same way as you would add a mailbox or contact. You may then want to hide the PF from the GAL so that it only receives items sent to the list. Also, make sure that folder permissions allow list members to add items, since otherwise Exchange will not be able to write new posts into the folder.

With such a volume of data to manage, be sure to appoint someone as the editor of each public folder repository. Without editing, the public folder will become an accumulation of data, where you will find it hard to locate anything. The editor should regularly review the messages delivered to the public folder and remove messages such as the "me too" posts, which we all see too often on email-based lists. Additionally, the editor can compress message threads down to a smaller number of items by removing duplications, which makes it easier for all to navigate through the folder and find information.

3.5.8 Using groups for permissions

Because Exchange treats them like any other recipient, mail-enabled security groups are a useful way of maintaining permissions on public folders, much along the same lines as delivery restrictions. When you give permission to a group, all members of the list inherit the permission. The advantage lies in the fact that it is much easier to grant permission to a single entity, the group, than it is to manage separate permissions for each individual in the group. Better still, when people join a group, they automatically inherit the permissions held by the group and so have access to all of the public folders that are available to the group. Later on, when you remove some members from the group, Windows revokes the permissions they inherit from the group and there is no danger that someone will gain access to confidential information after he or she no longer needs this privilege.

3.6 Query-based distribution groups

Large companies such as HP use distribution groups (or lists) extensively to create email-addressable objects that reach many people who share a common need or interest. However, it is typical to find a proliferation of distribution groups in any large email deployment, leading to a situation where people spend a lot of time updating the groups to make sure that the right people receive the right data all the time. For example, the HP GAL includes over 57,000 distribution groups, all of which have different maintainers. Some maintainers are very conscientious about how they maintain membership and the group is always accurate; others are less so and you can never be sure that the group contains everyone that it should.

Good maintainers remove members who no longer want to receive messages sent to the group or those who have left the company. Others simply leave the groups to degrade gently until they are no longer wanted. At that point, system administrators have to clean up the directory by removing redundant groups. However, cleaning up the directory or maintaining group membership is a low-priority task for hard-pressed administrators, so they are easy tasks to overlook. The result is a directory cluttered with obsolete groups and groups that do not reach the right membership. Exchange 2003 introduces support for query-based distribution groups to help you automate list maintenance. However, only Exchange 2003 and Exchange 2000 (SP3 onward) servers running in native-mode organizations support query-based distribution groups, connected to the AD on Windows 2000 SP3 or Windows 2003 servers, that have the necessary schema extension to support these lists (object type ms-Exch-Dynamic-Distribution-List). You can use the LDIFDE utility to gain an insight into the information that the AD holds for query-based groups. Figure 3.32 shows an edited version of LDIFDE output for a query-based group.

As you can see, many of the attributes that you expect for any other distribution group, including email addresses, exist for query-based lists. The big difference is the value of the msExchDynamicDLFilter attribute, which holds the LDAP filter that the AD resolves to determine the dynamic membership of the list. The use of new attributes to define a query-based distribution group means that you cannot use the Exchange 2000 version of AD Users and Computers to work with these groups.

When users submit messages addressed to query-based distribution groups, the categorizer (even on an Exchange 2000 server) identifies that the group requires a query and then resolves it by making an LDAP query against a GC. After the GC returns all the recipients, the categorizer builds the recipient list and decides how to route the message. The need to build a list before submission increases load on the GC and routing server and delays the message slightly, but this is a justifiable tradeoff between usefulness and overhead.

The only difference a user sees between a query-based group and a normal group is that you cannot view the membership of a query-based group from its GAL properties. This is quite logical, because the GAL has no way of resolving the LDAP query to determine group membership. From an administrative perspective, you cannot use query-based groups to control access to objects such as connectors, and you cannot nest these groups inside other distribution groups.

3.6 Query-based distribution groups

Figure 3.32
LDIFDE output for a query-based group.

```
C:> LDIFDE -v -d "cn=Exchange2003EMEA,cn=users,dc=xyz,dn=com" -f
dn: CN=ExchangeEMEA,CN=Users,DC=xyz,DC=com
changetype: add
objectClass: top
objectClass: msExchDynamicDistributionList
cn: ExchangeEMEA
description: Exchange 2003 Users in EMEA
distinguishedName:
 CN=ExchangeEMEA,CN=Users,DC=xyz,DC=com
instanceType: 4
displayName: Exchange 2003 Users - EMEA
proxyAddresses: SMTP:Exchange2003EMEA@xyz.com
proxyAddresses: X400:c=US;a= ;p=HP;o=Exchange;s=Exchange2003EMEA;
mailNickname: Exchange2003EMEA
name: ExchangeEMEA
showInAddressBook:
 CN=Default Global Address List,CN=All Global Address
Lists,CN=Address Lists Co
 ntainer,CN=HP,CN=Microsoft
Exchange,CN=Services,CN=Configuration,DC=xyz,DC=
 com
legacyExchangeDN:
 /o=HP/ou=First Administrative Group/cn=Recipients/cn=Exchange2003
objectCategory:
 CN=ms-Exch-Dynamic-Distribution-
List,CN=Schema,CN=Configuration,DC=xyz,DC=com
msExchRequireAuthToSendTo: FALSE
textEncodedORAddress: c=US;a=
;p=xyz;o=Exchange;s=Exchange2003EMEA;
mail: Exchange2003EMEA@xyz.com
msExchHideFromAddressLists: FALSE
msExchDynamicDLBaseDN: DC=xyz, DC=com
msExchDynamicDLFilter:
 (&(!cn=SystemMailbox{*})(&(&(& (mailnickname=*) (|
(&(objectCategory=person)(o
 bjectClass=user)(|(homeMDB=*)(msExchHomeServerName=*))) )))))
```

3.6.1 Creating new query-based groups

Before creating a new query-based group, you should know what purpose you want the group to serve as well as the attributes that you will use to query the AD and build the group. Some administrators like to create one or more AD organizational units (OU) to hold the query-based groups instead of holding them with other objects in "regular" OUs. For example, you might call this OU "Groups" to make its purpose obvious. This decision is a matter of taste and policy and is not a requirement to use these groups.

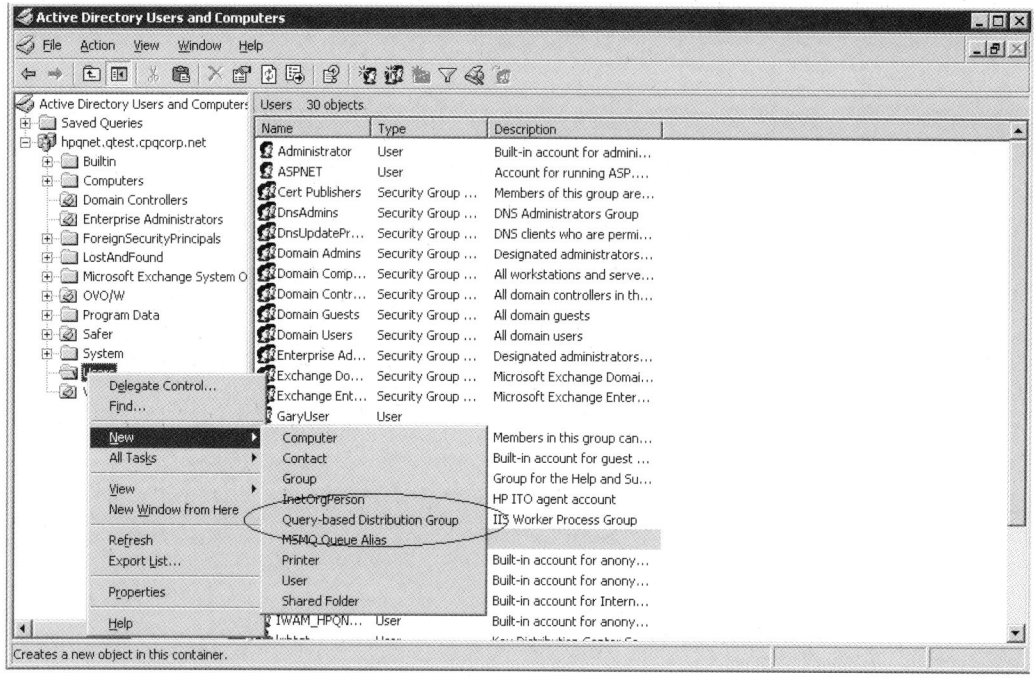

Figure 3.33   *Creating a new query-based distribution group.*

To create a new query-based group, open the AD Users and Computers console[4] and select the OU where you want to create the new object; then select "Query-based Distribution Group" from the menu, as shown in Figure 3.33. The next stage is to determine group membership. The AD uses LDAP queries to build group membership any time an application requests this information. As shown in Figure 3.34, you have to decide:

- The AD level to apply the filter—for the forest or a particular domain and its subdomains

- Objects to include in the group—these can be users with Exchange mailboxes, users with external email addresses, other mail-enabled groups, contacts with external email addresses, and mail-enabled public folders. In this context, an external email address means an address that an external correspondent can use to send a message to an object.

- Whether to apply a customized filter to further refine the search

---

4. The installation of Exchange 2003 updates the AD Users and Computers console to provide support for query-based lists.

3.6 Query-based distribution groups

You can use a wide range of AD attributes to build the query to collect a specific set of recipients. The AD supports different attribute sets for users, contacts, public folders, and distribution groups, but the most common examples across all object types include:

- Objects in a particular department or set of departments
- Users who have mailboxes on a specific Exchange server
- Users and contacts who have a specific title (e.g., all marketing managers)
- Users who are temporary employees or full-time employees, identified by using a customized attribute to locate the members of either set. You might like to combine the new security feature to restrict the ability to send to a group to certain users or groups (see Figure 3.31). For example, you could limit the ability to send messages to full-time employees to authenticated users so that someone outside the company cannot send a message to all employees.
- Objects in a particular country
- Queries that use values in the set of customized attributes reserved for your own deployment purposes. For example, you could store employee job codes in one of the customized attributes and search against these values.

After you select the type of objects to include in the query, you can set filters for the query by clicking on the "Customize" button. Select the "Advanced" page and begin adding the filters by selecting the available fields from the "Field" drop-down list and the conditions that the AD uses when it resolves the query. For example, the query shown in Figure 3.34 selects any Exchange recipient (someone with a mailbox on an Exchange server in this organization) whose Country field is "Ireland" and City field is "Dublin."

You can add as many criteria as you like to a query, but each criterion can slow the query. The AD always resolves exact matches against properties faster than it can resolve properties that start with a certain value. It can also resolve present/not present values quickly. In other words, you can look for users who have no value in a specific attribute or those who have something in the attribute. You will not notice any performance difference from inefficient or slow queries on small deployments, but creating efficient queries is critical when the AD contains more than a few thousand entries. The golden rule is to make queries as simple as possible and then test the query to make sure that you get the expected results. It is also best practice always

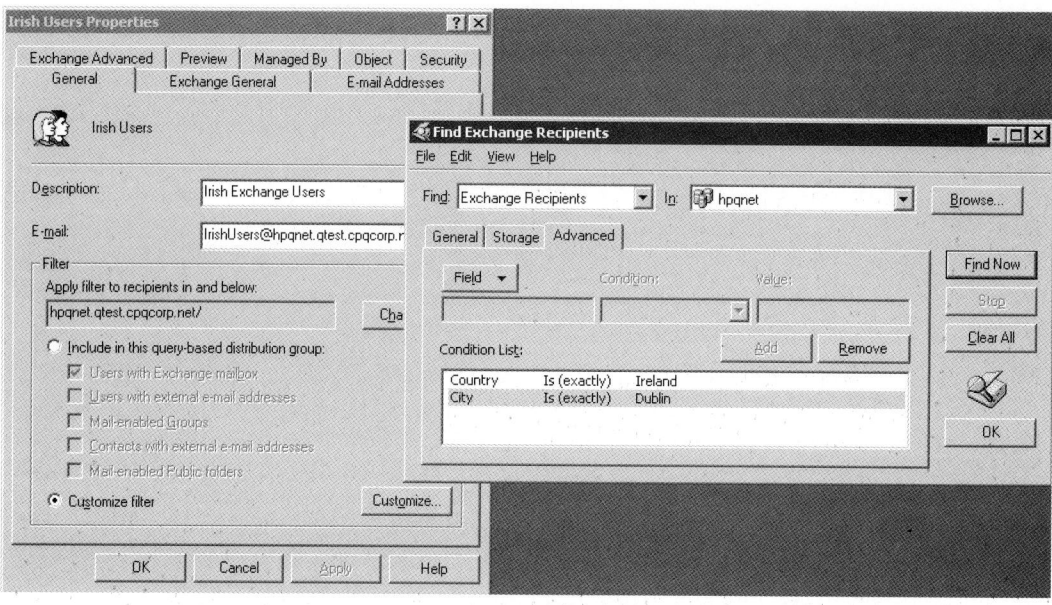

Figure 3.34   *Setting query parameters.*

to test a query-based group to ensure that the query actually works and will return some objects when the categorizer executes it to route messages. You can certainly address messages to a query-based group that resolves to no addressable recipients and you receive no indication that Exchange is unable to deliver the message. Behind the scenes, the message flows as normal until it reaches the categorizer, which executes the query, finds there are no addressees for the message, and then terminates processing because the message has (in fact) reached its final destination.

When you have defined the query parameters, you can test a query with the "Find Now" button on the dialog that you use to set filter criteria (Figure 3.34) or by selecting the query-based group from AD Users and Computers and viewing the preview property page (Figure 3.35). The preview page also shows the LDAP query that the AD executes to resolve the query.

Executing the LDAP query to view the contents of a list gives an insight into the way that the Exchange Routing Engine expands a query-based list. The process is simple: Find the AD entry for the list through its Distinguished Name (DN), then convert the DN to the Relative Distinguished Name (RDN), and then expand the contents of the list with an LDAP search. As with other searches, to ensure best performance the Routing Engine looks at the DSAccess cache first to see if the list exists there.

3.6 Query-based distribution groups

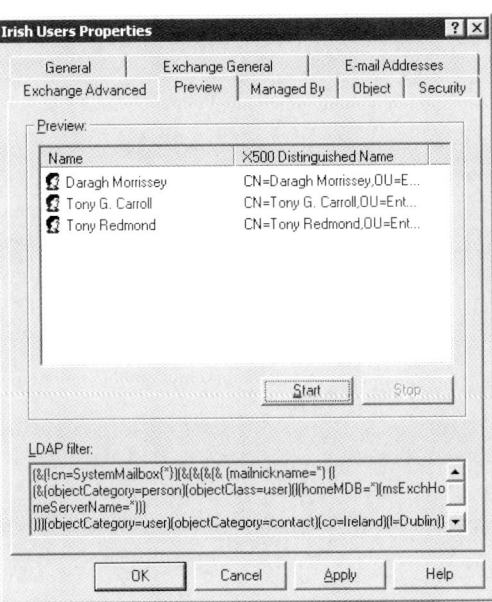

Figure 3.35
Previewing the results of the query.

3.6.2 Using custom attributes in query-based groups

Exchange has always provided a set of custom attributes that you can use to store information about users in the directory. It is highly unlikely that the designer of any directory will ever incorporate a set of attributes that satisfies every possible customer, so the Exchange 5.5 Directory Store and the AD both have 15 custom attributes that you can populate according to your needs. The Exchange 5.5 Administration program user interface only reveals 10 attributes, but there are 15. You just have to populate the last five programmatically if you ever want to use them. Fortunately, the AD reveals everything, and you can fill in the attributes by first selecting the advanced view for AD Users and Computers and then viewing the "Exchange Advanced" property page (Figure 3.36).

Before you begin to add values to the custom property set, you should clearly define what these values will hold and how to populate them. Otherwise, one administrator may think that custom attribute 1 holds an employee badge number, whereas everyone else uses custom attribute 2 for this purpose. Other common uses for these attributes include cost center identifiers, whether a user is a permanent or temporary employee, Social Security numbers (some countries bar you by law from holding personal information such as this in a general-purpose directory), job codes, and so on.

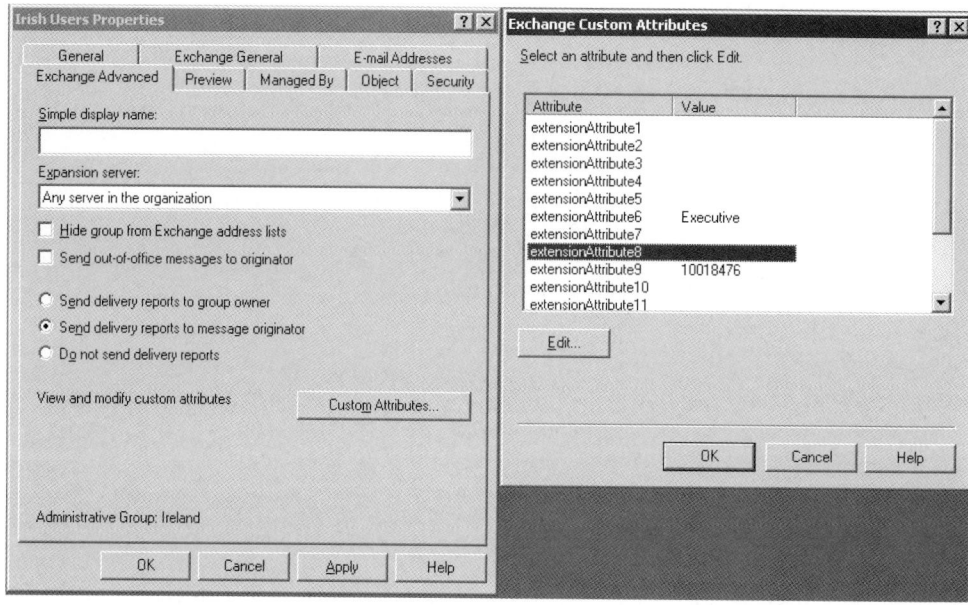

Figure 3.36 *Setting values for custom properties.*

3.6.3 Using query-based distribution groups

If you use Outlook, query-based groups look and behave like any other distribution group, and you can address messages to the group in the normal manner. The only indication that the group is any different is a different icon displayed when you browse the GAL, as well as the fact that you cannot view the membership if you look at the properties of the group through Outlook's Address Book (Figure 3.37). The inability to see group membership frustrates some users who are then unwilling to send messages to the group simply because they do not know who will end up receiving copies. It is possible that an administrator will make a mistake with the query that results in a message going to people who should not receive it, a fact that also worries users (if they realize what is happening in the background).

The Exchange 2003 version of OWA is also able to deal with query-based groups correctly, although you cannot view group membership through this client, since the OWA UI does not support it.

Outlook Express does not know about the query-based group object type, so it has some problems when you attempt to address or send email to

Figure 3.37
Viewing a query-based distribution group from the GAL.

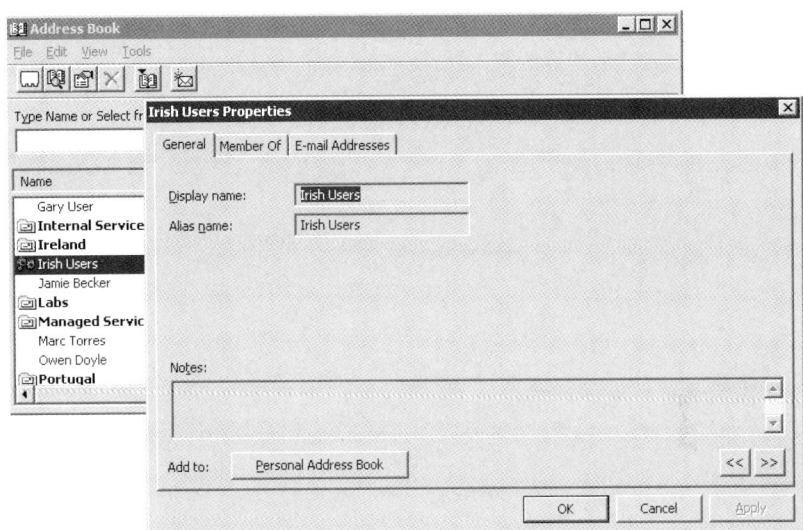

these groups. For example, you cannot use the CTRL/K feature with Outlook Express to check the name of a query-based group against AD. In addition, the Outlook Express interface to AD (a straightforward LDAP search) cannot find these entries, so it is best to create personal contacts that include the query-based group's SMTP address if you want to use query-based groups often. You can then use the contact or type the SMTP address into a message header, and Exchange will safely deliver the message by expanding the group membership after the Routing Engine resolves the address on the incoming message against the AD.

Because a query-based group only "exists" when an application such as Exchange resolves its membership against the AD, it follows that you cannot maintain group membership in the same way as users can update membership of regular groups by selecting the list from the GAL and then modifying its properties using Outlook. You have to make any change to a query-based group through AD Users and Computers.

Query-based distribution groups do not hold Windows security principals, so you cannot use them to control access to public folders or other resources such as file shares. In a similar manner, you cannot use query-based groups to place restrictions on objects such as connectors. In addition, you cannot nest query-based groups or add them to global or universal distribution groups; they stand on their own. Finally, the data captured by Exchange to chart the progress of a message sent to a query-based group in a server's message tracking log is the same as for regular groups.

The success of query-based groups obviously depends on a high degree of consistency in directory data. For example, if you want to create a query group to address all users in a particular country, the group can only be successful if you identify every user in that country by updating the user objects with the necessary information in the directory.

Query-based distribution groups are a useful feature that enables administrators to create self-maintaining groups. As with anything that depends on a directory, the accuracy of directory information will dictate the effectiveness of query groups.

3.7 Summarizing Exchange basics

The architecture of Exchange 2000/2003 delivers much greater granularity for management operations. Companies migrating from Exchange 5.5 start with an organization where each site is represented by an administrative group and a routing group. It is unlikely that the Exchange 5.5 site design is the most efficient or effective design in Exchange 2000/2003 terms, but evolution to an improved infrastructure is only possible by creating new administrative groups and moving mailboxes to the servers in those groups and then removing old administrative groups. Once in native mode, you can create multiple routing groups under a single administrative group and gradually separate the management of the routing topology away from day-to-day system management. Greater flexibility is possible when you design new Exchange infrastructures but only during the design phase. The same restrictions on server movement and organizational restructure exist after you deploy servers.

4

Outlook—The Client

Messaging servers cannot do very much unless clients connect to allow users to create and send messages. The range of clients available to Exchange continues to expand from the basic Exchange viewer released with Exchange 4.0 to everything from smart cell phones through PDAs to the Web browser, the most widespread client in terms of platform coverage.

Clients do much more than simply create and send messages. Most clients track tasks, appointments, and meetings as well. Some clients are customizable, ranging from the reasonably complete development possibilities in Outlook through simple disabling of feature sets as implemented in OWA.

From a design and deployment perspective, you have to understand the potential of each client from features through supported platforms as well as the implementation and support costs. Some worry about the protocols and application programming interfaces used to build clients, since they would like to select clients that are not going to be outdated and become unsupportable. While it is good to consider this point, in reality it is not an issue for two reasons. First, the decision to deploy client software is often highly influenced by the selection of desktop hardware and software. For instance, if you elect to upgrade desktops to Windows XP Professional, you will probably upgrade hardware as well and may find that the new PCs come with software already loaded or that a bundling deal includes new versions of office application suites. Users end up with the latest version of a browser, Internet mail client such as Outlook Express, or Outlook. It is hard to stop people from using software that they find on their desktop.

The second reason why protocol dependency is not an issue to get too hot about is the fact that Microsoft has a good record of accomplishment in backward compatibility. Every Exchange client shipped since 1996 can connect to the latest version of the server. Almost every browser can connect to Exchange and be an OWA client; and even the earliest POP3 client can still connect to Exchange. None of these clients may be able to use the complete range of features supported by the server, but they will certainly be able to take care of the basics.

Integrating new client types is the biggest challenge facing Exchange administrators today. It is hard to work out how best to incorporate cell phones, PDAs, Pocket PCs, and purpose-built messaging devices such as RIM's BlackBerry into the messaging infrastructure. Every client type connects in different ways; each may require specific hardware or software pieces to relay messages on the desktop or server, and each increases support complexity—not to mention the potential issue of breaking client connectivity when a service pack or hot fix is applied. User desire to possess the latest communications device compounds the difficulty, since it often results in senior management (who tend to be early adopters of new technology even if they do not realize it) demanding support for the latest gizmo. The situation should get easier as devices merge (otherwise, we will all end up resembling a Star Wars storm-trooper equipped with a belt full of different devices) and the myriad wireless protocols used around the world are consolidated, but don't expect this to happen overnight. Client gizmos will remain a challenge for Exchange administrators for quite some time yet.

4.1 MAPI—Messaging Application Protocol

Despite not being under active development for many years, MAPI remains the most functional and rich client application programming interface (API). As a platform, MAPI's role within the server has steadily declined since it reached its zenith in Exchange 5.5. The development group now favors either Internet protocols (SMTP, LDAP, HTTP, HTTP-DAV, etc.) or other Microsoft protocols (such as ADSI) whenever possible. In this respect, we have to make a distinction between the on-the-wire protocol used by clients and the API, since they are sometimes intermingled during a discussion about clients. For example, Outlook uses MAPI as the API to manipulate mailbox contents both locally and on the server and generates RPCs to fetch information from the server. RPCs can travel across different network protocols and now, with Exchange 2003 and the necessary Windows supporting infrastructure, you can even wrap RPCs in a layer of HTTP to navigate the Internet. Things can get quite complicated in the blizzard of protocol acronyms.

To return to the beginning, MAPI is Microsoft's Messaging Application Programming Interface, which first appeared in 1993 as part of Microsoft Mail. The implementation in Microsoft Mail was incomplete, as Microsoft had not yet fully fleshed out all the functions and interfaces that deliver the rich functionality available in today's clients. In fact, just enough functions were available to build a basic messaging system, so the version of MAPI in Microsoft Mail is "Simple MAPI," "sMAPI," or "MAPI-0." Simple MAPI is composed of 12 functions, including those necessary to log on to a server and then to create, address, send, and read messages. Extended MAPI or MAPI V1.0 is a far more comprehensive interface designed to meet the needs of many different messaging systems. Microsoft has removed support for Simple MAPI in Exchange 2003 and now the server only supports Extended MAPI.

It is worth emphasizing that there are two distinct versions of MAPI: one for the server and one for the client. It is wrong to assume that Microsoft keeps the two versions in lock step, because this has never happened and is the reason why you see some problems if you install a MAPI client such as Outlook onto an Exchange server. Almost everything works, but Microsoft is quite adamant that this is a bad idea. If you want to log on to the server and run an Exchange client (perhaps to check that email is flowing properly after you apply a service pack), it is better in most cases to use a client such as Outlook Express or Outlook Web Access, which does not require you to install the client-side MAPI components on the server.

While MAPI continues to provide the base platform for Outlook, it has weakened in terms of its predominant position for server-based functionality. There are three reasons for this. First, Internet protocols have become more important to Microsoft, so they do not always look at MAPI as the only solution for a problem. For example, Microsoft uses HTTP-DAV in the Exchange 2003 version of ESM to fetch information about public folders—something that the developers would previously have done with MAPI. On the client side, the Entourage for Macintosh Client has also begun to use HTTP-DAV in conjunction with IMAP4 to provide Exchange-based calendar and scheduling functionality without going anywhere near MAPI. Second, the architecture of Exchange has evolved to accommodate a division of work between front-end and back-end servers, but only when Internet clients are connected. Third, the introduction of other programming interfaces to the Store means that programmers have easier alternatives to MAPI when they need to work with Exchange.

In some respects, Microsoft has simply ignored MAPI, because it has not developed MAPI to any degree since it released Version 1.0. Microsoft has fixed bugs as they appeared, but the original intention for MAPI to be the foundation for Microsoft messaging products has long since disappeared. If you ask any Microsoft developer to assess an API that has no program manager or development resources assigned to it, he or she would tell you that this is "functionally mature technology" or even apply the dreaded "legacy" label. However, while noting that MAPI is now in the category of legacy APIs, it is also true that many independent software vendors (ISVs) continue to use MAPI to build add-on server-based products for Exchange. These companies will move from MAPI, but only after Microsoft provides an equally functional server-based API to replace MAPI.

The strategy of moving rapidly away from a highly functional and stable API such as MAPI to focus on Internet interfaces has some risks, but it is a good example of Microsoft flexibility in action. Microsoft is able to say that Internet protocols provide the foundation of Exchange, while still being able to use its own highly functional but proprietary interface for its own leading client, and it has improved the way that Outlook and Exchange communicate together with the Outlook 2003/Exchange 2003 combination with the introduction of cached Exchange mode. I suspect that Microsoft has half an eye on the future with respect to the next generation of clients and servers. HTTP-DAV seems to offer the best route forward, because it exploits HTTP, generates no requirement to open up new ports in firewalls, is cross-platform out of the box, and is lightweight, but perhaps it can never be quite as functional as MAPI. We see some movement in Outlook 2003 and new Microsoft clients for Macintosh OS X, but it is still early days.

MAPI's glory days are perhaps past, but it is still critical to the overall success of Exchange and will be the most popular client access protocol for years to come, if only because it takes so long for companies to deploy new clients to user desktops.

4.1.1 Outlook

Outlook is the predominant client for Exchange. Tens of millions of people (some estimates go as high as 200 million, with well over half of those connected to Exchange) use Outlook on a daily basis. The size of the Outlook community and its support for multiple protocols has naturally attracted companies to develop servers that compete with Exchange. It is much easier to sell a mail server if you can say that it supports Outlook, because it instantly means that anyone who uses Microsoft Office becomes a potential client. Typically, ISVs build client-side MAPI components to enable Outlook to connect to their email server in exactly the same way as you connect to Exchange. For example, HP builds a MAPI driver to connect Outlook to the HP OfficeServer for OpenVMS server. Connecting to the server is a matter of creating a new MAPI profile that points to the server, ensuring network connectivity (usually over TCP/IP), and connecting. The sole clue that a user may see to indicate that he or she is not connecting to Exchange is the need for multiple passwords, if the email server does not support single sign-on functionality using Windows credentials.

Other examples of integrated email servers that support Outlook include Samsung Contact and Oracle Collaboration Suite, while a number of Linux-based email servers use the Bynari InsightConnector to gain Outlook support. Among these offerings are the SCO Office Mail Server and Xchanger from Backwatcher. The fact that companies compete on the basis that they support Outlook for their email servers is a tribute to Outlook's functionality and the strong foundation provided by MAPI.

4.1.2 Supporting MAPI clients

MAPI clients vary from the original "Capone" client distributed with Exchange 4.0 in 1996 to the latest Outlook client. You can connect even the oldest MAPI client to Exchange 2003 without problems. Simply configure a MAPI profile to point to the name of the Exchange server and start the client, selecting the name of the profile that you have just created. You access the Outlook 2002 option to set up a profile through Tools.E-Mail Accounts, or use the Tools.Services option for all previous MAPI clients.

Figure 4.1 shows the Windows registry editor, REGEDIT.EXE, viewing details of an Exchange profile on a Windows XP Professional desktop. The registry key that points to all the profiles created on a PC is:

```
HKEY_CURRENT_USER\Software\Microsoft\Windows NT\
CurrentVersion\Windows Messaging Subsystem\Profiles
```

The information held in a MAPI profile is reasonably complex, because it stores many options describing the services (e.g., the mailbox and directory) that the client uses. In addition, the registry holds some of the profile data in binary format. However, it is worth your while to understand how you can tweak the way that Outlook works through the profile and consider whether you want to deploy a standard profile to restrict user options or enforce specific behavior. While Microsoft does not document all available registry settings in a single place, you can find most described in Knowledge Base articles, so a trawl through the Knowledge Base often unearths an unexpected jewel.

Table 4.1 lists some useful registry settings to illustrate the point. These settings are valid for Outlook 2002 (a specific service pack may be required)

Chapter 4

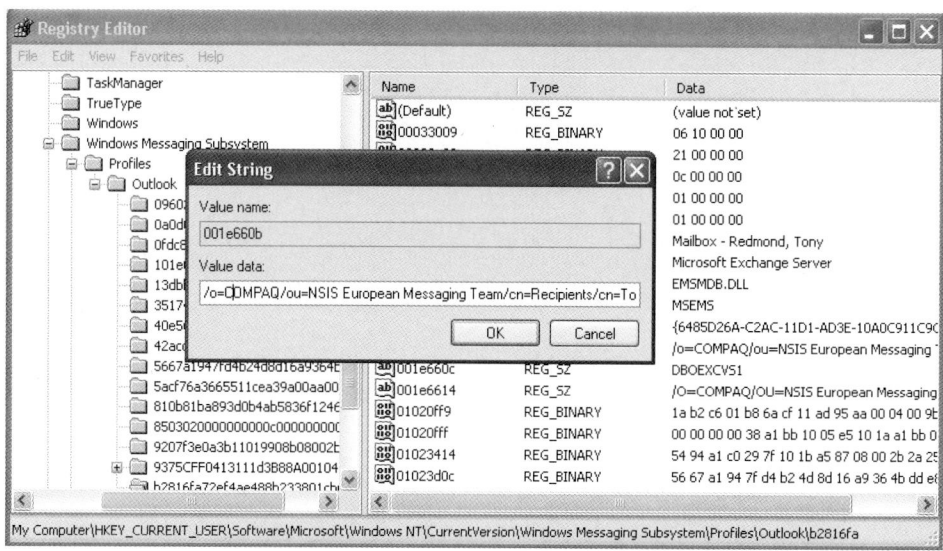

Figure 4.1 *Details of a MAPI profile.*

Table 4.1 *Outlook Registry Settings*

Root	Value	Earliest Outlook Version	Meaning
—	NoOutlookFormsDesigner	XP RTM	0 = prevents use of the Outlook forms designer
HKLM**	DisablePst	XP SP2	0 = prevents user from opening PST files
Outlook\Options\	DisableHTTP	XP RTM	0 = prevents user from adding HTTP account (such as hotmail) to Outlook
Outlook\Options\	DisableIMAP	XP SP2	0 = prevents user from adding IMAP account
Outlook\Options\	DisablePOP	XP SP2	0 = prevents user from adding POP3 account
Outlook\Options\Mail\	ReadAsPlain	XP SP1	1 = force all mail to be read as plain text
Outlook\PST\	PSTNullFreeOnClose	XP RTM	1 = Outlook overwrites deleted data in PST and OST files on exit

and Outlook 2003. To enforce, you create the necessary DWORD value under the root:

```
HKCU\Software\Microsoft\Office\<version>\Outlook
```

where "10.0" is the version number for Outlook 2002 and "11.0" is the version number for Outlook 2003. The only exception is "DisablePST," because it goes under the HKLM root.

Inputting these values on an individual PC is simple, but updating a few hundred PCs to attain consistency takes a lot more effort. For years, Microsoft has provided a limited set of tools (PROFGEN and NEWPROF) that you can use to generate profiles automatically, and it is possible to use these tools to create a new profile the first time a user logs on from a PC. Several third party software vendors engineer excellent utilities that make this task much easier. My current favorite is Profile Maker (www.autoprof.com). Outlook 2003 provides a suite of new options in the Office Custom Install Wizard that replaces PROFGEN and NEWPROF and allow you to automate many installation and deployment options. You may still prefer your existing tool set, but the Office Custom Install Wizard deserves your attention. Microsoft's Outlook Resource Kit (ORK) is an invaluable tool for any system administrator who has to support Outlook clients. You can download the ORK from Microsoft and then use it to configure client settings that you apply through group policies, set at either the domain or OU level within Active Directory. You can prevent users from accessing specific commands or stop them from customizing their environments. For example, you can stop users from going anywhere near Visual BASIC for Applications by applying the standard "Disable Access to VBA" template included in the ORK.

4.1.3 Profile changes after moving between administrative groups

The information in a MAPI profile is tied to the server that the mailbox is located on, so if you move a mailbox from one server to another, the profile must change. Exchange takes care of the profile update, so in most cases users never notice that their mailbox has moved. However, in a mixed-mode organization, where both Exchange 5.5 and Exchange 2000/2003 servers exist, the different directories make it more difficult for Exchange to perform profile redirection, so up to the release of Exchange 2003 SP1, you had to update the profile manually or create a brand new profile. In a native-mode organization, the same difficulty does not exist, because a single definitive directory (the AD) exists.

Microsoft addresses the problem in SP1 with the provision of the Exchange Profile Redirector program (ExProfRe—downloadable from the Exchange Web site), which runs on Windows 2000, XP, and 2003 platforms and supports any version of Outlook. ExProfRe is a command-line utility that allows you to control the GC server to reference to determine the new mailbox server and whether to create new Outlook client-specific files (the OST, OAB, favorites, and nicknames files). ExProfRe can only run when Outlook is not active.

ExProfRe's default behavior is to recreate files such as the OAB. However, you need to be cautious here, because this may not be good for server or network load, since downloading a complete replica of a mailbox and a new OAB to allow a client to operate in cached Exchange mode slows down the ability of the user to resume working. In any case, if you move a mailbox with an organization, there is no need to download a new OAB unless it is out-of-date. The same is true of the OST, but the Profile Redirector will not attempt to create the OST if the client is Outlook 2003 configured to run in cached Exchange mode. It is, therefore, an advantage to upgrade clients to Outlook 2003 before you move users between administrative groups in mixed mode.

4.1.4 Authentication

MAPI clients traditionally authenticate themselves through the NTLM (NT LAN Manager challenge-response) mechanism, using cached credentials if they are available and the user has set the option to use these credentials in the profile. As shown in Figure 4.2, Outlook 2003 clients can perform native-mode Kerberos password authentication when they connect to Exchange 2003 servers. This feature is important in cross-forest deployments, where user accounts exist in one forest while the Exchange servers belong to another forest and you have created cross-forest trust relationships. NTLM works across cross-forest trusts, but it is less efficient than Kerberos, which is also the preferred authentication mechanism for the future.

It is not a good idea to switch Outlook to use Kerberos authentication unless every Exchange server that the client might connect to runs Windows 2003 and user accounts are all in AD. This includes servers that host public folder replicas and applications. In the meantime, you are safest to continue using NTLM authentication.

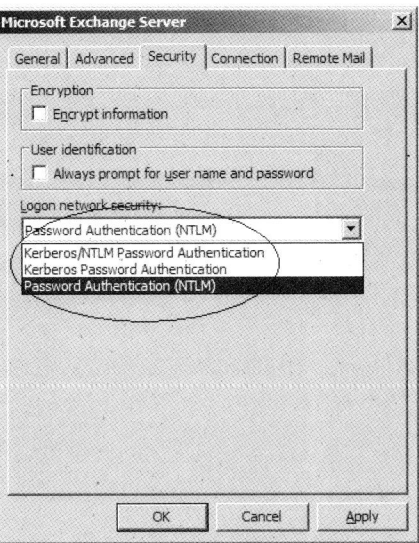

Figure 4.2
Outlook authentication modes.

4.2 Making Outlook a better network client for Exchange

Traditionally, Exchange has only supported MAPI RPCs over protocols such as TCP/IP over NetBIOS. This model assumes that clients connect to servers across perfect networks, or at least the consistent standard of service available in a corporate LAN. Many of us have experienced the frustration of watching Outlook report its chatty interchange with Exchange when we connect over slower or high-latency links such as an RAS dial-in. The RPC interchange is also fragile and prone to timeouts and failure. In fact, many things can interrupt the flow of data between client and server and lead to user frustration. While you might assume that RPCs are the root cause of the problem, in fact, Outlook has traditionally been a server-oriented application and as such generates a heavy communications load between client and server. Any interruption in communications due to temporary network glitches or other reasons caused Outlook problems. To address this issue and to accommodate new network devices such as the Tablet PC, the Outlook team focused on making Outlook 2003 far more tolerant to latency, reducing server communications, and not assuming that it is always possible to connect to a server. This design philosophy leads to features such as the local cache and on-the-wire compression. These factors, along with the constant need to remain competitive and add features in tandem with the rest of the

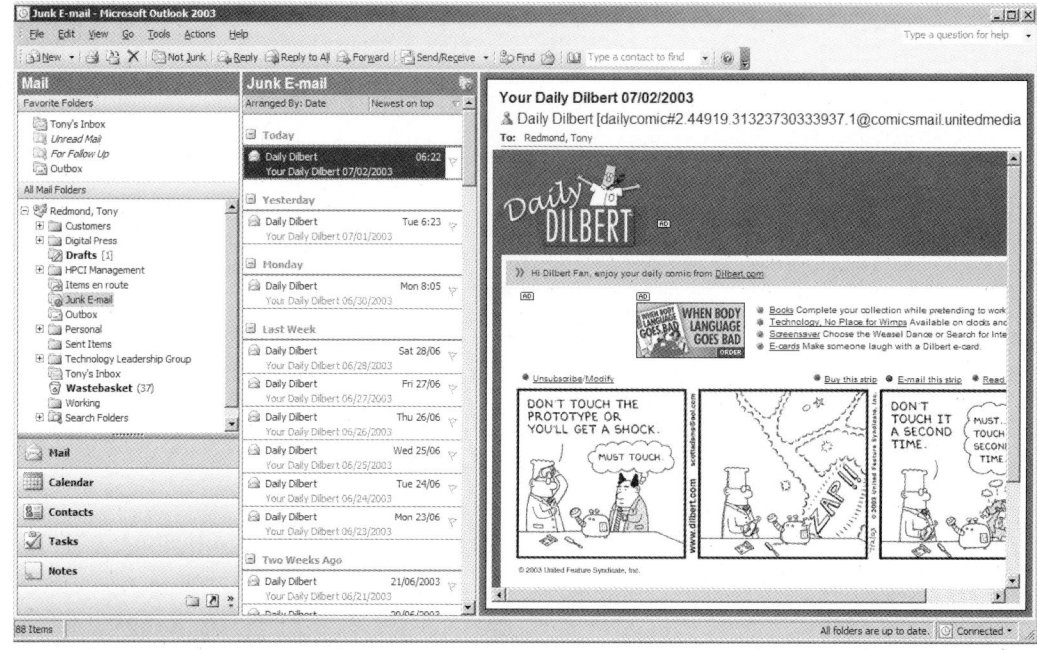

Figure 4.3   *Outlook 2003 interface.*

Office suite, drive some of the improvements we see in Outlook 2003. Because Microsoft developed Exchange 2003 and Outlook 2003 in tandem, it is easy to understand why Outlook 2003 can take advantage of some unique features in Exchange 2003, but some of the features are backward compatible with previous versions of Exchange, so you can get some value through a client upgrade even if you want to remain with Exchange 2000. In passing, it is worth noting that Outlook 2003 only supports TCP/IP, so Microsoft has discarded some of its history in this release.

Figure 4.3 illustrates the Outlook 2003 interface.

4.2.1   Why RPC latency is important to Exchange

As with any other communications mechanism, RPCs are sensitive to network latency, something that can affect both Exchange clients and servers. From a client perspective, problems with RPCs (most of which are due to excessive latency) become apparent when you see the pop-up window reporting that Outlook is waiting for Exchange to respond. Note that Outlook may communicate with several Exchange servers in a single session as users move between their mailboxes and public folders, and latency can affect any or all of these connections; so seeing pop-up windows appearing is not necessarily an indication that a network problem exists between the client and the mailbox server. The pop-up windows are only supported from Outlook 2002 onward, and they are welcome because you can decide to cancel a "hanging RPC" and terminate an operation, which is preferable to the previous situation where you had to kill the whole Outlook process if the client and server lock in a deadly embrace. Outlook is not always to blame here, since often Exchange simply fails to process the RPC and communicate back to the client in a timely manner.

You can use very low bandwidth networks to connect Outlook to Exchange (e.g., many people use 9.6-Kbps dial-up connections via cell phones) and transfer large items across the link, albeit slowly. All network protocols handle transfers over low-bandwidth links by splitting large items into multiple packets and then transmitting the packets in parallel. Unfortunately, applications may have to wait for the RPCs to complete and a response to arrive back, which is what you often see in Outlook to Exchange communications across high-latency links. You can now opt to have Outlook use the local cache to access information locally rather than fetch it from the server. While you work with local data, Outlook continues to fetch data from the server in the background to update the cache. The scheme works, but you sometimes see hiccups, so there is still some room for improvement.

Latency and slow connections can combine to generate interesting behavior for Outlook that can disconcert users. If you use a slow dial-up connection or perhaps a VPN link that disconnects and reconnects automatically, clients (prior to Outlook 2003) are sometimes slow in displaying new messages as they arrive in the Inbox. Users often notice this effect when they change folder view (by switching to another folder), only to notice that a number of messages suddenly appear in the Inbox, all seemingly delivered at different times. The underlying cause is that the connection between client and server is unreliable, and the synchronization necessary between Outlook and Exchange to process the RPCs sent by the server to the client to signal the arrival of new messages does not always work. It is uncommon to see this behavior over LAN connections when the link is reliable and neither latency nor bandwidth is a problem. However, it can happen if the server to client UDP notifications to trigger the update of the view fail.

Network gurus will cheerfully argue the factors that govern the point at which latency becomes a problem. Products such as Cloud (www.shunra.com) allow you to perform practical tests on a line to quickly measure where problems occur in your own environment. For example, you might set a limit of 300 ms for round-trip delays between Outlook and Exchange and test the line to determine whether you see pop-up windows during a variety of operations (create meetings, access public folders, send large messages, and so on). If problems occur, you can change the setting and test again. An approach such as this helps to quantify whether you need to upgrade your network and avoid user satisfaction issues, especially if you want to consolidate servers into central locations.

Note that it is important to distinguish between end-to-end latency and round-trip latency before conducting any tests, since otherwise you may confuse the issue. Obviously, a test result of 300 ms for round-trip response is equivalent to a 150-ms result for a trip between the server and client, but a quick glance at the headline figures may focus on one figure to the detriment of the other. In addition, any network analysis is very subjective and the measurements you take are highly sensitive to actual operating conditions, so the results attained in laboratory conditions may not be viable in the field. For that reason, it is wise to add some wiggle room to the figures to arrive at an acceptable standard.

4.2.2 Networking improvements in Outlook 2003

Among other improvements that it wanted to make in Outlook, Microsoft recognized the need to make the client smarter about the way it consumes network resources through its internal experience and customer feedback. The increasing demand for connectivity for mobile devices that connect using wireless networks, or even by using the latest cell phone networks, is another influence. In addition, devices such as the Tablet PC pose interesting challenges for applications that expect persistent high-quality connections to servers and get upset if they experience a network interruption. Previous versions of Outlook fall squarely into this category.

Microsoft had to do something to make Outlook a smarter network client, and the four major improvements in Outlook 2003 are:

- The introduction of Cached Exchange Mode in the form of locally cached mailboxes and the replication mechanism required to synchronize the local copy with the server mailbox: Outlook 2003 is able to fetch data from Exchange 5.5, Exchange 2000 and Exchange 2003 servers to maintain a local cache that the client then uses to access messages and attachments. Cached Exchange mode is now the default option for Outlook when you create new profiles for users. The intention here is that cached Exchange mode creates a condition where the user becomes unaware of the current network state and whether he or she has a connection to the server. Because they work with local data, performance is more consistent and acceptable than the previous model.

- Improved replication semantics, including header-mode downloads, compression, and "best body support": New code in Outlook 2003 optimizes the flow of RPCs exchanged with the server to reduce the amount of data sent over the wire during synchronization operations. The fact that Microsoft found opportunities to optimize Outlook's chatty interchanges with Exchange should come as no surprise to anyone who has monitored the flow of bytes across a dial-up connection as client and server patiently moved messages from one to the other. Better compression and smarter use of network resources mean that you see less dialog boxes popping up to report that Outlook is waiting for Exchange to respond.

- Outlook 2003 can use three types of replication behavior (download headers only, drizzle mode synchronization, always fetch full items) across any network connection: Some new code puts Outlook into "header only" mode when you use a slow connection, but you can override this option. Outlook detects changes in network state, including failover to new networks, transition between online and offline mode, and restore from standby and reconnect to the server. The client uses code different from that used across slow high-latency link to replicate data across fast LAN-type connections (note that high latency is not unique to slow connections).

- Using HTTP to transport RPCs: To do this, Outlook 2003 puts an HTTP or HTTPS wrapper around the MAPI RPCs sent to Exchange. You can connect Outlook 2003 to an Exchange 2003 server any time you are able to connect OWA to Exchange, with no requirement to remap RPC ports or establish a VPN. You must deploy Outlook 2003 on Windows XP SP1 (or above) on the desktop and connect to Exchange 2003 servers to enable secure authentication. In a front-end/back-end configuration, the front-end Exchange 2003 servers in the DMZ can proxy the RPCs to back-end Exchange 2003 servers. Because Microsoft made some changes to the network stack protocol to allow RPC requests to travel over HTTP, the Exchange 2003 servers must run on Windows 2003, as must the GCs and DCs used by Outlook. To make everything work, you also have to configure various ports (6001 to 6004) to allow proxies to work. While being able to connect Outlook back to Exchange over essentially any Internet link is a great feature, especially if you have to

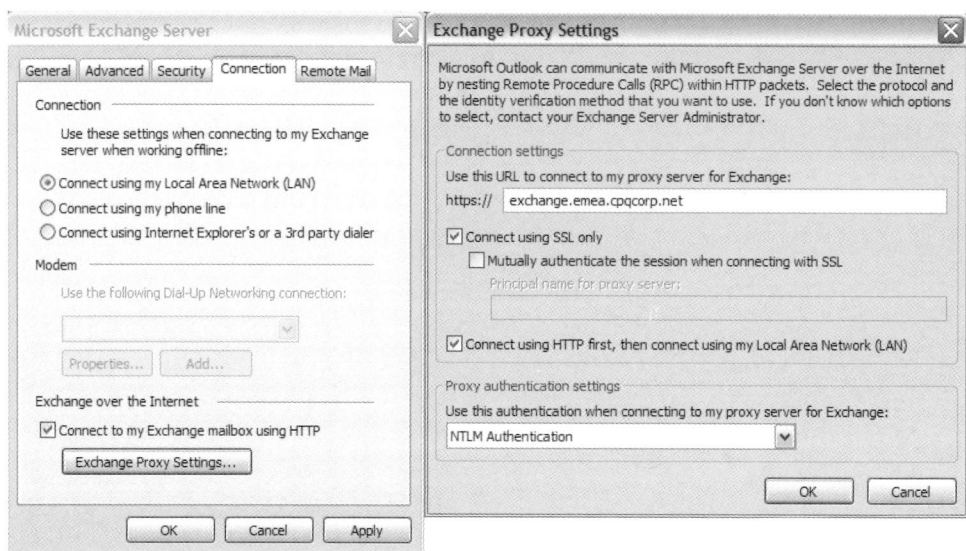

Figure 4.4 *Configuring Outlook 2003 to use RPC over HTTP.*

support a large community of traveling users, there are prerequisites and setup work that you must do before you can implement RPCs over HTTP. In some cases, it can be quicker, easier, and even cheaper for you to install a normal Virtual Private Network (VPN). Apart from anything else, a VPN allows users to access other resources on your internal network after they connect, whereas the RPC over HTTP feature only accommodates email.

If your PC runs Windows XP SP1[1] or later, you can select to connect to the server over HTTP, specifying the URL to the RPC proxy server (such as http://server/). When Outlook connects to Exchange over HTTP, the standard UDP-based mechanism for new mail and calendar notifications changes to use polling instead. In a manner similar to OWA, Outlook polls the server regularly to detect whether it needs to notify the user of some new event rather than waiting for updates. The Outlook Custom Installation wizard and Custom Maintenance wizard also allow you to specify RPC over HTTP connections in client deployment kits. Figure 4.4 shows how you configure Outlook to use RPC over HTTP. Clicking the "Exchange Proxy Settings" button shows the screen on the right, where you enter the URL to connect to Exchange, the type of authentication to use, and

---

1. Even with Windows XP SP1, you also need to install the hot fix described in Microsoft Knowledge Base article 331320, or deploy Windows XP SP2. Outlook grays out the HTTP option if your PC is not running the right software versions.

whether Outlook should automatically revert to "normal" RPCs if it fails to connect over HTTP. You can force Outlook to use HTTP always and never revert by setting a new registry value, as shown in the following code segment. Set the value to 1 to disable use of "normal" RPCs.

```
Key:    HKCU\Software\Microsoft\Office\11.0\Outlook\RPC
Value:  DisableRpcTcpFallback (DWORD)
```

Outlook 2003 includes the ability to compress graphic attachments (Figure 4.5). This is particularly useful when you send screen shots or other images to illustrate a point. In the example shown, the original bitmap is over 2 MB. Before it sent the message to Exchange, Outlook compressed the file to an 89-KB attachment (using the medium compression option), which makes a huge difference in transmission and delivery times. Usually, Outlook achieves the highest compression ratios for bitmap (BMP) files, and the exact degree of compression varies across different graphical and other formats. This feature is client-side, so it works also with Exchange 5.5 and Exchange 2000 servers.

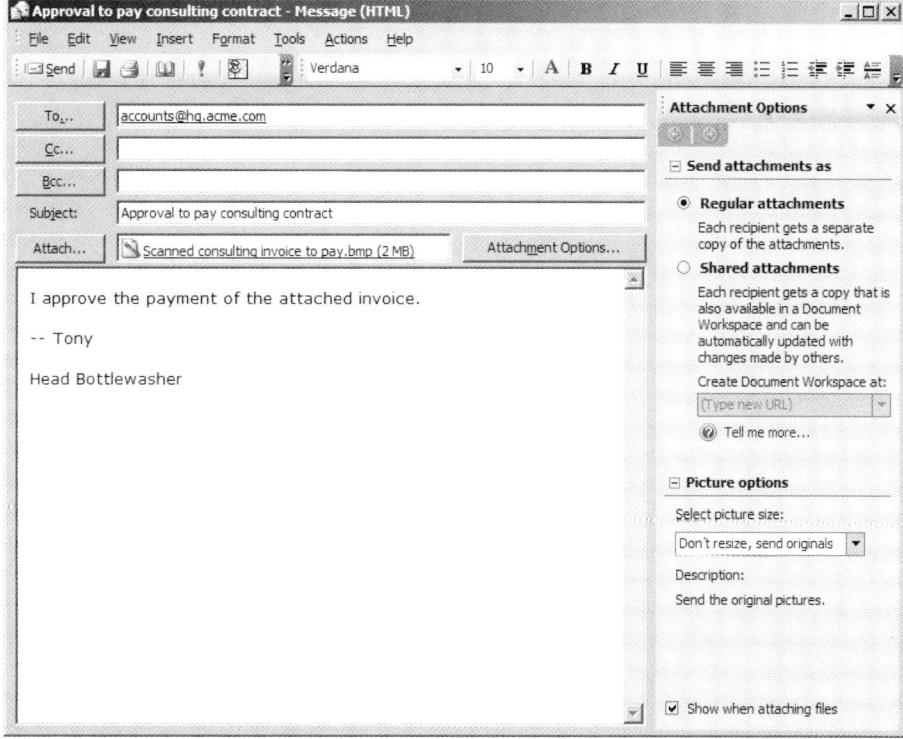

Figure 4.5   *Outlook options to compress graphics.*

"Best body support" means that Outlook can ask Exchange to provide native-mode content instead of forcing the server to convert message bodies into RTF. When an older Outlook client connects to Exchange, the server cannot be sure what format messages the client can support. For example, Outlook 97 and 98 do not support HTML format message bodies. If Exchange receives an HTML message, it could not take the chance that a client requesting synchronization supports HTML, so the server automatically converts the HTML into RTF and sends both copies down to the client. Every MAPI client and Exchange server support RTF, so it is effectively the lowest common denominator in any transfer operation. Sending two copies of every message body increases the amount of data that passes between server and client and makes OST files far larger than they need be. When Outlook 2003 connects to a mailbox on an Exchange 2003 server, it requests the server to send its best body part and the server can transmit just one copy without conversion. Not only does this change reduce network traffic, it also relieves a large processing load off the server, because messages do not have to be converted. Instead, if the client ever detects that it needs to convert the format of a message body, it can perform the conversion locally rather than going back to the server to request a new copy of the data.

It is difficult to quantify what benefit accrues to Exchange here, since everything depends on the percentage of HTML format messages received by the server. Outlook's default format has been HTML since Outlook 2002, so if you use recent clients you will have more HTML in the overall format mix. In addition, you will not realize full advantage of best body support until you upgrade every client to Outlook 2003.

Synchronization is the process of keeping one or more replicas in lock step with each other, normally based on a master copy. In Exchange, the server copy of a folder is always the master. The prospect of corrupt data always exists when computers want to send data to each other, and synchronization is no different. In previous versions of Outlook, when the client encounters a "bad item" in its replica of a mailbox or public folder, it places the item in the synchronization failures folder, logs an error in the synchronization log, and keeps on going. However, Exchange fails and halts synchronization if it hits a bad item when it attempts to synchronize down to the client. It is also possible to see loop conditions, where client and server merrily send data to each other with no effect except clocking up network traffic. Outlook 2003 incorporates a "bad item check" to validate that items are complete (formed with a body part and full set of properties) before it attempts to synchronize into the OST.

4.2.3 Cached Exchange mode

Previous versions of Outlook work in either online mode or offline mode. When online, the client connects to Exchange and you can work with any item in any mailbox folder, as well as public folders. All user actions generate server transactions and round trips between client and server. When offline, the client uses an offline store (OST), which you must first synchronize items to before Outlook can use it. All activity is local until you connect Outlook to Exchange to synchronize changes between server and local folders. Working offline is acceptable if you can do nothing else and cannot connect to Exchange, but it means that you have no access to the up-to-date GAL, cannot perform free and busy lookups for meetings, and do not have access to folders unless you marked them for synchronization and then performed synchronization. Organized road warriors prepare for trips by making sure that they download the OAB and synchronize their folders, but many people have found themselves off site with no connectivity and a set of unsynchronized folders. Before the advent of Outlook 2003, offline mode had some big traps to fall into if you did not prepare for every road trip by synchronizing all folders and downloading an up-to-date copy of the OAB. Things are a little easier now.

You can use the combination of Outlook 2003 and Exchange (5.5, 2000, or 2003) to implement "cached Exchange mode" for client/server communications, which is now the default mode for Outlook 2003 clients to connect to Exchange. Essentially, this is a combination of online and offline working, where clients continually fetch data from the server in a background thread while processing user actions against data held in a local cache. The default for new profiles is to use cached Exchange mode. If you already have a profile that you used with a previous version of Outlook, you have to set the properties of your Exchange server profile to use cached Exchange mode (a local copy of your mailbox), as shown in Figure 4.6. After selecting cached Exchange mode and logging out of Outlook, you log back on to Exchange in the normal way (to enable new mail notifications and so on), and begin using cached Exchange mode. Administrators can force existing users to move to cached Exchange mode through group policy settings, but this is not something to rush into until you understand the consequences for the server that must then handle the load generated by clients when they connect to build the cache.

After changing your profile to select cached Exchange mode, Outlook must build the local cache. If you already used an OST with a previous version of Outlook, it is likely that you did not synchronize every folder in

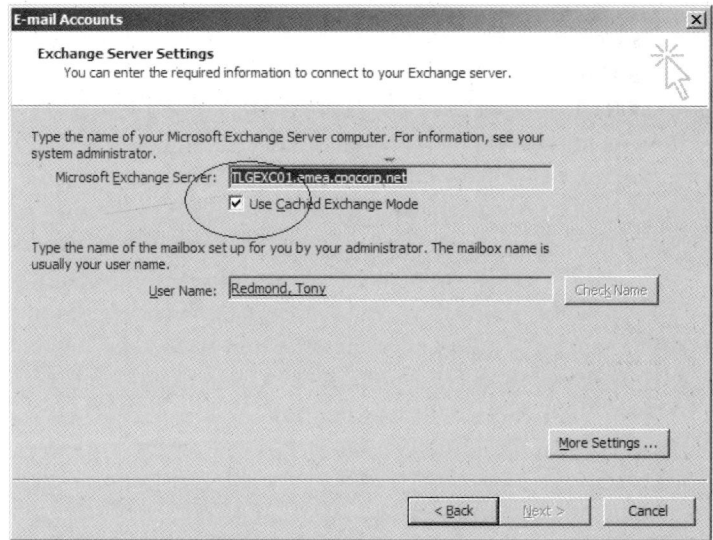

Figure 4.6
Setting up cached Exchange mode for Outlook 2003.

your mailbox. Outlook therefore populates the content in those folders so that you end up with a complete local replica of your mailbox. If you did not use an OST, Outlook builds the local cache from scratch into a new OST file. In either case, building the local cache and making sure that it is completely up-to-date requires a substantial amount of processing and network activity, and you may find that your PC's performance is a little sluggish (largely due to disk I/O) until Outlook finishes downloading content from the server. This operation can take an hour or more to complete, depending on the configuration of your PC, other work that you are doing during the download, the speed of the network connection, the size of your mailbox, and the number of folders it holds.

In addition, the size of your OST file on your local hard disk inevitably grows bigger than your mailbox. OST storage is not as efficient as the Exchange database, so the usual result is a file that is approximately 20 percent to 30 percent larger. However, some conditions can force dramatic expansion. For example, my 686-MB mailbox exploded to become a 1.8-GB OST. Initially, I could not explain the vast increase in size unless it was due to the mixture of RTF, plain text, and HTML-format messages in my mailbox. Certainly, having a complete copy of all folders available for offline work gives users an excellent opportunity to clean out old material and reduce the size of the OST, but in reality, few will take this chance. Best body support, which is only available when you connect Outlook 2003 to an Exchange 2003 server, reduces OST bloat by only downloading a single copy of each message. Later, it became obvious that an early beta release of Outlook 2003 had synchronized full copies of every one of my public folder favorites, including some folders that held well over 10,000 items. After removing some old favorites, the file shrunk back to about 1.5 GB, and when I removed all public folder favorites, the OST reduced to 890 MB and settled down at this level, shrinking and increasing in line with the size of my mailbox. The shipping version of Outlook 2003 leaves public folder favorites alone, and you can control whether to synchronize the contents of public folder favorites into the cache through the advanced options for the mailbox. If you enable cached Exchange mode, you can expect to see OSTs that are 120 percent of the size of a mailbox, which is a reasonable overhead to pay for the facility of having a complete mailbox cached locally. You should try to keep an OST less than 1 GB, because past this point Outlook incurs a heavy I/O overhead to keep the OST synchronized.

4.2.4 Drizzle synchronization

By default, Outlook downloads full items into the local cache, just as it has always done when you synchronize items into an OST. Now, you can opt for Outlook to use two other download modes to better match current network conditions: header only and headers first followed by the full content of items. In the latter case, Outlook uses an algorithm called "drizzle synchronization." The idea behind drizzle-mode synchronization is to keep the local cache always up-to-date. Drizzle-mode replication is also more suited to the type of slow, high-latency roaming network links used by mobile devices (wireless and cell phones) and especially suits the "grab and go" nature of a wireless-enabled Tablet PC. The scenario here is that you can take a Tablet PC from its docking station that is equipped with a traditional Ethernet connection and immediately switch to a wireless link while Outlook stays connected to Exchange. With previous versions of Outlook, you need to shut down and restart Outlook to make a smooth switch between network connections, but Outlook 2003 takes network switches in its stride.

Windows XP plays a part here, too, because the operating system tells Outlook if the state of network connectivity changes, such as when you undock a tablet and move from a LAN connection to a wireless link. The situation is different with Windows 2000 Professional, which does not support a feature called Network Location Awareness (NLA) and does not update Outlook if a network change occurs. Instead, Outlook has to poll the network connection every 15 seconds to see if anything has changed. If Outlook detects a network change, it may decide to change its connection state to Exchange. For example, if a higher-speed connection is available, Outlook will use that. If no connections are available, Outlook changes to a disconnected state. Finally, if you use an RAS or VPN connection, Outlook gives that precedence over other connections. The logic here is that you probably established the RAS or VPN connection to reach an Exchange server outside the current LAN.

You can control how Outlook synchronizes your mailbox by using the "Cached Exchange Mode" option to instruct Outlook to download headers only (to restrict network activity), headers followed by content, or full items immediately. You can also ask Outlook to switch automatically to header-only mode if the client detects a slow network connection. However, if you connect Outlook 2003 to Exchange 2000 or 5.5 servers, the user interface forces you to download full items. This is because these servers do not support selective or header-only download.

My preference is to download headers followed by full items, because this means that I have a chance to review the contents of the Inbox immediately after Outlook fetches the headers and then take the decision to delete unwanted messages (such as spam). If you use a hard delete (press shift and delete together) to remove these items, Outlook will not move them through the Deleted Items folder and therefore will not download the full content when it updates that folder. Once I have reviewed new messages in the Inbox, I can begin working with messages and Outlook will download the full content behind the scenes. Without too much effort on my part, the mailbox is in a completely populated state any time I remove my PC from the network. Another small change in download behavior is that the most recent items appear first in the Inbox rather than the oldest items.

The advantage of cached Exchange mode is to deliver excellent client performance while retaining access to all of the server features. People will still want to work in traditional offline mode and configure suitable send/receive synchronization groups to preserve network resources, especially across expensive dial-in links from hotel rooms or similar locations, but most users will find cached Exchange mode a benefit.

4.2.5 Download activity

On slow connections, you can opt for Outlook to download only headers. Outlook does not attempt to calculate throughput to decide whether a connection is fast or slow. Instead, it requests the network adapter speed from Windows and uses that as the base. You can assume that a modem connection

Figure 4.7
Outlook progress bar and Exchange connection types.

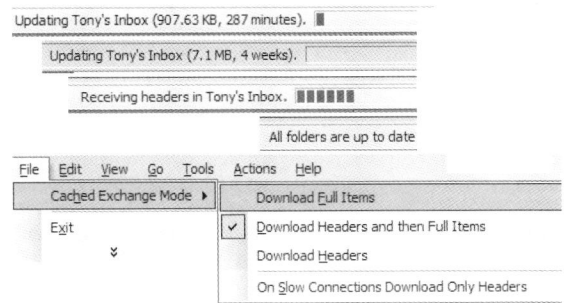

is going to be slow and a LAN connection is fast, and the decision point is approximately 144 Kbps.

The top set of screen captures in Figure 4.7 illustrates how difficult it can be for software to predict the time necessary to perform any action. Outlook can ask Exchange how much data remains for the client to download and then estimate a time based on network speed and current throughput, but sometimes things just go wrong. Even the slowest connection can probably download 7.1 MB in less than four weeks! Fortunately, these screen captures come from beta versions of Outlook 2003 and the final shipping product is more accurate. The bottom part of Figure 4.7 shows the options available from the "Cached Exchange Mode" choice on the File menu, which allows you to determine how Outlook fetches information from the server. If you move to a folder that Outlook has not updated yet, it immediately begins to download the items into the folder so that you can work. Left to itself, Outlook will eventually download the headers for new items for all folders.

After you begin using a local cache, Exchange notifies the client to ask it to initiate synchronization any time new content arrives in your server mailbox. If you use an HTTP connection, Outlook polls for new items instead of waiting for notifications. The default interval to poll for new mail is 60 seconds, and Exchange provides this value to Outlook when the client connects. You can adjust this on the server by creating a new registry value at:

```
HKLM\System\CurrentControlSet\Services\MSExchangeIS\
ParametersSystem
```

The new DWORD value is called Maximum Polling Frequency and its default value is 60,000 milliseconds, or 60 seconds.

Using the local cache introduces some additional synchronization overhead when Outlook starts, because it has to check every server folder in the mailbox to determine whether changes exist. Outlook also has to perform some housekeeping, such as registering for notifications on all folders, retrieving security settings, and so on. Outlook's initial connection to Exchange 2003 is faster than to previous versions of the server because Microsoft has optimized the housekeeping routines, but you should not see any evidence of extra processing except a small amount of network traffic.

After receiving a notification or detecting new items, Outlook downloads the message header (including the first 254 bytes of the message body) so that you know who sent the message, and the reading pane (previously called the preview pane) can function. The header also includes the data necessary to render views and to process rules together with an indication of whether any attachments are present. It does not download information about the number of attachments, their names, or sizes, but the message header does contain the overall message size, which is enough for a user to make a decision as to whether he or she wants to download the complete item. This data is stored in the local cache. If the user decides to read the message and view the attachments, Outlook fetches the information from the server, displays it, and stores it in the local cache. To keep everything synchronized, each time you connect to the server, Outlook checks each folder to make sure that its contents are up-to-date in the local cache and makes whatever adjustments are necessary.

Everything works without any obvious impact on mail delivery, and, apart from a brief pause while new messages are processed, users are not aware that Outlook is operating in a different manner. Indeed, you only realize that Outlook delays new message delivery slightly if you run two clients side by side and monitor delivery into the mailbox. Invariably, messages appear in the Inbox faster if Outlook connects to Exchange in a traditional noncached manner or if you use another client, such as OWA. This is expected, because the server notifies the client as soon as new mail arrives. When Outlook operates in cached Exchange mode, there is an interval between Exchange signaling Outlook that a new message has arrived in the Inbox (and seen by other clients) and Outlook downloading the message into the local cache and notifying the user with a pop-up display. At times, you may see a slightly extended delay in notifications, since Outlook attempts to bundle item synchronizations together if it receives notifications from Exchange that a number of new messages have arrived together.

If you decide to leave messages for later processing and Outlook connects to Exchange with a fast link, a background thread ultimately synchronizes the full message content, including any attachments into the local cache. Outlook uses up to five threads for synchronization: four dedicated to background synchronization and one reserved for immediate or foreground activity. This mechanism allows Exchange to distinguish between actions that it needs to respond to immediately and those that it can process with a little less speed. For example, if you spot a message from the list of downloaded message headers and want to read it immediately without waiting for Outlook to download full content, you can click on it to force the fifth thread to kick in and fetch the message. Exchange notes that the foreground thread is waiting for a response and puts the background synchronization threads on hold while it services the foreground thread and then resumes.

If a network interruption occurs during synchronization, Outlook can continue working with the local cache and wait for the network to come back before recommencing synchronization to update the local cache. Unlike previous versions of Outlook, where any network interruption severely disrupts client operations, Outlook 2003 is able to detect when the network is available again and reconnect to Exchange. This improvement is particularly noticeable across wireless connections, which often drop and reconnect automatically, or if you put a notebook computer into suspend mode and then restart it. When you work over a slow link, you can instruct Outlook to download headers or headers followed by full items. Downloading headers is often a good option, because it allows you to scan new items in the Inbox and delete some before you proceed to download email that you really need. You can still use the F9 command to perform folder synchronization as before, but this is now a feature used as an exception rather than a rule—for example, if you download headers for all folders and then decide to use F9 to invoke the default Send/Receive group to send and receive mail, or if you use Shift+F9 to synchronize a particular folder.

Once Outlook has downloaded messages to the local cache, the cache becomes its primary storage and Outlook never goes to the server unless absolutely required—for example, to fetch the content for a message whose header is in the cache.

Because Outlook focuses on data in the local cache, it can ignore temporary server outages or network interruptions. Clusters deal with hardware failures by transitioning resources such as storage groups from the node where the failure occurs to another node in the cluster. With previous versions of Outlook, the cluster state transition is noticeable, because the client "freezes" during this period, which can last from ten seconds to a couple of minutes or even longer. Outlook 2003 continues working during a cluster state transition and so can contribute to a higher service level for users, which may make the combination of Outlook 2003 and Exchange 2003 clusters more popular for system designers seeking the highest possible level of system availability.

The philosophy of using the local cache even extends to Outlook's address book. After all, if the client uses a local copy of the mailbox to avoid round trips to the server, should it not also use the local copy of the address book to avoid making LDAP queries to the GC? This is exactly what Outlook does when you work in cached Exchange mode after you have downloaded an OAB, as you can see by examining the GAL properties by opening the address book and then right-clicking on the "Show Names from the:" drop-down list (Figure 4.8).

Of course, if you work offline and use the OAB to validate addresses, it is important that you update the OAB regularly by either including the OAB in a send/receive group or by downloading it explicitly on a weekly basis. To eliminate more reasons to consult the server, Outlook 2003 introduces a new unicode-format OAB that holds more information about recipients (such as multiple values for telephone numbers) than the previous OAB. You do not have to upgrade to the unicode-format OAB, since Outlook 2003 also supports the previous version. Whichever OAB you use, Outlook 2003 always attempts to fetch information from the OAB and only goes to the server if the user accesses data not held in the OAB. For example, if you look up a user in the GAL, Outlook first displays the General page. All of the data shown here comes from the OAB. If you now click on the Organization tab, Outlook has to go to the server to fetch organizational data (the person's manager and direct reports), because these links to other directory objects are not stored in the OAB. The user is not aware

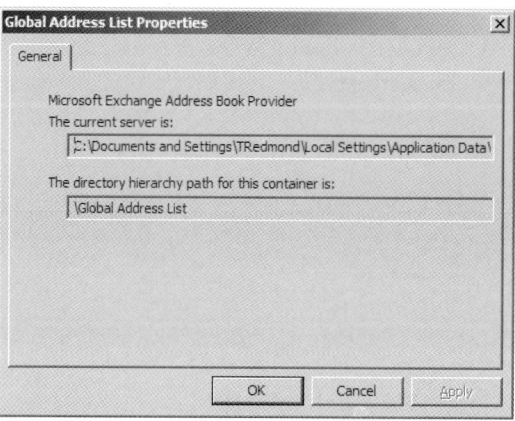

Figure 4.8
Using the OAB as the preferred address book provider.

that Outlook switches between local and network data, because the client aggregates the results before presenting data to the user. Apart from the normal download process, there is no way to insert information on a selective basis about new GAL entries into the OAB or to remove entries for deleted users, groups, or contacts. If you want to access a new entry that does not exist in your copy of the OAB, you have to download an updated OAB or use the new object's SMTP address if you want to send a message to it. Fortunately, as explained later in section 4.6, Outlook only downloads the differences between the client OAB and the server version to minimize bandwidth consumption.

Outlook cannot possibly cache every piece of mailbox data, and server access is still required to work with some information—for example, if you want to browse free and busy information when you schedule meetings or when you use delegate access to another user's mailbox.

It is possible that the advent of cached Exchange mode will drive some change in user behavior around the use of folders. Up to now, you probably kept many messages in your Inbox and sent items folders simply because Outlook automatically synchronizes these folders for offline access. The result is often folders holding a huge collection of items relating to many different topics. The items are available offline, but it can be hard to find a specific item and you normally end up with a lot of junk stored alongside the valuable data. Now, if you have a complete copy of all server folders, you may be more inclined to refile messages out of the Inbox and send item folders to a more appropriate location. Of course, unless you help people understand how to use folders effectively by setting up a logical folder structure, they will not be able to take advantage of this capability. In addition, it takes hours to go through large folders to refile items, and it is hard to justify the return for such diligent filing.

4.2.6 Incremental synchronization

Outlook uses an algorithm called Incremental Change Synchronization (ICS) to set checkpoints to determine the data that it has replicated with Exchange during synchronization sessions. Up to Outlook 2003, Microsoft set large checkpoint windows with ICS, which was good for performance but meant that any interruption of connectivity between client and server forced Outlook to restart synchronization from a checkpoint that might be well back in the past. Outlook went back to the last full folder that the client had downloaded, something that could be a long way if you experienced a network interrupt when synchronizing a large Inbox. Microsoft has improved the algorithm (now called "advanced ICS") and now checkpoints after every successful network buffer download to ensure that Outlook has to recopy less data if an outage interrupts synchronization. The increases in performance elsewhere more than compensate for the small decrease caused by smaller checkpoint windows here.

4.2.7 Deploying cached Exchange mode

Microsoft argues that cached Exchange mode improves client performance, because Outlook works with local data while also reducing network traffic and server load by replacing the normal client/server traffic and server transactions with a constant trickle down to the client. At the same time, server performance improves, because client operations smooth out over time and do not encounter the same peaks in demand that you see with traditional client/server email systems. For example, the impact of several thousand people logging on at 9:00 A.M. each morning to read their email is significantly different if the clients download messages to the local cache to allow users to process the messages locally. You trade constant and unpredictable demands from clients as people go through their new messages (which might involve multiple downloads of specific messages and attachments) in favor of the one-time phased hit required to make single download and any processing required by the server to send new messages. If Microsoft's arguments are valid, it may be possible to support larger user communities on a particular server. However, consolidation to a smaller set of servers is impossible until you deploy Outlook 2003 clients and Exchange 2003 servers everywhere to implement cached Exchange mode and take advantage of automatic data compression, a feature only supported by the combination of Outlook 2003 and Exchange 2003.

There are instances where cached Exchange mode does not work well. For example, users who roam from PC to PC cannot really use cached Exchange mode, because Outlook would have to rebuild the local cache on each PC the user visits. Not only would this drain network bandwidth, it also increases server load. In addition, the user would not be very happy, because his or her mailbox would be in a state of constant refresh. It is best to advise roaming users to continue to connect to their mailboxes and work online. This is also inappropriate for someone who only uses a workstation infrequently, because every connection will provoke a massive download. Obviously, someone who uses Outlook through a Windows Terminal Services or Citrix Metaframe thin client connection cannot use cached Exchange mode either.

Outlook's ability to recover deleted messages from Exchange's deleted items cache is useful, and it has helped me innumerable times to retrieve a message that I deleted that suddenly became important again. Unfortunately, some users forget that cached Exchange mode means that you are working with a local snapshot of your mailbox, so retrieving a message from the deleted items cache is not as fast as with previous versions of Outlook. After you select an item for Outlook to retrieve, the client must execute the request on the server and then synchronize the recovered message down into the local cache. The net effect is that deleted item recovery appears to be much slower with Outlook 2003. It is a small problem, but one that has caused some users to believe that something has gone wrong.

Another example where cached mode can cause problems is users with large mailboxes. There are people who have mailboxes over 2 GB—some over 5 GB—and it probably does not make sense to create a complete replica of such a large mailbox on a laptop, especially given the increase in the size of the OST, even with the size of disks in most modern laptops. If you want, you can now create an OST that uses unicode format and increase the OST to a virtually unlimited size. This is not a very good idea, because OST performance suffers due to excessive local disk traffic generated by Outlook to synchronize the local cache if you use a file larger than 1 GB. In particular, Outlook has to do a lot more work to insert new messages in the OST after it passes 1GB, so it is best to keep OST file sizes less than 1GB if possible, unless you store the OST on a high-performance disk. Most laptops are not equipped with disks in this category, but desktop systems may be.

There is no way to convert an existing OST to use the new unicode format. Instead, you have to delete your existing OST and then create a new MAPI profile. When you do this, the default option is to create a unicode-format OST (Figure 4.9). However, you then have to recreate the entire local cache into the new OST, so moving from old to new format takes time.

Users who have very large mailboxes are often better off working with an OST in offline mode, because they can apply filters in their send and receive groups to restrict the amount of data that Outlook synchronizes with Exchange. However, you can advance the argument that the large disks now installed on most laptops make it easy to trade some disk space for the advantages accrued from a complete local cache, especially if your PC is fast enough to handle the increased overhead implied in keeping the local indexes in the cache updated and accurate. As in most situations, users will make up their own minds.

To check the impact of these changes, Outlook 2003 includes the ability to track and report RPC performance data. Outlook posts the data it captures periodically to the Exchange 2003 server, which collates the data

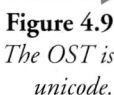
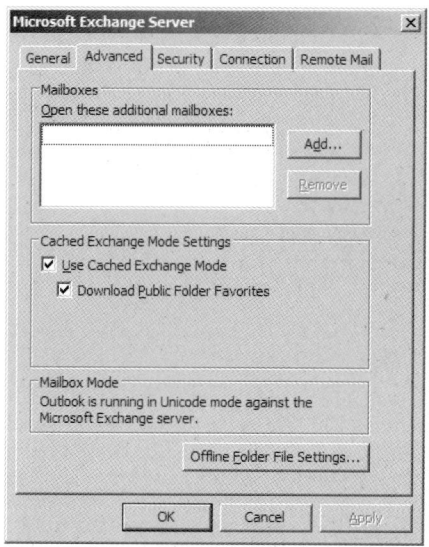

Figure 4.9
The OST is unicode.

reported by all of the connected clients. You can interrogate this data programmatically using WMI, or use the Performance Monitor utility to view it in real time. Table 4.2 lists the major counters that you can monitor, all of which belong to the MSExchangeIS (Information Store) object, some of which are very useful to determine service availability and responsiveness—two aspects that are not always easy to measure. For example, if you find that Outlook reports RPC failures, this may mean that connections have broken down between server and client, which may indicate a loss of service availability, albeit one that Outlook 2003 masks better than other clients through cached Exchange mode. If Outlook reports large numbers of RPCs with latencies greater than five or ten seconds, then you could be in a situation where Exchange is not providing good response to client queries. Again, cached Exchange mode helps to mask the problem, but users can still experience excessive latency when they need to connect to the server to fetch noncached data, such as when they view directory information about a GAL entry. Clients do not notice any difference in performance to collect data, and collation consumes some network resources when Outlook sends the data to Exchange.

From a deployment perspective, you may have to be careful about how you introduce cached Exchange mode. Apart from testing third-party add-on products to ensure that they keep working when Outlook uses cached Exchange mode, you have to phase in the new client behavior to minimize any impact on system performance. For example, if you deploy Outlook 2003 to a large number of desktops overnight and create new profiles to

4.2 Making Outlook a better network client for Exchange

Table 4.2 *Performance Counters Updated by Outlook 2003*

Performance Counter	Meaning
Connection count	Count of current client connections to the Store
Client: latency > 2 seconds RPCs	Total number of client RPCs with latency > 2 seconds
Client: latency > 5 seconds RPCs	Total number of client RPCs with latency > 5 seconds
Client: latency > 10 seconds RPCs	Total number of client RPCs with latency > 10 seconds
Client: RPCs attempted	Total number of client RPCs attempted since the Store initialized
Clients: RPCs attempted/second	Current rate of attempted RPCs per second against the Store
Client: RPCs failed	Total number of client RPCs that have failed since the Store initialized
Client: RPCs failed/second	Current failure rate per second of RPCs against the Store
Client: RPCs succeeded	Total number of client RPCs that have succeeded since the Store initialized
Client: RPCs succeeded/second	Current success rate per second of RPCs to the Store
Client: Total reported latency	Total count (in seconds) of latency of all client RPCs since the Store initialized
Client: RPCs failed: access denied	Total RPCs that have failed due to access denied
Client: RPC failed: call canceled	Total number of RPCs failed because client canceled the call
Client: RPC failed: server too busy	Total number of RPCs failed because the server was too busy to respond
Client: RPC failed: server unavailable	Total number of RPCs failed because the server did not respond
Client: RPC failed: all other errors	Total number of RPCs failed for some other reason

force users into cached Exchange mode, you will see a colossal load suddenly generated on the servers the next morning as the clients connect and begin to populate their cache. Best practice suggests that you should limit the number of clients that turn on cached Exchange mode to less than 30 a day (per server). Of course, every company is different and the degree of load depends on several factors, including:

- The number of clients
- The average mailbox size—the larger the mailbox, the bigger the load required to build the local cache
- User filing behavior—if people refile messages from the Inbox to other folders and have not synchronized these folders to their OST in the past, then Outlook must fetch more data from the server to build

the cache. On the other hand, if users keep most of their messages in the Inbox and Sent Items folders, then those folders already exist in the OST and less load occurs.

- The network connections that clients use to connect to the server—slow network links will extend the time that the additional load exists but may lessen the magnitude of the load.
- How quickly you deploy Outlook 2003—a phased rollout spreads the load
- The mix of Outlook and non-Outlook clients that you deploy

As with any other technology, it is wise to think about how it might influence your infrastructure before you rush to deploy.

4.2.8 Compression and buffers

MAPI clients request servers to provide data in chunks or buffers. To optimize communication between client and server, the size of the buffers varies depending on the client version and the type of network in use. For example, Outlook uses large 32-KB buffers on LAN-quality networks and reduces the buffer to 8 KB or even 4 KB as the connection slows. (See Table 4.3.)

In addition to the changes made for local caching, Outlook 2003 tweaks the buffer size and is now able to compress data. Exchange 2003 includes

Table 4.3 *Outlook Network Activity Connected to Exchange 2000 or 2003*

Version	Mode	Data Flow	Network	Client Buffer Size	Data Buffer Size	Size on Wire
Outlook 2002	Online	Download/Upload	LAN	32 KB	32 KB	32 KB
	Online	Download/Upload	WAN	4 KB or 8 KB	4 KB or 8 KB	4 KB or 8 KB
	Offline	Download/Upload	Any	32 KB	32 KB	32 KB
Outlook 2003	Online	Download	All	32 KB	32 KB	< 32 KB
	Online	Upload	All	32 KB	32 KB	< 32 KB
	Cached	Download	All	96 KB	> 96 KB	96 KB
	Cached	Upload	All	32 KB	32 KB	< 32 KB
	Offline	Download	All	32 KB	> 32 KB	32 KB
	Offline	Upload	All	32 KB	32 KB	<32 KB

4.2 Making Outlook a better network client for Exchange

Table 4.4 *MAPI RPC Compression Parameters*

Value	Description
RPC Compression Minimum Size (DWORD)	Defines the minimum size a packet is to compress (default is 1,024)
RPC Compression Enabled (DWORD)	Flag to allow or prevent compression. The default is 1, which enables compression. Set the value to 0 if you want to use a Network Monitor to track the actual data that passes between clients and server.
RPC Packing Enabled (DWORD)	Flag to enable or disable RPC packing. The default is 1, which enables packing.

the same compression technology,[2] so compression is full duplex rather than one way. However, compression only occurs when an Outlook 2003 client connects to Exchange 2003. The server only knows if a client can receive compressed data if it uses a special MAPI call to request data. Older clients do not use this call, so Exchange 2003 therefore reverts to noncompressed transfers.

Exchange incurs a performance penalty to perform compression and decompression, but Microsoft believes that the penalty is more than offset by the gain, because the server needs to process less network packets. You can influence how Exchange 2003 performs compression for RPCs to Outlook 2003 clients with the registry values described in Table 4.4, which you insert at the key:

```
HKLM\System\CurrentControlSet\Services\MSExchangeIS\
ParametersSystem\
```

Whenever possible, Exchange 2003 compresses complete messages, including attachments. In much the same way that ZIP utilities achieve different compression ratios for different file formats, the ratios produced by Exchange vary across different message types and attachments. For example, HTML and plain text body parts compress to between 60 percent and 80 percent of their original size. Word documents and Excel spreadsheets compress well, while PowerPoint presentations are less amenable to compression. Exchange already compresses RTF message bodies, gaining a further saving in bytes transmitted on the network.

---

2. Microsoft calls the compression technology "XPRESS" and it is based on the Lempel-Ziv algorithm. Active Directory uses the same algorithm to compress data sent by RPCs between domain controllers.

Table 4.3 summarizes how Outlook 2002 and 2003 vary buffer sizes in different conditions. If you compare Outlook 2003 with Outlook 2002, you can see the wider range of buffer sizes in use. It is important to emphasize that the impact of this change on servers will vary with different user behavior and format mixes. For example, if you upgrade servers to Exchange 2003 and leave clients alone, you will not see any improvement. Upgrading each client to Outlook 2003 makes things a little better, but less so if everyone uses HTML as his or her message editor and sends large PowerPoint presentations to each other. You gain best results after everyone upgrades to the latest version of Outlook and sends a normal mix of HTML, plain text, and RTF messages with various attachments.

4.2.9 Conflict resolution

The nature of synchronization, where different versions of items can exist on client or server for good reasons, creates the potential for conflicts. A conflict occurs when some action modifies two or more replicas of the same item independently of each other, and Outlook then detects that different versions exist during the synchronization process. For example, you update an appointment using OWA and then update the same appointment with Outlook when you work offline, or you receive a reminder for a meeting on two devices (such as a Pocket PC and a desktop PC) and dismiss the reminder on both devices. When Outlook goes online again, it detects that the version of the calendar item on the server is different from the one in the client folder and a conflict occurs.

In previous versions of Outlook, the solution is to mark the item with the "crossed swords" icon to show the user that the conflict exists. Outlook keeps both versions and the user can decide which version is the definitive copy. Unfortunately, the process is manual and users may not be aware that any conflicts exist unless they attempt to open an item in conflict. In addition, applications such as ActiveSync do not handle items in conflict well, because they do not include code to resolve or otherwise deal with the problem.

Outlook 2003 includes a new conflict resolution engine designed to resolve conflicts automatically. The idea behind conflict resolution is to weed out spurious conflicts (caused when two versions of an item are identical) and improve the user experience when conflicts happen. Many conflicts occur because of predictable user behavior, such as dismissing reminders on two devices, and the conflict engine aims to resolve these conflicts without user intervention. Sometimes, as in the case of reminders, the conflict resolution engine resolves the problem by comparing the two

4.2 Making Outlook a better network client for Exchange

versions, seeing that they are identical, and discarding one copy. In other situations, it is harder to determine why a conflict occurs, so the conflict resolution engine applies an algorithm to determine which version of the items in conflict "wins." In this context, when a version of an item "wins" in the conflict resolution process, it remains in its original folder. The "losers" end up in the "Conflicts" folder, a subfolder of "Sync Issues." You have to click on the "Folder List" shortcut to see the Sync Issues folder in the tree view.

The items in "Conflicts" (Figure 4.10) are alternate versions to items that exist in other folders such as the Inbox and Sent Items, and you can review them to decide whether you wish to keep a version of a specific item instead of the version selected by the conflict resolution engine. To do this, select the item and open it, then right-click on the conflict information band in the header. Outlook then displays the options you can take (Figure 4.11), including replacing the item in the other folder with this version or even replacing any line breaks that Outlook removed during formatting.

Outlook maintains two other folders under Sync Issues: Local Failures and Server Failures. Local Failures holds items that Outlook was unable to synchronize up to the server, while Server Failures holds items that Exchange was unable to push down to the client. Obviously, you should

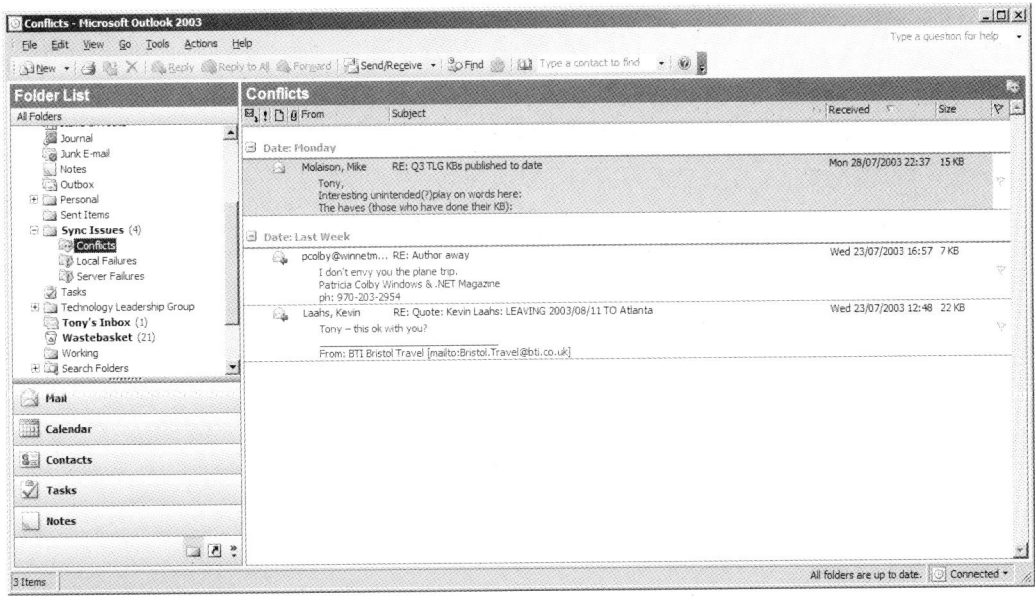

Figure 4.10 *Reviewing an item in conflict.*

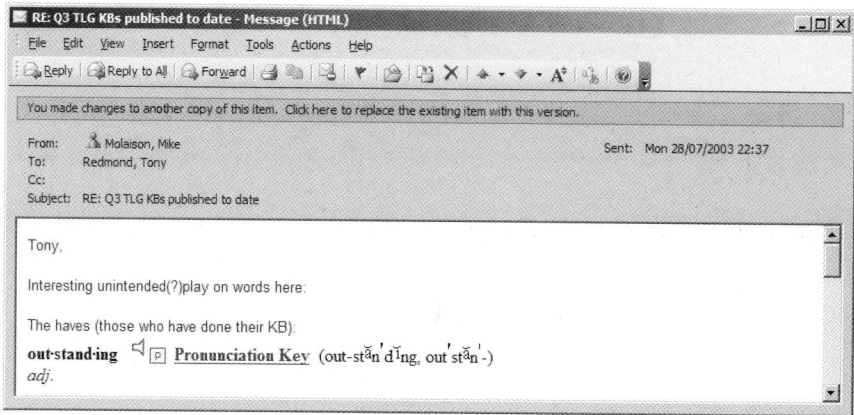

Figure 4.11   *Some items that Outlook had a problem with.*

not see many items in these folders, and if you do, item corruption is the probable cause. In previous versions of Outlook, the Local Failures folder is "Synchronization Failures," so Outlook 2003 renames the folder to bring it in line with "Server Failures," introduced as part of Outlook's "skip bad item" feature that allows the server and client to complete synchronization even if they encounter corrupt data during the process. Ideally, you never see any items appear in these folders. If they do, then you need to understand why. One way to find out more information is to enable mail logging through Tools, Options, Other, and Advanced (Figure 4.12), which instructs Outlook to generate synchronization logs in the Sync Issues folder for more operations. The information reported in the logs may help you understand the root cause of the conflicts, but it is more likely that you will pass this information on to PSS to help Microsoft debug the problem.

4.2.10   Is Outlook 2003 the best Exchange client?

Generally, I think Outlook 2003 is easily the best client for Exchange, but there are places where Microsoft can still make improvements in Outlook's networking layers and the efficiency of its communications with Exchange. While they are less common than with previous versions, Outlook 2003 still hangs (for a few seconds) from time to time when the client seems to stutter or pause for no good reason, even when connected across a high-speed DSL or LAN-quality link. After a while (perhaps once a time-out period has passed), Outlook begins working properly again. I suspect that the root cause for these interruptions is associated with proxies or some other connection between Outlook, IE, Messenger, and the other Microsoft products that share common components, but it is difficult to track down

4.2 Making Outlook a better network client for Exchange

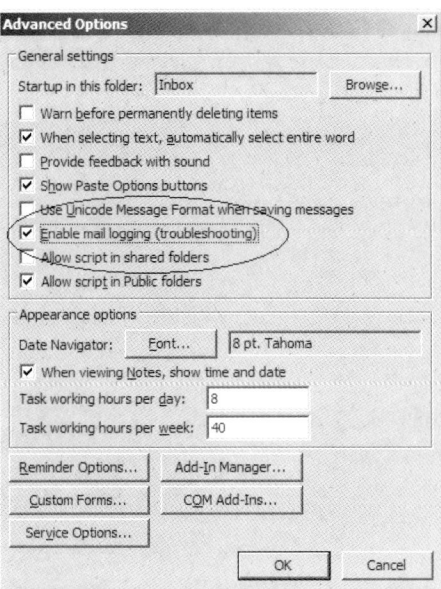

Figure 4.12
Enabling mail logging.

just what is happening. I also see more problems when using Word as the default editor, but I put up with this because Word is a far more functional editor and I like to use its features. It is also true that Outlook still seems to do an awful lot of communication with Exchange, especially if your mailbox has many folders, before it gets to transfer any messages. This problem is most evident on low-speed links.

In addition to its improved user interface, including features such as search folders, translucent pop-up notifications, and an improved reading pane, there is no doubt that Microsoft has done a lot of work to make Outlook the best network client for Exchange. The inevitable glitches take a little away from the overall impact, but they do not make the client less attractive. You can deploy Outlook 2003 only if you run Windows 2000 Professional (SP3 or later) or Windows XP, since these are the only operating systems supported by Office 2003. As shown in Table 4.5, you can exploit some of the features against Exchange 5.5 or Exchange 2000, but you can only realize the full benefits of the network improvements when you combine Outlook 2003 with Exchange 2003.

All of these changes are very welcome, but many companies will take several years before they can leverage smarter network behavior. It is common to find two- or three-year desktop refresh cycles, so the need to deploy a new version of Office and possibly upgrade the desktop operating system is a more difficult hurdle to overcome than installing Windows

Table 4.5 *Outlook 2003 Features Against Different Versions of Exchange*

Feature	Exchange 5.5	Exchange 2000	Exchange 2003
Search folders	X	X	X
Cached Exchange mode (full items)	X	X	X
Cached Exchange mode (drizzle and header synchronization)			X
MAPI RPC compression			X
Buffer packing			X
Kerberos authentication			X
Best body support			X
Performance tracking			X
ICS check pointing			X
Smart change synchronization	X	X	X
Skip bad items		X	X
Presynchronization reporting and improved progress reports			X
Integration with server-based antispam protection			X
RPC over HTTP			X
LIFO downloads—last in, first downloaded			X
Unicode OST and PST			X
Junk mail processing	X	X	X

2003 and Exchange 2003 on their servers. However, if your company has many mobile users, it is well worthwhile to accelerate an upgrade program for the user who can benefit most—users of notebook computers who travel extensively.

4.3 How many clients can I support at the end of a pipe?

Let us assume you have a group of users that work at the end of a 64-Kbps network link. Your design can place a server at the end of the link and either connect the server to an existing routing group or form a new routing group and connect via a routing group, SMTP, or X.400 connector. On the other hand, you can elect to connect the users into a centralized server. In most cases, designs seek to eliminate servers as far as possible in order to reduce ongoing administrative effort and cost. The question is whether the

64-Kbps link is big enough to provide reasonable response to the users at the end of the line.

The answer depends on three factors: the number of users, the type of work they do, and the software you deploy. Even if you do not have detailed analysis to back up designs, you can revert to some guidelines that are often used successfully in projects. For example, the classic rule of thumb for estimating MAPI client demand is as follows: Allow 3 Kbps for each "light" email user, 6 Kbps for every "medium" email user, and 10 Kbps for every heavy email user.

This is a simple rule that hides all sorts of complexity, since you then have to answer the question of how to define users as light, medium, and heavy. Generally, light users are people who receive far more email than they send and do not receive more than ten messages a day. Medium users are more balanced in terms of the send/receive ratio and generate up to 20 messages a day, along with some scheduling and other activities that create network traffic. Heavy users are online most of the time and probably deal with over 50 messages a day. These people tend to maintain their own distribution lists. Large distribution lists are not bad as such, but large personal distribution lists impose an extra penalty when the client expands their contents to add each recipient to the message header. This action increases the overall size of messages to a point where a simple message containing a couple of lines of text occupies 50 KB or more after all the individual recipients are in the message header. System distribution lists do not incur the same penalty, because Exchange keeps only a pointer to the list in the message header. Heavy users also tend to attach more documents than other users and are the people who explore the edge of the envelope when it comes to client options such as autosignatures. Every company varies, and you may find that your heavy users demand more than 10 Kbps.

Even the most detailed network analysis will not cover all possible situations. There are going to be times when a network connection slowly stops because of cumulative user load or due to an action taken by an individual. Early in the morning, when people log on at roughly the same time and connect to read new mail, is often a time of peak demand. Attaching a large file to a message can fully occupy a 64-Kbps link for some time. Obviously, other activities use up bandwidth too. Given the graphically rich nature of the Web, browsing often chews up much more bandwidth than you may realize, especially if users download files from the Internet.

The software factor is harder to quantify, because it depends on the intersection of user habits and corporate environment. If your user community is largely mobile, then the demands made on software are different from classic LAN-based populations, and it may be worthwhile to upgrade quickly to software designed to accommodate mobile connectivity, such as Outlook 2003. As explained previously, the success of Outlook 2003 varies depending on the version of Exchange the client connects to, so there are many different items to measure before you can get an accurate picture of the situation.

A useful place to begin when assessing potential client traffic is to read Microsoft's data for Exchange 2003 at http://www.microsoft.com/exchange/techinfo/outlook/CliNetTraf.asp. Remember that you need to put this data into context for your own network and user environment; do not accept it as absolute.

4.4 Blocking client access

Exchange 2000 SP1 (and onward) includes the ability for an administrator to block access to specific sets of MAPI clients or groups of MAPI clients through a registry setting on the Exchange server. The idea is that you may want to "encourage" users to upgrade their client to a specific version, perhaps to ensure that everyone has applied a service pack or hot fix by blocking access to his or her mailbox until an appropriate client is used.

All of the client-side code to connect to Exchange is in DLL, called the MAPI client provider—each version of Outlook has a slightly different version of this component, identified by Microsoft with a number that represents a sequential build number, which is incremented over time. For example, the build number for MSMAPI.DLL, the file that contains the MAPI client provider for Outlook 2002, is 10.0.3416 (Figure 4.13). The first figure in the list represents the major build number. It is sometimes associated with an internal number used by Microsoft to track releases of Office, as in the case where Office 10 is the internal number used for Office XP. Because Exchange used to ship its own client prior to the release of Outlook, some of the major build numbers prior to Office XP refer to releases of Exchange (4.0, 5.0) rather than Office.

When a MAPI client connects to Exchange, it passes details of its client provider version to the server. You can view this information through ESM by examining the users currently logged in and connected to a store database, as shown in Figure 4.14. Note that the version number reported here is a set of four digits rather than the three that you see when you examine the client provider build number. As you can see, you can sort by client type by clicking on the client version heading. In Figure 4.14, we have some

4.4 Blocking client access 233

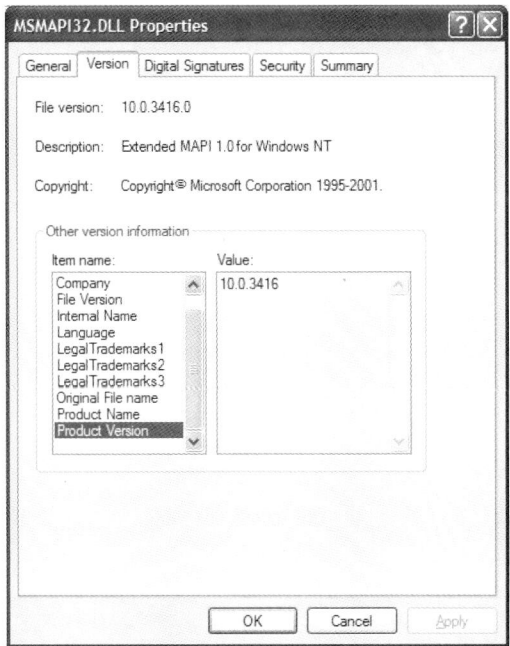

Figure 4.13 *Examining the version number of the MAPI provider.*

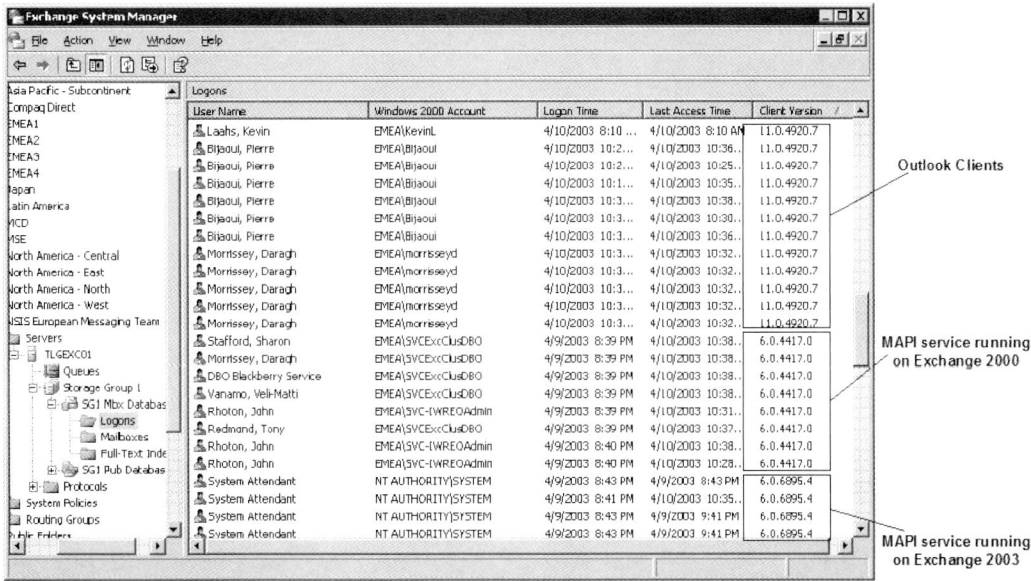

Figure 4.14 *Viewing the MAPI client version of connected users.*

Chapter 4

Outlook clients, some client logons from a service running on an Exchange 2000 server (a BlackBerry Enterprise Server), and some local Exchange 2003 services operated by the System Attendant. Outlook clients connect to the Store with multiple threads, so this explains why you see multiple entries per user for these clients. ESM also lists the Windows account used by each account, and we can see individual user accounts plus some privileged service accounts. For example, the System Attendant runs under the Windows LocalSystem account, while the BlackBerry service runs under a privileged account created for the purpose. Note that the SMTP Routing Engine connects to the Store via an SMTP provider, and other Exchange services (CDOEXM, WMI, etc.) access the Store via the OLE/DB provider, which provides an abstraction layer for MAPI.

The registry setting that blocks client access depends on client provider version numbers, so it is important to specify correct values for the clients that you want to block. Table 4.6 lists the complete set of MAPI clients shipped to date, together with values for the MAPI version shown when you view the Help/About option and the adjusted value required to block client access. If in doubt, connect a copy of the client that you want to block to Exchange, note the version number reported by ESM, and then discard the second digit. Figure 4.14 shows that a client is connected with

Table 4.6 *MAPI Client Versions*

Client	Value Shown in Help/About	Value Required to Restrict
Exchange 4.0	4.0.993.3	4.993.3
Exchange 5.0	5.0.1457.3	5.1457.3
Outlook 97 (Office version)	8.02.4212	5.1457.3
Outlook 97 (with Exchange 5.5)	8.03.4629	5.1960.0
Outlook 98	8.5.5104.6	5.2178.0
Outlook 2000	9.0.0.2711	5.2819.0
Outlook 2000 SR1	9.0.0.3821	5.3121.0
Outlook 2000/Office 2000 SP2	9.0.0.4527	5.3144.0
Outlook 2002	10.2627.2625	10.0.2627
Outlook 2002 SP1	10.3513.3501	10.0.3416
Outlook 2003	11.5614.5614	11.0.5604

4.4 Blocking client access

version 5.0.2819.0, resulting in 5.2819.0 after you discard the second digit. If you look for this value in Table 4.6, you can see that it belongs to an Outlook 2000 client.

Many Exchange services use MAPI to access the Store, so it is important that you do not block access to client providers that begin with 6. For example, the MAPI provider version number for Exchange 2000 SP1 is 6.4712.0, for SP2 it is 6.5716.0, and for SP3 it is 6.6429.0. The easiest way to find this value is to view the properties of MAPI32.DLL in the EXCHSRVR\BIN directory. If you include these values in the block, services such as the Exchange System Attendant will not work.

4.4.1 Blocking Outlook clients

You block Outlook client access to the Store by inserting a new REG_SZ value called "Disable MAPI Clients" into the system registry (Figure 4.15). Insert the value into the registry at the following location:

```
HKLM\System\CurrentControlSet\Services\MSExchangeIS\
ParametersSystem
```

The value contains the numbers of the MAPI providers used by the clients that you wish to block. Numbers can be stated as a range (to block multiple clients) or individually. For example, the value shown in Figure 4.15 prevents access by the Exchange 4.0, 5.0, and Outlook 97 clients, whereas a value of 5.2178.0 is sufficient only to block Outlook 98 clients. You can also prefix the version number with a hyphen to indicate that you wish to block all clients prior to the stated value. For example, to block access to all clients prior to Outlook 2000 updated with Office SP2 (5.3144.0), use the value:

-5.3143.0

Similarly, you can block access to clients higher than a specific value by placing a hyphen after the value. For example, to restrict access to clients greater than Outlook 2002 SP1 (10.0.3416), use the value:

10.0.3147-

Once you update the registry, you must stop and restart the Information Store service to implement the block on Exchange 2000 servers, whereas a background thread checks for a block every 15 minutes on Exchange 2003 servers, so you can wait for the Store to detect the change automatically. Afterward, clients that do not use an appropriate version of the MAPI client provider will be unable to open their mailboxes and will see the same error

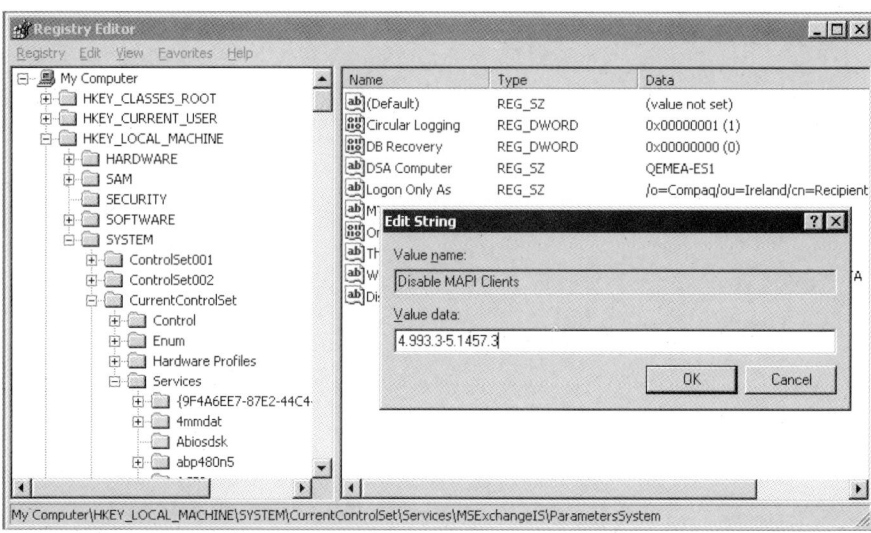

Figure 4.15 *Blocking a range of MAPI clients.*

message as if a network failure had occurred or they had provided incorrect NT credentials. Be sure to inform the help desk about how to check MAPI versions and verify that users have the correct software.

Exchange manages client access on a server level, so if you want to block access across a range of servers, you will have to update the registry on each server. In addition, make sure to review the settings after Microsoft releases either a new version of Exchange (including service packs) or a new version of the Outlook client.

4.4.2 Blocking clients for Internet Protocol access

Microsoft does not support an equivalent registry setting to block client access to Exchange via HTTP, POP3, or IMAP4. However, you can easily block access for these clients by either selectively disabling access by updating a user's account or by stopping the appropriate virtual server. To disable a protocol for a specific Exchange 2000 user, switch the AD Users and Computers console to "Advanced View" and then select the desired account. You can control access to the various protocols through the "Protocol Settings" button on the "Exchange Advanced" property page. Select the protocol you wish to control, click on the "Settings" button (Figure 4.16), and then disable access for that protocol. Alternatively, if you run Exchange 2003, use the Exchange Task Wizard to manage protocol access for users.

4.4 Blocking client access

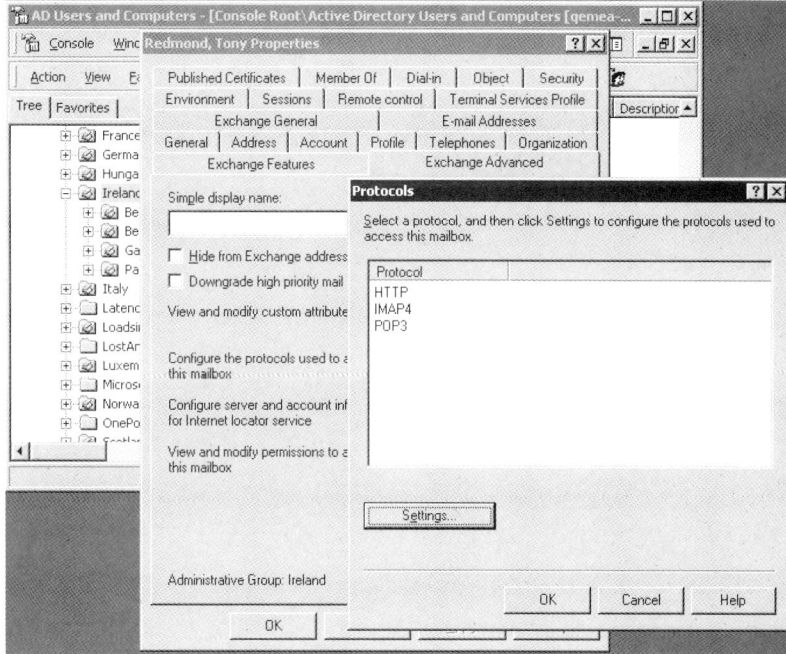

Figure 4.16
Disabling user access to specific protocols.

4.4.3 Selective blocks

From Exchange 2000 SP1 onward, you can impose a selective block, so that only a specific account is able to connect to the server, by setting the two values shown in Table 4.7 in the following location in the system registry:

```
HKLM\System\CurrentControlSet\Services\MSExchangeIS\
ParametersSystem
```

A sample value that you could use to stop anyone connecting to the Store except the account with its LegacyExchangeDN attribute set is in the following form:

```
/o=Compaq/Ou=Ireland/CN=Recipients/CN=TonyRedmond
```

After setting the appropriate registry values, you must stop and restart the Information Store service to begin blocking access. The Store process reads the registry when the service starts up, notes the presence of the values, and then verifies whether the AD contains an account with the LegacyExchangeDN attribute set to the value held in the registry. This is a fast search, because the AD indexes the LegacyExchangeDN attribute. If it matches an account in the AD, the Store begins to block access, but if the

Table 4.7 *Values Required for Blocking Access to Exchange 2000/2003*

Value	Meaning
Logon Only As (DWORD)	0 = Free Access; 1 = Block Access
Trace User LegacyDN (REG_SZ)	LegacyExchangeDN (distinguished name) of the account to allow access to; all other accounts are blocked.

value is null or invalid, the Store operates as normal and users can access their mailboxes.

To find the value of the LegacyExchangeDN attribute of an account, use the ADSIEDIT utility to examine the attributes of the account you want to access the Store. You can either note the value or simply cut and paste it from ADSIEDIT into the registry editor. Figure 4.17 shows how ADS-IEDIT displays the value of the LegacyExchangeDN attribute for a mail-enabled account, which you can find in the Domain NC container.

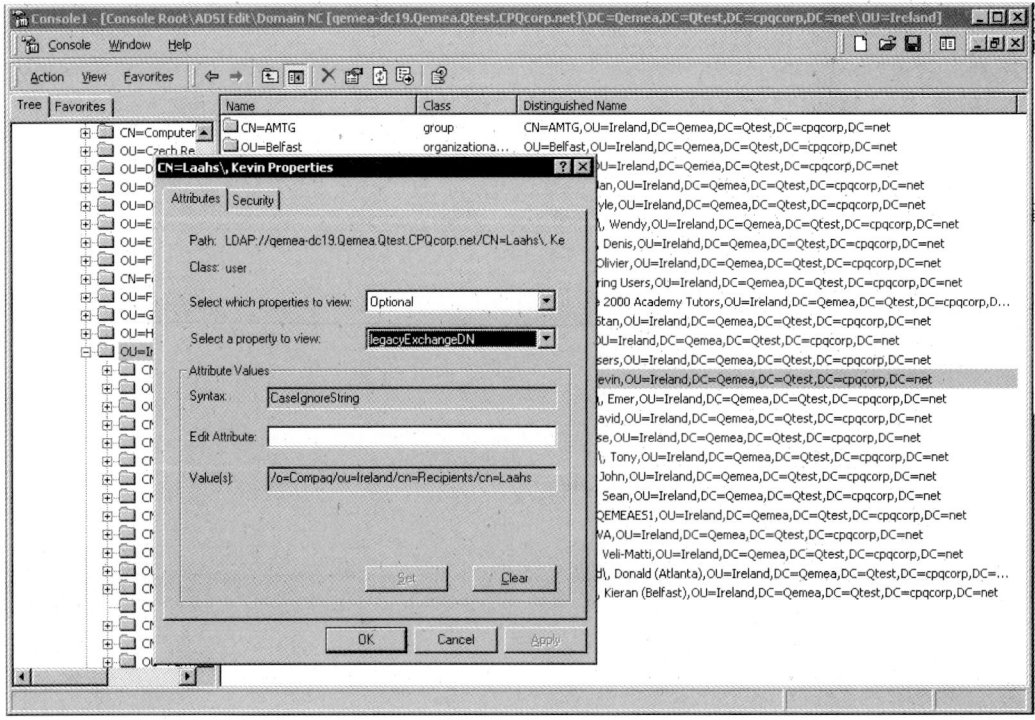

Figure 4.17 *Using ADSIEDIT to discover a LegacyExchangeDN.*

The block is removed by editing the registry and either deleting the Logon Only As value or changing its value to 0. Remember to stop and restart the Information Store service to complete the removal of the block.

4.5 New mail notifications

Exchange has always pushed new mail notifications down to MAPI clients and this behavior continues today. The decision to use push notifications instead of the classic polling is firmly based in Exchange's early history, when the designers had to come up with a scheme that did not impose a heavy network load and could work across multiple network protocols. TCP/IP was still in its early implementation phase when Exchange appeared in 1996 and many Exchange clients ran NetBEUI or IPX/SPX. A polling mechanism would work, but Microsoft's models demonstrated that the network chatter generated by clients constantly (usually once a minute) polling a server to find out if new mail had arrived could swamp the kind of networks that were then in place. The solution was to have clients register their interest in notifications with the server so that the server could then notify the client when it had something for the client to fetch. Outlook therefore sends Exchange a Universal Datagram Packet (UDP) containing the client's IP address. Exchange registers the IP address and sends a UDP back to Outlook whenever new mail arrives. Outlook then fetches the new mail. This scheme still works today with Outlook 2003, even in cached Exchange mode.

Network Address Translation (NAT) is an obvious problem here. With NAT, the communications between Outlook and Exchange are disrupted, because the client IP address is effectively hidden from the server. However, there is a workaround, since you can force Outlook to revert to polling Exchange with RPCs. See Microsoft Knowledge Base article 305572 for details. Note that Outlook always reverts to polling for notifications when you connect using RPC over HTTP links.

4.6 Junk mail processing

All versions of Outlook support rules to allow you to automate common tasks. In an Exchange environment, rules divide into two types: server-side rules and client-side rules. Exchange can execute server-side rules set on a mailbox without clients. For example, you do not need to log in for the Out of Office rule to send out of office notifications. Client-side rules normally require a user to authenticate by logging on to a mailbox and can only execute after the client connects to a mailbox and begins to download messages. Previous versions of Outlook attempted to suppress junk mail with rules, but the growing volume of spam and the more sophisticated techniques used by spammers to avoid detection mean that the rules-based approach is ineffective. The Outlook 2003 junk mail filter is brand new; it does not use the previous rules-based approach coupled with a static list of keywords to detect junk mail. Because the client executes the code to detect junk mail, messages remain in your Inbox until you connect Outlook, at which point processing begins. However, you can only use the junk mail processing feature if you configure Outlook 2003 in cached Exchange mode or connect to a server with POP3 (a protocol that always stores messages locally) or IMAP4. You can also elect to have messages delivered to a local PST and the junk mail filter will work then, but this method of delivery is now somewhat outdated by the advent of cached Exchange mode and is only useful if users have very small mailbox quotas.

Outlook could connect in the traditional manner and process messages online, but would need to fetch the message content from Exchange before the client could filter the messages. This approach works for small messages, but the network communication overhead required to fetch messages for checking is excessive, so Outlook limits this feature to messages stored in the local cache.

4.6.1 Detecting junk mail

Some junk mail is easy to detect. Messages that come from people in Nigeria who offer you incredible opportunities to earn millions of dollars if only you send them a couple of thousand to grease the wheels of commerce. Messages from young women who want to perform a range of personal services. Then there are the messages from those who have many interesting drugs to enhance your performance. The list goes on.

Spam detection software relies on a mixture of detection techniques to identify unwanted messages, including looking at originator addresses to block messages from well-known spammers (the blackhole lists) as well as message content to pick up phrases such as "Viagra" and "porn." Detection software also analyzes message structure. In the past, Outlook rules were not capable of performing the sophisticated filtering that anti-SPAM software can, but Outlook 2003's junk mail feature can suppress a very high percentage of the spam that creeps through corporate defenses and penetrates your Inbox. In this respect, you can view Outlook's junk mail filter as implementing another layer for defense in depth against spam, much as you run a desktop antivirus tool to supplement the antivirus software run on servers.

4.6.2 How Outlook's junk mail filter works

If you opt for some level of junk mail protection, Outlook begins to process new messages waiting in the Inbox as soon as it starts up and checks incoming messages as they arrive. If you do not want Outlook to look for junk mail, select the "No protection" level at the Junk E-Mail Options dialog reached from Tools.Options (Figure 4.18). The default protection level is "Low," meaning that Outlook will only detect obvious spam. Based on the level of spam that arrives in my Inbox, I prefer to set the protection level to "High," meaning that Outlook aggressively checks for spam and moves any message that seems to be spam into the Junk Mail folder. Outlook automatically creates the Junk Mail folder if it does not already exist, and you do not have the option to select another folder. However, you can opt to delete junk mail immediately (the equivalent of using the shift-delete option to remove messages without going through the deleted items folder). This is a recommended option only if you have a very high level of confidence in the filters that Outlook uses to catch spam. In my case, I found that the junk mail filter is able to intercept the bulk of offending messages. I used to capture 100 or so junk messages each month until I decided that the filter was effective enough that I did not need to see the messages in the Junk Mail folder, so I now have Outlook delete spam immediately.

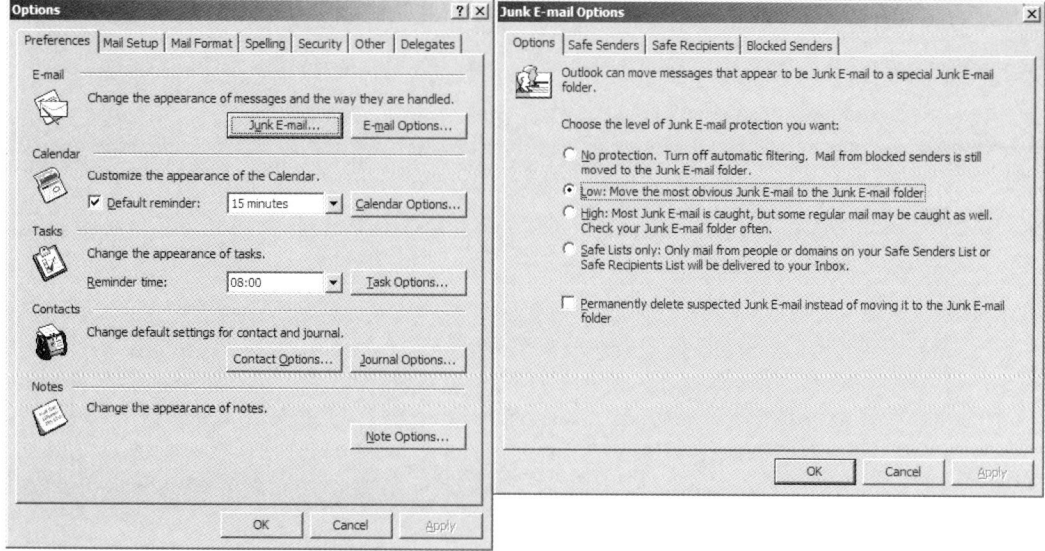

Figure 4.18 *Junk mail options.*

You cannot change the algorithm Outlook uses to decide whether a message is spam, but you can help Outlook improve its level of accuracy by creating lists of safe senders and blocked senders. Safe senders are email addresses that you recognize and do not want Outlook to mark as spam. Blocked senders are the precise opposite and are addresses that you gather from spam that elude Outlook's filters. To mark a message as spam, right-click and then select the Junk E-mail option, then "Add Sender to Blocked Senders list." Outlook adds the sender's email address to its list of known spammers, as shown in Figure 4.19. You can add anyone you like to this list, including colleagues. However, Outlook rejects any attempt to add a sender from within your organization (those who appear in the GAL) to the junk senders list. This is a pity, because there are always a few individuals who generate mail that you really do not need to read.

Outlook's junk mail filter works as follows:

- Checks email against your contacts and assumes that any message from a contact is safe to deliver.

- Checks email against the corporate GAL and assumes that you are willing to read messages from anyone in the GAL.

- Checks email against the user's "Safe Senders list" and passes any matching messages through.

- Checks email against the user's "Safe Recipients list" and passes any matching messages through.

- Checks email against the user's "Blocked Senders list" and transfers any matches to the Junk Mail folder.

- Runs the spam filter.

The filter generates a ranking (think of the ranking as being a number from 1 to 100) to determine whether a message seems, behaves, and feels like spam. The higher the number, the more spam-like Outlook believes a message to be. After a value is determined, Outlook decides whether to refile the message into junk mail. If you set a low protection level, messages with relatively high spam values will get through. If you set a high protection level, Outlook removes any message that even smells of spam. Sometimes, the high protection level is too aggressive and Outlook refiles legitimate messages into the Junk Mail folder. This is a good reason to check the messages in the Junk Mail folder from time to time before deleting them, just in case. If you find that Outlook is consistently picking out messages from specific correspondents, you can add them to your "Safe Senders list" to take care of the problem.

4.6 Junk mail processing 243

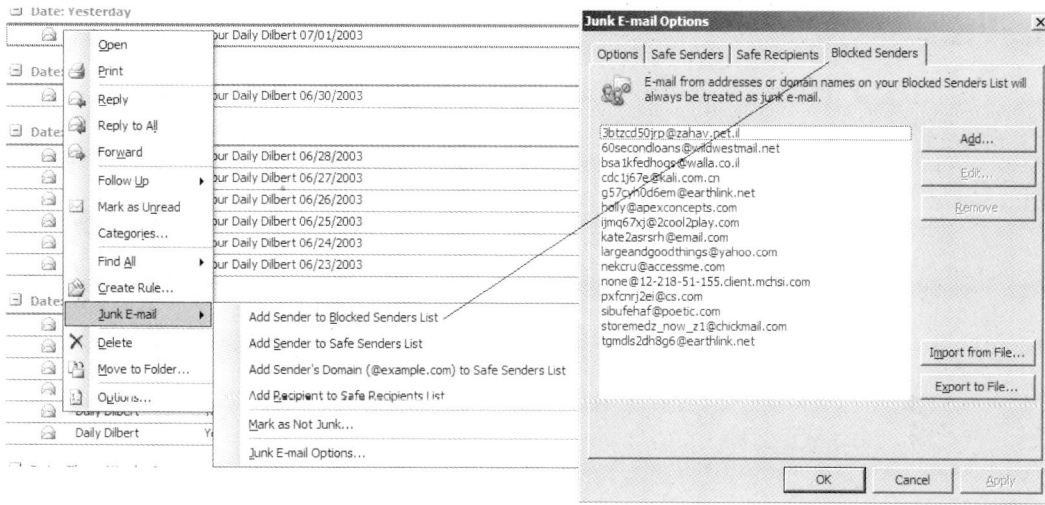

Figure 4.19   *Adding a message to the Blocked Senders list.*

Behind the scenes, Outlook depends on a file called Outlfltr.dat, which holds a large dictionary that contains keywords and phrases that the junk mail filter uses to detect spam. Apart from adding spammers to the Blocked Senders list, you cannot train the filter to improve its detection rate in any other way, so the filter implicitly relies on the accuracy and completeness of the dictionary to ensure that it catches the maximum amount of spam. Microsoft has committed to update the contents of this file on a regular basis to improve the accuracy of the filter and issued the first update in December 2003, with subsequent releases every few months afterward. You can fetch dictionary updates from the Microsoft Office support Web site (http://office.microsoft.com/officeupdate).

Microsoft released Office 2003 Service Pack 1 in July 2004. This version tweaks Outlook's junk mail filter slightly by allowing you to add the mail addresses of people to whom you send mail to the Safe Senders list automatically. In addition, a new "International" tab allows you to filter messages from international Internet domains and those whose text is in various character sets. For example, Russia has an unfortunate reputation as the home country for many spammers and, certainly, a lot of spam arrives in the Russian Cyrillic character set. You could elect to block anything from a *.ru domain that uses the Cyrillic character set.

The use of the Blocked Senders and Safe Senders lists is apparent: The purpose of the Safe Recipients list is less so. Essentially, a safe recipient is a way to identify messages sent to a particular destination (often a distribution

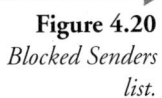
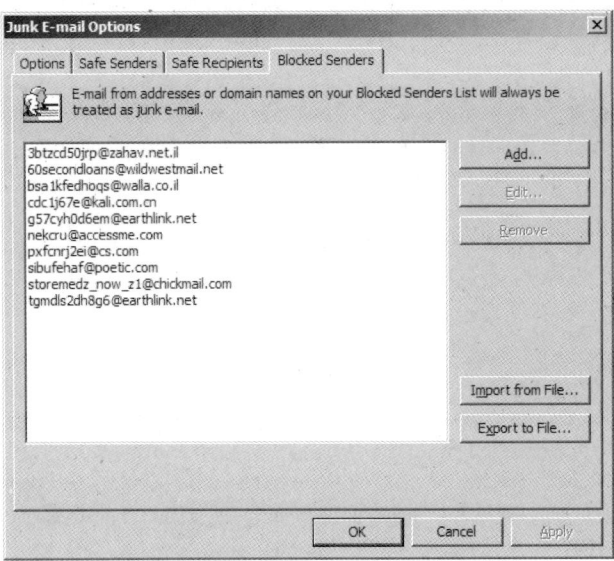

Figure 4.20
Blocked Senders list.

list or newsgroup) that you receive copies of and want to receive. You do not control the membership of the distribution list or newsgroup, but you assume that the administrator will make sure that no one uses the list for spam. Therefore, you want to tell Outlook that these messages are OK and you do this by identifying the email address of the list as a safe recipient.

After a while, you will accumulate a list of spammers that you may want to share with others. You may also want to share lists of safe recipients and safe senders. You can export or import data into any list. Figure 4.20 shows a list of people who sent me spam. Taking the "Export to file" option generates a simple text file that you can manipulate with any text editor. You can append lists gathered from different users and share updated lists of known spammers from a central location so that anyone can load them into Outlook. Note that you can also add complete domains to your Blocked Senders list to block any attempt to send you email from any of those domains. However, be careful not to be too enthusiastic about adding individuals or domains to the Blocked Senders list, since large lists will only slow down processing.

Even the best implementation of bastion servers to protect networks against incoming spam will let some messages through. There are just too many messages circulating to block everything, and the spammers come up with new tricks regularly that fool corporate defenses temporarily. If you take the time to capture details of spammers as junk mail arrives, gradually you improve Outlook's ability to recognize and block new spam. With previous versions of Outlook, rules can slow down delivery to a mailbox, especially when they call for complicated processing such as the type necessary to detect spam. Outlook 2003 caches the different lists it uses and implements the junk mail filter in compiled code, so performance is acceptable. By this, I mean that I perceived no great difference on mail delivery with the junk mail filter in place. Note that if you use cached Exchange mode, Outlook does not perform junk mail filtering until it has fully downloaded the header and content of new messages.

While it is good for Outlook 2003 to have its own junk mail block, the client leverages some Exchange server features too. Outlook stores the safe and blocked lists as well as its junk mail settings in user mailboxes to allow OWA to use the same data when it checks for junk email. Exchange can also exploit this information with antispam tools, which run on the server, and Exchange honors the Blocked Senders list to redirect email into the junk mail folder as soon as it arrives on the server without Outlook getting involved. Outlook 2003 and OWA also both block external content to prevent spammers from getting hold of valid email addresses; they use your Safe Senders list to ensure that you can see any content that you receive from sources that you know to be safe. See section 5.4 for more details.

The Blocked Senders and Safe Senders lists established with the junk mail filter also work in tandem with the Exchange Intelligent Mail Filter (IMF), if the mailbox store is on an Exchange 2003 server. Any message that passes through the IMF is assigned a spam confidence level (SCL) rating. Exchange blocks the message at the gateway if its SCL is too high and passes the remaining messages onward for delivery. Exchange 2003 mailbox servers perform a second test using the SCL when the messages arrive at the inbox and use the Blocked Senders and Safe Senders list to decide whether the Store should deliver messages that meet the SCL threshold set for mailbox stores. See Chapter 9 for more details on the IMF.

Occasionally, Outlook moves messages that originate from an authentic source and contain valid content to the Junk Mail folder for no apparent good reason. On the other hand, Outlook sometimes leaves messages that are obviously spam in the Inbox. Either situation causes users to question the effectiveness of the junk mail filter. Here are some reasons why these situations occur:

- Outlook regards internal business process messages as spam: Internal business process messages include expense reports, subscription updates from SharePoint Portal Server, and other messages that applications generate, typically by making an unauthenticated SMTP connection to a server to submit email. The important point here is that the connection is unauthenticated—so even if the messages have internal email addresses (in HP's case, they come from a server within the hp.com or cpqcorp.net domains), Exchange regards these messages as potentially generated by an external sender and Outlook therefore processes them through the junk mail filter. When this happens, the filter often thinks the messages are spam, because they contain little text content, have URL links to other content, or do not have a "From:" field specified in their header. The solution is to add the sender address to the Safe Senders list. If you are the administrator of the application that generates these messages, you could change the application to authenticate the SMTP connection and have Outlook then think that all messages from this address are valid.

- Obvious spam is not filtered: Spammers update their tactics continuously to try to fool filters. For example, they add text around the content that only serves to get the message past filters and into user inboxes. International content poses another difficulty for any language. English language filters have a hard job of deciding whether Russian content masks spam in the same way that Russian filters are challenged by English content. The only solution is to keep the junk mail filter file up-to-date with the latest version released by Microsoft.

- Messages move between folders: It is possible that mailbox rules will move new messages to specific folders after Outlook downloads headers (which contain enough information for Outlook to process rules) followed by a subsequent move to the Junk Mail folder after Outlook downloads the complete message content (to allow the junk mail filter to execute). This behavior is logical, but it can confuse users. You may be able to negate part of the problem by reviewing rules that are in place to process new mail and eliminating any that are no longer used.

No filter will be perfect, and it will always be a fight between spammers and maintainers to maximize the benefit that users gain through filters.

One other related change included in Outlook 2003 is the suppression of graphics included in HTML format messages that Outlook has to download from a remote site before it can display the full message. Spammers use these downloads as a "Web beacon" to know when someone has read the message, indicating that they have successfully sent the message to a real address. To have Outlook download the graphics, you can explicitly request a download after Outlook signals that it has blocked some graphics, add the sender to the Safe Senders list, or change the settings for automatic picture download (Figure 4.21) through the Tools.Security option. Strangely, if you do not download the graphics in an attempt to thwart a spammer, Outlook

4.6 Junk mail processing

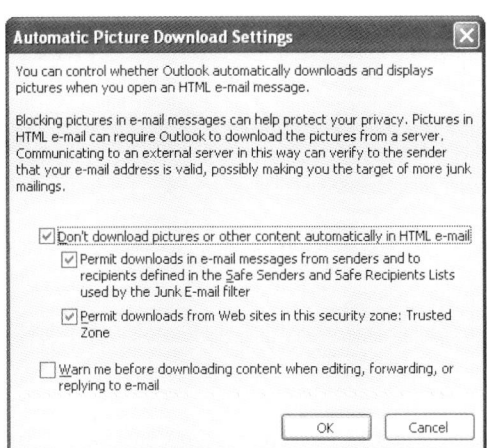

Figure 4.21
Outlook automatic picture download settings.

will go ahead and download them anyway if you subsequently forward or print the message. There must be some logic here, but I cannot quite fathom it. We will return to discuss Web beacons in Chapter 5; Outlook Web Access also blocks downloads (see section 5.4).

If, like me, spammers generate intense annoyance and you want to take action against people who send you unwanted email, you can take out an account with an antispam company and use it to report spammers to the carriers that facilitate their email. It is important to use a "blind" email account to report spam, because spammers generally welcome responses, since they prove that their messages are getting through. In my case, I use a www.spamcop.net account. To report a message, you paste details of the message's path from its header into a form on the antispam site, which then analyzes the header data to determine whether the originator is a known spammer or otherwise exhibits the attributes of a potential spammer. You can then decide to send messages to the administrator of the domains that carried the message along its path to your domain. As shown in Figure 4.22, I used the Options menu when viewing a message to see the header information and then pasted it into spamcop.net, which reported that the message came through a site included on several lists of well-known spammers. Fighting spammers by protesting their activities through sites such as spamcop.net seems to reduce the amount of spam, possibly because these people do not like anyone to report their activities to ISPs that host their activities.

Of course, Outlook's junk mail processing technology is not available to you if you do not have Outlook 2003. If you use an earlier version of Outlook and want to suppress spam, you have to consider third-party add-on products such as Sunbelt Software's IHateSpam (www.sunbeltsoftware.com),

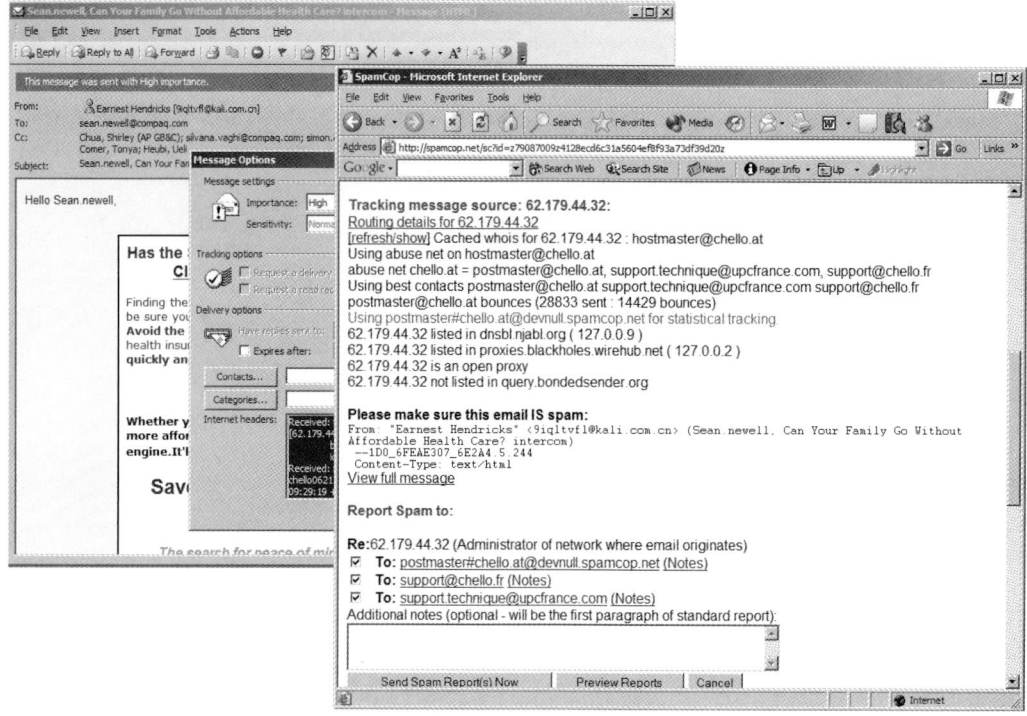

Figure 4.22   *Checking a suspected Outlook message for spam.*

which supports Outlook 2000 and 2002. Deploying add-on products is not a popular option with system administrators because of the purchase cost, work to deploy the utility to desktops, and ongoing support, but it is certainly something you may have to look at if spam becomes a major problem. The alternative is to plan an early upgrade to Outlook 2003, an option that also incurs cost but at least you end up with the functionality that is part of the base Outlook product supported by Microsoft.

4.6.3   More about rules

Outlook 2003 does not deliver much in terms of extra functionality for rules and you are still restricted to a 32-KB limit for the maximum size of server-side rules for a mailbox. Exchange lore suggests that this limit is because of a MAPI RPC restriction, but, in fact, it is due to the Store, which assumes that data passes in chunks of 32 KB or less. However, no equivalent limit exists for the number of client-side rules that Outlook supports. Outlook 2003 does allow users to create rules based on a message. The idea is that it is a lot easier for users to pick a message and say that they

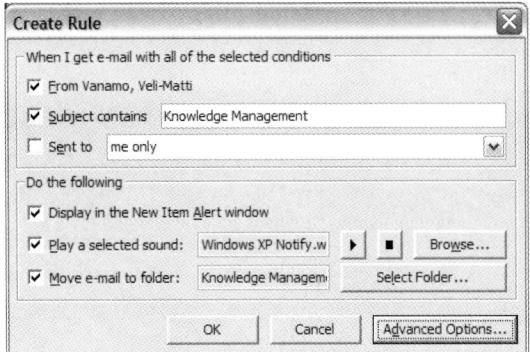

Figure 4.23
Creating a rule from a message.

would like to process similar messages automatically. You can, therefore, select a message and then right-click and take the "Create Rule" option to begin creating a rule based on the message. As you can see in Figure 4.23, Outlook prepopulates a dialog with information extracted from the message. You can amend the details, like defining a folder for Outlook to refile the message into, or click on Advanced Options to work with the normal Rules Wizard.

4.7 The Offline Address Book (OAB)

The OAB is a point-in-time snapshot that holds address and other information about mail-enabled objects fetched from the AD. MAPI clients can download the OAB to enable offline validation of addresses in message headers. In fact, you have to download the OAB before you can do more than just read email offline. Apart from restricting access to a smaller set of properties for users and contacts than they can see in the online GAL, users perceive no practical difference between the GAL and OAB, since the AD is the common source. If you opt to download full details from the OAB, all the information presented on the pages that hold General (Figure 4.24), Phone/Notes, and email address properties is available online or offline. However, any data that depends on pointers to other directory objects is unavailable offline. This includes organizational data, such as pointers to AD objects for managers and their direct reports, and group (distribution list) membership. Distribution groups are collections of pointers to other user, contact, and group objects. Customized attributes that you may have added to the AD, such as an employee number or location code, are also unavailable in the OAB. OWA shares some of the same restrictions, so you cannot, for instance, view the contents of a distribution group through the GAL that OWA presents.

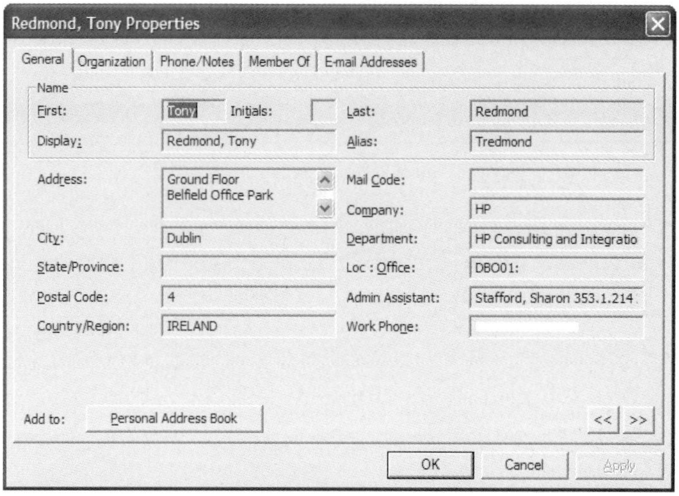

Figure 4.24
Viewing details of a user in the OAB.

Outlook clients fetch the OAB with the Tools–Send/Receive–Download Address Book option, which invokes the dialog shown in Figure 4.25. You can minimize the amount of data downloaded by selecting the "No Details" option, but this makes the OAB much less useful. You can still validate email addresses, but other useful data, such as the X.509 certificates that contain public keys for users registered for advanced security, is only available when you select the "Full Details" option.

As with other synchronization operations, Outlook 2000 and XP use a background thread to download the OAB files, allowing users to continue working while the download proceeds. By comparison, earlier clients "lock"

Figure 4.25
Options to download the OAB.

4.7 The Offline Address Book (OAB)

the PC by exclusively downloading until everything is complete. Since any download can take a long time if files are very large, or when you have to use a slow dial-up connection, using a background thread is a much better approach.

Outlook 2002 introduces the concepts of "Send and Receive" groups, which you can use to define how you want synchronization to proceed: which folders to synchronize, filters to apply, and whether or not you want to download the OAB. The default is to download a new copy of the OAB each time you synchronize folders. This is good in that you always have an up-to-date OAB, but any synchronization will take much longer if the OAB is large. After you move to Office XP, review what your send and receive groups are set up to actually copy before launching any synchronization. My preference is to make OAB download an explicit action, so you either should define a special send and receive group that includes the OAB or use the Tools–Send/Receive–Download Address Book option whenever you want an updated copy.

Outlook 2003 downloads the OAB automatically, but only if you elect to use the local cache and have a fast connection. In this case, Outlook checks daily (you cannot change the frequency of this check) to see whether the OAB has changed. The time that these updates occur varies from client to client to ensure that Exchange is not swamped by many clients attempting a download at the same time.

If updates are available on the server, Outlook automatically downloads the differences and applies them to the local OAB. If Outlook 2003 discovers that it does not have an OAB available when it first creates an OST file, it attempts to download the OAB from the server. If the download fails, Outlook continues to attempt downloads of updates to the OAB every hour until it succeeds. If Outlook needs to fetch a full OAB, it will only attempt this once in a 13-hour period. In both cases, an attempt is counted if Outlook can connect to Exchange and begin a download.

The description to date is true for LAN-quality or "Fast" connections. If you connect over a slow connection, such as a dial-up telephone link, you must explicitly instruct Outlook to download the OAB in the normal manner. In either case, you can disable automatic OAB downloads by setting the "DownloadOAB" DWORD registry value to 0 at the following registry location:

```
HKCU\Software\Policies\Microsoft\Office\11.0\Outlook\
Cached Mode
```

Chapter 4

Administrators can include a setting in a group policy to control automatic OAB downloads. In this instance, the "DownloadOAB" DWORD value is placed at:

```
HKCU\Software\Policies\Microsoft\Office\11.0\Outlook\
Cached Mode
```

If set, users who do not have administrative permission on the PC will not be able to affect the way that Outlook downloads the OAB. In either case, you can configure Outlook to flag a warning before it begins to download the OAB through the "Allow Full OAB Prompt" DWORD value at:

```
HKCU\Software\Microsoft\Exchange\Exchange Provider
```

Set the value to 1 to see the prompt. The default behavior is 0, meaning that you never see a prompt.

Some companies that have large user populations that typically work offline and connect over slow links include the OAB as part of a standard client kit along with Windows and other applications. Each time they install a client kit onto a new PC, it gets a copy of the latest OAB so the user does not have to download the OAB. This approach is very viable, because the OAB is just a set of files and all you have to do is make sure to place the files in the right folder on the PC. People still have to download updated versions to ensure that they can address email to new users, but at least they will only have to download the differences rather than the complete OAB. For me, the inability of Outlook to escalate searches intelligently to the online GAL (if required by the user) to discover (and insert into the OAB) details of new users causes frequent annoyance and spoils the impact of the OAB somewhat. You can make a registry change to force Outlook to use the online GAL, but this then works for every lookup and not just for those that cannot be found in the OAB (see section 4.7.2). While poor search escalation seems a small complaint, it is surprising how often this situation occurs, and I cannot address messages to the newly added users, contacts, or groups until after Exchange regenerates the OAB and I download the updates. Of course, it is possible to send messages to the SMTP addresses of the new entries, if you know the addresses, which is not always possible. Given that Exchange generates updates daily and that an Outlook 2003 client downloads changes daily (by default), the maximum time between a change appearing in AD and then downloaded to the OAB is 48 hours. However, this means that the client would have to download the OAB just as the server is updating the OAB files from AD, and this is unlikely. It is more common to make changes in the AD during the day; Exchange then builds the OAB the following morning, and clients download updates the following day, resulting in a delay of approximately 24 hours before you see new or updated entries in the OAB.

An outdated OAB can result in incorrectly addressed messages, either sent to users who are no longer in the organization or who have changed their email address for some reason. It would be good if the Outlook download options provided some idea of the age of the OAB by displaying the date of the last download, since you would then know if the OAB needs a refresh. Even better, Outlook could generate a reminder to download the OAB according to a user-defined schedule or if Outlook considered the OAB to be too outdated to use. Maybe we will see these options appear in a future version, but until then you will have to remember to download the OAB at regular intervals. In most organizations, it is sufficient to download monthly, although it may be a good idea to download more frequently during a migration or other period of flux, such as when companies merge or divest business units.

As you can see in the bottom part of Figure 4.26, the six ANSI format *.OAB files that contain the HP OAB (in June 2004) span approximately 211.4 MB. Hidden recipients are not included in the OAB, so this data represents the 285,000 entries (mail-enabled accounts, contacts, and groups) in the HP GAL. Note that Windows hides OAB files by default, so if you want to see them, you have to set Windows Explorer to reveal hidden and system files. From this data, we can conclude that a reasonable back-of-the-envelope calculation to work out the likely size of an OAB for an organization is roughly 1 MB for every 1,000 entries.

The top part of Figure 4.26 shows the OAB files on the server, where they are stored in a public folder. The public folder is a replica of the master folder, which is located on the server that generates the OAB. We will discuss the process of OAB generation later on in this chapter. For now, all we need to know is that the server holds the OAB in a series of items within the folder. Exchange compresses the files, so that they are roughly one-third the size they occupy on disk. For example, you can see a 60 MB file in the bottom of the public folder contents. When expanded, this becomes the 144 MB UDETAILS.OAB file on disk. Note the URL used to view the contents of the public folder through OWA. You can use a similar URL to view the data on any server that holds a replica of the OAB folder.

UDETAILS.OAB (or DETAILS.OAB) is usually the largest file, since it contains all of the detailed information displayed in the GAL (email addresses and so on). During a full OAB download, Outlook creates a temporary file called DETAILS.TM_. In this case, the compressed details file was approximately 70 MB. After it downloads the compressed versions of

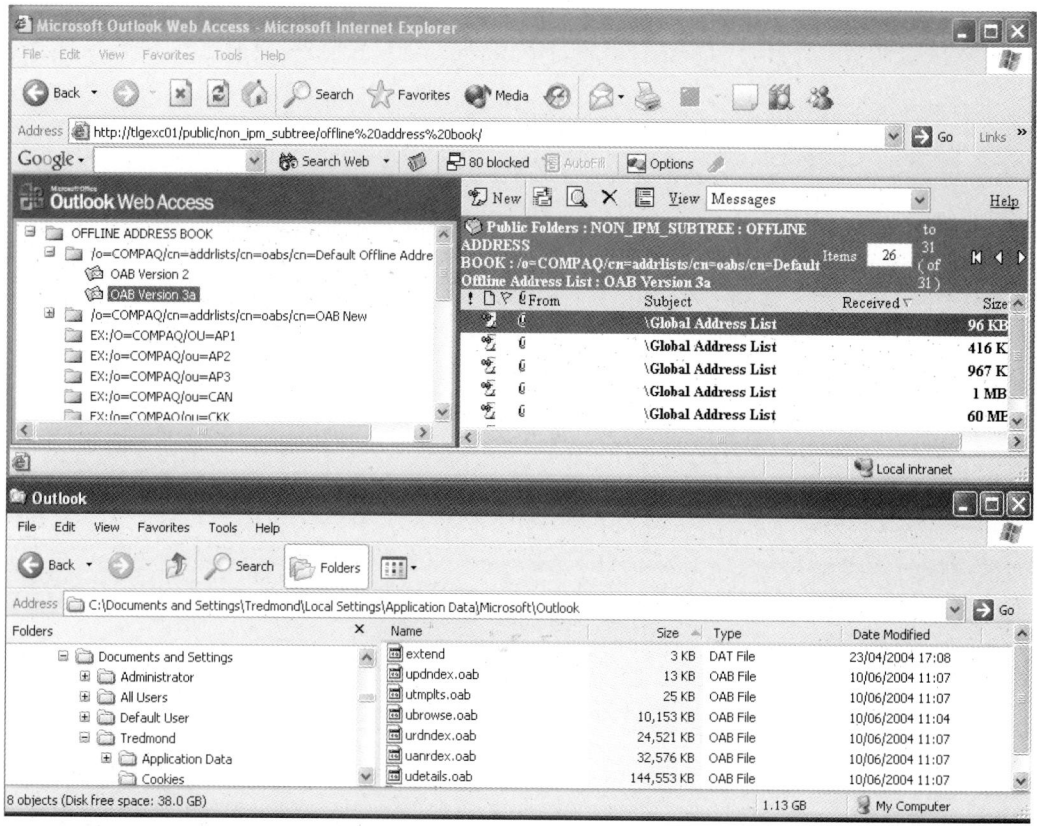

Figure 4.26   *OAB files.*

the six OAB files, Outlook expands them to create a set of .TMP files, such as DETAILS.TMP. Outlook 2003 works differently, since it creates the .TMP files immediately and then populates their contents. If the download is successful, Outlook renames the .TMP files to replace the old .OAB files, and, as you can see, the 70-MB compressed version of the details file expanded to approximately 124 MB. By comparison, a details file that does not contain the detailed information for GAL entries (an oxymoron) is 65 MB, so you can expect to double the size of the file if you download the full version.

Even with compression, downloading such a large OAB can take a very long time to complete, especially over a slow connection. At HP, even over a WAN link, downloading a complete copy of the OAB can take up to 15 minutes. The time required to fetch the OAB depends on the closeness of the nearest public folder server that holds a replica of the OAB. Clearly, if

4.7 The Offline Address Book (OAB)

you have to navigate a transatlantic link to fetch a copy, the time necessary to connect and download increases. In situations where you have very large OAB files or the AD changes to such an extent that clients have to fetch large files or even complete OABs regularly, you may want to use the registry changes described earlier to limit automatic daily downloads and instead ask users to download on an as-needed basis. The problem here is that users will invariably forget to download updates and so will operate with outdated OABs, but this may be a lesser evil than having to cope with excessive demand on the server or network as they cope with client downloads. It is, therefore, a good idea to monitor server and network load as you add Outlook 2003 clients to your system.

To speed downloads, Exchange 2003 reduces the size of the OAB by eliminating a number of certificates that OABGEN includes when you download an OAB with "full details." Microsoft realized that Outlook never uses these certificates, so there is no point in including them in the OAB. In some organizations, this simple change reduced the size of the OAB by 25 percent to 30 percent, while others will see a smaller reduction. In HP's case, the reduction was around 10 percent.

Unless your OAB is very out-of-date or corrupt in some way, you normally do not need to download the complete OAB. Instead, select the option to download changes since the last download, which means that Outlook downloads a smaller differences file and then applies updates to the local OAB files. The size of the differences file depends on the number of changes applied to the directory, but it should always be much smaller than a full download. For instance, the typical differences file at HP is around 5 MB. However, because it is more efficient, Outlook always downloads a full copy of the OAB if changes have been made to more than 12.5 percent (approximately) of the total directory entries since the last full download. For example, when HP merged with Compaq, the directories from the Exchange organizations run on both companies[3] synchronized to form a common GAL. Obviously, the next time users attempted to download changes to the OAB, a lot more than 6 percent of the directory had changed, so they had to download a complete copy of the OAB. Adding a new administrative group to the organization also causes clients to download a complete OAB, even if only a few changes have occurred to other GAL entries. Table 4.8 lists the files that form the OAB. Refer to Figure 4.26 to see the relative sizes of these files.

---

3. At the time, HP ran Exchange 5.5 and Compaq ran Exchange 2000.

Table 4.8 *OAB Data Files*

File	Use
BROWSE.OAB or UBROWSE.OAB	Browse file
DETAILS.OAB or UDETAILS.OAB	Details of users and contacts
RDNDEX.OAB or URDNDEX.OAB	Index
PDNDEX.OAB or UPDNDEX.OAB	Index file
ANRDEX.OAB or UANRDEX.OAB	Index (search) file for ambiguous name resolution
TMPLTS.OAB or UTMPLTS.OAB	Addressing templates

Outlook 2003 uses a "divisor" to know the percentage of change that must occur within the OAB before it invokes a full download. The default divisor is 8, or 12.5 percent. You can change this value to alter download behavior. To do this, use regedit to create a new (or update an existing) DWORD value called "OAB Dif Divisor" under the key:

```
HKLM\Software\Microsoft\Exchange\Exchange Provider
```

Set the value of the DWORD to be the divisor you want to use to govern full OAB downloads. For example, a divisor of 4 means that you only want full OAB downloads after 25 percent of the full OAB changes. A value of 2 means that you are happy to wait until 50 percent changes, and so on. If the value is set to 0, Outlook uses 16 (6.25 percent) to avoid any problems caused by attempting to divide by 0.

Within the OAB, distinguished names in the format used by Exchange 5.5[4] (rather than the format used by the AD) identify objects, and clients write the distinguished names fetched from the OAB into message headers after they validate addresses. Using distinguished names in this way allows the display names of users, contact, or group to change without rendering OAB entries invalid. Using Exchange-format distinguished names may seem strange, but it allows Microsoft to maintain backward compatibility, not only in the OAB but also in MAPI profiles, and allows users to reply to messages originally sent on older servers. An attribute called Legacy-ExchangeDN provides the magic. This attribute stores the older form of distinguished name for AD objects and participates in address validation through the ambiguous name resolution process. Therefore, when an Out-

---

4. For example: /O=Organization/OU=Site-Name/CN=Recipients/CN=Tony-Redmond.

look client reconnects after creating some offline messages, Exchange revalidates the addresses by searching the AD using the LegacyExchangeDN attribute.

4.7.1 OAB generation process

One selected server generates the OAB for an organization, storing the OAB in a system public folder. By default, this is the first server installed in an Exchange organization, but you can move the OAB generation process to any server you like. A component called OABGEN, which runs as part of the System Attendant process, generates the OAB according to the schedule determined for the Default Offline Address List. By default, the OABGEN job executes at 4:00 A.M. every morning, but you can schedule this for a different time. Most companies are happy to generate an update nightly, especially during periods of migration when mailboxes move between servers or other user details are changing rapidly. After the migration completes and things settle down, you may wish to schedule a less frequent update depending on the rate of change within the corporate directory. There is no compelling case to generate an OAB more than daily, since this only incurs an additional server overhead to build the OAB files and network overhead to replicate the updates around the organization.

You can modify the properties of the Default Offline Address List to change the OAB server, include other address lists (the default is to build the OAB from the GAL—see Figure 4.27), or change the schedule that the System Attendant follows when it updates the OAB. You can also force an immediate rebuild of the OAB by selecting the list and using the "Rebuild" option from the context-sensitive menu. For example, you may find that the public folder does not contain any OAB data (some bugs have caused this in the past), or you might have added a large amount of new directory entries and wish to generate a fresh OAB.

On an Exchange 2000 server, the System Attendant process generates the OAB files as posts (with attachments) in a public folder called "OAB Version 2" (Figure 4.28). Version 2 indicates that an earlier format exists, but this format is now obsolete and you only need an OAB in this format if you have to support Exchange 4.0 and 5.0 servers. In an Exchange 2003 environment, you will also find an "OAB Version 3a" folder to contain the new unicode-format version of the OAB, which is currently only supported by Outlook 2003. Each time OABGEN runs, it creates a new, full version of the OAB in one post and another post that contains the differences

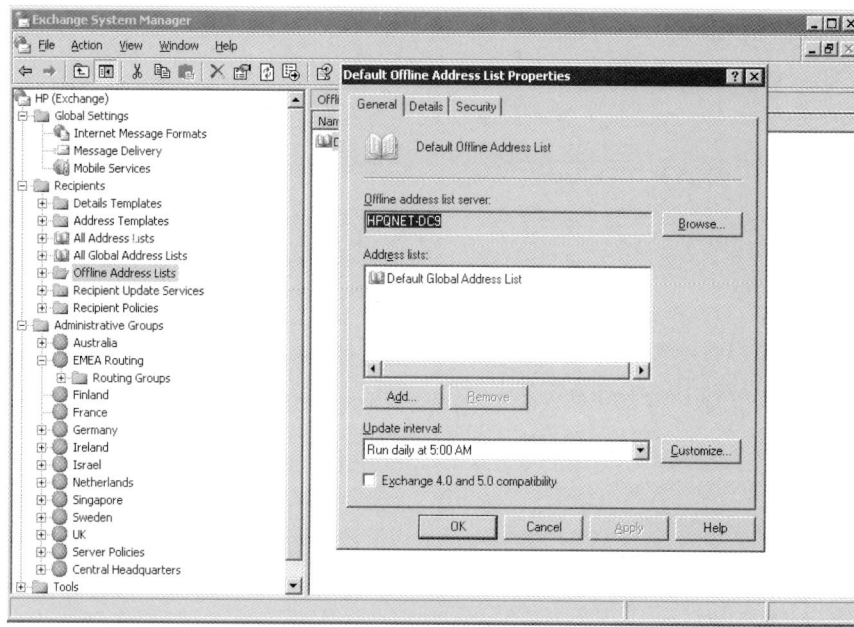

Figure 4.27   *OAB properties via ESM.*

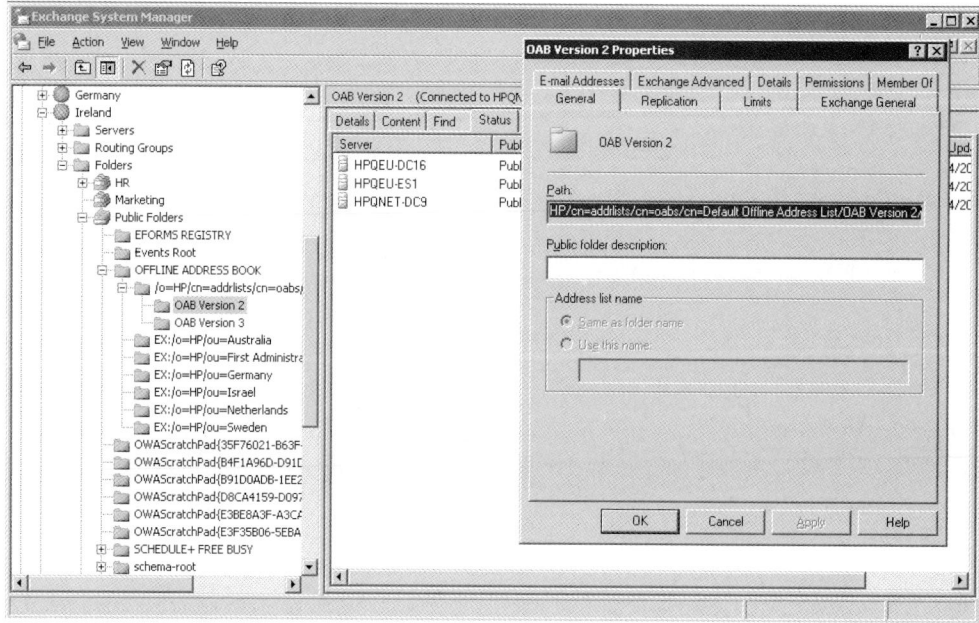

Figure 4.28   *The OAB public folder.*

between the current full version of the OAB and the previous version. Thus, the public folder ends up containing a set of posts: one for the full OAB and one for the set of differences. Attachments to the posts contain the full detail information that clients can opt to download.

When clients connect to request an OAB download, they fetch either the full OAB or just the message objects in the OAB folder that contain the differences since the last time they updated their on-disk copy of the OAB. The OAB system folder has a default aging limit of 30 days, so it can keep up to 30 days of changes as older generations are automatically removed. If a client, therefore, needs to download more than 30 days of change data, he or she will be unable to find all the necessary data and must download a complete copy of the OAB. The client downloads the OAB data to temporary files in the directory where it stores the OAB files, and then decompresses the information before applying changes to the client files. Alternatively, if a full OAB is required, the client downloads the data and decompresses it into the set of OAB files on disk. Note that Outlook 2003 and Outlook 2003 allow only one type of download per day. In other words, if you opt to download the OAB with no details and then decide that you really should have taken the full OAB, you have to wait until the next day before Outlook is able to download the full OAB.

If you have multiple administrative groups in your organization, you will probably want to create copies of the OAB on more than one server, so that users can connect to a server in a local routing group to fetch a copy of the OAB. Exchange uses normal public folder replication to replicate copies of the OAB data to different servers around the organization. To minimize network traffic and speed client downloads, you should arrange to replicate copies of the OAB to a server in every routing group. To view the current replication status, proceed as follows:

- Select the administrative group that holds the default public folder hierarchy.
- Select "View System Folders" from the context-sensitive menu.
- Expand the Offline Address Book folder.
- Select the folder named o=org/cn=addrlists/cn=oabs/cn=Default Offline Address List (the internal pointer to the OAB Version 2 and OAB Version 3 folders) and view its properties.

Figure 4.29 shows the view of the OAB folder through ESM (Exchange 2003). In this case, there are two subfolders: one for the version of the OAB used by pre-Outlook 2003 clients (OAB Version 2) and one for the unicode-format version that Outlook 2003 can use (OAB Version 3a). You can

Figure 4.29
OAB replica synchronization.

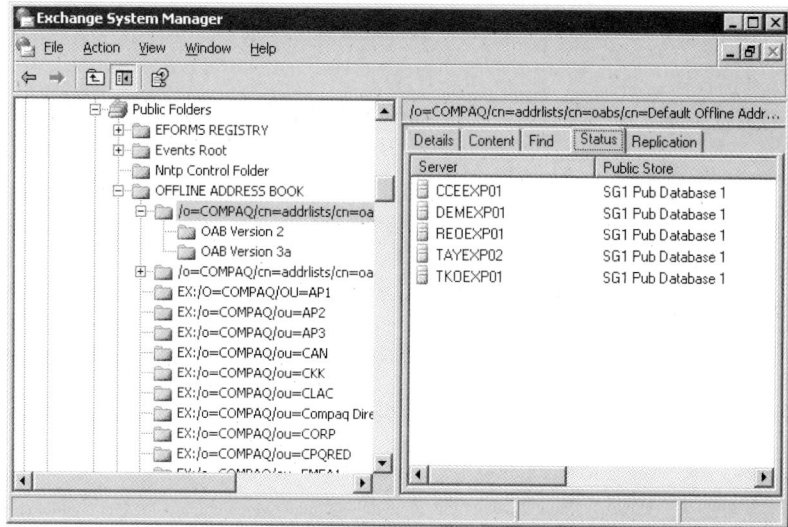

click on the Status tab to list the current servers to which Exchange is replicating the OAB. To add a new server, select the OAB, view its properties, and then use the Add button to add a server to the replica list. Replication normally proceeds at the same schedule used for other public folders. In some cases, administrators place public folders in a specific administrative group to isolate the management tasks associated with public folders, such as replication. This is a good technique to use if you want to restrict public folder management and stop people from creating excessive replication traffic or setting up multiple public folder hierarchies.

In passing, it is worth noting that the other entries (beginning with EX:/O=) listed underneath the Offline Address Book folder shown in Figure 4.29 are legacy versions of the OAB generated by Exchange 5.5 sites. The Exchange OAB is an organizational-wide entity, while previous versions generated an OAB per site. Once an administrative group is fully migrated to Exchange 2000 or 2003, you can safely remove the OAB for the original Exchange 5.5 site.

If you have problems generating or replicating the OAB, you may have a corrupt set of files in the system folder. You can either regenerate the OAB through the "rebuild" option or delete and recreate the offline address list in the Offline Address Lists container. In either case, you should increase diagnostic logging to maximum for the OAL Generator component for the MSExchangeSA (System Attendant) service beforehand to see if anything is reported in the event log.

4.7.2 OAB name resolution

In section 2.8.4, we discuss the concept of ANR, or Ambiguous Name Resolution, the process that the AD uses to resolve addresses when they contain some ambiguous information—for example, if a user enters "Tony" and multiple matching entries exist in the directory.

The OAB is a subset of the information contained in the AD, so it should come as no surprise to learn that Outlook can use fewer fields to resolve addresses when it works with the OAB than when it works with an online GAL. Table 4.9 lists the fields involved in address resolution for the GAL and OAB.

The normal behavior for Outlook 2003 is to resolve names against the OAB. However, you can force Outlook to include the online GAL and so be able to resolve addresses against additional fields. This might seem to be a good idea, but there is a substantial downside, because you obviously have to transmit data to a GC server for resolution. Each time you address a message, you generate some RPCs between Outlook and the GC, which can be a huge performance hit. It is, therefore, not a good idea to use online

Table 4.9 *Name Resolution with the GAL and OAB*

Field	Online GAL	OAB
Displayname	Yes	Yes
Mail	Yes	No
givenName	Yes	No
legacyExchangeDN	Yes	No
mailNickname	Yes	Yes
physicalDeliveryOfficeName	Yes	Yes
proxyAddresses	Yes	No
Name	Yes	No
SAMAccountName	Yes	No
Sn	Yes	Yes
Primary SMTP address	Yes	Yes
Primary X.500 address	Yes	Yes

address resolution unless you absolutely must, possibly because of user demand for validation against custom attributes or another attribute not present in the OAB. If you want to take this step, run regedit on the client PC and create a new DWORD value called "ANR Include Online GAL" under the key:

```
HKCU\Software\Microsoft\Office\11.0\Outlook\Cached Mode
```

Set the value to 1 to include the online GAL. The default value is 0.

4.8 Free/busy information

As important as the OAB is, the free and busy folder is the one that Outlook users use on a far more constant basis to synchronize free and busy data from the calendar folder in the users' accounts with data in the hidden system free/busy folder on the server.

As the name implies, free and busy information is used to track whether someone is available (free) or not (busy) when someone attempts to arrange a meeting at a specific time. As you can see in Figure 4.30, the name of the free and busy system folder is "SCHEDULE+ FREE BUSY," and it acts as a container that holds a separate folder for each administrative group in the organization. By default, a server holds a replica of the folder for the administrative group it belongs to as well as a folder for each of the other administrative groups in the organization. Initially, these folders are just placeholders, but you can replicate free and busy information between administrative groups to facilitate fast lookup of the data. Replication of free and busy information does not incur a huge overhead in terms of data, but it does generate a consistent stream of updated transactions because people usually update their calendars frequently. For example, the free and busy folder for a large administrative group in HP's Exchange organization holds 17,580 entries (one for every MAPI client that connects to a server in the administrative group), amounting to 5.9 MB of data. In public folder terms, this is not a lot of data. Figure 4.31 shows that folders for six administrative groups are present on this server. You will also notice that the naming convention for the folders follows the Exchange 5.5 structure for distinguished names to preserve backward compatibility with older MAPI clients.

Clients publish their free and busy information by updating an item in the system folder and the item takes up approximately 100 bytes in the folder. Updates happen when changes occur in a user's calendar, at regular intervals in between, and when Outlook is logging off from the server. The Outlook calendar options allow users to control how much data the client

4.8 Free/busy information

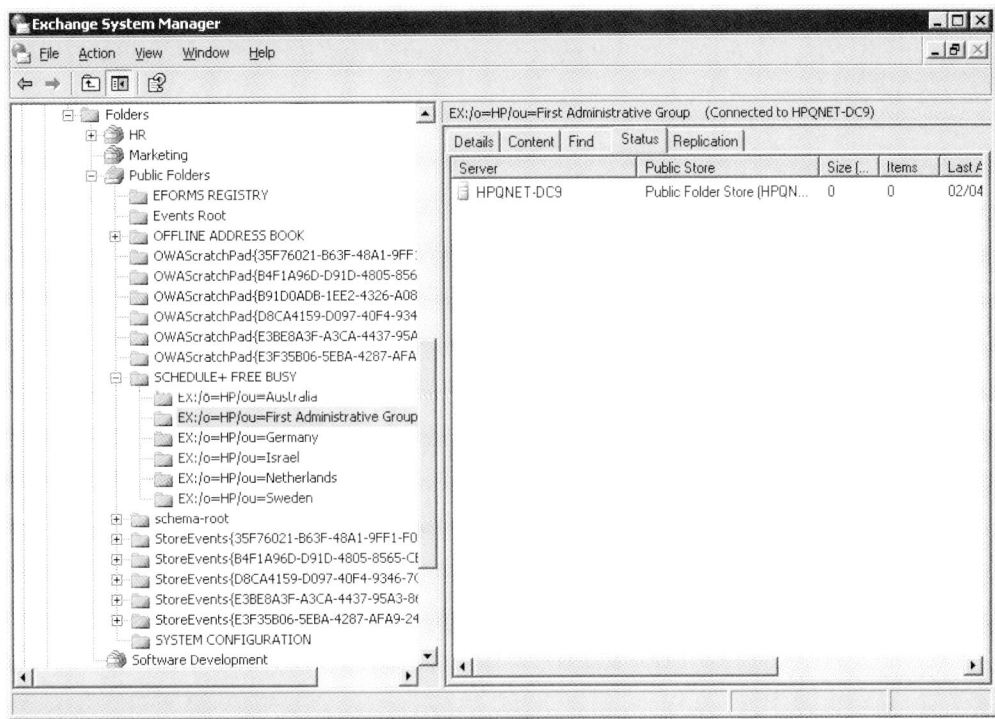

Figure 4.30 *System folders for free and busy information.*

publishes and how often it is refreshed (Figure 4.31). Note the option to publish and search using the Microsoft Office Internet Free/Busy service, which allows you to publish your free/busy information to a server maintained by Microsoft, identifying yourself with a .NET passport. The point here is that users in other Exchange organizations can then see your free/busy information when they schedule meetings. This may not seem like an advantage, but it can be a useful facility for companies that need to work together and cannot formally link their organizations, such as in the due diligence period when companies discuss a merger. Exchange maintains a separate item in the free/busy folder for each user. Technically speaking, Exchange treats the item as a "note" (IPM.Note) and identifies it through its subject, following the convention:

```
USER-/CN=<recipients container>/CN=<mailbox alias>
```

For example, the free and busy item for my user account has a subject line of:

```
USER-/CN=RECIPIENTS/CN=REDMOND
```

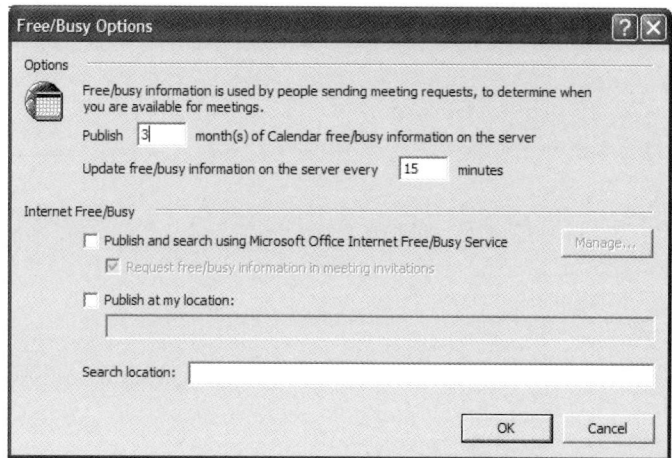

Figure 4.31
Controlling how Outlook publishes free and busy information.

Exchange derives information about the recipients container and mailbox alias from the LegacyExchangeDN attribute in the user's AD account. As you will recall from earlier discussions about distinguished names, the LegacyExchangeDN attribute is used to hold a distinguished name in Exchange 5.5 format to allow applications, such as early versions of Outlook, to continue working with Exchange 2000 and 2003.

Even on large servers that host thousands of users, the naming convention allows Outlook to locate a specific user's record quickly when you attempt to schedule a meeting. To do this, Outlook fetches the target user's distinguished name from the AD through the DSProxy service, which returns a value in the format expected by Outlook (the value held in LegacyExchangeDN). Outlook then reformats the value to create the key to use to search the folder and then attempts to find the record. If it can find no record, Outlook concludes that the user is available for the meeting and displays "No Information" in the Attendee Availability window to show that it could not validate this against free and busy data. This may happen for new users, who have an account but have not yet connected to the server, or for people who use clients that do not support free and busy publication. For example, if you use Outlook Express all the time, your free and busy information will never be updated, so you're always available for meetings!

By default, the age limit for items kept in a free/busy folder is 100 days. Exchange ages out items that clients do not update by connecting to the server and removes the items 100 days after the last update. You can alter the age limit and set a longer or shorter period, but there is no good logic to do so. For example, if you set the age limit to 20 days, people who took

4.8 Free/busy information

long vacations would find that their free and busy information was removed from the server during their vacation. The amount of data that a free and busy folder uses is very small in context of the overage storage of a server, so it is best to leave this folder alone.

Apart from writing some code, there is no obvious way to access the content of the free and busy folder and check that items exist for specific users, or even delete items for accounts that are no longer required. The latter point is moot anyway, because the age limit ensures that the Store removes obsolete records 100 days after you delete an account.

The MDBVU32 (mailbox viewer) utility can be used to examine the internal contents of a mailbox without the user interface applied by a normal client. In other words, you can see the raw data in much the same way as ADSIEDIT allows you to look at information in the AD. MDBVU32 is included in the Platform SDK and uses MAPI calls to log on to a mailbox (you must have the appropriate rights for this) and then walks down through the folder tree to examine the contents of a folder or the properties of an item.

When MDBVU32 starts, it asks for a profile. Any MAPI profile will do. To access the free and busy information, follow these steps:

- Select "OpenMessageStore" from the MDB menu.

- Select "Public Folders" and click the Open button.

- Select "Open Root Folders" from the MDB menu. Two folders are displayed: IPM_SUBTREE and NON_IPM_SUBTREE. The first root hosts all the normal public folders that users expect to see; the second is used for system folders such as the free and busy information. Select NON_IPM_SUBTREE.

- Select "SCHEDULE+ FREE BUSY." You should now see all of the administrative groups in your organization in the child folders window. Select the name of the administrative group you want to examine. If you select an administrative group that does not replicate its free and busy information to your server, the folder will be empty.

You should now be able to see the items in the free/busy folder in the "Messages in Folder" pane. You can now select the free and busy information for a user by double-clicking on the item (using the name, as explained earlier), after which you can look at its properties and so on.

You can also use MDBVU32 to perform maintenance operations, such as deleting old free and busy information. Short of writing your own utility,

MDBVU32 is the best way to see the free and busy information maintained on a server. For example, you can use MDBVU32 to examine the search folders in a mailbox.

By default, free and busy information is not available when Outlook works in offline mode. The data maintained in a local copy of the calendar folder (in the OST) allows users to look at current appointments and create new ones when working offline, but scheduling meetings can be a hit and miss affair, because you never know whether the people you want to meet are busy. A freeware utility called "Offline Free/Busy Application" uses CDO to solve the problem by replicating free and busy information to the PC and providing a custom form to consult the offline data. Of course, the accuracy of the data depends on when it was downloaded to the PC, but the solution is certainly better than nothing. At the time of writing, the utility is available from http://www.slipstick.com/addins/gallery/offlinefb.htm.

4.8.1 Other system folders

Returning to Figure 4.30 for a moment, you can see a number of other system folders along with those that hold free and busy information. These include the following:

- Eforms Registry: a folder used to register electronic forms. This is a holdover from the old-style Exchange forms and is not used much today.

- Events Root: a folder used to hold details of registered events and the users who are allowed to execute or otherwise work with events.

- Schema: a folder used to hold the base Exchange XML (Extensible Markup Language) schema used to reference Exchange objects and their properties in code implemented in server-side events and other consumers of the schema. The folder is populated by a server event from a set of XML files on the server CD.

- Store Events (followed by a GUID): per MDB registry for store event handlers. Before you can activate an event, you must register it in the associated folder or set of folders.

- Offline Address Book: a folder used to hold the files for the Offline Address Book.

- System Configuration: Exchange 5.5 also uses this folder, and it acts as a repository for messages that contain information about basic system configuration that the Store replicates to other servers. Currently, the messages hold information about expiration settings (age limits for public folders) that are active on a server, but Microsoft could expand the folder's use for other purposes in the future.

In most cases, system administrators do not have any reason to do much with the system folders. Leave well enough alone, unless you know what you are doing, is the golden rule here.

4.9 Personal folders and offline folder files

The Exchange Store is the repository for messages and other items created by users. The Store has many notable attributes: high performance, single place to check for incoming virus attacks, availability from any client, and so on. However, from a user perspective, the drawbacks of server-based storage are that each mailbox has a set quota enforced by the Store and that mailboxes are only available when the server is running and the network can connect clients to the server.

You can use personal folder (PST) files to provide additional storage to users, while offline folder files (OST files) enable people to work when a network link is unavailable or they cannot otherwise reach the server.

4.9.1 Personal folders

PSTs reside on either a PC drive or space allocated to users on a network share. You can even create a PST on a floppy disk, a feature that you can use to transfer small amounts of folder data from one PC to another. The concept behind PSTs is a "personal repository," differentiating storage from the server-based mailbox and public folders. PSTs allow users to create and manage their own private document archives. All servers have some storage limitations in terms of either the total available physical disk space or the mailbox quota allocated to individual users. It is easy to run out of space, especially if you are in the habit of creating or circulating messages with large attachments. In these situations, users can reduce their mailboxes under the quota by moving files to a PST.

Up to Outlook 2003, an ANSI-format PST can grow to a maximum of 2 GB, and the new unicode format allows PSTs to expand to fill disks, if you allow them to. The new default size limit is 20 GB (more than enough for even the most fastidious of human packrats), although administrators can limit this to even less than 2 GB by setting the registry keys described in Table 4.10 at:

```
HKEY_CURRENT_USER\Software\Policies\Microsoft\Office\
11.0\Outlook\PST
```

Table 4.10 *Registry Values to Control PST and OST File Sizes*

Name	Value Range	Default Value	Meaning
MaxLargeFileSize	0x00000001–0x00005000	0x00005000 (20,480 in decimal or 20 GB)	Maximum size of a unicode PST or OST
WarnLargeFileSize	0x00000001–0x00005000	0x00004C00 (19,456 in decimal or 19 GB)	Size when Outlook issues warning that a PST or OST is becoming too large
MaxFileSize	0x001F4400–0x7C004400	0x7BB04400 (1.933 GB)	Maximum size for an ANSI-format PST or OST
WarnFileSize	0x00042400–0x7C004400	0x74404400 (1.816 GB)	Size when Outlook issues warning that a PST or OST is becoming too large

All values are DWORDs and expressed in megabytes (unicode format) or bytes (ANSI format). Administrators can control all these values through policies.

Clearly, there are many older Outlook clients in use, so a danger exists that users could attempt to store more than 2 GB in a PST and corrupt the file. Microsoft released preventative fixes in Office XP SP1 and service release 1A for Office 2000. The Office XP fix issues a warning when a PST gets to 1.8 GB, while the Office 2000 fix just stops the file from growing. If you get into a situation where a PST grows past the supported limit, you can use a Microsoft utility called PST2GB[5] to truncate the file. However, truncation will lose data, so it is best to keep PSTs small.

You cannot convert an existing PST file to unicode format, so if you want to use a PST larger than 2 GB, you have to create a new file and populate it from scratch, including dragging and dropping items from older PSTs. People often use PSTs to transfer documents between each other, so remember that older versions of Outlook cannot open unicode-format PSTs and use older format files whenever you need to swap files in this fashion.

Unless it is password-protected, no security credentials are required to open a PST, so you can browse a PC or net share, find a PST, and then open it with any MAPI client, even if it is not associated with your own mailbox. You can set a password on the PST when you create the file (Figure 4.32) or by changing the properties of the PST afterward. You must then provide

---

5. See http://www.microsoft.com/downloads/release.asp?releaseid=44353.

4.9 Personal folders and offline folder files

Figure 4.32
Properties of a PST.

the password before the client can open the file. Microsoft's official policy is that there is no way that they can recover data from a PST if the user forgets his or her password. However, this is a legal rather than a technical issue and you can easily break into a PST through utilities such as PS19UPG, which circulate freely around the Internet. Of course, if an accident happens and you corrupt the PST by using an unsupported utility, you are on your own and Microsoft support will be very unsympathetic.

Encouraging users to work with PSTs is fine as long as they use the same PC all the time and understand their responsibilities to manage and protect data. However, if users move from one PC to another they will leave information behind them. In these situations, server-based storage (which is accessible from any PC, and from any client) is a better solution. One way to accommodate roaming users is to place their PSTs in their directories on a networked file server. If you do this, remember to tell users to always fully log out from each PC they use; otherwise, they will not be able to connect to their PST when they move to another PC. Microsoft did not design the internal structure of a PST to support multiple concurrent accesses.

4.9.2 Mail delivery to personal folders

You can configure Outlook to deliver new messages to a PST through the Delivery tab of the client Tools | Options menu option (Outlook 98 or 2000) or by selecting the PST file as the preferred mail delivery location, as shown in Figure 4.33 (Outlook 2002 and later). Rushing to divert messages from your mailbox to a PST is not a good idea, and you should consider a few points before you make what is, to some extent, a radical change in a basic function of the messaging system. When you select the option to

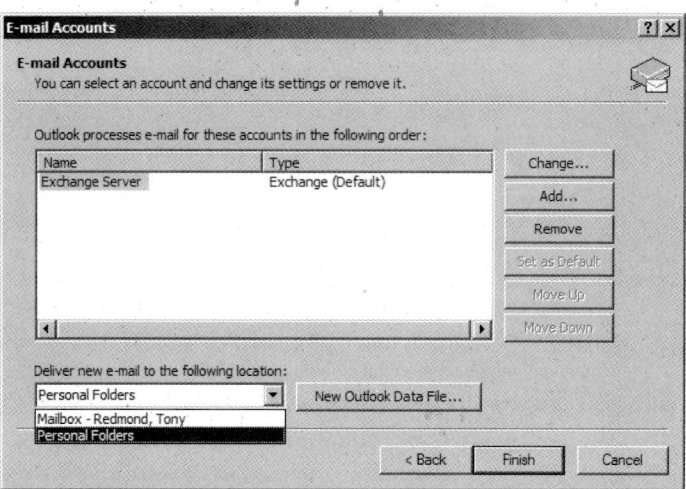

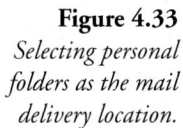
Figure 4.33
Selecting personal folders as the mail delivery location.

deliver messages to a PST, the messages remain in the server mailbox until you connect to the server. Outlook then transfers the messages from the server Inbox folder to an Inbox folder in the PST. After the messages transfer, Exchange deletes them from the mailbox. Some users do not expect this to happen and are very surprised when they look at their server-based Inbox to find that all their mail has apparently disappeared! Of course, the messages are available in the PST, but users often overlook this fact, leading to any number of frantic calls to the help desk to demand the return of the missing messages.

Delivering mail to a PST is similar in concept to the traditional POP3/IMAP4 email model provided by ISPs. This model holds some attractions if you want to build Exchange servers to host very large numbers of mailboxes with a restricted amount of storage. The economics behind hotmail.com would be very different if each user had mailbox quotas of 50 or 100 MB, common allocations in corporate messaging systems.

If server-based mailboxes are used, the space available to each user is constrained by his or her mailbox quota. If PSTs are used, the server's storage is largely transient, because Exchange only holds messages on the server until users connect to fetch messages. Users can therefore be allocated relatively small quotas within the Store (10 MB or less), allowing many more users to be supported on a single server. Delivering messages to PSTs or using PSTs as secondary storage was much more common in the early days of Exchange, but cheaper hardware and software that is more functional have reduced the attractiveness of these options. Given the relatively low cost of disk storage and the ability to partition the Store, most Exchange designers now choose to deploy server-based storage and have downgraded the importance and need for PSTs (in this respect).

Additionally, multiple client access has become increasingly important. Exchange 4.0 offered a single client and single access protocol (MAPI). Exchange now supports MAPI, IMAP, POP3, and Web clients, but only MAPI clients can use PSTs. If you opt to deliver mail to a PST, then you immediately restrict your options for client deployment, so you lose much of the value of being able to make an occasional connection to your mailbox with Outlook Web Access, since only new messages are kept there. Diverting incoming email to a PST also eliminates the effect of the shared message model, which is not quite as important now as it was in the past.

The arrival of email-enabled viruses creates yet another factor for administrators to consider. There are many server-based antivirus agents, all of which are able to protect thousands of mailboxes from a single point. Microsoft has utilities to scan a complete mailbox store to find and disinfect viruses, but no utilities exist to scan multiple PSTs for viruses. If a virus arrives and passes by an outdated virus detection pattern and is intended for delivery to hundreds of PSTs, you will have a huge amount of work to track down each instance of the virus and eliminate it.

It is a fact that you can only read a message delivered to a PST if you have physical access to the PST. In other words, an administrator who can access the contents of server-based mailboxes cannot see the messages in the PST unless he or she can access them. The only messages that remain in the mailbox are those that have arrived since the last time the user connected and picked up mail.

In cases where the PSTs used for mail delivery are located on networked file services, the responsibility for backing up the PSTs remains with the system administrators. Backing up individual PSTs is easier than backing up a very large mailbox store, chiefly because there is a wider range of backup software available that is capable of processing individual files (the PSTs). Restoring an individual file from a backup tape is much easier than restoring a user mailbox from a backup of the Store, and this fact alone makes the use of PSTs something to consider if you do not run a backup program that supports bricked backups and restores (and, indeed, uses the facility).

While on this point, it is interesting to note that MAPI clients automatically disconnect from a PST after 30 minutes of inactivity, allowing system administrators to plan to take file-level backups of PSTs stored on a network share even if users leave their PCs logged on (hopefully protected by a password-enabled screen saver). The next time a client operation commences that uses an item in the PST, the client automatically reestablishes the connection.

Table 4.11 lists the pros and cons of using PSTs.

Some installations encourage users to view their server mailbox as a repository for working documents, a place that holds information that must

Table 4.11 *Pros and Cons of Using PSTs*

Pros	Cons
A PST can be stored on any available device, including floppy disks.	You cannot share a PST between users. For example, you cannot use a PST to share documents between a manager and a secretary. Users who leave a PC logged on can inadvertently block their own access to a PST if they move to another PC.
PSTs can be used to transfer files between users, including users in different Exchange organizations.	You can encrypt a PST to protect its content against other users, but if the password is lost, there is no supported way to recover it. However, unsupported utilities exist that can crack PST passwords.
An "old format" PST can expand to any size up to a theoretical 2-GB limit, subject to available disk space. The largest PST in use is well over 1 GB (there is a limit of 64,000 items in a single folder). A unicode-format PST can grow much larger than 2 GB. Thus, PSTs allow users to hold more information, so they become a more attractive personal archive.	Delivering mail to a PST removes the benefit of single-instance storage (within a single mailbox store). In addition, unless you use Outlook 2003, double the space is required to store a message, because the PST holds items in both RTF and ASCII format.
You can back up PSTs with any file-level backup utility.	If you use PSTs, make sure that someone is actually backing up the files on a regular basis. There is an increased chance of message corruption, because there is no rollback/transaction log mechanism available for PSTs, so you may need to go back to a backup to recover data.
PSTs are easier to restore than a complete mailbox store.	You cannot send deferred mail messages unless you connect the client to the server.
The Auto-Archive feature in the Outlook client uses PSTs to store archived items.	Inbox Assistant rules are not processed unless the client is connected to the server.
PSTs provide an easy way for Microsoft Mail users to move to Exchange, because they can convert MMF files to PSTs.	There is a decreased ability for system administrators to monitor disk use, because messages and other items can be stored on the server and scattered across user PSTs.

4.9 Personal folders and offline folder files

Table 4.11 *Pros and Cons of Using PSTs (continued)*

Pros	Cons
The EXMERGE utility uses PSTs to move mailbox contents between servers.	Extra network traffic is generated to move information to and from PSTs. Messages for delivery to a PST are held on the server until a client connects, and if a lot of mail is waiting the initial connect can take a long time.
	You can only access PSTs from MAPI clients.
	The ESM "Move Mailbox" option does not move items stored in PSTs. If you move users to a new server, you may also have to move their PSTs to a suitable local file share.
	It's difficult to come up with a good strategy to clean items infected by a virus if they are delivered to a PST.
	PSTs may not be available to roving users—for example, people who want to work with the same data at home and in the office.

be available no matter which client they use to connect to the server. According to this model, users are supposed to move items to a PST once the files are no longer current or become less important. The model assumes a fair amount of discipline on the part of users, something that is not always easy to find. It also devolves responsibility for data security to users after data transfers to user control. One of the undoubted advantages of server-based storage is the assurance that someone else will take care of backing up all your important data. People are not that good when the time comes to create backups or copies of local data on a PC.

4.9.3 Configuring PSTs

Users are not limited to connecting to a single PST, and you can configure multiple PSTs for use, perhaps having one file on a networked file service and another on the local PC disk, with maybe a third on a floppy disk. Putting a PST on a floppy disk may seem strange, but it is certainly a valid method to transfer files from one PC to another or from one user to another. You must configure each PST individually in the MAPI profile. By default, the display name of each PST is "Personal Folders," so things can get slightly confusing if you do not change the name afterward to reflect the intended use of the PST. For example, use names such as "Network Personal Folders," "Archived Folders," "Mail Folders," and so on. You can eas-

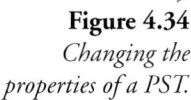

Figure 4.34
Changing the properties of a PST.

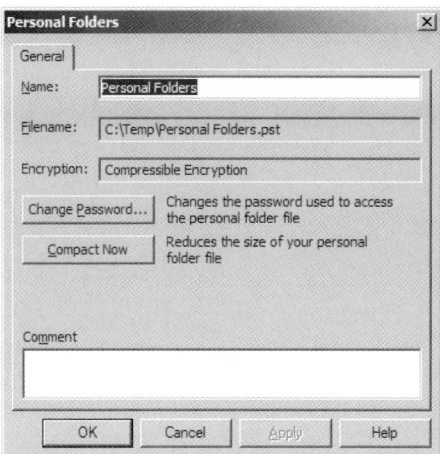

ily change the display name of a PST through Outlook by selecting the PST and then bringing up its properties, as shown in Figure 4.34. Administrators are unable to configure or control PSTs through ESM. Remember: These are *personal* folders.

Users moving to Exchange from old LAN-based mail systems such as Microsoft Mail or Lotus cc:Mail often find PSTs a very natural extension of the mode of working they are used to. It is normal with LAN-based email systems for clients to download messages from a post office to a local mailbox file. With Exchange server, the opposite is true, since the recommended way of working is to leave messages on the server rather than moving them to the PC. Users can move messages to a PST if they wish, albeit through a drag-and-drop operation rather than having the mail system do it automatically. Installations moving from LAN-based email systems should carefully consider whether they want to migrate megabytes of user messages to Exchange. In my opinion, it is best to leave messages where they are—on the PC by converting the older format mailbox to a PST. Apart from reducing the demand for server resources, this approach means that users can be migrated to Exchange much more quickly.

Training sessions clearly offer an opportunity to encourage good work habits such as the effective use of PSTs. Trainers can use hint or cheat sheets to brief users on how you would like them to work and so relieve some pressure on server-based resources. As with most features, there are pros and cons that you need to understand before you can make the most effective use of them. Make sure that you understand the impact of these issues before you rush into using PSTs.

4.9.4 PST archiving

Users, despite the suspicions of many system administrators, are only human. As such, they will accumulate mail messages and other items in their mailboxes in the same way as they collect anything else. Some people will be very neat and tidy, maintaining an efficient and effective folder structure. Others will let chaos exist, with messages piling up in folders created for a purpose long forgotten. Most users exist between the two extremes. They do their best to keep their mailboxes reasonably clean, eliminating dead wood from time to time, but, generally, there is a lot of excess information hanging around mailboxes, all occupying valuable space on the server.

Archiving attempts to provide automatic clean-up assistance to users by allowing them to define criteria to control when to move items from the "live" (server-based) store to a "passive" (PST) store. Archiving obsolete email helps to increase overall system performance by reducing the number of items in folders and the overall size of the mailbox stores. The more items in a folder, the slower it is to access. This is especially so for folders such as the Inbox, Journal, and Calendar.

Archiving criteria are age based. In other words, messages become archival candidates after they exceed a certain age: 28 days, 15 weeks, or maybe 6 months. The net effect of moving messages from the live store is to reduce the amount of information held on the server, although you do not reduce the actual physical size of a mailbox store unless you rebuild the database with the ESEUTIL program. Of course, reducing the space occupied by databases is good from a system administrator's point of view. More space is available for new items, optimal use is made of disks, and you reduce backup times.

In Exchange, archiving is client driven and the server plays no great role, apart from processing client requests during the archival process. Outlook is the only client that includes archiving features, either on an automatic basis or on an explicit basis according to criteria defined by the user.

Outlook can archive messages in two ways. First, access the "Archive" option on the File menu to invoke the dialog shown in Figure 3.35 (Outlook 2002 running on Windows XP Professional). The default option reviews the contents of selected folders (and subfolders) and archives any items contained in the folders that are older than a specified date. The items are archived immediately into the archive file, which is a PST located on any available disk.

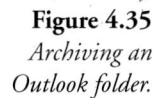

Figure 4.35
Archiving an Outlook folder.

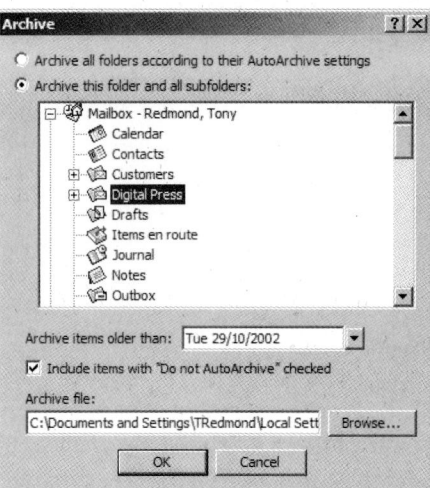

Alternatively (by clicking the first radio button in the dialog), you can scan all folders in the mailbox and process items according to the auto-archive settings (Figure 4.36). Auto-archive settings can be set on an individual folder-by-folder basis, or you can apply the same criteria to all folders. Note that Outlook archives items based on a message's last modified date rather than the received or created date. The following actions change an item's modified date:

- Forwarding
- Replying
- Replying to all
- Editing and saving
- Moving or copying

The second option you can take is to auto-archive, which Outlook runs according to a schedule that you create (Figure 4.36). The default interval is 28 days. When Outlook starts, it checks to see if auto-archiving is enabled and then how long it is since it archived items. If archiving is enabled and the time interval has elapsed, Outlook prompts to determine whether it should begin to process folders.

Auto-archiving can take a long time. The initial implementation of archiving (prior to Outlook 98) suffered because moving items from server to a PST is a slow process. Users who hit the "OK" button when they were given the option to archive quickly learn that the process could take up to 30 minutes to complete (depending on the folders and the number of items

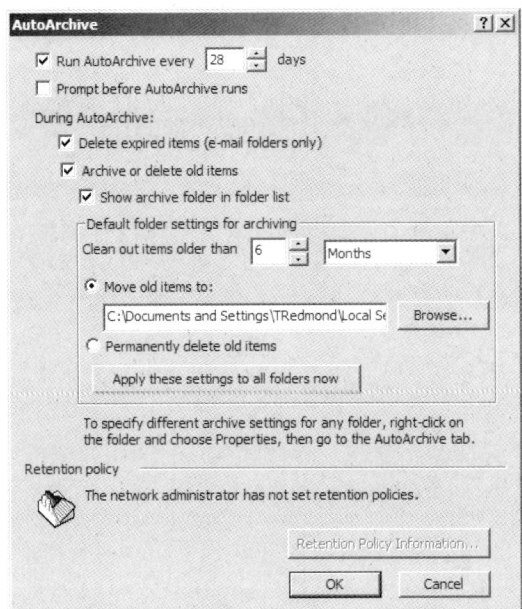

Figure 4.36
Outlook 2002 auto-archive options.

in each folder), and during that time they could do nothing else. Current versions of Outlook perform archiving in a background thread, much like background synchronization. Users can continue to work while archiving proceeds, albeit with reduced response times.

4.10 Offline folder files

We have already met OSTs (offline folder files) and described how Outlook 2003 uses them to support cached Exchange mode. MAPI clients have always used OSTs to work with items without connecting to the server. OST folders are slave replicas of server-based folders. You can compare them to snapshots of the server folders taken at a particular point in time. Essentially, OSTs use the same basic technology as a PST, with the noticeable exception that they automatically encrypt their contents and so require authentication before a client can connect and use the file. The encryption key (based on the MAPIEntryID GUID for the mailbox) exists in two places: in the mailbox on the server and in the user's MAPI profile in the PC's registry. Every time you attempt to work offline afterward, Outlook reads the profile to determine whether the key exists in the registry and matches the value in the OST. As long as the two keys exist and match, you can open an OST with Outlook and synchronize with a mailbox. If you cause them to differ, for example by recreating a profile, the OST becomes invalid and you cannot access its contents.

Not using the right profile is the most common reason for not being able to access an OST. Deleting and recreating the server mailbox is another cause, since this operation changes the master ID, even if the alias, distinguished name, account, and other account properties match. In this instance, the next time you connect to the server, the master ID for the server mailbox will not match the data held in the profile, and Outlook will refuse to load the OST. You can find an "OST recovery utility" at http://www.officerecovery.com/exchange/.[6] The utility works by reading the OST and writing out a PST, which can then be opened as usual. No guarantee is given that you can open every OST and Microsoft does not support its use.

Instead of being a separate and distinct repository, such as PSTs where the contents of the files have no connection to anything on the server, OSTs hold replicas of server-based folders. Outlook automatically creates an OST when you configure a MAPI profile to enable offline to work. The name of the OST is visible by selecting the "Offline Folder File Settings" option when viewing details of the Exchange service in the profile. Table 4.12 contains a more exhaustive list of the basic differences between OSTs and PSTs.

4.10.1 OST synchronization

When Outlook creates an OST, it automatically adds the set of special mail folders (Calendar, Tasks, Inbox, Journal, Notes, Outbox, Sent Items, and Deleted Items). These folders allow you to process messages while disconnected from the server. For example, you can create and send messages or set up meeting requests. Outlook holds the messages in the Outbox folder and automatically sends them through a synchronization process the next time you connect to the server, after which Outlook moves the messages into the Sent Items folder. Outlook automatically checks an OST for outgoing messages that are waiting to be sent each time it connects to Exchange.

By default, unless you use cached Exchange mode with Outlook 2003, the folders in your mailbox are not available offline, so you must select each folder you want individually and then change its synchronization properties. You can also apply a filter so that Outlook only synchronizes selected items. For example, you could decide that you only want to have items less

---

6. At the time of writing, the recovery utility cannot handle a unicode-version OST.

Table 4.12 *Differences between PSTs and OSTs*

	Personal Folders (PSTs)	Offline Folders (OSTs)
Valid Locations	Any DOS device, including floppy diskettes (however, you need read/write access to the media).	Any DOS device.
Storage Type	Permanent, persistent user-managed storage.	Transient storage that is inextricably linked to the contents of the master (server) folders.
Can Be Opened By:	Any MAPI client, using any MAPI user profile.	Any MAPI client but only using the same MAPI profile that originally created the OST.
Synchronization	None—all movement between the PST and other stores is user initiated and performed manually.	Automatic for changes made to offline folder replicas upon each connection to the server. Specific synchronization must be set up for replicas of public folders, or for any user-created folder when connected to the server.
Encryption Options	Optional encryption with a separate password (individually defined for each PST).	By default, OSTs are automatically encrypted. No password is used (because of OST association with the server mailbox).
Managed Through:	By configuring a Personal Folders information service (see the Tools | Service option).	Offline Folder File Settings tab from Advanced properties for the Exchange service (Tools | Services).
Concurrent Access Possible to Multiple PSTs/OSTs?	Yes	No. A PST and OST can be open at the same time, but you cannot open two OSTs concurrently.

than three months old in your offline folders. To do this, you create an appropriate filter for the folder. Note that you can only mark folders from your primary mailbox for synchronization. In other words, if you connect to another user's mailbox to access one of his or her folders (such as the calendar), you cannot replicate any of the folders in that mailbox for use offline. Using a public folder to hold shared calendar or other items is a good workaround because you can synchronize these folders.

You must first mark a public folder as a "favorite" before including it in the synchronization process. Everyone is different when it comes to making decisions about the folders he or she wants to be able to access offline. When the disks on notebook PCs were small (under 2 GB), you certainly couldn't afford to synchronize large numbers of folders, because the resulting OST could quickly fill the entire disk. Now that notebook disks are far larger, the same limitations do not exist and I probably synchronize too many folders. The set includes a group calendar, archive folders that store messages posted to various distribution lists, and public folders that contain presentations and other reference material that are useful to have when on the road. It is very convenient to be able to browse messages sent to large distribution lists when offline, as it is to have copies of folders that contain project information.

You synchronize public folder favorites in the same way as mailbox folders by adding them to a send and receive group (Figure 4.37) or by including them in cached Exchange mode. At the same time, you can specify a filter to restrict the amount of information that Outlook fetches from the public folder. For example, you may only want to synchronize last month's contributions to a distribution list, or ignore items that have attachments larger than a specific size, and so on. The filter becomes active the next time you connect to a server. While Figure 4.37 features Outlook 2002, all clients since Outlook 98 support folder filters for offline synchronization. If in doubt, go to the folder properties and you will be able to set the filter there.

Because OSTs are slave replicas of server folders, you can use them to recover information from accidentally deleted mailboxes. For example,

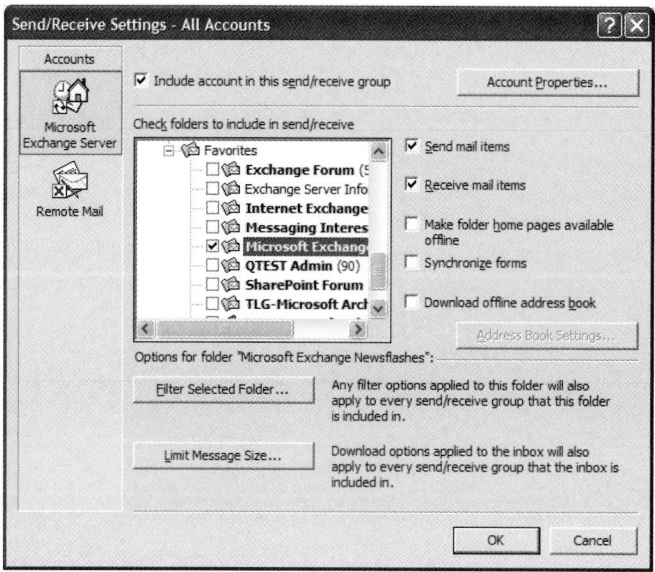

Figure 4.37
Adding a favorite public folder to the offline store.

assume that a system administrator deletes a mailbox, only to discover that it should not have been deleted. If an OST is available, you can start Outlook, work in offline mode, and recover items by copying them from the OST to a PST. Once the copy is finished, log out of Outlook, delete the OST file, and reconnect to the server using a new MAPI profile. The old OST is invalid, because the mailbox ID changes when you recreate the mailbox, so there is no point in attempting to use it. The recovered messages are in the PST, and you can drag and drop the messages from the folders in the PST to folders on the server after you connect to the mailbox. Following that, synchronizing with the newly populated server folders will rebuild a new OST. This technique only works for folders synchronized with the OST, and the server-based "Recover Deleted Mailbox" option should be your first step in situations such as this.

Outlook synchronizes offline folders when you select the Tools | Synchronize option, or by pressing F9. You can synchronize a single selected folder or all folders at one time. Of course, Outlook only synchronizes the special mail folders plus any other folder that you have marked for offline access when you select the "all folders" option. Outlook's journaling feature normally generates a lot of synchronization activity, so this is a good reason to disable it unless you absolutely need the journal.

Over a typical 28.8-Kbps dial-up connection, any version of Outlook prior to Outlook 2003 can take up to five minutes to send 20 or so messages of various sizes, and much longer if you include some large attachments. Improvements mean that Outlook 2003 easily generates the lowest network demand, but otherwise you will wait as you download new messages and perhaps a few public folders. All this activity may result in spending 15 to 30 minutes waiting for the job to complete. Even with widespread availability of VPNs in airports, hotels, and other public locations, it is still good to restrict synchronization activity by limiting the number of folders that you mark for offline access and by limiting the number of items in these folders. If you find yourself spending a lot of time synchronizing, and you have not already upgraded to Outlook 2003, it is time to change—but only if Exchange 2003 is running on the server.

Outlook automatically synchronizes changes you make to offline folders when it connects to a server, transmitting any waiting messages to the server for onward delivery and applying deletes or other changes in the folders marked for synchronization. Outlook also synchronizes changes made to offline replicas of public folders back to the server-based folders. If synchronization errors occur, Outlook captures details in a message in the Deleted Items folder. The most common error is caused by a client not having sufficient permissions to access the contents of a folder; typically this is a public folder, but you can see this error for system folders such as that holding the OAB.

Apart from their obvious use in processing messages, offline folders are very useful for anyone who travels. For instance, you might want to take a copy of all documents relating to a particular project before going on a trip. During the trip, you can browse the data and make any changes that you wish, and when you get back to base, you can synchronize the changes back with the data held in the server-based folder. Conflicts can occur when synchronization is attempted. If this happens, you will have to resolve the conflicts manually by deciding which copy of an item you should keep.

4.10.2 Restricting synchronization traffic

Prior to Outlook 2003, item synchronization occurs at an object level. In other words, if any property of an item is changed, Outlook synchronizes the complete item between the server and OST. This is a logical arrangement, but it does incur a synchronization overhead to update the flags that Outlook maintains to indicate whether you reply to a message or forward it to another user. For example, let us assume that you receive a message containing a 1-MB PowerPoint attachment to review. You connect and synchronize your Inbox and then work offline to read the message. You then decide to reply to the originator with your comments. When you next connect, Outlook sends the reply and must then synchronize a complete copy of the original message because its "replied to" flag is changed. Instead of a quick connect to send a short message, you must incur the overhead as Outlook synchronizes the 1-MB message again. The same is true if you forward the message, since Outlook must update the "forwarded" flag.

Outlook 2003 has a much smarter synchronization mechanism, but you may not be able to deploy this version quickly. Even so, you can make synchronization less demanding by instructing earlier versions of Outlook not to maintain tracking flags by adding a new value to the registry. Begin at:

```
HKEY_CURRENT_USER\Software\Microsoft\Office\
```

Then navigate to the appropriate key for your version of Outlook, as shown in Table 4.13. Add a new DWORD value called "RFNoTrack" and set it to 1. Afterward, Outlook will not attempt to track the forwarded and replied flags and this will reduce the overall traffic between server and client.

Table 4.13 *Registry Values to Stop Outlook from Synchronizing Object Properties*

Version	Key
Outlook 97 and 98	…\8.0\Outlook\Options\Mail
Outlook 2000	…\9.0\Outlook\Options\Mail
Outlook 2002	Not supported
Outlook 2003	Not required because of smart synchronization

Outlook 2003 includes the smart change synchronization feature, which is Microsoft's way of admitting that it made a mistake by synchronizing complete copies of items if only one or two properties such as the "forwarded" and "forwarded date" flags change. Smart change synchronization treats reply and forward header information as special attributes, and Outlook 2003 does not synchronize complete copies of items when their headers change.

4.10.3 The local calendar

Normally, you must configure an OST file and synchronize it with server folders before you can access folder contents offline. However, if you use Outlook 98 or Outlook 2000 without configuring an OST, you will find that Outlook has created one in the background to store a local copy of your calendar. The idea is to speed up access to calendar data, which is composed of many different individual items held in the Calendar folder on the server, by maintaining a local copy in an OST. If you already have an OST configured, the calendar data is stored there, but otherwise Outlook will create an OST in the following location (Windows XP Professional):

```
C:\Documents and Settings\User name\Local Settings\
Application Data\Microsoft\Outlook\Outlook.Ost
```

Every time the user updates his or her calendar, Outlook waits ten seconds before starting a background thread to synchronize the change in the local copy with the calendar held in the server mailbox. Changes can also arrive at the server—incoming requests for meetings or updates to meetings that a user has organized—and when these arrive at the server, Exchange notifies Outlook, which is then able to start a background thread to collect the new data and update the local copy. All of this happens automatically, and users are not usually aware that synchronization is progressing unless they monitor data transfer over a very slow network.

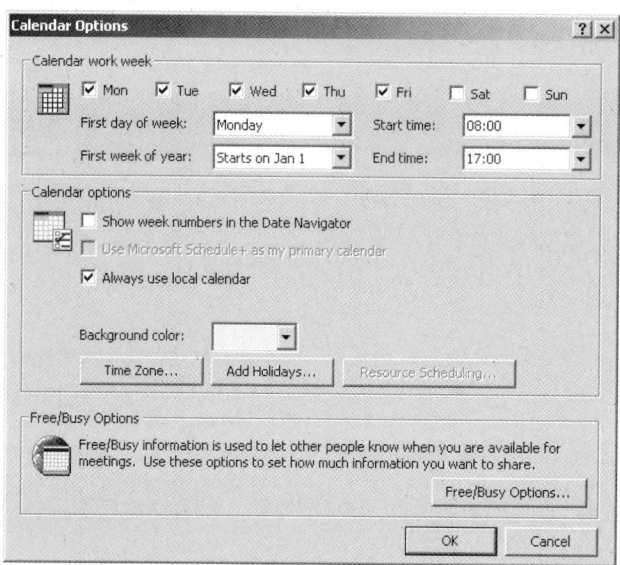

Figure 4.38
Telling Outlook 2000 to use the local calendar.

Accessing data held locally is much faster than making frequent requests to the server. Browsing through a well-populated calendar could involve fetching hundreds of items representing appointments and meetings from the server. Outlook 2000 added the option to allow users to access the local copy of the calendar for all requests (Figure 3.38), relying on background synchronization to keep the server and local copies up-to-date—a more primitive version of the same mechanism used by Outlook 2003 to populate its local cache. As with any folder synchronized to the local cache, selecting this mode reduces network traffic and speeds up access to the calendar, especially for people who use calendaring heavily, so it is an option you should consider if you deploy Outlook 2000 clients. An exception to this advice is for users who share calendars, such as in the case of managers and their assistants, who may find conflicts that arise from changes made to multiple copies of offline calendars. In this case, it is probably best to continue to rely on everyone accessing the online calendar whenever possible, since this will channel all updates through a single definitive copy of the calendar.

Unfortunately, the demise of the "local store" feature that Microsoft promised to ship in Office XP had the effect of removing the ability to use the local calendar by default. Microsoft intended to replace the OST with the local store, and engineers had removed some of the options that leveraged the OST, such as local calendar access, before Microsoft made the decision not to include the local store. Not enough time was available to replace local calendar access (for all activity) in Outlook 2002. The arrival of local caching in Outlook 2003 means that the same idea exists in a different format, so only Outlook 2002 clients cannot use a local calendar.

4.11 SCANPST—first aid for PSTs and OSTs

ESEUTIL and ISINTEG are available to maintain the contents of server-based stores. There is also a need to ensure that users can fix any inconsistencies in local OST and PST files that occur through normal operation. Even when errors exist in their structure, the files might continue to work in an apparently normal manner, but eventually a problem becomes apparent.

Over time, you can expect that Outlook and Exchange (or vice versa) will experience communications failure. Network interruptions will occur, there may be errors reading or writing data to the hard disk, or you might find that someone powered off a PC while Outlook was running with an open PST or OST. Most of the problems that I have encountered with OSTs (as obvious in this chapter, I do not like PSTs very much) have occurred because a network connection terminated during synchronization.

If a fundamental problem occurs with an OST and you find that Outlook cannot read the file, the easiest solution is to recreate the file. Unlike a PST, it is easy to recreate an OST, albeit with some minor problems. After you restore or replace the disk, use Outlook's Tools | Services option to access the properties of the Exchange service. The Advanced tab allows you to define the name of a new OST. Enter a name or accept the default and click on OK. Outlook then creates the file, but you have to reconnect to Outlook before you can use the new file. A hidden benefit is that if you use Outlook 2003 and connect to an Exchange 2003 server, Outlook creates a unicode-based file, but only if you recreate your profile.

However, recreating an OST removes the folder properties controlling whether a folder is available offline for all folders except the special folders (Inbox, Calendar, and so on). Before synchronizing the other folders (including public folder favorites), you must mark each folder you want to use in offline mode and apply any necessary filters. Alternatively, you can use Outlook 2003 and a fully cached mailbox, which means that Outlook synchronizes all folders automatically. Obviously, synchronizing a brand new OST can take a long time, especially with a large mailbox or over a dial-in connection.

You need to rebuild the OST any time you get a new laptop PC. If you do rebuild a PC, remember that you also need to download the OAB to cre-

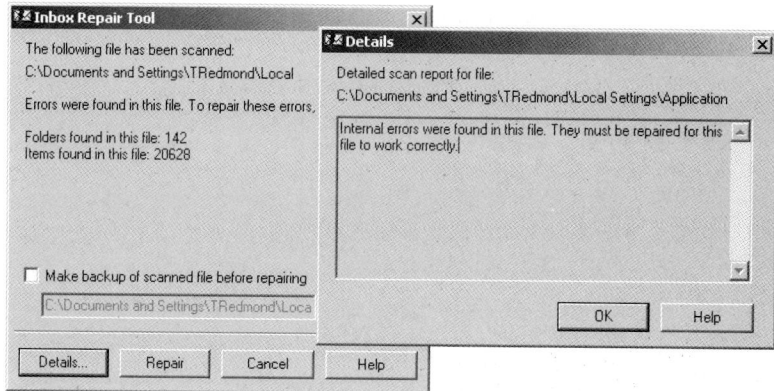

Figure 4.39
The result of scanning an offline store.

ate the complete offline environment. As discussed earlier, some OABs are very large (HP's is over 183 MB when uncompressed), so this operation can take some time to complete.

Problems in a PST take on a different dimension, because the folders in a PST are not slave replicas of online folders so the data does not exist elsewhere. Instead, they are the sole containers for the data they hold. A tool that is able to "fix" a PST to get around the problem is, therefore, an important weapon in an implementation team's armory. That tool is SCANPST.EXE, and you find it in the same directory as the MAPI client software.[7]

You can only run SCANPST if the program can gain exclusive access to the PST or OST you want it to process. After SCANPST opens the target file, it performs a series of eight tests to establish whether any inconsistencies exist in the internal structure of the file and the links between folders and items stored within. If SCANPST detects any inconsistencies, you can proceed to repair the file, or, in the case of a successful run, the program reports the number of items processed and will go no further. Mostly, as in the case shown in Figure 4.39, SCANPST finds errors and there is no option but to carry on and repair the file. In this instance, my OST is large (20,628 items in a 650-MB file) and had been in continual use for over four months, so it was not too surprising to find that a few errors had crept in. SCANPST offers to detail the problems within a file, but, as you can see, the detailed information that the utility presents is hardly enlightening!

SCANPST creates a small log file in the same directory as the PST or OST that you have processed. While the file reveals some of the processing

---

7. On PCs running Windows XP Professional, the program can be found in \Program Files\Common Files\System\MAPI\NT.

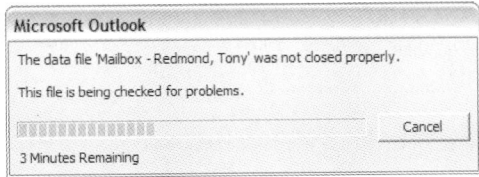

Figure 4.40
Checking for OST errors.

done by SCANPST, it is not too revealing either. Because Outlook 2003 depends on an OST to implement its cached Exchange mode, it runs code to validate that the local cache is consistent every time you start the client. If Outlook detects that the local cache is inconsistent for some reason (again, network interruptions of forced client shutdowns commonly lead to inconsistencies), it attempts to make the cache consistent by checking the contents of the OST, validating the local indexes, and ensuring that the correct links exist between tables. While this happens, you have an opportunity to get an extra cup of coffee. Figure 4.40 shows why.

In general, there is no need to run SCANPST unless you find a problem with either a PST or OST. But there is no harm in running the program, and it does provide a certain peace of mind for those of us who form the more paranoid element of the Exchange community.

4.11.1 The value of an OST

I can live without PSTs, but the loss of offline capability would severely affect my daily working life. Before Outlook 2003, my OST typically contained between 20,000 and 30,000 items in a variety of folders and occupied up to 650 MB of disk space. I am certainly not the record holder in this respect, since I know of people who keep hundreds of thousands of items offline, using more than 3 GB of space. Now, with Outlook 2003's cached Exchange mode, my OST is much larger because it holds a complete copy of my mailbox and all my public folder favorites, so the OST is even more useful.

With all versions of Outlook, offline folders complement the client's dial-up capability and make it easier for road warriors to get their job done. Without the ability to browse and reply to messages offline, I would not have much chance of getting through the hundreds of messages I receive each week. Offline access also makes it much easier to keep up-to-date with the events in heavily trafficked distribution and mailing lists.

4.12 Working offline or online

Even in today's world of high-speed Internet connections available at home and in hotels and other public locations that permit VPN access to the office, there are still times when a slow dial-up connection is the only possible link. Taken together, the combination of OAB and OST allows a user to work offline quite comfortably and take maximum advantage of the slow link when it is available.

However, there is a downside to offline working, since you lose some functionality, including:

- There is no access to free and busy information when scheduling meetings.
- You cannot create new public folders.
- You cannot set permissions on folders, including granting access to your Inbox and calendar.
- The group calendar feature (Outlook 2002) is not available.
- You cannot create new mailbox rules.
- You cannot create an out of office notification.
- The information available in the OAB may be restricted if you opt not to download full details.

These restrictions do not matter to some users, especially those who concentrate on email.

As explained earlier, Outlook synchronizes messages that you create offline and sends them when you connect to the server. You can also synchronize to download new messages and update other folders, and then disconnect to work offline. However, some users, including me, like to work online briefly to quickly review new messages and process urgent messages. To optimize bandwidth use, I follow some simple rules:

- Include the message size field in the folder view so that messages with large attachments can be quickly located. Make a decision whether these messages are urgent, and move any that can wait to a folder that is not synchronized. You can then process these messages the next time you have access to a high-speed connection.
- Turn off the reading pane. Outlook must download a complete copy of a message before the client can display the message in the pane and this soaks up precious bandwidth. The Auto Preview facility offers

almost the same feature at the cost of just 254 bytes per message (Auto Preview only displays the first couple of lines from a message), so use it instead of the preview pane.

- Always download a full copy of the OAB before starting on a road trip to ensure that any messages you create and send offline have valid addresses.

- Treat any new Outlook feature with suspicion until you know it works without demanding too much bandwidth.

These simple steps save bandwidth and reduce the time you spend on dial-up connections.

4.13 Outlook command-line switches

Outlook supports a number of command-line switches to solve problems. These are listed in Table 4.14.

Table 4.14 *Command-Line Switches*

Switch	Effect
/CleanFinders	Restores Outlook 2003 search folders back to the default state.
/CleanFreeBusy	Cleans and regenerates free/busy data.
/CleanReminders	Cleans and regenerates reminders.
/CleanSchedPlus	Deletes all Schedule+ (old calendar format data) from the server.
/CleanViews	Restores default views for folders.
/ResetFolderNames	Resets the language of the default folders to the language of the Outlook client.
/ResetOutlookBar	Rebuilds the Outlook bar.
/ResetWunderBar	Rebuilds the new Outlook 2003 control bar.

5

Outlook Web Access

Experienced Exchange administrators are all too aware that the speed of client deployment limits how quickly they can deploy Exchange within an enterprise. Outlook is a highly functional client, but deploying Outlook takes a lot of work, especially if you want to tailor the options to suit your company's requirements. To some degree, the utilities in Microsoft's Office Resource Kit, including the Outlook Custom Installation Wizard, and tools from company like ProfileMaker (www.autoprof.com) help to speed deployment. However, there are often situations where you simply do not need to provide Outlook to user communities that, for one reason or another, only need relatively simple features.

The major advantage of a Web-based client is that it does not need an administrator to download code or otherwise configure a user PC. Simply point the browser to the correct URL to launch the application, and the browser downloads whatever code is necessary. Of course, there is nothing new in this strategy, because it has existed under a different name (mainframe computing) almost since the dawn of computing. Those who decried mainframe and minicomputer email systems with the term "green screen email," at the advent of PC-driven client/server email applications such as Exchange and Lotus Notes, now seem to be quick to embrace the concept of a Web client, possibly because they have been burned by the effort and expense required to deploy, maintain, and update PC clients.

With Web clients, users can move from PC to PC and access their email without interfering with data belonging to other users who might have previously used the PC. There is obvious flexibility in this approach but at a cost. Network traffic is higher because all data, including application code, must come from a server. Working offline is not possible, because there is no way to support the user data needed to work offline. Web clients do not usually satisfy people who need to work offline regularly, such as road warriors.

Road warriors love their ability to work anytime and anywhere with or without network access.

From a strategic aspect, delivering a highly functional Web client is important to Microsoft for a number of reasons:

- The size of the potential market (and therefore paid client access licenses) for Exchange is only limited by the number of browsers in use.

- Browsers support many platforms that Microsoft does not build clients for, so clients are available for Exchange on platforms that it would not otherwise cover.

- Browsers do not require the same hardware performance or capabilities as full-featured clients, so it is much less expensive to deploy a browser-based messaging system.

- Browsers provide a ubiquitous low-maintenance, zero-configuration, low-support client that can be quickly deployed for schools, universities, or in any other situation where people want messaging, but perhaps not to the degree of sophistication available in purpose-designed clients.

- A browser is the client of choice for many ISPs, largely because they can control the user interface and can incorporate revenue-generating advertisements, which in turn pay for the free email service usually offered as an inducement to subscribe. The success of hotmail.com or any of its competitors is evidence of the popularity of browsers in the ISP world.

- Microbrowsers in new devices such as cellular phones can link to Exchange over a suitable network connection such as GPRS.

People often talk of browsers as stateless clients, because they do not leave traces of their presence on a PC in the same way that a client such as Outlook does. The browser downloads some files (cookies, .html, and .asp pages plus associated graphics) into the local cache, but this is nothing in comparison to the footprint left by Outlook. Before Outlook can start, you need to create a profile, which involves making changes to the system registry. During operation, Outlook creates and uses other files, such as offline stores, personal folders, the offline address book, the Outlook bar, and so on. If different users access the same PC, they can interfere with each other's data and settings, albeit unwittingly. The usual solution is to either make sure that PCs are purely personal devices only used by a single individual, or to keep as much data as possible on servers and download to client PCs after they have logged on to the network. Either approach works, but the first requires you to deploy at least the same number of PCs as you have users (and probably more), while the second can only be implemented through hard work and good system management. Both options add to the overall cost of deployment.

The first release of the Outlook Web Access (OWA) application was in Exchange 5.0. This release supported basic messaging and public folders but did nothing for calendaring, task management, or setting options such as passwords. OWA worked, but it was slow and clunky when compared with Outlook, and there were many missing features, since OWA could not support more than 300 (approximate) concurrent users on a well-configured server. Matters were somewhat improved in Exchange 5.5, but the architecture used could not deliver the required combination of performance, scalability, and functionality, so a fundamental rewrite was required.

5.1 Second-generation OWA

The architecture for the first generation of OWA (Exchange 5.0 and 5.5) uses active server pages. Exchange 2000 increased the capabilities and performance of OWA by leveraging:

- Increased browser functionality from IE (Internet Explorer) 5 onward, including the support of new protocols such as XML, XSL, and HTTP-DAV (or WebDAV[1]).

- More experience in hosting Web applications and the necessary architecture to increase scalability. In particular, Microsoft realized that if it wanted to make OWA scalable, it needed to move as much processing into the Store as possible.

- IIS to support a set of Internet protocol stacks including HTTP.

In addition, by giving every object in the Store an addressable URL, the code required to build a browser interface is easier to write, more supportable, and more easily customized to meet specific needs.

Customer acceptance of Exchange 2000's OWA client delivered a pleasant surprise to Microsoft. The speed and functionality delivered by OWA forced many companies to reconsider how best to deploy and use browser clients, and this led to a flood of requests to add some of the missing features. Microsoft has responded to these requests by incorporating new features in service packs. For example, Exchange 2000 SP2 provides support

---

1. See http://www.webdav.org/ for information on the DAV extensions. DAV is now described in RFC 2518.

for new mail notifications and calendar reminders as well as a basic logoff option. When the time came to develop Exchange 2003, Microsoft had done the work to make OWA a highly acceptable client at an architectural level in Exchange 2000, but it needed to build on the foundation to eliminate some rough points and hone OWA's edge. Accordingly, the major themes for OWA 2003 are:

- Performance: Because OWA always connected to a server, Microsoft concentrated on reducing network traffic through techniques such as compression, more intelligent download of page elements, and so on.

- Cross-client compatibility: Outlook 2003 boasts a user interface, and OWA takes many of the same improvements, such as the reading pane, and brings them to the Web world. Apart from generating a better-looking interface, implementing much the same interface across both clients makes it easier for users to move from one to the other. The race between the two clients will continue, because Outlook also continues to improve, but the difference is now very close.

- Security: In common with the general improvement in security across Exchange, OWA increases security through features like controls over the download of Web beacons and specific attachment types as well as the ability to encrypt and sign messages.

- User requests: Microsoft has received many enhancement requests for OWA, so it responded by supporting server-side rules, spell checking, junk mail processing, and so on.

Over the last two releases, Microsoft has made enormous progress to develop the OWA user interface to a point where it comes close to Outlook. Even as the interface becomes richer, performance improves as Microsoft engineers fine-tune communications between client and server to improve responsiveness, especially over slower connections. New controls provide essential elements of the user interface, including the folder list, and restrict the need to communicate with the server.

5.1.1 The strategic relationship between IIS and Exchange

It is important to underline the extremely close interrelationship that exists between IIS and Exchange. Shortly after the Nimda virus struck in September 2001, Gartner analyst John Pescatore issued a recommendation[2] that

---

2. Gartner document FT-14-5524 (September 19, 2001).

Microsoft customers should look at using another Web server instead of IIS. Gartner's recommendation was because the Nimda virus spreads through file shares and known vulnerabilities that exist in an unpatched version of IIS 5.0. Microsoft's patchy history of security holes in Windows and IIS to that point did not help, and many people seriously considered how they could move away from IIS.

Microsoft's immediate response was a "lockdown" tool for IIS. You should apply this tool on all Windows 2000 servers that run IIS 5.0, with the notable caveat that you need to throttle back the restrictions imposed by the lockdown tool, since otherwise OWA cannot work because dynamic content is blocked. See Microsoft Knowledge Base article Q309508 for more information. More importantly, Microsoft has done a lot of work since Nimda appeared to block holes and prevent the same problems from occurring. The result of this work is in IIS 6.0, which is more scalable and has a much better security record than IIS 5.0 or 4.0. Exchange 2003 leverages the Worker Process Isolation Model (WPIM) in IIS 6.0 to protect the interaction between the Store and OWA clients.

You can, of course, follow the Gartner advice and look elsewhere for Web servers, but this decision has enormous consequences for Exchange. As we know, apart from OWA, IIS provides all of the Internet Protocol support used by other components of Exchange. Therefore, if you remove IIS, you remove Internet Protocol support for Exchange. You will still be able to start the Store and connect MAPI clients to mailboxes, but that marks the extent of the server's functionality, and you will be running a configuration that Microsoft is unlikely to support. It is better to implement a proactive security policy that performs the following functions:

- Monitors signs for potential attacks (e.g., by checking sites such as http://securityresponse.symantec.com/ [Symantec's Security Response] and http://www.microsoft.com/security/default.asp [Microsoft's own security site]) daily to keep an eye on what's happening in the world of viruses.

- Establishes how you can learn about new virus attacks if your email server is affected.

- Defines how patches (IIS, Exchange, and Windows) are tested and then applied to production servers; many of the servers afflicted by Nimda and other viruses are not properly maintained and run outdated software.

Another sad fact is that many Exchange administrators do not know IIS well enough to realize when something is wrong and needs fixing. IIS is now a critical component of Exchange, so perhaps the Nimda attack is the necessary wake-up call for all of us to understand IIS better than we have done in the past.

5.1.2 IIS changes in Exchange 2003

The close working relationship between IIS and Exchange is obvious, but the sheer number of attacks involving IIS required Microsoft to make changes in IIS 6.0, some of which affect Exchange. IIS 6.0 implements a different architecture designed to improve management, performance, scalability, reliability, and security. The most important developments are:

- Implementation of the kernel-mode HTTP:SYS listener, which OWA exploits to protect communications with the Store via the epoxy layer. The HTTP:SYS listener replaces the InetInfo process in this role.

- The user-mode service administration and monitoring agent.

- Worker Process Isolation Mode (WPIM), which prevents applications from affecting each other following a failure by requiring administrators to restart the W3Svc process. Exchange supports its Web-based applications such as OWA through WPIM.

You can install Exchange 2003 on Windows 2000 servers, in which case OWA works with IIS 5.0 and you do not gain the benefits outlined here (IIS 6.0 does not run on Windows 2000 servers). However, even on Windows 2000, you still get the improved client interface. Running Exchange 2003 on Windows 2003 introduces IIS 6.0 (remember that you have to install IIS before you install Exchange), and you gain better security, more reliability, and faster performance—all very desirable improvements. Time will tell whether hackers continue to attack IIS, but at least the improvements made in IIS 6.0 lay a good base for the future.

5.2 The OWA architecture

Figure 5.1 illustrates the basic components of the OWA architecture as it functions on a back-end server. If we follow the interaction between a browser and Exchange, we see the following:

- A browser issues an HTTP request: The request contains a URL that identifies the server name that will process the request. Another part of the URL identifies Exchange as the application that will eventually

5.2 The OWA architecture

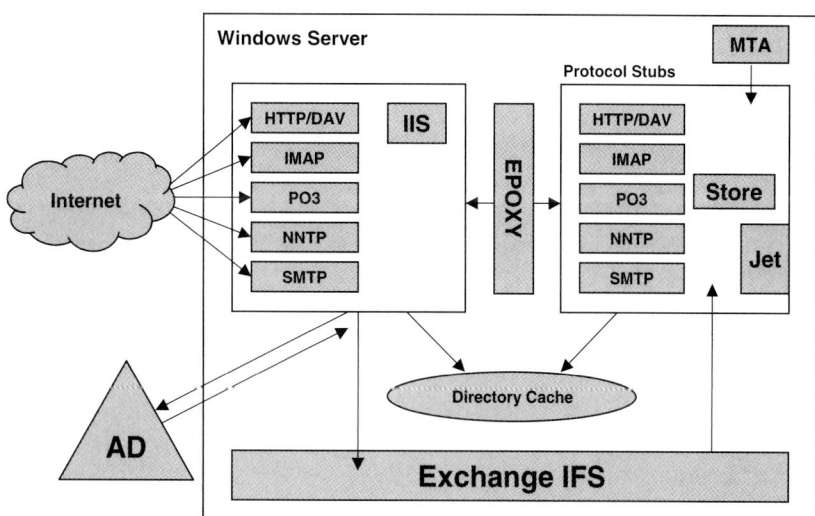

Figure 5.1
Outlook Web Access architecture.

provide the data. As far as the browser is concerned, it is just asking a server for some data.

- The HTTP request flows back across the network to the IIS server referenced in the URL. Note that it is possible to direct OWA communications across a secure HTTPS connection rather than a standard HTTP link. You can also integrate solutions such as RSA's SecurID to increase security further, especially in the area of user authentication.

- Exchange registers itself with IIS as a valid application, so IIS knows that it should redirect any URL coming in that includes "Exchange" to the entry point for the application. In this case, the entry point is davex.dll, an ISAPI extension that includes the functions necessary to communicate with the Store. Exchange also registers Davex.dll with IIS as the component to handle all incoming requests for the Exchange application.

- Davex.dll interprets the request (open a folder, return some content from an item, etc.) and contacts the Store through the epoxy interprocess communication channel. Communication goes to the HTTP epoxy stub.

- Because the interprocess communication uses shared memory, epoxy can only operate when both the IIS and Store processes operate on the same physical computer. Each protocol has its own epoxy stub that runs in the Store process. The use of the epoxy layer removes the need for RPCs, which previous versions of OWA use for IIS Store communications. The overhead imposed by RPCs was the root cause of some scalability issues.

- The HTTP epoxy stub communicates with the general data entry point for the Store (exoledb.dll), which fetches the necessary information from the Store.

- OWA uses ExIFS if it wants to access information from the streaming file. ExIFS streams the data out straight to the browser. OWA fetches the properties for messages from the EDB file.

- OWA takes a reverse path to return the data to the browser, which sees the information coming back in its native format (HTML) across the HTTP protocol.

Microsoft continues to work hard to improve OWA performance, and the code in Exchange 2003 is roughly 30 percent faster than Exchange 2000. Along with the new interface, the additional performance helps OWA to be a more acceptable client for many users.

OWA is a core component of Exchange, so the Exchange installation procedure automatically installs OWA onto every server. Windows 2000 servers include IIS automatically, but in line with the new philosophy for Windows of never installing a component on a server unless an application needs it, you have to install IIS on Windows 2003 servers before installing Exchange. You do not have to do anything special after the installation to enable Exchange to serve clients with OWA. The virtual root for Exchange becomes part of the base Web site on the server. If you want to disable OWA, you must disable the virtual root, but you must be aware that this action will prevent any HTTP access to any mailbox or public folder hosted on the server.

5.2.1 HTTP-DAV extensions

OWA uses HTTP-DAV as the base set of browser commands to build its functionality. In addition to the base set of HTTP 1.1 commands, DAV provides methods (commands) to:

- Manipulate files: MKCOL, COPY, MOVE, LOCK, UNLOCK
- Manipulate document properties: PROPFIND, PROPPATCH
- Perform searches: SEARCH
- Publish: SUBSCRIBE, POLL

5.2 The OWA architecture

Taken together, the additional commands enable a certain degree of document management features for browsers. HTTP-DAV is able to process files as single entities or as collections. The MKCOL command makes a collection, or selection, of objects, such as a set of files in a directory, a set of items in a folder, or it creates a folder. Being able to process collections is clearly more efficient than being required to fetch and process individual items.

Browsers traditionally process documents rather than individual attributes or properties of the document. XML describes a schema for documents, and HTTP-DAV uses the PROPFIND and PROPPATCH commands to manipulate document properties described in the schema. The PROPFIND command allows browsers to retrieve properties of documents, such as their author or subject. PROPPATCH sets values for properties, so a browser can now change the title of a document. Changing the time of an appointment provides a good example of how HTTP-DAV can manipulate properties. A number of properties need to be updated to change an appointment—the start time, end time, and perhaps the details of the appointment such as the subject and place. The PROPPATCH command is used to change the properties to update the appointment. Indeed, rich browsers are able to update the screen with the new properties without having to issue a call to the server, whereas older browsers have to click on the refresh button.

In some respects, SEARCH is the most interesting command, because it allows a browser to use SQL-type syntax to enumerate the contents of folders or the properties of an item and then receive the result of the search in the form of raw XML data that the browser can sort and view in different ways. Rich browsers use Extensible Stylesheet Language (XSL) style sheets to format the data for display. The XSL style sheet that OWA uses comes from the requested Outlook view. The server generates the view on the fly and downloads it once to the browser, which then applies the view to each page. Reach browsers do not support XSL, so their views are built with HTML tables.

The point here is that the browser does all the work to manipulate data locally once the client receives data from the server, and this is the magic that allows OWA now to support different views or sorting by columns without needing to go to the server and fetch new data after a new view or sort is requested. You can easily see XML processing in action if you expand and collapse a view, or opt to sort a view by a different field. If you elect to use a new view on a folder such as "By Conversation Topic," a slight delay may occur while the browser downloads and then sorts the data, but

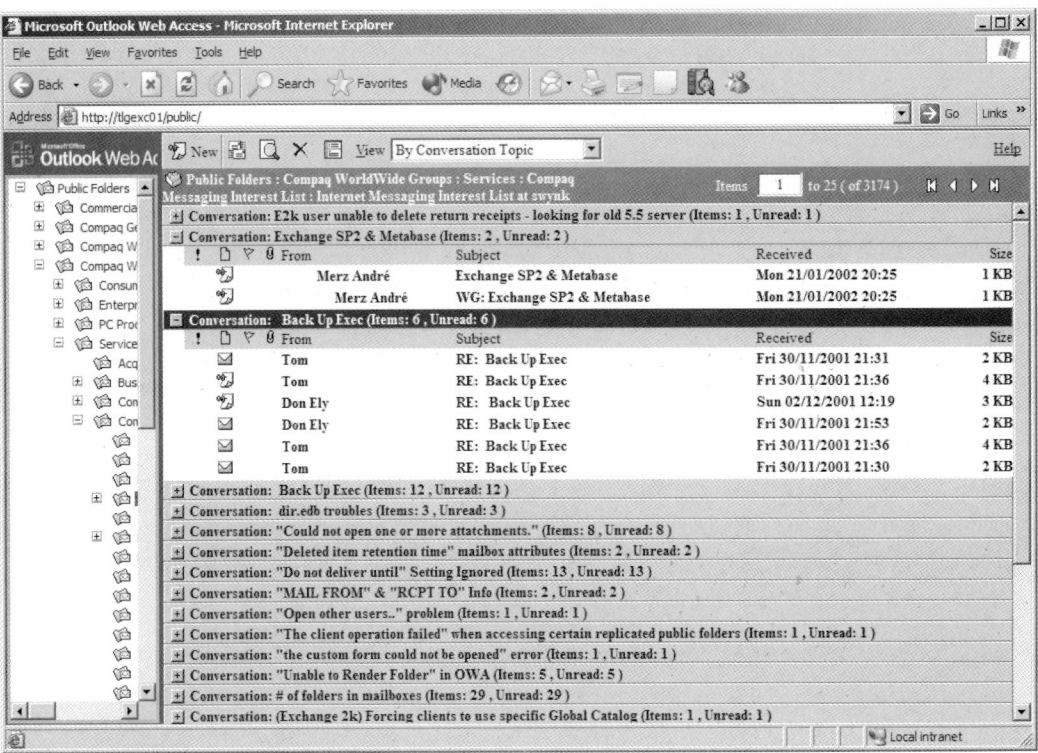

Figure 5.2 *Applying a view to a large public folder.*

performance is very acceptable even for large folders. As an example, Figure 5.2 shows OWA accessing a large public folder that takes in a feed from the public msexchange mailing list on www.swynk.com. A large number of messages arrive in the folder daily—over 30,000 in a year. Even with so many items to process, the XSL and IE combination in OWA 2000 or 2003 delivers more than acceptable performance. By comparison, in Exchange 5.5, OWA refreshes data from the server each time it needs to change the way it presents data (similar to a view change), but cached XML data means that the browser can collapse or expand a view or sort data in a view without going to the server. Now, even with large folders, OWA is able to switch views almost instantly without placing any additional burden on the server.

Note that caching does not imply that data remains for long periods on the PC. The design of OWA views data as transient and the user interface as more persistent. To accomplish this, the headers for HTML and XML data specify the "nocache" keyword to ensure that the browser does not leave user data on the PC for potential examination after a user session is over and to ensure that OWA never displays stale data. Style sheets and behaviors that influence the user interface are more persistent.

5.3 Functionality: rich versus reach or premium and basic

Browsers that support the XML, XSL, DHTML, and HTTP-DAV protocols have the largest available OWA feature set. All Microsoft browsers since IE5 (including IE5 for UNIX) support these protocols, and you will probably have these browsers in place on many desktops purely because they are part of the operating system. Any desktop that runs Windows XP automatically has IE6, for example. Note that IE6 is required if you want to run OWA in some languages (Hebrew or Arabic, for example). Check with Microsoft to determine the latest status on language support if you are unsure whether you need IE6 in your own environment. There have been many security attacks against IE, and the best advice is to use the most up-to-date version and keep a close eye out for any updates that Microsoft releases.

If you do not use the latest version of IE, possibly because you have made a decision to use browser technology from another company (such as Opera or the Netscape browser), you will find that basic messaging and calendaring functionality work quite well on all downstream browsers. You do not have to replace every browser just to take advantage of the extra stability and performance delivered by OWA. Indeed, even downstream browsers benefit from some of the architectural changes that Microsoft began to make in Exchange 2000, because OWA uses less frames, script, and applets to build the user interface, so performance is snappier. Using less scripted code has another benefit in that there is less chance of OWA encountering compatibility problems with different browsers. In terms of OWA, we define a downstream browser to be any browser that does not support the protocols built into IE5 or later. Any browser shipped after IE5 should be able to exploit the full set of OWA features, but you do need to test to confirm that this is the case for any particular browser.

Over time, Microsoft has used different terms to describe the various types of browsers that OWA can support. The original terms were rich and reach, with rich meaning that the browser is capable of supporting the full OWA feature set. Reach indicates that the browser cannot support all of the OWA features for some reason, usually protocol support. If you look at the OWA logon screen that allows users to select the type of client they want to use, you see that Microsoft uses premium and basic to describe the client types. These terms reflect the way that ASPs price OWA connectivity

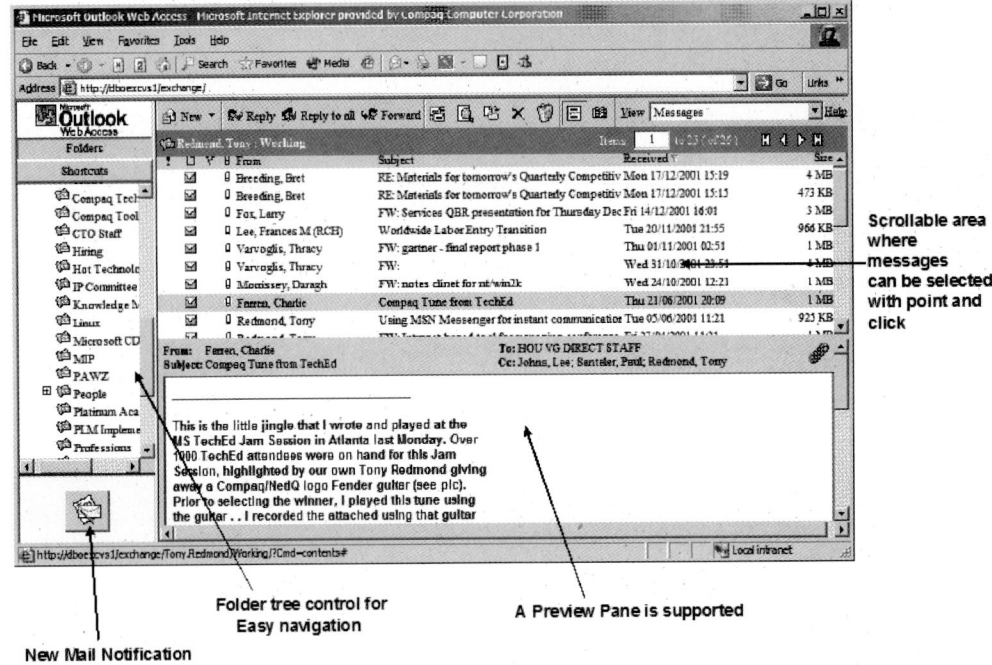

Figure 5.3 Outlook Web Access and IE6 (Exchange 2000).

to users, so they are reasonably logical. Note that the support of feature segmentation makes it easier for ASPs to differentiate service delivery, even if you connect with an advanced browser.

While the words have changed, they mean the same thing. The concept of a reach browser means that even basic browsers can connect to Exchange to read and send messages, but you will only get limited functionality in browsers that cannot support extended protocols such as rich DHTML behaviors and XML-HTTP. Even relatively recent browsers such as IE4 fall into the reach category, because they do not support the extended protocol set. All current versions of Netscape Navigator fall into the same category. In one way, you can think of the feature set for the reach client as the lowest common denominator for a browser. Even with this caveat, the feature set supported by the reach client is impressive when you compare it with other browser-based email systems such as the Squirrel Mail client.

IE5[3] was the first "rich-level" browser, meaning that the browser is capable of processing many user interface operations without reference to the

---

3. IE5 is available on the Sun Solaris and HP-UX platforms. If you connect to Exchange 2000, you can use the rich OWA client, but Exchange 2003 restricts you to the reach client.

5.3 Functionality: rich versus reach or premium and basic

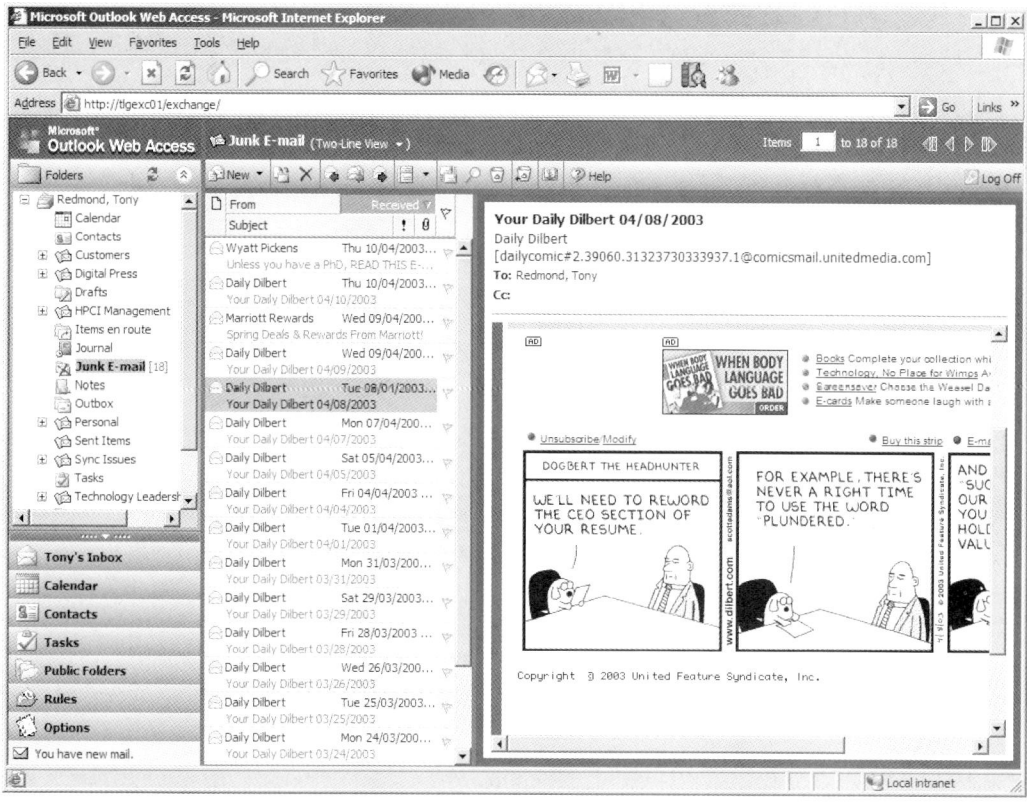

Figure 5.4 *Outlook Web Access and IE6 (Exchange 2003).*

server. Figure 5.3 shows the kind of environment you can expect when you combine IE6 with OWA from Exchange 2000, while Figure 5.4 demonstrates the improvement in user interface design and implementation that Microsoft achieved in Exchange 2003. It is obvious what kind of impact a couple of extra years' development can make on a user interface when coupled with a huge amount of user feedback. By offloading the processing of views, rich clients reduce load on servers. A server is therefore capable of supporting more concurrent browser connections, and performance tends to be higher because the OWA architecture eliminates the server to browser time lag for all but the initial download of data.

The goal for OWA is to create a user interface that is as close as possible to the full-function Outlook client, and this is possible only with rich browsers. Each release builds on the last to move toward the goal, and Microsoft is very close to it with Exchange 2003, which boasts a more attractive and streamlined user interface. Aside from the new user interface,

Microsoft learned from its experience with Exchange 2000 and tweaked browser-server communications to make OWA more responsive. For example, if you delete an item in a folder with OWA 2000, the browser requests the server to perform a folder refresh, including a check for any new items that might have arrived in a folder such as the Inbox. With Exchange 2003, OWA does not refresh a message list until you delete more than 20 percent of the list's content (based on the user's own determination for the number of items on a page), so item deletion is more responsive. For example, if you set OWA to display 50 items per page, it will not refresh until after you delete 11 items.

OWA makes use of IE "behaviors" to build part of the user interface. Behaviors are a way of making DHTML pages easier to build by separating the code that implements the user interface from the data. The separation of code and data makes HTML pages more manageable and the user interface more predictable. The code that defines behaviors is typically shipped in an .htc file. A number of .htc files used by OWA are located in the \exchsrvr\exchweb\controls directory. Examples include features such as "drop-menu" (which defines how to respond to the right mouse button when it is clicked by displaying a drop-down menu), and you can find the hierarchical tree control to display folders in a mailbox or public folder hierarchy in the same directory.

IE uses behaviors to extend the functionality of an HTML element by adding new attributes, methods, and events for the element. For example, you can define behavior to control how a LIST element expands and collapses or how a command button changes color when the mouse passes over it. Outlook clients make extensive use of lists or views that collapse and expand, so it is easy to see the attraction of this feature from an OWA developer's view.

Because their main function is to display data pushed down by a server, browsers often just handle static displays. Microsoft has attempted to mitigate some of the static nature of browsers by forcing updates of screen content when an application creates new items. For example, if you create a new appointment, OWA knows that it has to refresh the view and does so automatically to show the new item in your calendar. It is easy for a browser to know that a refresh is required when Exchange has added a new item to a folder, but new mail notifications are a different matter because you never know when new mail will arrive. To solve the problem, OWA (Exchange 2000 SP2 onward) uses the HTTP-DAV SUBSCRIBE and POLL methods to enable new mail and calendar notifications. The feature works by subscribing to the Inbox and calendar folders when OWA initializes, and then polling for new email or upcoming appointments every two minutes.

5.3 Functionality: rich versus reach or premium and basic

The set of features supported by rich browsers includes:

- Point-and-click selection of objects from a scrollable list.

- Drag and drop from one folder to another. Unlike Outlook, you cannot drag and drop files from the Windows Explorer to an OWA 2000 message to add an attachment to a message or drag a file and drop it into a folder to copy it to the folder, but you can with OWA 2003 after you install the S/MIME control. In addition, you cannot drag and drop an item from the Inbox to the Contacts folder and expect to create a new contact, since this functionality is not yet available.[4] Drag-and-drop support does include resizing calendar appointments to fit a time slot.

- OWA supplies context-sensitive toolbars for different folders. For example, a different toolbar is displayed when the Inbox is active than when the calendar is displayed. In addition, context-sensitive menus are available. For example, if you right-click on the Deleted Items folder, you see an option to empty the folder.

- As with Outlook, OWA supports grouped views such as "Group by Conversation Topic" to allow items to be collapsed and expanded according to the criteria defined for the view.

- Sort folders by different attributes, such as date, author, subject, and so on.

- View the first bodypart of a message through the reading pane. In addition, the Exchange 2003 version of OWA allows you to position the reading pane to the right, bottom, or delete it from the screen, just like Outlook 2003.

- Calendar and contact items can now be stored in other folders, including public folders. This offers some interesting possibilities for group calendars or group contact folders. Personal contacts are now used to validate email addresses.

- A rich text editor is available to generate HTML content. However, unlike Outlook, you cannot call Word for Windows and use it to edit the content of messages.

---

4. Some of the reasons why a file can't be dragged and dropped into a folder lie in the way that browsers deal with files. RFC 1836 specifies how a browser uploads files to a server for storages and the mechanism that OWA uses to transmit files to Exchange. Uploading in this manner is designed to be secure rather than support user interface features such as drag and drop and explains why drag-and-drop support in OWA 2003 is linked to the S/MIME control.

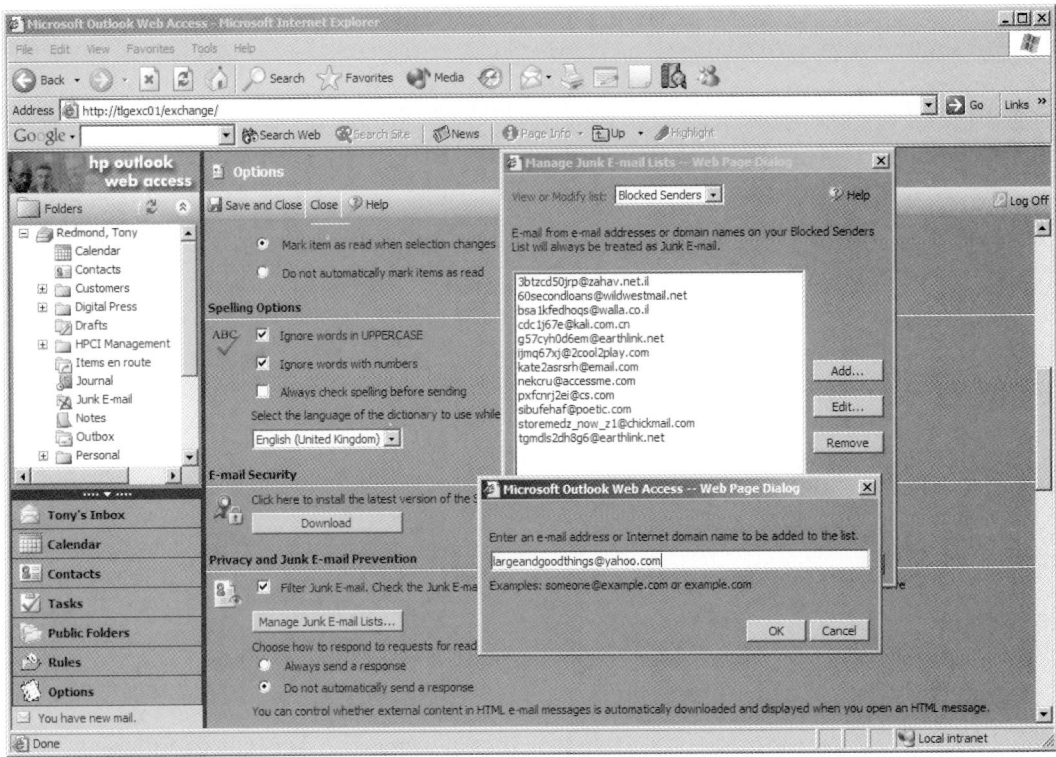

Figure 5.5 *Setting up a Blocked Senders list with OWA.*

- You can set server-side rules (but only when connected to an Exchange 2003 server).

- OWA supports the server-side processing of junk mail, but it does not download messages and review content to detect spam in the same way as Outlook 2003 does. However, you cannot import or export the Blocked or Safe Sender lists as you can with Outlook. Exchange holds these lists as mailbox properties on the server. The maximum size of the lists is 512 KB, so you can add roughly 1,024 safe senders and 1,024 blocked senders to the list (Figure 5.5).

- OWA includes a logoff button (from Exchange 2000 SP2 onward) to close off the browser session. This option does not remove any temporary files that you may create on the PC during an OWA session, but Exchange 2003 will flush the browser password cache when you log off. Apart from implementing session timeouts through the forms authentication feature, OWA has no method to force a user to log off, leading to a situation where someone might leave a browser con-

5.3 Functionality: rich versus reach or premium and basic

nected to his or her mailbox when he or she leaves. Third-party solutions provide other options that you might like to investigate.[5]

- OWA supports the CTRL/K keystroke to resolve the names entered in message headers. OWA displays any ambiguous matches to the user when it checks addresses. OWA 2003 makes the display of unrecognized and ambiguous addresses easier for users to resolve and supports more keyboard shortcuts to speed up email processing. You can use these shortcuts when you position the cursor in the list of messages. The shortcuts are:
    - New message (or post for public folders): Ctrl+N
    - Reply to selected message: Ctrl+R
    - Reply all to selected message: Ctrl+Shift+R
    - Forward selected message: Ctrl+Shift+F
    - Mark selected messages as read: Ctrl+Q
    - Mark selected messages as unread: Ctrl+U

- OWA supports spell checking from Exchange 2003 onward. This feature imposes a certain load on the server because OWA must upload the message text and check it on the server, but this is unlikely to cause any performance concerns for modern servers. The spell checker is not too good when asked to deal with Shakespearean sonnets, but it is as capable as the Outlook spell checker is and supports six languages (English, French, Italian, German, Spanish, and Korean). Exchange 2003 SP1 adds Arabic, Danish, Finnish, Hebrew, Swedish, and Norwegian.

- OWA performs a check for password expiration after the initial connection and notifies users if a password change is required soon (within 14 days).

In addition, if you run IE6 (SP2 or later) and connect to an Exchange 2003 server, data passed between the client and server can be compressed using the GZip compression algorithm.

If you run IE6 on Windows 2000 or Windows XP workstations, you can also create, read, and sign S/MIME encoded messages using a control that you have to download to the browser.[6] The control is specific to a PC, so you must download the control to every PC where you use OWA and plan to sign messages or encrypt messages. OWA signs and encrypts messages according to the S/MIME V3 standard, but it can also read S/MIME V2

---

5. For example, SecureLogOff for OWA from MessageWare http://www.messageware.com/.
6. Two DLLs are downloaded: EXSMIME.DLL and MIMECTL.DLL.

encrypted messages. Options to control whether OWA signs and/or encrypts messages by default are available along with the other OWA options, and you can opt to sign or encrypt a message on an individual basis in much the same way as with Outlook. However, OWA does support S/MIME encoded read receipts. Figure 5.6 illustrates some of the OWA encryption and signing features in action. The top screen shows a signed and encrypted message, which you can recognize by the presence of the padlock (encrypted) and rosette (signature) on the right-hand side. The bottom screen shows the GAL properties for one of the recipients, where we can see that AD holds a valid digital ID (certificate) for this user.

Before you can start using message encryption with OWA, you have to deploy a public-key infrastructure. You can use the Windows Certificate Server to issue certificates to users or use those issued by other certification authorities such as Verisign. In either case, you have to arrange for users to get the certificates and perform administrative operations such as key revocation through other tools, because OWA only makes use of certificates; it

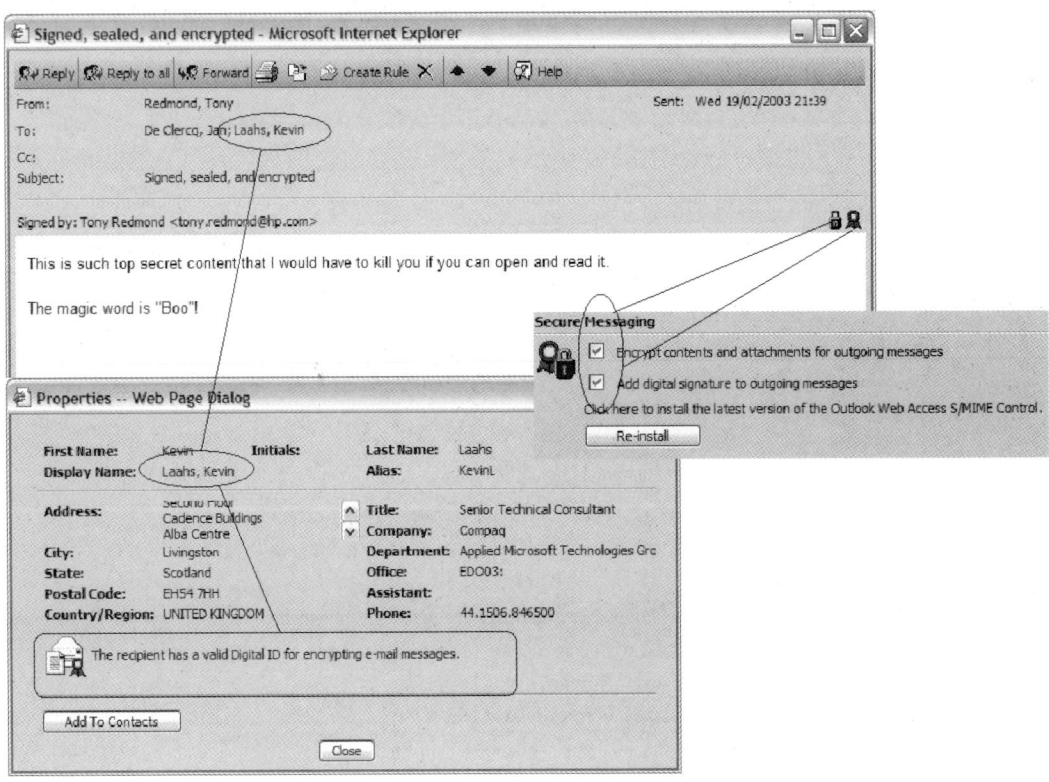

Figure 5.6 *Signed and encrypted OWA email.*

includes no functionality to control, manage, or otherwise work with certificates. Exchange 2003 performs all certificate validation (e.g., to determine that certificates are still valid and are not on a revocation list). The certificate can be in any location accessible to the Windows CryptoAPI, including the local certificate store and smart cards. If you attempt to sign or encrypt a message and OWA cannot find a valid certificate, it prompts you to provide a key by inserting a hardware-based device. In addition to your own certificate, recipients must possess certificates that Windows can access before OWA can generate signed or encrypted messages. The certificates can be attributes of user AD objects, or you can store certificates along with other contact information. In either case, if OWA cannot find the certificate for a recipient, it will warn you that the recipient may not be able to read the message if you continue to send it.

You may decide not to download the S/MIME control on the basis that you do not want to send or encrypt messages, but, in fact, the control also enables more sophisticated message handling. For example, after you load the control, you can:

- Click on the attachment icon in the toolbar and attach files without going through the normal two-step attach and post dialog.

- Drag and drop messages from one folder to another. However, if you drag a message to the calendar folder, OWA does not populate the necessary attributes to create a new appointment and you cannot see the item in the calendar views.

- Drag and drop messages onto new messages.

- Drag and drop files from Windows Explorer to a message to become an attachment. If you make a mistake, you can right-click on an attachment to remove it.

- Use all of the fonts installed on a PC instead of the default five.

On the surface, you may find it hard to understand why OWA links the S/MIME control to additional message handling functionality, but it has to do with security. With the control added, OWA deems you to have a more secure browser, so it allows you to work with local files more easily and the PC can compose the message rather than dispatching components to the server for assembly and dispatch. For example, you can drag and drop attachments into a send message window rather than going through the more extended (but safer) process of opening a separate "Select Attachment" window to select the attachment you want to send. Assuming that everyone has access to keys and has downloaded the S/MIME control, you can force users to encrypt and/or sign messages by creating two new registry values, as follows:

```
HKLM\System\CurrentControlSet\Services\MSExchange\OWA\
AlwaysSign
```

```
HKLM\System\CurrentControlSet\Services\MSExchange\OWA\
AlwaysEncrypt
```

Set these DWORD values to 1 to force signing and encryption. The default is 0, which allows users to choose. It is unwise to force these settings unless you are sure that users have the S/MIME control installed and understand how to use digital signatures and message encryption. For example, they need to know that they can sign messages addressed to anyone, but they need to have access to a recipient's public keys before they can encrypt an outgoing message.

5.3.1 Updating slowly

It is great to know that IE supports all the protocols necessary to implement the full OWA feature set, but Microsoft cannot expect everyone to upgrade to the latest version of IE overnight. It is a nice dream, but it will not happen. Backward compatibility is necessary, yet the challenge exists to upgrade and improve the performance of reach browsers when they connect to Exchange without using any of the new protocols. OWA does this by reducing the amount of data downloaded from the server, cleaning up the script code in the ASP pages, simplifying the user interface to use a smaller number of frames, and taking advantage of the additional performance delivered by the new architecture.

Almost all of the basic messaging functionality available to rich browsers is available to reach browsers, but there are some major differences in the user interface. For example, OWA provides references to objects as hot links, so you have to select an item and then double-click it before activating the item. Rich browsers use the same point-and-click, scrollable, multiselect model used by Win32 clients. Figure 5.7 provides a good view of the user interface of a reach browser connected to Exchange 2003. A quick comparison with the rich interface shown in Figure 5.4 demonstrates the difference between the two interfaces. You can see the effect immediately, since the user interface is much flatter and the advanced features such as the reading pane are not available. In addition, extended features such as spell checking and S/MIME support are only available to rich browsers.

However, the difference is only truly obvious when you attempt to use the reach interface after using the rich interface for a while. It is an unfair

5.3 Functionality: rich versus reach or premium and basic   311

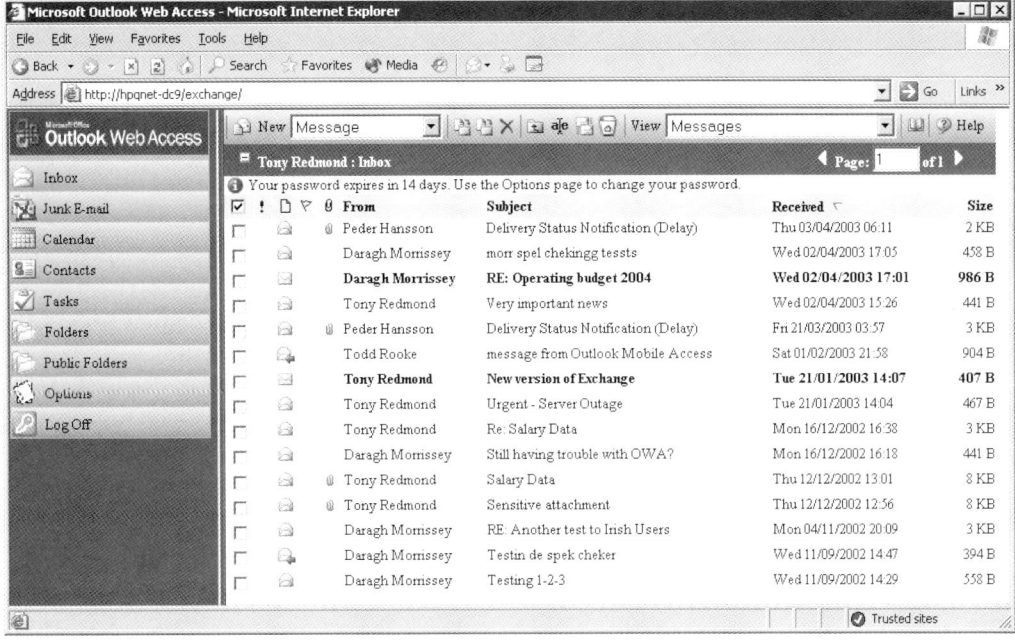

Figure 5.7   *IE6 runs the reach interface (Exchange 2003).*

comparison, because there is no way that the reach interface can approach the usability of an interface that Microsoft has worked on for many years. Today's rich browser client is streamlined and attractive, whereas the reach client is clunky and dated. Still, if you need the reach client to access your Inbox or are forced to use it in a situation such as a public kiosk, it is more than capable of delivering.

There are instances when you may want to opt selectively to use the reach interface—for example, when you connect across a slow link and want to check email quickly. The Exchange 2003 version of OWA allows you to use the reach client even if you have the latest version of IE installed. However, once you have experienced the rich OWA client, you will not want to go downstream again.

5.3.2 Limiting richness

Sometimes, you may want to limit the abilities of clients and force them to connect in reach mode, perhaps to achieve consistency across all desktops and ease support and training requirements. Another reason is that some firewalls may not support the transmission of HTTP-DAV verbs. Microsoft built the ability for administrators to selectively downgrade, even for a short period, into Exchange 2003. You cannot apply a selective downgrade, since it affects every client that connects to a server as long as the downgrade is in effect.

You can control OWA downgrading by setting the registry value:

```
HKLM\SYSTEM\CurrentControlSet\Services\MSExchangeWEB\
OWA\ForceClientsDownLevel
```

The default value is 0, meaning that OWA decides if a browser can support the rich client. Set the value to 1 to force Exchange to offer down-level support only. You do not need to restart the Store or IIS to make the change effective, since it kicks in the next time a client connects. In a front-end/back-end configuration, you have to make this change on the back-end servers, because these servers control the user interface that clients see.

5.3.3 Spell checking

OWA spell checking works as an ISAPI extension[7] that links to the relevant language library found in the same folder. When a client requests Exchange to spell check a message, it uses a POST verb to send the text to the ISAPI extension. Exchange checks the text against its dictionaries and generates an XML document that contains all possible corrections. Exchange then sends the XML document down to the client, which displays the text and corrections to the user through the interface shown in Figure 5.8. After the user has selected whatever corrections he or she wants to accept, OWA makes the amended text into the message body. This mechanism is effective, but it limits you to checking the entire text of a message rather than being able to check selected areas. As with Outlook, users can select options to control how to perform spell checking (language, ignore uppercase words, ignore words with numbers). Exchange stores these options as mailbox properties to ensure that users can move from PC to PC and retain their preferences.

It is conceivable that spell checking could affect overall server performance, but only if the server is already experiencing performance problems and is literally "on the edge" and unable to accept any further load. If this happens, you can throttle back the resources that users can consume with spell checking with a number of registry values at:

```
HKLM\System\CurrentControlSet\Services\MSExchangeWEB\OWA
```

Table 5.1 describes the available values.

---

7. exchweb/bin/spell/owaspell.dll.

5.3 Functionality: rich versus reach or premium and basic

Figure 5.8
OWA spell checking.

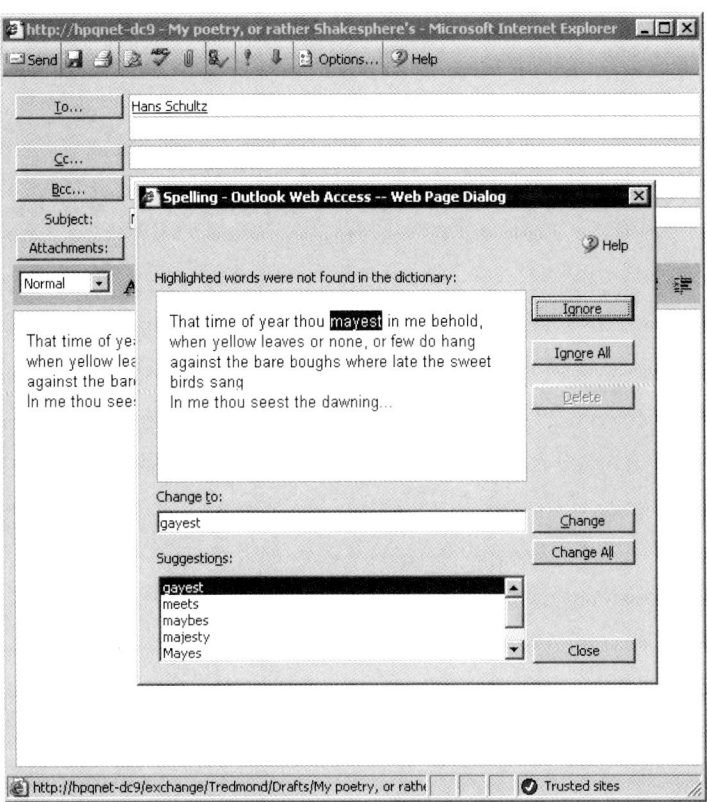

Table 5.1 *Registry Values to Control OWA Spell Checking*

Value	Meaning
MaxSpellDocumentSize	The maximum size (in KB) of a document that an OWA client can send to Exchange for spell checking. If a user sends a larger document, Exchange returns an error.
MaxSpellErrors	The maximum number of errors that Exchange will generate in a document, after which spell checking ceases. If too many errors exist in a document, Exchange spell checks until it meets the limit set, then returns the document to the user and notes that it is only partially checked.
MaxUniqueSpellErrors	The maximum number of unique errors that Exchange will generate in a document, after which spell checking ceases. The same error can exist multiple times, in which case it counts against MaxSpellErrors. In this case, Exchange looks for unique errors and counts each instance once. After a document exceeds the limit, Exchange returns it to the user and notes that it is only partially checked.

Table 5.1 *Registry Values to Control OWA Spell Checking (continued)*

Value	Meaning
DisableSpellCheckOnSend	DWORD value set to 1 if you want to prevent users from spell checking messages before sending. The default allows users to use this feature.
MaxSpellRequests	The maximum number of spell checking operations that Exchange will accept from OWA clients at one time. If the server exceeds this limit, OWA clients that subsequently attempt to check a document see a dialog saying that the spell check server is busy and they should try again later.

5.3.4 Subscriptions

OWA clients use subscriptions to enable notifications for new mail and the calendar. When OWA initializes, it uses the SUBSCRIBE method to the URL for whatever folders the user has enabled reminders for (through OWA Options—see Figure 5.9). If you want email notifications, you take out a subscription for the Inbox folder, but if you want calendar notifications, a subscription is taken out for the Calendar folder.

The subscription specifies the type of reminder that the user wants. For example, a simplified form of the HTTP message sent to the server to enable new mail notification for my account is:

```
SUBSCRIBE/Exchange/TRedmond/Inbox HTTP/1.1
Notification-Type: pragma/<http://schemas.microsoft.com/
exchange/newmail>
Host: Server-name
```

The request asks for a subscription on the Inbox folder that watches for new mail arriving. In response, the server replies with an OK and gives the client a subscription identifier and a subscription lifetime (in seconds). The client must renew the subscription before it expires if it wishes to continue receiving notifications—all OWA subscriptions have a default lifetime of one hour. It is the responsibility of the client to poll the server to receive subscription updates. The POLL command is very simple and passes the folder and subscription identifier:

```
POLL /Exchange/TRedmond/Inbox
Subscription-Id: 1099
Host: Server-name
```

The response is a stream of XML data that contains reminder information. New mail notifications are straightforward—a simple indication

5.3 Functionality: rich versus reach or premium and basic   315

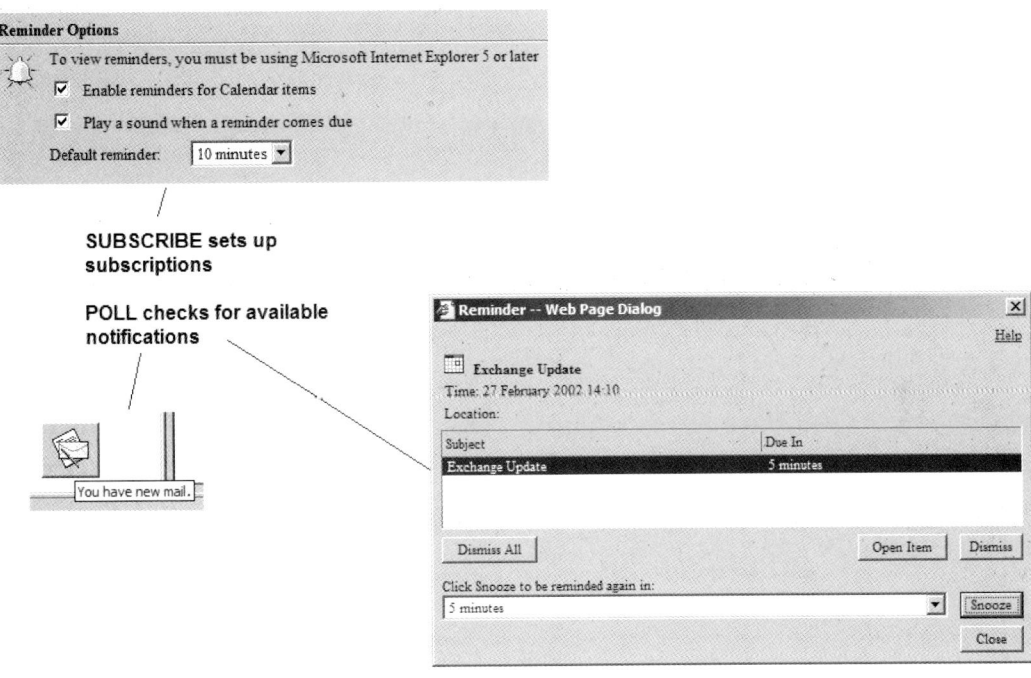

Figure 5.9   *OWA subscriptions.*

that new mail has arrived. Calendar notifications include information about the meetings or appointments and may include multiple reminders. OWA uses this data to show the user the calendar reminder dialog shown in Figure 5.9.

By default, OWA checks for new mail every 2 minutes and checks for new calendar reminders every 15 minutes. You can set different default intervals on the server by updating the system registry at the following key:

```
HKLM/System/CurrentControlSet/Services/MSExchangeWeb/OWA
```

Change the values (in minutes) of NewMailNotificationInterval (new mail) and ReminderPollingInterval (calendar) to whatever settings you desire. Note that the default reminder time stated here is different from the time shown in the OWA Options dialog; OWA uses this value to create reminder times for new appointments and meetings. However, remember that increasing poll activity generates more work for the server, so do not change the intervals unless you are sure that this will accomplish a well-defined goal.

5.3.5 Forms or cookie authentication

Exchange 2003 supports a logon security feature called "forms-based authentication" (also known as cookie authentication) to enable secure connectivity for browsers. The typical configuration is a front-end/back-end deployment (it is also possible to deploy forms authentication in a pure back-end or normal server configuration) to host connections from browsers running in kiosk-type environments. In this case, the form we refer to is the OWA logon form (owalogon.asp), which you can find in the language-specific folder under the \exchweb root. The logon page gathers user credentials. Behind the scenes, OWA uses cookies to gather the credentials and then attach them back to HTTP requests issued by the browser. An ISAPI filter and ISAPI extension check the incoming HTTP requests and validate that the credentials are correct before they permit any access to Exchange. IIS reroutes any HTTP request that does not contain the necessary credentials back to the logon form to maintain session security. Forms-based authentication increases the level of security within the OWA client by:

- Disabling the ability for users to instruct the browsers to remember their passwords

- Enabling a session inactivity timer, so that users must reauthenticate themselves if they are inactive for more than a specified period

- Causing the logout button to return users to the logon screen and disabling their ability to use the browser "back" button to return to their mailbox without reauthentication

- Allowing users to select between the rich and reach client interfaces during the OWA logon procedure

- Forcing an SSL connection—forms authentication only works on HTTPS traffic

When you configure a system to be a front-end Exchange 2003 server, it means that you want IIS to take any incoming HTTP requests for Exchange and proxy them onward to the back-end server that hosts the user's mailbox. Behind the scenes, Exchange switches the ISAPI extension for the "Exchange" Web application from DAVEX.DLL to EXPROX.DLL to replace direct Store access with proxying. In addition, integrated Windows authentication is replaced by basic authentication to allow IIS to forward requests to back-end servers. We can then proceed to enable forms-based authentication. Because forms authentication changes the way that

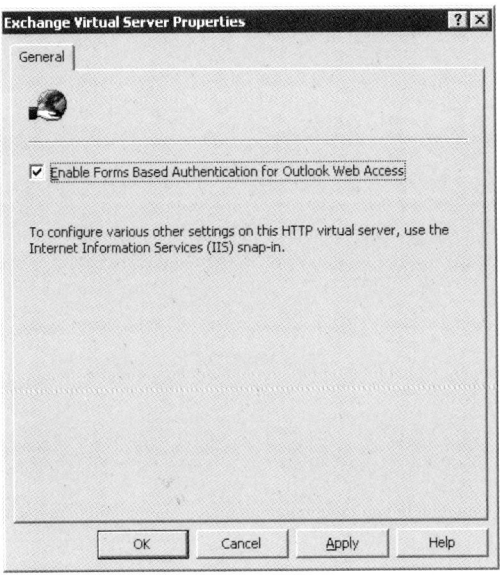

Figure 5.10
Enabling forms-based authentication.

OWA works, Exchange disables it by default. However, you can enable it by:

- Enabling SSL on the front- and back-end Exchange 2003 servers that host the mailboxes you want to access through forms-based authentication

- Using ESM to enable the feature for the Exchange virtual server (navigate through the Protocols node to select the HTTP Protocol, and then click on the properties of the Exchange virtual server, as shown in Figure 5.10)

Once again, Exchange has to make a number of changes to its Web application to make forms-based authentication work. It registers a new extension (OWAAUTH.DLL) to handle processing of user credentials, changes the default domain for the virtual directories to "\" to allow users to pass UPNs when they log on, enables the \exchweb\bin\auth virtual directory and sets its default document to be OWALOGON.ASP (Figure 5.11), and enables anonymous access to the directory.

Once everything is in place, processing works like this:

- To access his or her Exchange mailbox, the user enters a URL pointing to the Exchange application on the front-end server—for example, https://front-end/exchange. Note that the filter only traps SSL requests.

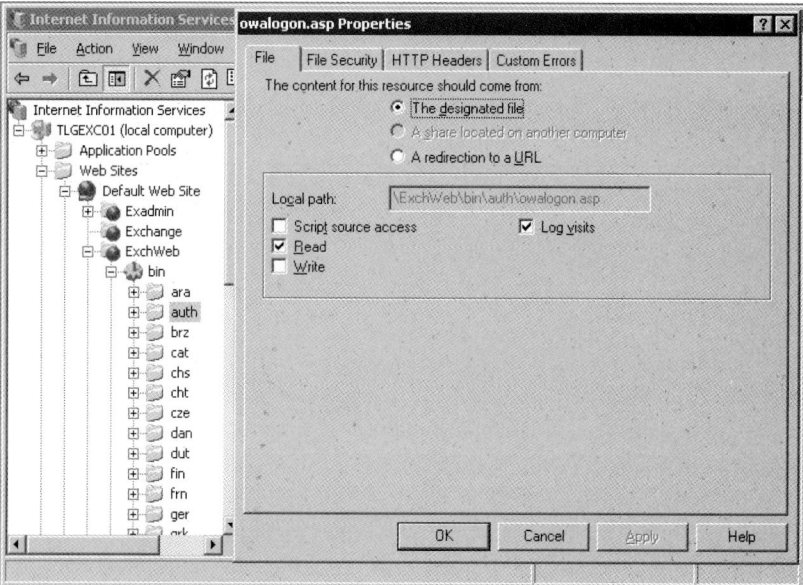

Figure 5.11 *OWALOGON.ASP properties.*

- The ISAPI filter intercepts the request and attempts to extract the user's logon credentials from a cookie that it looks for in the request.

- The user has not yet provided any credentials, so the ISAPI filter forwards the request to the Exchange Web application.

- Exchange will not allow the user to access a mailbox without credentials, so it responds with a "401" (unauthorized access to page) error. The ISAPI filter redirects the connection to display the OWA logon page to collect user credentials.

- After the user enters his or her credentials, the logon page sends a POST request to the OWAAUTH extension, which creates an encrypted cookie and redirects processing back to the URL that the user originally entered. At this point, IIS needs to be able to interact with a domain controller to validate the credentials that the user entered, so if the front-end server is in a DMZ and the controller is behind a firewall, you need to open the necessary ports to allow RPCs between IIS and the controller.

- The ISAPI filter is now able to extract a cookie, so it attempts to decrypt its content using a set of symmetric keys that Exchange regularly generates. Exchange keeps the current key and the last two

5.3 Functionality: rich versus reach or premium and basic

previous keys to ensure that we do not encounter a situation where keys become invalid because of a change in a time boundary. If the credentials exist, the ISAPI filter attaches them to the HTTP request and forwards the request to Exchange.

- Exchange recognizes the credentials and grants access to the mailbox, and normal OWA processing begins.

- To speed matters up, OWA prepopulates a hidden frame by downloading toolbars and other graphics as a user goes through the authentication process, so that it can display its user interface as quickly as possible after authentication occurs.

You can configure the session inactivity timer (in minutes), which controls how often Exchange generates the symmetric keys used to encrypt the cookie contents, by setting the DWORD registry value KeyInterval at:

```
HKLM\System\CurrentControlSet\Services\MSExchangeWeb\OWA\
```

The maximum value you can set is 1,440, or 24 hours. While you might put in a value such as 20 to indicate a 20-minute timeout, OWA cannot implement timeouts with such exactness. The browser does not constantly poll the server to know what the value is. Instead, the value represents a root value to determine the maximum and minimum inactivity time. OWA calculates the maximum and minimum values by multiplying the key interval by three and two, respectively. For example, if you set the key interval to 5, the maximum inactivity period is 15 minutes and the minimum is 10. Thus, the time when OWA requires reauthentication may occur any time after 10 to 15 minutes of inactivity.

Implementing forms-based authentication secures OWA access for kiosk-style environments but has some problems in intranet access. For example, single sign-on no longer works. In addition, you configure ISAPI filters on a per–virtual server basis, so after you set things up to support forms-based authentication, the effect is to channel all HTTP traffic for the server through the filter and not just the traffic for Exchange.

5.3.6 Some missing features in OWA

Even when you use OWA with a rich browser, some features are still missing. Microsoft has been adding new features through service packs, so you will attain maximum functionality if you connect to OWA on a server that has the latest service pack installed. Even so, working offline is notable for its absence and there is no way to access personal folder files (PSTs).

Figure 5.12
Working with rules in OWA 2003.

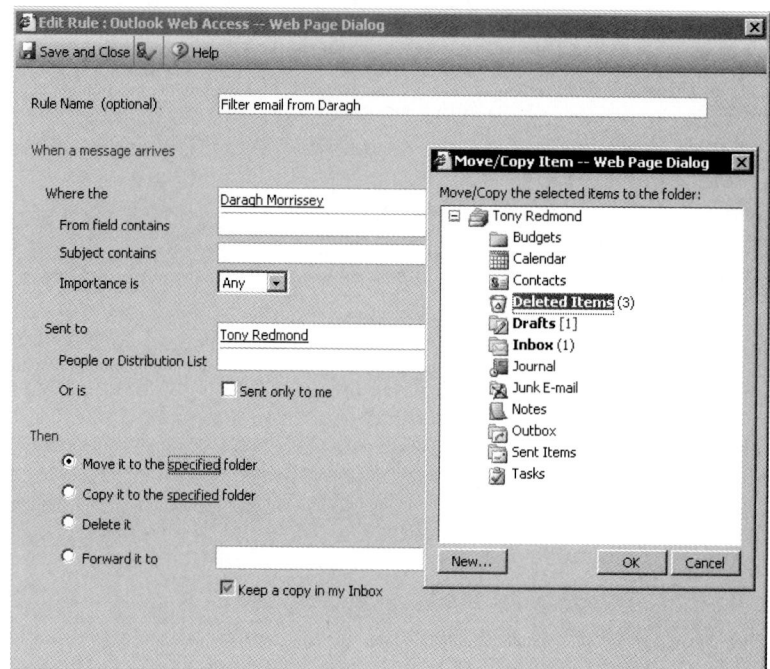

With Exchange 2000, you cannot set server-side rules through OWA, although the server will honor any rules set through an Outlook client. Microsoft implemented item type processing for Tasks in OWA 2003, but OWA does not support the Journal. You can use OWA to create new items in the Journal folder, but OWA does not include the client-side processing that makes these items function as journal entries.

With Exchange 2003, you can use the rich OWA client to work with server-side rules (Figure 5.12) and process S/MIME messages, as well as use other features missing in Exchange 2000, such as auto-signatures, search folders, support for tasks, attachment blocking, and content filtering. Tasks, auto-signatures, and attachment blocking are now also available to reach clients. However, do not expect to recall a message, set up a new public folder or set permissions on a folder, or maintain distribution lists, because those options are still missing from the OWA user interface.

Providing some mechanism to allow working offline is possibly the hardest problem to crack, at least from a philosophical point of view. Remember that Microsoft designed OWA as a "stateless client," with no need to deposit or keep user-specific data on a desktop. How does this goal measure up with the storage required to facilitate working offline? Once an application downloads local data onto a PC, you run into problems of

5.3 Functionality: rich versus reach or premium and basic

people moving around using multiple PCs. This does not usually affect personal email systems such as those offered by the free email providers, because a single PC tends to be used by one person or shared within a family; but it is certainly an issue in corporate environments, when a PC might be used first by a senior manager and later by a relatively junior employee. The prospect of someone discovering sensitive or confidential information accidentally is enough to remove any interest in this feature. Outlook solves the problem in some respect by restricting access to offline stores to the mailbox and profile that created the store, but the extent of the problem can be seen if people deliver messages to personal folders (PST files), which can be accessed by anyone who cares to browse a disk.

Access to the GAL works well, but because OWA uses LDAP instead of MAPI and does not support address list views, the access is less smooth than in Outlook and you cannot browse the GAL to locate a recipient. This is not surprising, because LDAP is a search rather than a browse protocol, so it delivers the results of the searches you execute as discrete operations. MAPI incorporates the concept of cursor locations within a data set, allowing you to browse forward and back from any particular point in the GAL. In addition, OWA does not permit users to update the contents of distribution groups, so you have to pass on this work either to people who use Outlook or to administrators.

Given Microsoft's track record in adding new features with each release of OWA, some of the missing features should appear in the future, but don't hold your breath waiting for anything that might compromise the stateless nature of the client or the ability of OWA to support multiple platforms.

5.3.7 Password updates

New Exchange 2003 servers do not allow OWA users to change their passwords, but servers upgraded from Exchange 2000 do. The logic here is that system administrators had to perform several steps on Exchange 2000 servers before users could change their passwords, so it was easiest to disable password changes in Exchange 2003. Microsoft says that this avoids end-user confusion, but I am not so sure. In any case, Microsoft Knowledge Base article 327134 explains the steps that you have to take to enable password changes for OWA users in Exchange 2000.

As with so many things in Exchange, a registry value controls how this feature works. The DWORD value is at the key:

```
HKLM\System\CurrentControlSet\Services\MSExchangeWEB\OWA
```

The value is DisablePassword. The default value is 1, meaning that users cannot set passwords. To enable this feature, set the value to 0. The upgrade procedure maintains settings on Exchange 2000 servers during the upgrade to Exchange 2003.

5.4 Suppressing Web beacons and attachment handling

Web beacons are code inserted in HTML messages as an invitation for users to transmit a "heartbeat" or indication that they have received a message back to the originator. Beacons began as very small transparent graphics included in HTML pages that are hard to notice. Web designers used beacons for a laudable purpose to track the number of visitors to a page by counting the number of downloads for the beacon's graphic file.

Today, the most common implementation of a beacon is as a URL included in a message that links back to a graphic file on an Internet site. When you open the message, the client responds to the HTML commands for the beacons and connects to the site to download the graphics. Programmers can exploit these links to send back information about you when you view the graphic, and spammers often use this technique to separate real email addresses from the guesses that they often use to populate their distribution lists. Once they know that they have a real email address, they can include it in other distribution lists that they sell, and you end up getting more spam. Links to view graphic content are implicit links, because you cannot do anything about them if you want to view the graphic. Links to other sites labeled, for example, "Click Here for more information" are explicit, because you have the choice to click or not.

Outlook 2003 and OWA 2003 both include Web beacon suppression. However, the two clients take slightly different approaches. Outlook can work offline, so it assumes that any content from intranet sites is OK and allows you to specify whether you automatically download pictures from trusted sites. The very nature of OWA is to work online always, so if it encounters links inside message content, they might be Web beacons, even from known sites. Therefore, OWA always suppresses this content and leaves it to you to decide whether you want to view it.

Figure 5.13 illustrates the story. A new message has arrived in the Inbox and OWA displays it in the reading pane. OWA detects that the message contains some content that could be a Web beacon, so it suppresses the display and flags this in the message header. Clicking on the warning tells

5.4 Suppressing Web beacons and attachment handling   323

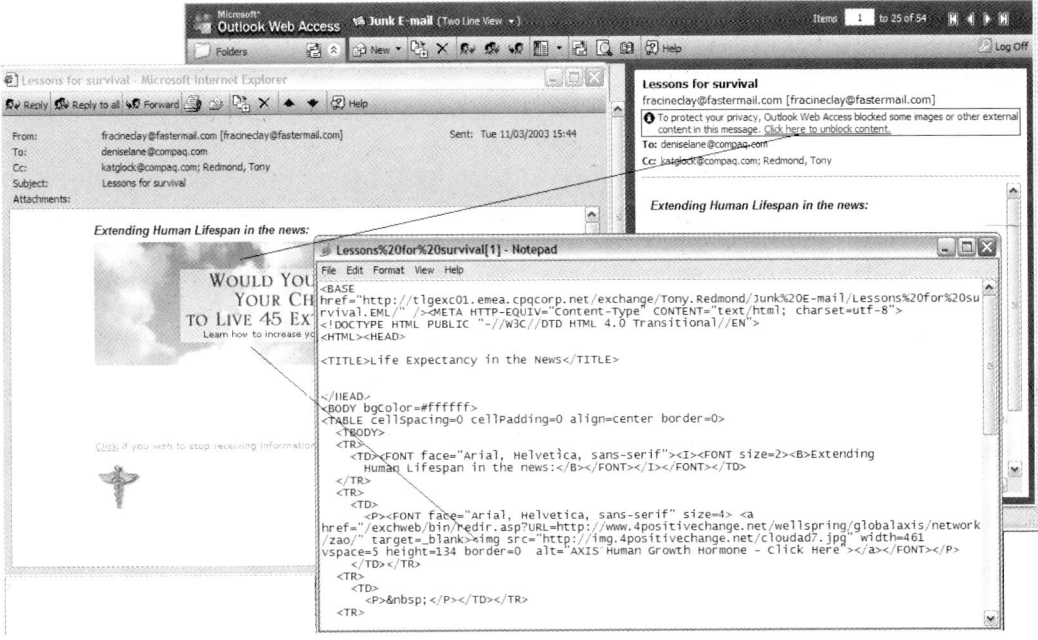

Figure 5.13   *OWA and Web beacons.*

OWA to fetch the suppressed content and display the message in a separate window. We can then view the HTML source to see where the problem might be, although at this point the data has already gone back to the originator if a programmer included the necessary instructions in the source. Note that the message has both implicit and explicit links. (See Table 5.2.)

The description so far is how OWA works OOTB. As in so many places in Exchange, a number of DWORD registry values exist that you can create

Table 5.2   *Options to Control How OWA Processes External Content*

Key	Meaning
FilterWebBeacons	0: List external content in OWA options and let the user decide (the default as shown in Figure 5.14)
	1: Force filtering and remove the UI
	2: Disable filtering and remove UI
WebBeaconFilterMode	0: Display filtered images as broken images
	1: Display filtered images as clear GIFs (default)

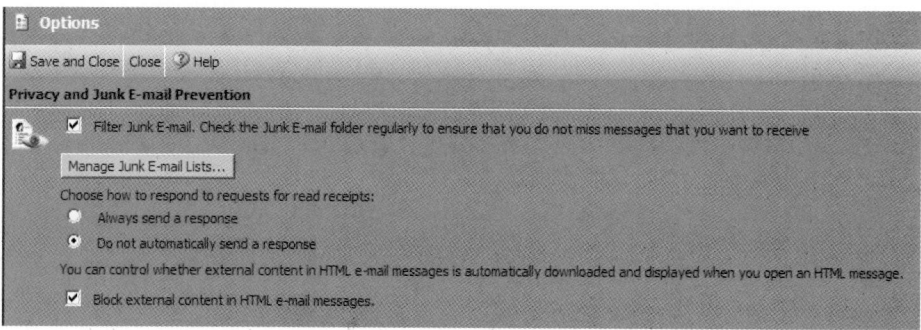

Figure 5.14 *User interface to control how OWA handles external content.*

at `HKLM\System\CurrentControlSet\Services\MSExchangeWeb\OWA` to modify behavior.

Attachments can also cause great damage if they contain malicious code and sneak past your organization's antivirus barriers. OWA 2003 implements the same type of attachment handling as Outlook and splits attachment types into three levels:

Level 1: OWA blocks all access to these attachments.

Level 2: OWA allows users to save the attachment, but they cannot open the attachment without first saving it.

Level 3: OWA processes the attachment using whatever method is available.

OWA identifies attachment types by their file extension and their MIME type. It is relatively easy to imagine the attachment types that you want to block from users, including EXE (executables) and BAT (Windows batch files). Other attachments are potentially dangerous if users execute them without thinking—VBS (Windows scripts) and URLs are usually in this category. Normal office files such as Word documents (DOC) and Excel spreadsheets (XLS) are usually in level 3.

Once again, you can see how OWA deals with attachments through some registry values at:

`HKLM\System\CurrentControlSet\Services\MSExchangeWeb\OWA`

OWA does not apply attachment blocking for every possible attachment that you might want to stop, so you have to configure a server if you want to implement these blocks. Table 5.3 lists the registry values that you can use.

Table 5.3 *Configuring Attachment Blocking for OWA*

Key	Meaning
Level1FileTypes	String value containing comma-separated list of blocked attachments—for example: `EXE, COM, BAT`
Level1MIMETypes	String value containing the MIME types of blocked attachments—for example, to block Macromedia Shock and Director files, input (or add to the existing list): `application/x-shockwave-flash, application/futuresplash, application/x-director`
Level2FileTypes	String value containing comma-separated list of potentially dangerous attachments—for example, the list to block Macromedia Shock and Director files is: `swf, spl, dir, dcr`
Level2MIMETypes	String value containing the MIME types of potentially dangerous attachments—for example: `text/html`
DisableAttachments	DWORD value set to: 0: Respect values defined in File and MIME attachments 1: Block all attachments no matter what their type 2: Only block attachments when client accesses the mailbox through a front-end server
AcceptedAttachmentFrontEnds	String value containing comma-separated exception list for front-end servers to ignore when you set DisableAttachments to 2. This allows you to configure some front-end servers that permit attachments, probably for use in an internal network.

5.5 OWA administration

From the sections we have just gone through, it is obvious that you can tweak the way OWA works through many registry settings. OWA administration is not as graphic an experience as running ESM to change settings for an Exchange server. Instead, we have to deal with a mixture of registry settings: ESM to view properties of the HTTP virtual server and the Exchange IIS applications, and IIS. The Exchange installation procedure adds a number of applications to support OWA to the IIS default Web site. These applications (Figure 5.15) are:

- Exchange: The root used to enable browser access to user mailboxes. Exchange also maps the mailbox root to drive M: through ExIFS. On an Exchange 2000 server, you can expand this root with the IIS snap-in to see a list of mailboxes. You cannot use this route to gain access

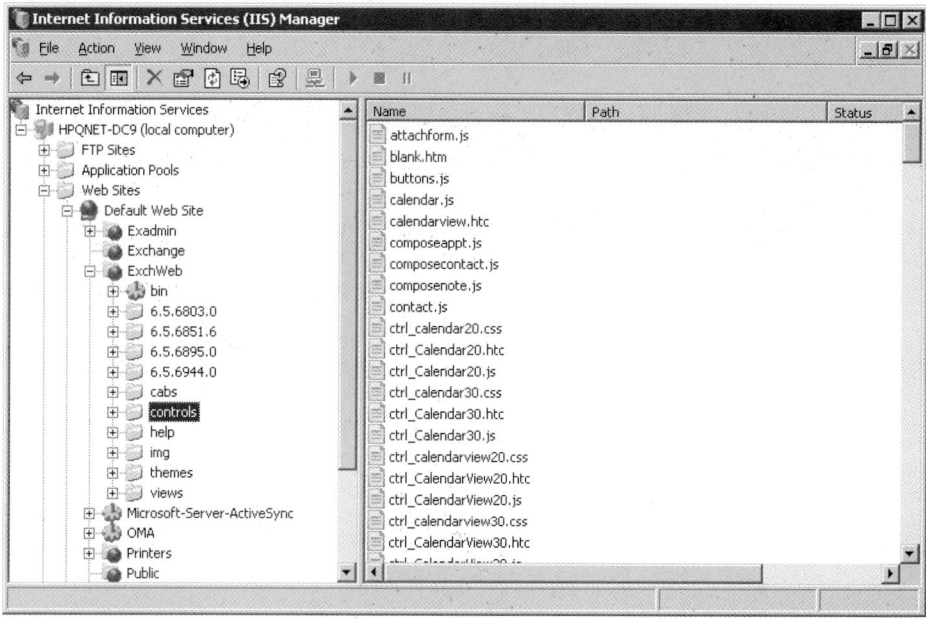

Figure 5.15 *Exchange IIS applications.*

to mailbox contents because the IIS snap-in cannot provide the necessary credentials to authenticate itself to Exchange. Exchange 2003 blocks this route to mailboxes.

- Exadmin: This root holds the ASP and other files required for Exchange administrative operations.

- Public: The root for browser access to public folders. The root is mapped to the default Public Folder hierarchy within the organization and on an Exchange 2000 server, you can navigate the public folder hierarchy from this point. In ExIFS terms, this equates to M:\organization name\Public Folders. Exchange 2003 servers do not reveal any details of public folders here.

- Exchweb: The code for the Exchange application. You can change access controls on the files through this interface, but Microsoft does not intend this to be the way to develop or customize Web components for use with Exchange.

Exchange 2003 introduces new virtual roots for "OMA" and "Microsoft-Server-Active-Sync" as part of its Exchange Mobile Services initiative. These components used to be part of the Microsoft Mobile Information Server. During the installation process, SETUP registers the

5.5 OWA administration

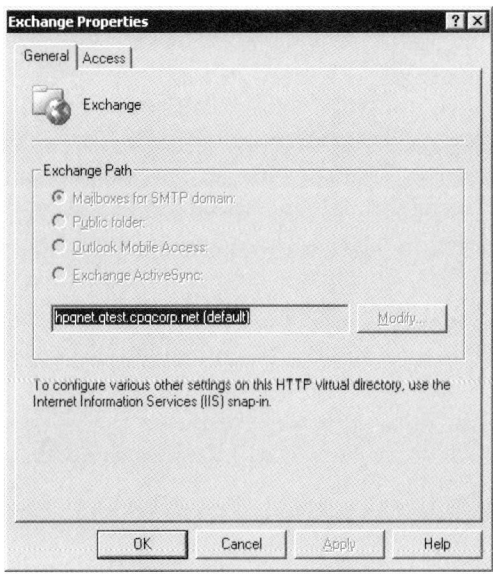

Figure 5.16
Viewing Exchange IIS application properties from ESM.

Exchange ISAPI application in the IIS metabase, the repository used by IIS to hold configuration data about applications. Properties of the application are also accessible through the ESM. However, because ESM reads its data from the configuration naming context in the AD, a potential gap clearly exists between the two sets of data.

Best practice is always to perform management for the Exchange IIS components through the IIS administration program. This marks a subtle change for Exchange 2003, since Exchange 2000 is happy to change settings through ESM and have a component of the System Attendant process, called DS2MB. perform updates to the IIS metabase behind the scenes by replicating changes made to the AD into the IIS metabase.[8] Some updates are on a demand basis, but DS2MB updates the metabase every 15 minutes by synchronizing changes made to the Exchange configuration in the AD into the metabase. As you can see in Figure 5.16, the Exchange 2003 version of ESM now directs administrators to use the IIS administration program, because it is safer and more reliable to use the one program to perform all updates.

OWA is an IIS application, so you can apply some of the management techniques and tweaks used with other IIS applications to OWA. For example, the OWA application combines many small files that create the user

---

8. DS2MB runs in a service called MSExchangeMU, where "MU" means metabase update.

interface on the browser. As with all Web applications, you have icons and other small images together with the behavior files, style sheets, and so on. Each PC maintains a local cache of Web files, and the browser checks the cache first before attempting to download a file from a server. The cache removes files based on the timeout setting defined for the application, or after the size of the files exceeds the space allocated to the cache, or if the user elects to delete the contents of the cache. In the case of OWA, the default timeout setting is one day, meaning that the browser will check a file in the cache and fetch a new copy if the cached version is older than one day. The advantage of a short timeout is that browsers always use up-to-date application files, which is clearly important for an application that does not use compiled code. However, too short a timeout forces the browser to generate extra network traffic to fetch new copies of files that probably have not been updated on the server. The trick is to look for a timeout that provides updated files reasonably quickly after a server update while reducing network traffic to an acceptable level. (See Figure 5.17.)

Some administrators argued that the default one-day timeout for OWA files used by Exchange 2000 is too short because the application is unlikely to change between service packs. Apart from installing hot fixes, this assertion is true, and you can therefore consider extending the timeout to a more appropriate value. Microsoft changed the default timeout period to 30 days in Exchange 2003 and you can increase it further if you wish. Figure 5.18

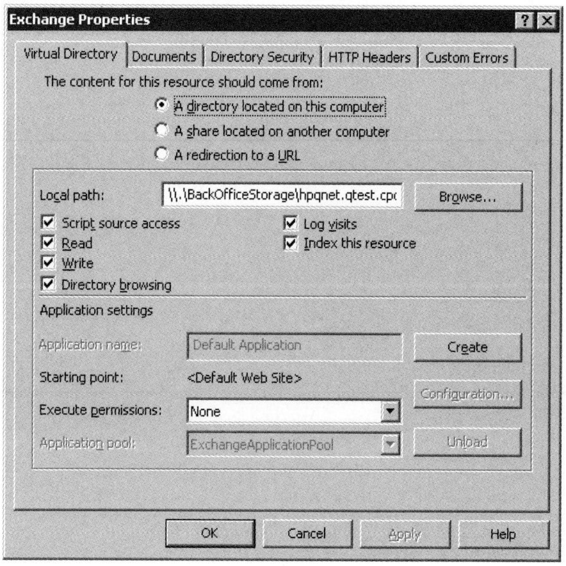

Figure 5.17
Properties of the IIS Exchange application.

5.5 OWA administration

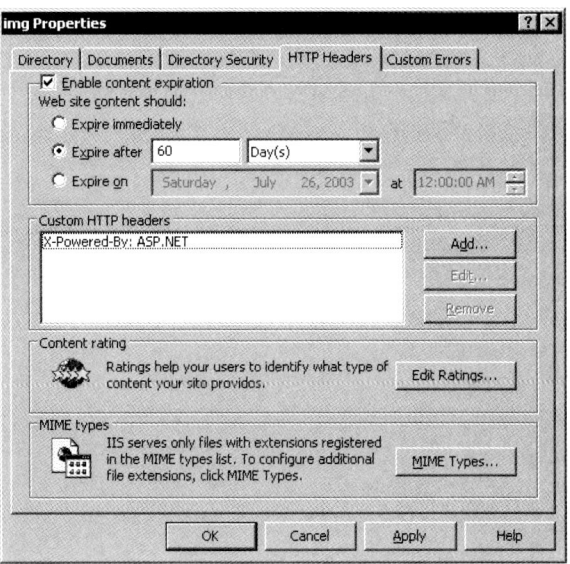

Figure 5.18
Changing the content expiration timeout for OWA.

shows a timeout of 60 days applied to the \img directory of the exchweb application (the \img directory holds all the images used by OWA). Sixty days is probably an excessively long timeout, but it serves to prove the point that you can apply standard IIS administration techniques to OWA, once you understand the impact of any of the changes you propose to make.

As you probably gather after going through so many mentions of tweaks that you can apply to the registry to change the way OWA works, OWA has no equivalent of ESM as an administration utility. Microsoft has steadily increased the functionality of OWA since it first appeared in Exchange 5.0, but singularly failed to provide any OWA administration tools of note. Working with the registry brings its own risks, and it is a real pain to attempt to make consistent registry changes over several computers unless you do this through a GPO. However, that is not always possible if you do not have the right level of administrative permission for the AD. Microsoft, therefore, introduced Outlook Web Access Web Administration (OWAWA) in a tools Web release in May 2004. You can download OWAWA from Microsoft's Web site.

OWAWA provides a Web interface to the vast majority (there will always be some hidden tweaks) of changes that administrators need to apply, including the ability to control how junk mail processing works or apply corporate branding to the OWA UI. Feature segmentation is also far easier to control through OWAWA.

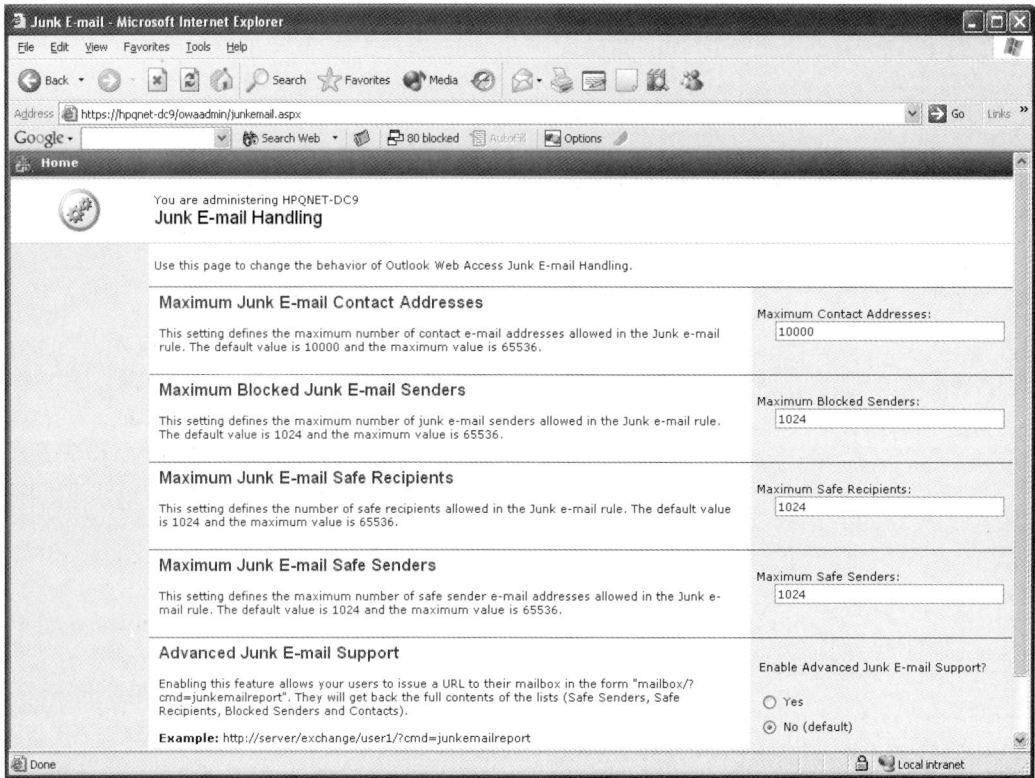

Figure 5.19 *OWA Web Administration.*

To run OWAWA (Figure 5.19), you need to run IE6 or above on the client, and you have to install Version 1.1 (at least) of the .NET framework and ASP.NET on the server where you install OWAWA. Naturally, the server also has to run IIS. Once you have everything in place, connect to the server with a URL such as:

```
HTTPS://server_name/OWAAdmin
```

If you have only one OWA server, OWAWA connects you automatically to it; otherwise, you can select the server to manage from a drop-down list. Note that the URL is HTTPS, implying the use of the Secure Sockets Layer. You can only administer servers in the same domain as the server that you connect to.

OWAWA is simple, it works, and it solves a problem for administrators, so it achieves all the hallmarks of a good tool. However, as with any tool, it is a good idea to understand what goes on behind the tool when you change something, so take the time to research the effect of a change before you update anything on a production server. Be aware that OWAWA usually implements changes immediately—there are a few instances where the changes do not apply until IIS is restarted, but OWAWA flags these as you make them.

5.5.1 OWA scalability

A long time ago, Microsoft's original development goal for OWA was to support approximately 80 percent of an equivalent MAPI client workload on a server, so a server that is capable of supporting 2,000 active MAPI clients should support 1,600 OWA connections. This has proved to be the case, and, in fact, OWA continues to narrow the gap with MAPI. Exchange 2003 is better than Exchange 2000, and the trend of increased usability with better performance will continue for OWA. In terms of network, testing indicates that OWA requires more bandwidth than MAPI, but the net requirement varies from deployment to deployment. It all comes down to the characteristics of the workload generated by users. How many messages are sent and processed every day, calendar activity, and the size and complexity of messages (attachments, distribution lists, etc.) all influence bandwidth consumption.

Cost comes into the equation too. In the United States, where network costs are typically much cheaper than anywhere else in the world, it is often possible to justify upgrading network links to support OWA on the basis that the cost is offset by the reduced deployment expenses and the reduced number of calls the help desk can expect with OWA instead of Outlook. Elsewhere, the cost of bandwidth can be much higher, and designers seek to connect as many clients as possible across available links. The bottom line is that you need to do some testing to validate the right solution for your own situation. Use the published performance tests as a guideline, but always validate the results or, if you do not have the time or capability to run tests, add 50 percent to the results as a contingency (the "fudge factor") to ensure that you err on the side of caution.

Some people will worry that the URL namespace permits anyone to use OWA if he or she has a mailbox. You might not want this to happen, perhaps because you want people to use an IMAP client or a customized version of Outlook, or you think that OWA will use too much bandwidth on a saturated network link. As we have already seen, you could disable the virtual root for the Exchange ISAPI application, but this will disable all HTTP access to the Store. The best way to disable OWA access is by restricting access on a server or mailbox level by disabling the HTTP protocol.

Every user is different, so your mileage may vary according to workload and the nature of the messages that OWA processes. In particular, calendar manipulation tends to generate heavier system load than processing an Inbox. You can explain this by the fact that the calendar is composed of multiple appointments, all of which the browser must fetch from the server and then format for display in a daily, weekly, or monthly view. Users read messages on an individual basis, and even displaying a page of data from a folder usually only involves retrieving details of 15 to 20 messages. Daily views are the least demanding, because they tend to have only two or three appointments scheduled at most. Logically speaking, a monthly view is composed of a collection of daily views, so it is the most demanding view to build. My calendar for October 2002 contains 52 separate appointments. October was a busy month, because it featured sessions and events at two Exchange conferences (United States and Europe), but it serves to illustrate the point. If the user community (such as management teams) makes heavy use of calendars, you will support less concurrent connections than a user community (such as technical staff), which mainly sends messages.

Data about the number of client connections, the pages they fetched, and the browsers that are used can be retrieved from the IIS logs. It is possible to write a script to parse the data and format it into a report. The Exchange development team does this to ensure that they get the necessary coverage of browsers (Windows, UNIX, Macintosh, Microsoft, and non-Microsoft) during their testing.

The IIS logs are stored in WINNT\System32\Logfiles\W3SVC1 with file names of "EX" followed by the date in YYMMDD format. For example, the log file for March 24, 2003, is EX030324.LOG. A typical session starts off with a client connection being recorded with the date and time, the login domain and account, the IP address of the client, and a series of GET commands as data is downloaded to the browser (any missing GIF files or other controls such as dropmenu.htc, which control the behavior of drop-down menus). When it has fully initialized the user interface, OWA then fetches data from the server to fill in folder contents. As the session proceeds, IIS logs the commands that OWA issues as it works with data. You'll see entries for SEARCH commands, where OWA is scanning through a folder; GET commands to download XSL data, where OWA is retrieving information to the browser (only for rich clients) before it is sorted locally; and PROPFIND to locate the properties of an object.

You can retrieve other valuable data by monitoring the performance counters for the "Exchange server HTTP Extension" object, which monitors the number and effect of commands such as PUT and GET, and the

5.6 Exchange's URL namespace

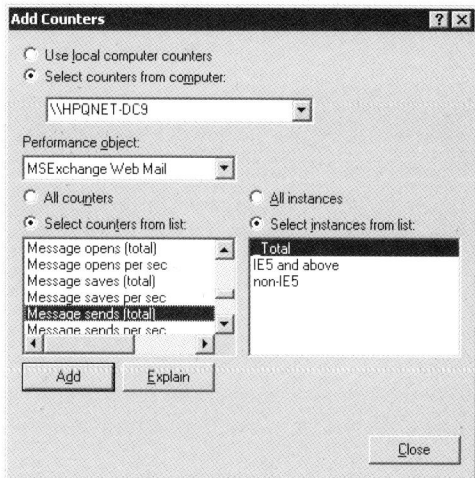

Figure 5.20
Adding a performance counter for OWA operations.

"Exchange Store Driver (IIS)" object, which monitors the interaction between browsers and the Store. The "MSExchange Web Mail" counter is also interesting, since it drives down into a level of detail such as:

- The number of appointments being accepted and declined
- Resolutions against free and busy information
- Authentications
- Folder operations
- Message operations

As you can see in Figure 5.20, Microsoft has also provided separate instances to track statistics for rich and reach browsers, or the total from both browser families.

5.6 Exchange's URL namespace

The Store automatically generates a URL for every item that it holds. Initially, the URL for an item comprises the server name, the alias for the mailbox, the folder name, and the subject. The Store adds an .eml extension,[9] to let the browser know that it is able to process the file by reference to the application that controls the file system where the item is located. In this case, the application is Exchange, which takes responsibility for displaying information for any of the standard item types, such as note, appointment,

---

9. The .eml extension stands for "Exchange Message Link."

or message. For example, if I post an item with a subject of "OK" in a folder, the URL is:

```
http://server_name/exchange/alias/folder_name/OK.eml
```

If you know it, you can use an item's URL just like any other URL, and, as long as you have permission to access the item, OWA will display its contents. In Figure 5.21, you can see an item in the Drafts folder displayed by OWA after I typed in its URL. Note that OWA does not display some of the command buttons that you would expect to see if you opened the Drafts folder normally (such as Reply and Reply All).

The Store does not finalize an item's URL until a client first accesses the item through the ExIFS interface. At this stage, the Store writes the file name part of the URL into the owning EDB as a property of the item. Even if the subject of the item changes after this time, the file name part of the URL will remain constant. For example, if an item starts with a subject called "Treasure Island," its initial URL is http://server_name/exchange/alias/folder_name/Treasure Island.eml. If you then rename the item to

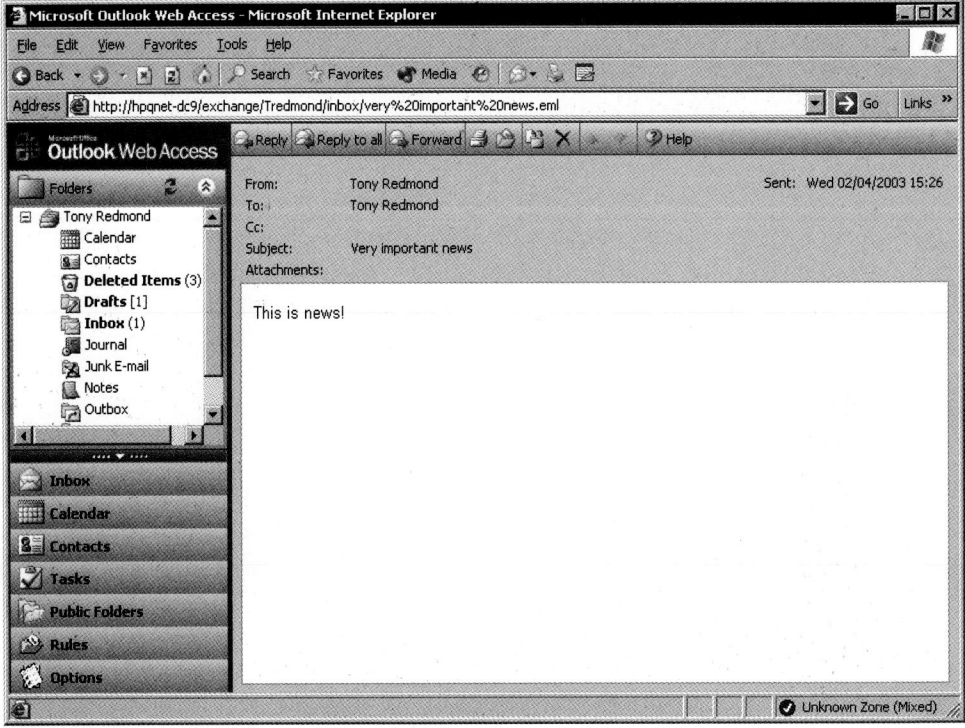

Figure 5.21 *Accessing an item with a URL.*

5.6 Exchange's URL namespace

"Treasure Cove," the Store automatically adjusts the file name part to be "Treasure Cove.eml." If ExIFS is used to access the item (from a Web browser or IMAP client, for instance), the file name is committed into the Store and remains constant from that point on, even if the item was then renamed back to "Treasure Island." Deferring writing the file name property in this manner avoids the need to update the store with properties for all known items during either the Exchange installation procedure or when a user opens a mailbox the first time after the upgrade. In the case of duplicate subjects for items held within a folder, Exchange adds a number to create a unique URL for each item. For example, if I have two items called "Operating Budget" in the "Plans" folder in my mailbox, the Store generates the following URLs:

```
http://server_name/exchange/tonyr/Budgets/Operating
Budget.eml

http://server_name/exchange/tonyr/Budgets/Operating
Budget-2.eml
```

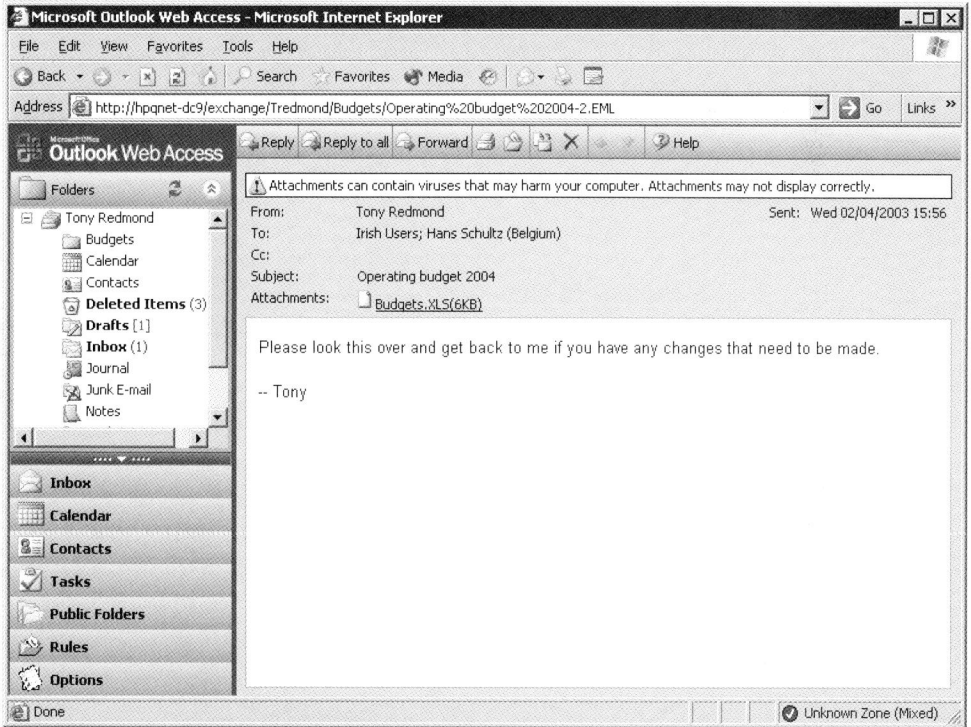

Figure 5.22 *Creating unique URLs for duplicate item names.*

If other items are added with the same subject, the trailing number is incremented by one each time, resulting in URLs ending in -3, -4, -5, and so on. The Store updates item URLs as they move between folders. Interestingly, if the Store gives an item a trailing number to create its URL, the item keeps the number as part of the URL unless some other reason occurs to force a readjustment, such as the discovery that an item with the same name already exists in the folder. Thus, you can take an item with a URL of "Budget-3.elm" and move it into another folder and the Store keeps the same file name. Figure 5.22 shows the scheme in action. The "%20" characters in the URL represent space characters.

The Store generates slightly different URLs for items that originate from Office and other applications. Instead of the .eml extension, Exchange uses the extension that already exists when the user imports the file into the Store. For example, if you drag and drop a BMP file into a folder, the generated URL uses the .bmp extension. The same occurs for common file types, such as Word (.doc), Excel (.xls), PowerPoint (.ppt), and Abode Acrobat (.pdf). When a browser requests items that belong to an application outside Exchange, OWA either loads them into the browser window (if the browser supports this feature) or downloads the content to a local file and launches the appropriate application.

5.6.1 FreeDocs

FreeDocs is the Microsoft term for documents that users add to public folders by dragging and dropping from Windows Explorer or the desktop. Users can then double-click on the document to launch the associated application and load the content from the public folder. The same type of access is possible through OWA if you pass a URL pointing to the document in the public folder. For example:

```
http://server-name/public/Budgets/2004-Budget.doc
```

In this instance, the URL points to the file 2004-Budget.doc in the top-level Budgets public folder. Exchange 2000 supports this type of access (referred to as a translated HTTP request) by default, but Microsoft disabled it in Exchange 2003 to close off a potential route where a user could put some malicious content in a public folder and infect other users with a virus or take another action to damage files or steal data. Some applications depend on translated HTTP requests, so you can reenable this feature by adding a new DWORD registry value at the key:

```
HKLM\System\CurrentControlSet\Services\MSExchangeWEB\OWA
```

The supported values are:

- 0: Default. OWA does not support translated HTTP requests.
- 1: OWA supports translated HTTP requests, but only from a back-end server.
- 2: OWA supports translated HTTP requests, but only from a back-end server or via a front-end server when the host header matches one of the format types specified in the AcceptedAttachmentFrontEnds registry value.
- 3: OWA supports translated HTTP requests everywhere.

The best course of action is to leave OWA in its default state unless you discover that an application needs to use this feature, in which case you can test various scenarios to discover the setting you need to make on the server.

5.7 Customizing OWA

Application developers found the first generation of OWA to be relatively straightforward to customize in terms of appearance and even to add a certain degree of functionality, because Microsoft provided a large portion of the source code in the form of active pages, which you can easily change with even a simple text editor. Ease of access and customization brings its own problems, the most obvious being that you had to reapply customizations on a server after you installed each new version or service pack for Exchange.

The current OWA architecture is quite different. OWA now uses a much higher percentage of compiled code and the source is not available outside Microsoft, which would prefer that you do not attempt to customize OWA except by using approved methods. The implementation of the URL namespace means that you can insert references to Exchange data inside any Web page, and, if required, you can use OWA command qualifiers to refine the URLs. You can now specify a specific view, sort items in a certain order, or start off a calendar at a set date. For example, the following URL displays my calendar in monthly view starting at March 1, 2003:

```
http://server_name/exchange/redmond/
calendar?View=Monthly&Date=20030301
```

Another example:

```
http://server_name/exchange/Redmond/
calendar?Cmd=New&Type=Appointment
```

This URL instructs Exchange to go to the calendar folder in Redmond's mailbox and execute the "New" command to create a new item of type "Appointment." Table 5.4 lists a sample of the available commands. The set of commands expands as Microsoft adds new features to OWA, so check the Microsoft Web site for details on the current set.

Table 5.4 *URL Suffixes*

URL Suffix	Function
Cmd=Navbar	Display the navigation bar in a frame
Cmd=Contents	Display the contents panel in a frame
Cmd=New	Create a new item (of a specified type)
Cmd=Options	Display the options panel (set out of office notification, etc.)
Cmd=Open	Open an item for reading
Cmd=Edit	Open and edit an item
Cmd=Reply	Reply to the sender of the current message
Cmd=ReplyAll	Reply to everyone in the header of the current message
Cmd=Forward	Forward the current message
Cmd=Delete	Delete the current item
Cmd=Options	Display the OWA options form
Cmd=ShowDeleted	Show deleted Items
Type=Message	Set the item type to be a message
Type=Post	Set the item type to be a post form
Type=Appointment	Set the item type to be an appointment
Part=1	Generates simplified views for inclusion in Web parts
Page=x	Display page x (of a set of pages)—for example, page 3 of the Inbox folder
View=x	Use a specified Outlook view—for example, View=Daily will display the Daily view in the calendar
Sort=x	Sort by the specified column—for example, Sort=Subject
Date=x	Display the specified date in the calendar. Dates are always passed in the YYYYMMDD format—for example, 20030317 is March 17, 2003.

5.7 Customizing OWA 339

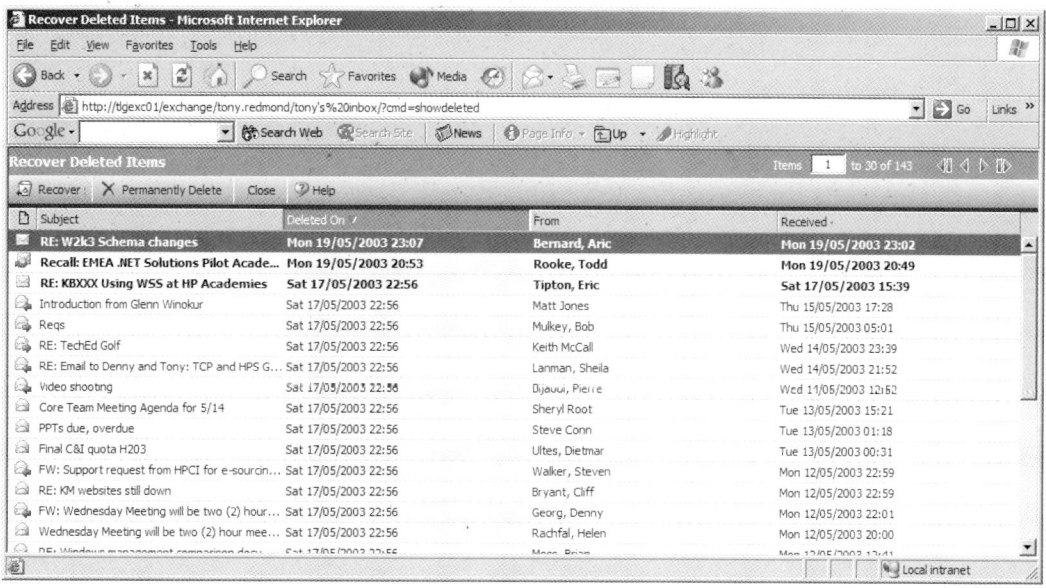

Figure 5.23 *Viewing the deleted items cache for a folder.*

Using the Exchange 2003 version of OWA, you can also create a message addressed to a specific user by using the following URL format:

```
http://server-name/exchange/username/drafts/
?cmd=new&mailtoaddr=user@domain.com
```

Exchange 2003 also allows you to look at the contents of the deleted items cache for any folder by using a command line such as:

```
http://server-name/exchange/username/folder-name/
?cmd=showdeleted
```

Figure 5.23 shows the effect.

Command-line qualifiers provide a basic level of customization. If you want to change the look and feel of OWA by applying different colors or styles, hiding the command button, or revealing or hiding folders, you have to change OWA source code components. These include the .htc, .js, and .xsl files held in the exchsrvr\exchweb folder. Table 5.5 lists the various components that interact to build the OWA user interface and the directories where you can find the files.

Microsoft does not supply a code management system to isolate and identify the changes you make to OWA files, so always work on a development system and be sure to note the changes that you make to different files

Table 5.5   *OWA Components and Directories*

Directory	Contains
Exchsrvr\bin	Wmtemplates.dll—responsible for defining the default templates used to render OWA. This component cannot be customized.
Exchsrvr\exchweb\bin	Exwform.dll—handles custom form processing
Exchsrvr\exchweb\cats	Localized (language-specific) Exchange multimedia control and associated .cab files
Exchsrvr\exchweb\controls	Holds the .css (cascading style sheets), html files, and client Jscript libraries. For example, OWA uses calendarprint.css to print calendar views.
Exchsrvr\exchweb\help	Localized versions of the OWA help files
Exchsrvr\exchweb\img	OWA image files. For example, navbar.img contains the images used in the navigation bar.
Exchsrvr\exchweb\views	XSL style sheet files used to build the standard OWA folder views. For example, v_cal.xsl is used to generate client-side views of calendar data.

to create customized code. You will have to test and then reapply changes after you install a service pack or hot fix, and you may find that the Exchange developers have altered the way that OWA works and broken one of your customizations after Microsoft produces a new service pack or hot fix. Additionally, since OWA supports well over 20 languages, you may have to make changes in multiple places to accommodate different languages. With no code management system in place, it is inevitable that reinstallations will overwrite customizations, and this is the basic reason why you are on your own if you decide to change the OWA files. The following customization changes can be made:

- Show specific Exchange components (such as the calendar) in a browser frame
- Modify the navigation bar to add or remove options
- Modify the folder tree view control to remove public folders
- Hide toolbars from folder views
- Modify the colors used with OWA style sheets
- Change the icons used by OWA
- Add new forms for use with OWA

5.7 Customizing OWA

- Change the XSL style sheets used for client-side view generation
- Logoff customization

This list is not exhaustive and is likely to change as Exchange evolves. However, customizing OWA is a double-edged sword. You may accomplish your goal, but you will create extra work in the end to maintain and reapply customizations after service packs and other upgrades.

5.7.1 Branding

You can customize the appearance of OWA 2003 through themes. OWA provides a set of five default color schemes (blue, olive green, silver, burgundy, and dark blue) for users to select from, but programmers can customize the CSS style sheet to define their own color scheme and the image files used in the OWA interface and so build their own theme. For example, you can combine a company's preferred color scheme and logos to generate a "house style" for OWA. Figure 5.24 demonstrates an "hp-branded" version of OWA, including the new mail notification pop-up. This feature is

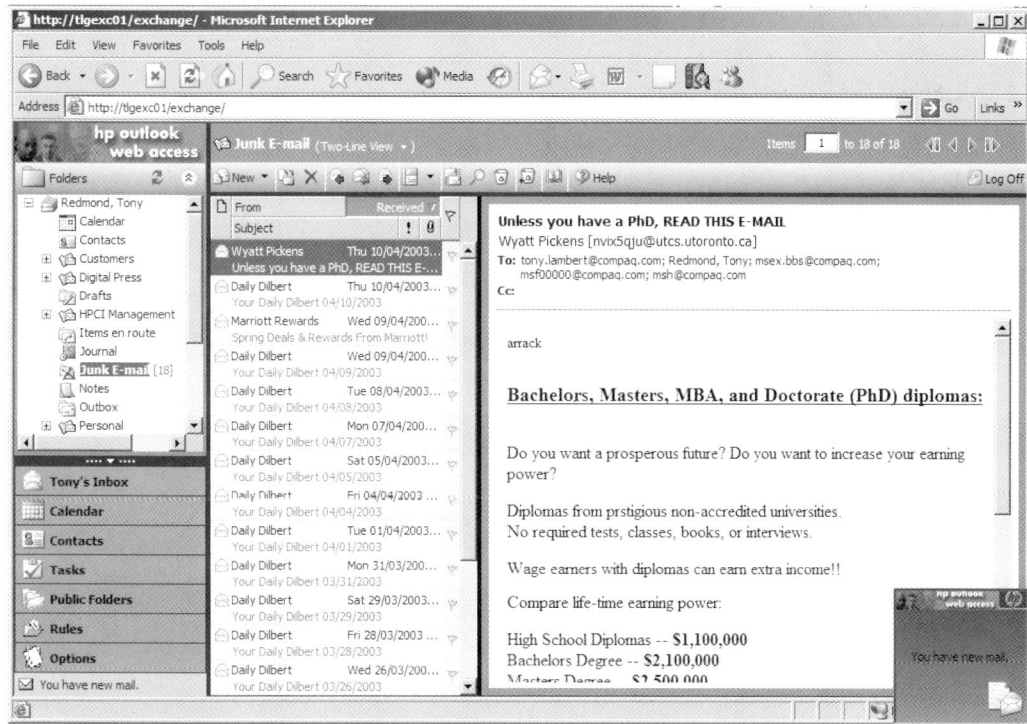

Figure 5.24   *Branded OWA.*

likely to be popular with companies as well as ASPs, who can now generate "branded" versions of OWA. However, the branding only works for mailbox access, since OWA uses a different interface for public folders.

5.7.2 Segmenting OWA functionality

Application Service Providers often want to divide OWA functionality to control the components available to users. For example, users who pay for calendar access can see the calendar, while those who only want to use email cannot. You might also decide to limit client functionality to reduce the load on the server. Exchange 2000 SP2 onward allows administrators to segment OWA functionality on a server or individual user basis. You can control the most important areas of OWA functionality as follows:

- Messaging: If enabled, users can send and read email messages and access all mailbox folders.

- Calendar: If enabled, users see their Calendar folder and if Messaging is enabled, they can create and accept meeting requests.

- Contacts: When enabled, users can see the Contacts folder and create and use contacts (including to validate addresses on messages).

- Tasks: When enabled, users can see their Tasks folder.

- Journal: When enabled, users can see their Journal folder.

- Notes: When enabled, users can see their Notes folder.

- Public folders: If enabled, users can access public folders and OWA displays the links to public folders. If not, OWA shows no evidence that public folders exist.

- Calendar reminders: If enabled, calendar meeting reminders are signaled; otherwise, they are suppressed.

- New mail notifications: If enabled, OWA signals new messages with a notification pop-up; otherwise, notifications are suppressed.

- The interface: If enabled, clients are able to use the OWA rich interface; otherwise, the reach interface is used. Note that the rich interface requires Internet Explorer 5.* or later.

You control segmentation by setting bits in a bit mask. Each feature is controlled by a separate bit value, and when that bit is set to 1, the feature is enabled. Conversely, you disable the feature if the bit is set to 0. Values are set in a bit mask using increasing powers of two, so you enable the desired set of features by totaling the unique value for each feature and using the

5.7 Customizing OWA

Table 5.6 *OWA Segmentation Bit Values*

OWA Feature	Value	Exchange 2000	Exchange 2003
Messaging	1 (1 hex)	X	X
Calendar	2 (2 hex)	X	X
Contacts	4 (4 hex)	X	X
Tasks	8 (8 hex)	X	X
Journal	16 (10 hex)	X	X
Notes	32 (20 hex)	X	X
Public folders	64 (40 hex)	X	X
Calendar reminders	128 (80 hex)	X	X
New mail notifications	256 (100 hex)	X	X
Rich user interface	512 (200 hex)	X	X
Spell check	1,024 (400 hex)	—	X
S/MIME secure email	2,048 (800 hex)	—	X
Search folders	4,096 (1,000 hex)	—	X
Auto-signature	8,192 (2,000 hex)	—	X
Rules	16,384 (4,000 hex)	—	X
Themes	32,768 (8,000 hex)	—	X
Junk mail filters	65,536 (10,000 hex)	—	X
All available functionality	FFFFFFF (hex)	—	X

cumulative total. Table 5.6 lists the values for the available features. For example, to enable Messaging, Calendaring, and their notifications while using the rich OWA interface, the calculation is:

1 + 2 + 128 + 256 + 512 = 899

You apply OWA segmentation to a complete server by adding a new DWORD value called DefaultMailboxFolderSet to the system registry under the HKLM\System\CurrentControlSet\Services\MSExchangeWeb\OWA key. Input the calculated value in hexadecimal, then stop and restart the Information Store service and the World Wide Web service. Test that the desired change is effective by connecting to the server with OWA. Note that the browser controls some degree of segmentation. For example, it does not matter if you allow people to have full access to all features if they run a down-level browser. Along the same lines, some dependencies exist between different functions. For example, messaging is a fundamental component for calendaring and you will not be able to send out meeting notifications without it, so there is not much point in enabling calendaring without messaging, and, indeed, OWA 2003 will not let you! In addition, if you do not explicitly specify the rich client interface, you will see the reach interface, which in turn means that you cannot use functionality that the reach interface does not support.

You can also apply feature segmentation at an individual user account level or, more probably, for a selected group of user accounts. The user setting overrides the server setting, which is a useful feature. However, for Exchange 2000 SP2 onward, the big problem is that you need to update the AD schema to add the necessary attribute (msExchMailboxFolderSet) before you can apply segmentation to an account, and you input the necessary bit mask by selecting the account and updating its attribute with ADSIEDIT. The new attribute holds a list of folders that a user is able to access. This is not a major issue if you apply schema updates at the start of a deployment, but adding an attribute that the AD must then publish to every GC server in the forest will cause a complete refresh of GC data, something that you must plan carefully if your forest is already in full production. You do not have to worry about the schema update for Exchange 2003 if you use Windows 2003 domain controllers, since the Windows 2003 version of the schema includes this change.

Function segmentation works only for OWA and does not affect the options available to other clients.

5.8 OWA firewall access

It is reasonably common to encounter a requirement to allow access to mailboxes on Exchange servers through a firewall, perhaps to accommodate the needs of traveling users who wish to connect across the public Internet without a VPN. In one scenario, you have one or more front-end servers placed in the DMZ to accept incoming requests from clients and then relay or proxy them onward to the mailbox servers. Another common scenario is to deploy a proxy server such as Microsoft Internet Security and Acceleration (ISA) server in the DMZ and keep the front-end servers safely behind the firewall. Because ISA includes components specially designed to support secure OWA access, it is the most popular choice for OWA deployments.

5.8 OWA firewall access

The front-end servers authenticate user credentials but do nothing with the traffic, since their purpose is to accept the incoming request and channel it to the appropriate back-end mailbox server. To protect communications, firewalls are in place to control external traffic into the DMZ and from the DMZ to the internal network. To make this all work, you open the ports used by Exchange and other associated components on the internal and external firewalls, limiting the open ports to the smallest possible set in order to reduce the potential for hacker attacks. A full set of ports used by Exchange and other infrastructure components is shown in Appendix C.

In most front-end/back-end scenarios, you use Outlook Web Access as the client, although you can take the same approach with Outlook 2003 when it connects to Exchange over HTTP. Figure 5.25 illustrates the basic layout of the front-end/back-end scenario. This is a very simple example that is suitable for small deployments. It is quick and easy to set up, but the basic configuration is not secure because the front- and back-end servers do not encrypt the HTTP streams. You can certainly use IPSec to protect the interserver traffic, but even so, you still must maintain a large number of open ports on the internal-facing firewall, which attackers could exploit if they manage to penetrate the DMZ.

Larger deployments, such as those used by Application Solution Providers, often deploy proxy servers in the DMZ to process client connects before they reach the Exchange front-end server. You can deploy software (such as ISA) or hardware-based proxy servers (a network appliance such as those made by Nortel and Cisco) to achieve the major advantage of being able to move the front-end server out of the DMZ to behind the internal

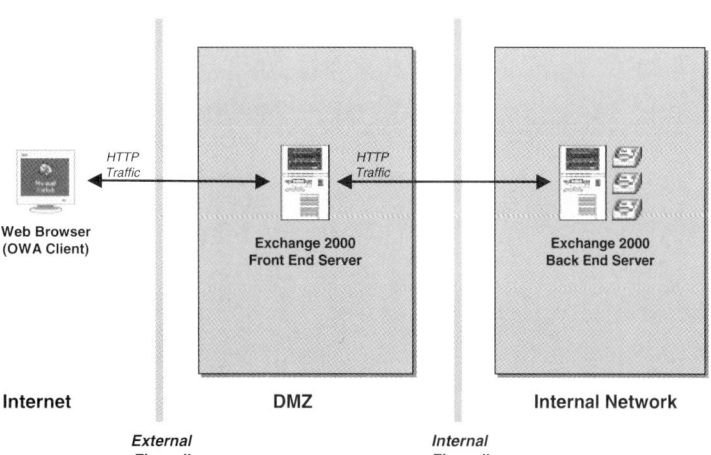

Figure 5.25
Basic layout of OWA access through a firewall.

firewall. Typically, you couple software-based proxy servers with SSL/TLS accelerator cards to offload some of the encryption activity and increase throughput. Hardware-based proxy servers deliver the best performance but they are far more expensive than software equivalents, so the volume of connections you expect to handle often dictates your choice.

Once the front-end server is in the internal network, you do not have to worry about opening ports in the firewall and therefore have less risk of an attack. In addition, clients can use an end-to-end HTTPS connection over port 443 through the DMZ to the front-end server and so protect all traffic from prying eyes.

The proxy server can provide two variations of protection: tunneling and bridging. With tunneled connections, the proxy server passes communications straight through from client to front-end server, and the front-end server does all the processing to decrypt the HTTPS traffic. With bridging, the proxy server intercepts the proxy server client communications and establishes a new connection between the proxy server and the front-end server. You can continue to protect the new connection with SSL, or you can have the proxy server perform the decryption and pass an HTTP stream to the front-end server and so offload the decryption workload from that server. With no need to decrypt traffic, the front-end server is capable of supporting far more client connections. Another advantage is that when the proxy server intercepts the original client connections, it can inspect the packets, decide whether any are suspicious, and terminate their passage.

The requirements for secure access differ from company to company. If you decide that you need to support browser access back through the public Internet, then it is worth taking the time to investigate all of the potential solutions, since technology moves fast in this area. You should also look at alternatives to support other clients, such as implementing a VPN to allow older versions of Outlook and other clients to connect. Given the widespread availability of public LANs (both wired and wireless) in hotels, airports, and other facilities, having VPN access is a great way for users to be able to work online and connect to all corporate resources instead of just being limited to email.

5.8.1 Securing OWA

Mention of firewalls inevitably leads to a discussion about security and the vulnerability of IIS to hacking exploits. The OWA architecture is firmly rooted in IIS and IE, both products that have a checkered history when it comes to hacker exploits. A large number of buffer overflow bugs afflicted both IIS and IE and at times it seemed that a new exploit was reported weekly, followed by a new patch to be applied to either server or browser. To its credit, Microsoft responds as quickly as possible whenever someone reports a new potential security issue (not all reports turn out to be real issues; some are due to lack of knowledge or misunderstanding about software functionality), but this is not the problem: Companies are concerned that deploying IIS and IE will open up holes for future exploits. Outlook is also open to abuse, as is evident in the large number of virus attacks based on macros and other loopholes experienced in the last few years.

Administrators can mitigate their exposure by including IIS and IE in the list of components regularly reviewed for security within the overall messaging infrastructure. You must review and then apply (as appropriate within your environment) Microsoft's tools for increased security, such as the IIS Lockdown tool for IIS 5.0. Be sure that any tool is fully tested before you deploy it into production, since overzealous protection will stop IIS from serving dynamic content and thus halt OWA. Better yet, you can deploy IIS 6.0 and take advantage of its much improved security model. On the client side, the latest versions of IE are more secure, but that is no reason to fail to check for current browser patches and hot fixes that close off reported problems.

5.8.2 IPSec

If you run a front-end/back-end configuration to support clients such as OWA or IMAP4, you probably use a variation of the classic configuration that places the front-end server in the DMZ and the back-end mailbox servers behind the firewall. Exchange does not support SSL encryption of the traffic flowing between the front- and back-end servers and it is a bad idea to leave the traffic unprotected, just in case a hacker manages to penetrate your external firewall and enter the DMZ. You can certainly use a solution such as Microsoft's own Internet Security and Acceleration (ISA) server to bridge SSL traffic across the firewall, but this complicates the configuration by adding additional components and introduces some extra cost. Of course, if you have other uses for ISA, then you can exploit its existence, but if not, you should look at IPSec as a free way to protect the traffic.

IPSec is a set of transport layer extensions to the basic Internet Protocol that binds the Internet together. Because IPSec operates at the transport layer of the network stack, applications do not have to provide special code to take advantage of its existence. Instead, the applications "see" a communications path that is protected, even if they do not know this (or need to). IPSec includes two protocols that complement each other: the Authentication Header Protocol and the Encapsulating Security Payload (ESP) Protocol. From an Exchange perspective, we are more interested in ESP, because we can use it to encrypt datagrams as they pass between servers. Servers that use IPSec use another component, the Internet Key Exchange (IKE) Protocol, to exchange cryptographic keys and negotiate to discover the type of encryption (algorithm and key length) that the two servers support. Once this is done, the servers establish a secure channel between them and encrypted application data then begins to pass across this channel.

When administrators approach IPSec, they often find that the most complicated part of the implementation is the policies that Windows uses to control IPSec. This is a situation where excessive complexity can easily creep in, especially if security wizards attempt to close down every possible channel. However, there is an easy answer, because Windows includes three IPSec policies that you can use immediately. These policies begin to solve the problem for the majority of implementations, so you should always start with them. The three policies are:

- Client Respond Only: This policy lets target servers (such as the mailbox servers) respond to requests from other servers that want to negotiate a secure channel.

- Server Request Security: This policy instructs servers to always attempt to negotiate a secure channel when connecting to another computer. If the negotiation fails (perhaps because the target server does not support IPSec), communication can continue, but it is not protected.

- Secure Server Require Security: This policy forces the server to require the use of IPSec. Be careful with this policy, because it can stop a server from communicating with all but a limited set of servers, or even none, if you make mistakes.

To apply IPSec, we can use the Client Respond Only policy for the back-end mailbox servers, applying the policy to each server using the IP Security Management MMC console. Make sure that the IPSec Policy Agent service is running before you attempt to do anything with IPSec policies. If the service is not running, you will not be able to apply policies to servers and secure channels will not work. Securing the front-end servers takes a little more work, because you need to use the IP Security Policy wizard to create a policy that states:

- The traffic you want to protect flows through port 80

- The IP addresses of the source (front-end) and target (back-end) servers
- Traffic flows across a LAN and does not use a tunnel
- TCP is the required protocol

These are the basics of the required policy. It is wise to leave IPSec policies to an expert if you have not created and applied one before, or make sure that you read up on the subject and do some serious testing before you go anywhere near a production server. When the policies are in place, use the IPSECMON tool from the Windows Resource Kit to ensure that traffic is flowing as expected by viewing the secure channels that are in place. In addition, check that users can access their mailboxes as normal.

5.8.3 Leaving sensitive files around

Some administrators worry that users might leave sensitive information on a PC after an OWA session. Attachments are the usual worry. When users receive an attachment in a message, they can open it, save it, forward it, or delete it just as they can do with any other client. With other clients, they probably use the same PC all the time, so it does not matter if the file remains on disk; but it may matter if someone else comes along, discovers the file, and opens it to read something that he or she should not see.

In the same way that you are powerless if a user forwards confidential information to someone else by mistake, you cannot do much if a user elects to save a file to disk. All you can hope is that the user knows what he or she is doing and will not do anything stupid. OWA minimizes potential problems by setting an already past expiration date on all files that it creates temporarily when users open attachments for viewing. This means that the browser automatically removes the files (because they are expired) when it closes (Figure 5.26). Behind the scenes, OWA creates a file in the user's Temporary Internet Files folder. If you check the time and date of the message (13:01 on December 12, 2002) against the file's expiration date (12:02 on December 12, 2002), you can see how things work. The bottom line is that the software attempts to mitigate problems as much as it can, but you cannot legislate for user behavior, which is where most security problems originate.

5.8.4 IE enhanced security

If you connect to OWA with a mailbox on an Exchange 2003 server running on Windows 2003, you may be annoyed to discover that you have to

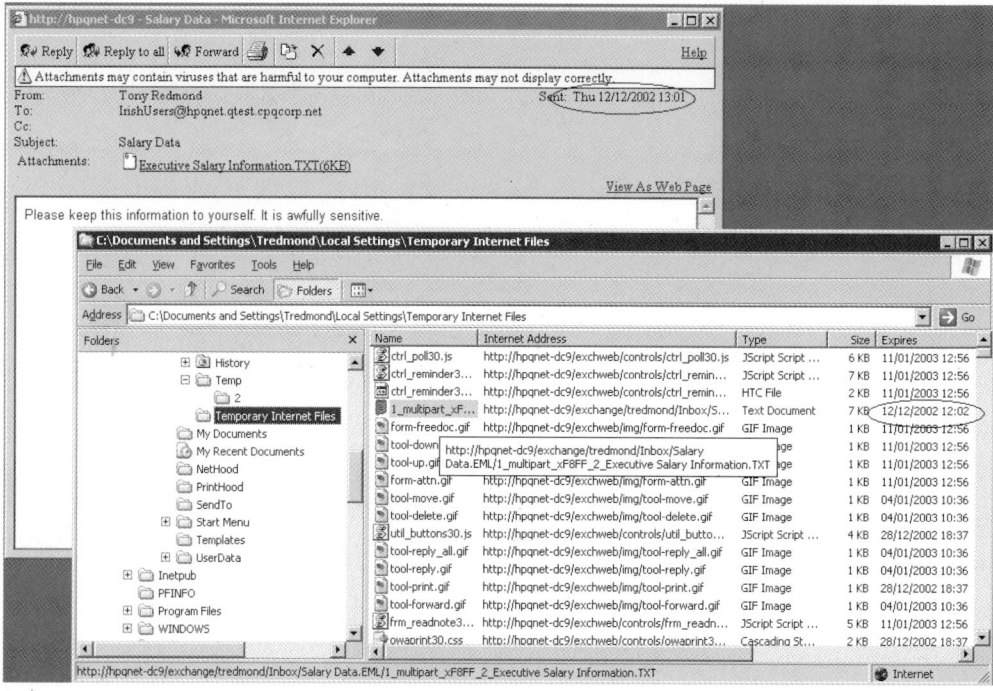

Figure 5.26   *OWA expiration dates for attachments.*

log on before you can access your mailbox (Figure 5.27). By default, Windows 2003 implements enhanced security for IE, meaning that users must provide explicit credentials before they can access secure sites.

You can stop IE from prompting for credentials in a two-step process. First, you use the Add/Remove Programs applet to remove Internet Explorer Enhanced Security Configuration from the set of Windows components. Second, you add the Exchange server that hosts your mailbox as a trusted site for IE (use Internet Options under the IE Tools option to do this).

5.9   OWA for all

Can you throw away Outlook and replace it with OWA? Probably not, if your user community has become used to the way Outlook works and exploits some of the features not supported by OWA, such offline access. Outlook 2003, especially operating in cached Exchange mode, performs better from a user perspective especially if you tend to switch between folders frequently and the folders contain many messages. This kind of activity

5.9 OWA for all   351

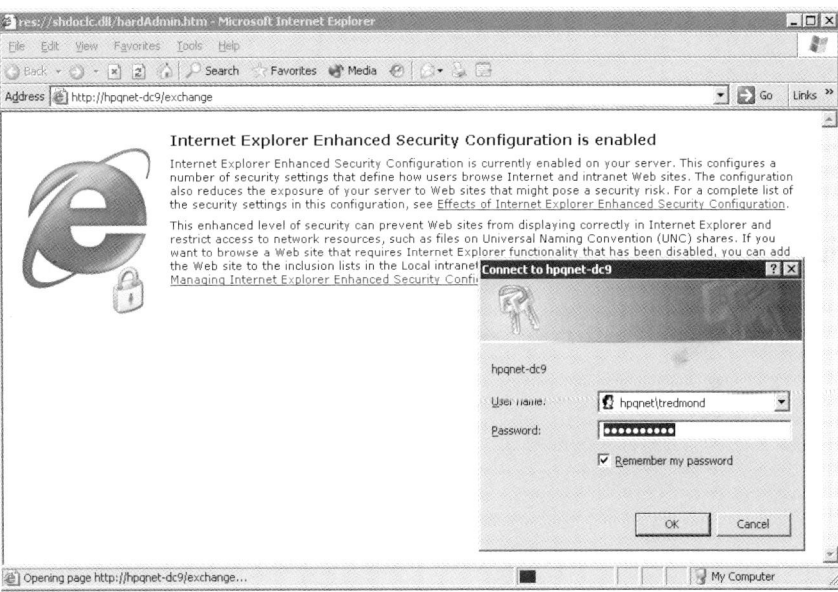

Figure 5.27   *IE6 enhanced security and OWA logon.*

exposes the Achilles Heel of OWA because it demands heavy client-server communications whereas Outlook can exploit its local cache. Nevertheless, OWA offers a very real alternative to companies that want to deploy Exchange to serve user communities without going through the pain of client deployment and maintenance.

OWA is very useful even if you are quite happy with Outlook. OWA provides a great way to connect when Outlook is not available, such as when traveling, at home, or when using someone else's PC. OWA is also tremendously valuable when you have an unreliable or slow network connection that cannot support the network traffic generated by Outlook. For example, if you use a telephone link to connect Outlook to an Exchange server, the client and server exchange a substantial amount of bytes to establish context, check reminders, and so on. If the link disconnects and you reconnect, roughly the same traffic flows across the line to reestablish context. In comparison, if you use OWA and the line disconnects, you can reconnect and begin working again almost immediately. Outlook 2003 has made great improvements in usability, performance (cached Exchange mode) and flexibility (RPC over HTTP connections), but OWA has also improved so it is a ding-ding battle between the two as to which is the more efficient client.

There is no doubt that Microsoft has improved support for browser clients enormously since its initial effort in 1996. Microsoft continues to expend substantial development effort on OWA, so it will be interesting to see how the OWA versus. Outlook debate evolves over the next few years.

6
Internet and Other Clients

While Outlook remains the most popular choice to connect to Exchange mailboxes, Microsoft has encouraged other clients to connect to Exchange by supporting popular Internet protocols such as IMAP4 and POP3. Microsoft also has clients such as Outlook Express, Pocket Outlook, and the Macintosh clients that you can connect to Exchange; with Exchange 2003, we have a new set of smartphone and other mobile clients that can join the party.

Any large organization is likely to have a number of client platforms in operation, especially when you factor in mobile clients like the Pocket PC and other handheld devices. From an Exchange perspective, these are all just clients that funnel in to one place (the Store), but clearly it is a challenge for administrators to support the many different client types that users want to exploit. In this chapter, we look at the Internet and mobile clients and discuss some of the points you need to consider as you build corporate messaging environments.

6.1　IMAP4 clients

IMAP4 (Internet Mail Access Protocol Revision 4) represents the state of the Internet art for a messaging client protocol, and any recent IMAP client can connect to Exchange. The latest version of Outlook Express (6.0 or later, as shown in Figure 6.1) is a very functional Exchange client. Best of all, Outlook Express is free and comes as part of the Internet Explorer package, and it's well integrated with other Microsoft Internet software such as MSN Messenger.

Outlook Express scores over Outlook for users who spend a lot of time on the road and connect over slow telephone links, since it requires much less bandwidth to send and fetch messages from Exchange. My own very

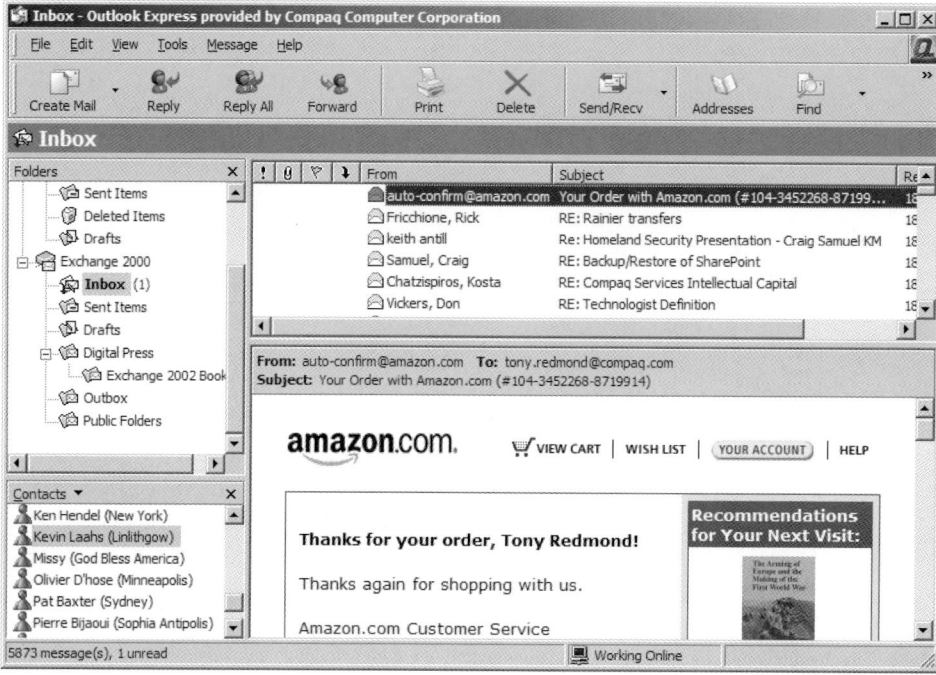

Figure 6.1   *Outlook Express.*

basic and totally nonscientific observations are that Outlook Express is at least twice as fast as Outlook 2002 in connecting and downloading messages, and this feeling can be explained by the fact that communication between Outlook and Exchange is always via RPCs, even over a dial-in link using cached Exchange mode. Because RPCs are a "heavy" network protocol, which assumes that the network is reliable and available all the time, channeling RPCs over a telephone link can be an intensely painful experience, especially when the client seems to want to report every small step to the server! By comparison, IMAP is like other Internet protocols in that it does not assume perfect high-quality networks, so its transmissions are less costly and tend not to have the same number of retries that RPCs accumulate. To see what I mean, monitor the number of bytes transmitted between Outlook and Exchange after making a connection using dial-up networking. You will be amazed at the amount of data that Outlook sends just to log on to Exchange and display the contents of the Inbox. Outlook 2003 makes better use of network resources, especially when it connects to a mailbox on an Exchange 2003 server; cached Exchange mode improves user perception of performance, but Outlook Express still has a lighter touch.

It is also possible to configure Outlook to connect to Exchange 2000/2003 via IMAP. Outlook 2002 (and later) allows concurrent use of both MAPI and Internet protocols to access multiple mailboxes—even to connect to the same mailbox. You must configure earlier versions, such as Outlook 2000, in Internet mode before it can use either POP3 or IMAP4 to access Exchange.

Outlook and Outlook Express share a number of components, such as the IMAP engine and the HTML rendering engine. Aside from messaging functionality, the major difference between the two clients is that Outlook incorporates many more PIM (tasks, journaling, and notes) features than Outlook Express. Users gain some advantages with Outlook Express—for example, you are able to ignore mailbox quotas to continue sending messages, because Exchange enables mailbox quotas through the Store and not in the SMTP virtual server, which Outlook Express uses to transmit messages.

Despite the feature deficit, some companies prefer Outlook Express, because it requires less memory and disk space after installation. Outlook Express is also a superb client for newsgroups. Outlook, along with the rest of the Office suite, requires many megabytes of disk space to run. The actual Outlook.exe file is only 46 KB,[1] but all the DLLs that the client needs to run spread out to occupy a lot of disk space. Finally, it is easier to train and support Outlook Express, because it is inherently simpler than the full-feature Outlook. Each extra option, command button, and property page represents potential support calls and extra time to train users. Outlook Web Access is certainly another good client alternative that scores over any IMAP client, because it can better handle calendars, public folders, tasks, and other extended features. However, even the latest version of Outlook Web Access is less functional than Outlook Express if you need offline access.

Essentially, if you just want email, then all of the basic and most of the extended messaging features found in Outlook are present in Outlook Express, so you should consider whether you should deploy Outlook or Outlook Express. Either client will do an excellent job for email, but Outlook should be selected if you need calendaring, workgroup features, sophisticated offline access, and the ability to customize the user environment through electronic forms, views, and CDO-based code.

Figure 6.2 shows the major properties that you must define to connect Outlook Express (left) and Outlook 2002 (right) to an Exchange mailbox. The properties are very similar in both cases. Note that the same server

---

1. Size taken for Outlook 2002, executable version 10.0.2627.1.

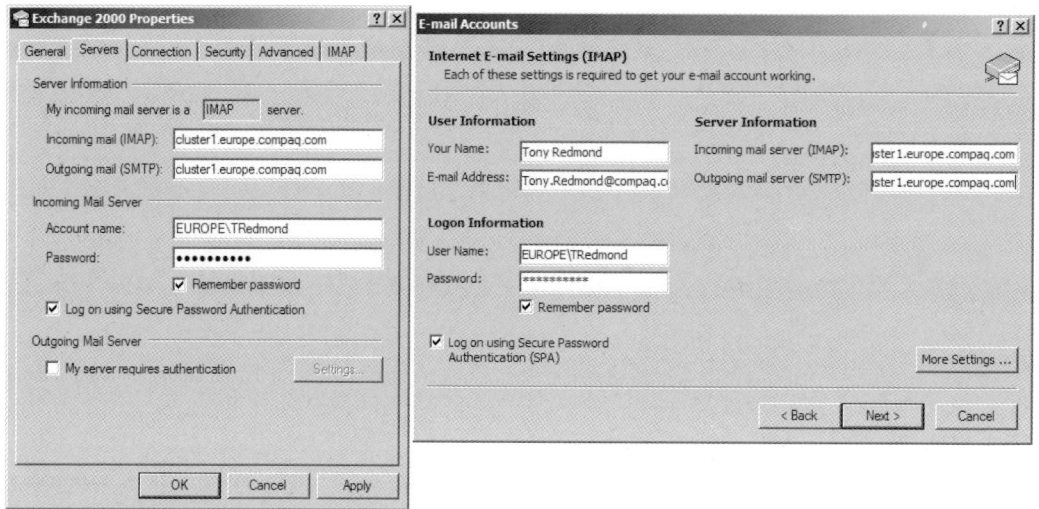

Figure 6.2   *Configuring IMAP access to Exchange.*

processes both incoming and outgoing mail and that SMTP sends outgoing email, since IMAP is only a message processing protocol. Every Exchange server has the ability to send and receive SMTP messages, so you can use the same server for client access and message transmission.

Generally, if you are interested in just email and do not need to use any of the workgroup functions provided by Outlook, IMAP is a good solution and is the fastest way to access messages on an Exchange server. Clients such as Outlook Express support advanced features such as secure email (and can use the same X.509 certificates as Outlook, so interoperability is not an issue), auto-signatures, an HTML format message editor, spell checking, and the ability to work offline. Outlook Express even supports rules processing (Figure 6.3), albeit in not quite as sophisticated a manner as that supported by Outlook. IMAP loses some of its appeal whenever you want features outside basic messaging, such as calendaring and applications hosted by Exchange public folders. You can certainly access the contents of public folders by adding them to the list of default folders that the client will automatically access, but you will not be able to use any customized forms or code created to drive the content held in the folder.

Losing access to electronic forms and code is not a disaster for the vast majority of Exchange installations, simply because not many companies have deployed applications that exploit public folders. Perhaps administrators focus more on delivering the messaging service and have not decided

6.1 IMAP4 clients

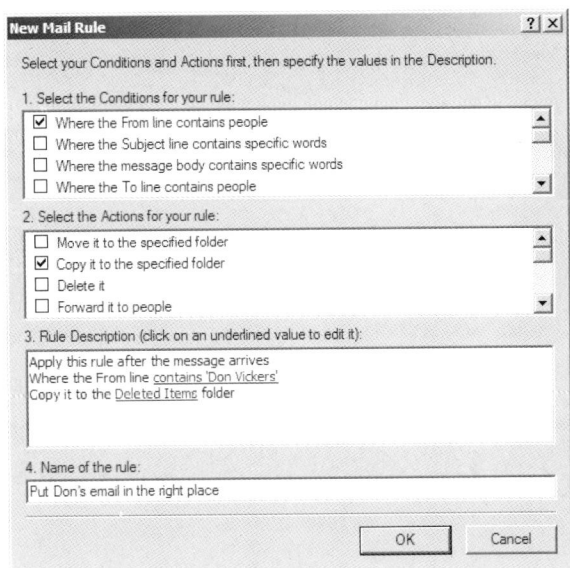

Figure 6.3
Outlook Express rules processing.

how best to use public folders, or perhaps there is a general reluctance to use Exchange as the basis for applications. Every company is different, so you need to check exactly how your company uses public folders before you can assess whether IMAP is a viable candidate for deployment.

Even organizations that use Outlook as their default client can find a use for IMAP, sometimes in surprising ways. Although Outlook 2003 now supports RPC over HTTP to allow you to connect to Exchange via the public Internet through relatively simple firewall configurations, you need to upgrade a lot of your infrastructure before you can deploy this feature. Users find themselves in many situations when they can access the Internet, usually with a Web browser, but do not have access to the corporate network. It is common to find public Internet access available in hotels, airports, libraries, and so on. To allow users to access their Exchange mailboxes, you can deploy a system running an IMAP server outside your firewall and route incoming client connections back to the appropriate Exchange mailbox server. For example, HP users can connect to an IMAP server and provide their logon credentials in the form of their email address and Windows password. After a security server authenticates their credentials, they can access their Exchange mailbox through secure (SSL) IMAP using a browser interface. The magic in the middle comes from an open source IMAP server called Squirrel (see www.squirrellink.com) and a single sign-on capability implemented by HP's IT department. As you can see in

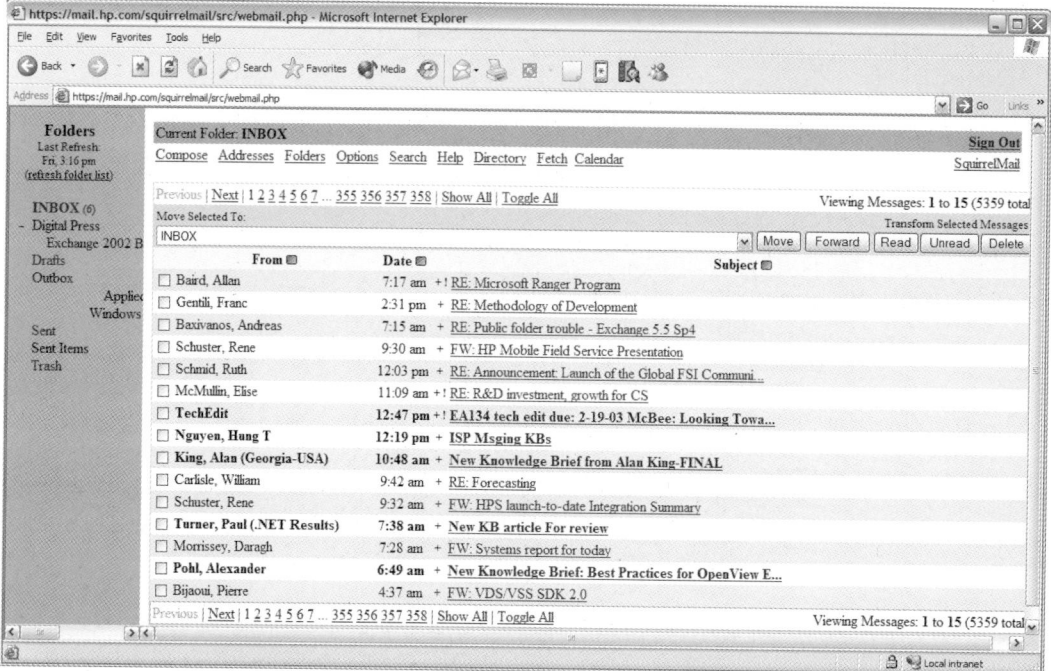

Figure 6.4   *The Squirrel IMAP client connected to Exchange 2003.*

Figure 6.4, the user interface is certainly not up to the standard of even the Outlook Web Access reach client. However, it is both simple and effective and a great way to browse a mailbox from a public access point.

6.1.1   IMAP virtual server settings

IMAP clients access Exchange through an IMAP virtual server. Every Exchange server is equipped with a default IMAP virtual server, so clients can connect immediately.

In most cases, the IMAP server's default properties are enough to provide good service to IMAP clients, but it is still interesting to look behind the scenes to determine whether you can tweak any of the properties to improve service. Among the changes that you might consider are:

- Cutting down the number of public folders returned to IMAP clients (Figure 6.5): The default is to return all public folders, but if the public folder hierarchy is large or IMAP users are not interested in public folders, you can leave the checkbox blank.

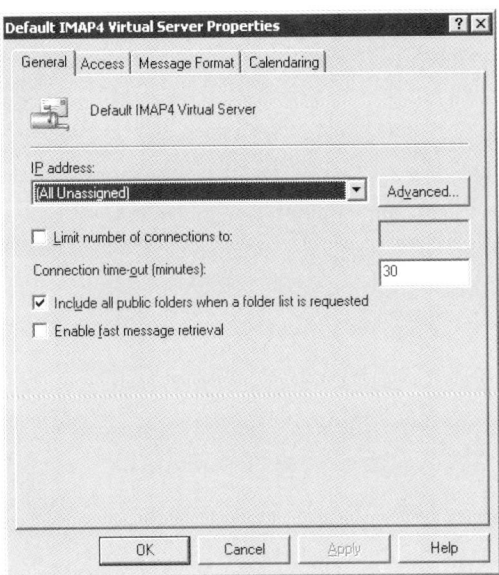

Figure 6.5
Properties of an IMAP virtual server (part 1).

- Enabling fast message retrieval (Figure 6.5): By default, Exchange calculates the size of each message so that it can inform IMAP clients of their size. Calculating message size slows down message retrieval, but only slightly. If your IMAP clients do not make use of the message size property, you can speed up retrieval by turning it off. Outlook Express does not show message size by default, but the field is available for users to add to their folder view if they want.

- Provide message contents as plain text or HTML (Figure 6.6): Different IMAP clients are able to deal with varying message formats. The more modern clients have no problems handling HTML content, which is the default provided by Exchange, but some of the early clients will probably choke if they attempt to process HTML messages. If this is the case, you can force Exchange to provide plain text copies of messages along with the HTML (so the client can choose which to process), or just plain text.

As with all the other protocol virtual servers supported by Exchange, the IMAP virtual server is the place to go when you want to find out what type of server load a client population is generating. To see the users who are currently connected, click on the IMAP virtual server to expand the node, and then click on "Current Sessions." ESM then lists details of connected clients in the right-hand pane, as shown in Figure 6.7.

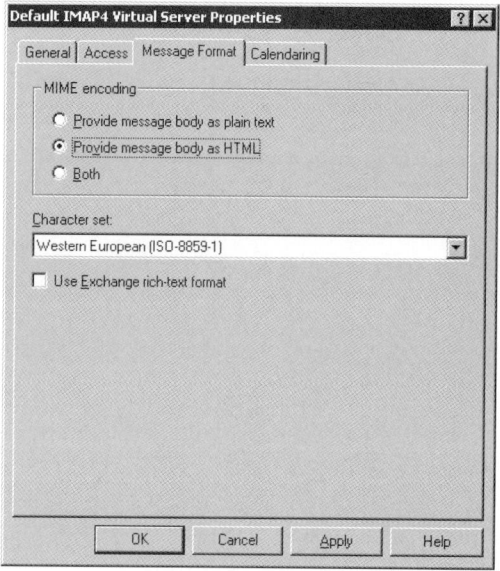

Figure 6.6 *Properties of an IMAP virtual server (part 2).*

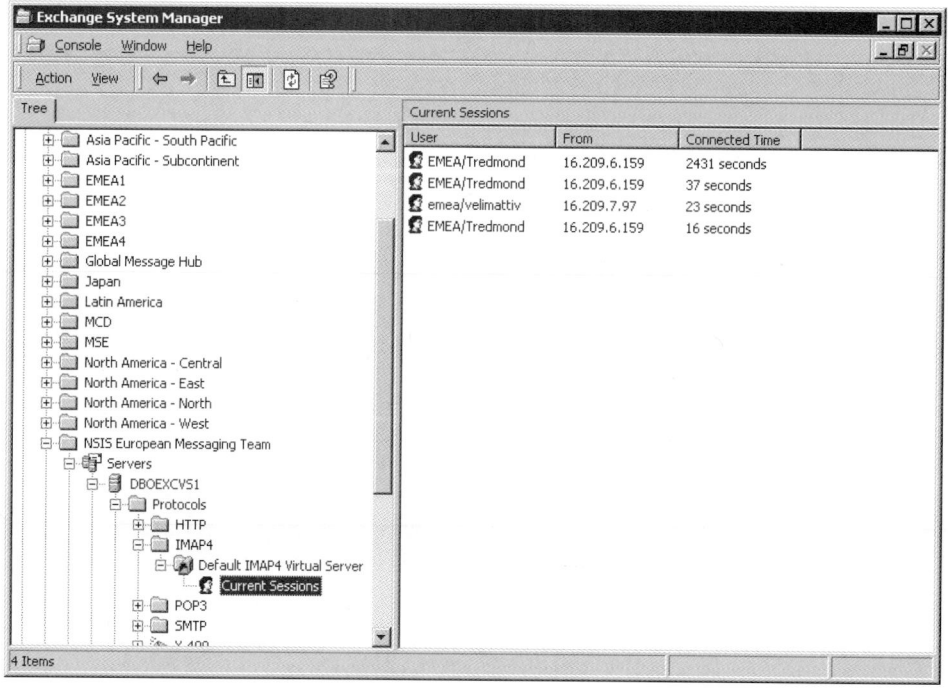

Figure 6.7 *Details of connected IMAP clients.*

ESM lists my account three times, so does this mean that Outlook Express generates three connections to process email? The answer is both yes and no. Normally, one connection is made by each client, so multiple connections probably mean that a user has logged in multiple times, but Outlook Express is also able to create additional connections for specific purposes, such as background synchronization of folder content or to fetch details of mailbox folders from the server. The additional connections disappear as soon as the activity ceases.

6.2 POP3 clients

POP3 is the "Post Office Protocol," the first general-purpose email client protocol approved by the IETF. POP3 client access has been supported since Exchange 5.0, but the protocol's use has steadily declined to a point where there is no good reason to ever connect a POP3 client unless you really want to. POP3 is a very simple protocol that revolves around a single server-based folder—the Inbox—and limits client functionality to a basic set of messaging operations. You can certainly read messages by using POP3 to download the messages to the client, but functionality rapidly runs out afterward.

POP3 is also a receive-only protocol, so the client sends outgoing messages by making an SMTP connection to a server, which may be the same physical computer as the POP3 server but does not have to be. Indeed, in an ISP environment, it is very common to have a bank of mailbox servers accessed by POP3 for message retrieval and a separate (usually smaller) set used for SMTP traffic. Exchange normally acts as the SMTP server for both POP3 and IMAP4 clients.

In passing, Windows 2003 servers now include a basic POP3 service that you can use with POP3 clients. Because POP3 is so basic, Windows delivers the same features as Exchange, but Exchange scores on administration, multi-protocol access to mailboxes, and so on, so it is much preferable to use Exchange as the server if you need to support more than a few POP3 clients.

6.3 LDAP directory access for IMAP4 and POP3 clients

IMAP4 and POP3 are exclusively messaging protocols and do not incorporate a directory service. The assumption is that a client will use another protocol such as LDAP to access a separate directory service. The AD provides the directory service for Exchange and you must configure access to the directory separately.

By default, Outlook Express includes a placeholder entry for Active Directory in the list of directory services installed with the client. However, the entry is just that—a placeholder—and you must update its properties to add the necessary details to allow the connection to proceed. Figure 6.8 illustrates an example of the required changes, in this case to connect to a Global Catalog Server within the hp.com domain.

On the "General" property page, enter the FQDN of a Global Catalog Server in the "Server name" field, usually the same Global Catalog as used by the Exchange server that hosts the user mailbox. Secure connections to the AD are required, so you must state logon credentials in the form of the user's Windows account and password. The account name can be specified in the form of a User Principal Name (similar to the email address shown in Figure 6.8) or in the form Domain Name\Account Name (e.g., DOMAIN1\REDMOND). You can also instruct Outlook Express to use the directory to check names before sending messages. Only messages addressed to names are checked, and the client ignores fully qualified email addresses such as John.Doe@xyz.com.

The settings on the "Advanced" property page control how the client makes the LDAP connection to AD. The IP port number is specified (3268

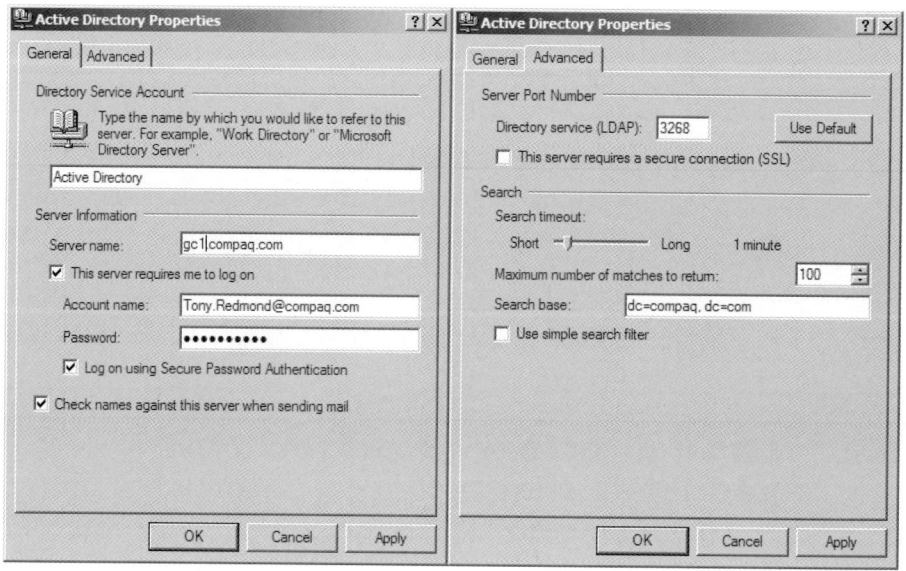

Figure 6.8   *Configuring access to the Active Directory.*

6.3　LDAP directory access for IMAP4 and POP3 clients

is the default), along with the timeout and maximum number of matches to return. The default values for these parameters are a one-minute timeout and return 100 matches, which is acceptable in most situations. If configured correctly, AD responds quickly to LDAP searches, and exceeding a timeout points to a badly specified search. For example, if you execute a search for everyone called "John" in a directory holding 50,000 accounts or more, it is likely that the search will return many more than 100 entries and take a long time to go through the directory, so both parameters are likely to be exceeded. Users have to be educated to be as specific as possible when they search the directory. Unlike MAPI, LDAP offers no ability to browse the GAL, so you cannot begin from a position within the directory and move backward and forward to find the right entry.

The "Search base" field establishes the root of the search within the AD. You can use this field to limit searches to a specific domain or organizational unit, if required. The value shown in Figure 6.8 means that searches begin from the dc=compaq, dc=com address, which indicates that you might be looking for someone with a compaq.com email address.

The Outlook Express client executes directory searches by invoking the "Find People" option. Figure 6.9 shows the results of a search, including the criteria used to limit the search. Even when executed against a directory

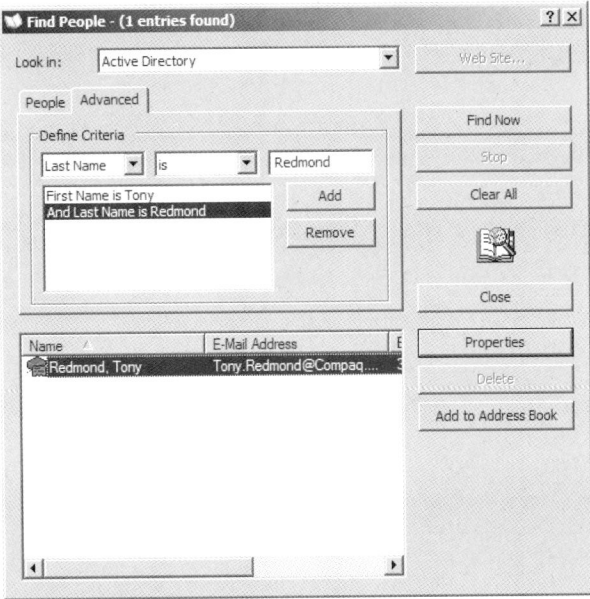

Figure 6.9　*Executing an LDAP search against Active Directory.*

containing over 150,000 accounts, the search responded in less than a second. By comparison, the search with the criterion "Name contains Tony" timed out after a minute, because the directory could not respond within the default timeout interval. LDAP does not differentiate between accounts, contacts, and distribution groups and treats them all as mail-enabled directory entries that you can search for using first name, last name, name, email address, or organization.

Unlike Outlook, which can use the OAB to validate and search addresses offline, IMAP and POP clients cannot use LDAP to interrogate addresses offline. Some clients, such as recent versions of Outlook Express, "remember" recently used email addresses and incorporate an auto-complete feature to fill in email addresses from this list as you type. This is certainly convenient, but power users will have to populate their own personal address books with email addresses they want to use offline. The problem with any personal address book is that it is very personal—and no facility exists to synchronize the data with a definitive directory to keep email addresses updated.

6.4 Supporting Apple Macintosh

Four options are available to connect Mac users to Exchange. These are:

- Outlook for Mac: Microsoft released Outlook 2001 as part of Office 2001 for Macintosh in November 2001.
- Entourage: the new Mac PIM and email client
- Web browser: the obvious candidate being IE
- Any other IMAP4 or POP3 client that is available for the Mac. Microsoft provides a version of Outlook Express for the Mac. Eudora (www.eudora.com) is another popular option.

Another less obvious option is to install Citrix terminal services and use a Mac thin client to run Outlook on the server. This method allows users to access all of the features of Outlook at the expense of substantial extra load on the server. Your options may be constrained by the version of Macintosh that you run. For example, Outlook 2001 is only available for Mac OS 8.6 or above, and Microsoft designed the latest version of Entourage for Mac OS X. Older Macs may be limited to a browser or POP3 client.

Entourage is part of the Microsoft Office Version X application suite. It is broadly equivalent to Outlook and supports email, address book, calendar, tasks, and notes. Entourage connects to Exchange via POP3 or IMAP4 and can use LDAP for directory access, just like Outlook Express. However, because Entourage does not support MAPI, it suffers from the same limitations as other IMAP clients around extended MAPI-centric functionality, such as calendaring.

Outlook for Mac is closer to its Windows cousin than Entourage and supports features such as PST files that are format compatible with Windows. The latest version is a huge improvement over the initial releases, which were slow, buggy, and featured a bad port of the Windows interface. Unlike Entourage, Outlook connects to Exchange with MAPI, so its messaging functionality is more powerful and complete. Outlook is also better at sharing calendars with other Exchange users across the Windows and Mac platforms. Outlook is a Mac OS 9 program, so you have to run it in "classic" mode on OS X, which slows performance. In addition, some of the changes that Microsoft made to get MAPI to work over the network make Outlook a bad choice for OS X users.

Microsoft Office 2004 for Mac (which requires you to run at least Mac OS 10.2.8 on the client) includes a new version of Entourage that uses IMAP4 to connect to Exchange for messaging and HTTP-DAV for calendar and scheduling, which addresses one of the major problems that Entourage users had. Entourage 2004 includes some of the features first seen in Outlook 2003, such as junk mail filters and the three-pane view, but still lacks features such as voting buttons (explained by the difference in functionality supported by the MAPI and HTTP-DAV protocols). Exchange 2000/2003 support connections from Entourage 2004 via HTTP-DAV, but if you use earlier versions, you need to run Exchange 2000 SP2 (at least) and install a special Exchange update for Entourage X. In all situations, you need to enable the HTTP-DAV and LDAP protocols on your Exchange server to allow Entourage clients to connect.

In some respects, Microsoft has caused confusion in the user community through the presence of Entourage and Outlook for Mac. Outlook exists because of its history as part of the Office suite, but Entourage is the only email and PIM application included in the Office suite for Mac OS X. Entourage does not use MAPI, so Outlook for Windows users find it limited in functionality. It is clear that Microsoft's long-term focus is on Entourage, and the new release will go a long way to delivering the equivalent functionality to Outlook for Windows on the Macintosh platform. For more information on the options available to connect Macintosh clients to Exchange, see http://www.microsoft.com/mac/support.aspx?pid=exchange.

6.5 Supporting UNIX and Linux clients

We have already discussed how to use OWA as a suitable client for UNIX (including Linux) workstations. In many cases, this is the obvious solution, because it is both free and easy to deploy. Other options include:

- Deploy native UNIX clients that support IMAP4 and POP3. Many such examples exist, including popular applications such as Eudora.

- Run Microsoft applications (Outlook or Outlook Express) on a UNIX or Linux workstation through Windows emulation software (Wine, an implementation of the Win16 and Win32 APIs for UNIX, see www.winehq.com). You can certainly run specific versions of Outlook under Wine, but expect a time lag between Microsoft releasing a new version of an application and full support under any emulator, which is not usually a good solution.

- CodeWeaver's CrossOver utility is an alternative to Wine when it comes to supporting Microsoft applications on Linux desktops. For example, the SuSE Linux Office Desktop uses this technology to support Office 97 and 2000 on top of the SuSE Linux 8.1 OS.

- Deploy a thin client connected to Terminal Services and run Outlook on the server.

- Use a native UNIX application that emulates Outlook and supports its functionality when connected to Exchange: For example, the Ximian Evolution application is a full-featured email client in its own right and supports an optional connection to Exchange through the Ximian Connector for Exchange.

In all cases, you need to perform testing to determine what users can do and what they cannot do. Be especially careful with add-on software. For example, if a user wants a wireless device to connect to his or her mailbox, such as the RIM BlackBerry, does the client software support this? In addition, you need to test the client to ensure that it does not expose any vulnerability (security or virus) to other users. While it is true that UNIX clients have received far less attention from hackers than Outlook in the recent past, this is not a reason to suppose that an enterprising hacker would not attempt to exploit a route exposed by a UNIX client in the future.

In the long term, Microsoft will no doubt watch the progress of efforts such as the "Chandler" project from the Open Source Applications Foundation (OSAF),[2] as teams attempt to develop Outlook-like products that combine email, calendars, tasks, contacts, and other collaboration functionality into a single client based on open source code and Internet protocols. Apart from its functionality, the major attraction of something like the OSAF project is its platform independence, so it may be possible to deploy a single client across all desktop platforms. It is also interesting to note that the brains behind OSAF include Mitch Kapor, a cofounder of Lotus Development and one of the original developers of products such as Lotus 1-2-3 and Lotus Notes.

Ray Ozzie, the other cofounder of Lotus and the "father" of Lotus Notes, has taken a different tack in the product he now builds and focuses on interoperability between Groove,[3] his peer-to-peer collaboration tool; Outlook; and other Microsoft technologies such as SharePoint. However, Groove only runs on Windows.

6.6 Exchange Mobile Services

Exchange Mobile Services, a new feature of Exchange 2003, aims to make mobility a core part of Exchange by allowing people with Pocket PCs, smartphones, and other handheld devices to access Exchange resources, such as their Inboxes, contacts, and calendars. Mobile Services supports two ways to connect devices: always on (Outlook Mobile Access, or OMA) and synchronization, based on Microsoft's ActiveSync technology. As we will see later on, you can also use a desktop version of ActiveSync to connect a Pocket PC to your mailbox and synchronize mail, calendar, contacts, and tasks using a desktop cradle. In a more general sense, the network capability of a specific device and the software that runs on the device determines which mode is more appropriate to establish a mobile connection to Exchange.

Exchange 2003 integrates Mobile Services directly into the server. There are three basic components. First, a new global setting controls how the organization supports mobility (Figure 6.10), and it is here that you decide whether you support Exchange ActiveSync (synchronization), browser access through Outlook Mobile Access (OMA), or both modes.

The ability of Exchange to send notifications to mobile devices via SMTP really depends on whether the target cell phone carriers support such notifications. Many European carriers allow users to send SMTP messages to GSM/GPRS phones, typically using SMTP addresses of the form: Mobile-phone-number@provider-smtp-address—for example, 0868246057@sfr.fr.

---

2. http://www.osafoundation.org/.
3. http://www.groove.net.

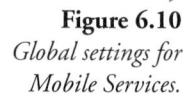
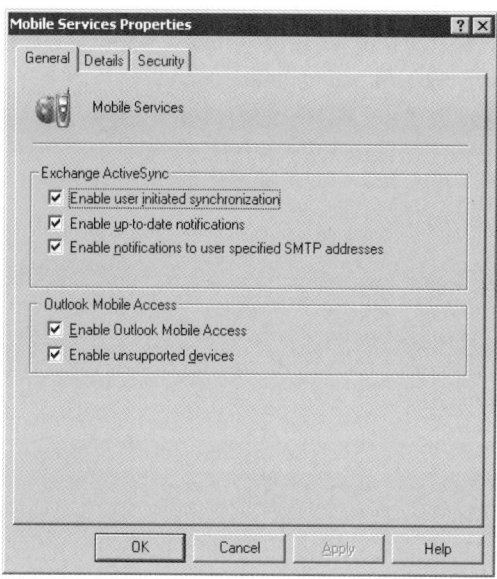

Figure 6.10
Global settings for Mobile Services.

Some carriers can accept the notifications generated by Exchange Mobile Services and interpret the number of the mobile device to deliver the notification to from data held inside the message. Others require you to use MSN notification services as a bridge. In this context, MSN takes a message from Exchange and transforms it into the form required by the carrier. MSN might strip out forwarding headers, remove white space, and compress the data to make it easier for the carrier to process. Still other carriers accept new message notifications via SMS but expect you to use a WAP connection to read the content, possibly by connecting to a special phone number that incurs additional charges. As you can see, this area is full of different implementations, so you need to contact your own carrier to work out how it supports notifications and how you connect Exchange Mobile Services to its notification mechanism.

You can also decide whether you want to limit OMA to the set of devices that Microsoft fully supports or allow users to connect an unsupported browser, such as Opera or even IE6 running on a desktop PC. Extensions to the AD schema allow you to control settings for individual users, as shown in Figure 6.11. Finally, two new Web applications run under the control of IIS to allow users to synchronize with ActiveSync or run OMA browser sessions. Figure 6.12 shows the properties of the OMA Web application as viewed from the IIS manager console. As you can see, it looks very similar to the properties of the standard "Exchange" Web application for OWA.

6.6 Exchange Mobile Services

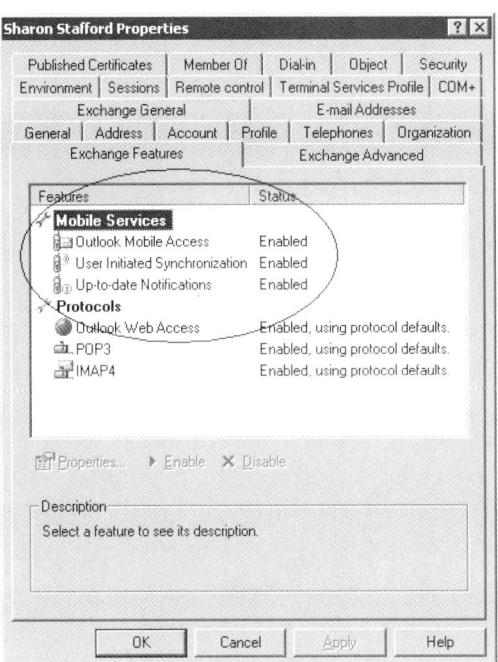

Figure 6.11
Controlling OMA access.

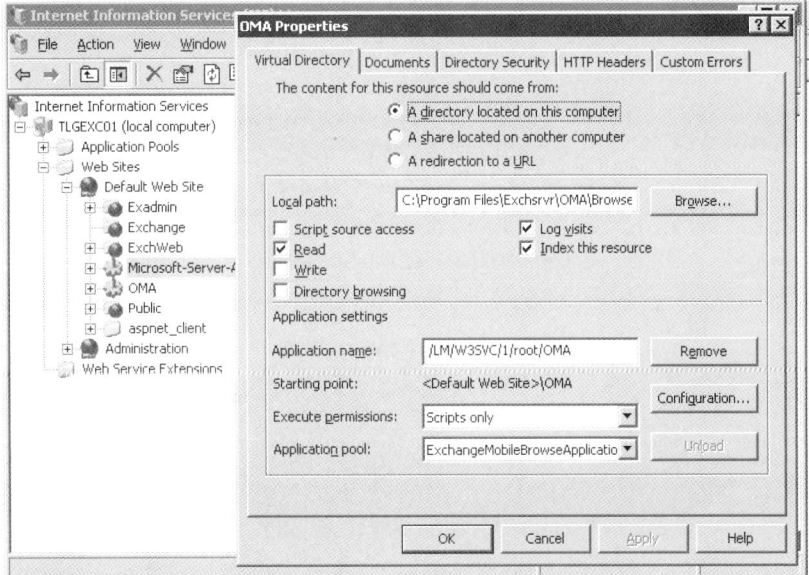

Figure 6.12
Properties of the OMA Web application.

Chapter 6

For Pocket PCs, Microsoft also supports synchronization through a server-based version of ActiveSync running with Microsoft Mobile Information Server (MMIS) 2002, which you can use with Exchange 2000.[4] However, it is much easier to support mobile devices with Exchange 2003, because you can use the Mobile Services functionality integrated into the server (e.g., you have to install a separate set of schema extensions for MMIS, whereas the Exchange 2003 installation procedure installs the mobility schema updates along with its other extensions).

It is important not to confuse OMA with OMM (Outlook Mobile Manager), a client-side add-on to Outlook 2002 that creates a partnership between Outlook and a mobile device. In this scenario, the OMM module processes incoming messages and decides whether to forward them on to the mobile device. If it forwards a message, OMM also strips it of white space to make the message as small as possible. You can certainly use OMM, but its long-term future is uncertain and you have to deploy it client by client. With this in mind, Exchange Mobile Services seem like a better foundation to serve mobile devices.

Microsoft upgraded the MMIS feature set to create Mobile Services for Exchange 2003. The new features include:

- Support for data transfer to smartphones using XHTML, HTML, cHTML, or WML over WAP 2.0 or i-Mode connections. This range of protocols means that Microsoft can support a wide range of smartphones globally. Given the nature of the cell phone market and the amount of new models introduced to the market, it is impossible to provide an up-to-date list of supported phones here. Check with Microsoft for the latest information. Table 6.1 lists some of the devices supported at the initial release, known as Device Update (DU) 2. Expect new DU releases every six months or so. For example, Exchange 2003 SP1 includes DU4. Microsoft maintains a list of supported devices at http://go.microsoft.com/fwlink/?LinkId=24847.

- Support for continuous updating of Pocket PC and smartphone clients by notifying devices when new messages, contacts, or calendar data arrives at an Exchange 2003 server.

- Improvements in the way that clients negotiate with the server to establish credentials and determine the client's capabilities (a smartphone is different from a Pocket PC).

---

4. Because its functionality is now incorporated into Exchange 2003, Microsoft is phasing out MMIS, so the best plan is to install an Exchange 2003 server and run OMA on it if you want to support large populations of Pocket PCs.

6.6 Exchange Mobile Services

Table 6.1 *Supported Models for Initial Release of OMA*

Manufacturer	Model	Browser	Rendering	Network
Sony-Ericsson	T68i	AU R201A, R301A	xHTML	GSM
All	X503is	Compact Netfront 2.0 by Access	cHTML	iMode
All	X504i	Compact Netfront 2.0 by Access	cHTML	iMode
Microsoft	All	PIE 3.02	HTML	All
Toshiba	J-T51	J-Phone 4.x	xHTML	J-Phone
Sharp	J-SH51	J-Phone 4.x	xHTML	J-Phone
Casio	A3012CA	—	xHTML	KDDI
Sanyo	A3011SA	—	xHTML	KDDI
Toshiba	C5001T	—	xHTML	KDDI
Sony-Ericsson	P800	All	xHTML	GSM
Sony-Ericsson	T68i	All	xHTML	GSM
Microsoft	All	PIE 4.01	HTML	All

- General improvements in efficiency of folder synchronization between Exchange and wireless devices to optimize the use of network bandwidth—something that is very important for wireless networks, especially given the amount of data some users want to move to and from their mailboxes!

6.6.1 Exchange ActiveSync

ActiveSync is the synchronization process that transfers mailbox and calendar data from Exchange to handheld devices through Microsoft's ActiveSync protocol, including Pocket PC or other devices that run variants of Windows CE, like phones that run Pocket PC Phone Edition or the new smartphones that run Microsoft Windows CE for Smartphone 2002. You work with messages and other information held in local storage on the device and then connect to Exchange whenever you want to send or retrieve data or when the server informs you that it has new information for you, like new mail. This mode of working requires the device to have the capability of processing information offline and the ability to accept incoming notifications from the server. Synchronization can also occur through a PC-Pocket PC "partnership" where the PC (desktop or laptop) acts as a conduit for the Pocket PC to access Exchange data. We will cover this type of connection later on in this chapter.

Exchange 2003 includes the ActiveSync server, an application that runs as managed code under ASP .NET, as part of Exchange Mobile Services. You can use two distinct synchronization modes:

- Traditional or explicit synchronization: you connect the PDA or other ActiveSync client (including smartphones) to Exchange and the device synchronizes its local data with your mailbox. For example, the device uploads messages for Exchange to send and downloads messages waiting in the inbox. In this mode, you typically use a cradle (usually a device connected via USB to connect the PDA to the network and other resources via an intermediate PC) or a wireless link. Unless it is a slow GSM/GPRS connection, a wireless link is usually faster than a cradle when synchronizing, but you may not notice the difference unless you have many messages and other data to download.

- Notification-driven or implicit synchronization (sometimes called Always Up to Date, or AUTD): the smartphone receives a notification that the Exchange server has new content and connects to download the content, or makes a connection to upload new data. The connection is over a network such as GPRS, while notifications usually originate as SMTP messages sent to the network carrier for delivery to the phone as SMS messages.

As noted earlier, Microsoft introduced server-mode ActiveSync support for clients in Microsoft Mobile Information Manager, so this is tried and tested functionality. The major differences are that Microsoft has now integrated mobility as a key part of Exchange and that Exchange 2003 supports notification-driven synchronization.

Smartphones generate a lot of attention because they integrate the ubiquitous connectivity of the cell phone with versions of Office applications. A battle exists between Microsoft's platforms and the Symbian OS, supported by many phone manufacturers such as Nokia. Over time, the capabilities of the different platforms will probably merge and you will be able to connect to Exchange as easily with one as you can with the other. For now, Microsoft's own platforms have the edge because they come with out-of-the-box compatibility. Once you decide that you want a phone that runs a Microsoft OS, you then have to make a choice between a Pocket PC with phone capability and a smartphone that supports some of the features of the Pocket PC. The T-Mobile-branded phone running Pocket PC Phone Edition 2002 (Figure 6.13) is a good example of the first category, while the Orange SPV smart-

6.6 Exchange Mobile Services

Figure 6.13
The Smartphone interface

phone is the first production example of Microsoft's smartphone platform, with Motorola and Samsung the second set of companies to produce smartphones. Obviously, Microsoft is keen for other companies to produce similar smartphones and you can expect other versions to appear, especially in North America, in the future.

Both platforms synchronize with Exchange via ActiveSync for email, contacts, and calendar information. Both support server-mode and cradle-mode ActiveSync, so you do not have to deploy server-mode ActiveSync if you only need to deploy a few units. Different aspects of the platforms attract. For example, if you are accustomed to use cell phones to send SMS messages, you will probably enjoy the ability to work with Pocket Outlook on a smartphone because smartphones have the same T-9 predictive text entry mode to help users compose messages. On the other hand, if you want to work with Word or Excel documents, you need a Pocket PC platform because the smartphone does not currently support these document types. The larger screen size of Pocket PC-based devices is more suitable if you need to read more than a page or so from messages or documents and a bigger screen makes it easier to navigate through a large inbox. Both platforms include versions of Pocket Explorer, so you can access the Web, albeit slowly sometimes. Both include VPN capability too, so you can access resources within your internal network if you add the necessary certificates to the device's certificate store.

6.6.2 Outlook Mobile Access

Outlook Mobile Access enables real-time, bandwidth-constrained, browser-based connections for devices such as the latest generation of smartphones. Unlike synchronization, these connections are "always on" and are similar to the connection that you would use with a WAP browser on a cell phone. For OMA, a smartphone is something like a Sony-Ericsson T68i, which is capable of connecting to Exchange using a supported microbrowser that can render mailbox and calendar contents. The T68i uses xHTML to render data that it fetches with a GSM connection. Microsoft's own smartphones also connect with GSM and use HTML to display information via a version of Pocket Information Explorer. The Japanese iMode cell phones also support OMA now, and you can expect to see many more phones with this capability in the future. As with any other piece of functionality, once one manufacturer supports a feature such as games or WAP, the other manufacturers respond to the competitive advantage, and, over time, the feature becomes a standard part of all cell phones.

You do not have to support OMA on every Exchange 2003 server, and you may decide that you do not want to because users have quite enough opportunities to access email without using their phones. If you do go ahead and implement OMA, it is good to know that you can verify that OMA is functioning from any desktop that runs IE. This method is useful if you are having difficulty connecting a smartphone and want to make sure that Exchange is functioning correctly. To do this, proceed as follows:

- Navigate to http://exchange-server-name/oma.

- Enter your logon credentials for a mailbox that exists on the server that you can access.

- Click on the OK hyperlink when you receive a warning that your device (such as IE6) is not supported.

- Access OMA. You should see a display similar to that shown in Figure 6.14.

If you compare the view of the mailbox provided by OMA in Figure 6.14 with the view that you expect through OWA, it is obvious that much of the data you would normally see is missing. This is by design and demonstrates the "fit for function" mode that OMA implements to deal with the bandwidth and screen estate challenges set by cell phones. Even in its reach client, OWA expects to use a reasonable network connection back to the server. OMA makes no such assumptions, because the link could be something like a relatively puny 9.6-Kbps GSM dial-up connection from a modem connected to a cell phone. Therefore, OMA strips out any unnecessary text or graphics and provides a minimum folder list to reduce the data that the server must transmit to the client. In addition, many OMA clients will have limited screen estate (think of the standard screen on a cell phone), so the target platform is a 320 × 320 screen rather than the 640 × 480 base minimum provided by any PC.

No one pretends that you are going to enjoy processing a large Inbox through OMA. Given the small screen, lack of keyboard, and stripped-

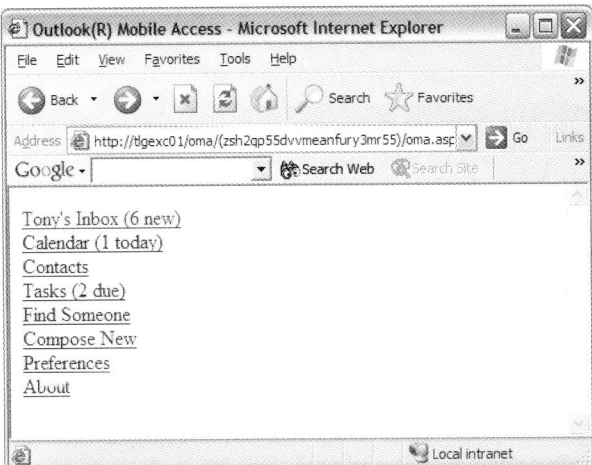

Figure 6.14
OMA running on IE6.

down data, it is unlikely that you will be able to deal with hundreds of messages, but that is not the intention. Think of OMA as a way to triage new messages as they arrive in your Inbox, to be able to identify the messages that you need to respond to immediately and those that you can ignore (or better still, delete without reading). In terms of responses, you will not compose a long reply, but you can certainly forward a note to someone else for his or her action or reply briefly using terms such as "OK," "No," "For action," and so on. Because OMA provides only a limited view of your folder list, you are not able to work with most of your mailbox, and, indeed, you cannot move messages from the Inbox to another folder.

Because they are relatively new, smartphones may receive the majority of attention for OMA. However, OMA is not just for smartphones, and devices such as Pocket PCs can benefit greatly from the mobile synchronization capabilities now built into Exchange 2003. Unfortunately, because OMA uses Microsoft's own AirSync standard for synchronization instead of the more common and more popular SyncML protocol, mobile devices that do not run the Pocket PC O/S have to be upgraded to support AirSync before they can benefit from OMA.

6.7 Pocket PC clients

For years, I have watched the evolution of Windows CE-powered handheld devices, and I always discounted their use for email after looking at their speed, applications, and interface. The prospect of peering at a dim screen while trying to navigate the Inbox or compose notes and memos through a hunt-and-peck stylus or handwriting recognition that could not understand my feeble attempts at writing was not very attractive, and I could always get my job done more effectively with a notebook PC.

While I have not yet concluded that it is time to turn in my notebook (even for a Tablet PC), there is no doubt that the latest combination of Pocket PC hardware, operating system, and applications is much more usable.

6.7.1 Connection options

Depending on the hardware configuration and the software provided with the Pocket PC, different models offer a variety of ways to connect to your Exchange mailbox. The normal options are either server-based synchronization service provided by either Microsoft Mobile Information Server (for Exchange 2000) or Exchange Mobile Services (Exchange 2003), or desktop-based synchronization using client-side ActiveSync. Naturally, if you want to use server-based synchronization, you have to be able to connect the Pocket PC to the server over the network, using wireless or even a dial-up connection. Server-based synchronization becomes the preferred option as soon as you upgrade to Exchange 2003, but until then users will probably remain with client-side connections, so I will focus on this method for now.

With client-side ActiveSync, you make a hosted connection through a USB or serial port that connects a cradle that holds the Pocket PC to a desktop or notebook PC, which runs both Outlook[5] and the ActiveSync application, which we will cover in a little while. Think of the host PC as an intermediary for the Pocket PC, acting as a gateway to data that is either on the PC's drives or available on a network resource that the PC can connect to. In Pocket PC terms, this is referred to as a "partnership," meaning that the Pocket PC and the PC combine to access network resources and perform maintenance operations. For example, if you want to install a new application or software onto the Pocket PC, you first install the software onto the host PC, which then downloads the necessary information to the Pocket PC the next time that the two connect.

The cradle acts as a docking station for the Pocket PC. When you place the Pocket PC into the cradle, it is able to use the USB or serial port connection to communicate with the host PC and synchronize data. An infrared connection is only possible if both the Pocket PC and the host PC have

---

5. While earlier versions of Outlook can be used, best results are obtained with Outlook 2000 onward.

infrared ports. If this is the case, you can line up the two ports, establish an infrared link and synchronize data across the link. You can also use an infrared connection to link the Pocket PC to a cell phone and make a dial-in connection. However, the connection can be both very slow and very expensive, especially if the inbox holds a large number of messages or you attempt to download some large attachments. Infrared is convenient when nothing else is available, but it is much slower than a USB or serial connection.

Along with Bluetooth connectivity, the latest models of the Pocket PC like the HP h5500 or h5400 series sport integrated wireless 802.11b LAN capability, so you can connect these devices into corporate networks very easily. If the Pocket PC does not have wireless capability, you can usually enable it with an add-on card that goes into the Pocket PC or an expansion pack. Expansion packs are jackets or sleeves that wrap around the Pocket PC to allow the Pocket PC to use add-on devices. The jacket adds to the bulk and thickness of the Pocket PC, but it does allow it to use almost any type of PCMCIA card that you would use with a standard notebook PC, including wireless cards and even a GPS card.[6] Some models resemble a smartphone because they integrate a fully functional GPRS phone into the Pocket PC. My personal experience of these devices is mixed, because their voice quality is often not as good as a regular cell phone. Obviously, wireless connectivity is only interesting if you work at a location that has been equipped with wireless base stations, which allow devices equipped with wireless cards into the network. Once connected, wireless devices enjoy the same type of access to the network as you have with traditional Ethernet cards. I work at a facility that is equipped with a wireless LAN, so I use a wireless card to connect to Exchange and other network resources. Both Pocket PC 2002 and Windows Mobile 2003 include MSN Messenger, a Terminal Services client, and the ability to navigate Windows file shares, so you can use the Pocket PC for much more than email and Web browsing. They also support Virtual Private Network (VPN) connectivity, so you can connect across a VPN using wireless networks installed in public locations such as airport lounges.

If you deploy Exchange 2003, Exchange Mobile Services is the obvious way to connect wireless-enabled Pocket PCs to user mailboxes, but if you chose to remain with Exchange 5.5 or 2000, there are other products to consider. For example, InfoWave's Wireless Business Engine for Exchange (http://www.infowave.com/) provides good connectivity to mailbox and calendar data for both Pocket PCs and laptops. The InfoWave server compresses the traffic that passes across the link and maximizes the relatively

---

6. See http://www.teletype.com/pages/gps/receivers.html.

low connection speeds available with second-generation cell phones (typically 19.2 Kbps or less) to deliver adequate performance when browsing your inbox. You can use High Speed Circuit Switched Data (HSCSD) to increase the throughput of GSM connections to 28.8 Kbps or above, if your phone and carrier offers this feature. GPRS cell-phone connections allow much higher throughput and maintain an "always-on" connection, thus avoiding the need to constantly connect and authenticate to a server.

6.7.2 Accessing email with the Pocket PC

Network or dial-up connections differ from those established via a cradle in that an intermediate PC is not required. Instead, you make a dial-up connection to servers over RAS in exactly the same way that you would dial in from a notebook PC. Once connected, Pocket Outlook can use the link to connect to your Exchange mailbox using the IMAP4 or POP3 protocols. In effect, you make exactly the same type of connection as you would with a client such as Outlook Express. IMAP4 is a more functional protocol, which supports features such as multiple folders and server-side storage, and it is therefore preferred if you are going to use a traditional network connection. As with ActiveSync, you can customize the connection to state how many days of email to download to the Pocket PC and how much of each message to bring down, including attachments.

6.7.3 Security and passwords

When you use a client-side partnership, ActiveSync connects to an Exchange mailbox using the default MAPI profile created for Outlook. The MAPI profile identifies the server where your mailbox is located and the name of the mailbox, and, together with the cached Windows credentials held on your PC, this is enough to make a connection to Exchange and synchronize information. The Pocket PC does not support the NT authentication sequence, so you will never see a screen demanding a domain name, account name, and password. If a password (a four-digit code) is active on the Pocket PC, you must provide credentials. However, if you insist, you can tell ActiveSync to remember the password, so that you do not see a prompt for your password when the Pocket PC connects. Keeping credentials cached is not very secure, because only a four-digit PIN protects the device. If you want better password protection and sign-on security, you can use software extensions such as HP's Security Enhancements for Pocket PC or hardware devices such as the integrated biometric fingerprint reader in the HP iPAQ 5400 series.

If you forget your password and use the standard PIN, you can take the batteries out of the Pocket PC to force a reset, which will allow you to change the password. You can then provide the new password to ActiveSync the next time the Pocket PC connects to the server. Resetting the device will usually require you to resynchronize all data, because you recreate the partnership.

Even if you have configured your system to support multiple MAPI profiles and set the Outlook option to ask which profile to use when it starts up, ActiveSync will only use whatever profile is currently in use, which is normally the default profile. In a way, this approach is sensible, because the copies of your Inbox, calendar, notes, and tasks folders on the Pocket PC are similar to the replica folders held in an offline store (OST). Both are tied to a particular configuration, and just as you have to rebuild an OST if a MAPI profile is deleted or changed to point to another mailbox, you'll force a complete resynchronization of all items on the Pocket PC if you log on and use another profile to connect to Exchange.

6.7.4 Explaining Pocket PC synchronization

Synchronization is the process of comparing the contents of folders in an Exchange mailbox (Inbox, Calendar, Tasks, and Notes) and the Pocket PC and resolving differences. During the synchronization process, ActiveSync downloads new messages, sends any messages waiting on the Pocket PC, and makes whatever adjustments are required to the calendar. You can define how synchronization occurs through the Sync Mode option (Figure 6.15). Since I keep my Pocket PC in its cradle whenever I am in the office, I use continuous mode.

Others may prefer to have synchronization only on first connection or control the process manually, but I like to be able to take my Pocket PC away with me in the knowledge that synchronization is up-to-date. The choice depends on the speed of your connection. Over a USB link, updates occur in a matter of minutes, even if I have been away from the office for a couple of days and have not bothered to update the Pocket PC in that time. Things happen much more slowly over a serial connection, and are even slower over infrared, so it may pay to limit connections in these situations.

The nature of synchronization means that conflicts can occur, often because different versions of the same item are on both devices. ActiveSync also flags conflicts when it cannot copy items to the Pocket PC without user intervention. For example, it is possible to input a large amount of data into the Notes field of an Outlook calendar item. I often use this feature to capture details of a meeting, such as the agenda. Pocket Calendar supports very

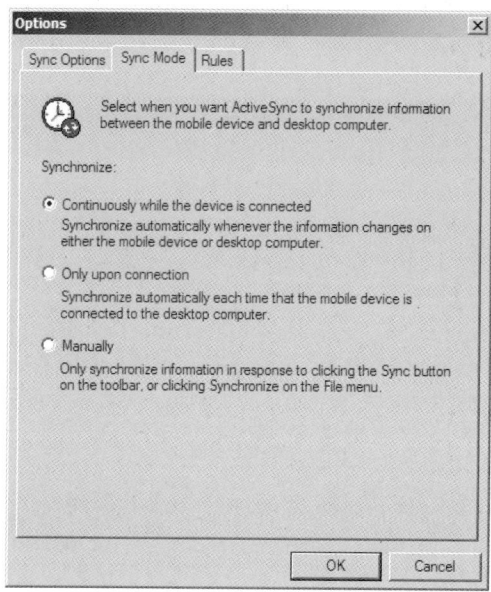

Figure 6.15
ActiveSync synchronization settings.

limited notes for its items, so any Outlook item that has a large note is flagged as a conflict. You can decide to synchronize the item without its notes data, and this is usually the best way to resolve matters. Figure 6.16 shows how ActiveSync brings conflicts to your attention. In this case, two appointments are in conflict, and you have the choice to skip the items or resolve by accepting the version kept in either location.

To make things easier, you can tell ActiveSync to resolve conflicts automatically (Figure 6.17) through the Rules option. As you can see, I prefer to resolve conflicts manually, possibly due to my paranoid nature that leads me to distrust allowing computers to make decisions about any of my personal data!

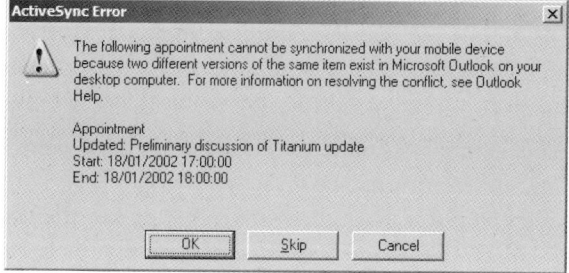

Figure 6.16
Synchronization conflict.

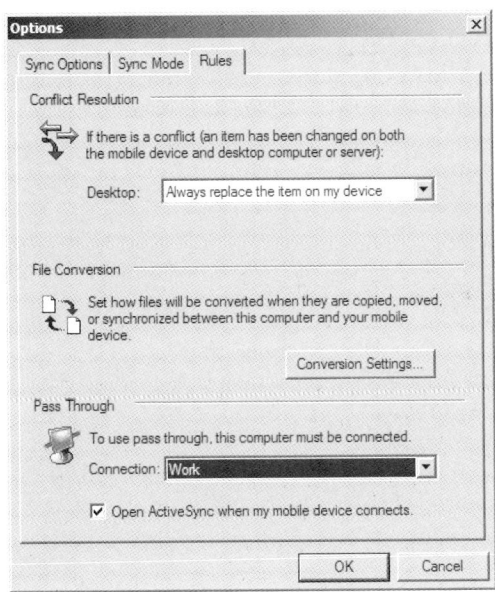

Figure 6.17
Synchronization rules.

As with a POP3 client, Pocket Outlook 2000 supports the Inbox and Outbox folders, but you can only view the Inbox, since the Outbox folder is a holding point for messages waiting to go to the server. Pocket Outlook 2002 is a major advance, because it can synchronize any folder in your Exchange mailbox.

As with any other attachment, you can open and view graphics files on the Pocket PC if a suitable application is available, but the contents of ZIP files remain inaccessible. Pocket Outlook downloads S/MIME encoded messages but cannot display their content. Instead, all you see is an attachment called "smime.p7m"—the bodypart containing the encoded text. This is quite reasonable, since the Pocket PC has no way to access the keys necessary to decode the content. Pocket Outlook 2002 deals with calendar meeting requests, but it does not support access to public folders except through third-party products such as Extended Systems (www.extendedsystems.com) or PumaTech's IntelliSync server (http://www.pumatech.com/intellisync.html). Public folders are often associated with electronic forms or special views, which are used to display or organize data in the folder, so do not assume that these products will deliver exactly the same user experience on the Pocket PC. The best advice is to get hold of a copy and test it out against your data to validate whether the products work in your environment.

6.7.5 Using the Pocket PC

Even the earliest Pocket PCs had enough horsepower to deal with the Pocket PC versions of Microsoft Outlook, Word, and Excel. Today's versions have upgraded CPUs, more memory, and most importantly, vastly superior communications capability through integrated infrared, Bluebooth, wireless, and GPRS. The devices are slimmer and lighter and are capable of running a wider range of applications and you can now use a small keyboard with the Pocket PCs, which is a huge advantage when dealing with lots of email. The operating system and applications have also improved, and Windows Mobile 2003 and the latest versions of the Pocket Office application are superior to the earlier versions

Synchronizing the server inbox with the Pocket PC is usually the first step that users take. The ActiveSync Options menu allows you to define settings for each type of data to synchronize, including the Inbox (Figure 6.18). Here you can specify how many days of email to copy, the maximum number of lines to copy for each message, and whether or not to copy attachments. The golden rule is that the more data moved to the device, the more memory you occupy. Just like working with an offline store (OST file), any message that you create on the Pocket PC is automatically sent when you next connect and synchronize.

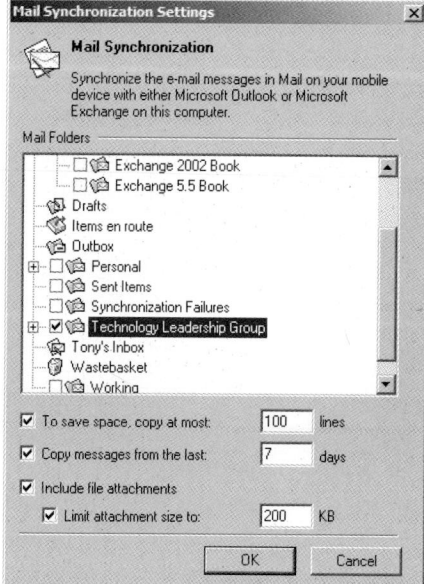

Figure 6.18
Synchronization settings.

When you compare the Pocket PC with other handheld devices, its strongest card is the compatibility between Microsoft Office applications and the Pocket versions. You can certainly download e-mail or your schedule to a Palm Pilot, but things get interesting when you try to read an attachment. It is true that there are minor incompatibilities between Word and Pocket Word (complex tables, graphics, and any special type of formatting including fill-in forms pose particular challenges), and you will not find many pivot tables in Pocket Excel, but the standard features are supported and the content of most documents and spreadsheets are accessible.

Some attachments are just too large ever to download to a Pocket PC. However, you probably do not want to read 150-page 3-MB Word documents on the Pocket PC's relatively tiny screen. Microsoft does not support a pocket version of PowerPoint yet, so presentations remain a challenge. However, third-party utilities[7] are available to convert presentations to a format suitable for the Pocket PC and then display them, even driving an external screen or projector. Microsoft Reader is provided to read electronic books, but there are still some tasks that are best left to either a large PC screen or a printed copy, and work remains to be done before the Pocket PC can elegantly cope with a large document or a complete book.

The best things about a Pocket PC are that your inbox, contacts and calendar are available at the touch of a button and that you can work with Word and Excel attachments if required. Up until recently, the major pain points are the lack of even a "two-thumb" integrated keyboard and the fact that handwriting recognition is a mystery that some users cannot get their minds (and fingers) around. However, you can now buy good keyboards for Pocket PCs to solve the first problem. I also dislike the weight of the device if you attach various gadgets like a GPS receiver, but the latest generation of iPAQs have slimmed down, full of features, and small enough to fit into a shirt pocket.

The advent of wireless-enabled Tablet PCs has caused some people to question whether the Pocket PC has a future. After all, the Tablet PC is a "real PC," uses full-sized keyboards and other peripherals, and is light enough to carry around from meeting to meeting. Some Tablet PCs even come with BIOS-level browsers that display Outlook data (calendar, contacts, and to-do items) as soon as you turn them on, to get past the normal need to boot Windows or restore it from hibernation before you can access your calendar. This feature gives the Tablet PC some of the "instant-on" capability that a Pocket PC enjoys. Long term, it is likely that the Pocket

---

7. www.pocketgear.com is a good location to start looking for Pocket PC utilities, including PowerPoint viewers.

PC will slim down further to become more like the single integrated device combining a phone, pager, and Office applications that everyone will want to carry. Some early forms of such devices, based on Pocket PCs, already exist, but they need more refinement and battery life to become truly compelling. It will happen; the only question is when.

6.8 Palm Pilots

People often ask whether the Pocket PC is better than the Palm Pilot family of portable computers. The answer is not simple, because it all depends on what you want the device to do. The Palm Pilot is tremendously popular and traditionally outsells other handheld computers by a considerable factor, perhaps as a reflection of the slowness and lack of capability, including applications, of the original versions of the Pocket PC software and hardware. With typical Microsoft persistence, the current generation of the Pocket PC is very usable, and costs have come down enough to permit the assembly of a reasonably high-powered specification for low cost. Palm finds the market much more challenging than before and has had to drop prices and increase functionality to stay competitive, so we now have more choices than previously.

Many people connect their Palm Pilots to Exchange to download email, contacts, and the calendar. At this point, if you count cell phones, Pocket PCs, pagers, and other smart email-capable devices, users may have too much choice for lightweight stay-in-touch devices and the choice often comes down to familiarity. If you have used a Palm Pilot for years, then you are probably going to continue to use a Palm. After users are hooked by an application or have built up data on a device, relatively few people migrate from one device to another unless they can get better functionality and keep all their data. As long as Palm continues to evolve and stay competitive, it will retain a substantial user base. The danger is that the architecture of the Pocket PC allows for more expansion in a world of .NET applications and Palm may struggle to compete. Time will tell.

6.9 Mobile BlackBerries

You know that a device is popular when you see it in the hands of users in airports and other public places. RIM's (www.rim.net) BlackBerry device certainly passes this test and many BlackBerries connect to Exchange servers. People like the simplicity of the device and appreciate being able to receive email anywhere connectivity is offered by a network provider. RIM has been selling BlackBerry devices connected to corporate messaging systems such as Exchange and Lotus Domino, as well as IMAP/POP messaging systems, for years. In North America, you can use three wireless networks—Mobitex, DataTac, and GPRS—while elsewhere the GSM/GPRS mobile phone protocol has expanded the scope and reach of these devices worldwide. For example, O2 and T-Mobile, major European cell providers, supply BlackBerry devices for their GPRS networks, including roaming capability, in many European countries.

Roaming between countries and across different network providers enables you to stay in touch all the time, but it is easy to run up large monthly connection charges, especially if you do a lot of international travel. GPRS roaming is only possible if your home provider has an agreement with a local network provider, and this is not always the case. The GPRS version of the BlackBerry supports SMS, the international standard for Short Message Services, which means that you can send messages to cell phones by using the phone number as the address for messages. It is much easier to compose an SMS message on a BlackBerry than through the limited keypad of a typical cell phone. Sometimes, roaming agreements between providers do not permit full GPRS connections, but you can still connect via GSM. In this situation, you can use the BlackBerry to send and receive SMS messages, just as you would do with a normal cell phone, but you cannot send and receive email. However, it is often possible to scan for all available networks and select one that does support GPRS rather than accepting the default or preferred network that the device automatically registers with when it starts up.

Another difficulty is that GPRS networks in the United States use a frequency different from those in Europe and Asia, so you cannot yet enjoy full roaming capability unless you have the proper equipment. RIM introduced its first tri-band international models (the 6230 and 7230) in June 2003. These devices support 900-, 1,800-, and 1,900-MHz GSM and GPRS networks, so assuming that a roaming agreement exists you can now use your BlackBerry around the world.

BlackBerries also support PIN-to-PIN communications, which means that you can send messages between devices using the personal identification number of the target device to transfer the message across the carrier network. PIN communications are unfriendly, because the addresses are not normal email addresses or phone numbers. Instead, they are strings, such as "200212F4," that are difficult to remember. The big advantage of PIN communications is that it works over the base network, so you can get messages to other users when your Exchange server is down. Note that the carriers always encrypt email communications across their networks, PIN messages are scrambled, and SMS messages are in plain text. This may not be an issue, because if Exchange is down and you need to get a message through to someone, you probably do not mind that the text is relatively insecure.

The BlackBerry is a great solution if you just want to send and receive email and live somewhere that a carrier provides a suitable wireless service, which can be in surprising places. While we can expect airlines to provide in-seat Internet access in airplanes in the near future and you can now use very expensive in-plane phones to connect and read email, airplanes still are the last bastion of the unconnected world. It is interesting to see people tapping away at their BlackBerries in a plane, furiously processing Inboxes while hiding their activities from the cabin crew. Depending on the reach of the network, you can read and send messages at 30,000 feet and above in the United States, while European GPRS networks do not extend quite so high, and I have only been able to send messages at relatively low levels just after take-off or before landing.

6.9.1 BlackBerry Enterprise Server (BES)

You can get messages from your email account to a BlackBerry using a desktop redirector or an Enterprise server. Individual users who do not belong to a large messaging infrastructure owned by a single company tend to use the desktop redirector, while the Enterprise server is a better option when you need to connect more than small workgroups. One good reason why this is the case is because BES can deliver or accept messages even when your PC is turned off, whereas if you rely on the desktop redirector, you have to keep a PC powered up and logged in to Exchange. BES channels messages delivered to the mailboxes of registered users to their handhelds via the wireless network. You install BES on a Windows 2000 or 2003 server and can connect it to mailboxes on Exchange 5.5, Exchange 2000, or Exchange 2003 servers. The BES software uses a privileged account running as an NT service to access mailboxes and process mail. In many respects, this is an approach similar to that taken by MAPI-based antivirus products, which also need to monitor incoming messages. A single BES can handle mailboxes for up to four Exchange servers if the account BES runs under has the necessary permissions to access the mailboxes on all servers. In addition, much like any other client that uses MAPI, BES needs reasonable connectivity to the Exchange servers it handles. You can certainly have a BES connect to a mailbox across a WAN connection, but if the connection is not reliable or suffers from high latency, then BES may not be able to deliver messages to user handhelds.

There are a few minor issues to consider before you install a BES:

- You cannot run Outlook on the same server, because the versions of CDO and MAPI used by Outlook and BES are different. Indeed, you have to apply a CDO patch before you install BES. The current use of CDO and MAPI limits the number of concurrent sessions that a single BES can support. Tests performed by HP show that the limit occurs at around 800 concurrent sessions. The new Exchange System Objects (XSO) interface supported by Exchange 2003 is more efficient than the MAPI/CDO combination, and a future version of BES based on XSO is likely to be more scalable.

- You need to have a Microsoft database engine on the server to allow BES to register and hold user details. MSDE is OK for small user communities, but SQL 7.0 or SQL 2000 are better choices if you have large populations or you have already installed and licensed SQL.

- Given the speed of current systems and the relatively low resource consumption of BES, it can run alongside other applications, including SQL, unless those applications already stress system performance.

- BES uses Server Routing Protocol (SRP) to communicate with external servers, normally those used by the wireless network to accept messages and dispatch them to users. SRP uses port 3101, so you have to arrange to open this port in your external firewall. Often, the internal discussion about opening a firewall port takes longer to resolve than any other issue in a BES deployment.

- RIM releases patches and service packs for BES, so it is wise to check whether an updated release is available before you start deployment. The same is true for the RIM desktop software, and you definitely need to verify if an update is available to support new versions of Outlook. As an example, the beta versions of Outlook 2003 broke the calendar synchronization code in the desktop redirector.

- BES transfers messages to handhelds by monitoring user mailboxes for new messages. The server is multithreaded and is capable of monitoring hundreds of mailboxes while maintaining fast response in terms of processing new messages sent or received by users. When messages arrive, BES uses a mixture of CDO and MAPI calls to create copies of the messages (in this respect, BES operates in a manner similar to a

Figure 6.19
User properties from BES.

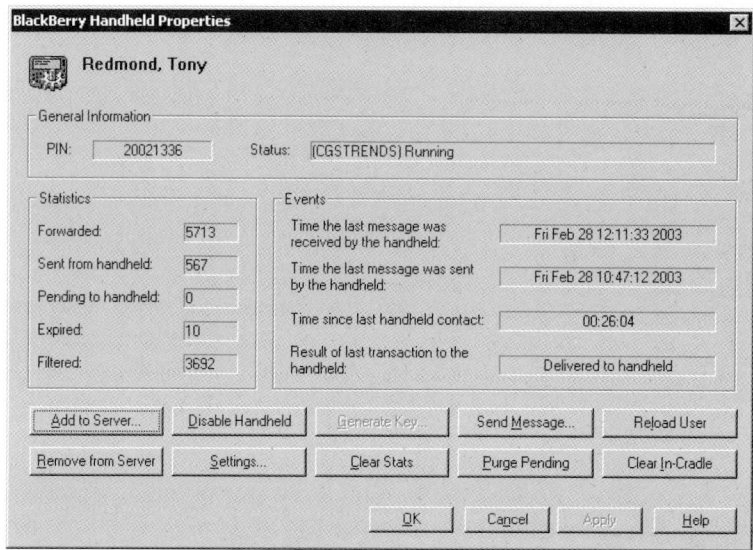

first-generation Exchange antivirus scanner), converts them to plain text, and then sends the first 2,000 bytes to the handhelds. If users need to read more than 2,000 bytes, they can request BES to send more information. Typically, the messages first pass through the corporate firewall to a relay server operated by the network provider, which then transmits the messages onward for final delivery.

- After you give people their handheld devices, you have to register them with a BES to establish communications. Figure 6.19 shows details of some of the information held in the BES user database, including statistics about the number of messages forwarded to the handheld device and sent by the user from the handheld device. Pending messages that cannot be delivered because of a network outage or because the handheld device is turned off are also noted, and the administrator can purge these messages to prevent the user from receiving a flood of new messages after the device is turned on.

You probably do not want BES to redirect every message that arrives in your mailbox to the handheld device. The Redirector Settings option of the Desktop Manager allows you to create filters or rules to stop some messages at the server. In most situations, it is sufficient to set filters to restrict messages to the ones where you are a TO: or BCC: recipient, but you might also like to see messages when you are a CC: recipient. These are the filters shown in Figure 6.20. In action, these filters will not forward messages that arrive in your Inbox because you are a member of a distribution list, unless

6.9 Mobile BlackBerries

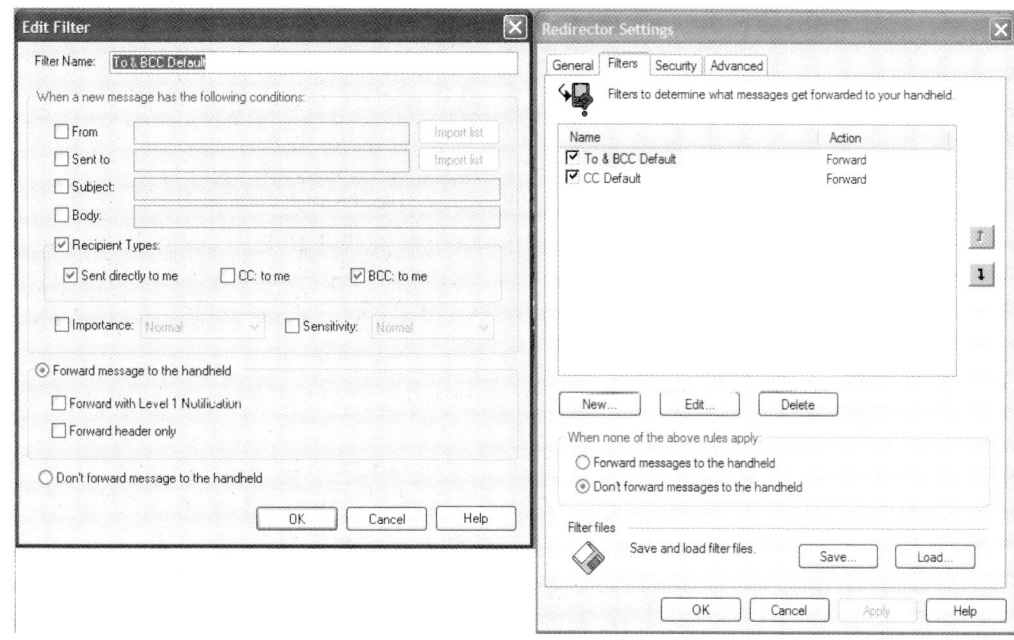

Figure 6.20 *Setting BlackBerry filters.*

Outlook has expanded the distribution list or it is a personal distribution list. Because UCE generators often address messages to huge distribution lists, the default filters block the majority of spam, although some gets through. As you can see from the statistics for my account in Figure 6.19, in the measurement period, BES filtered 3,692 messages and forwarded 5,713, which gives you an idea of the amount of traffic I receive that is not addressed directly to me. Deciding how much mail to block is a matter of preference, and there are advantages in letting everything through. Some messages that look like spam might be important, and you can open even the most virus-ridden message on a BlackBerry in the knowledge that it cannot infect your PC.

You can create as many filters as you want and have specific instructions for messages sent to special lists or from special people, such as your boss. The final filter is the catchall instruction to tell BES what to do with messages that do not match any filter. You can either have these messages blocked (the default option) or delivered to your handheld device. Note that BES only monitors messages arriving in your Inbox. If you want it to check other folders, you have to instruct BES to watch selected folders by entering this information in the "Folder Redirection" filter setting available through the Advanced tab. You might want to do this if you have created server-based filters for Exchange to refile messages as they arrive in your Inbox.

6.9.2 Using the BlackBerry

Although the BlackBerry keyboard is small, many find it easier to use two thumbs to drive a keyboard to create message text than tapping out the characters with a stylus or through handwriting recognition. You will not be writing *War and Peace*, nor will you "thumb out" anything more than a couple of hundred characters, but this is enough to respond to urgent messages, even if you mistype a lot of what you enter when you respond, as I am apt to do. Albeit with a different user interface (point and click with a stylus), the same is true of the Pocket PC. You can add a keyboard to a Pocket PC if you want, but it is just another piece of equipment to take on the road. The improved handwriting recognition engine from the Tablet PC will appear in the Pocket PC eventually, which will remove some of the recognition issues in Pocket PC 2002.

The simplicity and size of the BlackBerry make it easy to take anywhere. As an email device, you cannot get anything more compact and straightforward to use, and because it is so small, it is easy to check email anywhere—even when on the move. Another advantage is that the BlackBerry device is much easier on batteries than a Pocket PC. Even in constant use, the charge on a BlackBerry lasts up to a week (in my hands), whereas the Pocket PC drains much more quickly.

For users, the major advantage of the BlackBerry is the speed with which you can process an Inbox and deal with urgent messages. However, RIM inevitably had to compromise to create a device that clings to a belt, incorporates a keyboard, and is designed to do a few things extremely well. When compared with a Pocket PC, you find that BlackBerry handhelds limit the amount of data they download at any time to restrict network traffic. In most cases, the full content of messages arrives, but you may have to retrieve multiple "chunks" to read the complete content of large messages. This is not a problem, but some users forget to fetch more data and end up reading only part of the message. You can also restrict Pocket PC synchronization to limit the amount of data downloaded for each message, but because it downloads full messages (up to a predetermined limit) and attachments, the Pocket PC usually transmits and receives far more data than the BlackBerry does.

Even if you enable Outlook's Junk Mail processing feature or use other client-side rules to intercept offending messages en route to your Inbox,

BES will forward them to your handheld, because Outlook is unable to execute a rule to delete the messages unless it is connected to your mailbox. This is more of an annoyance than a problem, because you simply delete spam as soon as it arrives. However, if your network provider charges by the byte rather than a fixed monthly fee, there is a case to argue that spam is costing you money. On the other hand, some people use their handhelds to view suspect messages before they open them with Outlook, because, so far, virus or other attacks have not targeted the BlackBerry.

Up to the advent of Service Pack 1 for BES 3.5, you could not view Word, Excel, PowerPoint, or other attachments on a BlackBerry. Instead, you could install additional software to process attachments by printing on a fax or by sending messages to a conversion server, which returns the attachment in plain text. MetaMessage for Wireless from Onset Technologies[8] is a good example of such a product. These solutions require additional hardware for the server that handles the conversion workload. In many cases, users find it simpler to wait until they get back to the office because the conversion either loses so much formatting information that you cannot easily read the document or the document is so large that navigation on the handheld device is challenging. RIM introduced its own Attachment Server in BES 3.5 SP1 to allow users to request BES to send either the table of contents or the complete content of attachments to the Attachment Server, which then converted them to a format suitable for transmission to and viewing on the handheld. The Attachment Server supports common formats like Word, Excel, PDF, and WordPerfect and RIM plans to add more formats over time. However, while it is great to be able to view an attachment, many of the complex formatting features used within documents do not show up well on the handheld's restricted screen. In addition, you may have to update the firmware on your handheld before you can select the option to request attachments. On the server side, the work to convert large documents can impose a heavy load on the computer that hosts the Attachment Server. You can also delay transmission of newly arriving messages to handhelds if you ask for large attachments and it is easy to run up big bills if your wireless contract is limited to a certain amount of "free" data traffic per month and you exceed it with attachments.

As mentioned earlier, the nature of the thumb-driven keyboard will prevent you from composing long messages. You probably only want to create quick and simple replies to incoming messages, so the fact that the editor is rudimentary in the extreme (no formatting, no spell checking, and restricted cut-and-paste functionality) will not cause any problem. You can

---

8. http://www.onsettechnology.com/.

move within the text of a message and insert special symbols after you master the necessary keystrokes, which becomes second nature for some people. However, as with most cell phones, the editor includes an auto-text facility to help compose text quicker. New users typically take some time to become accustomed to the unique BlackBerry interface and learn the shortcut keys to take full advantage of the device. Adding to the task of mastering the device, the backlit screen and keyboard are sufficient to work with messages in the dark, but it is a challenge to read text on sunny days.

Compared with a Pocket PC, the BlackBerry has limited space to hold messages, and, similar to the Pocket PC, the BlackBerry clears out old messages to make space for new. The length of time that the device holds messages is very dependent on the amount of email you receive. Even though I delete many messages immediately after sending or receiving them, I find that I can keep about four weeks' worth of email on the device. If you need to, you can save important messages for longer. The BlackBerry does not support multitasking in the same way that a Pocket PC does. You work with one application at a time, switching to others as the need arises.

Synchronization between the BlackBerry and Exchange is not quite as thorough as ActiveSync is for the Pocket PC. The normal mode of working is for the handheld to receive new messages only if it is out of its cradle, so the copy of the Inbox on the BlackBerry is never complete. The same is true of Sent Items, where the BlackBerry only has copies of messages sent from the handheld rather than the complete collection. By comparison, if you synchronize a folder with ActiveSync, you can copy the entire contents of the folder. However, on balance, the synchronization is good enough to make email, calendar, and contacts available on the BlackBerry.

6.9.3 The Good option

While RIM created the form factor and established BlackBerry-type devices as a "must-have" device in large parts of corporate America, it is not the only player in this market. Good Technologies (www.good.com) sells a comparable service that runs on RIM's own 950 and 957 handhelds as well as its own G100 device, which connects to your PC via USB instead of a cradle. This makes the G100 device easier to take on the road when you want to bring as little clutter as possible. As the second entry in the field of corporate email handhelds, Good was able to take advantage of the wider availability of wireless networks by concentrating on wireless communications for downloads and synchronization and ignoring the cradle-centric approach taken by RIM. In RIM's defense, while cradles are inconvenient at times, they allow people who do not have a corporate email account to sign up with an ISP-delivered email system and still have wireless email.

The Good handheld software is platform-independent and is therefore not limited to the current RIM or G100 device form factor. The software can run on devices such as the Treo 600, powered by an ARM processor and running the Palm 5 operating system or indeed on a Pocket PC under Windows Mobile 2003. RIM responded by announcing its intention to support the BlackBerry software on Palm OS devices in May 2004 and by porting their client to the Pocket PC. The Pocket PC option is especially attractive if the Pocket PC comes equipped with a minikeyboard, an option that is increasingly available. The Pocket PC option is especially attractive if the Pocket PC comes equipped with a mini keyboard, an option that is increasingly available. The interaction between the Good handheld software and the GoodLink server is easier to set up than Exchange Mobile Services and works for Exchange 5.5, 2000, and 2003 mailboxes. Running Good's software on a Pocket PC instead of Pocket Outlook and ActiveSync might seem to compete with Microsoft's own products, but it does increase the number of wireless devices that can connect to Exchange, including sites that do not want to implement Exchange Mobile Services to support just a few users. The combination becomes even more compelling if you attach a keyboard to the Pocket PC to allow users to work better with email and Office documents. While teenagers have no difficulty composing long SMS messages with cell phones, it can be a challenge to face a large Inbox equipped solely with a stylus and a touch screen.

The GoodLink server software is comparable in function and purpose to BES 3.6 and includes the ability to handle attachments. Overall, the synchronization between handheld and email accounts seems smarter, possibly because Good came second to the market and knew where it could create a difference. For example, if you delete a message on a Good handheld, the GoodLink server deletes the message from your server mailbox—something that was a surprising problem for RIM until the release of BES 3.6. In North America, you can connect Good devices to Exchange 5.5, 2000, and 2003 mailboxes over the Cingular Mobitex wireless service. However, you cannot yet connect Good devices to Exchange over GSM or GPRS networks, so this is strictly a North American offering until Good manages to sign up international telecom providers to support its service in other countries (expected to begin in 2004). Non-U.S. coverage always was an issue for Good until it expanded into the United Kingdom as its first European venture in 2004. Given the current situation, the best advice when you consider deploying BES or the Good service to support corporate

Exchange users is to test both and see which one provides most value to your organization and then go with that option.

6.9.4 Is a handheld better than a Pocket PC?

I have known people to move from the BlackBerry to a Pocket PC and vice versa. The choice is very personal and depends on the work that the user does and how mobile he or she is. From a purely mobile perspective, devices such as the BlackBerry or the G100 are still the best way to stay in touch with your email and calendar anywhere a wireless network is available. However, if you want truly portable email and applications, then the combination of the Pocket PC and Exchange is the thing to have, especially if you can use a reliable wireless connection. The interesting thing here is the move by RIM and Good Technologies to replace Pocket Outlook with their own email clients, both of which are capable of connecting across different wireless networks deployed around the world. For example, the HP iPAQ h6300 series Pocket PCs (Figure 6.21) are equipped with everything that you expect from a Pocket PC plus a reasonable keyboard. Configurations differ from market to market, but this kind of Pocket PC is the one that I find most useful. Deployed in tandem with Exchange 2003 Mobile Services, Pocket PCs like the iPAQ 6300 are a very real competitor (for the first time) to BlackBerry and Good handheld devices.

There is no doubt that the classic Blackberry-style device is an extremely functional way to access your email, especially if you receive large numbers of messages daily. The Microsoft smartphone is more graphic, runs Windows, and does a reasonable job of getting to your inbox, but once high-speed wireless connectivity becomes reality everywhere, the extra features and growing maturity of the latest generation of the Pocket PC make the battle between the different access devices even

Figure 6.21
A modern Pocket PC: The HP iPAQ 6300 series.

harder to call. At the end of the day, it all comes down to which features make most sense for you—the device you are most comfortable with, the one that is easiest for you to carry, or the one that integrates best with your own messaging environment.

6.10 Sending messages without clients

Sometimes a need exists to create and send messages without starting up a client. Now that every Windows server supports SMTP, you can use simple batch command files to connect to port 25 and then build messages through SMTP commands. Another way of approaching the problem is to use a program or script to output a file containing text lines with the necessary SMTP commands to create and send a message. You can then place the text file in the appropriate "pickup" directory for the SMTP virtual server that you want to use on the server and Exchange will send the message for you. Create the message as a simple text file, giving the file a temporary name (the virtual server discards the file as soon as it sends the message) and format the contents according to RFC 822. For example:

```
Date: 2 Jun 03 1210 GMT
To: "Tony Redmond" Tony.Redmond@hpconsulting.com
From: "John Smith" John.Smith@acme.com
CC: "Jane Jurvis" Jane.Jurvis@acme.com
Subject: Notification of System Status

Warning. You should attend to the system because I think
all hell is about to break out!
```

You can include HTML commands in the file if you want to emphasize information. However, to accomplish this goal, the text becomes more complex, because you have to create a multipart MIME message that respects the rules that allow SMTP to transmit more than just plain text. It is not difficult to create the necessary commands, and after you have done it once it is easy to automate the process in a program or script. Here is the text file used to create the message shown in Figure 6.22.

```
Date: 2 Jun 03 1210 GMT
To: "Tony Redmond" Tony.Redmond@hpconsulting.com
From: "System Monitor" System.Manager@hpconsulting.com
Subject: Notification of System Status
MIME-Version: 1.0
Content-Type: text/html; charset="iso-8859-1"
Content-Transfer-Encoding: quoted-printable

<h1>Important Status Report </h1>
```

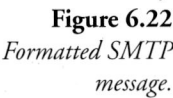

Figure 6.22
Formatted SMTP message.

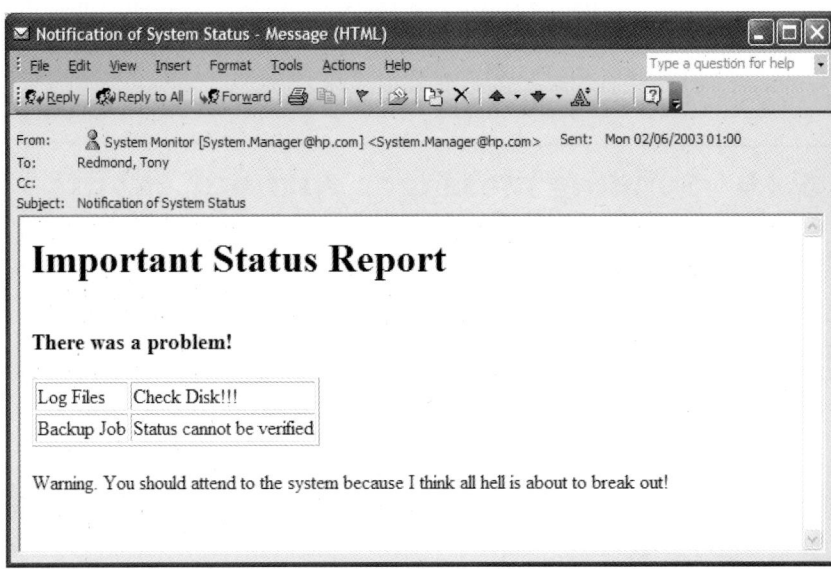

```
<br>
<h3>There was a problem!</h3>
<table border>
<tr><td>Log Files</td><td>Check Disk!!!</td></tr>
<tr><td>Backup Job</td><td>Status cannot be verified</
td></tr>
</table>
<p>
Warning. You should attend to the system because I think
all hell is about to break out!
```

It is easy to make a mistake when you generate commands to create MIME-formatted messages, so it is wise to verify that everything works by putting a message into the pickup directory and seeing whether it arrives. If Exchange delivers the message to the right Inbox, you know that the commands are right. On the other hand, if the message ends up in the virtual server's "badmail" directory, you know that an error is present. Usually, there is something wrong in the basic SMTP directives in the message header (To:, Cc:, and so on), but a malformed MIME bodypart can also cause problems.

If you do not want to mess around with programs, scripts, or SMTP commands, you can use the MAPISEND utility, which is part of the Exchange Resource Kit, to create and send messages. MAPISEND works by connecting to a mailbox to send a message. For example, the command:

6.10 Sending messages without clients

```
MAPISEND -u "Exchange" -r John.Doe@xyz.com -s "The moon
is full" -m "The moon is full tonight. Look outside your
window" -v
```

performs the following actions:

- Log on to the mailbox identified in the profile called "Exchange." Just like all other MAPI clients, a profile must exist on the client before MAPISEND can make a connection. If security credentials are already present (in other words, an account has already been logged in to), they are used for authentication. Alternatively, you can pass the password with the –p parameter.

- The message is addressed to the recipient John.Doe@xyz.com. You can pass any address that Exchange can resolve, including the name or email address of a distribution group.

- The message subject is set to be "The moon is full."

- The text of the message is set to be "The moon is full tonight. Look outside your window."

- The –v command switch tells MAPISEND that it must verify that it successfully sent the message.

As with all simple utilities, there is not much more to say. You cannot format the message text by adding colors, emphasis, or different fonts, but it is more than enough to send a short note. Typical uses include informing administrators that important system housekeeping jobs are finished, or sending a message to a pager or via SMS to a GSM phone to let the recipient know that a problem has occurred.

If you prefer not to use MAPISEND, the BLAT[9] utility or a commercial product such as Postie (available from www.infradig.com) offers another alternative. For example, here is the command line to use BLAT to send a text file called "mail.txt" to the recipient Jane.Doe@hp.com from a user called John.Doe@hp.com. The message subject is set to be "Urgent Message." Messages to notify system administrators that a problem has occurred with a program or other task are often sent in this manner, and since you can use any valid SMTP address, the messages can be sent to pagers, cell phones, and other devices.

```
BLAT mail.txt -t jane.doe@hp.com -f john.doe@hp.com
-subject "Urgent Message"
```

---

9. See http://www.interlog.com/~tcharron/blat.html.

New utilities appear all the time, so browsing the various support forums dedicated to Windows and Exchange may turn up another program that is closer to your needs.

6.11 Client licenses

No matter what client you connect to Exchange, you need a client access license (CAL), so there is no direct saving in software licenses if you elect to deploy a "free" client that connects via POP3, IMAP4, or HTTP.

Outlook Express is certainly a very good free client, but because Outlook is part of the world's most popular office application suite (Microsoft Office), many companies simply end up with the software anyway. Never base the decision solely on the cost of software licenses. Instead, look at the overall cost of ownership, including support and deployment costs. Outlook is the most functional client you can connect to Exchange, but because it is so functional, Outlook is usually harder and more expensive to support, and this represents another cost that you must factor into the equation.

7
The Store

> *As with most media from which things are built, whether the thing is a cathedral, a bacterium, a sonnet, a fugue, or a word processor, architecture dominates material. To understand clay is not to understand the pot. What a pot is all about can be appreciated better by understanding the creators and users of the pot and their needs both to inform the material with their meaning and to extract meaning from the form.*
>
> —Alan Kay

The Store (or Information Store) has always been at the heart of Exchange. If you doubt this adage, stop the Store service and discover just how quickly users protest. As with any critical component, we have to understand, manage, maintain, and protect the Information Store, or Store. Much of the strength of the Store comes from its solid architectural base.

7.1 Structure of the Store

Figure 7.1 illustrates the internal structure of the Exchange Store, which is unchanged in Exchange 2003. The Store Kernel is the component that builds features unique to Exchange on top of the generalized Jet Blue engine. These features include single-instance storage, views, and automatic indexing of items as clients add items to the Store. The Jet Blue layer builds on top of the generalized ESE database engine. This layer takes responsibility for managing low-level internal structures such as the B-trees and class tables. ESE has no knowledge of high-level structures such as the schema used in any particular database. Instead, ESE operates at the page level to manipulate database contents.

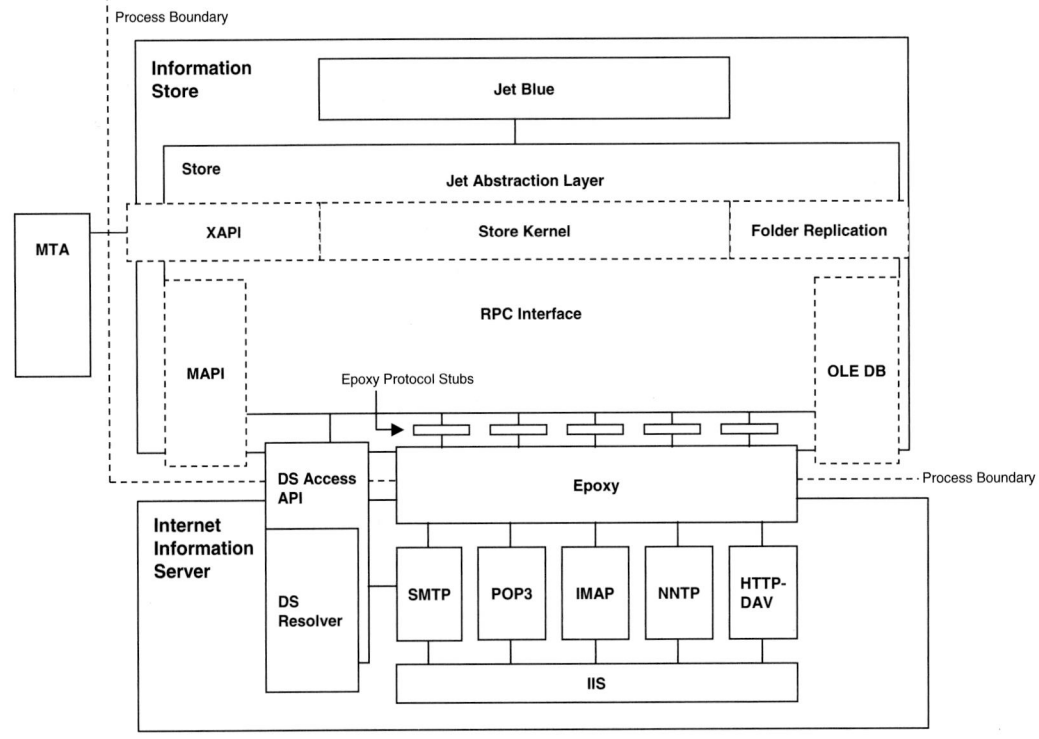

Figure 7.1 *The structure of the Store.*

We have referred to Jet, which stands for Joint Engine Technology, a generalized Microsoft database engine that Microsoft builds off of to form variants that drive products as diverse as the Store and Access. ESE is a much-enhanced development of the basic Jet engine now used by the AD and the DS. Apart from Exchange and Access, there are many other examples of Jet in use within Microsoft products. For example, Windows use Jet databases to hold WINS and DHCP data, and these databases share many of the characteristics you see in Exchange, including transaction logs and reserved logs. The original plan was for Jet to evolve to become a common technology platform for Microsoft databases, but this never materialized. In the future, Microsoft wants to achieve the vision of a unified database platform through the Yukon engine. Future versions of Exchange will use a variant of Yukon, much as the current version of Exchange uses a variant of Jet.

By definition, ESE is a multiuser ISAM database with full Data Manipulation Language (DML) and Data Definition Language (DDL) capability. Applications such as Exchange use ESE to store and index records in an efficient manner and in different ways. Microsoft has optimized ESE for highly scalable performance through fast retrieval of data, with a priority given to accessing data held in memory caches instead of going to disk whenever possible. The massive numbers of simulated MAPI users supported on Exchange servers demonstrate just how scalable ESE is. Even if you would not want to connect 30,000 users to a single eight-way server, the fact that the database is able to cope with the load generated by so many simulated users is an impressive testament to its inherent scalability.

Microsoft refers to the version of ESE implemented in Exchange 2000 and 2003 as ESE98 to differentiate it from previous implementations, such as that used in Exchange 5.5, which share the same basic engine (ESE97) as the AD. However, there are some subtle differences between ESE97 and ESENT, the variant used by the AD, the most obvious of which are the different sizes of pages and transaction logs.

Because of the common link to Jet, it is easy to make the erroneous conclusion that Exchange and Access share the same database engine. This story has become one of the street fables around Exchange and surfaces every so often in Internet newsgroups. Microsoft designed the variant used by the Store to deal with the hierarchical nature of the mailbox/folder/item model found in messaging and document management systems. A hierarchical model is much more appropriate than a relational model for clients such as Outlook, which navigate to data using a tree structure similar to a file system. Internally, there are certainly many relationships maintained within the Store. Folders have a relationship to mailboxes, and subfolders have a relationship to their parent folders. Folders hold items, and users own mailboxes. The need to deal with loosely formatted semistructured data is another major difference between the classic database engines and ESE. One message transaction is a simple email sent to three users, but a user might send the next transaction to a massive distribution list, and the message could contain four attachments, each of which is larger than 5 MB. A database designed to handle structured transactions, such as those typical of financial applications, is not necessarily going to be able to handle the type of transactions seen in a messaging system.

7.2 Exchange ACID

Microsoft designed the Store to meet the ACID (Atomicity, Consistency, Isolation, and Durability) test for database transaction integrity. Transactions are only applied if they are compete and intact. Microsoft makes great efforts to ensure consistency throughout the Store; transactions are isolated from each other, and there are many features implemented in the Store to make it a reliable and robust repository.

A transaction is a series of modifications to a database that leaves the database in a consistent state. These modifications are called operations. Sending a new message requires several operations that form the single logical transaction we consider when we think of someone sending a message and Exchange delivering it to recipient mailboxes.

An operation is the smallest change made to an ESE database. Operations include insert, delete, replace, and commit. A database is left in an inconsistent state if not all of the operations that make up a transaction are committed. For example, if a server experiences a sudden failure during normal operation, it is quite likely that a number of transactions are outstanding and have not yet been completely committed to the database. Exchange can return its databases to a consistent state by processing the contents of the transaction log files. When the Store makes the database consistent, ESE may ignore some transactions because the Store was not able to complete all of the operations necessary to finalize some transactions when the system crash occurred.

ACID transactions mean that ESE must fulfill the following requirements, as described in *Transaction Processing: Concepts and Techniques* (by Gray and Reuter, 1983):

- Atomic: An atomic transaction is one where all its operations are indivisible. Either all of the operations that make up a transaction are committed to the database or none is committed. There is no halfway stage.
- Consistent: Transactions move the database from one consistent state to another. In other words, after a transaction is fully complete, the database is consistent.
- Isolated: Changes made to the database are not visible to users until all operations that make up the transaction are completed. At this point, the transaction is committed to the database.
- Durable: Committed transactions are preserved even if the system crashes.

We will examine many of the features that contribute to ACID compliance in this chapter, including:

- The single-instance storage model
- Transaction logging

- Recovery from server crashes
- Throughput

Operational experience demonstrates that many system administrators do not understand the way that the ESE database model works. Knowing how transactions occur and are stored is fundamental to understanding Exchange, as is the concept that transactions are stored in three different locations: the on-disk databases (content and properties in the EDB database and potentially content in the streaming file), a cache managed in memory, and a separate set of transaction logs for each active storage group. Before we look at how the features of the Store help Exchange to achieve these goals, we need to review how ESE organizes data within the database.

7.3 EDB database structure

From Exchange 2000 onward, the Store uses two types of database: the EDB and the STM (a database set). The EDB is the traditional database and is organized into a set of 4 to 8–KB pages, numbered in sequence. Microsoft also refers to the EDB as a "property database," because its original function was to hold MAPI properties for messages and other items. Exchange holds message content and attachments as MAPI properties, although there is a limit to the amount of content that a particular property can hold, so the Store often uses extensions to hold large amounts of data. Exchange only needed a MAPI database as long as it only supported MAPI clients, but once Internet clients appeared some change was necessary to support the way they retrieve data. Exchange 5.0 and 5.5 handle Internet clients as if they were modified MAPI clients, but this is an inefficient mechanism, because it forces the Store to convert streamed data to MAPI always.

Microsoft then introduced the STM, or streaming database, in Exchange 2000 to handle the native MIME content generated by POP3 and IMAP4 clients. Every EDB database has a matching STM, and the Store manages the interaction between the EDB and STM databases invisible to clients. Whenever possible, the Store maintains content in its original format and only converts it when necessary, avoiding permanent conversion if not needed. For example, if an older MAPI client that cannot support MIME reads a message held in the STM, the Store converts the content to MAPI. If the client then decides to amend the content, the Store writes the MAPI content into the EDB and updates pointers so that if the user retrieves the message again, using whatever client, he or she gets the MAPI content. Because you can use different clients to access your mailbox, a mailbox can contain both MAPI and MIME content, and, again, the Store

Chapter 7

makes sure it hides this complexity from view. Sometimes conversions happen when you do not expect them. For example, if you use AD Users and Computers (or the Exchange 2003 version of ESM) to move a mailbox from one server to another or from one database to another on the same server, any MIME content in the mailbox transfers automatically into MAPI. The net effect is that the size of the EDB file can grow alarmingly if you move many mailboxes, and the time taken to perform the moves is sometimes longer than you might expect.

7.3.1 EDB page structure

The first two pages in an EDB are the database header. The remaining pages hold data, so the third physical page is logical database page 1, the fourth is logical database page 2, and so on. The Enterprise Edition of Exchange allows a single ESE database to store up to 232 pages, meaning that the maximum possible size for a single database is 16 TB (the standard edition restricts databases to 16 GB). Of course, this limit is largely theoretical, since no administrator would allow a database to grow so large because the database would be difficult to back up, not to mention restore, unless snapshot technology were used. The largest operational Exchange database has grown 20-fold from 10 GB in 1996 to over 250 GB in 2001; if we observed a similar rate of increase, the largest database might be 4 TB by 2006, a monster that would be a challenge in terms of backup and (especially) restore. Fortunately, the advent of Store partitioning across multiple databases has restricted databases to more manageable sizes.

Each page has a 40-byte header, which includes the page number, a count of free bytes available in the page, and a checksum. As we will see later on, the checksum plays an extremely important role in the way that ESE ensures data integrity. The page header for data pages also holds information about the adjacent pages on either side, which helps ESE to navigate through pages quickly and is a characteristic of the B+tree implementation. While there is an extra overhead in calculating the adjacent page numbers, they allow for faster sequential reads through data.

7.3.2 Within the trees

ESE organizes database pages into balanced trees. Balance tree technology is not new, nor is it particular to Exchange.[1] Balanced trees allow fast

---

1. The concept of B-trees was first described in a paper entitled "Transaction Processing: Concepts and Techniques" by Bayer and McCreight in 1972.

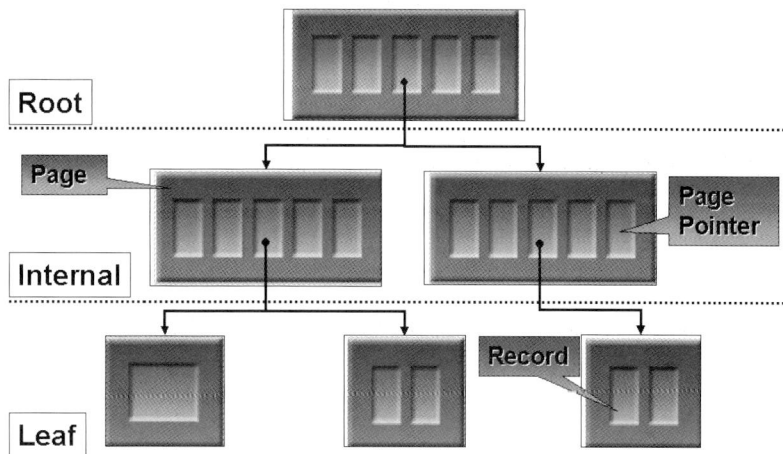

Figure 7.2
The B-tree structure within an ESE database.

access to data on disk and reduce the number of I/Os the engine requires to find a specific piece of information. Data in balanced trees is sorted in whatever way is required by an application. ESE uses a variant called B+tree (B-plus-tree), which provides a higher degree of efficiency by minimizing the extent of the database's internal hierarchy. In turn, limits are also set on how wide the branches within the database can grow and how many levels deep they go.

Pages can hold data or act as pointers to other pages, and both page types are intermingled within the database. ESE is able to cache pages in memory to improve performance and reduce disk I/O. The Exchange buffer manager, one of the Store components, using a well-known public domain algorithm called Least Recently Used Reference Count (LRU-K), manages the pages in memory. In other words, ESE flushes pages from the cache if it calculates that they have not recently been used, while pages that have been referenced are retained whenever possible.

To find anything in the tree you start at the root page and navigate down to the leaf level (see Figure 7.2). The internal pages (not at the leaf level) only contain pointers to leaf pages. An individual page can contain between 200 and 300 pointers to leaf pages. Because ESE compresses the pointers into a reasonably small number of pages, the height of the tree that ESE must navigate is never very large. Inside ESE, there is normally never more than four levels to navigate. Put another way, no more than four LRU-K I/Os are required to get to the data you require, and each I/O can be eliminated if the relevant page is in cache. Most heavily trafficked pages will be in the cache. Records are stored at the leaf level. The actual record depends on what type of tree you access. The Store allocates space in a series of 16 consecutive pages to minimize I/O activity further. Pages cannot belong to different data tables or hold data from two different trees.

ESE uses three major types of B+trees: index, data, and long value trees. Indexes provide different sort orders on the data held in data trees. They allow secondary index keys to map the primary index at a small additional cost. Sorting is performed using MAPI properties. Unlike other databases, ESE has the capability to add or delete new indexes dynamically.

7.3.3 Database tables and fields

ESE organizes mailbox and public folder data into tables, which are then made up of records and then columns (fields). Within a database, we therefore have many thousands of tables—at least one for every folder in every mailbox. Statistically and as you would probably expect, message and attachment tables occupy at least 90 percent of the space within a typical database. The maximum size of a record is approximately 4,050 bytes (the 4-KB page minus the header overhead). Thus, a record equates to a page. Apart from a few exceptions, ESE only assigns space to a column if data is available. You do not have a situation where a large number of columns are blank, because some message attributes have not been completed by a user. The header information for most messages fits into the space within a page, but, obviously, there are going to be times when records need to grow past a 4-KB boundary. For example, if you send a message whose body text is larger than 4 KB, it cannot be stored in the data page allocated to the MAPI PR_BODY property. The same is true when dealing with attachments larger than 4 KB, since attachments are also stored in another MAPI property. ESE solves the problem with long value trees. Each table can have a long value tree, which is created on an as-needed basis. If a piece of data is too big to fit into the data tree, it is broken up into a series of 4-KB chunks stored in the long value tree. Each chunk is assigned a table-wide identifier within the long value tree. When required, data can be located very efficiently in the long value tree through a combination of the identifier and offset within the tree.

By comparison, the AD organizes information into 8-K pages. You can understand the difference by the fact that the AD might have to store hundreds of attributes about a user or other object, so the average size of an object is probably going to be greater than 4 KB. If the AD used 4-KB pages, it would result in many page splits, which would not make the internal structures very efficient.

7.3 EDB database structure

Strictly speaking, the internal structure of the EDB is not a relational database, but that model is the closest you would come to when making comparisons between Exchange and other databases. Much of the interaction is carried out on a hierarchical basis, as users navigate within the folders and subfolders inside mailboxes, but the access to individual items within a folder depends on many relationships maintained inside the database. Many different types of tables are defined for use inside the Store, but the majority of these tables are used internally and are not very interesting to users or system administrators. The ISINTEG utility provides an insight into the number of tables, but not their use, when you run the utility in verbose mode.

Internally, ESE does not represent a table by one tree. Instead, each table is a collection of trees. The system catalog stores the information about the trees that collectively make up a table. The trees set in a table includes the root pages, information about the columns that make up the table, and the indexes used by the table. Views are secondary indexes for folders. Users can generate views at a whim by clicking on one of the field headings when browsing a folder through a MAPI client (POP3 or IMAP clients do not support views). When this happens, a new view is created (e.g., sort by author name) and added to the table. A slight delay may be encountered when a view is first built, but afterward the view is available as part of the table, and switching views happens very quickly. Views are aged out after seven days and discarded at that point if they are no longer in use. This approach prevents the Store from being cluttered with old and obsolete views, which may have been used only once.

ESE uses a special table called the system catalog to track its internal operations. Because the system catalog is so vital to ESE, the Store keeps two copies, called MSysObjects and MSysObjectsShadow. The repair process carried out when you run ESEUTIL with the /P qualifier is able to access the backup copy of the system catalog and fix problems should they occur in the original system catalog.

Data trees store the actual records where the Store holds information such as message and attachment content. These pages do not form a very complex structure. After all, there are only so many steps you can take to organize data within a repository. It is worth noting here that arranging data in 4-KB pages is satisfactory if the data remains small. Once the size of messages goes past 4 KB, ESE must split the content across multiple pages; there is no guarantee that all the pages are stored contiguously in the database. There is an additional processing overhead required to assemble message content from multiple pages, and the overhead grows in line with message size. This is one of the major influences behind the decision to split storage between the EDB databases and the streaming file.

7.3.4 Tables in a Mailbox Store

Despite its hierarchical nature, navigation within a mailbox depends on relationships between different tables within a Mailbox Store. The most important of these tables are as follows:

- The mailbox table: One row holds properties for each mailbox on a server.
- The folders table: One row exists for each folder in every mailbox.
- The message table: One row holds content for every message.
- The attachments table: One row holds content for every attachment.
- A set of message/folder tables: A separate table exists for every folder.

Public Folder Stores and the AD also organize their data into tables and rows. Everyone is familiar with mailboxes, and Mailbox Stores get most use on any server, so it is the most appropriate example to use for illustrative purposes. This discussion is based on the interaction that occurs within a single database. The Store manages the retrieval of data from multiple databases, if these are involved in transactions.

Pointers link one table to another within the Store. This interaction forms the basis of single-instance storage and delivers a unified view of Store contents to clients. The processing that takes place when a client opens a mailbox, and then opens and reads a message, illustrates how pointers tie the tables together.

Let's examine what happens when an Outlook client opens a mailbox. Sample data is used to illustrate the explanation, and the data has been simplified for clarity.

The Store supports nested folders. In other words, folders can contain subfolders. Clients construct a tree view of folders by reading data from the Folders table. Each folder has a unique identifier, and the Store recognizes subfolders by the existence of a parent folder ID, which also serves to link subfolders back to the parent folder. The sample data in Table 7.1 shows that the "Articles" and "Newsflash" folders are both subfolders of the "Magazine" folder. Clients use the count of new items to decide when to bold folder names as a visual sign to users that they should review the contents of the folder.

7.3 EDB database structure

Table 7.1 *Sample Contents of the Folders Table*

Folder ID	Folder Name	Folder Owner	Count of Items	Count of New Items	Parent Folder ID
10445872	Inbox	TonyR	195	10	0
10427756	Magazine	TonyR	15	0	0
10427558	Articles	TonyR	29	1	10427756
10475586	Newsflash	TonyR	5	0	10427756
10479514	Deleted Items	TonyR	85	0	0
10475866	Inbox	BillR	100	15	0
10557660	Deleted Items	BillR	16	0	0

A separate table holds header information (all of which are MAPI properties) for each folder. Maintaining header information in a separate table allows each folder to have its own sort order. The alternative is to request data from a much larger table, albeit sorted and indexed. The scheme used by Exchange minimizes the data transmitted between client and server when clients wish to display information about a folder. For example, when an Outlook client builds the folder list, it proceeds to display header information from the currently selected folder (usually the Inbox) in the right-hand pane in its main window. Fetching data similar to that shown in Table 7.2 from the appropriate message/folder table performs this operation.

The MTS-ID (message identifier) links a row in a message/folder table to the actual content of a message. When a user selects an item and double-clicks to read it, the message ID is used to fetch content from the message table, and the combination of header and content information is used to populate the form used to display the complete message.

Table 7.2 *Contents of a Message/Folder Table*

From	Subject	Received	Size	Priority	Attachment Flag	MTS-ID
Don Vickers	Florida holidays	01-Sep-2003	4 KB	Normal	No	42955955
Larry LeMan	Clustering Exchange	29-Sep-2003	3 KB	High	Yes	48538505
Ken Ewert	Titanium Baby!	30-Sep-2003	948 bytes	Low	No	42552902
Kieran McCorry	Customer trip report	30-Sep-2003	22 KB	Normal	No	49919495
Administrator	New cafeteria	01-Oct-2003	2 KB	Normal	No	41848910

Table 7.3 *Contents of the Message Table*

Message ID	To	Message Body Content	Use Count	Attachment Pointer
48538505	Tony Redmond	Exchange supports multiple databases …	4	—
49919495	Tony Redmond	On my recent trip I visited …	25	66456776
52195995	Kieran McCorry	Has anyone tried the new fish dish in …	1	—

Table 7.3 illustrates the type of data we might find in the message table. The message body content is stored in Rich Text Format (RTF). If attachments exist for the message, a pointer appears in the attachment pointer field and the client can use this to retrieve the attachment(s). If message content originated from an IMAP client, it may still be stored in the streamed database. However, tables in the EDB database always hold the properties of the message. The Store retrieves content automatically from the streamed database if necessary and provides it to MAPI clients in RTF format. If the MAPI client then alters the content, the Store removes it from the streamed database into the message table.

The use count field is very important. It contains the count of folders that contain a reference to a message. The count decrements over time as users delete their references to messages. When the use count reaches zero, the Store removes the row from the table.

From reading this brief description of some of the tables inside the Mailbox Store, it is obvious that clients retrieve data from a number of tables when they read messages. Clients are not aware of all the work, because the Store masks the entire interaction through the appropriate service provider. Thus, the MAPI service provider assumes the responsibility of fetching the necessary information whenever Outlook reads a message, as illustrated in Figure 7.3.

7.3.5 Search Folders

Databases allow you to create many different views of data held in their tables. Search folders (or "smart folders") are Exchange's equivalent of database queries, because they are particular views of data based on underlying tables. Outlook clients have traditionally supported search folders in the "Advanced Find" function, which allows users to search their mailboxes for specific items. However, the resulting search folders are temporary, and, as such, they are volatile because the Store destroys them as soon as the client

7.3　EDB database structure

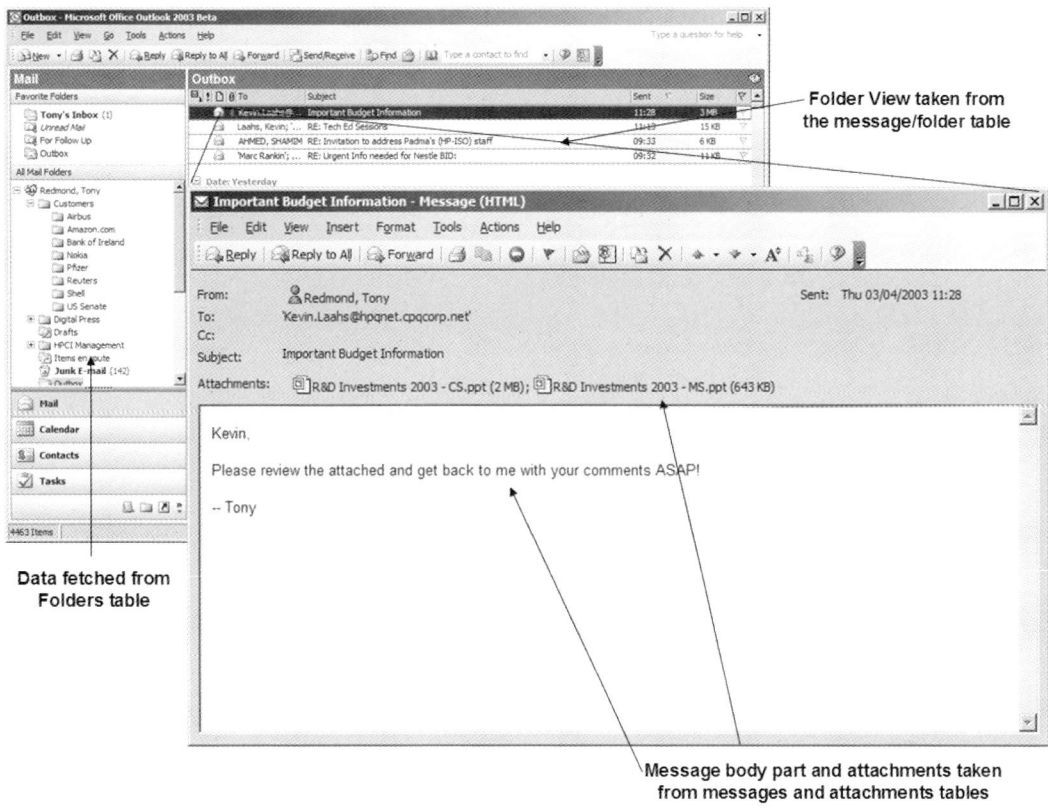

Figure 7.3　*How Outlook accesses database tables.*

exits. Outlook 2003 and OWA 2003 now support persistent search folders and incorporate these folders into the standard user interface. Search folders work against Exchange 5.5, 2000, and 2003 servers, but only Exchange 2000 and 2003 allow you to perform a search within a search folder. Clients process items in search folders in exactly the same way as normal folders. In other words, if you delete an item from a search folder, the Store removes it from the underlying table in its "real" folder.

On the surface, search folders seem like a great idea and they are, but they create an additional load for the Store. Active search folders soak up CPU cycles, because the Store has to maintain the temporary search folders. In fact, if you create many search folders in your mailbox, you may slow down the delivery of new messages, because the Store has to check every new message against all the search folders to see whether it has to update the views for any of the temporary folders.

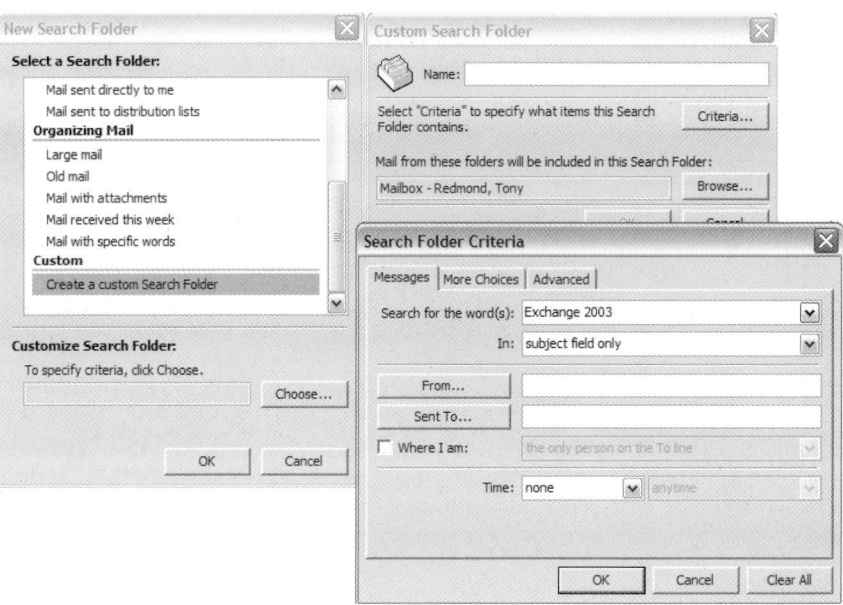

Figure 7.4   *Creating search folders.*

While you can still create search folders from an "Advanced Find" operation, you can also set out to create them from scratch. As you can see in Figure 7.4, you can create search folders based on many different fields, such as messages sent by specific people or to selected distribution groups, message size or age, or messages with flags set. For example, I have a search folder to identify messages that I send to my direct reports, while Outlook 2003 comes with predefined search folders for unread messages (extracted from any folder), large messages (anything larger than 100 KB), and those that are flagged for follow up. The rich OWA client for Exchange 2003 also supports search folders. Apart from identifying the queries for the Store to build folder contents, search folders also register themselves for notification when new items appear in the underlying folders. Thus, if a new message arrives with a large attachment, the Store knows that it must notify the "Large Messages" search folder so that it can update its content.

It is worth noting that search folders exist in the Store and in client-side OSTs. If you create a new search folder on the server, the synchronization process copies the folder to the OST, but the new folder replica is in an "inactive" state, and it remains the responsibility of the "owning" store to populate the search folder. In other words, the synchronization process only moves the query part of a search folder from server to offline store; it does not replicate the results of the query. Therefore, you have to click on the

7.3 EDB database structure

Table 7.4 *Registry Values to Control Search Folders*

Value	Meaning
SearchMaxNumberOnline	Controls maximum number of online search folders. Set to 0 to suppress user interface and stop users from accessing search folders.
SearchOnlineKeepAliveDays	Controls the lifetime of online (Store) search folders. If the user does not click on the folder in this time, the Store deactivates the folder (disables notifications) and clears its content. If you set the value to 0, it means that the Store clears the folder contents as soon as the user moves to another folder, which forces repopulation every time a user accesses the folder, thus creating a heavy load for the server.
SearchOfflineKeepAliveDays	Controls lifetime of offline (OST) search folders.
SearchNoCreateDefaults	Controls whether Outlook creates the three OOTB search folders (such as "Large Messages"). Set the value to 1 to suppress creation.

search folder when connected to the server to force the Store to refresh the folder contents, and you have to do the same thing to force Outlook to refresh a client-side search folder when you work offline.

Table 7.4 lists the registry values that you can use to control some aspects of search folder behavior for Outlook 2003. Create the SearchNoCreateDefaults value at:

HKCU\Software\Microsoft\Office\11.0\Outlook\Options\Setup

while the others are created at:

HKCU\Software\Microsoft\Office\11.0\Outlook\Options\General

Search folders exist in two states: inactive and active. An inactive folder is one that has no notifications registered, so the Store does not maintain its contents. Active folders have notifications registered, so the Store maintains the views for the folder by watching for new items that enter the mailbox and deciding whether they match the underlying folder query. If so, the Store adds the new items to the folder. Users activate search folders by clicking on them. This action registers the notifications and executes the search query against the complete mailbox to populate the folder view. This is the most intensive processing that a search folder imposes on the Store. When you review the search folders in a mailbox, you can recognize the inactive folders easily because Outlook italicizes their names. For example, in Figure 7.5, the "Sent to HPCI CTO DR" folder is inactive, while the other folders are active. In addition, the Store observes normal convention of marking search folders with unread items in bold. If you click on a folder and select

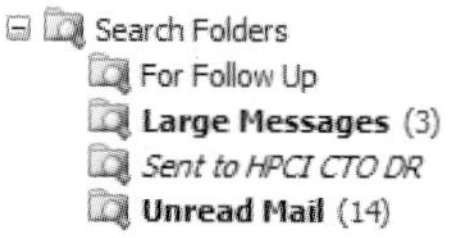

Figure 7.5
Search folders.

```
Search Folders
    For Follow Up
    Large Messages (3)
    Sent to HPCI CTO DR
    Unread Mail (14)
```

"Properties," you can tell Outlook to display the total number of unread items or the total number of items in the folder. Note that OWA only supports access to active online search folders and has no user interface to support the creation of new search folders. Naturally, OWA has no access to offline search folders.

By default, a search folder has a lifetime of two months after creation. If the folder is not used, the Store will send a request to the client to ask it to remove the folder to avoid the possibility that old and outdated views continue to absorb performance. However, it is possible for a client to log on once, create a set of search folders, log off, and never reconnect. In this case, the search folders remain active forever, because the Store's request to remove the folder goes into a blank void. There is no way for an administrator to disable search folders, so the only way to minimize their potential impact on performance is to use clients that do not support the feature.

7.3.6 The checkpoint file

ESE maintains a checkpoint file for each storage group. During normal operation, ESE writes transactions in the in-memory queue into databases when system load allows. The checkpoint file (E00.CHK for the default storage group) keeps track of the last committed buffer through a pointer. ESE uses the checkpoint file during "soft" recoveries to determine the point at which to begin replaying transactions. However, if ESE cannot access the checkpoint file, or it does not exist, ESE can examine the transaction log set to determine the replay point.

Exchange adds a further safeguard through a new header in a database that records the generations of log files that are required to make the database consistent, should a recovery operation be necessary. Recovery will stop with a –543 error if a required transaction log file is not available.

You can "force" ESE to flush transactions out of memory and write them to the database by stopping the Store service. This happens when you shut down a system gracefully. If you force Exchange to stop abruptly, such as in the case of a power outage, it is likely that some outstanding transactions remain that the Store has not committed to the physical database. We can gain some insight into the purpose served by the checkpoint file by

7.3 EDB database structure

Figure 7.6
Header dump from a checkpoint file.

```
Microsoft(R) Exchange Server(TM) Database Utilities Version 6.0
Copyright (C) Microsoft Corporation 1991-2000. All Rights Reserved.

Initiating FILE DUMP mode...
     Checkpoint file: e00.chk

     LastFullBackupCheckpoint: (0x0,0,0)
     Checkpoint: (0x7DD6,2012,B2)
     FullBackup: (0x7DBF,8,16)
     FullBackup time: 04/09/2002 20:30:24
     IncBackup: (0x0,0,0)
     IncBackup time: 00/00/1900 00:00:00
     Signature: Create time:07/18/2000 11:36:36 Rand:2804053 Computer:
     Env (CircLog,Session,Opentbl,VerPage,Cursors,LogBufs,LogFile,Buffers)
(    off,    252,   37800,    1740,   12600,    128,   10240,    98184)

Operation completed successfully in 1.31 seconds.
```

dumping it with the ESEUTIL utility. Use the ESEUTIL /MK switch for this purpose, which generates a listing similar to that shown in Figure 7.6.

The most important field is "Checkpoint," which contains a hex value (0x7DD6) indicating the transaction log generation where the checkpoint is currently positioned. The other values in this field (2012, B2) are internal offsets that only have meaning to the database. The backup fields hold information about the date and time that the last full (April 9, 2002, at 20:30) and incremental backups were started, and the "00/00/1900" date indicates that an incremental backup has never been performed for this storage group. The checkpoint indicates that transaction logs up to generation 7DBF were included in the last full backup. If you compare the signature in the checkpoint file against the storage group signature, you can see that they are identical, so you know that this checkpoint file belongs to that storage group.

During a soft recovery operation, ESE uses the data in the checkpoint file to determine which transactions to replay by comparing the timestamp in the checkpoint file against the transactions in the log files. If the transactions in the logs are newer than the timestamp in the checkpoint file, ESE replays them and writes the transactions into the Store. ESE discards any transactions that do not end in a commit operation, because they are incomplete. Note that replayed transactions do not just include new messages and attachments; they can also include deletions and updates. If ESE has to replay a large number of transactions when a system powers up, the Store update can take a few minutes to complete.

While it is convenient to have the checkpoint file available before beginning a recovery operation, it is not a prerequisite. If ESE finds that the checkpoint file is not available, the logs in the transaction logs directory are scanned (starting at the lowest available generation) to determine the point at which transactions had been committed to the database.

Removing the checkpoint file before a recovery operation is not a good thing to do, because it eliminates a safeguard that ensures it recovers the right transactions.

7.3.7 Page checksum

Along with its number, each page holds a checksum in its header. Every time the Store writes a page from memory to disk, it first calculates the checksum, using a very simple algorithm based on the stream of bits in the page, and then writes it into the page header before the page is committed to disk. Calculating the checksum imposes no great overhead on the system. Later, when the Store reads the page from disk, the checksum is recalculated using the same algorithm to ensure that the data in the page has not been changed since it was written. If the calculated checksum does not match the checksum stored in the page header, the page is suspect and a problem may have occurred. In reality, the only way that the checksums can be different is if the page were not written correctly to disk or had not been read correctly from disk. ESE attempts to get around the second issue by rereading the page up to 16 times before concluding that a problem actually exists, but it is obviously much harder to fix a page that the Store never writes properly to disk.

Note that it is the responsibility of the Windows file system and hardware to write data to disk. Exchange simply hands the data to Windows and requests the write. Everything that happens from that point is under the control of first Windows (to pass the write to the hardware) and then the device drivers for the controller and disk hardware (to perform the write). The majority of database problems encountered with Exchange are due to poor quality or poorly maintained hardware. For example, the potential for further problems to occur obviously exists if administrators do not apply firmware updates to either controller or disks to address known bugs.

Some commentators have identified write-back caching as an area that can generate errors for Exchange databases. While it is true that some controllers incorrectly signal the file system that data has been successfully committed before the data is actually written to disk, high-end controllers manage the process by securing data in cache memory that is protected by battery backup. Thus, even if the controller fails, the database can be updated with outstanding transactions through the cached data. You should never use write-back caching with Exchange if unprotected controllers are used. Exchange cannot predict that a problem will occur; it can only report that a problem exists and that it is due to a failure that occurred sometime in the past.

7.4 The streaming file

In daily life, you most commonly encounter streamed data in the form of audio or video files. Streamed files are normally very large, so clients access them in a continuous stream. Even a DVD video, which allows much more selective sampling of a film than is normally available in a standard video format, breaks up a film into scenes, each of which may be hundreds of megabytes in size. Audio files are no different, especially if they are recorded at a high sample rate to achieve the best possible quality. If you use the "Record narration" feature of PowerPoint to record notes for a presentation, you will be surprised at just how quickly your hard disk fills.

Even if we do not want to encourage users to send massive attachments to each other, the simple fact is that they do. Every holiday, a new variation on the electronic greeting card is made available somewhere on the Web, and it ends up being mailed millions of times to different users. In the days of "green screen email," we had cards composed of video escape character sequences. The escape characters instructed the terminal to display a series of primitive graphic characters in the correct order to create a picture. With a lot of dedication and trial and error, people produced amazing effects, and the electronic card was born.

The internal structure of EDB databases is not very suitable for storing large attachments that clients access in a continual stream. Think of how the Store needs to divide a 10-MB attachment containing the latest electronic greeting card into 2,500 separate pages inside the database. No guarantee is given that these pages will be contiguous to each other; so reading the data requires that the Store perform substantial processing. Internally, the streaming file is organized into clusters similar to an NTFS on-disk structure. This structure is more suited to the fast streaming of information than if you had to retrieve data from multiple points within a file, which is the case with the EDB. Originally, Microsoft referred to the STM as an SLV database, because it is designed to hold "super-long-value" content, which gives you an insight into the intention behind its introduction.

Table 7.5 shows the split in responsibilities between the streaming file and the EDB databases. The streaming file holds native content generated by Internet clients such as Outlook Express or Web browsers, while MAPI clients such as Outlook ignore the streaming file and continue to use mailbox or Public Stores as before. The Store handles all the necessary processing to hide the interaction between the two databases when MAPI clients need to retrieve content stored in the streaming file by Internet clients. The streaming file only stores content to enable fast access to data that is not

Table 7.5 *Differences between the EDB and Streaming File*

EDB Database	Streaming File
Holds content (HTML or RTF) generated by MAPI clients	Holds content generated by Internet clients and manages data created for the ExIFS
Holds indexed message properties (author, date sent, etc.) generated by all clients. The Store promotes properties automatically for items held in the streaming file into the EDB database as they are accessed.	Does not hold any message properties
Holds attachments generated by MAPI clients (native format)	Holds attachments generated by Internet clients (MIME format)
Access organized in 4-KB pages	Access via data streaming in 4-KB pages

suitable for storage in a Mailbox or Public Store. In terms of processing, it is costly to retrieve attachments such as the 25-MB *Star Wars* trailer when the Store has to fetch data from multiple individual pages that are unlikely to be stored contiguously. Of course, you can stop users from sending such large attachments by setting message limits on connectors, as we will see in Chapter 8.

The streamed database solves this issue by allowing clients to access data in a continuous stream. The properties of all messages, such as the subject, author, and recipients are stored in a Mailbox or Public Store, where ESE indexes item properties automatically to make them available for searching. The indexing referred to here is different from full-text indexing, which is an optional feature and is controlled by a property set on each database.

7.5 Transaction logs

Transaction logs are very important and are fundamental to the proper operation of an Exchange server. The way Exchange commits transactions to the database on an asynchronous basis means that it is entirely possible for users to read and write messages entirely in memory. You can receive and read a message without ever going near the database. This is the major implication of the write-ahead logging model used by Exchange, and it is something that every administrator needs to understand.

Messages do not appear in the databases until they have been committed, so until commitment the only place the data exists is in memory and the transaction logs. A system failure renders the memory cache and version useless, and the transaction logs then form the only repository that ESE can use to recover data. It is important to underline and understand this situation. Too many Exchange servers have experienced disk failures in the past, only for the system administrator to find out that the data had been lost because it was not adequately protected in the transaction logs.

Every time the Store service starts up, ESE automatically checks the databases to see whether they are consistent. A flag in the database header is set to "consistent" or "inconsistent," depending on whether the database was shut down cleanly and ESE managed to flush all the data in the cache to disk. The flag is always set to "inconsistent" when a database is active, implying that data exists in the transaction logs that has not yet been committed into the database. If you are unsure whether a database is consistent, you can run the ESEUTIL utility with the /MH flag to check the database header.

Any trace of inconsistency prompts ESE to refer to the transaction logs to identify any outstanding transactions that need to be committed to the database. This operation is referred to as a "soft recovery," or the need to locate and play back missing transactions from the logs. ESE interleaves transactions from all of the databases in a storage group within a transaction log set, so it needs to accomplish some sophisticated and complex processing to locate and then recover transactions. However, ESE masks the complexity from the administrator. You will not, for instance, find any event log messages to tell you that ESE recovered 15 messages from a log for one database and 17 for another.

The only way you can be sure that the Store is fully consistent is to perform a controlled shutdown of the Information Store service. When a shutdown occurs, the Store ensures that there are no transactions still outstanding and commits all the pages in the cache to disk. Taking a full online backup creates a similar effect insofar as the backup represents the database at a particular point in time (when the backup finished). However, it is important to note that you need the combination of transaction logs and database files from the backup tape in order to be able to restart the database and be sure that no data is lost.

7.5.1 Managing transaction logs

Exchange deals with the set of transaction logs as if they formed one large logical log, divided into a set of generations for convenience. To make the transactions easier to manage, ESE divides the logical log into a set of 5-MB log files, referring to each as a "generation." A single large message with one or multiple attachments can span several log files. For example, a message with a 6-MB PowerPoint attachment might force ESE to write the message content and the first 2 MB of the attachment into the current transaction log, and then switch to a new log to write the last 4 MB of the attachment. Each log file has an internal generation number to allow ESE to know the order to access the logs in the event that it needs to replay transactions. The current transaction log is always the highest generation. These generation numbers allow ESE to begin replaying a transaction that starts in one log file and continue through as many logs as necessary until it reaches the end of the transaction.

On a very busy server, millions of transactions might flow through the log files daily, and it is common to see hundreds of log files created during the working day. Apart from normal messaging activity, log file creation also comes about when you import large amounts of data into the Store, perhaps by using the ExMerge tool to move mailboxes from another server, or when you run the Migration wizard to import mailbox data from another email system.

Transaction logs are "tied" to their storage group in two ways. First, ESE writes a unique identifier (the "signature") into each log file as it creates the log. The log identifier must match the signature of the storage group before ESE can use the log contents to recover transactions. Second, ESE records the database directory path in the logs, so ESE knows where it should find the logs when the time comes for recovery. Identifiers and other interesting information can be found by running the database maintenance utility with the /ML switch to dump the header information from a transaction log.

Earlier versions of Exchange number log files sequentially using a file-naming scheme of EDBxxxxx.LOG, where xxxxx is a hexadecimal number from 0 to f. The hex naming scheme allows for over 1 million logs in a series (0xFFFFF = 1,048,575) before logs begin to reuse numbers. Since the Store architecture in Exchange 2000 onward supports multiple storage groups, ESE now uses a naming convention of the storage group prefix followed by the hex number. When it creates a new storage group, ESE allocates the separate prefix, and you can view the log prefix through the storage group properties (Figure 7.7). You cannot allocate your own prefix to a storage group. The default (first) storage group uses "E00," the second "E01," the third "E02," and so on. The current transaction log for the first storage group is always E00.LOG, and the current transaction log for the second storage group is E01.LOG. The recovery storage group introduced in Exchange 2003 uses a special "R" prefix for its logs. Figure 7.8 illustrates a typical set of transaction logs.

7.5 Transaction logs

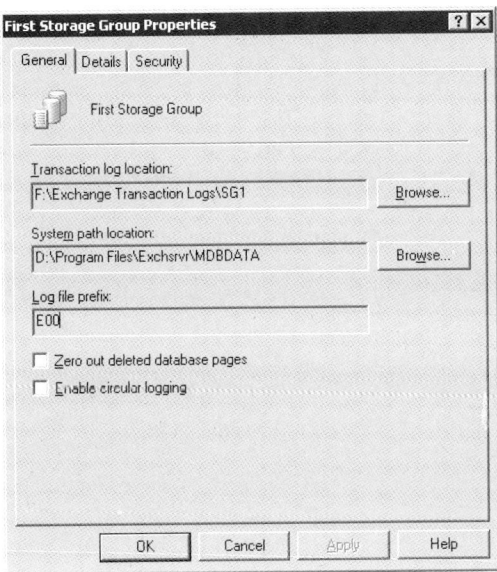

Figure 7.7
Viewing the storage group prefix.

Giving each storage group a separate prefix allows you to keep log files from multiple storage groups in a single directory without running the risk that ESE might overwrite a log from one storage group with transactions from another. However, it is best practice to isolate transaction log sets away from each other by placing each set in a separate directory. Large servers that host many thousands of mailboxes split across three or more storage groups should allocate separate drives to each transaction log set to avoid creating an I/O bottleneck.

7.5.2 Creating new generations of transaction logs

If circular logging is enabled (not recommended for production servers), it means that ESE uses a set of four or five log files to hold transactions (more will be created if required by server load), so the Store switches in old logs to become the current log as transactions are committed to the Store. Otherwise, with circular logging disabled, when ESE fills the current transaction log, it must create a new log. ESE performs the following steps to create a new log file and switch out the existing log file.

First, ESE advances the checkpoint in the checkpoint file to indicate that the transactions in the oldest log have been committed into the database. If they have not, ESE cannot overwrite the oldest log and must therefore proceed to create a new log and continue to write transactions to that

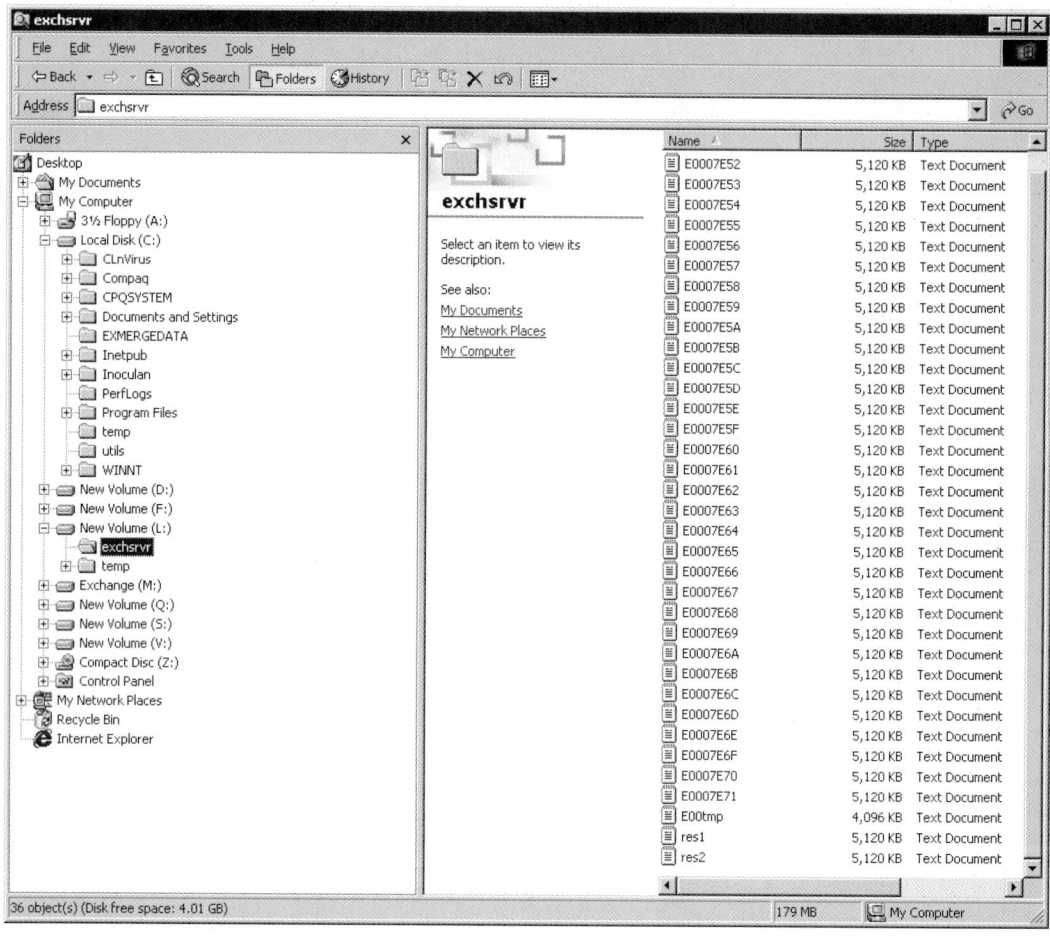

Figure 7.8 *A set of transaction logs.*

file. At this point, you can delete all of the log files that contain transactions older than the checkpoint to return space to the file system.

Up to Exchange 2000 SP2, the potential for a slight delay in processing existed before the new transaction log became available. Microsoft addressed this issue through asynchronous log creation, which means that ESE creates a temporary log file and keeps it available to swap in to become the current transaction log immediately after it fills the current transaction log. The change makes little difference on the majority of systems, but it does speed up log processing on heavily loaded servers. The name of the temporary log file is <storage group prefix>tmp.log—for example, E00tmp.log.

It is best practice never to use circular logging on production mailbox servers, so ESE maintains a complete set of log files between full backups. This scheme requires more disk space, but it is infinitely more secure in terms of data retention. When circular logging is disabled, ESE attempts to create E00TMP.LOG immediately. If the file creation fails, it means that space is not available on the disk where the transaction logs are located.

At this point, E00TMP.LOG should be available. ESE then initializes the log header with the generation number, database signature, and timestamp information before proceeding to rename the current transaction log from Eprefix.LOG (e.g., E00.LOG) to Eprefixgeneration.LOG (e.g., E0007E71.LOG). ESE then renames E00TMP to Eprefix.LOG so that it becomes the current transaction log. ESE does not attempt to write data to the transaction log while these operations are proceeding, so once the new transaction log is available, it proceeds to flush waiting transactions to disk. Switching E00TMP.LOG to become the current transaction log happens very quickly.

Apart from the temporary file, which begins at zero bytes and gradually grows, every transaction log is 5 MB.[2] If you see that a log is anything other than 5 MB (5,242,880 bytes), it is a good indication that the log is corrupt. In this case, you should check the event log for errors, take an offline backup, and then stop and restart the Information Store service. These actions should erase all the log files that contain fully committed transactions and bring the database into a consistent state. In addition, check whether the event log contains any indications that the disk holding the log files is experiencing hardware problems.

Transaction log turnover on mailbox servers varies with user activity, but it is a good rule of thumb to expect servers under heavy workload (i.e., users who are very active) to create one transaction log per user daily. User behavior also influences transaction log turnover. Clearly, if people use email to circulate messages with large attachments instead of using file shares, the number of transaction logs increases to hold the attachments. Thus, a mailbox server supporting 2,000 users who create and send 50 messages a day, 50 percent of which contain attachments, might generate 2,000 transaction logs, or approximately 10 GB of data, amounting to new messages, calendar appointments, moving messages from the Inbox to other folders, system

---

2. The 5-MB size is used in all versions since Exchange V4.0. The ever-increasing size of messages once prompted me to ask some Exchange engineers why the log file size had not increased further, so that more messages could be stored in each log. The answer was that the overhead incurred to create a new log file was so small that it wasn't worthwhile changing the size now. The Active Directory uses 10-MB log files.

messages, and deletes. This does not mean that the Store databases will grow by this amount, because the single-instance storage model is a very efficient way to capture and store data; ESE will reuse deleted pages in the database to store new messages.

Other servers (such as those hosting a lot of public folders) that engage in heavy replication activity turn over transaction log files quickly, as can those that handle large incoming NNTP news feeds. Bridgehead servers and NNTP servers are both candidates to use circular logging if they do not host mailboxes.

Replication is the process by which servers update each other about the contents of public folders. Servers can be very "chatty" if allowed to be so. For example, servers will send each other frequent details of the public folder hierarchy, just to make sure that everyone knows where all the different public folders are located. Servers circulate snapshot information in special messages, in exactly the same manner as interpersonnel mail. You can cut down on the number of messages generated by replication by limiting replication to occur at particular times of the day rather than whenever Exchange feels the need. Scheduling in this manner also reduces traffic through whatever connectors you use to link servers together, thus preventing any potential delays for interpersonnel mail that might otherwise creep in.

7.5.3 Reserved logs

Each storage group uses two special log files (RES1.LOG and RES2.LOG) to reserve 10 MB of space in case no free space is available on the disk where the transaction logs are located. In this situation, ESE suspends normal processing and uses the space occupied by the special logs to capture details of current transactions into the reserve logs, which become the current transaction logs. The Store then proceeds into an orderly shutdown, and you will have to free space on the transaction log disk before you can start the Store again.

No facility exists to write more than 10 MB of data. On large or heavily trafficked servers, such as those that host thousands of users or act as central switches for distributed organizations, it is quite common to see hundreds of log files created daily. This means that administrators must take care in selecting a location for the log files. This is a very good reason why you should monitor free space on all disks that hold transaction logs. Best practice allocates a separate disk for transaction logs to avoid this problem. Another rule of thumb is to allocate ten times the amount of space usually generated by transaction logs daily on the basis that this provides sufficient buffer space if anything goes wrong with backups to stop the backup operations from removing obsolete logs. The extra space also deals with situations when unexpected traffic generates additional logs, such as when you need to move mailboxes between servers.

7.5.4 Locating transaction logs

The \MDBDATA directory under the Exchange root is the default location for both the transaction logs and the databases in the default storage group. You can choose to place either the transaction logs or individual databases to other locations when a new storage group or database is created, or this can be done afterward. Changing the location of the transaction logs will force Exchange to dismount and remount all of the databases in the storage group (and update the configuration data in the AD), and you should take a backup immediately after you move databases, since the move nullifies any previous transaction logs because the location information in the log headers is now invalid. Changing the location of a database will only stop operations to that database, but, once again, you should take a backup, since all of the databases in a storage group share the transaction logs, so you want to put everything into a consistent state. Naturally, you should only attempt to move databases or transaction logs when the system is at its quietest so as not to impact users and your uptime statistics.

ESE automatically purges transaction log files whenever you take full or incremental online backups. Cleaning up log files in this manner is logical. After a successful backup, you have a consistent version of the databases on the backup medium, and the database on disk contains all the transactions to the point that the backup started. The backup also contains the log files that exist at the start of the backup, so there is no longer any need to retain these log files. Since log files can take up quite a bit of disk space, the automatic deletion is welcome, but if you want to be cautious, you can always take a separate backup of the log files before you commence the database backup.

On an Exchange server that is also a DC or GC, you have at least two sets of transaction logs: one for each storage group and one for the AD. This is similar to the situation that exists in Exchange 5.5, which maintains separate sets of transaction logs for the Store and DS. Obviously, because Exchange 5.5 and Exchange 2000/2003 use different versions of ESE, you cannot apply Exchange 5.5 transaction logs to an Exchange 2000/2003 database, or vice versa. It is normal to expect that Microsoft will upgrade the database engine through versions and even perhaps in service packs, so you should expect that there is no way to roll back transactions after you

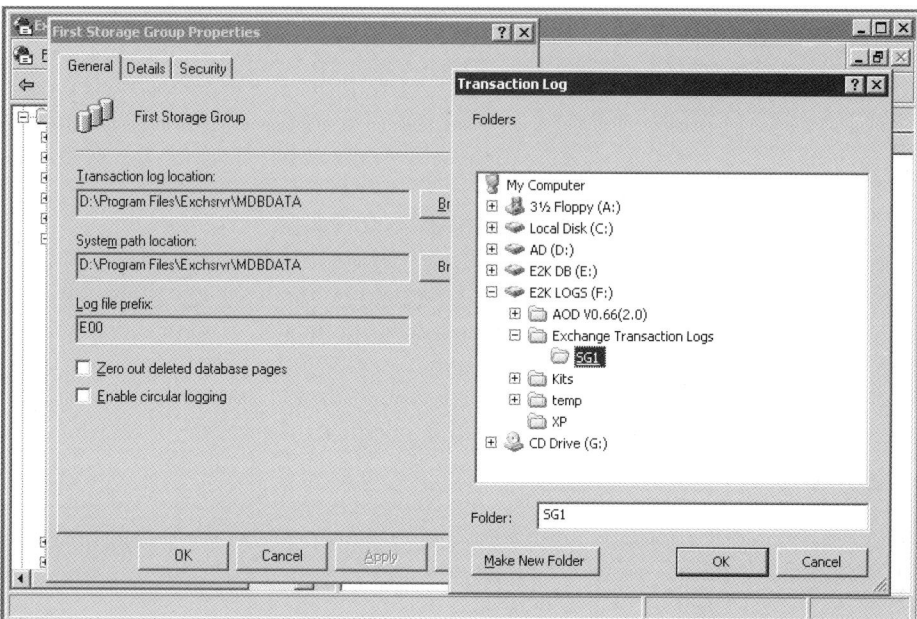

Figure 7.9 *Select new location for transaction logs.*

upgrade a server. For this reason, always take full backups before you begin to upgrade a server, and because paranoid behavior is often good around databases, you should take a full backup immediately after the upgrade is completed.

To relocate the transaction logs to a suitable volume, first create the target directory and then use ESM to select the storage group that they belong to and view its properties. Click on the "browse" button opposite the current log location and navigate to the new location, as shown in Figure 7.9. Press OK to proceed. ESM now asks you to confirm that it should make the change and warns that it must dismount all the databases in the storage group before it can move the logs. Click on the Yes button to confirm the move. ESM then dismounts the Stores, moves the logs to the new location, and then remounts the Stores. You should take a full online backup at this point to ensure that you can recover, should a future problem occur.

7.5.5 Transactions, buffers, and commitment

After a client submits a message, an ESE session that is responsible for the transaction follows a well-defined order to apply the transaction to the Store. First, ESE obtains a timestamp using the internal time (called a "db-time"—

7.5 Transaction logs

an 8-byte value) maintained by the database in its header. In order to modify a page, ESE must calculate a new db-time based on the current value. Equipped with the timestamp, ESE writes the record into the current transaction log (e.g., the default storage group uses E00.LOG). The first write is into an internal log buffer in memory, and after this operation completes, the session can go ahead and modify the page. Page modifications occur in an in-memory cache of "dirty pages," so ESE may first need to fetch the physical page from the database and page it into memory.

Eventually, ESE flushes the modified pages out of memory and writes them into the database. Note that ESE always writes transactions into the current log file first and has an internal mechanism to ensure that it processes log buffers before their corresponding pages. This implements the write-ahead logging mechanism and ensures data protection. The final entry in the log file extract, shown in Figure 7.10, commits a transaction from session 8. The commit forces ESE to flush the entire set of log records up to and including the commit record for session 8 to disk. ESE performs this process synchronously, so no other operation can proceed for the session until the write to disk is complete. Enabling write-back caching on the disk that holds the transaction logs improves performance by allowing the write to complete in the controller's memory and releasing the synchronous wait. The controller is then responsible to ensure that it actually writes the data to disk.

The arrival of a single mail message usually causes ESE to modify many pages, since all of the tables involved (Inbox, message folder table, and so on) are updated. ESE must also update the index for each table, and if the message contains a large attachment, its content will be broken up into several long value chunks, all of which generate log records. The net effect is

Figure 7.10
Data in a transaction log.

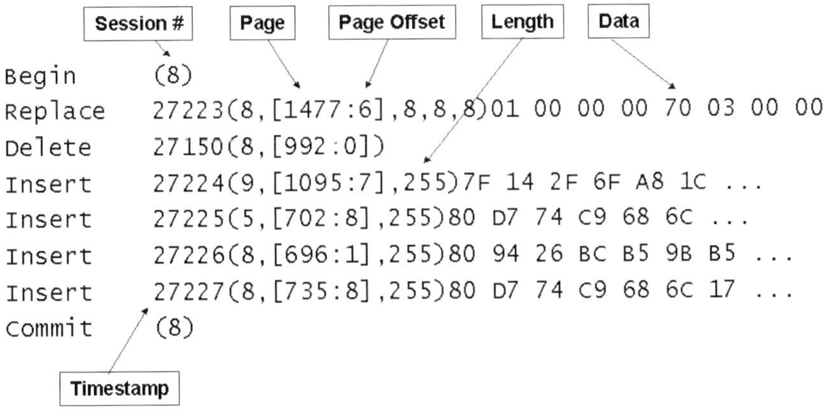

```
                Session #    Page      Page Offset   Length    Data
Begin     (8)
Replace   27223(8,[1477:6],8,8,8)01 00 00 00 70 03 00 00
Delete    27150(8,[992:0])
Insert    27224(9,[1095:7],255)7F 14 2F 6F A8 1C ...
Insert    27225(5,[702:8],255)80 D7 74 C9 68 6C ...
Insert    27226(8,[696:1],255)80 94 26 BC B5 9B B5 ...
Insert    27227(8,[735:8],255)80 D7 74 C9 68 6C 17 ...
Commit    (8)
          Timestamp
```

that delivering a single message results in dozens of log records. Remember that the log records detailing the message delivery are interspersed among the records generated by other sessions. Replaying a transaction is not simply a case of reading and replaying a contiguous chunk of transactions. There is no way to look at the contents of a log file and determine what transactions belong to a single occurrence. Transactions occur at a much lower level than the high-level view contained in the statement that a "new message has arrived." It is, therefore, impossible (in a practical sense) to recover a single transaction from a log file. All you can do is allow Exchange to replay and execute the transactions in exactly the same way as they originally occurred, and that is exactly what happens when the Store executes a "soft" recovery.

7.5.6 Examining a transaction log

You can use any Windows editor to open a transaction log, but it is unlikely that you will be able to interpret much of the contents. Figure 7.11 shows Notepad editing a transaction log. Some of the text in a message header is visible, so you can make sense of the contents, but most of the information is binary and represented by nonprinting characters.

The internal contents of a transaction log can be broken down into the header section and data associated with transactions. The header information contains a hard-coded path to the database it is associated with, a timestamp showing the creation time of the log, a unique "signature" from the

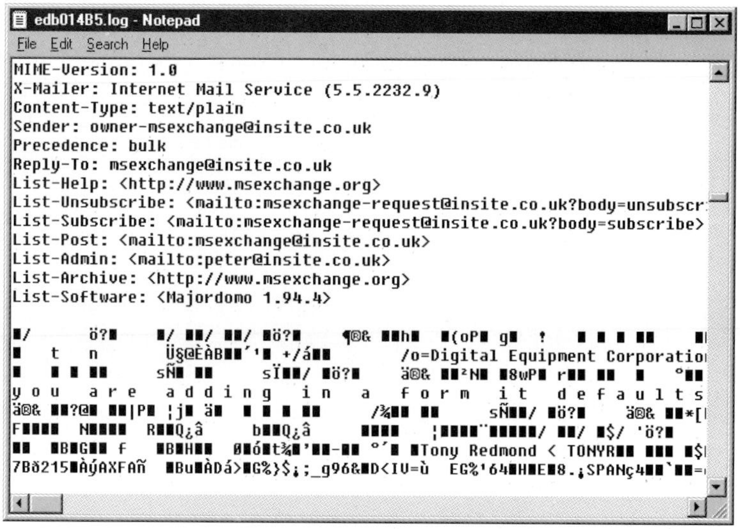

Figure 7.11
Editing a transaction log with Notepad.

database, and data relating to the generation the log belongs to. Signature information is important, because it prevents any attempt to replay transactions to the wrong database. Applying transactions from the wrong log file will have disastrous implications for a database! The signature information for a database changes if you need to rebuild or repair the database with the ESE database maintenance utility (ESEUTIL), rendering all the transaction logs invalid. This is the reason why you must take a backup immediately after you rebuild or repair a database.

7.5.7 Dumping a transaction log

You can dump the header of a log file to view this information with the ESEUTIL utility, as follows:

```
ESEUTIL /ML E0101969.LOG
```

When we look at the dump of the log, the checkpoint, log generation, timestamp, and signature are reasonably obvious. Other important data includes the name of the database the log belongs to as well as the disk location for the database. In the example shown in Figure 7.12, the log comes from the Store. Exchange maintains a single set of transaction logs for every storage group. The names of all the databases in the group are included in the log. The other information is reasonably esoteric, but the important point is that Exchange understands it and can use the data to replay transactions from the log when required. To explain further, we can examine the contents of the transaction log header shown in Figure 7.12.

The most important fields in the transaction log header are:

- lGeneration: The generation number (can be equated back to the name of the log file). The example log is generation 32,213, so 32,212 previous log files exist. Exchange uses a hexadecimal naming scheme to create file names for the logs, and 7dd5 (hex value for 32,213) is used to create a transaction log name of E0007dd5.LOG. The Store allocates a transaction log prefix to each storage group. The default (first) storage group is always allocated prefix "E0," meaning that all transaction logs for this storage group have file names beginning with the prefix. Thus, we know that this transaction log belongs to the default storage group.

- Checkpoint: The position of the checkpoint when the transaction log was created. In this case it is "NOT AVAILABLE"; this does not imply a problem, since ESE can retrieve the checkpoint information by examining other logs.

Figure 7.12
Dumping the header of a transaction log.

```
Microsoft(R) Exchange Server(TM) Database Utilities Version
6.0|Copyright (C) Microsoft Corporation 1991-2000.  All Rights
Reserved.

Initiating FILE DUMP mode...

      Base name: e00
      Log file: e0007dd5.log
      lGeneration: 32213 (0x7DD5)
      Checkpoint: NOT AVAILABLE
      creation time: 04/10/2002 12:12:04
      prev gen time: 04/10/2002 11:28:55
      Format LGVersion: (7.3704.5)
      Engine LGVersion: (7.3704.5)
      Signature: Create time:07/18/2000 11:36:36 Rand:2804053
Computer:
      Env SystemPath: F:\EXCHSRVR\mdbdata\
      Env LogFilePath: L:\exchsrvr\
      Env Log Sec size: 512
      Env
(CircLog,Session,Opentbl,VerPage,Cursors,LogBufs,LogFile,Buffers)
(    off,    252,  37800,   1740,  12600,    128,  10240,  98184)
      Using Reserved Log File: false
      Circular Logging Flag (current file): off
      Circular Logging Flag (past files): off
    1 F:\EXCHSRVR\mdbdata\priv1.edb
      dbtime: 336642779 (0-336642779)
      objidLast: 164351
      Signature: Create time:07/18/2000 11:36:52 Rand:2829026
Computer:
      MaxDbSize: 0 pages
      Last Attach: (0x7CB7,1563,1FF)
      Last Consistent: (0x7CB7,1554,15)
    2 S:\MDBDATA\Mailbox Store 2 (DBOEXCVS1).edb
      dbtime: 100102776 (0-100102776)
      objidLast: 68693
      Signature: Create time:04/17/2001 16:29:15 Rand:1031433187
Computer:
      MaxDbSize: 0 pages
      Last Attach: (0x7CB7,1564,CD)
      Last Consistent: (0x7CB7,155B,C3)
    3 S:\MDBDATA\pub1.edb
      dbtime: 255603408 (0-255603408)
      objidLast: 137393
      Signature: Create time:07/18/2000 11:36:51 Rand:2806806
Computer:
      MaxDbSize: 0 pages
      Last Attach: (0x7CB7,1625,110)
      Last Consistent: (0x7CB7,1562,16A)

      Last Lgpos: (0x7dd5,27FF,0)

Operation completed successfully in 1.31 seconds.
```

7.5 Transaction logs

- Creation time and prev gen time: The date and time when the transaction log was created and the date and time when the previous generation was created. Times that are close together indicate that the Store is under load, since it is creating 5-MB transaction logs at a rapid pace. In this case, almost 44 minutes separates the two logs, so the server is not heavily loaded.

- Env SystemPath: The location of the checkpoint and TEMP.EDB file for the storage group that owns this transaction log.

- Env LogFilePath: The location of the transaction logs. You should check that the log files are not in the same location as the databases (there are three databases in the storage group detailed at the bottom of the listing), since this would mean that best practice of separation of logs and databases is not being applied. Always separate transaction logs from their databases.

- Signature: This data comes from the signature of the databases this transaction log is associated with. All of the databases in a storage group have a signature, and the storage group itself has another signature, which ESE uses to ensure that it only applies valid transactions to a database.

- Circular logging: Circular logging is disabled for this storage group, so ESE will continue to create transaction logs as it needs and will not reuse logs that contain committed transactions.

- Database Information: Transaction logs belong to a storage group, not an individual database. The dump lists details of all of the databases in the storage group. In this case, we can see that three databases, two Mailbox Stores, and a Public Store are associated with this transaction log. Therefore, we can expect to see transactions from those databases interleaved in the log.

7.5.8 Data records

The data section of a transaction log contains records of the low-level physical modifications to the databases. Each log contains a sequential list of operations performed on pages in memory. ESE captures details of when a transaction begins, when it is committed, and if it is rolled back for some reason. Each record in the log is of a certain type. Record types include begin (a transaction is starting), replace (some data in a page is being updated), delete (data is removed), insert (data is added), and commit. In addition to interleaved transactions from multiple databases, transactions from multiple sessions are interleaved throughout a transaction log, so the begin record type also identifies the session that performed a transaction. You can think of a session as a thread running within the Store process. The session forms the context within which ESE manages the transaction and all of the associated database modifications. Each session could be tied back to a particular client, but the database has no knowledge of individual clients (MAPI or otherwise), since all it sees are the threads that operate on its contents.

Regretfully, there is no tool provided to interpret a log file. Figure 7.10 illustrates how a set of transactions might appear in a log. In this example, the first transaction in session 8 (or thread 8) is replacing a record in the database. Every physical modification to a database is timestamped. ESE uses timestamps later if it has to replay transactions from a particular point in time. The page number and an offset within the page are also recorded. The length of the data to be replaced is then noted and followed with the actual binary data that is inserted into the page. The next transaction is a record delete. The set of insert transactions demonstrates that transactions from multiple sessions are intermingled within a log. Sessions write data into the log file as they process transactions. Any dump of a log file from even a moderately busy server will record transactions from scores of sessions.

7.5.9 Transaction log I/O

ESE always writes transactions in sequential order and appends the data to the end of the current transaction log. All of the I/O activity is generated by writes, so it is logical to assume that the disk where the logs are located must be capable of supporting a reasonably heavy I/O write load. In comparison, the disks where the Store databases are located experience read and write activity as users access items held in their mailboxes. You should never place transaction logs on a compressed drive, since Exchange will have to decompress them each time it needs to access the content, which only slows down processing.

On large servers, the I/O activity generated by transaction logs is usually managed by placing the logs on a dedicated drive. This solves two problems. First, the size of the disk (today, usually 36 GB or greater) means that free space should always be available. If you have managed to accumulate 36 GB of logs (7,200 individual log files), it means that either your server is under a tremendous load or you haven't taken a full online backup in the recent past. Full online backups remove the transaction logs when they successfully complete. Second, in all but extreme circumstances, a dedicated drive is capable of handling the I/O load generated by transaction logs. I cannot think of a reason why a dedicated drive could become swamped with I/O requests from log activity. In any case, if such a load were ever generated on a server, the I/O activity to the Store is probably going to be of more concern than the log disk.

Of course, having a dedicated drive for log files is a luxury that you might not be able to afford. But the logic applied to justify the drive — reserve enough space for log file growth and keep an eye on I/O activity— should be remembered when you decide where the logs should be stored on your system. For example, it's a bad idea to locate the logs on the same drive as other "hot" files, such as a Windows page file. Also, never place the logs on the same drive as a database. Keeping the logs with their database may seem like a good idea, but it risks everything. If a problem afflicts the disk where the stores are located, the same problem will strike down the transaction logs and you will lose data.

7.5.10 Protecting transaction logs

Apart from the fundamental first step of separating the transaction logs from their databases through placement on different physical volumes, best practice is to deploy the necessary hardware to provide the Store databases with maximum protection against disk failure.

You also need to protect transaction logs, but they certainly do not need RAID 5, since the overhead generated by RAID 5 will slow the write activity to the logs. RAID 0+1 is overkill too. All you need to do is buy two disks for the transaction logs and create a mirror set. You can run the logs on an unprotected drive, but if you do this, you must understand that any problem on that drive may render the logs unreadable. In this situation, if you then have to restore a database for any reason, you will not be able to replay transactions from the logs into the restored database and data will be lost.

As discussed earlier, the default behavior for ESM is to create transaction logs and databases on the same volume. Exchange places the default storage group and its transaction logs on the same volume when you first install a server. You should, therefore, review log placement on a regular basis with an aim of assuring both maximum protection and performance.

I may seem a touch paranoid when I discuss protection for the databases and transaction logs, but I look at it in a different way. Consider how much money it costs to recover data if a drive fails. Now factor in the cost in terms of loss of productivity, the strain on everyone involved, and the sheer lack of professionalism that exists in any situation where you might compromise data integrity. With these points in mind, I think I am right to be paranoid about protecting data!

Chapter 7

7.5.11 Transaction log checksum

Every transaction log contains a checksum, which ESE validates to ensure that the log data is consistent and valid. Microsoft introduced the checksum to prevent logical corruption from occurring, since the Store replays transactions into a database during a recovery process. The checksum also prevents administrators from replaying a selective set of logs back into the Store after a restore, something that used to be possible up to Exchange 5.5. Selective replays are a bad idea, because the Store interleaves transactions from all databases in a storage group into a single set of logs, so it is possible to miss parts of a transaction if the Store does not replay the complete set.

ESE uses a type of "sliding window" algorithm called Log Record Checksum (LRCK) to validate checksums for a selected group of records in a log to ensure log integrity. ESE reads and verifies these checksums during backup and recovery operations to ensure that invalid data is not used. If ESE detects invalid data through a checksum failure, it logs a 463 error in the system event log. If ESE fails to read the header of a transaction log and is unable to validate the checksum, it signals error 412, as shown in Figure 7.13. Transaction log failure inevitably leads to data loss, since the only way to recover from this error is to restore the last good backup. All of the transactions since that backup will be lost.

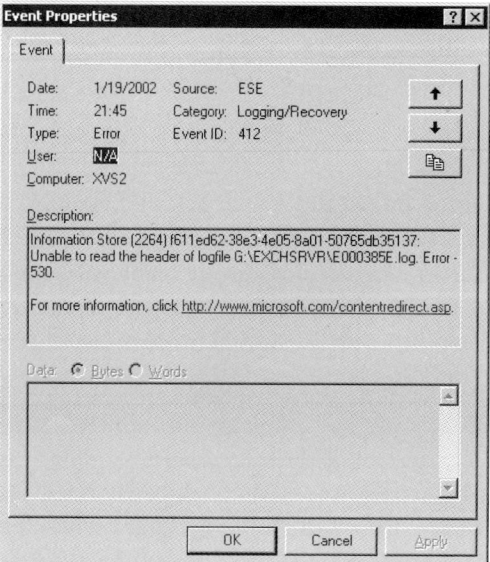

Figure 7.13
Transaction log checksum failure.

7.5.12 Circular logging

Many Exchange servers support relatively small user communities. In the early days of Exchange, when companies migrated from PC LAN email systems such as Microsoft Mail and Lotus cc:Mail, disk resources were scarce, so Microsoft implemented circular logging to prevent the Store from halting because the transaction logs filled all available disk space. Circular logging saves disk space by reusing transaction logs. Instead of gradually accumulating a set of logs that represents the complete set of transactions that have occurred since the last full backup, when you enable circular logging for a storage group, the Store marks a log file for reuse after all of its transactions have been committed to the database. The checkpoint determines when a transaction log is available for reuse. When the Store advances the checkpoint to a point where the transactions in a log have been committed, the log file is no longer required for a recovery operation and can therefore be marked for reuse. You could delete the file, but if the log is left alone, the Store will rename the file and make it the next transaction log when the current log is filled. In normal operation, circular logging uses no more than five or six files, or 25–30 MB.

On first appearance, circular logging sounds like a wonderful idea. The benefits are obvious: a reduced disk space requirement and no need to monitor the disk where the logs are stored to ensure it does not run out of space. The downside is less obvious. Exchange keeps logs to allow you to recover transactions in case you ever have to restore a database from a backup. However, if the Store has reused the logs, it is obvious that it has had to overwrite transaction data in the logs that you can never recover. Thus, if you use circular logging, you should be aware that any time you come to restore an Exchange database, a very large possibility exists that some data will be lost. This is because you can restore the database, but you have lost the ability to roll forward any transactions that have occurred since you took the backup. The transactions in the current set of logs are useless, because a gap exists in the generation of logs created since the last full backup. The Store can only recover transactions if all generations are available during a recovery operation.

You might be able to argue a compelling case to enable circular logging on small systems, such as those that run Exchange with Microsoft Small Business Server. Indeed, the version of Exchange 2003 included in Small Business Server enables circular logging by default (however, the Backup Wizard disables circular logging, presumably using the logic that if you take backups, you do not need to use circular logging). The best rule of thumb is

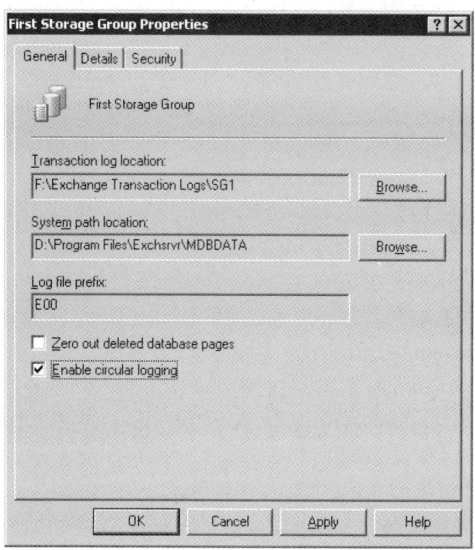

Figure 7.14
Enabling circular logging for a storage group.

that any production server that supports mailboxes and creates more than five log files a day should never enable circular logging.

Circular logging is a property of a storage group and can be enabled or disabled by accessing the properties of the storage group and setting or clearing the checkbox, as shown in Figure 7.14. The Store will implement the new behavior the next time the databases in the storage group are mounted. Note that Exchange disables circular logging by default.

7.5.13 Database zeroing

Figure 7.14 also illustrates the interface used to enable database zeroing, another property of a storage group. Zeroing means that the Store writes zeros to replace the data as it deletes deleted pages to prevent any possibility that someone could look through the database and work out what the pages contain. Zeroing adds a small amount of overhead to Store processing and is not enabled by default. Generally, administrators do not bother with zeroing pages unless they are very concerned that a malicious third party could compromise and reuse the data in deleted pages in some way.

7.6 Store partitioning

Early Exchange servers used systems built around slow processors, limited memory, and slow disks. The system configuration imposed natural limits for mailbox support, and most deployments did not worry about the 16-GB limit that Microsoft then imposed on a Store database. After all, if you only allocated a 10-MB or 20-MB quota per mailbox, you would not hit the 16-GB limit unless the server had to support thousands of mailboxes, and no server was able to handle the load. There were notable exceptions to the rule—especially enterprise customers who scaled using the extra power of the Alpha processor to handle thousands of mailboxes. Enterprise deployments ran into the 16-GB limit and demanded change.

Over time, improvements in hardware and software—faster CPUs, better disk controllers, Windows NT 4.0, and especially the vastly superior multithreaded capability of the Exchange 5.5 Store—meant that the 16-GB limit became a scalability bottleneck faster than Microsoft could imagine. The initial response was to remove the limit and allow databases to grow to a theoretical 16-TB size in the Exchange 5.5 Enterprise Edition. However, no one could even think about approaching the 16-TB limit, because of storage costs and (more importantly) the issue of how to handle backup and restore operations for huge email databases. Everyone's mailbox was held in a single database, so if it failed, the administrator had to work out how to get the database back online as quickly as possible. With backup rates running at up to 40 GB/hour and restore rates half as fast, most administrators drew the line at 50 GB and split mailboxes across multiple servers when storage needs increased past this point. The very bravest administrators explored the outer limits and some databases went past 250 GB—but at this size, any database maintenance operation becomes something that you must carefully plan and schedule and then perform flawlessly.

The result is that the limitations imposed by a single monolithic mailbox database became the single most pressing reason why Microsoft had to update the Store architecture. Their answer is to partition the Store across multiple databases, collecting the databases into "storage groups" as a convenient point for management operations.

7.6.1 The advantages of storage groups

Exchange gains many advantages through Store partitioning. First, you can control the size of databases on a server much more easily. Instead of having to move mailboxes to a new server after the database reaches its desired limit, you simply create a new Mailbox Store and move mailboxes over to the new Store. An added benefit is that smaller databases lead to faster management operations. Second, management operations are accomplished at a database level rather than at the Store level, meaning that you can work with an individual database (e.g., restore it from backup) without affecting the other databases, all of which can stay online and maintain service to users. Because you can back up and restore each database individually with all other databases working online, Exchange is able to deliver a better and more resilient service to users. Note that you can perform multiple backup operations when you deploy multiple storage groups. Inside a storage group, backup operations proceed serially as the backup application processes each database in turn. Third, you can arrange databases and transaction logs across the available disks and controllers in the storage subsystem to manage I/O most effectively and to ensure that you protect data from failure. The last point is very important, because I/O management becomes increasingly important as the number of supported mailboxes scales up on large servers.

Of course, you cannot attain any of these advantages unless you put good system management practices in place and then see that administrators carry them out. You can partition the Store into 20 databases, an action that results in a dramatic increase in complexity for every administrative operation. No improvement in software will ever improve uptime or quality without matching effort from the people who run the computers. Some administrators, who rushed to partition the Store without thinking through the consequences, have discovered this to their detriment.

You can define a storage group as an Exchange management entity within the Store process that controls a number of databases using a common set of transaction logs. By default, when you install Exchange, the Store is composed of a single storage group that contains the pair of Mailbox and Public Stores that you would expect to see on an Exchange 5.5 server, together with newly created streaming files for each Store. In fact, when you think about it, it can be argued that the concept of a storage group already exists in Exchange 5.5, because its Store is a single storage group that controls two databases using a common set of transaction logs. Note that the standard edition of Exchange is still restricted to a single storage group and cannot grow databases past the original 16 GB.

7.6.2 Planning storage groups

Theoretically, the internal architecture of the Store permits up to 15 storage groups to be active on a single server, plus a special 16th storage group used for recovery operations. You can create up to six database sets in each storage group. A database set is either a mailbox or public database together with its associated streaming file. Thus, simple mathematics suggests that

7.6 Store partitioning

you could deploy up to 90 databases on a single server. One of these will be the default Public Store, so, on a purely theoretical basis, you could partition user mailboxes across 89 Mailbox Stores. If you only support MAPI users, you could remove the local Public Store and point users to a Public Store on another server and get 90 Mailbox Stores. All good theory, but Microsoft discovered that it was not possible to implement a server that hosts 15 storage groups.

Architectures usually exhibit some practical limitations when the time comes to deploy on real-life computers, and the Store is no different. In this case, the major limitation comes from the 32-bit nature of Exchange. Virtual memory is used to mount each database, so the more databases that are in use, the more virtual memory is taken up for this purpose. In addition, the system has to perform more context switches within the Information Store process as Exchange brings more storage groups and databases online. Testing performed during the development of Exchange 2000 demonstrated that the practical limitation is around 20 databases spread across four storage groups, which led Microsoft to impose this limit in the software. In other words, each storage group hosts a maximum of five database sets (while the storage group can support six databases, one of these is reserved for recovery and maintenance operations such as restores or using the ESEUTIL utility). Future versions of Windows (with suitably tweaked versions of Exchange) may support higher virtual memory limits and so be able to support higher numbers of databases. Even the 64-bit version of Windows 2003 Enterprise Server is unlikely to solve the problem until Microsoft upgrades Exchange to become a true 64-bit application. Otherwise, we will be in the same situation as when Microsoft compiled the 32-bit Exchange 5.5 code to run on the 64-bit Alpha platform: The code runs, but it cannot take advantage of platform extensions.

While it might be disappointing not to be able to probe the outer limits of the Store architecture, 20 databases are quite enough to deploy and manage to meet 99.9 percent of today's requirements. To put things into perspective, administrators can now deploy 20 times as many mailbox databases on a server as they could in Exchange 5.5, so properly managed systems should be able to support 20 times as much data. Given that the largest Exchange 5.5 systems support over 200 GB in a single mailbox database, it is conceivable that you could expect to support more than 4 TB of mailbox data on a single server. The server configuration would not be simple: To protect this amount of data you would deploy a highly resilient cluster with the best possible storage subsystem you could buy, together with an appropriate backup solution. Relatively few companies will be interested in such a configuration, although it may be an issue for some of the larger ISPs that want to deploy very large servers.

Storage groups require some additional planning on clusters. A cluster is composed of virtual Exchange servers, each of which takes control of different resources that run on the physical servers that compose the cluster. From a planning perspective, you can consider storage groups as a cluster resource and, since they usually support large numbers of mailboxes, the majority of clusters deploy multiple storage groups. To be technically accurate, a cluster supports a Store resource that manages the storage groups. If a virtual server fails, the cluster attempts to transition the resources that were running on the failed virtual server to another node in the cluster. This cannot happen without multiple storage groups, and the basic rule is that each virtual server supports at least one storage group. In a two-node cluster, each virtual server might support up to four storage groups, and in a four-node cluster, each server might support two or three storage groups. Of course, you must factor other considerations into these configurations—for example, the version of Windows you run on the server and the ability of the version of Exchange to support different numbers of active nodes in the cluster.

The per-server limit for storage groups occurs because all of the active storage groups on a node run under the single Store process. Apart from the obvious problem that a transition may overload a virtual server by transferring too much work to a single system, you should also ensure that a transition would not force the cluster to exceed the limits of databases or storage groups. For example, in a four-node cluster, where three nodes are active and one is passive, each virtual server supports two storage groups. If one server fails, the cluster transitions the two storage groups to the passive server. After the transition, the three active nodes still support two storage groups, so the cluster still respects the limitations for Exchange cluster transitions. If a second server fails, the transition moves the two storage groups from that server to the two remaining servers, which end up with three each. In a doomsday situation, a third server failure will force the cluster to attempt to move the three storage groups from the failed server to the remaining server. This would result in six storage groups on that server, but the Store cannot support six storage groups, so the transition will stop after one storage group transitions. Users whose mailboxes are in the two remaining storage groups will lose service. A failure that knocks three nodes out of a four-node cluster is clearly serious and highly unlikely to occur except in unusual circumstances. However, it does underline the need to think through potential cluster failure scenarios. The advent of eight-node cluster support for Exchange 2003 makes the exercise a little trickier.

7.6 Store partitioning

Keep these numbers in mind whenever you plan storage group deployment, so that you do not run the risk of exhausting virtual memory or other restrictions; exceed them and you might. To reinforce the message, Microsoft hard coded the maximum limits into ESM. You can certainly get around the limitation by writing some code to use Exchange Management Objects to create new storage groups, but this will create an unsupported system configuration.

Testing continues as new versions of both Exchange and Windows become available, along with different hardware configurations, and the maximum number of either storage groups or database sets may change over time, so you should check with Microsoft's Web site and hardware vendors before making a definitive judgment on any particular configuration. For example, you can find a good Exchange clustering guide at www.microsoft.com/exchange. Plenty of people have experience with low-end systems, but relatively few know how to combine software and hardware together into high-end systems. You should, therefore, be cautious when building very large systems, and base everything you do on experience.

Exchange treats storage groups as a management entity. In other words, the Store manages all of the databases within the group according to a common set of properties and policies. While it is nice to have multiple storage groups on a server, each requires separate management as well as its own set of transaction logs. Dividing mailboxes within databases in the same storage group is the first and most effective step to Store partitioning. You only need storage groups when you need to apply different settings to the databases. For example, you might want to create a separate storage group to host one or more public stores that accept inbound feeds for newsgroups. Circular logging and database page zeroing are usually not appropriate for databases that contain information that expires on a weekly or monthly basis, so the storage group that hosts these databases operates under a policy different from that pertaining for a group that includes Mailbox Stores.

7.6.3 Does single-instance storage matter anymore?

Single-instance storage (SIS) was a hyped feature of Exchange 4.0 when it shipped in March 1996. SIS is the feature where Exchange keeps a single copy of a message in a database no matter how many users appear to have a copy of the message in their mailboxes. Individual users access the content through a set of pointers and other properties that enable the same content to take on different identities. For example, one user can file a message in his or her Inbox folder, while another user puts the same message in quite a different folder. The Store maintains an access count for each message that is incremented by one for each mailbox that shares the content. The Store then decrements the count as users delete their pointer to the message. Eventually, when the count reaches zero, the Store removes the content from the database.

Exchange is not the first email system to use SIS. ALL-IN-1, a corporate messaging system sold by Digital Equipment Corporation from 1984 onward, used a similar scheme. The major difference between the implementations is that Exchange holds everything—content, pointers, and item properties—within a single database, whereas ALL-IN-1 uses a database for the pointers and properties and individual files for messages and attachments. In both instances, engineers designed SIS into the architecture to reduce the demand for disk space and eliminate redundancy. PC LAN–based systems, such as Microsoft Mail and Lotus cc:Mail, typically deliver separate copies of messages to each mailbox, an approach that is perfectly adequate when a server never has to process more than 50 copies of a message. However, as servers scale up to support hundreds or thousands of mailboxes, creating individual copies imposes a huge drain on system resources and can swamp the ability of the I/O subsystem to handle the workload. Things only get worse as messages and attachments become larger.

There are a number of obvious advantages in a shared message model—for instance:

- Disk I/O activity is reduced, because the system does not have to create, delete, and otherwise manage multiple physical copies of messages. This is especially important when message content is large, and the average size of messages is increasing. Think of the I/O generated to create 100 copies of a 100-KB message. Now, scale up to 2,500 copies of a message (perhaps one circulated to everyone in a company) that has a very large attachment. Without single-instance messaging, a server would quickly find itself on its knees due to the I/O activity from a single message sent to a very large distribution list.
- Disk space required for message data reduces, because the Store creates no redundant copies of messages.

The net effect of these points is that the single-instance storage model is easily the most effective and scalable storage mechanism available to high-end messaging servers.

Apart from making effective use of storage, the single-instance model also effectively increases the maximum size of the Store from the physical

7.6 Store partitioning

limit imposed by available disk space upward toward a higher logical plateau. Charging the size of a message (and its attachments) against the quota of each mailbox creates more apparent logical storage than is physically available. In some respects, this is a smoke and mirror trick, since users believe that their mailboxes occupy more space on a server than is actually used within the database. For example, if you send a 10-KB message to three recipients, then 10 KB is used in the database, but a total of 40 KB of storage is logically occupied (10 KB for each recipient and the sender). In other words, message content is stored once and a series of pointers allows individual mailboxes to share the single copy of the content. Single-instance storage cannot occur if a user makes a change to a message's content, such as altering its properties to allow Outlook or OWA to download embedded graphics. Once this happens, the Store creates a separate copy of the message in that user's mailbox. All other recipients continue to share the original copy of the message.

In the early days of Exchange, anyone who created an Exchange implementation plan worried about SIS. Perhaps this was because analysts considered SIS to be a major bonus of the Exchange architecture, especially as servers took on the load of multiple PC LAN post offices that they replaced. However, I think the real reason was the need to conserve hardware resources. Consider that the systems in use in 1996–1997 were much smaller than today; disk space was more restricted and a lot more expensive, and network bandwidth had to be conserved. Now, the systems are a lot faster and come equipped with more memory, the software makes better use of features such as multiple CPUs, copious disk space is available, and network bandwidth is cheaper. I have not met many administrators or system designers recently who think about SIS when they come to assess system design. The world has changed, and Microsoft considerably undermined the feature when they introduced Store partitioning.

What factors influence the SIS or sharing ratio that you see on a server? Here are a few that come to mind: Messages sent to many users or large distribution lists increase the ratio because more users share a single copy of a message. If you can arrange for users who tend to send messages to each other to share a server, you have a higher sharing ratio. Apart from achieving a higher sharing ratio, keeping messages on a server whenever possible reduces network traffic and speeds message delivery. For much the same reason, the sharing ratio tends to be higher on larger servers than on smaller servers.

Messages sent to external Internet recipients tend to be less shareable than internal messages. This is a generalization, but if you look at the mes-

Chapter 7

sages you send to Internet recipients, you will probably find that the majority go to a single recipient. Incoming Internet messages are usually addressed to a single recipient on the target server, which further reduces the sharing ratio.

Mailboxes transferred between servers using the standard "Move Mailbox" option (both Exchange 5.5 and Exchange 2000/2003) preserve SIS as much as possible. Checks are performed using message properties to see whether a message already exists in the store on a target server, and, if the message exists, the Store creates a new pointer. However, if the message does not exist (because it was never delivered to a mailbox on the target server or all copies have since been deleted), a new copy of the content is created. Mailboxes transferred using the ExMerge utility always create a new copy of message content. ExMerge does not check for existing message content, because it is a simple export-import utility designed to extract or import data from mailboxes.

Exchange servers that run multiple Mailbox Stores have lower sharing ratios than those with a single Mailbox Store. The reason is simple. As soon as you split mailboxes across Stores, you increase the potential that Exchange must deliver any message to multiple databases. The more Stores you have on a server, the lower the overall sharing ratio will be. The implementation of multiple Stores offsets the higher sharing ratio that you tend to see with large servers.

Servers that host connectors tend to have lower sharing ratios than mailbox servers do. Messages passing through connector servers are transient and the servers often do not host many mailboxes, so the sizes of the Mailbox Stores are small and the sharing ratio is low.

It is easy to check what the sharing ratio is on your server. Exchange provides performance counters for the MSExchangeIS Mailbox object to do the job. A separate counter is available for each Mailbox Store, and there is a counter to track the overall sharing ratio as well. The Store calculates the counter by dividing the total number of entries in the message table by the total number of entries in the message folder table. The Store keeps individual messages as rows in the message table. Each message is one row, no matter how many folders the message is in. The Store holds the folder from all mailboxes as rows in the message folder table. Putting this structure together, if Exchange delivers a message to 20 users whose mailboxes are in the same database, the Store only needs to create a single row in the message table for the new message. Rows already exist for the 20 Inboxes in the message folder table, so the Store can update the message folder tables with a

7.6 Store partitioning   445

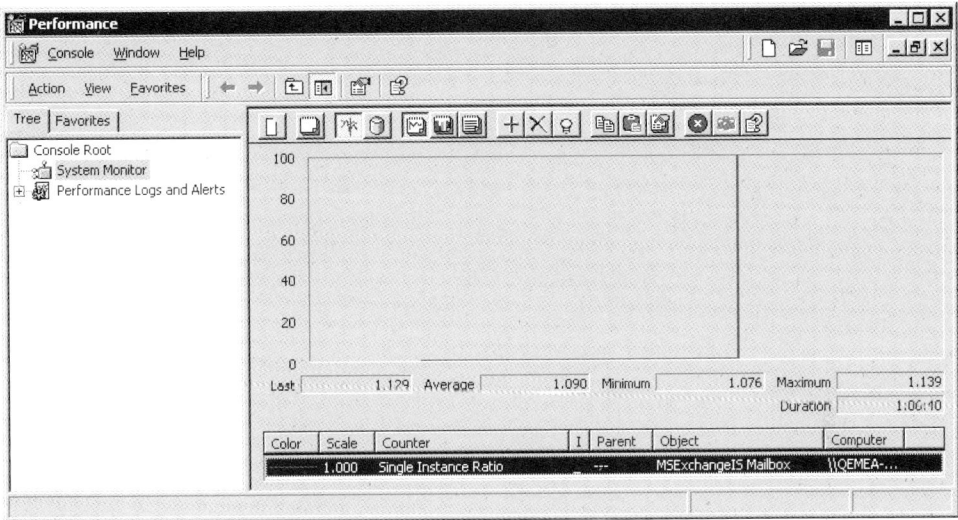

Figure 7.15   *Monitoring SIS on an Exchange 2000 server.*

pointer to the new message. Gradually, as users delete messages, the Store first moves pointers to the Deleted Items folder, and then finally removes the data when users empty the Deleted Items folder. This is a simplified description of what happens, because the Store can "hide" messages and keep them for an additional period if a deleted item retention period is set on the database.

Figure 7.15 shows the SIS performance counter on an Exchange 2000 server with a single Mailbox Store. The highlighted figure indicates a low sharing ratio (1.129), meaning that there are 1.129 references on average to every message in the Store. This ratio is at the low end of the expected scale and is indicative of a server where many users tend to send messages off the server or to users whose mailbox is in another Store. High ratios (such as 4.0 or above) usually indicate that users are human packrats who do not delete messages as often as they should. Sharing ratios seen across hundreds of Exchange servers deployed at HP range from approximately 1.2 to 3.5. Anecdotal evidence gathered at conferences or through discussions in forums such as the msexchange list maintained at www.swynk.com indicates that you can consider a range of 1.5 to 2.5 as normal.

Do not expect real-time updates for these performance counters. It would be unreasonable for Exchange to dedicate valuable resources to have the Store constantly monitor the number of messages and folders in a database. The values are unlikely to vary dramatically, unlike other performance

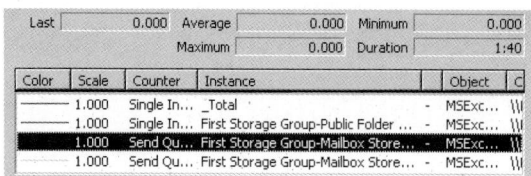

Figure 7.16
No sharing at all!

counters such as CPU use. If you want to keep track of the sharing ratio on a server, record the value at a regular interval (weekly or monthly is enough). Looking at performance monitor reporting the same ratio for hours on end is very boring.

Exchange also provides a sharing instance ratio counter for items in the Public Store. On my Exchange server, the counter reported a figure of 22, implying that each item in a public folder had an average of 22 references. Mailboxes do not exist in a Public Store, so it is hard to imagine how a single item is referenced more than once unless it is stored in multiple public folders. However, attaining an average sharing ratio of 22 means that there is an awful lot of cross-indexing in public folders. Only 123 instances of public folders exist in the Public Store, but I cannot figure out how this result occurred. There are other instances when the counters do not make sense. For example, Figure 7.16 proudly reports that a Mailbox Store has attained an average sharing ratio of 0.000, which is a touch on the low side. This value appeared following a cluster transition, when the Store moved some storage groups between two physical nodes, so I assume it is due to a glitch in the cluster transition code.

7.7 Managing storage groups

The Store process controls all of the storage groups that are active on a server. Exchange 5.5 uses a single client instance to the Store, used by the Store process to access the Private and Public Stores. Exchange 2000/2003 uses the client access mechanism to access the Store and Site Replication Services (SRS). However, these applications run in the context of separate processes, such as SRSMAIN.EXE, so they do not affect the Store. For Exchange, each storage group is a client instance running inside the Store process. As a separate instance, each storage group has its own set of transaction logs and checkpoint files.

The basic architectural concepts set down for the Store, including the atomic transaction model, logging, pointers, and use counts, are still valid

7.7 Managing storage groups

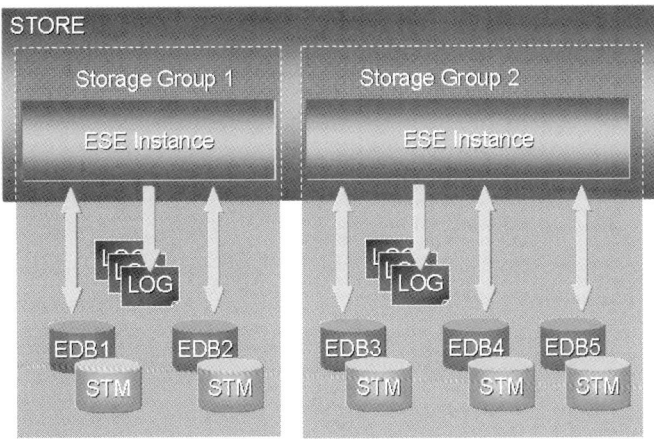

Figure 7.17
Storage groups.

for multiple storage groups. Operating multiple databases brings its own set of challenges, and we have to expand the established concepts to incorporate how storage groups work.

Figure 7.17 illustrates how storage groups help to make the current version of Exchange more resilient than earlier versions. Two storage groups are active on our sample server. If a problem affects the disk holding the EDB4 database, then you must take Storage Group 2 offline to fix the problem. Storage Group 1 remains active, and users whose mailboxes are located in any of the databases in Storage Group 1 will not be aware that a problem has occurred. You must take a complete storage group offline to fix a problem, even if a hardware problem only affects a single database. This is because the Store captures data for all of the transactions for the storage group into a single set of log files.

Splitting the Store into multiple databases makes Exchange more tolerant to database failure at system startup too. The Exchange 5.5 Information Store service will refuse to start if it detects any problem with either the Private or the Public Store. The problem could be minor, and it is frustrating to find that an important service will not start up until everything is perfect. Once Exchange introduced storage groups, additional granularity was required inside the Store. Beginning with Exchange 2000, if Exchange detects a problem with a database, the Store marks the database as "offline" and continues to load the next database. The problem only affects the mailboxes or public folders held in the offline database. When the problem is fixed, you can bring the repaired database back online to restore full service.

7.7.1 Store status

You can put an Exchange database into two different states:

- Mounted: The database is online and available for use. This is the state during normal operation. The Store will not attempt to manage a database unless it is mounted.

- Dismounted: The database is offline and unavailable to clients. This is the state when you need to perform certain maintenance operations, such as a database rebuild or hard recovery, on databases. Exchange is able to start the Information Store service without mounting any databases, which might be the case during a restore operation.

You mount and dismount databases using ESM, as shown in Figure 7.18. You can also use the Computer Management console (Manage Applications and Services) to manage databases, and you can set a property of a database so that Exchange will not attempt to mount it as the Information Store service starts up (Figure 7.19).

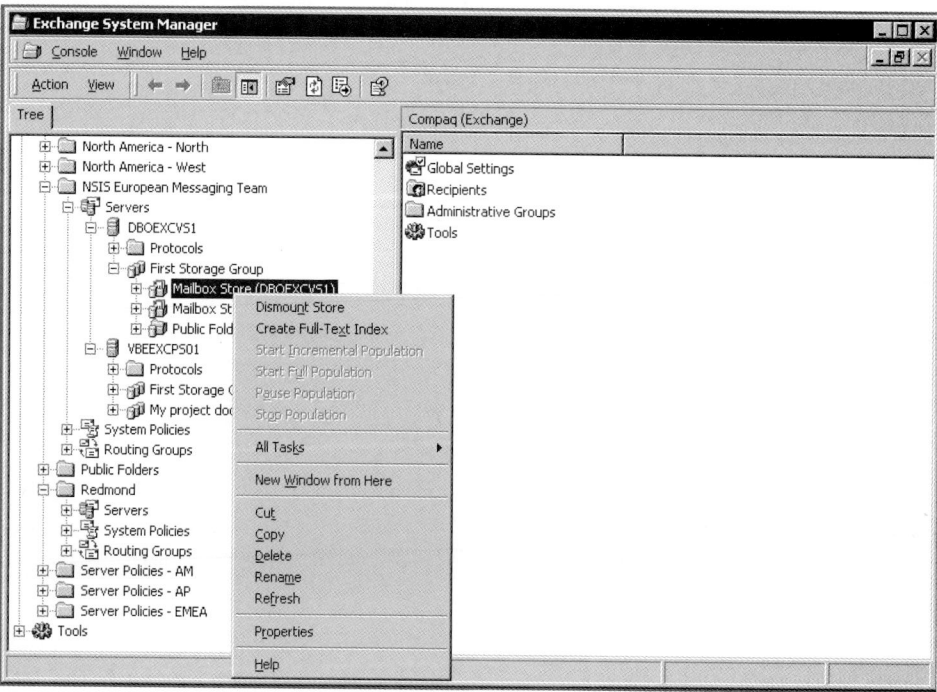

Figure 7.18 *The option to dismount a Store.*

Figure 7.19
Do not mount a Store at startup.

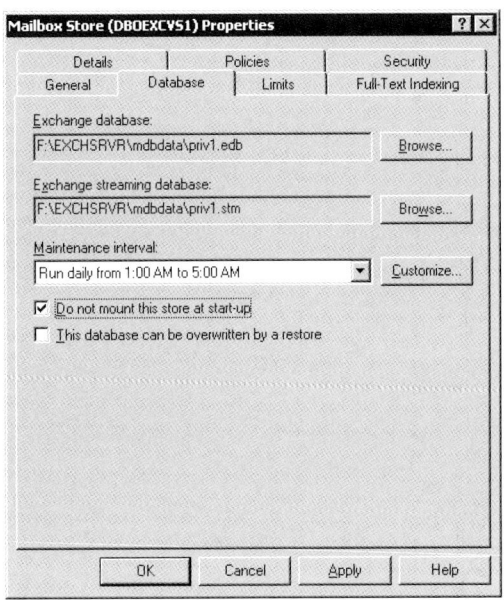

Exchange maintains a set of parameters to control the functioning of the Store. You can find the global parameters in the system registry at HKLM\Software\Microsoft\ESE98\Global\System Parameter Overrides. However, be very careful about making any changes to these parameters unless you are sure of what you are doing. Exchange holds the parameters for a storage group as properties of the storage group. Global parameters, applied to all storage groups, include the size of the cache allocated to the buffer manager and the version Store. Storage group properties include the locations for databases, transaction logs, and temporary databases.

7.7.2 Planning storage groups

It is unwise to rush to create additional storage groups and databases unless you have good reason to extend the Store. For example, you might want to isolate important users into a separate database where they have increased mailbox quotas. Alternatively, you might decide to split a Mailbox Store to reduce backup time after it reaches a specific size, such as 50 MB. Of course, if database size prompts you to create a new Mailbox Store, you need to move some mailboxes to the new Store to prevent the old Store from growing further, and you may want to run the ESEUTIL utility to rebuild the old Store and return space to the file system.

Exchange servers that host multiple companies may find it convenient to create multiple storage groups. With Exchange 5.5, all the companies share a common Information Store, but it is much better to be able to provide each company with its own SG or database, allowing you to create a storage firewall between each company's information.

Even the largest server is unlikely to use more than 20 databases in the near future, so it seems reasonable to come up with some rules of thumb that you can factor into planning exercises for Exchange deployments. For example, it is reasonable to pick a storage limit as the point at which you will consider partitioning the Store. In my experience, the average size of databases in production today on medium to large servers (500 mailboxes and upward) is still under 20 GB, so perhaps it is reasonable to say that 25 GB is a good starting point at which to consider creating a new Mailbox Store. The new Mailbox Store will still be in the default or first storage group. You could then decide that you will create a new storage group when an existing group contains three databases.

Alternatively, if you want to distribute I/O load and create additional resilience from disk failure, you might decide that you will create a new storage group after you have two fully populated 25-GB Mailbox Stores. Each storage group increases the administrative complexity of the system, especially in terms of backup and restore, so only consider moving to multiple storage groups if you have more than 50 GB to manage. As you add storage groups and databases to a server, be sure to use a reasonable naming convention to identify the storage entities and their directories. Figure 7.20 shows the convention used at HP for storage groups and databases. Note

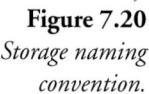

Figure 7.20
Storage naming convention.

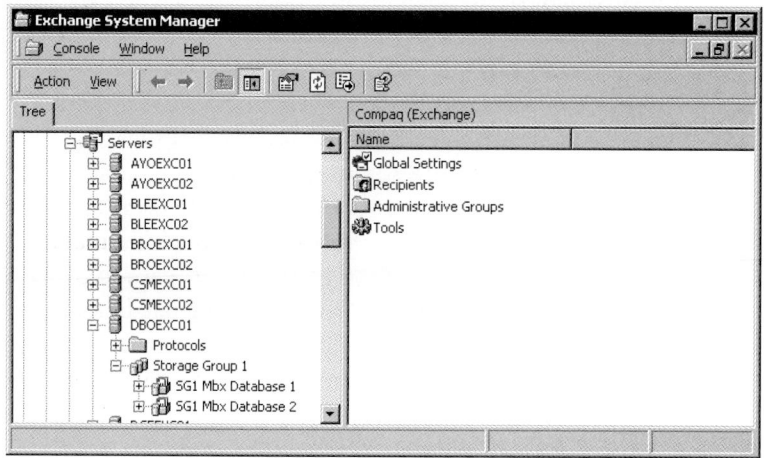

Table 7.6 *Naming Convention for Storage Groups*

Storage Group 1	File and Folder Names
Transaction Logs	L:\Exchsrvr\SG1_TransactionLogs\
Database Folder	S:\Exchsrvr\SG1_Mdbdata\
Mailbox Store 1	S:\Exchsrvr\SG1_Mdbdata\SG1MBX1.EDB
Streaming Store 1	S:\Exchsrvr\SG1_Mdbdata\SG1STM1.STM
Mailbox Store 2	S:\Exchsrvr\SG1_Mdbdata\SG1MBX2.EDB
Streaming Store 2	S:\Exchsrvr\SG1_Mdbdata\SG1STM2.STM

the way that the databases are associated with the storage groups through naming and the way that the database type is indicated in the name ("Mbx" = mailbox). To make it easier to identify important files using Windows Explorer, you can carry this naming convention forward into the physical file and folder names used for storage groups. Table 7.6 outlines a suitable naming convention. We use drive L: for transaction logs and S: for the Store databases to create a logical association between the drives and their purpose. Again, it is best to use the same drive letters for the same files on all servers.

Service-level agreements are another point to consider, since an SLA may call for a recovery time for database outages that can only be satisfied by distributing mailboxes across multiple databases and perhaps multiple storage groups.

Every storage group and database that you add to a server makes demands on system resources. Databases take up disk space, and every storage group maintains its own set of transaction logs. Windows uses approximately 10 MB of physical memory to load the internal structures (tables and indexes) for each database into memory. Apart from the physical memory, Windows needs contiguous chunks of virtual memory to map the Store's internal structures. Large servers are normally equipped with plenty of memory, but it is still important to realize that loading up multiple databases will occupy resources from an unexpected quarter. For example, a server that splits processing across ten databases requires 100 MB of physical RAM just to start up. Windows and the other Exchange components also require memory and might consume 500 MB just to get a server up and running.

For maximum resilience and I/O performance, you should distribute each set of transaction logs to a separate set of disk spindles. As with Exchange 5.5, it is essential to separate the transaction logs from their associated databases to ensure that a hardware failure on a disk will not affect logs and databases at the same time. Protect each of the spindles used for transaction logs with RAID 1. There is no need to use RAID 5 to protect transaction logs, since this will just slow down I/O performance.

You affect Exchange's single-instance storage model when you deploy multiple databases. If you send a message to three recipients, and each of the recipients' mailboxes is located in a different Store, then the Store must create a separate copy of the message for each recipient. Obviously, the potential to create multiple (somewhat redundant) copies of messages is one reason why you want to restrain the urge to create multiple databases unless you have good reason to do so.

Exchange 2000 supports two-node (on Windows 2000 Advanced Server) or four-node active/active clustering (on Windows 2000 Datacenter Server). Exchange 2003 supports up to eight-node clustering. Clusters treat storage groups as resources, so they can move or fail over storage groups from a failed node to run on the remaining active nodes in the cluster. Clusters will run multiple storage groups, but you have to take care to ensure that the individual nodes in the cluster are able to support the load of all the storage groups in the case of failure. For example, in a two-node cluster you should not stress each server past 50 percent of its rated performance, because it will have a double workload if the other server fails. In the same way, use up to 66 percent of the rated performance of a server in a three-node cluster or 75 percent of rated performance in a four-node cluster. The last thing you want is for a server to collapse under the load when everything transitions to it after its cluster partners fail.

7.7.3 Creating new storage groups

Creating a new storage group is very straightforward. Indeed, Microsoft has made the operation so simple that the danger exists that an unwary system administrator will create new storage groups or databases without going through the necessary planning process. You can do all of the work to create a new Store or storage group through ESM, as shown in Figure 7.21.

When you create a new storage group, you provide a name and a location for its transaction logs (Figure 7.22). Place the logs on physical disk volumes separate from their databases. Servers that support several thousand mailboxes are likely to be equipped with multiple controllers and

7.7 Managing storage groups

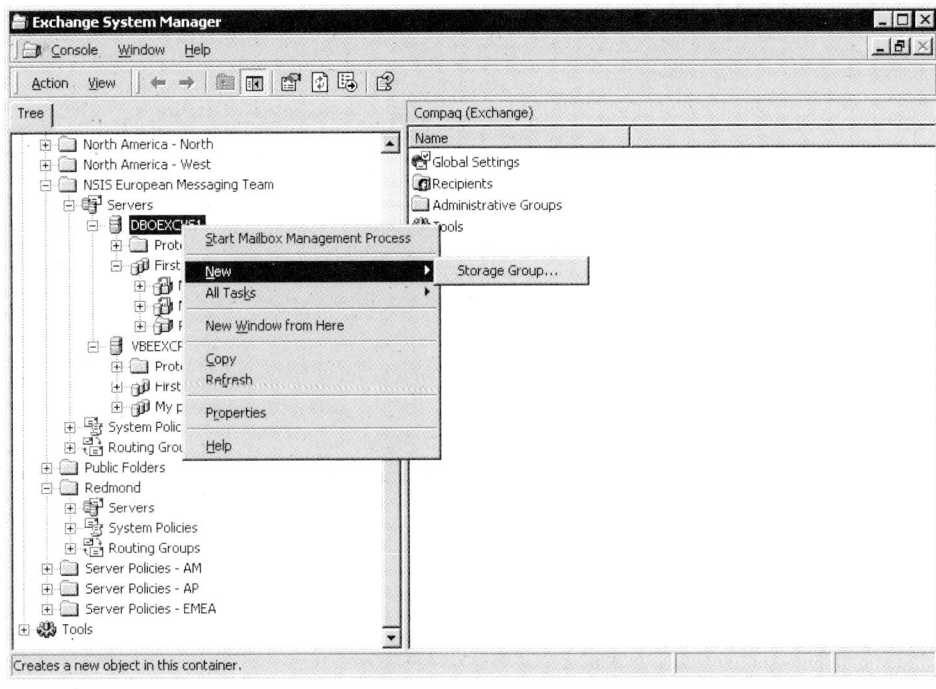

Figure 7.21 *Creating a new storage group from ESM.*

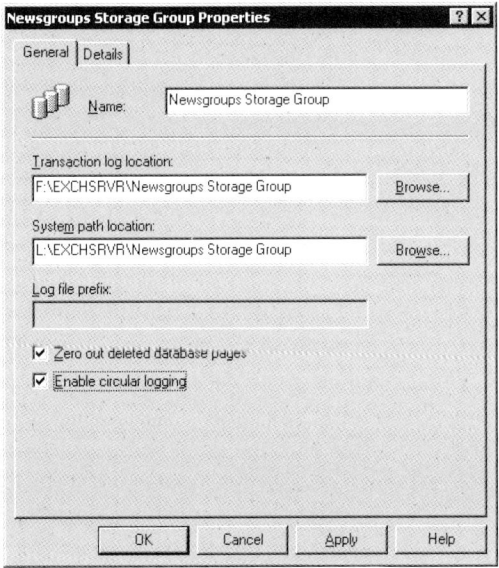

Figure 7.22 *Specifying details of a new storage group.*

Chapter 7

many physical disks, and you should take every step to place files in such a manner that a failure on any individual drive will not affect multiple databases or sets of transaction logs.

Always disable circular logging for storage groups that support mailboxes. However, it is possible to have circumstances where you would want to have circular logging turned on. Let us assume that you have a server that accepts an NNTP newsfeed from many different Internet newsgroups. The traffic to newsgroups can be very heavy, which results in a large and rapid buildup of transaction logs as the Store replicates newsfeed content to public folder replicas on other servers. Newsgroups typically store transient information that is removed after a short interval, typically 7 to 14 days, so the need to recover transactions if a database is restored is clearly not as high as for mailboxes or regular public folders. In this situation, it is quite acceptable to create a new storage group specifically to host newsgroups and enable circular logging.

Note the checkbox to control "zero out deleted database pages" in Figure 7.22. Some companies wish to ensure that there is no possibility to recover message content after users delete items and empty their deleted items folder. If this checkbox is set, Exchange will overwrite the pages that contain deleted messages with a bit pattern that effectively zeros out deleted pages to remove any chance that anyone could ever look at the data again. Zeroing out pages places a little extra overhead on the system, so it is best to leave the checkbox alone unless you really need to use this feature. It is best practice to perform a full backup after enabling this feature, since the biggest impact of page zeroing occurs during backup time when ESE actually writes the pattern to zero database pages.

After the Store creates the new storage group, you can proceed to create the Stores that the storage group will manage. Figure 7.23 shows the properties for a new Mailbox Store before creation. Note that each database has a separate maintenance schedule for activities such as background defragmentation. This is to ensure that background maintenance does not swamp a server by running maintenance tasks for multiple databases concurrently. Background maintenance tasks are less likely to affect multi-CPU servers, but it is still something to keep an eye on. Figure 7.23 clearly shows the locations of the two files that make up the new Mailbox Store. The first is the familiar EDB database that Exchange has used since 4.0. The second is the name and location of the streaming file that holds Internet content. Remember, the Store creates a streaming file for every EDB database.

Often, administrators find that they need to relocate store databases to a new volume. Perhaps you have just commissioned a SAN and want to move

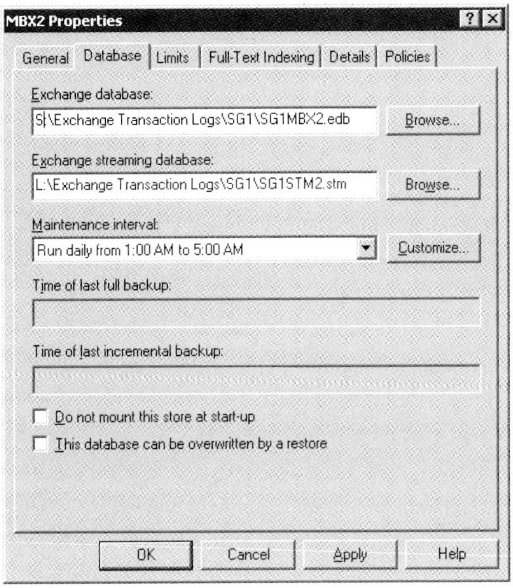

7.7 Managing storage groups

Figure 7.23
Viewing database locations for a new Store.

databases over to use the new storage, or maybe you have just increased capacity on one of the existing volumes. In whatever circumstances, ESM has to dismount Mailbox and Public Stores before it can move them. You can also dismount the stores manually by selecting the Store through ESM and then selecting the "dismount" option, but it is easier to let ESM do all the work.

To move a Store, select it through ESM and access its properties. Go to the database property page and use the browse button to select a new location for the EDB and streaming file files, and then click "OK" or "Apply" to make the move. ESM then warns you that the move affects existing backups, because ESE can no longer apply data in the transaction logs from the backups to the database after the move, if you need to recover transactions after a hard restore (Figure 7.24). For this reason, you should always take a full backup immediately after you move a database.

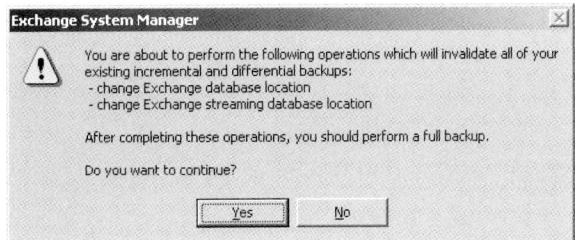

Figure 7.24
Warning before moving a database.

7.8 ESE database errors

Three types of errors can occur in an Exchange database:

- Application (Exchange or ESE) level
- JET (database) level
- Physical or page level

Table 7.7 describes the most common errors. See Microsoft Knowledge Base article 314917 for more information.

A −1018 error occurs when the ESE engine makes a request to Windows to fetch a particular page from the database and ESE then returns unexpected data, normally a different page number or checksum. ESE flags the error to prevent further access to the page and to let administrators know that action is required. Continuing to attempt to access a damaged page (or damaged section of a database) usually results in even more data loss than may occur if you immediately notice a problem and take appropriate action. For example, if you take a backup of a flawed database, you will not be able to restore it.

Many different underlying problems can cause a wrong page to be returned, including a disk or controller error or faulty SCSI cable termination. In the past, Microsoft has also pointed the finger at antivirus software and questioned whether the methods used to access the Store to detect incoming viruses are the root cause of some −1018 errors, especially when vendors use nonapproved APIs for the Store. While no conclusive answer to this question has ever been determined, you can eliminate the antivirus

Table 7.7 *Exchange Database Errors*

Error	Meaning	Indication
−1018 (JET_errReadVerifyFailure)	The checksum read from disk is not the same as the checksum that was originally written, or the page number does not match the page number that is expected.	Page-level corruption may have occurred.
−1019 (JET_errPageNotInitialized)	A page that is expected to be in use is not initialized or empty.	The page may be corrupt.
−1022 (JET_errDiskIO)	A generic error indicating that the requested page cannot be read by ESE.	A physical disk error is probable.

issue, since the major antivirus vendors now support Microsoft's VS (Virus Scanning) API. Thus, if a problem occurs because of an antivirus product, the issue is now likely to be in Microsoft's own code rather than in the add-on product.

Microsoft has worked hard to eliminate false errors that caused much concern in earlier versions and to institute better problem reporting for errors. For example, Figure 7.25 shows how Exchange reports a problem reading a page. In this instance, the Store requested a certain page number and ESE returned a page whose page number was different. While this is not a –1018 error, a condition now exists that will eventually result in a –1018 error if its underlying cause is not some transient hardware condition. In either case, the sheer fact that the Store is having difficulty in reading pages accurately is enough for a system administrator to become concerned.

Another example is the retry logic introduced in Exchange 5.5 SP2 (and used since) in an attempt to solve the problem where a temporary hardware glitch would cause a –1018 error to be reported. Instead of immediately accepting that a problem exists, the Store pauses and then enters a retry pattern, where it attempts to read the failed page up to 16 times before concluding that a problem is real. The Store makes no further attempt to reference the page after the failure occurs, since this might cause further corruption.

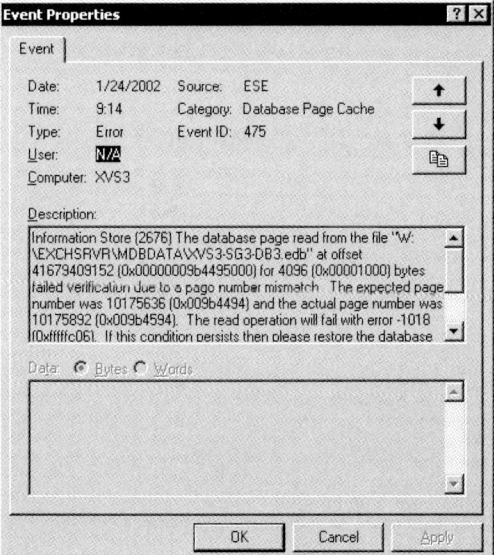

Figure 7.25
Error 475 precedes a potential –1018.

Even if a retried read is successful, the Store still flags a −1018 error to the event log along with details of the failed page and the number of read attempts, because you must investigate even a transient problem to ensure that it is not an indication of a deep-rooted problem that will eventually corrupt a database. You should check for loose SCSI cables, controller boards, and any other connections to ensure that they are not the root cause. Also, make sure that firmware upgrades for disks and controllers are applied so that known bugs are not maintained.

While failing hardware is often the cause of transient errors, sometimes they are associated with times of heavy system load where the software cannot keep up with the demand. However, you will not see this type of problem with current versions of Exchange. Such −1018 errors may also be generated during online backups. The Store verifies checksums as it streams each page out to the backup media and halts the backup if a page fails a checksum test to ensure that the backup does not contain corrupt data.

ESE signals −1019 errors when it attempts to read a page that it expects to contain data only to find that the page is not initialized or it is empty. Pointers within the database may be corrupt, so that a link exists to an incorrect page or a bug has caused bad data to be written. ESE generates a −1022 error when it cannot read a page because of an I/O problem. This is a catchall error, which usually means that the database is damaged for one reason or another and you need to repair it. This is when a solid knowledge of Exchange disaster recovery techniques is invaluable.

7.8.1 Hard and soft recoveries

Recovery is the process that the Store goes through to make a database consistent. Databases become inconsistent when the Store process terminates abruptly without having the chance to commit all outstanding transactions into the database. Replaying transactions after a power outage or similar failure is referred to as a "soft recovery." The database is available and just needs to be updated from the transaction logs. As outlined previously, ESE can determine what transactions are outstanding by reference to the checkpoint file and the transaction logs. A hard recovery means that a hardware failure has meant that you have to recover data from a backup. Exchange performs different processing during hard and soft recoveries.

Soft recovery is an automatic process that requires no human intervention. ESE always checks that its databases are consistent before it commences normal operations. ESE takes the following steps each time a client (such as the Store) starts an ESE instance with the JetInit function:

- ESE locates the current transaction log by reference to the checkpoint file.
- ESE verifies the signature in the transaction log to ensure that it matches the database.
- ESE consults the checkpoint file to detect whether it needs to roll forward any transactions.
- Normal operations begin and client connections are accepted.

The same sequence takes place when a soft recovery occurs. Many system administrators are probably unaware that it has happened, although evidence exists if you care to look for it in the application event log.

Soft recoveries

An inconsistent database must go through a successful soft recovery process before the Store is able to mount it. If the soft recovery does not work, you have to run ESEUTIL to repair the database and then attempt to mount the fixed database. Apart from entries in the application event log, the vast majority of soft recoveries pass without the need for administrator intervention, since the Store checks to see whether it must perform a soft recovery for each database every time the Information Store service restarts.

During a soft recovery, the Store checks the database header to determine the log files that are required to make the database consistent. This information is held in the "Log Required" field, which records the log generations that are needed.[3] The Store then checks the signature in each log to ensure that it belongs to the database and then searches the logs for transactions that have not been committed to the database. ESE reads each page referenced in a transaction and compares its timestamp. If the timestamp on the page is earlier than the timestamp in the log record, ESE replays the operation. If the timestamp is equal or higher, ESE ignores the transaction. While it processes transactions, ESE tracks the transactions that it begins and the ones that it fully commits. At the end of the pass, any uncommitted transactions will have all of their operations rolled back. Adjusting the database in this manner is sometimes referred to as "physical redo, logical undo." ESE must process all transactions before the Store can allow clients to connect.

Note that programs that operate on the database at low level, such as the ESE maintenance utility, also check transaction logs for outstanding trans-

---

3. The database stores log generations in decimal. You have to convert these values to hex to determine the log file names that are needed.

actions before they commence operation. The only exception to this rule is when you run ESEUTIL/P to repair a database. When you repair an inconsistent database, ESE ignores the log files and they cannot be used afterward, since the internal structure of the database is changed as ESEUTIL repairs the database to make it consistent.

As can be seen in Figure 7.12, transaction logs contain hard-coded paths to the database. If you move the database to a new location before a recovery operation begins, ESE ignores the logs when the Information Store service restarts. If you attempt a recovery using logs that do not match the location of the database, ESE flags a –550 error. From a hardware perspective, the time taken to recover a log depends on the speed of the CPU and disk I/O subsystem, but even the smallest system should be able to recover logs at better than one log/minute. Surprisingly, it is faster to process a few messages with large attachments rather than a set of smaller messages. This is because ESE has fewer pages to read and process. The more pages to read, the longer recovery will take. The speed of current CPUs largely disguises this fact. Naturally, recoveries that do not have to actually process (or redo) many transactions, because the database was largely up-to-date when the crash occurred, are much faster than recoveries that have to process thousands of outstanding transactions. This is because each redo operation results in a "dirty" page, which must be written out to disk, thereby increasing the I/O load. Any time a log generates many redo operations, you will see a spike in the I/O load on the server.

Not all log files are necessarily required during a recovery operation. Some logs contain details of transactions that have been fully committed to disk and exist in a database. ESE uses the checkpoint to determine whether a transaction has not been fully committed. It is often a good idea to copy all of the transaction logs to a holding directory before beginning any recovery operations, just in case you run into a problem with the recovery and have to go back and start over again.

Recovery can only occur if the target database is in a consistent state when the operation begins. Do not expect success if you restore a corrupted database. You will cause further damage if ESE attempts to replay a transaction for a record on a page that does not exist. In this case, ESE proceeds to locate whatever data is in the specified location and delete it. The replay operation will then proceed and perform whatever instruction is in the log file. For instance, ESE might insert new data into the page. The new data has no relationship to the other contents of the database that depended on the original data, so the result is a logical corruption. The requested record might not exist because ESE never wrote the page to the database due to a hardware or software problem. Perhaps physical corruption occurred after the page was written and the header had been altered.

The problems that occur after you restore a database only to find it is corrupt are all the justification you need to verify backups on a regular basis. You should further protect your system by monitoring the event log to discover and respond to any database errors that ESE reports in the application event log. Never attempt to replay transaction logs against a database other than the original. You cannot, for instance, take transaction logs from one server and replay them on another in an attempt to recover messages after a crash. You should not rename transaction logs or attempt to create a missing log to complete a set (perhaps by copying another log file). The checkpoint file should stop any attempt to circumvent the protection mechanisms built into database recovery, but only if it is available. If you delete the checkpoint and then mess around with transaction logs, you are playing with fire. It is quite possible that the ESE engine will limp its way through the logs, cheerfully corrupting your database to an unrecoverable state, and then report "Recovery complete." Of course, recovery is not complete and all you have managed to create is a useless set of data.

The current transaction log must be available before any recovery operation can succeed. If a hardware failure corrupts this file, it may be possible to rename the previous log to become the current transaction log and proceed with the recovery, but at your own risk. It is highly likely that modifications made by transactions span the corrupt log file and the file that you rename. Some of the modifications may have been committed into the database, but when you run the recovery, you will end up in a situation where incomplete transactions are committed. There is no way to complete the transaction due to the missing log. There is no way to redo or undo these transactions, so you will end up with a corrupt database. In this situation, no clue will exist in the event log, since ESE has been "tricked" by renaming the transaction log and has no idea that transactions are incomplete. The effect of the corruption may only become evident later when further transactions attempt to manipulate the affected pages.

You can experience much the same type of corruption if you use write-back caching on a controller that does not protect its cache if a failure occurs. Write-back caching tells an application that a write operation is complete when data is written into the cache. In this case, ESE will assume that it can flush pages and will proceed to do so. If the controller then fails, some data will remain in the cache. This is not a problem if the controller protects the cache or you can transfer the cache to a replacement controller, but it certainly is if you replace the cache along with the controller. In this case, when you restart the system the cache is empty and ESE cannot recover the outstanding transactions, which results in a severely corrupted database. Never use a controller that does not support a fully protected and removable cache equipped with good battery backup, and always remember to move the cache to the new controller after installation.

Hard recoveries

Hard recoveries need human intervention. Exchange cannot deal with a hard disk failure on its own. After you replace the failed disk, you need to restore the last full backup as well as any incremental backups that have occurred since. Essentially, you need to assemble a complete set of transaction logs containing all the transactions that have occurred since you took the last full backup. The aim is to provide Exchange with the opportunity to replay details of every transaction that has occurred since the last full backup, and you need a complete set of logs for this to be possible. When you have recovered the databases and all of the necessary transaction logs, you can restart the Store service, which then begins to replay any outstanding transactions found in the logs.

To make things as simple as possible, I normally recommend that installations take a full backup each night to avoid the requirement for multiple restore operations. Given the speed of the backup hardware and software available today, servers that use less than 50 GB for the Store databases should always take a full daily backup. Larger databases deserve more attention, because the time required to take a backup is usually much longer, and a substantial investment in backup hardware may be required to shorten the backup period. It is best practice in many large companies to take steps to attempt to keep any online backup to less than four hours. The logic here is that if the backup takes four hours, then a restore will take eight hours (restores usually take twice as long as backups). Eight hours is one working day, and service metrics will take a very large hit if you cannot restore a server to good health in one day. You can use a simple equation here. You know the size of the databases that must be backed up—let us say that the total size of the databases amounts to 60 GB. The backup hardware and software combination must therefore be capable of processing data at 15 GB/hour to remain inside the desired four-hour period. If this is not possible, you need to upgrade the backup hardware or software (or perhaps both) until the goal is met. Striped arrays of DLTs provide the best performance in terms of throughput, but they are expensive. The true value of the hardware investment here is often not realized until the second day of a disaster recovery, at which time it is too late to rescue the career of the unhappy system administrator.

Exchange does not allow soft recoveries to proceed against databases that need hard recoveries. You might, for instance, restore a backup and then run ESEUTIL /P to repair the database and make it consistent again. After ESEUTIL is complete, the database header shows the database to be consistent, but recall that up to Exchange 2000 SP2, a backup contains the database and the patch file that holds information about pages that user activity has changed after the backup application originally wrote the pages to the backup media. Running ESEUTIL /P ignores the patch file, so ESE will never apply the details contained there back to the database, which provides a potential to create a logical corruption. This sequence of events is unusual, and the removal of the patch file from backup operations in SP2 simplifies matters, but it certainly can happen if unwary administrators think they are doing the right thing to "fix" the database after a restore. Exchange protects itself by noting whether a hard recovery is required and issuing error –544 if you attempt to repair a database after a restore.

Because hard recoveries rely on the availability of log files, it is obvious that if the log files are on the same drive as the database you run the risk that any failure will affect both database and log files. Without log files any recovery becomes impossible. This is a fundamental reason for you to separate the database and transaction logs on any Exchange server intended for production work.

7.9 Background maintenance

All databases have internal structures that have to be maintained in some way or another and the Exchange Store is no different. You can take a database offline to rebuild it with the ESEUTIL utility or verify its internal structures with the ISINTEG utility, but these operations require you to deprive users of access to their mailboxes. Since Exchange is designed to be highly available with as little downtime as possible, it is obvious that some online maintenance operations are required. The Store performs online maintenance as a background task nightly to ensure logical consistency within the mailbox and public store databases and to remove unwanted data. As shown in Table 7.8, the Store performs 11 background maintenance tasks nightly.

While the Store controls background maintenance, it actually only executes the first ten tasks. The last is performed by calling the ESE database engine to perform defragmentation, an action the Store takes after at least one of the ten tasks is complete. In concept, the difference between the tasks performed by the Store and those executed by ESE is similar to how

Table 7.8 *Background Maintenance Tasks*

Task	Mailbox Store	Public Store
Purge indexes	Yes	Yes
Perform tombstone maintenance	Yes	Yes
Purge the deleted items cache	Yes	Yes
Expire outdated public folder content	No	Yes
Expire tombstones in public folders	No	Yes
Public folder conflict aging	No	Yes
Update server versions	No	Yes
Secure folders	No	Yes
Purge deleted mailboxes	Yes	No
Check for obsolete messages	Yes	Yes
Store defragmentation	Yes	Yes

ISINTEG understands the structure of tables and indexes that the Store assembles pages into while ESEUTIL deals with pages in the database at a lower level. Obviously, these tasks can generate a huge amount of updates to Store contents. As with any other update, the Store captures details in transaction logs, which accounts for why you will see more transaction logs generated during the maintenance window than you can account for through user activity (which is usually low at this time) or even public folder replication. Note that the "secure folders" task is now obsolete, since it only applies for public folders that are homed in Exchange 5.5 sites. Once you establish a native Exchange 2000/2003 organization, the need for this task goes away.

You can take backups at the same time as background maintenance, but background defragmentation does clash with backups; if you attempt to take a backup while online defragmentation is running, the Store suspends processing until the backup finishes. If the Store cannot complete all the tasks during the allocated time, it finishes the last running task and records where processing stopped so that it can pick up from that point at the next maintenance period.

By default, Exchange schedules background maintenance for between 12:00 P.M. (midnight) and 5 A.M. local time. You can set up a separate custom schedule for each server by selecting the database through Exchange

7.9 Background maintenance

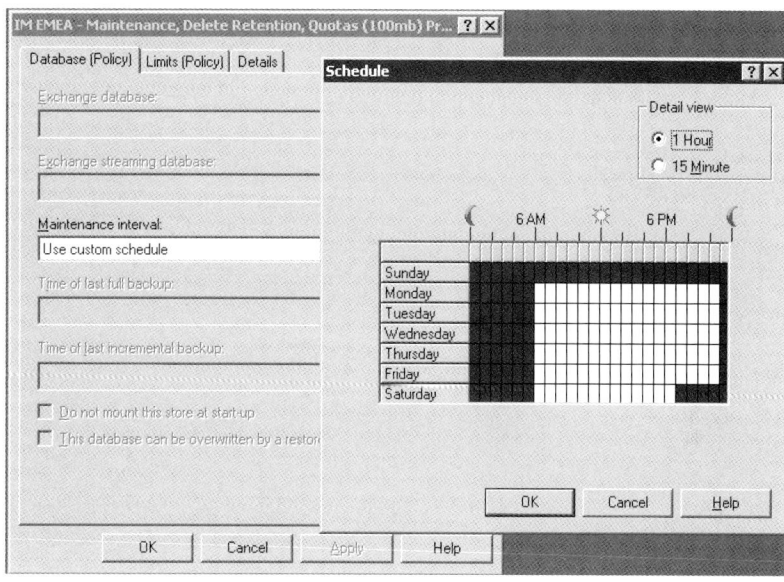

Figure 7.26
Setting an IS maintenance schedule through a server policy.

System Manager, viewing its properties, and then selecting the Database tab. Alternatively, you can create a server policy and apply it to databases on many servers at one time, which is obviously the best approach in large Exchange organizations. Figure 7.26 shows a custom schedule set through a server policy. In this case, the schedule allows the Store to run background maintenance from 11:00 P.M. to 6:00 A.M. on weekdays, and from 6:30 P.M. on Saturday through all day Sunday. Creating such a long maintenance period during the weekend is logical, since it ensures that the Store can complete even the longest operation during a time when user activity is low. Note that you can create a schedule to allow background maintenance to run "Always," which means literally that the Store is free to conduct maintenance operations constantly, including online defragmentation. This is not a great idea unless you know that your server has the capacity to accept the load that background maintenance generates, remembering too that online defragmentation and backups clash with each other.

7.9.1 Background tasks

Now that we understand what happens during background maintenance and when it happens, we can consider some of the detailed processing.

Clients such as Outlook make extensive use of ESE's ability to dynamically generate indexes or views. For example, if you decide that you want to view your inbox by author rather than by date, Outlook requests the Store for this view. If the Store has previously generated the view and has it cached, the response is very quick, but the Store is able to process quickly (through ESE) even a request for a brand new view. Over time, the Store accumulates large numbers of views—each folder in every mailbox can have several views—and this is not desirable, because each view occupies space within the database and some views are only used once. To manage the situation, the Store assigns each view an expiration time and keeps track of the views in an internal table called the index aging table. When background maintenance runs, the Store scans the index aging table to discover views that are older than 40 days (the value is 8 days on Exchange 5.5 servers) and removes any view that has expired. Of course, if a client accesses a view, its expiration time is reset.

The next task is to perform tombstone maintenance. The Store maintains a list of deleted messages for each folder and a list of "tombstones" to indicate that a message was deleted. The tombstone list is most important for replicated folders, such as public folders, because it provides the Store with a list of message delete operations that it must replicate to every server that holds a replica of the folder. After successful replication, the Store can clear the entries from the tombstone list. Background maintenance ensures that the lists are accurate.

When a client deletes a message, the Store sets a flag to hide the message from the mailbox (this is known as a soft delete). Clients can retrieve messages from the deleted items cache by clearing the flag, thus causing the message to reappear in the mailbox. During background maintenance, the Store examines every message that has the deleted flag set (the entire contents of the deleted items cache) to determine whether its retention period has expired. If this is true, the message is removed permanently from the Store (a hard delete). You can set retention periods on a per-mailbox, per-store, or per public–folder basis and can control this setting globally through a server policy. For example, Figure 7.27 shows the limits set on a public store. You can see the deleted retention time is set at seven days. Exchange also allows you to set a retention period for content in a public folder either per store or per folder. The idea here is that you may use some public folders to hold content that ages out in a systematic way, such as a feed from an NNTP service. By aging out the content, you impose a check on how large the folder grows. Background maintenance also checks for deleted folders that have exceeded their retention period and removes them as well. Much the same processing occurs for deleted messages in public folders, and the Store checks for messages that have expired and removes them. The Store also checks for deleted mailboxes, which have a default

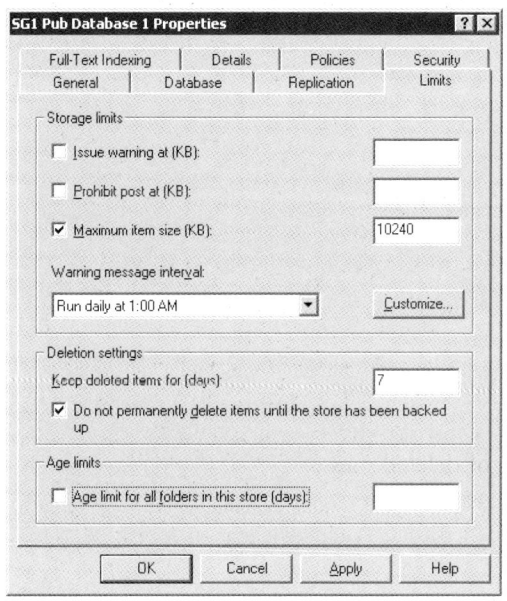

Figure 7.27
Public store limits.

retention period of 30 days, and removes any that have expired. Removing obsolete folders and mailboxes cleans up the internal table structure of the database and increases efficiency.

The next check is for deleted public folders that have expired. By default, if you delete a public folder, the Store creates a tombstone for the folder. This allows the replication mechanism to propagate the deletion properly to servers that hold replicas. Because replication may not occur quickly in some circumstances, the Store retains the tombstone for 180 days (default value). If replication has not propagated the tombstone in 180 days, your organization is experiencing fundamental replication difficulties and a few erroneous tombstones are of little concern. During background maintenance, the Store checks for folder tombstones that have expired and removes them. However, the Store only removes a maximum of 500 tombstones per 24-hour period.

Public folder replication is somewhat of a black art and it is easy for conflicts to occur—for example, if multiple users modify the same item in different replicas of a public folder or if multiple users attempt to simultaneously save an item in the same replica. When a conflict happens, the Store sends a conflict resolution message to the users who caused the problem to ask them to resolve the issue. It is easier for human beings to decide which change is more important and so resolve the conflict. While the human beings decide what to do, the Store maintains the different versions of the items in conflict. However, if the human beings fail to respond, the Store examines each item in conflict and resolves them automatically, usually by accepting the most recent version. It is possible to control the resolution process programmatically by manipulating the MAPI PR_RESOLVE_METHOD property on the folder. Most administrators are likely to leave Exchange to its own devices.

The next task is to update server versions for the public stores. This process updates any version information that is necessary to maintain the system configuration folder. The Store incurs no great overhead, and you cannot control the process. Background maintenance also checks that no duplicate site folders exist within public stores in an Administrative Group and removes any duplicates that it detects.

The Store uses a single-instance storage model, meaning that it keeps a single copy of message content and uses pointers in user mailboxes to the content. The Store tracks the number of mailboxes that have pointers to content through a reference count and physically removes the content from the database when the reference count reaches zero. In any database, there is the potential for pointers to become unsynchronized, so background maintenance checks for lingering messages that have a zero reference count and then removes up to 50,000 of these items per day. The Store does not report how many items it has removed, so a large growth in transaction logs is the only indication that this type of activity is ongoing. If you observed that the Store generated more than the normal quantity of logs in the midnight to 6:00 A.M. period, it could be an indication that you should run ISINTEG against the mailbox store.

The final and most compute-intensive task is for the Store to invoke ESE to perform online defragmentation. See section 7.10.1 for a discussion about the differences between online and offline defragmentation.

7.9.2 Some registry settings to control background maintenance

Exchange would not be Exchange if there were no registry settings that you could twiddle to change the way things work. As shown in Table 7.9, background maintenance has a selection for you to experiment with, if you like playing with fire. It is good to know that these settings exist, but you should only set these values if you have an extremely good reason to do so.

7.9 Background maintenance

Table 7.9 *Registry Values to Control Background Maintenance Tasks*

Task	Registry value	Meaning	Key
Purge indexes	Aging Keep Time	The amount of time in milliseconds to keep unused indexes and views in the database. Default is 40 days.	PS
Purge indexes	Aging Clean Interval	The interval in milliseconds at which the Store attempts to purge unused indexes.	PS
Purge indexes	Reset Views	If you set this value to 1, the Store removes all indexes regardless of age during the next background maintenance cycle. Afterward, clients will have to rebuild previously cached views.	M/P
Purge Deleted items	Deletion Thread Period	The interval (in milliseconds) at which the Store attempts to purge unused indexes.	M/P
Public folder expiration	Replication Expiration	The interval (in milliseconds) at which the Store removes items that have exceeded the retention period.	P
Tombstone expiration	Replication Folder Tombstone Age Limit	The interval (in days) to keep tombstones.	P
Public folder aging conflict	Replication Folder Conflict Age Limit	The interval (in days) that the Store allows items in conflict to exist.	P
Online defrag	OLD Minimum Run Time	The minimum amount of time that ESE spends on online defragmentation after the Store completes at least one of its background maintenance tasks. The default is 15 minutes.	M/P
Online defrag	OLD Completion Time	The amount of time in seconds beyond the scheduled maintenance window that ESE is allowed to continue with online defragmentation. The default value is 1 hour, or 3,600 seconds.	M/P

All of these registry values are DWORD. They go into three separate places in the registry, as indicated by the key shown in Table 7.9, where PS means ParametersSystem, M is the key for a mailbox store, and P is a key for a public store. In previous versions of Exchange, the common practice was to place registry settings in the ParametersSystems key under MSExchangeIS, but because Exchange 2000/2003 supports store partitioning, we now have a key named after the server with separate keys for each

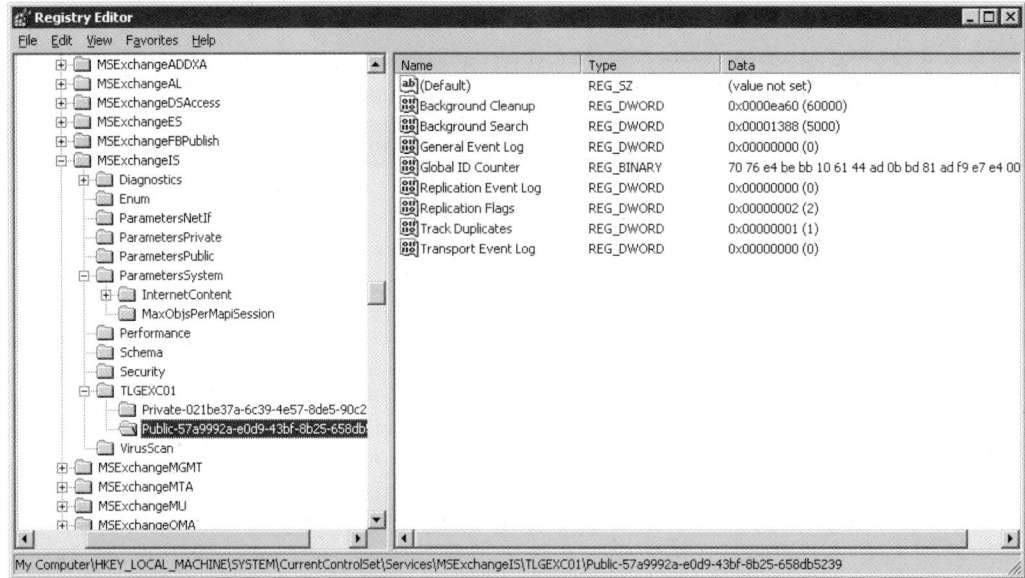

Figure 7.28   *Registry settings for maintenance tasks.*

lower store. Figure 7.28 shows the complete path to registry settings that govern how the Store deals with a public store on a server.

PS   `HKEY_LOCAL_MACHINE\SYSTEM\CurrentControlSet\Services\MSExchangeIS\ParametersSystem`

M   `HKEY_LOCAL_MACHINE\SYSTEM\CurrentControlSet\Services\MSExchangeIS\<ServerName>\Public-<Public Folder GUID>`

P   `HKEY_LOCAL_MACHINE\SYSTEM\CurrentControlSet\Services\MSExchangeIS\<ServerName>\Private-<Public Folder GUID>`

7.9.3 Tracking background maintenance

As with any other operation in Exchange, the selected level of diagnostics logging determines how much information the Store writes about maintenance operations in the Application Event Log. You set the level for diagnostic logging by selecting a server in Exchange System Manager and then viewing its properties and selecting the Diagnostic Logging tab, as shown in Figure 7.29. You need to adjust the Background Cleanup setting for the MSExchangeIS Public Folder and Mailbox objects from its default logging level of "None" to "Minimum" or above. I find it useful to set the level to "Maximum," because, unlike other settings (such as public folder replica-

7.9 Background maintenance

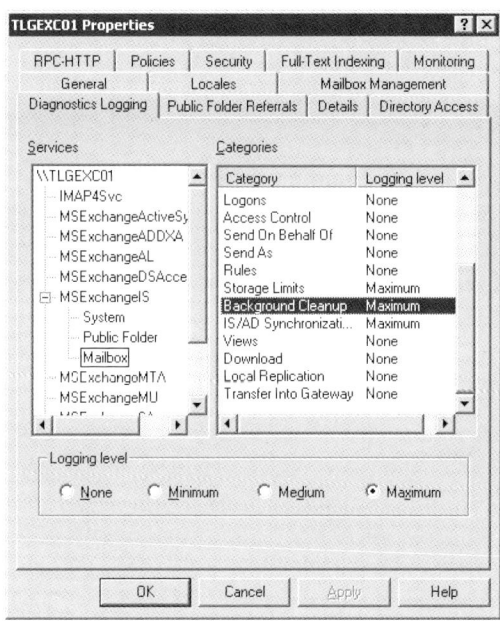

Figure 7.29
IS maintenance diagnostics setting.

tion), background maintenance does not generate a flood of events even at the maximum level, and you can always learn something from the extra detail generated at this level. Once you are familiar with the different operations and know what to expect, you can reduce the setting to "Minimum."

After applying the new setting, the Store begins to generate events the next time it runs background maintenance. Table 7.10 lists the most common events that you will see, and Figure 7.30 illustrates some typical examples.

Table 7.10 *Common Background Maintenance Events*

Event Identifier	Meaning
1208	The Store begins to execute background maintenance tasks
1209	The Store has completed background maintenance tasks
1210	General event noting that one of the maintenance tasks is complete—for example, tombstone maintenance, site check folder, or deleted mailbox cleanup
1206	Beginning to clean up mailbox items in the deleted items cache past their retention date
1207	End of cleanup of mailbox items in the deleted items cache
1100	Report of folders deleted during background cleanup

Chapter 7

Table 7.10 *Common Background Maintenance Events (continued)*

Event Identifier	Meaning
9531	Start cleanup of deleted mailboxes
9535	End of cleanup of deleted mailboxes
700	Background defragmentation begins
701	Background defragmentation completes a full pass of a database within the maintenance window
702	Background defragmentation restarts an interrupted pass
703	Background defragmentation completes a resumed pass
704	Background defragmentation for a database is interrupted

Except on very large or heavily loaded servers, many of these tasks complete quickly. The obvious exception is background defragmentation. This is the most intense activity and can last many hours, depending on background load, server capacity, and the amount of data to process. For example, my quad-CPU 900-MHz server with 1 GB of memory takes 4 hours to process a 14-GB mailbox store.

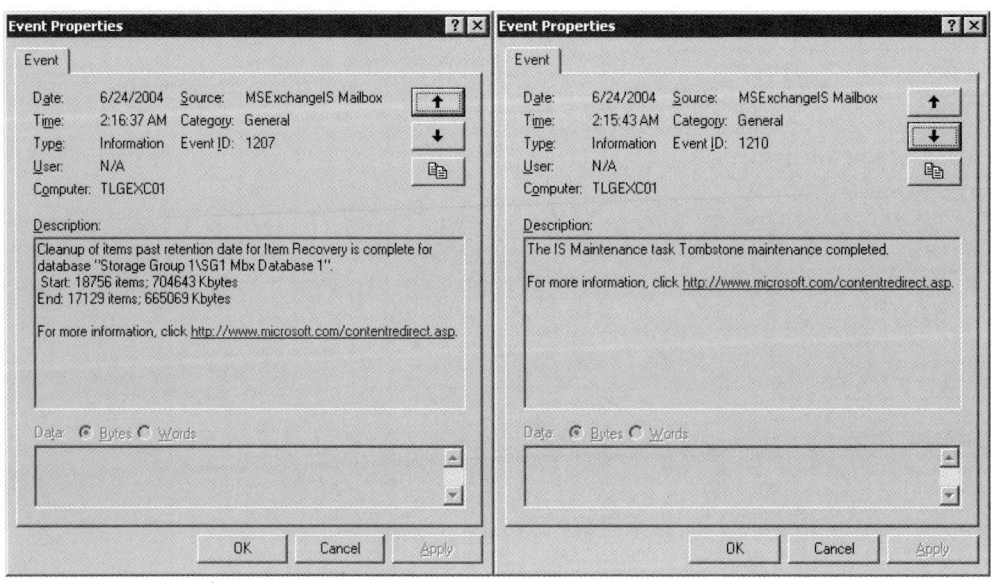

Figure 7.30 *Background maintenance events are recorded.*

7.10 Database utilities

Table 7.11 lists the three utilities you can use to maintain or verify Exchange databases.

A great deal of mystique has grown up around the ESEUTIL and ISINTEG utilities over the years, with some administrators believing that running either or both is sufficient to cure all database ailments. The truth is somewhat different. ESEUTIL can certainly help to get a database running again, but it cannot fix fundamental damage or corruption caused by hardware failure. In these circumstances, if you encounter a series of –1018, –1019, or –1022 errors in the event log, the best procedure is to restore the database from the last good backup and roll forward all subsequent transactions by replaying the transaction logs. Thankfully, the advent of automatic single-bit error correction in the Store in Exchange 2003 SP1 means that we will see fewer database errors, but the fact remains that database errors will occur during the lifespan of the majority of Exchange servers, so you have to be prepared to deal with them.

ISINTEG verifies the application-level structures (tables and pointers), but it depends on a good database. Thus, if ESEUTIL cannot fix the problems in a database, ISINTEG will not be able to work any magic either.

These utilities have been present in Exchange for many versions now. Indeed, ISINTEG and ESEUTIL first appeared in Exchange 4.0, so it is a constant source of personal bemusement to see that Microsoft persists with such command-line utilities when almost every other complex operation in the product has at least a graphic interface or even a wizard. Wizards do not stop you from making mistakes and they would not prevent administrators from fixing databases that do not need fixing, but they would at least provide another layer of protection. Experience shows that many administrators do not fully understand the damage they can do with utilities such as

Table 7.11 *Exchange Database Utilities*

Utility	Purpose	Location
ESEFILE	Verify checksums of ESE pages	Server CD (see the SUPPORT\UTILS\i386 folder)
ISINTEG	Check folders and other application-level structures	Included in Store
ESEUTIL	Verify physical page structure	EXCHSRVR\BIN

ESEUTIL (in particular), and I am sure that Microsoft receives many support calls each year about database recovery operations that have gone wrong because of a misapplication of ESEUTIL. Microsoft has done some good work in the disaster recovery area with the provision of the Recovery Storage Group (see section 11.6), and it is surprising that it continues to leave ESEUTIL bereft of a suitable interface, ready for unwitting administrators to fall into the black hole of data loss. With this warning in place, let us consider just how ESEUTIL works.

7.10.1 Running ESEUTIL

ESEUTIL has no knowledge of database contents and operates on a page level in different modes. When recovering from a database problem, the two most important modes are /D (defragmentation) and /P (repair). Always take a file-level backup of a database before you begin working with ESEUTIL. Only use the version of ESEUTIL compatible with the version of Exchange running on the server.

You can only run ESEUTIL against a dismounted database. In an Exchange context, offline defragmentation means that the ESEUTIL utility rebuilds the database, page by page, and administrators usually perform an offline defragmentation to recover disk space to the file system. Best practice is to have at least 120 percent of the database size available in free space to accommodate the temporary files used during processing, although this figure can vary depending on the degree of internal fragmentation within the database. If necessary, to find the required disk space, you can redirect the location of the temporary files to a disk that has sufficient free space. You can even run ESEUTIL on a computer that does not have Exchange installed by transferring the necessary program files and databases to that computer. All of this work takes time, and users cannot access their mailboxes while processing takes place.

The Store runs an online defragmentation process nightly for every database on a server to "shuffle" pages internally so that linked pages are kept together in the most logical sense; that data is compressed into the smallest and most efficient number of pages (to reduce I/O), and the "white space" (unused pages) is placed at the end of the database. The process calls the ESE engine to examine individual tables in the Store and attempt to reduce the number of pages that the table occupies. For example, if a message table currently uses 100 pages that are half-full, the defragmentation process will aim to compress the table into approximately 50 pages. Online defragmentation never returns space to the file system and the overall size of the database is not reduced. Even though the database size remains the same

7.10 Database utilities

physical size, online defragmentation contributes to the overall efficiency of the Store, because the reduced number of pages means that the Store expends less I/O to access information.

Early versions of the online defragmentation process were not very efficient, which led to recommendations that administrators should rebuild their databases on a regular basis to prevent the databases from becoming too large. From Exchange 5.5 onward, the online defragmentation process is much more efficient and effective, and you should not need to perform an offline defragmentation (rebuild) unless you have good reason to suspect that you can recover a large amount of disk space. Note that nightly online defragmentation does not affect the STM file, because Exchange does not attempt to rearrange the internal structure of this file.

After online defragmentation, the Store reports the amount of unused pages in the application event log as event 1221 (see Figure 7.31). In the left-hand screen (Exchange 2000 on Windows 2000), ESE reports that 4,633 MB of white space is available in a 9.32-GB Mailbox Store, which means that you could recover the space occupied by almost half of the database if you use ESEUTIL to perform an offline defragmentation. However, this is an exceptional occurrence due to many mailbox moves to another server. The right-hand screen (Exchange 2003 on Windows 2003) shows more typical results, with only 50 MB recovered in a 9-GB Mailbox Store.

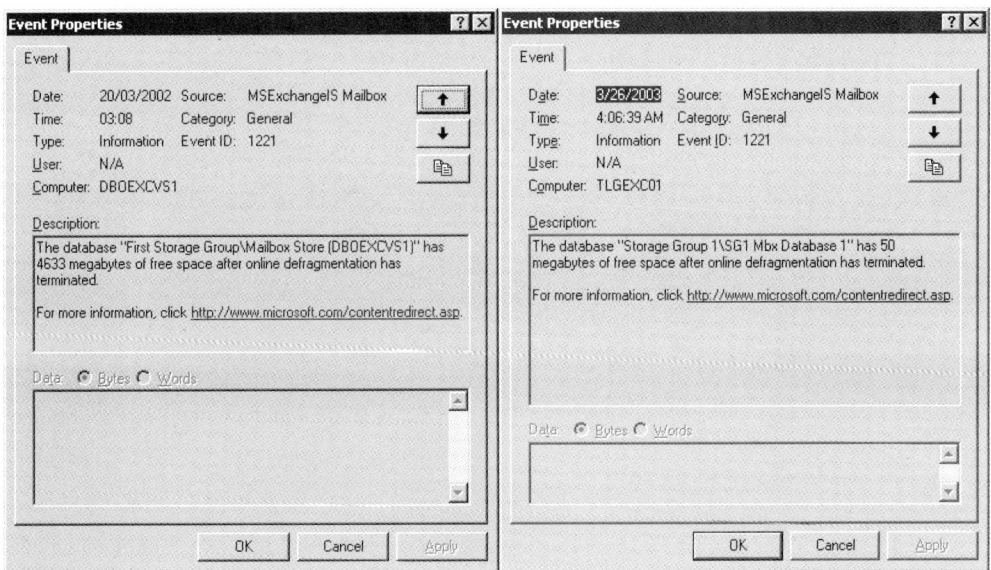

Figure 7.31 *Result of online defragmentation.*

The expected range of white space on Exchange 2003 mailbox servers ranges from 1 percent to 10 percent, depending on how long the Mailbox Store has been operational since the last offline rebuild.

You can check events 700 (start of run) and 701 (end of run) to determine how long online defragmentation takes. In this case, processing lasted three hours and eight minutes, or roughly 3 GB/hour. Throughput varies with processor speed; I/O capacity; and system load, including other management operations that may be proceeding at the same time, such as the emptying of the deleted items cache, defragmentation of other databases, and the generation of the Offline Address Book.

Using ESEUTIL to rebuild a database (/D)

You have to take a database offline before you can rebuild it using ESEUTIL/D. The immediate impact is removing service from users, because they cannot access their mailboxes until you bring the rebuilt database back online. This fact alone makes a rebuild a bad idea unless you have a very good reason (such as PSS advising you that a rebuild is necessary) to go ahead with the procedure. Typically, you should not consider running ESEUTIL to perform an offline rebuild unless more than 30 percent of the pages in the database is free space, a situation that normally only exists after a number of mailboxes are moved from one database to another, moved to another server, or if the database has been left in use for many months. Previous versions of Exchange accumulated reasonably large quantities of white space (unused pages) within databases, but the combination of better reuse of white space and a more efficient background defragmentation process performed nightly means that you are far less likely to encounter a database with a large amount of white space in it today. As noted in the previous section, you can check event 1221 in the event log after the nightly defragmentation run to see how much space is available for recovery.

The standard version of Exchange restricts database sizes to 16 GB. This is usually enough space for the intended users of the standard edition, largely in the small to medium business sector, but sometimes it is possible for these systems to approach the 16-GB limit. If this happens, the Store will stop running and you will have to take steps to free up space. Rebuilding the database is an immediate fix, since it will usually bring a database under the 16-GB limit, but you will have to take more fundamental steps afterward to prevent the problem from reoccurring. The best long-term fix is to upgrade the server to the Enterprise version of Exchange, but you can also consider implementing reduced mailbox quotas on users and enforcing good cleanup habits with the help of the Mailbox Manager.

7.10 Database utilities

The major advantage that you gain by rebuilding the database is the elimination of all white space in the file, leading to the recovery of disk space to the file system. Backups will therefore complete faster, since they have less data to process and it is more likely that the pages that constitute a mailbox and its contents are contiguous within the database, so they can stream out faster to the backup media. Some commentators have also observed that large databases often cause NTFS to extend the size of the file several times. The more extents there are on a disk, the longer Windows takes to run CHKDSK to verify the disk after an unexpected reboot. Hopefully, servers will not have many unexpected reboots, so removing Exchange from service to perform an offline rebuild to speed up CHKDSK does not really deliver a lot of benefit weighed against the disruption to users.

While a fully defragmented database occupies less space on disk, you must understand that the database will begin to expand almost as soon as it comes back into production use. It may, therefore, grow to reoccupy all of the recovered disk space in a short period. Another problem is that the rebuild renders all transaction logs null and void, because the rebuild changes the internal database signature that ties transaction logs to the database.

To rebuild a database with ESEUTIL, you proceed as follows:

- Take a full online backup.

- Dismount the target database and so remove service from users whose mailboxes are in the Store (or remove service to public folders).

- Run ESEUTIL /D.

- Remount the database after ESEUTIL completes successfully,

- Take a full online backup, since you can no longer roll forward transactions in previous transaction logs to the newly rebuilt database.

Note that ESEUTIL defragments both the EDB and STM databases in the same operation.

When it runs, ESEUTIL reads a page from the source database, verifies its content, and writes the page to the new copy of the database. ESEUTIL ignores empty pages, so if the problem exists in an empty page, ESEUTIL can fix it because it does not write the problem page into the new database. However, if the page contains data, ESEUTIL will not be able to complete the defragmentation and you will have to resort to repair mode. Figure 7.32 shows how ESEUTIL reports the successful rebuild of a 42-GB database. In this instance, the source and target volumes were a 36-disk set and the process took 164 minutes, or approximately 15.38 GB/hour.

Chapter 7

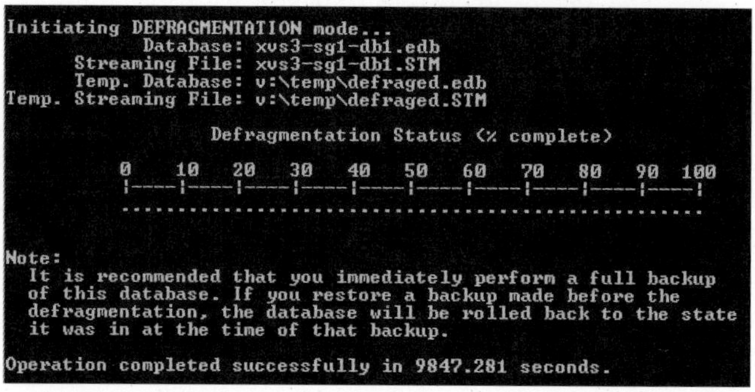

Figure 7.32
ESEUTIL succeeds in a database defragmentation.

```
Initiating DEFRAGMENTATION mode...
         Database: xvs3-sg1-db1.edb
    Streaming File: xvs3-sg1-db1.STM
    Temp. Database: v:\temp\defraged.edb
Temp. Streaming File: v:\temp\defraged.STM

         Defragmentation Status (% complete)
    0    10   20   30   40   50   60   70   80   90   100
    !----!----!----!----!----!----!----!----!----!----!
    ...................................................

Note:
  It is recommended that you immediately perform a full backup
  of this database. If you restore a backup made before the
  defragmentation, the database will be rolled back to the state
  it was in at the time of that backup.

Operation completed successfully in 9847.281 seconds.
```

You can find out how much space you can recover in a database by running ESEUTIL with the /MS switch. At the bottom of the output (lower right-hand side), you will find a total number, which is the number of pages that ESEUTIL expects to free. To see how much the STM will shrink, look for a section called "SLV Space Dump" and then for the figure reported as "Free Total." Since both figures represent pages, you need to multiply them by 4,096 to get the number of bytes and then transform the bytes to megabytes or whatever other figure you want to use.

The order in which you state the qualifiers in the command line is important. Always put the major option first (rebuild, repair, integrity check, etc.) followed by any options that affect how ESEUTIL runs.

ESEUTIL repair mode (/P)

When we refer to a database repair, we mean that you run ESEUTIL in a mode where it discards any problem page if it fails a checksum test. Sometimes, we refer to running ESEUTIL in this mode as performing a "hard" repair, because there is no middle ground in the decision to keep or reject pages, so data is easily lost if it exists in pages that ESEUTIL discards as it repairs the database. The only pages that end up in the new copy of the database are those whose checksums can be verified by ESEUTIL. The impact of discarded pages depends on the data they contain. Discarded leaf pages mean that important system or user data is no longer available, so complete folders may disappear from mailboxes. However, if ESEUTIL discards the pages containing system catalog data, the database may be unusable.

Repairing a database is a last-chance option that you should only proceed with if a good backup is unavailable. ESEUTIL is not a fast utility and typically processes data at up to 8–10 GB/hour depending on the system configuration, so running ESEUTIL against a moderately sized file will

7.10 Database utilities

take hours to complete and you have no guarantee that the repair will be successful. A real-life example involves a corrupt 192-GB database, roughly 20 GB of which was white space. When the Store experienced problems, the administrators discovered that they had not taken a full backup for a week and had some 300,000 logfiles that Exchange would have to replay to update the database (a process that could take ten days to finish). Instead, they made the decision to attempt to fix the database with ESEUTIL/P using a four-processor HP Proliant DL580G2 with 4 GB of memory and an HP XP512 SAN. ESEUTIL completed the rebuild after 36.5 hours, or roughly 5.2 GB/hour. Add on the time required to take backups before and after, and the whole operation took two days. The best thing you can say is that this is better than ten days, but it does prove the need to take full backups on a frequent basis and to monitor carefully for potential database problems.

Before starting a repair, ensure that you check out all possible hardware faults that may have contributed to the corruption in the first place. There is no point in spending hours waiting for ESEUTIL to repair a large database only to find that either the repair job fails or the newly repaired database runs into immediate problems because the storage subsystem is flaky. After you check out the hardware, check out Windows and Exchange to make sure that the failure is not due to a simple problem that you can fix. A server reboot will probably not fix the problem, but it does not hurt just to try (just how many Windows problems are fixed with a reboot?). You should also check the event log to see if there are any clues there to point to the underlying root cause for the failure and then check the Microsoft Knowledge Base to see whether you can fix the problem without using ESEUTIL. Make sure that you take a copy of the database before you run ESEUTIL, just in case you want to go back to the original version. In fact, it is a good idea to copy all of the files associated with the failing database, including the transaction logs and STM file, to a safe location before you do anything else.

If you successfully repair a database with ESEUTIL, the resulting database will function properly and Exchange will run. However, it is possible that some lingering problems persist in the database's internal structures that make it prone to future problems, and the internal indexes and space allocation may not be optimal. For example, a corrupt structure may cause the Store process to consume excessive CPU or memory. For this reason, it is a good idea to run ESEUTIL again, this time to rebuild the database (with /D, or the defragment switch), since this operation will rebuild all the internal structures (and shrink the size of the database). In addition, when

Chapter 7

you have a newly rebuilt database, you should run ISINTEG (in -fix -all-tests mode) to ensure that the internal tables are accurate. Remember that ESEUTIL treats an Exchange database in terms of pages and low-level structures and has no idea what the pages contain or their importance to Exchange. When everything is complete, take a backup to preserve your work.

The time required to execute these steps to repair, rebuild, and fix the database may be just too long for the users to operate without access to their email. For this reason, some administrators consider it better practice to restore service immediately with a new database to allow users to start working again, albeit with blank mailboxes. Meantime, behind the scenes, the administrators attempt to repair the failed database files and then recover the mailbox data and reload it back into the online databases. You need a separate recovery server for this exercise with Exchange 2000, but you can use the new Recovery Storage Group feature (see Chapter 11 for details) in Exchange 2003 to do everything on the same server, providing you have enough spare disk space to run the recovery utilities. While swapping in new databases and fixing failed databases elsewhere invariably results in a "clean" database (and probably one that is better for long-term use in production), it cannot fix an underlying disk or storage subsystem problem that may have caused the corruption in the first place. In addition, the rebuild causes considerable disruption to users, including the potential loss of some data that ExMerge is unable to export and import. For this reason, creating new databases is very much a step that you should take only as the absolute last resort when you know that you cannot get back to a supportable situation in any other way.

Note that from Exchange 2000 SP1 onward, you can specify the /create-stm switch for a repair operation to force ESEUTIL to create a brand new STM file if the current STM file is unrecoverable due to corruption. Do not take this step unless you are sure that the STM file is irreversibly damaged, since you immediately lose data when ESEUTIL creates the STM. Remember to take a full backup of the repaired database after ESEUTIL completes processing.

ESEUTIL and low disk space

Sometimes you will encounter a situation where you want to run ESEUTIL to rebuild but you do not have enough free disk space on your server to allow for the temporary storage used by ESEUTIL when it processes the database. In order of ease of use, there are three possible solutions:

7.10 Database utilities

- Map a network drive on a temporary basis, move the databases to the newly mapped drive, run ESEUTIL, and then move the files back to their original location.
- Copy the databases to another server that has enough available disk space and run ESEUTIL there.
- Redirect the location of the temporary files to some network storage.

You can specify a location for ESEUTIL to create the temporary database created during an offline defragmentation (/D) or repair (/P) operation with the /T qualifier. When the operation is complete, ESEUTIL moves the temporary database back to take the place of the original database, unless you use the /P qualifier to instruct ESEUTIL not to replace the original.

Using another server to run ESEUTIL is useful when you want to perform other work (such as applying an operating system upgrade) on the server where Exchange normally runs. You do not even have to use a server that has Exchange installed, since it is possible to move ESEUTIL.EXE and a small set of associated DLLs to a target server and run ESEUTIL there. Microsoft Knowledge Base article Q244525 describes the necessary steps. In all cases, remember to take a backup before and after you run ESEUTIL.

7.10.2 ISINTEG

ESEUTIL repairs a database on a page level but does not address any logical faults that exist within the tables that form the content of the database. For example, in some versions of Exchange 2000, it is possible for the Store to report inaccurate mailbox quotas if clients convert MAPI format messages to MIME, a reasonably common situation when you run a mixture of Outlook and Internet clients. ISINTEG can address problems such as this by examining the contents of the Store and then updating attribute values to reflect the true situation. Think of ISINTEG as a utility that can take the physical pages in the database and organize them in a way that makes sense to Exchange. ISINTEG checks that the internal tables are logical and do not contain errors so that Exchange can present them to clients as mailboxes, folders, and items.

You can check a database for logical faults by running ESEUTIL with the /MH switch to check the database header. Look for the "repair count," and, if this is greater than zero, run the ISINTEG utility to fix the logical errors, as follows:

```
ISINTEG -S [server_name] -FIX -TEST ALLTESTS
```

Unlike versions of Exchange prior to 2000, the ISINTEG utility is merely a stub image that invokes the code to perform the tests. This code is part of the Store.

Despite rumors to the contrary, ISINTEG cannot fix problems caused by hardware corruption. If you have a damaged database caused by hardware corruption and you cannot repair the problem with ESEUTIL (even at the expense of discarding damaged pages and losing data), it is not worthwhile to run ISINTEG. The only solution is to restore the database from the last good backup and replay transaction logs to recover any outstanding transactions. Note that if you do repair a database with ESEUTIL, it is possible that some of the relationships between tables in the database will become inconsistent because of the repair. In this situation, running ISINTEG after ESEUTIL successfully processes a database completes the fix-up by restoring lost links.

7.10.3 ESEFILE

ESEFILE serves two major purposes. First, it can be used (/C qualifier) to copy large files in a very efficient manner. While the utility helps to move large EDB databases from disk to disk, perhaps to run ESEUTIL on another computer, it can actually copy any Windows file. Do not use ESEFILE to move databases to a new location for any purpose other than running ESEUTIL. Always use ESM if you want to move a database's location, since this ensures that you update Exchange's configuration data in the AD.

The second purpose is to perform a checksum test against a complete database (/S qualifier) or to verify a selected page (/D qualifier). As already noted, Exchange uses a simple algorithm to generate and verify checksums, so ESEFILE can process very large databases quickly. Backup products that mimic snapshots by stopping the Store, breaking a mirror copy, and then restarting the Store sometimes use ESEFILE to validate that the databases on the mirror are valid and intact. This is important, because the database copy on the mirror is a "crash consistent copy," similar to a database after an unexpected exit and may contain errors such as torn pages. For this reason, it is much better to use the combination of Windows 2003 Volume ShadowCopy Services (VSS), Exchange 2003, and suitable hardware and backup software to take fully supported hot snapshot backups. See Chapter 8 for more information on VSS.

Microsoft replaced ESEFILE with an extension to ESEUTIL in Exchange 2003, so you can run ESEUTIL /K on an Exchange 2003 server to accomplish the same functions.

7.10.4 Error Correcting Code—Exchange 2003 SP1

Manufacturers of memory modules commonly implement Error Correcting Code (ECC) algorithms in their products. ECC algorithms automatically detect and correct single-bit or "bit flip" memory errors, which occur when a single bit of data that should contain a zero changes to one, or vice versa. When the ECC code detects that a bit has an unexpected value, it can correct the value and proceed. Microsoft's own data indicates that up to 40 percent of –1018 errors are simple bit flips, so there is obvious value in being able to reduce the number of –1018 errors on a server by implementing an ECC algorithm for the Store and by updating the format of pages inside the EDB database. Up to SP1, each page in the EDB database starts with a 4-byte page number, which the Store uses to ensure that it reads the correct page off disk or commits the right page into memory. SP1 replaces the 4-byte value with an 8-byte checksum, which is actually two separate 32-bit checksums. The first is an XOR checksum that the Store calculates much in the same way as before. The Store uses the second 32-byte checksum as an ECC check to correct single-bit errors on the page. Together, the extra intelligence in the Store and the expanded checksum processing allows the Store to self-heal some –1018 errors as they occur.

Microsoft expects that the new code will reduce the number of –1018 errors in line with the statistical evidence. However, ECC can only handle single-bit errors, so problems can still happen when the Store attempts to process a page and encounters a hardware problem caused by a disk or storage controller presenting bad data. In these instances, Exchange flags a –1018 error, and you will have to take action to fix the underlying hardware problem and then recover the database.

As with any other change to the Store, the introduction of ECC slightly complicates the SP1 upgrade procedure. Exchange does not attempt to upgrade the entire Store at one time when you apply SP1 to a server, because this would take too long for anything but small servers. Instead, the Store upgrades the page format to accommodate ECC as users access and update individual pages and are then committed back into the database. Over time, the Store will process all of the pages and complete the database update. The phased approach makes it easy for administrators as long as they remember that you cannot take a backup from an SP1 server and expect to restore it on a pre-SP1 server, because the pre-SP1 Store does not understand the ECC data that SP1 adds to each page in the database and therefore considers the pages to be corrupt. Note that if you want to update a database immediately after you install SP1, you can run the ESEUTIL utility with the /D parameter to rebuild the database, and the rebuild process will update each page. Be sure to take a full backup before and after the rebuild, since this operation renders any transaction log generated previously invalid.

Exchange 2003 SP1 also includes a subtle change in the way that the Store processes online backups. The Exchange backup API has always validated each page as it streams out of the database into the backup saveset. If the backup encounters a –1018 error, the Backup API terminates processing, because you do not want to take a flawed backup, so if an online backup is successful, you know that an Exchange database has no detectable problems. From SP1 on, if the backup finds a single-bit error, it reports the problem but continues with the backup, so the backup saveset can contain a number of known errors. However, if you have to restore the backup, the Store will deal with these errors as it updates the pages. If it meets a –1018 error, the backup is aborted as before. Exchange reports all –1018 problems in the event log as event 474.

To help administrators, Exchange flags single-bit errors in the event log. The most common event is a 399 warning, which indicates that the Store encountered a single-bit error and was able to correct it in memory (the error may still exist on disk, because the Store only corrects a problem on disk when it updates a page and commits it back into the database). A 398 error is more serious, since this occurs when the Store has corrected a single-bit error in a page but subsequently believes that the page is still invalid. Microsoft believes that a 398 error will be very rare.

7.11 The epoxy layer

Epoxy is a special interprocess communication layer designed to offset the inevitable degradation in performance that you can expect when work is divided across multiple processes. Interprocess communication normally results in many context switches, which are expensive under Windows. Epoxy uses shared memory to manage the data that must pass between the Store and IIS, and the Exchange development team claims that this technique reduces the performance loss to less than 1 percent of normal interprocess communication. The development team believes that any performance loss is bad, but the slight degradation is offset by improvements made elsewhere within the Store. Epoxy cannot operate across remote links, implying that the IIS must be local or installed on each server that hosts Store databases.

On a strategic level, creating a division between protocol access and storage helps toward the long-term goal of scaling Exchange to be able to handle the user and message loads generated by typical ISP environments. Based on today's technology, even the largest clustered server is probably not going to be able to handle hundreds of thousands of mailboxes and the attendant load generated by tens of thousands of concurrent user connections. Building a virtual server composed of front-end protocol servers and back-end storage servers is a good solution, and you cannot do that if storage and protocol access is totally integrated.

7.12 The Public Store

Mailbox Stores hold purely personal information. By comparison, the Public Store is a shared repository whose content is available to anyone, subject to the access controls you impose on individual public folders or on folder trees (where subfolders inherit permissions from parent folders).

On the surface, public folders seem to add a lot of functionality to Exchange. It is good to have a place to hold shared information that you can make available to all users or selected groups of users who can access the folders using MAPI, IMAP4, or as Web clients (you can also direct NNTP feeds into public folders). It is even better that you can associate electronic forms with public folders to build applications, even if those forms are usually limited to MAPI clients, unless you take the time to develop a set to accommodate browsers.

The problem is figuring out how and when to use public folders in an Exchange deployment. When is it best to use public folders and where are network file shares more appropriate? Should I consider public folders to be a dead-end street and focus on deploying SharePoint Portal Server or a straightforward Web server instead? What training must I give to users to help them create and use public folders? What impact will public folder replication have on the network and what steps can I take to manage the traffic? For public folders, there are often more questions than answers.

7.12.1 The goals for public folders

To some degree, system designers and administrators do not know what to do with public folders and perhaps the fault is Microsoft's, because it has never been able to state just what public folders are good for. Before Microsoft launched Exchange in 1996, public folders seemed to offer an exciting platform for electronic forms and collaboration. You could take EFD, a Visual BASIC–like electronic forms designer program, and build all manner of forms to serve many purposes, such as travel requests, tracking expenses, reporting sales calls, and so on. You could set up public folders to be the base for online discussion forums, something that was in line with Microsoft's original name used during development, "public fora," or places where people can come together to share and exchange information, an electronic version of the original Roman Forum.

However, the result was not good. EFD was reasonably easy to work with, but it produced 16-bit code that ran slowly, especially when the folder contained more than a few items. In passing, it is worth noting that the old rule always to run demos with just enough data to get your message across holds true for public folders. You could not question Microsoft's earnest evangelism for public folders, but slow performance and the inability to support all platforms marked a quick end for EFD. Remember, in those days, Exchange supported a DOS client, so 16-bit was an important platform! The situation with electronic forms has certainly improved over the years and you can now generate sophisticated and powerful forms with Outlook. Folder performance is better too, but do not expect sparkling access to a folder that contains several thousand items, especially if the replica you use is not collocated on your mailbox server.

The other major use of public folders is as a replacement for network file shares, the logic being that it is much easier for users to navigate through public folders than a fragmented set of network shares. Public folders can successfully take the place of network shares, but only if you take care to create an appropriate folder hierarchy and maintain the folders, which is not always the case. It is not wise to use public folders to hold documents that change frequently, such as project updates, because of the replication load that this generates. Exchange performs public folder replication on an item level and does not support delta changes, so if you change a single word in a large PowerPoint presentation or a document, Exchange has to replicate the complete item, instead of just the changed data, to all of the servers that hold folder replicas. Public folders do make good repositories for static information such as policy and procedure information, since Exchange does not begin content replication unless someone changes an item in a folder.

Few administrators rush to store more than a couple of hundred files in a network share, whereas they seem to be quite happy to accumulate many more items in a public folder, although maybe not quite as many as Outlook believes exist in Figure 7.33. Perhaps the number and size of files held

7.12 The Public Store

Figure 7.33
How many items can you hold in a public folder?

in network shares is more obvious. Just like mailbox folders, public folders can hold thousands of items. For example, any public folder that acts as an archive for a busy email distribution list can quickly capture large numbers of items. Figure 7.34 shows one of the public folders used to capture contributions to an email distribution list at HP.

Thankfully, public folder administration is easier today than ever before. Some of the early disaster areas such as the need for the infamous DS/IS Consistency Checker (which caused so many problems for Exchange 4.0 and 5.0 administrators), have been eliminated and replication normally

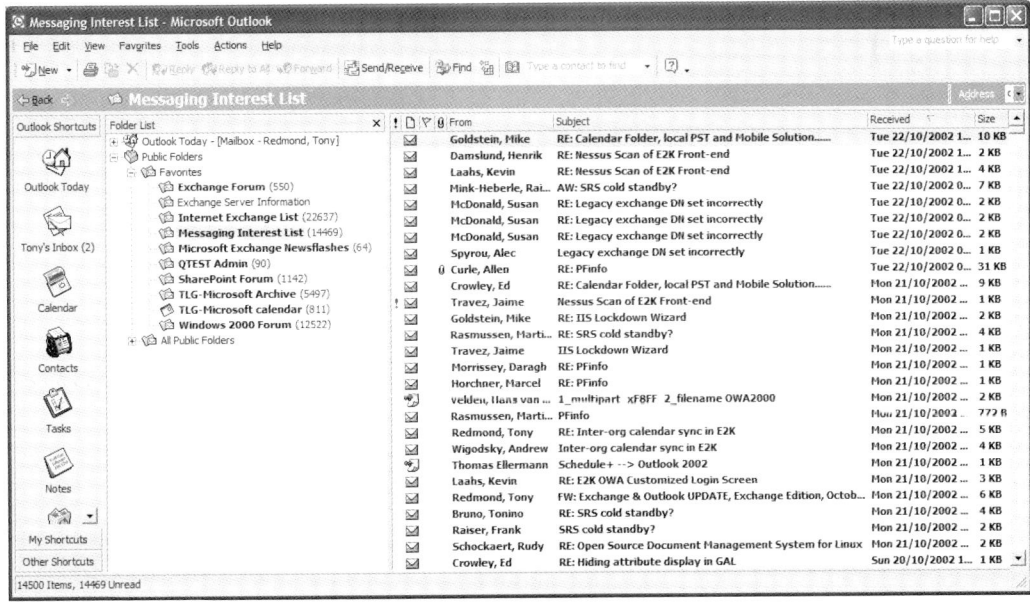

Figure 7.34 *Viewing the contents of a large public folder.*

flows smoothly. For instance, you do not have to guard against some other administrator rehoming all of the public folders from their original site into his or her site, or removing a complete set of folders from the hierarchy in a well-intentioned attempt to clean up things. As usual, everything depends on a solid design, so that is where we should begin.

7.13 Laying out a public folder design

As with any other repository intended to be a source of information to users, you need to put in some work to design a good structure for public folders. A well-designed hierarchy is easy for users to navigate and easy for administrators to manage. The design should address the following points:

- Top-level folder layout: What are the folders immediately under the root and who has the permission to create new top-level folders?

- Folder organization: Do you want to organize folders on a geographical, business unit, or other basis? The hierarchy is difficult to reorganize once it is in place, so it is a good idea to get it right the first time. You should establish a taxonomy for folder organization and communicate it to anyone who is responsible for creating or managing public folders. If you use other repositories (file shares, SharePoint Portal Server) in the company, it is a good idea to lay down rules for what content is stored and where and how it is organized and named.

- Folder naming convention: Are folders named in such a way that people can immediately understand what the folders might contain? Figure 7.35 illustrates a PF hierarchy that is easy for users to follow, because it is divided into organizational units (such as divisions) and geographies, so it should be easy to find information.

- Folder administration: Who is responsible for creating new folders? What logic drives folder creation? You do not want to restrict public folders so much as to force users to complete 14 forms before an administrator creates a new folder, but equally you do not want to grant the freedom to all to create folders unchecked. Some large companies have allowed such freedom and the resulting chaos takes months to sort out.

To manage public folders better, you may wish to move the default public folder container into a separate administrative group and assign the permissions to manage the administrative group to a limited set of users (it is best if you manage these users as a universal security group). In addition, what expectations do you have about how folder owners manage the con-

7.13 Laying out a public folder design

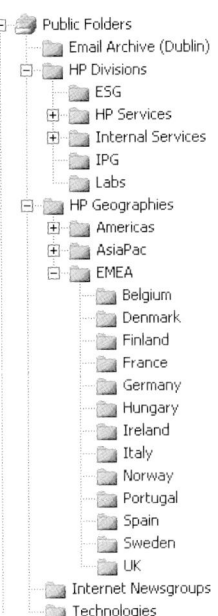

Figure 7.35
A well-laid-out PF hierarchy.

tent held in the folders? It is best practice to deny the ability for any user to create new top-level folders. Every time you introduce a new Exchange server into the organization, the installation procedure grants the ability to create new top-level public folders to "Everyone," which is not a good idea. Microsoft fixed this bug in Exchange 2003, but while you continue to deploy Exchange 2000 servers, you should check that the correct permissions remain in place after each installation and that folder creation remains restricted. It is a good idea to install all public folder servers during the early part of the deployment in order to sort out permissions, replication schedules, ownership, and so on, taking the following points into consideration:

- Folder control: What are the default values for deleted item retention, storage quotas, age limits, and so on? You have to make a decision to impose these values on an individual server-by-server basis or use a system policy to impose a policy across multiple servers. Unfortunately, the mailbox manager does not process public folders, so age limits and quotas are the only way to restrict what people can keep in public folders.

- What clients will access the public folders? If you exclusively use MAPI clients, you are restricted to a single top-level hierarchy. If you use IMAP4 or Web clients, you can create and use new hierarchies, but you need to have a good reason for doing so.

Chapter 7

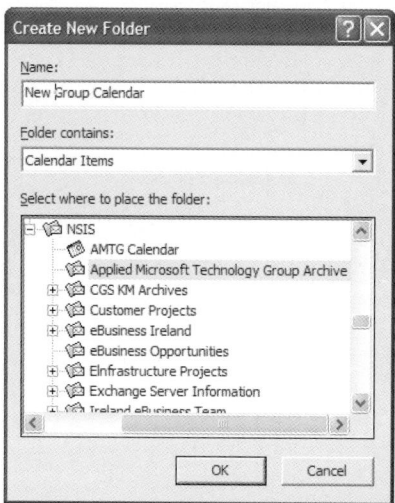

Figure 7.36
Creating a new calendar folder from Outlook.

With Exchange 2000 and 2003, you can create new folders through ESM or Outlook, and you can post items into the folder using the Exchange 2003 version of ESM (previously, posting is only supported by clients). However, if you want to use a public folder to host a shared calendar, you should create it through Outlook and select the appointment item option from the Create New Folder dialog box (Figure 7.36).

Whatever public folder design you use, make sure that top-level folder creation is restricted to a very small number of users, preferably secured through a single universal security group. If you allow people to create a folder anywhere in the hierarchy, they will, and you end up with a horrible mess.

7.13.1 Top-level hierarchies

The first versions of Exchange organize public folders into a single top-level hierarchy (TLH). In other words, there is a root (called "Public Folders") and the Store arranges the folders under the root. A single hierarchy is easy to access and the root is the obvious point to start looking for public folders, but the more folders you add, the harder it can become to navigate to the right place. Sometimes, the Exchange documentation refers to a TLH as a public folder tree.

You create a default TLH, called "All Public Folders," when you install the first Exchange server in an organization. If you migrate from Exchange 5.5, the default TLH comes over too. Today, you can create multiple TLHs, albeit with the one major caveat that the new hierarchies are invisible to

7.13 Laying out a public folder design

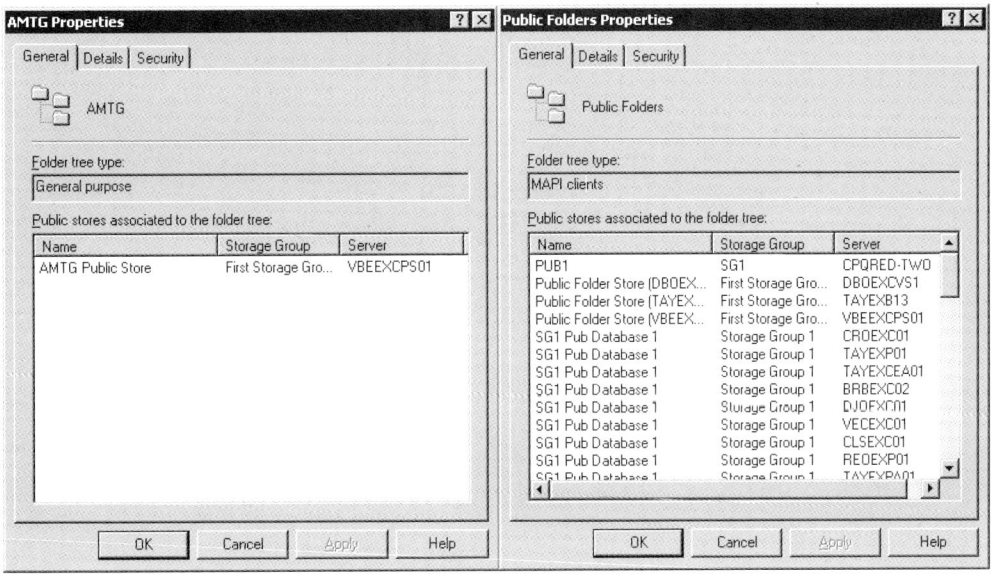

Figure 7.37   *TLH properties.*

MAPI clients, since the original MAPI design does not accommodate multiple hierarchies.

There are two problems here. First, the vast majority of clients remain MAPI, so the new hierarchies are only available to a minority of users. Second, IMAP4 and Web clients typically only use email, which further reduces the potential user community. You can use ESM to examine the properties of a TLH to know what clients it supports. Figure 7.37 shows the properties of two TLHs. The left-hand screen is marked "general purpose," which means that MAPI clients cannot see it and use the contents of its folders, while the right-hand screen is marked "MAPI clients," which means any client can access the hierarchy and content. Confused? Consider too that each TLH is associated with one or more Public Stores, and you cannot have two Public Stores on the same server sharing the same tree. In addition, the two types of TLH are very different, and you cannot change a MAPI TLH to become a general-purpose TLH or vice versa, even by manipulating their properties programmatically.

Apart from ASPs that host multiple companies in a single Exchange organization and need to offer public folders to each company, it is hard to think of major deployments that have made extensive use of multiple TLHs and equally hard to come up with reasons to argue for their creation; however, here are a few:

- Administrative control: Dividing folders across multiple TLHs allows you to assign different administrative control over complete hierarchies. For example, you could create a hierarchy for HR folders and assign permissions over the TLH to specific users. However, you could also create a subroot for HR folders under the default TLH and assign control from the subroot down. Dividing folders into multiple TLHs is really only of value when you host multiple companies in one organization and must maintain a clear separation of data between the different companies.

- Scalability: While you can create multiple Public Folder Stores, you cannot combine folders belonging to multiple TLHs in one Store. When you create a new Public Store, you associate it with a single TLH. Naturally, just as multiple Public Stores on multiple servers share the default MAPI hierarchy, you can create new Public Stores on other servers to share the same general-purpose TLH. While few companies generate enough MAPI public folders to cause scalability concerns, you can easily create a scenario where multiple companies hosted by the same Exchange organization need to use tens of thousands of folders. Here you need to create multiple TLHs to ensure that Exchange can scale to provide good service to clients when they access the folders.

- Reduce the impact of failure: If you put all your eggs into one public folder basket, any corruption of a database affects everyone who depends on a folder in the database. Dividing folders across multiple hierarchies and multiple databases mitigates the potential impact of any problem.

These factors affect few deployments, so the general advice is to pause long and hard before you create a new TLH. Remember that Outlook clients cannot see folders in general-purpose TLHs, so you have to use a redirect method by associating a link (URL) from a MAPI public folder to the folder in the other TLH. Do this by first finding out the URL to the folder with OWA and then inputting the URL in the Home Page property for the folder. When Outlook next attempts to open the folder, it will use the URL to access the contents.

7.13.2 Should you deploy dedicated public folder servers?

Older Exchange designs invariably feature dedicated servers that are set aside to host and manage public folders. This is an anachronistic hangover of old design practices that attempted to isolate mailbox and public folder traffic, largely because older servers are unable to cope with the load generated by users and background replication activities. The situation is different now. Current servers are so powerful and have so many disks available that you can usually host both mailboxes and public folders on the same server without worrying too much.

On the other hand, you can argue the case that deploying some dedicated public folder servers makes replication easier to manage because there are less Public Stores to work with. A further advantage is that by concentrating public folders on a small number of dedicated servers, you eliminate the replication traffic that Exchange generates to update folder hierarchies to every server in the organization that holds a Public Store. In a large organization, these replication messages can amount to tens of megabytes daily. You can also make a case to allocate a dedicated public folder server to host a newsfeed from USENET, if you want to host USENET feeds.

If you do decide to deploy dedicated public folder servers, make sure that your design allows Outlook clients to connect to a nearby server. Do not seek to minimize the design so much as to force clients over extended network connections each time that they need to access a public folder. Another design point is that at least one server in every administrative group must hold the default MAPI public folder tree to allow access to system folders. In addition, make sure that you replicate the system folders, such as the Schedule+ free/busy information, offline address book, and eforms registry, to the dedicated servers.

Figure 7.38 shows the replication schedule for a free/busy folder. The screen shot does not show the full name of the folder, but the hint that it is a free/busy folder comes from the folder name shown in the title bar. This begins with EX:/ followed by the distinguished name of the administrative group that owns the free/busy information. While the name might not be important, the schedule is, and in this case we can see that Exchange replicates content from this folder according to the default schedule (typically every 15 minutes) for the Public Store. You can check the replication schedule for your free/busy folder through ESM by looking through the free/busy section of the system folders. Select the folder for your administrative group and then view its properties to see the information shown here.

Even if you use dedicated public folder servers, anyone upgrading from Exchange 5.5 should review the number and configuration of existing public folder servers to determine whether you can reduce the number

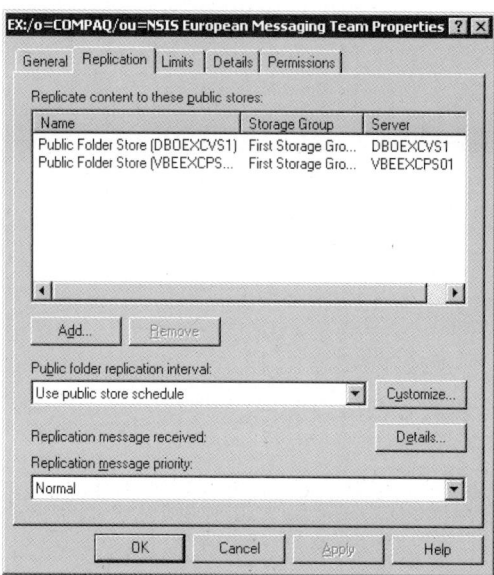

Figure 7.38
Replication for the Schedule+ free/busy folder.

of servers in the organization and reduce replication activity by removing the public folder server. Naturally, before you remove any public folder server, ensure that replicas of all the folders it hosts exist elsewhere in the organization.

7.13.3 Auditing public folders

Some companies have tens of thousands of public folders, but you have to wonder whether anyone knows what the folders hold, who manages the content and access control for the folders, why the folders were originally created, and who has a full understanding of what bandwidth the folder replication traffic consumes. These questions point to a need for public folder management that is often ignored in production when keeping email flowing becomes the major concern for administrators. Apart from the options available through ESM, you can use other utilities to manage public folders.

PFTREE (part of the Exchange Resource Kit) counts the number of folders, subfolders, and items in the default MAPI TLH, but not much else (Figure 7.39). However, it is a good way to get some statistics about the number of public folders and the information that they hold. If you record these statistics regularly, you can track the growth in public folder use. If you record statistics, you should also track the growth in size of the Public Store.

7.13 Laying out a public folder design

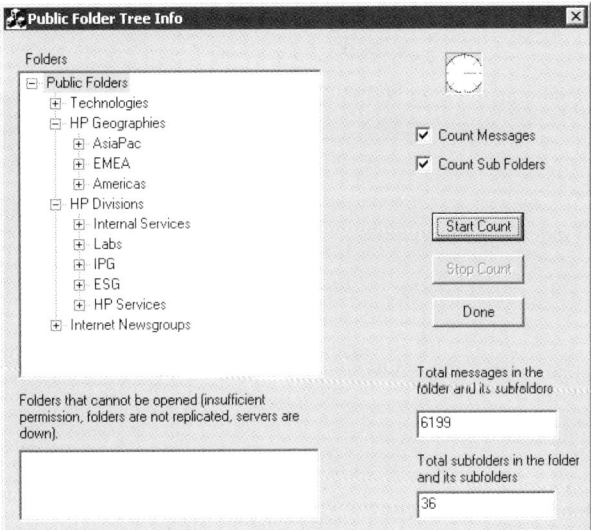

Figure 7.39
PFTREE.

The Outlook Folders program (Figure 7.40) is a more interesting utility, because it exports details of the public folders that it analyzes, which you can then open with Excel or load into a database such as Access for further analysis. This program replaces the older PFINFO utility, which was part of the Exchange Resource Kit. Outlook Folders can export a file that you can then use as input to PFADMIN, a command-line utility that you can use to create new replicas, list existing replicas, rehome a folder (Exchange 5.5 only), or even search for specific file types (e.g., find all AVI files in any public folder). The syntax used with PFADMIN is cryptic, so it is a good idea to practice on a test server before launching yourself upon a full set of production public folders. Better again, you can ask Microsoft for a copy of PFDAVADMIN (or download it from ftp://ftp.microsoft.com/pss/tools/exchange%20support%20tools/pfdavadmin/), which is an upgraded version of PFAFADMIN based on the .NET Framework, has a better user interface, and addresses some of the bugs in PFADMIN. PFDAVADMIN is good at fixing permissions that are broken on public folders, because an administrator set NT permissions through drive M: (see Microsoft Knowledge Base article 313333) and it is a good tool to use to document just what public folders you have. All of these tools use MAPI, so they do not process any folders held in alternate TLHs. Remember that these tools are not part of the Exchange product, so if they do not meet your needs, you can consider commercially available programs that report on different aspects of Exchange. For example, MessageStats from Quest Software is able to generate reports on folders and replicas.

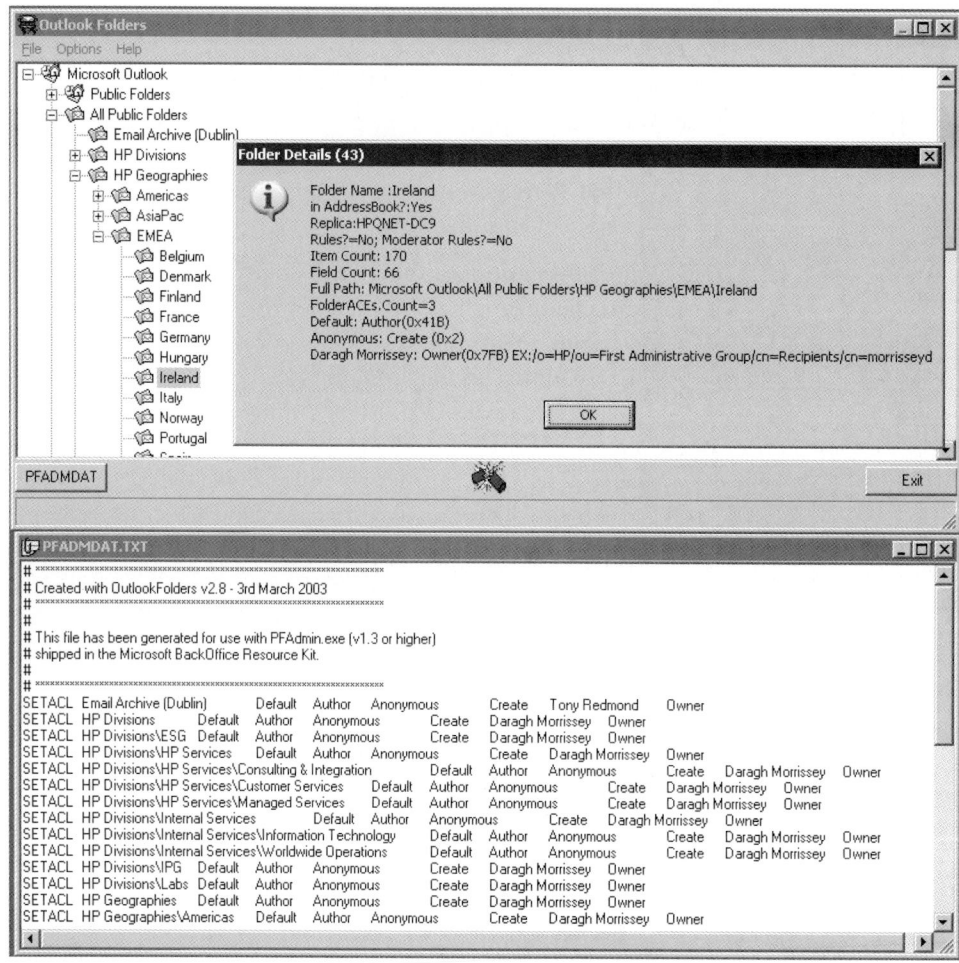

Figure 7.40 *Outlook Folders utility.*

7.13.4 Mail-enabling a public folder

A mail-enabled public folder has a set of email addresses similar to mail-enabled users and contacts, so to mail-enable a public folder Exchange must create suitable addresses (by reference to recipient policies) and stamp the addresses into the public folder object in the AD.[4] When you mail-enable a folder, it can appear in address lists and its address can be used to send and receive email. In addition, unlike MAPI and OWA clients, you need to

---

4. The AD stores the folder objects in the Microsoft Exchange System Objects OU. You can only see this OU if you use the Advanced View for AD Users and Computers console or an LDAP utility.

7.13 Laying out a public folder design

mail-enable a public folder to allow IMAP4 clients to access its contents. Windows also assigns an ACL for the folder. In most cases, you do not want to see public folders in the GAL, so the normal approach is to hide the folder from address lists.

Up to Exchange 2000, public folders were automatically mail-enabled when created. In a mixed-mode Exchange environment, folders are also automatically mail-enabled for backward compatibility with Exchange 5.5. Once you move to a native-mode Exchange organization, you have to explicitly mail-enable a new public folder if you want users to be able to post information to the folder by sending it messages. To mail-enable a folder, select it from ESM, right-click, and select "Mail Enable" (Figure 7.41).

Users do not automatically have the right to enter data into a public folder even if it has email addresses. You must also grant users the permission

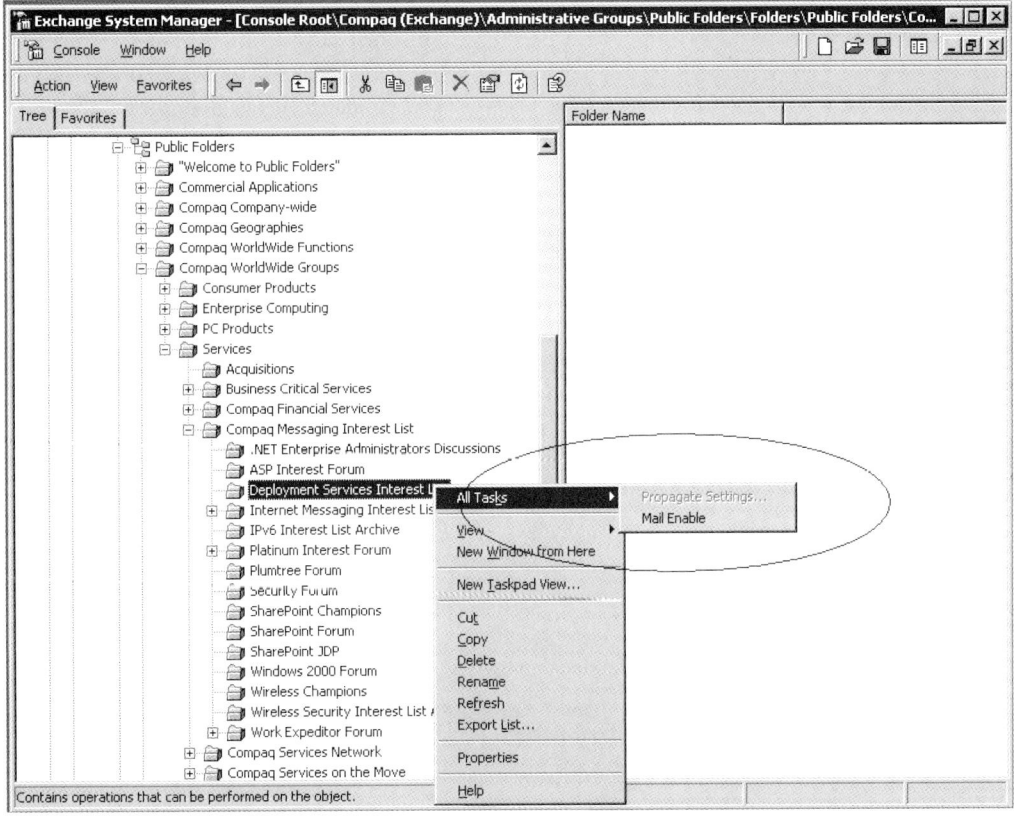

Figure 7.41   *Mail-enabling a public folder.*

to create new content in the folder. For example, if you mail-enable a public folder because you want to include it in a distribution list so that it receives a copy of every message sent to the list, you have to either add the distribution list to the folder's access control list or allocate the "contributor" role to the special "anonymous" user.

7.13.5 Public folder favorites

Because large organizations can have thousands of public folders, it would be unreasonable to ask users to navigate a complex hierarchy each time they want to access a specific folder. Public folder favorites, a unique feature of MAPI clients, allow you to access marked folders with a single click by placing them into a set of folders stored as properties of your mailbox (Figure 7.42).

Apart from being easier to access, you can also take public folder favorites offline by synchronizing them to an OST (something that happens automatically if you use the local cache in Outlook 2003). Offline storage is convenient, but it can have undesired effects. For example, let us assume that you have permissions to delete items from a folder. The same permission is active when you work offline, and situations have occurred when users have unwittingly "cleaned up" a folder offline under the impression that the delete commands only influence the OST. Unfortunately, the next time they synchronized the folder with the Store, Exchange executed all the delete commands and removed the affected content from the online folder.

Cleaning out a folder when you work offline is OK if it is a folder that holds transient content, such as newsgroup postings, but this can create difficulties if you delete copies of the current budget, operations plan, or similar documents. Fortunately, Exchange supports deleted item recovery for public folders, but only if you set a deleted item retention period for the folder. You can set a specific deleted item retention period for a folder or

Figure 7.42
Public folder favorites.

Figure 7.43
Setting a deleted item retention period.

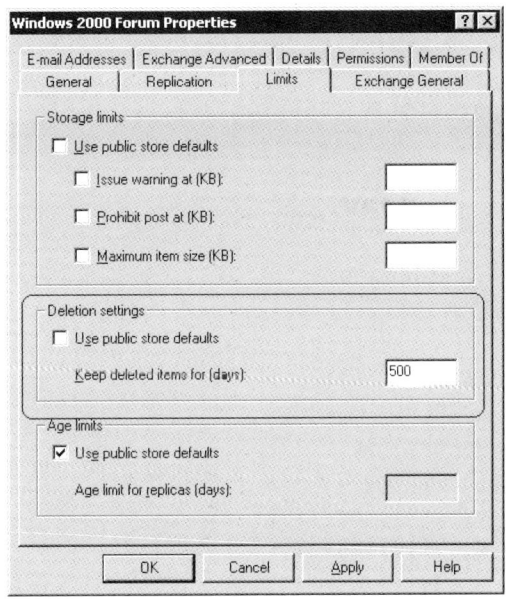

inherit the general value set for the Public Store database, and you can set the same value across multiple stores by applying a system policy. Figure 7.43 shows how you set the retention period for a folder. Five hundred days is probably a little excessive and 30 days is a more typical value.

7.13.6 Public folder permissions

You access public folder permissions through folder properties. The "permissions" page separates permissions into three separate groups (left-hand screen in Figure 7.44): client permissions, directory rights, and administrative rights.

Client permissions define which users can access the folder and the privileges they have when working with folder content. To make things easier for users, Exchange masks the complexities of Windows ACLs and security descriptors by representing permissions as a set of roles, each of which represents the collection of permissions that a user must possess to be able to perform specific actions on a folder. You can only assign folder permissions to AD objects that hold a security principal: mail-enabled accounts and mail-enabled security groups. You can assign permissions to a mail-enabled universal distribution group (UDG), but Exchange will automatically convert it to a mail-enabled universal security group (USG) afterward. This happens as soon as you use a distribution group to assign permissions to

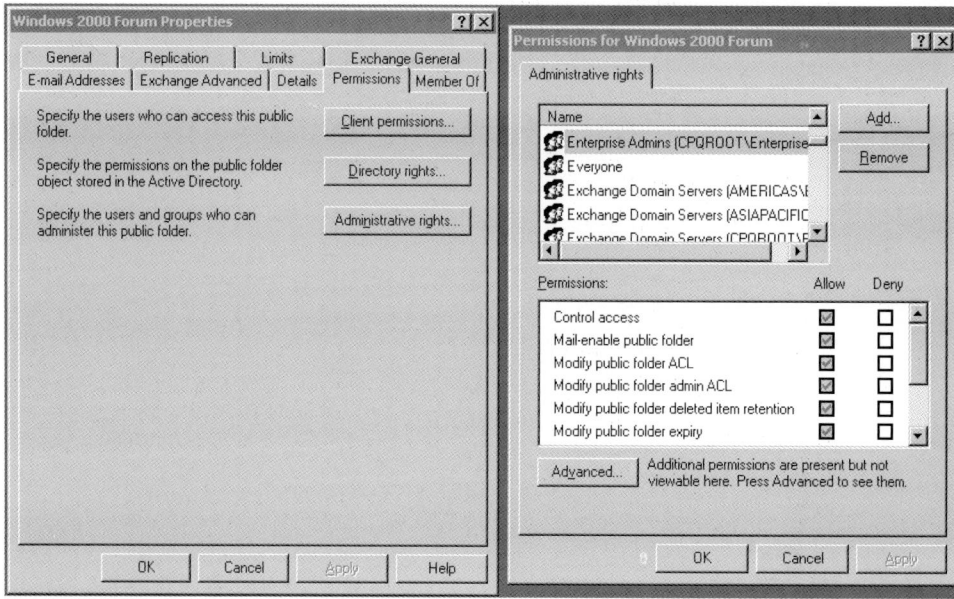

Figure 7.44   *Setting administrative permissions on a public folder.*

any AD object, and the Store updates the AD to transform the group into a universal security group. You can stop automatic group conversion by using ADSIEDIT to set the value of the "MsExchDisableUDGConversion" attribute of the Exchange organization to either 1 (to block client-initiated conversions) or 2 (to block all conversions). The default value (0) permits conversions.

The roles are:

- Owner: Users can create, read, change, and delete all items. They can create subfolders. When you create a new folder, you automatically become the owner of the folder and retain that role until you assign it to another user. More than one user can be folder owners. The folder owner is also a folder contact.

- Publishing editor: Users hold the same rights as the owner, except that they are not marked as a folder owner or contact.

- Editor: Users can create, read, and change items, but they cannot create subfolders.

- Publishing author: Users can create items and subfolders and can read everything, but they are only able to edit items that they author.

7.13 Laying out a public folder design

- Author: Users can create and read items, but they can only edit items that they author.

- Nonediting author: Users can create and read items, but they cannot edit any items, even those that they author.

- Reviewer: Users are only able to read items.

- Contributor: Users are able to create new items, but they cannot read or edit them afterward. This is the correct permission to allocate to the Anonymous user to allow anyone to post items into a public folder that you set up as an archive for a distribution list.

- None: Users cannot access the folder.

If none of these roles meets your needs, you can build a custom role and associate the set of permissions necessary for users to do their work. You only see the "Directory Rights" button if the folder is mail-enabled. When you mail-enable a folder, AD creates a folder object in the System\Exchange container under the domain root. You can see these objects by turning on Advanced View for the AD Users and Computers snap-in, and then expanding the System and Exchange containers. Folders can appear in the GAL after they are mail-enabled, but it is usual to hide folders from address lists (this option is available through the Exchange Advanced property page).

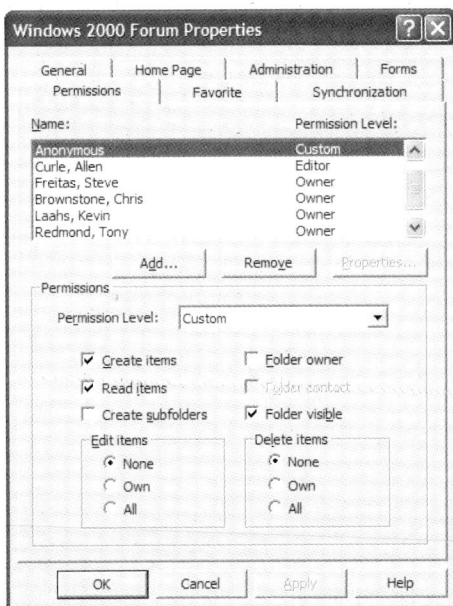

Figure 7.45
Controlling public folder access from Outlook.

Administrative rights (right-hand screen in Figure 7.44) allow you to allocate the ability to set quotas and item retention periods for the folder, modify the ACL on the folder, mail-enable the folder, and so on. You can also use Outlook to control user access to a public folder (Figure 7.45). This feature, which is unique to MAPI clients, allows you to delegate day-to-day control over a folder to someone else, usually the folder owner. However, you can obviously only use this feature with a folder that MAPI can access, so it must be in the default TLH.

Public folder ACLs can be afflicted by zombies, lingering remnants of permissions belonging to objects that used to be in a directory but do not exist today. Usually, zombies arise through a migration from Exchange 5.5, and the ACEs refer to directory entries that have not yet been migrated or no longer exist. In either case, the Exchange 2003 Store is able to detect zombies and remove them to clean up public folder permissions.

7.14 Public folder replication

A public folder exists in an organization as a single instance on its home server or as replica copies hosted by multiple servers. The Store performs replication on top of the messaging infrastructure, so connectors must be in place before any replication can take place. When multiple replicas exist, Exchange uses an email-based replication mechanism to move updated content between the replicas. Any replica can generate replication requests, because users with the appropriate permission can apply updates to any replica.

Two types of replication activity exist for Exchange: hierarchy and content. The Store replicates the public folder hierarchy to ensure that all of the servers in the organization that share a public folder tree have a common view of the folders in the tree and their properties. Hierarchy replication involves changes to the hierarchy, such as new folders, folder renames, folder deletes, and any changes that users make to folder properties. You cannot manage hierarchy replication, since this is totally under the control of Exchange. However, you can configure content replication on a folder-by-folder basis to copy the contents placed in the folder (together with all their properties) to all replicas. The Public Folder Replication Agent (PFRA), a process that runs inside the Store, manages both hierarchy and content replication. Note that the Active Directory takes care of replicating the mail-enabled properties of public folders, such as their email addresses.

7.14 Public folder replication

Microsoft designed public folder replication to:

- Bring data close to users by allowing them to connect to a local replica.

- Make data more available and resilient by keeping multiple copies around the organization.

- Avoid excessive network traffic that would otherwise be required to pull information from single points in the network.

The last point is interesting, because the single point of contact is the model adopted by Web sites and portals. The most obvious disadvantages of public folder replication are that maintaining several copies of information increases the data storage requirements of the system, and it is possible to swamp a network with public folder replication if you allow it to grow in an unmanaged fashion.

The responsibilities of the PFRA are to:

- Maintain folder replica lists so that it knows which servers host replicas of public folders.

- Monitor replication schedules and dispatch replication messages to distribute content according to the schedule.

- Send status messages to other Exchange servers to ensure that data has arrived and content does not need to be backfilled.

- Generate any necessary backfill requests if required to complete the content in any of the folder replicas that it manages.

- Respond to incoming backfill requests generated by other servers.

Replication is an advantage that public folders have over network shares. You can put documents in a public folder and Exchange will replicate the contents to other servers in the organization. You can even replicate documents in public folders between organizations using the InterOrg Replication Utility. Not many deployments have a need to use this program, because a single organization suffices, but it is useful if you need to share data between two or more organizations in the case of mergers and acquisitions, or if you simply need to operate multiple organizations, perhaps because you need to deploy different AD schemas. The free/busy system folder is the favorite replication target, because this allows users in both organizations to see each other's availability for online meetings.

The art of system design is to maximize advantages and minimize disadvantages. Obviously, you do not want to channel thousands of users toward

Chapter 7

a single folder on a remote server somewhere, but you also do not want to distribute replicas of every public folder to every server in the organization. Therefore, the trick is to create an appropriate number of replicas for each folder you want to share, and then make sure that content replication takes place at the right intervals.

When you consider the replication interval for a folder, you need to think of who are likely to want to access a folder and where they are located, and then consider creating a replica on or close to (in network terms) the server where these users' mailboxes are located. Think of the use that the folder will get. Maybe the folder is going to contain items that users frequently update, or, on the other hand, the folder may contain documents such as policy and procedure statements that the owners review and update once a year. Perhaps the folder holds items for a forms application that requires users to receive updates as quickly as possible, or it captures new items from an Internet mailing list or newsgroup for users to browse. All of these are factors that help you determine how many replicas to create, the servers where the replicas are located, and the replication schedule.

Figure 7.46 illustrates the replication status information for a public folder as displayed by ESM. The local replica (server TLGEXC01) is "In Sync," which means it is fully synchronized with its peer replicas. The other servers report "Local Modified" status, meaning that some data originated from these servers at the noted time and replicated to the connected server. However, I take these status reports with a pinch of salt, since they have never been totally accurate. The only way that you can be sure that replication works is to add an item to one replica and see how quickly it appears in

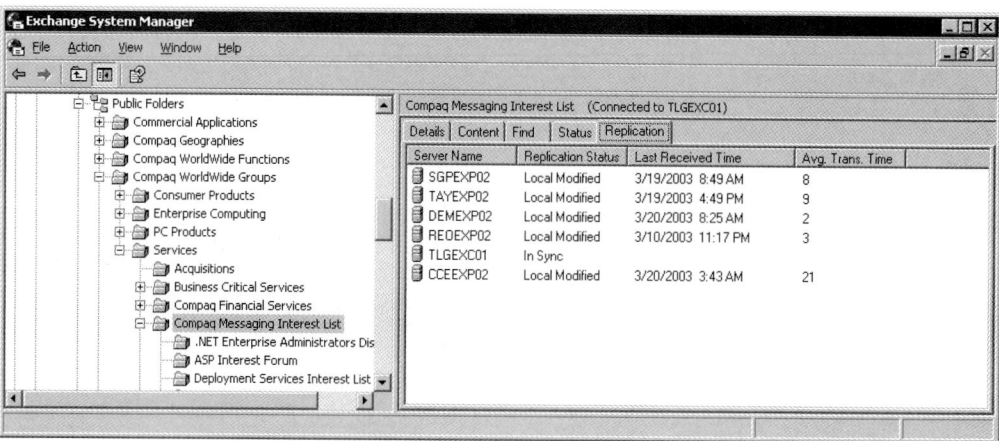

Figure 7.46 *Viewing public folder replication status.*

another. Alternatively, wait until someone says there is a problem and then find out if a replica is missing data and why.

7.14.1 Creating new replicas

You create new folder replicas by either pushing or pulling. Pushing means that the administrator of the system that hosts a public folder decides on which other servers a new replica of the folder should be created. The system administrator of any server that already holds a replica can push out new replicas of folders to other servers. You do this by selecting the desired folder, opening the Replication property page, and then selecting the new target server(s) to host the new replicas. For example, in Figure 7.47, you can see that the replica already exists on five servers, and the administrator has the option of creating a new replica on another server by selecting it from the list.

The administrator of the target server is not aware of this action. Any administrator can decide to push a replica toward another server. Because Exchange performs replication using the messaging system, as long as there is a valid messaging path between the servers and the "pushing" administrator has the necessary permissions over the receiving server, the content goes to its new home. The only indications that a new replica has been established is an increase in the number of replicas and a growth in the disk space

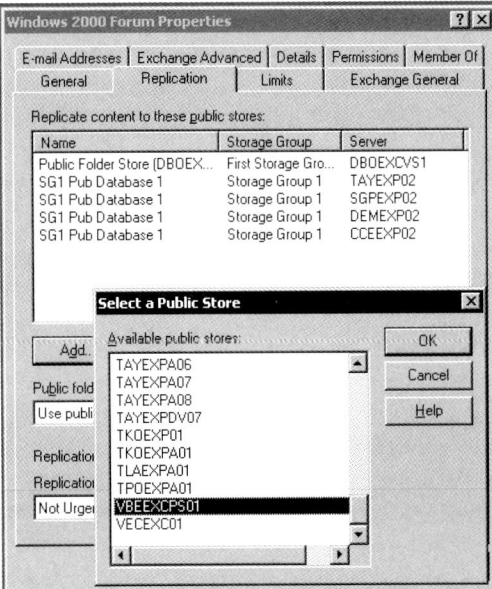

Figure 7.47
Pushing a new public folder replica.

occupied by the Public Store on the target server. Most administrators will not even be aware that a new replica has arrived!

The "push" model is only viable when you have a server that already hosts a replica (remember that Exchange treats all replicas as equivalent masters). Servers that do not already have a copy use the "pull" model. In this case, the system administrator of the server that wants to create a new replica browses through the public folder hierarchies until the desired folder is located. At this stage, you can add the replica using the same sequence as outlined previously. As soon as the change is applied, Exchange will proceed to request the host Public Store to begin transmitting the folder contents to the requesting server. Folder content arrives in a series of messages sent to the Public Store on the target server by the PFRA on the host server, so it may take some time before the local replica is available for user access.

Does it matter whether you pull or push? The answer is that either action is valid and useful, as long as you want to create the new replica and understand the consequences of your action. In most cases, the consequences are no more than an increase in the volume of messages generated within the system. The more replicas, the more messages are required to ship data around for all changes—additions, deletions, and amendments. If you allow the public folder hierarchy to grow without restraint, you create the potential that the sheer number of folders within the hierarchy cloaks valuable data. In the same way, if multiple replicas are created without restraint, a danger exists that valuable network bandwidth is absorbed by unnecessary messages being transmitted between Exchange servers.

It is interesting to reflect on the philosophy inherent in a system that allows uncontrolled distribution of replicas to occur. There is no way that a system administrator can prevent an administrator of another system from deciding that a folder created on his or her system should be pushed over the network, or indeed to create a local replica and pull content from your system. The reverse is true too. There is no method to prevent a remote system administrator from rejecting an attempt to create a replica on his or her server. The replica may arrive, but as soon as the local administrator notices its presence, he or she can remove it, sending the folder back to where it came from.

Implementation plans should address this issue by stating clear guidelines for the creation of replicas. In other words, who can create replicas and the conditions that must exist before you create new replicas. Regular checks should also be performed to see how many replicas exist for each folder, especially those that might contain sensitive information, and where those replicas reside. Finally, you should keep some basic statistics to track the growth of the number of public folders, their use, the users who access the folders, and who manages the access control list for the folders. It is also useful to know who is creating the public folders and have a procedure to allow people to inherit control of folders when the original owners move on to other responsibilities.

7.14.2 Public folder referrals

Replication gets data close to users. The alternative is to force users to come to data held on a remote location, which is what happens when you refer an attempt to access public folder content on a server in another routing group across a connector. One or more replicas of the target folder may exist in the organization. Referrals are most useful if you want to maintain a single definitive set of data rather than replicating it to several or all sites. However, client access to remote data is usually slower than when clients can access a local replica. MAPI clients use RPCs to attempt to connect to a public folder via referral. It therefore makes no sense to refer public folder accesses to a server linked via an extended X.400 or SMTP connection. If you can manage to maintain just one replica of a folder in the organization, then referrals offer a number of potential advantages over replication, including:

- No network overhead is incurred to replicate new and updated content to different servers throughout the organization.

- No latency occurs between the time when changes are made and the same data is available to everyone throughout the network.

- There is no need for conflict handling.

- You do not duplicate information in multiple locations.

By default, connectors permit referrals. Unlike Exchange 5.5, where public folder affinity is a property of a site and you can allocate different sites varying weightings to determine the order in which Exchange will try to reach a public folder replica, Exchange 2000 depends on the weighting allocated to a connector to know how to attempt referrals. If there is only one connector available for a server to use, Exchange attempts to contact a server that holds a replica in the routing group that the connector links to; otherwise, it selects a server in the routing group served by the lowest cost connector. Note that a connector is just a path for messages and plays no role in the actual connection to public folder content, since a point-to-point client to server connection establishes this using MAPI RPCs. If an

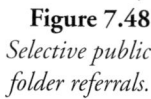

Figure 7.48
Selective public folder referrals.

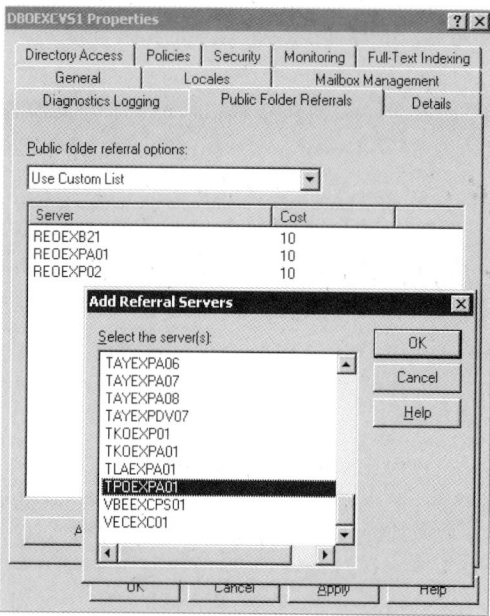

administrator has set the properties to block referrals across that connector, then the public folder is unavailable. If two connectors are available and both support referrals, the connector with the lowest cost is used.

The situation is different in Exchange 2003, because you can choose how public folder referrals behave on a server-by-server basis. The default referral mechanism continues to use the routing group topology. However, if you know that a server should always connect to a specific public folder server to fetch content, you can select the server in ESM, select the "Public Folder Referrals" property page, and then opt to use a customized list of public folder servers for referrals, as shown in Figure 7.48. This is known as a "forced referral." In all instances, whether you distribute public folders or access their content via referrals, system administrators can see the folders and replicas that exist in each administration group by browsing through the TLHs to find individual folders that seem interesting. They are then able to create a new replica on their server. The only way to prevent this behavior is to block administrative rights to the folder and deny access to everyone except a small group of users.

The case for referrals is hard to argue in terms of user convenience, and this fact is borne out by experience. Most companies that have tried to centralize public folders have not persisted because of slow network access. The most obvious advantage is the fact that a single network-wide copy represents definitive data. This cannot be said of a replicated folder, because the possibility always exists that a change to the content has been made somewhere in the network and has not yet arrived on the local server. The concept of a single definitive source of information attracts many organizations, especially when that information is critical corporate information. You have to make a decision regarding whether your network is able to facilitate fast (or at least acceptable) access times to the information. If there are many slow links in the network, replication is usually a better solution.

7.14.3 Scheduling replication

The PFRA replicates public folder data according to whatever schedule you set on a Public Store. Each Public Store has its own schedule, and you can set a specific replication schedule on a folder, so it is possible to schedule on a "fit for purpose" basis. For example, you can schedule replication for a folder that holds policy documents that you do not change very often once a week at a time when the network is quiet. On the other hand, you probably want to replicate a folder that holds data used by a forms application every 15 minutes or less to ensure that users see up-to-date information across all replicas.

Figure 7.49 illustrates both options. You can see the schedule for a Public Store on the right-hand side, while the schedule for a specific public

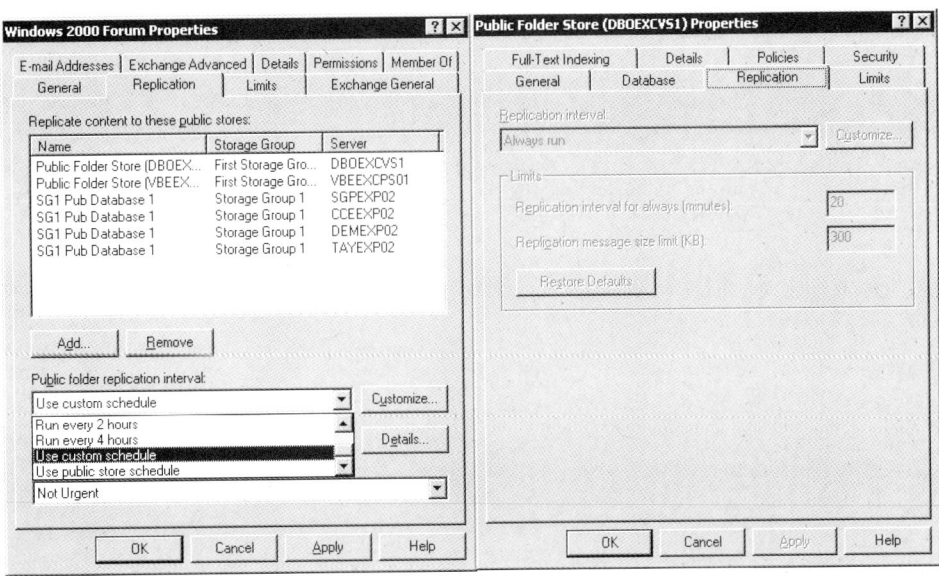

Figure 7.49 *Public folder replication schedules.*

folder is on the left. We can see that some of the fields are grayed out, which indicates that this Store is under the control of a system policy. You cannot change the replication interval, schedule, or size for this Store until you remove it from the list of Stores covered by the system policy. Note that you are able to define a precise Store schedule by changing the "always" interval to whatever value you like. In previous versions, this interval meant "every 15 minutes."

You can also adjust the size of replication messages, which is set to 1 MB in this instance. This does not mean that Exchange can only replicate items up to a maximum of 1 MB, since this would prevent replication of items such as a 5-MB PowerPoint presentation. Instead, the limit indicates the size of messages generated by the PFRA when it packs items together to send to another server. For example, if the limit is 300 KB and there are ten 90-KB messages for replication, the PFRA packs three of the 90-KB messages into a 270-KB message and sends it off, meaning that Exchange transfers four messages between servers (three of 270 KB and one of 90 KB). If a

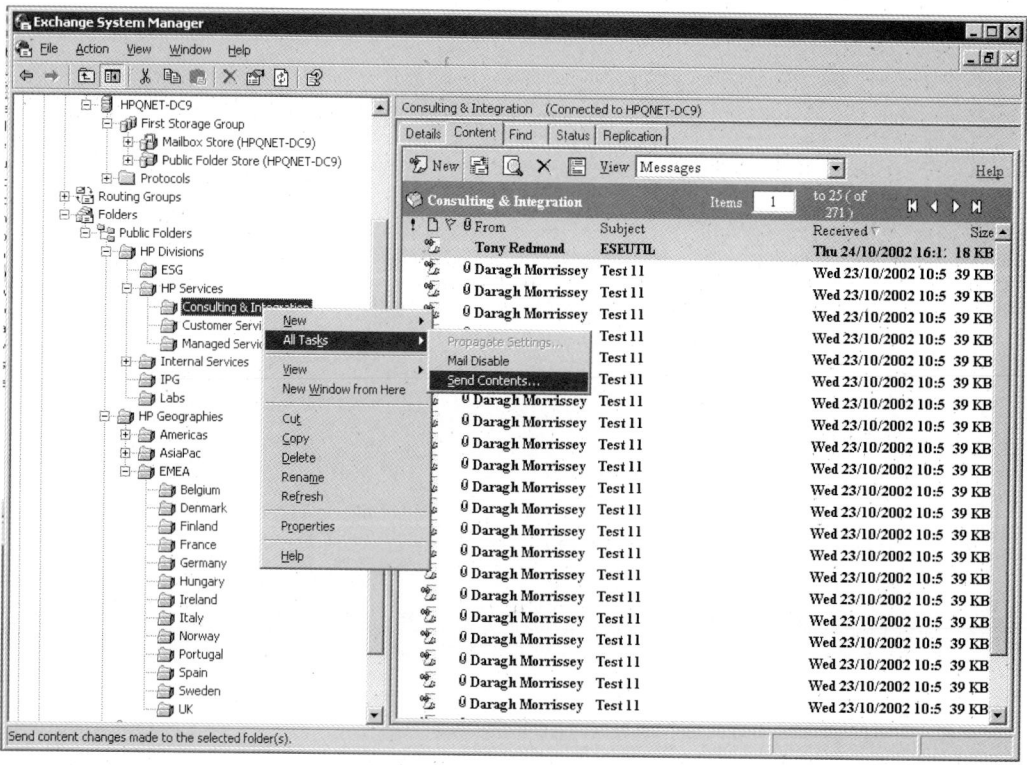

Figure 7.50   *Send public folder contents.*

user then places a 400-KB item in the folder, the PFRA cannot pack this item into a 300-KB message, but replication still needs to occur, so the PFRA takes the item and sends it on intact to replication partners.

If you want to prevent users from adding very large files to public folders, use the "Maximum Item Size (KB)" field in the Limits property page. You can also apply limits and replication settings for Public Stores through a system policy, which is the best way to ensure that multiple servers use the same settings.

Exchange 2003 includes a new "Send Contents" ESM option (Figure 7.50) to allow an administrator to select a folder and instruct Exchange to replicate any changed content immediately. You can use this option to distribute urgent information by starting an immediate replication cycle to all replicas. Replication still occurs via messages, so nothing goes unless the messaging system works.

7.14.4 When public folder replication happens

The following events cause public folder replication activity to occur:

- An administrator creates a new public folder in a public folder hierarchy.
- An administrator creates a new replica of an existing folder.
- A user adds some content to a public folder.
- The Store generates status requests.
- You add a new server to the organization and the new public store generates replication requests to build its view of the public folder hierarchy.
- The Store generates backfill requests to complete a replica.

All the servers in an administrative group automatically share the same set of public folders and top-level folder hierarchy (TLH). You can host multiple replicas of folders on servers within an administrative group, but you should only do this if users are unable to connect to a single replica per administrative group. Each replica adds replication traffic and increases the complexity of public folder management.

7.14.5 How replication occurs

The PFRA takes care of monitoring changes made to public folders but only for folders where replicas exist. The Store maintains a list of servers that hold replicas, or instances, as a property of each folder. After users add or change content in a folder, the PFRA takes care of dispatching details of the changes to all of the other servers that hold replicas, using messages sent from the Public Store to the Public Store on the recipient servers.

In addition to the relatively simple task of sending updates to other Public Stores, the PFRA maintains historical information about the state of each message in each replicated folder. The Store uses a mechanism called Change Number Sets (CNS) for this purpose. Each folder has a unique set of change numbers, based on a GUID (global unique identifier, based on 64-bit hex strings). Conceptually you can think of the number set being incremented by 1 as each change is made to a folder (addition, modification, deletion). Thus, the first item added to a folder becomes change number 1, the second number 2, and so on. The CNS for the folder is now 1–2 (the actual values are more complicated). If someone now creates a replica, the Store sends the CNS in a status message to inform the Store on the receiving server that it must backfill its new replica with the content represented by CNS 1–2. The name of the server is included to make the CNS unique. Thus, you could think of the CNS as being something like:

```
EXCH-SRVR\PUBIS\0174345
```

The change number shows that this is change number 174,345 generated by the Public Store on the EXCH-SRVR server. Of course, real change numbers are in an encoded fashion that makes sense to computers, not humans, so this example is purely to illustrate the point. The PFRA maintains a list of all predecessor change numbers for a Public Store, meaning that the agent is able to recognize the most recent or current message.

The Store generates a status message containing the current CNS for each replicated folder daily and sends it to all servers that hold replicas. This message serves to prime the replication system and ensure that any servers that receive the message will check the folder replication status and request backfills for any missing data. The CNS is also included in every message that contains replicated content, a step that ensures that backfill will occur even if a server misses any status messages for some reason.

The simplest replication task involves new items. When a user adds a new item to a folder, the PFRA creates a new change order and sends it along with the content of the new item to all of the other servers that hold instances of the folder. The receiving servers check the incoming replication message to determine whether they have already received the content. If the checks pass, the local Public Store inserts the new item into its copy of the folder. Deletions follow a similar path, except that the PFRA only sends instructions to remove the items. Updates are slightly more complex, because the local Store must verify that the incoming change is for the same version or a later version of the message that it holds.

If permissions allow, all servers are entitled to modify items. The Store always applies modifications to local instances, so the local PFRA takes responsibility for informing the other servers that a change has occurred. When a modification message arrives to a Public Store, it replaces the original content, but only if the modification is more current than the existing message. The Store uses the change number on the message and the predecessor change list to determine whether it should apply the message. If the Store discovers that it has content that is more up-to-date than the content in the replication message, it realizes that a potential conflict exists, and a conflict resolution process begins. "Process" is too powerful a word here, because it implies that Exchange uses some form of artificial intelligence to resolve concurrent updates applied to the same content from multiple points. This is not the situation, because the process is manual. The users who attempt to update the content receive a conflict notification and copies of all the changes. They can proceed to resolve the conflict manually by reviewing all the changes and merging them together into an agreed-upon copy, or just take the option to apply their original change—which is what normally happens!

7.14.6 Monitoring the flow of replication

Replication should flow smoothly as long as messages pass between Exchange servers. The inability of users to access a folder is the most commonly reported problem, and the reason for this is usually one of the following: The user does not have the necessary permission to access a folder, or a local replica does not exist and a referral to a remote replica is not possible across a connector.

Insufficient permissions are the most common problem, but if not, replication might not be working. The easiest way to check if a problem exists in the messaging infrastructure is to send a message to a mailbox on the server that hosts the replica. Set a delivery receipt on the message so Exchange notifies you when the message reaches the server. If you get a delivery notification, you know that messages are flowing between the two servers and you can assume that Exchange can send and receive replication messages. You can use the Message Tracking Center to follow the path of the message, providing that administrators have enabled the message tracking on all servers along the message's path. However, if you receive a deliv-

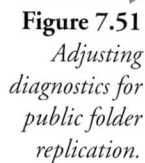
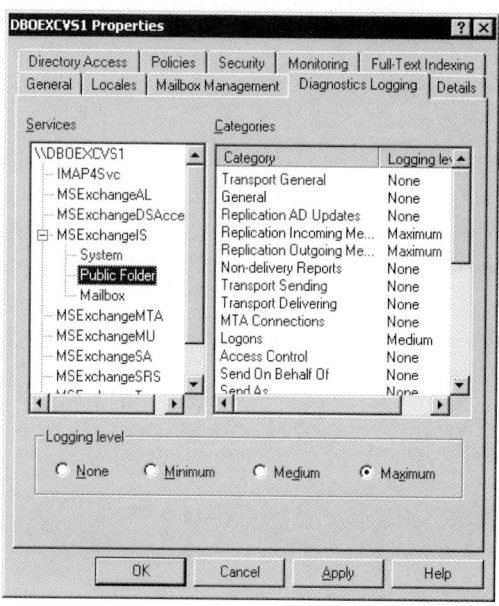

Figure 7.51
Adjusting diagnostics for public folder replication.

ery notification, this step is not necessary unless you have another reason to track the progress of a message.

The next step is to turn up the diagnostics setting for the "MSExchange IS\Public" object and then examine the collected information. The normal diagnostics setting is "None," meaning that Exchange only records errors in the Application Event Log. You can set the various replication categories (such as "replication incoming messages") to "Medium" or "Maximum" to see how Exchange processes replication requests (Figure 7.51). Be warned that a large volume of events will accumulate quickly on servers that host busy public folders or servers that replicate content at short intervals.

Once you have increased the diagnostic level, you can add an item to the public folder to force replication to occur. Select the folder that the user cannot access and set its replication interval to "Always." Add some content to the folder and observe the information written by the Store in the event log.

Figure 7.52 illustrates two typical replication events as reported in the event log. The left-hand screen (event 3028) reports that the Store has processed an incoming replication message for a subtree in the Compaq Worldwide Functions folder. You can clearly see the minimum and maximum values of the CNS (1-2e2-4690CDA to 2e2-4690DED), which makes little sense to people. The message type is 0x2 (2), meaning that this message

7.14 Public folder replication

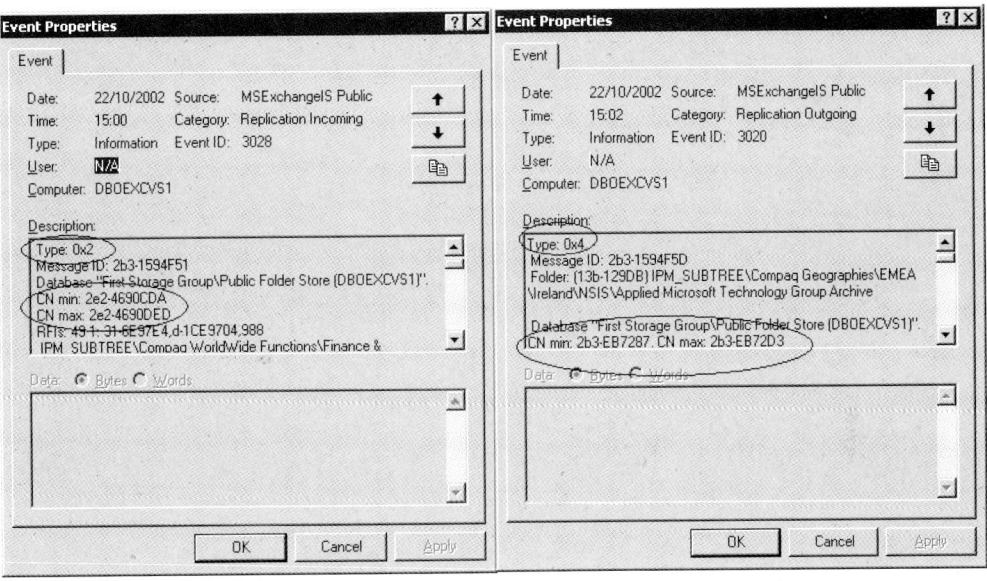

Figure 7.52   *Typical replication events.*

contains new folder information being replicated from this server to another server. In other words, a user has created a new folder under the Compaq Worldwide Functions folder. By contrast, the right-hand screen (event 3020) reports details of an outgoing replication message. The message type is 0x4 (4) and you can see the full path to the folder where someone added, changed, or deleted content. Again, the event reports details of the CNS.

Other valid message type codes are:

8: Backfill requests—a server is requesting some backfill data to complete its replica.

10: Status message—the server is reporting the CNS for one or more folders to other servers.

20: Status request—the server is looking for a replica of a folder to retrieve information or is reporting that it is still active.

Matching the diagnostic information collected in the event log with the knowledge you have of the public folder hierarchy and replication intervals provides invaluable background knowledge of how the PFRA works. This is a subject often ignored by system administrators, only to become a hot topic when things go wrong and everyone is wondering why replication is not working, or why too much replication activity is going on.

7.14.7 Backfilling public folders

Backfilling describes the process by which a server updates the content in a public folder replica with information that is missing for whatever reason. Backfilling also occurs when you create a new folder replica to populate the folder with content. System outages include hardware crashes, which may cause an administrator to restore a Public Store on a server. A restored database is often out-of-date in some respect, and may lack some content replicated from other servers since the server's last full backup. The Store usually recovers most of the missing content when it replays transaction logs to make the database consistent, but often some content was en route when the outage occurred. Therefore, when you restart the server, the Store checks incoming replication messages from other servers and then uses the change numbers in the messages to update its predecessor change list. Examining the change numbers reveals if any gaps exist in the predecessor change list, and, if this is the case, the Store begins the process of filling the gaps, or backfill.

The Store begins by generating a backfill entry, which is literally a placeholder inserted into the database to indicate that some data is missing. It then proceeds to dispatch requests for assistance to two other servers (chosen at random) that also hold replicas of the folders that are missing information. The request specifies what the missing content is and requests the receiving server to generate a message containing the content and send it back to the requesting server.

Exchange never executes backfill messages immediately after receiving a response from a remote server. Instead, it keeps the messages in a queue for up to two hours to await the arrival of messages containing the original content that was marked as missing. If the waiting period elapses, it sends a message containing the backfill request to the store on the folder's home server. When the home server receives the backfill request, the Store examines its detail to determine what content is required, as defined by the CNS. The Store then generates one or more messages with the missing data and sends them off. The Store also sends a status message that contains details of the current CNS from the home server to inform the replica what the current situation is. The Store continues to make backfill requests until the CNS of the replica is the same as the CNS on the home folder.

With Exchange 2003, you can set the preferred server for backfilling public folder content by updating the AD with the GUID of the preferred server in the msExchPreferredBackfillSource attribute on the target Exchange servers' Public Store objects. Alternatively, you can update the registry, again using the GUID. Neither approach is exactly people friendly, since it is all too easy to make a mistake when you type in a GUID. Microsoft PSS has scripts to help you, so if you ever need to force backfill behavior in this way, contact PSS and ask them to help.

Sometimes, replication happens in odd ways. For example, after you install a new server into an organization, the Store mounts the new public store and begins the process of building a copy of the public folder hierarchy. To do this, the Store has to broadcast status request messages to other servers that host public folder stores in the organization. So far so good, and you would expect that the nearest public folder store (perhaps one in the same administrative group) would process the request and return the necessary data. However, Exchange uses a security mechanism to ensure that it does not respond to unauthorized requests. The mechanism consists of checking that the sender's address exists in the AD (in this case, the sender is the public store on the new server). To avoid potential performance problems, Exchange performs the check against a local cache of known public store, but, of course, the new server may not exist in the cache because Exchange only refreshes the cache hourly. Two problems now kick in. First, local servers may not respond to the incoming status request, because they do not know about the new public store. Second, a remote server (in some cases, a very remote server) may be the server that initiates the request and begins replication. This may not seem a problem, because it does not take much data to replicate a complete public folder hierarchy. The problem becomes more apparent when the new server begins to issue backfill requests to its newly discovered replication partner and ignores servers that are local in network terms because they ignored the initial status request. After an hour or so, this temporary condition should pass, as the public store caches refresh, and further backfill requests should flow more efficiently.

7.14.8 Replicating public folders with Exchange 5.5

You have to create a public folder connection agreement with the ADC before you can replicate public folders between Exchange 5.5 and Exchange 2000/2003 servers. A public folder CA replicates details of the public folders so that each type of server knows about the information held on the other. For example, the CA creates entries for Exchange 5.5 public folders in the Microsoft Exchange System Objects OU of the AD (Figure 7.53). Because public folders are "owned" by sites in an Exchange 5.5 organization, you need a separate CA for every site to create a full set of public folders in the AD. Public folder CAs are always two-way to ensure that public

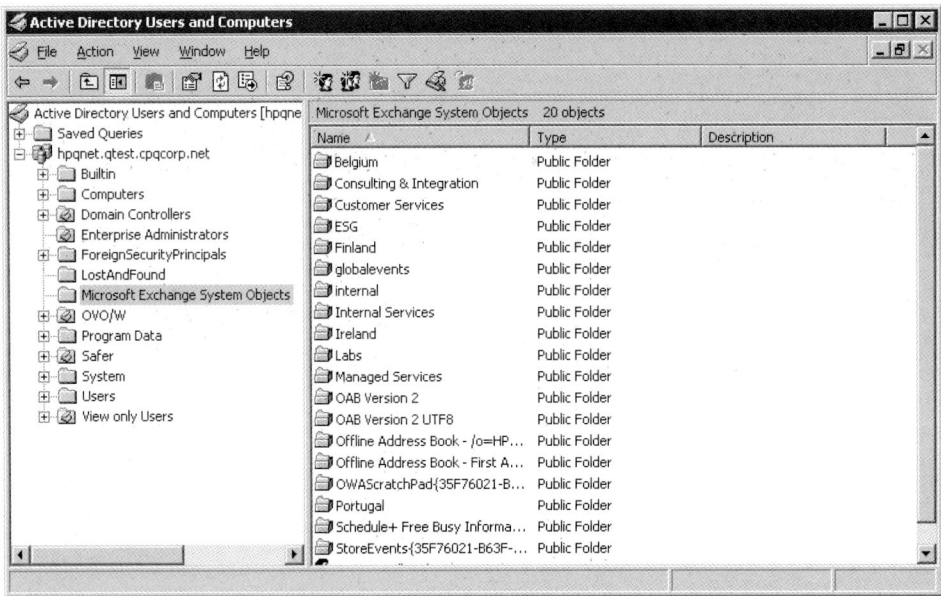

Figure 7.53   *Public folders in the AD.*

folder information is consistent on both sides, and, unlike user CAs (which replicate information about users, contacts, and groups), you cannot change the source and target destinations, since these are predefined.

7.14.9 Erasing zombies

The upgrade from Exchange 5.5 to Exchange 2000/2003 incorporates a fundamental change in security, as Windows ACLs replace the old Exchange-specific public folder permissions maintained in the DS. Permissions form part of the attributes of a folder, and the Store automatically converts the old format to the new as you upgrade servers. However, occasional inconsistencies can creep into the process (typically a failure to convert old Exchange permissions to Windows ACLs), which can lead to user problems, such as the inability to see public folders or bad performance when browsing the public folder hierarchy. Even after you complete the upgrade from Exchange 5.5, you can still experience problems if public folder ACLs contain lingering Exchange 5.5 permissions that, for one reason or another, failed to convert in the past. These attributes are zombie permissions, because they can never go anywhere, since there are no Exchange 5.5 servers to resolve the old format permissions.

If you suspect that you have a problem with zombie permissions, perhaps because users report that they cannot see folders, you can set a registry value to instruct the Store to ignore zombie Exchange 5.5 permissions always. To do this, open the registry and then navigate to the following key:

```
HKLM\System\CurrentControlSet\Services\MSExchangeIS\
ParametersSystem\
```

Then, create a new DWORD value called "Ignore zombie users" and set it to 1. While it is nice to eliminate zombies, you should not set this parameter unless you have eliminated any other possible cause for the reported problem. The parameter is valid on Exchange 2000 SP3 and Exchange 2003 servers. See Microsoft Knowledge Base article 327167 for more information.

The PubFoldCheck utility (part of the ExDeploy toolset) allows you to scan public folders and remove nonuser accounts from public folder ACLs, in much the same way as the old DS/IS Consistency Checker (some would say "wrecker") cleans up public folder permissions. This is an effective way of removing potential zombie accounts from public folders as you migrate Exchange 5.5 servers to Exchange 2003. To use PubFoldCheck to remove the zombies, execute the following command:

```
ExDeploy.exe /t:PubFoldCheck /s:"server"
```

where "server" is the name of the Exchange 5.5 server that you want to run the utility against. Typically, this is a dedicated public folder server.

7.14.10 Problems with public folder replication

The problems with public folder replication are many and varied. First, you have to decide how many replicas are required. Next, you have to distribute the replicas throughout the organization in such a way that you do not flood servers with replication traffic but still maintain fast access for users. Third, you have to decide how to channel user access. In Exchange 5.5, the site model determines access, and Exchange uses a simple preference algorithm that favors server, location, site, and then a remote replica. Public folder affinity defines how Exchange selects replicas on different servers. In Exchange 2000/2003, routing groups supersede the site model and referrals to remote replicas via connectors replace affinity. Planning referrals or affinity can get quite complex in a large, distributed organization, and it is probably one of the least understood administrative concepts for Exchange.

Assuming that you manage to place a sufficient number of replicas out in the organization, have no replication issues, and users can always get fast access to folder content, the next issue that looms is replication clashes. Exchange has no way to check documents for exclusive access, and public folders follow a multimaster replication model where all masters share equal status in terms of the definitive copy of an item. Thus, you can get into a situation where two or more users decide to edit the same item concurrently, each connecting to a different replica. The problem does not occur if there is only one replica, because the Store can then prevent two users from attempting concurrent edits. Now let us assume that the users finish their work and commit their changes back into the public folder. The Store recognizes that a change has occurred and replicates update information to the folder replication partners, but at the same time, other servers take the same action, which leaves the Store in a "replication clash" scenario when the competing changes arrive. Exchange does not possess artificial intelligence or insight into the minds of the respective authors, so it throws its hands up in disgust and lets the people sort out the problem. Naturally, any user believes that his or her change is absolutely the most important information, so the user accepts the update and discards the others—a scenario that is likely to occur on other servers.

In early versions of Exchange, it was possible for administrators to browse the public folder hierarchy, find folders that seemed to hold interesting information, and instruct Exchange to create a new local replica on their server. Exchange 5.5 allowed administrators to eliminate this practice by setting a property on public folders to limit administrative access to the home site. In other words, if you set the property, remote administrators could not then decide that they would like to set up a new replica. Practical experience demonstrated that many administrators missed this subtle but important point and replica numbers continued to expand in most deployments.

The migration from Exchange 5.5 to Exchange 2000/2003 is an excellent opportunity to conduct a full review of public folders and replicas. At the same time, you can look at each folder to decide whether its original purpose is still valid, and you should keep the folder or delete it to help clean up the public folder hierarchy. While you check each folder, take the time to review who the folder owner is, whether he or she still wants to be the folder owner (some people forget they have ownership if they take up new responsibilities), and the other people who access the folder. It is best practice to use distribution lists to control access to public folders, since this reduces the number of entries in the access control list, and it is easier to grant or deny access to folders through a simple edit of a distribution list. When you move public folders from Exchange 5.5 to Exchange 2000, the Store upgrades the access control list from Exchange-specific permissions to Windows 2000 permissions, and cleans up the access control lists by removing users who no longer need access to make the migration less complex.

7.14.11 Long-term options for public folders

When public folders first appeared, they offered some significant advances over network shares as document repositories and included such things as electronic forms, document routing, workflow, and so on. After nearly a decade, public folders have aged badly, and Microsoft has not succeeded in developing their capabilities to a point where every Exchange installation can point to a successful and useful deployment. The attempt to broaden acceptance through multiple top-level hierarchies has foundered through excessive complexity and the lack of MAPI support, plus the simple fact that public folders are just too hard to manage in large deployments. It was always doubtful that it was a good idea to add extra hierarchies without a suite of management tools to control and rationalize existing public folders and so it has proved to be in reality. Finally, public folders are hard to search, so looking for a specific item can be like looking for the proverbial needle in a very large haystack.

Perhaps Microsoft never really believed in public folders or maybe it lost interest after the original vision faded. It is also true that other imperatives took engineering attention as Microsoft fought a bitter email war against Lotus. Indeed, you can argue that Microsoft lost complete interest in public folders as soon as it could claim that it had beaten Lotus for corporate messaging prominence, since public folders have seen very little progress since.

However, I think that the real reason is that Microsoft has better technology that it can sell outside Exchange. This technology features document versioning, check-in and check-out facilities, basic approval routing, a good search engine, the ability to index public folders (backward compatibility), browser and Windows Explorer interfaces, good integration with Microsoft Office applications, and it's easy to deploy. While no version of SharePoint Portal Server (SPS) yet supports replication—possibly the only real advantage that public folders now hold—you can argue that the advantages of replication are overvalued given that most companies have sufficient bandwidth to allow users to access a single definitive source of information and do so by deploying Web sites all the time. In addition, the management problems that replication can bring make the prospect of deploying multiple replicas around an organization less attractive.

On the other hand, public folders are free with Exchange and deploying SPS incurs additional cost, since you must license every client. You also have to deploy some client software if you want to access documents in an SPS portal through Windows Explorer and Office applications, and there is the small matter of additional hardware, because you cannot deploy Exchange and SPS on the same server, plus the cost of different antivirus and backup tools, and so on. The good news is that migration utilities (see http://workspaces.gotdotnet.com/spimport for a copy) now exist to export the contents of public folders as file libraries or discussion lists with attachments and then import them into an SPS 2003 portal as topic areas or into a Windows SharePoint Services site. Similar migration utilities exist to move data from other repositories, such as Windows file shares, Lotus QuickPlace, and eRoom, so it is possible to look at SPS as a catchall repository. The migration utilities are not perfect, but they are a start and the developers plan future enhancements to improve the accuracy of the export and import operations.

SPS is, therefore, no silver bullet to address all the inadequacies found in public folders, but it is an option for organizations that want to deploy lightweight document management or department-level portals. With some care in planning, SPS is capable of serving very large organizations too, although its management tools are still raw.

The future of public folders is unclear. You cannot anticipate a massive investment in engineering time from Microsoft to make public folders a comprehensive platform for document-centric applications, and short of a complete redesign, it is difficult to see how they will progress. For this reason, it is best to treat public folders as an ad-hoc repository for documents and messages and look to other solutions like SharePoint Portal Server for anything more sophisticated.

7.15 ExIFS—the Exchange Installable File System

When Exchange 2000 shipped, it came with a new installable file system called ExIFS, or the Exchange Installable File System. Since then, people have spent a lot of time figuring out just how useful ExIFS is. Apart from the technical aspect of being able to navigate the contents of mailboxes and folders in the same way you can move within the NTFS directory structure, it is difficult to pinpoint exactly how ExIFS enhances Exchange.

Originally, Microsoft's grand plan for the second generation of Exchange, beginning with Exchange 2000, was to transform the Store from an application-specific repository to be an enterprise repository. This meant that you would be able to hold much more than simple email items and attachments in the Store and that many more clients would emerge to become consumers of the Store. Of course, the Store has been able to deal with any type of attachment since day zero, but the consumer side was limited to email clients. Over time, the client set grew, but never went past an email focus. At one time, some at Microsoft believed that public folders could be a candidate to replace network shares and tried to sell this idea to anyone who would listen. However, the grand plan foundered, because public folder access is limited to MAPI, IMAP, and browser clients, and most public folder implementations suffered from poor performance as soon as you stored more than a couple of hundred items in a folder. Other issues existed to limit the universal usefulness of the Store, but performance and client access are large problems to solve.

Another issue is the long-term direction for the Store. When Microsoft designed ExIFS, the Microsoft .NET initiative had not taken root and the concept of presenting data and application services based on common standards such as XML did not exist. Basing Store access on a rudimentary file access protocol such as SMB does not make sense in a .NET world, so there is not the same need or interest for something like ExIFS.

Hindsight is a wonderful way to look at anything. Given today's knowledge, it might not seem that Microsoft took a bold move in Exchange 2000 when it introduced ExIFS in an attempt to open up the Store, but at the time, ExIFS was an interesting and worthwhile advancement. Microsoft reasoned that if it engineered support for the SMB protocol into the Store, then any application that used SMB to access a file system (normally FAT or NTFS) would be able to use the Store. These applications might want to access messages, attachments, and other items held in the Store, but, more attractively, developers might make the decision to use the Store as the preferred repository for application-specific data. Another attraction for application developers is that they can use ExIFS to access the Store without generating RPCs. Applications such as Web browsers and the Internet Protocol virtual servers (POP, IMAP, etc.) that Exchange uses deal with files using standard NT file operations. The presence of ExIFS allowed these servers to continue with the normal approach of passing buffers, sockets, and file handles to what seemed to be a normal file system, whereas Exchange hides behind the screen. Apart from anything else, performance is better if you manipulate files like this instead of via RPCs, because Windows has no user-mode processing to perform.

ExIFS works by mapping the Store and representing it in a form that applications supporting SMB can understand. In Exchange 2000, this means that applications see drive M: (you can change the drive letter if required) as the entry point to the Store. If the application has sufficient permission, it can navigate down through drive M: to access the contents of mailboxes and public folders.

HTTP-DAV presented another issue for ExIFS. Getting to a file is one thing; getting to a file and all the metadata that surrounds it to make it a mail message or attachment is another. HTTP-DAV allows programmers to avoid MAPI RPCs and is more in line with the .NET direction, so the combination of performance and access to more data means that it is hard to argue for ExIFS as a general-purpose programming interface.

ExIFS still survives in Exchange 2003, albeit in a more restricted and background role. Most of the reasons for this positioning are that the experience gained with ExIFS since the launch of Exchange 2000 has not been good. Sure, applications can certainly access the contents of the Store through ExIFS, but instead of using this ability in a good and productive manner, applications tended to use ExIFS as a way around the protection that Exchange normally gives to the Store when you access it through a client such as Outlook or an API such as CDO or ADO. Well-behaved applications respect permissions, but examples exist where applications have used ExIFS to try to work around permissions and break security, attempt to take backups, or even use ExIFS as a well-intended route to protect mailboxes against viruses. Backups are a specific instance, where the file-level-type access available to backup utilities via ExIFS is enough to destroy all of the contextual information that Exchange needs to know, including where data fits into stores, mailboxes, and public folders. You can certainly take a backup through ExIFS, but you have little chance of being able to reassemble all the pieces from the resulting save set if you ever need to restore. Some people have tried, all have failed, and all have had a hugely frustrating time when they discovered just how important contextual information is.

The net result from these experiences is that Microsoft now views ExIFS as merely an internal file system that Exchange can use for its own purposes to perform optimal streaming and I/O activities such as data transfers across process boundaries. The Store also uses ExIFS in some of its interactions with the STM file.

The net result of this experience is that Microsoft took the decision to hide the ExIFS drive from view in Exchange 2003, and you have to reveal it if you decide that you have some applications that could use ExIFS. In most cases, it is best to leave well enough alone and let ExIFS sink back into the mists of hidden processing performed on an Exchange server.

7.15.1 The role of ExIFS

Even though ExIFS no longer has the future originally mapped out by Microsoft, it is still interesting to explore the technology because it is still used by Exchange 2000 and Exchange 2003. ExIFS allows Win32-based programs to map mailboxes and public folders in the Store as if they were just another network drive, and this fact is leveraged extensively by the virtual protocol servers hosted in the INETINFO (IIS) process to perform file-type data manipulation on Store data with minimal overhead.

Figure 7.54 shows how ExIFS links Win32 programs to the Store. Common Win32 file manipulation functions (CreateFileEx, ReadFileEx, FindFileFirst, etc.) called by programs such as Windows Explorer that want to use Store data are directed to a logical device that is managed by a kernel-mode driver called EXIFS.SYS, which also handles programmable access to content via the FileSystemObject object. Note that programs access the STM file using ExIFS, because its storage is file oriented rather than the traditional database page-style layout used in the EDB. The role of ExIFS is to intercept and redirect the function calls made by the applications to the Store. As far as programs such as Windows Explorer are concerned, they make calls to retrieve and process data stored on a DOS device. In essence, ExIFS makes the contents of the Store appear to Win32 applications as a collection of folders and individual files in exactly the manner they would expect to see when browsing any other DOS device. ExIFS also supports all the file system–related functions exported from KERNEL32.DLL.

Figure 7.55 shows ExIFS in action. In this case, I have logged on to my mailbox with Outlook Express and can scroll through the items in the Sent

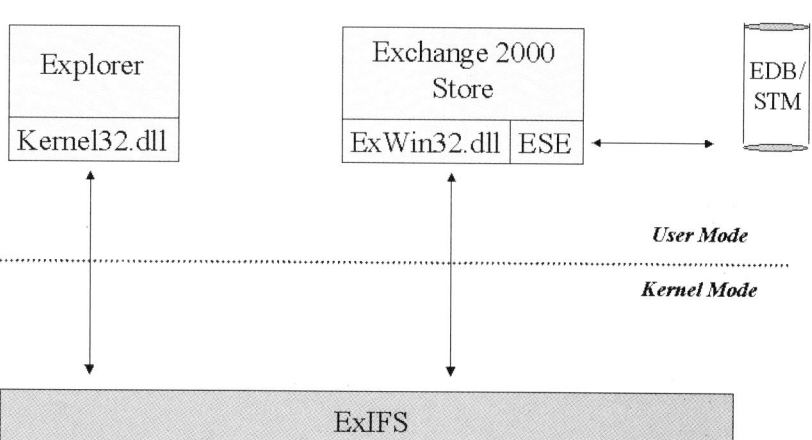

Figure 7.54
ExIFS architecture.

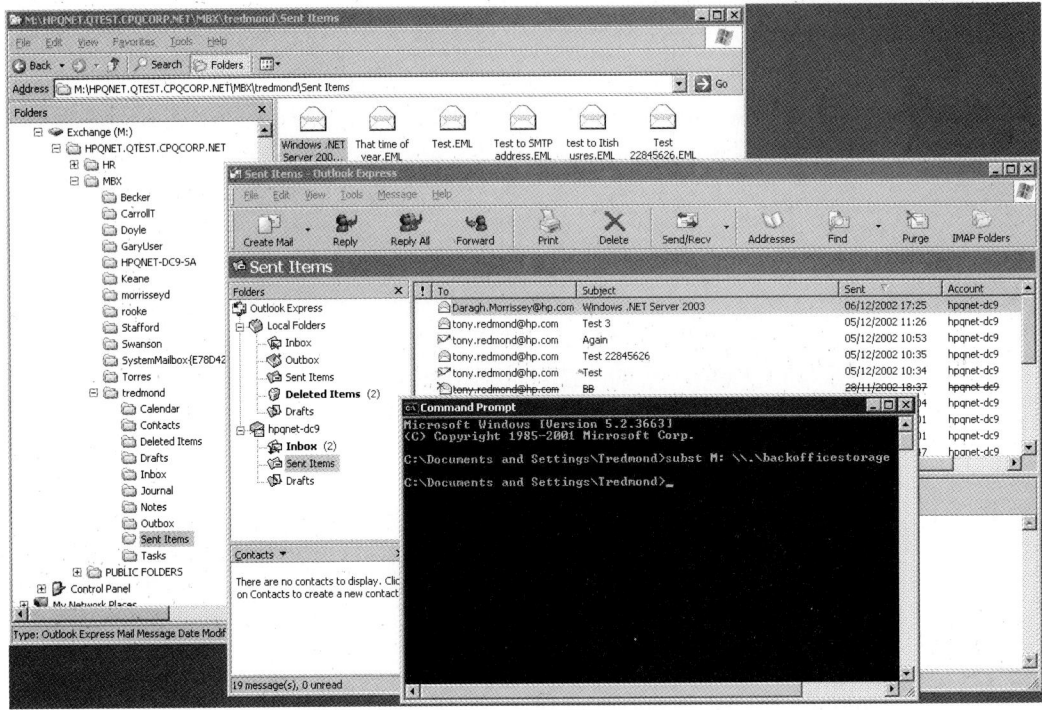

Figure 7.55 *Viewing the same items through Windows Explorer and Outlook Express.*

Items folder. In the background, Explorer browses the same items using its normal interface. Outlook Express connects with IMAP; Explorer sees the mailbox content via ExIFS.

The right-hand Explorer pane shows the "MBX" folder. This is the logical root for all mailboxes on the Exchange server and individual mailboxes show up as folders under MBX. Standard Windows permissions prevent unauthorized access to a mailbox via ExIFS. All the mailboxes are visible (in the same way as you can see other users' mailboxes in the GAL), but any attempt to access a folder in someone else's mailbox is firmly denied. However, unlike the GAL, ExIFS lists folders for hidden mailboxes.

After you install Exchange 2000, users can map to their own mailboxes by using the M: drive as a network share. M: is the default drive letter allocated by ExIFS when it loads, connects to the Store, and initializes the file system. If a server already has allocated drive M: for another purpose, ExIFS selects the next available letter. Apart from the fact that Microsoft Mail used an M: drive and that "M" stands for "Mail," there is no great architectural reason why Microsoft selected M: as the default letter for ExIFS. Probably each one of the engineers involved in the design has his or her own version of why this particular letter was chosen. In practical terms, M: avoids the most common letters allocated on servers (the selection of C:, D:, E:, F:, G:, and H: probably cover the letters allocated to volumes on 80 percent of all servers), but Microsoft could equally have selected another letter toward the other end of the scale (such as X:). However, administrators often allocate letters toward the end of the alphabet to network shares and the easiest way to avoid conflict is to select a letter in the middle.

ExIFS creates a folder for a user under the M: drive root the first time an item appears in his or her mailbox. If users wish, they can map another DOS drive to their own mailbox or public folder, and, indeed, issue a NET USE command to make a folder available to other users as if it were just another network share. There is no doubt that being able to map a mailbox like a DOS drive is very cool, and it does hammer home the message of "access from anywhere" in an effective manner. Taking our analogy of a database as file system a little further, the picture is complete now because ExIFS allows you to view the content of messages and other items within the Store represented as individual files arranged within a file system. The biggest advantage delivered by ExIFS is that you do not have to install any additional software on a client system before you can use ExIFS as long as the standard network redirector is available.

The Store and IIS must be operational before you can access the contents of the M: drive. If either of these components is not running, the M: drive is unavailable to applications and users. Thus, if you have an application that depends on the M: drive (perhaps to create a document in a particular folder) and access the drive through a network share, you have to make sure that you share out the drive each time Exchange 2000 is started. However, it is not a good idea to use ExIFS as the basis for any application access, because there is no guarantee that Microsoft will continue to support ExIFS in future releases of Exchange.

Unlike Exchange 2000, both SharePoint Portal Server and Exchange 2003 hide the ExIFS drive. You must expose the ExIFS drive temporarily or permanently to access its contents from the command prompt or Windows Explorer. In addition, if you run Exchange 2000, you can go the reverse route and hide the ExIFS drive by following the instructions in Microsoft Knowledge Base article 305145.

To expose ExIFS temporarily, use the SUBST command from a command prompt to map the special backofficestorage mechanism, as follows:

```
C:> SUBST M: \\.\backofficestorage
```

Exchange 2000 uses drive M: by default, so it should be available without the need to make a change to the server. You can select any other unused letter if you prefer, although it is a good idea to have a common approach across all servers. You have to update the registry to change the drive letter used by ExIFS or on an Exchange 2003 server if you want to expose the ExIFS drive permanently. Do not reenable the ExIFS drive unless you have a good reason to do so. To enable the drive or change the existing allocated letter, go to the key:

```
HKEY_LOCAL_MACHINE\SYSTEM\CurrentControlSet\Services\
EXIFS\Parameters
```

Then select the "DriveLetter" value or add it if it does not exist, and type "M" or whatever drive letter you chose into the value. Figure 7.55 shows the SUBST command and the same data viewed from Outlook Express and Windows Explorer. In this case, we are looking at the Sent Items folder. In Windows Explorer, the items have a .EML extension and a message icon, while Outlook Express displays them as normal.

Figure 7.56 illustrates the point. In this case, we access the contents of an Exchange folder via DOS. In DOS terms, the folder path is the Windows domain name followed by the "MBX" root, mailbox alias, and then folder name. Once mapped, you can use DOS commands to manipulate the items and folders within the mailbox. For example, you can add a new file by copying it into the mailbox from another directory on another drive. To demonstrate this point in action, Figure 7.57 shows the result when I

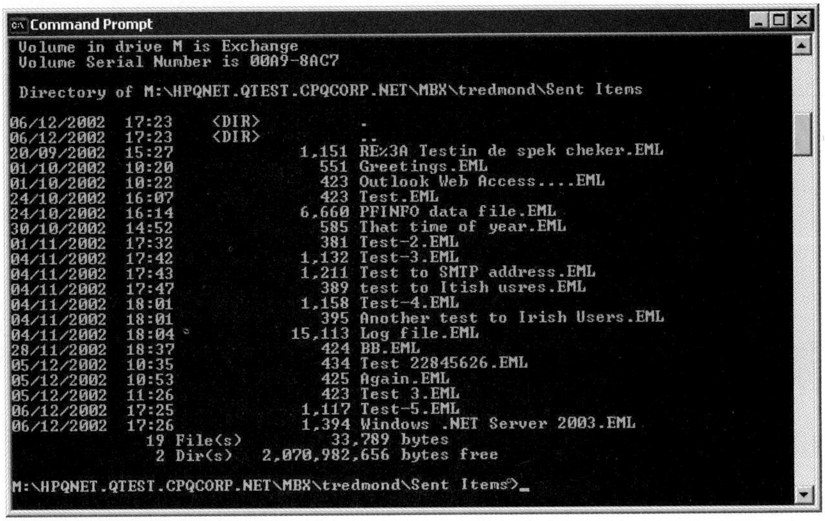

Figure 7.56
Listing an Exchange mailbox folder with the DOS DIR command.

used the TYPE command to display the contents of an email, which Exchange identifies by giving the item an .eml extension when it generates its DOS file name.

Figure 7.57
Example output from DOS TYPE command (Outlook Express 6.0).

```
From: "Tony Redmond" tredmond@hpqnet.qtest.cpqcorp.net
To: mmecti@hp.com
Subject: Access to MSDN and TechNet
Date: Fri, 6 Dec 2002 17:52:17 -0000
MIME-Version: 1.0
Content-Type: multipart/alternative;
    boundary="----=_NextPart_000_0023_01C29D50.37DC1570"
X-Priority: 3
X-MSMail-Priority: Normal
X-Mailer: Microsoft Outlook Express 6.00.3663.0
X-MimeOLE: Produced By Microsoft MimeOLE V6.00.3663.0

This is a multi-part message in MIME format.

------=_NextPart_000_0023_01C29D50.37DC1570
Content-Type: text/plain;
    charset="iso-8859-1"
Content-Transfer-Encoding: quoted-printable

Folks,

With reference to yesterday's message about the new arrangement for HP =
employee access to MSDN and TechNet, the question was asked if you would =
have electronic access to the Microsoft MSDN site. We have checked this =
and confirm that all registered employees will have access. =
= 20
------=_NextPart_000_0023_01C29D50.37DC1570
Content-Type: text/html;
    charset="iso-8859-1"
Content-Transfer-Encoding: quoted-printable

<!DOCTYPE HTML PUBLIC "-//W3C//DTD HTML 4.0 Transitional//EN">
<HTML><HEAD>
<META http-equiv=3DContent-Type content=3D"text/html; =
charset=3Diso-8859-1">
<META content=3D"MSHTML 6.00.3663.0" name=3DGENERATOR>
<STYLE></STYLE>
</HEAD>
<BODY bgColor=3D#ffffff>
<DIV><FONT face=3DArial size=3D2>Folks,</FONT></DIV>
<DIV><FONT face=3DArial size=3D2></FONT> </DIV>
<DIV><FONT face=3DArial size=3D2>With reference to yesterday's message =
about the new=20
arrangement for HP employee access to MSDN and TechNet, the question was =
asked=20
if you would have electronic access to the Microsoft MSDN site. We have =
checked=20
this and confirm that all registered employees will have access.= 20

</LI></UL></SPAN></DIV></BODY></HTML>

------=_NextPart_000_0023_01C29D50.37DC1570----
```

While it might seem obvious, it is important again to emphasize that ExIFS deals with Store data just like files, so a lot of metadata goes missing when you use ExIFS. Some message metadata is always present, because it is part of the information held alongside message content in the STM file. Essentially, this is the data specified by RFC 822, such as message subject, recipients, originator, and so on, so this explains what you see when you use TYPE to view the message. When Exchange fetches message data with ExIFS, it also fetches the metadata from the EDB file through the epoxy layer and ends up with a complete message. DOS-like programs such as TYPE have no knowledge about epoxy, metadata, or anything to do with messaging, so they ignore this data. The Store performs the work to combine STM data with EDB data and with information such as priority, flags, attachments, and so on and presents the message body part in the correct format (plain text, RTF, or HTML). Clients do not need to be aware that these complexities exist and can concentrate on the user interface.

The output listed in Figure 7.57 comes from a short note sent to a distribution list. If you view this output through a DOS command box, the content scrolls continually to the screen until it reaches the end and is impossible to follow, so it is better to redirect output to a text file to examine the message structure. In this case, Outlook 2000 generated the message in RTF format (it could also have been generated in HTML) and stored it in a mailbox. When ExIFS receives the request from DOS to provide content, it retrieves the message and converts it into a readable format.

For many good reasons, including the experience Microsoft gained of ExIFS in action and the advent of Microsoft .NET, while a good foundation was laid by enabling file system access to Store data in Exchange 2000, Microsoft decided not to develop the technology further in Exchange 2003, so we are left with an incomplete work. For example, ExIFS does not support all possible Win32 calls. Enough is there to allow programs to insert and retrieve messages and attachments from the Store exactly as they request information held on an NTFS or FAT drive. As a demo, the technology works and proves the point that SMB-compliant applications can map and access Store data, but Microsoft did not understand the ramifications of the access well enough.

In the examples, where we use the DOS TYPE command to examine the content of a message, you see raw content without formatting or reference to any of the properties that clients merge with content to represent the totality of any item in the Store. No support is available for DOS-level access to calendar, tasks, or journal items. You can see the file names of

7.15 ExIFS—the Exchange Installable File System

these items, but any attempt to access a file results in the message "The system cannot find the file specified."

Because of its flaws and shortcomings, it is best if you leave ExIFS alone to its internal function, where Exchange can take care of all of the interaction between EDB and STM, Store and IIS, client and server. ExIFS is an interesting demonstration, showing that technology can bridge the gap between data and wildly different representations (DOS and Outlook, for instance), but it is not a prime time component any more. HTTP-DAV is often the best solution if you want programmatic access to Exchange data.

8

Performance and Clusters

It is easy for system designers to become preoccupied by performance. It is good to know that a specific system configuration can cope with a specific workload, and you can run performance tests until the cows come home to demonstrate that Exchange is able to cope with thousands of mailboxes. Unfortunately, this position guarantees that you miss two facts. First, because it is difficult to assemble thousands of real-life users and get them to create a workload for a server, the normal course is to run performance tests with a simulated workload. Of course, this demonstrates that the server can cope with a simulated workload and therefore creates a certain amount of confidence before deployment, but it is no guarantee that the system will achieve the desired performance in production. Real users have an annoying habit of doing things that no self-respected simulated user would, such as deciding to send a message with a 10-MB attachment to a huge distribution list, and this type of behavior skews system predictability.

The second factor is raw CPU performance. An Exchange benchmark exceeded the 3,000 mailboxes per server level in 1997, yet few system designers rush to put more than 3,000 mailboxes on a production server even though CPU clock speed has increased dramatically since. Benchmarks now suggest that you can easily support tens of thousands of Exchange mailboxes on the latest servers, but few go past the 3,000 sticking point unless they are sure that they have the right combination of rock-solid operations procedures wrapped around industrial strength server and storage hardware. The fact is that the steady increase in server speed reduced the need to worry about Exchange performance long ago. Most modern servers will cheerfully handle the load that your user population generates, and you can crank up the number of mailboxes on a server to levels that seemed impossible just a few years ago. Of course, increasing mailboxes on a server is not wise unless you know that you can manage them, but that is not the fault of either the software or the hardware.

A discussion about Exchange performance is, therefore, more about how you can run performance tests and the type of hardware configurations that you might deploy at the high end rather than a pursuit of the last possible piece of speed. Therefore, that is what we cover in this chapter: aspects of Exchange performance, the performance tools, high-end standard servers, the role of storage, and a discussion about clusters. Performance changes with hardware and developments in this area evolve rapidly, so it is best to use this chapter as a guideline for places you need to investigate rather than to expect the definitive text (which would fast become outdated).

8.1 Aspects of Exchange performance

The earliest Exchange servers were easy to configure. You bought the fastest processor, equipped the server with as much direct connected storage as it supported, and bought what seemed to be a huge amount of memory (such as 128 MB). System administration was easier, too, since the number of supported mailboxes on servers was not large. Table 8.1 charts the evolution of typical "large" Exchange server configurations since 1996 and especially illustrates the growth in data managed on a server. Today, we see a trend toward server consolidation, as companies seek to drive down cost by reducing the number of servers that they operate. The net result of server consolidation is an increase in the average number of mailboxes supported by the typical Exchange server, an increasing desire to use network-based storage instead of direct connected storage, and growing management complexity with an attendant need for better operational procedures and implementation.

The growing maturity of Windows and the hardware now available to us help server consolidation, but the new servers that we deploy still have to be balanced systems suited to the application in order to maximize results. A

Table 8.1 *The Evolution of Exchange Server Configurations*

Version	CPU	Disk	Memory
Exchange 4.0	Single 100-MHz/256-KB cache	4 GB	128 MB
Exchange 5.5	Single 233-MHz/512-KB cache	20 GB	256 MB
Exchange 2000	Dual 733-MHz/1-MB cache	>100 GB	512 MB
Exchange 2003	Quad 2-GHz/2-MB cache	SAN	4 GB

8.1 Aspects of Exchange performance

balanced system is one that has the right proportions of CPU power, storage, and memory. After all, there is no point in having the fastest multi-CPU server in the world if you cannot provide it with data to process. Storage and good I/O management are key points in building Exchange servers to support large user communities.

Exchange performance experts often aim to move processing to the CPU and keep it busy on the basis that a server that hums along at 10 percent CPU load may be underloaded because it is waiting for I/Os to complete. This illustrates the point that a system is composed of multiple elements that you have to balance to achieve maximum performance.

8.1.1 Storage

Storage becomes cheaper all the time, as disk capacity increases and prices drop. However, configuring storage is not simply a matter of quantity. Instead, for Exchange servers, you need to pay attention to:

- Quantity: You have to install enough raw capacity to accommodate the space you expect the O/S, Exchange, and other applications to occupy for their binaries, other support files, and user data. You also need to have sufficient capacity to perform maintenance operations and to ensure that the server will not run out of space on important volumes if users generate more data than you expect.

- Resilience: You have to isolate the important parts of the overall system so that a failure on one volume does not lead to irreversible damage. The basic isolation scheme is to use separate physical volumes to host the following files:
    - Windows O/S
    - Exchange binaries
    - Exchange databases
    - Exchange transaction logs

- Recoverability: Tools such as hot snapshots need a substantial amount of additional space to work.

- I/O: The sheer capacity does not matter if the storage subsystem (controller and disks) cannot handle the I/O load generated by Exchange.

- Manageability: You need to have the tools to manage the storage, including backups. Newer techniques such as storage virtualization may be of interest if you run high-end servers.

You can build these qualities into storage subsystems based on direct-connected storage to the largest SAN. The general rule is that the larger the server, the more likely it is to connect to a SAN in order to use features such as replication, virtualization, and business continuity volumes. Indeed, you can argue a case that it is better to concentrate on storage first and build servers around storage rather than vice versa, because it is easier to replace servers if they use shared storage.

Best practice for Exchange storage includes:

- Always keep the transaction logs and the Store databases isolated from each other on different physical volumes.

- Place the transaction logs on the drives with the optimal write performance so that the Store can write transaction information to the logs as quickly as possible.

- Protect the transaction logs with RAID 1. Never attempt to run an Exchange server in a configuration where the transaction logs are unprotected.

- Protect the Store databases with RAID 5 (minimum) or RAID 0+1. RAID 0+1 is preferred, because this configuration delivers faster performance (twice the speed of RAID 5) with good protection.

- Multispindle volumes help the system service the multiple concurrent read and write requests typical of Exchange. However, do not attempt to add too many spindles (no more than 12) to a RAID 5 volume. Deciding on the precise number of spindles in a volume is a balancing act between storage capacity, I/O capabilities, and the background work required to maintain the RAID 5 set.

- Use write cache on the storage controller for best performance for transaction log and database writes, but ensure that the controller protects the write cache against failure and data loss with features such as mirroring and battery backup. You also need to be able to transfer the cache between controllers if the controller fails and you need to replace it.

Storage technology evolves at a startling rate and we have seen the price per GB driven down dramatically since Exchange 4.0 appeared. New technologies are likely to appear, and you will have to make a decision regarding whether to use the technology with your Exchange deployment. Sometimes vendors make it unclear whether Microsoft fully supports the technology, and this is especially so with respect to database-centric applications such as Exchange and SQL. For example, Network Attached Storage (NAS) devices seem attractive because they are cheap and allow you to expand storage easily. However, at the time of writing Microsoft does not support NAS block-mode devices with Exchange and does not support any file-mode NAS devices. There are a number of reasons for this position, including network latency for write operations and redirectors introduced between the Store APIs and the Windows I/O Manager (see Microsoft Knowledge Base articles 314916 and 317173 for more information, including Microsoft's support policy for NAS devices). The Hardware Compatibility List (available from Microsoft's Web site) is the best place to check whether Microsoft supports a specific device, and it is also a good idea to ask vendors whether they guarantee that their device supports Exchange. Another good question is to ask the vendor to describe the steps required to recover mailbox data in the event of a hardware failure. However, technology changes and newer devices may appear that eliminate the problems that prevent Microsoft from supporting NAS and other storage technology. For this reason, you should consult a storage specialist before you attempt to build a storage configuration for any Exchange server.

8.1.2 Multiple CPUs

Given the choice, it is better to equip Exchange servers with multiple CPUs. Since Exchange 5.0, the server has made good use of multiple CPUs. Best practice is to use multi-CPU systems instead of single-CPU systems, with the only question being how many CPUs to use. Here is the logic:

- It does not cost much to equip a server with additional CPUs when you buy servers, and adding a CPU is a cheap way to extend the lifetime of the server.

- The extra CPU power ensures that servers can handle times of peak demand better.

- Add-on software products such as antivirus scanners consume CPU resources. The extra CPUs offload this processing and ensure that Exchange continues to service clients well.

- New versions of Windows and Exchange usually include additional features that consume system resources. If the new features support SMP, the extra CPUs may allow you to upgrade software without upgrading hardware.

- Adding extra CPUs after you build a server can force you to reinstall the operating system or applications.

- The performance of any computer degrades over time unless you perform system maintenance, and, even then, factors such as disk fragmentation conspire to degrade performance. Some extra CPU power offsets the effect of system aging.

Note that secondary cache is important for symmetric multiprocessing. Secondary cache is a high-performance area of memory that helps prevent front-side bus saturation. Large multi-CPU servers are inevitably equipped with a generous secondary cache, with the general rule that the more, the merrier.

With these points in mind, it is a good idea to equip small servers (under 1,000 mailboxes) with dual CPUs, and large mailbox servers with four CPUs. Going beyond this limit enters the domain of high-end systems and is probably not necessary for the vast majority of Exchange servers. Few people find that something like a 32-way server is necessary to support Exchange and that it is easier and cheaper to deploy servers with fewer CPUs. If you are tempted to purchase a system with more than eight CPUs, make sure that you know how you will configure the system, the workload it will handle, and the additional benefit you expect to achieve.

8.1.3 Memory

The various components of Exchange, such as the Store, DSAccess, Routing Engine, and IIS, make good use of memory to cache data and avoid expensive disk I/Os, so it is common to equip Exchange servers with large amounts of memory, especially since the price of memory has come down. It is always better to overspecify memory than install too little, since server performance is dramatically affected by any shortage of memory.

The Store is a multithreaded process implemented as a single executable (STORE.EXE), which runs as a Windows service and manages all the databases and storage groups on a server. As more users connect to mailboxes and public folders, the number of threads grows and memory demands increase. The Store is reputed to be a particular "memory hog," because it uses as much memory as Windows can provide. However, this behavior is by design and is due to a technique called Dynamic Buffer Allocation, or DBA, which Microsoft introduced in Exchange 5.5. Before Exchange 5.5, administrators tuned a server with the Exchange Performance Wizard, which analyzed the load on a running server and adjusted system parameters. Specifically, the wizard tuned the number of buffers allocated to the Store to accommodate an expected number of connections. However, the wizard used no great scientific method, and much of the tuning was by

8.1 Aspects of Exchange performance

guesswork and estimation. If the actual load on a server differed from the expected load, the tuning was inaccurate.

Microsoft implemented DBA to provide a self-tuning capability for the Store and ensure that the Store uses an appropriate amount of memory at all times, taking the demands of other active processes into account. DBA is an algorithm to control the amount of memory used by the Store and is analogous to the way that Windows controls the amount of memory used by the file cache and the working set for each process. To see the analogy, think of I/O to the Store databases as equivalent to paging to the system page file.

DBA works by constantly measuring demand on the server. If DBA determines that memory is available, the Store asks Windows for more memory to cache more of its data structures. If you monitor the memory used by the Store process, you will see it gradually expand to a point where the Store seems to use an excessive amount of memory, a fact that can alarm inexperienced system administrators who have not experienced it before. For example, in Figure 8.1 you can see that the Store process occupies a large amount of memory even though the system is not currently under much load. This is the expected situation and if another process becomes active that requires a lot of memory, the Store process shrinks if Windows cannot provide the required memory to that process.

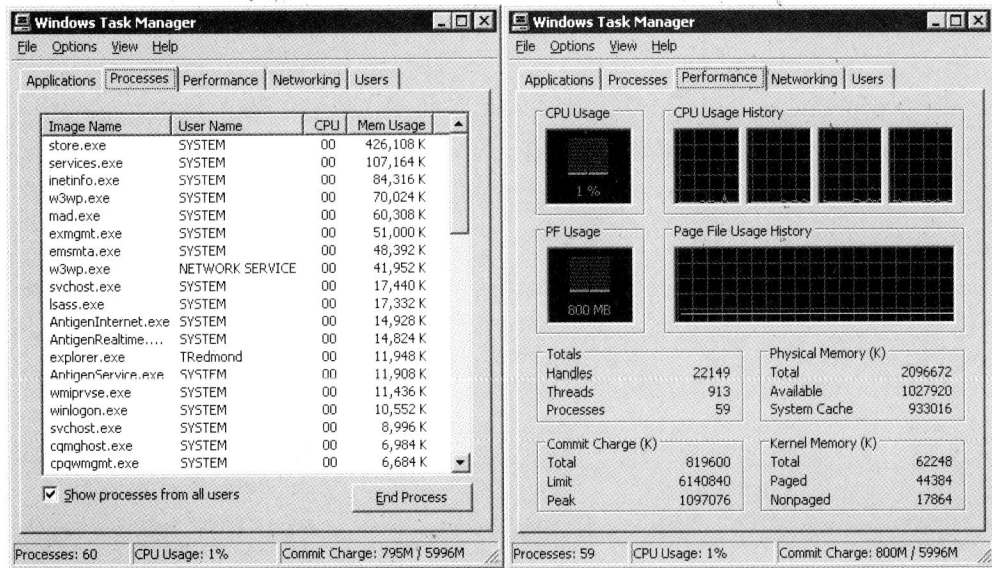

Figure 8.1 *Memory used by the Store.*

Chapter 8

There is no point in having memory sitting idle, so it is good that the Store uses available memory as long as it does not affect other processes. DBA monitors system demand and releases memory back to Windows when required to allow other processes to have the resources they need to work; it then requests the memory back when the other processes finish or release the memory back to Windows. On servers equipped with relatively small amounts of memory, you can sometimes see a side effect of DBA when you log on at the server console and Windows pauses momentarily before it logs you on and paints the screen. The pause is due to DBA releasing resources to allow Windows to paint the screen. DBA is not a fix for servers that are underconfigured with memory, but it does help to maximize the benefit that Exchange gains from available memory.

8.1.4 Using more than 1 GB of memory

Exchange servers running Windows 2000 Advanced Server (or any version of Windows 2003) that are equipped with 1 GB or more of physical memory require changes to the default virtual memory allocation scheme to take advantage of the available memory. Usually, Windows divides the standard 4 GB available address space between user and kernel mode. You can set the /3GB switch to tell Windows that you want to allocate 3 GB of the address space to user-mode processing, which allows Exchange to use the additional memory, especially within the single Store process that probably controls multiple Store instances on large servers (one for each storage group). Although using this switch allows you to provide more memory to Exchange and therefore scale systems to support heavier workloads, Windows may come under pressure as you reduce kernel-mode memory to 1 GB, which may cause Windows to exhaust page table entries—in turn, leading to unpredictable system behavior.

To make the necessary change, add the /3GB switch to the operating system section of boot.ini. For example:

```
[Operating Systems]
multi(0)disk(0)rdisk(0)partition(2)\WINNT="Microsoft
Windows 2000 Server" /fastdetect /3GB
```

Windows 2003 provides an additional switch for boot.ini (USERVA). When used in conjunction with the /3GB switch, you can use the USERVA switch to achieve a better balance between the allocation of kernel- and user-mode memory. Microsoft recommends that you use a setting of /USERVA=3030 (the value is in megabytes) for Exchange 2003 servers. This value may change as experience grows with Exchange 2003 in different

8.1 Aspects of Exchange performance

production configurations, so check with Microsoft to determine the correct value for your server configuration. Its net effect is to allocate an extra 40 MB of memory to the Windows kernel for page table entries, in turn allowing Exchange to scale and support additional users without running out of system resources.

Based on experience gained in the way the Store uses memory, Exchange 2003 attempts to use available memory more intelligently than Exchange 2000 when you set the /3GB switch, and you should set the switch on any server that has more than 1 GB of physical memory. If you do not, Exchange reports a nonoptimal configuration as event 9665 in the event log (Figure 8.2) when the Information Store service starts. This is just a pointer for you to remember to set the /3GB switch.

In Exchange 2000, the Store allocates a large amount of virtual memory (858 MB) for the ESE buffer. The Store always allocates the same amount of virtual memory, regardless of the system or memory configuration. The one size fits all approach is convenient, but it can lead to situations where smaller systems exhaust virtual memory. In Exchange 2003, the Store looks for the /3GB switch and uses it as the basis for memory allocation. If the switch exists, the Store assumes that lots of physical memory are available, so it allocates 896 MB for its buffer. If not, the Store tunes its virtual memory demand back to 576 MB.

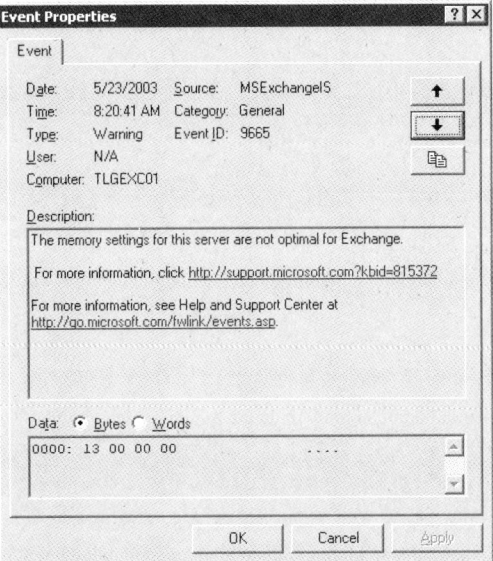

Figure 8.2
Exchange reports nonoptimal memory.

Finally, even though the Datacenter Edition of Windows 2003 supports up to 512 GB of memory, there is no point in equipping an Exchange server with more than 4 GB, since the current 32-bit version of Exchange cannot use the extra memory. This situation may change over time, so it is a good idea to track developments as Microsoft improves its 64-bit story.

8.1.5 Advanced performance

People want the best possible performance for their servers, so each new advance in server technology is eagerly examined to see whether it increases the capacity of a server to support more work. In the case of Exchange, this means more mailboxes. As we have discussed, other factors such as extended backup times or not wanting to put all your eggs in one basket (or all mailboxes on one server) can influence your comfort level for the maximum number of mailboxes on a server, but it is still true that extra performance always helps. Extra CPU speed can balance the inevitable demand for system resources imposed by new features, any lack of rigor in system management and operations, and the drain from third-party products such as antivirus scanners. Apart from speedier CPUs, the two most recent developments are hyperthreading and 64-bit Windows.

Hyperthreading (or simultaneous multithreading) is a technique that allows a CPU such as recent Intel Xeon processors to handle instructions more efficiently by providing code with multiple execution paths. In effect, to a program, a server seems to have more CPUs than it physically possesses. Not every program is able to take advantage of hyperthreading, just as not every program can take advantage of a system equipped with multiple CPUs, and not every program can exploit a grid computer. As it happens, Exchange has steadily improved its ability to use advanced hardware features such as multithreading since Exchange 5.0, and Exchange 2003 is able to use hyperthreaded systems. Indeed, experience shows that enabling hyperthreading on the 400-MHz front-side bus found in high-end servers creates some useful extra CPU "head room," which may allow you to support additional mailboxes on a server. Therefore, if you have the option, it is best to deploy a hyperthreaded system whenever possible.

With the arrival of the first native 64-bit Windows operating system,[1] people often ask how Exchange will take advantage of the extended memory space and other advantages offered by a 64-bit operating system. The

---

1. Windows NT ran on the 64-bit Alpha chip from versions 3.1 to 4.0, but Windows 2000 was never ported to Alpha for production purposes. Microsoft used 64-bit versions of Windows 2000 on Alpha for development purposes only.

answer is that Exchange runs on the IA64 platform, but only as a 32-bit application running in emulation mode in the same manner as first-generation Exchange supports the Alpha platform. Porting a large application such as Exchange to become a native 64-bit application requires an enormous amount of work, and given that the third generation of Exchange uses a new database engine, it was always very unlikely that Microsoft would do the work in Exchange 2003. Thus, the next major release will be the first true 64-bit version of Exchange. In the meantime, you can certainly deploy Exchange 2003 on IA64 systems with an eye on the future.

Waiting for a future 64-bit version to appear does not mean that Microsoft will stop fixing problems in the current Store, nor will they stop adding features. Instead, the true meaning is that Microsoft is now dedicated to developing a new company-wide storage strategy that will accommodate Exchange alongside other products rather than focusing on the current ESE-base Store. The net effect is that we still have a while to wait before we can expect to use a version of the Store that fully exploits a 64-bit architecture to achieve better performance and higher scalability.

8.2 Measuring performance

As with any venture, the first question to ask is why you want to measure performance. Perhaps it is to validate different system configurations so that you can make a choice between one system configuration and another. For example, should you use a two-CPU system or a four-CPU system? Or perhaps it is to test a particular variant of an Exchange server under realistic working conditions, such as a cluster (to test how long failovers take after a Store failover) or how front- and back-end servers work together with clients accessing the servers through firewalls, a DMZ, and so on. For whatever reason, it is wise to begin the exercise with four points in mind:

- The "realistic" workload that you generate through simulation software is only representative of the workload that simulated users produce. Real users can do weird and wonderful things to upset system performance. In fact, they are rather good at doing this.

- A balanced system is more important than the fastest system on earth. This means that you have to concentrate on achieving the best balance between the speed of the CPU, the number of CPUs, the amount of storage, the type of storage and controller, and the amount of memory.

- Performance measured on a server that only runs Exchange is about as valid as a three-dollar bill in the real world of operations. No Exchange server simply runs Exchange. Instead, real servers run a mixture of Exchange and other software, including antivirus and antispam detectors, and so on, all of which steal some CPU cycles, memory, and I/O.

- New advances, such as hyperthreading and 64-bit Windows, will continue to appear to drive performance envelopes upward. However, operational considerations often limit the number of mailboxes that you want to support on a single server. The old adage of not putting all of your eggs in one basket holds true today. Against this argument, it is generally true that organizations operate far too many servers today and server consolidation is a trend that will continue for the foreseeable future.

Because its ability to deliver great performance decreases the further you get from the datacenter, even the best-balanced and most powerful server will not satisfy users all the time. The reasons for this include:

- Network speed and latency: If users connect across slow or high-latency links, their perceived access and performance are gated by the amount of data transferred across the link. You can install faster computers, but it will not make much difference to the users at the end of such links.

- Clients: Each client differs in its requirements. A POP client makes minimal demand when compared with Outlook, but the latest version of Outlook can work in cached Exchange mode to speed perceived performance on the desktop. Outlook Web Access is highly sensitive to bandwidth.

- User workload: If users are busy with other applications, some of which also use network links, the performance of their Exchange client might suffer and they might blame Exchange.

All of this goes to prove that no matter how well you measure performance and then configure systems before you deploy Exchange, user perception remains the true test.

8.2.1 Performance measuring tools

Microsoft provides three tools to assist you in measuring the performance of an Exchange server:

- LoadSim

8.2 Measuring performance

- Exchange Stress and Performance (ESP)
- JetStress

LoadSim is the oldest tool, since Microsoft first engineered it for Exchange 4.0 to generate a measurable workload from MAPI clients. ESP serves roughly the same purpose for Internet clients (including Outlook Web Access), while JetStress generates low-level database calls to exercise the I/O subsystem. You can download these tools from Microsoft's Exchange site at www.microsoft.com/exchange.

LoadSim and ESP both work by following a script of common operations that you expect users to take (creating and sending messages, scheduling appointments, browsing the GAL, and so on). You can tweak the scripts to create heavier or lighter workload. Usually, one or more workstations generate the workload to exercise a server, each of which follows the script and generates the function calls to perform the desired operations. The workstations do not have to be the latest and greatest hardware, since even a 700-MHz Pentium III-class machine is capable of generating the equivalent workload for 600 or so clients. Note that LoadSim does some things that make it very unsuitable for running on any production server. For example, when LoadSim creates accounts and mailboxes to use during the simulation, it gives the new accounts blank passwords. You can imagine the opinion of your security manager if you create hundreds of accounts with blank passwords in your production environment. For this reason, always run LoadSim on test servers, but equip those servers with hardware that is as close as possible, if not identical, to the configuration used in production.

JetStress falls into a different category, because you do not use this tool to measure the overall performance of a server. Instead, JetStress exercises the storage subsystem by generating calls to stress the physical disks, controllers, and cache to identify if a configuration is capable of handling a specified workload. Another way of thinking about JetStress is that it mimics the work done by the Store process, whereas the other tools aim to exercise a complete Exchange server. While the Store is central to Exchange, many other components affect the overall performance of an Exchange server, such as the Routing Engine. The Store places the heaviest load on the storage subsystem and that is what JetStress attempts to measure. Unlike the other tools, JetStress does not come with a pretty interface and does not generate nice reports. You have to be prepared to interrogate the system performance monitor to capture data that you later analyze. In addition, while LoadSim and ESP work on the basis of operations (such as sending a message to two recipients) that you can easily associate with time, JetStress requires detailed knowledge of Windows performance and storage fundamentals if you are to make sense of its results. It is probably fair to say that any Exchange system administrator can run and understand LoadSim, but JetStress requires you to do more work to understand how to change hardware configurations to improve performance based on the data it generates.

8.2.2 The difference between vendor testing and your testing

Hardware vendors typically use a standard benchmark workload called MMB2 for Exchange 2000 and MMB3 for Exchange 2003[2] when they test new servers. MMB2 is a modification of the original MMB workload and represents the workload generated by average office workers, if you could ever find one of these strange beasts. MMB3 is an evolution of MMB2, but differs in that it attempts to reproduce the different load generated by Outlook 2003 clients that use cached Exchange mode. Client-side caching changes server workload and may affect overall system performance, but it is only one aspect of Exchange 2003 performance. Microsoft has incorporated other factors into MMB3 (such as the use of rules, query-based distribution groups, and search folders) that increase client demand on a server, so a typical MMB3 result (in terms of number of mailboxes supported by a server) is lower than MMB2. Therefore, you cannot take a server result for Exchange 2000 and compare it with a result reported for Exchange 2003, because it is not an apple-to-apple comparison. You need to use the LoadSim 2003 version to perform benchmarks based on the MMB3 workload. A similar situation occurred when Microsoft changed the original MMB benchmark to MMB2 with the introduction of Exchange 2000.

All benchmarks attempt to prove one thing: that a server can support many more Exchange mailboxes than any sane administrator would ever run in production. To some extent, the benchmarks are a game played out by hardware vendors in an attempt to capture the blue riband of Exchange performance. It is nice to know that a server will support 12,000 mailboxes, but you always have to realize that, despite Microsoft's best effort to refine the MMB workloads, real users generate workloads very different from simulations for the following reasons:

- Real servers run inside networks and experience all of the different influences that can affect Exchange performance, such as losing connectivity to a GC.

---

2. Microsoft does not endorse any benchmark results gained by running MMB2 against Exchange 2003 servers.

8.2 Measuring performance

- Real servers run much more than Exchange. For example, antivirus detection software can absorb system resources that inevitably affect overall system performance. Some informal benchmarking of leading antivirus software shows that it can absorb 20 percent to 25 percent CPU, as well as virtual memory, with an attendant reduction on the number of supported mailboxes. Multi-CPU systems tend to be less affected by add-on software, because the load is spread across multiple processors.

- Benchmarks usually test the performance of single servers and ignore complex configurations such as clusters.

- Benchmarks do not usually incorporate complex storage configurations such as SANs, but shared storage is a prerequisite for any server consolidation exercise. Storage can significantly affect server performance, especially for database applications such as Exchange, which is the reason why vendors avoid complex storage configurations in benchmarks. They also tend to use RAID 0 volumes to hold the Store databases. This ensures performance, but you would never use RAID 0 for Store databases on production servers.

- The Store databases on real-world servers include a much wider variety of attachment types than found in the measured setup of a test database. For example, you do not typically use test databases that include huge PowerPoint attachments, yet any corporate Exchange server is littered with these files.

- The performance of all servers degrades over time due to factors such as disk fragmentation.

If you just read these points, you might conclude that there is no point in paying any attention to vendor benchmarks and running your own benchmark tests may not deliver worthwhile results. This is an oversimplification of the situation. The results of a vendor benchmark performed using a standard workload (remember that the MMB3 workload is preferred for Exchange 2003) gives you a baseline to measure different system configurations against each other. You can understand the impact of installing multiple CPUs in a server, the difference an increase in CPU speed makes, or how different storage controllers and disks contribute to overall system performance. All of this assumes that vendors perform the benchmarks according to the "rules" laid down by Microsoft and do not attempt anything sneaky to improve their results. Many consultants take the benchmark results reported by vendors and adjust them based on their own experience to create recommendations for production-quality server configurations.

Other factors, such as the "keeping all your eggs in one basket" syndrome and the time required to take backups (and, more importantly, restores) of large databases, reduce the tens of thousands of mailboxes that some benchmarks report to a more supportable number. For example, an HP quad-CPU (2 GHz) Proliant DL580 with 4 GB of memory benchmarks at 13,250 mailboxes, but you would never run this number in production. Experience of most corporate-style deployments indicates that 4,000 is closer to a long-term supportable number.

The decision to run your own benchmarks is harder to make because of the effort required. You can run LoadSim on a server just to see how it responds, but this will not generate a measurement that you can use in any serious sense. To create a proper benchmark you need:

- Dedicated servers to host Exchange and the Active Directory (DC and GC), as well as the workstations to generate the workload.

- A similar software configuration on the Server Under Test (SUT) that you intend to run in production. In other words, if you want to run a specific antivirus agent on your production servers, it should be installed and running on the SUT too. The same is true if you intend to host file and print services or any other application on the production servers—these have to be factored into the equation.

- Access to the same storage configuration that you plan to deploy in production. If you want to use a SAN, then you must connect the SUT to the SAN and use the same controller and disk layout as planned for production. Because Exchange performance is so dependent on the Store, you can drastically affect overall performance by changing storage characteristics.

- Apart from basic disk layout of the Exchange files (database, logs, and binaries), you should place the SMTP and MTA work directories and the message tracking logs in the same locations that they have in production.

Apart from all of this, all you need is time to prepare the test, run the benchmark, and then analyze the captured data. Do not expect to get everything right on the first run, and be prepared to run several tests, each of which lasts six hours or more (one hour to normalize the load, four hours to measure the SUT being exercised, one hour to complete the test).

During the same time, you may want to take advantage of the realistic configuration you create for the test servers to validate that assumptions about backup and restore times are correct, that antivirus and archiving tools work, that operational procedures are viable, and so on. You may also want to use other tools, such as Intel's IOmeter, to measure the base performance of storage volumes or other components.

Of course, you can take the view that every server available today is easily capable of supporting thousands of Exchange mailboxes and ignore benchmarks completely. This is a viable option if you then buy high-quality server hardware based on attributes other than just speed, including:

- Vendor support
- Additional features, such as the ability to boot or otherwise manage the server remotely
- Form factor (some sites prefer blade servers because of their reduced rack size or form factor)
- Server compatibility with the storage infrastructure

Even if you do ignore benchmarks, it is still worthwhile to build some test servers based on the desired configuration and validate it before proceeding to full deployment.

8.3 Cloning, snapshots, and lies

The traditional approach to backups saves an offline or online copy of data to tape. Tape throughput, better software, and increased automation have all improved and increased the ability to manage backups, but the amount of data to be processed has increased at a faster rate. The tape drives and libraries deployed to back up Exchange 5.5 servers with 10-GB Mailbox Stores may struggle to handle the demands of a modern Exchange server with multiple large databases. If you cannot back up your databases in a reasonable time or, more importantly, quickly restore your databases from a backup set should a disaster occur, then you inevitably need to limit database sizes. Limiting database size then restricts the number of mailboxes you can support on a server or limits the size of the mailboxes you can provide to users. Given that most users struggle to cope with a small mailbox, especially in corporate environments, and that administrators want to consolidate small servers into larger servers, we need a way to back up and restore large databases as quickly as possible. This has been a requirement since Exchange 5.5 lifted the 16-GB limit for a database, and the need has become increasingly urgent as servers become more powerful and storage costs decrease.

Backups to disk are always faster than tape and you can use disk instead of tape if that is your preferred backup medium. However, it is difficult to keep enough free disk space available to process backups, so it is unusual to find this implementation. Volume cloning and snapshots—sometimes referred to as "hot backups"—have attracted a lot of attention in the last few years. The marketing term for cloning is Business Continuance Volumes (BCV), which describes the intention behind the technology: reduce the possible downtime due to data unavailability to a minimum. Up to now, you need to deploy specific storage technology to be able to take snapshots, and some limitations exist in application support. Now, the availability of Volume ShadowCopy Services (VSS) in Windows 2003 brings this technology into the mainstream.

Clones and snapshots use different mechanisms to duplicate data so that you can create point-in-time copies. Clones are physical copies of data and are based on RAID 0+1 technology, so the technology to create a clone has been in storage architectures for a long time. You create a clone by establishing a new member of a RAID 0+1 mirror set so that the controller duplicates any data written to the mirror set automatically to all member drives. To create the clone, you split one of the members from the mirror set. The application can continue working, because the mirror set still exists and you can proceed to back up the newly created clone to create a backup save set for long-term storage. When the backup is complete, you can then reintroduce the drive into the mirror set to restart the cycle. Clones hold a complete copy of the data on a volume, so you can use a clone to very rapidly recover data should the need arise. The right-hand pane in Figure 8.3 shows the concept in action after you split off the clone from the mirror RAID set containing production data.

As its name implies, a snapshot is a point-in-time picture, or mapping, of the physical blocks on a volume. You can also think of a snapshot as a logical copy of data. When you create a snapshot, the blocks mapping the original file on disk are maintained, and the snapshot is created from a combination of the original blocks (the starting point) and any blocks of data that hold data that has changed since. The left-hand panel in Figure 8.3 illustrates how a snapshot is built from original and changed blocks.

Implementing hot backup technology is not simply a matter of plugging in appropriate storage technology. Storage systems commonly support many operating systems, so they include the necessary hardware and firmware support for cloning and snapshots. The operating system then implements the necessary support within its file system and drivers and then applications come along to take advantage of whatever they can from the new facilities. Applications include backup utilities as well as the applications that generate data. A complex collection of relationships and depend-

8.3 Cloning, snapshots, and lies

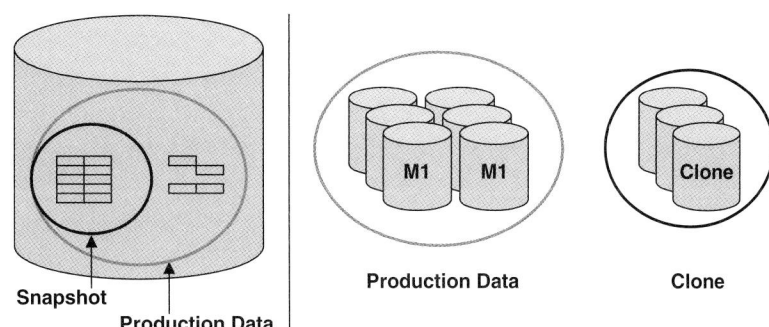

Figure 8.3
Snapshots and clones.

encies needs to come together before you can truly generate and depend on hot backups.

The Exchange developers knew that Windows would eventually include the necessary support for hot backups, so they never sought to build their own implementation into the Exchange backup API or ESE. From 1997 onward, storage vendors decided not to wait for Microsoft and began to build their own implementations. These solutions enabled pseudo hot backups for both Exchange 5.5 and 2000 by working around the essential fact that the Store is a transactional database with no way to become fully consistent unless it shuts down. Some solutions addressed the problem by closing down the Store process before they take a hot backup. This forces the Store to flush any outstanding transactions and creates a consistent version of the database on disk. The normal flow is to break the mirror set as soon as the Store process shuts down, followed by a fast restart of the Store process to restore service to users. You can then mount the disk that contains the clone on another server and begin a tape-based backup to take a copy of the database. Users usually do not notice the interruption in service if you schedule it early in the morning or at a time of low demand. The time taken to close down the Store, break the mirror set, and restart is a matter of a few minutes, and these operations are usually automated through vendor-provided scripts that can handle backup and restore operations.

Recent variations on this theme involve breaking the mirror set while the Store is still running and then taking a backup of the database copy plus all its transaction logs. While this technique works—most of the time—it exhibits inherent flaws, because the Exchange Store does not support backups made in this manner. In effect, what you are doing is creating a backup of an inconsistent copy of the database from disk. In this scenario, the database copy is always inconsistent, because the Store has not had the chance to commit outstanding transactions, so you rely on the roll-forward capability to capture transactions in the logs whenever you need to make the database consistent—if you ever need to restore and use this copy of the database. In addition, because you halt Store processing in a very abrupt manner, there is no guarantee that the internal structures are intact, because you never know what the Store was doing at the exact moment that you take the hot backup. Finally, unlike normal backups, the Store does not perform checksum validation on pages as it writes them out to the backup media, so you could easily take a copy of an already corrupt database and make it even more corrupt. It is not surprising that Microsoft does not support this technique for Exchange 2000 and leaves any support issues that occur, such as recovering a corrupt database, to the vendor that supplied the storage, scripts, and other technology used to take the backup. If you insist on using such a method to take backups, you should also take frequent full tape backups, so that you are sure that you always have something to recover. Or, even better, upgrade to Windows 2003 and Exchange 2003 and find storage and backup vendors that support the Volume ShadowSet-Copy Services API and take proper, fully supported hot backups.

Once you have split a mirror set to create a copy of the database, you need to take a file-level backup to copy the data to tape. In this respect, backups take roughly the same amount of time as they would when you take an online backup of the Store, but restores can be dramatically faster if you can use an on-disk copy of the database. For example, tests performed by HP using its Rapid Restore Solution for Exchange demonstrated that it is possible to restore a 41-GB storage group (two Mailbox Stores and one Public Folder Store) in 6 minutes from a clone, compared with 1 hour 45 minutes from tape. Clearly, restoring a database or storage group takes the same amount of time if the disk clone is not available and you have to use the tape backup.

There is no doubt that hot backups work when properly implemented and integrated into a backup and restore plan. Everything works extremely well at the storage hardware level and all of the issues occur with the application. Exchange knows nothing about the hot backup, because you must stop the Store to remove the clone of the database. The other problem is the variety of approaches and implementations taken by vendors, because they build off their own platform. This is not a problem when you always work with a single technology, but it can be a problem where different groups deploy a variety of technologies inside a large organization.

8.3.1 Volume ShadowCopy Services

VSS provides the necessary architecture for application and storage vendors to support hot backups using a common API. VSS incorporates application

8.3 Cloning, snapshots, and lies

synchronization (how to control the taking of a hot backup), discovery and listing of shadow copies (both clones and snapshots), and a plug-and-play framework for backup components from different vendors.

Vendors use the VSS API to develop provider processes that maintain data about physical clones and snapshots and can expose them to the operating system and applications. VSS processes can contain kernel-mode (device drivers) and user-mode code (the user interface and processing to take a hot backup). Windows 2003 contains a software-based VSS provider as part of the operating system. Storage vendors such as HP and EMC have hardware providers to allow their storage technology to participate in VSS backups.

In addition to VSS providers, vendors also develop VSS requesters. These applications coordinate the processing required to take a backup or perform a restore. VSS providers and writers do the actual processing to create a backup or perform a restore. Typical processing incorporated in a requester includes the identification of the volumes to include in a backup, requesting data from different writers (Exchange, SQL, Oracle, other applications), and communication through a user interface. You can think of the requester as the center coordination point for hot backup operations. It has to communicate with the applications to ask them to provide data and with the providers to identify how to back up the data from volumes under their control. Traditional backup applications such as Legato and Backup Exec are likely VSS requesters.

In VSS terminology, the applications that control data permit writers to allow VSS requesters to include data from the applications in shadow set copies. Exchange 2003 is the first version to support VSS and incorporates the necessary support to be a VSS writer in the Store process. Each application controls its own data and may use dramatically different ways to access and maintain that data, but this complexity is hidden from requesters by the ShadowCopy interface, which ensures data integrity and consistency across applications. During ShadowCopy processing, application writers perform operations such as prepare (get data ready for processing), freeze (prevent writes while processing proceeds), thaw (allow I/O to begin again), and normalize (complete operations). Each writer defines its needs through a set of XML metadata that the requester can interpret and process during a backup or restore operation. For example, the metadata published by Exchange 2003 includes details of the databases and storage groups to include in an operation (the components), whether a reboot is required after the operation completes, what type of restore operations are possible, and so on.

The fact that the VSS framework exists means that a common way of implementing hot backups exists, but you must upgrade many components before you can take hot backups. The storage hardware, operating system, applications, and backup software must work together, so it is important that you have the correct versions installed to make everything work.

8.3.2 Using VSS with Exchange 2003

Assuming that you have the right combination of backup software and hardware, you can plan to incorporate snapshots into your backup strategy. VSS backups for Exchange are always taken at the storage group level, so a full VSS backup contains the complete set of databases in the storage group and the transaction logs, and the log set is truncated (old logs are deleted) after a successful backup. Exchange also supports VSS copy backups at the storage group level, with the major difference being that the transaction logs are not truncated. Incremental and differential backups only copy transaction logs, and, once again, everything is done at the storage group level, with the difference being that the logs are either truncated (incremental) or not (differential). Exchange writes the information about the components assembled into the backup in an XML document that it then provides to the VSS requester, which then proceeds to copy the information stated in the document.

In a restore situation, the backup application is only responsible for extracting information from the backup and restoring it to disk. The Store is responsible for making the database consistent through log replays using the normal soft recovery process, which the Store initiates when you remount databases after recovering them from a backup set.

You should view snapshots as complementary to tape backups, but not as a complete replacement. Streaming to tape retains some advantages that snapshot backups do not have. For example, the Store calculates a checksum for each page as it streams data out to the backup media, but obviously this does not happen when you take a snapshot. The same is true for empty page zeroing (or scrubbing), which the Store can do as it processes pages during a backup, but it cannot be done for a snapshot. As long as you are confident that your databases are in good order, you can proceed to take snapshots with confidence, but it is still a good idea to take an old-fashioned tape backup from time to time, just to be sure.

Software and hardware vendors are likely to collaborate to create special packages to handle VSS-based Exchange backup and restores in an automated manner. Because every hardware and software backup vendor will now use a common API to take hot backups, the benefit in these packages comes from the ease and speed in which the software and hardware combination processes backup and restore situations. Before buying any solution, investigate how easily it handles various disaster recovery situations, such as corrupt databases or logs, as well as the routine of daily backup operations. If a disaster occurs, you will be grateful if the solution automates the entire recovery process instead of leaving you to figure out how best to restore service.

8.4 Virtual Exchange servers

VMware's[3] ESX Server is a popular option for server consolidation on Intel systems. The idea is simple. Buy the biggest server you can find and then run software that creates logical partitions that support virtual servers. The software (VMware) runs on top of either Windows or Linux and allows you to install different operating systems and applications to form the virtual servers. Once you have virtual servers going, you can install applications to make the virtual servers productive. In concept, this seems very similar to the way that Windows clusters work. After all, Exchange runs as a virtual server supported by a physical server that is part of the cluster.

Is it a good idea to deploy some very large multi-CPU servers and consolidate smaller Exchange servers onto the system, running each as a virtual server? Different people will give different answers, but, at the end of the day, supportability rather than feasibility will probably influence your decision more.

There is no doubt that you can build Exchange servers (including clusters) on top of a VMware virtual server, so the question of feasibility does not occur. Many companies use VMware to test server operating systems and applications, but they do not necessarily take the next step to deploy the same configuration into production. This is where the question of supportability occurs.

As of mid-2003, Microsoft's position on the subject is clear.[4] It will only support a problem reported on a virtual server if you can replicate the same problem on a standard server. Microsoft does not include virtual servers in its test procedures, so it is difficult for it to provide support for complex applications such as Exchange and SQL in an environment that it does not test. In addition, most production Exchange servers do not simply run

---

3. www.vmware.com.
4. See Knowledge Base article 273508 for details.

Exchange. Instead, they support other utilities, such as migration tools, messaging connectors, antivirus checkers, backup products, and so on. It would be possible for Microsoft to test and validate Exchange on a virtual server, but including all possible permutations into a test plan for a platform that it does not build is asking a little much.

The answer today is that virtual servers are a good idea for testing complex applications, and they have a role to play for server consolidation projects for simple facilities, such as file and print services. However, until Microsoft fully supports virtual servers without the requirement to replicate problems on standard servers, it is difficult to argue a case to use virtual servers in production. Microsoft's purchase of the Connectix technology (to become the Microsoft Virtual Server product) in early 2003 will generate some interesting scenarios as product groups grapple with the need to support a Microsoft-branded virtual server. Interesting days lie ahead.

Server consolidation is a good idea, and, because many Exchange servers support relatively small user populations, Exchange is definitely a candidate for consolidation. This is especially true since network costs have come down, because it can be cheaper to pay for the increase in bandwidth to bring clients back to a small set of large servers in a datacenter than to keep a set of smaller servers distributed to multiple locations. Early Exchange deployments, those that have run since Exchange 4.0 and 5.0, are specific candidates for consolidation, a project that you might care to undertake in conjunction with a deployment of Outlook 2003 so that you can take advantage of its more efficient network use.

8.5 A brief history of clustering Exchange

> *A cluster is a parallel or distributed system that consists of a collection of interconnected whole computers that are utilized as a single, unified computing resource.*
>
> —Gregory Pfister, *In Search of Clusters,* 2d ed. 1998.

Microsoft introduced Exchange clusters in November 1997, when it released Exchange 5.5, the Enterprise Version of which supported Wolfpack 1.0, or Windows NT cluster services. Exchange's implementation as a clustered application—at least one that could take full advantage of active-active clustering—was incomplete and not every Exchange service could run on a cluster. In particular, a cluster could not host many of the connectors to legacy messaging systems such as Microsoft Mail. However, you could deploy the basic messaging infrastructure on clusters and use them as mailbox servers.

The two servers in an Exchange 5.5 cluster must match in terms of CPU and memory, and you need licenses for the enterprise editions of Windows NT 4.0 (or Windows 2000) and Exchange 5.5 for both servers. Additionally, the hardware must be certified by Microsoft and be included on the cluster Hardware Compatibility List (HCL). Because Exchange 5.5 only supports active-passive clusters, one of the servers is usually inactive, although some customers used the passive server either to run file and print services or host another application. The net result was that an Exchange 5.5 cluster is an expensive solution that requires substantial expertise to deploy. Cluster state transitions were often extended, and although Microsoft worked to eliminate the causes (RPC timeouts and other software glitches) and improved matters in service packs, Exchange clusters never took off, and only a small percentage of customers evaluated them—with an even smaller percentage (estimated at less than 1 percent of corporate customers) moving into deployment.

The low penetration achieved by clusters had a domino effect, since ISVs were reluctant to make their code work on an Exchange 5.5 cluster. Thus, while you could deploy clusters as mailbox servers, you could not protect them against viruses or install other popular ISV software, such as backup agents, fax connectors, and so on. This situation gradually improved, as ISVs updated their code to support clusters, but the lack of third-party software presented a huge hurdle for potential cluster deployments to overcome.

8.6 Second-generation Exchange clusters

The release of Exchange 2000 promised a new beginning for Exchange clusters. Many factors had changed to improve matters, including a new version of the underlying cluster software provided by Windows, the partitioning of the Store into storage groups to allow greater granularity during transitions, support of four-way active-active clusters, and the experience of almost three years of real-life deployments. Unfortunately, some of the same hurdles to customer acceptance of clusters remain, including:

- Complexity
- Cost
- Lack of support for third-party products

The lack of support from third parties is entirely due to market acceptance of clusters. Because clusters remain strictly a minority interest within the general Exchange community, third-party developers focus their efforts on supporting mainstream standard servers. The result is that it is often difficult to find a version of an add-on product for Exchange that supports a clustered environment.

Soon after Exchange 2000 shipped, customers began to report problems with memory management on clusters. The problems appeared on active-active clusters and caused Exchange to freeze and be unable to service client requests. Administrators also reported similar problems on high-end standard Exchange 2000 servers that handle heavy workloads over extended periods. SharePoint Portal Server 2001, which uses a modified version of the Exchange database engine and Store, can also run into memory management problems under heavy load.

Microsoft has steadily improved the quality and robustness of Windows clusters and the applications that support clusters, including Exchange. However, even six years after Microsoft first shipped Exchange clusters, the two biggest problems that cause operating issues with Exchange clusters are still the overall complexity of the solution and operational management. Microsoft now says that all support above two nodes must be active/passive. In other words, you must always keep a passive node available to handle failovers. To those used to other cluster implementations (such as VMSclusters), the need to keep a passive node around is a condemnation of Microsoft clustering technology.

8.6.1 The complexity of clusters

Successful operation of Exchange clusters requires:

- Appropriate hardware
- Attention to detail
- Administrator knowledge of Windows, Exchange, and cluster services
- Cluster-aware operational procedures and third-party products

Cluster hardware should include high-quality servers with balanced configuration of CPU and memory to allow the servers to handle workload equally. A SAN is almost mandatory for anything but entry-level clusters, so you need to pay attention to controller configuration and resilience, basic disk technology (speed and placement), file layout across available volumes, and so on. Commissioning procedures differ across storage technologies, so be sure that you take the right approach for the chosen technology.

Clusters depend on a complex interaction between hardware, operating system, applications, and people. You need to pay attention to detail to ensure that you properly install and configure the cluster before you introduce any application into the equation. This is particularly important when you deal with a SAN, since technology differs greatly across SANs provided by different vendors—and almost every production-quality cluster uses a SAN.

Applications often follow a different installation procedure on clusters. It is not enough to assume that Windows and Exchange behave only slightly differently on a cluster—practice makes perfect! For example, in the case of Exchange, you must manage the basic services that make up the application through the cluster administration tool rather than performing actions such as stop and start services through the Services Manager utility or ESM. However, because clusters are expensive, it is often difficult for administrators to get the necessary experience on clusters before deploying the first production cluster. Few test environments incorporate a fully configured production-quality cluster, but it is perfectly possible to commission an entry-level cluster and use that for testing. Many companies use virtual systems to test clusters, which is an effective approach to solve the need.

Administrators must understand how Microsoft has implemented cluster services for Windows and then what modifications occur for applications to support cluster services. For example, you can only install Exchange on a cluster in a mixed-mode site if another Exchange 2000/2003 server is already present, because some of the services (such as SRS) required for mixed mode cannot run on a cluster. Administrators must understand the differences between standard servers and clusters and understand how to manage and troubleshoot both environments, including how to correctly back up and restore a cluster, as well as how to cope with various disaster recovery scenarios, such as a catastrophic hardware failure.

It is essential that you modify operational procedures developed for standard servers for clusters. The software used to monitor servers and applications may not support clusters and may require a change or replacement. Some third-party software may not be supported and may force you to change the operational procedures to accommodate a different package. In addition, clusters are sensitive to change, so you must carefully plan and test any upgrades and installations of new software before you make changes to production environments.

8.7 Microsoft cluster basics

Microsoft clusters use the shared-nothing model, which means that each server owns and manages local devices (e.g., disks) as specific cluster resources. Clusters include common devices that are available to all of the nodes, but these are owned and managed by only one node at one time. For example, an Exchange virtual server that supports one storage group usually places its transaction logs on a volume, which we will call L: for the moment. The L: volume is visible to all of the servers in the cluster, but only the server that currently hosts the Exchange virtual server running the storage group can access L: at one time. If a failure occurs and the cluster transitions the virtual server to another physical server in the cluster, that server takes ownership of the L: volume.

8.7.1 Resources

Microsoft cluster management services take care of the complex interaction between the physical servers in the cluster, the virtual servers they host, and the resources such as disks that they use, including the management of the different network addresses (names and IP addresses) used by clients to access cluster resources. In this context, a resource is any physical or logical component that you can bring online or take offline within the cluster, but only a single server can own or manage the resource at one time. A network interface card (NIC) is an example of a physical resource, while an IP address is an example of a logical resource.

Each server in the cluster has its own system disk, memory, and copy of the operating system. Each server is responsible for some or all of the resources owned by the cluster, depending on the current state of the cluster. For example, in a two-node cluster, where one node has just failed, the single surviving node hosts its own unique resources (such as its system disk) as well as all the shared cluster resources and the applications that depend on those resources. When the failed server is available again, the cluster redistributes the shared resources to restore equilibrium.

8.7.2 Resource groups and other cluster terms

The number of resources used in a cluster can be quite large, so cluster services use resource groups as the fundamental unit of management within cluster; they also represent the smallest unit that can fail over between nodes in a cluster. Resource groups hold a collection of resources for both the cluster (its network name, IP address, etc.) itself as well as applications. For management purposes, clusters define Exchange virtual servers as resource groups. The shared-nothing model prevents the different nodes within the cluster from attempting to own resources or resource groups simultaneously, so all the resources that make up an Exchange virtual server must run on a single node. In fact, if you have enough processing power, you can run multiple Exchange virtual servers on a single physical computer—something that is interesting in the software laboratory but not recommended for production.

Resource groups can contain both logical and physical resources. For Exchange, the logical resources include the name of the virtual server and its IP address as well as the set of services that make up Exchange. The physical resources include details of any shared disks (used to hold the binaries, Store, and logs). Resource groups often have dependencies on other resource groups—conditions that must be satisfied before the resource group can come online. The properties of a resource or resource group state any dependencies that exist. For example (Figure 8.4), an Exchange virtual server cannot come online unless it has a valid IP address to allow clients to connect. You can only bring Exchange resources online in dependency order.

Dependencies also exist on standard Exchange servers, the best example being the Information Store service, which cannot start if the System Attendant is not running. Note that dependencies cannot span resource group boundaries, since this would complicate cluster management enormously

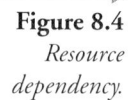

Figure 8.4
Resource dependency.

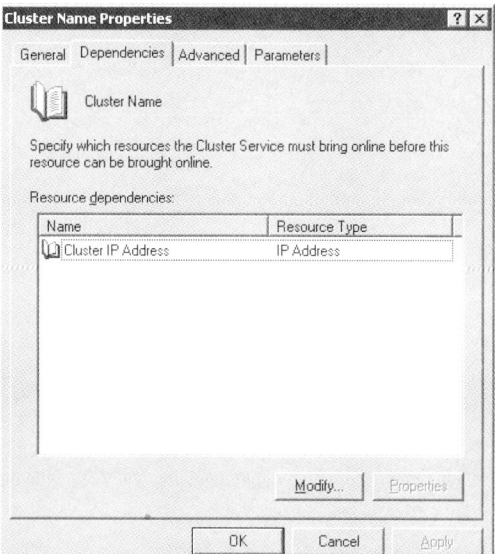

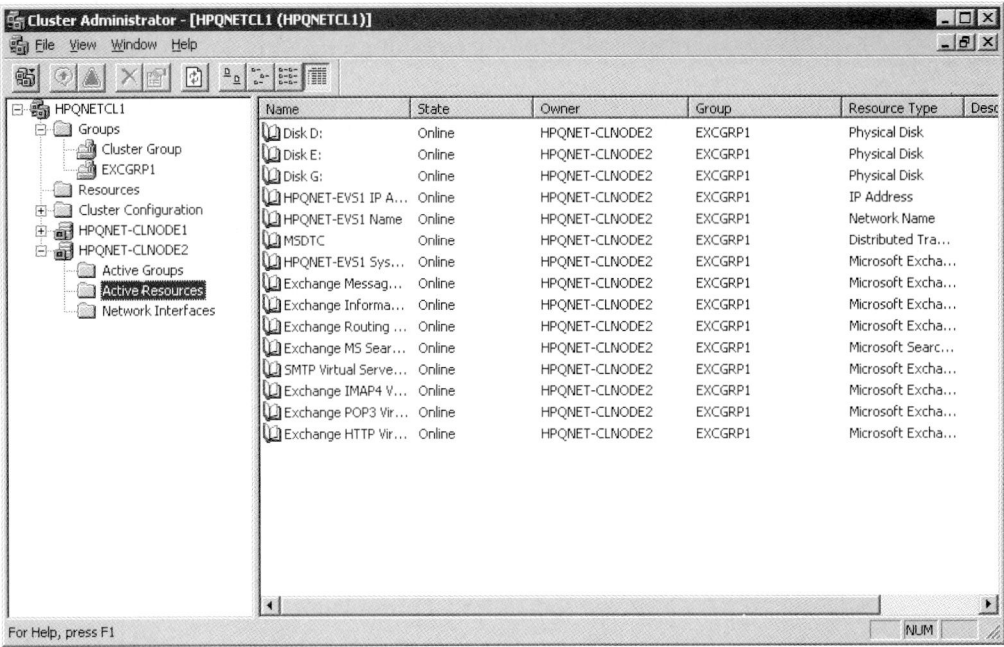

Figure 8.5   *Cluster groups and resources.*

and create situations where resource dependencies might be scattered across various physical servers. In our example, you could not create a dependency for an Exchange virtual server on an IP address that is part of a different resource group.

Figure 8.5 shows the resource groups and resources for a very simple cluster. In this case, the cluster consists of one physical server. Even on a single-node cluster, the basic principles of a cluster still apply, so we can see details of cluster resources as well as the resources that make up an Exchange virtual server. Notice that Exchange represents all of the services that you would expect to see on a standard Exchange server to the cluster as resources. The resources also include some elements that are under the control of IIS, such as the different protocol virtual servers used by Exchange (IMAP, SMTP, POP3, and HTTP).

Before going too far, we should first explain the various names used in a cluster, which include:

- The name of the cluster (in this case, HPQNETCL1)

- The names of each of the physical servers (nodes) that make up the cluster—here we have two physical servers (HPQNET-CLNODE1 and HPQNET-CLNODE2), which are the computers that Windows, cluster services, and applications such as Exchange run on.

- The names of each of the virtual servers that the cluster hosts: Clients do not connect to the cluster, nor do they connect to a physical computer. Logically, they look for the name of the Exchange server that holds their mailboxes. This cluster supports only one Exchange virtual server (HPQNET-EVS1), which runs on a physical server that is part of the cluster. Cluster services move a virtual server from one physical server to another within the cluster. Moves do not affect clients, because the cluster services take care of redirecting incoming client requests to the combination of hardware and software that represents the virtual server within the cluster at that point in time.

It makes sense to decide upon and use naming conventions for cluster systems and virtual servers so that their purpose is obvious at a glance. Some practical definitions of other important cluster terms include:

- Generically cluster aware: A mode where an application is cluster aware by using the generic cluster support DLL, meaning that the application is not specially upgraded to support clusters and can only operate on one node of the cluster at a time. Microsoft supplies the generic cluster support DLL to allow vendors (including its own development groups) to run applications on a cluster with minimum effort.

- Purpose-built cluster aware: A mode where an application is cluster aware through special application-specific code, which enables the application to take full advantage of cluster capabilities, and the application can run on all nodes of the cluster concurrently. Exchange implements its support for clusters through EXRES.DLL, which the setup program installs when you install Exchange on a cluster. EXRES.DLL acts as the interface between the Exchange virtual server and the cluster. At the same time, setup installs EXCLUADM.DLL to enable the cluster administration program to manage Exchange components so that they respond to calls such as "come online," "go offline," and so on. With these components installed, the core of Exchange can run on all nodes in a cluster (active-active mode), but some older or less frequently used code does not support this mode or cannot run at all on a cluster.

- Cluster registry: A separate repository to the standard system registry used to track the cluster configuration and details about resources and resource groups. The quorum resource holds the cluster registry.

A mechanism called "global update" publishes information about cluster changes to members of the cluster.

- Members (or nodes): The physical computers that make up the cluster. In production, clusters range from a two-node cluster to an eight-node cluster (on Windows Server 2003 Enterprise Edition), although you can build a single-node cluster for training or test purposes.

- Quorum resource (Figure 8.6): Most Windows clusters use a disk quorum, literally a physical disk that holds the registry and other data necessary to track the current state of the cluster plus the necessary information to transfer resource groups between nodes. While Exchange 2003 does not have any direct involvement with quorums (this is the responsibility of the OS), you can install Exchange clusters with disk quorums as well as local and majority node set quorums. A local quorum is only available to a single-node cluster (also known as a "lone wolf" cluster), which you would typically use in a disaster recovery scenario, while a majority node set quorum is usually found in stretched clusters where multiple systems use a disk fabric to communicate across several physical locations. In this situation, network interrupts may prevent all the systems from coming online at the same time, so majority set quorums allow the cluster to function once a majority of the nodes connect. For example, once five nodes in an eight-node cluster connect, a quorum exists.

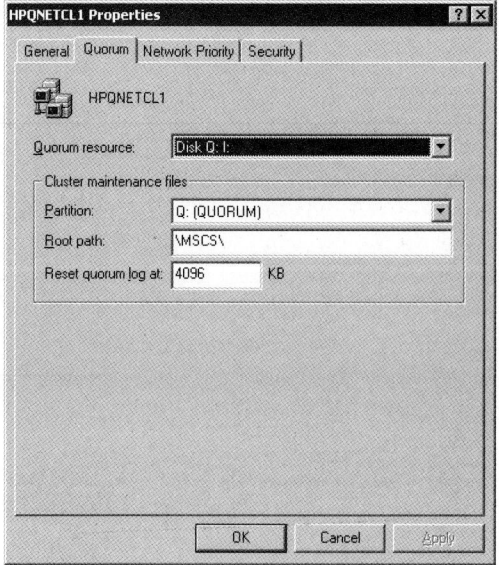

Figure 8.6
The cluster quorum.

8.7.3 Installing Exchange on a cluster

Cluster purists may not agree with some of the definitions offered here. However, they are functional rather than precise and provide enough foundation to proceed.

You must have the following resources to install Exchange on a cluster:

- An IP address and a network name for each virtual server. You cannot use dynamic IP addresses.
- The physical hardware for the cluster nodes, ideally balanced in terms of CPU (number and speed) and memory.
- Physical shared disk resources configured to hold the Store databases and transaction logs.

It is best to create a separate resource group for each Exchange virtual server in the cluster and then move the storage used for the databases and so on into the resource group. Installing Exchange on a cluster is no excuse to ignore best practice for the Store, so make sure that you place the databases and the transaction logs on separate physical volumes. Interestingly, the number of available drive letters may cause some design problems on very large Exchange clusters, since you have to allocate different drive letters to each storage group and perhaps the volume holding the transaction logs for each storage group. This problem does not occur when you deploy Exchange 2003 on Windows 2003 clusters, because you can use mount points to overcome the lack of available drive letters. By convention, clusters use drive Q: for the quorum resource and M: for ExIFS (such as all other Exchange servers).

Remember that on Windows 2003 clusters, you have to install components such as IIS and ASP.NET on each node before you can install Exchange. Exchange 2003 requires Microsoft DTC, so you have to create it as a cluster resource before you install Exchange.

Equipped with the necessary hardware, you can proceed to install the cluster and elect for an active-passive or active-active configuration (for a two-node cluster) up to an eight-node cluster where seven nodes are active and one is passive. Installing the cluster is reasonably straightforward, and defining the number of storage groups and databases is the only issue that you have to pay much attention to afterward. The enterprise edition of Exchange 2000 or 2003 supports up to four storage groups of five databases. Each virtual server running in a cluster can support up to these limits, but such a configuration runs into problems when a failure occurs, because Exchange cannot transfer the storage groups over to another cluster node. Consider this scenario: You have two virtual servers, each configured with three storage groups of three databases. A failure occurs and Exchange attempts to transfer the three storage groups from the failed server to the virtual server that is still active. The active virtual server can accept one storage group and its databases and then encounters the limit of four storage groups, so a full transition is impossible. Cluster designs, therefore, focus on failure scenarios to ensure that remaining virtual servers can take the load and never exceed the limits. In a very large cluster, where each virtual server supports two storage groups, you may only be able to handle a situation where two or three servers fail concurrently, depending on the number of storage groups each virtual server supports.

8.7.4 What clusters do not support

The vast majority of Exchange code runs on a cluster, but you should think of clusters as primarily a mailbox server platform, because of some limitations on connector support. In addition, you never think of clusters for front-end servers, because these systems do not need the high level of resilience and failover that clusters can provide and they are too expensive.

Most of the components not supported by clusters are old or of limited interest to the general messaging community. These are:

- NNTP
- Exchange 2000 Key Management Server
- Exchange 2000 Instant Messaging
- Exchange 2000 Chat
- MTA-based connectors (GroupWise, Lotus Notes, cc:Mail, Microsoft Mail, IBM PROFS, IBM SNADS)
- Exchange 2000 Event Service
- Site Replication Service

You can break down these components into a set of old connectors, which, depending on the MTA, are being phased out in favor of SMTP connections; subsystems such as Instant Messaging, which Exchange 2003 does not support; and the Site Replication Service, which is only needed while you migrate from Exchange 5.5. The exception is NNTP, but very few people use Exchange as an NNTP server or to accept NNTP newsfeeds simply because other lower-cost servers are better at the job. In addition, using a cluster for NNTP is total overkill.

8.7.5 Dependencies

Figure 8.7 illustrates the resource models implemented in Exchange 2000 and Exchange 2003. The resource model defines dependencies between the various components that run in a cluster. The Exchange 2000 resource model centers on the System Attendant and the Store, so if either of these processes fails, it affects many other processes. By comparison, the Exchange 2003 resource model removes many of the previous dependencies on the Store and makes the System Attendant process the sole "must-be-alive" process for a cluster to function. The change improves failover times by reducing the processes that have to be stopped and restarted if a problem occurs; this is entirely logical, because the protocol stacks have a dependency on IIS rather than the Store.

8.7.6 Clusters and memory fragmentation

When Microsoft released Exchange 2000, system designers looked forward to a new era of high-end email servers built around active-active clusters, a promise that was further embellished when Exchange 2000 SP1 provided the necessary support for Windows 2000 Datacenter Edition to enable four-way active-active clusters. System designers look to clustering to provide high degrees of both system resilience and availability and often as a

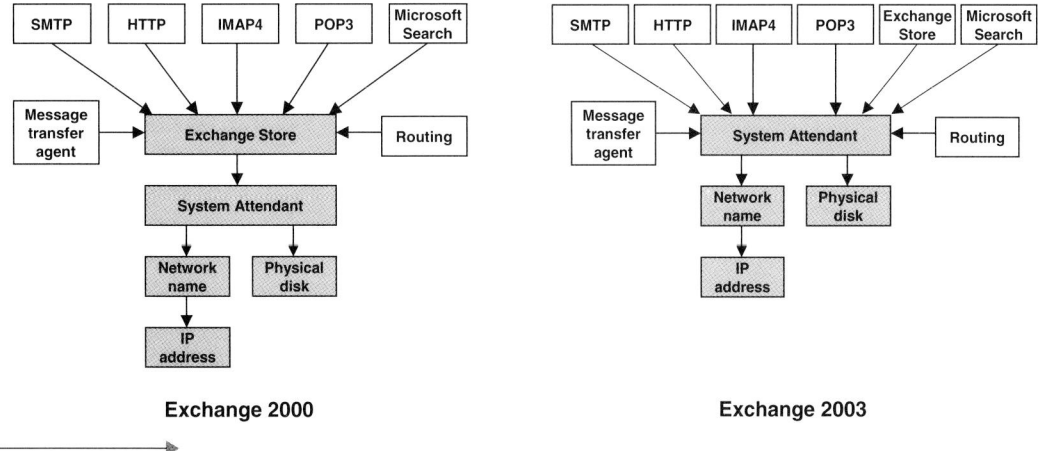

Figure 8.7 *Exchange cluster resource models.*

way to consolidate a number of servers into a smaller set of large clusters. Exchange 5.5 supports active-passive two-node clustering, meaning that one physical system or node actively supports users while its mate remains passive, waiting to be brought into action through a cluster state transition should the active system fail. This is an expensive solution, because of the need for multiple licensed copies of the application, operating system, and any associated third-party utilities (e.g., backup or antivirus programs), as well as the hardware. Active-active clusters provide a better "bang" for your investment, because all of the hardware resources in the cluster are available to serve users.

Unfortunately, active-active clusters ran into virtual memory fragmentation problems within the Store, and this issue prevents Exchange from taking full advantage of clustering. The way that Exchange implements Store partitioning is by establishing a storage group as a cluster resource that is transitioned (along with all its associated databases and transaction logs) if a problem occurs. However, while everything looked good on the theoretical front, clustering has not been so good in practice. Exchange uses dynamic buffer allocation (DBA) to manage the memory buffers used by the Store process. DBA sometimes gives administrators heart palpitations, because they see the memory used by STORE.EXE growing rapidly to a point where Exchange seems to take over the system. This behavior is by design since DBA attempts to balance the demands of Exchange to keep as many Store buffers and data in memory as possible against the needs of other applications. On servers that only run Exchange it is quite normal to see the Store take large amounts of memory and keep it, because there is no other competing applications that need this resource.

During normal operation, Windows allocates and deallocates virtual memory in various sizes to the Store to map mailboxes and other structures. Virtual memory is sometimes allocated in contiguous chunks, such as the approximately 10 MB of memory that is required to mount a database, but as time goes by it may become difficult for Windows to provide the Store with enough contiguous virtual memory, because it has become fragmented. In concept, this is similar to the fragmentation that occurs on disks, and usually it does not cause too many problems—except for cluster state transitions.

During a cluster state transition, the cluster must move the storage groups that were active on a failed node to one or more other nodes in the cluster. Storage groups consist of a set of databases, so the Store has to be able to initialize the storage group and then mount the databases to allow users to access their mailboxes. You can track this activity through event

8.7 Microsoft cluster basics 569

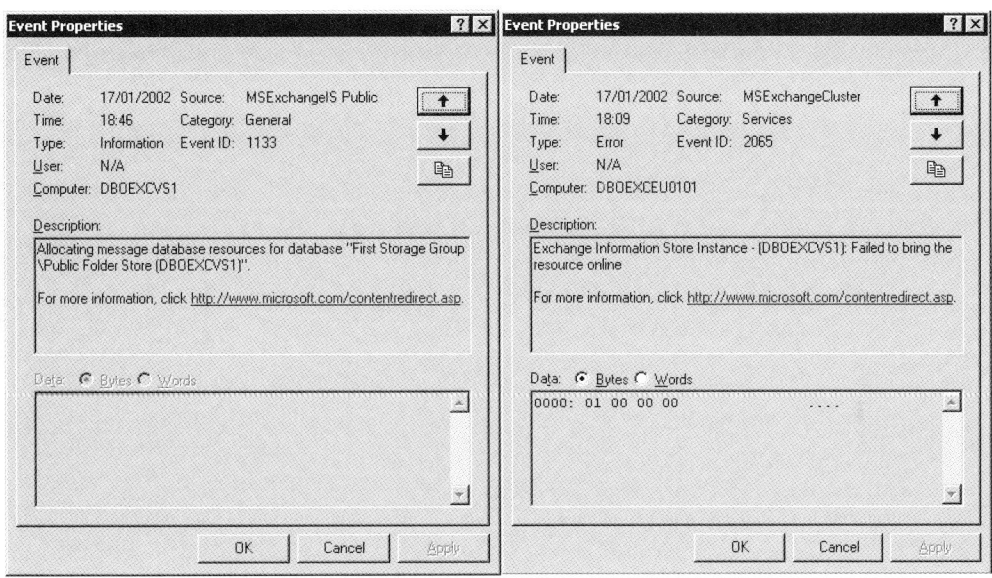

Figure 8.8 *Allocating resources to mount a database, and a failure.*

1133 in the application event log (see left-hand screen shot in Figure 8.8). On a heavily loaded cluster, it may be possible that the Store is not able to mount the databases, because no contiguous virtual memory or not enough contiguous virtual memory is available, in which case you will see an event such as 2065, shown in the right-hand screen shot in Figure 8.8. Thus, we arrive at the situation where the cluster state transition occurs but the Store is essentially brain dead, because the databases are unavailable.

Now, it is worth noting that this kind of situation only occurs on heavily loaded systems, but you will remember that server consolidation and building big, highly resilient systems is one of the prime driving factors for system designers to consider clusters in the first place. After receiving problem reports, Microsoft analyzed the data and realized that it had a problem. It began advising customers to limit cluster designs to lower the numbers of concurrently supported clients (1,000 in Exchange 2000, 1,500 in SP1, and 1,900 in SP2, going a little higher with SP3[5]) when running in active-active mode.

Because MAPI is the most functional and feature-rich protocol, MAPI clients usually generate the heaviest workload for Exchange, so these num-

---

5. At the time of writing, Microsoft has not yet completed its testing to identify suggested levels of mailbox support for Exchange 2003.

bers reflect a MAPI load. Outlook Web Access clients generate much the same type of demand as MAPI. The functions exercised through other client protocols (such as IMAP4 and POP3) typically generate lower system demand and may result in a lesser workload for the server, so it is possible that you will be able to support more client connections before the virtual memory problem appears. Your mileage will vary, and a solid performance and scalability test is required to settle on any final cluster configuration. The test must be realistic and include all of the software incorporated in the final design.

From Exchange 2000 SP3 onward, the Store includes a new virtual memory management algorithm, which changes the way it allocates and frees virtual memory. The key changes are:

- JET top-down allocation: Prior to SP3, the JET database engine allocates virtual memory for its needs from the bottom up in 4-K pages. Other processes that require virtual memory (Store, epoxy, IIS, etc.) are also allocating virtual memory from the bottom up, but they allocate memory in different sizes. This method of managing memory can result in virtual memory fragmentation when multiple processes are continuously requesting and releasing virtual memory. SP3 changed the JET virtual memory allocation to a top-down model to eliminate contention for resources with other system processes. In practical terms, the top-down model results in less virtual memory fragmentation, because small JET allocations pack together tightly. It also allows the Store process to access larger contiguous blocks of virtual memory over sustained periods of load.

- Max open tables change: When the JET database engine initially starts, it requests the virtual memory necessary to maintain a cache of open tables for each storage group. The idea is to have tables cached in memory to avoid the need to go to disk and page tables into and out of memory as the Store services client requests. SP2 allocates enough memory for each storage group to hold 80,000 tables open, which requires a sizable amount of virtual memory. SP3 reduces the request to 27,000 open tables per storage group. The reduction in the request for memory does not seem to affect the Store's performance and increases the size of the virtual memory pool available to other processes. In addition, lowering the size of MaxOpenTables leads to fewer small allocations by JET.

Experience to date demonstrates that servers running SP3 encounter less memory problems on high-end clusters. Thus, if you want to run a cluster or any high-end Exchange server, make sure that you carefully track the lat-

8.7 Microsoft cluster basics

est release of the software in order to take advantage of the constant tuning of the Store and other components that Microsoft does in response to customer experience.

The problems with virtual memory management forced Microsoft to express views on how active clusters should be. Essentially, Microsoft's advice is to keep a passive node available whenever possible, meaning that a two-node cluster is going to run in active-passive mode and a four-node cluster will be active on three nodes and be passive on the fourth. Of course, this approach is most valid if the cluster supports heavy load generated by clients, connectors, or other processing. Clusters that support a small number of clients and perhaps run only a single storage group with a few databases on each active node usually operate successfully in a fully active manner, because virtual memory fragmentation is less likely to occur.

By definition, because a "fresh" node is always available in an active-passive configuration, clusters can support higher numbers of users per active node, perhaps up to 5,000 mailboxes per node. The exact figure depends on the system configuration, the load generated by the users, the type of clients used, and careful monitoring of virtual memory on the active nodes as they come under load. There is no simple and quick answer to the "how many users will a system support" question here, and you will need to work through a sizing exercise to determine the optimum production configuration. See the Microsoft white paper on Exchange clustering posted on its Web site for more details about how to monitor clustered systems, especially regarding the use of virtual memory.

8.7.7 Monitoring virtual memory use

Exchange incorporates a set of performance monitor counters that you can use to check virtual memory use on a cluster. Table 8.2 lists the essential counters to monitor.

Figure 8.9 shows the performance monitor in use on a cluster. In this case, there is plenty of virtual memory available, so no problems are expected. If available virtual memory begins to decline as the load on a cluster grows, Exchange logs a warning event 9582[6] when less than 32 MB of available memory is present and then flags the same event again, this time with an error status, when no contiguous blocks of virtual memory larger than 16 MB exist inside STORE.EXE. After the Store reaches the

---

6. Article 314736 describes how incorrect use of the /3GB switch in BOOT.INI on Exchange 2000 servers can also generate event 9582.

Table 8.2 *Performance Counters to Monitor Virtual Memory*

Performance Object	Performance Counter	Description
MSExchangeIS	VM largest block size	Size in bytes of the largest free virtual memory block
MSExchangeIS	VM total free blocks	Total number of free virtual memory blocks
MSExchangeIS	VM total 16 MB free blocks	Total number of free virtual memory blocks larger than or equal to 16 MB
MSExchangeIS	VM total large free block bytes	Total number of bytes in free virtual memory blocks larger than or equal to 16 MB

threshold, the cluster can become unstable and stop responding to client requests, and you will have to reboot. Microsoft Knowledge Base article 317411 explains some of the steps that you can take to capture system information to assist troubleshooting if virtual memory problems occur.

You may also see event 9582 immediately after a failover to a passive node, if the passive node has ever hosted the same virtual server that the cluster now wishes to transition. Each node maintains a stub STORE.EXE process, and the memory structures within the Store process may already be

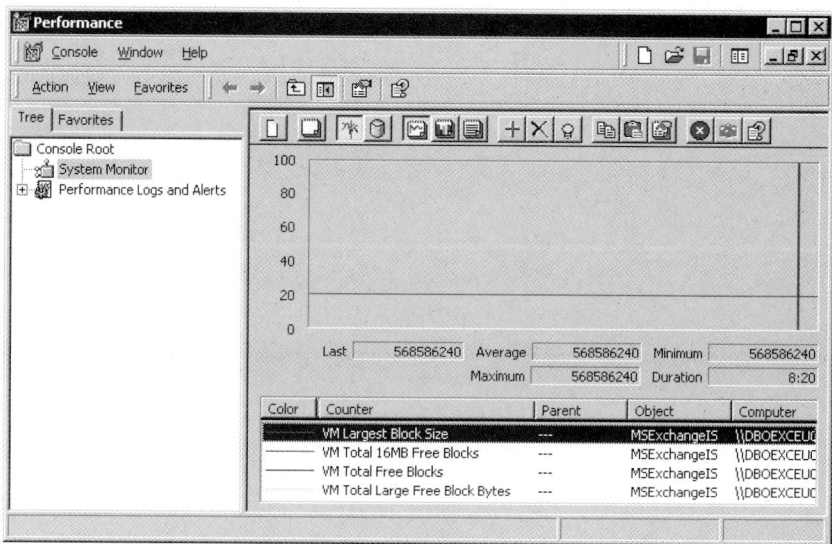

Figure 8.9
Monitoring virtual memory.

fragmented before a transition occurs, leading to the error. You can attempt to transition the virtual server to another node in the cluster and then restart the server that has the fragmented memory, or, if a passive node is not available, you will have to restart the active node. The rewrite of the virtual memory management code included in Exchange 2000 SP3 generates far fewer problems of this nature, and you are unlikely to see event 9582 triggered under anything but extreme load.

Microsoft made many changes to virtual memory management in Exchange 2003, and, generally speaking, the situation is much better and you should not see 9582 events logged as frequently as on an Exchange 2000 server. In addition, Microsoft incorporated a new safety valve into the Store process that kicks in if the Store signals the warning 9582 event. When this happens, the Store requests a one-time reduction (or back-off) of the ESE buffer to free up an additional 64-MB block of virtual memory. The net effect is that the Store can use this memory to handle the demand that caused the amount of free virtual memory to drop to critical limits. However, because the Store releases the virtual memory from the ESE buffer, server performance is affected and you cannot ignore the event. Instead, you should schedule a server reboot as soon as convenient. The advantage of the one-time reduction is that you have the opportunity to schedule the server reboot in a graceful manner, but it is not an excuse to keep the server up and running, because the 9582 error event will eventually occur again and you have to conduct an immediate reboot.

Note that some third-party products—particularly virus checkers—can affect how the Store uses virtual memory. If you run into problems, check that you have the latest version of any third-party product and monitor the situation with the product enabled and then disabled to see if it makes a difference.

Even though Exchange 2003 has improved virtual memory management, this is still not an area that an administrator can ignore, especially on heavily used servers. Once a server supports more than 1,000 concurrent mailbox connects (a rule of thumb, because server configurations vary dramatically), you should monitor virtual memory use to determine whether fragmentation is likely to be an issue for the server.

8.7.8 RPC client requests

The RPC Requests performance counter for the Store (MSExchangeIS) tracks the number of outstanding client requests that the Store is handling. On very large and heavily loaded clusters, the workload generated by clients may exceed the capacity of the Store and requests begin to queue. Normally, if the server is able to respond to all the client workload, the number of outstanding requests should be zero or very low. If the value of the RPC Requests counter exceeds 65, you may encounter a condition where Exchange may lose connectivity to the Global Catalog Server, resulting in clients experiencing a "server stall." Outlook 2003 clients that operate in cached Exchange mode experience fewer interruptions during cluster transitions or when servers have other problems, so you may want to deploy Outlook 2003 clients alongside Exchange 2003 clusters to isolate users as much as possible from server outages.

8.7.9 Upgrading a cluster with a service pack

Upgrading clusters always seems to be a stressful activity and the application of service packs to clusters is probably the worst culprit, possibly because of a now normal dependency on hot fixes. Microsoft has published a reasonable guide regarding how to apply service packs (see Microsoft Knowledge Base article 328839) that should be your first port of call for information. Exchange 2003 SP1 is a good example of how to go about applying a service pack to an Exchange cluster. The steps are:

1. Investigate any hot fixes for Windows that you need to apply to the cluster and install the fixes before beginning the upgrade.
2. Make a backup.
3. Install the service pack on the passive node of the cluster and reboot (if required).
4. Once the upgraded passive node is online, use the Cluster Administrator to move an Exchange virtual server over from an active node to the node that is now running the service pack.
5. Upgrade the inactive node using the "upgrade Exchange Virtual Server" option in the Cluster Administrator.
6. Continue to move virtual servers around to allow upgrading of each node in the cluster until they are all done.

After all nodes are complete, take another backup (just in case) and check that failover works correctly.

8.7.10 Stretched clusters and Exchange

Given the importance of email to many corporations and the need to ensure resilience against disaster, it comes as no surprise that there is an

8.7 Microsoft cluster basics

interest in using stretched clusters with Exchange. Stretched, or geographically dispersed, clusters use virtual LANs to connect SANs over long distances (usually between 10 KM and 20 KM, but sometimes over longer distances). For the cluster to function correctly, the VLAN must support connectivity latency of 500 ms or less. Exchange generates quite a specific I/O pattern, so if you want to use a stretched cluster, it is important that you deploy storage subsystems that support Exchange's requirements:

- The hardware must be listed in the multicluster section of Microsoft's Windows Server Catalog (search microsoft.com for "Windows Catalog" and navigate to "multicluster").

- The replication mechanism in the disk storage system must be synchronous (at the time of writing, Microsoft had not completed testing of systems that use asynchronous writes).

- The disk storage system must honor the ordering of writes.

In most cases, if Exchange suffers problems on the cluster, Microsoft will look at the storage system first, so it is good to have a high-quality relationship with your storage vendor and have some members of your team skilled in the technology.

Stretched clusters deliver resilience, but only in terms of geographical isolation. By themselves, they add nothing to the regular reliability functions delivered by running Exchange on any cluster. Indeed, stretched clusters come with a downside, because they can support fewer users than their regular counterparts due to the synchronous nature of the I/O. The exact reduction depends on workload and configuration, but you can expect to cut the number of supported users by half. This aspect of stretched clusters may improve over time as the technology gets smarter, but, for now, it is an issue to consider.

Hardware-based stretched clusters are the only implementation method that Microsoft supports. Software-based stretched cluster implementations do exist, but some evidence indicates that these solutions are less than perfect within an Exchange environment, so they are not recommended.

8.7.11 Deciding for or against a cluster

Assuming that you have the knowledge to properly size, configure, and manage an Exchange cluster, Table 8.3 lists some of the other factors that companies usually take into account before they decide to put clusters into production.

Table 8.3 *Pros and Cons of Exchange Clusters*

Pros	Cons
Clusters allow you to update software (including service packs) on a rolling basis, one node at a time. This ensures that you can provide a more continuous service to clients, because you do not have to take the cluster totally offline to update software.	If you plan software upgrades properly, schedule them for low-demand times (e.g., Sunday morning), and communicate the necessary downtime to users well in advance, so you can take down a server to apply an upgrade without greatly affecting users. Routine maintenance is necessary for all systems, so planning a software upgrade at the same time is not a big problem. Microsoft hot fixes are often untested on clusters when released to customers, so it is a mistake to assume that you can apply every patch to a cluster. In addition, third-party product upgrades do not always support rolling upgrades, and you can only apply the upgrade to the active node.
Clusters provide greater system uptime by transitioning work to active members of the cluster when problems occur.	Clusters are expensive and may not justify the additional expense over a well-configured standard server in terms of additional uptime.
Active-active clusters are a great way to spread load across all the servers in a cluster.	Memory management problems limit the number of concurrent clients that an active-active cluster supports, so many clusters run in active-passive mode to ensure that transitions can occur.
Clusters provide protection against failures in components such as motherboards, CPUs, and memory.	Clusters provide no protection against storage failures, so they have an Achilles heel.
	Because clusters are not widely used, a smaller choice of add-on software products is available for both Windows and Exchange.
	Clusters require greater experience, knowledge, and attention to detail from administrators than standard servers.
	Clusters do not support all Exchange components and therefore are only useful as mailbox servers.
	Failures in the shared disk subsystem remain the Achilles heel of clusters: A transition from one node to another that depends on a failed disk will not work.

When many companies reviewed their options for Exchange server configurations, they decided not to use clusters and opted for regular servers instead. Common reasons cited by administrators include:

- Not all locations in the organization require (or can fund) the degree of uptime that a cluster can provide. Deployment and subsequent

8.7 Microsoft cluster basics

support is easier if standard configurations are used everywhere and the total investment required to support Exchange is less.

- Administrators can be trained on a single platform without having to accommodate "what if" scenarios if clusters are used.
- The choice of third-party products is much wider if clusters are not used.
- The hardware and software used by the cluster are expensive.
- Experience of Exchange 5.5 clusters had not been positive.

Every company is different, and the reasons why one company declines to use clusters may not apply elsewhere. Compaq was the first large company to achieve a migration to Exchange 2000 and opted not to use clusters. As it happens, the Exchange organization at Compaq does include a couple of clusters, but they only support small user populations and support groups that have the time and interest to maintain the clusters. In addition, none of the clusters at Compaq uses active-active clustering. On the other hand, many companies operate two-node and four-node production-quality clusters successfully. In all cases, these companies have dedicated the required effort and expertise to deploy and manage the clusters.

8.7.12 Does Exchange 2003 make a difference to clusters?

The combination of Windows 2003 and Exchange 2003 introduces a new dimension to consider when you look at clusters. The major improvements are:

- The dependency on Windows 2000 Datacenter Edition is gone, so you can now deploy up to eight-node clusters without the additional expense that Windows 2000 Datacenter edition introduces. Now that the Enterprise Edition of Exchange 2003 supports up to eight nodes in a cluster, administrators have a lot more flexibility in design.

- Windows 2003 and Exchange 2003 both make changes that contribute to better control of memory fragmentation, which may increase the number of MAPI clients that a cluster supports. Windows and Exchange also make better use of large amounts of memory, because Microsoft has gained more experience of how to use memory above 1GB when it is available.

- You can use drive mount points to eliminate the Windows 2000/ Exchange 2000 restriction on the number of available drive letters, which limits the number of available disk groups in a cluster. This is important when you deploy more than ten storage groups spread across multiple cluster nodes.

- Assuming that you use appropriate hardware and backup software, you can use the Volume ShadowCopy Services (VSS) API introduced in Windows 2003 to take hot snapshot backups. This is critical, because clusters cannot attain their full potential if administrators limit the size of the databases they are willing to deploy, in turn limiting the number of mailboxes that a cluster can host.

- The Recovery Storage Group feature lets administrators recover from individual database failures more quickly and without having to deploy dedicated recovery servers.

- The Store is faster at moving storage groups from failed servers to active nodes.

In addition, if you deploy Outlook 2003 clients in cached Exchange mode, there is potential to support more concurrent MAPI clients per cluster node because the clients generate less RPC operations against the server, since much of the work that previous generations of MAPI clients did using server-based data is now executed against client-side data. However, we are still in the early days of exploring this potential and hard results are not yet available.

To Microsoft's credit, it is using clusters to test the technology and help consolidate servers. For its Exchange 2003 deployment, Microsoft has a "datacenter class" cluster built from seven nodes that support four Exchange virtual servers. Four large servers (HP Proliant DL580 G2 with quad 1.9-GHz Xeon III processors and 4 GB of RAM) take the bulk of the load by hosting the Exchange virtual servers, each supporting 4,000 mailboxes with a 200-MB default quota. A passive server is available to handle outages, and two other "auxiliary" servers are available to perform backups and handle other administrative tasks. Microsoft performs backups to disk and then moves the virtual server that owns the disks holding the backup data to the dedicated backup nodes, a technique necessary to handle the I/O load generated when they move the data to tape for archival. All the servers connect to an HP StorageWorks EVA5000 SAN, and the storage design makes heavy use of mount points to allocate disk areas for databases, transaction logs, SMTP work areas, and so on. Supporting 16,000 mailboxes on a large cluster demonstrates that you can deploy clusters to support large numbers of users. Of course, not all of the users are active at any time, and the administrators pay close attention to memory defragmentation in line with best practice, along with normal administrative tasks.

One thing is certain: It is a bad idea simply to install a cluster because you want to achieve highly reliable Exchange. An adequately configured and well-managed standalone server running the latest service pack is as likely to attain a "four nines" SLA as a cluster.

8.7.13 Clusters—in summary

Microsoft did its best to fix the problems with memory fragmentation, but there is no doubt that Exchange 2000 clusters have been a disappointment. As with Exchange 5.5 clustering, which initially promised a lot and ended up being an expensive solution for the value it delivered, the problems have convinced many who considered Exchange clusters to look at other alternatives, notably investing in standalone servers that share a Storage Area Network (SAN). In this environment, you devote major investment into building resilience through storage rather than clusters. If you have a problem with a server, you still end up with affected users, but the theory is that the vast majority of problems experienced with Exchange are disk related rather than software or other hardware components. Accordingly, if you take advantage of the latest SAN technology to provide the highest degree of storage reliability, you may have a better solution to the immediate need for robustness. Going with a SAN also offers some long-term advantages, since you can treat servers as discardable items, planning to swap them out for newer computers as they become available, while your databases stay intact and available in the SAN.

Fools rush in to deploy clusters where experienced administrators pause for thought. There is no doubt that Exchange clusters are more complex than standard servers are. Experience demonstrates that you must carefully manage clusters to generate the desired levels of uptime and resilience. Those who plunge in to deploy clusters without investing the necessary time to plan, design, and deploy generally encounter problems that they might avoid with standard servers after they have installed some expensive hardware. On the other hand, those who know what they are doing can manage clusters successfully and attain the desired results. At the end of the day, it all comes down to personal choice.

The early reports of successful deployments of Exchange 2003 clusters, including Microsoft's own, are encouraging and we can hope that the changes in Windows 2003, Exchange 2003, and Outlook 2003, as well as improvements in server and storage technology and third-party software products, all contribute to making Exchange clusters a viable option for more deployments. The challenge for Microsoft now is to continue driving complexity out of cluster software and administration so that it becomes as easy to install a cluster as it is to install a standard server. That day is not yet here.

I remain positive about clusters. Providing that you carefully plan cluster configurations and then deploy those configurations, along with system administrators who have the appropriate level of knowledge about the hardware, operating system, and application environment, clusters do a fine job; I am still content to have my own mailbox located on an Exchange cluster. The problem is that there have been too many hiccups along the road, and clusters have not achieved their original promise. Work is continuing to improve matters, but in the interim, anyone who is interested in clustering Exchange servers should consider all options before making a final decision.

Getting the Mail through—Routing and Message Delivery

As a messaging system, the primary task for Exchange is to deliver messages in a reliable and robust manner. The Routing and Transport Engine is responsible for this work. Message routing encompasses three major tasks:

- Server to server message delivery
- Routing between different groups of servers
- External and local message delivery

Exchange has always been good at routing and delivering messages. First-generation servers hold information about all of the other servers in the organization, including how the servers connect together in the Exchange Directory. The X.400-based Message Transfer Agent (MTA) uses this information to route messages quickly and effectively, and most of the time things work well. The wide range of available connectors helps Exchange to link up with its major competitors; many of the connectors also handle directory synchronization, which is of major assistance when you need to migrate from another email system. The combination of comprehensive connectivity and high-fidelity directory synchronization has been the cornerstone of Exchange's success in the enterprise messaging market. On the down side, when things go wrong with the MTA, administrators can tear their hair out to discover where the problem lies. Because of its age and the complexity of its code, Microsoft never upgraded the MTA to be a cluster-aware component.

Exchange 2000 and 2003 still support X.400, but the focus is now firmly on Internet protocols as the foundation for messaging—with SMTP being the most important message transport protocol. As elsewhere in Exchange, the AD is the repository for user email addresses, system information, and the routes served by connectors. Exchange uses a mixture of LDAP and ADSI calls to fetch information from the AD. Unlike other SMTP email systems, Exchange does not use DNS MX records to decide how best to route messages within an Exchange organization; but Exchange does use MX records whenever Exchange needs to send messages to an external SMTP server. The logic here is that MX records simply indicate that a server can accept email, and an Exchange server already knows this fact about other Exchange servers in the same organization.

To some degree, Microsoft took a huge risk when the MTA was superseded by the Routing Engine in Exchange 2000, but the strategy worked, because Exchange is now able to process more messages faster using the SMTP engine than ever before. The X.400 MTA is still present in Exchange 2003 and Exchange can still route messages across the older set of connectors, but only after the Routing Engine has examined the messages and concluded that they cannot be processed any other way.

9.1 SMTP and X.400

Originally defined in 1982 in RFC 821, SMTP has since been widely used as the de facto standard for email exchange—first within the Internet and then between different corporate bodies. At the beginning of the 1990s, SMTP battled with X.400 to become the generally accepted protocol for email exchange. X.400 had many champions, mostly in Europe and including industry bodies such as the Electronic Mail Association (EMA), but the overwhelming force applied by the Internet juggernaut catapulted the SMTP/MIME combination into the lead position.

The X.400-based MTA is the core of first-generation Exchange servers. The presence of X.400 at the heart of these servers reflects the view in 1992–1995 that corporate messaging systems could really only be built around a solid, well-defined, and comprehensive protocol. When Exchange 4.0 was in development, no one could argue the case that SMTP had reached the same level of development as X.400, which at that stage had evolved through several sets of recommendations and been deployed in many corporations around the world. In comparison to the maturity of X.400, SMTP had not yet evolved to accommodate nontext bodyparts (in essence, binary attachments). In real terms, this meant that X.400 was the only way that people were able to send each other attachments, such as Word documents or Excel spreadsheets, without resorting to complex encoding schemes that required manual intervention. Forcing people to encode a document before attaching it to a message is OK in the technical community, but few office-type users have the patience to go through such a laborious procedure.

The MTA executable (EMSMTA.EXE), the Windows NT service (the Microsoft Exchange Message Transfer Agent), and the X.400 connector collectively formed the backbone of the majority of first-generation Exchange enterprise-scale deployments. The pervasiveness of X.400 within Exchange—even today—is the reason why you cannot delete the X.400 addresses created for every mail-enabled account. Without an X.400 address, the MTA cannot route messages to an Exchange 5.5 mailbox. While X.400 is not a very approachable protocol, there is no doubt that the MTA delivered fast message processing. Even the earliest versions of Exchange running on system configurations now deemed puny were able to accept messages from the Store, assess their destination addresses, and route them very quickly. In addition, you cannot underestimate the importance of the MTA during mixed-mode operation, because it is the primary communications mechanism between Exchange 5.5 and Exchange 2000/2003, unless you decide to deploy SMTP connectors instead.

The speed and throughput of the MTA increased steadily as the first generation of Exchange rolled out. Of course, the added power of the computers and use of symmetric CPUs made their contribution, but the MTA provided the underlying speed. Over three releases, multiple service packs, and many hot fixes the MTA grew in reliability and robustness. However, the rapid evolution of the Internet protocols and the general acceptance of SMTP as the way to accomplish global messaging marked the end for the "X" protocols. In today's Exchange infrastructures, the use of the MTA is limited to dealing with messages sent to older Exchange servers or those destined for other X.400 systems. As companies phase out their use of X.400 in their messaging environments, it follows that the number of messages handled by the MTA is in steady decline, whereas the message volume handled by SMTP grows all the time.

9.2 The evolution of SMTP

The earliest implementation of SMTP provides a very rudimentary means of transferring messages from one system to another. RFC 821 (and the closely associated RFC 822) only allows for the transfer of 7-bit ASCII text messages. If you monitor the traffic going to port 25 on an Exchange server, you can see that the interaction between SMTP servers is very straightforward. The protocol defines how to contact a server, how to transmit data to set up the connection and establish the link necessary to transfer messages, how to transfer the message content, and then how to sign off.

The major virtue of content simplicity is that nearly every email system can understand 7-bit text, and SMTP lived up to its name in its ability to send simple text messages between people. Success in the commercial email world depends on meeting user requirements, and the success of Windows as the desktop platform of choice introduced many new file types to the equation. Clearly, something had to happen to enable SMTP to transport the huge array of PC files that people wanted to send to each other. Equally important, while 7 bits are acceptable in a U.S.-English environment, many characters in daily use outside the United States are not included in 7-bit ASCII.

A new protocol developed to overcome the serious limitations in SMTP. MIME, or Multipurpose Internet Mail Extensions, supports binary attachments and guarantees message fidelity across SMTP gateways. Although specified in RFCs 1341 and 1342, MIME does not replace RFCs 821/822. Instead, MIME is fully backward compatible with early implementations of SMTP and is designed to extend the basic messaging functionality defined by SMTP. In some cases, you can still use UUENCODE as an alternative mechanism to transmit attachments. The MIME protocol defines a mechanism for declaring the different parts that might be included in a message, such as the header, body text, and attachments. At the same time, MIME defines the methods required to transform complex content so that a messaging system can transport this data as easily as if it were simple text. MIME meets its goals by introducing a number of new message header fields, including fields to specify the content type (text, multipart, application, message, video, and so on) and the content encoding scheme. Most MIME-encoded messages seen in an Exchange environment use the Base64 encoding scheme, which allows binary data to travel across transports originally designed for 7-bit transmission.

The collective evolution of SMTP and MIME provides the foundation for the Exchange Routing Engine, but only after extension of the basic protocols. The key development here is the definition of ESMTP (extended SMTP) in RFC 1869. ESMTP allows new commands to extend the basic protocol, either those defined in another RFC and so generally supported within the SMTP community, or commands intended for use by specific applications. Exchange uses ESMTP to support a wide array of the industry-standard extensions, as well as an extension of its own to support the propagation of link state routing information between servers. The S/MIME extensions allow the basic MIME protocol to accommodate the requirements of secure email. S/MIME enables the reliable transmission of encrypted messages and the keys necessary to decrypt the messages between SMTP gateways. Exchange has supported S/MIME since Exchange 5.5 SP1.

9.2.1 SMTP extensions in Exchange

Performance and scalability are very important to Exchange. The most important ESTMP extensions supported by Exchange 2000/2003 are:

- Pipelining: The ability for an SMTP client to issue many commands without waiting for the server to acknowledge each command, in the knowledge that the acknowledgments will eventually arrive in the same order that they are issued. The original RFC 821 states that an acknowledgment (usually in the form 250 OK) is sent after each command. This implementation was necessary in the early days of computer networks, but is less important as the reliability of networks improved. Pipelining, defined in RFC 2197, avoids the overhead of waiting for command acknowledgments, speeds up communication between SMTP clients and servers, and so increases message throughput.

- 8-bit clean: The SMTP transport complies with the 8-bit MIME standard (defined in RFC 1652), so it is able to pass and accept 8-bit MIME content without having to interpret it. Exchange servers send messages in 8-bit MIME format within a routing group, but downgrade to 7-bit format (Base64 encoded) inside a mixed-mode organization that contains an older Internet Mail Service (IMS). The logic here is that Exchange might eventually have to redirect the message via the IMS, and it is safer to ensure that all parts of the messaging system can transport the content from start to finish instead of constantly checking as the message passes through different servers. Exchange 2003 servers are able to make full use of 8-bit clean mode when communicating between bridgehead servers to eliminate the overhead of converting to and from 7-bit MIME format. Seven-bit MIME requires approximately 30 percent more overhead than 8-bit, so avoiding the conversion saves CPU cycles and network bandwidth.

- Delivery Status Notification (DSN): The ability to tell you whether the messaging system has successfully delivered to its final destination. Exchange supports delivery status notifications as defined in RFCs 1891, 1892, and 1894. The Routing Engine parses DSN data to ensure that clients interpret and display delivery information in a manner that may be specific to the client. For example, Internet clients such as Outlook Express receive DSNs formatted exactly as laid

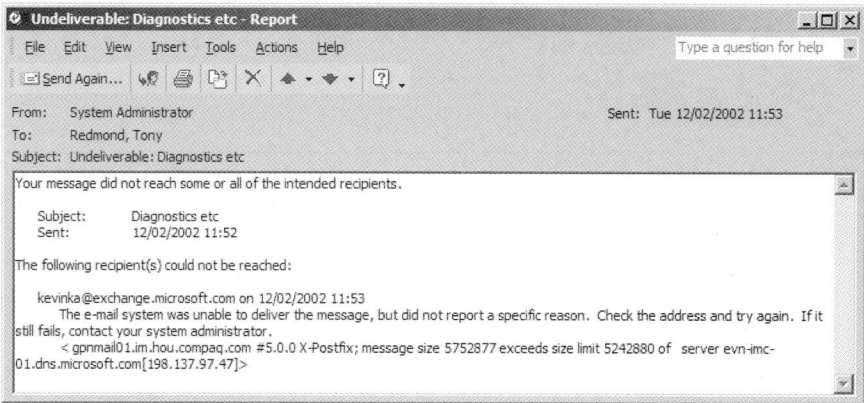

Figure 9.1 *A DSN displayed by Outlook 2002.*

out in the RFCs, while Outlook receives DSNs formatted in the style used since the original MAPI clients. Microsoft upgraded DSN processing in Exchange 2000 SP2, and work continues in this area to ensure that users receive information that is understandable and clear. For example, Figure 9.1 shows a delivery notification that tells the recipient that Exchange was unable to transmit the message because it exceeded the acceptable size (5 MB) on the destination SMTP server. Enough human-readable detail is provided to allow a help-desk representative to interpret why the message was undelivered and to perform the steps necessary to get the message through. Engineers and users tend to disagree exactly where to draw the line between readability and technical accuracy, and ongoing work is required to cater to all possible causes that prevent message transmission, but Exchange is good in this respect. See Table 9.1 for a list of DSN error codes.

- Chunking or BDAT: Normally, servers transmit the content portion of SMTP messages as one or more DATA statements. Each statement (or line) terminates with a CR/LF, full stop/CR/LF sequence. This implementation works well for small text-based messages but is less successful when dealing with very large encoded attachments of the type that circulate in corporate messaging systems today (PowerPoint presentations, large Word documents, MPEG files, and so on). RFC 1830 defines BDAT (or binary data transfer) as part of the "chunking" ESMTP specification and replaces the standard DATA command. BDAT always passes an argument, which specifies the number of octets contained in a message bodypart, and then proceeds to

Table 9.1 *DSN Error Codes*

DSN	Meaning
4.2.2	Mailbox quota exceeded.
4.3.1	Flagged as a memory exceeded error, but is usually caused by a disk full condition somewhere (such as the disk holding the SMTP drop folder).
4.3.2	The administrator has manually caused the message to be nondelivered.
4.4.1	Host is not responding—could be a transient network error or the target server is down.
4.4.2	Connection dropped between servers.
4.4.6	Message exceeded maximum hop count.
4.4.7	Message expired in queue.
4.4.9	An SMTP connector has a non-SMTP address space defined, and Exchange attempted to use the SMTP connector to route the message.
5.0.0	Hard categorization error, normally indicating that the message is corrupt. The error can also be provoked if SMTP cannot route the message, because no connector can handle the address on the message. You can often resolve this problem by ensuring that at least one SMTP connector can handle an address space of *.
5.1.0	Generic categorization error, normally caused by a missing attribute on the message.
5.1.1	An unresolved address—based on its SMTP or X.400 address, the address seems to belong to this Exchange organization, but a lookup cannot resolve the address against the directory.
5.1.3	The address on the message does not conform to RFC 821 specifications (bad address syntax).
5.1.4	More than one object in the directory has the address on the message, so it is ambiguous and the categorizer cannot resolve it.
5.1.6	The recipient is in the directory, but does not have an associated Exchange server (home server or home Mailbox Store), so the categorizer cannot deliver the message.
5.1.7	The sender of the message has a missing or malformed address in the AD, so the transport engine cannot deliver the message.
5.2.1	The message is too big for delivery or the recipient's mailbox is disabled.
5.2.3	The originator attempted to send a message larger than permitted or the recipient cannot accept a message of this size.
5.3.3	The remote server does not have enough disk space to accept incoming messages.
5.3.5	Loop back detected. The server is configured to loop back on itself.
5.4.0	DNS lookup error (host not found, smarthost entry incorrect)
5.4.4	Routing hop not found.

Table 9.1 *DSN Error Codes (continued)*

DSN	Meaning
5.4.6	A forward loop exists in the categorizer for this recipient.
5.4.8	The categorizer was processing a message for a recipient with a mailbox on a remote server, but the FQDN of the remote server matches a local domain.
5.5.0	An SMTP protocol error—you normally find an explanation about why the protocol error occurred in the DSN text. The 5.5.0 error in Figure 9.1 shows that the message size exceeded a limit set on a connector somewhere along the message path.
5.5.2	SMTP commands are executed out of sequence.
5.5.3	The sender of the message cannot address a message to so many recipients. You can configure recipient limits on both a per-user and an organization-wide basis.
5.7.1	Access denied because the originator cannot send messages to this recipient. Alternatively, the user may be attempting to send a message on behalf of another user without the appropriate permission.

stream content to the server until all the data is transmitted. No attempt is made to interpret or understand the content, and the server only has to wait until the expected amount of data has arrived to know when transmission is complete. This approach allows the SMTP virtual server to send and receive messages much more quickly than by using the DATA command. Exchange servers always attempt to use BDAT after they have created outbound connections to another SMTP server. If the other server cannot support BDAT,[1] Exchange automatically downgrades the connection to use the standard DATA command. Connections between Exchange 2000/2003 servers always use BDAT. Together with the streaming file, chunking allows Exchange 2000/2003 to process messages containing audio or video content very efficiently. Chunking provides SMTP with a big advantage over X.400, which is relatively chatty in terms of acknowledgments and checkpoints as large messages pass across the wire. Opening up a connection and streaming data until the correspondents reach an agreed-upon point allows the SMTP server to transfer data faster. However, if a message fails in the middle of transmission, chunking does not allow servers to restart from a checkpoint, and they must resend the complete message.

---

1. Exchange looks for the "chunking" keyword in the response to its initial EHLO command. If the keyword exists, Exchange knows that the other SMTP server supports BDAT and is able to accept binary transmission.

9.2 The evolution of SMTP

In addition, Exchange (and the basic SMTP service provided by Windows) supports the following:[2]

- VRFY (RFC 821): verify or ensure that the server can deliver a message to a local recipient. While the verb is present, Exchange does not use it because its sole purpose is to verify that an address is valid, which is great for spammers and not so good for administrators. If you need this command, you have to enable it, and there is no out-of-the-box way to do this except via a purpose-written event sink.

- EXPN (RFC 821): expand a distribution list into individual recipients. The command asks the server whether the recipient is a distribution list and, if so, to return the membership of the list.

- ETRN (RFC 1985): an extension of the standard TURN command, which reverses sender and receiver roles. The standard TURN command enables clients to download messages for a domain but does not include any validation mechanism. Thus, it is possible that a rogue system could attempt to download messages held on a server (normally managed by an ISP) for a site or domain other than itself. ETRN provides a mechanism for a client SMTP system to request download for a specific queue of messages. The host server can then decide whether to honor the request and dequeue the messages.

- SIZE (RFC 1870): provide an indication of how large a message is. SIZE also advertises the maximum size of a message a server will accept.

- TLS (RFC 2487): a method to use transport-level security to protect the communications between SMTP clients and servers.

- AUTH (RFC 2554): a method to allow an SMTP client to negotiate an agreed-upon authentication mechanism with a server. As shown in Figure 9.2, Exchange supports GSSAPI, NTLM, and LOGIN as authentication and encryption mechanisms. Exchange 5.5 supports NTLM (NT Challenge/Response) and TLS (Transport-Level Security), both of which implement an SSL-secured connection.

The list of commands may vary in the future with support packs and updates to both Windows and Exchange. To verify the current list of commands supported by SMTP on your server, TELNET to port 25 on the server and issue an EHLO command. The server returns a list of keywords

---

2. The Internet Mail Consortium maintains a chart comparing functionality of different SMTP servers. The chart is available at http://www.imc.org/features-chart.html.

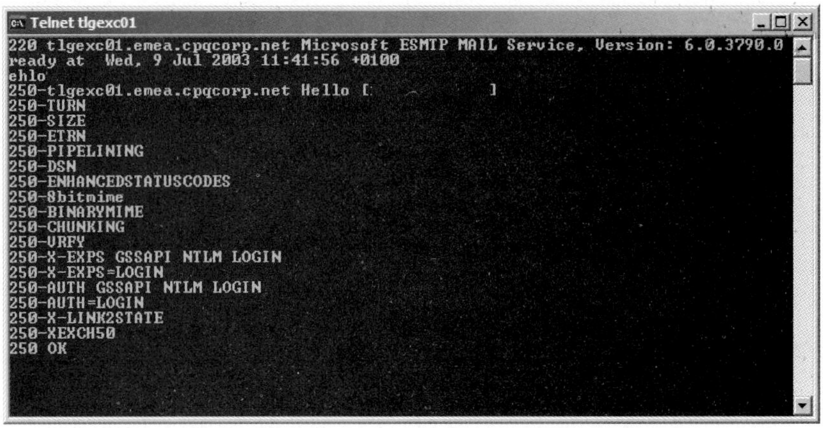

Figure 9.2
Extended SMTP commands supported by Exchange.

```
Telnet tlgexc01
220 tlgexc01.emea.cpqcorp.net Microsoft ESMIP MAIL Service, Version: 6.0.3790.0
ready at  Wed, 9 Jul 2003 11:41:56 +0100
ehlo
250-tlgexc01.emea.cpqcorp.net Hello [          ]
250-TURN
250-SIZE
250-ETRN
250-PIPELINING
250-DSN
250-ENHANCEDSTATUSCODES
250-8bitmime
250-BINARYMIME
250-CHUNKING
250-VRFY
250-X-EXPS GSSAPI NTLM LOGIN
250-X-EXPS=LOGIN
250-AUTH GSSAPI NTLM LOGIN
250-AUTH=LOGIN
250-X-LINK2STATE
250-XEXCH50
250 OK
```

for the commands supported by the server, as shown in Figure 9.2. The version number reported at the top of the screen tells you which version of Exchange is on the server.

Note that the commands listed by a particular server may not be the complete set. For example, the server queried in Figure 9.2 does not list the STARTTLS or TLS commands, because a certificate is not available for the server to use to encrypt traffic. Servers issued with certificates will display these commands when they respond to an EHLO query. Apart from the list of commands, Figure 9.2 also reveals some information about the server. The version number reported by the SMTP server reveals the version of IIS that is running on the server, in turn revealing some information about Windows. In this case, we see that the server reports version 6.0.3790, meaning that this server runs IIS 6.0 on Windows build 3790, which turns out to be the RTM build of Windows 2003. You can discover similar information about the version of Exchange running on a server if you TELNET to port 110 (POP3) or 143 (IMAP4) and examine the version number. For example, a version number starting with 6.0 means an Exchange 2000 server, while anything starting with 6.5 means Exchange 2003. The numbers after 6.0 or 6.5 reveal the service pack level, so 6.0.6249.0 indicates a server running Exchange 2000 SP3, and 6.5.6944.0 is the RTM build of Exchange 2003. Why does one protocol reveal information about Windows and another informs about Exchange when IIS controls all the protocol stacks? Well, SMTP is a basic Windows service, so its version number depends on Windows. POP3 and IMAP are services provided by Exchange, so their version number depends on Exchange. See section 9.2.4 for a discussion on how to suppress banner information reported by protocol servers.

9.2 The evolution of SMTP

Windows and Exchange both depend heavily on SMTP to transport messages between servers. Indeed, the Exchange development group provides the code for CDONTS, which ships with every Windows server as part of IIS. The basic SMTP functionality in Windows is similar to that in many UNIX servers and is a no frills messaging server. The basic SMTP server does not include the capability to send messages between mailboxes. Instead, the SMTP server provides Windows and other products with a well-known transport that can carry information between applications. The best example of this is intersite AD replication, and SharePoint Portal Server is another good example, since it uses the SMTP service to send subscription messages to users after users add new documents to its repository.

Administrators manage the SMTP service through the Internet Information Services MMC console, and IIS holds its configuration data in the IIS metabase. The SMTP service runs as part of the INETINFO process, in the same manner as all the other protocols supported by IIS. Because the AD holds the Exchange configuration data, a background process managed by the System Attendant synchronizes the AD with the IIS metabase. The same situation is true for all protocols.

The SMTP service supports many of the extended functions defined by ESMTP as well as virtual servers and scripting. Clients can generate and send messages programmatically or by communication through the standard SMTP listener port (25). Alternatively, applications can generate text messages in SMTP format and submit them for processing by placing them in the SMTP drop directory.[3]

Apart from the functions available through the IIS MMC console, no management capabilities are available to control or manipulate the SMTP service. You can, therefore, conclude that the SMTP service is so basic that either it is working or it is not. In other words, if you can create and send messages, then the SMTP service is operational. If problems occur, you usually have to restart the SMTP service to correct matters.

When Exchange is installed, the base SMTP service is upgraded (not replaced) to add the features for advanced queuing and routing and the new SMTP command verbs to enable link state routing updates. Exchange upgrades SMTP capabilities by adding a new event sink and some transport and protocol events that allow SMTP messages to flow into the Store via ExIFS. Transport events extend the function of the transport core, while protocol events extend the SMTP protocol. After the upgrade, the most

---

3. The mail drop directory for the default SMTP virtual server is \exchsrvr\mailroot\vs1\pickup. The directory is moved from the Windows default location when Exchange is installed on a server.

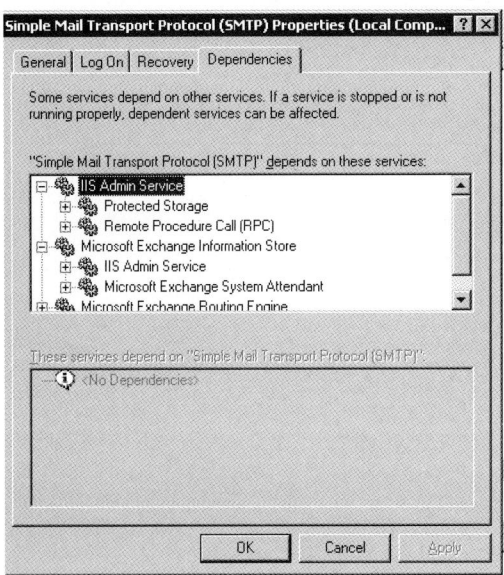

Figure 9.3
Dependencies of the SMTP service.

important difference is that the extended SMTP service understands how to process messages sent to mailboxes.

Because Exchange upgrades the basic SMTP service to add its own set of events, it follows that the SMTP service becomes a very large dependency for Exchange. In fact, Exchange also becomes a dependency for the SMTP service, as you can see in Figure 9.3. Interdependencies mean that you have to be careful when you manage components. For example, you should not reinstall the SMTP service from the Windows distribution kit without also reinstalling Exchange.

9.2.2 SMTP virtual servers

Windows and Exchange both implement SMTP protocol support in the form of virtual servers managed by IIS. A virtual server is composed of an IP address, IP port, and protocol. This is a major difference from the previous implementation in first-generation Exchange servers, where a connector (the Internet Mail Service) binds SMTP protocol access to a specific port. Once bound, SMTP remains associated with that port, and only one instance of the protocol can exist on a server. For example, the Exchange 5.5 IMS usually binds to port 25, so port 25 is the only port that can accept SMTP traffic. Now, the default virtual server for SMTP is a combination of the SMTP protocol, a port, and one or more IP addresses. The virtual server handles all SMTP traffic sent to those IP addresses and port.

Exchange takes the same approach with the virtual servers for the other Internet protocols. For example, the default virtual server for HTTP is composed of HTTP and port 80, and so on.

When you upgrade an Exchange 5.5 server that hosts an Internet Mail Service (IMS), the default SMTP virtual server takes over the role played by the IMS. The address space defined in the configuration of the IMS becomes an SMTP connector that runs as part of the virtual server. You can have more than one SMTP connector on an individual server, a useful configuration if you want to process outbound mail to different destinations in a different manner. For example, you might decide to create a special SMTP connector to handle messages going to nonurgent personal Internet mail services such as hotmail.com, msdn.com, aol.com, and so on. You can then configure the connector with a schedule to pass messages outside normal business hours, so that messages sent to commercial destinations receive a higher priority.

Routing group and SMTP connectors both use the SMTP protocol and are therefore associated with a virtual server. All of the connectors tied to a virtual server respect its properties, which control how the virtual server operates. You can view and work with the properties of the virtual server through ESM by selecting the hosting server, opening the protocols container, and then selecting the virtual server. Apart from logging, you do not have to restart a virtual server or connector before a change to a property becomes active. ESM signals any updates as events that the virtual server recognizes, so the effect of making a change to a server's properties is almost immediate. Table 9.2 outlines the default settings for SMTP virtual servers.

If you run in a heterogeneous messaging environment that includes UNIX or Linux servers, you should also check that the FQDN of the server is a value that SMTP MTAs running on the UNIX and Linux servers can resolve. The RFCs that govern DNS (1034 and 1035) do not accommodate the underscore character in server names, but Windows is quite happy if you use an underscore to name a server. For example, the name EXCH_SVR is perfectly valid for Windows, but when it appears in an FQDN (EXCH_SRVR.abc.net), some SMTP MTAs may refuse connections and will not transfer messages. In this situation, you probably do not want to rename the server, so it is good that you can work around the issue by accessing the Delivery property page for the SMTP virtual server, then Advanced, and then change the server's FQDN to remove the underscore (in this case, to EXCHSVR.abc.net). Now, whenever the SMTP virtual server connects, it passes the name you define, rather than the default value,

Table 9.2 *Important Settings for an SMTP Virtual Server*

Virtual SMTP Server Property	Default Value	Other Possible Values
Outbound security	Allow anonymous connections. Exchange servers ignore this setting, since they establish their own credentials before sending messages.	Require basic authentication (clear text) or TLS (encrypted) with an X.509 server certificate
Inbound security	Allow anonymous connections (must be set to allow IMAP and POP clients to send messages)	Require basic authentication or TLS
Port number	25	Any free IP port
Limit message size	2,048 KB (2 MB)	
Limit number of messages per connection	Unlimited	
Limit number of recipients per message	Unlimited	
Outbound retry intervals	First, 15 minutes; second, 30 minutes; third, 60 minutes; then 240 minutes until timeout	
Delay notifications	Send after 12 hours	
Expiration timeout	2 days	
Local delivery delay	12 hours	
Maximum hop count	15	
Smart host name	FQDN or IP address of smart host server	
Connection controls	All servers can connect	Define a list of servers that are allowed to connect to this server
Relay restrictions	All servers that can connect can relay (submit messages for onward delivery)	Define how servers handle attempts to relay messages

and the remote MTA is happy. You may also want to update the DNS PTR record for the server to the new name so that it can be resolved externally.

9.2.3 Relays

The default SMTP virtual server is the basic building block for the routing group and SMTP connectors, the two preferred ways to link Exchange serv-

9.2 The evolution of SMTP

ers together. You do not need to define a second virtual server unless you really have a good reason to use another. Performance is not one of the reasons. Virtual servers are multithreaded anyway, so creating a second virtual SMTP server does not increase the ability of the computer to process SMTP messages any faster. Remember, all incoming messages arrive at port 25 and are then processed by the default SMTP virtual server. You can create another virtual SMTP server that sends outgoing messages through another port, but you have to ask yourself why you want to add any more complexity to your administrative environment than you already have. You only need to configure separate virtual servers when a requirement exists to handle messages sent to specific domains in a different manner, or when you want to handle messages above a certain size or messages with a particular priority.

Table 9.2 lists many of the important settings that you can apply to an SMTP virtual server. The settings give some insight into the reasons why you might want to create a new virtual server. For example, let us assume that you want to allow a specific set of external systems to use your server as a relay, but you only want them to be able to send messages of a certain size, and an authentication connection is necessary. You could apply these settings to the default virtual server, but then they would affect all connections, and you might want to allow messages sent locally to be larger, have more recipients, or not require an authenticated connection. Remember that you must clearly define the address space for each virtual server so that it can process email for various domains.

Mail relays are an integral part of the SMTP architecture, so the fact that a server allows relaying is not bad in itself. Relays are fine, as long as they are controlled and used for the purpose that you want to use them for, such as allowing IMAP4 clients such as Outlook Express to send messages by making a connection to an SMTP server. The Internet is a great place, but it has some seedy quarters and practices, most notably spam or unsolicited commercial email.

9.2.4 Changing SMTP banners

SMTP servers respond to incoming connections with a banner message, which contains information about the type of server and the version of the software it runs. For example, if you TELNET to port 25 on an Exchange 2000 server, the default response of the SMTP server is:

```
220 server name.domain name Microsoft ESMTP Mail Service,
    Version 5.0.2195.2966 ready at <time>
```

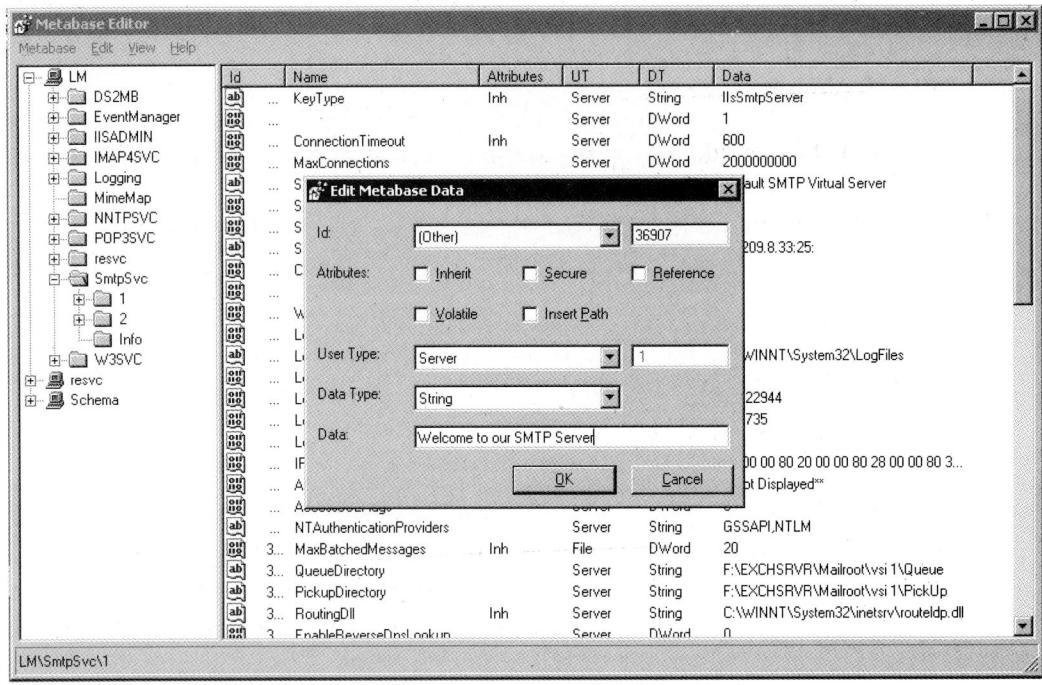

Figure 9.4   *Editing the IIS metabase to change an SMTP banner.*

A hacker may be able to use this information to determine how best he or she can attack the server. The response tells the hacker the version of the software (5.0.2195 indicates the RTM build of Windows 2000, with 6.0.3790 meaning the RTM build of Windows 2003). Hackers also know that the server is ESMTP capable and so will respond to a wider set of commands. You can frustrate hackers by changing the banner to whatever string you like by editing the IIS metabase. This is a good example of the dependency that Exchange has on the IIS, since there is no way to edit the banner through ESM or any other Exchange-specific utility. Follow these steps to change the banner:

- Download an IIS metabase editing tool such as MetaEdit[4] and install it on the server where you want to change the SMTP banner.

- Open the utility and navigate to the node for the SMTP virtual server. Remember, a physical server can support multiple virtual protocol servers, and the IIS metabase contains separate information for

---

4. Microsoft Knowledge Base article Q232068 explains how to download and install the MetaEdit utility.

9.2 The evolution of SMTP

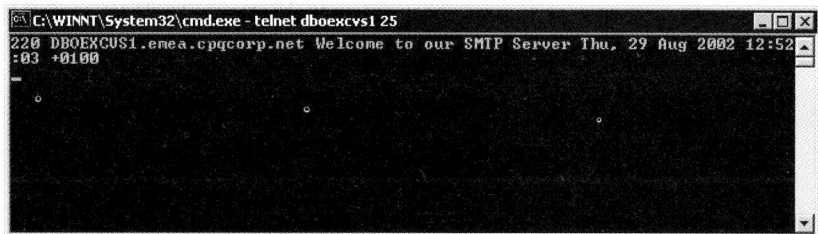

Figure 9.5
The SMTP banner is successfully changed.

each virtual server. The node for the default SMTP virtual server is Lm\Smtpsvc\1.

- Click on the Edit option, click New, and then click on String to add a new string value.

- Verify that the entry in the ID box is Other, and type 36907 in the space to the right of the ID box (Figure 9.4). The identifier for the string used in the banner is 36907.

- Type the new banner string in the Data box and click on OK.

- Exit the metabase edit utility.

- Use ESM to stop and restart the SMTP virtual server. On a cluster, you have to do this with the Cluster Administrator utility.

TELNET to port 25 on the server to test that the new banner is effective. You should see the default banner replaced by the string that you input into the metabase. Figure 9.5 demonstrates that the string input in Figure 9.4 has replaced the default banner.

Remember that you must manually implement this change on every server that connects to the Internet before your SMTP network is prevented from offering information to potential hackers.

9.2.5 Installing Exchange servers in the DMZ

When you design your messaging infrastructure, you need to look at how to connect Exchange to the Internet. Large enterprises typically create a DMZ to isolate the internal network from the external network and place only the servers necessary to accept and transfer messages to and from the Internet into the DMZ. You have to decide whether to put an Exchange server into the DMZ and make it the first point of contact for incoming SMTP messages or use another option.

Many complex issues drive this choice, including the overall computing and messaging infrastructures, security, and antivirus and spam protection.

However, the essential decision is whether to use Exchange or another mail server in the DMZ. Because Exchange relies so heavily on the AD, if you want to use Exchange, you have to open up additional ports in the internal-facing firewall to permit the Routing Engine to resolve email addresses and read configuration data. Reducing the number of open ports is important, because the less open ports you have, the less chance hackers have to exploit holes in the firewall. For this reason, many enterprises choose to install an SMTP relay host in the DMZ and keep all their Exchange servers in the internal network. The most common relay host configuration is one or more UNIX or Linux servers running software such as sendmail or postfix. An alternative approach is to create a special Exchange organization and AD forest for email routing and put it into the DMZ.

The relay server may take on several roles, including:

- Acting as the entry point for incoming SMTP messages
- Acting as the exit point for outgoing SMTP messages
- Acting as a block for incoming spam
- Acting as a block for incoming inappropriate messages or outgoing messages that may contain sensitive or commercially secret information
- Acting as a check to ensure that the intended recipient works for the company by validating email addresses against the enterprise directory

You can do all of these things with Exchange, so functionality is not the issue. If you want to deploy Exchange into the DMZ, make sure that you understand the consequences of maintaining the necessary open ports.

9.2.6 The ongoing role of the X.400 MTA

The Routing Engine now performs much of the work done by the MTA for first-generation Exchange servers. Table 9.3 compares the function served by the MTA in Exchange 5.5 with its current workload.

By default, Exchange allocates an X.400 address to every user with a mailbox. The X.400 address is critical within a mixed-mode organization, because older Exchange servers use the X.400 address to route messages to mailboxes. You should not delete the X.400 addresses from mailboxes unless you are positive that they will never be required again. Given that the addresses take up little space in the AD, it is best to leave them alone.

An Exchange organization that operates in native mode transmits all messages via SMTP, so you might assume that you can disable or remove the MTA from servers. However, while it is possible to remove the MTA,

9.3 The transport core

Table 9.3 *Difference in MTA Roles between Exchange 5.5 and Exchange 2000/2003*

MTA in Exchange 5.5	MTA in Exchange 2000/2003
Controls intrasite RPC message management	Routing groups replace sites as the basis for routing. Exchange uses SMTP to send messages between routing group members. The MTA is still responsible for controlling RPC communication to Exchange 5.5 servers in mixed-mode organizations.
Controls intersite traffic across site and X.400 connectors	The MTA can connect old Exchange sites to routing groups. You can also use an SMTP connector, which may be faster.
Determines message routing (the GWART)	Routing is determined by the link state table, which is managed by routing group masters. In a mixed-mode organization, the SRS provides data for inclusion into the GWART for Exchange 5.5 servers to use.
Manages connections to X.400 messaging systems (1984, 1988, 1993)	The MTA continues to manage connections to X.400-based messaging systems.
Manages Exchange Development Kit (EDK) connectors	The MTA still manages connections made by connectors built using the EDK. Most fax connectors fit in this category.

the ramifications for server operation are unpredictable, because Microsoft has not completely tested all possible scenarios for servers with a removed MTA. For this reason, while it would like to be able to run Exchange in a pure SMTP configuration, Microsoft does not support servers if you remove the MTA.

Over time, Exchange collected many different connectors, ranging from fax connectors to those that support other messaging systems. Microsoft never upgraded some of the older connectors to use SMTP, including its own IBM PROFS and IBM SNADS connectors, which are now obsoleted in Exchange 2003 along with connectors for Lotus cc:Mail, Microsoft Mail, and so on.

9.3 The transport core

The transport core is the heart of Exchange message routing. It is broken down into the following four major components:

- Advanced Queuing: This component manages messages as they enter and exit the different queues within the transport core. The queuing engine supports domain-level queues, where messages are grouped according to their final destination (such as any message sent to recipients at hp.com), as well as link queues, where messages are grouped according to the next hop that they will be routed across to get to their final destination. For example, messages sent to hp.com might have to travel across a link to an ISP. As explained later in this chapter, Exchange maintains destination queues for messages sent to domains such as hp.com, as well as link queues for messages waiting to travel on the next link to their final destination. For example, if you send messages to hp.com via a connection to an ISP, Exchange maintains a link queue for the ISP and places any messages going to hp.com there along with messages for any other address that the ISP handles. A message can pass from server to server and move from link queue to link queue, but it will stay on the same domain-level queue. The queuing engine is supported by the QueueAdmin API, which is used by the Exchange System Manager snap-in to view queue status. You can use this API to stop and start queues as well as to enumerate queue contents. The Advanced Queuing component is also responsible for generating delivery service notifications.

- Categorizer: The categorizer analyzes message headers and properties to decide how to best process messages. Senders and recipients are resolved against the AD to ensure that Exchange respects any administrator-imposed restrictions and that it can route messages to addresses in the headers. A limited version of the categorizer is included in the basic Windows SMTP server to enable it to expand mail-enabled groups. The version provided with Exchange 2003 adds support for features such as checking for mailbox quotas, whether a mailbox can receive mail from a specific sender, which Mailbox Store a mailbox is located in, whether a user can send messages across a specific connector, and so on.

- Exchange Store Driver: This is the interface between the Advanced Queuing component and the NTFS file system. Windows ships with a basic Store driver, which allows it to save incoming SMTP messages as formatted files; these are later processed to accomplish tasks such as AD replication. The Exchange Store driver is an upgraded version, which includes ExIFS support; this enables Advanced Queuing also to have direct access to messages in the Store.

- Routing Engine: This component replaces the RID master and GWART used to determine routing paths within an Exchange 5.5 organization. It is a much more sophisticated routing mechanism and

9.3 The transport core

is capable of assessing incoming updates about the state of the network and adjusting the path messages will take. Exchange can route messages according to their size, the sender of a message, and their priority. This information is taken into account, together with the cost associated with the various links defined between servers in the organization and the current state of the links, to decide how a message is eventually routed.

Exchange uses a modified version of Dijkstra's algorithm to determine routing decisions. The method used to route messages is explained in section 9.7. Figure 9.6 illustrates how the different parts of the transport core work together. While the diagram looks complicated at first appearance, the detailed workings of the transport core present a far more complicated picture than that depicted here. However, it is sufficient to reveal the essential workings of Exchange's transport core. To explore how the parts of the Routing Engine work together, we can follow the path of a message as the Routing Engine processes it within the transport core:

- Messages can enter the transport core from the SMTP service, the MTA, or the Store. Messages coming from the SMTP service originate from other Exchange servers or external systems and arrive as NTFS files, which are then processed via ExIFS. MAPI mailboxes

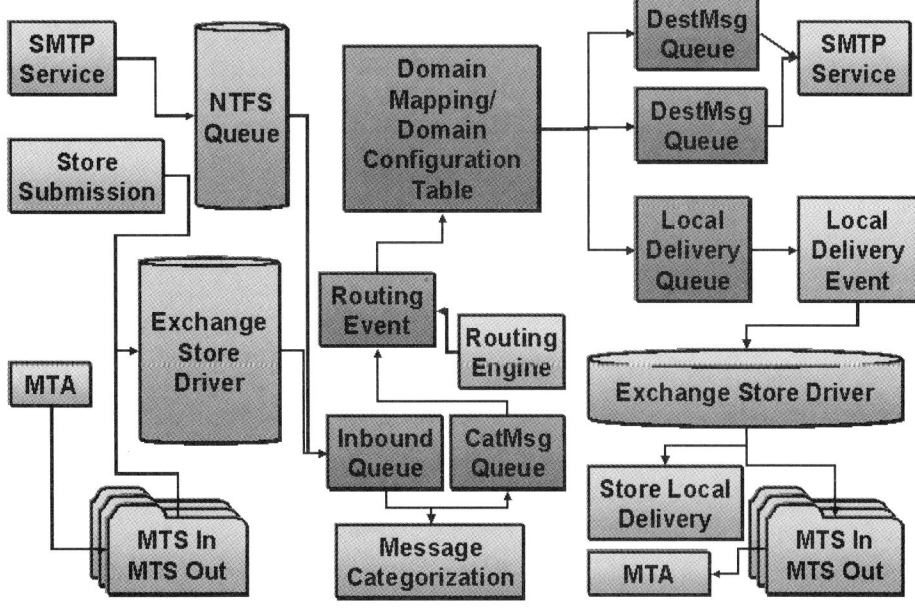

Figure 9.6   *The Exchange transport core.*

submit messages through the Store, and messages arriving from Exchange 5.5 servers come in through the MTA. IMAP and POP3 clients submit messages through the SMTP protocol stack in IIS, which, in turn, uses ExIFS to create the message bodies and insert them into the streaming file. HTTP-DAV clients can access ExIFS directly without going through the SMTP protocol stack. Message properties are promoted into the appropriate Mailbox Store. In all cases, the messages are placed into the Inbound Queue.

- The queuing engine manages processing of the inbound messages and passes them to the Message Categorization code. Message Categorization performs checks such as mailbox quota limits for recipients and verifies that the message can be routed onward. The individual addresses in distribution groups are expanded at this time.

- The message goes on to the Categorized Message Queue. The transport core now checks to see whether any routing event should be triggered for the message. For example, if an event implements a check to ensure that outgoing messages should not contain profanities, it would be possible to scan the text of the message and its attachment. The message could then be routed onward or returned to the originator if some problem words were found. Routing events are designed to facilitate the fastest possible delivery of messages to the final destination, so checking for profanities is not a particularly good example of how a routing event is used. Nevertheless, it does demonstrate that events open up all sorts of new possibilities to developers.

- A lookup is performed against the Domain Mapping and Configuration Table. This table tells the transport core to route the message for local delivery or to one of the SMTP virtual servers that are active on the system.

- Messages intended for local recipients are placed on a local delivery queue. "Local" means anything that is not another SMTP server (including remote Exchange servers). Remember that the MTA is still tightly integrated with the Store, so any message that must be dealt with by the MTA has to be routed through the Store. At this point, another event could be triggered before the message is actually delivered to a mailbox. For example, a copy of the message could be sent to a special recipient if it came from a user in a particular department. The message is then passed to the Exchange Store driver, which either delivers the message to a local mailbox or passes it to the MTA for onward transmission to an Exchange 5.5 site or legacy connector.

9.3 The transport core

- Messages for other SMTP servers are allocated to the destination queues for the SMTP virtual servers allocated to handle messages for the different domains. The Connection Manager monitors the links to other SMTP servers for the destination message queues and adjusts routing as required. For instance, if the link state table were updated to reflect the fact that a hub server was currently not available, the Connection Manager might reroute messages that pass through the affected server via another hub. To improve message throughput, Exchange 2003 performs DNS resolution for SMTP addresses synchronously instead of the asynchronous processing done by Exchange 2000.

- All outgoing messages are dispatched to their final destination using the standard Windows SMTP service.

The introduction of query-based distribution groups can pose a huge processing challenge for the Routing Engine, which must resolve the LDAP query to build the complete recipient set represented by a query-based group before it can decide how to route a message. Consider a query that generates 400,000 recipients (a real-life example). The two biggest problems are the time taken to generate the list (between six to eight hours on a fast server) and the fact that Exchange does not checkpoint the recipient set, so the Routing Engine has to start over if any problem prevents it from generating the complete list. The combination of Exchange 2003 (which fetches 1,500 recipients at a time in LDAP queries instead of 1,000 for Exchange 2000) and Windows 2003 provides the fastest performance for query-based distribution groups, but even so, you should arrange to submit messages addressed to groups that expand into very large collections at a time of low user demand. One further issue is that there is no way for an administrator to track the progress of list expansion, so once a message is submitted, it goes into a black hole until it comes out again. Message tracking can help you follow the course of a message through the transport core. Exchange 2003 upgrades message tracking to capture even more information than before.

9.3.1 Domain and link queues

Exchange uses two different queues in the final stages of routing SMTP messages. The Routing Engine maintains queues on a per-domain basis. In other words, all the messages for a specific SMTP domain (such as *.com) are held together on one queue. The Routing Engine takes messages off domain queues and places them on link queues, which Exchange maintains on a per-hop basis. This means that the Connection Manager moves messages to the most suitable link queue for final routing. You can equate queues to links in some respects, but it is not 100 percent accurate to think that both are the same. A link is an object that is associated with multiple queues, each of which can provide messages that will use the link. Another way of thinking of this is to define a link as an outbound connection to a single host that can be used by multiple queues.

Per-destination queues allow Exchange to handle hold-ups in message delivery to specific destinations. The Exchange 5.5 IMS implements a different solution by holding all messages in a single queue until they are sent. If problems are encountered transmitting messages to a domain, then all messages are blocked until the problem is resolved. For example, let's assume that the IMS is used to connect Exchange 5.5 sites in Dublin, London, Dallas, and New York. Messages normally go from Dublin to Dallas via New York. If the network link goes down between Dublin and New York, messages are rerouted if another route exists. If not, they remain on the queue until the link is fixed. This underscores the importance of factoring in multiple available routes between routing groups, if possible, when you consider the design of an Exchange organization. Note too that only the messages on a single link are ever blocked by a failure that closes off communication to a specific destination. Messages going to all other destinations continue to flow unless they have to pass along the link affected by the failure.

The Routing Engine will know that the link between Dublin and New York is down and will attempt to discover alternate routes. If links are available between Dublin to London, and London to Dallas, then messages can be moved to the per-link queue for London and be routed via that location. Rerouting happens automatically and does not have to be manually reconfigured when problems occur.

9.4 Processing incoming messages

Messages can arrive into an Exchange server through a variety of different routes. The initial submission mechanism and processing performed to get the message into the system is different for each route, but they all come together when messages arrive at the categorizer.

9.4.1 SMTP messages

SMTP servers act as clients to other SMTP servers when they transmit messages. Clients submit messages to port 25, one of the ports monitored by

IIS. The SMTP service creates a thread to process the new message. Protocol events might fire before a message is fully accepted. For example, the SMTP service may need to check the sender of the message with a DNS lookup to ensure that the sender comes from a valid server in an attempt to defeat spammers. If valid, the SMTP service can accept the message and the transaction continues.

The Routing Engine fires a Store driver event when it accepts a message. Currently, Exchange uses an enhanced version of the standard Windows NTFS Store driver to access NTFS files instead of a driver that accesses the Store directly using ExIFS. The developers took a deliberate decision not to use ExIFS to avoid creating a dependency on the Store service or, more specifically, to attempt to access a folder in a database that the Store might not have mounted when a message arrives. NTFS is always available when a server is running, and the drop directory is available if the disk where it is located is mounted. In addition, directing messages into an NTFS folder rather than the Store avoids problems that might occur when administrators move or delete Mailbox Stores.

The new message goes onto the OnSubmission queue, which fires an event. If an error occurs at this point (e.g., the SMTP service receives a badly formed SMTP message or an unauthorized source attempts to relay through the server), a failure DSN message (a nondelivery notification) is generated and sent back to the originator. If Exchange cannot generate the DSN, perhaps because the sender is unknown, the message goes into the badmail directory (typically \exchsrvr\mailroot\badmail). The message also ends up in the badmail directory if Exchange rejects the DSN message or cannot deliver it. If you leave your server available as an open SMTP relay, spammers can use it to "inject" messages and send them around the world. Spammers address messages to lists that they assemble, and the nature of the beast is that a lot of spam goes to invalid recipients and ends up by generating NDRs. If Exchange cannot deliver the NDRs, they may end up in your badmail directory and steadily absorb disk space until you close off the open relay. This is one reason why you should always check Exchange servers for open SMTP relays.

You can change the location of the badmail directory through the "Messages" property page for the SMTP virtual server, as shown in Figure 9.7. The fired event then causes the transport core Store driver to create a special object called an ImailMsg and then populate the structure with various properties extracted from the incoming message. Similar to an X.400 message, the ImailMsg structure divides into two main parts. A set of properties such as the sender, subject, and recipients composes the message envelope,

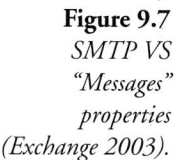

Figure 9.7
SMTP VS "Messages" properties (Exchange 2003).

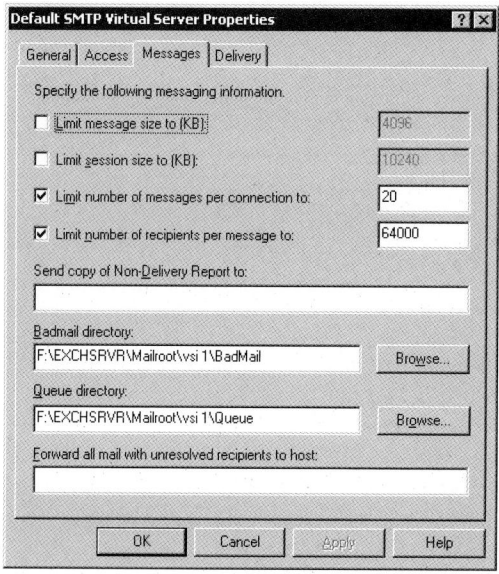

while a file on disk in the Queue directory holds the message body and any attachments. The transport core Store driver returns the pointer to the file created on disk and inserts this pointer into the ImailMsg structure.

After the ImailMsg structure is fully populated, the SMTP service returns it to the Advanced Queuing component, which then places the message in the Pre-Categorizer queue. If an error occurs at any point while the transport core is processing an incoming SMTP message, it is removed from the queue and dumped into the badmail directory, as described previously. (See Figure 9.8.) Note that it is easy for a busy server that acts as an SMTP gateway to accumulate large numbers of messages in the badmail directory over time. Because of the danger posed by Denial-of-Service (DoS) attacks, which could flood a server with undeliverable mail that Exchange would then deliver to the badmail directory, Microsoft changed the default behavior for the SMTP protocol server in Exchange 2003 SP1 in two ways. First, by default, Exchange suppresses the generation of badmail messages because Microsoft's experience was that most of these messages related to undeliverable DSN (delivery status notification) or NDR messages, which administrators do not care about anyway unless they are attempting to diagnose a message delivery problem. Second, SP1 includes support for a set of registry values under HKLM\System\CurrentControlSet\Services\SMTPSVC\Queueing to allow administrators to control how Exchange manages the badmail folder. (See Table 9.4.)

9.4 Processing incoming messages

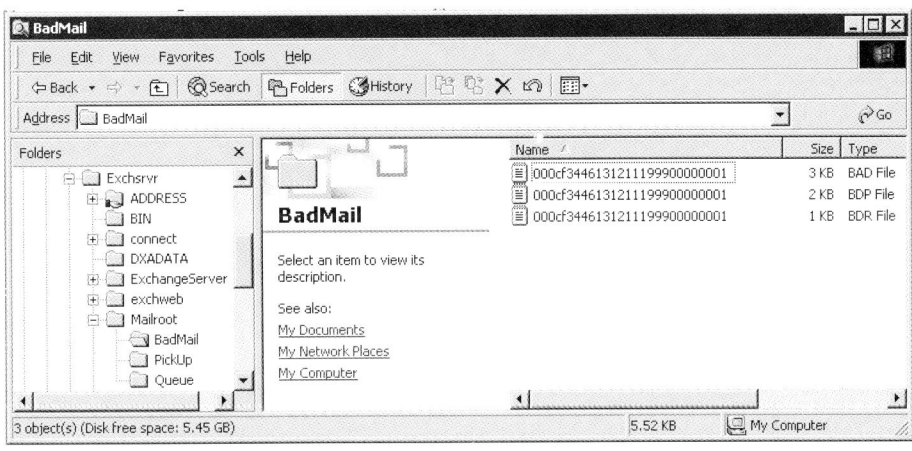

Figure 9.8 *SMTP messages that cannot be processed.*

You can also use Microsoft's badmail deletion and archiving script to move messages from the badmail directory on an automatically scheduled basis. Alternatively, you can simply delete all of the messages in the badmail directory manually, perhaps after a quick scan to ensure that nothing important is present.

If the queuing engine determines that the message is for local delivery, it must insert the message into the Store. To do this, IIS obtains a file handle to a virtual file and writes the incoming data directly into the file through ExIFS. ESE provides data in 2-MB contiguous chunks to ExIFS when it requests space, which then becomes "reserved space" until it is finally used. New messages are written into a set of pages in the reserved space. After it receives each message, ExIFS returns the list of pages the message was written to and its properties are promoted into the EDB database. The message

Table 9.4 *Badmail Registry Settings*

Value	Type	Meaning
MaxBadMailFolderSize	DWORD	Controls the maximum value in KB that Exchange allows the badmail folder to grow to before Exchange stops placing messages in the folder. Default value is 0, meaning that Exchange never puts email into the badmail folder. A value of –1 reverts Exchange to capture badmail as before and the growth of the badmail directory is unchecked.
BadMailSyncPeriod	DWORD	Controls how often (in minutes) Exchange checks the size of the badmail folder. The default is 12 hours.

transaction is logged into the current transaction log, and, after this occurs, the pages in the streaming file are deemed to be committed and are moved out of the reserved set. Outgoing messages are handled the same way, being read out by IIS from the Store via ExIFS.

9.4.2 MAPI messages

MAPI clients do not travel via an IIS protocol stack. Instead, MAPI clients make a direct connection to the Store and submit messages in much the same manner as Exchange 4.0. The notable difference is that submission is no longer the point at which Exchange generates nondelivery notifications or delivery receipts. After a message is accepted, the Store puts the message into a special folder called "SendQ" and fires an event to notify the transport core Store driver that a new message is waiting. The transport core Store driver then processes the MAPI content and builds an ImailMsg structure for submission to the Advanced Queuing component.

MAPI messages sent between Exchange servers are rendered in Transport Neutral Encapsulated Format (TNEF). TNEF is a format that Exchange can very quickly transform back into MAPI properties and content, so this is a low-overhead method to transport MAPI messages across SMTP. The messages are formed from an RFC 822–compliant header and an application-specific MS-TNEF MIME bodypart. Exchange servers communicate together using SMTP, which implies that the TNEF content needs to be rendered into MIME before it can be transported. Exchange solves the problem by transporting the messages as if they were binary content, so they do not need to be converted. Messages that are destined outside the organization are converted into MIME using the Base64 coding scheme, so they end up being between 25 percent and 30 percent larger.

9.4.3 HTTP messages

OWA clients generate and send messages over HTTP-DAV; these messages arrive into the Store through a direct connection similar to MAPI.

9.4.4 X.400 messages

The MTA handles all inbound X.400 messages, but it does not attempt to perform any routing or assessment of addresses, such as distribution list expansion. After the message is accepted by the MTA, it is simply put into the MTA Out folder within the Store, from where the message is then placed on the OnSubmission queue before it is fetched by the transport

9.4.5 Foreign connectors

Any connector that attaches to Exchange maintains its own MTS Out folder in the Store. It is the responsibility of the connector to process incoming messages and ensure that they are validly formed and ready for further processing. When the connector is satisfied, it places the message in the MTS Out folder, which causes the transport core Store driver to move the message to the OnSubmission queue for processing by the Advanced Queuing component.[5]

9.5 Categorization and routing

All inbound messages that arrive on an Exchange server are eventually processed by the Advanced Queuing component. They then move to the Pre-Categorizer queue, where a Categorizer thread picks them up for further processing. A number of operations are then performed on the message:

- The address of the message sender is extracted from the envelope. A search is then conducted against addresses held in the AD (using the proxyAddresses attribute) to determine whether it can be resolved.

- Each entry in the recipient list held in the envelope is examined and a lookup performed against the AD to determine whether the recipient can be resolved. If the recipient is a distribution group, the group is expanded to include the members of the group in the recipient list, but only if expansion is allowed on the server. If a recipient cannot be resolved, it is marked "unknown."

- A check ensures that the resolved recipients can accept messages, according to any restrictions that might currently apply for the recipients, such as quota exceeded on a mailbox.

- Any per-sender and per-recipient limits are checked.

- Internet message format settings (such as whether the target domain can only accept plain text messages) are checked and properties set to ensure that recipients receive messages in a format they can deal with.

---

5. A problem with the Lotus Notes connector is that it does not operate correctly in a routing group that contains mailbox servers. You therefore need to create a special routing group to host the Lotus Notes connector, which should run on a server that has no mailboxes. The problem is fixed in Exchange 2000 SP1.

- Occasionally multiple copies of a message may need to be created, because different recipients must see different versions of the message. A good example of where this happens is if the Routing Engine can find one recipient in the AD that has a mailbox on an Exchange server and another recipient that does not. In this instance, Exchange creates one version of the message for delivery inside the organization (which might, for example, send TNEF content as a binary bodypart) and another for delivery outside the organization (which might have the same bodypart encoded in Base64).

- Each recipient is then marked as either "gateway" or "local." Gateway recipients are reached via the MTA or a connector, while "local" recipients have mailboxes on an Exchange server in this organization.

After categorization, messages are placed in a prerouting queue, and the routing event is called to create a "next-hop identifier" for the message. The Routing Engine writes information about categorization processing into the XEXCH50 properties of messages so that subsequent Exchange servers along the path do not repeat work. The next-hop identifier tells the queuing engine which per-domain queue will handle the message.

9.5.1 Handling messages for protected groups

Exchange 2003 allows you to protect mail-enabled objects, including query-based distribution groups, so that they will only accept messages from authenticated users. This feature requires changes in the SMTP service, Routing Engine, and categorization to ensure that Exchange stamps incoming messages with authentication data and then checks to validate that the message does in fact come from an authenticated user.

Exchange 2003 processes incoming SMTP messages as before, but now appends some authentication data[6] in the "Mail From:" field as defined by RFC 2554. This data is retained as long as the message passes between Exchange 2003 servers (as in front- and back-end servers), but drops if the message goes to an Exchange 2000 or earlier server. Exchange uses the same mechanism to transmit data for the "Sent by" field when a user sends a message on behalf of another user.

After the SMTP service accepts the message, it passes it to the transport engine, which detects that authentication data is present and then performs a security check to validate the data. If the check succeeds, the transport engine adds a flag to indicate that this is a trusted sender. Note that the

---

6. The format is AUTH=user@namespace as in AUTH=Tony.Redmond@xyz.com.

Store sets the same flag on messages that come from authenticated users, which means that every message that originates on an Exchange 2003 server has the trusted flag set. After the security check, the categorization engine then takes responsibility to evaluate the message and decide whether to deliver it to its destination (the group). The following process occurs:

- If we have an authenticated user, and delivery to the group requires authentication, the categorization engine proceeds as normal.

- If we have an authenticated user, and the group is open to anyone, delivery proceeds as normal.

- If the user is unauthenticated, and the group is restricted, the categorization engine logs event 9007 (the restricted group name is logged, but not the sender that failed) and dumps the message.

- If the user does not authenticate, and the group is open to accept messages from anyone, delivery proceeds as normal.

9.5.2 Moving messages off queues

The Routing Engine identifies recipients on other Exchange servers by examining the HomeMDB attribute in their AD entries. If this attribute holds the distinguished name of a Mailbox Store, Exchange knows that the recipient belongs to the same organization and it can deliver the message by routing the message to the server that hosts that Mailbox Store. The Routing Engine can examine the routing table to determine how to route the message and write this information into the next-hop identifier. If the Mailbox Store is located on the same server, Exchange can make a local delivery by placing the message in the local delivery queue.

When you view a queue, you are looking at data structures that the SMTP service keeps in memory. The actual messages that form the contents of the queues remain in the Store or an NTFS directory (\exchsrvr\mailroot\queue—see Figure 9.9) until they are transmitted. You get best performance when the queue is located on a fast drive, preferably away from its standard location, which is to go on the same drive as the Exchange binaries. In Exchange 2000, you have to edit the configuration of the SMTP virtual server with ADSIEDIT and insert the path to the new folder into the value for the msExchSmtpQueueDirectory attribute. Even worse, you have to make the same edit for every virtual server on every server that you want to tune. With Exchange 2003, you simply select the SMTP virtual server through ESM, choose the "Messages" property page, and then browse for the directory where you want to relocate the queue, as shown in Figure 9.7.

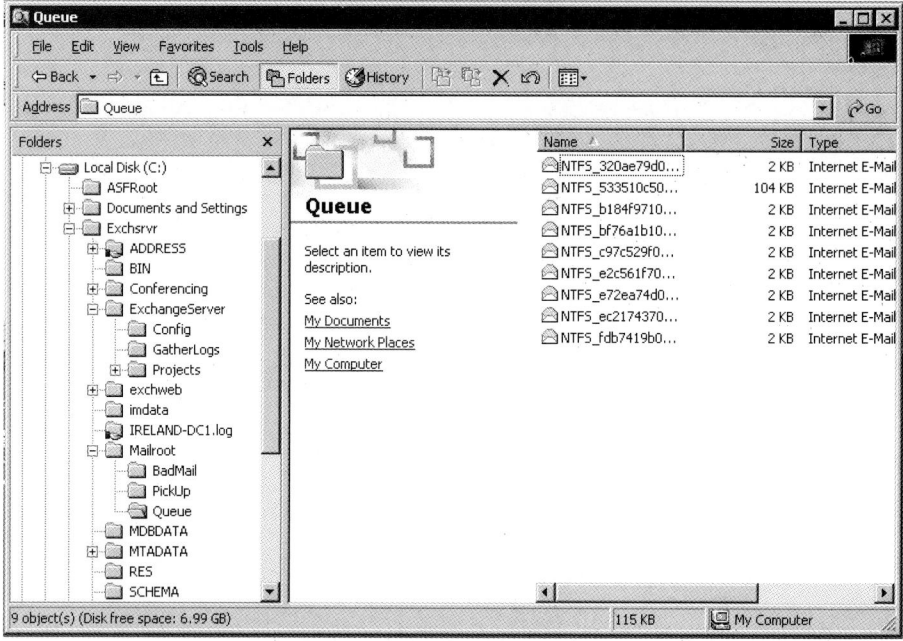

Figure 9.9 *Messages waiting to go.*

Changing the queue directory is not something you need to worry about for small servers, but it can deliver a real benefit for any server that handles significant SMTP traffic, such as bridgehead servers for large routing groups, or any server that acts as an SMTP entry point for the organization.

Exchange uses SMTP to deliver messages to other Exchange servers in the same routing group or to servers connected by a routing group connector, as well as messages going to external SMTP addresses. In these instances, Exchange places the messages on the relevant queues, where they remain until the connectors retrieve them for onward dispatch.

Figure 9.10 shows how Exchange 2000 lists messages waiting on queues, while Figure 9.11 shows the streamlined and much improved queue viewer interface in Exchange 2003. The improvements made in Exchange 2003 include:

- All queues are viewed together rather than as per virtual server (or MTA).

- There are new queues for "Deferred" messages (awaiting delivery at a future time), "Retry" (delivery failed because of a problem that might be transient), and "DSN" (messages checked against DSN but still

9.5 Categorization and routing 613

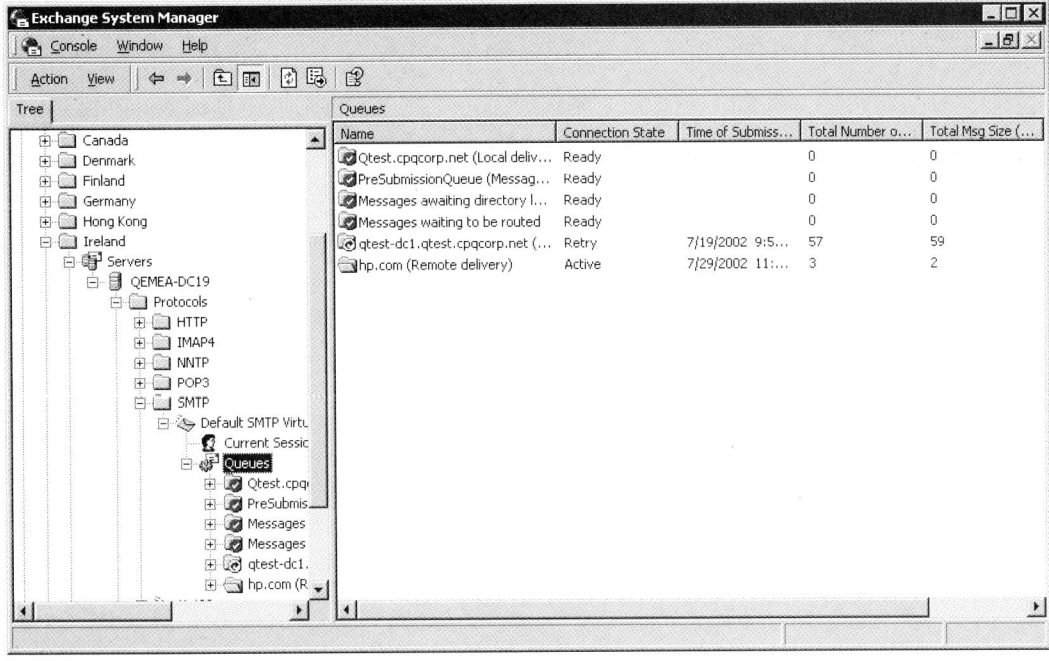

Figure 9.10   *Viewing queues—Exchange 2000.*

not routed). These queues give a more complete view of the current routing situation.

- You can disable outbound mail at one point.
- You can set a queue refresh interval (default is two minutes) through the "Settings" command button.
- You can select a queue (obviously one that has messages on it) and then search based on criteria such as sender, recipient, and message state (e.g., "frozen"). (See Figure 9.12.)

Collectively, these changes make the Exchange 2003 queue viewer easier to work with and more functional. Table 9.5 lists the major queues that you can expect to see in the Exchange 2003 queue viewer. Obviously, any queue with more than a couple of messages waiting deserves some attention to determine why the messages are on the queue.

The queue viewer reports a state for each queue. These states are:

- Ready: The queue is ready to accept messages.
- Disabled: The link between this server and the next-hop server is not available.

Chapter 9

9.5 Categorization and routing

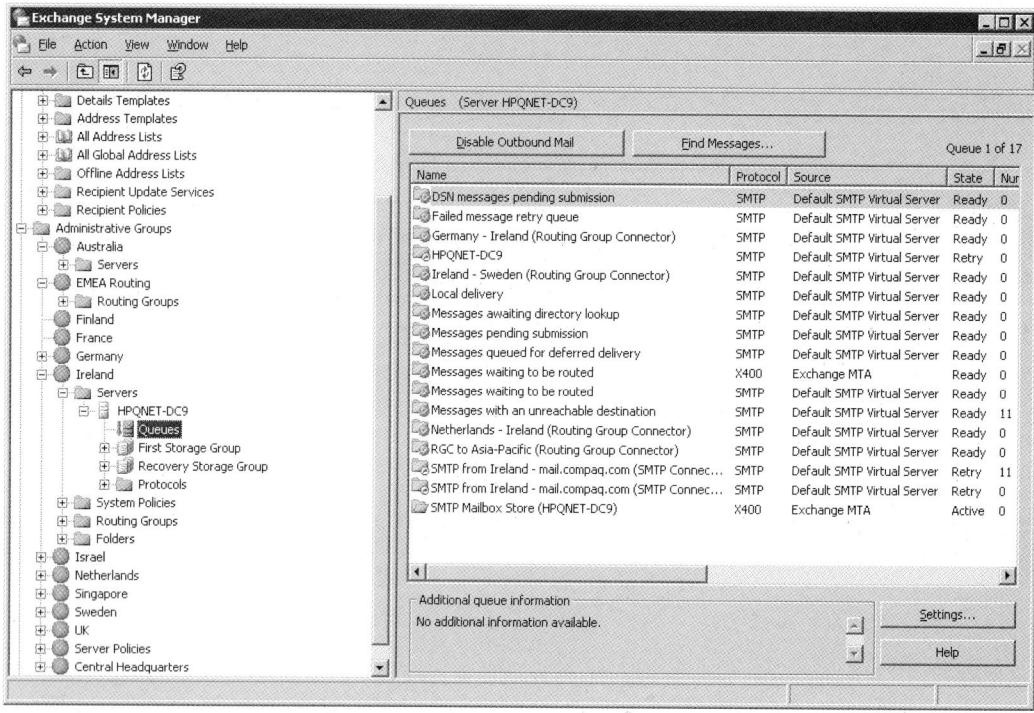

Figure 9.11   *The Exchange 2003 queue viewer.*

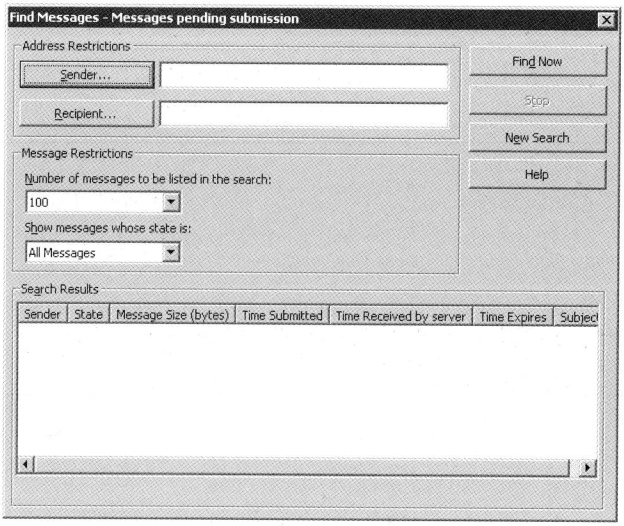

Figure 9.12   *Search message queues.*

9.5 Categorization and routing

- Active: There is an active connection between this server and the next-hop server.

- Retry: Previous connection attempts have failed and the server is waiting for another attempt. You can use the Force Connection command to change a queue in the Retry state to Active, which causes the Routing Engine to begin processing messages on the queue again. If the problem that caused the original retry state still exists, you will see the queue revert from Active to Retry very quickly.

- Scheduled: The queue is waiting for the next scheduled connection attempt.

- Remote: The queue is waiting for a remote server to execute a dequeue command (TURN/ETRN) to fetch the queued messages.

- Frozen: An administrator has frozen the queue. The Routing Engine can add new messages to the queue, but it will not attempt to process them onward. Freezing an Active queue immediately terminates the transport sessions for that queue.

Table 9.5 *Exchange 2003 Queues*

Queues	Protocol	Description
Local domain name (Local Delivery)	SMTP	Contains messages queued for delivery to a mailbox on the local server. Queues are named for "Local Delivery" or the name of the local server.
Messages awaiting directory lookup	SMTP	Messages waiting for address validation against AD—for example, expanding the contents of a distribution group.
Messages waiting to be routed	SMTP and X.400	Messages waiting for the Routing Engine to determine the next link queue.
Messages with an unreachable destination	SMTP	Messages that the Routing Engine cannot currently find a route to, possibly because a connector to a specific foreign email system is unavailable.
Failed message retry queue	SMTP	Queued messages that failed in the initial submission
DSN messages pending submission	SMTP	DSN (service) messages waiting to be submitted to the categorizer
Presubmission	SMTP	Messages that the Routing Engine has accepted but has not yet begun processing
PendingRerouteQ	X.400	This queue is empty unless there are messages pending reroute after a temporary connection problem.

Table 9.5 *Exchange 2003 Queues (continued)*

Queues	Protocol	Description
READY-IN	Foreign	Messages that have arrived from a foreign email system (e.g., cc:Mail) via an MTA connector. The connector has converted the message format (e.g., content conversion, attribute mapping, etc.), but the recipient addresses have not yet been resolved.
MTS-IN	Foreign	Messages that have arrived from a foreign email system and the routing engine has validated their addresses
MTS-OUT	Foreign	Messages going from Exchange to a foreign email system via an MTA connector and still awaiting address resolution
READY-OUT	Foreign	Messages going from Exchange to a foreign email system with resolved addresses (but message format transformation may still be outstanding)
BADMAIL	Foreign	Messages that an MTA connector cannot process for some reason. The messages remain on the queue until an administrator removes them.

All the queues shown in the viewer are per-link queues, so they reflect the next step in the routing path for messages. The names used in the queues are the connectors that will transfer the message the next step along its journey. You might expect that the queue viewer would list domain queues, so that you could see all of the messages going to a particular final destination, but the link queue is actually more interesting; it shows queued messages waiting to depart from a specific server, and you know where the messages are destined to go next.

There is a situation when you might see two queues for the same link. This occurs when routing information has changed—you may have added a new connector, the properties of an existing connector were adjusted, or Exchange has updated the link state table because of a network problem. In this situation, the Routing Engine invalidates the old queue and reroutes messages from the old queue to other queues, one of which it might have created for the same link. Exchange then cleans up the old queue and removes it.

Normally, if all network links are available and messages are flowing freely, very few messages are queued. The SMTP transport processes messages very quickly, and there should be little delay between a message entering the queue and its final transmission. Because they do not handle directory replication traffic, current Exchange queues are usually much

9.5 Categorization and routing

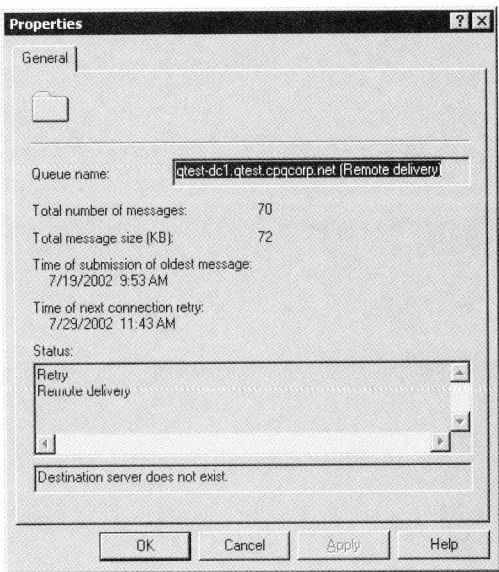

Figure 9.13
Properties of a queue.

smaller than Exchange 5.5 queues. Some Exchange 5.5 servers, normally those in hub sites, process hundreds of thousands of directory replication messages daily; all of the replication message traffic is now under the control of the AD. (See Figure 9.13.)

Exchange ensures that routing information is as accurate as possible by replicating configuration data along with other link state information. If you change the configuration of a connector, the changes replicate along with other link state updates, so they will get through if the servers can contact each other via SMTP, irrespective of whether AD replication works properly. See section 9.7 for more information on the link state routing mechanism.

Potential still exists to swamp message queues with large quantities of public folder replication traffic, especially if you replicate the contents of large Internet newsgroups around an organization. Keep an eye on the queues, and take action to restrict public folder replication schedules if queues build up and seem to include a lot of public folder traffic. If you see messages building on a queue, you can use the "enumerate" option (Exchange 2000) or the "Find Messages" option (Exchange 2003) to list the messages and reveal more details, as shown in Figure 9.14. Again, this is the Exchange 2003 user interface.

You can then select an individual message from the set and examine its properties (Figure 9.15). At this point, you can also decide to delete the

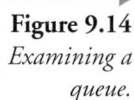

Figure 9.14
Examining a queue.

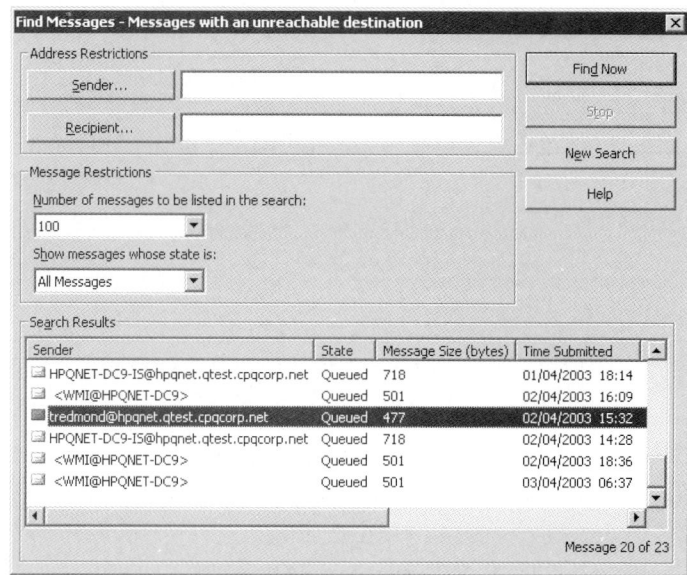

message from the queue and opt to send an NDR back to the originator. You can also choose to delete the message invisibly (no NDR).

Of course, there are reasons why messages build up. The most common cause is that a server is unavailable because it is down or the network link is saturated and Exchange cannot make a connection to the remote server. Other, less common, reasons include the possibility that a server might be underpowered and unable to provide the raw processing power to deal with

Figure 9.15
Properties of a message on a queue.

9.5 Categorization and routing

messages sent to it, or the sheer number of messages has exhausted the capacity of the SMTP transport to process them quickly enough to reduce the queues. The messages might be very large and require a substantial amount of time to transfer to the target server, or the target server might be slow to process incoming traffic. The most common problem is that a network link or server is unavailable when Exchange attempts to make a connection.

In Figure 9.10, we see that the queue for "qemea-dc1.qemea.qtest.cpq-corp.net" is currently in a retry state, meaning that the SMTP service has failed in an attempt to transfer messages to this destination and is now waiting to make a retry. Viewing the properties of the queue, as seen in Figure 9.13, reveals more detail about the likely cause of the problem. In this case, we can see that Exchange believes that the remote server does not exist! While it is possible that someone has removed the server from the network, a more likely reason for this error is that Exchange (and, more specifically, the SMTP service) is not running on the server, so all attempts to contact the server to pass messages have failed.

9.5.3 Unreachable domains

Any time a domain is unreachable, the SMTP service registers a warning in the system event log. You can use these events to determine what domains are proving troublesome and take steps to try to establish better connectivity. Sometimes problems are purely transitive and result from servers going offline or network errors. Other problems may point to an issue in your infrastructure, such as DNS updates that are not properly applied or propagated, or perhaps a server that is not routing messages to the correct smart host.

In the case shown in Figure 9.16, we can see that the warning was issued because the SMTP service tried to send a message to a recipient with a Compaq.com address, but the message could not get through because the domain was unreachable. Sending a simple "PING" command to a troublesome domain will usually determine whether the problem still exists, or you can use the NSLOOKUP utility to validate whether Exchange is using the correct name servers to resolve the domain. Remember that a successful PING only indicates that the computer is available on the network; it does not mean that you can send data to the computer. Something else might be causing SMTP to fail to connect: the Exchange services might not be running on the target computer or a disk might even be full. During virus outbreaks, system administrators often disable network connectivity to servers

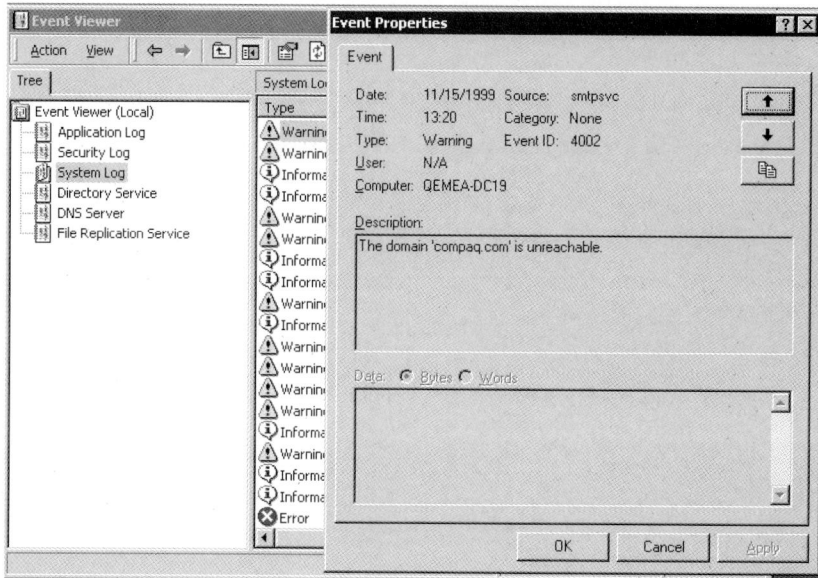

Figure 9.16
SMTP error in the system event log.

while they clean the system, so this is another thing to check if you see queues building up for a specific server or domain.

Exchange servers do not need MX records to enable SMTP message interchange across routing group connectors, because they use routing information held in the configuration naming context in the AD rather than DNS MX records. Exchange servers do need MX records if they communicate with each other across an SMTP connector, unless you route everything through a smart host. See the discussions about creating routing group connectors in section 9.8.1 and creating SMTP connectors in section 9.9. Note that Exchange does use DNS "A" records to resolve server names to IP addresses.

We have already said that the queue viewer displays link queues, but surely you can regard a domain such as hotmail.com as a final destination? The answer is: yes and no. It is true that an address such as hotmail.com is the final destination for a message, but it is also the next hop or link along the message's path. Let us assume that you configure an SMTP connector with an address space of *, meaning that the SMTP connector is able to route messages to any Internet domain. The message sent to hotmail.com is placed on the queue for the SMTP connector (its final destination), but its next hop is to hotmail.com, which is the reason why this queue is shown. Using the same logic, you can see link queues for messages going to a server in the same routing group. Again, this is a final destination, but it is also the next hop in the message's route.

Note that link queues are transient and only appear when they are in use. If you go back to refresh the queue viewer after Exchange has successfully transferred the message, the queue for hotmail.com may not be visible. Queue cleanup happens each time a message goes through the system, and unused or unwanted queues are removed at this point.

When you look at queues, you will see two special queues—the "Messages awaiting directory lookup" queue and the "Messages waiting to be routed" queue. The first holds messages that the Categorizer has not yet processed. The second queue holds messages that Exchange has not yet analyzed to determine on which link queue to put the messages. If messages show up on this queue, it is an indication that something is not working as planned, so it is a good idea to check the application event log and review any errors shown there.

Messages to other routing groups connected by an X.400 connector transfer via the MTA. Sometimes, an interim routing group is along the route to the eventual X.400 connection, and, if so, the Routing Engine dispatches the message to that routing group, where the message is then reassessed and routed to X.400. Once the message arrives at the server that hosts the X.400 connector, it is placed on the local delivery queue and processed by the transport core Store driver, which assesses the recipient list again and makes any local deliveries for mailboxes on this server. The message is then placed into the MTA's MTS Out folder in the Store, which is the final stop before it is dispatched out via the X.400 connector.

The same type of routing occurs for foreign connectors. The Routing Engine assesses the route to the connector and either dispatches the message directly to the connector, if it is available locally, or routes it via another routing group to reach the connector.

All mail-enabled users, including those who have their mailboxes on Exchange 5.5, also have a value in their HomeMBD attribute, which points to the distinguished name of the Mailbox Store for their mailboxes. The Routing Engine can use this information to consult the routing table to determine whether the server exists in the same routing group; a mixed-mode site; or in another Exchange 5.5 site, which must be routed through a connector hosted by an Exchange 5.5 server. Delivery to an Exchange 5.5 server in the same site is routed via the MTA and executed with RPCs.

Mail-enabled contacts do not have a HomeMDB attribute, so the Routing Engine consults the TargetAddress attribute, which should contain a routable address in the form "ADDRESS-TYPE: ADDRESS"—for example: "SMTP: John.Doe@xyz.com." The categorizer encapsulates the found address inside an SMTP address, with the right-hand side of the address containing the FQDN of the server that has the most suitable gateway to process the address. Of course, if the address is an SMTP address, no rewrite is necessary and Exchange can route the message directly to the lowest-cost SMTP connector that is able to handle the address space specified in the address.

9.5.4 Exchange and MX records

In a classic SMTP environment, the MX records held in DNS indicate the preferred servers to handle mail traffic for a domain. MX records are not strictly required for mail to flow into a domain, and if the MX records are not present, external servers will attempt to connect to all the servers listed with "A" DNS records for the domain. In effect, therefore, the MX records enable us to channel messages to a set of servers that we can configure to handle mail effectively.

Exchange must accommodate two cases when it wants to send messages: connection to a server within the same Exchange organization or connection to a server outside the organization. The server outside the organization could be another Exchange server, but it could also be a UNIX server running sendmail or some other server that supports SMTP, such as Lotus Notes.

Exchange consults the configuration data in the AD to decide whether a target server is inside the organization. If it is, Exchange fetches the GUID of the server or connector from the AD and uses it to determine the next hop. The Routing Engine has a special protocol sink that can act as a DNS resolver, which returns the IP addresses of SMTP servers to Exchange. During this process, Exchange uses the GUID to reference the AD to retrieve the host name. The resolver responds with the host name of the server to connect to or one of the servers that can act as a bridgehead for a connector. The resolver then passes the name of the selected server back to the Routing Engine, which can then check DNS to get the IP address of the server and proceed to make a connection to port 25 to transfer the message. While the Exchange 2000 version of the DNS resolver works, experience proved its performance was not always efficient, so Exchange 2003 adds logic to improve resolution by using multiple DNS servers and retries if a server becomes unresponsive.

If a target server or domain is outside the organization, Exchange performs a standard DNS lookup to locate an MX record for the name. Three possibilities exist:

- An MX record is found. In this case, the Routing Engine uses the MX record priorities to locate the name of the server to send the message to, and then resolves the name to find the IP address to which an SMTP connection should be made.

- DNS responds with "authoritative host not found" for the record, which indicates that DNS was able to contact the root of the DNS tree and verify that not even an "A" record existed for the target domain. The most common cause is that the sender mistyped the address, turning, for instance, compaq.com into compak.com. The message is returned to the originator with a nondelivery notification.

- No MX record is found, but either the DNS root cannot be reached to make an authoritative determination or an "A" record is found for the domain. In this case, Exchange attempts to use a gethostbyname() call, which performs both a DNS lookup for the "A" record and also attempts a WINS/NetBIOS name resolution.

In all cases, the result should be that the Routing Engine knows where to send the message. In summary, Exchange servers do not need MX records to send messages to other servers either inside or outside the organization, but MX records are used if they exist and are defined in DNS. The Routing Engine is also able to retrieve information about servers and connectors from the AD and resolve this data into the basic IP address to transfer messages.

9.6 Routing groups

Servers in a routing group typically communicate through high-speed connections, so the definition of a routing group is very similar to that of an Exchange 5.5 site. In general, network links should be capable of supporting the transfer of even very large messages (>10 MB) within the routing group without causing concern. Within a routing group, servers form a point-to-point, fully meshed network to route messages over SMTP, and each server must be able to make a connection to another server in the group without waiting for a network link to become available. The sole exception to SMTP transmission is when legacy Exchange servers operate inside a routing group in a mixed-mode organization. In this situation, the MTA sends messages to the legacy servers via RPCs.

While the availability of high-speed connections is always a definite plus for a messaging infrastructure, the move away from RPCs to SMTP means routing groups are able to span across low-speed connections as well. RPCs are prone to failure over high-latency connections, where SMTP is able to connect quite happily. Thus, it is possible to build large routing groups that incorporate a mixture of different network connections.

Initially, organizations that migrate from Exchange 5.5 begin with a routing group for every Exchange 5.5 site. After the organization moves into native mode, you can consider modifying the routing group structure to improve the topology. Consider reducing the number of routing groups to simplify the routing topology, or perhaps move servers into special administrative groups that only contain routing groups to isolate routing management away from other administrative tasks.

Many older designs use a hub and spoke approach, with sites that contain mailbox servers connecting into hub routing sites. Designers create hub sites to introduce resilience and provide multiple paths for messages. However, the dynamic nature of link state routing and the way that the Routing Engine now directs messages between routing groups reduces the need for hub sites, affording a further opportunity to simplify the routing topology.

In order of importance, the factors that influence the decision to create new routing groups include:

- Availability of stable network links
- Available bandwidth that can support the automatic on-demand connections made by servers within a routing group
- A need to schedule connectivity between servers
- A need to control the transmission of large messages
- A need to restrict the use of connections to particular users, or to deny a connection to particular users

The first three factors also pertain to older Exchange designs, while the last two are specific to Exchange 2000/2003. The Routing Engine is flexible, but it depends on network consistency. You will never attain efficient routing if the links between routing groups go up and down all the time. In this scenario, the link state table will be in "continuous update mode," and messages will bounce from one connector to the next. The safest approach is to group servers into islands of highly available connectivity, which then become your basic routing group structure. Later on, as experience with network conditions, traffic, and message throughput grows, you can make selective changes to the routing group design by creating new groups and moving servers into them, or transferring servers between existing groups. The Routing Engine is flexible and will adapt to new conditions as quickly as the AD can replicate the updated configuration data, so do not be afraid to make changes. You can reduce any possible impact on users by making changes to routing groups at times of low user demand. Any temporary queues that build up due to slow replication should clear before peak time occurs again.

Network use and message delivery times are the key indicators that you need to make some changes to the routing topology. If network links become saturated, you should attempt to reduce the traffic that goes across the link. If message delivery times become extended (more than 15 minutes between individual routing groups, or more than 1 minute between servers in a routing group), changes in the routing topology may be called for, depending on the goals of the organization. Some companies require message delivery times of less than one minute everywhere, while others will be happy if messages get through in less than an hour. Understanding the expectations of users for message delivery time is an important piece of data for a routing group design.

Always remember that Exchange depends on a solid Windows infrastructure, particularly the underlying network and AD replication. If the network fails, and configuration data and the AD cannot replicate information about servers and connectors, no amount of tinkering with routing groups will result in a dependable routing structure.

9.6.1 Routing group master

One server in each routing group acts as the routing master. By default, the first server installed in a routing group takes on the role of the routing master and remains as such unless altered by an administrator. You can assign the routing master role to any server in a routing group, and the most important and critical task the server then takes on is to maintain the link state table (LST). The routing master builds the LST from two sources: basic configuration data about the Exchange organization fetched from the DSAccess configuration cache and routing updates that come in from other routing groups. The routing master attributes a higher importance to routing updates than the somewhat static configuration data that comes from AD. This is only natural, because servers generate and communicate link state updates dynamically.

After it builds the LST, the routing master shares the LST automatically with all the servers in a routing group. As bridgehead servers in the routing group become aware of information about connections (their link state), they relay the data to the routing master, which uses the data to create an updated LST every time an update arrives from any source. After it updates the LST, the routing master broadcasts change information to all the servers in the routing group, and the servers adjust their own copy of the link state table.

You can move the routing master role easily between servers, as shown in Figure 9.17. Select the server that you want to take on the role and right-click to bring up a context-sensitive menu. Then select the "Set as Master" option.

Occasionally, the routing master is unavailable due to maintenance or a system outage. When this happens, the other servers in the routing group continue to route based on the last known LST. Routing in this situation may not follow an optimal path, because Exchange may send messages to a server whose link is unavailable, or there may be a better route available. However, even in its suboptimal state, the last LST is likely to be far more up-to-date with network information than the GWART used by the MTA

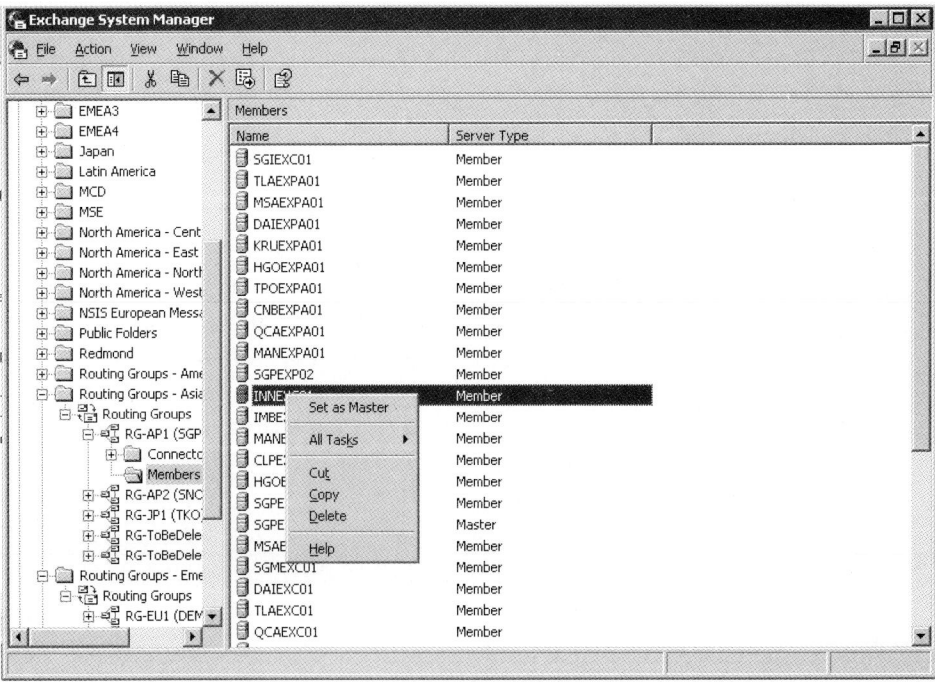

Figure 9.17 *Defining a routing master.*

to route messages in Exchange 5.5. The MTA normally generates the GWART once a day—after a new server or connector joins a site or if an administrator decides to request the MTA to generate the GWART. As such, the GWART is relatively static. Routing problems usually do not surface with the GWART when the network is stable, but if connectors or servers go offline it can be difficult to regenerate an accurate picture of the network and get messages to flow optimally again.

9.6.2 Creating new routing groups

Creating a new routing group is easy, mostly because a new routing group is just a container in the Exchange organization. Unlike an Exchange 5.5 site, which is instantiated when you install the first server into the site, you can create a routing group in the organization long before you move the first server into the group. This is a useful feature, because it allows you to configure the routing group structure for an Exchange organization at the start of the deployment and instruct administrators as to which routing group to use for new server installations. It also avoids the complications that occur in Exchange 5.5 when you remove the first server originally installed into a site and need to reconfigure homes for all the site objects (such as the default set of system folders).

To create a new routing group, select the routing groups container and take the "New" option from the right-click menu, as shown in Figure 9.18. You can do this even when your organization is operating in mixed mode—the sole requirement is that a routing group container already exists in the Administrative Group. If you have not yet created a routing group container, click on the Administrative Group; take the "New" option from the context-sensitive menu, and then the "Routing Group Container" choice. This mechanism makes it obvious that a routing group is just another container within the configuration container for an Exchange organization, so the properties that you need to add at this point (the name of the new routing group) are not very exciting.

Exchange performs no validation to check that the routing group name you provide already exists in the organization. This is logical from the perspective of the hierarchy within the Exchange configuration. Remember that a routing group is a subcontainer within an administrative group, so you can create routing groups with the same names as long as they are in different administrative groups. Exchange is happy, because the resulting routing groups have a different distinguished name within their configuration containers, but an obvious chance for confusion now exists. If we look

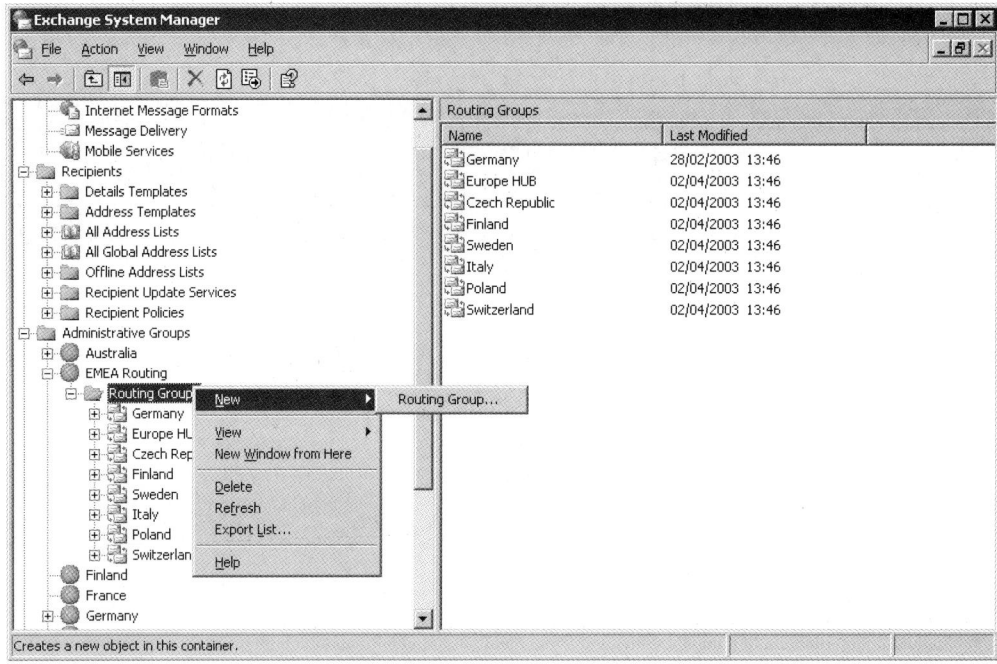

Figure 9.18   *Creating a new routing group.*

at Figure 9.19, we see "EMEA Routing" and "Ireland" administrative groups, both containing routing groups for "Finland." In addition, further confusion arises from the "Europe HUB" routing group in the "EMEA Routing" administrative group and the "European Hub" routing group in the Ireland administrative group. On the surface, both routing groups seem that they might act as a central hub for European-wide routing operations, but can you tell the difference? The ease in which you can create new routing groups and the fact that they are subcontainers that can have the same name as existing containers underlines the need to plan the routing topology from the start rather than allowing administrators to build the topology on a whim.

As with Windows sites, I favor naming routing groups after geographical terms so that their purpose and coverage is immediately obvious. The alternative is to come up with another naming scheme, but I do not see the point unless you really want to sit down and construct a set of complex names that only you and your fellow administrators understand. However, consider the case of a new administrator. Will he or she understand the naming and purpose of routing groups if you do not use simple names? In all cases, the important thing is that users remain unaware of

9.6 Routing groups

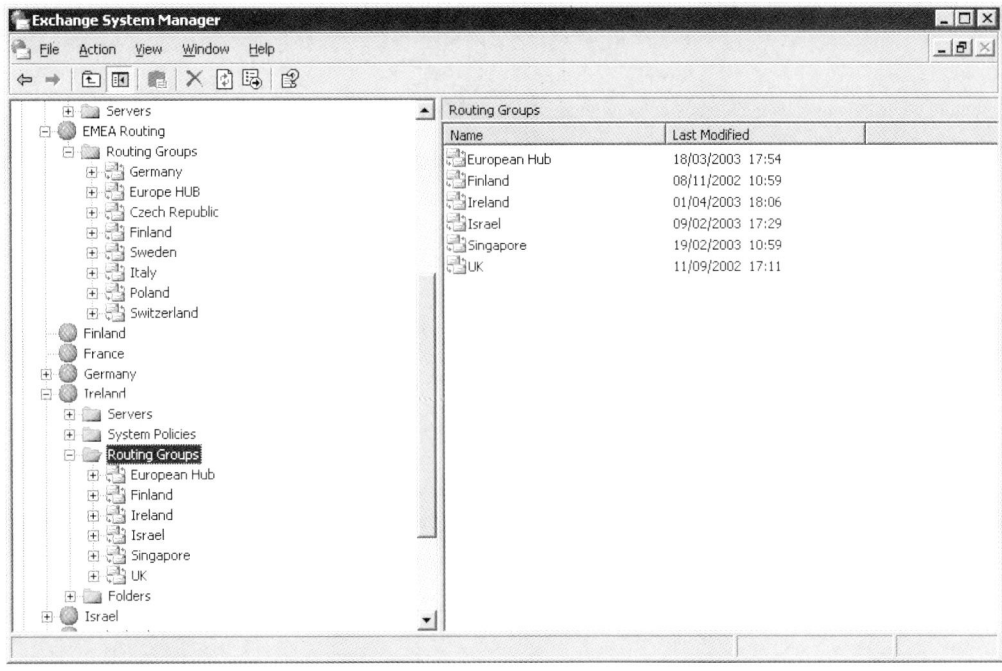

Figure 9.19   *Duplicate routing groups.*

whatever you do, because they cannot see all of the organizational detail about Exchange.

Best practice is to create a special administrative group to hold all the routing groups in the organization and to assign permissions over that administrative group to the people who are responsible for managing the routing topology. They should be the only people who ever create a routing group or connector, which then limits the potential for other routing groups to appear and cause confusion.

Figure 9.20 shows an example of the type of naming convention I recommend for routing groups: simple and easy to understand. After Exchange has created the new routing group, you can add servers to it by selecting a server and dragging it to the "Members" container of the new routing group. However, you can only drag and drop a server into a new routing group if you have Exchange administrator rights for the server's administrative group. You can also install servers directly into the new routing group.

Dragging and dropping servers between routing groups just to see what happens seems like a fun way to idle away a rainy afternoon, but it is only

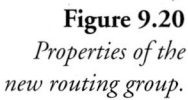

Figure 9.20
Properties of the new routing group.

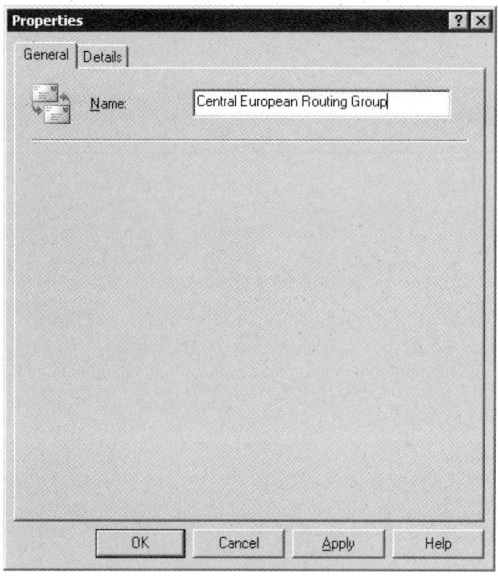

an exercise that you should perform in a software laboratory for test purposes. Never move a server unless you have to, and only perform the operation after everyone involved in the administrative group has approved. In other words, it is still good to have the discipline to plan server moves rather than move servers around on a whim.

Exchange imposes some restrictions on server moves. You cannot move a server to another routing group if the server is a bridgehead for a connector. Connectors and routing groups are fundamental inputs to the routing tables, and moving a server that hosts a number of connectors would have a huge impact on the way Exchange routes messages. While Exchange is now much more amenable to change and has a mechanism to discover changes in the network very quickly (link state routing), as well as taking updates through changes made to configuration data managed by the AD, it is still not a good idea to make wholesale changes. Figure 9.21 illustrates the type of error you will see if you attempt to move a server that still has active bridgeheads. In this instance, the server is in the Netherlands routing group and has a connector to Ireland. The server also hosts an SMTP connector, and its name indicates that it handles external communication, so it is likely to be quite an important connector for the whole organization. If a server is the only member of a routing group, you will have to delete all connectors in the group (a connector must have at least one bridgehead server allocated to it) before you can move the server to a new routing group.

9.6 Routing groups

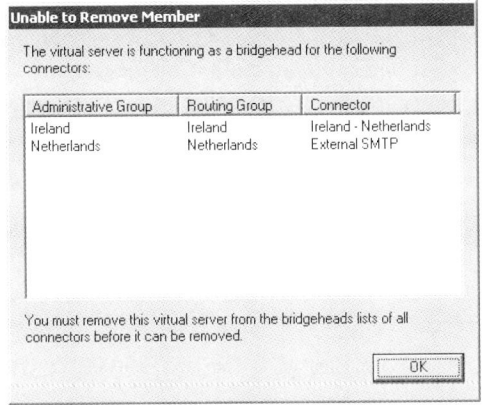

Figure 9.21
Error when moving a server to a routing group.

If you want to decommission routing groups, best practice is to gradually move the servers from the defunct routing group to other routing groups and relocate or delete connectors as required. Leaving one or two days between each server move is sufficient to allow AD replication to occur in large organizations and to reveal any flaw or problem in routing behavior provoked by the move. After you move the final server from the defunct routing group, you can rename the routing group to indicate that it is no longer used and leave it for a week or so before final deletion. Figure 9.22 illustrates the concept.

9.6.3 Routing groups and public folder referrals

Apart from routing messages, routing groups also control access to public folder replicas through referrals. The AD holds a list of available replicas for every public folder with the other Exchange configuration data. When a client attempts to access a public folder, Exchange looks for a replica on the

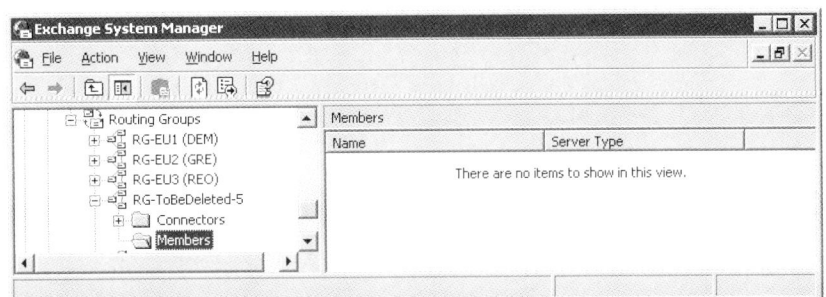

Figure 9.22
A defunct routing group awaits deletion.

same server as the user's mailbox, and then for a replica on a server within the same routing group. If Exchange cannot locate a local replica, it looks for a replica in other routing groups connected by connectors that allow public folder referrals.[7] Exchange 2003 improves matters by allowing you to specify the servers that you want to handle public folder referrals.

If you do not provide Exchange with a preferred list of referral servers, the cost of a connector determines which replica to access if replicas exist in multiple routing groups. Content from the public folders does not flow across the connectors. Instead, the requesting client makes a direct network link to the server that hosts the public folder. Naturally, if this link extends across low-bandwidth connections, access to the public folder is slow. MAPI clients continue to use RPCs to access public folder content, while other clients use their native protocol (IMAP or HTTP-DAV). Most IMAP clients do not support referrals, because the protocol does not include any mention of this functionality.

9.7 Link state routing

Any large messaging infrastructure is usually in a state of flux. While network links are normally available all the time, human, computer, or network error can conspire to interrupt traffic on a circuit and block the flow of messages. The more distributed and extensive the network, the more likely it is that some part of the network is currently unavailable.

As mentioned earlier, Exchange 5.5 uses the GWART to maintain a list of the routes messages can take to a final destination, including gateways. The GWART does not attempt to keep track of temporary network outages and merely consists of information about routes, so it is essentially a list about point-to-point connections that may or may not be available to route messages at any point in time. If a block occurs along the route for any reason, large queues can quickly build up in the MTA or connectors. Exchange now sends link state information between servers to provide an up-to-date picture of available routes messages can take. Exchange sends link state information using two methods:

- Within a routing group, the routing service on each bridgehead server binds to port 691 via the IIS on the routing master to send and receive link state table updates. Communication occurs using a

---

7. The "Do not allow public folder referrals" checkbox on a connector's general property page controls referrals. The default is to allow referrals across the connector.

9.7 Link state routing

special protocol called LSA,[8] specially developed by Microsoft for this purpose. In its turn, after receiving updates from bridgehead servers, the routing master broadcasts changes to all the servers in the routing group, again via port 691. If the IETF eventually sets out a common mechanism for email servers to share routing information, Exchange's current routing architecture is flexible enough to accommodate multiple protocols.

- Exchange sends link state table updates between bridgehead servers in different routing groups whenever an update is available. The bridgehead server then passes the data on to the group's routing master. If Exchange uses an RGC or SMTP connector to link routing groups, it sends SMTP messages between the servers using port 25 instead of the LSA protocol across port 691. The connection starts with an "EHLO" to tell the server that ESMTP is going to be used, and then an "X-LINK2STATE" command to advertise the fact that the server is capable of exchanging link state information. If the receiving server acknowledges the command, the two servers then trade link state information. Exchange passes link state data in a highly compressed format and only requires a single DWORD to pass the up/down information; so little overhead is required to accommodate the basic data. Configuration data updates take up a little more space, and Exchange also sends the GUID and digest for the organization, but the overhead usually remains small.[9] X.400 connections use a field to store and transmit link state information. Before Exchange sends any information, servers check that they belong to the same Exchange organization by verifying that they share the same organizational GUID and digest. The digest contains a hash of the organization name and version number and Exchange uses this to generate a string value that it can check quickly against a value generated by another server. If the check passes, the servers proceed with the update.

Exchange 2003 improves the performance of link state routing updates, especially for slow links such as those used by remote offices. For example, in a hub and spoke network, where routing groups in the spokes have only one possible link back to the hub, it does not make sense to generate new

---

8. LSA is the protocol currently used by Exchange, and Microsoft may propose it in the future as the basis of an implementation for link state updates between SMTP servers to the IETF. If this proposal is accepted and turned into a formal RFC, it's likely that LSA will continue to be used in future releases. However, if another protocol is defined, it can be inserted instead of LSA. The X-LINK2STATE command is implemented as an ESTMP extension. See Figure 9.2 for a list of the ESMTP commands supported by Exchange 2000/2003.
9. The WinRoute utility shows the actual link state data transmitted between servers.

routing tables if that link fails, so Exchange 2003 now suppresses updates in these circumstances.

In addition, Exchange 2003 attempts to dampen the number of updates that "oscillating" connections (those that come up and down frequently) cause within the network, which reduces bandwidth consumption because Exchange transfers fewer routing updates between servers. To accomplish the goal, Exchange 2003 makes two changes. First, where Exchange 2000 has a strictly binary view of whether a connector is available (up/down), Exchange 2003 attempts to analyze whether the connector is experiencing a transient failure that might clear up before it decides that the connector has really failed. Second, Exchange 2003 suppresses "minor" link state updates (which flag a connection being up or down) and only transmits "major" updates. Major updates are caused by the installation of a new connector and similar changes to the routing infrastructure.

If you need to, you can suppress link state updates on an Exchange 2000 server by creating a new DWORD value called SuppressStateChanges in the registry at:

```
HKLM\SYSTEM\CurrentControlSet\Services\RESvc\Parameters
```

Set the value to 1 to suppress link state updates. This is not something to rush into unless you understand the consequences of suppressing the updates and are confident that the net saving in bandwidth will make a difference.

Anything to reduce bandwidth consumption always helps and you can gain a further boost by running on Windows 2003 servers, because, Exchange can then use the updated Windows DNS resolver code, which is less sensitive to slow response to DNS queries than the previous DNS resolver. In large organizations that have good network links and stable DNS environments, you may not notice these improvements, since they become most obvious when servers and links change state frequently. You can obtain some insight on the flow of SMTP communication between two Exchange servers from Figure 9.23, which shows two typical transactions between servers.

The first transaction is with the server with IP address 19.209.12.154 and consists of a HELO/MAIL/RCPT/DATA/QUIT command sequence. These commands establish a link, set up a recipient for the message and some originator details, pass some message data, and then terminate the connection. We know that the server we are corresponding with is not second-generation Exchange, since the initial connect is made with the HELO command rather than EHLO. The next transaction is with the server with

9.7 Link state routing

Figure 9.23
Extract from SMTP log file.

```
11:39:47 19.209.12.154 HELO - 250
11:39:47 19.209.12.154 MAIL - 250
11:39:47 19.209.12.154 RCPT - 250
11:39:47 19.209.12.154 DATA - 250
11:39:47 19.209.12.154 QUIT - 0
11:41:02 19.40.65.204 EHLO - 250
11:41:02 19.40.65.204 x-link2state - 200
11:41:02 19.40.65.204 MAIL - 250
11:41:02 19.40.65.204 RCPT - 250
11:41:02 19.40.65.204 DATA - 250
11:41:02 19.40.65.204 QUIT - 0
```

IP address 19.40.65.204 and begins with EHLO. This does not automatically mean that this is a recent Exchange server, since many other SMTP servers support extended SMTP, but it is a good start. The extract does not tell us how the remote server responded to the EHLO command, but the fact that Exchange then issues an X-LINK2STATE command is a very good indicator that we have connected to another Exchange server. As it happens, the remote server is a bridgehead for another routing group. Bridgeheads always take the opportunity to update each other every time they talk.

Assuming we have a LAN-quality connection, sending link state information does not take very much time (less than a second in this case), but it is always done first to allow the remote server to update its LST if the need occurs. After Exchange passes the link state information, the two servers settle down to the normal sequence of commands necessary to send a message and the transaction then ends.

It is possible that you may want to restrict LST updates within an organization, especially if the servers are connected using low-bandwidth links. To suppress LST change updates, create the following DWORD value (and set the value to 1) in the system registry on all Exchange servers that you want to control:

```
HKLM\System\CurrentControlSet\Services\RESvc\Parameters\
SuppressStateChanges
```

The LST holds information about connection availability and cost for an entire organization. The picture of the network changes as you add, remove, and update servers and connectors or adjust connection costs. The major value of the dynamic nature of the LST is when an organization evolves, as in when you upgrade the servers in an organization, or when a company goes through a period of acquisition, merger, and divestiture. In these scenarios, the LST is often in a state of dynamic flux as the routing group master updates it with information coming in from other servers in the same routing group plus information from other routing groups.

Table 9.6 *Example Link State Table*

Link States for London Routing Group	State	Cost	Version 125
Link from London RG to Dublin RG	Up	20	
Link from London RG to Paris RG	Up	20	
Link from London RG to Frankfurt RG	Up	20	
Link from London RG to New York RG	Down	10	
Link from London RG to Copenhagen RG	Up	20	
Link States for New York RG	**State**	**Cost**	**Version 146**
Link from New York RG to San Francisco RG	Up	20	
Link from New York RG to Boston RG	Up	20	
Link from New York RG to Houston RG	Up	20	
Link from New York RG to London RG	Down	10	
Link from New York RG to Copenhagen RG	Up	50	
Link States for Copenhagen RG	**State**	**Cost**	**Version 343**
Link from Copenhagen RG to London RG	Up	20	
Link from Copenhagen RG to New York RG	Up	50	
Link from Copenhagen RG to Stockholm RG	Up	20	

You can envisage the LST in many different tables, one for each routing group, as shown in Table 9.6. The concept of availability extends beyond the boundaries of Exchange, since external connections are also included. This prevents the Routing Engine from continually attempting to send messages across a connection such as an external Internet gateway when a network link is down. When a particular link fails, a retry is attempted. If the retry fails, the Routing Engine fires an event to tell the server that it must issue a link state update to the routing group master.

Every routing group maintains a version number for its link state information. The version number can only be incremented by the routing group master, and this happens whenever the information changes because of a link state update. Routing groups use the version number to compare information about the state of the network. You can think of this data as the unique view of the network known to each routing group, and if the versions do not match during link state operations, the servers know that they have to update each other.

The reason for maintaining dynamic link state information is to allow the Routing Engine to find the optimum path for messages, basing the decision on the LST data. Exchange uses a modified form of Dijkstra's algorithm, a commonly used method to determine the shortest path between two points in a network, to assess the available routing paths. Open Shortest Path First (OSPF) is another name for this type of routing, and many network routers use a variation of the same algorithm to send packets between computers in the most efficient manner.

Inside a network, Exchange determines the optimum route using factors such as delay, throughput, and connectivity. Messaging is a little different, because other factors come into play, such as the eventual destination of a message (e.g., does Exchange have to route the message across a specific connector to reach another email system), its size, the sender, and message priority. During the decision process, the Exchange organization is modeled as a network, with each routing group represented as a network node and each connector as a link between nodes. The basic decision that has to be made is: Given a message and its properties (current location, sender, recipient, priority, and size) and the network infrastructure (link state and cost), what is the next best hop to route the message? As already discussed, Exchange allows connectors to be limited to handle particular sizes of messages or only accept messages from specific email addresses.

Avoiding message "ping-pong" and the type of rerouting that occur in Exchange 5.5 are major reasons for implementing link state routing. The GWART is static, so messages can be routed to an inoperative connector. When this happens, the MTA checks the GWART to discover whether another route exists and attempts to send the messages across the alternate route. If this connector is also unavailable, the MTA will attempt other routes until it exhausts all possible routes, in which case the messages remain queued until a route becomes available. It sounds OK to reroute messages in this fashion, but the messages ping-pong around sites and connectors until all available routes are exhausted, and in a large organization containing many sites and connectors, it can take some time before the MTA decides that it has tried all available routes. Another complication arises from the fact that connectors built with the Exchange Development Kit (EDK) maintain their own queues, and once the MTA has passed responsibility for a message to a connector by placing it onto the connector's queue, no further rerouting can take place. The IMS is the best example of how this can cause a problem. If an Internet connection is down, then all of the messages queued to the IMS that serves the connection will remain on that queue until the connection comes back up. Because manual intervention is required to force a GWART update (by increasing the cost to use the IMS that is down), and time is required to replicate the GWART to all sites, messages continue to accumulate on the queue until every site is updated.

Dynamic updates address the problem. The key advance is to propagate updates fast so that all routing groups learn about downed connectors so that messages do not have to travel to the connector only to discover that they need to be rerouted. Each routing group maintains its own LST and has a copy of the LST from every other routing group. Updates can occur literally each time a bridgehead server communicates to another bridgehead server, and the LST is updated as quickly as the bridgehead server can make a connection across port 691 to the routing master. Exchange uses the updated LST immediately as the basis for subsequent routing decisions, so message queues do not accumulate. Best of all, despite the fact that the routing group connector and SMTP connector are both SMTP based, they both allow rerouting, so even if an SMTP connection is unavailable, messages can be rerouted quickly as soon as a connector is deemed to be unavailable, assuming that an alternate path exists. This makes the routing system very efficient, because less processing is expended to route messages to their final destination. Note that an SMTP connector configured with a "*" address space is never marked as unavailable. This is logical, because such a connector is capable of handling traffic to any SMTP domain, and a failure to send to one domain (such as a.com) does not necessarily mean that the connector cannot transfer messages to other domains.

The MTA does not have the same central role in message routing in Exchange 2000/2003 as it had in previous versions. However, the MTA continues to perform this role for Exchange 5.5 servers, even in mixed-mode sites, and it is able to take advantage of the faster notification of downed connectors to make better routing decisions. Think of the new role of the MTA as the protocol interface for X.400 and the gateway (via the Store) to EDK connectors, such as those for IBM PROFS and SNADS, and the wide variety of available fax connectors. Eventually, as these connectors are phased out (and the fact that they are no longer supported by Exchange 2003 is a good signpost for the future), the MTA will gradually disappear—if Microsoft can find all the places where the MTA is referenced in the rest of the Exchange code base.

Microsoft originally intended that the Exchange routing master should automatically take over the RID master role (also known as the routing calculation master) in sites in mixed-mode organizations. The RID master is the server that builds a GWART within a site and publishes it to the other servers. Acting in this role, the routing master would be able to combine its knowledge of the routing table and GWART data provided by other Exchange 5.5 sites (obtained by replication through the site replication service and the ADC) and generate a GWART for sharing with the Exchange 5.5 servers in the site. The advantage of this mechanism is that the Exchange 5.5 servers are able to take some advantage of the dynamic nature of the LST. Exchange uses static routing to other Exchange 5.5 sites, because the GWART data from those sites remains essentially static, but the updates flowing into the link state routing table flow into the GWART generated in mixed-mode sites. One little flaw affected the plan.

Exchange 5.5 supports the concepts of subsites through locations that you assign as properties of servers. The availability of connectors can be limited by setting their scope, one of which limits a connector to the subsite or location into which you install the server. The routing master supports connector scopes, but administrative and routing groups have replaced sites, so the concept of subsites has gone away. If you use the routing master to generate the GWART, it will ignore subsite scopes, so if you use this feature in Exchange 5.5 you do not want the routing master to generate the GWART. Fortunately, you can assign any server in a mixed-mode site to act as the Exchange 5.5 routing calculation master. You set the server to act as the Exchange 5.5 routing calculation master through the Site Addressing properties of the site object, as shown in Figure 9.24.

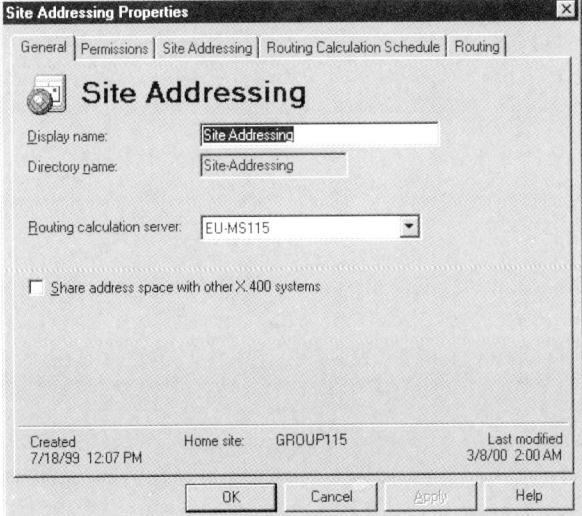

Figure 9.24
Exchange 5.5 routing calculation.

There is obviously a big difference between the way the MTA handles address spaces in the GWART and the new link state routing mechanism. If you have deployed connectors that limit their scope to a single site, you may find that you need to review the connectors before you start to deploy Exchange 2000/2003 servers.

9.7.1 Routing, retries, and updates

To explain what happens when a failure occurs on the network and how Exchange updates the LST, we can use the LST data outlined in Table 9.6 to follow the path of a message generated on a server in the Dublin routing group sent to a mailbox on a server in the Boston routing group. Figure 9.25 shows how the routing groups are connected. Network connectivity is similar to the type of links used in large corporate deployments. The network is organized into a series of hubs (New York, London, and Copenhagen), with the major links between New York and London and London and Copenhagen. A backup transatlantic link is available between Copenhagen and New York, but it is costed to prevent traffic from going across the link unless no other route is available.

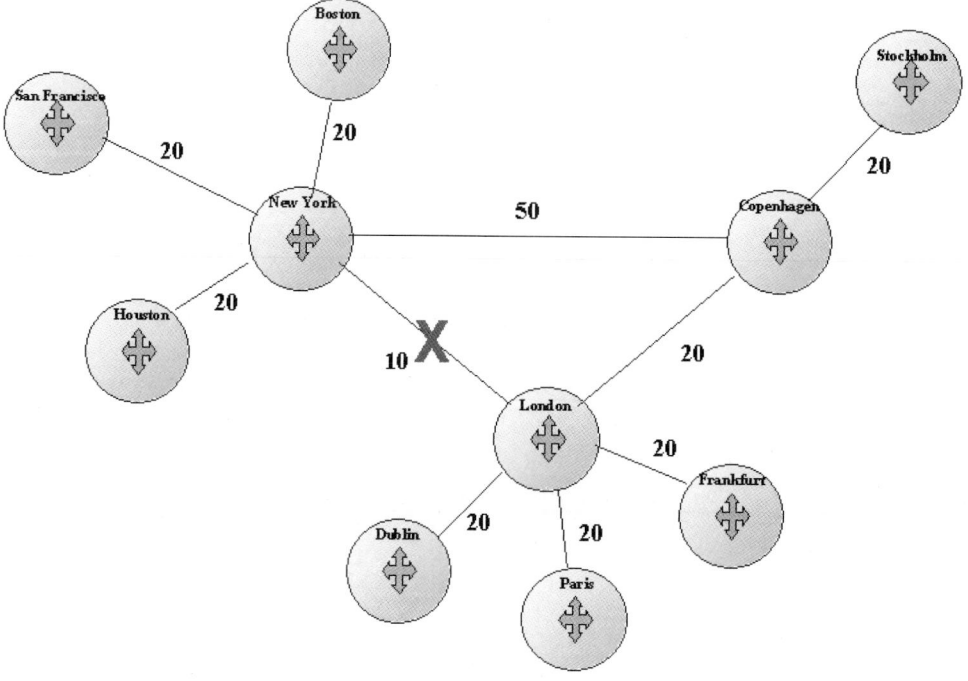

Figure 9.25   *Link state routing and network outages.*

The message starts by routing to the bridgehead server in the Dublin routing group. Exchange automatically generates a direct SMTP link to route the message from the originating server to the bridgehead, which then attempts to create a connection to the bridgehead server in the London routing group. After London successfully receives the message, Exchange analyzes the address information in the message header to determine how to route the message for the next hop to New York. London then attempts to open a connection to a bridgehead server in New York, but the attempt fails because of a network outage. If there are multiple bridgehead servers defined for New York, the London bridgehead will attempt to open a connection to each. All attempts fail.

The London bridgehead now goes into a "glitch-retry" state. This means that the server has recognized that a problem exists but will try to establish a connection in 60 seconds in case the fault is temporary. After 60 seconds, an event fires to tell the server to try again. Exchange attempts to contact each bridgehead server in New York but fails due to a continuing network problem. The London bridgehead goes through the "glitch-retry" sequence three times before applying the retry schedule set on the SMTP virtual server. The messages that caused the retry are rerouted as soon as a problem is detected and do not have to wait for the "glitch-retry" sequence to finish. The connection is then marked as "down," and the bridgehead server informs the routing group master in London about the problem.

After receiving the update, the routing group master updates its LST and sends updates to all of the other servers in the London routing group. The bridgehead server consults the updated LST (Table 9.6) and decides that an alternative, higher-cost route is available via Copenhagen. The server then sends link state updates to the other routing groups via the ESMTP X-LINK2STATE command to inform them that the London to New York link is currently unavailable. The update occurs before an attempt is made to send any other messages to prevent servers in the Dublin, Frankfurt, Paris, Copenhagen, and Stockholm routing groups from attempting to send messages to London for onward processing. The routing groups that receive the link state update compare the version number on the update against the data held in their own tables. If the version number is higher, the update is applied and a new LST is created for the routing group.

Connectors are one way, so the London routing group first detects the problem when it attempts to send a message. At the other side of the Atlantic, a message sent to London will prompt the bridgehead server in New York to go through the same discovery process and update its own routing group master with a "down" status. Exchange then publishes the updated link state information to servers in the New York, Boston, and San Francisco routing groups, which proceed to update their copies of the LST.

The link between New York and Copenhagen becomes the preferred transatlantic connection until a bridgehead server in either London or New York determines that the link between the two routing groups is now available. The retry schedule on the SMTP virtual server determines when attempts are made to investigate the current status of the connector, and as soon as a connection is successful, the link is marked as "up," in which case a series of LST updates begins again to inform all routing groups that the connection is back and available for routing.

9.7.2 Looking at routing information

Short of trawling through memory and making some excellent guesses about what you find there, there is no out-of-the-box way of getting a detailed view of the LST on a server. The WinRoute tool provides the best insight (see section 9.11.1), with information displayed through the Status node in the Monitoring and Status section of ESM the next best thing. As Figure 9.26 shows, the Status option lists all the servers in the routing group that a server is connected to plus their status. In this case, our server (HPQ-NET-DC9) provides a view of the current routing environment as it sees it. We can see that the HPQEU-DC4 and HPQEU-DC24 servers are unavailable for some reason, possibly because the set of Exchange services is not running. In any case, Exchange cannot route messages to these servers now.

The top portion of the display shown in Figure 9.26 lists all the connectors available to the servers. Lack of attention to naming conventions has made the output in Figure 9.26 a real mess, and there is no immediate indication of the purpose some of the connectors serve. For example, what is the difference between the "SMTP to Internet" and "External SMTP" connectors? We also seem to have two connectors for "Netherlands – Ireland" (albeit in different routing groups). However, a little work to apply a consistent naming convention and remove any unnecessary connectors will create a much more informative view.

Details of connectors are stored as AD objects, and you can rename them at any time. A short delay occurs before the rename is effective and displayed in the status window. This is because ESM keeps a cache of configuration data to stop it from having to go back to the AD each time it repaints a window. Within ten minutes of renaming your connectors, the new names should appear in the list, which is shown in Figure 9.27. By

9.7 Link state routing

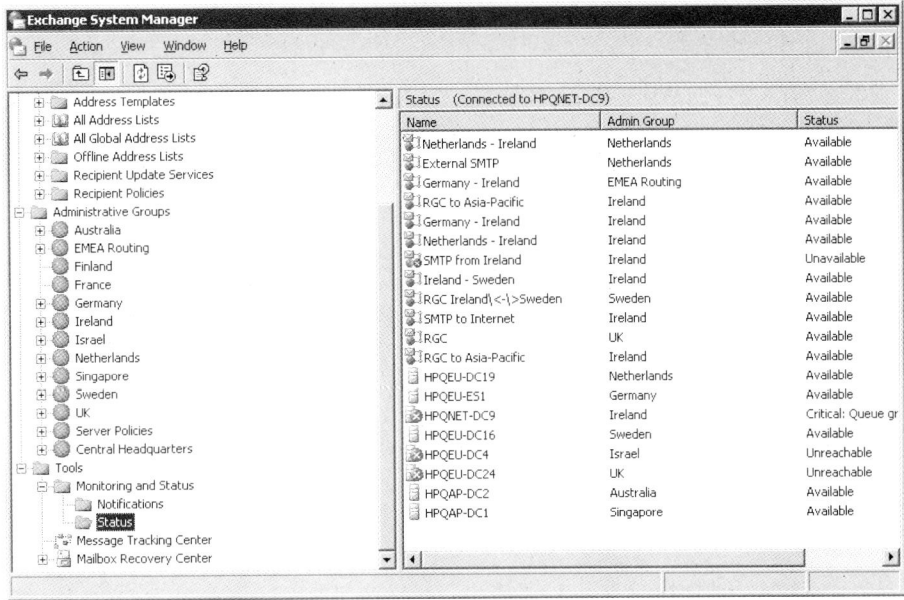

Figure 9.26 *Taking a snapshot of the routing environment.*

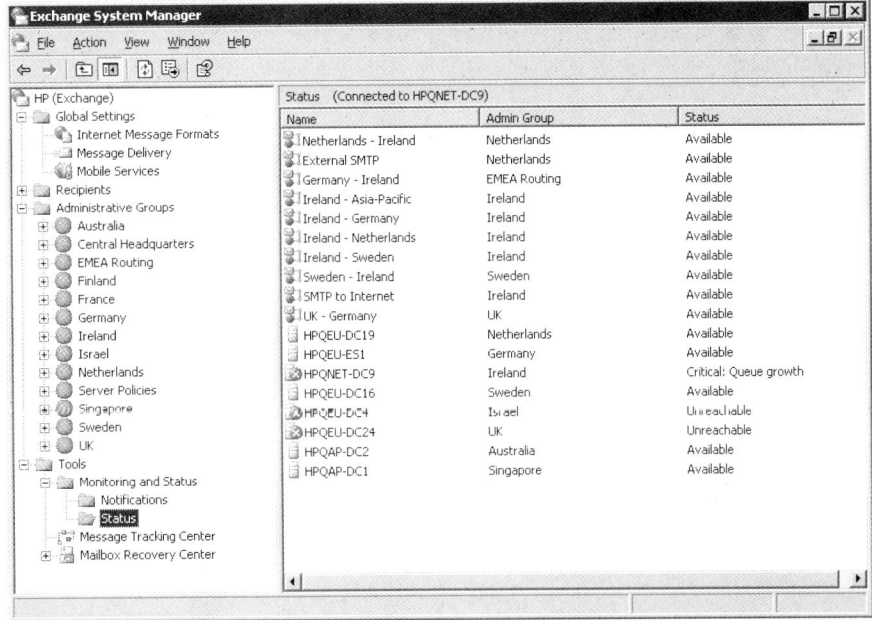

Figure 9.27 *Improved naming conventions.*

simply following a naming convention, we improve the information that an administrator sees at a glance, because all the connectors have names identifying their location and purpose. You do not have to use a strict naming convention, and it is possible to rename the connectors after creation by clicking on the name within the routing group and typing in a new name. Nevertheless, if you do not adopt a naming convention from the start, administrators will forget and will not go back and clean up the names afterward, which may result in confusion later on. According to Murphy's 233rd law of computing, that confusion will inevitably occur during a crisis, just as you are trying to debug an onerous routing problem.

If you are unsure about the route that Exchange is currently using to send messages, select a message that was recently sent between two routing

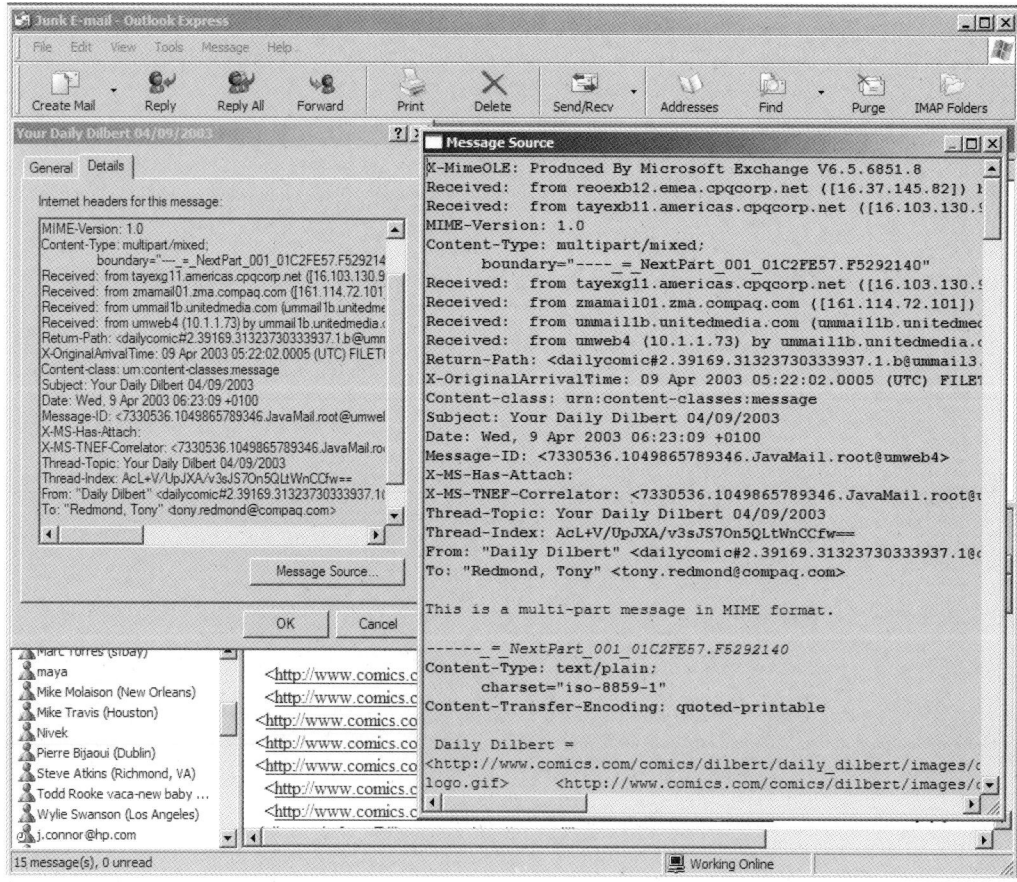

Figure 9.28 *Examining the headers of a message.*

groups and examine the message header. All of the servers that handled the message en route are captured in the header. Figure 9.28 illustrates the point. In this instance, we are using Outlook Express to examine the properties of a message that had some delivery problems. The "details" tab of the properties reveals the route information, and it is often easier to follow this data by clicking the "Message Source" button to view the complete message in a resizable window.

9.8 Connecting routing groups

Routing groups connect together through routing group Connectors (RGCs), X.400 connectors, or SMTP connectors. The RGC is very similar to the RPC-driven "Site" connector in Exchange 5.5, since it is the fastest and easiest connector to set up. As with the Site connector, you achieve convenience at the expense of giving up a certain amount of control over how messages are transmitted, such as the fact that the RGC cannot be configured to prevent messages of a certain size from being delivered. You can configure both of the other connector types to a much tighter degree. This fact is probably not important if you simply want to send messages between two routing groups located in a well-established and stable network, but it might be if you wanted to route mail between two routing groups over the public Internet.

The RGC uses SMTP to pass messages between servers, and an SMTP connector can also do this. There is not a conflict here, because the RGC takes care of internal communications within an Exchange organization, while the SMTP connector handles external communication. You should use the SMTP connector instead of the RGC when:

- You need to connect to Exchange 5.5 sites that use the IMS as their connection mechanism.

- You need to authenticate a remote bridgehead server before sending messages.

- You need to schedule message exchange with another server, perhaps to pick up messages across a link that is only available at particular times. Connecting to an ISP for message pickup is perhaps the best example of such a scenario.

- You want to use DNS MX records as the basis for routing messages instead of the Exchange configuration data held in the AD. In an organization that only has Exchange 2000/2003 servers, the Routing Engine never needs to use DNS to route messages, because all of the information about servers and routing groups is held in the AD, and the link state table contains all the data required about the lowest available cost path. Exchange uses DNS to translate server names to IP addresses, but ignores the MX records.

Some people will use SMTP or X.400 connectors to tie routing groups together, but the RGC is the most popular choice for connections today.

9.8.1 Creating a routing group connector

An RGC links one or more bridgehead servers in one routing group to one or more bridgehead servers in another. This is different from the Site connector in Exchange 5.5, which allows you to select either one server to serve as a bridgehead for a site or use any server in a site. The "any server in a site" option is often not desirable when you deal with very large sites and you want to control how messages flow within the network. You should configure multiple bridgehead servers whenever you want to achieve better resilience across a link or when the volume of messages requires that the load is balanced across multiple servers. Exchange automatically balances message load if you configure multiple bridgehead servers in a routing group.

The RGC is unidirectional, which means that you must configure the connectors on both sides before messages can flow between two routing

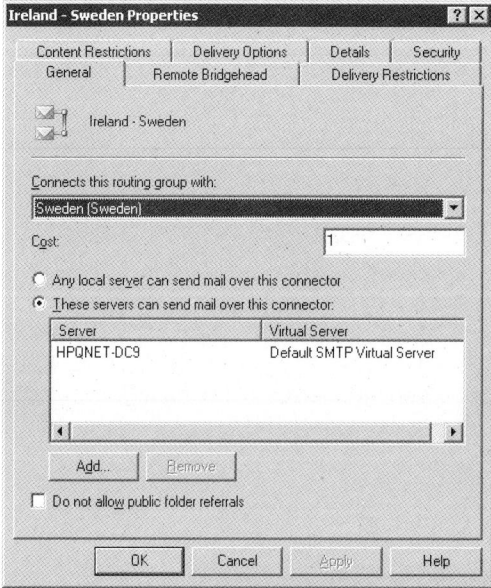

Figure 9.29
General properties of a routing group connector.

9.8 Connecting routing groups

groups. As with the Site connector in Exchange 5.5, when you set up an RGC on one server, you can have the RGC configured in the target routing group at the same time, providing you hold the appropriate administrative permissions for that routing group. The RGC is protocol independent. SMTP connects Exchange routing groups together, but in a mixed-mode environment, where an RGC links an Exchange routing group to an Exchange 5.5 site, RPCs flow across the connector. This is logical, because SMTP is an optional protocol on an Exchange 5.5 server, and RPC is the only protocol that you can absolutely guarantee to have available for interserver communications.

Creating a new RGC is very straightforward, and Figures 9.29 and 9.30 illustrate the two major screens you need to complete. Before starting, you need to know:

- The server to act as the local bridgehead
- The server to act as the bridgehead in the routing group you want to connect to. You can specify more than one bridgehead, if you want to spread the messaging load across multiple servers.
- The cost allocated to the connection
- The name of the connector, which can be up to 64 characters long

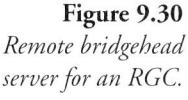

Figure 9.30
Remote bridgehead server for an RGC.

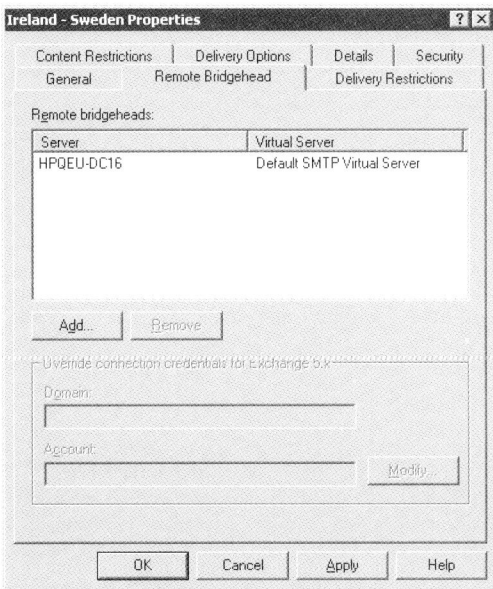

The default cost for connections is 1. Best practice suggests that you set a default cost of 10 for all major connectors and use steps of at least 10 for minor connectors. Because the concept of "major" and "minor" links varies greatly from company to company and depends on network connectivity and the way that routing groups are created, it is very difficult to offer hard and fast definitions. For most purposes, you can define a major connector as a link that you expect to handle heavy traffic. For instance, a connector that links a central routing group and a hub routing group in a hub and spoke network falls into this category. Minor connections are defined as links that carry less traffic. A connection that serves a downstream routing group (one that not connected directly into a hub routing group) falls into this category. If you look at the organization illustrated in Figure 9.25, the major connection is between London and New York and has a cost of 10. The links between the routing groups off the two hubs all have a cost of 20.

After Exchange creates the local RGC, Exchange prompts you to create the corresponding RGC in the target routing group. This is equivalent to the way that you create Site connectors for Exchange 5.5, where, if you have the necessary permissions in the Windows NT domain that hosts the remote site, you can create connectors in both sites in a single operation.

The Content Restrictions, Delivery Restrictions, and Delivery Options property pages allow you to exert additional control over messages that flow across the link. Content restrictions determine what priority of messages can be transmitted: High, Normal, or Low. Delivery restrictions allow administrators to create lists of users who are either permitted or barred from using the link. The combination of Content and Delivery restrictions is enough to create a scenario where a link is only able to handle high-priority messages from a select group of users. In most cases, administrators will not want to create such a restrictive environment, but many will be interested in the Delivery options.

Everyone wants the messages to go as quickly as possible, but sometimes people send messages that you really wish were left until after office hours. Most of the time, these messages are very large. Delivery options allow you to determine when the connector is available and set a different schedule for messages that exceed a certain size. Figure 9.31 shows that the connector is always available (the default) and that a separate schedule governs when messages over 2 MB (approximately 2,000 KB) can be transmitted. Given the size of many PowerPoint presentations sent by major corporations today, 2 MB may be too small a limit, but it serves to illustrate the point.

9.8 Connecting routing groups

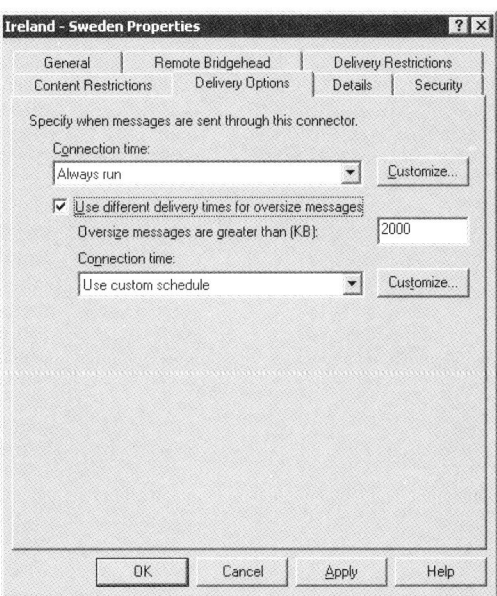

Figure 9.31
Delivery options for an RGC.

Exchange keeps any messages that exceed the limit on the queue for the connector until the schedule allows their dispatch.

After creating a new connector, it is always a good idea to check that it works by sending a message with a delivery confirmation to a mailbox on a server in the target routing group. Of course, the nature of link state routing is such that Exchange will deliver the message by any possible route, so your test may work even if the connector does not if another route is available. You can use message tracking to verify the route that the test message takes, just to be sure.

Connectors are one way, so it is important to remember that any change you make to an RGC only applies in the routing group that the connector belongs to. If you impose a restriction on who can use the connector or the size of messages that can be processed and only make the change on one side of the link, it is quite possible to end up in a situation where users can send large messages from one side to the other, but not the other way around.

The best way to avoid potential problems is to ensure that you maintain the same configuration for the RGC from both sides of the link. After you have configured the RGC on both sides, you should be able to see both connectors in their respective routing groups (Figure 9.32).

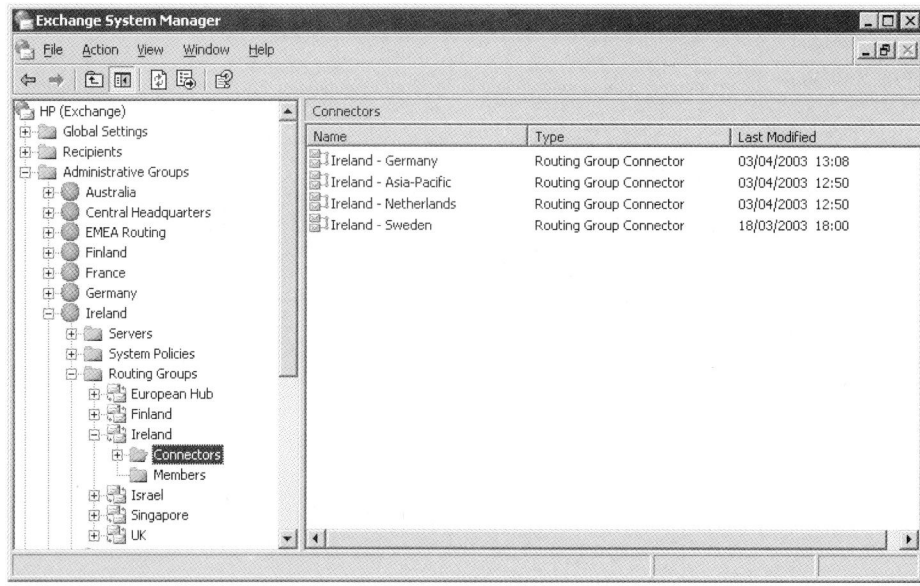

Figure 9.32   *Routing group connectors.*

9.9   Creating an SMTP connector

The RGC uses SMTP, so why is there a separate SMTP connector? The answer is simple: There is a huge SMTP world out there where Exchange is a relatively small presence today. People want to communicate with other SMTP domains, and they would like to do so in as functional a manner as possible. In addition, RGCs can only connect to other routing groups and cannot send email to an SMTP server that is outside the Exchange organization, so another connector is required to link Exchange to the wider SMTP world. Exchange 2003 includes an Internet Mail Wizard to help you create SMTP connectors, but it is more fun to do the work yourself.

As with the RGC, the SMTP connector runs under the context of an SMTP virtual server. The RGC uses the Exchange configuration data held in the AD to route messages, but Microsoft designed the SMTP connector to use standard SMTP routing techniques such as the Mail Exchanger (MX) records held in DNS. You should, therefore, use an SMTP connector whenever you want to route messages to a "smart host" system, and use MX records as the basis for routing or to send messages outside Exchange (including to the IMS running on older Exchange servers).

9.9 Creating an SMTP connector

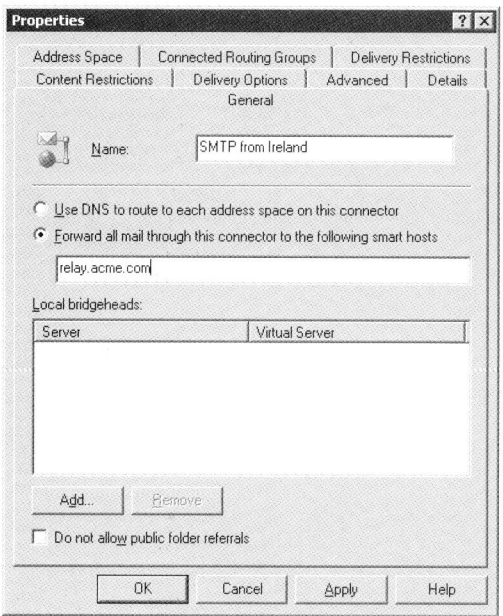

Figure 9.33
General properties of an SMTP connector.

Figure 9.33 shows a good example of an SMTP connector in action. The connector is configured to send any message to "relay.acme.com." Smart hosts are mail servers that often act as central collection and dispatch points for SMTP mail for an enterprise. You can specify either a fully qualified domain name (as in this case) or a specific IP address to point to the smart host. If you use an IP address, remember to enclose it in square brackets—for example, [22.18.19.20].

Bringing messages together to a central point before they are sent outside a company allows for centralized checking for viruses or profanity, as well as verification that users are complying with company standards such as disclaimer text on messages or even that classified information isn't being sent to external correspondents. The Clearswift Enterprise Suite (www.clearswift.com) is a popular example of software that often runs on smart hosts.

Setting up the connector to route all mail to a smart host is the first step toward achieving control over SMTP routing. You can achieve finer control by defining routes for specific domains through the address space property page, where you define the SMTP domains that can be reached through the connector. The default is "*"—meaning that all domains can be reached, but in some cases you might want messages for a specific domain to be handled in a certain manner. Figure 9.34 shows how you configure the address space for a specific domain, in this instance acme.com. With this configuration, the connector is only able to handle messages addressed to a recipient in acme.com, and all other messages will have to find another route.

At the bottom of Figure 9.34, you can see how Exchange controls the scope of a connector. The feature (also available in Exchange 5.5) allows administrators to restrict the availability of a connector to other servers. You can restrict a connector to servers at a location, site, or the organization. With Exchange 2000/2003, you can apply restrictions at either the routing group or organizational level. In our example, the connector is only available to the servers in the local routing group. Setting a scope on an SMTP connector is most useful when several connectors exist in an organization, each of which has very different capacities, possibly because of varying costs of Internet connections via ISPs from country to country. For example, assume that you have two SMTP connectors created in routing groups in Paris and New York. ISP charges are typically cheaper in North America, so if the New York connector ever goes down, you may not want to reroute messages across the Atlantic to Paris, since this would drive up the use of the ISP connection there and might result in heavier fees. In this case, you could set the scope for the SMTP connector in Paris at the level of the routing group.

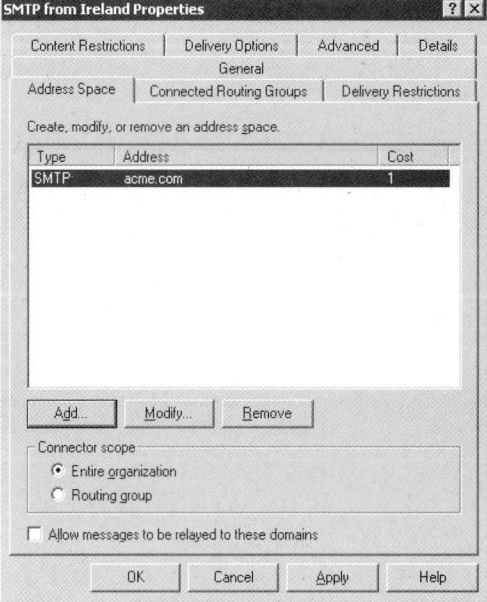

Figure 9.34
Specifying the address space for an SMTP connector.

9.9 Creating an SMTP connector

Microsoft built scope control into Exchange for a reason, so it is a good idea to consider this option for every SMTP connector that you create.

The SMTP connector has many advanced properties that you can manipulate, but you can rely on the defaults if you simply want to connect together SMTP-based email systems, or link Exchange to the Internet through a permanent connection. For example, as with the routing group connector, the Delivery Options property page allows you to check the "Use different delivery times for oversize messages" box to tell the SMTP connector to send messages (perhaps over 1 MB) according to a different schedule, which is a reasonable approach to giving priority to "normal" traffic. Of course, there are other ways to allocate different priorities to protocol-based traffic. For instance, Packeteer's (www.packeteer.com) PacketShaper product allows you to set bandwidth allocation policies for protocols such as LDAP, SMTP, and HTTP, so you could favor SMTP traffic over HTTP, or vice versa. You can even create special virtual links for applications such as Exchange to use to guarantee bandwidth. These solutions ensure that you can provide a defined quality of service for applications, which can be vital if you sign up for service-level agreements.

Companies that depend on ISPs to provide a message drop service will be happy to find that the SMTP connector is much easier to work with than the Exchange 5.5 IMS. The connector supports all the features

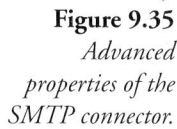

Figure 9.35
Advanced properties of the SMTP connector.

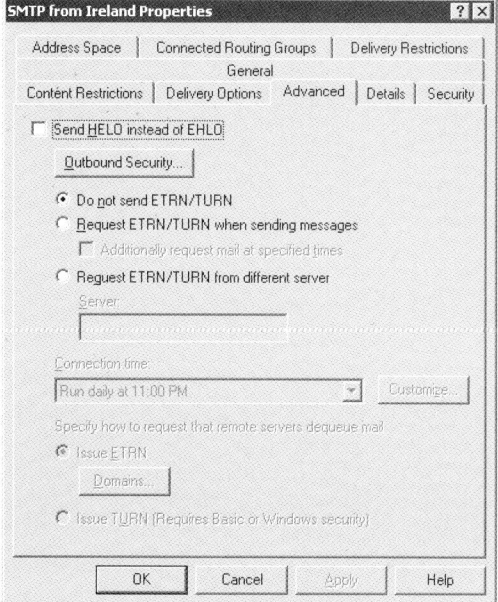

required to make a connection to an ISP and pick up messages using the SMTP ETRN or TURN commands (Figure 9.35). Creating a connection between Exchange and an ISP can be a specialized business that requires much more discussion than can be afforded in a book such as this, so those interested in the topic should consult a specialized Web site such as that at www.swinc.com.

9.9.1 Encrypted SMTP communications

SMTP messages are sent in plain text, so unless the actual content is encrypted using Exchange advanced security or some other secure scheme, the possibility exists that the data could be intercepted and examined by someone who you'd rather not. The Exchange 5.5 Site connector uses encrypted RPCs, so obviously security is somewhat downgraded when you switch site connectors over to RGCs or SMTP connectors.

The solution is to establish a secure connection for SMTP traffic to flow between the servers. The preferred and recommended solution is to do this with IPSec (which you can apply to specific ports or IP addresses), although it is also possible to create an encrypted connection with TLS. However, IPSec incurs far less overhead than a TLS connection and is built into Windows 2000 and Windows 2003; you can apply IPSec to a large number of servers through group policies. An IPSec connection secures all IP traffic across the link, another advantage gained by selecting this approach.

9.9.2 Delivery restrictions for SMTP-based connectors

SMTP provides the foundation for both SMTP and routing group connectors. As shown in Figure 9.36, the Delivery Restrictions property page on a connector defines the set of users who can submit messages to the connector or who the connector will explicitly reject messages from.

You access the Delivery Restrictions property page by selecting a connector through ESM and then viewing the connector's properties. For the default set of Exchange connectors, the MTA controls the restrictions placed on the X.400 connector, while a combination of the Routing Engine and SMTP service controls the restrictions on routing group and SMTP connectors. As you can see in Figure 9.36, you can use individual mailbox names or distribution groups to define who can use a connector.

Unfortunately, for whatever reason, Microsoft decided that applying restrictions through ESM was not sufficient. To complete the job and make the restrictions effective, you also have to change the registry to instruct the

9.9 Creating an SMTP connector

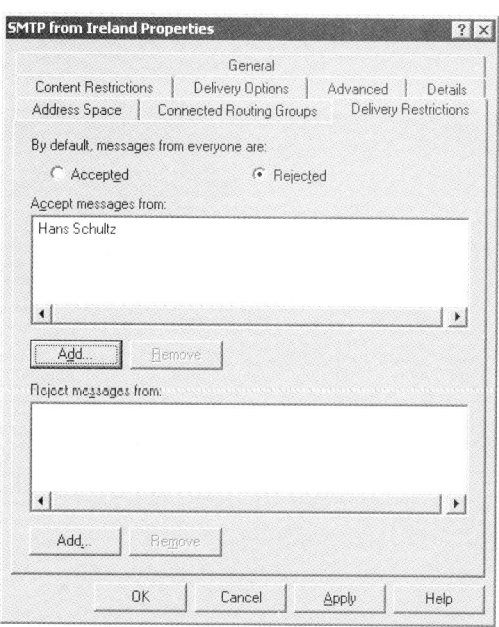

Figure 9.36
Limiting users on an SMTP connector.

SMTP service that restrictions are in force and tell the Routing Engine that it should validate submitters and recipients. The logic behind this two-step approach is probably that turning on restrictions causes additional overhead for the Routing Engine as it checks names against the restricted list. The Routing Engine validates email addresses against the Active Directory, so it is a bad idea to turn on restrictions on a bridgehead server that is already under load or has an extended connection back to the nearest GC. Remember that Exchange uses the GC to validate names, because the GC holds a copy of all mail-enabled objects in a forest. However, in production situations, bridgehead servers are typically located close to GCs, and many of the names that the Routing Engine needs to check will be in the local directory cache, so the additional overhead is not large.

Two DWORD registry values (Table 9.7) control how checking is performed. Place these values in:

```
HKLM/System/CurrentControlSet/Services/RESvc/Parameters
```

Once you have inserted the two values, stop and restart the SMTP service and the Routing Engine service to make the blocks effective. The restart is necessary to allow the two services to recognize that restrictions are in place and read the information about users you want either to permit or bar from using the connector. Once set, the restriction is active for all SMTP-based

Table 9.7 *Registry Values to Implement SMTP-Based Connector Restrictions*

Value	Meaning
CheckConnectorRestrictions	Set to 1 to enable checks.
IgnoreRestrictionforNullDSN	Set to 1 to ignore restrictions for delivery service messages (such as nondelivery messages). If set to 0, DSNs will be blocked from going across a restricted connector.

connectors on a server. You should then test that the restrictions are in place by attempting to send a message from an account on the blocked list. If the block is effective, you will receive a nondelivery notification.

Of course, any change made to the system registry can only influence components that are active on that server. If this is the only server that hosts connectors such as a shared organization-wide SMTP connector, then the block is effective for the entire organization. However, if a message can take multiple routes to get to a destination, then you need to implement the restriction at every bridgehead server along these routes.

9.10 Creating an X.400 connector

With all the focus on SMTP, you might assume that an Exchange administrator would never have to create an X.400 connector again. This may well be the case in many companies, especially those in the United States, where SMTP links have always been more popular. The largest constituency for X.400 connectivity remains companies that operate X.400-based backbones that integrate many different messaging systems. In addition, some companies use the X.400 connector to link multiple Exchange organizations together, especially when the organizations are of different vintage.

Many administrators regarded the X.400 connector as one of the more complex components in previous versions of Exchange. This is an unfair label, and it is largely because the X.400 connector had more property pages than either the Site or the SMTP connectors. The truth is that you can safely ignore the majority of the pages if you want to set up a connection between Exchange sites or organizations or link to an X.400 backbone (including the X.400 service offered by large service providers such as AT&T). The X.400 connector offers more opportunity to tune the way that connections are established and operated, but that is no reason to consider it complex.

9.10 Creating an X.400 connector

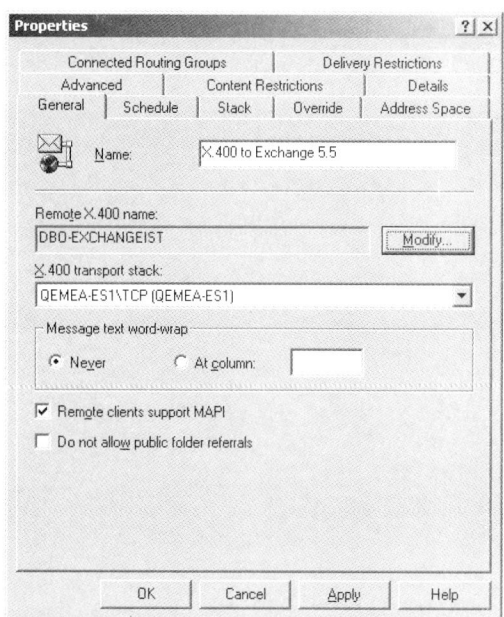

Figure 9.37
General properties of an X.400 connector.

To illustrate how easy it is to create an X.400 connector, let us look at the steps required to set up an X.400 connector to link Exchange to an Exchange 5.5 organization. While SMTP is the easiest way to link Exchange 2000/2003 to Exchange 5.5, it may be the case that you want to operate a scheduled connection (on both sides), and X.400 is able to offer this facility.

Figure 9.37 illustrates the general properties of the X.400 connector. The important items here are:

- The name of the remote MTA: This is usually the name of the remote bridgehead server that you want to connect to. Unlike the RGC or SMTP connectors, you can only define a single bridgehead server for each side of an X.400 connection. However, you can install multiple X.400 connections within a routing group to provide fault tolerance if the server that hosts the primary connection fails.

- A password for the remote MTA: Usually blank, unless you wish to secure the connection by forcing each MTA to authenticate itself to its partner by exchanging passwords each time the MTA attempts to make a connection. Note that the password is sent in plain text.

- Message text word wrap: Since this connection is going to another Exchange organization, it is safe to send messages without forcing lines to wrap at a set position. Older X.400 systems (usually those that support the 1984 X.400 recommendations) may insist that each line is wrapped at column 75 or 78, or another value.

- Remote clients support MAPI: Again, since the connection is going to an Exchange 5.5 organization, we can expect that any client that connects to the servers will understand MAPI, or the server will provide the client with a translated version of the messages (as in the case of POP3, IMAP, or OWA).

- Do not allow public folder referrals: If the X.400 connector is used to link routing groups together in the same Exchange organization (including a mixed-mode organization), it is safe to allow public folder referrals to flow across the connector. However, in this case we are using the X.400 connector to link two different Exchange organizations, one of which is running Exchange 5.5. You cannot share public folders between two different organizations, so the checkbox is completed.

The X.400 transport stack defines the method used to establish the X.400 link and the server that will act as the bridgehead. Most X.400 connections within the Exchange community flow across a TCP/IP link, although we could equally use an X.25 dial-up link. The details of how X.400 works across a TCP/IP link can be found in RFC 2126 (an update to RFC 1006), which defines how OSI software can connect over IP (messages are routed through port 102). X.25 dial-up links are usually confined to situations where a telephone connection is the only possible link. In these circumstances a dial-up SMTP connection, either direct to a central hub or via a connection managed by an ISP, is now a better option. SMTP supports authentication and encryption, whereas X.400 only supports basic authentication (MTA passwords), and, as we have seen, SMTP is the way of the future, so it's best to move if at all possible.

You must configure a suitable transport stack on a server before it can support an X.400 connector. Figure 9.38 shows how to begin the process of configuring a new stack. The properties of the stack are very simple and merely require you to provide a name for the new object plus values for the TSAP, SSAP, and PSAP used in OSI address information. TSAP, SSAP, and PSAP stand for Transport, Session, and Presentation access points and represent the different points within the OSI model used by the X.400 connector. This is a real opportunity to make things complex. You can keep things simple by specifying blank values, which means that incoming MTAs can also specify blank values when they make a connection, or you can complicate matters by playing around with different hex and text values in each

9.10 Creating an X.400 connector

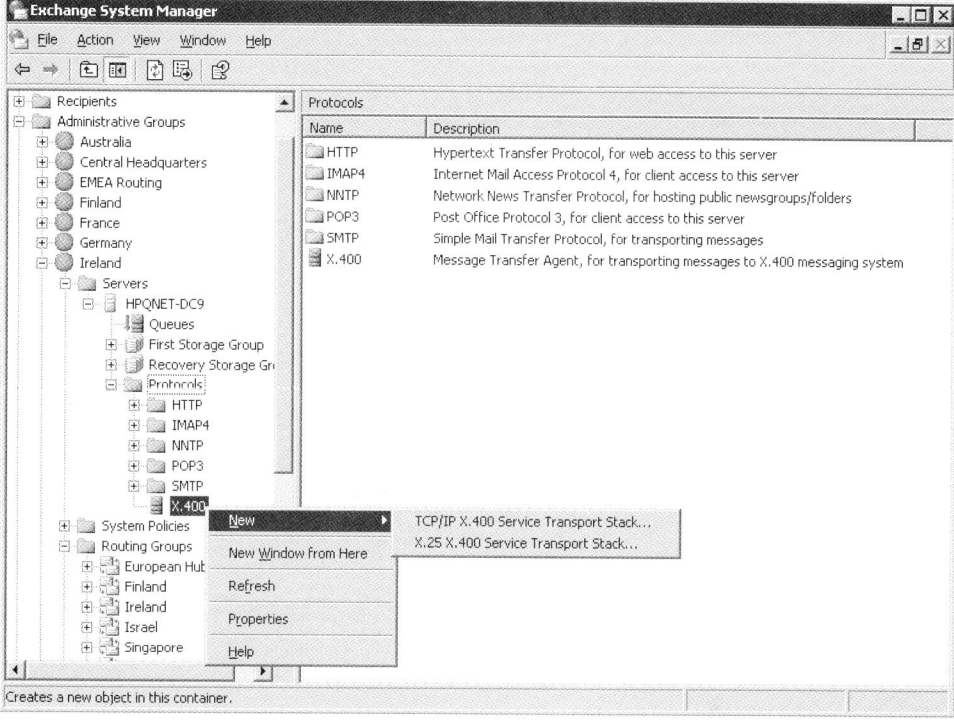

Figure 9.38 *Installing a new X.400 transport stack.*

access point. Of course, you are much more secure now, because you have created a situation where incoming MTAs absolutely must be able to pass the required access point information before a connection is established. This is sometimes required, especially when communicating with X.400 backbones, but if you're only going to communicate with other Exchange servers you should use blank values. Over the years, there has been more frustration and bad words spoken during attempts to make Exchange servers talk to each other across X.400 connections. Normally, the reason is that the MTAs have mismatching access points. Life is too short to get involved in such situations.

Figure 9.39 illustrates the properties defined in the Stack page. We define two major pieces of data here. First, you need to specify either the name of the host server you want to connect to or its IP address. It is best practice to use the fully qualified domain name of the host server, since this allows the IP address to be changed if necessary. Just to prove that I do not always follow best practices, I have used the IP address here. This is safe to do if you are sure that the address is unlikely to change. Using

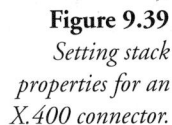

Figure 9.39
Setting stack properties for an X.400 connector.

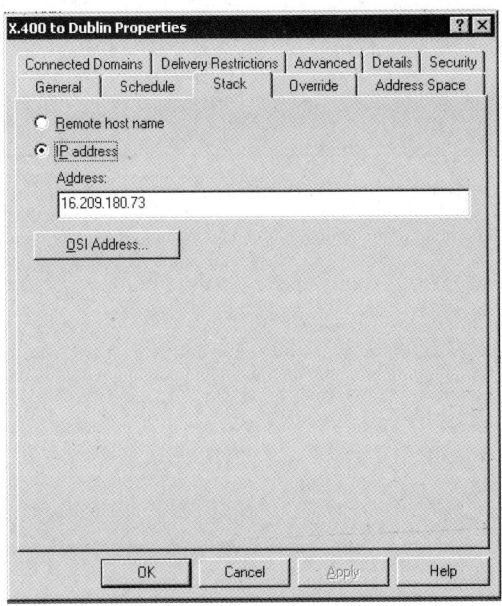

the IP address offers a major advantage in that connectivity can still be established if DNS is unavailable to resolve the host name. However, if DNS is unavailable, your Windows 2000 infrastructure will be experiencing some major problems of its own, and sending email across an X.400 connector is likely to be one of the lower-priority items on an administrator's to-do list.

The OSI address information can be entered in hex or text format. Computers and some people understand hex well enough to be able to accurately interpret data entered in hex, but I don't and can't be bothered to work it out, so I take the easy option and go for text and then leave the values blank whenever possible. You can enter outgoing and incoming OSI information for the TSAP, SSAP, and PSAP selectors. Exchange sends the outgoing information to the remote MTA when it establishes the connection, while the local MTA expects the remote MTA to provide the specified OSI data when an incoming connection is initiated. If the information does not match expectations, the connection will be determined. Between Exchange servers there is no real need to specify OSI selector information, so it's best to leave these fields blank. Connecting to other X.400 systems may require you to know the OSI selectors the remote MTA will broadcast, so be sure to find out this information before you set up the connector.

9.10 Creating an X.400 connector

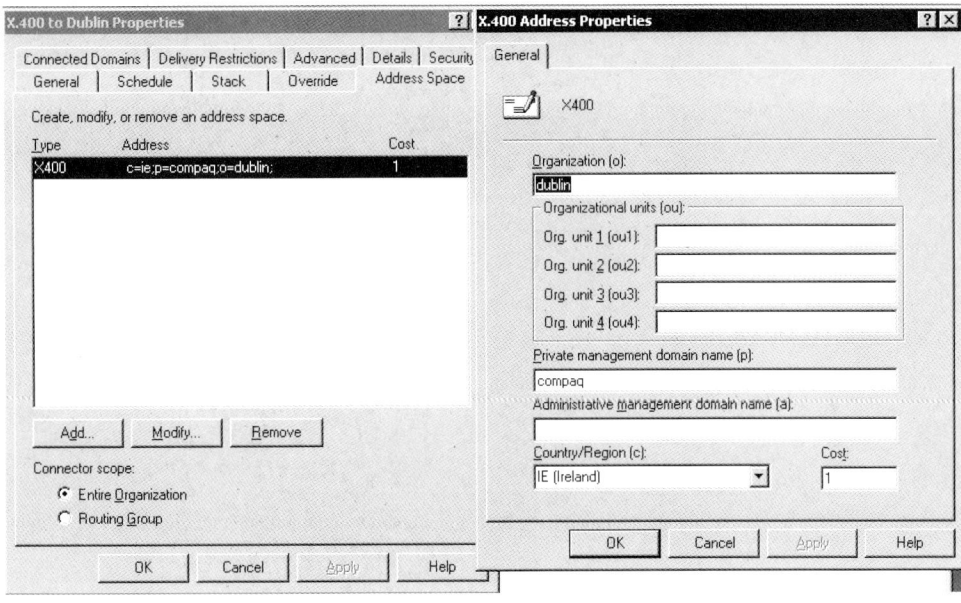

Figure 9.40 *Defining an address space for an X.400 connector.*

All Exchange connectors specify an address space. The address space determines how messages are routed to the connector. In the case of the X.400 connector, we need to define what X.400 addresses can be handled by the connector. The routing core will then send any message it finds that matches the address space to the connector. Figure 9.40 shows two screens. The left-hand screen lists all of the address spaces defined for the connector, while the right-hand screen shows how an address space is defined. In this case, the definition means that any message with an X.400 address starting with:

```
C=IE;A=;P=compaq;O=Dublin
```

will be routed through the connector. Most users do not know (and do not want to) how to generate X.400 addresses, but it is useful to know how so that you can send a test message to an address on the other side of the connection to make sure that everything works. Using a MAPI client, you can enter an X.400 address by enclosing it in square brackets and prefixing the address with X400, as follows:

```
[X400: C=IE;A=;P=Compaq;O=Dublin;S=Redmond;G=Tony]
```

Be careful with blank values. In the previous example, the A (administrative domain) part of the address is blank, meaning that no value is passed at all. In some situations, a single space character may represent a "blank,"

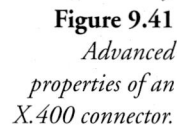

Figure 9.41
Advanced properties of an X.400 connector.

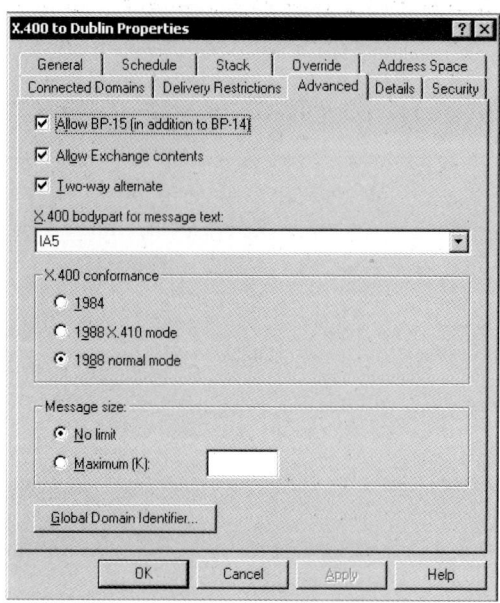

and you might have to test several variations of address formats before you determine the correct format.

Figure 9.41 shows the advanced properties of our X.400 connector. These properties are easy to determine when you connect to another Exchange server, since you can accept the default values. However, when you connect to a foreign X.400 system, you will have to know what the other system supports.

"Allow BP-15" means that the remote MTA supports bodypart-15, which means that Exchange can send file names instead of an X.400 OID (object identifier) for each attachment. In other words, if you send a Word attachment, the message header includes file name information such as "document1.doc" instead of a binary value. Most modern X.400 systems support BP-15. Note that the responsibility for interpreting the file names and processing the attachment with the correct application lies with the client, not the MTA, so clients that attach to the receiving MTA must be able to understand the file names that Exchange will send.

"Allow Exchange contents" means that the message will contain MAPI content (header properties, message text, and attachments). If the clients attached to the remote MTA understand MAPI, you can check this box.

"Two-way alternate" means that the two MTAs can send and receive messages alternatively. Some older MTAs can only accept or send messages in a connection. IA5 is the most common encoding scheme used for text bodyparts. Older X.400 systems may support the 1984 recommendations. However, these systems are rare now, and you will normally find that the remote system supports 1988 mode.

The values used to configure X.400 connectors in first-generation Exchange are the same as those required now. If you already have X.400 connectors in use, they should continue to function perfectly after you upgrade.

9.10.1 Deciding when to use an X.400 connection

The X.400 connector is just one of the options that you can use to connect Exchange servers together, or to connect Exchange to another messaging system. The question is when should you use an X.400 connector? Here are a few scenarios that call for the X.400 connector:

- An enterprise uses a well-established X.400 backbone to link diverse messaging systems together. The temptation may exist to move to an SMTP backbone, but the other messaging systems may not support the same level of rich SMTP extensions as Exchange. On the other hand, because X.400 has been in use since 1984, it is probable that systems now in use support a rich set of features, as defined in the 1988 or 1992 X.400 recommendations. In this case, it is best to operate on the basis that you should not fix something that is not broken and continue to use the existing backbone. As new versions of the other messaging systems become available that might support extended SMTP, you can test their interoperability with Exchange and decide whether the time has come to move to a new backbone. Similarly, you may want to connect to a public email service that uses X.400. Most public systems now offer SMTP, but there are a few (reducing all the time) that still rely on X.400.

- The bandwidth available between routing groups is 16 Kbps or less. The Advanced properties page for an X.400 connector allows you to tune how messages are transmitted to achieve a finer degree of control than is possible with the SMTP or RG connectors. Fine control becomes very important when bandwidth is low.

- No technical reason might exist, but your organization may decide that X.400 is the preferred protocol for connections. This might come about because system administrators are more familiar and comfortable with X.400 and still believe that SMTP is only for simple messaging, or a decision taken some time ago to use X.400 is still in place and you have not yet had the chance to review the role of SMTP in your messaging interoperability strategy.

It is possible that SMTP will experience problems for some reason, such as a smart host server failing. In this case, you can configure X.400 connectors to communicate stating IP addresses for servers (rather than FQDNs), disable the SMTP connectors, and force the Routing Engine to channel messages across the X.400 connectors. This can be a short-term workaround to avoid messages building on queues, which proves that it is always useful to have multiple ways to solve a problem or, in this case, to route messages.

One esoteric but important point is that Exchange does not support the X.400 MIXER (RFC 2156) functionality (Exchange 5.5 offers this support). MIXER allows full mapping of SMTP and X.400 for recipients and originator addresses in the envelope (P1) and content (P2) of a message. If you need this functionality to communicate with an X.400 email system, you will have to maintain an Exchange 5.5 SP3 (or later) server in the organization until the requirement disappears. Despite the charge toward Internet protocols, X.400 will be in use for some time yet. SMTP will eventually win in the battle of the messaging protocols, but achieving final victory for the SMTP camp will be a long, drawn-out affair.

Finally, the MTACHECK utility is still around and supported for Exchange 2000 and 2003. MTACHECK validates the MTA's internal database that it uses to track messages and ensures that all necessary files are available.

9.11 Understanding routing

Most of the time, things just work and messages flow reliably, so you do not have to worry about all the behind-the-scenes processing. When things go wrong, it is useful to have a set of tools to use to understand how the Transport Engine and the connectors process messages. WinRoute helps you understand the link state table, while SMTP logging and archiving capture information about the flow and format of messages processed by Exchange.

9.11.1 WinRoute

The link state table only exists in memory. Most administrators are not equipped to interrogate data held in memory, and viewing queues is not always the best way to understand how routing works. WinRoute began as a Microsoft support tool and is now part of the shipping product (see the \

9.11 Understanding routing 665

support\utils\i386 directory on the server CD); it is the best way to gain an insight into how the Exchange routing topology works.

You can launch WinRoute from the server CD, but it is more convenient to move the executable into the same directory as the rest of the Exchange binaries. You can also run WinRoute on a Windows XP Professional workstation. Apart from some bug fixes, the version of WinRoute provided with Exchange 2003 is no different from the version used with Exchange 2000.

WinRoute works by connecting to an Exchange server as if it were another Exchange server and then requesting the current link state table. WinRoute then interprets the data before displaying it, as shown in Figure 9.42, which illustrates data taken from the HP production environment. You can see some of the native link state data in the lower panel. It is composed of a series of GUIDs and other binary information that Win-

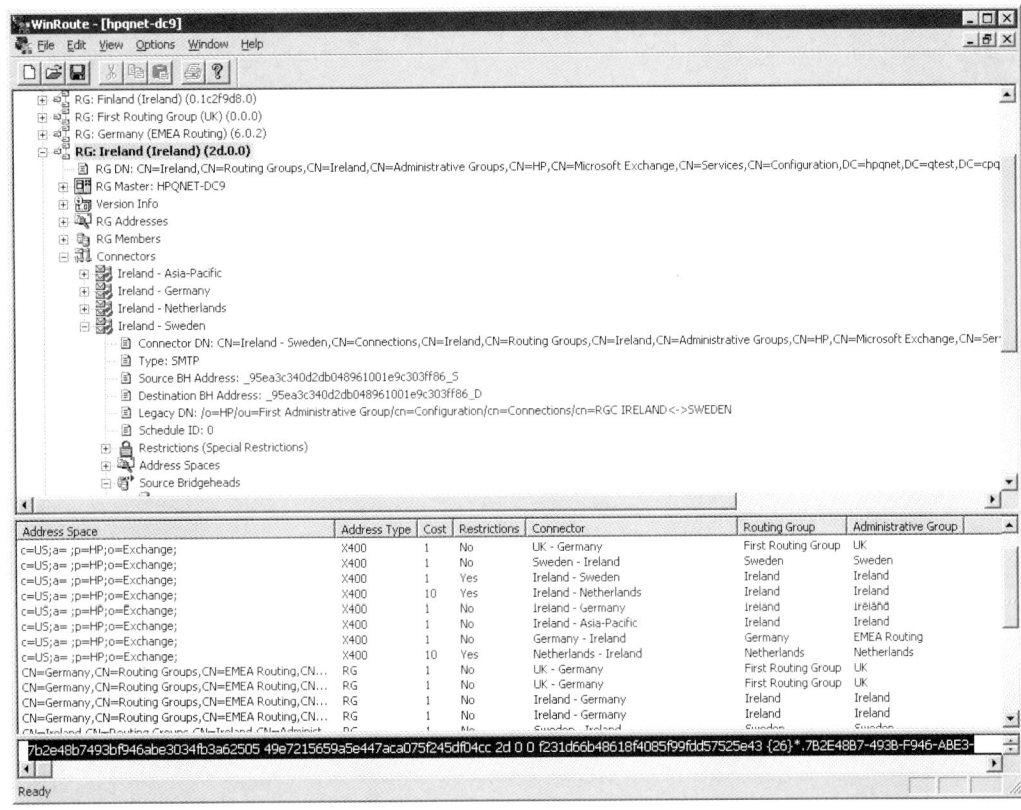

Figure 9.42   *The WinRoute utility.*

Chapter 9

Route resolves by reference to the configuration data in the AD. Sometimes WinRoute cannot resolve the GUIDs and you will see "object_not_found_in_ds" displayed instead of connector names. Normally, this is due to temporary glitches between Exchange and the AD, perhaps because you removed a server that was a routing group master or hosted a connector and replication is not yet fully complete. In this situation, WinRoute may encounter some outdated information and is unable to turn the contents of the link state routing table into people-friendly displays. Replication latency is the root cause in the vast proportion of such instances, and the errors in interpretation do not affect effective message routing. You can either ignore the glitches by waiting for replication to complete, or flush the cached data that WinRoute depends on by stopping and restarting either IIS or Exchange. This is acceptable practice on a test box but not on a production server, so most administrators overlook this small WinRoute bug.

The upper two panels are most important in interpreting WinRoute information. The top panel displays the routing topology as normally visualized through ESM, with the organization broken down into routing groups and connectors. You can expand objects to discover information such as version numbers, details of bridgehead servers, restrictions, and so on (Figure 9.43). All of this information is available through ESM, but WinRoute makes it available more quickly and in a format that allows you to capture the data to a .rte file for later analysis with the File/Save option, perhaps even when working offline. This facility is also useful when problems occur, since you can give the WinRoute file to Microsoft PSS to help isolate the problem or identify a bug. Analysis of the data in a captured .rte file can also verify that the expected routing topology is in use.

The middle panel reveals the set of connectors known by the server. You can sort the data by address space, address type, cost, restrictions, connector name, routing group, and administrative group. Address type includes standard values of "RG" (routing group), "SMTP," and "X400,"

Figure 9.43
Details exposed by WinRoute.

9.12 SMTP logging

as well as types used by nonstandard connectors, such as "FAX," "SMS," and "NOTES."

As with any tool, WinRoute is not a solution in itself. However, its value increases with the size of the Exchange organization. Anyone can understand the routing topology of a single server organization, and it is not difficult to comprehend how messages flow between two or three routing groups, especially if you only use routing group connectors. Organizations that span 20 or more administrative groups, that incorporate nonstandard connectors, or that operate multiple SMTP connectors for external communications are a different matter, and it is almost impossible for a person to grasp the full picture through ESM. WinRoute is, therefore, an invaluable tool for enterprise Exchange administrators.

9.12 SMTP logging

You enable logging on an SMTP virtual server to gain an insight into how Exchange conducts SMTP conversations with other servers or as an aid to debug a problem. After you enable logging for a virtual server, Exchange records details of communications generated by all the connectors that use the virtual server.

You have to enable logging separately for each SMTP virtual server. To start logging, select the virtual server and view its properties, then check the box and select the log format, as shown in Figure 9.44. Afterward, stop and restart the virtual server to begin the logging process. You do not need a restart if you change logging properties afterward—for example, if you decide to change the interval for log file rollover from hourly to daily. Note that you need to stop and restart the virtual server through the cluster administration tool if Exchange is running on a cluster.

By default, you find SMTP logs C:\WINNT\SYSTEM32\LOGFILES\SMTPSVCx\, where "x" is the number of the server that you want to work with. The default SMTP virtual server is 1. Exchange can generate SMTP logs in four formats: IIS Log File Format, NCSA Common Log File Format, and W3C Extended Log File Format are all text-based formats. ODBC Logging requires a connection to an ODBC-compliant database, such as SQL, which then generates a small additional load on the server. The major advantage of using a database is its ability to handle very large amounts of data, which is useful if you want to analyze data captured from a very busy server, which can easily amount to several hundred megabytes. Most of the servers in use today can comfortably support the load generated by directing logging data to a database, but you may not want to get

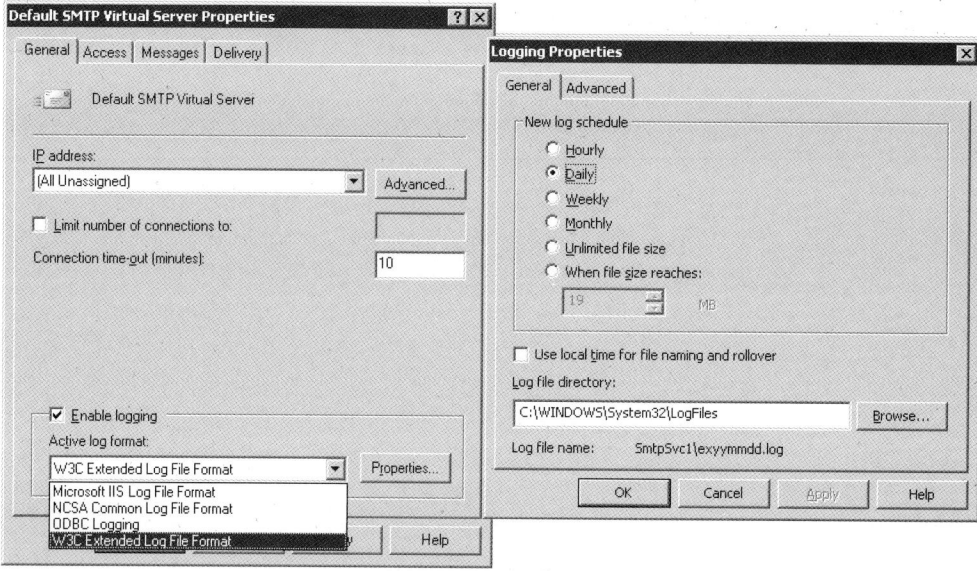

Figure 9.44 *Enabling logging for the default SMTP virtual server.*

involved in the additional complexity of configuring the database. Unless you really need to capture data in ODBC format, use a text format—preferably W3C—since this gives you maximum control over the fields written into the log through the Extended Property page (Figure 9.45). The other text formats supply a predefined set of data that you cannot change.

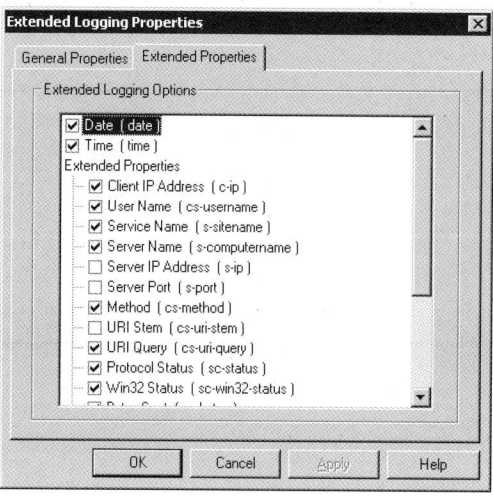

Figure 9.45 *Extended properties for an SMTP log.*

9.12 SMTP logging

Even if you begin logging with a text format, it is possible to convert a log file into a database to perform analysis. Indeed, administrators often use Excel for this purpose, because it will read any of the text formats; it is sometimes easier to use Excel to navigate large quantities of data than to simply edit it with a text editor.

Any production Exchange server generates a lot of SMTP traffic, so it is unwise to keep the log files on the same drive as the Windows binaries. Select another drive that handles little I/O and has sufficient free disk space. A server that handles email and public folder replication traffic can generate 500 MB or more of logs daily (any of the text formats). While logging stops if disk space is exhausted, so does everything else that uses the same disk. This is the fundamental reason not to use the same drive as Windows. Note that neither Exchange nor Windows purges these logs, so this is another manual task.

You can configure when Exchange switches log files through the General property page. The most common option is daily, using local time to control file naming and rollover. This means that Exchange creates a new log file at midnight and names it according to the selected file format. For example, the file ex030101.log is a daily log in W3C format for January 1, 2003, whereas in030101.log is from the same date in IIS format. Hourly logs add the hour number (in 24-hour format) to the end of the log file name. For example, ex03010113.log is the log file beginning at 1:00 P.M. on January 1, 2003.

If you elect not to use local time, the rollover time differs depending on format. W3C uses midnight GMT, while IIS and NCSA use local midnight. To avoid confusion and to ensure that you have a good idea where to look for data if you need to trace a specific connection, use the same log format and rollover time throughout the organization. The fields written into a W3C format log file are controlled through the Extended Properties page, as shown in Figure 9.45. Since virtual servers run under IIS, some of these fields do not hold useful data for tracing SMTP communications.

Figure 9.46 illustrates sample data that you can expect to capture in an SMTP log. In this case, the DBOEXCVS1 server initiates a connection to the DEMEXB12 server with the EHLO command. DEMEXB12 responds and the two servers establish a secure connection using the GSSAPI command. The certificate data used follows the GSSAPI command. After successful authentication, DBOEXCVS1 issues an X-LINK2STATE command to exchange link state data, so we know that this connection is between two Exchange 2000/2003 servers across a routing group or SMTP connector. After the exchange of link state information, DBOEXCVS1 begins to send a

9.12 SMTP logging

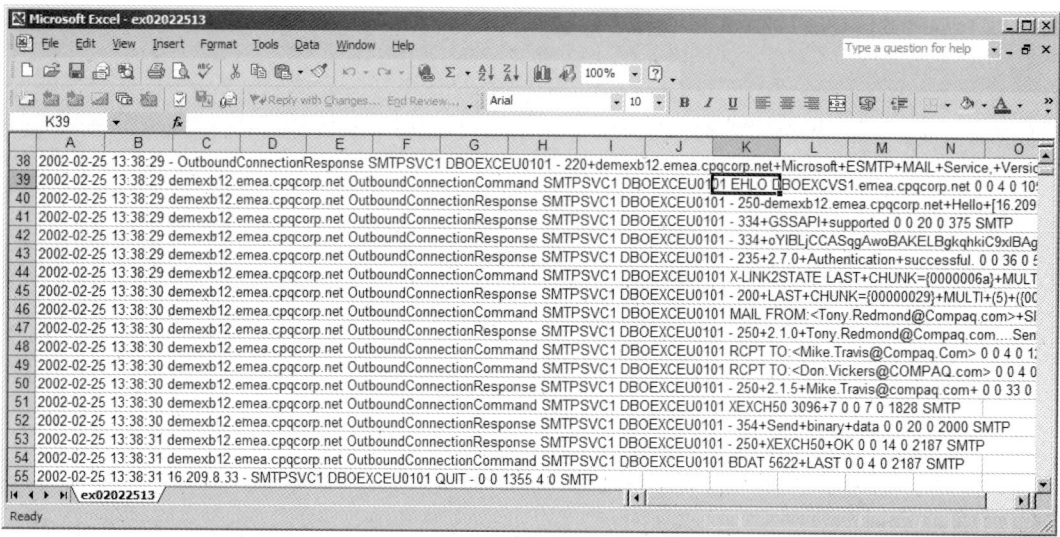

Figure 9.46   *Examining an SMTP log file.*

new message by issuing the MAIL FROM command, following with an XEXCH50 command to establish that the receiving server can accept Exchange-specific data (MAPI properties). Finally, Exchange uses the BDAT command to send a stream of binary data containing the message content, followed by the QUIT command to terminate the message.

Note that an SMTP virtual server can handle concurrent transactions from multiple sources and write data from all transactions into the log as they occur. Thus, you end up with a log containing interleaved transactions rather than a set of clearly segregated transactions. As it happens, the extract shown in Figure 9.46 refers to a single message from the initial EHLO to the BDAT command that sends the message content. Dealing with interleaved content is not a major problem as long as you know that this is the case, but it can sometimes be confusing when you attempt to follow the exact steps that a transaction has taken. To avoid confusion, try to use a known fact about the message that you want to track (such as the sender, the originating server, the time when the message was sent) to ensure that any particular entry belongs to the targeted message. It is also a good idea to work through some sample data taken from test servers that relate to well-understood scenarios (e.g., a message going to recipients in another routing group) before you attempt to interpret logs from production servers. Apart from anything else, you will have a known reference point to consult if you ever meet entries that you do not understand.

As mentioned earlier, SMTP logs occupy lots of space, so you should not enable logging on a production server unless necessary. Use data recorded by test servers to understand the normal flow of messages and to know what you expect to see in a log. This will make it much easier to debug problems when the need arises.

9.13 SMTP archiving

SMTP archiving is different from message journaling, which takes a copy of every message flowing through a server and stores it in a preset destination, normally a mailbox or public folder. SMTP archiving is a debug tool that you can use to capture the entire content of SMTP messages, including all the header information that details the passage of a message through various servers, as files in an archive directory. You can then examine the content to determine where problems lie. For example, an application might generate malformed SMTP messages, which do not strictly follow the SMTP formatting rules as laid down in the RFCs, and so will not be displayed correctly by a client.

Exchange implements SMTP archiving through an event sink, which traps two transport events fired by messages as they move through the Routing Engine. The events are "OnMessageSubmission," which fires once by every message as it is submitted. After a message is categorized (all the recipients are known, including distribution list), the "OnPostCategorize" event fires and could potentially generate an additional copy of a message to handle the situation where some recipients must receive messages in a predetermined format. Capturing messages after submission is an effective way to capture copies of all traffic on a server, while enabling postcategorization capture ensures that Exchange can capture copies in all formats. By default, the archive sink only captures messages after submission.

Only turn on SMTP archiving when you have good reason. A busy server generates thousands of messages hourly, perhaps far more than you anticipate, because you are not 100 percent aware of all the traffic that the server handles. By default, SMTP archiving does not capture system-generated messages such as replication messages. To enable the archive sink, you go to the directory that contains the Exchange binaries and run the archivesink_setup.vbs script, as follows:

```
C:> cscript archivesink_setup.vbs 1 install c:\exchsrvr\bin
```

The "1" referenced here means the default SMTP virtual server; if you have multiple virtual SMTP servers on a system, you need to enable

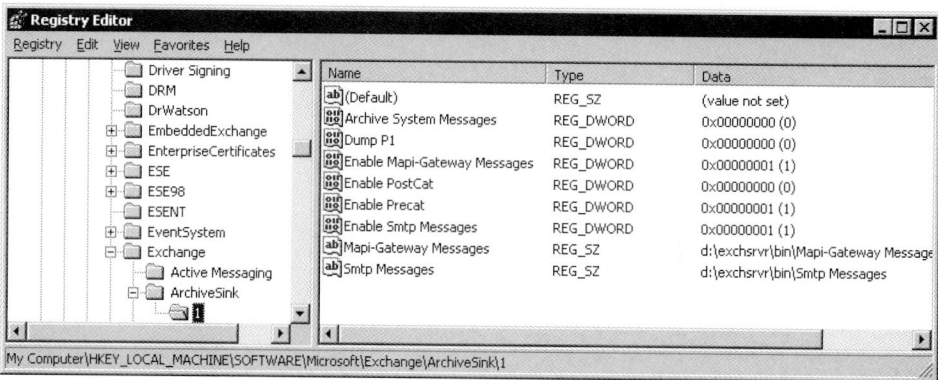

Figure 9.47   *SMTP archive registry entries.*

archiving for each server. The code for the archive sink is in archivesink.dll, and Microsoft originally provided it in the Exchange resource kit. However, the archiving sink is part of the Exchange kit from Exchange 2000 SP2 on. Exchange 2003 upgrades its functionality slightly by ensuring that the sink can capture messages addressed solely to BCC recipients. This is a useful upgrade, because it is common practice to address messages to large distribution lists added as a BCC recipient to prevent users from causing a mail storm by replying to everyone on the list when they want to ask a question about the content of the message. When activated, the sink attaches itself to the two transport events and begins to capture messages. The archive sink also writes a set of entries to the system registry to control its operations, as shown in Figure 9.47. Again, you need to make the set of registry entries for each SMTP virtual server. You can modify the registry settings to tweak the archive sink, as shown in Table 9.8.

Note that the Exchange 2000 version of the archive sink does not capture messages sent to BCC: recipients. However, if you run Exchange 2000 SP3 and install the post-SP3 roll-up patch (see Microsoft for details), you can configure the archive sink to capture BCC: recipients by creating a new DWORD value in the system registry at the following location:

```
HKEY_LOCAL_MACHINE\System\CurrentControlSet\Services\
MSExchangeTransport\Parameters\JournalBCC
```

Set this value to 1 to capture BCC recipients. The default is 0, meaning that the archive sink only captures TO: and CC: recipients. The Exchange 2003 version of the sink captures all recipient types.

Apart from considering whether to capture BCC: recipients, the most obvious change you should make to the default settings is to move the

9.13 SMTP archiving

Table 9.8 *Registry Settings for SMTP Archive Sink*

Setting	Default Value	Meaning
Archive System Messages	0 (off)	Set to 1 to force capture of system messages.
Dump P1	0 (off)	Set to 1 to force inclusion of P1 (envelope) data in message copies.
Enable MAPI-Gateway Messages	1 (on)	Capture messages submitted by MAPI clients, including OWA and the MTA.
Enable PostCat	0 (off)	Set to 1 to force capture of messages after the categorization process.
Enable PreCat	1 (on)	Capture messages after submission.
Enable SMTP messages	1 (on)	Capture messages submitted by SMTP clients (including SMTP-based connectors, other Exchange servers in the same RG, and IMAP4 and POP3 clients).
MAPI-Gateway Messages	Directory	Location to store messages originating from MAPI clients
SMTP Messages	Directory	Location to store messages originating from SMTP clients

archive directories away from their default location under the directory holding the Exchange binaries. It is best to place these directories on a disk that has a lot of free space, just in case the archived messages fill the disk (perhaps because you do not turn archiving off) and stop some other process. The archive sink does not respond to changes made to registry settings until the next time IIS restarts. Effectively, because of the dependency that exists between Exchange services and IIS, this means that you have to stop and restart Exchange.

The archive sink captures messages in their raw format. Figure 9.48 shows two sample messages and the type of file names that you can expect. All of the files have an .eml extension. The top message came in through a routing group connector, so it is a standard SMTP/MIME structure. Note that these messages include both plain text (which you can see) and MIME content (below the portion shown in the screen shot). The bottom message is a response to the first message generated using Outlook's "reply" function. In this case, Outlook sends the message in MS-TNEF, the internal format that Exchange uses to transfer messages if there is no need to convert the

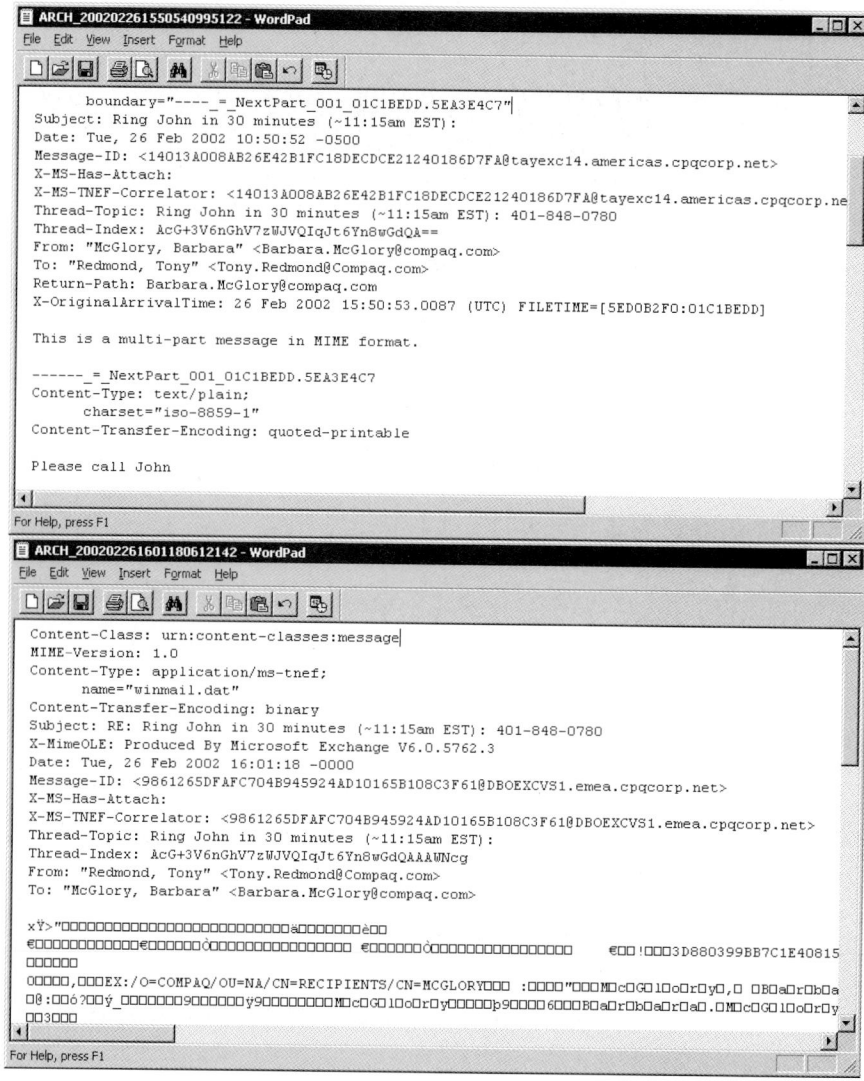

Figure 9.48   *Reading SMTP archived messages.*

content to MIME. Exchange transports this content as an attachment called WINMAIL.DAT. People cannot read MS-TNEF or the attachment, so you will not see useful data in these messages unless the originator decides to use a client-specific option to generate plain text format.

Archiving uses a lot of disk space, so be sure to disable it as soon as you have captured enough messages to analyze any potential fault. Remember that archived messages may contain confidential and sensitive material, so

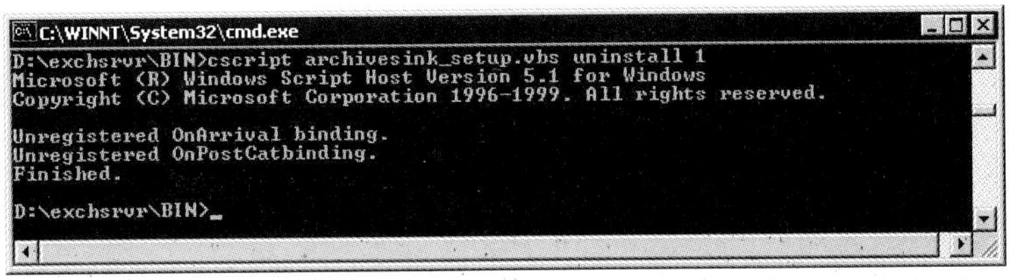

Figure 9.49
Disabling the SMTP archive sink.

```
D:\exchsrvr\BIN>cscript archivesink_setup.vbs uninstall 1
Microsoft (R) Windows Script Host Version 5.1 for Windows
Copyright (C) Microsoft Corporation 1996-1999. All rights reserved.

Unregistered OnArrival binding.
Unregistered OnPostCatbinding.
Finished.

D:\exchsrvr\BIN>_
```

you should also ensure that the archive directories are secure from prying eyes. To disable archiving, you run the archivesink_setup.vbs script again as follows (also shown in Figure 9.49):

```
C:> cscript archivesink_setup.vbs 1 install c:\exchsrvr\bin
```

The archivesink_setup.vbs script removes all of the registry entries that control archiving when it deinstalls the archive sink. In Exchange 2003, you can stop the sink without removing it. Because of a bug, this is not possible in the version provided in Exchange 2000.

9.14 Global messaging settings

Exchange allows administrators to establish global messaging settings that apply throughout the organization. These settings avoid the previous situation in Exchange 5.5, where administrators had to agree on settings across an organization and then apply them on individual servers and SMTP connectors. The value here is that you have consistency throughout an organization for the formats Exchange uses when it generates outgoing messages, originators that can send messages to the organization, how Exchange blocks spam, and so on. The global settings are:

- Internet message formats, which define the formats that Exchange uses when it sends SMTP messages to specific domains.

- Global message delivery settings, which define limits for the size of incoming and outgoing messages as well as any filters that you want to apply to incoming messages. Exchange 2003 offers far more sophisticated filter capabilities for incoming email.

- If you run Exchange Instant Messaging in an Exchange 2000 organization, you can set global parameters for IM here.

- On Exchange 2003 servers, you can define global settings for Mobile Access, such as whether you even want to support mobile devices.

This section explains how you can exploit global messaging settings in an enterprise implementation.

9.14.1 Internet message formats

The range of Internet message formats defined within an organization can be as granular as you wish. At one end of the scale, it is possible to define a single default format that Exchange uses whenever it sends messages to any other SMTP domain, such as compaq.com, microsoft.com, hp.com, and so on. At the other end, you can define a separate format for each of the SMTP domains with which the organization communicates. Few organizations find the need to achieve quite such granular control over message formats, and, as the world of messaging becomes less heterogeneous through the widespread acceptance of SMTP as the de facto standard for message interoperability, it is perhaps less important to be able to exert such a level of control. That is, until you meet a situation where servers cannot exchange messages until you change a particular setting for just one domain by defining a separate message format for that specific domain.

After you install the first server in an organization, only the default message format is active. As you can imagine, the default message format is very basic, and you need either to update the default format or add domain-specific formats to achieve the highest possible degree of interoperability with other email domains. Figure 9.50 illustrates two typical message formats defined in an enterprise-class organization. The left-hand screen shows a

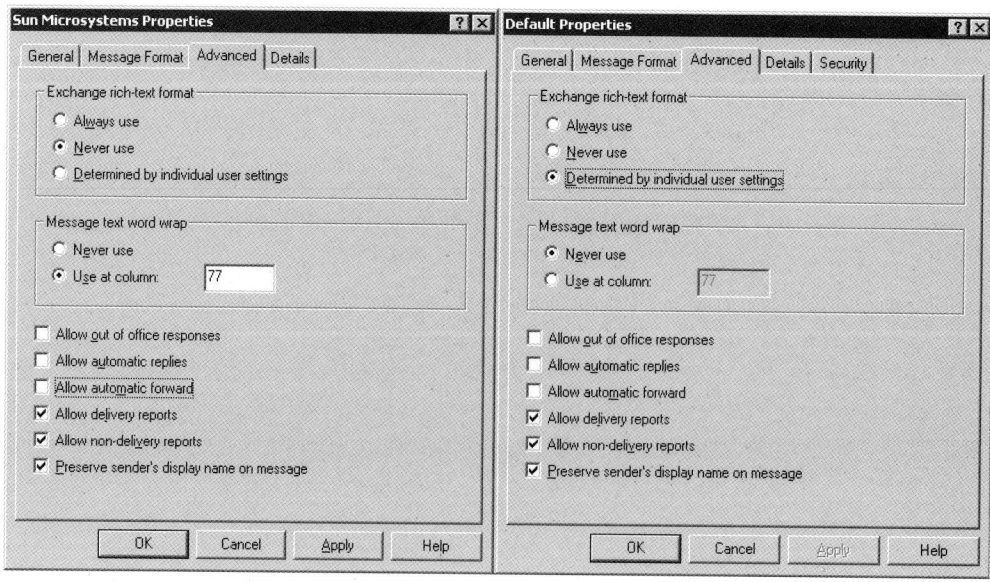

Figure 9.50   *Internet message formats.*

9.14 Global messaging settings

format that allows a limited set of interoperability with a domain that we know probably does not support all of the Exchange features. This domain could be a legacy Exchange organization served by the Exchange 5.5 Internet Mail Service, or another mail system that receives messages through an SMTP connector. The messages to this domain are in Exchange rich text format and always go in plain text; the text wraps at a set column position. The format purposely sets a lowest common dominator bar to ensure that recipients in the domain can read our messages, while allowing for the full range of delivery and nondelivery notifications. However, we suppress information contained in out of office replies.

The right-hand screen in Figure 9.50 shows the default format that Exchange uses if you do not define domain-specific formats. In this instance, we allow users to specify the format Exchange sends the message in, according to an option set through the client. Because we do not know where messages will go, automatic SMTP reply messages are disabled. However, we allow out of office notifications as well as delivery and nondelivery reports, and we allow the display of the sender's display name.

Many organizations implement far more restrictive default message formats. For example, delivery reports and out of office messages are blocked and display names are suppressed, because it is possible that a recipient can learn some confidential details of an organization's structure if division names, job titles, or locations are included in display names. Administrators often restrict this type of information for "free" email domains, such as hotmail.com, aol.com, and msn.com, to try to limit the amount of spam sent to the organization. Spammers often use delivery reports and out of office notifications to validate the email addresses that they use. Once they know that an email address is valid, a spammer is happy to add the address to every list he or she maintains and sell it to other spammers, which then leads to an increase in incoming spam.

You can also see that we have blocked automatic mail forwarding in both cases illustrated in Figure 9.50. This means that users are not able to set up rules that forward new messages to addresses in the SMTP domains covered by these formats. The logic why is easy to understand, as you probably do not want users to forward messages outside the company without thinking about why they are taking this action. After all, it is all too easy for confidential information to escape through forwarded email. Under some circumstances, you may want to allow specific users to automatically forward email. For example, someone may be travelling and want to read their email but is not going to be able to access the corporate network. You set up a rule to automatically forward specific messages to another email service but you do not want to grant open access for everyone to forward messages to this domain. To get around the problem, you can create a mail-enabled contact that points to the target email address. Then, use the Delivery Options (on the Exchange General property page) to update the user's own AD account to add the new contact as a forwarding address and set the option to have Exchange deliver copies of the message to both their mailbox and the forwarding address. Remember to hide the new contact so that users do not see it in the GAL and to turn off the forwarding when the user returns from their trip.

The Message Format property tab allows further control for messages that Exchange sends to non-MAPI clients, such as Outlook Express connecting to a server via IMAP4. Figure 9.51 shows the settings for a well-known UNIX domain, sun.com. Because of its UNIX heritage, we can anticipate that this domain has few—if any—MAPI clients, and the vast majority of clients use POP3, IMAP4, or HTTP to connect to their mail server. The UUencode coding standard is likely to guarantee the highest degree of compatibility and allow older UNIX clients to understand attachments, so it is good to select this setting for this domain. Newer UNIX clients are happy with MIME, so the choice depends on the client mix you have to support. Note that you can pass messages in BinHex format, required for some older Apple Macintosh clients. You could opt to use MIME encoding and pass messages in plain text format, since almost every email client is able to understand plain text. Newer Internet-style clients,

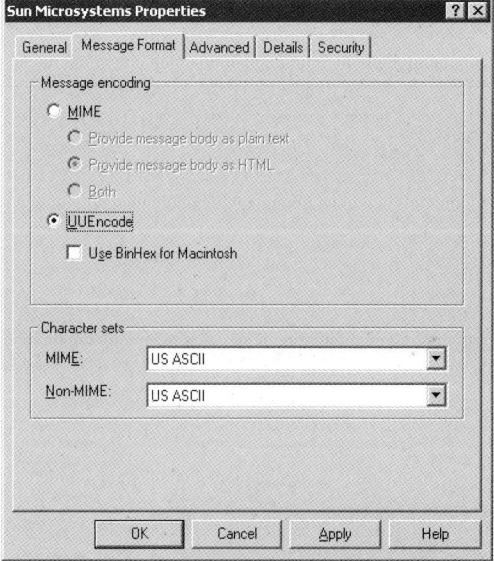

Figure 9.51
Message Format properties for a typical UNIX domain.

9.14 Global messaging settings

such as Outlook Express 5.0 or later, also support HTML format messages, but you may encounter problems with older clients if you select this option. You can select both, meaning that Exchange will generate separate body-parts in plain text and HTML, but this will at least double the overall size of the message. Some users consider it rude to send HTML format messages to Internet mailing lists, because some of the recipients on the list may not be able to read the message. In this case, you can create a specific message format for the address of the list (e.g., msexchange.swynk.com) and define that messages for this domain go in plain text format.

Because it is reasonable to expect that the majority of clients connected to Exchange understand MIME, you can usually specify MIME for messages sent to other Exchange email domains. However, you should select plain text if you know that the other domain supports a mixture of clients, including some older versions that cannot read MIME messages. You can also elect to use HTML, if the clients are all late-generation Outlook Express (5.0 or later), rich-mode OWA, or Outlook (98 or later). The MIME and UUencode settings only apply to MAPI clients. If set, the "Apply content settings to non-MAPI clients" forces Exchange to convert messages submitted by non-MAPI clients to the specified formats by first translating content into MAPI and then into the specified encoding format before transmission. In a perfect world of MAPI, this approach makes sense. In today's heterogeneous messaging environment, it does not, since it simply slows down message throughput by introducing the need for an

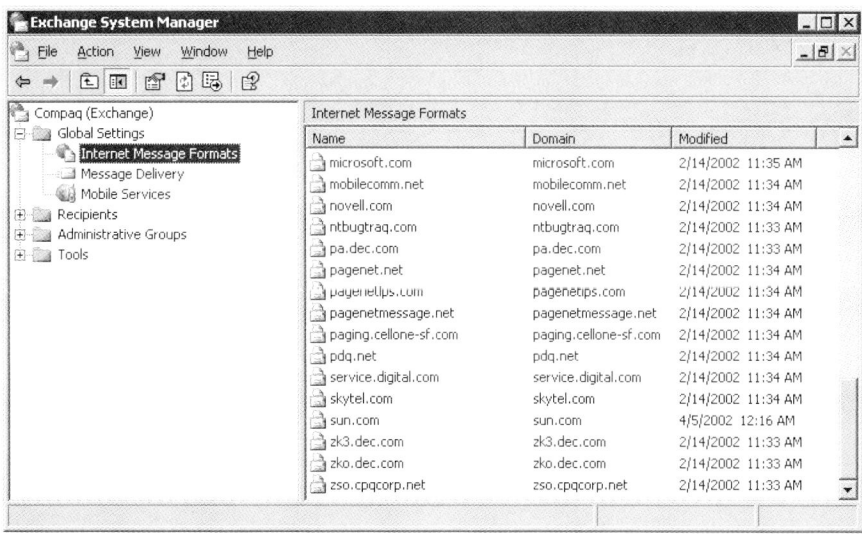

Figure 9.52   *A selection of Internet message formats used at HP.*

additional format conversion. In large enterprise deployments, such as HP's (Figure 9.52), where messages are sent to many different email domains (both internal and external) that use different servers and clients, the pursuit of total fidelity leads to a large number of message formats.

9.14.2 Global message delivery settings

Global message delivery settings allow administrators to set default values for the size of incoming and outgoing SMTP messages, the number of recipients in a message header, and to implement some primitive antispam protection through message filters.

The default values for message delivery permit unlimited message sizes and set a 5,000 recipient limit, which allows users to send messages with huge attachments, such as the famous 25-MB *Star Wars* trailer. Accordingly, most organizations impose stricter limits. For example, Figure 9.53 shows 5-MB limits set for incoming and outgoing messages. Note that the default values are just that—default. An administrator can override the default by setting explicit values for message sizes through the "Messages" property page of an SMTP virtual server. The logic here is that messages arrive and go through SMTP virtual servers, so the properties of a specific SMTP virtual server always take precedence. Note that these settings only affect messages that flow through SMTP virtual servers. Messages sent within an

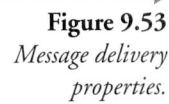

Figure 9.53
Message delivery properties.

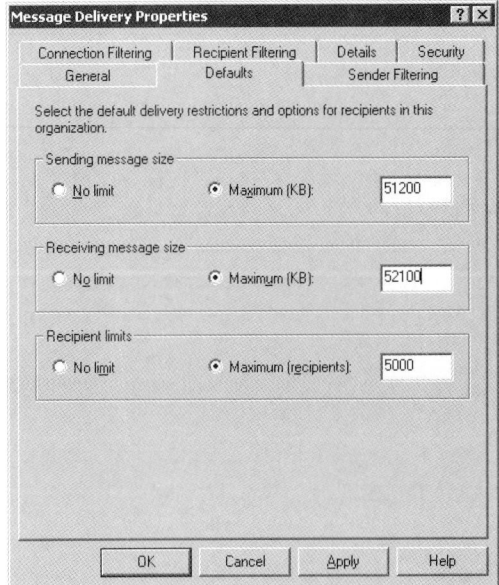

organization, whether across a routing group connector or via the MTA, do not respect these limits.

Global settings allow administrators to set standards for an organization. While this capability is not important for small installations, it becomes increasingly essential as the number of Exchange servers in the organization grows.

9.15 Combating the menace of spam

The first reported instance of spam was a message sent to ARPANET subscribers on May 3, 1978. The author was Gary Thuerk, a marketing manager with Digital Equipment Corporation, who wanted to tell people all about the new computers in the DECsystem-20 family. The note offered people the chance to come along to demos in Los Angeles and San Mateo and is possibly the first example of a marketer using email to project its message across a wide geographical distance (Digital was located on the East Coast of the United States, the target customers were on the West Coast). The message generated fury and dismay on the part of its recipients, including notes from the military officers who then ran the ARPANET.

Spammers generate huge quantities of unwanted messages that clutter up mailboxes; they send messages to lists of users whose addresses they just guess, to addresses harvested from messages posted to public forums, or lists that they purchase from intermediaries.[10] The messages usually offer something that you cannot resist, such as the chance to get rich with no work whatsoever. Other popular topics include enlargement of various body parts, the chance to enter into intimate relations with highly detailed pictures of the human body, chain letters, urban legends, and outright hoaxes. According to some surveys, users can receive up to 1,470 pieces of spam annually (see www.imm.com for further data). While it is very annoying to have to deal with this rubbish when it arrives in your Inbox, consider just how many copies of these messages spammers have sent. Even worse, the amount of spam rises all the time, so we can only expect more of it to circulate. HP is a very large and well-known company, so it is not surprising that HP is a choice target for unwanted email. In 2002, the bastion servers guarding HP's email system dropped 30 percent of all the messages addressed to @hp.com recipients, because they came from a known spammer or contained suspicious content (such as a known virus payload), and

---

10. A company that provides lists of addresses to spammers is referred to as a "Spamhaus." You can get a list of well-known companies in this category from www.spamhaus.org or www.spamsites.org.

this ratio of "blocked" to "good" email traffic rises all the time. Just one year later, in mid-2003, the percentage of dropped email had risen to 70 percent, or approximately 21 million messages per month.

If you doubt that spam is a growing menace, open up a new email account on a free service such as hotmail and wait to see how many unwanted messages turn up in your mailbox after a couple of days. In this environment, administrators have a duty to protect their servers from taking part in this activity by making sure that spammers cannot take over servers and use them as relays.

Spammers often like to use other people's systems as an intermediate relay to disguise the originator of the messages and to speed up their delivery through additional processing power (provided by your server). You may not realize that your system has been "borrowed" by spammers unless you receive complaints about email that you know has not come from one of your users, or you see sudden spikes in system load caused by an external program that may send messages to millions of recipients. Apart from the annoyance caused by spammers, if your system is used to send messages to unwanted recipients, your organization runs the risk that it will be entered on a list (sometimes called a real-time blackhole list, or RBL) of known spammers, such as that maintained by MAPS at www.mailabuse.org or the Distributed Server Boycott List at www.dsbl.org. In comparison to a blacklist, a whitelist contains the names of trusted domains that you are always happy to accept email from.

If a monitoring service adds your domain to a list of known spammers, you will have to do a lot of work to get the domain removed from the list, and other servers may begin to block all messages—including legitimate email—that originate from your domain because of your reputation as an "open relay." Antispam software uses lists of known spammers to monitor incoming email and evaluates arriving email to determine whether the message comes from a known spammer or meets some criteria that means it might be unwanted. For example, the software might do the following:

- Use simple keyword filters to examine the message subject. If the message subject contains "Get rich quick," it probably means that the message has no great business value.
- Use scoring systems or contextual analyzers that look for patterns in subjects and text that you typically find in spam. For example, the exclamation point seems to be very attractive to spammers, who feel compelled to emphasize their messages with lots of exclamations. If the scoring system finds a message that contains 20 exclamations, it

could be spam. On the other hand, it could be from an enthusiastic member of your marketing department.

- Look for "fingerprints" of known spam. Antispam vendors track the characteristics of spam by analyzing message content to create a fingerprint that a filter can use to recognize similar messages.

Because these approaches vary in usefulness from environment to environment, it is a good idea to install the software and test it for a couple of weeks before you commit to a purchase. During your test, check how effective the software is at stopping spam and how it reports and disposes of spam. Does it merely block spam and provide the administrator with a list of all blocked messages and their destinations? Does it pass the message through after marking it in some way, such as changing the subject field to include "spam"? On the other hand, does it place all of the blocked messages in a quarantine filter to await your attention and perhaps allow you to redirect the messages to users after you have had a chance to examine their content and decide whether they actually fall into the category of spam?

In Exchange 2003, you can take advantage of lists of known spammers and open relays and use them as a filter to prevent spam from arriving on your server. You can also take advantage of the new junk email detection functionality that Microsoft includes in Outlook 2003 to allow users to set up their own black- and whitelists to take care of any spam that creeps through the corporate filters. (See section 4.5 for details.) Another interesting trend is for antivirus software vendors to incorporate spam filters in their products. This is a very logical progression. After all, if you check incoming email for viruses, you might as well check them for spam. Ever since Exchange 2000, antispam products can implement a transport sink with code to examine messages as they arrive at the SMTP service and before Exchange accepts them for categorization and further processing. Sybari's Spam Manager for Antigen, which integrates into its Antigen antivirus product, is a good example of this technology in action. Relatively few software developers took up the challenge of using this technique to combat spam, largely because viruses were the major threat to servers. Viruses are still a threat, but the dramatic increase in spam prompted Microsoft to introduce a new "hook" for antispam products. This is the SCL, or Spam Confidence Level, a new Store property that antispam products can update using whatever techniques or algorithms they care to engineer into their transport sink. The SCL Processor, a new component within the Store, can examine SCL values on messages as they arrive and take action based on those values, such as to delete or refile the messages. See section 9.16 to learn how the Exchange Intelligent Message Filter sets and uses SCL values.

Chapter 9

The higher the SCL value, the higher the probability that the message is spam. Antispam utilities use different algorithms to analyze the data in message headers and contents to determine the SCL value. You can deploy multiple antispam utilities if you like or an antispam product that utilizes a number of different scanning techniques (similar to the way that some antivirus products use multiple virus detection engines to ensure that they catch a higher percentage of suspect messages). In all cases, the desired outcome is either to discard spam or to allow messages to pass on for further processing with an SCL score included in their properties to help client-side utilities process the messages. For example, Outlook 2003's Junk Mail processing feature allows you to choose to delete known spam messages (the default is to place these messages into the Junk Mail folder). Normally, Outlook's own junk mail processing algorithm makes the decision to refile spam messages into the Junk Mail folder after they arrive in the user's mailbox, which allows Outlook 2003 to work with Exchange 5.5 and Exchange 2000 servers. On an Exchange 2003 server equipped with suitable antispam software that sets the SCL property on incoming messages, the Store can make the decision to refile messages that an antispam utility has determined to have a high SCL value before the messages go anywhere near the client. This is better, because the client does not have to download messages, which saves bandwidth and processing.

9.15.1 Blocking relays

The most straightforward and simple defense of your system is to restrict its capability to relay. By default (Figure 9.54), only authenticated connections, such as when an Exchange server connects to another Exchange server, are able to relay messages. This may not be what you want, since you may want to support the transmission of messages from other non-Exchange servers, so review the situation and make whatever adjustments you think are necessary to secure your systems. To test whether someone can use your server as a relay, issue the following commands from a DOS prompt, selecting a non-local recipient as the addressee:

```
TELNET server IP address (or FQDN) 25
HELO (or EHLO)
MAIL FROM: Bill.Gates@Microsoft.com
RCPT TO: Your address@external-domain.com
DATA
I think you have done an incredible job with Exchange.
Well done!

Bill
```

9.15 Combating the menace of spam

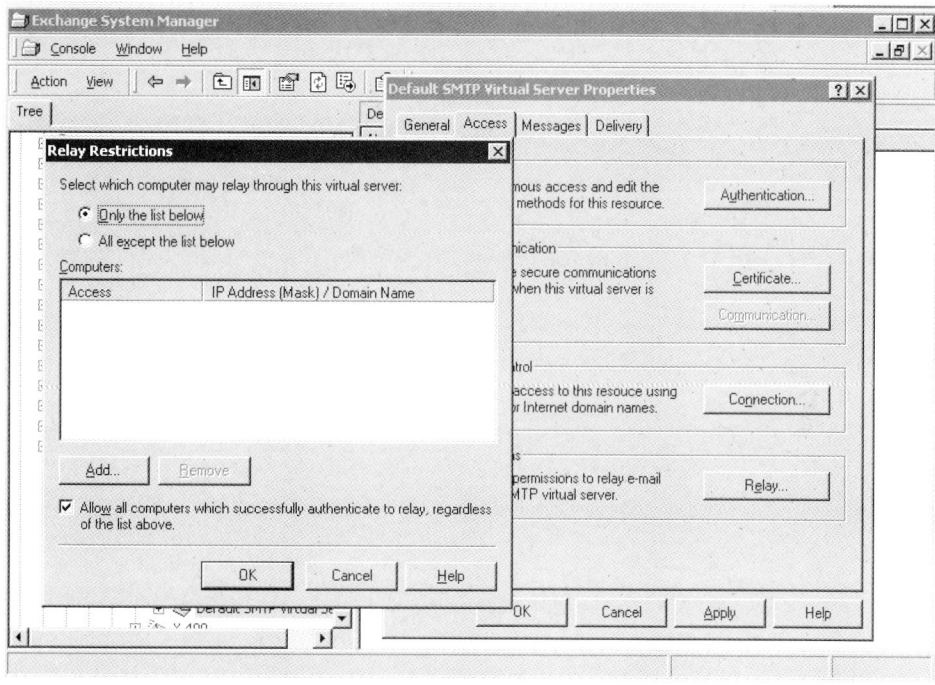

Figure 9.54 *Setting relay restrictions.*

Terminate the message with a carriage return, full stop, and another carriage return. If the message is accepted, you have just proved that your system is open to relaying, but at least you now have a way to prove that Bill Gates approves of your plans to deploy Exchange. The message is not very pretty, and you can tidy it up by adding a message subject and formatting the text properly to help convince the recipient that it came from Bill Gates.[11] A server that responds with a status code of 550[12] after the recipient address is typed indicates that relaying is prohibited, while a 551 code means that the recipient is not local and the server will not allow you to relay to it. However, if you get a "250 OK" response to the RCPT TO command, you know that the server is open to illicit relays.

You set restrictions on message relays by changing the properties of an SMTP virtual server through ESM. (See Figure 9.55.) First click on the Access tab and then on the "Relay" button. When ESM displays the Relay Restrictions properties, by default you see that an SMTP virtual server has

---

11. Those interested in knowing how to create SMTP messages from programs, including the addition of subject lines and adding attachments and text, might like to browse a copy of John Rhoton's book, *Programmer's Guide to Internet Mail*.
12. Error code 550 is defined by RFC 2505 to mean "relaying prohibited."

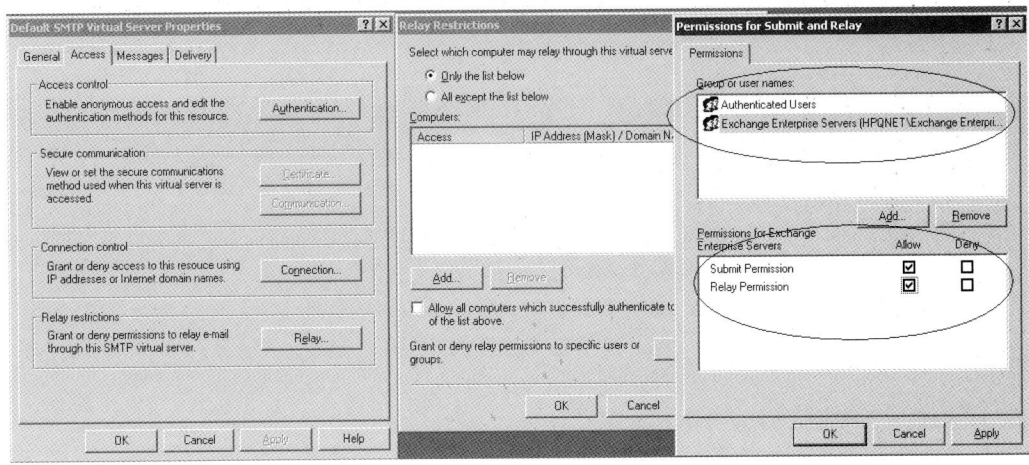

Figure 9.55   *Setting relay permissions.*

the "Only the list below" option set, and the computer list is empty, which effectively disables SMTP message relays. Exchange 2003 provides you with another weapon to prohibit mail relays in security principle-based submit and relay. Exchange 2000 servers control relays based on IP address, IP subnets, or DNS domain names, but Exchange 2003 servers can set an ACL to define relay restrictions for individual users or security groups. Using the same Relay Restrictions property page, you can set the relay ACL by first unchecking the "Allow all computers which successfully authenticate to relay, regardless of the list above" checkbox to enable the "Users" button. You then select the users and groups that you want to add to the ACL, which populates the ms-Exch-SubmitRelaySD attribute for the SMTP virtual server. Be careful of setting ACLs that can influence message flow. This is definitely something to test thoroughly in the laboratory before introducing into production.

Exchange servers do not use the settings that control external SMTP mail relays for internal traffic, even if messages flow across an SMTP connector. This is because Exchange servers authenticate together when they begin a connection with the ESMTP "X-EXPS" Kerberos authentication verb. If an SMTP server advertises this verb, Exchange will attempt to issue an X-EXPS command. Authentication will succeed if both servers are members of the "Exchange Domain Servers" security group. The Exchange installation procedure automatically adds the Exchange servers in a domain during the installation procedure. This means that you only need to allow anonymous connections on servers specifically designated to act as the inbound target for Internet or intranet SMTP connections from non-

Exchange servers. "Allow anonymous" is enabled by default on all Exchange 2000/2003 servers.

There's no doubt that messaging administrators are aware of the danger that illegal relaying and spamming pose, but even with all the publicity and comment, the most recent report from the Internet Mail Consortium[13] found that just over 17 percent of servers tested still allowed mail relays in July 1999 (the situation has not improved much since). Every one of these servers is an open target to spammers, who are all too quick to take advantage of the open door policy afforded to them. For this reason, it is a good idea to check servers on a regular basis and close off any loopholes that might have opened up.

9.15.2 Defining message filters

Microsoft does not pretend that the message filtering capability in Exchange 2000 supports the same range of functions as fully fledged content management products, such as the Clearswift Enterprise Suite (www.clearswift.com). These products, which can protect enterprises against spam, inappropriate content, and loss of confidential information, are targeted at large enterprises and the better examples integrate into the Routing Engine through techniques such as transport sinks to ensure that they can check every message that passes through the server. Both large and small companies use Exchange, and the message filtering capability is there to allow even the smallest company to gain some degree of protection.

The situation is better with Exchange 2003, since this version supports filters for connections to enforce real-time blocks to check email from known spammers as it arrives on your server, as well as sender and recipient filters to check for known senders of spam and specific types of recipients. Exchange has had great SMTP capabilities for several years, so the addition of features such as connection, sender, and recipient filters makes Exchange 2003 a more valuable component in a messaging infrastructure. These features are critical for smaller companies that cannot afford to deploy multiple layers of servers to defend their networks and want everything done by a single server. Note that Outlook 2003 and the Exchange 2003 version of OWA both include client-side junk mail filtering, so you can impose blocks on both the client and server. On an Exchange 2000 server, you can enable basic message filtering in two steps. First, you establish a global message filter policy, which includes the following features:

---

13. See http://www.imc.org/ube-relay.html. The report is dated July 5, 1999, and may have been revised by the time you read this.

- Prevents acceptance of messages with a blank sender: Many spammers send messages that do not include the sender's name. Thus, you can stop a certain proportion of spam by blocking messages with a blank sender.

- Accepts messages without notifying sender: Spammers may depend on nondelivery or other notifications to know whether their messages are getting through. Your policy can accept messages and move them into a virtual blackhole, where the originator does not know that Exchange has filtered the message or delivered the message to a user mailbox.

- Archives filtered messages: You may wish to learn how successful your filtering policy is, and you can do this by capturing copies of filtered messages into the \filter directory of the SMTP virtual server's working directory (for the default virtual server, the full specification is exchsrvr\mailroot\vs1\filter). On any reasonably busy server, files will quickly accumulate in this directory, so it is not a good idea to archive filtered messages for an extended period. Use the archive to test the effectiveness of your policy, and then disable archiving.

- Establishes a filter list: Figure 9.56 shows a simple filter for a specific user, but you can also use the wildcard (*) character to set up filters such as *@hotmail.com, which blocks all hotmail messages, or *guy*@aol.com, which blocks any message from aol.com generated

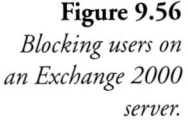

Figure 9.56
Blocking users on an Exchange 2000 server.

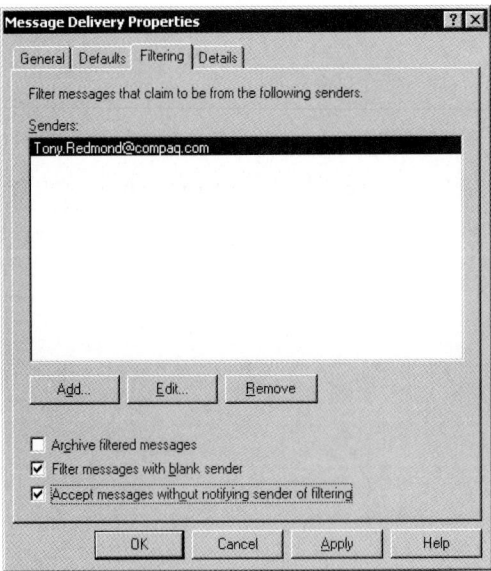

9.15 Combating the menace of spam

by someone with the word "guy" in his or her user name. Using the real-time blocks supported by Exchange 2003 is a more sophisticated and complete version of the technique.

After setting up the policy and waiting for the System Attendant to replicate its details to the IIS metabase, you must then enable filtering on individual servers by changing the properties of the targeted SMTP virtual servers. If a message arrives at a server before you enable filtering, Exchange will process it as before. As shown in Figure 9.57, you enable filtering on an SMTP virtual server by selecting the server (from ESM), viewing its properties, and then clicking on the "Advanced button" on the General property page. Then, click the "Apply Filter" checkbox for each of the IP addresses that you wish to filter on, remembering that an SMTP virtual server can be bound to multiple IP addresses. As we will see later on, you take the same approach to apply the more extensive filter set supported by Exchange 2003.

After you enable filtering on the SMTP virtual server, you can test the effectiveness of the policy by using the TELNET utility to connect to port 25 (or whatever port is bound to the SMTP virtual server) to create and send a dummy message, using one of the addresses you want to filter. If the filter is successful, Exchange captures the message in a .tmp file in the \filter directory. Figure 9.58 shows the contents of a sample message that you might capture.

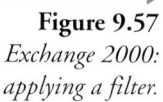

Figure 9.57
Exchange 2000: applying a filter.

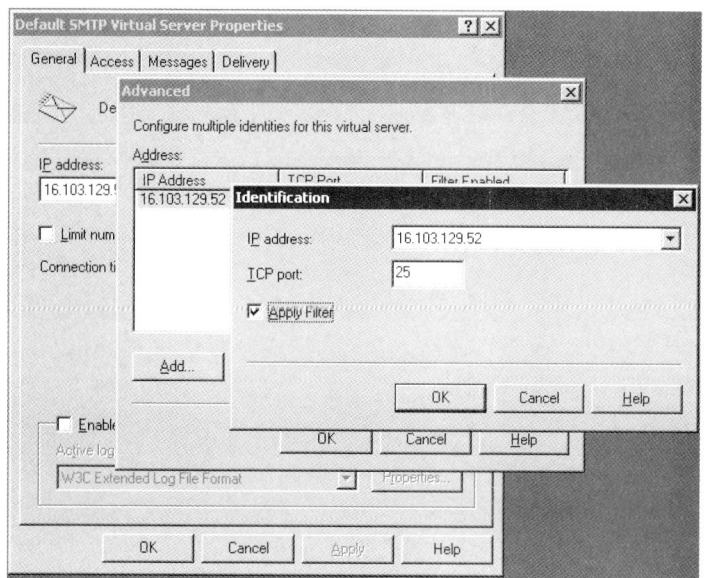

Figure 9.58
Sample filtered message.

```
Received: from ([207.209.6.159]) by exch-server.abc-server.abc.net
with Microsoft SMTPSVC(6.0.3590.0);
    Thu, 14 Feb 2003 15:33:14 +0000
From: Tony.Redmond@abc.net
Bcc:
Return-Path: John.Smith@xyz.com
Message-ID: zpIqUfO21CM00000005@exch-server.abc-server.abc.net
X-OriginalArrivalTime: 20 July 2003 15:33:16.0528 (UTC)
FILETIME=[EC199700:01C1B56C]
Date: 20 July 2003 15:33:16 +0000

Something that you needed to know, but really don't have to.
```

If you run Exchange 2000 servers and have no plans to deploy Exchange 2003 soon, you should investigate some of the third-party antispam tools that support Exchange. Table 9.9 details some of the well-known antispam products that support Exchange. If you consider installing an antispam product for Exchange 2003, be sure that it supports the SCL hook to maximize spam suppression.

9.15.3 Connection filters and real-time blackhole lists

Unlike the majority of SMTP add-on services or extensions, no RFC governs how real-time blackhole services work, how domains qualify for inclusion on the lists, or how you eventually decide to trust domains again and remove them from a list. Instead, you depend on third-party service providers that manage lists of the IP addresses used by known spammers that are available on the Internet as a public service. There are a number of different blackhole providers available (see http://www.declude.com/JunkMail/sup-

Table 9.9   *Antispam Add-On Products for Exchange*

Company	Product
Brightmail (www.brightmail.com)	Anti-Spam Enterprise Edition
GFI (www.gfi.com)	GFI MailEssentials for Exchange
Intellireach (www.intellireach.com)	Message Manager Suite for Exchange
NetIQ (www.netiq.com)	MailMarshal for SMTP
Sybari (www.sybari.com)	Sybari Spam Manager
Trend Micro (www.trendmicro.com)	InterScan eManager
Sunbelt Software (www.sunbelt-software.com)	iHateSpam Server Edition
McAfee (www.macfeesecurity.com)	Spamkiller for Exchange

9.15 Combating the menace of spam

port/ip4r.htm), but perhaps the best known of the real-time blacklist providers is MAPS, a not-for-profit California organization (http://mail-abuse.org/); many large companies use MAPS to protect their email infrastructures. The idea behind a blackhole is straightforward: If a known spammer contacts your server and attempts to pass messages, you detect the connection and either divert it to a null network device (to put messages into a "blackhole") or just drop the connection.

A service provider such as MAPS typically offers five services:

- RBL: lists of domains known to generate and send spam

- RSS (Relay Spam Stopper): lists of open relay SMTP servers that spammers can take over and use to send their messages

- DUL (Dial-up User List): lists of IP addresses that have dial-up connections (normally to ISPs) used to send spam

- NML (Nonconfirmed Mailing List): lists IP addresses that have demonstrated to be sources of mailing lists that do not verify email addresses on their lists

- RBL+: provides one-step access to a combination of databases, combining RBL, RSS, and DUL through a single query. Large organizations most commonly use this service.

Mail servers such as sendmail have traditionally incorporated support for blackhole lists in their configuration. Many commercial products use RBL information to detect and suppress spam. Up to Exchange 2003, administrators wishing to block spam can deploy bastion servers to intercept and examine SMTP traffic coming into a company from the Internet before relaying acceptable messages to Exchange for final delivery. In HP's case, the bastion servers are Linux systems running Postfix software, equipped with RBL support. In an enterprise environment, it is probably best to keep the bastion servers in place and use them as the first line of defense against spam, and then configure Exchange 2003 to trap any spam that arrives at an SMTP virtual server as a second line of defense. If you choose, you can add yet another layer by deploying the spam suppression features that a number of antivirus products that support Exchange, such as Sybari Antigen, are adding. And, of course, there are always the junk mail features built into clients such as Outlook.

Exchange 2003 implements connection filtering in an SMTP transport sink that reads information about connection policies from the AD. You set the connection filter policies through ESM, where they become properties of the "Message Delivery" object under "Global Settings" for the Exchange organization. Once the policy is set, each time a remote SMTP server connects to a virtual SMTP server hosted by Exchange 2003, it caches its IP address and forwards it as a DNS query to the RBL service provider defined in the connection policy. The RBL service provider then actions the DNS query by checking its lists, which hold data about known spammers as special DNS service records. The RBL service provider then returns a result code to Exchange, which then checks the policy to decide whether it should accept the incoming connection. The result code is specific to a service provider and indicates why the service provider recognizes the domain (on a blacklist as a known spammer, known open relay, so it can transmit spam on a dial-up IP address). In enterprise environments, it is common for companies to purchase a service from a blacklist provider to allow them to maintain local copies of their lists (and perform lookups through a delegated DNS zone) that they update through downloads on a regular basis.

A connection policy can use multiple service providers, and Exchange checks each provider in the order listed by ESM, halting after it finds the first match. The implementation allows checking to proceed even if one of the service providers is unavailable; it also includes service providers that might specialize in detecting specific types of spammers.

9.15.4 Configuring a connection filter policy

You configure a connection filter policy by first selecting the Message Delivery object at the Global Settings node in ESM, and then selecting "Connection Filtering." The policy is broken down into a set of blacklist service configurations, or rules. You give each rule an arbitrary name to convey its purpose, and then specify the service provider (usually a DNS suffix to get the latest version of the list) that the rule will contact to check incoming traffic. The position in the list shows the priority that the rule has when Exchange checks traffic. Some lists are better at blocking specific sites than others, so you can combine as many lists as you like to attain the desired degree of protection.

A policy that is composed of two blacklists with a blacklist that provides a general block against most known spammers is backed up by a check for what you might call "bad habits." Note that you can customize the error message that Exchange returns to a submitter. The default message is SMTP code 550 with a DSN of 5.7.1 and the text "This email was rejected because your domain is reported by a DNS Blacklist Provider." In Figure 9.59, we changed the default error message to be:

```
The %0 mail server is on a black list owned by %2
```

9.15 Combating the menace of spam

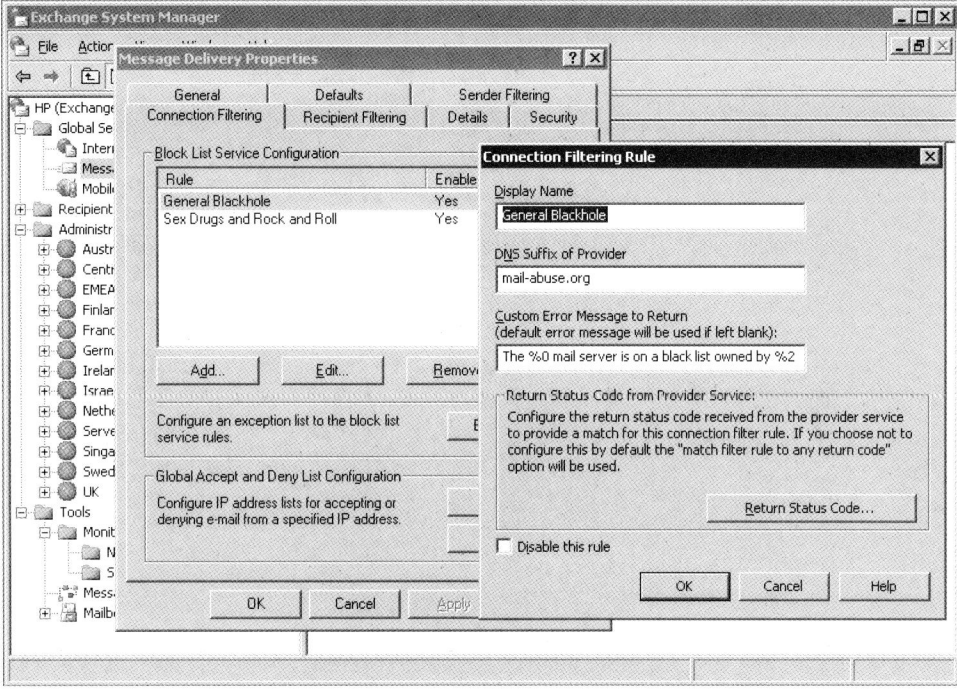

Figure 9.59 *Defining a connection filter.*

When Exchange sends this response, it fills the "%0" substitution string with the IP address of the SMTP client that attempted to connect and the "%2" string with the DNS suffix of the RBL service provider. You can also include a "%1" string if you want to insert the display name of the connection filter.

9.15.5 Return status codes

You can configure how Exchange reacts to the return status code from the service provider by clicking on the "Return Status Code" button. The simplest (and default) behavior is that Exchange responds, or matches the filter, if any return code comes back. In other words, if the RBL service provider recognizes the IP address of the incoming SMTP client for any reason, Exchange will immediately end the SMTP session.

The MAPS service provider uses a well-known set of status codes:

```
1: On a blacklist
2: Known Open Relay
4: Dial-up IP address
```

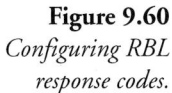

Figure 9.60
Configuring RBL response codes.

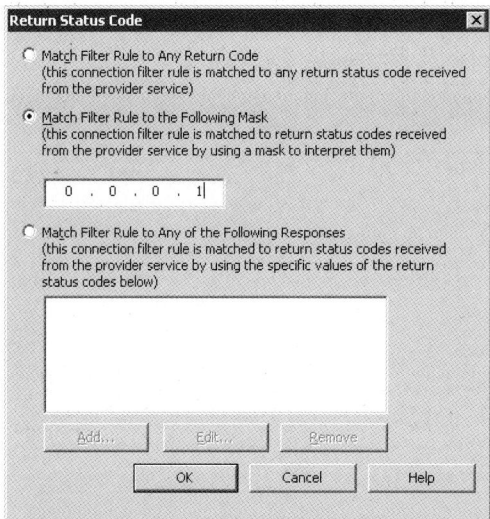

If you decide that you only want to block connections from IP addresses on known blacklists, you match the filter against a mask of "0.0.0.1," as shown in Figure 9.60. The reason why the filter mask is in this format is that matches occur as the result of logical "anding" the binary bits in the last octet of the return status, which is always in the form 127.0.0.n, where n is a number between 1 and 254. For example, if we want only to block known open relays, we know that the response is going to be 127.0.0.2, so the value of the mask needs to be 0.0.0.2. If we want to catch domains on blacklists or open relays, then we use a mask of 0.0.0.3.

Exchange does not apply filters to messages addressed to "Postmaster@your-domain," because these messages notify an organization that someone has put it on a blacklist, so it is important that the messages get through. If it does not exist, the Exchange 2003 installation program assigns a secondary SMTP proxy address of "postmaster@your-domain" when you install Exchange 2003. You can allocate this address to a more appropriate recipient afterward.

As with many other system management features, it is good to be able to define special cases or exceptions where filters will not apply. You may know that a blacklist service provider has placed one of your trusted partners on a list for some reason. Negotiations are ongoing regarding removal from the list, but if you do not enter an exception, connection filtering will block any of this email. You can decide to enter an explicit exception for an email address, or you can enter an IP address mask to tell Exchange that you are willing to accept traffic from these sources. Equally, you can enter an IP

9.15 Combating the menace of spam

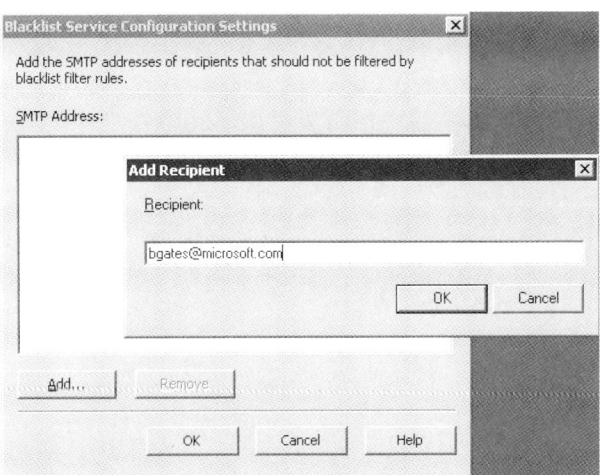

Figure 9.61
Configuring an exception.

address mask and decide that you never want to accept traffic from that source. Figure 9.61 shows how to enter an SMTP address as an exception. Enter IP address masks to deny or accept traffic as properties of the connection filter.

After you have configured the connection filter, you need to select the virtual SMTP virtual servers that will use the filter. Typically, these are the SMTP virtual servers that handle Internet traffic for the organization, and you probably do not need to configure the filter on any SMTP virtual servers that handle traffic to other internal SMTP systems, such as sendmail on Linux.

Use ESM to find the Exchange 2003 server that hosts the SMTP virtual server you want to apply the filter to and expand its properties. Click on the Advanced button and then add an identity (the TCP port that the SMTP virtual server monitors) or edit the existing identity for port 25 (the default SMTP port). You can then select to apply a sender, recipient, or connection filter. In this case, you need to check the "apply connection filter" box and then click the OK button. Figure 9.62 shows the complete set of screens that you see after you select a virtual server and apply the filter.

9.15.6 Sender filters

If your mailbox is anything like mine, you have a number of persistent correspondents who insist on sending you details of great offers that you would prefer not to receive. You can use Outlook's junk mail filter to purge your Inbox of these messages and swap lists of known offenders with other users,

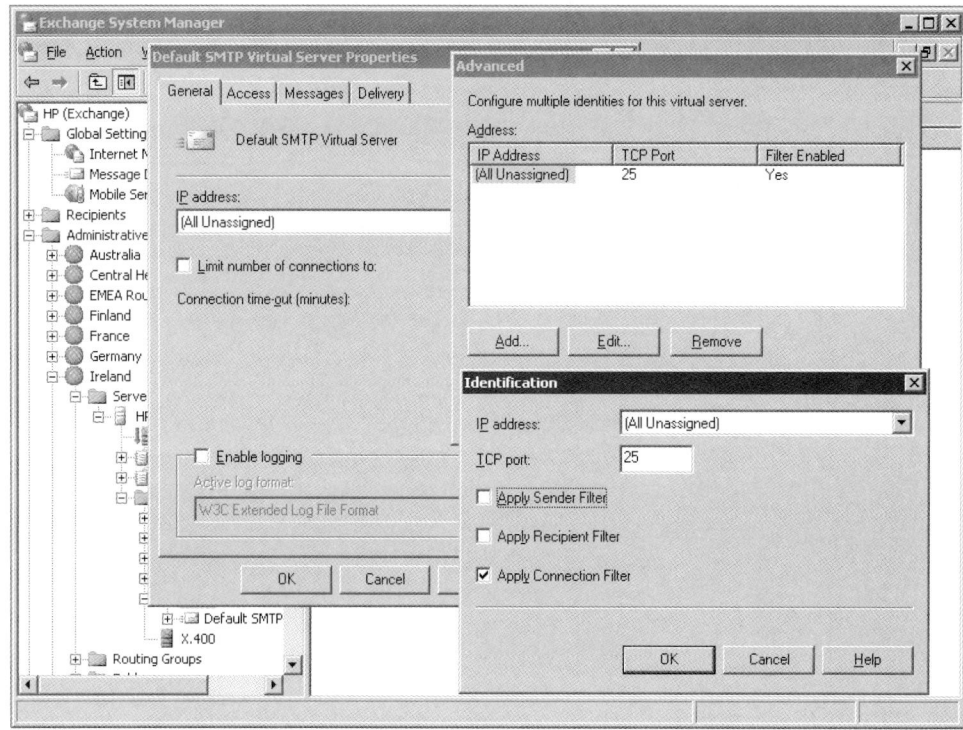

Figure 9.62 *Applying the connection filter to an SMTP VS.*

but it is much more effective to be able to block this traffic as soon as it appears at the gate of your messaging infrastructure.

Connection filters eliminate a lot of spam, and Exchange 2003 supports sender filters too. A sender filter is a list of known email addresses that you never want to receive messages from. You can poll users to collect their "most hated spammer" lists or assemble the list yourself. The list illustrated in Figure 9.63 contains email addresses of people who have sent me unwanted messages, so please do not get upset if you find yourself listed.

You create a sender filter list from the Message Delivery section of ESM. You can decide to filter messages that arrive with blank sender information (a typical trick of the spamming fraternity) and archive any messages that match the filter, which means that Exchange puts the message into its dump directory but does not deliver it to its intended recipient. Once you have a sender filter list, you need to apply the filter to any SMTP virtual servers that handle external traffic in exactly the same way as you apply a connection filter. If you look back to Figure 9.62, you can see that the option to apply a sender filter is the first checkbox in the set of available filters.

9.15 Combating the menace of spam

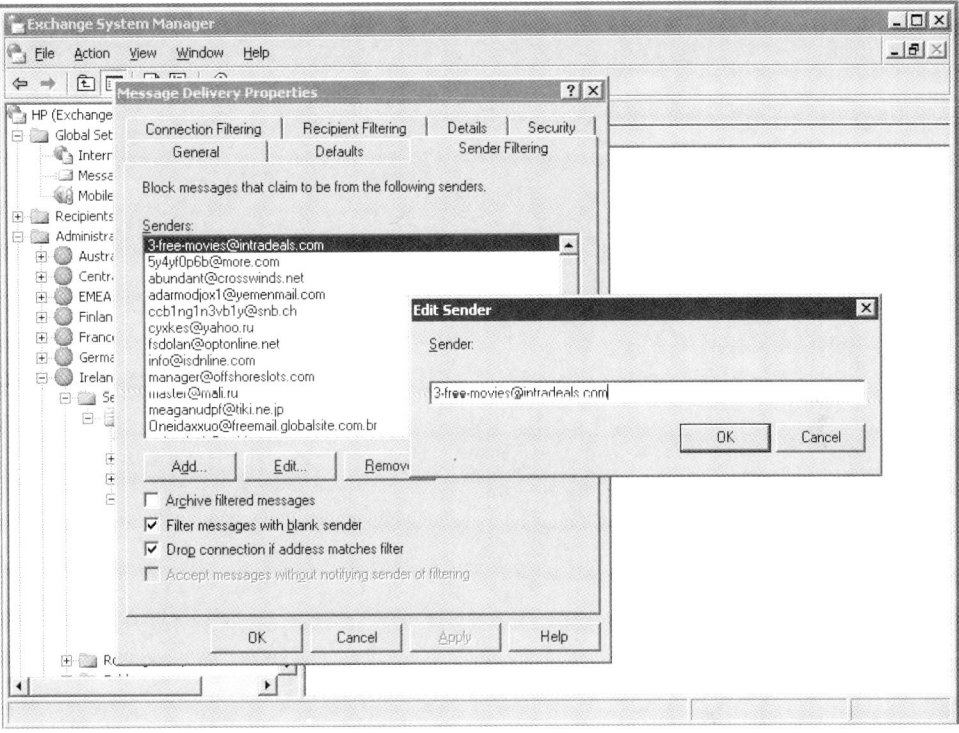

Figure 9.63 *Setting up a sender filter.*

9.15.7 Recipient filters

Exchange 2000 is happy to receive incoming SMTP messages from any domains specified in your Internet message format policies. Given the amount of malicious content floating around the Internet, such an open framework poses some management challenges to control the content arriving on a server. Recipient filtering is the ability to block incoming email by dropping the SMTP connection if the "Mail From:" or "RCPT TO:" fields contain a string that matches addresses defined by the administrator. Exchange 2003 implements recipient filtering in a transport sink (sometimes called the "Turf List" sink), which blocks messages addressed to a specific list of addresses (even if they exist as mail-enabled objects in the AD) that come from anonymous clients, as well as messages sent to addresses that Exchange is unable to locate in the AD. Messages coming in from (nonanonymous) SMTP clients, authenticated users, and Exchange servers within the same organization bypass recipient filtering.

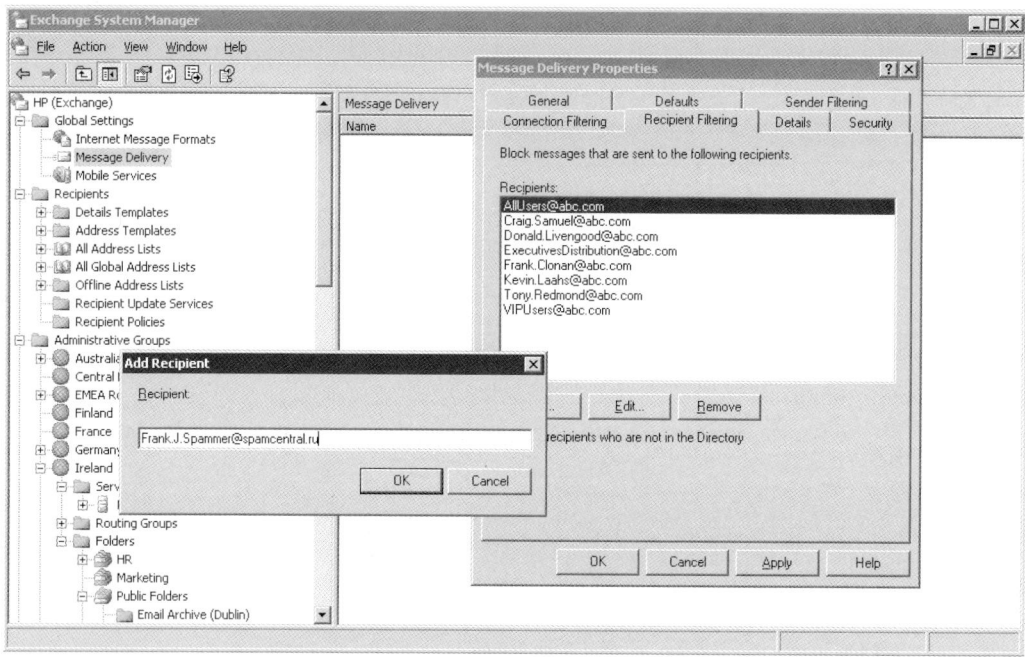

Figure 9.64 *Recipient filtering.*

Figure 9.64 shows how you create the list of recipient addresses to block. ESM does not validate the addresses against the AD as you enter them, but it does insist that the address includes the "@" sign. You can include the SMTP address of any mail-enabled object that you want to protect, including distribution groups. Note that you can also protect distribution groups against unauthenticated senders by setting a property of the group. The list is global in scope and is used by any SMTP virtual server to which you apply the filter.

After you enable the recipient filter on a virtual server, each time a message is presented from an anonymous sender, the sink compares the "RCPT TO:" data in the message header to the list. If the sink discovers a match against one of the specified addresses, it returns error code 550 with a DSN of 5.7.1 ("Requested Action not taken: mailbox not available) to the SMTP client. Exchange will deliver the message to any recipient in the message header who is not in the blocked list.

If you elect to check incoming messages against the directory (set the checkbox), much of the same processing occurs and the sink validates that each of the addresses in the message header exists in the AD. If any address fails, Exchange responds with the same error code and DSN as for a blocked addressee. On first reading, you might assume that Exchange will reject any message that arrives to an addressee that is not in the directory, and you would be correct. In this case, Exchange accepts the message and performs the necessary checks to validate the address when the Routing Engine determines how best to route the message. At this stage, the Routing Engine flags the address as invalid and generates an NDR. If you set the checkbox to filter messages against the directory, Exchange checks the message as it is presented by the remote server and rejects it immediately, thus avoiding the overhead of processing the message through the Routing Engine. The net effect is, therefore, that you avoid wasteful processing by implementing the check.

9.16 Exchange Intelligent Message Filter (IMF)

IMF, shipped in summer 2004, is the first product to use Microsoft's "SmartScreen" technology that Bill Gates announced in his Comdex 2003 keynote. IMF builds on the better filtering introduced in Exchange 2003 and the client-side junk mail processing delivered in Outlook 2003 to follow best practice by maximizing the amount of unwanted mail suppressed at the point where spam attempts to enter an organization. The logic is that this approach conserves maximum bandwidth and reduces the impact of spam on users once it "escapes" within an organization. Intercepting spam close to the network edge also allows administrators to enforce enterprise-wide policies and avoids the need to update many different network locations with data to counter new spam exploits, a problem that desktop administrators have to solve to deploy updated filter files to every client.

Given that Exchange 2003 already has increased antispam protection, why has Microsoft released IMF? The reason is straightforward—better protection for gateway systems. It is true that administrators can deploy the full array of filters available in Exchange 2003 to combat the bad guys, but filters rely on external input such as real-time blackhole lists and a reasonable degree of expertise to configure the filters correctly. Even with all the filters in place and correctly configured, you are unlikely to trap a large percentage of spam because spammers change their tactics and techniques on a very frequent basis to evade detection. For example, spammers switch domains to avoid suppression by being on blackhole lists, and they constantly play with the text of their messages to stop antispam tools from recognizing them too readily. Spam in foreign languages is an increasing annoyance too. The spate of prosecutions launched by major ISPs against known spammers based in the United States in March 2004 may be frustrated by moving spam operations to foreign locations where the law does not prohibit spamming. Because there are so many active spammers that generate so much email, it is almost impossible to keep pace. The value proposition of the antispam industry is for specialized companies to do the hard work for email administrators in tracking the latest spam techniques, where spam comes from, and figuring out the most efficient way to suppress the spam while generating the fewest possible "false positives" (messages identified incorrectly as spam) and not slow down overall mail transmission and delivery.

IMF originated in Microsoft Research (where it is know as "SmartScreen"), which developed the patented machine learning technology to recognize the distinguishing characteristics of both legitimate email and spam based on a huge collection of different messages gathered from inside and outside Microsoft. Microsoft designed IMF to scan messages and make an assessment as to whether they are spam or legitimate based on the characteristics it developed. Microsoft believes that IMF is highly accurate, because of the huge sample of messages used to develop the characteristics and because it included both legitimate and spam in the sampling. Similar to antivirus products, IMF depends on intelligence (code) and data (such as spam patterns and indicators) to assess messages and decide whether they are spam. Given that spamming techniques change constantly and that spammers will attempt to discover how IMF works and how best to avoid detection, Microsoft needs to update both the IMF intelligence and data regularly. In its initial release, administrators will have to download regular updates for IMF from Microsoft's Software Assurance Web site and apply the updates manually to maintain the effectiveness of IMF's antispam protection. Microsoft anticipates that it will automate this process in the future, perhaps following the release of the Exchange Edge Server edition in 2005. It is worth noting that modified versions of SmartScreen technology are featured in Outlook 2003's junk mail filter and Microsoft Entourage 2004 for Mac OS X.

IMF only detects spam that comes into an organization through connectors hosted by SMTP virtual servers—so it will not protect against spam arriving through X.400 or other connectors. This is reasonable, because spammers are, by their very nature, unknown to an organization, and X.400 and other messaging connectors are only used to link well-known messaging systems together. On the other hand, SMTP is the lingua franca of the Internet, and spammers operate by sending messages to SMTP addresses they have harvested from public repositories, such as newsgroups, Web sites, or addresses that they generate for targeted domains. For

9.16 Exchange Intelligent Message Filter (IMF)

example, it does not take much spammer imagination to generate a set of addresses for a domain such as winnetmag.com using common naming schemes such as first name.last name@winnetmag.com and use those addresses to spam everyone in the domain.

After IMF is activated, it examines the messages passed by any filters you have deployed on the Exchange servers that host SMTP connectors to the Internet. Exchange applies connection, recipient, and then sender filters to messages in that order before passing them to IMF. IMF examines and evaluates messages against known characteristics of spam and legitimate mail and determines the outcome as a rating known as the spam confidence level (SCL), which ranges in value from 1 to 9. Exchange uses two other values internally: 0 indicates legitimate email and –1 indicates that the message originated inside the same Exchange organization and requires no further validation. You can find information on how to manipulate SCL values programmatically in the Solutions section of the Exchange 2003 Software Development Kit on MSDN.

To retain the rating as the message passes within the organization, Exchange stores the SCL as a message property. Generally, the lower the SCL, the less likely a message is to be spam, so if a message receives an SCL higher than 5, it is a reasonable guarantee that it is spam. Exchange 2003 introduced the concept of SCL and made the necessary changes to support the property in the Store, including adding new attributes in the Active Directory schema to control UCE processing, but the original version of Exchange 2003 did not provide the user interface for administrators to determine what happens to a message based on its SCL rating. IMF processing generates SCL ratings for messages, suppresses some of those messages at the gateway if they meet a threshold, and then allows mailbox stores to perform further processing, based on the SCL ratings on messages delivered by the gateway, to ensure that it respects user preferences for blocked senders and safe senders.

9.16.1 Where to deploy IMF

You can deploy Exchange servers to host SMTP connectors to the Internet as standalone servers in the DMZ or deploy the servers behind the firewall, in which case you need to install other servers to operate in the DMZ as the initial SMTP connection for the organization. For example, many companies deploy UNIX or Linux systems in this role, running email MTAs such as Sendmail or Postfix to provide basic handling of messages in and out of the company. If you elect to deploy Exchange inside the DMZ, it is best practice to put the servers in their own Exchange organization to reduce the potential for a security breach. These servers should ideally be managed by separate administrators, and not host mailboxes. Instead, their sole function is to accept incoming messages, perform checks (for viruses, spam, unwanted senders) to ensure that messages really should be accepted, and to pass (or relay) the messages to other servers behind the firewall for delivery to the destination mailbox. Separate organizations imply separate forests, because you can only have one Exchange organization per Active Directory forest, so there is added cost implied here to provide the server infrastructure to host the Active Directory. When you deploy IMF with Exchange servers in separate organizations in the DMZ and behind the firewall, you must enable cross-forest authentication to allow Exchange to send SCL rating information between the organizations. In other words, the connectors that link the two forests must use authenticated accounts instead of making unauthenticated connections, which is the norm. Authenticated connections allow Exchange to transmit extended properties of messages between the forests, including the SCL rating. Of course, you may decide that you will rely only on the IMF gateway filtering and not use Store filtering, in which case you can revert to unauthenticated connections.

It is relatively unusual to see Exchange servers deployed in the DMZ, but the increased level of security in Windows 2003 and Exchange 2003 makes Exchange a reasonable choice for this purpose. Indeed, Microsoft plans to ship a specialized version of Exchange 2003 designed to operate as a dedicated "edge" server in early 2005. Exchange Edge Server includes some changes to the SMTP stack to help it process incoming messages more efficiently. For now, the more likely scenario is to have one or more Exchange gateway servers behind the firewall with SMTP connectors linked to the DMZ server and these are the target servers for IMF.

Note that if you operate more than Exchange servers in your messaging infrastructure and you pass messages between the two systems via SMTP, you should deploy IMF on the Exchange 2003 servers that host the gateways to the other mail system to ensure that Exchange catches any spam that gets through that system.

9.16.2 Installing IMF

Microsoft only supports IMF on standard Exchange 2003 servers—you cannot install it on a clustered Exchange 2003 server and it does not support earlier versions such as Exchange 2000. The installation is simple, and the only sign that anything has changed is the addition of the Intelligent Message Filter tab for Message Delivery under Global Settings in Exchange

9.16 Exchange Intelligent Message Filter (IMF)

System Manager (ESM) and a new Intelligent Message Filtering node under the SMTP protocol on the Exchange server where you have installed IMF. Once you install IMF in an organization, administrators can set thresholds and establish actions for Exchange to take with spam by modifying the global Message Delivery settings and then activating IMF for SMTP virtual servers on the servers where you have installed IMF. Figure 9.65 shows the IMF administrative options that you can access through the Message Delivery properties in ESM.

After you install IMF inside your Exchange 2003 organization, you can see the Intelligent Message Filter tab. There are three basic decisions for an administrator:

- What is the gateway SCL threshold?

- What should be done when messages exceed the gateway SCL threshold?

- Which SCL threshold (Store Junk E-Mail Configuration) should be set for mailbox stores? Note that ESM does not allow you to set the mailbox store threshold to be the same or greater than the gateway threshold—it must always be lower.

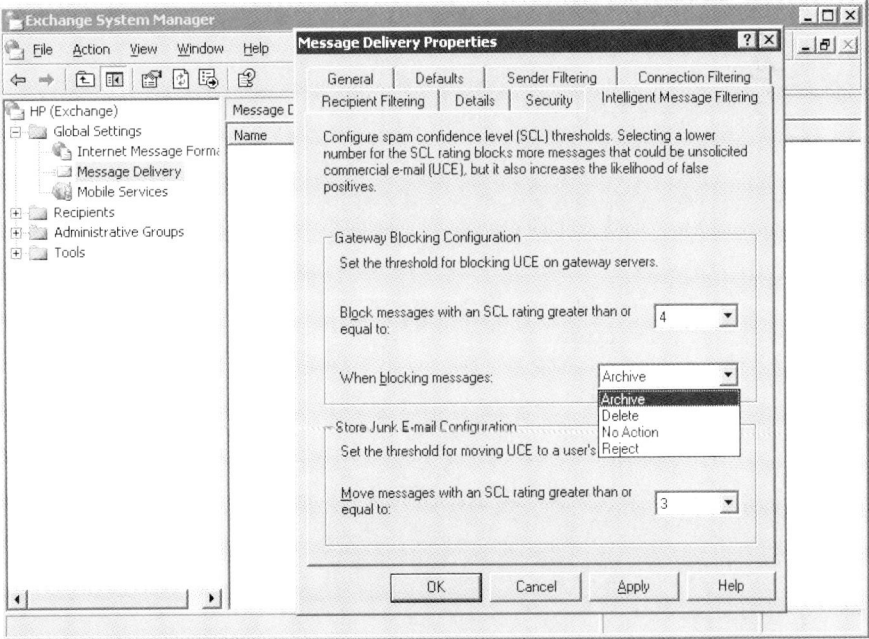

Figure 9.65 *Configuring IMF.*

As with other Global Settings, changes made to SCL ratings for gateways and mailbox stores apply to all servers within an Exchange organization.

The gateway SCL threshold (sometimes referred to as the "block" threshold) controls the action that Exchange takes on the server that hosts the SMTP connector. There is a balancing act for administrators here. If you set the SCL threshold too low (say at 2), then you run the risk that legitimate messages will be treated as spam. On the other hand, if you set it too high (say at 7), then your users may experience more spam than they care to read. The tolerance level of every company is different, and some believe that it is better to accept some spam into mailboxes in order that every legitimate message gets through as fast as possible. Others believe that it is better to filter as much spam as possible and then have a reliable process for administrators to deal with the false positives that are blocked. The best idea is to start with thresholds that are slightly higher than you think you need, check on the volume of false positives that you see over a couple of weeks, and ensure that users are happy because they do not receive many spam messages. You can then reduce the threshold gradually until you arrive at a steady state, where IMF is blocking the maximum amount of spam without generating floods of false positives for administrators to process.

The next issue is what the gateway server does with the message if its SCL is greater than or equal to the threshold. The options here are Archive, Delete, No Action, and Reject. The Delete action is straightforward, since IMF immediately drops the messages without a trace. No Action means that Exchange allows the message past the gateway, although the destination mailbox server might still delete it. Reject means that the gateway returns the message to its originator. To avoid the expense of transporting spam around their networks, most companies have a policy to delete identified spam as soon as it arrives on a system.

IMF processes messages in memory and does not commit anything to disk unless it archives a message. Archiving messages that meet the SCL threshold on a gateway gives administrators an opportunity to check messages for false positives. By default, Exchange moves archived messages to a directory called Exchsrvr\Mailroot\vsi n\UCEArchive, where vsi is the instance number (1 is the default) of the SMTP virtual server. You can review messages captured in this directory by opening them with Notepad or Outlook Express, and you can resubmit a message that you discover to be a false positive by moving it to the Exchsrvr\Mailroot\vsi n\Pickup directory, which forces the SMTP virtual server to process it onward.

9.16 Exchange Intelligent Message Filter (IMF)

Note that Exchange removes the SCL rating from archived messages unless you change the registry to add a new DWORD value called ArchiveSCL (set its value to 1) under HKLM\Software\Microsoft\Exchange\ContentFilter. This change instructs IMF to write the rating into the X-SCL attribute in message properties. You may not want to do this, because if you review a message and decide that it is safe for delivery to the destination mailbox, you do not want the mailbox store to drop the message because its SCL meets the mailbox store threshold!

Of course, a potential problem immediately appears with archiving messages to the disk where program and other files are also located. Apart from the physical effort required to examine archived messages to locate and then process false positives, you have to be careful that the disk holding the archive location never exhausts free space, unless you want your SMTP service to crash. You are unlikely to meet this problem on a test system, but once you put IMF into production on a server that handles heavy message traffic you should consider relocating the archive directory to another disk (or decide to delete messages that IMF identifies as spam). Unfortunately, there is no user interface to move the archive directory, so you have to do this with a registry change. Create a new string key value called ArchiveDir under HKLM\Software\Microsoft\Exchange\ContentFilter and set its value to be the full directory path where you want to store the archived messages—for example, F:\Exchsrvr\Archive. You need to stop and restart the SMTP service before the change becomes effective and you have to apply the same change on all Exchange servers that host IMF.

Archiving is a good feature to have, but the IMF implementation gives you the bare minimum. Other antispam systems, such as NetIQ Mail-Marshal, provide a more comprehensive set of features for archiving suspect messages, such as the ability to search the archive set, view messages by date, and so on. You may wonder why Microsoft cannot provide the necessary UI to make basic management changes such as this and avoid the need to mess with the system registry. The answer is linked to internal Microsoft rules that govern when products can update the UI and is driven by many factors, including documentation, support, translation into multiple languages, and so on. You can anticipate that Microsoft will update the UI in the future, perhaps in a future service pack for Exchange 2003. It is also possible that some developers may provide add-on or third-party tools to manage the IMF archives, and several developments are already under way, so it is worth checking with your local Microsoft office to see if it knows about tools to manage the archive directory.

9.16.3 Message Stores and SCL

The Exchange gateway server takes no action for messages that have an SCL lower than the threshold, so Exchange routes these messages as normal to the mailbox server that hosts the destination mailbox. When the messages arrive on the server, the transport engine delivers them to the Store, which then takes responsibility for checking the messages against the Store threshold and the blocked senders list configured by users through Outlook 2003 or Outlook Web Access 2003. Note that if you use earlier versions of Outlook or other clients, the Store does not perform any further checking. The existence of the blocked senders list for a mailbox tells the Store that it has to check messages.

You may wonder why Exchange implemented Store-level checking in addition to gateway processing. There are a couple of reasons. First, non-Microsoft antispam server-based products that calculate and set SCL ratings for messages might be used instead of IMF. Second, it is always good to give users the ability to block messages from people they do not care to communicate with or give a definite indication of correspondents they always want to receive mail from. Blocked Senders and Safe Senders lists are implemented in the latest clients, but the data that enforces user checking is held in the Store alongside other mailbox information. Of course, even if you have not upgraded users to Outlook 2003, any user whose mailbox is on an Exchange 2003 server can fire up a browser and connect with Outlook Web Access to create a Blocked Senders or Safe Senders list. Click on the "Options" button and then on "Manage Junk Email Lists" to select the Blocked Senders list using Outlook Web Access.

Assuming that the mailbox is on an Exchange 2003 server, the Store looks at the SCL rating on each message and either of two things happens. If the SCL rating is lower than or equal to the Store threshold and the sender of the message is not on the Blocked Senders list (or the Store cannot access the list), the Store delivers the message to the user's Inbox, but only if the sender is in the mailbox's Safe Senders list. If the user has blocked the sender, then the Store takes the action defined in the user's junk mail option (deliver to junk mail folder or delete permanently). On the other hand, if the SCL rating is higher than the Store threshold, the Store checks the user's Safe Senders list to ensure that it does not block messages from a correspondent the user knows to be safe. If the Store can find the sender's email address in the list, it knows that the user wants to receive the message so the Store delivers it to the mailbox. If the message does not come from a safe sender, the Store handles it according to the user's junk mail option, as discussed previously.

9.16.4 Applying IMF to SMTP virtual servers

After you have configured the global IMF settings, you have to activate IMF on the SMTP virtual servers that actually handle message traffic. In concept, this is exactly the same operation that you take to enable connection, sender, or recipient filtering except that you do it through a slightly different interface. The difference is that you can apply IMF to multiple SMTP virtual servers in one place, whereas you normally apply filters to servers one by one.

As mentioned earlier, after you install IMF on a server, a new Intelligent Message Filter node appears under SMTP in the "Protocols" stack (Figure 9.66). If you view the properties of the node, ESM lists all of the SMTP virtual servers that are active on the server and indicates whether IMF is active on each virtual server. Figure 9.66 represents what you see on the vast majority of Exchange 2003 servers—a single default SMTP virtual server associated with TCP port 25 and handling all IP addresses. Exchange can support multiple SMTP virtual servers assigned to different ports and handling different ranges of IP addresses all on a single physical server, but

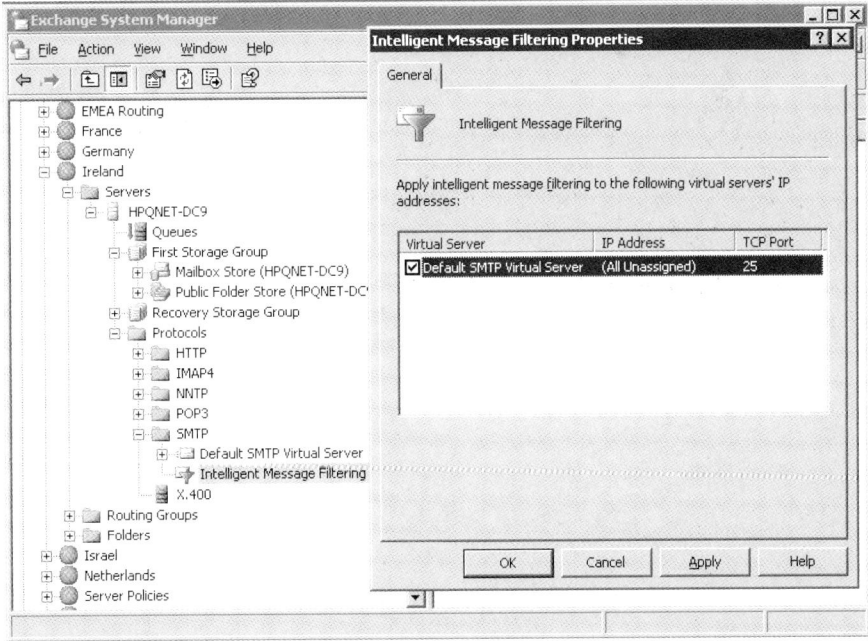

Figure 9.66 *Configuring an SMTP virtual server to use IMF.*

making changes such as this is unnecessary, unless you have a well-understood requirement.

IMF is a simple service, which is either running or not. Behind the scenes, IMF writes a number of new events to the Windows Application Event log when specific actions occur. For example, you can search for event 7512 to view information about messages that the gateway has rejected or deleted. More interestingly, IMF writes event 7515 whenever it cannot process a message, possibly due to it being malformed or corrupted in some way.

Event data tends to be sparse, so you can get some insight into IMF's activity level by viewing the performance counters that Microsoft installs under the MSExchange Intelligent Message Filter object. You can discover the total count of scanned messages, scan rate per second, and totals for messages rejected, deleted, and archived. You can also discover how many messages IMF assigns to each SCL value. A separate counter reports the percentage of the total of scanned messages that IMF believes are spam and another tells you the percentage of spam received in the last 30 minutes. While Microsoft is not providing any API to connect IMF to management frameworks such as HP OpenView, it is possible for these frameworks to retrieve the IMF performance data and analyze it for their own purposes.

9.16.5　IMF licensing

Microsoft's original plan was to limit IMF to customers who enroll in Microsoft's Software Assurance program, a recent change to licensing that allows customers to spread their costs across three-year periods, during which Microsoft provides free upgrades for products covered by the license. Therefore, if you have an Exchange 2003 server license covered by a Software Assurance agreement you receive an IMF license. Microsoft does not sell IMF as a separate product, so the idea was to use it as a compelling reason for customers to sign up for Software Assurance. However, calmer minds prevailed and you can now download IMF from the Microsoft Exchange download center on the Web. Alternatively, if you want to erect an antispam barrier without using IMF or before you deploy Exchange 2003, you can simply use a third-party antispam product, such as Brightmail Anti-Spam for Exchange, Symantec Mail Security 4.5, or Sybari Spam Manager or Advanced Spam Defense.

Of course, apart from the positive publicity that it gains by providing yet another protection mechanism through IMF, Microsoft also makes the upgrade proposition more attractive for people running Exchange 5.5 or

Exchange 2000, neither of which supports IMF. You can deploy IMF on Exchange 2003 gateway servers to protect a set of Exchange 5.5 and 2000 mailbox servers. This is likely to be an early deployment scenario in some companies, but such an implementation delivers only half the benefit, because the message stores on Exchange 5.5 and 2000 servers do not understand the SCL value set by IMF in message headers and can take no action to suppress spam that gets through the gateway. You achieve better protection if you upgrade all servers to Exchange 2003, so there is a subliminal message here—maintain your support contracts, run the latest version, and stay protected through whatever developments the product team generates during the contract lifetime; stay on older versions or buy Exchange 2003 without taking out Software Assurance and battle spam by yourself.

Now that Microsoft has provided an antispam service for Exchange, is this the end of the third-party market for antispam products? The answer is no and there are several reasons why, beginning from the point that you have to be licensed under the Software Assurance program to benefit from IMF. After that, there is the undoubted truth that there are many other email systems than Exchange 2003, including its biggest current competitor—Exchange 5.5. Next, we have the situation where many enterprise administrators prefer not to connect Microsoft servers directly to the Internet, and it will take time before Windows becomes the platform of choice for edge connectivity; there is the time lag before IMF proves its competence in production. Finally, it is unlikely that you can block 100 percent of spam at a single point in a messaging infrastructure. In the same way that it is best practice to implement multiple layers of antivirus protection, you can eliminate maximum spam from user inboxes by deploying blocks at the network edge, mail server, and client. Microsoft certainly provides two good solutions for the edge and client, but there is an interesting middle ground to be fought over.

Third-party antispam vendors will not be idle and will realize that IMF now provides the basic standard for antispam protection in an Exchange environment. Their products have to offer extended features, such as easier management (especially in distributed and heterogeneous infrastructures), better reporting (such as daily statistics for throughput and spam detection) and data management (of captured messages), regular updates to counter new spam techniques, integration with antivirus protection, and fewer false positives. It will be interesting to see how this piece of the Exchange add-on market evolves over the coming years now that Microsoft has made the statement about IMF that "spam protection is important—and part of every Exchange deployment."

10

Managing Exchange: Users

Installing Exchange is only the first step along a very long path. The server needs continued care and maintenance to deliver a reliable messaging service to users and to interact with other servers in the organization. At a conceptual level, Exchange is not particularly difficult to manage. The server is reasonably straightforward and the management interface is mature and meets the majority of administrative needs. However, Exchange does not function in a vacuum, and complexity mounts through its interaction with and dependency on the operating system, third-party products, other Microsoft servers and services, and so on. In addition, complexity increases further as the number of servers grows in the organization. In this chapter, we will look at the challenges involved in day-to-day Exchange operations, covering topics such as setting up and managing the user community, quotas, and so on.

10.1　ESM and other consoles

Exchange divides basic administration into two areas: users and servers. On Exchange 2000 servers, you perform user management through Active Directory Users and Computers, and server management through the Exchange System Manager console (ESM). The logic here is that you are acting on quite different objects. Users, which include contacts and groups, are AD objects that may or may not be mail enabled. Users are stored in AD organizational units (OUs). Servers are also AD objects, but the AD holds server details in quite a different naming context or location. Along with other organizational data such as connectors, details of Exchange servers are stored within the Microsoft Exchange container in the AD configuration NC.

ESM (Figure 10.1) brings all of the common server administrative tasks together into one place and is the closest equivalent you can find to the

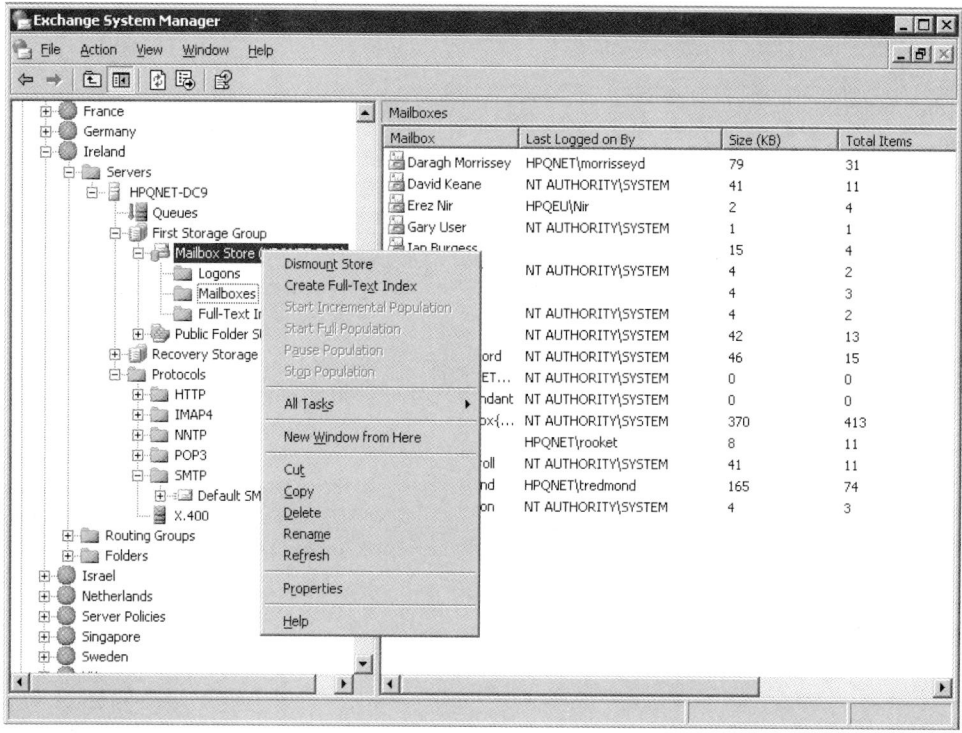

Figure 10.1   *Managing Exchange through ESM.*

previous Exchange 5.5 administrator program. The original intention, as expressed in Exchange 2000, was that a clear separation existed between the tasks that Exchange administrators perform and the work that AD administrators do. Therefore, Microsoft designed ESM as the primary tool to manage the overall shape of the Exchange organization (administration and routing groups), as well as organization-wide components such as recipient and server policies. It is certainly true that such a separation exists in some companies, but it is more common to find that an Exchange administrator also takes care of Exchange-related AD account maintenance, so dividing tasks across multiple consoles occasionally confused administrators. For this reason, Microsoft changed ESM in Exchange 2003 by supporting the option to perform "Exchange tasks" (such as move mailbox) within ESM. Previously, you had to do this through AD Users and Computers. When you think about the subject, it is more logical to be able to move mailboxes from ESM, because you view mailboxes grouped in stores rather than the user-centric view presented by AD Users and Computers. Note that you

10.1 ESM and other consoles

can move multiple mailboxes in one operation, including the ability to schedule the move during off-peak hours.

Microsoft recognized that ESM functionality was weak in some other areas, so it upgraded ESM in Exchange 2003 to include the following features:

- Support extensions to existing options, such as public folder creation and population. Previously, you could only view the public folder hierarchy and view the status of folders. Now you can use ESM to work with public folders in much the same way as the Outlook Web Access client.

- Enhance the UI and functionality of other options, such as the Queue Viewer and the Message Tracking Center.

- Show whether a server is a standard (basic) server, front-end, or virtual server running in a cluster. ESM also displays the edition of Exchange running on the server. As you can see in Figure 10.2, the routing group contains a standard server running an evaluation version of the Enterprise edition of Exchange 2003 and a virtual server on a cluster. Note that clusters never report an evaluation copy, even if they run this software. Exchange 5.5 servers always report that they run the standard edition, even if they run the enterprise edition.

- Support new options, such as Exchange Mobile Services, the Mailbox Recovery Center, and the antispam measures now available through connection, recipient, and sender filters.

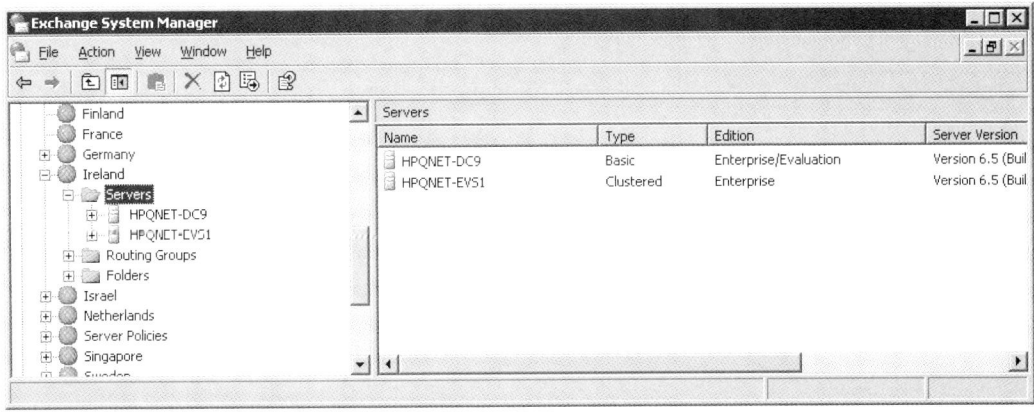

Figure 10.2 *Server types shown by ESM.*

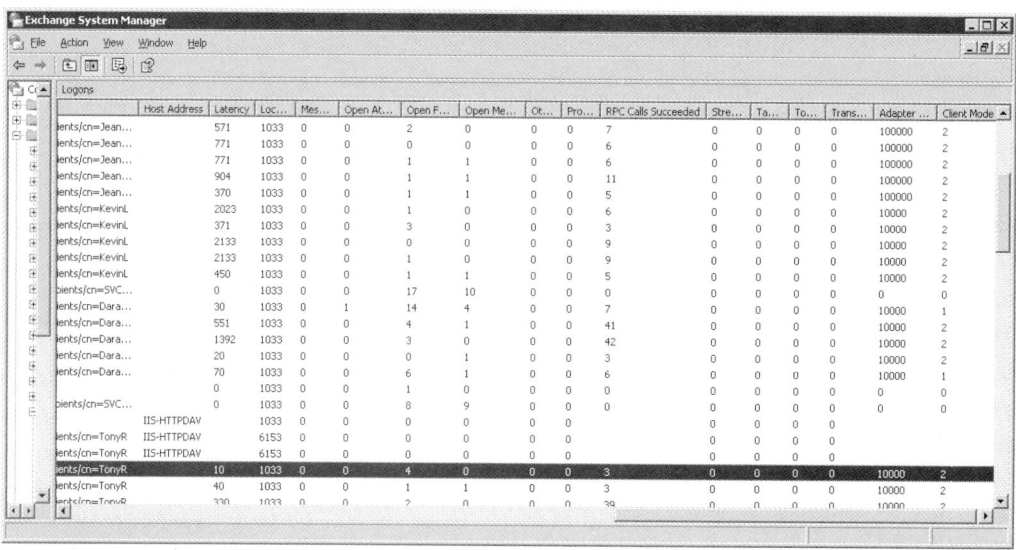

Figure 10.3 *New ESM columns.*

- Add an Internet Mail wizard to help inexperienced administrators (or those who simply need some help along the way) to create and configure email links to the Internet. Microsoft's analysis of calls reported to its support groups identified this as a major source of problems, so it made sense to automate the process.

- Add extra information gathered from clients to the columns available in ESM. Currently, only Outlook 2003 clients populate this information, but this may change in the future. Figure 10.3 shows some of the information you can expect to see, while Table 10.1 lists the most important of the new fields. The Exchange 2003 WMI providers expose this information to system management applications, so you can write your own code to take advantage of the data.

Somewhat surprisingly, ESM does not use the DSAccess component to discover the best DC to fetch configuration data from. Instead, ESM makes an ADSI call to perform a serverless binding to the directory and selects a DC from the result. Using DSAccess might be more consistent, but most of the time it does not matter—unless you have replication problems between sites and ESM binds to a DC in one site, while DSAccess selects a DC from a different site and you end up looking at two sets of data because replication is incomplete. The larger your organization, the more work ESM has to do to fetch and interpret the configuration data from AD and then display the data in the console. The version of ESM provided with Exchange

Table 10.1 *Additional Columns Available to ESM 2003*

Column	Meaning
Adapter Speed	NIC speed reported by the client in Kbits/second
Client IP Address	IP address of the client
Client Mode	Three values: 0 (unknown)—possibly a server application such as an antivirus agent; 1 (online); 2 (cached)
Client Name	FQDN of the client workstation
Latency	Last round-trip latency for RPC between client and server, reported in milliseconds
MAC Address	Hardware address of the client
Locale ID	Number of the locale ID of the client (1033 = English)
Full Mailbox Directory Name	AD distinguished name of the mailbox
Full User Directory Name	AD distinguished name of the user account connecting to the mailbox
Open Messages	Current number of messages open by the client
Open Attachments	Current number of attachments open by the client
Code Page	Code page used by the client
Host Address	Blank for Outlook clients; OWA clients report IIS-HTTP-DAV

2000 is often slow to respond in large organizations. The difference between working in large and small organizations is quite remarkable, especially when you want to look at the properties of an object such as a Mailbox Store. Exchange 2003 is better, but you could not describe it as superquick if you want to retrieve properties of an object from the AD. Clearly, a faster server makes ESM more responsive, and a multi-CPU system is more responsive than a single-CPU system, while a slow or unreliable network connector to the DC used by ESM to retrieve configuration data from the AD slows console performance. Exchange 2003 replaces some RPCs with HTTP-DAV calls to fetch information about items such as public folders, which leads to improved performance, especially with large collections of data. For example, Figure 10.4 shows a new feature in ESM for Exchange 2003: public folder management. In this instance, we review the contents of a large public folder (16,053 items), and ESM uses the same type of calls as OWA to fetch the PF content from the server.

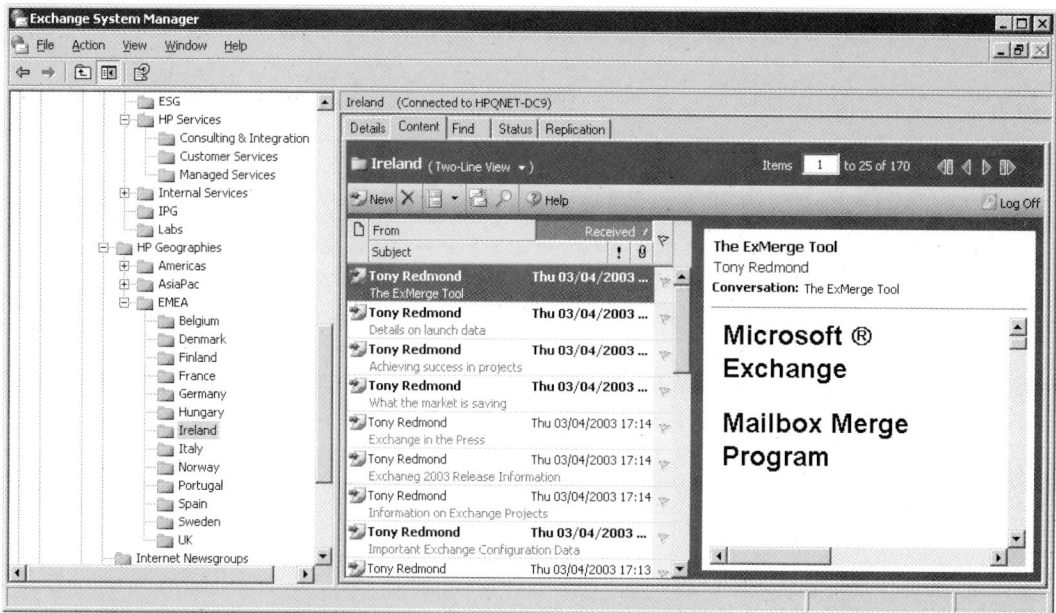

Figure 10.4   *Managing public folders with ESM.*

10.1.1 Other Exchange management snap-ins

Exchange provides a set of MMC snap-ins to allow you to create your own management environment. Each of the snap-ins can be loaded into a console file, or you can combine them together. The basic idea is to implement a granular approach to system management by allowing you to support different management scenarios by combining the snap-ins together into consoles that you can then allocate to different levels of support staff. For example, you can give a front-line support person staffing a help desk a console that allows him or her to maintain user accounts and mailbox properties but not view details of Mailbox Stores. To do this, you build a console that includes the snap-in to manage AD user objects (or even local users and groups, if you wanted to confine management to a single computer that is not a DC).

Implementing granular system management solves a major problem often encountered in early Exchange deployments. The only way to perform any administration of a first-generation Exchange server is through the administration program—even simple operations such as changing someone's telephone number or title. Building a single, monolithic program to do everything is acceptable for small implementations, when typically

10.1 ESM and other consoles

one or two people perform all system management—from setting up the network to configuring user workstations to managing applications such as Exchange. In larger companies, when you have different levels of staff doing different jobs, the all-in-one approach does not work so well. Why, for instance, should someone working in a front-line help-desk role who takes care of basic user management (update directory entries, monitor mailbox quotas, and so on) be able to change the configuration of an Internet connection? Exchange was not the only application that suffered from this problem. Windows NT suffers from exactly the same problem. User Manager for Domains is a good program when you want to perform all account management operations, but it is not very flexible and you cannot restrict its access to the SAM in any way. The lack of granularity and flexibility is indicative of two things: the roots of Windows NT as a LAN-based operating system and the need for Microsoft to serve small user communities that have evolved from Microsoft Mail. Exchange has moved on a lot since its early days and now offers much more flexibility for large implementations.

Moving forward, people who act as second-level support staff might need to deal with server properties, including routing groups and storage groups, so they would use a different console. Third-level support might have access to a console that contained all of the snap-ins or have total administrative access to computers and the network. Each company is different, so you need to devote some thought to consider exactly who will have access to the different snap-ins. There is a large degree of flexibility in Exchange administration now and you can be far more selective in allocating responsibilities to individuals. Be careful that you do not go overboard and stop people from doing their jobs in your efforts to restrict access to critical components such as routing groups. As always, common sense and

Table 10.2 *Exchange MMC Snap-Ins*

MMC Snap-In	Use
Advanced Security	Manage the process to enroll users and provide the keys necessary to encrypt and decrypt messages.
Chat Networks	Manage the Exchange chat network (Exchange 2000 only).
Conferencing Services	Manage online data conferencing service (Exchange 2000 only).
Folders	Manage public folders and hierarchies.
Message Tracking Center	Track the progress of a single message across an Exchange organization.
Exchange System Manager	The standard ESM console (Figure 10.1)

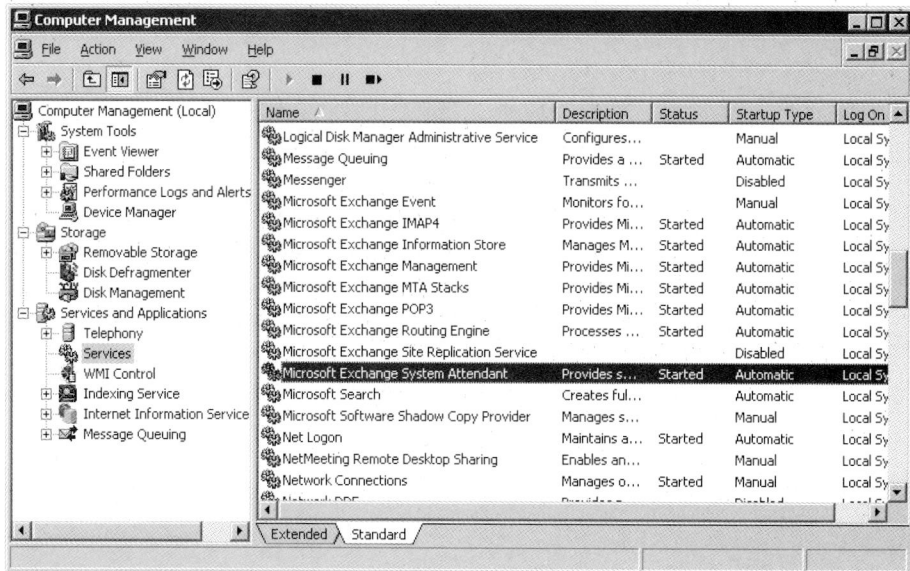

Figure 10.5 *Managing Exchange through computer management.*

knowledge of what support people do to be effective will go a long way toward ensuring successful system management.

Table 10.2 lists the different Exchange snap-ins that you can incorporate into an MMC console. ESM includes all available snap-ins. Just to spice up the management environment a little more, you can also manage part of Exchange through the Computer Management MMC snap-in (Figure 10.5). This snap-in allows you to manage Exchange on a server that you log on to, but you lose access to the other servers in the organization. Additionally, you cannot work with administrative groups or routing groups.

10.1.2 Finding out about server versions

Sometimes administrators find it difficult to determine just which version of Exchange is running in an organization. This is easy to do if you have a small number of servers to deal with, but it becomes more difficult to track as organizations grow and servers become more distributed. The easiest way to determine the version number for an individual server is to select it through ESM and view its properties. If you look on the General tab, you will see the build number shown in a form: Version x.x (Build xxxx.x: Service Pack x), as shown in Figure 10.6.

10.1 ESM and other consoles

Figure 10.6
Viewing a server build number.

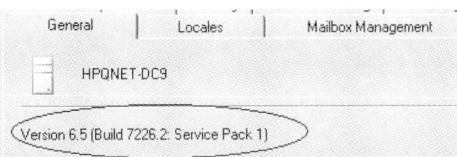

In this example, Version 6.5 means that the server is running Exchange 2003 (Exchange 2000 is version 6.0, which would have followed on from the previous 5.5 version had Microsoft not decided to change the way that it numbered Exchange versions). To check that you have the correct build for a service pack and that you are not running a test version, you can compare the build number against the data listed in Microsoft Knowledge Base article 158530, which lists the build number for every version of Exchange and its service packs since the original Exchange 4.0 release (4.0.837) in 1996.

Checking individual servers is acceptable for one or two servers, but not for an entire organization. You can retrieve build information for a complete administrative group by expanding the group to display server data, as shown in Figure 10.7. You can also save the data to a text file by right-clicking on the "Servers" node in the group and selecting the "Export List" option. Unfortunately, ESM does not offer an option to do this automatically for every administrative group in an organization, so you have to select each administrative group in turn and then combine the text files to form

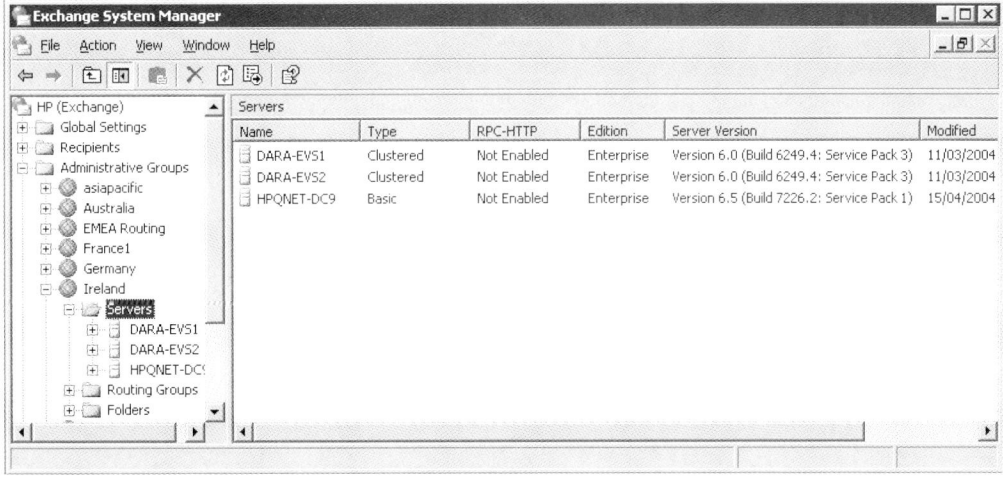

Figure 10.7 *Using ESM to determine build numbers.*

Chapter 10

the overall view of the organization. Alternatively, if you like programming, you can use WMI to interrogate the Exchange configuration held in the Active Directory and build whichever report you choose.

10.1.3 Running ESM on workstations

You can run ESM on both a server and on a workstation. Originally, Microsoft only provided formal support for ESM on Windows 2000 workstations. However, after dragging its feet for awhile (possibly understandable, since it did not want to use valuable testing resources to figure out what it needed to change to support Windows XP), Microsoft eventually released a patch in April 2003 to make ESM for Exchange 2000 work properly on Windows XP (SP1 or later). To get the patch, go to www.microsoft.com/downloads and search for Exchange2000-KB815529-x86-ENU.exe.

Out of the box, Exchange 2003 is quite happy if you run ESM on a Windows XP SP1 workstation with the Windows 2003 Management Pack (which includes the NNTP and AD Users and Computers snap-ins), albeit after you configure the Windows XP SMTP service on the workstation, because ESM has a dependency on some of the SMTP components. While you must install the SMTP service on the workstation before you install ESM, you do not have to run the SMTP service after installation. Note that the workstation must be part of same forest as the Exchange servers, so you cannot install a workstation into a standalone or test domain and then connect the workstation to manage Exchange. Things are a little easier with Windows XP SP2, because you do not need to install the SMTP component, since it comes along with the IIS snap-in. However, if you upgrade an XP SP1 workstation that already has the IIS snap-in installed to XP SP2 and then attempt to install ESM, you may have problems with the SMTP component, because the IIS snap-in did not include SMTP prior to XP SP2. Confused? Well, it all has to do with different Microsoft teams shuffling components around. We cannot fix this issue, but we can get ESM working again by reinstalling the IIS snap-in after upgrading to XP SP2 to ensure that all of the required components are now present.

In addition to these requirements, because of the conflicts between the MAPI components used by ESM and those used by Outlook, you cannot run Outlook and ESM on the same PC. With these restrictions in place, many administrators do not attempt to install ESM on workstations and instead use the Remote Desktop Connection feature included in Windows XP to connect to servers and manage them remotely. In passing, it is worth noting that facilities such as HP's Remote Insight Lights-Out Edition (RILOE) cards for Proliant servers help administrators keep servers online, because you can perform server management operations such as reboots through a Web browser interface without having to go anywhere near the server.

Note that you should not use the Exchange 2000 version of ESM to administer Exchange 2003–specific features such as Outlook Mobile Access or the Recovery Storage Group. It is logical to expect that the older version of ESM has zero knowledge of the new capabilities and may not function correctly because of this fact. With this in mind, it is best to upgrade all administrative workstations to use the Exchange 2003 version of ESM as soon as possible. Assuming that you deploy the Exchange 2003 version of ForestPrep, you can then use Exchange 2003 features of ESM against Exchange 2000 servers, such as:

- The new Move mailbox functionality
- The integrated Queue viewer
- Internet Mail wizard
- Some of the public folder management enhancements
- The Mailbox Recovery Center

10.2 User access

Users are the most important part of any system, and perhaps especially so in the case of systems that automate common office tasks and enable better people interaction. Without users, there is simply no point in running an electronic messaging system. Actually, setting out with a goal of "managing" users is probably the wrong attitude for a system administrator to have. The people who connect to mail servers are consumers of a service. As with any other consumer, users have the right to expect that Exchange will deliver a service in a reasonably predictable manner and that they will not go through too much pain to access and employ the service. Anyone who has ever managed a mail server knows that you have to register people in some way before they can use the system. Exchange is no different in this respect. You have to set up users with a mailbox and allocate them some quota to hold their messages, establish the email addresses that they can use for external communication, and determine the protocols they can use to connect to Exchange. The AD holds the details of users, contacts, groups, and public folders (Figure 10.8), and you can manipulate these objects like any other AD object. The objects that are important to Exchange are as follows:

- Mail-enabled users: This is the most common type of mail-enabled object. Everyone who wants to use Exchange to send and receive interpersonal messages must be able to access a mailbox. With the appropriate permissions, you can access multiple mailboxes as well as have people processing email on behalf of other users. Windows 2003 introduces support for the iNetOrgperson object, which you may need to create instead of user objects to interoperate with LDAP-enabled applications that depend on such objects. iNetOrgperson objects only exist in a full-function Windows 2003 forest and are a variation on the user object supported since Windows 2000, so you can think of it as a user object with some extra attributes. If you mail-enable an iNetOrgperson object, Exchange treats it in the same way as a user object.

- Mail-enabled groups (distribution lists): A group is a collection of recipients of any valid type. When you send a message to a distribution group, Exchange expands the group and sends a copy of the message to each recipient.

- Mail-enabled contacts: Recipients on other email systems that you can address from Exchange—for example, an Internet user who receives mail via SMTP, or someone who receives messages sent via an

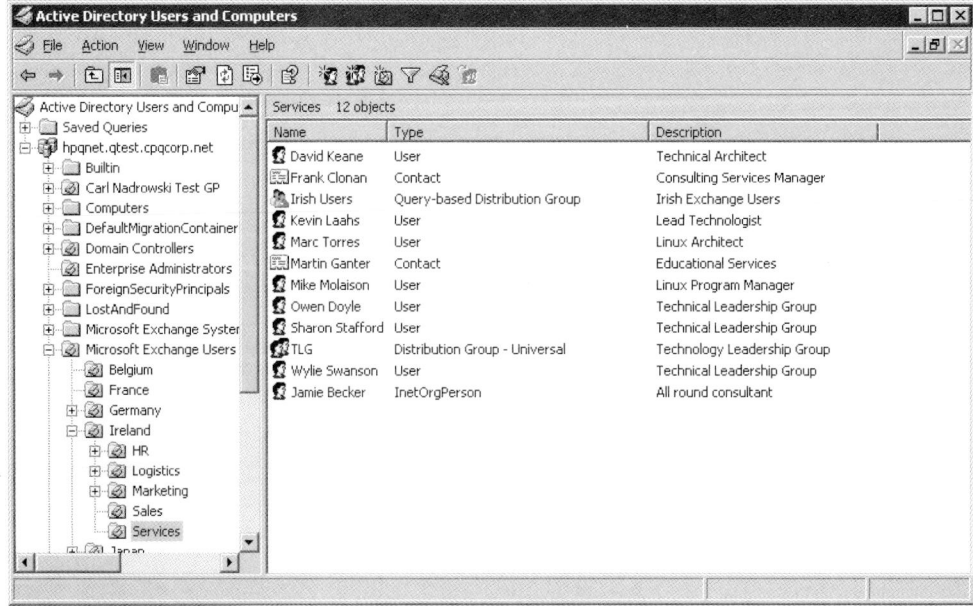

Figure 10.8 *Users, contacts, and groups in the Active Directory.*

10.2 User access

X.400 link between Exchange and another SMTP-compliant messaging system, such as America Online (AOL).

- Mail-enabled Public folders: You can mail-enable public folders to allow users to post information into the folders by sending them email.

You can place mailboxes, groups, and contacts in any organizational unit within the AD, or use AD Users and Computers to move them between organizational units within the same domain by simply selecting the object and then selecting the Move option and the organizational unit to receive the object, as shown in Figure 10.9.

Organizational units are more than just a subdivision of the AD. They play an important role in how you implement security within a Windows environment, since you typically use group policy objects to apply security settings at the level of an organizational unit. It is important to have enough organizational units to be able to apply proper security at a sufficiently granular level, but it is also important not to have too many organizational units, since this will result in an overly complex structure within the directory. Best practice is to limit the depth of organizational units to no more than four from the domain root. Every company is different, and requirements vary greatly, but some good general recommendations for organizational unit design are:

- Base the top level of organizational units on something that makes sense for your company. If you organize the company on a geographical basis, then use location names. Figure 10.8 shows an example in which organizational units map countries as the basis for the hierarchy.

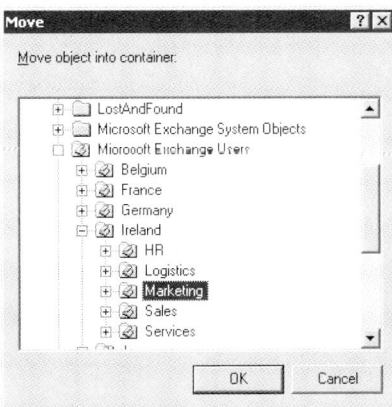

Figure 10.9
Moving to another organizational unit.

Chapter 10

- You can then create subsequent levels to establish subgroupings within the major organizational units. Sometimes, the decision on how to do this is easy, since there already are well-established departments such as marketing, sales, HR, and so on. In Figure 10.9, we are moving an object into the "Marketing" organizational unit.

- Use names that make sense. The current set of administrators may understand code names for departments, locations, or buildings, but this is not necessarily going to be the case for new administrators who join the company in the future. There is no need to save a couple of bytes by shortening names to codes, so try not to do it. Users never see the organizational unit names.

Another point to remember is that organizational units provide a great basis to enforce standards through group policy objects.

10.2.1 Creating accounts and mailboxes

After you have the organizational unit structure designed, creating new user accounts is easy. The AD schema is extended with the necessary attributes to support Exchange when you install the first Exchange server in the forest or when you run the /ForestPrep option for the setup program. Afterward, the property pages required to add an Exchange mailbox and to define properties such as email addresses and mailbox quotas are automatically available whenever you work with accounts. Windows activates the Exchange property pages dynamically when you start AD Users and Computers.

You can add new mailboxes by connecting to any domain controller (DC) in the domain to hold the account. While the AD Users and Computers console offers the option to copy an existing user to create a new one, you should always create a mail-enabled user from scratch to ensure that all of the necessary attributes that Exchange depends on are correctly set. The three most important properties given to a new account when you create it are:

- The account name: This includes the down-level Windows NT account name and the UPN, or User Principal Name. For example, my NT account name is TRedmond, while my UPN is Tony.Redmond@acme.com.

- The SMTP email address: This can be the same value as the UPN, and it is most convenient for users when it is. The Recipient Update Service generates the SMTP address and any other proxy addresses according to policies that you establish. The AD validates any email address against the directory to ensure that it is unique within the organization. Some companies generate user records as the result of automated HR processes and synchronize information into the AD to add the account. These procedures can cause email clashes if the code does not check for duplicates.

- The display name: Users see this name most often, because it is the name shown in the GAL and other address lists.

It is a good idea to determine a set of policies to set standards for account and email addresses before you add any accounts or mailboxes. Plunging forward to create accounts in an uncontrolled manner may be artistic, and indeed this approach will probably work for a small operation, but it is inappropriate for a corporate-style implementation. If administrators do not comply with standards, you will see increasing problems as you add more accounts, particularly with display names in the GAL. It is inevitable that different administrators will name accounts according to a variety of different styles, and no one will be quite sure how to find people in the directory.

Some companies have well-meaning but unworkable ideas for how to create account names. For example, if your organization allocates numbers to staff members, it may seem sensible to use the same staff numbers as the basis for allocating account names, or even SMTP addresses. In reality, such a scheme is not feasible, since the resulting addressing scheme is very hard to use when you want to find someone. In HP's HR systems, my badge number is 100150847, but I would hate anyone to think of me as a mere number or to have people be forced to address messages to me as 100150847@hp.com.

National Social Security or insurance numbers are unique and are sometimes proposed as the basis for an even more unfriendly account naming convention. Thankfully, it is illegal to use Social Security numbers in this way in many countries. Even worse naming conventions are in use, and, strange as it may seem, there are organizations that think it is a good idea to use cryptic, esoteric naming schemes. I have received messages from people forced to use addresses such as AAA19974X@org.com,[1] and wondered how the email administrators in that company dreamed up such a charming naming convention. Perhaps it is an attempt to keep corporate secrets or stop people from guessing what an email address might be. Even more

---

1. Creating non-user-friendly email addresses is more common than you might imagine. Even Scott Adams's "Dilbert" cartoon strip has poked fun at people who come to computer conventions equipped with business cards that have very long and complex email addresses. Naturally, Dilbert and his friends laugh hysterically when they see these addresses.

bizarrely, there are companies that support logical addressing schemes for incoming mail, and then insist on putting esoteric reply addresses on outgoing messages. For example, you might be able to send mail to Tony.Redmond@xyz.com, but get a response from Red0134246@xyz.com! Mixing addresses in this manner does not deliver a consistent external presence for a company.

The most sensible principles to remember when considering the most appropriate account naming scheme for your organization are:

- Logical: Users should not have to go through mental contortions to remember their own email addresses. Equally, they should find the GAL easy to look through when they need to find someone. As we have just discussed, the naming convention for external addresses should also follow a logical structure. The Electronic Messaging Association (EMA) recommends "first name.last name@domain" as the preferred convention for external SMTP email addresses.

- Friendly: Some logical schemes are, well, too logical. Look for a compromise between logic and user friendliness.

- Straightforward: Avoid complexity at all costs.

Administrators often consider surnames as the first and most obvious basis for planning a naming scheme, and it is often possible to use this approach in small to medium email systems. However, the statistical fact is that the more users a system supports the more chance there will be that common surnames exist. In a small system supporting 50 users you might only have one "Smith" (or the equivalent most common name in a country or language), but I'll guarantee that in a system supporting more than 100 or so users there will be more than one surname clash to contend with. Surnames are also a western convention that does not always apply well in international deployments. There are places in the world, including Malaysia, Iceland, and parts of India, where the concept of a surname is not universally observed, and others (China) where the surname is the primary name.

A good account naming policy covers:

- The naming convention used for new accounts, including the down-level NT account name, the UPN, and the alias used for the Exchange mailbox. The account names must be unique within the domain.

- The email addresses allocated to the new mailbox and instructions about how to resolve duplicate addresses. The Recipient Update Service creates email addresses automatically, but you may want to differenti-

10.2 User access

ate addresses when two or more users with duplicate names exist. For example, if there are two Jane Smiths in a company, what SMTP addresses will you allocate? Most companies use a middle initial to split the two, resulting in names such as Jane.F.Smith and Jane.D.Smith. This is fine until you have two people with the same middle initial, so be prepared to be inventive. Whatever you do, do not add numbers to the ends of people's names. It is not nice to have an email address such as Jane.F.Smith2@org.com!

- The Mailbox Store to host the new mailbox.

As mentioned earlier, the natural choice for display names, and the one that is probably most used in the English-speaking world is: "Given Name Last Name," as in: Tony Redmond.

This convention is fine for small implementations, but it is not appropriate for very large deployments. The basic problem is that there is a smaller number of first names in use than last names, so if you create display names in this manner it can be very difficult to find users in the GAL. There are just too many people named "John," "Peter," or "Tom" in large companies. For this reason, large companies often use a naming convention of: "Surname, Given Name" as in: Redmond, Tony.

The resulting GAL is usually easier to search (if you know someone's surname). The naming convention also needs to specify how to identify users who share the same name. The usual approach is to append some unique information to help identify users, often their location or department. Some implementations use initials, but correspondents tend not to know someone else's initials, although they often have an idea where the person works or which department the person works for. Thus, the complete naming convention is: "Surname, Given Name (Identifier)."

Figure 10.10 shows an extract from the HP GAL, in which I searched for anyone who shares my surname. As you can see, the second from top entry is an example of how to use a location identifier to identify an individual. HP now places the surname first in display names. This was not always the case—the first implementation of Exchange at Digital in 1996 sorted the GAL by first names. Everything was fine until we had 10,000 mailboxes in the directory and people started to notice that it was not as easy to locate other users anymore, since there were just too many "Johns," "Janes," and "Joes" in the company. We reversed the naming convention quickly to put surnames first and this approach has been successful ever since, surviving even the upheaval within the directory caused by two very large corporate mergers. The HP GAL contains over 250,000 entries,

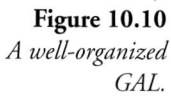

Figure 10.10
A well-organized GAL.

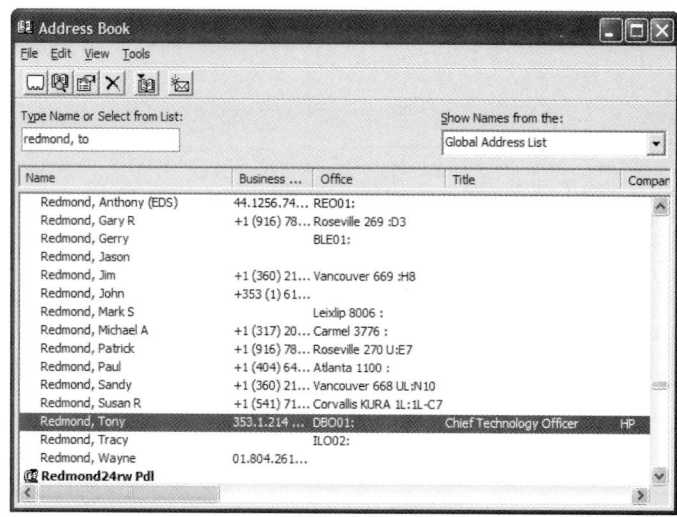

including mailboxes, contacts, and distribution groups, so you can appreciate that it is important to use a good naming convention with such a large number of entries.

Note that groups and contacts also need a naming convention for display names, preferably a convention similar to the one selected for user accounts. Group names should convey the reason why the group exists and should not use a cryptic name. Figure 10.10 also includes an example of a group name (toward the bottom of the screen) that is totally esoteric and unmeaningful. Using a meaningful prefix (such as DL--) keeps all groups together in one place in the GAL and provides an obvious hint to users that they are sending to a group.

Policies will allocate a default set of email addresses to a new account. The policy will ensure that the default addresses comply with corporate standards, but you may need to adjust the automatically generated addresses if the policy cannot generate an appropriate address, because the default address will conflict with an address already held by an account elsewhere in the organization.

10.2.2 Maintaining mailbox details

Administrators can enter lots of information about user accounts into the AD, and users can access most of this information through the GAL. Some companies restrict the number of properties that they update, because they do not want the overhead of maintaining the data (perhaps because it is

10.2 User access

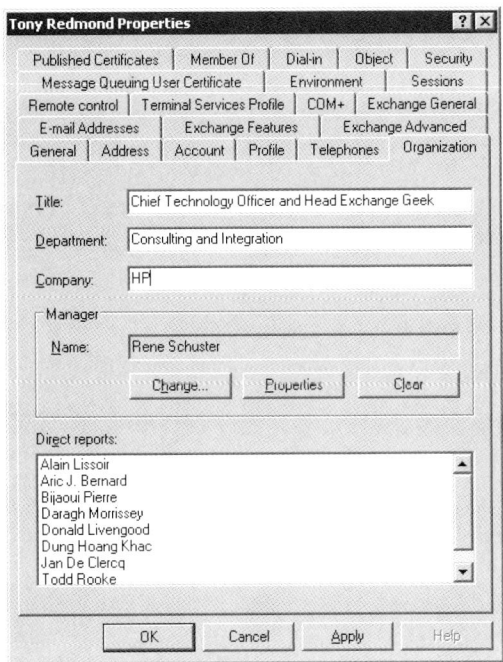

Figure 10.11
You can populate AD with organizational information.

held in many other directories within the company) or they fear the replication traffic that might be created. Others go to extremes and try to use the AD as the definitive repository of information about user accounts, including updating details such as organizational data (managers and their direct reports), as shown in Figure 10.11. However, going to this amount of trouble to populate the directory is rare, largely because it is so difficult to first find the data and then ensure that it is valid.

The AD Users and Computers snap-in requires only a user logon name and first name to be specified when you create a new account. Everything else, including a password, is optional. If you want the account to be able to use Exchange, you have to specify a minimum number of details—whether to create a mailbox, the server in which the mailbox is located, and the mailbox database to use—but aside from this, administrators often omit a lot of information when they create accounts. They might have to go back afterward and populate properties such as phone numbers, titles, addresses, department names, add the accounts to groups, and so on. You might update the accounts manually or through a directory synchronization process with something like an HR database that already holds these details. Left to their own devices, most administrators "forget" to complete the job. After all, once you create an account it is ready for its owner to use. Why should the administrator bother completing every possible attribute, assuming that he or she knows the value that should be in each attribute? The answer is that if you want to have a directory containing useful and consistent data, you have to populate and maintain the entries according to standards. These standards should define the properties (e.g., whether full department names are used or abbreviations, whether to include organizational detail such as the manager's name, what phone numbers are included, and so on).

Once you create accounts, it is a major challenge to keep the data in the directory accurate. All companies experience ongoing change. People take on new responsibilities, they change offices, get new phone numbers, and join new departments. Departments split and merge to form new entities. If you do not take care, the directory will quickly become outdated and stale. In this respect, Exchange suffers from the same flaw as all its predecessors. Users probably make a forgivable assumption that administrators or other privileged users will make all the necessary amendments. Because the AD is replicated everywhere through an organization, it is important to exert control over updates. However, it is silly to prevent users from being able to make changes to properties that are not very sensitive, such as their telephone numbers. In situations in which users cannot update their own directory information, it usually falls to help-desk staff to process update requests, which then leads to a need for tools to maintain directory information. Access to the AD Users and Computers snap-in is sufficient to maintain account and mailbox details, and you can impose suitable access control lists on an organizational unit basis to restrict update privileges to specific staff.

It is possible to avoid using the standard Windows administration tools, but you will have to build your own programs or buy a commercial directory maintenance program. On a programmatic basis, you can use either ADSI or LDAP calls to update the directory in a controlled manner, or generate an LDIF output file that contains the necessary commands to update the directory, which you then process through a batch run under the control of a privileged account. It is also possible to create LDIF output from other programs, such as an HR database, to update the AD with information. You can use a similar approach to allow users to update their own mailbox information. A program or Web browser can fetch information from the AD and display it to the user, who then updates whatever fields need to be changed. Ideally, the program will enforce standards for the entered data and make sure that it complies with standards. The program could write out an XML or other formatted file and email it to an administrator for verification and checking or simply update the directory using ADSI.

Other implementations of corporate messaging systems allow users to update their own directory details, so is this a competitive disadvantage for Exchange? Perhaps so, but allowing users to update their own directory data may affect the quality of the information in the directory. A lot depends on corporate culture and experience from previous messaging systems. If you have only ever used Exchange, then the fact that you cannot update your directory data will not come as a surprise. If people expect to be able to change their telephone numbers or make sure that their titles are correct, then Exchange can be a little frustrating. To deal with users' frustrations, it is best to explain why it is important that control is exerted over the directory, and then make sure that some mechanism is in place to allow users to update information in a controlled manner.

10.2.3 Restricting mailboxes

You do not have to reveal all mailboxes in the GAL. The "Hide from Exchange Address Lists" checkbox on a user account's Exchange Advanced property page controls whether a mailbox is included in address lists. You only see the Exchange Advanced property page (Figure 10.12) if you select the "View.Advanced Features" option for AD Users and Computers. Senior management or other individuals occupying sensitive posts are often excluded from directory listings, the email equivalent of an ex-directory telephone number. Exchange 2003 moves the "Protocol Settings" option from this property page to the Exchange Features property page.

The Delivery Restrictions button on the Exchange General Property page defines who is able to send messages to a mailbox. This is another common restriction requested by senior management, who sometimes do not want to have messages arriving from anyone outside their immediate staff or a selected group of users. In fact, many senior managers arrange to have two mailboxes. One appears in the GAL and is available for anyone to send messages to, while the second is hidden and known only by the set of people who can send messages to it. The second mailbox is used for business-critical email, while the first is usually monitored on a daily basis to see whether any staff complaints, suggestions, or other email has arrived and needs to be answered. As shown in Figure 10.13, distribution or security groups are an excellent way of managing those permitted to send messages to a mailbox, with exceptions made on an individual basis thereafter.

You can impose further restrictions on the mailbox quota and the size of messages that a user can send. Indeed, you can get even more restrictive by not letting particular users send messages via specific connectors. All of this

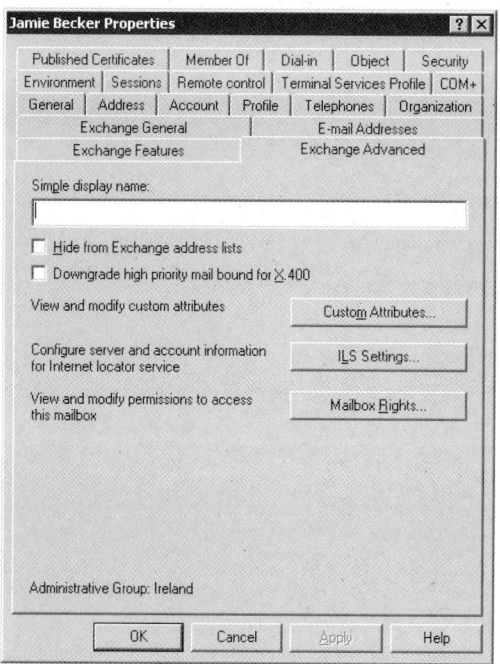

Figure 10.12
Exchange Advanced options for user accounts.

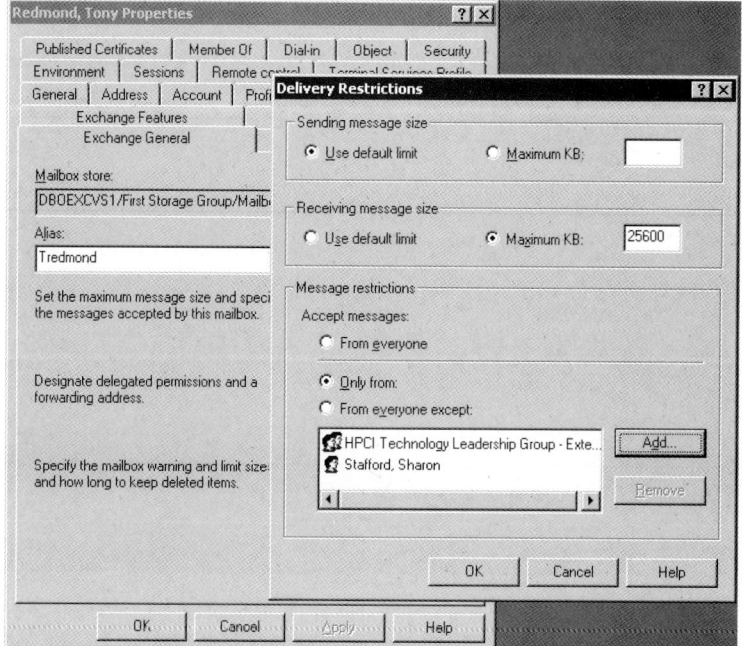

Figure 10.13
Defining who can send messages to a mailbox.

may sound a little paranoid, since you might think that it is best to allow free and complete communication across the whole user community. The spirit of this sentiment is admirable, but there are always situations in large implementations where it is nice to be able to tighten the screw a little. Consider the case of contract workers who arrive to help with a project for a couple of weeks. It is good to be able to give them a mailbox so that they can communicate with the rest of the project team, but it is even better to be able to provide them with a secure working environment that allows communication while denying users the chance to send confidential information out to the Internet via an SMTP connector.

Exchange 2000/2003 Enterprise Edition allows you to create multiple Mailbox Stores on any server, but perhaps you want to restrict some Stores to particular user groups. For example, you might want to have a Store that holds executive mailboxes, or one for members of a particular department or office. In these situations, you need to control who can add or move mailboxes to the Stores. By default, Exchange does not provide an obvious method to apply such control, but there is a way.

Let us assume that you have two security groups for Exchange administrators. One is for the Enterprise administrators, who have access to everything, and one is for people on the help desk, who take care of most user issues but should not have access to the special Mailbox Stores. To block access to the special stores, you need to:

1. Use the ADSIEDIT console to open the AD configuration naming context and browse through the Exchange configuration data to the entry for the Mailbox Store that you want to protect.

2. Edit the security property for the container (the Mailbox Store) and add the security group for the help-desk administrators. Set access for the "Read" permission to "Deny."

After the change is applied, Exchange hides the Mailbox Store whenever an administrator in the help-desk group is adding a mailbox to a Store or moving a mailbox from one Store to another. The same technique works at the storage group level, so you can hide a complete storage group if you choose.

10.2.4 Mailbox quotas

You set mailbox quotas either on an individual mailbox basis or through system policies that you apply to selected Mailbox Stores. System policies allow you to implement the same settings across a large user population in

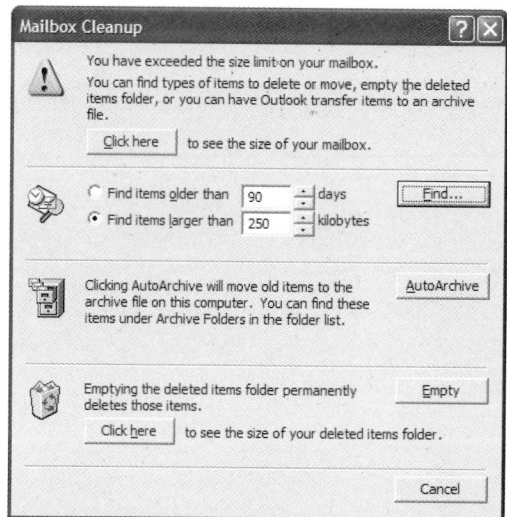

Figure 10.14
Actions Outlook users can take when they exceed quota.

a single operation, so it is a very convenient mechanism for administrators. Users are more concerned with the quota that you allocate, and they are especially concerned when they run into the brick wall of no more available quota and are unable to send or receive messages. The behavior of mail clients differs when a mailbox exceeds its quota. Some simply refuse to send or receive messages, while Outlook detects the condition and lets users know what they can do to clean up their mailboxes to free space (Figure 10.14). The easiest option is to empty the deleted items folder, but that may only free up a small amount of quota. The hardest and most time-consuming option is to go through your folders and figure out what you need to keep and discard everything else. Indeed, some companies believe that users waste so much valuable time on mailbox maintenance that it is easier and cheaper in the end to keep increasing quotas and adding disks to servers.

Determining appropriate values for mailbox quotas has long been a vexing question for Exchange administrators. If you use too low a value, users complain because they constantly exceed quota and have to stop work. Set it too high, and you end up with very large databases and extended backup times—and you can never be sure that all the data kept by users in their large mailboxes is vital corporate information. In fact, most of the time it is not, except in the eyes of the user. Three further issues increase the management problem: increased user demand for more graphical documents (so they are larger), the ease of attaching documents to messages in a simple drag-and-drop operation, and the fondness of users for including graphics such as corporate logos in their auto-signature files. These factors have increased the average size of a message on many corporate servers from circa 4 KB at the start of the 1990s to well over 100 KB today. Looking forward to an era when notes composed in digital ink on Tablets and handheld PCs may replace some of the typed memos sent today, it is safe to assume that the average size of a message will continue to increase. Certainly, one small digital ink note containing five or six lines of writing can easily occupy 200 KB, a good pointer to future demand. The larger the average message size, the fewer messages can be held in a set quota, and the more users complain. It is an ongoing battle that will continue, so a wise administrator might plan for 50 percent growth in mailbox space per year and be happy when actual growth dips under this amount.

Relatively speaking, disk storage is cheap today and continues to decline in price per GB, so the long-held argument that you need to restrict quotas to manage storage is not altogether accurate. When Exchange first shipped, it was common to find mailbox quotas of 20 MB or less. Now, even users of free email services can get this amount of space, and it is relatively uncommon to find such a low quota on a corporate Exchange server. Table 10.3 identifies mailbox quotas for different user types. Executive users justify their large mailbox sizes because they tend to receive more email than regular users and often have to keep email for legally defined periods. The largest single mailbox I have ever seen approached 3 GB, but I am sure that there are larger mailboxes in use.

Note that the AD Users and Computers UI and ESM (for both Exchange 2000 and 2003) impose a 2-GB limit on the values that you can assign to the cut-off points for storage warning, restrict send, and restrict send and receive. If you attempt to set a value past 2,097,151 (KB), AD Users and Computers signals an error and will not accept the value. Some

Table 10.3 *Mailbox Quota Allocation by User Type*

User Type	Mailbox Quota Range
Hosted (ASP)	5–15 MB
Standard corporate mailbox	30–100 MB
Heavy corporate user	100–250 MB
Executive user	250 MB–2 GB
Other users	Anything past 2 GB

users will need a larger quota, so you can either set the mailbox store or an individual mailbox to have no limit (in effect, the mailbox can grow as large as it needs) or set higher values by editing the values of the account's mDB-StorageQuota (storage warning), mDBOverQuotaLimit (prohibit send), and mDBOverHardQuota properties with ADSIEDIT. Exchange will respect changes made through ADSIEDIT, but you can only view the updated quotas through AD Users and Computers and will not be able to change them again except by using ADSIEDIT. Possibly, the logic behind the 2-GB limit here is due to the 2-GB limit for ANSI-format OSTs and PSTs, so you should be cautious about setting higher limits, especially if you use cached Exchange mode, unless you are sure that everyone uses Unicode-format OSTs and PSTs.

After you apply quotas, it is a good idea to take a proactive attitude to quota management. It is much better to know that a quota is about to expire and ask a user whether he or she needs more quota than to have a help-desk call logged by a frantic user who has suddenly discovered that he or she has run out of quota. You can also ask Outlook users to check for themselves on a regular basis, assuming that you tell them what their quota is in the first place! The simplest way to check current consumption is the "Show Folder Sizes" option, which generates a display similar to that shown in Figure 10.15. The difference between the "size" and "total size" fields is that the first value represents the size of all items in the folder itself, while the second represents the size of the items in the folder and all its subfolders (if any exist). Note that if you use Outlook 2003 in cached Exchange mode, you see tabs for "Local Data" (in your OST file) and "Server Data" (in your mailbox on the server). Exchange determines your quota based on data held in your server mailbox.

Figure 10.15
Viewing folder sizes from Outlook.

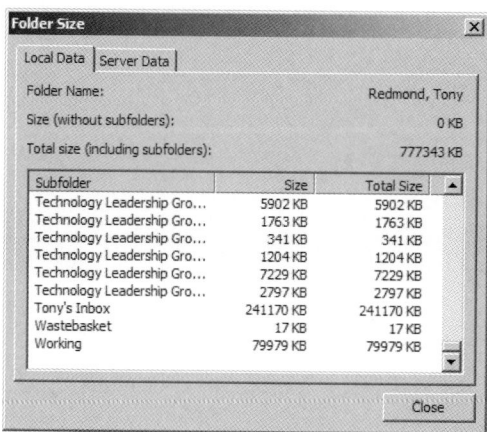

10.2 User access 737

The easiest way to review the status of user mailbox quotas is to expand the mailbox detail for a Store through ESM and use the "Export List" option to write the data to a CSV file, as shown in Figure 10.16. Unfortunately, you cannot export data from several stores or servers in one operation, so some manual intervention is necessary to combine data together for all users. If you are programmatically minded, you could dump this information into a database and perform ongoing analysis on quota use—an exercise that is always likely to result in a chart that shows a continued sharp upward rise in mailbox storage. (See Figure 10.16.)

You can also implement the Mailbox Manager to automatically scan, identify, and delete obsolete messages from mailboxes. This approach has the advantage that it preserves quota by eliminating junk from mailboxes. It also has a disadvantage in that users do not like automated tools making decisions about what messages to keep and what to delete.

Despite frequent requests, Microsoft does not support the customization of the text in the messages that the System Attendant sends to users when they exceed their mailbox quotas. It is possible to change this text, but only if you are willing to play with fire. You need a program called rlquiked.exe, which Microsoft publishes as part of its localization toolkit at

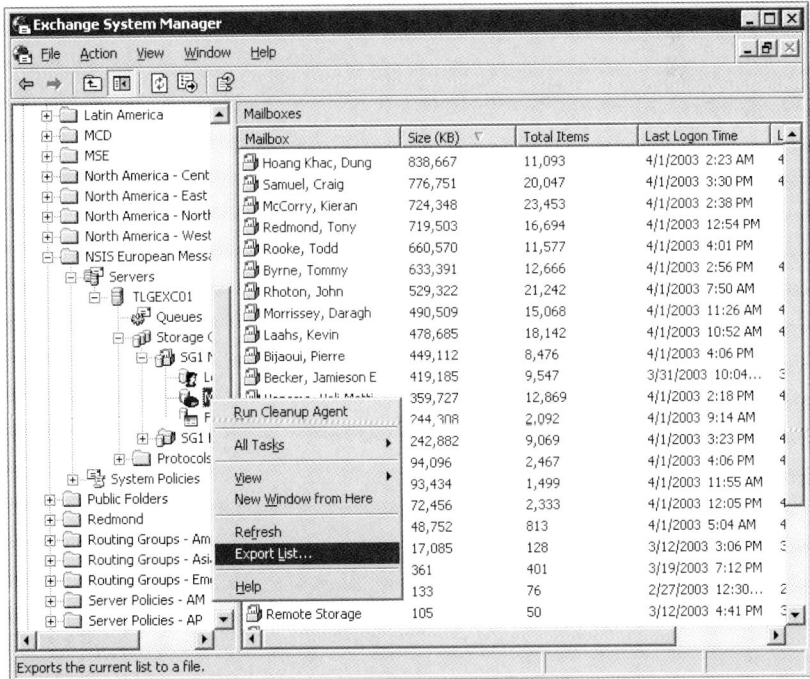

Figure 10.16
Listing mailbox quotas used in ESM.

Chapter 10

ftp://ftp.microsoft.com/softlib/mslfiles/rltools.exe. Engineers who generate language-specific versions of Exchange use this toolkit to replace English-language text with local versions, and you can use the same approach to generate your own text for system messages. To do this, proceed as follows:

- Note the text that you want to replace.
- Download rtltools.exe and extract rlquiked.exe.
- Take a copy of exchsrvr\bin\mdbsz.dll (the resource dll that contains all the strings) to make sure that you can go back to a starting point, just in case things go wrong.
- Run rlquiked.exe and open mdbsz.dll.
- Search for the text that you want to replace and make the change by double-clicking on the text string to open a text box where you can edit the content.
- Save the altered file to a temporary dll
- Stop the Information Store service and replace mdbsz.dll in exchsrvr\bin\ with the customized dll.
- Restart the Information Store service and check that everything works and that messages contain the customized text.

Perhaps as a response to the idea of people attempting to change message text without fully understanding how to go about it, the Exchange development group released some code called the Quota Service on http://www.gotdotnet.com/ in April 2004. This code works, but it is not fully polished. Nevertheless, it is a great start to the solution that hopefully will come in a future service pack or new version.

Playing around with code is not an exercise to practice on a production server, so try things out on a test server before you even attempt to put the customization into practice. Remember that Microsoft may overwrite mdbsz.dll in service packs, hot fixes, or new versions of Exchange, so any change that you make becomes another item to check before you bring new software into production. Finally, if you run into any problems with the Information Store, you will have to swap the original mdbsz.dll back before you can expect any help from PSS.

10.2.5 Mailbox surrogacy

Mailbox surrogacy or delegation means that users give permission to other users to take control of their mailboxes for specific purposes. The classic example is when managers grant access to a secretary or administrative assistant to process messages that arrive in their mailbox. Even today, some senior executives process their own electronic mail, but others are still at the stage where they demand that their assistants print out their messages each day for their perusal. They then mark the printed copies of the messages with their comments or replies and leave the marked-up messages with their assistants, who take care of sending the replies. Of course, you might think that these people are dinosaurs or belong to the "Pointy Haired Boss" class, but sometimes it is easier to read and understand printed copies of messages, especially for people who are uncomfortable with keyboard skills. Receiving email is great, but how often have you replied to a message after quickly browsing its contents only to realize shortly afterward that you completely misunderstood the point and have sent off some rubbish as a response?

In the early days of email, systems tended to be unsophisticated when compared with the systems we have today. The total feature set was limited to simple create, send, read, forward, and reply functions, and delegation was accomplished by telling other people your password. Your secretary could then log on and assume your identity, and as far as the system was concerned, it was you at the controls. System administrators rightly hated this method, because it totally compromised system security. Users do not tend to pay much attention to system administrators at the best of times, so they continued to do what was necessary to get through their work. Passwords have always been the bane of administrators' lives, especially when users keep passwords on convenient scraps of paper that they can store in desk drawers or paste underneath a keyboard for easy reference.

As email systems evolved, designers paid attention to eliminating security holes while they extended feature sets. Facilities to allow users to access other users' mailboxes in a controlled manner began to appear in the early 1990s, but even so, many users persist in these new-fangled ways and continue to exchange passwords quite happily. Exchange supports mailbox delegation, which means that a user is able to open more than one mailbox, subject to being granted the appropriate permission. MAPI clients are able to open multiple mailboxes concurrently by modifying the advanced properties of the Microsoft Exchange service provider (in the MAPI profile) to specify the names of the extra mailboxes they wish to open. Internet clients have to log on to each mailbox separately.

You can grant delegate access in two ways:

- Outlook users can grant access to their own mailboxes with the Tools | Options | Delegates option. Figure 10.17 shows the option in use

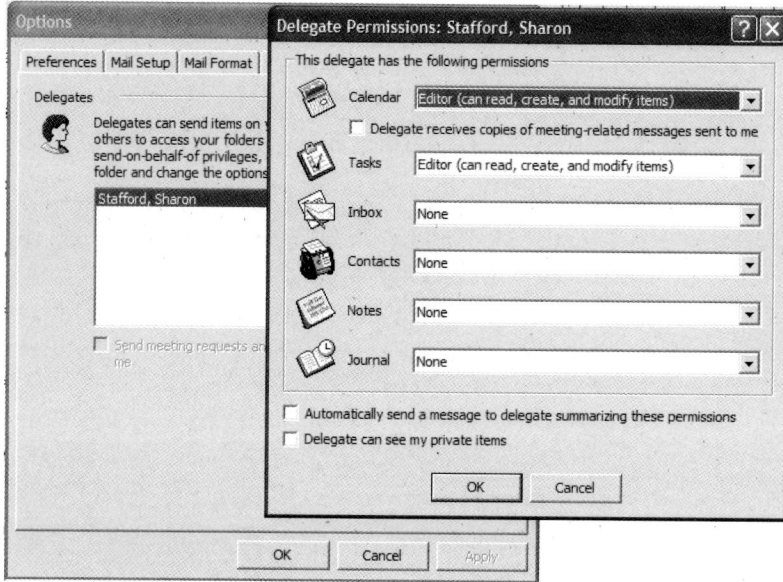

Figure 10.17
Granting delegate permission to folders from Outlook.

from Outlook 2000. Note that you can exert a certain amount of control over the options that another user can take within the mailbox. In most cases, administrative assistants or secretaries need to process calendar appointments and incoming email, but they do not necessarily have to set up new contacts. If you grant access to the Inbox folder, it means that delegates can move items to other folders as required.

- Administrators can grant the "Send on Behalf" access to a user's mailbox with the AD Users and Computers snap-in. Select the mailbox you want to grant access to, go to the Exchange General tab, and click the Delivery Options command button. Add the names of the accounts that will be allowed to access the mailbox and click OK (Figure 10.18). The degree of access control is much coarser, since you can't specify which folders a delegate has control over.

As with everything else in Exchange, Windows access control lists control delegate access. The Delivery Options screen also allows you to set a limit on the maximum number of recipients a user can add to a message. This is a feature intended to stop users from sending internal spam. The default value is "no limit," so in practical terms users can continue to add recipients to a message until they get bored. You can still send a message that exceeds a set limit, but the Routing Engine will reject the message when it examines the header to determine how to route the message. At this

10.3 User authentication

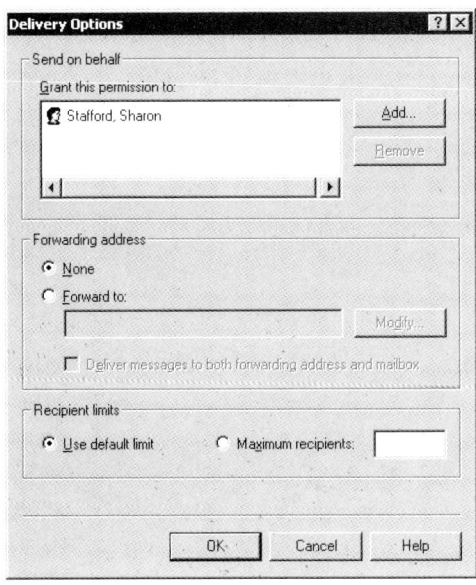

Figure 10.18
Allowing "Send on Behalf" permission for a mailbox from AD Users and Computers.

stage, the Routing Engine generates and sends a nondelivery notification to the originator.

Delegate access is a good example of a feature that is highly sensitive to local and company culture, and the attitude of users varies greatly, even after they have been trained on the use and benefit of the feature. Even busy executives sometimes resist allowing their assistants to have access to their mailbox. It may be that they wish to process incoming messages themselves, preferring to forward messages to be actioned when required. I certainly prefer this approach, mostly because my mailbox receives a mixture of confidential, personal, and normal business messages. Others are quite happy to allow their assistants to process all new messages and pass on those that require attention from the executive.

10.3 User authentication

Windows supports multiple authentication protocols. Kerberos V5[2] is the preferred and default protocol. Clients negotiate with DCs to decide on the authentication protocol to use, based on a common understanding. A DC will always attempt to use Kerberos first, and will revert to a down-level protocol if the client indicates that it cannot understand or support Ker-

---

2. Microsoft's implementation of Kerberos V5 is based on the definition as laid out in RFC 1510.

beros. If a server application supports Kerberos, it is said to be "Kerberized." Not all Windows applications have done the work to achieve this status; IIS has, but Exchange 2000 did not. This means that any client connection to an Exchange 2000 mailbox will use NTLM (the NT challenge/response mechanism), if clients need to authenticate their credentials before being allowed to connect to a mailbox. The situation is different if you run the combination of Exchange 2003 and Outlook 2003, since you can elect to use Kerberos authentication instead of NTLM. Do not rush to update your mailbox profile to specify Kerberos until you are quite sure that all servers, including those that host public folder replicas, are upgraded and can accept your Kerberos credentials.

Windows supports the concept of a single sign-on. This means that users should not have to enter their account and password information every time they wish to access an application or use a resource such as a file share. Instead, their credentials are established when they log on to a domain, and those credentials can be accessed and used by applications as the need arises. When a user logs on to a DC, he or she provides account name and password. In return, if the DC recognizes the credentials, Windows grants the user an access token that contains his or her Security Identifier (SID) and the SIDs of any group the user belongs to.

Every mailbox is associated with a Windows account. Unless you configure Outlook to prompt for a user name and password each time it connects, it will attempt to use the credentials established by your domain logon. You will only see a separate logon dialog for Exchange if the credentials fail. Figure 10.19 illustrates the password dialog that Outlook displays to collect new credentials. Outlook 2000 shows a need to support connections to Windows NT servers by imposing a 15-character restriction on the length of the domain name, a fact that might come as a surprise if you have implemented longer domain names (as is now possible in Windows 2000/2003).

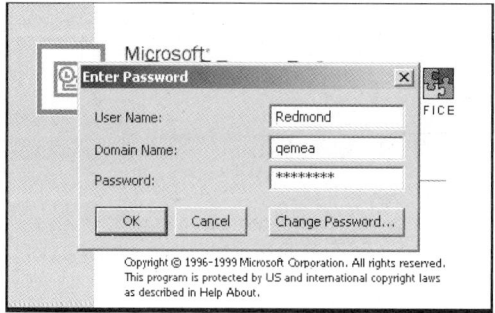

Figure 10.19
Providing a password to log on to Exchange 2000 (Outlook 2000).

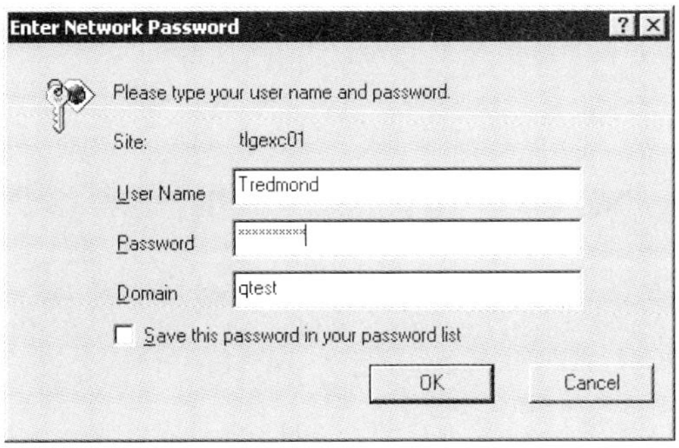

10.3 User authentication 743

Figure 10.20
Providing credentials to OWA.

By default, Outlook Web Access does not present users with a logon dialog to specify their mailboxes, servers, and domains before connecting to Exchange. Everything proceeds based on the URL specified to access the mailbox, which may already contain the name of the server and the alias for the mailbox. The browser is able to access the cached set of local credentials and pass these to IIS to authenticate when OWA makes the initial connection. If the credentials are invalid or not present, the browser presents a dialog to allow users to provide the necessary information, as shown in Figure 10.20.

Outlook Express and other POP3 or IMAP clients do not use profiles in the same way as MAPI. Instead, you specify details about the account you

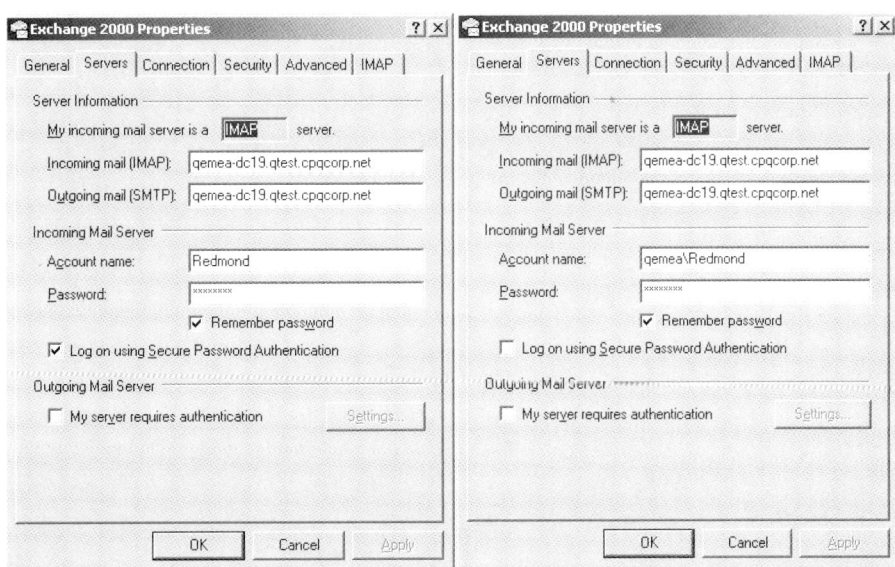

Figure 10.21   *Outlook Express account details.*

Chapter 10

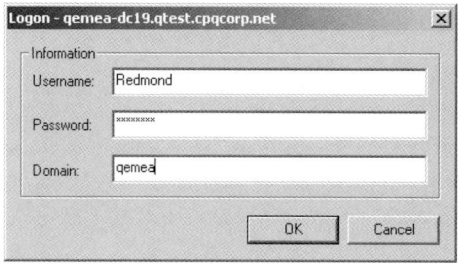

Figure 10.22
Secure IMAP logon to Exchange.

want to use through a client-specific option. In the case of Outlook Express, this is the Tools.Accounts option. Multiple accounts can be set up, so it is quite possible to have one account for business use that accesses Exchange and another that uses a free mail service such as hotmail.com for personal messages.

The account properties specify whether the client uses the POP3 or IMAP protocol to retrieve messages, the name of the server for incoming mail, and the name of the SMTP server that will send messages on your behalf. While they can be different, in most cases the names of the incoming and outgoing server are the same. As you can see in Figure 10.21, you can specify credentials in two ways. The left-hand screen has checked the "Log on using Secure Password Authentication," which means that you are required to provide credentials through a logon dialog (Figure 10.22). On the other hand, the right-hand screen has left the checkbox blank and has inserted some domain information in the account name field. The combination of domain name, account name, and password is enough to log on to the server without filling in any dialog.

MAPI clients access the AD via a pass-through proxy. All other clients use LDAP whenever they need to retrieve information from the directory, and a connection to the AD may require the client to provide password credentials.

10.4 Defining a document retention policy

The concept of a document retention policy first briefly appears in the discussion on Outlook archiving to a PST (section 10.8.1). Email archiving is a very personal activity and its execution depends entirely on users, so to some degree you have to educate users about how to process email effectively in terms of how they file messages and how long they decide to keep them.

10.4 Defining a document retention policy

In the past, department secretaries kept business records and performed filing to ensure that they could retrieve information. They also took care of tasks such as archiving, disposing of obsolete papers, clearing out file cabinets, and so on. Today, many secretaries have disappeared, and users, all of whom have the ability to implement their own document management policy within their own mailboxes, PC file structure, and other repositories, take care of information.

You may not be able to do much about how people organize data on their PCs, but you can influence user behavior by imposing draconian mailbox quotas to force users to keep clean mailboxes, or you can use the Exchange Mailbox Manager to automate mailbox cleanups with minimal user input. For many companies, Mailbox Manager is an essential part of document retention, because it allows you to exercise some control over people's packrat behavior. However, you must factor the Mailbox Manager into an overall document retention policy that you set down and communicate clearly. It is not enough to simply write down and send a policy around to everyone. If users are not educated about how they can implement the policy and the tools that are available to help them, it is unlikely that the policy will be successful. The components of a document retention policy often include the following:

- Setting mailbox quotas for different types of users
- Basic advice on how long users should keep messages and the tools used to help users stay within the policy
- How to decommission mailboxes when users leave the organization
- Whether you archive messages in some manner or permanently delete them

The reasons why you need a document retention policy include:

- Data management: You want to remove redundant or unneeded data from the Exchange Store so that you do not have to continue to manage it. In particular, it is very expensive to have to back up unwanted messages daily, so it makes sense to reduce the size of the Store databases by deleting messages as soon as they are no longer required.

- Compliance: Your industry may operate under the legal requirement to manage information in a specific manner. For example, financial traders in the United States must keep records of all communications with clients, including email, to comply with U.S. Securities and Exchange Commission (SEC) regulations.

- Disaster recovery: If a disaster happens, you need to know what documents are most important and should be recovered first and what you can leave for later.

- Support for litigation or defense against litigation: If you want to sue someone, you may need to recover or access email or documents and need to know where you can find them and then recover copies. The same is true if someone sues you, in which case the presiding judge may rule that you have to provide copies of messages sent by nominated individuals over some period. Do not assume that deleting messages means that they are unrecoverable, because a judge can require a company to retrieve information from backup tapes, search user files to discover printed copies, look through PSTs to find email that users archive themselves, or even find copies of messages that users sent outside the company. In this respect, email is similar to cockroaches: You think you have eliminated them from your environment only to discover that they can come back from backups or other sources. While purging systems and restricting users to small mailbox quotas is good idea, it is definitely not a defense against litigation.

- Document management and publication: You should decide how users most effectively communicate and share information via the different mechanisms that may be available, including email, instant messaging, network file shares, public folders, and document management systems (including SharePoint Portal Server). You might even consider giving advice to users about when it is appropriate to use email to communicate. Sometimes, a different tool such as Instant Messaging (IM) is a better choice. For example, if you want to ask someone a question and he or she is online, an IM conversation is a very convenient and effective communication mechanism. Even better, unlike email, unless you take steps to capture the content, IM conversations leave no trace on servers.

Every industry is different and requirements vary from country to country, so no hard and fast rule exists. One thing is for sure: If you give users free reign, they will swiftly fill every available disk with data—not all of which is vital.

10.5 The Exchange Mailbox Manager

The Mailbox Manager tool provides an automated way for administrators to enforce a basic email retention policy for mailbox contents. First introduced in Exchange 5.5 SP3, Microsoft totally rewrote the original MAPI code to use ADO and OLE/DB and integrated the Mailbox Manager with Exchange System Manager (ESM). Microsoft was not able to complete this work before it shipped Exchange 2000 in October 2000, so the Mailbox Manager made a delayed appearance in SP1. The Mailbox Manager is now an essential part of any administrator's toolkit, and for more reasons than just keeping mailboxes clean.

10.5.1 Email and discovery

The problem of embarrassing text appearing in discovered email is not new, as Oliver North so convincingly proved when investigators recovered incriminating email from an IBM PROFS mainframe system to display at the Iran-Contra hearings in 1987. Discovery actions are increasingly common, because lawyers understand that asking to scan internal email is a great way to find evidence that people create and store themselves. For example, New York State Attorney General Eliot Spitzer showed that email sent (on an Exchange system) by Merrill Lynch analyst Henry Blodget indicated he had not been as candid as he could with investors, and Jack Grubman's messages to WorldCom executives provided part of the case against Salomon Smith Barney. According to IDC[3] in late 2002, businesses generate 13 billion emails daily. Many of these messages end up in mailboxes waiting for users to clean them out or for lawyers to come along and peruse their contents. In addition, backup tapes hold billions of deleted messages that investigators can ask companies to recover during discovery actions.

The problem is that people do not consider emails to be business documents. The long-time rule is never to put anything into a message that you would not like the public to read, but everyone ignores this rule. Users are happy to send each other the most confidential and interesting information, including attachments that hold critical business or personal data. There is a comfortable informality about an email exchange with friends or business colleagues where users express emotions, lay out views about competitors or partners, or make statements that they would never say in public. Apart from the messages kept on servers, copies exist in offline replicas on laptops or partial replicas on hand-held devices such as Pocket PCs, smartphones, or other handheld devices—all of which are commonly stolen or lost. Most thieves only want to sell what they have stolen, but some are interested in what they find on a laptop and may even use the information for blackmail.

---

3. Quoted in Forbes.com, November 25, 2002.

In the United States, statutory requirements further restrict what companies can do. For example, the Sarbanes-Oxley act makes it illegal to destroy or attempt to destroy any document relating to a federal investigation, while the SEC mandates the capture of any electronic communication relating to trading activities.

You can certainly encrypt email, but investigators can demand that you recover the personal keys of users to allow them to read the messages. It is possible that the keys are not available, as is the case when users protect messages with personal encryption tools such as PGP; but it is not feasible to ask thousands of users to install such tools and then manage the process of distributing public keys to anyone they need to communicate with.

Some companies deploy solutions such as Secure Mail from Tumbleweed (www.tumbleweed.com) to scan messages for inappropriate content, key phrases that might indicate illegal actions, and so on. Companies in the financial sector that have to comply with various laws can scan outgoing messages to ensure that traders are not giving inappropriate advice to clients. In other situations, you may simply want to ensure that users do not include references to material such as pornographic jokes, which might seem amusing to the sender but can quickly lead to a lawsuit if the recipient finds the message distasteful. It is interesting to note that in some cases companies have found that network use has declined significantly as soon as they implemented email scanners, possibly because users quickly realized that the system would detect and report any potentially undesirable activities on their part. Of course, if you do implement an email scanner, it is only fair to inform users that the scanner is active as well as the type of content it is checking. Apart from anything else, letting people know exactly where the boundaries exist may avoid a future defense of "no one told me that this was forbidden" if you have to take action against an individual.

Other products, such as the Policy Manager product from Omina Policy Systems (http://www.disappearing.com/products/policy_manager/) integrate with Outlook to stop users from forwarding messages outside the company and implement strict retention and compliance policies. Another set of products, such as those from Authentica (www.authentica.com), focus on implementing "electronic shredding" by giving messages a set lifetime, after which they will automatically disappear, or preventing unauthorized users from reading messages by removing the ability to forward or print email or cut-and-paste content from one message to another.

Microsoft is entering the field with the introduction of its rights management protection initiative, which aims to protect electronic information through policies that you define for user access, as well as which actions

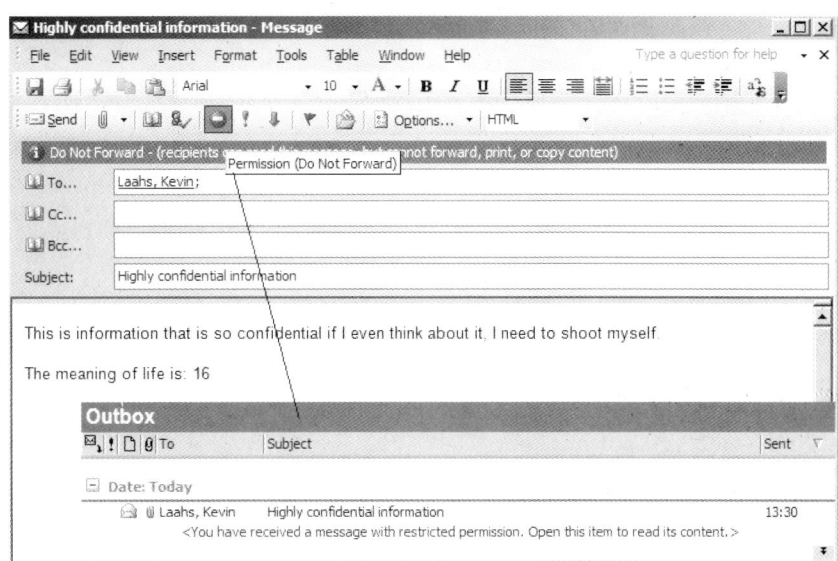

Figure 10.23
A secret Outlook message.

someone can take with information—for example, whether users can print, forward, or edit the data. Microsoft will implement this technology through its Windows 2003–based Rights Management Services (RMS), using XML and XrML (rights expression language standard) to define and manage the digital rights required to access and manipulate data. When you install and commission a rights management server, you can then install client extensions for Office applications and Web browsers to force them to comply with restrictions. For example, Figure 10.23 shows how Outlook 2003 incorporates an icon to allow users to mark messages that contain protected data. In this case, the recipient is able to read the message, but he or she cannot forward or print it or cut information out of the body and paste it into another file. Installing the rights management extensions for Office applications is only the start, since you also need to figure out how to manage the underlying infrastructure and support users who complain that they cannot access messages for one reason or another.

The important point is to establish a policy that clearly states what your company's stand is on the transport of confidential information inside email and how users should retain information. You can always delete some messages immediately after you read them; others you probably need to keep until the completion of a project or other activity. Implementing automated tools such as the Mailbox Manager can help keep mailboxes clean and remove messages after specific periods while leaving certain folders untouched.

10.5.2 Email retention policies

Mailbox management is only one part of an email retention policy, which may also include how to allocate and control mailbox quotas, how users deal with confidential information, virus protection, scanning for inappropriate content on outgoing messages, antispam protection, archiving, and so on. Most Exchange administrators begin with mailbox quotas, and we have seen a steady growth in the size of mailboxes from the average 25 MB or so allocated in 1996–1997 to an average of 100 MB today. You must protect every Exchange server against viruses. Servers that are unprotected by an integrated antivirus product have administrators who border on stupidity. Archiving continues to be of interest, with a lot of activity in the financial sector in order to satisfy legislative requirements. The most sophisticated archiving products implement policies that automate movement of data from user mailboxes into hierarchical storage mechanisms, together with appropriate mechanisms to inform users when data is archived, and to allow them to retrieve information as needed. At the other end of the scale, you can use Outlook's archiving feature to move items from server mailboxes into PSTs.

Every organization is different, and an email retention policy that fits all needs does not exist. The important point is to consider the type of policy that might be appropriate within an organization, integrate it with other sources of data such as network file shares and Web servers, and then work out how to implement the policy. Out-of-the-box tools such as the Mailbox Manager can help, but they are only fully effective when integrated into an overall plan for information management. However, even when an overall plan is not available, Mailbox Manager helps users to manage their mailbox quotas.

10.5.3 Defining a policy for mailbox management

You can divide a mailbox management policy into four main parts:

- The action enforced by the policy for items that meet the criteria stated in the policy. The available choices are:
  - Generate a report and send it to the mailbox owner and take no further action.
  - Move the items to the Deleted Items folder, where the items will either remain or be deleted the next time the user exits the mailbox (the exact action depends on a client setting).

10.5 The Exchange Mailbox Manager

- Move the items to a set of folders under "System Cleanup," from where users can move the items back into other folders if they wish.
- Delete the items immediately. Note that deleted items remain in the Deleted Items cache. Users can recover these items from the cache if they wish.

■ The criteria (such as the age of items) that the Mailbox Manager uses to check items in each folder. Individual criteria are set for the set of default folders that appears in every user's mailbox (Inbox, Tasks, Calendar, and so on) and you can add additional folders. A "catch-all" setting for all other folders is also set.

■ Whether or not to send a notification message to each mailbox's owner after the Mailbox Manager completes processing all the folders in the mailbox.

■ Whether the Mailbox Manager should exclude selected message classes from processing. Typically, you only need to take this option when Outlook uses customized message forms for applications such as expense or time reporting, in which case you may wish to exclude the message class used for these forms.

Note that you can only have a single active mailbox management policy for a recipient. You can certainly define multiple policies, but the System Attendant only respects the first that it finds.

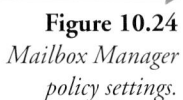

Figure 10.24
Mailbox Manager policy settings.

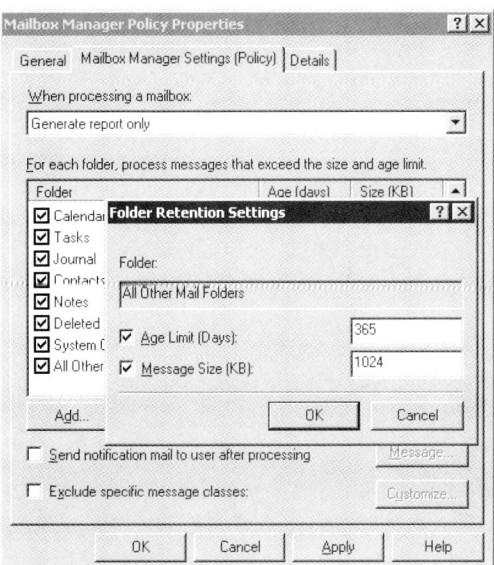

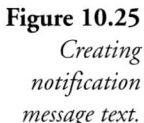
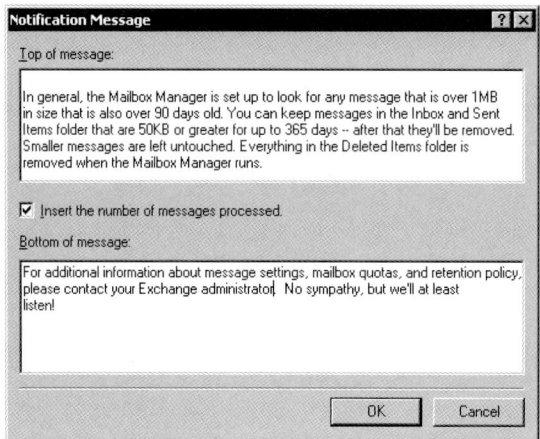

Figure 10.25
Creating notification message text.

Mailbox Manager can check items based on their size (in KB), age (since created or last modified), or either value on its own. These settings are folder specific. As an example, Figure 10.24 shows the check for "All Other Mail Folders" being set to 365 days and 1,024 KB. In other words, Mailbox Manager examines the folder to find any item that is older than one year and larger than 1 MB. Being able to establish criteria for every folder enables enormous flexibility, if you want to take advantage of this capability. For example, you could allow users to have a special folder that is never checked that acts as a "dumping ground" for large documents or items that the users want to keep. If defined in the policy, the System Attendant generates and sends a notification message to the mailbox owner to inform him or her what has happened during processing. You define the text of the notification message within the recipient policy, as shown in Figure 10.25. Note that the text is completely plain and the editor does not support bolding, underlining, or other text effects.

10.5.4 Running Mailbox Manager

After a suitable recipient policy is defined and applied, the Mailbox Manager runs according to a schedule set through the mailbox management properties of a target Exchange server (Figure 10.26), or it can be started manually (Figure 10.27). Note that you can start Mailbox Manager processing on a server, but nothing happens if you have not defined a suitable recipient policy to select the mailboxes on that server. Unlike the previous version of Mailbox Manager, which is able to process mailboxes on a remote server, the current version only processes mailboxes on the same server.

10.5 The Exchange Mailbox Manager

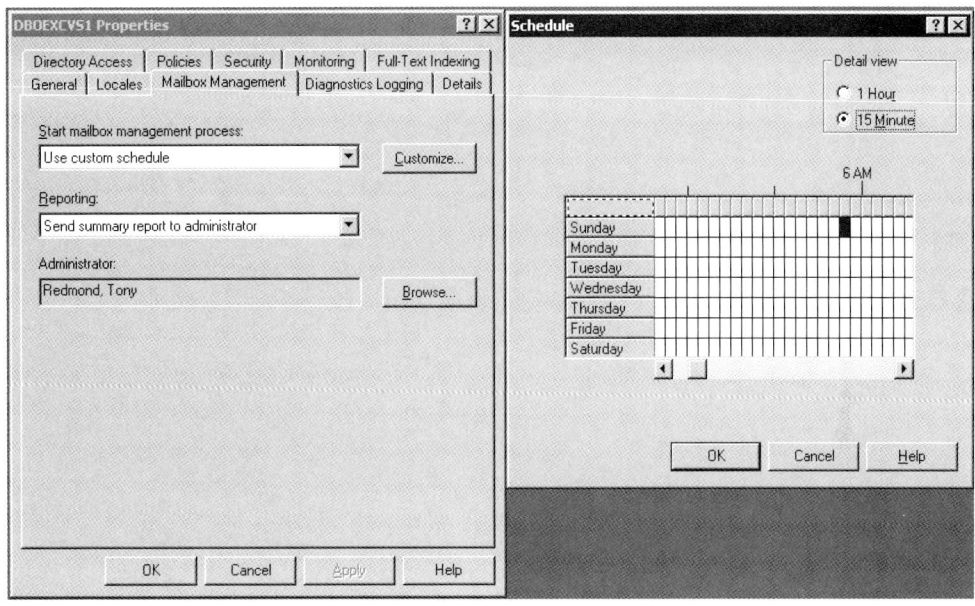

Figure 10.26 *Mailbox management server properties.*

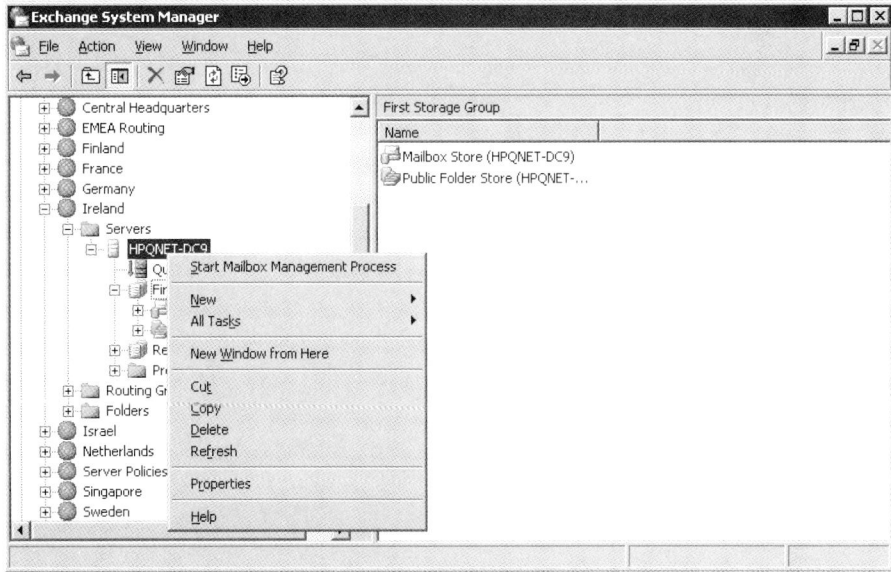

Figure 10.27 *Starting the Mailbox Manager.*

In general, Mailbox Manager processing generates a heavy load on a server, so it is unwise to start or schedule a run during peak user times. The standard options are to run the Mailbox Manager at midnight on either Saturday or Sunday, or to use a custom schedule. Anecdotal evidence suggests that the Mailbox Manager can generate an extra 20 percent load for a server when it is active, although your mileage will vary depending on server configuration, the number of mailboxes, the number of folders and items in the mailboxes, and the load generated by users during a Mailbox Manager run.

Users are likely to be surprised when you put the Mailbox Manager to use, especially if you have not made any great effort previously to control mailbox quotas. Apart from the concept that a system process can trawl through their mailboxes to (in their minds) arbitrarily select and delete items, users do not like sudden changes to their work conditions. It is, therefore, a good idea to educate users about the need for email retention policies and position Mailbox Manager as a way of helping to relieve users from the need to go through old messages themselves.

It is also a good idea to start slowly and build toward the type of email retention policy that you want to achieve. Users will probably protest if you start by deleting every item that is more than 30 days old, but they are unlikely to worry as much if you begin by looking for items that are six months old and larger than 1 MB. After running Mailbox Manager for three months, it becomes part of background system maintenance, similar to downtime due to planned server software upgrades, and you can tighten the retention criteria. Apart from anything else, starting with a loose retention policy restricts the possibility that you will make a mistake and end up deleting far more than you want. The concept of automated mailbox cleanup is not new and has existed in enterprise messaging systems since the mid-1980s. At that time, there were examples where enthusiastic system administrators deleted every message on a server. This results in very clean mailboxes and databases that are easy to maintain but also results in angry users. For this reason, you should run the Mailbox Manager first in report-only mode before progressing to a run that deletes items.

10.5.5 Mailbox Manager notification messages

The Mailbox Manager notes the number of messages that meet the set criteria as it processes each folder. The Mailbox Manager merges the complete results with the notification text from the recipient policy to create a notification message, which the System Attendant then sends to the mailbox owner. Figure 10.28 shows a sample notification message. Note that the

10.5 The Exchange Mailbox Manager

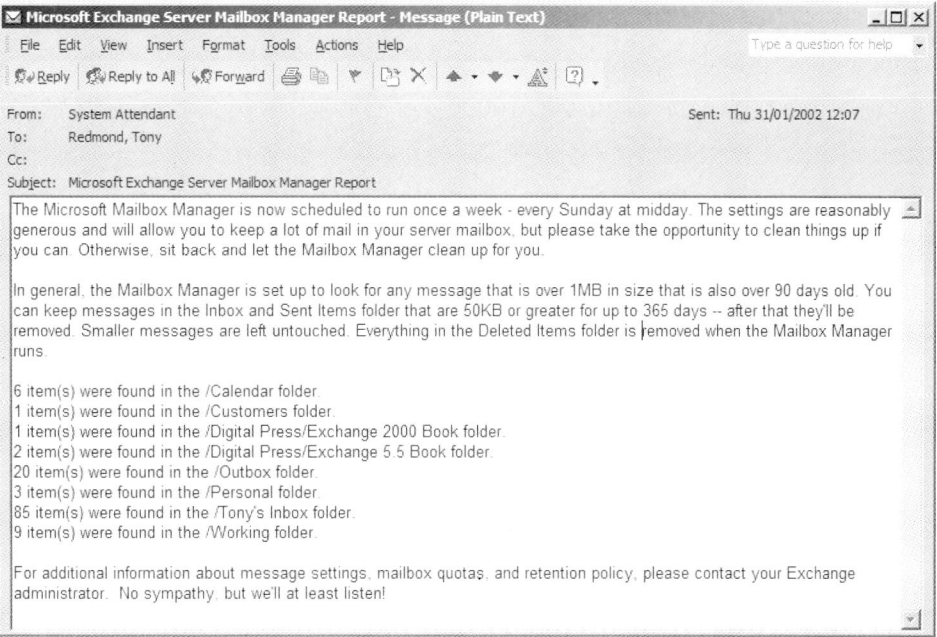

Figure 10.28 *User notification message.*

text from the recipient policy is inserted as a header and footer for the message. If no messages meet the criteria, the text between the header and footer is blank. Users may not realize that a background process is checking their mailboxes, so it is a good idea to customize the notification text both to inform users about what is happening and to tell them what to do if they have a problem. The example text explains that the Mailbox Manager looks for messages that are larger than 1 MB and over 90 days old and performs specific checks on the Inbox and Outbox folders. The remarks that close off the message are probably inappropriate in most environments, but some users may still possess a sense of humor after they receive a note such as this.

After Mailbox Manager completes processing all mailboxes on a server, it generates a summary message for the administrator, as set in the properties of the server. The summary message (Figure 10.29) states the start and finish times, the number of mailboxes processed, the number of messages that meet the set criteria for removal, and the total size of these messages.

You can gain maximum advantage by implementing the Mailbox Manager within an overall email retention policy, but even if you choose not to do this, the tool is a quick and simple way to implement a level of control over mailbox contents on an Exchange server. Before implementing, make

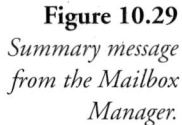

Figure 10.29
Summary message from the Mailbox Manager.

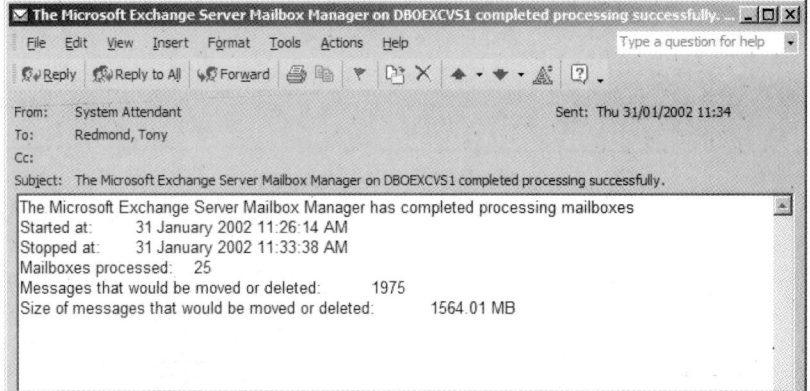

sure that you advise users that the Mailbox Manager will process their mailboxes, so that users are not surprised when they receive the notification messages.

10.5.6 Mailbox Manager diagnostics

As with all Exchange processes, the Mailbox Manager usually only logs important or critical events. The Mailbox Manager runs under the System Attendant process, so you have to increase the diagnostic logging level for the MSExchangeSA service if you suspect that things are not working. Figure 10.30 shows the properties of a server with the "Diagnostic Logging" page selected. The active services are listed, and you can select one of the service categories to increase logging—in this case, we want to increase logging for the Mailbox Management category, which is set to maximum. Exchange is a verbose application and logs a large number of events whenever you turn the logging level up. With maximum logging enabled, you will see the following events (with the number and meaning shown):

- (9214) Mailbox Manager processing starts on a server
- (9221) Start processing a mailbox (mailbox name is listed)
- (9220) Recipient policy is applied to the mailbox
- (9224) Total of items and their size found in the mailbox is reported
- (9225) Start processing a folder
- (9228) Number of items and size found in the folder is reported
- (9303) Number of items and size to be deleted is reported (see Figure 10.30)

10.6 Archiving messages

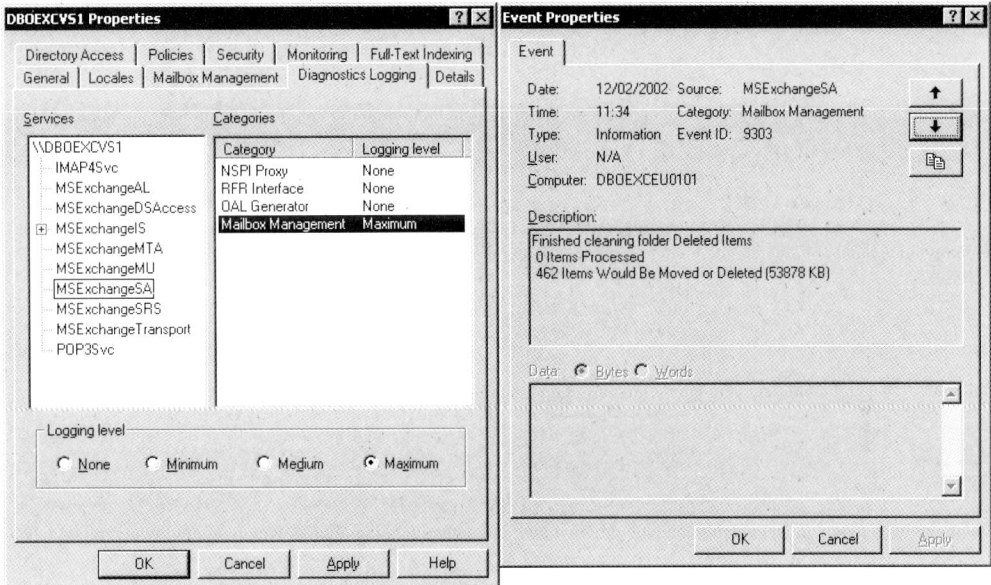

Figure 10.30   *Mailbox Manager diagnostics.*

- (9302) Finished cleaning a mailbox
- (9215) Mailbox Manager completes processing and reports how many items (and their size) it has removed

You may also see event 1022 followed by event 9231, which means that the Mailbox Manager is unable to log on to a mailbox. The usual reason is that an administrator has mail-enabled a user, but the mailbox is not yet created because Exchange only creates the mailbox when a user logs on for the first time.

10.6 Archiving messages

U.S. SEC rule 17-4A requires brokers and dealers to retain physical records of documents relating to transactions. The retention period is either three or six years, depending on the category of record. The SEC issued an amendment in February 1997 to cover email and stated that companies must treat email messages in the same way as paper correspondence. This requirement means that any company working in the U.S. financial community must retain all email messages in physical (printed on paper) or electronic form.

Other government agencies in the United States enforce similar requirements. For example, the FBI requires any company under investigation to retain messages for at least six months. The "Sunshine Law" enacted by the State of Florida requires that all government correspondence should be available to the public. This is similar to the situation in Sweden, where reporters are able to examine the prime minister's mail to see if anything interesting has arrived. The U.K. Civil Evidence Act (1995) lays down legal guidance for the admissibility of email as evidence in court cases. Other countries are likely to follow the lead established by the United States, United Kingdom, and Sweden, which poses an interesting problem for anyone who relies on email systems as a vital mechanism for internal communications. Indeed, the rise in popularity of Instant Messaging (IM) almost as a "behind the scenes" communication mechanism is largely because people say things when they communicate electronically that they would never say in public. The major advantage of most IM conversations is that they disappear into the ether as soon as the conversation is over, unless you use one of the IM applications that log conversations to comply with legal requirements.

As a concept, message journaling is not difficult to master. The major challenge is to determine the best place in the system to intercept messages to make copies. It is important that journaling can capture all email passing through the system—messages sent to local recipients as well as those sent to external recipients via a connector. A client-based solution is unacceptable, because it requires you to install and maintain code on every client. Server-side capturing is necessary to achieve any degree of scalability.

Message journaling was first featured in Exchange 5.5 SP1. Because it was part of a service pack (which means that no user interface changes are normally possible), Microsoft implemented journaling through a set of changes made to the Information Store, IMS, and MTA to force all messages to pass along prescribed paths so they could be copied into an archive location. There was no user interface, the documentation was sparse, you had to enable journaling through a set of system registry entries, and you could only capture messages rather than the complete set of items that can flow through an Exchange server. The journal location was normally a disk directory; you had to move manually the contents of the journal location to a more permanent location (such as a CD) on a regular basis.

Exchange 2000/2003 archiving allows you to:

- Archive or journal messages for a Mailbox Store: You can instruct Exchange to capture all messages that it delivers to mailboxes in a par-

10.6 Archiving messages

ticular Store by changing the properties of the Store to enable archiving and specifying where to capture messages. Archiving begins as soon as you click on the OK or Apply buttons, so this is something you do not want to do unless you are ready to handle the volume of messages that an Exchange server can capture daily. The destination can be either another mailbox (anywhere in the organization) or a public folder. You can also direct the messages to a contact that points to an SMTP or other external address, if you really want to have messages flow to an external location—which might be valid if some archiving software processes the messages when Exchange delivers them. However, you must enable archiving on each Store, since no server policy exists for this purpose. Best practice is to use a mailbox specially designated to capture and store archived messages, and this is required if you want to capture messages sent to BCC: addressees. Make sure that you allocate sufficient storage to whatever destination you use to hold archived messages and be sure to clear out the messages that accumulate regularly. (See Figure 10.31.)

- Capture incoming and outgoing messages: You can implement a transport sink to capture copies of all incoming messages as they pass through the transport engine. You will have to write the code in the transport sink yourself or seek a commercial product for this purpose.

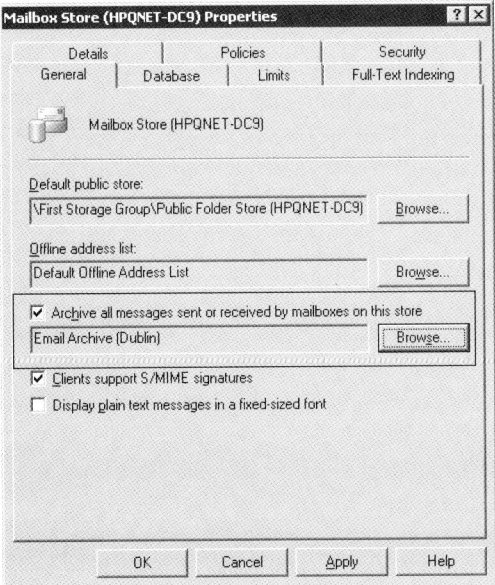

Figure 10.31
Enabling archiving on a Mailbox Store.

- Implement user-based Outlook archiving: Users can decide to archive their own messages to Personal Folder Files (PSTs) on a regular basis.

- Deploy third-party products and add-ons: A variety of commercial products exists to add full-feature archiving and retrieval functionality to Exchange, including the KVS Enterprise Vault (www.kvsinc.com), HP's ILM or Information Management Lifecycle (www.hp.com), and IXOS eCONserver (www.ixos.com). These products can capture large quantities of email traffic and utilize Hierarchical Storage Management (HSM) systems to enable fast access to specific messages. Apart from archiving messages, these solutions also focus on the benefits of clearing old messages out of user mailboxes to reduce the size of Store databases and thus the amount of administrative work required to maintain Exchange servers.

- Exchange 2003 SP1 adds the ability to journal to a custom recipient and expands distribution groups before messages are committed to the journal. However, these features do not make Exchange journaling a full-fledged data management product.

If you want to use the standard mailbox archiving, it is best to gather all the mailboxes that you need to capture mail for into a single Store or storage group rather than enabling archiving on many different Stores. Make sure that you allocate enough mailbox or public folder quota to the selected destination, since it fills up quickly, especially on a busy server. Encrypted messages pose a specific challenge for any archival system. Because the archiving software captures and stores messages in the same form as they pass through the messaging infrastructure, they end up in the archive in encrypted format. The archiving software cannot attempt to decrypt the content, because it has no access to the private keys used to secure the content. Administrators can recover keys for users who are enrolled in Exchange advanced security and can then use these keys to decrypt messages, but you can do nothing with messages secured with third-party tools such as PGP.

It is probably a good idea to differentiate at this point between SMTP archiving (see section 9.13) and message archiving (or journaling). The first and most obvious difference is that SMTP archiving works based on messages flowing through an SMTP virtual server (e.g., the VS that services an SMTP connector to the Internet), whereas you enable message archiving for every maiLbox Store that you want to journal messages. The next big difference is that SMTP archiving captures messages to a folder on the server, but you can direct message archiving to various destinations, all of which are usually easier to organize and search than a folder. One good way

10.6 Archiving messages   761

of thinking about these options is that SMTP archiving is really a debug or analysis tool designed to allow administrators to see which traffic is flowing across SMTP connectors, whereas message archiving allows organizations to capture messages to satisfy internal or external requirements.

Before making any decision about what style of archiving to implement, make sure that the selected technology (Exchange or third party) meets any legislative requirements your company is subject to as well as the needs of the company. In addition, ensure that you incorporate archiving into the standard operating procedures for Exchange, so that operators check that archiving is working properly daily, that the archiving destination does not fill up, and that any transfer to a more permanent archiving location such as an HSM works. You should also consider procedures to recover messages from the archive and the conditions under which such recoveries are possible. For example, can a user request or initiate a recovery operation if the recovery requires an operator to locate and mount a tape or other removable media? Does the user need prior authorization from a senior manager? How do you factor archives into the organization's overall data retention policy? How long do you maintain archives and how do you dispose of the archives? Finally, how do you maintain user privacy and prevent administrators and other privileged access holders from having access to confidential information that is probably present in the archive? Answers should be in place for these questions before you implement any archiving strategy.

10.6.1 Internal snooping (but nicely)

Government inspectors and other investigators love to review the contents of Mailbox Stores, public folders, and archives during discovery actions. These operations are carried out under legal order and according to strict standards, and there is normally nothing that you can do except comply with the order and make the necessary data available.

Sometimes, it may be necessary for you to do some snooping of your own—always with prior authorization and backing from your management and usually in response to a management request. For example, let us assume that your company has received a complaint that someone is sending messages to a domain that you do not really want to correspond with, such as lotsofgirlsforfun.com. Alternatively, you simply want to ensure that users do not send messages to competitors. The easiest way to keep an eye on outgoing traffic is to enable message tracking on all servers and analyze the data that Exchange captures. This will reveal who is sending messages, the message subjects (if you enable tracking of subject data), and where the messages go. Commercial products can even produce detailed reports show-

Chapter 10

ing where traffic goes, ordered by domain and traffic volume and analyzed by week, month, or other period. If you do need to track message traffic for an extended period, you may have to increase the retention period for the message tracking logs (normally between seven and ten days), so you need to set aside disk space for this purpose.

A more proactive approach is to install content scanning software on your network to examine messages as they pass en route to external destinations. You might want to watch for key phrases relating to trade secrets that you want to protect, inappropriate language, or anything else that might damage the reputation of the company or expose it to legal action. Most scanners operate on SMTP gateways and two holes exist. First, you will not be able to interpret encrypted messages. Second, you will not be able to examine any message sent from one Exchange server to another within the organization if the messages flow across routing group connectors. Different scanning products have different capabilities, and it is entirely possible that some products will be able to satisfy your needs, so take the time to investigate current capabilities and ask some questions to identify likely products and then test them thoroughly. A product that includes a scan for viruses, blocks suspicious attachments (you may not want to send out ZIP and EXE files or anything called "STRATEGY.DOC"), and checks contents of messages is ideal.

If you find that someone is sending messages to an undesirable destination and you find out who this person is, you can then proceed to recover messages to determine what the user has sent. If you have implemented an archiving solution, you can retrieve the information from the archive (a commercial application is much easier to use in this respect than Exchange's own archiving functionality). If not, you will have to access the user's mailbox and hope that the incriminating messages are still there or that they can be retrieved from the deleted items cache. If the message is not in the mailbox, you can restore a backup to a recovery server and access the mailbox there.

It is easy to grant yourself the permissions necessary to open another mailbox. Either use AD Users and Computers to grant your own account Send As and Receive As permissions for the mailbox or create a separate account and mailbox for inspection purposes and allocate the permissions to it. Log on to the account, create a MAPI profile to point at the mailbox, and you now have access and can read to your heart's content. OWA is also a good choice to open mailboxes without requiring a profile. However, if the other user opens the mailbox, he or she may pick up signs that someone is poking around. For example, if you read a new message and fail to set its status back to unread, users may wonder why they never saw that new message. You can change the status of unread messages to "read" unwittingly if the reading pane is active. You may forget to delete the welcome message that Outlook creates when a new profile logs on to a mailbox for the first time. Users may see some notifications (delivery and read) in their Sent Items folder and wonder why Outlook generated these receipts if they never read the corresponding message. The same is true of calendar responses. Someone else may mention that he or she received a response from the user when it was known that the user was out of the office and did not read mail. You have to be careful; software such as GrinningShark's[4] "WatchYourBack" product suppresses notifications.

Of course, if users have their email delivered to a PST on their laptop's hard drive, you will have difficulties checking their email with Outlook or OWA unless you can gain access to the PST.

The last situation is where you have a need to scan a complete server for content. Perhaps someone has taken an action alleging that your company has infringed a patent and a judge has ordered you to produce any email relating to the technology that may be the problem. Again, if you have an archiving solution in place, it should be easy to locate the relevant messages. If not, you can turn on full-text indexing for Mailbox Stores and go looking. Implementing indexing for a large Mailbox Store is not something to rush into, because it can affect server performance and generate a very large index, but if that is all you can do, you can certainly use a full-text index to locate messages. If you can focus in on a restricted group of users, you might be able to use the ExMerge utility to scan for messages with particular subjects or attachments. However, this is using ExMerge for a purpose well outside its normal scope; also, it is a crude instrument because it will not search content. The sole advantage of ExMerge is that it is free, but you can get much better functionality from commercial offerings such as GFI's MailEssentials for Exchange.[5]

By far the most intrusive snooping is when you deploy software such as Spector Pro from www.spectorsoft.com. This technology can record IM conversations, the full content of email, Web sites that users visit, and even online chat. It supports email systems as diverse as hotmail and Exchange (Outlook). I do not like such technology and would only deploy it in dire situations when I absolutely need to find out what is happening and when I have absolute protection from lawyers.

---

4. www.grinningshark.com.
5. www.gfi.com.

Accessing anyone's mailbox is not something that you should rush into, and people are not going to be very happy if they discover that you have been rummaging around in their mailboxes. Searching a mailbox is a huge breech of user privacy, which can result in legal action of its own if you do not protect yourself by seeking authorization before doing anything. You may also want to leave the actual investigation to someone else, such as the person who requested access and has a good reason to look for specific messages. You can set up the account, allocate the necessary privileges, explain how to look for the information, and leave the investigator to do the work. This way, if anything happens, you will not be the person who looked at the contents of the mailbox and you can defend your position.

Best practice is to proceed only under very specific circumstances that comply with local legal standards for data protection and user privacy. Legal standards differ from country to country and it is not safe to assume that the procedures used in the United States will resist legal scrutiny elsewhere.

10.7 Exploring the deleted items cache

When a user deletes an item, the Store moves the item into the Deleted Items folder. The item remains in the Deleted Items folder until the user makes an explicit choice to empty the folder or the client automatically empties the folder the next time the user exits. Clients such as Outlook and Outlook Express control this behavior through the option shown in Figure 10.32. Some users like to keep items in the Deleted Items folder for quite a long period, perhaps because they like to have the luxury to take time to review these items before they make the final decision to delete them. In some cases, I have known users to hold thousands of items in the Deleted Items folder. Some insist on synchronizing the contents of the Deleted Items folder to their offline Store—perhaps in order to review the contents offline. Given the transient nature of the majority of email, it is best to encourage users to make the decision to keep clean mailboxes by emptying the Deleted Items folder when they exit their client. You can give users "help" in this respect by using tools such as PROFGEN or ProfileMaker (www.autoprof.com) to generate profiles with a preset option to empty the Deleted Items folder when Outlook clients exit.

Up to Exchange 5.5, the story stopped here. Once deleted, items stayed deleted. However, users make mistakes and sometimes delete items when they should not. When this happened, administrators had a simple choice: Either tell the user that they could do nothing to recover the deleted item or go ahead and restore the mailbox database on another server, find the item,

10.7 Exploring the deleted items cache

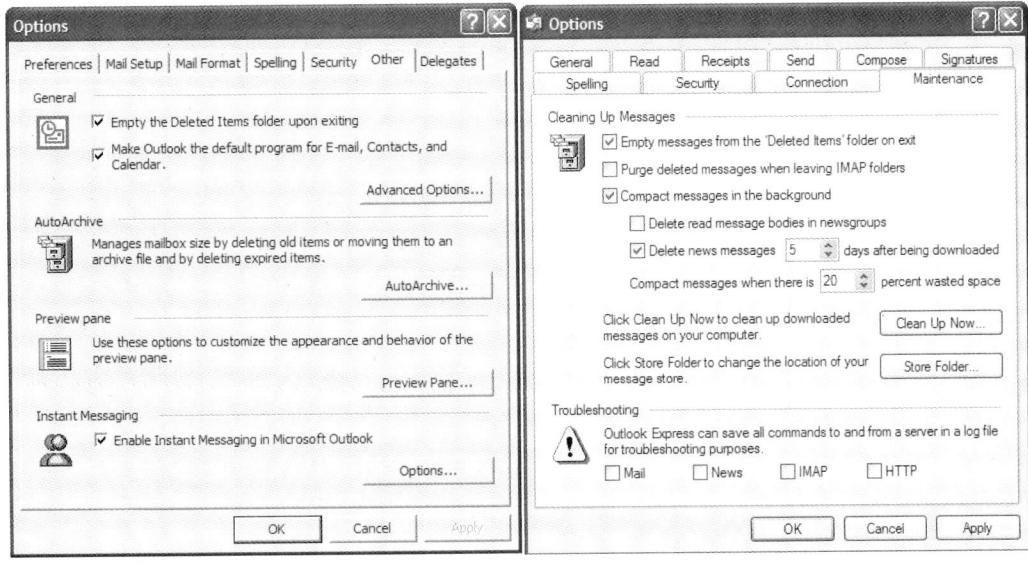

Figure 10.32 *Options in Outlook (left) and Outlook Express (right) to control the Deleted Items folder.*

export it to a PST, and provide it to the user. Given these options, most administrators chose to decline the chance to restore databases and users suffered—unless they held a sufficiently high position in the organization to convince the administrator to change his or her mind. All Exchange servers now support the option to maintain a cache of deleted items that remains in the Store until a set deleted retention period expires, at which point the Store removes the items from the database. This is a great feature for both users and administrators alike because it saves work for everyone.

10.7.1 Recovering items

Pushing work down to users is always popular with administrators. Appeals to the help desk to recover an important message can now be bounced back to the user, but only if he or she has the right client. MAPI clients from Outlook 98 onward include the option to recover deleted items from the cache through the Recover Deleted Items option from the Tools menu. From Exchange 2000 SP2 onward, OWA also includes the Recover Deleted Items option. You can only recover items when you are connected to a server. You then see a list of items in the cache (Figure 10.33), and, as you can see, you can recover all your deleted spam, just in case you missed reading some interesting information.

Chapter 10

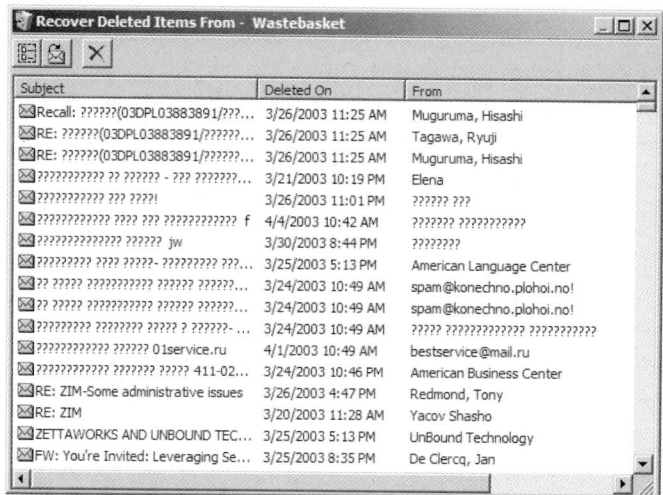

Figure 10.33
Recovering deleted items.

You can still recover deleted items if you use Outlook 2003 in cached Exchange mode, since this operation forces Outlook to connect to Exchange. However, recovered items do not appear in the Deleted Items folder immediately, because Exchange recovers them into the server-based folder, and there is a time lag before the client synchronizes the recovered items into the cache.

Before you can recover deleted items for public folders, the properties of the Public Folder Store must include a deleted item retention period, and the user who attempts to recover the items must have write permission for the public folder (see Knowledge Base article 811358 for full details). Note that you cannot use a public folder "favorite" to recover items, since this is merely a pointer to the actual folder. Instead, select the public folder from the hierarchy and then select the option to begin the recovery, which you accomplish by selecting the desired items and then clicking on the recover item. Outlook then moves the recovered items back into either the Deleted Items folder or the public folder.

If someone does not use a recent Outlook or OWA client, an administrator can log on to his or her mailbox with Outlook and recover the items. Certainly, this strategy can work for a limited period or if you only have a small number of clients in this situation and you have a plan to upgrade to the latest client software. However, it is not viable when you have to manage large populations of IMAP or POP clients.

By default, the Deleted Items folder is the only folder enabled for item recovery. However, clients can delete an item in place, meaning that the

10.7 Exploring the deleted items cache

item does not progress through the Deleted Items folder before it enters the cache (use the SHIFT/Delete combination to do this with Outlook). If users are accustomed to delete items in place, you may want to enable deleted items recovery for every folder to allow users to recover items in their original folders. To enable deleted items recovery in all folders, create a new DWORD value at the following registry location and set its value to 1—this works for all versions from Outlook 98 through Outlook 2003:

```
HKEY_LOCAL_MACHINE\Software\Microsoft\Exchange\Client\
Options\DumpsterAlwaysOn
```

While you can force the Outlook user interface to allow item recovery from every folder, you are not able to filter deleted items, so the Recover Deleted Items option only shows items originally deleted from a specific folder. In other words, when you select the Recover Deleted Items option, you see the complete contents of the cache—items deleted from all folders. This proves that Exchange keeps all deleted items in a single cache and does not maintain a separate cache for each folder.

10.7.2 Setting a deleted item retention period

The Store uses a flag (a MAPI property) to enable "soft" or two-phase deletes. When a client empties the Deleted Items folder, the Store hides the items from view by setting the flag, which has the effect of placing the items into the Deleted Items cache, the collection of items within the Store that have the deleted item flag set. The cache does not exist in a separate area in the Store. Instead, the items remain in the Deleted Items folder, but you cannot see them because the Store does not reveal their existence unless you use the "Recover Deleted Items" option. The Deleted Items folder does not exist for public folders, but you can still recover a deleted item by opening the public folder and then using the Recover Deleted Items option.

Deleted items remain in the cache until their deleted item retention period passes. A property of a Store database defines the deleted item retention period. You can set the deleted items retention period by individually setting the properties of each Store (Figure 10.34) or by applying a system policy to Stores on one or more servers that you select through ESM. The latter method is preferable in large organizations, since it allows you to impose the same policy on a large number of Stores at one time. It is nice to have the opportunity to control settings on an individual Store too, since you might have a situation where you need to apply a different policy. For example, you might decide that the Mailbox Store that holds executive mailboxes has a retention period of 90 days, just to ensure that you can

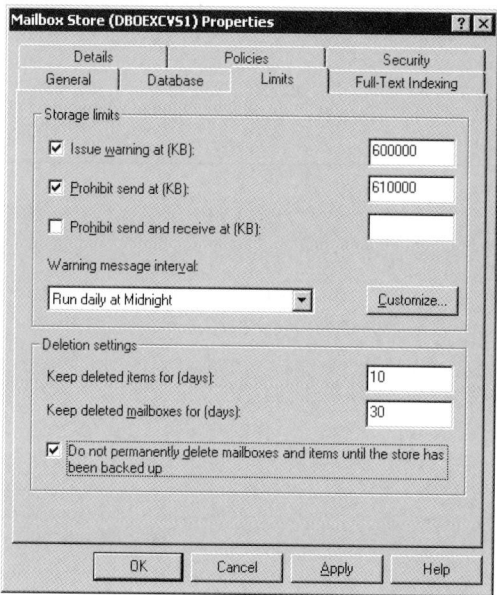

Figure 10.34
Setting the deleted items retention period.

always recover messages belonging to people who might be able to force a database restore. Note the checkbox in Figure 10.34 that refers to backups. You can opt to permanently remove items even if you have not backed up the Store, or you can keep them in the cache until you perform a successful backup. The second option is preferable, since you never want to leave yourself in a situation where you cannot recover an item.

You can also define specific retention periods for selected mailboxes by setting a property of the user account through AD Users and Computers (Figure 10.35). Because of the time-intensive nature of setting individual limits on mailboxes, this is not a recommended option and should only be taken when necessary. For example, during a legal discovery action, lawyers may compel you to retain all messages sent and received by particular users, such as the officers of the company or those involved in particular deals. You can either group all the affected users into a single Mailbox Store, apply the desired retention period to the Store, or edit each user's properties. The latter option is preferable if the target accounts use mailboxes on a set of distributed servers, perhaps spread across a wide geographical area.

Note that the Store does not calculate the size of items in the deleted items cache when it applies quotas to user mailboxes. Some users exploit this fact when they come close to exceeding their quota by selecting large items from their mailboxes, deleting the items, emptying the Deleted Items

10.7 Exploring the deleted items cache

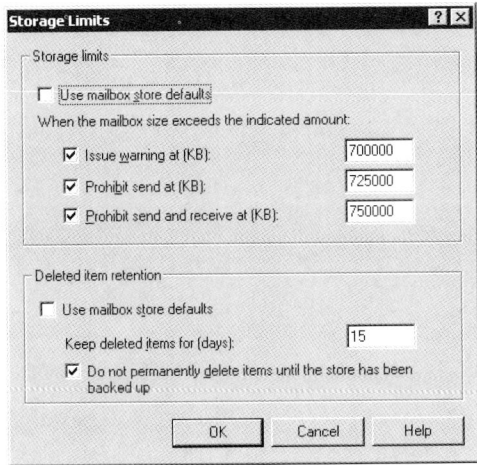

Figure 10.35
Setting a specific retention period for a mailbox.

folder, and then performing whatever actions they wish. Later on, when their quota frees up, they can recover the items from the cache.

Figure 10.36 shows how to add Stores to a system policy.

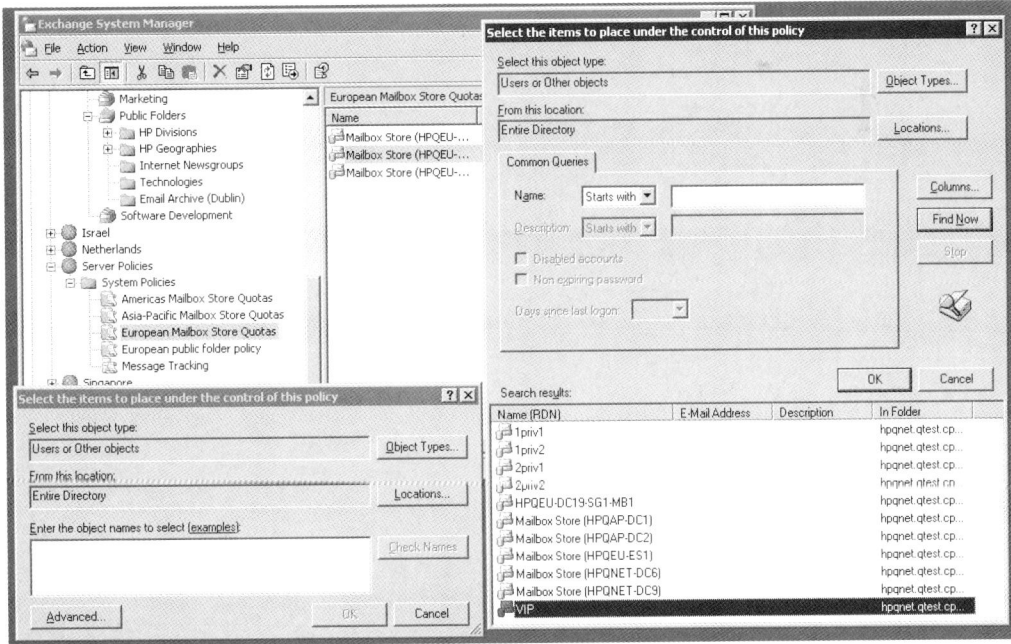

Figure 10.36 *Adding Stores to a system policy.*

10.7.3 Cleaning the cache

The background Store maintenance tasks performed by the System Attendant remove items in the cache after their retention period expires. The exact schedule that controls background processing is set through a database property, and it is usually started nightly just after midnight. In database terms, removing items from the deleted items cache is known as "hard deletes," because the Store removes the items from its database tables and you cannot recover them later without performing a database restore. You can get an idea of the clean-up processing done by the Store by looking for event 1207, which reports the number of items and their size in the cache before and after scanning for items with an expired retention period. As an example, Figure 10.37 shows that clean-up processing removed 487 items, which occupied 10,036 KB.

10.7.4 Sizing the cache

As soon as the deleted items cache appeared in Exchange, administrators began to worry about the impact of the cache on database sizes. After all, if the cache holds items instead of removing them from the Store, database sizes must increase. The question is, how much extra space will the cache occupy? Note that the maximum size of the cache is 4 GB per store, although you are hardly likely to accumulate so many deleted items unless your retention period is excessive.

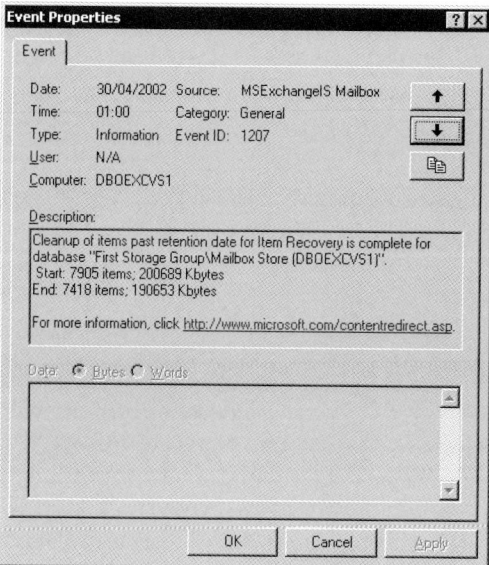

Figure 10.37
Items removed from the deleted items cache.

10.7 Exploring the deleted items cache

The cache begins to grow as soon as you install a server and it stabilizes over time. You can expect the cache to stabilize in size after twice the retention period. In other words, if you set the retention period to be a month, the cache should be stable in about two months. Once stabilized, the size of the cache will vary, but not dramatically unless user behavior changes. For example, if you double the default mailbox quota, users do not have to delete items to stay within the old quota and the deleted item cache will reduce. However, the size of the database grows to reflect the new quota.

Obviously, the retention period is the biggest influence on the cache size—the longer the retention period, the larger the cache. Most installations use retention periods between 7 and 15 days, the logic being that if someone does not realize that he or she has deleted an item in error in that time, the item probably is not very important. Other influences on cache size include:

- Mailbox quotas: Smaller quotas force users to delete items more quickly, so the cache tends to grow.

- Message volume: Higher message volumes create faster item turnover in user mailboxes, so the cache tends to grow.

- Organizational culture: If you train users to read messages and make a decision to delete or keep, the cache tends to grow (but users can work within lower quotas, so databases are smaller). Caches tend to be smaller when users keep everything and only delete items when necessary. You can use the Mailbox Manager to assist users by implementing a policy that automatically cleans out obsolete items from folders on a regular basis.

These rules of thumb have varying impact from company to company. You can make an accurate assessment by taking data from production servers to gain a view of actual cache sizes. You can then use the data to predict the likely impact on the cache size if something changes. Exchange provides a set of Performance Monitor counters to track the size of the deleted items cache. These are:

- MSExchangeIS Mailbox—total count of recoverable items

- MSExchangeIS Mailbox—total size of recoverable items

- MSExchangeIS Public—total count of recoverable items

- MSExchangeIS Public—total size of recoverable items

The Store maintains separate counters for every active database on a server as well as overall totals for Mailbox and Public Stores. As with other

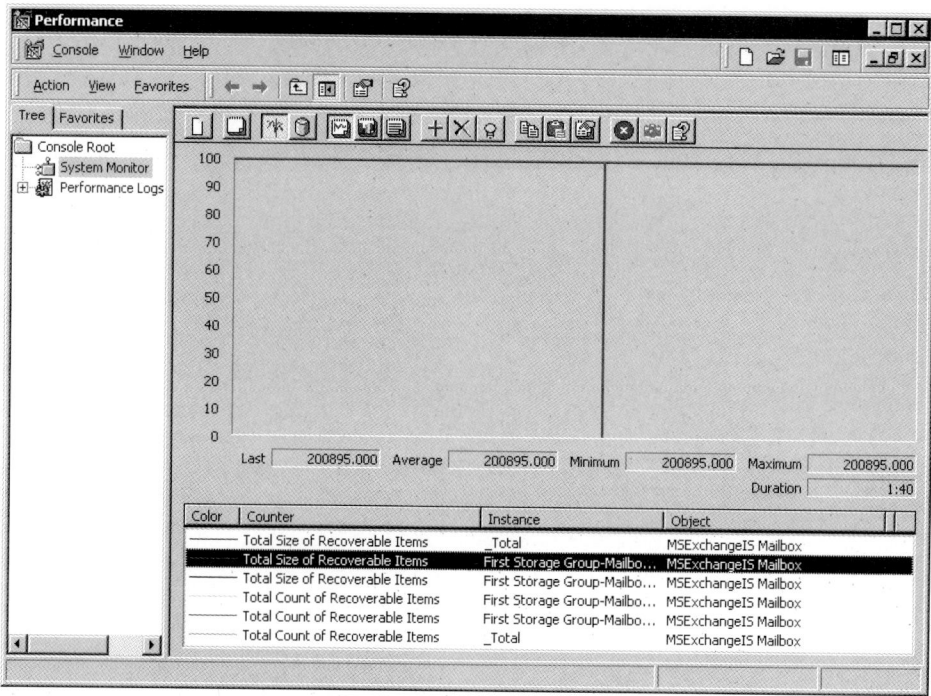

Figure 10.38   *Using Performance Monitor to track the size of the deleted items cache.*

performance data, the Store updates these counters on an ongoing basis, so you can track the growth of the cache over time. Figure 10.38 shows the Performance Monitor displaying the size of the deleted items cache for a Mailbox Store—200,895 KB is in the cache, equating to 10,052 items (reported by the count of recoverable items). Unless the server is very active, with users deleting items frequently, viewing cache data in this way is relatively uninteresting. The Store updates the counters as clients delete items, so you can see the cache size changing in real time. Treat the information as a snapshot that provides a quick overview of the cache or a data point that you can observe and record on an ongoing basis to track the size of the cache over time.

It is more interesting to look at the deleted item cache by user. You can do this through ESM by including the "Deleted Items (KB)" column in the data displayed in the console. This column is not one of the default column set, so you need to modify the view. Select a Mailbox Store, right-click, and then select "View" and "Choose Columns" to work with the columns displayed by ESM. Figure 10.39 shows how to add the column to the view. You may also want to move the columns around so that you can compare

10.7 Exploring the deleted items cache

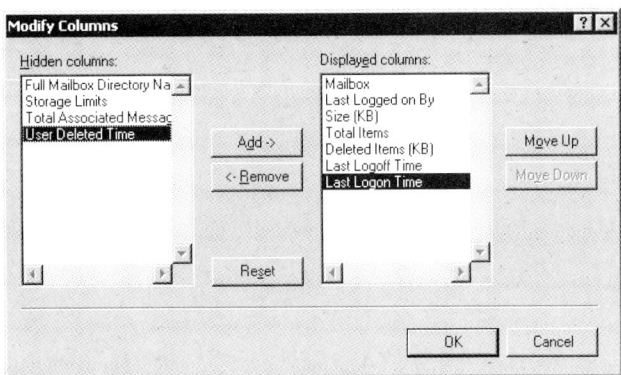

Figure 10.39
Adding the deleted items column to a display.

the size of the deleted items against the overall mailbox size. Figure 10.40 shows the resulting view.

After ESM displays the data, you can capture it by clicking on the context-sensitive menu, selecting the "Export List" option, and choosing the target file name and type—normally CSV (Comma-Separated Values). You can use Excel and other programs to create many different analyses from the captured data, but the essential data we require is a sum of the deleted items in each mailbox.

After you know the total size of the cache for an individual Mailbox Store, you can calculate it as a percentage of the overall database size. Remember to include the size of the EDB and STM files in the calculation. For example, the Mailbox Store illustrated in Figure 10.40 uses a ten-day default retention period and allows large mailbox quotas; the total size of the cache as reported by ESM is 437,178 KB. Using the file sizes reported by Windows Explorer, we calculate the cache as follows:

Size of mailbox EDB:	8.89 GB
Size of mailbox STM:	0.46 GB
Size of database:	9.34 GB
Total count of deleted items in mailboxes (reported by ESM):	0.54 GB
Percentage size of cache:	5.76%

The problem with this calculation is that it compares absolute database size on disk against the reported size of the cache, so "white space" is included in the calculation. White space is the set of unused pages in the database that used to hold deleted items. The Store reuses deleted pages to

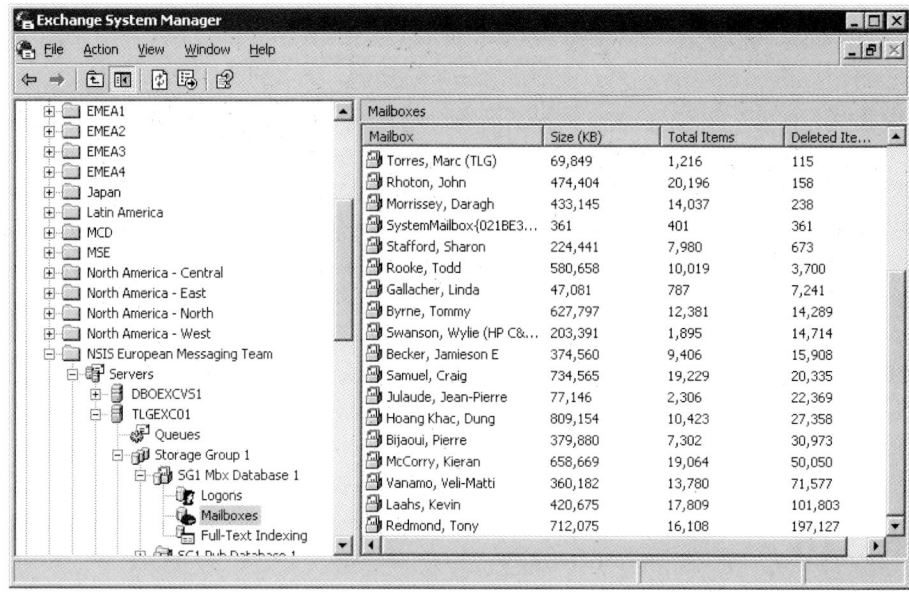

Figure 10.40   *Using ESM to view deleted items by mailbox.*

hold new items, but there is always a certain amount of unused space in any Mailbox or Public Store. You can reduce the amount to zero by rebuilding a database with the ESEUTIL utility, but it starts to accumulate as soon as the database goes back into use. Expect to see white space occupy between 5 percent to 15 percent of a database's reported size on disk, with larger percentages in databases where you have moved mailboxes to another database and you have not rebuilt the database. In our example, the reported size of all mailboxes in the database is 3.54 GB, so the deleted items cache actually represents 15.2 percent of this amount. You can decide to use this calculation to assess the likely impact of the deleted item cache on database size, but most administrators compare the reported size of the cache against the database size on disk, since they are more concerned about the absolute increase in database size.

With these points in mind, you can use the guidelines outlined in Table 10.4 to estimate the potential size of the deleted items cache on an Exchange server given a range of mailbox quotas. The percentage of the database occupied by the cache then varies according to user discipline. If users delete messages quickly, the cache will be at the lower end of the scale, but if they tend to retain messages, it is likely to be at the upper end.

It is important to emphasize that these are just guideline figures and your mileage will vary. Every organization is different, and the hard data

Table 10.4 *Estimating the Size of the Deleted Items Cache*

Cache Size	Large Mailboxes (200 MB+)	Medium Mailboxes (100–200 MB)	Small Mailboxes (50–100 MB)
5–10%	10 days	10 days	20 days
10–20%	20 days	25 days	35 days
15–20%	30 days	40 days	50 days

you gather from your own servers will provide guidelines that are more accurate. Known instances exist where the size of the deleted items cache is much larger than the 30 percent maximum shown here, but these are the exceptions that prove the rule. Remember that the larger the cache, the longer maintenance operations such as background Store defragmentation will take, and this is the reason why you should be concerned about the size.

The deleted items cache is a tremendous help to administrators, because it removes the need to recover databases if users delete items in error. Compared with its benefits, the additional burden in disk space requirement is not onerous.

10.8 Decommissioning mailboxes

Inevitably, some of a company's population leaves every year. Administrators need to be ready to secure accounts and mailboxes after users depart, prevent some messages from arriving in the mailbox, and then efficiently process any incoming messages that continue to arrive addressed to former users.

The easiest way to remove an account is to select and then delete it using AD Users and Computers. You can decide whether to remove the Exchange mailbox at the same time. Deleting a record in the AD needs replication to occur to all DCs in the forest before the deletion is completely effective. The AD maintains tombstones to mark deleted accounts and then eventually flushes the tombstones from the AD 60 days (the default) after the account deletion.

Deleting an account in this manner immediately denies access to the mailbox. However, it means that you may not be able to retrieve messages or other items in the mailbox, should the need occur. Note that even if you retain a mailbox with the intention of reviewing its contents to recover corporate information, any encrypted message will be inaccessible unless you know the recipient's private key.

Life would be simple if you could discard unwanted accounts as soon as the owner left the building. However, companies usually have processes to govern how people leave, including returning company property (e.g., laptops, phones, badges, and credit cards), handling of intellectual property such as documents, and access to computer accounts. The most basic step is to secure accounts against unauthorized access and preserve the information contained in any mailboxes used by the individual who is leaving.

You can quickly secure Windows accounts by disabling the accounts and changing passwords, and then testing to ensure that no one can gain access. Once you have the accounts and mailboxes locked down, it is a good idea to remove the user from internal distribution lists (groups) to prevent the generation of unnecessary messages. Since some Windows 2000 distribution groups are also security groups, this step ensures that you remove access from resources such as public folders and file shares. In addition, you should hide the user's mailbox from the GAL. Some administrators also add a comment to one of the fields in the account to indicate that the user has left and to set a date when they plan to delete the account permanently. For example, you can prefix the display name with something like "** 20031001" to show that the account is deleted and that you plan to remove it on October 1, 2003.

From a housekeeping perspective, unless you are compelled to keep accounts for longer, it is best to remove disabled accounts after a couple of months. If you put an expiration date on accounts as they are disabled, you can quickly scan the AD on a regular basis to locate expired accounts and permanently delete them. Two months is usually more than enough for an authorized user to review a mailbox's contents and decide whether to recover any information. Because the contents of a mailbox are personal and each country has its legal conditions that apply to situations in which representatives of a company access someone's mailbox, you should ensure that any access to the contents of a deleted mailbox can be defended under law.

10.8.1 Mailboxes and document retention

The next step depends on the type of document retention policy that is in place. While email can contain significant intellectual capital, some companies take positive steps not to retain information and move to delete mailboxes and any personal documents that belong to users who leave as soon as practically possible. The logic here is that opposition lawyers cannot discover deleted messages and documents during future legal actions, so it is a form of electronic shredding. Of course, smart lawyers know that backup tapes probably exist that contain copies of the information they are looking for, so deleting a mailbox is not a sure way of hiding anything.

Most companies keep mailboxes around for a set period after the user leaves, normally between 30 days and 3 months, to allow someone to examine the contents of the mailbox to determine whether anything of value exists that the company should retain. Before you finally delete the mailbox, you can use a tool such as ExMerge to export the contents of the mailbox to a PST, which you can then archive to a writeable CD just in case you need the information again. You can apply much the same policy to the user's PC, where a coworker reviews the contents of the hard disk before an administrator wipes the PC and reloads it with a fresh copy of the operating system and applications. Again, you can export documents and other interesting material to a CD before finally rebuilding the PC.

Other companies are constrained by legal requirements as to the actions that they can take with mailboxes. If a third party is suing your company, your lawyers may require the company to keep messages sent or received by any individual who may potentially be connected to the case. If one of those individuals leaves the company, you must retain his or her mailbox until the case concludes, just in case. Exporting a mailbox to a PST may meet the legal requirements, but you should check to make sure.

In situations where document retention policies are in place or you have to keep a mailbox to satisfy a legal requirement, you can use a forwarding address to direct new messages to another user, who will then process the message. Alternatively, you can create an Outlook rule to delete new messages as they arrive, or even send an informational message to tell people who attempt to send messages to the mailbox that the user has left the company.

10.8.2 Creating a blackhole for messages

If you do not want to go to the trouble of setting up a mechanism to process incoming messages, you can create a blackhole in the form of a "Disappearing Users" distribution group that has no members and then add the SMTP addresses of former users to the email addresses of the group. This creates a blackhole for messages to go into, since the Exchange Routing Engine will be able to locate a valid address to deliver messages to, but they actually arrive nowhere. This is an effective way to stop incoming spam addressed to users who leave your company. Remember that you must delete or change the SMTP address on the user's mailbox before adding it to the distribution group, since AD Users and Computers checks to ensure that an SMTP address is unique within the organization before adding it to an object. An alternative idea is to create a mailbox and add all of the email addresses for former users to it. The advantage gained in this approach is that you can then use Outlook rules to process and respond to incoming messages, as described later on in this section.

10.8.3 Redirecting messages

Forwarding addresses allows you to tell Exchange to redirect messages sent to another mailbox. The recipient can be any mail-enabled object in the Active Directory: another mailbox (the logical choice), a contact, a public folder, or even a distribution group. The same restrictions apply for Exchange 5.5, where the selected object must be in the Directory Store.

Forwarding messages to a public folder or distribution group does not make much sense, but there can be situations where it is appropriate to forward messages to a mail-enabled contact. For example, assume that someone who uses another email system assumes the responsibilities of the user who leaves. In this instance, you create a mail-enabled contact in the AD

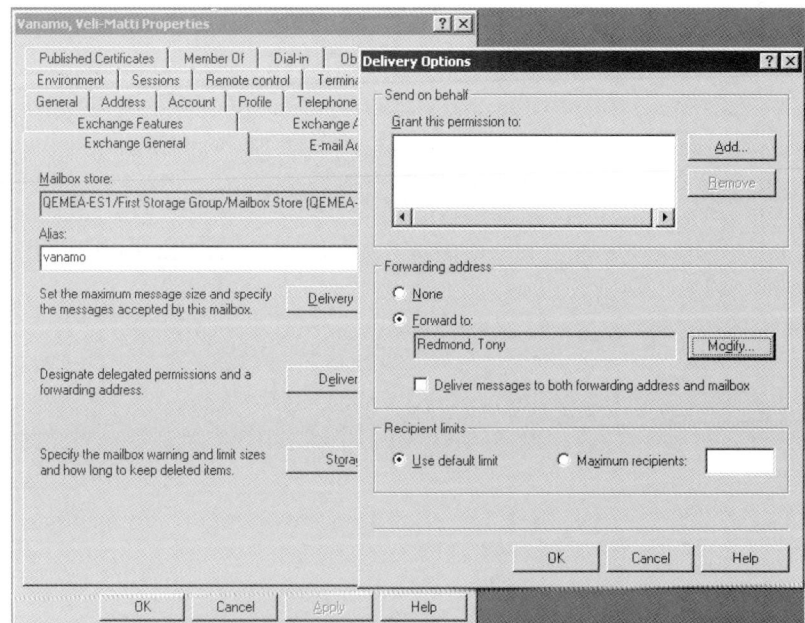

Figure 10.41
Specifying a forwarding address.

10.8 Decommissioning mailboxes

and then select the contact as the forwarding address when editing the Delivery Options for the user who has left, as shown in Figure 10.41.

Using a forwarding address is appropriate when the user is involved in many ongoing projects and you want to preserve continuity. However, it does place a certain load on the user to whom you forward the messages, since he or she will have an extra volume of email to process, including some messages that are probably not business related. The only clue that a recipient gets that a message was not originally sent to him or her is the address shown for the recipient, and it is easy to miss this!

10.8.4 Using Outlook rules to process messages

Outlook includes a powerful rules engine that you can use to perform many tasks. In this case, the rule for processing new messages is simple and consists of the following steps:

- Process all new messages that arrive in the mailbox.
- Move a copy of the messages to the Deleted Items folder.
- Optionally, send a response back to the originator to tell him or her that the user is no longer available at this address.

Figure 10.42 shows an appropriate rule as viewed through the Rules wizard. You create and edit text in the message containing the reply as you create (or later modify) the rule, and it is stored as a hidden item in the mailbox. You create or edit text in the message in exactly the same way as

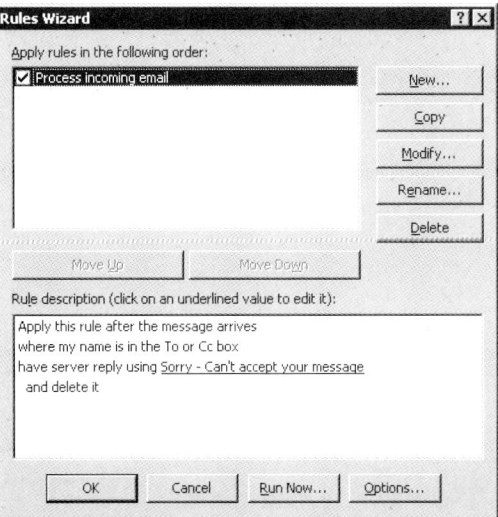

Figure 10.42
Creating a server-side rule to process new messages.

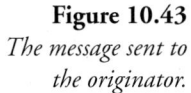

Figure 10.43
The message sent to the originator.

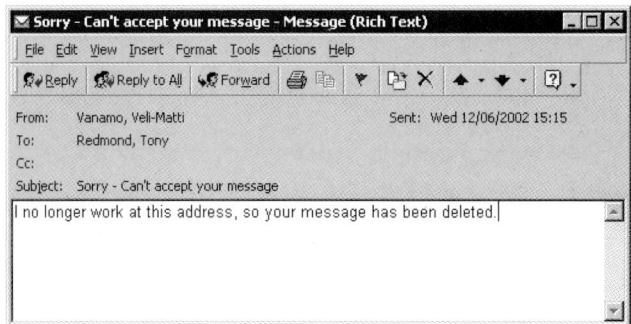

you create text for a regular message, so you can include any formatting required to get your message across. It is important to create a server-side rule to allow Exchange to process messages as they arrive. Otherwise, if you create a client-side rule, you have to keep Outlook running to execute the rule. Some conditions exist that force Outlook to create a client-side rule, including any attempt to delete an item permanently. For this reason, it is best to move incoming items into the Deleted Items folder, where an administrator can review and then delete the items or leave them for automatic cleanup by the Mailbox Manager.

Figure 10.43 illustrates how an originator receives the informational message that you associate with the rule. It is up to you as to how much information you include in the text. Some administrators like to include a forwarding address, but this is perhaps not a great idea if the user has gone to a competitor. If users subscribe to Internet mailing lists managed by list servers, it is likely that they will forget to unsubscribe when they leave the company. As stated, our rule will work and Exchange will automatically move any messages that come from the mailing list to the Deleted Items folder. However, Exchange sends the reply message to the list server, which will then forward it to all its subscribers in the same way that it deals with every other message sent to the list. Recipients will probably not appreciate receiving these messages, so we can add another rule to examine incoming messages to see whether they originate from a list server and then quietly delete any that do.

Of course, this approach means that the list is inaccurate, because it contains invalid subscriptions, but this is not the problem you want to solve. You could go through the mailbox to try to pick out messages generated by lists and send a note to the list administrator to ask him or her to remove the user. Some lists include unsubscribe instructions in the messages. This often requires that you send a message to the list server from the user's email

10.8 Decommissioning mailboxes

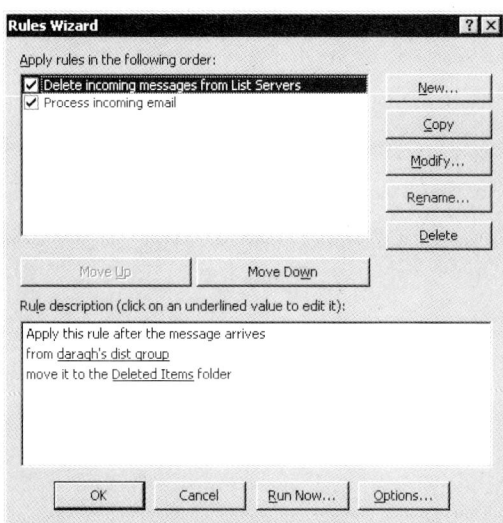

Figure 10.44
Processing for list server messages.

address; the easiest way to do this is to configure Outlook Express to send a message with the former user's old email address. If you feel that this is too much work, you can create a rule, similar to that shown in Figure 10.44, to delete the messages silently. Obviously, you must ensure that Outlook executes this rule first before it processes other messages.

10.8.5 User death

The requirement to handle mailboxes for users who die is something that we would perhaps not like to think about, but it does happen. In this instance, the need to preserve information that might be useful to the company still exists, but it is easy to cause some distress to coworkers of the recently departed if a rule or auto-reply generates a message that apparently comes from the user after his or her death. For this reason, take the normal steps to remove the mailbox from the GAL and distribution lists and then check that an auto-reply or rules are not in place.

Handling the mailboxes of former users is something you probably never think about before the need occurs. Apart from the technical aspects of how to handle new messages sent to former workers as they arrive, you may have to comply with legal or document retention policies. As with documents, mailboxes are part of the intellectual capital of an organization, so a well-thought-out method to decommission mailboxes that allows you to secure intellectual capital should be part of an Exchange administrator's toolkit.

10.9 Helping users to do a better job

Every email client has its unique features set. You have to manage them if optimum use is to be made of available system resources such as disk space and network bandwidth. In this section, we discuss some common issues that administrators should consider to help users optimize system resources, including:

- How to reduce the network load generated by clients
- How to limit the size of messages generated by clients
- Whether to add legal disclaimers to outgoing messages

Your company has a work culture of its own, so some give and take is required to achieve a balance between the perfectly managed systems valued by the administrators and the desire of the users to send messages without interference.

10.9.1 Eliminating bad habits to reduce network and storage demands

Every Exchange design pays a lot of attention to the number of servers deployed and how best to connect the servers together, along with plans to control public folder and directory replication. We often give less attention to the traffic generated by clients and how to reduce network demand, yet this aspect can be a very important part of a deployment project.

Users generate network load through their normal activities, such as sending and reading messages. Benchmarks such as LoadSim typically use standard messages ranging in size from 1 KB to approximately 10 KB that contain text, some attachments, and maybe a meeting request or two. However, real-life activity is always different from simulations and this is the reason why designs often demonstrate flaws when exposed to real-life pressure. People are very curious and use software in ways you could never imagine. If you do not educate users to respect the need to preserve network resources, they are unlikely to consider the ramifications of, for example, dragging and dropping a large PowerPoint presentation to a message and sending it to a distribution list.

Some of my personal dislikes regarding bad email habits are discussed in the following text.

Complex, object-ridden, auto-signature files

Because I work across low-bandwidth network links so often, bloated auto-signature files are the bane of my messaging life. The difference in connect times across 28.8-Kbps connections that results because people send messages that contain 2 KB of useful data but end up at 50 KB to accommodate a spinning, 3D, or other form of graphic-intense logo is annoying when you have just one message. The degree of annoyance becomes infuriating when 20 percent or more of the messages in your Inbox is similarly bloated. Apart from absorbing valuable bandwidth and slowing user ability to process email, graphics soak up storage and create pressure on mailbox quotas. It would be interesting to analyze the content of some Exchange Mailbox Stores to try to determine just how much graphics and other useless data they contain. We should calculate how much work administrators do daily to take backups of that data, not to mention the expense required to provide and manage the storage that the data occupies. For example, if you include a 50-KB graphic in your signature, then after you send 100 messages, your mailbox contains 5 MB of redundant, duplicated graphics. Would you or any other user accept a voluntary reduction of 5 MB in a mailbox quota? Yet many users cheerfully accept this overhead without thinking! Moreover, if you scale this up for 1,000 users on a server, you end up with 5 GB of useless data.

Auto-signature files convey some information about a message's sender; this feature appeared first in sendmail-based UNIX email systems. Normally, you add some auto-signature text to each message to provide details of your return email address, telephone and fax numbers, and perhaps some witty "thought of the day." Text-based data does not occupy much space and no one can really complain about auto-signatures until encountering some of the crazy ones that circulate today. Everyone is aware that cut and paste allows you to insert objects into message bodies, and it did not take people long to discover that they can do the same thing for auto-signatures. We can clearly see the intention behind auto-signature files in RFC 1855, which covers netiquette:

> *If you include a signature, keep it short. The rule of thumb is no longer than four lines. Remember that many people pay for connectivity by the minute, and the longer your message is, the more they pay.*

RFC 1855 appeared in 1995 and focused on a world where dial-up connects were the de facto standard, and people worried about paying telephone companies by the minute, a feature of life outside the United States.

The authors probably did not foresee a time when users could cheerfully include a spinning, multicolor, 3D logo into their email signatures.

If you are determined to use a graphically rich auto-signature, it is easy to include your favorite logo (which may not be the approved version of the corporate logo). Before you begin, find the logo you want to use and save it to a local directory. For Outlook, click on Tools and then Options to access the "Mail Format" properties, and then click on the Signatures command button. You can create a new signature or edit an existing signature file. When Outlook places you in the signature editor, you can click on "Advanced Edit" to force Outlook to launch an HTML editor. Usually, Outlook launches Microsoft FrontPage (Outlook 2000, 2002, and 2003) and you can paste the logo directly into the HTML content. After the logo is in the signature file, you can use the standard editor to change text information, such as your phone numbers, but you must use the advanced editor to make any change to the graphics. Outlook stores signature files in the C:\Documents and Settings\UserName\Application Data\Microsoft\Signatures directory.

I once inserted a digital picture of myself at the Microsoft Exchange Conference (2000) into my auto-signature, as shown in Figure 10.45. The net effect is that I added 250 KB of graphics to every outgoing message! Even with Outlook 2003's compression algorithms brought into action to reduce the size of the graphic, the outgoing messages are still 80 KB. If you must include a logo in your auto-signature file, then use a low-resolution GIF file to reduce the impact of the logo to an acceptable limit. For example, HP recommends users include a 1.11-KB GIF file in their auto-signatures. This is much better for all concerned than the other variations of corporate logos that are usually designed to be used in advertising or other graphically rich situations. Of course, even after providing a reduced graphic and making it known that the graphic is available to use, people still use whatever bloated graphic they can find.

Users often do not realize that email gateways might negate the desired effect of the logo on external correspondents if the gateways strip out graphics in message bodies (not attachments) as messages pass through. Companies are rightly concerned about viruses, and it is possible to hide a virus behind a graphic or embed instructions to launch a virus in a graphic, so it is also possible that antivirus scanners will remove the logos. Therefore, the result is that the only people you share the logos with are internal recipients, who probably already know what your company's logo looks like.

Another issue is the impact on recipients. While it may be acceptable for you to let everyone else in the company know what the current corporate

10.9 Helping users to do a better job   785

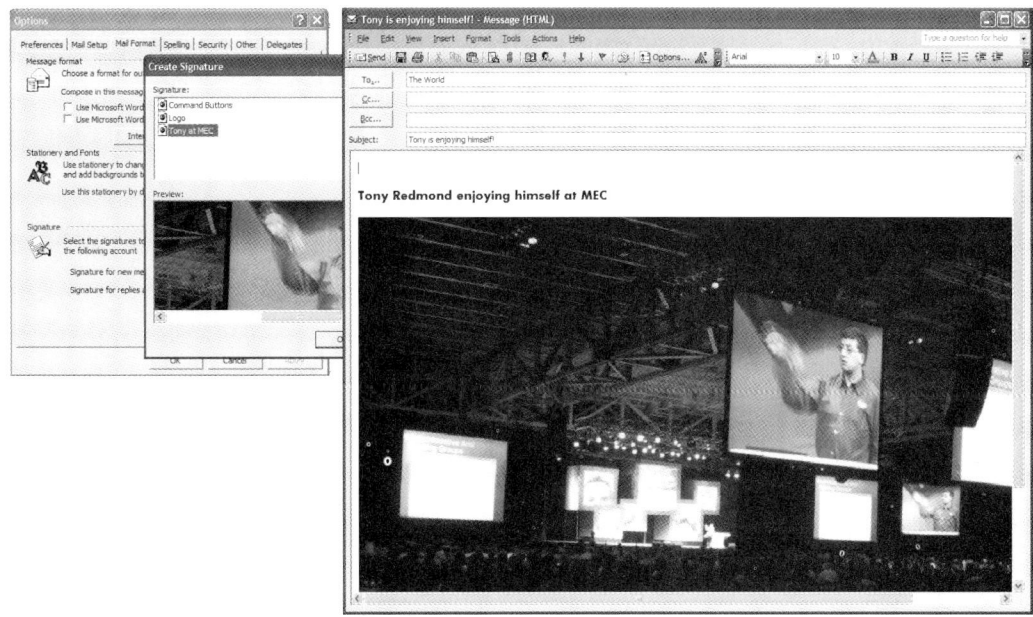

Figure 10.45 *Adding an outrageous graphic to an auto-signature file.*

logo looks like, it is a different matter when you send excessive data to other companies, because you are now consuming their network bandwidth, their time, and their storage to hold whatever you care to transmit. People already complain about spam, because these messages absorb resources that they have to pay for. Why would they not treat your graphically intense messages in the same light?

Apart from logos, trademarks, and other public information, such as a URL to the company's Web site, it is unwise to include corporate information in an auto-signature file. Titles and the name of your group are acceptable, as long as they make sense to the recipient, but if you send this information outside the company, you always have to be aware that recruiters or other people who want to learn about the company's organization for their own purposes could use the information. In addition, the GAL already contains all of the information you may want to transmit, so it is available to internal recipients. If required, they can click on the name of the sender or a recipient in the message header and view the properties of their entries in the GAL to discover details such as phone numbers, assistants, and even reporting relationships. Of course, the GAL is sometimes out-of-date, but it is usually the most reliable source of corporate information. Outlook 2003 makes things even easier by using smart tags (Figure

Chapter 10

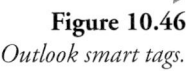

Figure 10.46
Outlook smart tags.

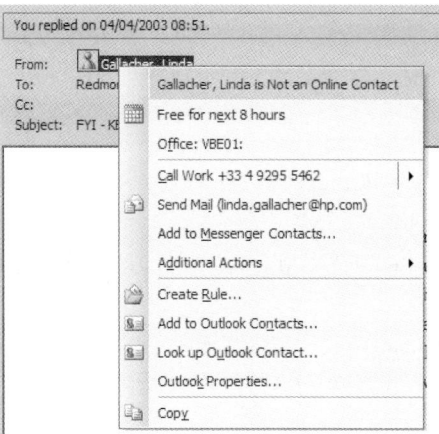

10.46), so you can click on a recipient to find out whether he or she is online (through instant messaging), available for a meeting (by checking free and busy information), and what his or her office phone number is (from the GAL).

Mail storms generated by "Reply All"

I'm sure that some sophisticated research into user interfaces has been conducted by messaging vendors over the years, but maybe they made the "Reply All" function a little too easy to use. The fact is, it is just too easy to reply to everyone while being blissfully unaware that thousands of people were circulated on the original memo. In addition, when many people add their own "me too," "good idea," or "I agree" contribution to the discussion, and reply to everyone else, we then have a fully fledged mail storm. With respect to bandwidth, two problems exist here. First, we have to deal with the sheer volume of messages generated by the contributors. Fortunately, there is an easy solution to this problem, because you can use the delete key to remove all the "me too" responses from your mailbox. I find that turning on the "View.AutoPreview" function in Outlook allows me to quickly scan my Inbox and identify candidate messages for instant culling.

The second issue is more invidious. Users tend to accept default options and do not want to mess too much with client settings in case they break things. By default, Outlook inserts the text of the original message into a reply, so you end up with messages that gently swell in size as Outlook adds each reply (short as it might be) to the thread. You can get rid of the "me too" replies by deleting them unseen, but this technique isn't so useful when the reply actually contains something meaningful and there is no real option except to download the full message, complete with the original text. As an example of the potential impact on message size generated by the "reply all syndrome," let us consider what happens in a typical email exchange.

- User A sends a message to seek opinions from ten colleagues. The original message is 5 KB.

- User B uses "Reply All" and includes User A's original text. This message is 10 KB.

- User C now responds with "Reply All" and includes the text from User B's message along with comments. The message has grown to 20 KB.

The cycle continues until everyone has contributed, and the final message that holds the complete thread might now be 100 KB. At this point, everyone involved probably has ten messages occupying 200 KB or more in his or her mailbox. The single-instance storage model in the Exchange Store helps to reduce the impact of this duplication, but you could end up with up to 2 MB of wasted space if the recipients' mailboxes are in different Stores. While tidy users will clean up and only keep the last message in a thread, many users only remove messages when forced to by reaching their quota and not being able to send any further email. The result is a lot of redundant information that is stored from here to the end of eternity, unless you use an automated tool such as the Mailbox Manager to clean up the mess.

There is no harm in inserting the original text in a reply, providing you use the text to add context or as the basis for edits. There is simply no case for including the original text just because it is there, so it is best practice to take the time to remove extraneous text before sending messages.

Attaching large files

We live in a drag-and-drop world. Users expect to be able to drag a document to their email client and drop it onto a message. Unless you compress an attachment, Outlook and Outlook Express take no further action to minimize the impact of sending large files with messages. This situation changes with the combination of Exchange 2003 and Outlook 2003, where compression techniques are used.

There is no doubt that the average size of messages has grown steadily over the last decade. Ten years ago, most corporate email accounts were on "green screen email" systems and the average message contained less than a page of text. Thus, fetching a message from the server generated no more than 4 to 6-KB traffic and we happily used 9.6-Kbps modems. If you track statistics from Exchange servers over a period, you will invariably find an increase in the average message size—to well over 100 KB in some companies. While messages with large multimegabyte attachments are the chief culprit, the reasons why today's email systems handle much larger messages include the following:

- The power of the drag-and-drop paradigm implemented in software such as Windows Explorer and Outlook makes it so easy to add an attachment to a message that people add attachments without thinking.
- People use graphics more extensively to convey ideas, so documents, presentations, and spreadsheets are full of diagrams, charts, and pictures.
- A wider range of software is used and few packages compress data.
- Especially in the United States, network bandwidth is more plentiful and far cheaper, so people take less care about bandwidth absorption.
- Users have better message editors (including Word), so they can include graphics in message content.
- Storage is also far cheaper, so the ever-growing size of files does not have a huge cost impact; users can have larger mailbox quotas, so they do not see the need to change the way they handle attachments.

You can try to educate people to use compression utilities such as WinZIP to process large attachments before adding them to messages. Word and basic graphic files such as bitmaps compress well, but compression utilities are less successful in reducing other file types (e.g., PowerPoint). However, users often forget to compress attachments, and the additional step makes the email system harder to use. In addition, administrators need to distribute copies of the chosen utility to all desktops.

If you are not able to deploy Exchange 2003 and Outlook 2003, you can still trade CPU cycles (to process the messages) against bandwidth and storage by installing an add-on product. For example, the Max Compression product from http://www.c2c.co.uk/ automatically compresses and decompresses attachments as users send and receive them through Outlook. Modules of the same product are available for Outlook Web Access working against both Exchange 5.5 and Exchange 2000 servers.

10.9 Helping users to do a better job

Examples of good email habits include the following:

- Because many people use smartphones, PDAs such as the BlackBerry, and Pocket PCs to read their email, it is best to write short messages or at least place the key points up front so that readers can understand what you want to say without going through multiple screens. It is also a good idea not to have important points or questions at the bottom of messages, because readers may never see them.

- To reduce the number of messages, do not respond immediately to a request if you do not have all the necessary information. Instead, wait until you have the information and then send a complete answer.

- The volume of email continues to rise, so it is helpful to use clear subjects so that recipients can pick the most important messages out of their Inboxes. Spammers pay a lot of attention to creating compelling message subjects and maybe this is something we can learn from them. If the topic being discussed changes during a message thread, alter the message subject to reflect the new discussion.

- Never use Word to compose a message and then send it as an attached document. Instead, use the advanced features of the message editor to format your text. Sending unnecessary attachments occupies valuable network bandwidth, ties up disk space, and makes the message hard for users of smartphones and hand-held devices to view.

The last good habit may save your job, or at least stop you from angering someone. It is always satisfying to compose the world's most cutting and sarcastic response to the inept ideas expressed in a message you receive, but it is even better to save your response as a draft and come back to it a few hours later. At that time, some mature reflection may convince you that it is a bad idea to send the text as written. Unfortunately, it is all too easy to send a message written in haste and then consider the consequences at leisure. Outlook includes a message recall function, but the speed with which Exchange transmits and delivers messages, plus the vast array of devices (smartphones, BlackBerries, etc.) that someone can use to receive the message means that the recall function has little chance of being able to retrieve the message before it is read. It is better to pause and save the message, leave it for an hour or so, and then review it before sending. Do not leave the message open, waiting to be sent, because it is easy to make a mistake and send the message inadvertently. If you do leave the message open, include an undeliverable address (such as "XXX") in the TO: or CC: line so that Outlook has to display an "unresolvable address" warning first.

10.9.2 Abusing disclaimers

The legal profession loves words. It especially loves words that establish a strict limitation of liability in as many circumstances as possible. Given the high profile of recent court actions that have featured email as exhibits, including the Arthur Andersen/Enron affair and the action taken by the U.S. Department of Justice against Microsoft, it is reasonable to assume that companies around the world have consulted their lawyers in an effort to restrict corporate liability for the actions of their employees.

The appearance of disclaimer text on the bottom of every outgoing message is evidence that managers are listening to the lawyers, but I often wonder whether this text has any effect. While the original disclaimers were blunt and to the point, some of the disclaimers are now bigger than the average size of messages they seek to protect. Apart from making messages larger, the disclaimers make messages harder and less friendly to read, especially if you insert the disclaimer into every reply as well.

On a purely facetious note, you might consider that implementing policies of this nature is a much-loved tactic of the PHB class. The real questions that we need to ask are whether recipients take very much notice of the dire legal warnings contained in the disclaimer and whether the warning has any legal meaning whatsoever in some of the places where people read the message. A legal warning that is valid in the United States is probably not effective in Eastern Europe, so all it does is keep managers and lawyers happy. On a more fundamental point, email is not like a fax, which someone can read as it arrives on a machine shared by a department or a complete building. Usually, email has a more precise delivery mechanism, since messages go to a known recipient who presumably must authenticate to a server before he or she can access the mailbox to pick up messages. However, these arguments do not usually hold much water when presented to the legal community. Your mileage will vary and policies differ from company to company.

As an illustration, here is a real-life example of a disclaimer seen in messages posted to the Internet mailing list for Exchange. I have removed the company name to protect the innocent. Of course, you have to question the wisdom of sending any message marked "confidential" to a public mailing list, but that is another matter.

This email and any files transmitted with it are confidential and are intended solely for the use of the individual or entity to whom they are addressed. If you are not the intended recipient, you have received this

10.9 Helping users to do a better job

email in error. Any use, dissemination, forwarding, printing, or copying of this email or any file attachments is strictly prohibited. If you have received this email in error, please immediately notify "Company Name" by telephone at 999 999 9999 or by reply email to the sender. You must destroy the original transmission and its contents.

"Company Name" has implemented antivirus software, and, while all care has been taken, it is the recipient's responsibility to ensure that any attachments are scanned for viruses prior to use.

Products such as Clearswift's MimeSweeper (www.clearswift.com) include features to add disclaimers on all outgoing messages. Alternatively, you can write your own SMTP transport event to do the job, remembering that you may have to install the event on all servers that handle email.

10.9.3 Out of office notifications

Out of office notifications (otherwise known as OOF) inform correspondents that a recipient will not be able to deal with their messages for some reason. As the name implies, the most common reason is that someone is traveling and will not have access to email for an extended period. Given the ability of people to reach their email via dial-in connections when they are on the road, out of office notifications are most useful when they tell you that someone is away on vacation. To be effective, the text of a notification should tell correspondents:

- A brief reason why the recipient won't be able to respond
- The next time the recipient is likely to be able to process email
- An alternate person they can contact for specific reasons, such as management of a project or to provide information on a product, together with contact details (email addresses and phone numbers)

Properly used, out of office notifications are very useful. The issue is whether to allow Exchange to send OOFs outside the company. You can control OOF transmission on a domain-by-domain basis by creating a separate Internet message format for specific domains or by amending the default "*" format if you use it. Once you make the decision to transmit OOFs, the trick is to get users to include the right information, as outlined previously. Unfortunately, short of creating a script to send messages to every user in the organization and collate what comes back, there is no automated way to check user OOF information. Best practice is to create awareness within the user community regarding the effect a sloppy, uninformative, or overly informative OOF can have.

In Exchange 2003, you have another tweak that you can apply to control OOF notices by inserting a registry setting to limit OOF generation back to the originator only if the recipient is explicitly mentioned as a TO: or CC: for the message. In other words, an originator will not receive any notices from messages going to non-Exchange distribution lists such as Internet mailing lists or even distribution lists that exist in another Exchange organization. To suppress the notices, add the "SuppressOOFs-ToDistributionLists" parameter as a DWORD value to the registry at the following location:

```
HKLM\System\CurrentControlSet\Services\MSExchangeIS\
ParametersSystem
```

Set the value to 1 to suppress OOFs, or leave it at 0 for normal behavior. You need to add this parameter to all mailbox servers before it becomes 100 percent effective.

10.9.4 Some other bad email habits

There are many other smaller points of email etiquette that cause people grief. These include:

- Replying to a message that you received as a BCC recipient when the author really would prefer you not to

- Forwarding a message to a new set of recipients without permission of the original author. This becomes an especially grievous fault if you send the message to external recipients, because you may disclose corporate information that should stay inside the company.

- Using an auto-reply (OOF) message where you do not give useful information to the recipient. It is nice to know that people are enjoying themselves on holiday, but it is even better to know where to go (preferably with a telephone number and email address) in their absence. Obviously, you need to balance informing internal correspondents with the requirement not to provide sensitive company information to external people who receive the OOF.

Minor breeches of etiquette usually cause frustration only and do not absorb additional resources. However, the frustration level can be intense, especially if you inadvertently tell someone about something he or she should learn about in another manner. For example, telling someone that you have heard that he or she is about to be promoted when you are not the boss is possibly acceptable, but telling a person that he or she is going to move to another job is not.

10.10 Email and viruses

Any Exchange server that runs without protection against email viruses is a disaster waiting to happen. New viruses spread quickly once they enter a messaging system and they circulate at an ever-increasing rate. In March 2004, MessageLabs, a notable provider of managed email services, reported that 2 percent of the messages that pass through its systems contained identifiable viruses—a percentage of messages containing potential problems that many large companies are likely to experience. Today's viruses exploit flaws in software (including Outlook) and the curiosity of human beings to propagate faster than ever before. People find it difficult not to read a message with an interesting attachment or respond quickly to a message that proclaimed that someone loves them.

A sizable proportion of the messages that circulate around the Internet today contain embedded objects or attachments, and many hide viruses. The pervasiveness of common Internet protocols means that you can confidently send attachments in the expectation that their contents will survive the transit between sender and recipient intact. Once in a mailbox, clients can download the attachment, and most PC-based clients can process the code in embedded objects unless security settings prevent this. Executables sent in attachments are an obvious source of potential contamination from viruses, whether included in messages received from outside the organization or those unwittingly passed on by people working inside the organization. It is frustrating to see normally sensible individuals send executables to their friends every Christmas on the basis that the executable contains nothing more than a suitable cheery message dressed up in holiday decorations. Despite warnings to treat executables with suspicion and not to send executables unless absolutely required, the same old Christmas card executables appear every year. Short of firing anyone who sends such an attachment, I suspect that it will be very difficult to eliminate these electronic greetings. Thankfully, electronic cards are an exception to the rule. Most users are now aware of the problems posed by executable-based viruses, and system administrators have taken steps to address the problem. For example, some sites disable floppy drives, while most have implemented some sort of automatic virus checking for system memory and .EXE and .DLL files whenever PCs are booted.

10.10.1 A brief history of office viruses

The first document-transmitted virus appeared in the Word for Windows "Prank" macro in 1995. The virus worked by inserting a macro called "Payload" into NORMAL.DOT, the default Word for Windows document template, and propagated itself by spreading the macro every time the user opened a document on the PC. This virus was primitive in concept and implementation and resulted in some irritation, but it was essentially harmless because you could eradicate the virus easily. All it ever did was display a dialog box, but it pointed the way for others to adopt the technique by extending the basic virus concept by including some more malevolent instructions. WordBASIC and Visual BASIC for Applications (VBA), the macro programming languages used in different versions of Word for Windows, are both capable of including calls to Windows API functions and file operations. In turn, virus writers can use these calls to inflict grave damage to user files. For instance, it is easy to write a macro that will automatically delete all sorts of important system files whenever the macro fires.

Many Windows products include a macro language, and the majority of these languages are already capable of making the same type of damaging system calls. You can create precisely the same effect as the "Prank" macro with an Excel macro written in VBA, or in a WordPerfect for Windows macro. Developers extend macro languages all the time to make them easier to use and less programming-centric. These developments make system administrators nervous, because users do not exercise the same level of care and attention when they deal with documents or spreadsheets. The lack of care when opening documents is perhaps natural, because so many documents flow around a messaging system, but it means that viruses created as document macros spread rapidly once they've been introduced into an installation.

10.10.2 The Melissa virus, Outlook, and variants

Everyone in the email world received a wake-up call when the Melissa virus appeared on March 26, 1999, as the payload in a message that had the ability to replicate itself and infect other servers. Melissa was the first virus to exploit features in MAPI and Outlook and caused a huge amount of concern within the Exchange community. Other similar viruses, such as "Papa," which used a variation on the approach to accomplish much the same effect, followed Melissa to add to the workload of harassed system administrators. The Melissa virus initially appeared in a message posted from an America Online account to the alt.sex bulletin board and spread rapidly, perhaps helped by the popularity of this Internet. Microsoft and other companies with major deployments of Exchange had to stop Internet connectivity until they could disinfect servers.

The New Jersey authorities tracked down David Smith, the author of the Melissa virus, in April 1999 and charged him with four counts of violating state computer laws for "interruption of public communication." His lawyer, Edward F. Borden, Jr., pleaded that Melissa did not cause damage because no data was corrupted or files deleted. Indeed, all the virus had done was to send a relatively innocuous message to 50 other people. No mention was made of the cost of isolating and removing the virus from documents around the world or the frantic overtime worked by system administrators to keep their messaging systems up under the strain of the attack. Smith eventually pleaded guilty in December 1999 and received a 20-month prison sentence with a $20,000 fine in May 2002, with the judge explicitly noting that a prison sentence was necessary to deter other would-be hackers.

The second major attack that exploited MAPI and Outlook came in early June 1999 with the Worm.ExploreZip virus, which launched a much more destructive attack on servers, because the virus deleted files on the infected PC, including any Word, PowerPoint, or Excel documents that it could find. The infected message deposited an executable on the PC to search out files on disks, including network file shares. Once located, the virus replaced files with useless zero-byte-length files.

Programmers also seemed to be high on the Worm.ExploreZip hate list, since common source code files for programs that you'd expect to find on PCs used for development (C language header and source files, assembler programs, and so on) were also infected. Users did not realize that the virus had affected their files because the files still seemed to be in place. It was only when users attempted to open the useless zero-byte-length files that the dreadful effect of the virus became apparent. Some companies lost gigabytes of information before they managed to stop the attack. Good backup procedures saved the day for some people, but many users lost the complete contents of their local drives.

The Nimda virus (2001) raised the bar higher by attacking servers on multiple fronts through file shares, IIS, Outlook, and Outlook Express. Nimda inflicted enormous damage on many corporations and stopped some operations dead. The threat continues, and there is no sign that the bad guys will stop their attempts to come up with new attack techniques any time soon.

10.10.3 Luring users toward infection

Apart from the impact wreaked by code in virus payloads, virus authors attempt to exploit human weaknesses by making their messages appear as normal as possible. The aim is to lure users into opening the infected attachment and so cause the attack to proceed. The first viruses, such as Worm.ExploreZip and Melissa, used the "trusted sender" technique to convince users to drop their level of vigilance. The payload message appears to come from a trusted correspondent and contains information that you might reasonably expect to receive. In the case of Worm.ExploreZip, the attachment had a WinZip icon and exploited the human fallibility that we all tend to open attachments we receive via email from trusted sources without thinking about what the attachment might contain. The attachment is not a true zipped file. Instead, the attachment is a hugely destructive program!

It is only natural for users to open any message with a subject that appears to be important, and curiosity is enough to make them complete the task by opening the infected document. The Melissa virus lured people to open the document by including the text:

```
"Here's the important document you asked for… don't show
it to anyone else ;-)."
```

Once the user opened the infected document, the virus lowered the security settings for Word to allow macros to run automatically when the user opened documents in the future. In other words, users would not be asked whether they wanted to run macros—the code would just execute! The author of the Worm.ExploreZip virus clearly studied Melissa and copied some of the techniques. In this case, the text that lured users is:

```
"Hi <User>

I received your email and I shall send you a reply ASAP.
Till then, take a look at the attached zipped docs."
```

How many users would have a second thought about opening the attachment? The Papa virus exploited another human failing: to trust instructions that come in messages, especially if they come from apparently trusted sources or the computer tells them to do something. This virus instructed users not to disable the macros in the Excel attachment when they opened the attachment. The aim here was to execute the virus contained in the VBA code. Other viruses instructed users to enable ActiveX controls in Internet Explorer to allow some processing to continue. It is relatively easy for administrators to warn users about messages with specific attachments or subjects, so current viruses make things

10.10 Email and viruses

harder by changing attachment names, subjects, and message content using randomly generated text. When this happens, people can no longer manually detect infected messages. Antivirus software recognizes viruses through patterns of data and other hallmarks and are not fooled by switching words around.

It did not take long before email viruses moved from being not particularly destructive to inflicting massive damage on a user's desktop. First-generation email viruses swamped email networks and often caused servers to come to a complete and total halt while administrators ran disinfection routines. Viruses continue to swamp networks, cause server shutdowns, and delete hundreds of important files. Each time a new virus appears, administrators have to disable external connections and disrupt the flow of email in and out of the company, which obviously has an immediate effect on communication. Users expect email to be available all the time, and they expect messages to go immediately. Once connections are closed, huge queues accumulate and it can take several hours for normal service to resume, with an obvious domino effect on user productivity and cost to the enterprise.

10.10.4 The dangers of HTML

HTML-formatted email has dangers of its own. A virus carried around in HTML code within an email has not yet appeared, but the danger exists. If you examine the VBscript code shown in Figure 10.47, you can see some simple HTML code that you can compose in FrontPage and then paste into an auto-signature file. As it happens, the code is not very exciting. It is an edited version of code from messages posted to the Internet mailing list for Exchange, so it is a real example of the types of messages that people are already sending. When executed, the HTML commands add a set of command buttons to the bottom of a message (Figure 10.48). The intention behind the command buttons is very laudable, since they act as pointers to different Web sites, but a real danger exists in the processing that could occur when users click on a command button when they do not know exactly what will happen next. For example, the code could connect to a Web site and download an executable to the PC. Equally, the command button could execute code to delete messages, send some email, remove all of your personal contacts, and other unfriendly acts. An infection could even add HTML code to everyone's auto-signature file and propagate itself in that manner.

There is no good way to stop users from including HTML code in their auto-signature files, although Outlook 2003 includes a feature called External Mail Content Control, which you can use to block users from loading

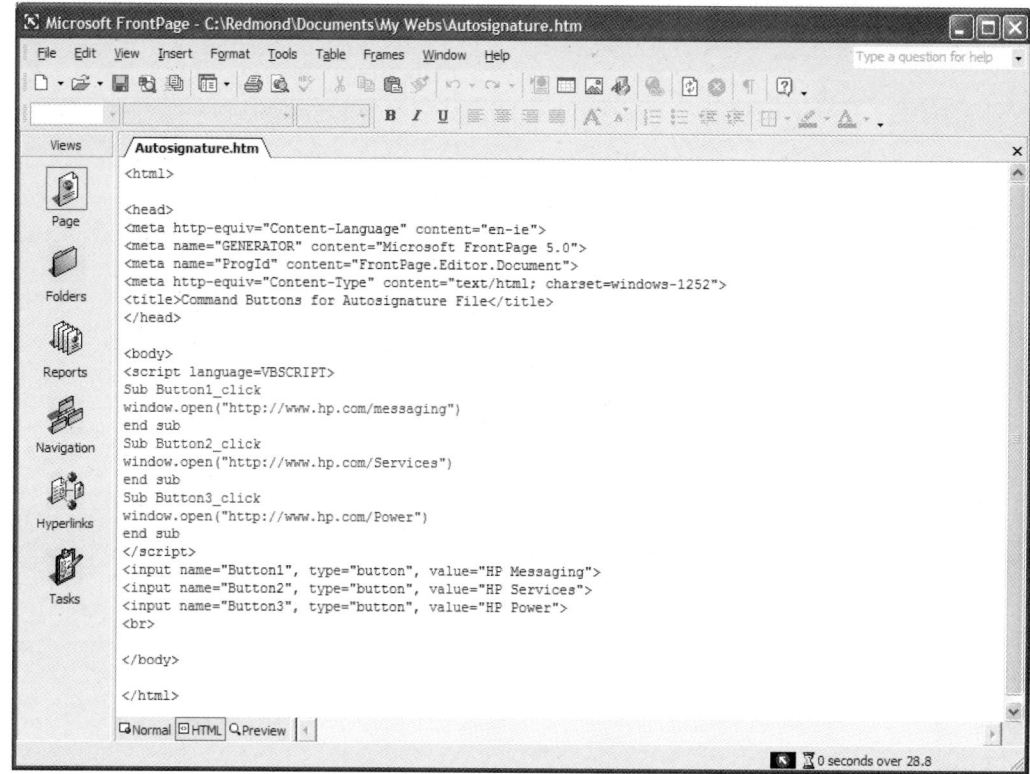

Figure 10.47   *Creating HTML code with Microsoft FrontPage.*

images and other external content referenced in HTML code inside messages. This feature blocks a trick that some spammers use to avoid detection, where they send messages that seem innocent but contain links to load content at viewing time. If spam can slip underneath your guard, it is fair to say that content that is more malicious can as well. If your antivirus tool does not proactively scan for dangerous HTML content, you can moderate some of the danger by:

- Education: Tell users not to click on command buttons displayed in messages.

- Administration: Since programmers and administrators are the most likely people to use HTML code in auto-signature files, you should provide guidance about the potential danger of such code to these people.

10.10 Email and viruses

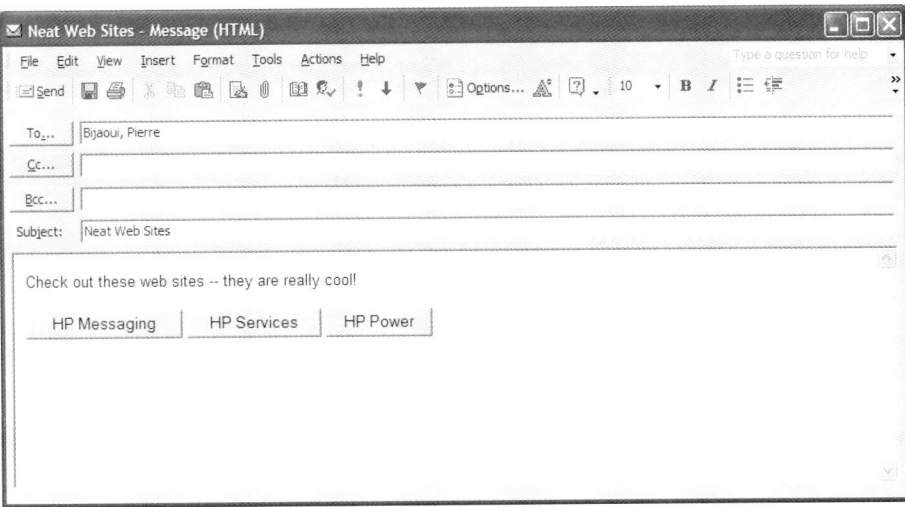

Figure 10.48 *HTML code creating command buttons in a message.*

- Enforcement: If necessary, you can amend Windows login scripts to search for HTML auto-signature files in user directories and delete any found. Auto-signature files are stored in the directory:

```
\Documents and Settings\Username\Application Data\
Microsoft\Signatures
```

Detecting HTML-enabled viruses transmitted in the body of messages is a challenge for antivirus products. Before making a decision on which antivirus software to deploy to protect Exchange, ask vendors how they deal with this danger, along with all the other points on your antivirus checklist. Good products will either be able to identify and disinfect problems in HTML or have clearly defined plans outlining how they will do this in the future. Vendors of second-rate products will not even be aware of the problem and will be unable to begin to discuss possible solutions, while vendors of leading-edge products will be working on a solution and will possibly combine message body scanning with other interesting features such as content management. This means that the scanners can examine the body of outgoing and incoming messages for profanities or other unacceptable content as well as potentially damaging code. It is an area that can be expected to develop greatly to keep pace with new probes and attacks from virus authors.

10.10.5 The damage caused by viruses

Despite the workload it generated for the many harassed system administrators, the Melissa virus and its followers did some good. It gave a wake-up call to everyone who was not running AV software and forced those who did to update their pattern files. More importantly, it illustrated the inherent danger that comes from a dependency on an integrated suite such as Office. In this instance, attackers used one component (Word) to exploit the fact that VBA code could use Outlook to dispatch infected messages. Melissa really did not do much damage—its effect could have been much worse, a point that rapidly became apparent when later viruses arrived.

Virus authors continue to explore new techniques or variants of previous attacks—all you can expect is for threats to continue to occur. Now that email is a proven viable method to distribute viruses, an increasing number of "me to" or developments of existing code-based virus attacks occur. The "Love Bug" virus, first reported in early May 2000, is a classic example of a combination virus and worm that caused enormous grief for major corporations, including Microsoft, and high-profile establishments such as the British Houses of Parliament. AV professionals regard Love Bug as a virus, because it inserts code onto a PC's hard drive to pull additional infective code from the network; it is a worm, because it replicates over the network. Unlike Melissa, the Love Bug virus depends on Windows scripting to locate Outlook on a PC and send it commands to generate messages to infect other users. A particularly nasty piece of the virus creates a new home page for a browser with code to steal passwords and email for the virus author. Unhappily (for the authors), the code is easy to interpret (save the code as a text file and open it with Notepad or another text editor to examine what it does), and the email address in the code gave the first clue regarding where to look for the culprits, eventually leading to a number of students in the Philippines.

The Love Bug attack was easy to detect, because not many people send each other Visual BASIC script files, so the arrival of such a file in a message titled "I love you" should have heightened suspicions. Unfortunately, many users have become so accustomed to receiving and launching attachments of all types in messages that they probably would not have known or noticed the Visual BASIC script icon on the attachment. The Love Bug virus set new records in terms of the speed of propagation and evolution of variants, with five additional variants reported in the wild in the days following the original attack. Variants seen since include an invoice for a Mother's Day gift, with the attack provoked when a user clicked on the icon to view the purported invoice, and others with subjects such as "Joke for you." In all cases, the viruses exploited human frailty and curiosity, relying on people's desires to read about interesting items that had nothing whatsoever to do with work. In some respects, the success of these viruses is similar to the success of hunters who lure animals into traps with tasty morsels of food.

Since Love Bug, we have seen many more attacks. According to Sophos, Klez and Bug Bear were the most widespread viruses in 2002. The persistence of viruses has changed. Love Bug appeared and disappeared very quickly, because virus checkers were able to eliminate infected messages very effectively. On the other hand, Klez topped the monthly chart for most popular viruses (an oxymoron in itself) for seven months in 2002. This proves both the extra persistence gained through better disguising of payloads and a worrying lack of discipline in terms of maintaining antivirus patterns that may have let viruses slip through long after the antivirus companies identified their signatures and released pattern files that companies could deploy to stop the viruses.

As horrible as the thought is, we may not have seen the worst yet. Imagine the damage if the code in a new virus searches your PC for documents marked "Important" or "Confidential" and then attached them to messages sent to your competitors or posted them to an Internet mailing list. We have already seen email-enabled viruses that are capable of mutating, when they change the contents and subjects of messages to get around the warnings issued to look out for specific attachments or message subjects.

User education about the dangers of viruses is not something that happens overnight, nor does it come about through a one-off class given to people when they become Exchange users. As we know from email viruses, new threats appear all the time, and administrators both owe it to their users and can save themselves a lot of time and effort through good communication and advice. As an example, here are four simple tips that can be given to users to help stop people from opening suspect attachments.

- Do not open an attachment if it does not seem to belong with the message. For example, if the message contains a small amount of text saying something like "Hi, how are you today?" and no attachment is mentioned, any attachment is suspect and should be treated with caution.

- Do not open an attachment if you would not expect to get it from the sender. The Melissa virus is transmitted through messages that state "Here's the important document you asked for... don't show it to anyone else ;-)." If you do not expect to receive an important document from the sender, then the attachment is suspect.

- Do not open attachments received from unknown correspondents. If you receive something, reply to the sender and ask him or her what the document is all about before opening it.
- Do not open an electronic greeting card from anyone, no matter how happy you feel about the sender or the particular time of year.

The last point is critical. Users should be encouraged to stop sending electronic greeting cards that attach executable programs. People have been sending these types of messages for years, but the early examples were composed of either simple text or escape character sequences that caused the terminal to display primitive graphics. No great harm came about from these messages, even if they took up almost 50 KB of valuable network to send. Today's executables, which are far more charming and cute, take up even more space and can hide a virus. Users need to be on their guard at holiday time, when electronic greeting cards are at their peak.

Microsoft has now addressed many of the concerns about how Outlook handles attachments that could contain harmful code, but there is no doubt that virus authors will attempt to exploit any possible weaknesses both in software and user behavior, so this is good enough reason to track any hot fixes that Microsoft releases for Outlook on a regular basis.

Email viruses are not very new. Back in the days of "green screen email," the IBM Education Networks BITNET and EARN and the IBM internal VNET networks were hit by a similar "worm" in 1987. Users received a message with a batch file embedded at the bottom of the file. The start of the file had instructions on how to save the message to disk and run it. It claimed it would then display a "Christmas Tree" on the user's terminal. What it actually did was mail itself to every one in the user's "Nickname" file, the equivalent of today's "Contacts" folder.

Administrators need to keep up-to-date with threats as they develop. You browse the security bulletins posted on sites such as http://www.ntsecurity.net/, http://www.cert.org/, or http://www.sar.com/, or have messages sent to you from alert lists.[6] Of course, an obvious problem with an email alert is that it may not get to you or to an administrator who can action the alert if a virus has already attacked your mail server. In general, independent security advice is better than that offered by AV vendors. There have been

---

6. You can subscribe to the Windows 2000 security alert list by sending an email to listserv@listserv.ntsecurity.net with the words "subscribe securityupdate anonymous" in the body of the message (without the quotes).

suspicions in the past that vendors have stirred the pot of controversy by announcing the arrival of new viruses that their product has detected first or maybe even uniquely! Sometimes these viruses are real, and sometimes the viruses never appear outside the vendor's software laboratory.

10.10.6 Multistage protection

Document-borne viruses are a major challenge for messaging system administrators, especially so in the case of systems such as Exchange, which place a high degree of importance on information sharing through distributed document repositories such as public folders. What can you do to defeat the best efforts of document virus creators? There are three basic ways to detect viruses:

- PC-based: Deploy AV software to all PCs to check as users create and copy files. These products do not understand the structure of Exchange files such as PSTs and OSTs, but they will stop users from creating infected files before attaching them to messages. Make sure that you regularly update AV pattern files on all PCs so that the software can detect new viruses.

- Store-based: Deploy Store-based AV software to ensure that any viruses that arrive via email are detected and disinfected before they have a chance to spread. Know if the AV software is unable to cope with specific format or message types and determine how you can protect your servers. For example, can the AV software scan for viruses in ZIP files? If not, maybe you want to block all ZIP files at the perimeter of your messaging infrastructure. How do you scan encrypted messages? There is no good answer for this problem today, but at least you can console yourself with the fact that the mass virus attacks do not usually cloak themselves in a layer of encryption, because the virus authors want to generate easily accessible messages.

- Perimeter-based: Consider deploying AV software that scans incoming SMTP traffic before messages arrive at Exchange. You can combine AV protection with other barriers, such as antispam measures, to ensure that only acceptable email penetrates inside the company. Note that these barriers will not stop infected messages from arriving through connectors such as X.400 or Lotus Notes. In these situations you depend on the administrators of those systems to deploy adequate protection to eliminate most viruses; you also rely on your Store-based AV software to detect any viruses that creep in.

If you use front-end servers, you probably do not need to run antivirus scanners on those servers, since you can leave the scanning and disinfection to Store-based products that run on the back-end servers. However, it is a good idea to consider running antispam and content scanners (including blocks for suspicious files and attachments) on the front-end servers, so that the only messages that pass to the back end are those that absolutely need to get through. Best practice is to erect barriers at multiple levels of the messaging system and desktop, so that if a virus manages to get past one check, checks at the next will detect the virus. Combining multiple levels of protection creates a more resilient solution, and the combination of Store- and perimeter-based checking is an excellent way to catch the vast majority of viruses. (See Figure 10.49.)

Despite recent virus attacks conducted via email, some managers balk at the investment required to deploy multitier virus checking. It is true that the licenses for virus checkers can be expensive, especially when you have to deploy across multiple servers, but this should not be a reason to attempt to take any budgetary shortcuts. The current generations of Windows and Exchange allow you to consolidate servers into a smaller number of computers, and if you take the opportunity to consolidate, you can save a great deal of money in software license fees for add-in products such as virus checkers. Even so, the cost to deploy virus checkers can still appear high to the untrained eye, especially when it does not make a direct contribution to

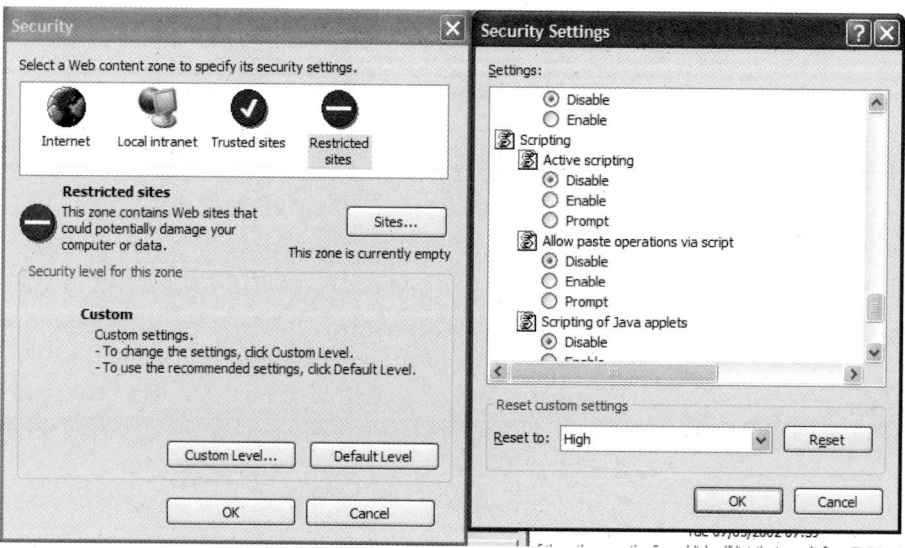

Figure 10.49 *Changing the security settings in Outlook 2002.*

the company's bottom line. With this in line, you need an argument to convince doubters that the investment is worthwhile.

Consider this scenario: Dealing with an infected message is a major hassle, and you may lose the email service for a day or so while you take servers offline for disinfection. However, sending an infected message to your business partners is a sure way to demonstrate that your company has a very low degree of attention to detail and does not care very much about secure business communications. A company that dispatches infected email regularly is clearly not one that you would care to do much business with; there is usually a competitor in the same business that manages its email correctly. No businessperson likes to think he or she might project a bad company image. Yet now that so much communication is via email, why take the risk of projecting an image of ignorance and bad management to customers? Enough said. Make sure that you scan every outgoing message for viruses in the same way as every incoming message is checked. Protect your business and your company's image by investing in good antivirus tools. From a purely organizational perspective, administrators need to agree on a common protection policy across the organization. It does not make sense to run multiple AV products, since this makes tracking updates more difficult. A simple policy includes the following:

- Agreement on the levels within the messaging infrastructure where antivirus products are installed: desktop, server, and backbone

- Agreement on how to secure servers by applying lockdown tools or closing off potential holes. For example, you should avoid creating file shares on an Exchange server to minimize the impact of a Nimda-type attack.

- Agreement on the antivirus products in use and the version of that product to use on production servers

- Full details of who is responsible for monitoring sources such as newsgroups, antivirus Web sites, and internal sources for information about virus outbreaks, as well as how this information disseminates to both administrators and users. It is easy for administrators to focus on the need to protect servers and stop new viruses from arriving. However, if you do not tell users that a virus is in the wild and active, their level of vigilance will remain low and more will become infected. Do not depend on email being available to distribute bulletins about new viruses, because it may be necessary to take down servers to disinfect databases or stop connectors between routing groups or to the Internet to prevent further spread. You should have some alternatives in place to ensure that as many people as possible know about a virus and can react accordingly.

- Be sure that you do not cause unnecessary panic by reacting to every new report of a virus attack, because an increasing percentage of such reports are hoaxes. Some hoaxes have advised users to delete specific files from their PCs on the pretext that the files are infected, only for users to discover later that the files are essential . . . such as a Java virtual machine.

- A mechanism to distribute new virus patterns across all servers in the organization

- Agreement on how to test new versions of antivirus products against new versions of Exchange and other associated products (such as new editions of IIS or Windows). Some products are sensitive to the version number of a specific component, such as STORE.EXE, and will stop working if you install a patch that increments the build number for the module. You need to be sure that the procedures for

Table 10.5 *Details of an Antivirus Protection Policy*

Protection	Achieved through . . .
Firewall Filter	All SMTP entry points into the company are able to filter, quarantine, or reject messages based on string comparisons against header or attachment names.
Store	Sybari Antigen runs on mailbox servers to protect against any infected messages that sneak through the firewall.
Store Cleaning	If the Store protection fails to detect a new virus, perhaps because the pattern file is out-of-date, utilities from Microsoft are available to remove messages from a Mailbox or Public Store based on strings in the header, message body, or attachment names. Jobs to clean a server can be launched from a central location.
Voicemail	After a virus attack begins, users receive voicemail notifications to warn them against opening infected messages.
Email	To back up the voicemail and inform users who may be out of the office, automated distribution lists are used to send flash messages to inform users that a virus attack is under way and tell them what action to take if they receive an infected message.
Global Response	When an attack happens, individuals from key internal functions around the world convene via con-call to collect data, determine the actual status, and coordinate an appropriate response. These individuals also check that the virus is not a hoax and check sites such as www.sophos.com to validate newsflashes about new viruses.
Desktop	Separate antivirus utilities run on Windows-based desktops to guard against infected files.

implementing a patch from Microsoft incorporate a check for antivirus support.

As an example of how to incorporate the principles outlined into a protection policy, Table 10.5 lists the steps used by a large company to protect its Exchange environment against attack. As you can see, they achieve protection through a combination of software and people action, all coordinated into multilayered protection.

One mistake with a virus can be very expensive, with damage running well into millions of dollars for even a small organization. Disinfecting a system, especially a large networked system, will take a lot of time and effort, and it is probable that the system will be unavailable to users while you eliminate the viruses.

10.11 Exchange antivirus tools

The world was very different when Exchange 4.0 first shipped in March 1996. At that time, most viruses were spread through infected floppy diskettes, and good floppy hygiene was normally sufficient to stop virus propagation. As people started to swap more and more attachments through the email system, the dangers of spreading infected files through email or postings to public folders became very evident. Trend Micro Inc. was one of the first companies to respond to the threat for Exchange and shipped its AV product soon after Exchange 4.0 appeared. Originally, Exchange was a very functional and feature-rich email system, but it was not very open to extensions. MAPI was the only API available to developers to build client and server extensions for Exchange, and Microsoft never designed MAPI to be a way to integrate antivirus protection into Exchange. Nevertheless, products such as Trend Micro's Antivirus for Exchange used MAPI to log on to user mailboxes and watch for newly arriving messages that contained attachments. As attachments arrived, the AV product sprang into life and checked the content for viruses.

10.11.1 The problems with MAPI

Implementing an AV solution through MAPI is not straightforward, and a number of problems exist for the developers to solve. First, after Exchange accepts an infected message and delivers it to the user mailbox, a race occurs between the user and the AV agent to get to the attachment first. While software usually responds much faster than people do, it is unlikely, but theoretically possible, that an infected attachment might get through. Second, the requirement to log on to each mailbox is an inefficient access mechanism and becomes more inefficient as the number of mailboxes scale up on a server. This was not important in the early days of Exchange, since few servers supported more than a couple of hundred mailboxes, but the scalability issue became increasingly important as Exchange servers started to support thousands of mailboxes. Third, if Exchange delivers the same infected attachment to many mailboxes, the AV software might attempt to disinfect the attachment many times, duplicating the work repeatedly until it eradicates the virus.

Even with all these issues, AV vendors persisted with MAPI, simply because there did not appear to be any alternative. Microsoft did not provide an AV interface and did not document the private interfaces it used within the product. Faced with this situation, the AV vendors made the best of what they had to work with and concentrated on steadily improving their products, including building management interfaces and tools to make AV software easier to manage, as well as adding capabilities to support Internet gateways and platforms other than NT. The first break in the MAPI wall occurred when Sybari shipped Antigen for Exchange in 1998. Sybari knew about the problems with MAPI, so it avoided the problems and perfected a technique (the famous "ESE shimmy") to swap out ESE.DLL (the DLL that drives the Extensible Storage Engine, the heart of the Store) for a brief period to load its code and then swap ESE.DLL back. Once loaded, Antigen monitors the attachments table in the IS to check attachments as new messages arrive. It is an effective and scalable technique, but one that Microsoft hated and refused to support until convinced otherwise by the success that Sybari had and the fact that other vendors, such as Trend Micro, started to use ESE instead of MAPI in their products.

10.11.2 VSAPI—virus scanning API

Microsoft's response to Antigen's use of ESE and the complaints about MAPI from other AV vendors is the Virus Scanning Application Programming Interface (VSAPI), a fully supported and documented interface designed to allow AV vendors to integrate their code directly into important Exchange components, such as the Store, MTA, and Routing Engine. However, the first release of VSAPI did not include all of the hooks required to support the feature set provided by existing products, so most vendors built test versions that used VSAPI but continued to base their "real" products (or rather, those that they recommended to customers) on MAPI or ESE.

Microsoft responded with updated versions of VSAPI 2.0 in Exchange 2000 SP1 followed by VSAPI 2.5 in Exchange 2003. The latest version allows AV software to tag infected messages so that Exchange does not deliver them to users. With VSAPI 2.0, AV software can remove malicious content, but a message always arrives in a user's mailbox. Users know that they have received an infected message and can contact the originator to determine whether he or she knows if there is an infection problem. However, especially in the middle of a heavy virus outbreak, you simply want to suppress everything and have messages stopped dead in their tracks, so VSAPI 2.5 allows AV software to control whether the Store aborts the delivery of infected messages. It is up to the AV vendor whether to enable this feature in its software. Another change in VSAPI 2.5 allows AV software to send a notification automatically to the originator of an infected message to tell him or her that there is a problem. Of course, all the features in VSAPI are of no help unless you run Exchange 2000 or 2003 with an AV product that supports VSAPI, but at least we now have a common API. All of the major AV vendors, including Trend Micro, McAfee, and Sybari, are committed to VSAPI.

All classes of virus checkers—even VSAPI—have difficulty with encrypted messages. The problem is simple. By definition, the encryption process protects the contents of an encrypted message against access unless you possess the necessary keys. AV software does not have the keys, so it cannot detect the patterns in content that allow it to recognize viruses. While you might consider that not being able to deal with encrypted messages is a shortcoming and a potential hole in antivirus protection, the impact is lessened when you realize that people who send an infected message to your company are unlikely to possess the necessary public keys to allow them to encrypt the content, unless you share private keys outside the company. Encryption is more of a problem if a virus gets into a company and then is circulated in encrypted messages. This is one situation when an insistence that all messages should be encrypted to protect against unauthorized access can introduce problems that the authors of such policies do not even dream of. If a problem with encrypted messages occurs, all you can do is attempt to disinfect the Store and remove all instances of the offending message. Microsoft provides the ISSCAN utility for this purpose for Exchange 5.5, and you can use the ExMerge utility to remove specific messages from Exchange 2000 or 2003 servers.

Any virus checker will steal some CPU cycles from your system. In most cases, the cost is between 5 percent and 10 percent, which is acceptable given the benefit gained through better protection. Your mileage may vary in line with message volume. In any case, if your system can't afford to give up 15 percent of its CPU capacity, it's time to upgrade your hardware, since the server is incapable of handling the peaks in demand that are inevitable in any messaging environment.

10.11.3 AV impact on multilingual clients

The language of the first client that connects to a mailbox determines the names of the default folders (Inbox, Deleted Items, and so on). Usually, this is not a problem, since the client runs software in the same language as Exchange and the server, but it can result in an interesting side effect in multilingual environments, where the antivirus software runs in a language different from the client's language. Exchange is available in far fewer languages than Outlook, and antivirus vendors follow the example set by Microsoft and limit the number of supported languages. Thus, you may find an English-language Exchange server supporting clients running in Portuguese, Spanish, Greek, and so on.

The problem occurs if the antivirus software performs a MAPI logon to connect to a mailbox before the user. To Exchange, the connection appears the same as any other MAPI logon, so the server recognizes the language specified in the connect request and creates the default set of folders in that language. Therefore, we may end up with folder names that the users do

Table 10.6 *Standard Folder Names and Identifiers*

Folder Name	Identifier
Deleted Items	3
Outbox	4
Sent Mail	5
Inbox	6
Calendar	9
Contacts	10
Journal	11
Notes	12
Tasks	13
Drafts	16

Figure 10.50
Setting folder names in VBScript.

```
Set myOutlookApplication = CreateObject("Outlook.Application")
Set mynamespace = myOutlookApplication.GetNameSpace("MAPI")
Mynamespace.GetDefaultFolder(3).Name="Wastebasket"
Mynamespace.GetDefaultFolder(9).Name="Diary
```

not recognize and cannot work with. The problem does not occur with AV software based on the VSAPI.

Outlook provides no way to reset the names of the default folders (this was possible with the earlier Exchange 4.0 and 5.0 clients), but you can change the folder names through some VBScript commands. Scripts typically execute in the context of an active Outlook session, so you should put the commands in a script that can be stored in a public folder for users to access. You need no special privileges to run the script. Table 10.6 lists the standard set of folder names in English, along with the identifier you need to reference in order to work with each folder.

Using these identifiers, we can build a script to modify the special folder names to whatever values we require. The script code in Figure 10.50 changes the Deleted Items folder to "Wastebasket" and the Calendar folder to "Diary"; this gives you an idea of what needs to be done to set the folders to whatever names you want, should the need occur.

10.11.4 Selecting the right AV product

With such a confusing vista of MAPI, VSAPI, and ESE protocols and multiple AV products on the market, what should you do to select the right AV product? Because every implementation of Exchange is different, the best idea remains to download trial versions of products from vendor Web sites and test the products in a test environment that accurately mimics the characteristics of the production systems, especially the hardware configurations and clusters that you plan to deploy. You should also test the special features of each product to decide whether these features are important in your situation. For example, you could test the multiple scan engine feature of Sybari's Antigen, or look at how easy it is to deploy AV software to new servers using Trend's management tools. You may also want to test performance to establish the additional load that the server must handle when an AV product is active. In addition, be sure to test how easy it is to fetch new virus pattern files from the vendor's Web site after it discovers a new virus. The ideal situation is to be able to download a new pattern file automatically a matter of hours after detection. After these tests, you should have the information you need to make the right decision.

In some cases, the factors that drive the buying decision are unrelated to Exchange. For example, Trend Micro's major strength is its range of products that support multiple platforms, so if you are interested in protecting platforms other than Windows, it might make sense to focus on vendors that can support all the platforms that you operate. Sybari is not a traditional antivirus vendor, because it does not produce its own virus-checking engine. Instead, Sybari licenses engines from other major antivirus companies, such as Norton, and concentrates on the management interface and the ability to run multiple engines from different companies. The logic here is that a new virus might get through the scan by one engine, but there is a better chance that you will catch a virus if multiple engines are scanning. Support for multiple engines is a major strength of Antigen, but the product only runs on Windows.

Table 10.7 lists three of the major players in the Exchange antivirus market. This is only a small selection. A more comprehensive list of AV products for Exchange is at http://www.microsoft.com/exchange/partners/antivirus.asp. The fact that the list contains so many alternatives is testimony to the relative approachability of VSAPI.

You do not even have to wait for an approved purchase order before starting to protect your system with a virus checker, since most vendors make 30-day test versions available for download from their Web sites. Whatever AV software you use, it is critical that you download updated pattern files on a regular basis. Pattern files contain details of the signatures or definitions that allow checkers to recognize viruses. The speed with which new viruses appear and propagate means that you can only defend your Exchange servers if you download and install the latest pattern files on a regular basis. Some virus-checking products, such as Antigen, allow you to download the latest pattern files directly from the product itself, which is a nice feature. It is even better when the new pattern is automatically installed and operational as soon as the download completes.

Table 10.7 *Major Antivirus Products for Exchange*

Company	Product	URL
McAfee	GroupShield	http://www.mcafeeb2b.com/products/groupshield-exchange2000/default.asp
Sybari	Antigen	http://www.sybari.com/products/antigen_exchange.asp
Trend Micro	ScanMail	http://www.antivirus.com/products/smex2000/

Companies often look for information about others that use products before they buy. Premerger, Compaq used Antigen to protect its Exchange servers, while HP used ScanMail. Does this make either product better than the other? No, but it does reassure customers if they know that another large company protects its email infrastructure with a product that they are considering.

Managing Exchange: Servers

Now that we know how to manage users and all the data that they produce, we need to move on to a discussion about how best to manage server-wide data, implement policies and procedures, and conduct daily operations. In this chapter, we look at essential management operations, such as backup and restore, as well as some of the more esoteric operations, such as message tracking.

11.1 System policies

Exchange defines a policy as a collection of configuration settings that an administrator can apply to one or more Exchange configuration objects of the same class. In practical terms, this means that you can define a policy and then apply it to every object of a certain class throughout the organization. For example, you could decide that the mailbox quota for users allocated to a special Mailbox Store should be set to certain values, as shown in Figure 11.1. Once created, Exchange applies the policy for all the users whose mailboxes are in the Store by adding the policy to the properties of the Store. You can also apply system policies to Public Stores, where the policies cover topics such as replication and full-text indexing.

Before you can create a system policy, you have to create a "System Policies" container for an administrative group. You do not have to have this container present in every administrative group, since it is quite feasible to create policies centrally and then deploy them to servers in different administrative groups, providing you hold the permissions to make changes to the configurations of the target servers.

Exchange supports two distinct types of policies: system and recipient. System policies affect server-side configuration objects. Exchange 2000/2003 supports three policy classes: Mailbox Store, Public Folder Store, and

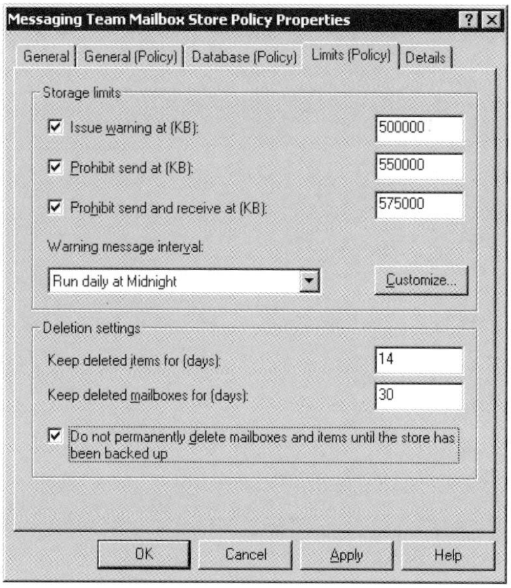

Figure 11.1
Creating a policy for storage limits.

server. Exchange applies changes made to system policies as soon as you press the "Apply" or "OK" button to update the properties of a policy. You can see that the policy to control message tracking logs is applied to servers in five different administrative groups, all of which could be managed on a day-to-day basis by several different people.

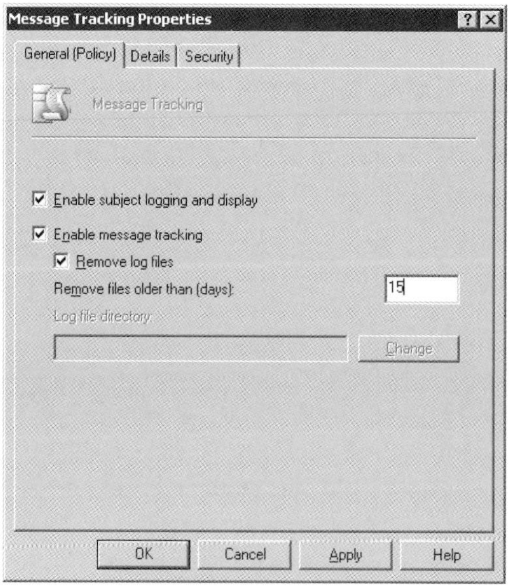

Figure 11.2
A system policy for server objects.

11.2 Recipient policies

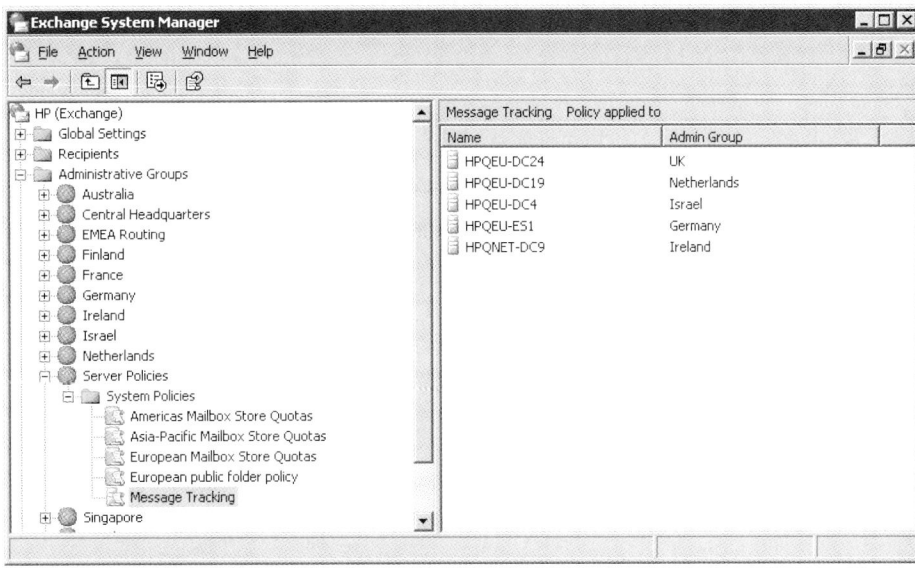

Figure 11.3 *Server policies displayed in ESM.*

Figure 11.2 is a good example of a system policy that you can apply to server objects. In this case, we want to enable message tracking across a range of servers. Instead of going to each individual server, we build a policy with the necessary settings. When the policy is ready, use right-click to view available options and select "Add." Windows scans the AD for any objects that you can apply the policy to and displays the matching items in a dialog. Select the desired servers and click on OK to apply the policy. Windows also adds details of the new policy to the appropriate configuration container within the AD, displayed through ESM (Figure 11.3). Exchange 2000 was obviously the first implementation of policy-driven settings, so there are many administrative operations that Microsoft has not yet covered, even in Exchange 2003. Expect to see operations added through new releases and even service packs.

11.2 Recipient policies

Recipient policies are organization-wide objects held in the "Recipient Policies" container, a subcontainer of "Recipients." The Exchange installation program creates a default policy and you can create as many policies as you want thereafter, although you must keep the default policy and cannot delete it. The major functions of recipient policies are as follows:

- Set the default value for the domain name used by Exchange to reference files via IFS (for example, hp.com). The default policy holds this value. Do not change this value.

- Control the generation of email proxy addresses: The Recipient Update Service (RUS) generates and sets email addresses on new mail-enabled objects, but you define the format for the addresses and the type of proxy addresses that the RUS generates through recipient policies.

- Control how the Mailbox Manager processes mailboxes.

- Enable SMTP virtual servers to accept incoming email for a domain. When you install Exchange, the SMTP virtual servers will accept email for the domain defined in the default policy, but you can add policies to cover additional domains if you want Exchange to accept incoming email for those domains.

Figure 11.4 shows a comprehensive set of recipient policies as viewed through ESM. In this case, a separate recipient policy exists for a number of country-level groups plus one for corporate users. You can have as many recipient policies as you like, providing that you can identify the target users with an LDAP search. Exchange uses the LDAP search when it applies the policy to the users. However, you can use the default recipient policy (or

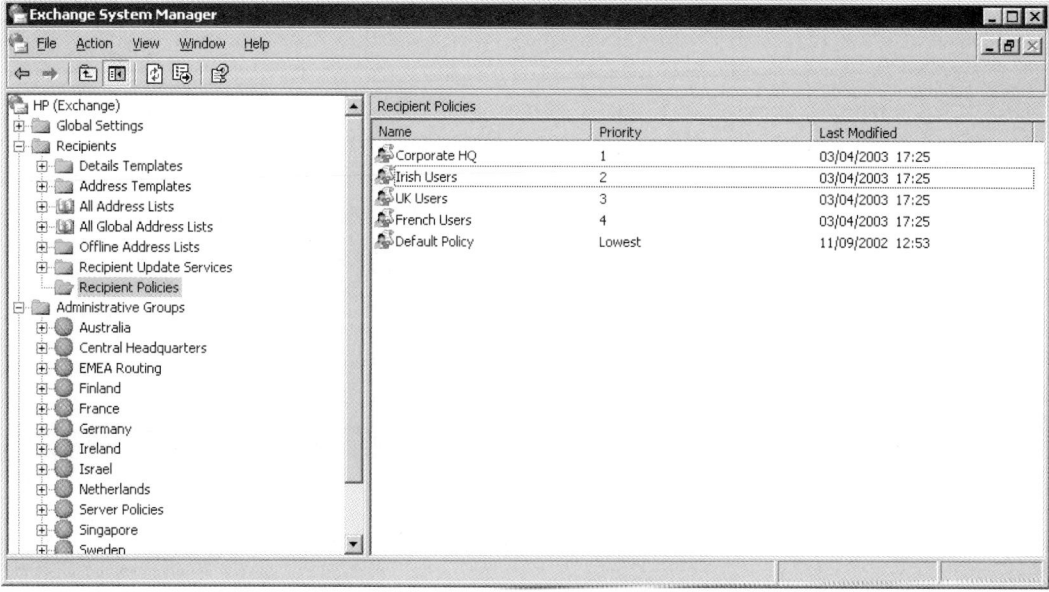

Figure 11.4   *Recipient policies.*

11.2 Recipient policies

create another one) and apply that to every mail-enabled object in an organization, a situation that usually exists in small organizations. ESM groups recipient policies in priority order, and you can move the policies up and down in the order. In Exchange 2000, ESM allowed you to define multiple policies at the same priority, but Exchange 2003 now assigns a number to each policy to indicate its order of precedence.

Exchange applies policies in priority order, so it is possible to create a policy that Exchange cannot apply, simply because a higher-priority policy takes precedence. It is quite normal to give the default policy the lowest possible priority to ensure that Exchange always applies first any policy that you want to apply for specific administrative groups or other groupings.

You edit a recipient policy by selecting and then double-clicking through ESM, or create a new policy by clicking on the Recipient Policies root and then select the "New…Recipient Policy" option. Older policies created before the Mailbox Manager was available may display only the property pages that collect administrative data (Details), control email address generation (Email Addresses), and establish the name of the policy and the target objects (General). You can add the property page to control the Mailbox Manager by selecting the policy and then selecting the "Change Property Page" option from the context-sensitive menu. Figure 11.5 illustrates how

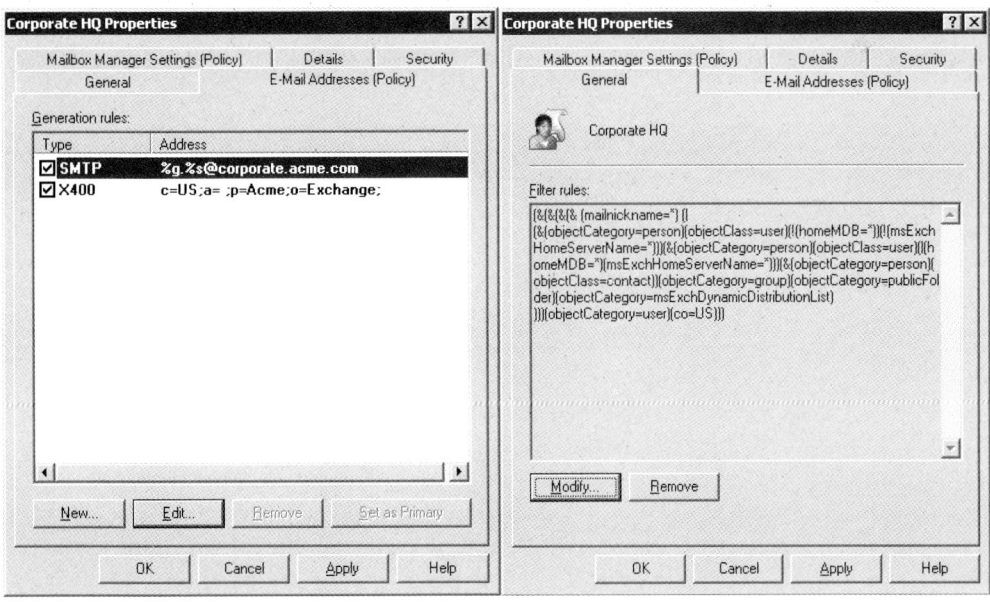

Figure 11.5 *Email addresses and LDAP query in a recipient policy.*

you define email addresses in a recipient policy (left-hand screen) and how to identify target objects through an LDAP query (right-hand screen).

Administrators implement default values for email address proxies by creating policies, defining the properties of the policies, and then defining LDAP queries to identify the mailboxes, accounts, or groups that Exchange applies the policies to. The LDAP query does not use a search base within the AD, so it is not easy to tie a recipient policy to a specific OU within the AD. One workaround is to create a group that includes all the users within the OUs to which you want to apply the recipient policy and then specify that group within the LDAP query. A mail-enabled object may have many different email proxies, including multiple values for the same type. However, you always have a primary address for each address type, and Exchange puts the primary address type in a message envelope when it leaves the organization. For example, an account may have multiple SMTP address proxies, because an organization has changed its name through merger and acquisition and you want to "grandfather" the older SMTP addresses so that Exchange can still deliver messages sent to those addresses. Thus, while my current primary SMTP email address in HP's Exchange organization is Tony.Redmond@hp.com, the AD still holds Tony.Redmond@compaq.com and Tony.Redmond@digital.com as alternate SMTP proxy addresses for my account. Storing multiple proxy addresses allows correspondents who may have the old addresses in their header to reply to messages from me; they can continue to use one of my old email addresses because that is how they know me. Because it is the current primary SMTP address, Exchange stamps Tony.Redmond@hp.com on all my outgoing messages. Of course, there is no point in defining addresses for domains if you do not have the necessary MX records in place to allow external servers direct email to your servers.

For incoming email, Exchange checks every possible email address held for users in the AD before it concludes that it cannot deliver a message, and, since the AD indexes proxy addresses, the check is very fast. As long as the AD stores the grandfathered email addresses as secondary SMTP proxies, Exchange is able to deliver incoming messages sent to these old addresses. This is a very useful feature, because it is quite possible that correspondents will send email to an address that they have in their address book, or by reference to an old business card, or by simply replying to an old message of yours that they have in their mailboxes. If Exchange did not support multiple proxy addresses, you would have to ensure that everyone knew your new email address and used it each time that the organization's name changed.

Some companies allow their users to define "vanity" email addresses as secondary SMTP proxy addresses, much as you can buy vanity license plates for cars. If I wanted to, I could ask my administrator to set up a proxy address such as ExchangePerson@company.com and Exchange would treat this address with the same importance and validity as any other address. Given the importance of SMTP as the primary mail transport for Exchange, most attention is usually dedicated to getting the SMTP address right, although the X.400 address is also important for routing if any legacy servers or connectors are used inside the organization. From a historical perspective, Exchange 5.5 and earlier versions use Site Addressing Defaults to define the default format for email proxies.

The right-hand screen in Figure 11.5 shows the LDAP query that Exchange uses to identify the set of Active Directory objects when it applies the policy. In this case, the LDAP query searches for all mailboxes on a named server. LDAP query syntax is reasonably complex, but you do not have to build the query by hand. Instead, the "Modify" button invokes a dialog (Figure 11.6) to collect search parameters. You can test the query with the "Find Now" button to ensure that the search finds the correct objects, and when you are happy, you can save the LDAP query with the "OK" button and return to the recipient policy. Just as with any LDAP query, it is best to be as exact as possible in the way that you reference fields. For example, in the example shown, the query looks for any entry where the Country field starts with "Ireland." We know that Ireland is unlikely to change its name anytime in the future and the name of no other country begins with Ireland, so setting up a search like this will return the right

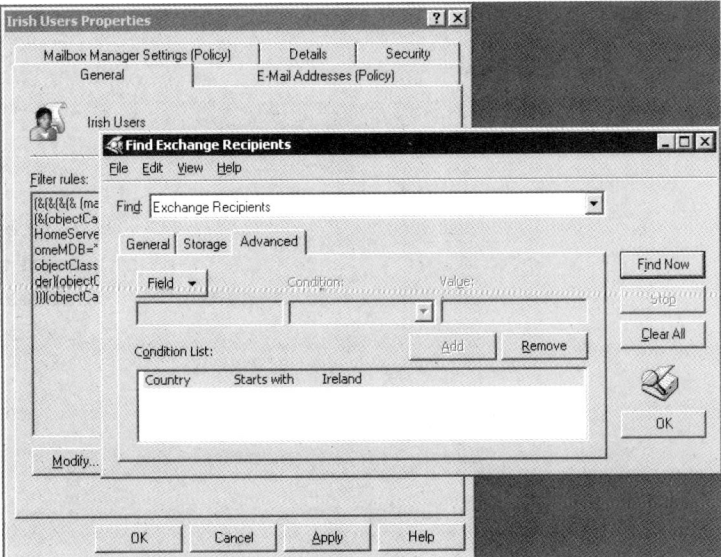

Figure 11.6
Building a search query.

results but in a much slower fashion than if we use a query such as "Country is exactly Ireland."

While the example shows an LDAP query that selects mailboxes from a specific server, it is far more common to create recipient policies for specific administrative groups.

11.2.1 Generating SMTP addresses

Recipient policies control the generation of SMTP addresses for mail-enabled objects through a pattern of replacement strings plus the email domain as laid down in the policy. For example, Figure 11.5 defines a pattern of %g.%s@corporate.acme.com. In this case, "%g" means "insert given name," while "%s" means "insert surname," so the default SMTP address implemented by this policy is "first name.surname@corporate.acme.com." Table 11.1 lists the set of valid replacement strings.

In addition to the basic strings, you can instruct Windows to use a specific number of characters by prefixing the string with a numeric value. For example, %3g means take the first three characters of the given name, %6d means take the first six from the display name, and so on. Exchange ignores invalid characters (as defined in RFCs 821/822) when it generates an SMTP address.

In the case of John Doe (first name = John, last name = Doe, display name = John Doe), the following replacement strings generate the email addresses shown:

```
%g.%s@acme.com      John.Doe@acme.com
%d@acme.com         JohnDoe@acme.com  (space removed as invalid
                                       character)
%2g%2s@acme.com     JoDo@acme.com
%r..%d@acme.com     JohnDoe@acme.com  (space removed by string)
```

The Recipient Update Service will apply the updated policy the next time it is active.

11.2.2 Changing display names

While you can define and apply different patterns for email addresses through recipient policies, you cannot do the same for display names. The default pattern for display names is %g %—in other words, first name <space> last name, or Tony Redmond. This is acceptable for small imple-

Table 11.1 *Replacement Strings for SMTP Address Generation*

Replacement String	Meaning
%s	Insert surname (last name)
%g	Insert given name (first name)
%i	Insert middle initial
%d	Insert display name
%m	Insert Exchange alias
%rxy	Replace all occurrences of character "x" with character "y"

mentations, where everyone knows each other and it is easy to find the correct recipient by browsing the GAL, but problems occur as the number of directory entries increases. On balance, more variation occurs in surnames than given names and users are accustomed to look through telephone directories by surname, so it makes sense to organize the GAL by surname. Think of a common given name, such as "John" or "Mary," and imagine how many times they occur in a large GAL. If the GAL is sorted by given name, you might have to look through several hundred entries before you locate the right recipient. It is easier to search using a surname, even with common surnames, such as "Smith" or "Ng."

Exchange builds the GAL from AD data, including display names. You can change the pattern AD uses to create display names by altering the properties of the user-display attribute of the Display Specified object in the configuration naming context with the ADSIEDIT utility. Follow these steps to make the change:

- Log on to an Enterprise administrator's account.

- If not already loaded, install ADSIEDIT and load it into an MMC console.

- Select the "cn=DisplaySpecifiers" node and expand it. Underneath, you will find entries for the entire set of locale IDs installed in the forest. Each locale ID has a separate value. Id = 409 is the identifier for U.S. English. Computers in multilingual environments support multiple locales. For example, id = 412 is the locale for Korean.

- ADSIEDIT lists the properties of the locale ID in the right-hand pane. Find the cn=user-Display attribute and click on it to select, then select the Properties option from the context-sensitive menu to display the properties of the object.

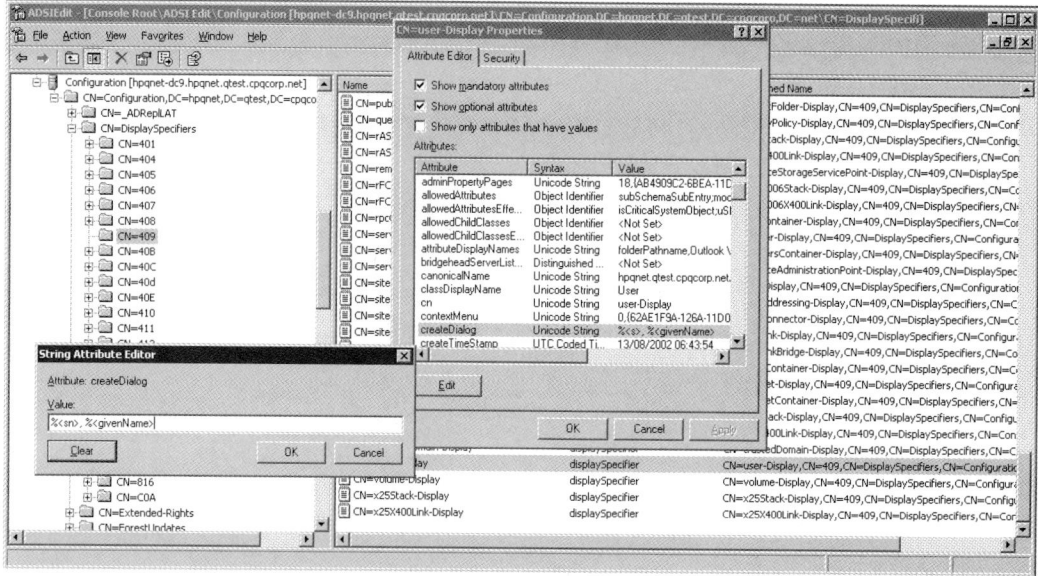

Figure 11.7 *Changing the user display name default format strings.*

- Select the createDialog property. This is an optional property.

- Set the attribute to be %<sn>, %<givenName> and then click OK to close the dialog and write the pattern into the directory. See Figure 11.7 for an example of how to input the pattern.

You can achieve similar results for new contacts by editing the createDialog property for the contact-display attribute for groups by editing the group-display attribute and for iNetOrgPerson objects by editing the iNetOrgPerson-display attribute. Few organizations alter the pattern for groups, but if you alter the pattern for user objects, you should also change the pattern for contacts. Otherwise, you will end up with contacts that follow a different sort order interspersed with users in the GAL.

Test that the change is effective by creating a new user. Complete the surname and given name fields and check that AD builds the full name field according to the new pattern. As shown in Figure 11.8, the pattern works. If you made a mistake when you entered the pattern, such as omitting the leading % sign for a value, or not terminating a value with a closing ">", the error will be obvious, since AD will be unable to correctly create the full name field.

Windows automatically replicates updates to the AD configuration naming context throughput the forest, so the new pattern will become

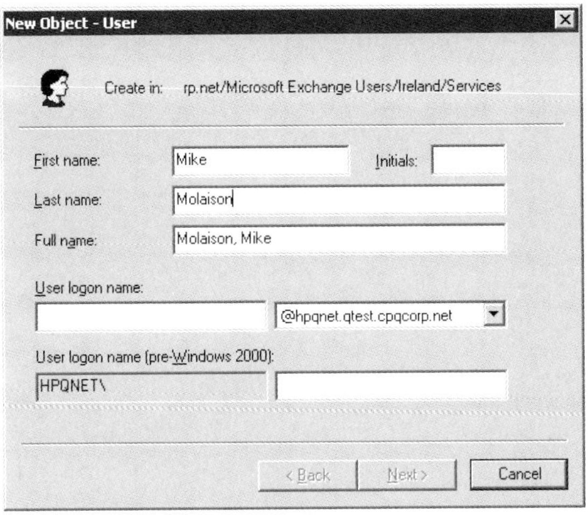

11.3 Recipient update services

Figure 11.8
Ensuring that the new default format works.

active as soon as replication completes. You can create a pattern based on any LDAP attribute held for an object (e.g., %<initials>), but, clearly, you should only use attributes that are provided when a user object is initially created. Any change made to impose a new pattern for user display names will not affect previously created user objects, so you will either have to change these objects individually or use a tool such as HP's LDSU to extract details of the objects, impose the new pattern, and then apply the change to the AD. Similar tools can be used if you need to change SMTP addresses (such as in the case of a merger or acquisition project) or to add secondary SMTP addresses. If you change SMTP addresses for any reason, it is best practice to grandfather the old SMTP addresses for at least one year after the changeover so that messages sent to old addresses can still be delivered.

Note that the display name pattern only governs the creation of objects, and you can change the display name afterward to input any value you like. For example, you could include a department name, location, job title, or other identifier to help resolve users that share the same name:

```
Smith, John (Glasgow)
Smith, John (Security Department)
Smith, John (VP, Technology)
```

11.3 Recipient update services

The Recipient Update Service (RUS) runs as part of the System Attendant process and, among other functions, is responsible for ensuring that mail-enabled objects appear in the correct address books, including the GAL.

The RUS performs this function by populating the necessary AD attributes for mail-enabled objects following initial creation or after modification. The RUS is very important to Exchange, because you cannot send messages to a newly mail-enabled account until RUS completes the process by stamping the necessary attributes on the object. In some cases, organizations choose not to use the RUS, because they have their own provisioning software that is capable of populating the attributes through an interface such as ADSI. Use of provisioning software is common in ASP environments where you may need to populate even more attributes than normal. For example, you can control access to the GAL for OWA users by setting the msExchQueryBaseDN with the value of the root DN where you want to begin searches (in this case, we assume that the AD contains entries from multiple companies, so you want to restrict access to the entries for a user's own company). Microsoft Knowledge Base article 296479 describes the processing that a provisioning tool must do to replace the RUS.

Two types of RUS operate in an Exchange organization. The first (the enterprise RUS) processes Exchange system objects (such as servers) in the Microsoft Exchange configuration container and permissions for the container as set by the Delegation Wizard; the other (a domain RUS) takes care of recipients in each domain spanned by the organization. Because all servers share a single configuration container across the organization, only one RUS is required to process system-wide objects. However, you need at least one RUS to process recipients per domain, and you may need multiple services if the domain is very large or distributed. During migration periods, when you need to create mailboxes in bulk, it is a good idea to set up multiple recipient update services in the domains that host the mailboxes to spread the load and ensure that the RUS can speedily enable mailboxes.

Figure 11.9 shows an organization with six recipient update services defined. Exchange servers are installed in three separate domains (HPQAP, HPQEU, and HPQNET), and a RUS is configured for each domain, with two additional RUS configured in the HPEU domain, possibly because of the number of accounts that the domain manages. The other RUS (the first in the list) is "Enterprise Configuration" and takes care of the system objects. The properties of the RUS (Figure 11.10) show the domain that it is responsible for, the name of the Exchange server that performs RUS processing, and the name of the domain controller that the RUS uses when it needs to read and write AD data.

RUS operates according to a schedule. It is most common to leave this as "always run," meaning that RUS processes changes to objects as soon as they are available. Other values include run every hour, every two hours,

11.3 Recipient update services

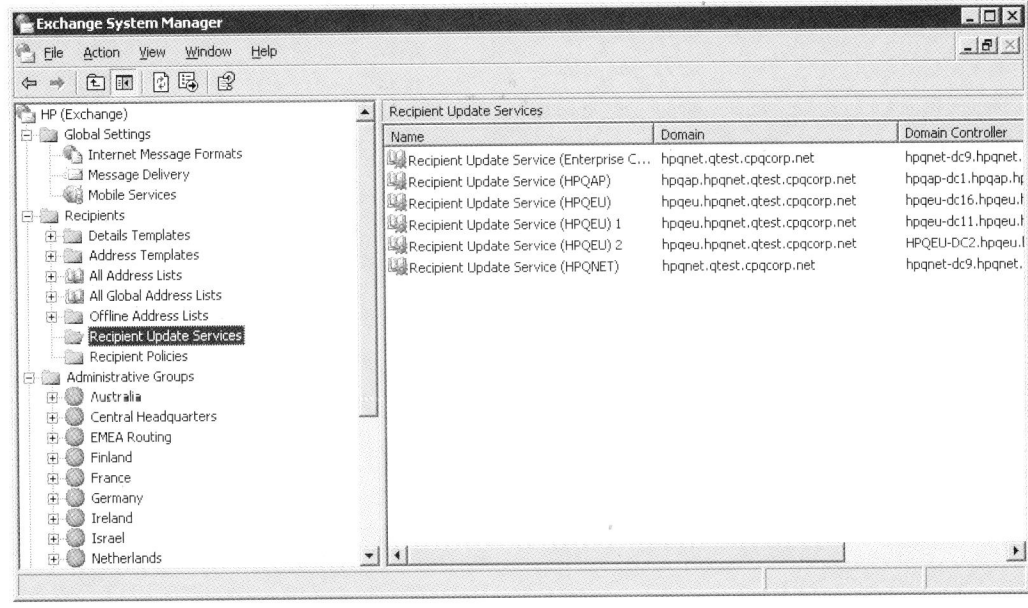

Figure 11.9 *Recipient Update Services.*

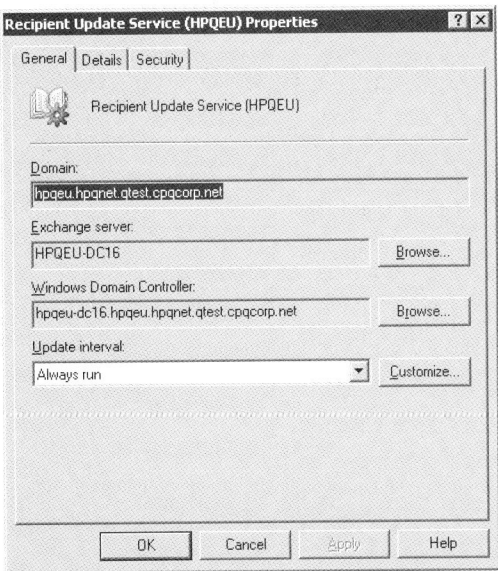

Figure 11.10 *Properties of a RUS.*

every four hours, never, or according to a preset schedule. The "Never run" option is usually only selected if you need to move RUS processing from one server to another. The "Update Now" option forces the RUS to run immediately to update any waiting objects for the domain. In some cases on Exchange 2000 servers, administrators report that the RUS mysteriously stops stamping new objects, which then means that they cannot begin to process email. The solution to this problem is to restart the System Attendant process.

The Exchange installation procedure creates the RUS for a domain when you install the first Exchange server in the domain. That server automatically hosts RUS processing and starts to maintain the address lists for mail-enabled objects in the domain. At the same time, Exchange selects an available DC to act as the source of AD data for the new RUS. The selected DC must be a GC server. You can move RUS processing to another Exchange server or select another DC by using the "Browse" buttons shown in Figure 11.10. The Exchange help text recommends that you select an Exchange server running on a DC to minimize network overhead. While it is true that such a selection will reduce network demand, best practice for enterprise installations is to avoid running Exchange on a DC, especially GC servers, so an adjusted version of the advice is to select a GC server that is in close network proximity to the Exchange server that hosts the RUS for a domain.

If multiple DCs and Exchange servers exist in a domain, you can divide RUS processing by creating multiple RUS for the domain. For example, if you operate a single worldwide domain with Windows sites in Australia and the United States, you may decide to create separate update services in Australia and the United States to avoid any possibility that RUS is unable to fully activate a newly created account in either location because it is unable to communicate with a remote DC. However, remember that this approach only spreads the processing load across multiple RUS threads: Exchange does not fully create a mailbox until a RUS thread has processed it. If you want a specific RUS to execute immediately, select it from ESM, right-click, and select the "Update Now" option. On the basis that simplicity is better than complexity, do not rush to create multiple RUS for a domain unless this is necessary. AD replication is often complex enough without introducing an increased number of "contributors."

11.3.1 Mail-enabling objects

In concept, the role of the RUS is simple, but in fact a lot of background work goes on to properly process different objects after you add them to the

11.3 Recipient update services

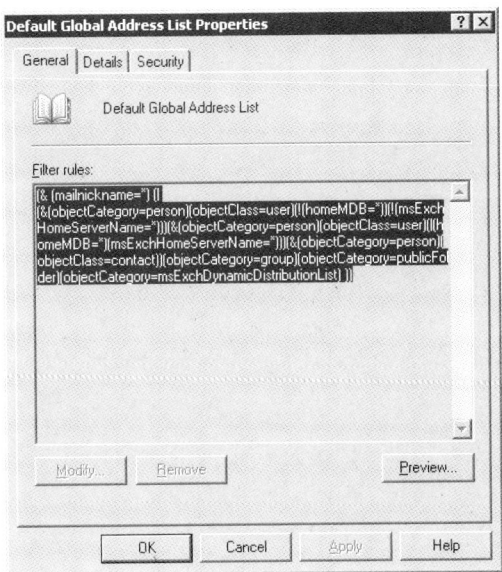

Figure 11.11
Default global address list.

AD. By default, a newly created AD object that you want to be mail enabled does not possess the full set of attributes to allow the user, contact, or group to participate fully in email activities. Some additional processing is required to add the necessary attributes, such as add the object to address lists, add email addresses, and so on. Indeed, the owner of a new mailbox cannot log on and connect to his or her mailbox until RUS completes its work. The exact interval between the time when an administrator creates an account and when a user is able to access his or her mailbox and receive mail depends on AD replication and the interval set for RUS processing; this can take up to 15 minutes. (See Figure 11.11.)

The set of attributes created by the RUS for all mail-enabled objects includes the legacyExchangeDN, all of the different email addresses for the object (SMTP, X.400, etc.) held in the proxyAddresses attribute, the primary SMTP and X.400 addresses, display names, and the mail nickname or alias. The RUS populates a set of additional attributes for mailbox-enabled accounts, including the distinguished names for the home server and Store and the security method to use when checking access to the mailbox. The RUS also defines the server responsible to expand the contents of a distribution group, if required. Table 11.2 lists the different AD attributes that the RUS maintains.

Additional attributes are required for mail-enabled groups. For example, you must set the msExchExpansionServerName attribute with the DN of

Table 11.2 *AD Attributes Maintained by the RUS*

Attribute	Use	Mail-Enabled Objects	Mailboxes
LegacyExchangeDN	Connection back to older Exchange objects	X	X
proxyAddresses	SMTP and other proxy addresses such as Lotus Notes (LN), GroupWise (GWISE), and so on. Addresses are stated in the form "prefix:address." The primary SMTP address is prefixed with "SMTP:"; secondary addresses have "smtp:".	X	X
textEncodedORAddress	Primary X.400 address	X	X
Mail	The primary SMTP address	X	X
MailNickname	Object alias. The alias forms part of the URL to point to a user's mailbox.	X	X
DisplayName	Display name (for GAL)	X	X
targetAddress	SMTP address	X (only contacts)	—
msExchHomeServerName	DN for home Exchange server	—	X
homeMDB	DN for home Mailbox Store	—	X
msExchUserAccountControl	Flag to indicate what SID to use when setting or reading permissions	—	X
msExchMasterAccountSID	Master SID for the account	—	X
msExchMailboxGuid	GUID pointing to user mailbox	—	X

the server that is responsible for expanding group membership. The showInAddressBook attribute is also required to ensure that objects appear in address lists. This multivalued attribute contains a list of the DNs for all the address lists that include the object. Assuming that you leave the RUS to complete the process of mail-enabling objects, it applies address list policies to determine which address lists an object should be in. The default address list policy ensures that a new mail-enabled object appears in the GAL, but organizations that host multiple companies can create a separate address list for each company that is restricted to the users within the company.

You do not need to change the default Global Address List to hide mailboxes unless you have good reason to exclude a whole set of mailboxes (which you can isolate with an LDAP filter) from the GAL. Instead, you can hide individual objects, including query-based distribution groups, by

11.3 Recipient update services

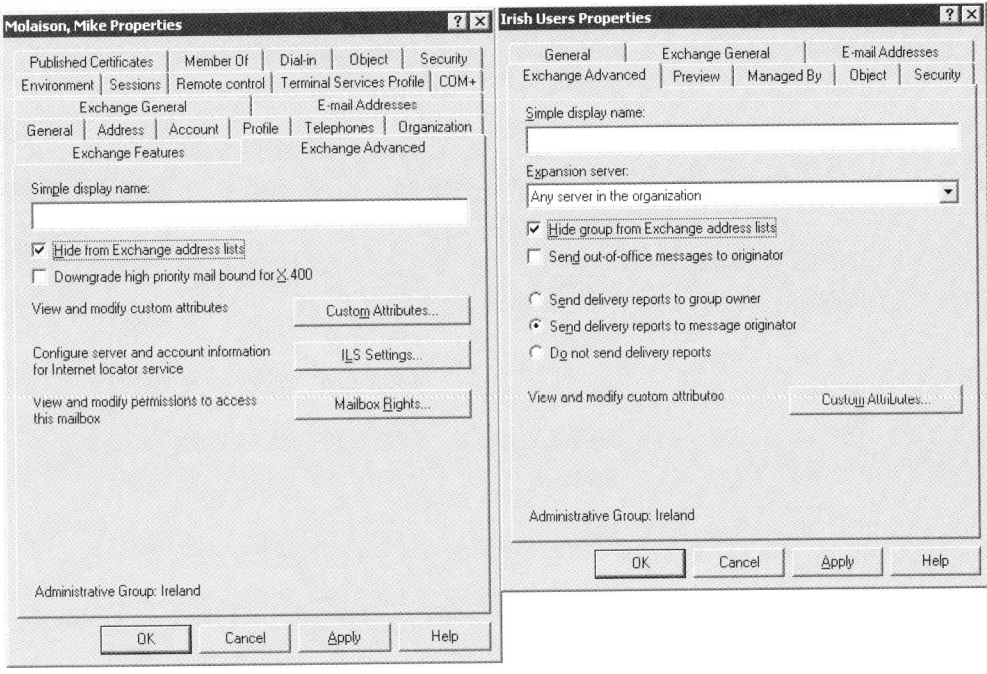

Figure 11.12 *Hiding mailboxes and distribution groups from the GAL.*

setting the "Hide from Exchange address lists" property (showInAddressBook) in the AD, as shown in Figure 11.12. The RUS also takes care of hiding or revealing the membership of distribution groups in the GAL, controlled by the hideDLmembership AD property. If hideDLmembership is set, the RUS sets a security descriptor on the group to allow Exchange servers to be able to expand the contents of the group (and so be able to deliver messages to all the group's members) while the membership remains hidden to clients. Once you create address lists, the RUS ensures that objects appear in the correct lists after they are added, modified, or deleted. Because they are more user friendly and easier to create and configure, the advent of query-based distribution groups in Windows 2003 and Exchange 2003 means that there is now less reason to create additional address lists.

11.3.2 Processing server details

The Exchange Domain Servers and Exchange Enterprise Servers security groups help secure information on Exchange servers. The Exchange Domain Servers group contains all of the Exchange servers in the domain, while the Exchange Enterprise Servers group contains the Exchange Domain Servers group for every domain where an Exchange server is present. These groups are local to each domain and are created by the Exchange installation program when the /DomainPrep process is run. RUS is responsible for the maintenance of the groups afterward. If you run Exchange 2000, you should use the EDSLOCK script (available from Microsoft) to ensure that servers are properly secured against unauthorized access. See Microsoft Knowledge Base article 309718 for further information.

11.4 Backups

A very wise person once said that an important difference between email and word processing applications is that the effect of a word processor failure is limited to a single user and perhaps a small quantity of documents. When an email system collapses, everyone is affected. Usually, people at the top of a company notice the problem fastest (and complain quickest). Having a large server go offline because of a hardware problem is a hassle. Not being able to recover the data because no backups exist or you cannot restore the data is a fundamental lapse in system management discipline that can lead to instant dismissal. There is simply no excuse for not taking backups, and there is no excuse for not ensuring that the data on the backup media is valid and restorable.

Email systems depend on many different hardware and software components to keep everything going. If any element fails to operate in the required manner, data corruption can occur. If the hardware suffers a catastrophic failure, or a disaster such as an electric outage afflicts the location where the computers are, you will need to know the steps necessary to get your users back online as quickly as possible. In all these instances, system backups are a prerequisite.

In their purest sense, backups are snapshots of a system's state at a certain point in time. All of the data available to the system should exist in the backup and should be restorable to exactly the same state if required. You can write backups to many different forms of magnetic or other media, although the most common medium is some form of high-density magnetic tape. DLT drives are the best option for Exchange.

Exchange has always supported online backups, which generally proceed without causing any discomfort or impact to clients connected to the server. There is no reason to take Exchange offline just to perform a backup. In fact, taking Exchange offline is not a good thing to do. First, it reduces overall system availability, because users cannot connect to their mailboxes.

Second, each time you bring the Store service online, the Store generates public folder replication messages to request updates from replication partners. Finally, the Store calculates checksums for each page before streaming them out to media during online backups, and if a checksum does not match, the Store will halt the backup operation. Best practice is always to perform online backups and to perform daily full online backups if possible, mainly because it is much easier to restore from a single tape than have to mess around with incremental backups.

When you install Exchange, the installation procedure enhances NTBACKUP.EXE, the standard Windows backup utility. These enhancements are as follows:

- Support for the transactional nature of the Exchange Store: in particular, the capacity to deal with the fact that the totality of the Store is in Mailbox Stores, transaction logs, and transactions that might still be queued in memory.

- Support for both the EDB and streaming file.

- Ability to perform online backups: in other words, to copy online databases to tape without having to shut down Exchange services. Users continue to work during backups.

- Extension of the NTBACKUP.EXE user interface to allow system administrators to select which servers and databases they wish to back up or restore.

- Microsoft has scheduled NTBACKUP from Windows 2003 SP1 to support hot backups of Exchange 2003 databases. Remember that you also need VSS-capable hardware to use VSS to take hot backups.

11.4.1 Creating a backup strategy

All hardware systems can expect hardware failures to occur over time. When it is your turn to experience a failed server, you will be glad that backups exist. System failures come in three broad categories.

- Disk or controller failure

- Other noncritical system component failure: for example, the video monitor for the server develops a fault

- Critical system component failure: for example, the motherboard or other associated component experiences a fault that you cannot quickly rectify

Any failure situation requires some fast but calm thinking in order to make the correct decisions to get everything online again. If you cannot bring the system back online, can you substitute another similar system and restore application data? If it is a particular system component, is a replacement available, or can you change the system configuration to work around the problem? Having backups around will not replace making the right decision, but they are a great safety net.

The Mean Time between Failures (MTBF) rate for disks improves all the time and new storage technologies guarantee an ever-increasing resilience to unexpected failure. The advent of hot snapshots through Volume ShadowCopyServices in Windows 2003 and Exchange 2003 also creates a new dimension for backup strategies. These developments do not mean that you will never experience a disk failure, but they do mean that you are less likely to have one over any particular period or that you can recover from failures more rapidly than before. A high MTBF is no guarantee that the disk will not fail tomorrow, so the challenge for system administrators is to have a plan to handle the problem when it occurs. Without a basic RAID array or more sophisticated storage technology, if something does go wrong with a disk you will have to stop and fix the problem or swap in a new drive. Once the hardware problem is fixed, you will have to restore the data, and, of course, this simple statement assumes that you have copies of all the application files that were stored on the faulty drive and that you possess the capability to move the data onto the new drive. The value of good backups is instantly obvious at this point! Of course, none of the protection afforded by storage technology is viable if you do not deploy the right hardware, such as hot-swappable drives and the best controller you can buy.

Having the capability to take online backups is one thing. Making sure that administrators take backups is quite another. Nightly backups of the databases, taken in tandem with full monthly backups of the server as a whole (i.e., including the Windows operating system, other applications, and all the Exchange files), must be taken if any guarantee as to the integrity of the messaging system is to be given to users.

The database-centric nature of Exchange poses a particular challenge for restore operations. There is no getting away from the fact that if a restore is necessary, it is going to take much longer than you may realize. The length of time that it takes an administrator to back up or restore databases from a large production Exchange server may come as a surprise to some. It is easy to forget just how long it takes to move data to backup media. Mailbox and Public Stores both have the capacity to expand quickly, so your backup times will grow in proportion. After a server has been in production for a number of months, you might find that it is time to consider looking for faster or higher-capacity media to help reduce backup times.

Remember, too, that it is not just the Exchange databases that you have to back up to ensure that you can recover a system. The AD, other Windows data, the IIS metabase, Exchange binaries, user data, and other application data all contribute to the amount of data and length of backup operations. In line with best practice, most Exchange servers are not DCs or GCs, so you may not have to restore the AD after a failure on an Exchange server. However, the IIS metabase is an important component that is easy to overlook. Exchange 2000 and 2003 depend on IIS for protocol access for Internet clients. The IIS metabase stores configuration data about protocols and virtual servers, including information about the SMTP, IMAP, and HTTP virtual servers used by Exchange. Since IIS is now such an integral part of Exchange, you must incorporate metabase recovery into any disaster recovery plan. Remember that clustered systems are different from standard servers, and securing data such as quorum resources, disk signatures, and so on is important for recovery operations.

It is also important to apply the correct levels of service packs to Windows and Exchange on the recovery server before commencing any restore operation. The internal database schema has changed a number of times in Exchange's history. In general, you cannot restore a database from a backup taken with a higher software revision level. In other words, do not expect to be able to restore a backup taken with Exchange 2000 or 2003 to a server running Exchange 5.5. This rule does not hold true for all combinations of service packs and versions, but there is enough truth in it to make a strong recommendation that you should maintain servers at the same software levels in order to ensure that you can always restore backups.

You must account for all of the factors discussed here in the operational procedures you employ at your installation. Restores are equally as important as backups, but all the attention goes to backup procedures and backup products. Administrators usually only look into the detail of restores when a disaster happens, which is exactly the wrong time to begin thinking about the issue. Consider this question: How long will it take to restore one gigabyte of data from your backup media using the backup software you employ? Now, how long will it take to restore 3 GB, or maybe 10 GB, or how about a full-blown 100-GB Mailbox Store? And what about a Public Store? Do you have procedures in place to handle the restore of the different permutations of the AD on a DC, GC, or Operations Master, as well as the data for all the other applications you may want to run on a server, such as the IIS metabase?

In most circumstances, even when suitable hardware is waiting to be hot-swapped into your production environment, the answer is in hours. Even when the restore is complete, you may have other work to do before Exchange is available for use again. For instance, the Store must replay transaction logs to roll forward messages and other items that are not fully committed to the database. The Store does this automatically, but applying masses of transactions at one time delays the startup operation (depending on processor speed and other load, 90 logs might take between 20 and 30 minutes to process on a slow server). Users will be yelling at you to get the system back online as quickly as possible, so it's going to be a time when stress levels are rising, which just adds to the piquant nature of the task. These are the facts of system management life. You must be prepared and able to conduct a well-planned restore of essential data in order to be successful. No one wants to explain to a CIO why the messaging system was unavailable for one or two days while staff fumbled their way through a restore. Knowing how to properly use and safeguard backup media is an important part of a backup strategy. Think of the following questions: After you perform backups, who will move the media to a secure location? Is the secure location somewhere local or remote? When will you use the tapes or other media for backup purposes again? How can you recover the backup media quickly if a disaster occurs?

11.4.2 Backups and storage groups

Store partitioning enables Exchange to take a granular approach to backup and restore operations. It is possible to back up or restore a single database instead of the entire Store. Figure 11.13 shows how you can select individual databases within a storage group for backup using the Windows Backup Wizard. When one or more databases from a storage group are processed, all of the transaction logs belonging to the storage group are also included in the backup media to ensure that the backup includes all transactions, including those that are not yet fully committed to the database. Therefore, it does not make sense to back up individual databases unless you have good reason to do so: Always process backups on a storage group level whenever possible. Note that NTBACKUP lists all of the servers in the organization, and you can perform a remote backup across the network, if you choose to do so. However, this is not a good option unless you have a very capable high-speed link between the source database and the target backup device.

Exchange reserves an additional special storage group for restore operations. When you restore a database, the Store overwrites the failed database

11.4 Backups 837

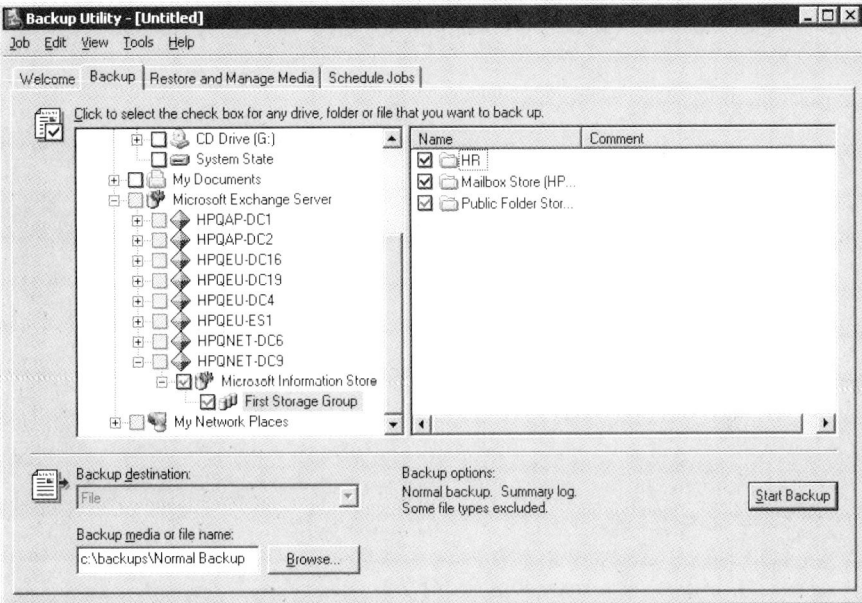

Figure 11.13 *Using the Windows Backup Wizard to select databases.*

with the database from the backup set and moves the transaction logs from the backup set into the temporary directory. The Store can then replay transactions from the logs, commit changes to the database, and make the database consistent and up-to-date. When the database is ready, the restore storage group turns over control to the normal storage group and operations recommence. This technique ensures that the other databases on a server continue to be operational when you have to restore a failed database.

11.4.3 Backup operations

A full backup of an Exchange storage group follows these steps:

- The backup agent (NTBACKUP or a third-party utility) performs its own processing to prepare for the backup. This includes establishing the type of backup (incremental, full, or differential) and the target medium (tape or disk).

- The backup agent makes a function call to ESE to inform the storage engine that it wishes to begin a backup. ESE logs event 210 to indicate that a full backup is starting.

- Up to Exchange 2000 SP2, the Store then creates a patch file for each database. For example, PRIV1.PAT is the patch file for the default

Chapter 11

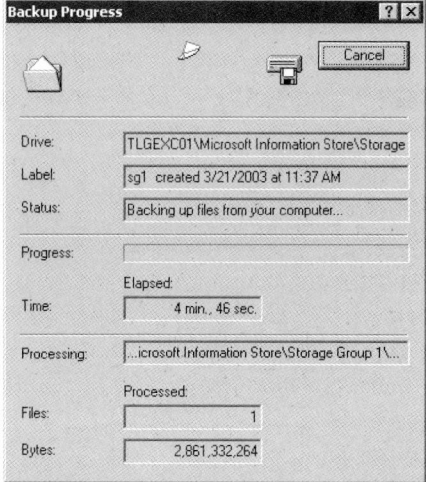

Figure 11.14
A backup in progress.

Mailbox Store. See the discussion about patch files later in this chapter for more information.

- The current transaction log is closed and the Store opens a new transaction log. The Store then directs all transactions that occur during the backup to a new set of logs that will remain on the server after the backup completes.

- The backup process begins (Figure 11.14). The backup agent requests data and the Store streams the data out in 64-KB chunks. ESE writes event 220 to the application event log (Figure 11.15) as it begins the backup of each database, noting the size of the file. On Exchange 2003 servers, the ESE backup API writes event 4028 to indicate the data transfer mechanism in use. For example, a backup to a disk file uses shared memory.

- As the Store processes each page, it reads the page to verify that the page number and CRC checksum are correct to ensure that the page contains valid data. The page number and checksum are stored in the first four bytes of each page, and if either is incorrect, the Store flags a −1018 error to the Application Event Log. The backup API will then stop processing data to prevent you from taking a corrupt backup. This may seem excessive, but it stops administrators from blithely taking backups of databases that potentially contain internal errors. There is no point in taking a backup if you cannot restore the data, and restoring a corrupt database is of little use to anyone. Note that this behavior changes from Exchange 2003 SP1, since the backup

11.4 Backups

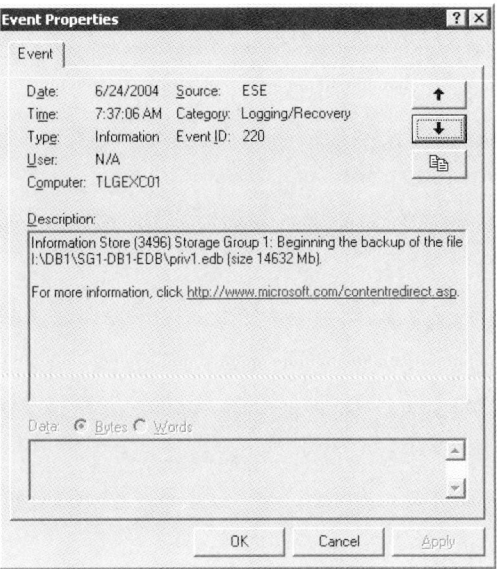

Figure 11.15
A full backup is about to start.

API can now distinguish between a single-bit error, which the Store can correct, and a more fundamental error, which indicates that the backup will be bad. See section 7.10.4 for more information.

- ESE logs event 221 as the backup of each database completes.

- After all the pages from the target databases (a complete storage group or individually selected databases) are written to the backup media, the backup agent requests ESE to provide the transaction logs, which are then written to the backup media. ESE then logs event 223.

- ESE only writes the set of transaction logs present when the backup starts to the backup media. If this is a full backup, ESE then deletes these logs (and notes the fact in event 224) to release disk space back to the system. It is quite safe to do this, since the transactions are committed to the database and are available in the logs in the backup set. Of course, if a situation occurs where a backup copy of a database is corrupted in any way (perhaps due to a tape defect), then you will need copies of every log created since the last good full backup to be able to perform a successful restore. For this reason, some administrators take copies of transaction logs to another disk location before a backup starts. Some may regard this behavior as a touch paranoid; others point to the failure rate for tapes and consider it a prudent step to ensure full recoverability.

Chapter 11

- The backup set is closed and normal operations resume. Successful completion is marked in event 213.

Exchange 2003 reports more detailed information in the event log. For example, you will see the size of the database files to back up plus details of the log files that the backup operation copies and then deletes. Windows 2003 servers report VSS events even though you do not use VSS backups. You can ignore these events and treat them as noise. When it completes processing, the backup utility usually reports the details of its work. For example, an NTBACKUP report of the successful backup of an Exchange storage group is as follows:

```
Backup Status
Operation: Backup
Active backup destination: File
Media name: "Storage Group 1 created 3/21/2003 at 11:37 AM"

Backup of "TLGEXC01\Microsoft Information Store\Storage Group 1"
Backup set #1 on media #1
Backup description: "Set created 3/21/2003 at 11:37 AM"
Media name: "Storage Group 1 created 3/21/2003 at 11:37 AM"

Backup Type: Normal

Backup started on 3/21/2003 at 11:38 AM.
Backup completed on 3/21/2003 at 11:53 AM.
Directories: 3
Files: 6
Bytes: 9,221,460,426
Time: 15 minutes and 22 seconds
```

Incremental and differential backups only copy transaction logs to backup sets. Incremental backups copy the set of logs created since the last backup, while a differential backup copies the complete set of logs created since the last full backup. Thus, to restore Exchange databases you need:

- The last full backup
- The last full backup plus all incremental backups taken since then
- The last full backup set plus the last differential backup

Obviously, a full backup is the easiest way to restore, because there are fewer tapes to handle and less opportunity to make mistakes. However, if you rely exclusively on full backups, it is possible that you will miss some log files if you need to recover back to a time before the last full backup. For this reason, it is best practice to take incremental backups between full backups, leading to a backup schedule where you might take a daily full

11.4 Backups

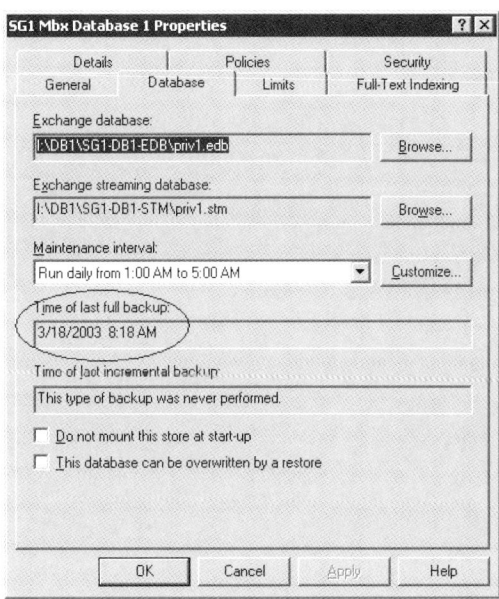

Figure 11.16
Last good backup timestamp.

backup at 6:00 P.M., with an incremental backup at lunchtime when system load is often lower.

Exchange 2003 places a timestamp on Stores after successful backups. You can view the timestamp by selecting a Store and viewing its properties through ESM. Exchange records times for the last full and last incremental backups, as shown in Figure 11.16. Apart from anything else, the existence of the timestamp gives you confidence that a successful backup exists, as well as telling you how old it is.

11.4.4 Backup patch file

Traditionally, Exchange servers generated patch files (*.pat) during backup operations. The function of the patch file is to record details of page splits that occur while a backup is in progress. ESE maintains a separate patch file for each database. During backups, ESE streams pages from the databases to the backup media. Since users continue to create and send messages while the backup is proceeding, the chances are that transactions will occur in a page that is already committed into the database. Because the logs capture these transactions, they do not affect the backup unless the transaction results in a page split. Page splits occur when ESE finds that it cannot fit all of the data for a transaction into a single page. Message headers that contain more than 20 (approximately) recipients often need two or three pages to fit all the header information. If a page split occurs, ESE notes details of the page in the patch file. Patch files only apply to operations to the EDB databases. Changes made to the streaming file do not cause page splits, so the data recorded in the set of transaction logs is enough to assure that ESE can reapply any changes.

ESE writes the patch files to the backup media at the very end of the backup to make them available in a restore situation. The first step in a restore is to apply the changes noted in the patch file to the database to make them consistent before rolling forward the transactions in the logs.

The patch file was a hangover from the original versions of Exchange and, to some degree, it complicated matters because administrators were never quite sure what its purpose was and how they should handle it. Microsoft solved the problem in Exchange 2000 SP2 by eliminating the patch file from backup processing. To remove the need for the patch file, ESE no longer advances the checkpoint and does not flush the Store buffers during full backup operations, which means that data can be recovered from the transaction logs, should the need occur. You no longer have to worry about the patch file, but its removal does mean that you cannot take a backup from an Exchange 2000 SP2 server (or later) and apply it to a server running an earlier version. This is both logical and correct, because all servers in an organization should run the same software level.

11.4.5 Checkpoint file

The checkpoint file (E00.CHK is the file used by the default storage group) maintains a note of the current log file position so that ESE knows the last committed transaction written to the databases in a storage group. ESE maintains a separate checkpoint file for each storage group.

The primary role played by the checkpoint file is during "soft" recoveries, when databases have closed down in an inconsistent manner through some system failure that has not resulted in a corrupt database. When the Information Store service restarts, ESE opens the checkpoint file and retrieves the location of the last committed transaction; it then begins to replay transactions from the logs from that point. While this is convenient, the checkpoint file is not mandatory for replays to occur, since ESE is able to scan the complete set of transaction logs to determine the point from which replays should commence. ESE does not write the checkpoint file to a backup set, because it serves no purpose during a "hard" recovery. In this scenario, you restore databases and transaction logs to different locations, so the ESE instance that controls the restore depends on the log information contained in the database header to work out what logs it should replay. In addition, ESE checks that all necessary log generations are present and available before beginning to replay transactions; it will not proceed if gaps exist. Other Windows components such as DHCP, WINS, and the AD that use ESE also maintain checkpoint files.

11.4.6 Restoring a database

Exchange 5.5 and earlier versions only support offline restores, meaning that the server can do no other work until the Information Store service is back online. Exchange now simply requires you to start the Information Store service before the restore can proceed; the Store can mount all of the unaffected databases, and users can connect to the mailboxes in those databases.

The Store is responsible for restore operations, and ESE uses a reserved storage group to enable online restores. The following steps occur:

- The database or storage group affected by the failure is dismounted by the administrator or is rendered unavailable by a hardware problem, such as a disk failure. In this case, you must fix the hardware problem before a restore can proceed. The Information Store service must be running.

- If you have a corrupt database in place, you probably want to overwrite the file on disk. Alternatively, you may prefer to take a copy of the corrupt database (EDB, STM, and associated transaction logs) before the restore overwrites the file and move it somewhere safe for later investigation. A database property controls whether the Store will allow the backup agent to overwrite a database. Either access the Store's properties and set the necessary checkbox, or simply delete the corrupt file before beginning the restore.

- The backup agent initializes and displays details of the backup sets that you can restore from the available media. Figure 11.17 shows NTBACKUP in operation. In this case, we have experienced a failure of the default Mailbox Store, so we need to restore the database plus the transaction logs copied to the backup set during the last backup. The backup set is from a full backup operation, because both databases and transaction logs are available. Incremental and differential backup sets only hold transaction logs.

- The backup agent notifies ESE that it wishes to begin a restore operation. The Store then launches an ESE recovery instance to manage

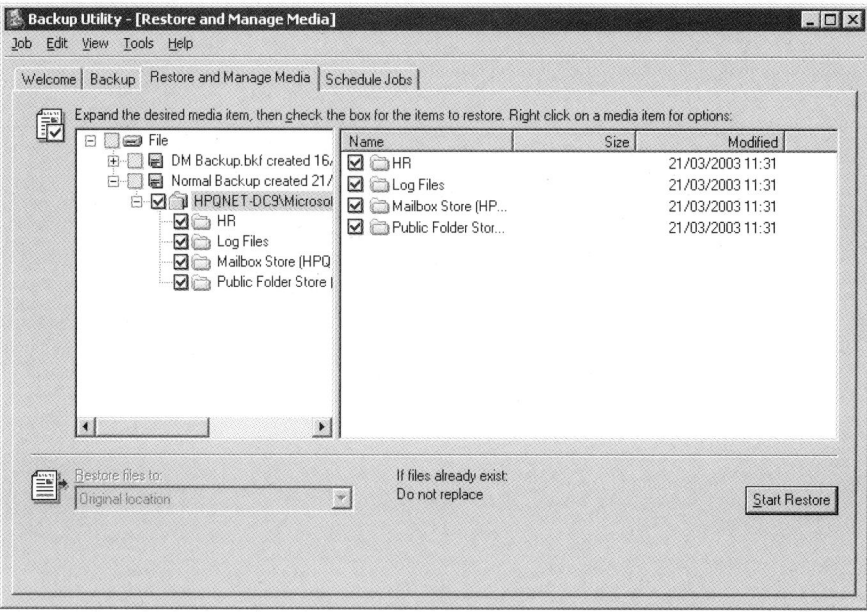

Figure 11.17   *Selecting a database for restore.*

the special recovery storage group. The recovery storage group only exists during restore operations.

- The backup agent begins to stream data out of the backup set into the necessary databases, using direct Win32 file system calls to copy the files into the appropriate locations. This operation proceeds under the control of the Store, which uses the special reserved storage group for this purpose. You restore differential and incremental sets first, followed by the most recent full backup. If you follow best practice, and always take full backups whenever possible, restore operations are much simpler. Figure 11.18 shows how you direct the backup set to the target restore server. Note that because this is the last backup set that must be restored, we can set the "Last Backup Set" checkbox to tell the backup agent that it does not have to look for any other backup sets and can complete the recovery operation once the databases have been restored. For NTBACKUP, this checkbox is a critical part of the restore operation, because ESE will perform none of the fix-up processing to make the database consistent until you tell ESE that it is OK to proceed by checking this box. However, if a database proves to be inconsistent after a restore, you

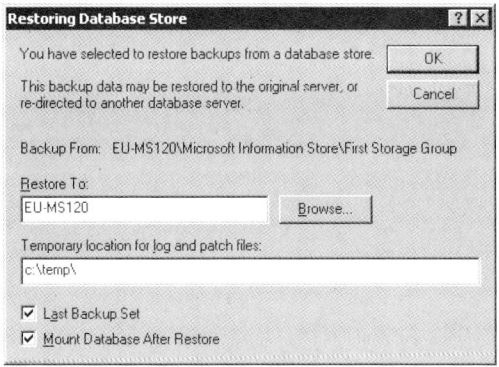

Figure 11.18
Setting parameters for the restore.

can use the ESEUTIL utility to try to correct any errors.[1] Note that the user interface of some third-party backup utilities does not include the "Last Backup Set" checkbox, because the utility controls the entire restore operation, including the decision when to begin postrestore fix-up processing. You can also check the "Mount Database After Restore" checkbox to get the restored Mailbox Store into operation as quickly as possible after the restore is complete.

- ESE restores the EDB and streaming files to the production directory, but not the transaction logs, since they might overwrite logs that contain transactions that ESE later needs to replay. You must, therefore, provide a temporary location to hold the transaction logs from the backup set for the duration of the restore. Make sure that the temporary location (e.g., C:\TEMP\BACKUP) has enough disk space to accommodate all of the log files in the backup set. (See Figure 11.19.)

- ESE creates a file called restore.env in the temporary location to control the processing of transaction logs during the restore. The restore.env file contains information about the databases, paths, signatures, and other information used by the restore and replaces the older registry key used by previous versions of Exchange to signal that a restore operation was in progress. ESE creates a separate file for each restore operation. You can dump the contents of restore.env with the ESEUTIL utility. Figure 11.20 illustrates a set of files used in a typical restore operation.

---

1. Usually, you end up with a restored database and a set of transaction logs accumulated since the time of the last backup, so you need to replay the transactions from the logs into the restored database. This is done with the ESEUTIL /CC /T<storage group instance> command.

Figure 11.19
A restore operation in progress.

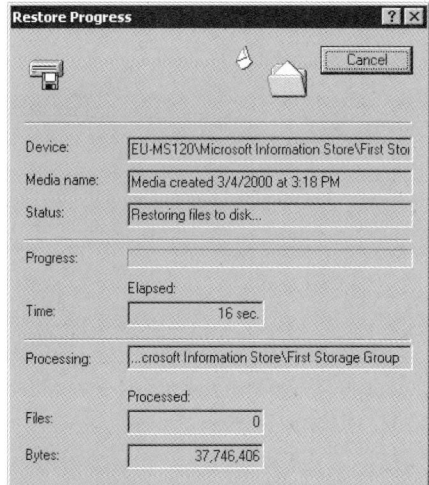

- Prior to Exchange 2000 SP2, after ESE restores the databases and transaction logs, it begins to apply any page splits to the respective databases. The application of page splits is not required after SP2. Next, the transaction logs are processed. During this process, ESE validates the log signature and generation sequence to ensure that the correct transaction logs are present and are available to recover transactions. If a log signature does not match the database signature, ESE returns error −610, and if it discovers a gap in the log generations, ESE signals error −611. If either of these errors is encountered, the recovery process is stopped. ESE has not yet replayed any transactions into the database, so you have a chance to fix the problem and start the restore again. Fixing the problem may require that you check the signatures on the databases and logs to ensure that they match, or discover why a gap exists in the log generations.

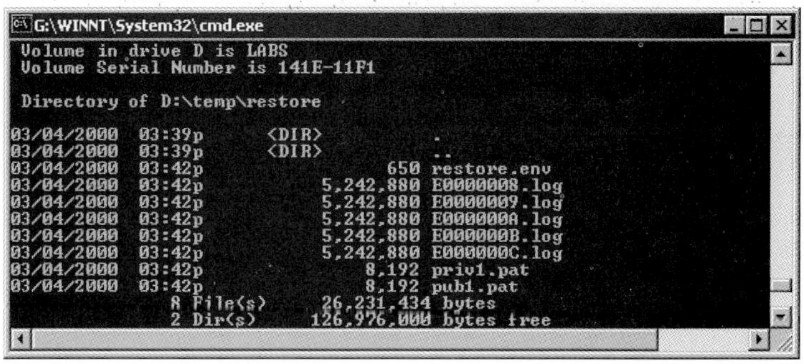

Figure 11.20
Files used by a restore operation in the temporary directory.

ESE actually reads two sets of logs during the restore. First, it processes the logs held in the temporary location, and then it processes the logs in the normal location that have accumulated since the backup. Transaction logs contain data for all of the databases in a storage group, so if you are restoring a single database, ESE must scan all the data in the logs to isolate the transactions for the specific database and then proceed to apply them. ESE ignores all of the other data in the logs. This phase of the operation may be the longest of all, depending on the number of transaction logs that have to be processed.

Once the data in the transaction logs has been applied, the recovery storage group performs some clean-up operations, exits, and returns control to the primary storage group (the storage group that is being restored), which is then able to bring the newly restored databases back online. ESE also deletes the files in the temporary location. ESE notes details of all of the recovery operations in the Application Event Log.

In the case of differential or incremental restores, only the transaction logs are loaded into the temporary location and processed there. At the end of a successful restore, ESE writes event 902 into the application event log. ESE also records the details of the restore operation in a text file (the file is named after the backup set). To be certain that everything is OK before you allow any users to connect to the store, check that ESE logs event 902 and that ESE has recorded no errors in the text file.

11.4.7 Third-party backup utilities

NTBACKUP is a basic backup engine and while you certainly can use NTBACKUP to perform backups of Exchange data, its interface and features lack functionality, especially when you are dealing with high-end servers. The same situation existed for Windows before Exchange came along, and for that reason, there are many highly functional and feature-rich backup third-party backup utilities available for Windows today. Most of these products have created add-on modules or new version releases to support Exchange, so NTBACKUP is not the only option.

Exchange provides two DLLs for use by backup utilities to access Exchange data. These are ESEBACK2.DLL, which interfaces with the service (Store, SRS, etc.) that the application wishes to connect to in order to take a backup or restore files, and ESEBCLI2.DLL, which provides the interface to the backup client. A system registry entry makes backup utilities aware of the client interface, and Exchange-enabled utilities such as

NTBACKUP look for the registry entry when they start up to determine whether they need to dynamically load and display Exchange resources.

The DLLs include the API necessary for backup utilities to process Exchange data. The following functions illustrate the flow of a backup operation:

- HrESEBackupPrepare: Establishes an RPC connection to Exchange and returns a list of the available databases available for backup.

- HrESEBackupSetup: Used by the backup utility to tell Exchange which storage group it wishes to back up. Each storage group uses its own backup set. You can perform a restore operation of a single database by selecting it from the list held in a backup set.

- HrESEBackupOpenFile: Opens the selected database for read access. Both EDB and streaming file are included.

- HrESEBackupReadFile: Reads the database in 64-KB chunks. This function also performs checksum calculation and verification.

- HrESEBackupCloseFile: Closes the database.

- HrESEBackupGetLogAndPatchFiles: Gets a list of all the log file names to include in the backup set. ESE backs up these files using the HrESEBackupOpenFile, HrESEBackupReadFile, and HrESEBackupCloseFile functions.

- HrESEBackupTruncateLog: Delete any obsolete transaction logs after a full backup. Truncation only happens after ESE successfully backs up all selected databases. If you do not back up all of the databases in a storage group for any reason, ESE cannot delete the logs.

- HrESEBackupInstanceEnd: End the backup for the instance (storage group or selected database).

- HrESEBackupEnd: Disconnect from the RPC connection to Exchange.

It is possible to run concurrent backup processes, with each process taking care of a storage group. Interestingly, Windows has a "FilesNotToBackup" registry key, which is used to record information about files that NTBACKUP should not include in a normal file-level backup (e.g., \exchsrvr*data*.*"—don't back up anything in the Exchange server data directories). The Exchange databases are a good example of such files, since the Store always has these files locked against access by other processes, and file-level backup utilities cannot, therefore, read these files.

Table 11.3 *Third-Party Backup Utilities*

Company	Product	Web Address
CommVault	CommVault	http://www.commvault.com
Veritas	Backup Exec	http://www.veritas.com
Legato Systems, Inc.	Networker for Windows NT	http://www.legato.com
HP	Omniback	http://www.hp.com
Computer Associates	ArcServe	http://www.ca.com
BEI Corporation	Ultrabac	http://www.ultrabac.com

Exchange provides a similar set of functions to restore databases from backup sets, including HrESERestoreOpen, HrESERestoreAddDatabase, and HrESERestoreOpenFile to support the restore of a single database or a complete storage group. While it is technically possible to run multiple concurrent restore operations, best practice suggests that it is safer to concentrate on a single restore at a time, just to reduce the potential for error. Taken together, the Exchange backup API is comprehensive and open to third-party vendors to exploit. Table 11.3 lists some of the major third-party backup products that support Exchange. Use the Web address to get information about the latest product features to help you decide which product best meets your needs.

It is always difficult to justify the additional expense of buying a package to replace a standard utility, especially when there is a standard utility that appears to do the job in an adequate manner. The cost of deploying, managing, and supporting the new utility across multiple servers also has to be taken into account. It is a mistake to run different backup products within an organization, since this makes it much more difficult to move data between servers. Due to the different ways that software can stream data out to tapes, it is highly unlikely that one backup software package will be able to read a tape created by another. Once you allow diversity, you create a potential situation where you cannot restore a backup for one reason or another. Moreover, Murphy's Law dictates that this situation occurs just after a server hosting thousands of users has crashed and you cannot bring it back online quickly.

For this reason, try to standardize on a single backup product and use the same backup media (tapes and drives) to gain maximum flexibility. You never know when you will need to move data onto a different server and it is embarrassing to discover that you cannot, because the target server is not equipped with a drive that can read the backup media.

A specialized package often provides very useful features that are missing in the standard utility. In practice, third-party backup products usually provide three major enhancements over the NTBACKUP program:

- Scheduling
- Speed
- Control

Specialized backup products tend to support high-end features, such as unattended backups, automated loading and unloading via tape libraries, and network backup to very large storage silos (CD-equipped juke boxes or similar). Such features are not critical to small or medium servers, but you need to consider them for any server that hosts large databases.

Microsoft designed the architecture of Exchange with online backups in mind. In other words, there is no requirement to stop the different services (Information Store, MTA, System Attendant, and so on) while the backup is proceeding. It might, therefore, appear that speed is of little concern. After all, you can start a backup each morning and have it running alongside users as the day proceeds. This is true, but it is only a partial picture. Backups can proceed online, but you can only perform restores by halting access to the database that you want to restore. If backup software processes data quickly, it is normal that restores are quick too. However, restores normally proceed at half the speed of a backup. Best practice is to plan for backups to take four hours or less to keep any subsequent restore operation to less than the length of an eight-hour working day. The online nature of backups is important too. Many products can take backups of files on a disk and some can take backups even if the files are open. In an Exchange environment, you can guarantee that some files are open, and products that support open file backups can write data for these files (such as the databases) to backup media. However, you have no assurance that a subsequent restore operation can deliver a usable file, because the files were "dirty" or in an inconsistent state during the backup. In all likelihood, you will have to restore the database and roll forward outstanding transactions, and, in some cases, you may not be able to make the files consistent again.

A combination of software and hardware improvements has increased performance and backup over the years. It is now possible to pump data out to devices faster than they can accept it. The Exchange developers know that the backup API can stream data out of the Store at very high rates to a null device. Hardware slows things down, but, even so, equipped with a dual-striped tape, developers were able to achieve real backup rates of more than 40 GB/hour. Some installations have exceeded this rate in production environments equipped with quad-DLT devices working in a RAID array, which can process data at much higher rates. It is important that you keep an eye on the quantity of data that you must back up over time. It is likely that the amount of data will grow, and if you do not increase the capacity of the backup hardware to handle increased amounts of data, your backups will take longer and longer.

Increased speed and reduced backup times make it more feasible to take full backups every day rather than the traditional cycle of full backups every week with incremental backups taken on the days in between. The advantage gained here will only accrue if you have to restore the server. You will be glad to find that it is much easier and faster to restore from a single full backup than to go through the hoops and loops of restoring from the last full backup followed by all the incremental backups since. With large servers that have multiple Stores, each of which might hold up to 50 GB, the backup times may be a touch too long to take full backups every day, but with smaller servers, it is certainly the best way to perform backups.

Better control over backup operations is the final advantage provided by third-party utilities. NTBACKUP is quite content to overwrite the same tape with a new backup every day if you leave the tape in the tape drive, as some people have discovered to their loss. Commands such as "eject tape after backup is complete" prevent accidents from happening and contribute to data security. This type of problem is unlikely to occur in datacenters where skilled operations staff work, but it is entirely possible in places where people only know how to insert tapes into drives. Effective tape handling is critically important for installations dealing with large stores that span more than one tape. You do not want to get into a situation where a backup never actually completes because someone forgot to take out the first tape and insert a new tape at the appropriate time. A number of the third-party backup utilities also allow you to back up the system registry, disks, and the Exchange databases in a single operation—much easier than having to make (and restore) three separate backup tapes.

It is important to understand that while third-party backup software can provide some valuable advantages, it is another piece to fit into your system configuration matrix. New releases of the backup software must be qualified against existing versions of Exchange and then against new versions of Exchange. You should also check the backup software against service packs of both Exchange and Windows. The Exchange development team cannot check its product against every third-party product or extension, so it is entirely possible that the installation of a service pack will introduce a problem that only becomes apparent when a backup operation is attempted. On the other hand, even worse, is a problem that suddenly appears during a restore. The complex interaction between Exchange, Windows, and any third-party product adds weight to the argument that you should test all combinations of software products (including patches) before they are introduced to production servers.

Good backups provide a parachute to administrators when problems occur, and if the backups do not work when you need them, then anyone involved may soon be looking for a new job, so it is reasonable to regard backup software as a very important part of the Exchange administrator's armory.

11.4.8 Backing up individual mailboxes

Some third-party backup utilities support a feature that allows administrators to back up one or more selected mailboxes instead of a complete Store, a feature known as a brick-level backup. NTBACKUP does not support this feature. Third-party products accomplish this feat by performing a privileged logon through MAPI to the user's mailbox and then reading out all of the items in the mailbox to the backup set. The application also records the necessary contextual (mailbox and folder structure) information to allow the items to be restored in the same order that they were retrieved. This is an arrangement very different from a normal backup, where ESE provides data in a continuous stream based on low-level internal database structures rather than the structure of mailboxes. Microsoft never designed MAPI for use as a backup interface, and the combination of MAPI and item-level retrieval does not result in fast performance. Backing up an individual mailbox can take between four and eight times as long as backing up the raw data using the Backup API, and there's no guarantee that you'll be able to restore an exact replica of a mailbox in terms of either content or format if the need occurs.

Some administrators believe that being able to take a mailbox-level backup is a useful feature, because it allows them to quickly restore a mailbox if the complete mailbox is deleted in error, or to restore specific items if a user happens to delete a number of important items by mistake. The usefulness of the feature was unquestioned with early versions of Exchange, since the loss of items by mistake or error required a complete restore of a database (normally on a test server) to retrieve the information. However, the provision of the Deleted Items Recovery feature in Exchange 5.5, the

Deleted Mailbox Recovery feature introduced in Exchange 2000, and Exchange 2003's Mailbox Recovery Center have largely removed the requirement to restore databases to fix problems caused by user or administrator error. Some argue, including me, that brick-level backups are now an anachronism of the past and that they are not worth the bother. Others, possibly those who have been forced to restore databases to retrieve large collections of messages, believe that these backups are valuable. It all depends on your operating environment, but, given the options, I think it best to set an extended deleted item retention period on Stores where users are likely to want to recover items (such as Stores used by executives) and avoid brick-level backups if at all possible.

11.4.9 Restoring an Exchange server

Coming in to find that your Exchange server is down and will not boot or has experienced a catastrophic disk failure is an experience that few system administrators relish. True, you can view the situation as a chance to demonstrate your calm, analytical skills in problem solving and deep knowledge of the hardware and software components that make up an Exchange server, but most of us react like human beings and panic.

As with most challenges, the people who have a well-thought-out plan usually do better than those who plunge in to try to get things working without putting their brains into gear. The history of Exchange is littered with examples where administrators caused further damage by failing to carry out procedures correctly, such as attempting to restore using an invalid set of transaction logs. Among the basic questions that you should ask at this time are:

- Is the basic server still working? Check whether Windows can boot and load applications. Note which applications are unable to start and check to see if any reasons are in the Event Log.

- Does any obvious sign exist that some hardware is unavailable to the server? Are multiple components affected by a single failure such as a controller problem that blocks access to multiple disks?

- Are all of the items required to perform a recovery available? These include replacement hardware (anything from a complete server to an individual disk). Can the server still connect to the network and access kits and other useful items on file shares? Do you have access to service packs, hot fixes, and third-party applications? Can you restore the backup tapes on the server?

- After you have sketched out the overall shape of the problem, you will find that the correct course of action is either:
  - Replace hardware components and restore any software and data affected by the failure. For example, replace a failed disk and restore an Exchange database and transaction logs.
  - Replace a complete server with similar hardware and rebuild the operating environment as quickly as possible.

Clearly, the second option is far more difficult to execute if only because more replacement components are usually necessary. You may have a server on stand-by and be able to take the disks from the failed server and insert them into the stand-by and restart. However, it is more likely that you will have to assemble hardware to form a server that is as close as possible in terms of processing power, memory, and storage to the original server, perhaps by cannibalizing the original hardware.

Once the server hardware is ready, you can begin to:

- Reinstall the same version of Windows, including any service packs and hot fixes.

- Restore the last full good backup of any applications and data for all disk drives. Obviously, you can leave some of the restores until you get Exchange back on the air and users are happily connected to their mailboxes.

- Restore the system state. This includes the system startup files, the all-important system registry, the IIS metabase, SYSVOL, and so on. The registry and the IIS metabase are critical to Exchange. If the system configuration is different, you may have to reboot a number of times in safe mode to get everything working properly.

- Ensure that the server can connect to the AD. If the server was a DC or GC, you will have to restore the last good backup of the AD from the server and wait for replication to backfill updates that have occurred since. The alternative is to perform an "authoritative restore" to wind back to a particular point in time. You can also demote the server from DC status using NTDSUTIL and then make it a DC again with DCPROMO. This will force a complete replication cycle to begin again. Many dangers lurk in these options, and the right answer varies from situation to situation and environment to environment. Either make sure that you know the best way to restore a server with AD or avoid problems by never running Exchange on a DC (normal best practice in large enterprises). The critical points here are to ensure that Exchange can connect to a DC and GC to access configuration data and that DNS is available.

- Run the Exchange setup program in /disasterrecovery mode. Microsoft designed this mode to read configuration data about the Exchange server from the AD and use the information to rebuild the configuration. This is the reason why you need AD connectivity, and the object for the server that you are restoring must exist in the AD before you attempt to rebuild Exchange. Remember to restore any optional component.

- Apply any service packs and hot fixes to Exchange. The Store is sensitive to version updates and may not be able to restore a backup taken with an earlier or later version of Exchange, so it is always safest to run exactly the same version as you had on the failed server.

- It is a good idea to set the Exchange MTA to start manually rather than automatically and also disable the SMTP virtual servers until you have completed all restore operations and the server works normally. This step will prevent email traffic from flowing into the server while you work. You do not want to get into a situation where you lose email because it arrives at a server that you then have to scrub because some problem occurs in the restore.

- Restart the server.

- Restore all of the storage groups that were on the failed server. Restore the last full good backup first, and then apply any transaction logs taken by copy backups since. Remember to check the Last Backup Set option for the last backup to force the Store to roll forward transactions from the logs. Hopefully, the transaction log disk will be intact and all of the logs taken since the last backup will be available.

- After each restore, check that the Store can mount the restored databases and that you can connect to mailboxes. Consider blocking client access to the server until all restores are complete and you are happy that the server is ready for use.

- Check that any connectors work and that you can send mail to people on other servers and outside the organization.

- If the server hosted the Site Replication Service, restore the component and the SRS database (only required in mixed-mode organizations).

- If the server hosted the Key Management Server, restore the component and then the KMS database (not required for Exchange 2003).

- Take a full backup.

- Announce another triumph of system administration and let users get back to their mailboxes.

Depending on whether you can put your hand on the items necessary to perform the restore, the whole operation may take from four hours (everything ready and immediately accessible) to as long as it takes to find replacement hardware. Be sure that you know how you are going to perform the steps before you commit to a Service-Level Agreement that calls for a server to be back online in a stated time. A number of critical points occur from this discussion. You need to:

- Have access to hardware or know how to get replacement hardware

- Have access to software, including service packs, hot fixes, and third-party applications. It is a good idea to create a disaster recovery CD that holds all of the necessary software to recover a server, but make sure that this is kept up-to-date and that you know where it is stored.

Unbelievably, it is now easier to rebuild an Exchange server than ever before. The reason is simple: Administrators have had a lot of practical experience in restoring servers over the years, and the Exchange development team has captured the knowledge gained in these situations regarding the way the software performs restores.

11.4.10 Recovery servers

Medium to large Exchange installations often maintain a dedicated server for recovery operations. You can use a recovery server as replacement hardware to get users back to work quickly after a catastrophic hardware failure (the need for this capability is reduced in Exchange 2003 with the introduction of the Recovery Storage Group), but the most common use of recovery servers is to retrieve specific information from an Exchange database taken from another server—for example:

- A mailbox that has been deleted in error and the deleted mailbox retention period is past

- A mailbox or items that you need to recover for legal or other reasons

- A public folder deleted when it is the only replica in the organization

- A specific item or items deleted by a user that he or she is unable to retrieve through the normal deleted items recovery option

11.4 Backups

- Recovery of mailboxes from a failed server to PSTs followed by subsequent reload of mailboxes to a server using new hardware

Given the increased frequency of discovery actions, which seek copies of email to prove points in legal arguments, lawyers have also used recovery servers to retrieve all the messages from several mailboxes. Sometimes, you have to recover messages sent over an extended period, which necessitates the restore of multiple backups to ensure that you do not omit a specific message. Recovery operations such as this are not pleasant to work on, so they are to be avoided at all costs. Unfortunately, lawyers usually make the decision when a recovery is required.

You can also use a recovery server to run database maintenance utilities against a backup copy of a database to check it for any lurking corruption or to test that you are taking reliable backups. For example, let us assume that you have noticed some -1018 events recorded in the application event log. Normally, these errors indicate that the drive where the database is located has a hardware problem. To check things out, you can restore a backup of the database to the recovery server and run the ESEUTIL utility to verify whether the database is in good health. If the database checks out (in other words, ESEUTIL reports no checksum or other errors), you can then arrange to verify the hardware to discover the root cause of the -1018 errors. If ESEUTIL fails, you know that a serious problem is in the database and that it will soon fail, even if you replace the hardware. Even so, you can arrange to transfer mailbox data to another server before the database fails, using the Move Mailbox option or the ExMerge utility.

Recovery servers are also useful if you want to test an add-on product against real-life data, especially backup and antivirus utilities. Far too many products work wonderfully in demo environments when they only have to process limited amounts of data only to encounter problems in production. Testing against a server loaded with real data allows you to determine whether the product will work when you put it into production.

You must allocate suitable hardware to the recovery server. This is not a production system, so you do not need the same type of multi-CPU, highly redundant disk subsystem configuration deployed in production. However, there are some prerequisites:

- Enough disk space must be available to restore the largest database that you might need to recover. Alternatively, the system should be capable of adding additional disks quickly should the need occur.

- The server should use the same backup software as used in production, and must be able to read the tapes created on the production servers.
- The server should be running the same version (including service packs and hot fixes) of Windows and Exchange.
- If you do not want to assign dedicated hardware to recovery servers, virtual servers can make excellent recovery servers providing they can connect to the various devices used in recovery operations.

Delivery of email to personal stores (PST files) poses another problem. Instead of recovering a single database, you now must recover all of the individual PSTs that are located on a failed disk. Not only will this operation require a surprising amount of disk (Exchange does not force users to delete email from their personal stores to stay within quotas, so they tend to keep more), the number of individual files makes this a tricky operation. While you might not think that it is the responsibility of an administrator to look after personal data, all bets are off when a server crashes, and you will probably find that you have to recover PST files as well. It is a good idea to factor in all aspects of email recovery in your disaster recovery plans. You can also use a recovery server to check how long it will take ESEUTIL to rebuild a database and whether you will save a significant amount of disk space after you have rebuilt the database. This is useful if you want to know how long you need to take a server offline to run the rebuild.

Having a recovery server available is only part of the equation. Knowing how to restore data quickly and effectively is the other. You cannot treat the two in isolation from each other, so make sure that you perform some trial runs and check that data can be recovered using production backups on the recovery hardware.

11.4.11 Recovering a Mailbox Store

Because Exchange depends so heavily on AD for mailbox and configuration data, you must take some specific steps to ensure that you can access mailboxes after you restore databases onto a recovery server. The basic requirements are that the recovery server is in a different AD forest than the original server. The forest name can be different and the two forests can share a network. However, you must install the recovery server into a different Exchange organization—but one with the same name. Remember that there can only be one Exchange organization in a forest, so by installing the recovery server into a different forest you prevent the recovery server from interfering with other servers in the "production" Exchange organization.

11.4 Backups

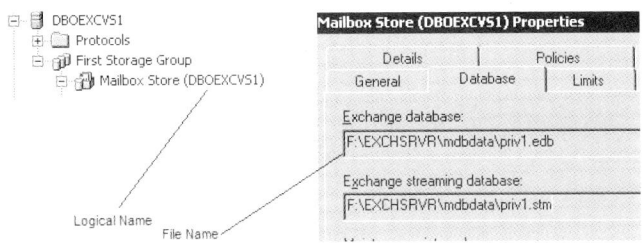

Figure 11.21
Database logical and file names.

You should also stop users from attempting to log on or otherwise access the recovery server while you are working.

Once you install Exchange on the recovery server, you can restore the databases using the normal restore procedure. Before proceeding with the restore, you must use ESM to rename the logical names of the storage group and the database to match the names of the storage group and database from the original server. The names should match exactly—including the name of the original server if specified—but it does not matter if the underlying file names (e.g., MAILBOX.EDB) are different. You can either create the storage group and databases with the correct names or rename them to the appropriate values. It is best practice to use the same storage group names and to follow a convention for database names throughout an organization to reduce the room for error during a recovery operation. Figure 11.21 illustrates the difference between the logical names of a Store as viewed through ESM and the underlying physical file names.

You are going to overwrite the database on the recovery server with the database from the original server, so you must use ESM to amend the target database's properties to allow the backup to overwrite the files. If you use an offline backup for the restore, you are copying data taken at a specific point in time, and there is no need for the Store to replay data in transaction logs to make the database consistent. Thus, you can delete the existing database and logs and overwrite them with the data from the backup set. However, you must set the properties of the database to allow the restore to overwrite the files, even when you use an offline backup.

Before restoring any data, check that the LegacyExchangeDN values for the administrative group and organization for original and recovery servers match. The LegacyExchangeDN AD attribute is used extensively by Exchange to identify objects, as well as ensuring backward compatibility with earlier versions. In this case, a successful restore depends on the Store being able to verify with the AD that a database it wishes to mount is registered with the AD. When you create a new database on an Exchange server, the Store stamps the database with the names of the organization and administrative group that it belongs to, and only a server that matches these names can mount the database thereafter.

The simplest approach to the problem is to specify the same values for the organization and administrative group as the server that you wish to retrieve data for when you install Exchange on the recovery server. If you have installed Exchange and used different values for the organization or administrative group, you can adjust the LegacyExchangeDN values before attempting to recover data by using the LegacyDN utility from the \utils\tools\i386 folder on the server CD. Essentially, you create a replica of the original environment for the restore to proceed correctly. You can make the necessary changes with other LDAP tools such as ADSIEDIT or LDIFDE, but it is much easier and quicker to use LegacyDN.

Warning: Do not run LegacyDN in a production environment, since it is very easy to make a mistake that will severely affect the Exchange organization. At worst, if you change LegacyExchangeDN values within an organization, you may have to restore the Active Directory and all Exchange servers.

Figure 11.22 shows the LegacyDN utility in action. In this case, the recovery server is "RESTORESERVER" and it is in the "RESTOREDOMAIN.COM" domain. We want to restore a database from the "NSIS European Messaging Team" administrative group in the Compaq organiza-

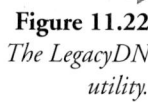

Figure 11.22
The LegacyDN utility.

tion. When you run the LegacyDN utility on a server, it scans the AD to find what administrative groups exist. You can then select an administrative group and change its base details (or LegacyExchangeDN stem) to reflect the values in the database that you want to restore. If you proceed with the recovery without changing these values, you will be able to restore the database from tape (or other media), but the Store will not be able to mount the restored database because the LegacyExchangeDN values do not match. To fix the values, we insert the names of the original administrative group and organization and click on the "Change Leg" button, then stop and restart the Information Store service to make the change effective. In this case, the net effect is to change the existing LegacyExchangeDN stem of:

```
/O=Compaq/OU=First Administrative Group
```

to:

```
/O=Compaq/OU=NSIS European Messaging Team
```

If you are unsure about the value of the LegacyExchangeDN attribute for the administrative group that the database comes from, you can use the ADSIEDIT utility to read the information about the administrative group from the Microsoft Exchange configuration container.

Figure 11.23 shows the result of using ADSIEDIT to drill down through the AD configuration naming context to the Services container and then the Microsoft Exchange container, followed by the organization container. Each administrative group is a subcontainer under the organization. Select the administrative group that the database came from and view its properties. Select the LegacyExchangeDN attribute from the drop-down list and note the value reported. In this instance, the value is:

```
/O=Compaq/OU=NSIS European Messaging Team
```

In Exchange 5.5 terminology, this equates to the name of the organization followed by the name of the site, so you can see how the "legacy" of the Exchange 5.5 naming convention is preserved in the attribute for use by Exchange. With all of the LegacyExchangeDN values adjusted, you can then:

- Dismount the target database on the recovery server.

- Restore the backup set from the original server to overwrite the database files on disk.

- Check the Application Event Log to ensure that the backup utility or ESE has reported a problem and that the Store has been able to mount the restored database.

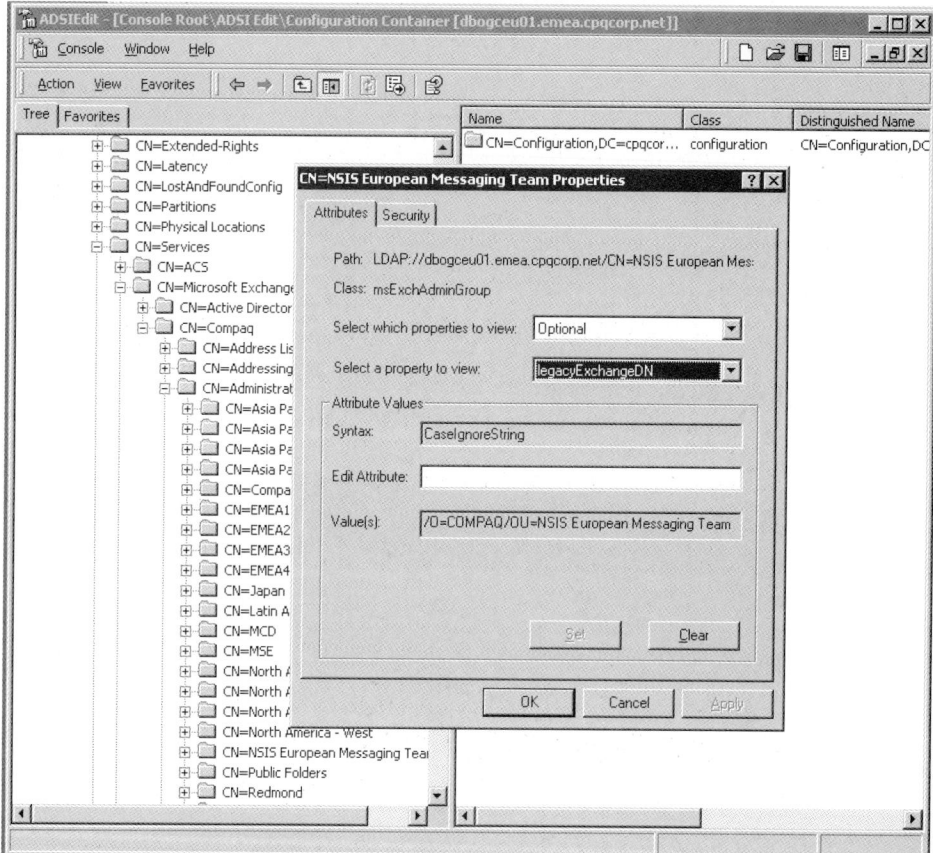

Figure 11.23   *Checking the LegacyExchangeDN value for an administrative group.*

The most common reason why the restore will not work is that the name of the database in the backup set does not match the name of the target database as shown in ESM. The most common reason why the Store fails to mount the database after the restore successfully creates the database is that the LegacyExchangeDN values do not match. In either case, the Store signals the errors in the Application Event Log. Look for event 1088 for details of a distinguished name mismatch—this will tell you that you need to adjust the LegacyExchangeDN values.

At this point, we have mounted a database that contains the mailboxes that we want to access, but we still need to associate them with AD accounts before we can use a client to open the mailbox and retrieve information. Remember that mailboxes are attributes of AD accounts rather than entities in their own right. Without an association with AD accounts,

11.4 Backups   863

mailboxes are repositories that you can see through ESM but cannot access with a client or other program.

In section 11.5.1, about the Mailbox Recovery Center, we will review how to link accounts with mailboxes. Some small differences exist when you use a recovery server. First, you must create the AD accounts (the names that you use do not have to match the original accounts). Second, you link the new accounts to mailboxes in the restored database. The easiest way to associate mailboxes with accounts is to use the Mailbox Cleanup Agent option in ESM. To invoke the agent, open the Mailbox Store and select "Mailboxes," use right-click to view the context-sensitive menu, and select "Run Cleanup Agent" from the menu. The Mailbox Cleanup Agent works by scanning a Mailbox Store to look for mailboxes that do not have a link to an AD account. Any mailbox that cannot be resolved is marked with a red circle with a white X in the center. Figure 11.24 illustrates what you might see after running the agent. All of the mailboxes are visible, but apart from the system mailboxes, a valid account is not shown in the "Last Logged on By" column. This implies that the Mailbox Cleanup Agent was unable to resolve the SID of the account last used to access a mailbox against the AD, so you know that a link does not exist between the mailboxes and AD accounts.

After the Mailbox Cleanup Agent finishes processing, you can select the mailboxes that you want to work with and use the Reconnect option (from

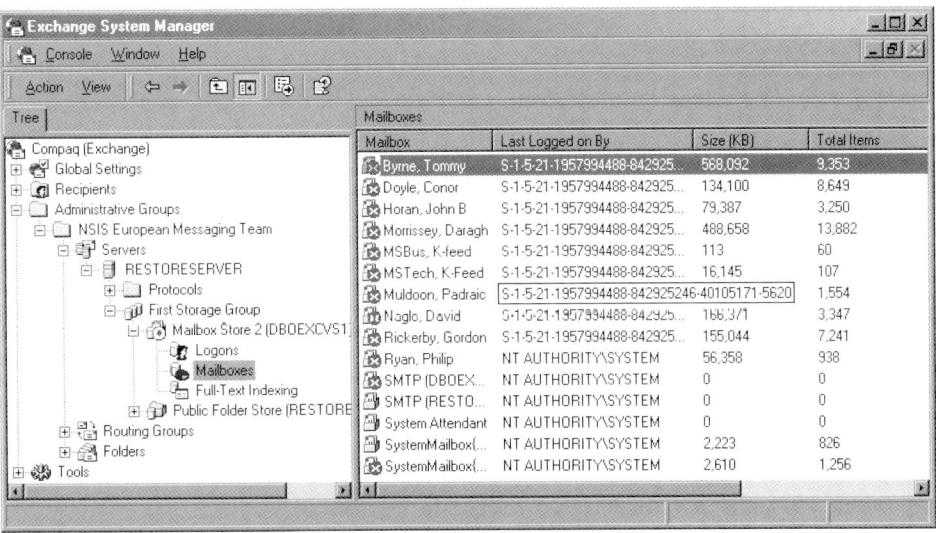

Figure 11.24   *Unassociated mailboxes after a restore.*

the right-click menu) to link them to an AD account. This is a satisfactory approach for a small number of mailboxes, but it quickly becomes tiresome if you want to connect hundreds of mailboxes. In this situation, you can use the MBCONN utility from the tools folder on the Exchange 2000 CD. Apart from being able to identify a complete list of mailboxes in the Store that do not have an associated AD account, MBCONN generates an LDF load file with details of the missing accounts. You can then use the LDIFDE utility to process the LDF file to recreate the accounts and run MBCONN again to reconnect the accounts with the mailboxes.

Once you connect accounts to mailboxes, you can use a client to log on to the mailbox and access the content. Default Exchange permissions block administrator access to mailboxes, so if you want to use your account to access the mailboxes, you must first change the permissions on each mailbox to allow access to that account. If you want to recover information for a user, you can select it from the mailbox and copy it to a PST, or use the EXMERGE utility to recover data for multiple mailboxes at one time. Remember that prior to Outlook 2003, you are restricted to a 1.8-GB maximum for PSTs, so you may not be able to export all of the contents from large mailboxes to a single PST.

The exact amount of time needed to perform the different steps to restore and access a Mailbox Store on a recovery server depends on the size of the database, the backup technology you use, and the amount of data you need to retrieve after the restore is complete. Use the figures listed in Table 11.4 as a guideline, but remember that you should verify the estimates in your own environment.

Clean-up operations are always the most popular work for system administrators. In this case, the recovery servers hold sensitive information in the recovered databases, so it is critical that you secure the data for as long as you need it and then delete it.

11.4.12 Rapid online, phased recovery

Rapid online and phased recovery (ROPR) is a technique used in conjunction with recovery servers to restore service very quickly to users. The idea is straightforward. Recover a failed server as quickly as possible with new hardware and reinstall Exchange, but then do not attempt to restore the databases on the newly installed server. Instead, Exchange will notice that the databases it expects are missing when the Store attempts to mount the files. This prompts Exchange to ask you whether it should recreate the databases. If you answer affirmatively, the Store recreates and mounts the data-

Table 11.4 *Task List for Mailbox Recovery*

Task	Estimated Time	Notes
Prepare recovery server by installing Windows 2000/2003, Exchange 2000/2003, all service packs and hot fixes, backup software, configuring DNS, and verifying all steps.	4–6 hours	Availability of suitable hardware (including correct tape drives), software kits, and licenses
Preparation of Exchange 2000/2003 environment prerestore	1 hour	—
Restore Mailbox Store	1 hour	Depends on size of database. In one hour, you should be able to restore 16–30 GB depending on the hardware and software combination.
Set up Active Directory accounts	30 minutes	Depends on the number of accounts to be used
Run Mailbox Cleanup Agent	10 minutes	The agent normally completes faster than this.
Reconnect mailboxes to AD accounts	1 minute per mailbox	—
Access mailbox and recover data	30 minutes per mailbox	You need to configure a client to access the mailbox, decide what data you want to recover, and then export to a PST. The actual time could be a lot longer if the mailbox is large.
Clean up server after recovery	1 hour	Delete files and prepare server for next recovery operation.

bases and you can then proceed to reconnect user accounts to their mailboxes. Of course, the mailboxes are completely empty, but users will be able to start to send and receive email immediately to complete the "rapid online" part of the exercise.

As soon as you restore service to users, you can recover the original databases to a recovery server and use ExMerge to export mailbox data to PSTs. Then, as ExMerge finishes processing each mailbox, you can provide the PST to its owner and tell him or her how to move messages from the PST back into the mailbox, which is what we mean by "phased recovery."

This technique is not perfect and there are many flaws. For example, ExMerge will not recover rules and other settings such as custom views, which Outlook holds in the mailboxes that you destroy when you force

Exchange to recreate the database. The biggest plus point is that users get online quickly, so the technique is far more applicable to situations such as an ISP rather than corporate environments where users expect a fully restored mailbox as soon as the server is available.

11.5 Recovering deleted mailboxes

Administrators make mistakes from time to time, and one of the most common mistakes is deleting a mailbox in error. The Exchange 2003 Mailbox Recovery Center makes it easier for administrators to fix the problem and restore service to users of deleted mailboxes. Unlike Exchange 2000, the Mailbox Recovery Center (MRC) permits centralized management and recovery of deleted mailboxes.

If an administrator deletes a mailbox on an Exchange 4.0–5.5 server, he or she has to restore the Mailbox Store on a recovery server to retrieve the mailbox and export its contents to a PST, and then import the contents back into a newly created mailbox. The process is easier for Exchange 2000, because administrators can set a retention period (the default period is 30 days) for deleted mailboxes as a Mailbox Store property. Thereafter, Exchange hides any deleted mailboxes and keeps their contents in their original Mailbox Store until the deletion period expires, at which time the Store deletes the mailbox content. This mechanism is possible because mailboxes exist within the database, and the link between users and mailboxes comes from attributes applied to mail-enabled AD user objects. When you delete a user mailbox, the effect is to clear the attributes so the user object is no longer mail enabled. As long as you do not delete the user object and Exchange has not cleared the mailbox contents upon expiration of the deletion period, you always have the opportunity to reestablish the link between the mailbox and the user.

To recover a deleted Exchange mailbox, you can browse the list of mailboxes in a Store and identify the deleted mailboxes, which the Store marks with a red icon (the marking is much more obvious in Exchange 2000—Exchange 2003 takes a more subtle approach). The Mailbox Cleanup Agent, which the System Attendant process runs nightly as part of normal background maintenance, is responsible for marking the deleted mailboxes. You can also force ESM to run the Mailbox Cleanup Agent by right-clicking on a Mailbox Store and selecting the option. After the agent finishes, refresh the mailbox list and you should see a display similar to that shown in Figure 11.25, where you can see three deleted mailboxes.

11.5 Recovering deleted mailboxes   867

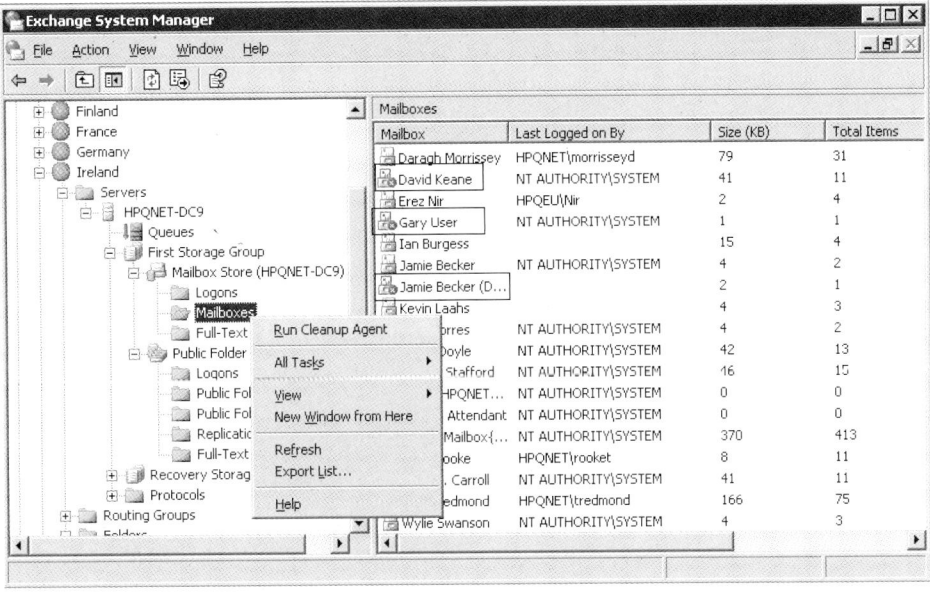

Figure 11.25   *Viewing deleted mailboxes.*

After you locate the mailbox that you want to recover, you right-click on the mailbox and select the "Reconnect" option (Figure 11.26). You can now browse the AD to select a user who does not currently have a mailbox. Click on OK, and Exchange connects the mailbox to the user by populating the necessary attributes for the user object. The next run of the Recipient Update Service for the domain then completes the process by ensuring that the newly connected user object has the proper email addresses. Note that if you find a disconnected mailbox that you absolutely do not want to keep, you can use the Purge option to remove it from the Store.

All of this sounds perfectly logical and the process works, but it is intended for processing single mailboxes rather than centralized management. You can argue that this is the way that Exchange should perform mailbox recovery. After all, only a few such cases occur yearly in even the

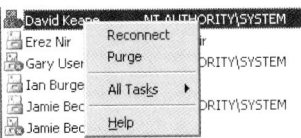

Figure 11.26   *Reconnect a deleted mailbox.*

Chapter 11

largest organization, and it is best for the administrator of the local server to handle the problem, but there are situations when you need to reconnect many mailboxes quickly, so it is good to be able to manage this process centrally. For example, in a disaster scenario, you may want to restore a database on a recovery server and then connect the mailboxes in the recovered Store to AD accounts to allow users to regain access to them. Microsoft provides the MBCONN[2] utility for this purpose, but MBCONN is not a supported part of the product, so some customers do not like to use it.

11.5.1 MRC: Mailbox Recovery Center

The Exchange 2003 MRC features are a new entry in the Tools section of ESM. In one way, you can think of the MRC as a souped-up version of MBCONN with a new UI that allows administrators to recover mailboxes from a central point, providing their accounts possess the necessary permissions to access the Stores that hold the deleted mailboxes.

You begin working with the MRC by identifying the Mailbox Stores that you want to work with. Open ESM and click on the MRC tool, then right-click and select "Add Mailbox Store." If you know the name of the Mailbox Store you want to work with, you can enter it now, or just type the first couple of characters in the Store name and click on "Find Now." ESM will then scan the AD to find all the Mailbox Stores that match and display a dialog to allow you to select Stores to work with, as shown in Figure 11.27. You can see that the names of all of the Stores listed start with "Mailbox," which is the default naming convention used by Exchange to name a new Store at creation.

If you are not quite sure about the Store you want to work with, click on the "Advanced" button to set search criteria. Figure 11.28 shows the result of browsing for all Stores that contain deleted mailboxes in an organization. After you select a Store, you see a list of deleted mailboxes. You can now select mailboxes and take three options:

- Find Match: Scan the AD to find user accounts that match the mailboxes.

- Resolve Conflicts: Resolve any conflicts that exist where you could connect multiple AD accounts to a mailbox.

---

2. See the \support\utils\i386 folder on the Exchange 2000 server CD. Apart from the MBCONN help file in the same location, you can find additional information about using MBCONN in Microsoft Knowledge Base article 271886. In some respects, you can think of MBCONN as being similar to the DS/IS consistency adjuster.

11.5 Recovering deleted mailboxes 869

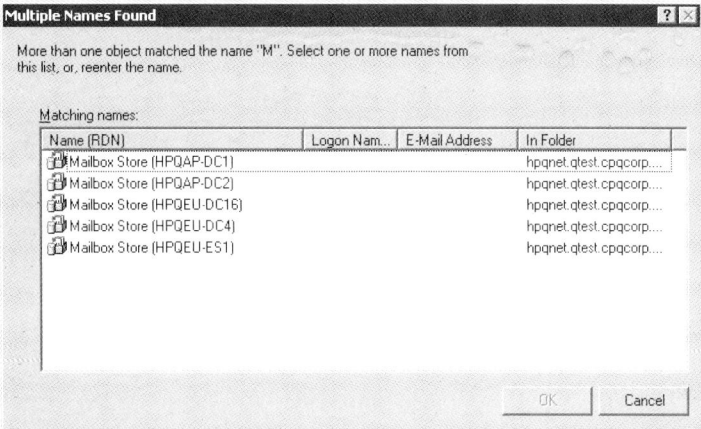

Figure 11.27
Viewing a list of Mailbox Stores.

- Reconnect: Reestablish the link between a deleted mailbox and an AD account. You have to match a mailbox with an account before you can reconnect.

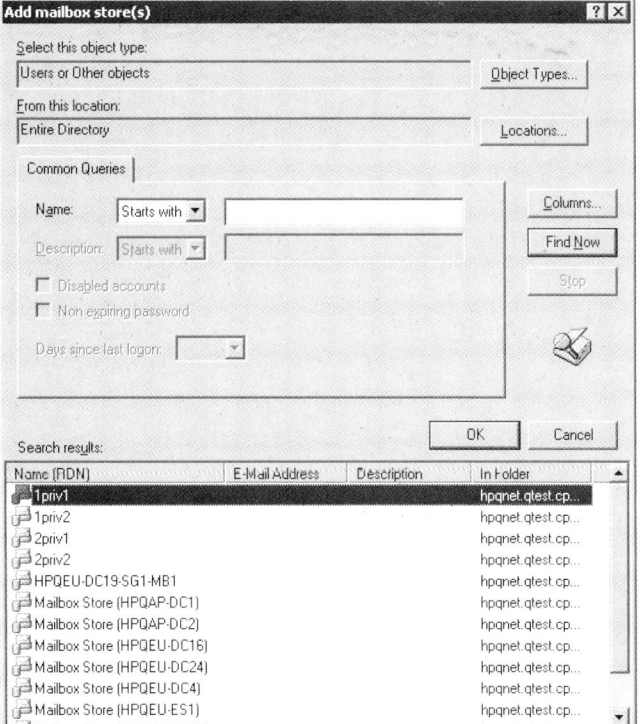

Figure 11.28
Finding a Mailbox Store.

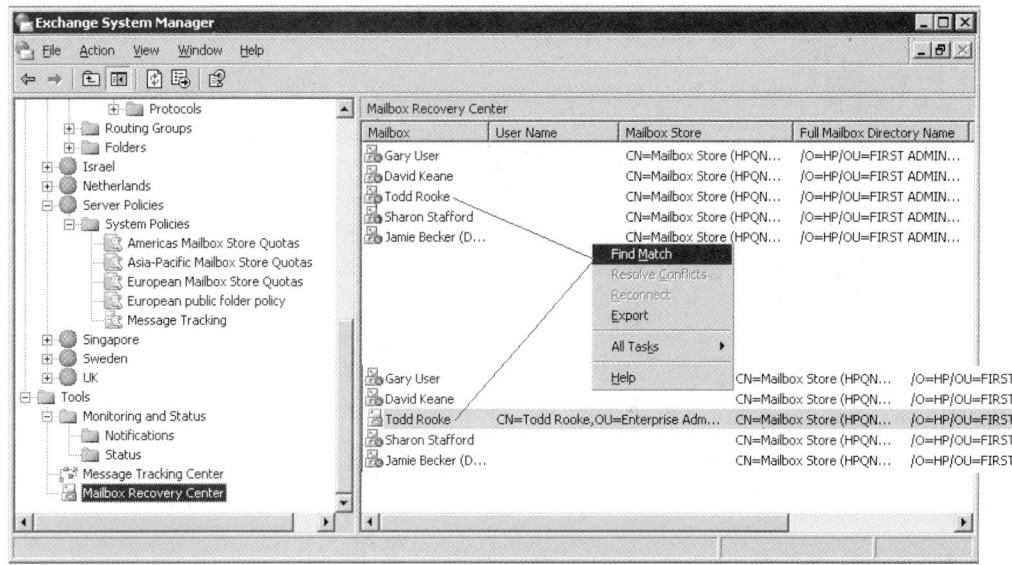

Figure 11.29   *Viewing a list of deleted mailboxes.*

Figure 11.29 shows ESM with a list of deleted accounts. The image in the bottom right-hand side of the screen shows the options, and you can also see the result of finding a match for Todd Rooke's mailbox because the user name column is populated with the DN for the AD account that ESM has matched the mailbox with. After matching the mailboxes, you complete the recovery process with the "Reconnect" option. You can connect a mailbox to an AD account different from that used previously if you need to. Upon successful completion, the user should be able to log on to his or her mailbox again. Note that once you establish a context for the MRC, you can use the refresh option to request ESM to examine the selected Stores and refresh the deleted mailboxes list. This action includes mailboxes deleted since the last listing and removes any reconnected mailboxes. The Mailbox Recovery Center builds on existing functionality to provide Exchange 2003 administrators with the ability to manage mailbox recovery on a centralized basis. While the feature might seem relatively unimportant, you will be glad it exists if you ever need to use it.

11.6   The Recovery Storage Group

During discussions about email outages, the concept of "dial tone" sometimes occurs in an attempt to convey the urgent need to restore service in the same way that phone companies keep telephone lines available. Of course, there is a world of difference between keeping the phone infrastructure running and bringing an email server back online, but the essential concept is similar. People depend on the service and want the service restored as soon as possible after an outage. Often, restores require hours of patient labor, a fact that users do not appreciate because they just want to access their email.

Up to Exchange 2003, the reliance on the Store means that any corruption, disk failure, or other outage that affects the ability of clients to connect to the Store renders Exchange inoperative until administrators can fix the problem and get the Store databases back online. If the database is more than 10 GB, running ESEUTIL to check a database and make it consistent can take hours. If you have a corrupted database, the only way to solve the problem is to restore the database files from backup media, which leads to extended outages and loss of user confidence. The need to avoid long outages that affect Service-Level Agreements is the reason why administrators evolved techniques such as "Rapid Online, Phased Recovery." While these workarounds are effective, they do not address the underlying system deficiencies and usually require extra hardware.

Exchange 2003 supports a Recovery Storage Group (RSG) to allow administrators to recover information from a failed database without the need to use another server specially assigned for this purpose and installed in a separate AD forest and Exchange organization. Large organizations can easily justify keeping a recovery server around to be able to respond to problems quickly, but this is an excessive cost for small organizations, so the ability to do everything on a single server is welcome. The RSG is a special form of storage group that you can use only for recovery operations, attaching up to five databases for recovery purposes. You can use the RSG in addition to the maximum of four standard storage groups supported by Exchange.

Despite the fact that the RSG supports access via MAPI (but no other protocols), users cannot connect to the mailboxes in the RSG database using a client such as Outlook. An administrator can recover data from the mailboxes with the ExMerge utility (Exchange 2003) or directly through ESM, if you run SP1 or a later release. In addition, any databases connected to the RSG are invisible to system maintenance utilities, such as full-text indexing, backup, or antivirus programs. Microsoft designed the RSG for mailbox recovery. In other words, if you need to recover data from a public Store, you still have to go through the classic recovery actions of setting up a separate recovery server and restoring the public Store there. The RSG is best used when you need to recover mailbox data from one or more databases but not a complete server, or when you need to recover AD data. Because of the way that Exchange references databases through the configuration data held in the AD, you cannot recover data from a backup if the configuration data has changed since the date of the backup. This is an excellent argument for taking full backups on a frequent basis. For much the same reason (possible mismatch of pointers such as the mailbox GUID), the RSG is not effective when you need to recover a deleted mailbox that the Store subsequently purged. In these instances, it is best to restore the database that contains the required data to a recovery server, use ExMerge to extract whatever you need, and then restore the data back into a newly created copy of the mailbox.

As an example of how to use the RSG, we encounter a problem with a database and want to restore service to users as quickly as possible (the dial-tone approach). We respond by creating a new database to allow users to continue working and then use the RSG to recover data from the most recent full backup set.

11.6.1 Encountering database problems

We begin with a database that is online and active. We also have a recent full online backup that we know is good, so we are in a position to restore if anything goes wrong. A problem now occurs and one of the database files is corrupted and ceases to function or goes offline. After we address any potential hardware problems, we then have to make a decision about how to handle the database:

- Attempt to mount the database and see whether the problem still exists. Sometimes, a hardware problem does not affect the databases and Exchange's normal soft recovery process is enough to make the database consistent when the Store mounts the database. In any case, it is unwise to attempt any recovery procedure if a lingering hardware problem persists.

- Immediately proceed to restore from backup media and make users wait until we complete the recovery process, including the replay of any outstanding transaction logs.

- Assuming that the Store cannot mount the database and some indication exists that the database is OK but perhaps inconsistent, we could attempt to fix the database with the ESEUTIL utility. On a small server, where the database is less than 4 GB or so, this may be a good course of action, especially if you have contacted Microsoft PSS and they advise you to run ESEUTIL. Because it takes so long to run

11.6 The Recovery Storage Group

ESEUTIL on larger databases, it is best to get users back online and plan to work with the database afterward.

- Immediately proceed to use the RSG.

In this instance, we want to use the RSG but also preserve the original database for analysis and perhaps to be able to run ESEUTIL on another server. Microsoft PSS may ask you to keep a database for them to look at. We therefore copy the problem database to a safe location, perhaps using a network location specially mounted for this purpose. After you are positive that you have copied the database safely, you can rename the original database file, and then proceed with the RSG-based recovery. The steps in the process are:

- Create a temporary database to host temporary mailboxes for users.

- Connect users to the temporary database to allow them to keep working during recovery operations.

- Create the Recovery Storage Group and attach the problem database to it. You can only attach a database from a server in the same administrative group as the server you use for recovery operations. In addition, you can attach multiple databases, but they must all belong to the same storage group.

- Recover the database files from the last good full backup plus any subsequent transaction logs.

- Due to some dependencies within the Store, the database that you want to attach must originate on a server that runs Exchange 2000 SP3 or above. The reverse condition is also true in that you cannot attach a database that comes from a server that runs a later version of Exchange. Note that if you attach a database from a server that runs a previous version of Exchange, the Store on the recovery server automatically upgrades the database to correspond to its version of the Store. This means that you cannot simply copy a database from the recovery server to its original server unless both servers run the same version of Exchange. For these reasons (among many others), it is obviously best if you can maintain the same version of Exchange on all servers.

- Use the RSG to ensure that you can see the data in the mailboxes in the recovered database.

- Switch the recovered database back into production. The temporary database is now under the control of the RSG.

- Use ExMerge to export the contents of the mailboxes in the temporary database and merge them back into user mailboxes in the production database.

- Close down the RSG and clean up the temporary files.

Most recovery operations tend to happen in pressure situations. People want their emails back online fast and are intolerant of any delay on the part of the system administrators. Because of the pressure, it is easy to make a mistake, even if Microsoft has made the recovery process easier to execute through the RSG. Do not wait for a real disaster to practice how to use the RSG. Take the time to perform a recovery at your own pace and on your own time to test all the recommendations made through various sources—Microsoft articles, MSDN, books, and magazines—and to make sure that they work in your environment.

11.6.2 Creating a temporary "dial-tone" database

The first step is to create a new database for users to access and start working with again. When the Store attempts to mount the database, it detects that the failed database is no longer present (you copied and then renamed the original file). The Store then offers to create a new database (Figure 11.30). Note the hint that you can leave the database alone and proceed to restore it from a backup. This is the classic recovery action to restore a database after file corruption, but in this case, it will take us too long to recover from backup and users want immediate access to their mailboxes.

The logic is that the temporary database is for short-term use and will only accumulate a small amount of data in its mailboxes, at least when compared with a production database. We therefore plan to switch users back to the production database as soon as we recover it from backup, and we will then recover whatever information they generate in the temporary database and merge it back into their mailboxes. The work to recover and merge happens behind the scenes. Users are aware that a problem exists and that they do not have access to their original mailboxes, but we should be able to switch the temporary database for production very soon after we recover the

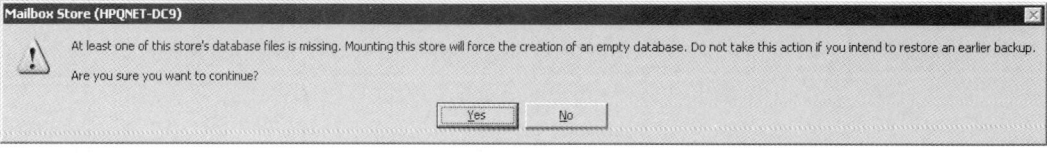

Figure 11.30   *The Store offers to create a new database.*

11.6 The Recovery Storage Group

last good copy of the production database from backup, so users will only lose access to their original mailboxes for that time. In the interim, they can process messages using the temporary mailboxes. The new Mailbox Store is empty, so users have no access to data previously held in their mailboxes. As soon as you mount the temporary database, clients can log on and begin working again. However, Outlook clients should turn synchronization off, because they are no longer working with the same mailbox context and the slave replica folders in the OST do not match the server folders in the temporary database. Outlook 2003 clients will detect that the Mailbox Store has changed, and they will be offered a choice to connect in online mode or connect to the OST and work offline. Alternatively, they can use OWA or another client temporarily. Clients can resume normal synchronization after you restore the production database. If you use ESM to view the mailboxes in the database just after mounting, you see that none appears to exist. This is because the Store only creates a mailbox within a new database (which is what we have) when a client first connects, so you will see the mailboxes appear only after users connect and begin to use their mailboxes.

Assuming that the volumes are available and the corruption is not due to hardware failure, we can place the database and transaction logs for the RSG on the same volumes that host the production files, as shown in Table 11.5.

Next, select the database and view its properties, going to the database page. Use the Browse option to change the paths for the database and transaction logs to the temporary directories and then press OK. Now remount the database. The new Mailbox Store is empty, so users have no access to data previously held in their mailboxes. As soon as you mount the temporary database, clients can log on and begin working again. However, Outlook clients should turn synchronization off and stop using cached Exchange mode with Outlook 2003, because they are no longer working with the same mailbox context. In both cases, the slave replica folders in the OST do not match the server folders in the temporary database. Clients can resume normal synchronization after you restore the production database

Table 11.5 *Locations of Production and RSG Files*

	Production	RSG
Database	D:\Exchange\SG1	D:\Exchange\RSG
Transaction logs	F:\Exchange Transaction Logs\SG1	F:\Exchange Transaction Logs\RSG

and swap out the temporary version. If you use ESM to view the mailboxes in the database just after mounting, you see that none appears to exist. This is because the Store only creates a mailbox within a new database (which is what we have) when a client first connects, so you will see the mailboxes appear only after users connect and begin to use their mailboxes.

11.6.3 Creating the RSG

With the dial-tone database in place, users can now create new messages and receive incoming email, but they do not have access to any of the information in the corrupted database.

The next step is to create the Recovery Storage Group. The process is much like creating a normal Storage Group. Select the server, right-click, select New from the menu, and then select "Recovery Storage Group," as shown in Figure 11.31. When you create the RSG, ESM proposes a default location to hold files during the recovery process. Typically, this is a directory under the Exchange root directory. Use the browse option (Figure 11.32) to change the locations to a more appropriate volume. Table 11.5 indicates the locations used in this example. Click OK to proceed and ESM instantiates the RSG. At this point, the RSG is just a placeholder in the Active Directory and no files exist. The next step is to tell ESM which data-

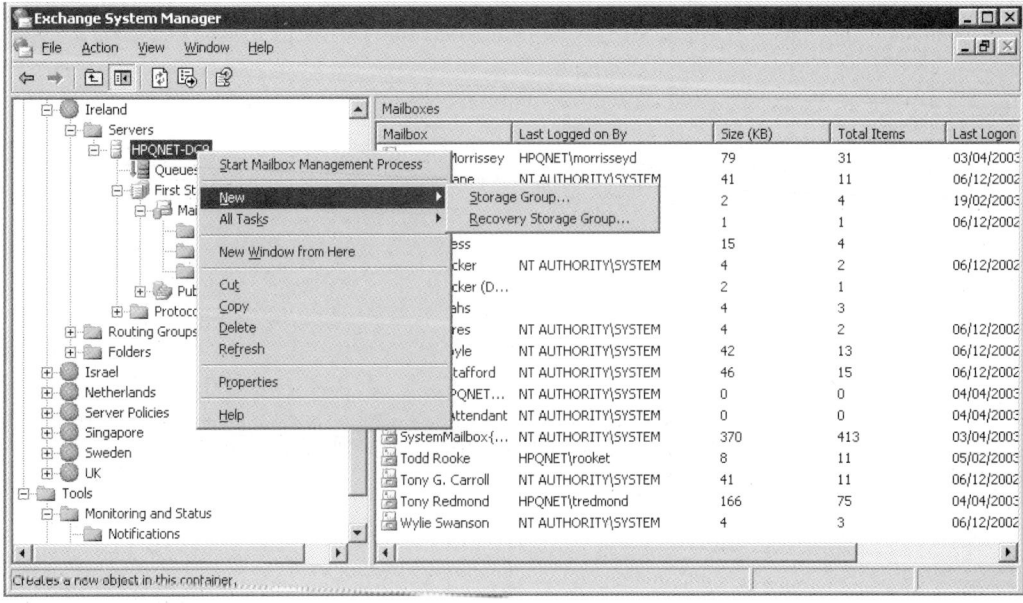

Figure 11.31 *Creating a new Recovery Storage Group.*

11.6 The Recovery Storage Group   877

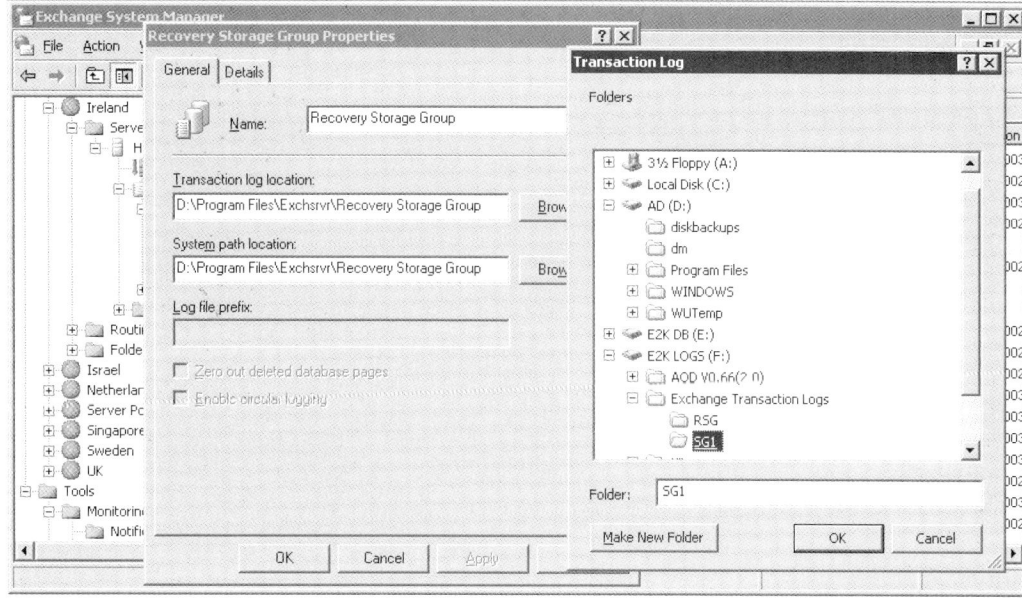

Figure 11.32   *Setting locations for the RSG.*

base you want to add to the RSG. The RSG only supports one database at a time, so if you have problems with multiple databases, you need to use either a recovery server or an RSG on another production server. Microsoft Knowledge Base article 824126 contains some useful information on the RSG that you should read at this point.

To add a database to the RSG, right-click on the RSG and select the "Add Database to Recover" option. ESM then checks AD to discover which databases exist in the administrative group that the server belongs to and displays the dialog shown in Figure 11.33. Select the database that you want to recover and click on OK.

We now have an association between the RSG and a database, in the same way as we have an association between a normal storage group and its databases. If we examine the properties of the RSG, we see that the database locations point to the directory we defined for the RSG. No files exist there yet, because we have not restored the backup. In fact, when you examine the properties, you will see that ESM generates default names for the databases, so they do not match the databases you want to restore. If desired, you can change these names to match the original databases with the browse option. As you can see in Figure 11.34, the properties of a Mailbox Store added to the RSG are similar to a normal Mailbox Store.

Chapter 11

11.6 The Recovery Storage Group

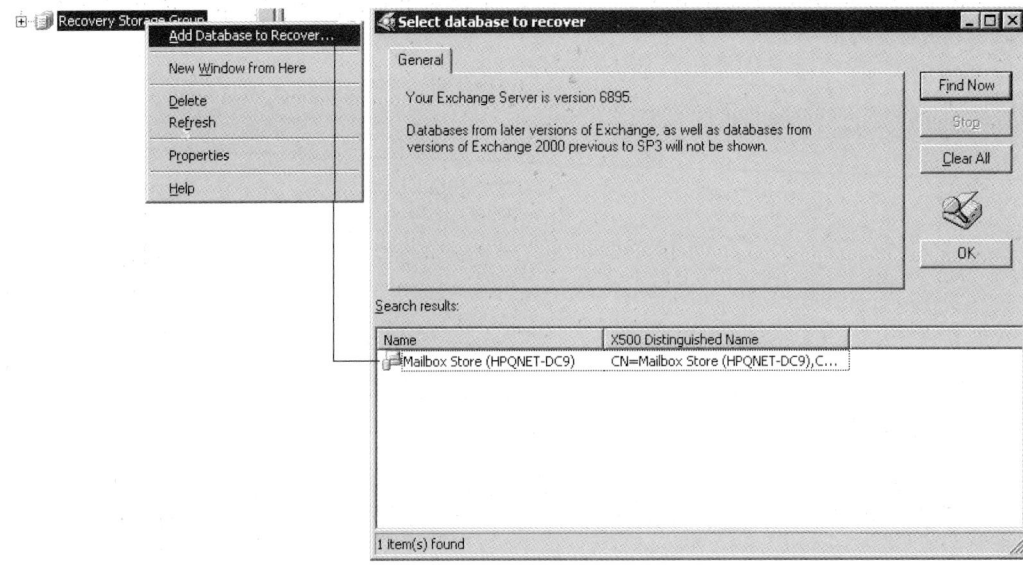

Figure 11.33 *Adding a database to the RSG.*

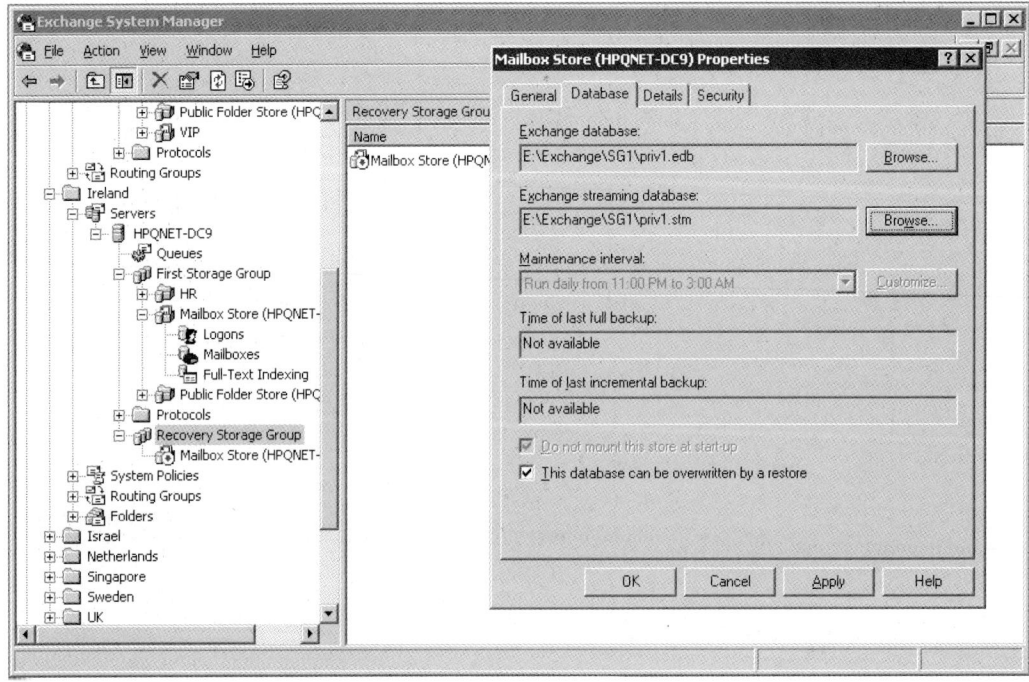

Figure 11.34 *Adding a database to the RSG is completed.*

11.6.4 Restoring the database

Restoring the backup copy of the failed database is the next step. In this instance, we use NTBACKUP to restore a copy from disk, but the same principle holds for other backup utilities and media types. We state a temporary directory for the restore operation to put the transaction logs in the backup. The "Last Restore Set" checkbox is set to tell NTBACKUP that we only want to process this set, meaning that the ESE will replay transaction logs at the end of the backup process to make the database fully consistent. (See Figure 11.35.) See Microsoft Knowledge Base article 824126 for more information on how to restore databases to the RSG using an online restore or by manually copying files into the correct location.

After a successful restore, the backup copy of the failed Mailbox Store is in the RSG directory. Go to ESM and mount the database in the RSG, then refresh the RSG entry to be able to list the mailboxes in the recovered database, as shown in Figure 11.36. All of the mailboxes have a red cross next to their names, because ESM cannot associate the mailboxes with AD accounts. End users cannot log on to these mailboxes and administrators cannot perform operations such as create new mailboxes in the RSG, but you can recover their contents, which is the major benefit. Running in production, we now have users connected to a temporary database that

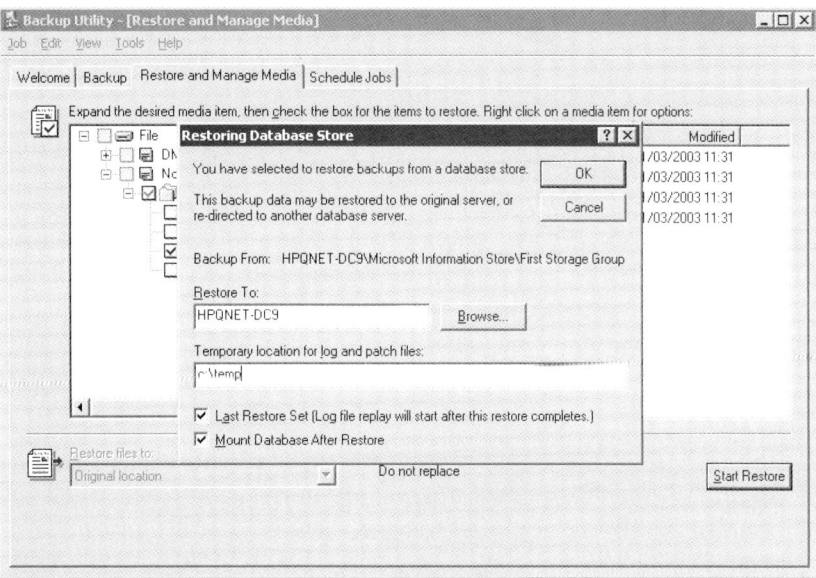

Figure 11.35   *Restoring the failed database from the backup set.*

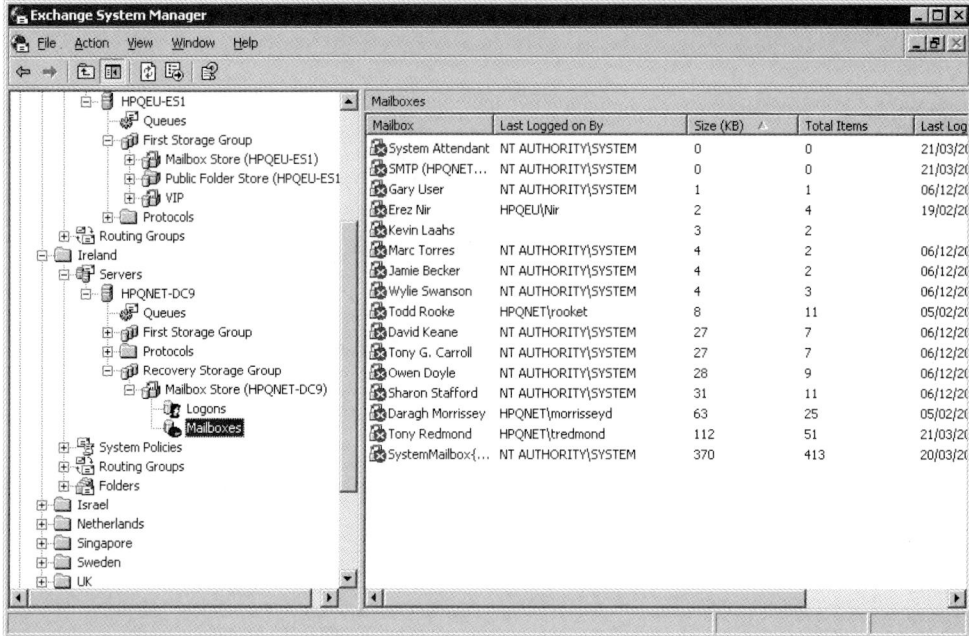

Figure 11.36 *Viewing the mailboxes in the restored RSG.*

holds little data (because it has not been in use much). The recovered database in the RSG holds far more data, so we now proceed to swap the two databases. The effect will be to provide users with all their data up to the time of the backup that we restored, while we move the data that they created after the problem happened into the RSG. Later, we will use the ExMerge utility to recover the data from the RSG and merge it back into the production database.

Exchange provides no user interface to swap databases, so we have to do it behind the scenes by editing database properties. These properties exist in the Microsoft Exchange configuration container in the AD, so we have to edit them with the ADSIEDIT utility.

Before we move anything, we have to dismount both databases to prevent any user access while we swap files. In addition, take the opportunity to set the "This database can be overwritten by a restore" checkbox for both databases so that the Store accepts that the underlying files have changed when you remount the databases after editing their locations. To edit the location for a database:

- Start ADSIEDIT and open the configuration naming context.

11.6 The Recovery Storage Group

- Navigate through Services | Microsoft Exchange | Administrative Groups to the server you are working with and then to the database in the storage group.
- Select the database and view its properties.
- Navigate to MsExchEDBFile (the location of the EDB database) and change its value to point to the correct location.
- Perform the same operation for MsExchSLVFile (the location of the streaming file).
- Select the database in the Recovery Storage Group and perform the same changes.

After making the changes, go to ESM and remount the databases. You should now be able to list the contents of the production database and view the mailbox contents at the time of the backup. Clients should be able to connect to their mailboxes and work normally. You should also be able to view the contents of the mailboxes in the recovery database, which holds the information that users generated while the temporary database was online. Figure 11.37 shows how to use ADSIEDIT to change a database location.

11.6.5 Using ExMerge to recover mailbox data

We now need to extract information from the temporary database and merge it back into the production database to provide users with a complete copy of their work before and after the problem occurred. As in a recovery server situation, you can retrieve data from mailboxes in the RSG with the ExMerge utility. It is important to use the version of ExMerge provided in the \support\utils\i386\exmerge folder on the Exchange 2003 server CD, since this version is able to bind to the mailboxes in the RSG with an appropriate level of security. Before attempting to run ExMerge, copy Exmerge.exe and Exmerge.ini into the \exchsrvr\bin directory to ensure that the executable can find exchmem.dll.

As with other ExMerge recovery operations, you have a choice between a one-step process and a two-stage process to recover data from mailboxes. A one-step process is most appropriate when the recovery and target servers are different. In this case, the two databases are available on the same system, so we can use the two-step process (extract and then import using interim PST files as the transfer mechanism). Make sure that you have sufficient disk space available for ExMerge to create the PSTs, planning on

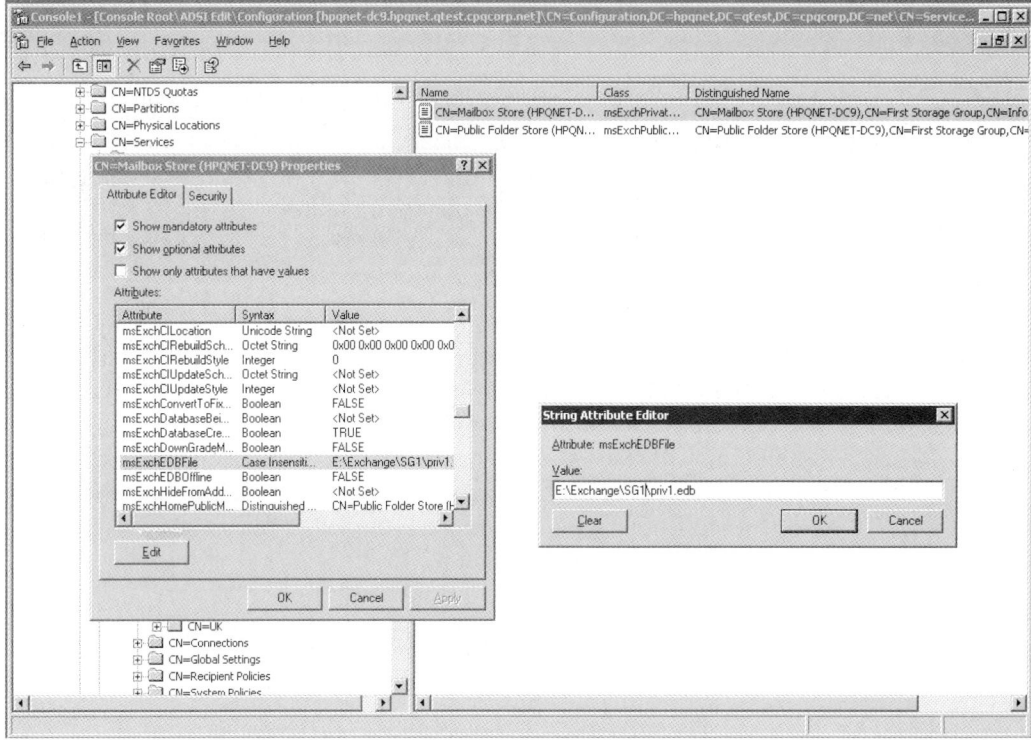

Figure 11.37 *Editing database locations with ADSIEDIT.*

the basis that the PSTs will occupy roughly twice the size of the reported mailboxes.

When ExMerge starts, it prompts for a server to connect to, and then the database from which you want to recover mailboxes. You want to export data from the mailboxes in the temporary database that is currently active, because you will eventually switch the restored database back into production; you are now saving information that users create while using the temporary database. For this reason, you should run ExMerge at a quiet time, when users are inactive.

After selecting the database, you can then select all or some of the mailboxes in the database; ExMerge will then begin to export mailbox data to the PSTs in the temporary directory. When this stage is complete, a separate PST exists for each mailbox. Figure 11.38 illustrates how to select the RSG database, how to select mailboxes in the database, and how ExMerge reports its progress.

11.6 The Recovery Storage Group

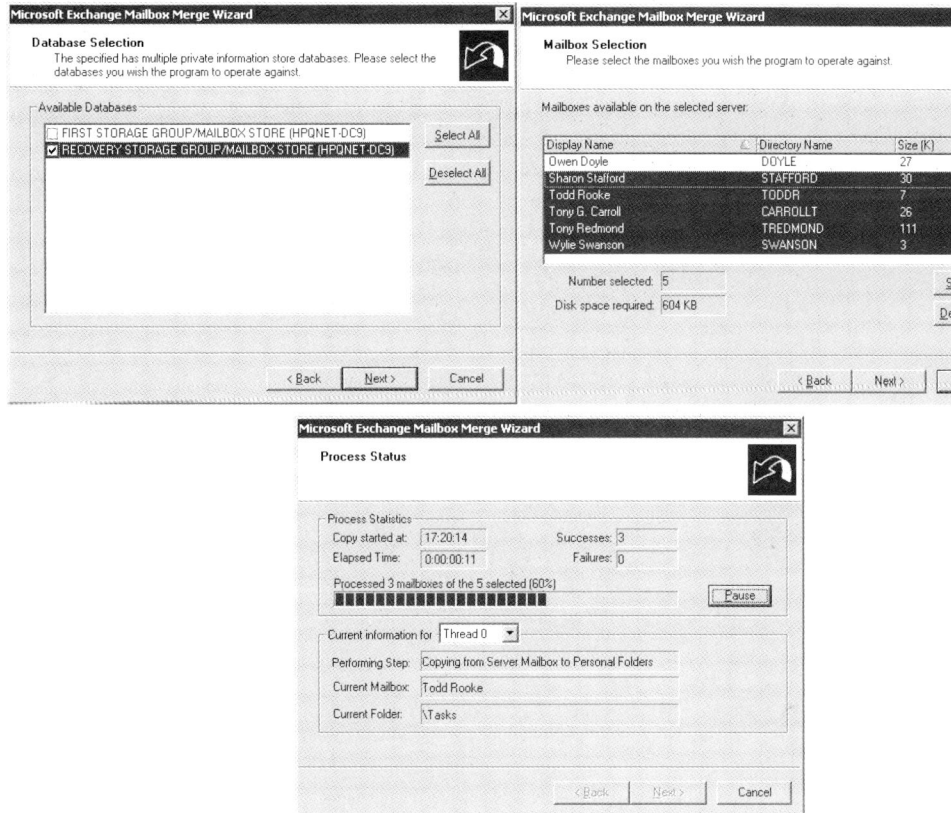

Figure 11.38 *Running ExMerge to recover mailboxes.*

Note that Exchange 2003 SP1 removes the need to use ExMerge to merge mailboxes. Once you have SP1 (or later) installed, you can use the Recover Mailbox Data option (in ESM) to extract data from the database that you load in the RSG.

11.6.6 Cleaning up

After you have recovered data from the temporary database and merged it back into the production mailboxes, there is no reason to keep the RSG active. To clean up:

- Dismount the temporary database in the RSG.
- Delete the database from the RSG.

- Delete the files from the RSG directory.
- Delete the Mailbox Store from the RSG.

It is also best practice to take a full online backup immediately after you merge data from the last mailbox in the temporary database back into the production database.

11.7 The ExMerge utility

Microsoft PSS originally created ExMerge in 1997 as a tool to solve a specific problem: to export data from a user mailbox to a PST and then be able to import the data from the PST into a new mailbox on another server. Since the original version, Microsoft has greatly enhanced ExMerge to a point where it is now part of the formal kit and is an essential piece of an Exchange administrator's toolkit. You can access a copy of the latest ExMerge utility from the \support\utils\i386\exmerge directory on the server CD. Note that the program depends on a number of DLLs from the Exchange kit (such as DAPI.DLL), so you will have to move the program into the \bin directory before it will run. In addition, the Exchange 2003 kit includes a new version of EXMERGE that you must use for any operations with an Exchange 2003 server (it also runs against Exchange 2000 servers).

Originally, the move mailbox option only worked within a site—a limitation imposed by the first-generation site model and the fact that the site name is included in a mailbox's distinguished name. Administrators used ExMerge to move mailboxes between sites to overcome this difficulty. It is much easier to move mailboxes between administrative groups, but only if sufficient bandwidth exists to transfer the contents of the mailbox to the target server. With most mailboxes being larger than 50 MB today, moving a mailbox across a low-bandwidth or saturated link is not an attractive proposition. ExMerge is a useful option in this situation, albeit even if you stop users from accessing their mailboxes during the export/move/import process.

ExMerge is also a useful tool in a disaster recovery situation. Imagine that a server has suffered a catastrophic hardware failure and you must rebuild it from scratch. The quickest way to restore service to users is to build the server with empty databases, since this avoids the need for users to wait while you restore databases from backup, verify that everything has worked correctly, take further backups, and so on. Once users are up and running, you can restore the databases to an offline recovery server and use

11.7 The ExMerge utility

ExMerge to export the contents of the mailboxes to PSTs. Then, you can move the PSTs over to the live server and use ExMerge to recover the contents of the mailboxes and merge them into the new mailboxes that are now in use. This technique works for both Exchange 5.5 and Exchange 2000/2003 servers.

Some administrators go so far as to use ExMerge as a form of "poor man's backup" to protect the mailboxes of users they deem to be important and deserving of extra protection. In this scenario, administrators use scheduled runs of ExMerge to export the contents of the important mailboxes to PSTs, which are then backed up to tape or other backup media. The advantage here is that you can easily recover a mailbox by restoring a PST. The disadvantage is the time required to export the data and back up the PSTs.

ExMerge uses the familiar wizard-based format to gather parameters and establish what it is going to do. Two basic approaches are available. Either you move mailboxes in a one-step process, where an initial export to a PST is immediately followed by an import to the target mailbox, or you can opt for the two-step process. In this scenario, you export mailbox contents first followed by a separate import operation, which you normally perform after you have had the chance to transfer the PSTs containing the exported mailboxes to the target server.

You can configure many options to determine how ExMerge exports and imports items, whether to include messages that are in the deleted message cache, how to handle permissions on folders, and how to specify a date range to limit the number of messages that are extracted. Figures 11.39 and 11.40 give some idea of the range of options available to control ExMerge processing. Comprehensive information about these options is available in the ExMerge documentation (a Word document), which you can find in the same directory as the ExMerge program files. You should read the documentation carefully before starting any complex operation, such as running ExMerge on a recovery server.

When ExMerge starts, you specify the name of the source Exchange server where the mailboxes are currently located. You can also instruct ExMerge to connect to either a local DC or GC to read mailbox information. If you connect to a DC, you can only process mailboxes belonging to accounts in the local domain. In most cases, an Exchange server only hosts mailboxes belonging to accounts in a single domain, so there is no real necessity to connect to a GC. If you do not specify a DC or GC, ExMerge uses the same controller information as the Exchange server that hosts the mailboxes, although the program seems to connect and fetch information

Figure 11.39
ExMerge options.

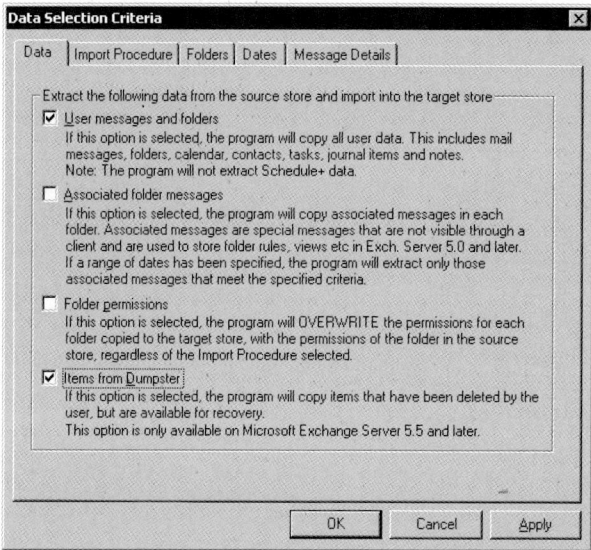

faster if you specify the name of a suitable controller. You can view this information through the Directory Access tab of the Exchange server properties. Note that while you can use ExMerge to view mailbox information, you need to use an account that has sufficient privileges to access and export mailbox data, since otherwise ExMerge will fail when it attempts to connect to the mailbox. An account that holds Exchange Administrator

Figure 11.40
Import options for ExMerge.

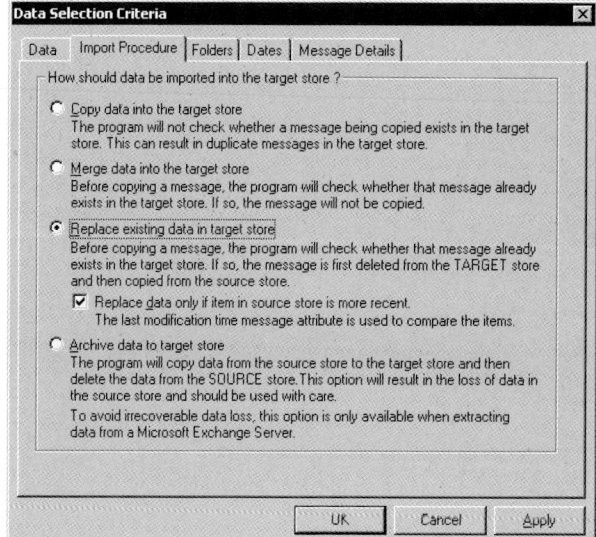

11.7 The ExMerge utility

permission on the source server is usually sufficient. In addition, the fields available to specify the names of the servers are not long enough to accommodate FQDNs.

After you specify the parameters for the export run, ExMerge displays the set of Mailbox Stores on the host server. You can opt to select mailboxes from a particular Store or all available Stores. ExMerge then fetches a list of the mailboxes and displays them for you to select the mailboxes for processing. You will not see mailboxes that belong to deleted accounts on the list, so if you want to take a copy of a mailbox as part of the procedure when someone leaves the company, make sure that you do this before you delete the account. Depending on the number of mailboxes in the Stores and the size of the AD, this step can take some time to complete and apart from a "Please wait" message, there is no indication that everything is working smoothly. However, if you are patient, ExMerge will return and you should see a display similar to that shown in Figure 11.41.

After selecting the mailboxes to process, the last step is to define where to create the PSTs. Exporting mailbox data can take up a lot of space, and you should estimate that the space reported by ExMerge for mailboxes will double when they are exported. For example, I exported a 550-MB mailbox and ExMerge created a 732-MB PST. While you can limit the amount of space used by not exporting items in the deleted items cache, the way that messages are stored inside a PST is the underlying reason why so much space is used; make sure that you have sufficient available space before you begin to process mailboxes. In addition, try to perform exports outside the hours of peak user demand, since the processing required to move items out

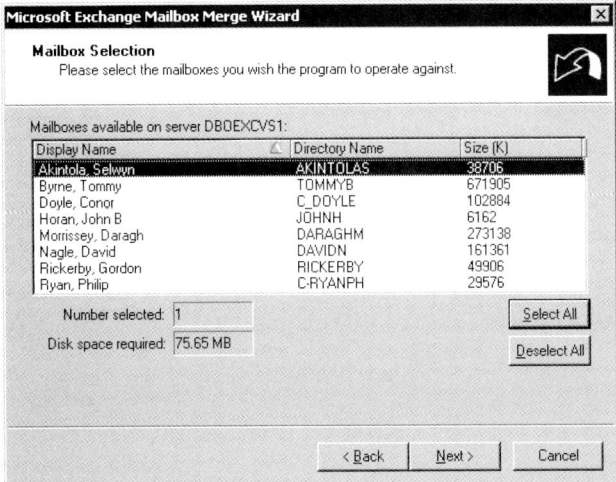

Figure 11.41
Selecting mailboxes to process.

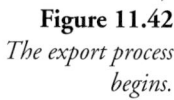

Figure 11.42
The export process begins.

of a mailbox to a PST is quite intensive. In the previous example, ExMerge took 29 minutes to process the 550-MB mailbox.

In addition to reporting ongoing progress (Figure 11.42), ExMerge logs details of all of its processing into a log file called c:\exmerge.log. The following code segment lists all the steps taken to export the contents of my mailbox. The level of detail here is typical of the standard (minimum) level of logging; you can increase the level of logging by specifying a command-line qualifier or changing the setting in the ExMerge.ini initialization file.

You can change the name of the standard log file by editing the ExMerge.ini initialization file and specifying the new name in the LogFileName section. Note that if multiple threads are running, each thread has its own log file named ExMerge-Thread1.log, ExMerge-Thread2.log, and so on.

```
*************************************************************
Microsoft Exchange Mailbox Merge Program, v6.0.5762.3
Start Logging: April 08, 2002   13:01:36
*************************************************************
[13:01:36] Logging Level: None
[13:01:36] Reading settings from file 'D:\exchsrvr\BIN\EXMERGE.INI'.
 [13:01:38] Accessing Domain Controller 'DBOGCEU01'
[13:01:38] 'DBOEXCVS1' is running Exchange Server 2000 or later
[13:01:38] Source server read from settings file is 'DBOEXCVS1'.
[13:01:38] Reading list of subjects for messages to be selected from file ''
[13:01:38] Reading list of attachment names for messages to be selected from file ''
[13:01:38] List of folders to be ignored has been read. 0 folders in the
```

11.7 The ExMerge utility

```
list.
[13:01:38] Current machine locale ID is 0x409
[13:01:38] Operating System Version 5.0 (Build 2195)
 [13:01:50] Accessing Domain Controller 'DBOGCEU01'
[13:01:50] 'DBOEXCVS1' is running Exchange Server 2000 or later
[13:01:53] Searching the Active Directory for mailboxes homed on the
following databases:
[13:01:53] CN=Mailbox Store (DBOEXCVS1),CN=First Storage
Group,CN=InformationStore,CN=DBOEXCVS1,CN=Servers,CN=NSIS European
Messaging Team,CN=Administrative Groups,CN=hp,CN=Microsoft
Exchange,CN=Services,CN=Configuration,DC=cpqcorp,DC=net
[13:09:54] Found 11 mailboxes, in the Active Directory, homed on the
specified databases.
[13:13:47] Using attribute 'PR_MESSAGE_DELIVERY_TIME' for date operations.
[13:13:47] Replacing data in the target store. The program will overwrite
existing messages in the target store, by first deleting these messages and
then copying the messages from the source store.
[13:13:47] Replacing only older items in the target store.
[13:13:47] Option to copy deleted items from the dumpster has been selected.
Recoverable deleted items will only be copied when extracting data out of
mailboxes on servers running Microsoft Exchange Server version 5.5 or later.
[13:13:47] Associated folder data will NOT be copied to the target store.
[13:13:47] Using 'English (US)' (0x409) as the default locale (Code page
1252)
[13:13:47] All mailboxes will be processed, regardless of locale
[13:13:47] Initializing worker thread (Thread0)
[13:13:47] Copying data from mailbox 'Redmond, Tony' ('TONYR') on Server
'DBOEXCVS1' to file 'D:\EXMERGE\TONYR.PST'.
[13:42:56] Number of messages processed for mailbox 'Redmond, Tony': 17914
[13:42:56] Number of folders processed for mailbox 'Redmond, Tony': 111
[13:42:56] Successfully completed copying mailbox 'Redmond, Tony' to file
'D:\EXMERGE\TONYR.PST'.
[13:42:57] Number of items copied from the source store for all mailboxes
processed: 17914
[13:42:57] Total number of folders processed in the source store: 111
[13:42:57] 1 mailboxes successfully processed. 0 mailboxes were not
successfully processed. 0 non-fatal errors encountered.
[13:42:57] Process completion time: 0:00:29:10
```

Many organizations use ExMerge to move mailboxes around during migrations, most often when they restructure the organization through server consolidation. While this is a good way for you to move a small number of mailboxes from server to server, you should be aware that the way ExMerge works impacts single-instance storage. The net effect is that the target Mailbox Store will grow faster than if single-instance storage were respected. In addition, there is limited support for rules, and you have to check that permissions are correctly in place after ExMerge imports mailboxes onto a server.

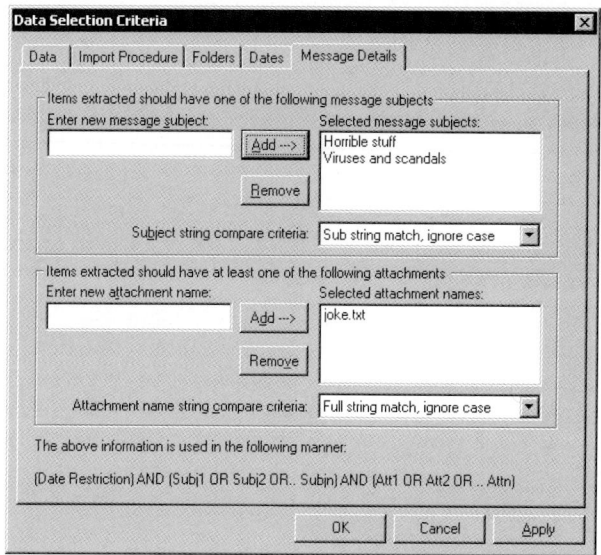

Figure 11.43
Looking for specific items.

Beyond its obvious uses, ExMerge offers some surprising features. For example, you can use the message selection feature to instruct ExMerge to scan a mailbox and select items based on subject, text string, substring matches, or names of attachments. You could then use ExMerge to "clean" Mailbox Stores by looking for specific items, extracting them to PSTs, and then removing the items from the mailboxes. Figure 11.43 shows how you can set up certain criteria, such as looking for an attachment called "joke.txt" (one of the well-known viruses sends its payload in such an attachment) or messages with certain subjects. ExMerge does not search nested messages and attachments, so it is by no means the perfect tool, but it is able to apply a certain degree of clean-up if required.

It is now very common for an organization to be required to provide copies of messages and documents to lawyers seeking information in a discovery action. You can use the ExMerge item selection (filtering) functionality to scan mailboxes to locate items that match criteria defined in the action. The lawyers will probably require printed copies of each message and may not accept that ExMerge cannot find every item that they want, but this is a good way to perform an initial scan to determine whether the Store holds any matching material.

Just as recovery servers hold sensitive information in recovered databases, you need to secure the PSTs created by ExMerge until you use them to recover mailboxes and then delete them. Given that any Outlook client can open a PST and that it is easy to crack a password-protected PST, it is unwise to leave PSTs containing user mailbox data anywhere that a casual browser can find them.

11.7.1 Running ExMerge in batch mode

Administrators most commonly run ExMerge interactively, but it also supports batch-mode execution, so you can schedule exports with batch jobs run by the Windows Scheduler. This is a useful feature if you want to do something such as remove all matching instances of a particular message or attachment from a large set of mailboxes. Instructions for batch mode are contained in the ExMerge documentation.

You can also script a run of ExMerge, providing a separate initialization file to process messages in a PST and import them into a mailbox. This technique is viable in migration projects, where you are able to export data from another messaging system to a PST. For example, the MailMover utility from Simpler Webb (www.swinc.com) can export mailbox contents from HP OpenMail systems to PSTs, and there are similar capabilities available for other email systems such as Eudora and TeamWare. As mentioned earlier, you can also use ExMerge to detect specific items in mailboxes. These items might be infected with viruses or contain offensive or sensitive material that you want to eliminate. To approach this problem, you would script ExMerge to run in batch mode (perhaps overnight) to examine targeted mailboxes, locate the desired items with filters, and then remove them. This is no substitute for installing proper protection against email viruses, but it is something that you can use to rid a server of offending items if they get through your defenses.

ExMerge is certainly a tool that has proved its usefulness to many system administrators, but it is unlikely that Microsoft will put more effort into future development. The Move Mailbox and Migration wizards have functionality that essentially eliminates the need for an ExMerge-like utility, and you can expect Microsoft to enhance these features over future service packs—for example, to support mailbox moves between different Exchange 2003 organizations.

11.7.2 Other recovery utilities

While they are less common than the other types of Exchange add-on utilities, there are tools that you can use to recover data from a Mailbox Store without ever having to install Exchange on a server. Remember that Store databases are just that—databases—and that a public API exists (MAPI). Put the two together and you can see how you could build a utility that uses

MAPI to connect to a database and read information for purposes such as item recovery, mailbox backup, searching messages, or retrieving information in response to legal discovery requests. The best known of these utilities is probably Ontrack's Powercontrols (www.ontrack.com). These tools are not especially expensive and they can save your skin if a problem occurs, so it is worth investigating the utilities that are currently available on the market to determine whether to incorporate them into your recovery toolkit.

11.8 Risk management

Security is all about risk management. The most secure system is the one installed in an ultra-secure room and disconnected from any network, preferably without any user access. You will never see a problem with this system, because it never does any real work, so it is unrealistic to consider such a situation. Therefore, securing Exchange servers means that you have to understand where potential risk comes from and prioritize it, so that you avoid risks while allowing people to work. The aim here is not to close down a system totally; instead, you need to know where you can open up in a secure manner—for example, how to enable firewall ports to allow clients to access Exchange in a secure manner.

All computers face attacks through the network. They also face internal penetration, where people use permissions that they should not have to access information they should not see. A discussion about Windows and network security (including wireless) is beyond the scope of this book, so we assume that you have applied basic security on all servers and that you install the latest service packs and security advisories. With this foundation, we can then look at Exchange-specific issues, such as:

- IIS weaknesses that may expose access to mailboxes or public folders through OWA
- Spam attacks that may cause denial of service
- Email viruses
- Administrative attacks, including unauthorized restores of Mailbox Store backup sets to recovery servers and elevating permissions to access other users' mailboxes

Microsoft's Baseline Security Analyzer (MBSA) is an excellent tool for system administrators to check Windows and Exchange servers for potential security weaknesses. You should download the latest version of MBSA from Microsoft's Web site and run it against all servers. The current version covers Windows 2000 and Exchange 2000, and even though Windows

2003 delivers a more secure out-of-the-box environment, it is likely that you will need MBSA or an equivalent tool to review server configurations, simply because there are just too many places to check manually.

Email systems have always been open to administrative probing, and the only way to stop a determined administrator who wants to read items in a mailbox is to encrypt all messages. Given that only a small percentage of Exchange deployments protect email in this manner, it is accurate to assume that your administrators have this ability. Some companies have a policy that users should never transmit confidential information via email, but this is unrealistic in today's world. Indeed, vast quantities of confidential data flow across the Internet daily, open to anyone who cares to read the SMTP traffic. To prevent unauthorized access by administrators, you need a policy that clearly states that breaking into a mailbox is unacceptable behavior, which will potentially lead to dismissal, and then back up the policy with monitoring.

11.9 The message tracking center

Exchange has always incorporated a facility called the message tracking center to track the progress of a message as it makes its way between servers in an organization. The feature depends on the availability of message tracking logs for interrogation by a requesting server that wishes to track a message.

The default properties set on Exchange servers allow message tracking. This means that a server maintains a set of message tracking logs, creating a new log daily, which is named according to the date—for example, 20030125.log (the log for January 25, 2003). Exchange stores the logs in a network share called *server_name*.log,[3] which is usually located on the same drive as the Exchange binaries. Figure 11.44 illustrates a typical set of message tracking logs. Note the difference in the size of data generated on typical workdays (such as 20030711 or July 11, a Friday) and the weekend (July 12 and 13). Clearly, Monday and Tuesday (July 7 and 8) were easy workdays or the users of this server did not generate much email then, perhaps because some were on vacation. Despite being the current day, the log for July 15 is largest, which indicates some heavy traffic going through the server for some reason. Logs generated by an Exchange 2003 server are slightly larger than Exchange 2000, because Exchange 2003 captures additional data as messages progress through the postcategorization, prerouting, and routing stages within the transport engine.

---

3. First-generation Exchange servers place their message tracking logs into a share called tracking.log.

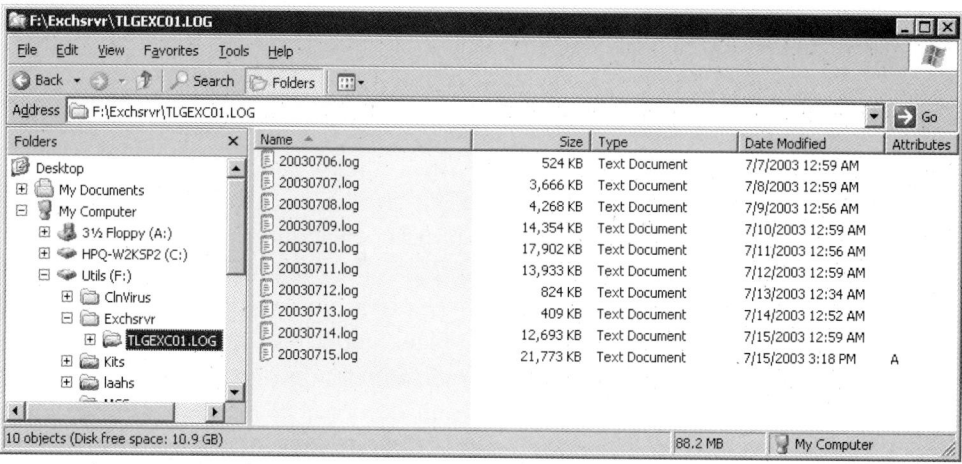

Figure 11.44   *Message tracking logs.*

Exchange 2003 uses the same network share to store its tracking logs but makes a subtle change to the permissions on the share. On an Exchange 2000 server, the share is open and any user can map it to access tracking log data. You can argue that few users are interested in looking at tracking log data, but it is conceivable that someone could browse the data to look for message traffic for a specific user—for example, to determine to whom a senior manager sends email or who he or she receives email from. Exchange 2003 therefore restricts access to the share to administrators. Remote

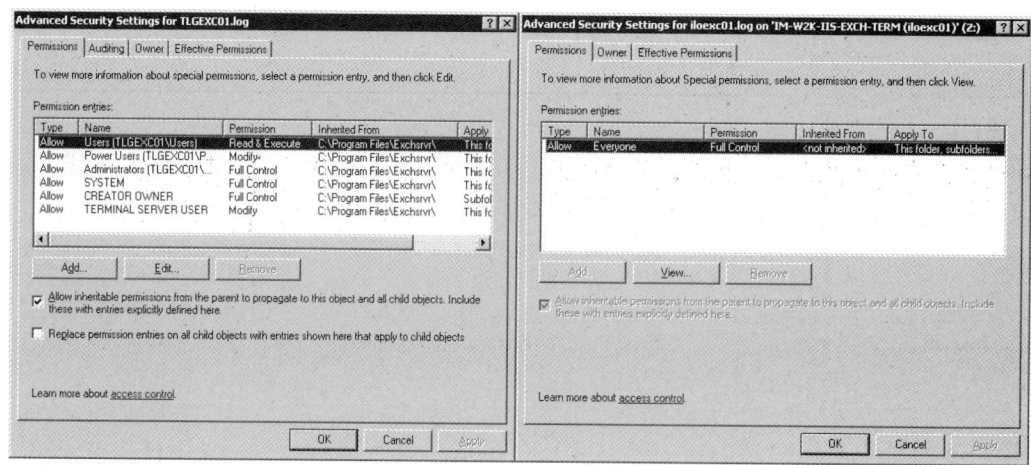

Figure 11.45   *Security on Exchange 2000 and Exchange 2003 shares.*

Exchange servers can continue to use the data, because they access the share through the local Exchange management service. Figure 11.45 shows the ACL on the tracking log share on an Exchange 2003 server (left) and Exchange 2000 server (right).

11.9.1 Tracking messages

Exchange generates a unique unifier for every message when a client submits the message to the server, and records the identifiers in the message tracking logs, thus making it possible to trace a message as it makes its way to its final destination. An example message identifier generated by a MAPI client is:

```
BE8B1DCC92D77E4C9CC70E141E3B583B02226F@EXCSERVER.acme.org
```

The only part of this identifier that makes any sense to people is the server name (EXCSERVER@acme.org in this case) at the end of the string. Everything else makes the computers happy when they track messages. Note that this identifier is not the same as the MAPI message identifier that you can see by viewing the properties of a message. POP3 and IMAP4 clients also generate their own message identifiers in the form:

```
000001c19dbf$78c6bf90$7705d110@acme.org
```

Aside from formatting, the major difference between MAPI and the message identifiers generated by non-MAPI clients is the omission of the originating server name. Client-specific message identifiers can be found in the Linked-MSGID field in the message tracking log. The messaging tracking center also displays the client-specific message identifier when you track a message and view its history.

You enable message tracking through three server properties (Figure 11.46). These properties can be set manually or across a set of servers (which may span multiple administrative groups) through a system policy (Figure 11.47). The properties are:

- Enable messaging tracking: This property instructs Exchange to begin creating and populating the message tracking logs. The transport engine logs every message that it processes and creates a new log every day. System messages, such as those that transport details of public folder hierarchies between servers are not logged.

- Enable subject logging and display: This property controls whether Exchange records information about message subjects in the message tracking logs and displays it when you track a message. Message

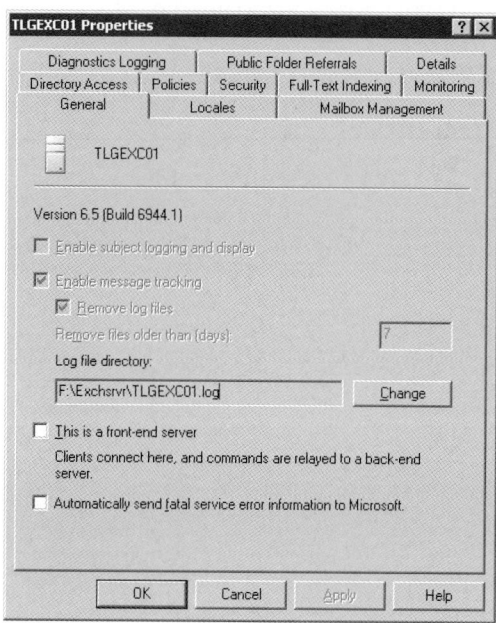

Figure 11.46
Server properties.

subjects can contain confidential information, which is the reason why some installations would opt not to collect this data. However, users should not really be putting confidential data into message subjects (they can secure confidential information through encryption, if it really is confidential), and the subject field is a good way to isolate the message you want to track if the user who has sent it generates a lot of traffic. In most cases, there is no harm in recording this data.

- Remove log files after a specific number of days: The default value is seven days, and the Exchange System Attendant process cleans up old logs daily and logs this activity with event 5008 in the application event log. With the amount of disk space installed on most servers today, the space occupied by message tracking logs is not usually a problem and you can opt to keep the logs for a longer period if you like. However, if a user has not asked you to track a message that he or she suspects has not been delivered to the intended recipient within a week of sending it, the message is probably not very important and you can probably ignore the request.

Obviously, you can only track messages if servers record details in the tracking logs. Within an organization, it does not make sense for some servers to implement logging and others not to, so it is a good idea to establish an enterprise-wide setting and apply it with a system policy. You should

11.9　The message tracking center 897

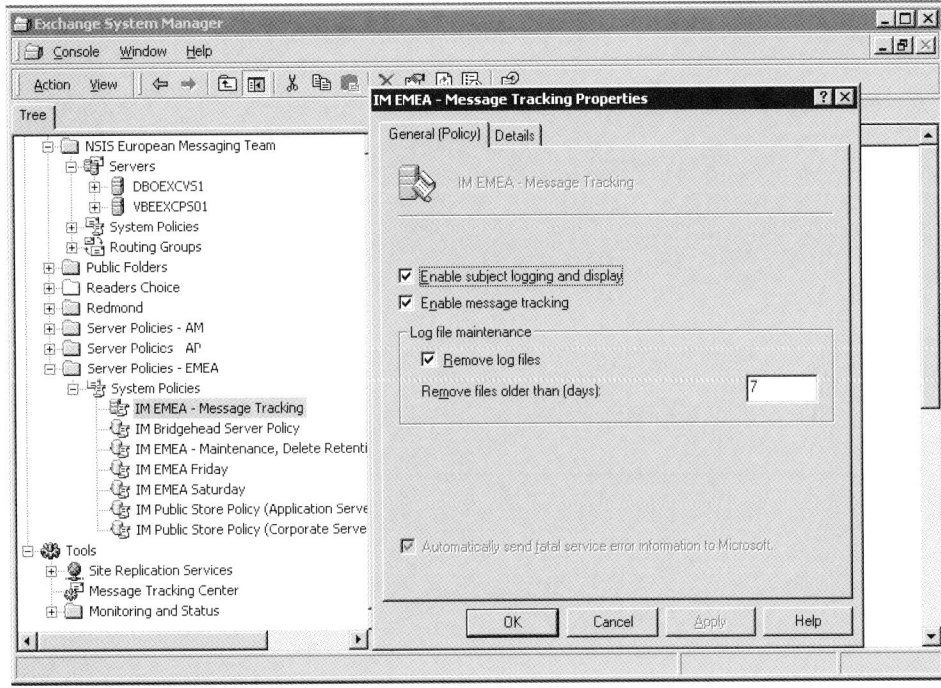

Figure 11.47　*A system policy for message tracking.*

either enable logging on all servers, or not at all. Best practice is to enable logging, because it provides a useful facility at very little cost.

11.9.2　Changing tracking log location

Exchange creates its message tracking logs in a network share called \\server_name\server_name.log—for example, \\QEMEA-ES1\QEMEA-ES1.log. The default permissions for the network share allow anyone to read the log data, while administrators and the local computer account have full control. Some commentators advise that you consider removing the "Everyone" permission from the share to increase security and prevent people who are not administrators from attempting to access the data. However, unless you enable subject logging, the message tracking logs usually do not contain anything that is of much interest to people who might be tempted to poke around a system, so this may be a step to increase security a notch too far.

No user interface is available to relocate the logs in Exchange 2000, so you must use ADSIEDIT to update the server properties to move the logs

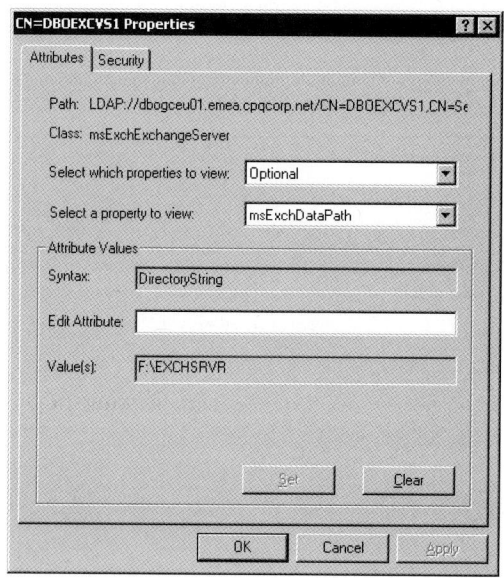

Figure 11.48
Changing the tracking log directory.

to a new directory and then update the system registry to relocate the file share. To update the server properties:

- Take all Exchange services offline by stopping the Microsoft Exchange System Attendant service.

- Create a new directory for the transaction logs (e.g., "T:\exchsrvr\"). This will be the root of the new tracking log directory.

- Copy the current tracking log directory "D:\Exchsrvr*ServerName*.log" to "T:\Exchsrvr\" (e.g., T:\Exchsrvr\SERVER1.log).

- Open the configuration naming context in ADSIEDIT and navigate to "Configuration, Services, Microsoft Exchange, Your Exchange Organization, Administrative Groups, your Admin Group, Servers, your Exchange Server."

- Select the Exchange server and click Properties.

- In the "Select a Property to View" box, choose "msExchDataPath," as shown in Figure 11.48.

- Input the new directory into the "Edit Attribute" field.

- Click "Set," then "OK."

- Open the Registry Editor and update the following key to match the new tracking log folder (e.g., "T:\Exchsrvr\Server1.log").

11.9 The message tracking center   899

```
Hkey_Local_Machine\System\CurrentControlSet\Services\
MSExchangeSA\Parameters\Log Directory.
```

- Restart the Exchange services and send a message. Verify that Exchange is writing details into the new tracking log as users send messages and that you can access the directory through the file share.

Fortunately, the situation is easier in Exchange 2003 and you can change the location of the tracking log directory through General Server properties, as seen in Figure 11.46.

11.9.3 Changes in Exchange 2003

The fundamental nature of message tracking does not change much in Exchange 2003. However, there are a few subtle details to understand. Exchange now records more information as a message makes its way through the Routing Engine. For example, notifications as messages pass through the postcategorization, prerouting, and routed stages. The net effect is that you see more information as you track a message. Tracking works between Exchange 2003 and Exchange 2000 servers, but, obviously, you see less information reported when a message's path crosses an Exchange 2000 server because some data is unavailable.

11.9.4 Starting to track messages

You track messages through the Message Tracking Center component of ESM. This is also available as a snap-in, which you can load into a customized console, but usually you access the Message Tracking Center via the "Tools" node in ESM. When you click on the Message Tracking Center, you can enter the criteria necessary to begin the search.

Clearly, the more information you have (who sent it, when it was sent, what was its subject) about a message, the better. Starting to search with some fuzzy details about a message that a user thought was sent four days ago to a group of people is much harder than looking for a message sent yesterday. Figure 11.49 shows the result of a search that has located two messages that I sent to a specific recipient. Note that in this instance, the server properties determine that message subjects are not included in the message tracking logs, so you will not see this information.

The Browse buttons for the Sender: and Recipients: fields allow you to search the AD for users, contacts, or groups that sent or received the message. The Message Tracking Center will not allow you to begin a search

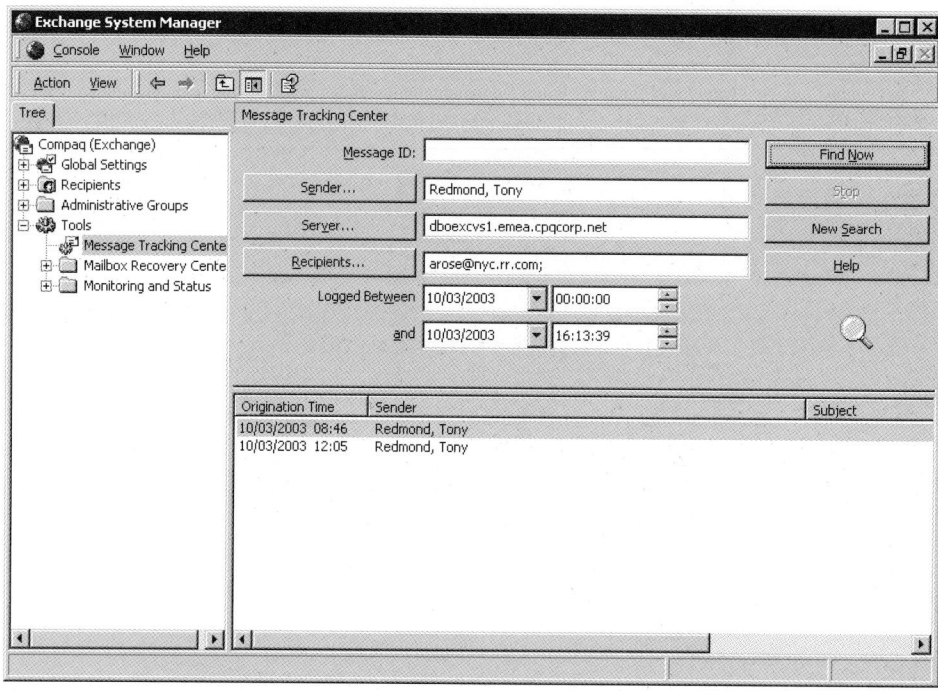

Figure 11.49 *Results of a message tracking request.*

until it verifies that you have provided valid sender and recipient data, using the logic that there is no point searching for anything based on invalid information. By default, you begin searching on the server that you connect to with ESM or the Message Tracking snap-in, but you can connect to another server to start searching if you need to. This is required if the person whose message you are tracking has his or her mailbox on another server. Even on large servers that handle heavy volumes of email, searching proceeds quite rapidly and you should have a result within a couple of minutes. Situations do exist when the Message Tracking Center appears to be unresponsive when it contacts other servers to retrieve data, especially if you search for a message addressed to a large distribution, but it will respond if left for processing to complete.

Apart from introducing a better user interface for the Message Tracking Center that resembles the "Find Message" functionality in Outlook, Exchange 2000 SP2 made an important architectural change to search processing. Prior to SP2, the server performing the search contacted each server in a message's path and retrieved all of the data from the remote servers before processing the search. From Exchange 2000 SP2 onward, the local server sends a search request to the Exchange Management Service running on each server involved in a message's progress. The Management Service processes the search request locally and then returns whatever relevant data it finds to the requesting server.

The number of messages found depends on the quality of the search criteria. In our example, we find only two messages, so it is likely that these include the message that we want. However, if you use some inexact criteria, it is possible that the MessageTracking Center will find ten or more messages, and it then becomes harder for you to decide which one is the message you really want. This is one reason why you should enable the capture of message subjects whenever possible; otherwise, it can be very difficult to isolate the exact message that you are interested in. You can view comprehensive details of the progress of a message through the Routing Engine by double-clicking on one of the found messages.

Figure 11.50 illustrates how Exchange tracks the path of a message as it interprets the tracking logs on each of the servers the message passes through. Note that we still cannot see the message subject, because server properties suppress this information. The tracking results show that after a client sends the message (the Store Driver reports that the Store submitted the message), the Advanced Queuing Engine and the Categorizer then process the message to determine on which queue to put the message. The result is a decision that the message is going to a remote SMTP recipient, so the Routing Engine transfers the message to a server that hosts an SMTP connector in order to use that connector to send the message to its

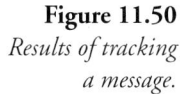

Figure 11.50
Results of tracking a message.

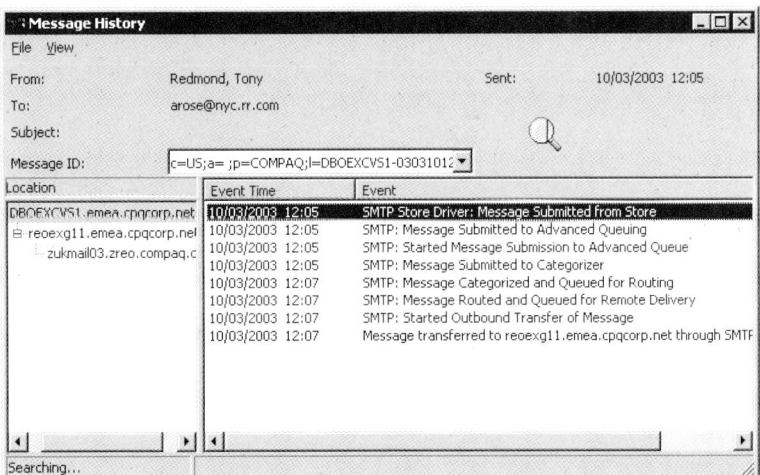

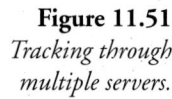
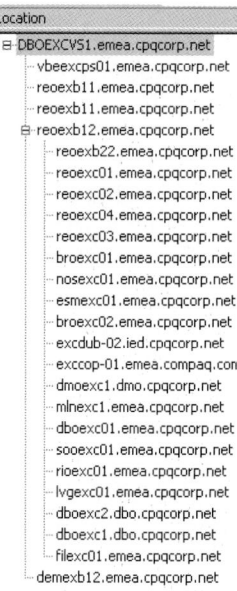

Figure 11.51
Tracking through multiple servers.

final destination. In situations where messages move to other routing groups, the Message Tracking Center lists the destination bridgehead servers in the routing group in a tree view in the "Location" (left-hand) panel. As tracking proceeds, the bridgehead servers expand to show all of the servers within the routing group that receive a copy of the message, as shown in Figure 11.51. You can click on any server to follow the progress of the message on that server (such as the delivery to local mailboxes or onward transmission via a connector managed by the server). However, you will not see any data if an administrator has disabled or otherwise blocked access to tracking logs on a server or your server has not completed the search process.

You may see that the Routing Engine transfers messages to the MTA for further processing. This implies that these messages are destined for an X.400 recipient, a mailbox on an Exchange 5.5 server, or for transmission via a legacy connector (such as IBM PROFS or Lotus Notes) for which the MTA has a responsibility to service. Messages to recipients in other routing groups go via SMTP to a bridgehead server in the same routing group for onward transfer or directly to another server in another routing group if your server hosts the routing group connector.

The Message Tracking Center may also list deliveries to mail enabled public folders. Organizations often use public folders as archives for messages sent to distribution groups and, in terms of delivery, Exchange processes these messages in exactly the same way as those sent to a local mailbox. The only evidence that the recipient is a public folder is its name, and you would have to know that this is the name of a public folder rather than a real person.

Tracking continues as long as the Message Tracking Center can follow the progress of a message. All of this functionality depends on administrators enabling message tracking on servers, preferably in a consistent manner across all servers in the organization. Creating a server policy to enable message tracking and then applying the policy to all servers in the organization, with or without the capture of the message subject, is the best way to achieve this goal. Obviously, if you do not enable message tracking, then Exchange will not create tracking logs and you will never be able to find out where a message goes.

11.9.5 Tracking log format

The message tracking log format for both Exchange 2000 and 2003 uses a set of tab-delimited fields (see Microsoft Knowledge Base article 246965 for more information), including:

- The date and time when the originating client sent the message. This value is set when the message is first submitted to the server, not when it first arrives on the server that hosts a message tracking log.

- The client IP address and client network name that generated the message

- The partner or messaging service that the message is handed to for processing—for example, the Store (for local delivery)

- The server IP address and server name that generated the message

- The recipient address: Upon submission, Exchange notes the address in its internal X.500 format. The address is shown in SMTP format after it is processed by the Categorizer (event 1023).

- An event identifier to indicate the specific processing that has occurred

- A unique message identifier that never changes, no matter how many servers the message travels through

- The priority of the message: −1 means low, 0 is normal, and 1 is high.

- The total size of the message in bytes

- A flag to indicate whether the message is encrypted. The flag is set to 1 if the message is signed, 2 means encrypted, while 0 means that the message is clear text.

- The version of the Routing Engine running on the server or the version of the SMTP server on a remote server

- Optionally, the subject of the message is recorded if permitted by server properties (see Figure 11.46). The subject is truncated to 256 bytes, if necessary.

- The number of recipients

- The originator's email address: This is the primary address of the originating mailbox, if known. It could be in X.400, SMTP, or a distinguished name format, depending on the transport that introduced the message.

11.9.6 Understanding message tracking log data

The easiest way to understand the data held in the tracking log is to take a copy of a log from a test server, load it into Excel (Figure 11.52), and then try to understand the different events as the Routing Engine processes a message from submission through to final dispatch. Of course, you can opt to review the data in a log from a production system, but typically these logs are very large (>50 MB daily), and it is harder to find a particular message and then track its progress, especially if the message goes to a large distribution list. The size of message tracking logs is not a particular concern for administrators, because it is unlikely that a collection of log files will ever cause a disk to fill up; the logs for ten days should be comfortably less than 750 MB on the largest server. However, large logs do slow down tracking, especially if you attempt to track a message across a number of different servers within an organization. Servers that host active public folders can generate heavy replication traffic, all of which Exchange captures in the message tracking logs. You can identify replication messages by the sender name, which is one of the following:

- The Exchange internal X.500 address for the Public Folder Replication Agent (e.g., EX:/O=Acme/OU=Central/CN=Configuration/CN=Servers/CN=Server1/ CN=Microsoft Public MDB)

- The SMTP address for the Public Folder Replication Agent (e.g., Server1-IS@acme.org)

For replication messages, the message tracking logs store the name of the destination server (the replication partner) in the "Recipient-Address" field.

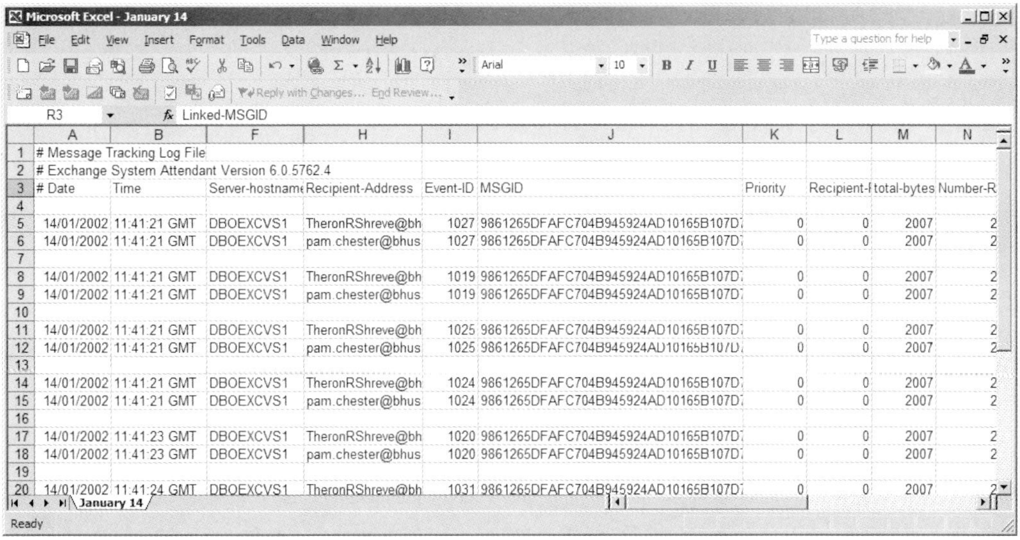

	A	B	F	H	I	J	K	L	M	N
1	# Message Tracking Log File									
2	# Exchange System Attendant Version 6.0.5762.4									
3	# Date	Time	Server-hostname	Recipient-Address	Event-ID	MSGID	Priority	Recipient-I	total-bytes	Number-R
4										
5	14/01/2002	11:41:21 GMT	DBOEXCVS1	TheronRShreve@bh	1027	9861265DFAFC704B945924AD10165B107D	0	0	2007	2
6	14/01/2002	11:41:21 GMT	DBOEXCVS1	pam.chester@bhus	1027	9861265DFAFC704B945924AD10165B107D	0	0	2007	2
7										
8	14/01/2002	11:41:21 GMT	DBOEXCVS1	TheronRShreve@bh	1019	9861265DFAFC704B945924AD10165B107D	0	0	2007	2
9	14/01/2002	11:41:21 GMT	DBOEXCVS1	pam.chester@bhus	1019	9861265DFAFC704B945924AD10165B107D	0	0	2007	2
10										
11	14/01/2002	11:41:21 GMT	DBOEXCVS1	TheronRShreve@bh	1025	9861265DFAFC704B945924AD10165B107D	0	0	2007	2
12	14/01/2002	11:41:21 GMT	DBOEXCVS1	pam.chester@bhus	1025	9861265DFAFC704B945924AD10165B107D	0	0	2007	2
13										
14	14/01/2002	11:41:21 GMT	DBOEXCVS1	TheronRShreve@bh	1024	9861265DFAFC704B945924AD10165B107D	0	0	2007	2
15	14/01/2002	11:41:21 GMT	DBOEXCVS1	pam.chester@bhus	1024	9861265DFAFC704B945924AD10165B107D	0	0	2007	2
16										
17	14/01/2002	11:41:23 GMT	DBOEXCVS1	TheronRShreve@bh	1020	9861265DFAFC704B945924AD10165B107D	0	0	2007	2
18	14/01/2002	11:41:23 GMT	DBOEXCVS1	pam.chester@bhus	1020	9861265DFAFC704B945924AD10165B107D	0	0	2007	2
19										
20	14/01/2002	11:41:24 GMT	DBOEXCVS1	TheronRShreve@bh	1031	9861265DFAFC704B945924AD10165B107D	0	0	2007	2

Figure 11.52 *Examining data from a message tracking log loaded into Excel.*

The message tracking logs also store data for incoming messages, including nondelivery notifications and delivery and read receipts, since administrators on other servers may want to issue a tracking request on your server.

Figure 11.52 shows the raw tracking log data used by the Message Tracking Center in Figure 11.50, as displayed through Excel. This is a relatively simple example, because the message originates from a MAPI client and goes to two external SMTP recipients. The logical processing performed by the Routing Engine is therefore very straightforward. The following steps are required: Accept the message, check the SMTP addresses, and route the message to an SMTP connector either on the same server (if present) or to the server that hosts an SMTP connector with the lowest possible routing cost. We can track the events in the message tracking log as follows, noting that entries exist for each address on the message:

1027: A client submits the message to the Store Driver.

1019: The Store Driver submits the message to Advanced Queuing to be processed.

1025: The message is processed by Advanced Queuing.

1024: The Categorizer begins to process the message.

1020: The Routing Engine places the message on a destination queue and is prepared for transfer from the server.

1031: The Routing Engine successfully transfers the message and processing completes.

In comparison, the sequence of events for a message delivered to a mailbox on the same server is as follows. The same events occur for deliveries to a mailbox in another storage group.

1027: The message is submitted to the Store Driver.

1019: The Store Driver submits the message to Advanced Queuing.

1025: The message is processed.

1024: The message is handed to the Categorizer.

1023: The Routing Engine places the message on the local delivery queue.

1028: The Store delivers the message to the mailbox.

Messages submitted from OWA clients log the same sequence of entries. Messages from POP3 and IMAP4 clients are submitted directly via SMTP to the Routing Engine and do not go through the Store Driver, so the sequence begins at event 1019. Other common entries include 1023 (successful delivery to a local mailbox) and 1029 (transfer to the MTA for onward delivery). Unlike the logs generated by Exchange 5.5, there is no special entry to mark the expansion of a distribution group. Instead, you will see 1020 (Exchange 2000) or 1033 and 1036 (Exchange 2003) entries written into the log for every member of the group after expansion. This applies to normal distribution groups and query-based distribution groups.

Complex messages addressed to a mixture of single recipients and distribution groups that resolve to local and remote addresses pose a particular challenge for email servers, especially if some of the recipients are included in multiple distribution groups. The fact that the properties of a group influence the number of messages that Exchange eventually generates for dispatch further complicates processing. For example, the properties of the group shown in Figure 11.53 reveal that any delivery reports for messages sent to this distribution group go back to the originator. In other words, if the group contains an invalid address (perhaps a contact whose email address is no longer valid or a mailbox with an exceeded quota), the originator will receive a nondelivery notification. You can set the properties of the group to suppress delivery reports, a situation that cuts down email traffic while creating a virtual blackhole where users are never quite sure if their messages get through. The Routing Engine performs the same per-message processing for out of office notifications, which you can also suppress or enable through the properties of a distribution group. Collectively, a num-

11.9 The message tracking center   907

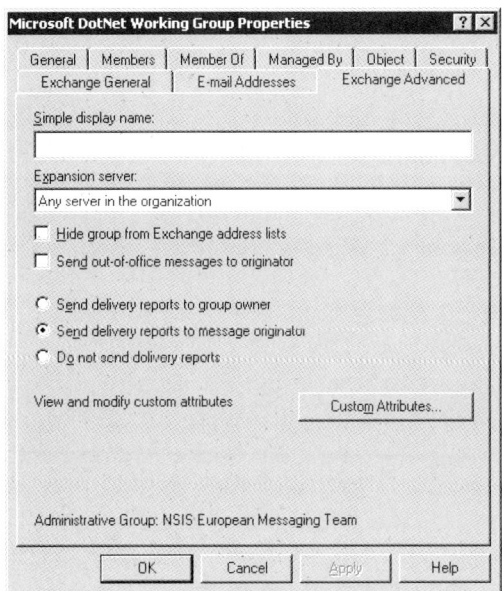

Figure 11.53
Exchange advanced properties of a distribution group.

ber of message generation permutations exist due to the different values of these properties.

Because Exchange processes delivery reports and out of office notifications on a per-message basis, if you send a message addressed to two groups, one that permits delivery reports and one that suppresses reports, the Routing Engine must generate two sets of messages. Thus, the recipients in one group will receive a copy of the message with its properties set to allow delivery reports, while recipients in the other group will receive a copy with properties set to suppress delivery reports.

You do not want users to receive multiple copies of a message, and it is easy to end up with this situation if the code does not handle all possible circumstances when the Routing Engine builds the recipient list for a message. To optimize the recipient list, the Routing Engine must expand all distribution groups, check the delivery reports and out of office notification properties of the distribution groups, and then generate the appropriate number of messages to meet the requirements as determined by the properties of each group. The result of the complex nature of recipient lists means that you may see multiple 1020 and 1028 entries for each address on a message when you look through tracking log data.

By comparison, the MTA expands distribution lists (or groups) for first-generation Exchange servers using a process called "fan-out," where the

Chapter 11

MTA builds the address list and then figures out how to send a single copy of the message to every addressee using the best possible route. First-generation Exchange servers do not support the same set of properties to control out of office messages and delivery reports, so building a recipient list is easier. In either case, if duplicate messages get through, the Store on the receiving server can identify their presence by reference to the message identifier and can then suppress the duplicates. This serves as a backstop to ensure that Exchange never delivers duplicate messages.

11.9.7 Analyzing Message Tracking Data

Details of the event identifiers used in message tracking logs are listed in Appendix B. It is easy to load a complete message tracking log into a program such as Access, where you can analyze the data to your heart's desire. However, if you're interested in using message tracking log data as the basis of any analysis, you are probably better off writing some code to reduce the data to its essential figures (such as number of messages sent during a period, the number of addressees, size of messages, and so on). Expect to process a large amount of data, since a single message sent to a large distribution group generates hundreds of entries in the tracking log. For example, a message sent to two common distribution groups that include 1,350 users (some duplicates) at HP generates over 4,000 entries. In addition, you have to separate entries that you are interested in (typically those belonging to user-generated messages) from those that you probably want to discard (e.g., system-generated messages such as public folder replication).

All versions from Exchange 2000 SP2 onward support the Message Tracking Logs WMI provider, a standard interface that allows programmatic read-only access to data held in message tracking logs. You can use this provider with programming languages that support COM scriptable objects (including WSH) to analyze the log data to your own requirements. Judging by comments made at conferences and Internet mailing lists, Perl is a particular favorite of those who write homegrown code to analyze message tracking log data.

Alternatively, you can buy a commercial product to do the job, such as Promodag Reports (www.promodag.com). MessageStats from Quest Software (http://www.quest.com/messagestats/index.asp) does a more sophisticated job of analyzing the contents of message logs to report on many different aspects, such as the most popular distribution list, the originator of most messages, and so on. Figure 11.54 is a good example of a common report of message traffic that you can generate with a product such as MessageStats, purely by analyzing the contents of the message tracking logs.

Server Volume Totals By Server

For 26/09/2002 to 02/10/2002

Server: DBOEXCVS1
Organization: Compaq
Site/Routing Group: NSIS EUROPEAN MESSAGING TEAM
Region:
Version: 2000

Date	Message Creation	Message Creation Volume (MB)	Average Size Message Creation (KB)	Received	Received Volume (MB)	Average Size Received (KB)	Sent	Sent Volume (MB)	Average Size Sent (KB)	Message Delivery	Message Delivery Volume (MB)	Average Size Message Delivery (KB)
02/10/2002	356	20	58	1,501	64	44	1,064	38	37	2,959	105	36
01/10/2002	305	37	124	1,247	75	62	829	42	52	1,836	105	59
30/09/2002	254	20	81	1,122	59	54	622	44	72	1,402	81	59
29/09/2002	25	0	0	295	5	17	103	2	20	357	5	14
28/09/2002	19	0	0	312	18	59	102	4	40	312	18	59
27/09/2002	317	77	249	1,406	141	103	842	131	159	1,818	195	110
26/09/2002	301	28	95	1,260	54	44	795	44	57	1,711	80	48
Total	1,577	182		7,143	416		4,357	305		10,395	589	
Average	225	26		1,020	60		622	44		1,485	85	

Found 7 item(s) corresponding to the search criteria: ([Date] BETWEEN '26/09/2002' AND '02/10/2002')

Figure 11.54 *MessageStats analysis of tracking log data.*

These utilities usually publish reports in Web format, so they are easy to access and analyze. Be careful to insist that whatever product you choose is capable of capturing data for all connector types, as well as messages sent to nested distribution lists, where the useful data results from the list expansion rather than the fact that a message went to a specific list.

While most administrators are happy to use message tracking data to report and understand traffic volumes, the data is sometimes used for other purposes. For example, if you have a suspicion that users are sending confidential information outside the organization, perhaps to a competitor, you can quickly check where they are sending messages by looking through message tracking logs for all their messages. While this will not tell you what the messages contain, it will tell you where the messages went, and, if you find enough evidence to warrant further investigation, you can then move the investigation to another level by turning on message archival or deploying other tools to capture copies of message traffic. Your management and human resources department must support these activities, since casual checking of people's message patterns is unlikely to be an approved system management activity in most jurisdictions.

11.10 ExchDump

Administrators and system designers have always had an issue with documenting Exchange servers. Microsoft PSS have exactly the same issue, because it is very difficult for them to help customers solve problems if they do not know the details of server configurations. Moreover, on the phone, people occasionally omit essential details. Having a utility to dump and report on the essential settings and other information about an Exchange server is incredibly useful. The only sad thing is that it has taken Microsoft so long to provide such a tool. Perhaps this was by design, to leave a gap for companies such as Ecora, with their Configuration Auditor for Exchange,[4] to exploit. However, when you think about it, a fundamental part of good system management practice is to know what configuration your servers run all the time. Fortunately, the situation is improved in Exchange 2003, because Microsoft has created the ExchDump tool, which you can download from its Web site (the description supplied here is based on prerelease software). Microsoft released an earlier version of the program, called ExchUtil, for Exchange 2000, but this never became general knowledge, so it is a hidden gem!

11.10.1 Running ExchDump

To run ExchDump, open a command window, navigate to the exchsrvr\bin directory, and type in the program name together with the command switches you want to use. ExchDump extracts information from both the IIS metabase and the Exchange configuration container in the AD, as appropriate. Table 11.6 lists the full set of command-line switches.

Table 11.6 *ExchDump Command-Line Switches*

Switch	Meaning	Runs: IPCONFIG and/or NETSTAT
/HTTP	Dumps configuration information about HTTP and Outlook Web Access, such as the Default Web Site and the Exchange virtual server.	IPCONFIG
/SMTP	Dumps SMTP configuration information, such as the log directory and authentication settings.	Neither
/RPC	Lists RPC connection information to Exchange components, such as the Store, System Attendant, and MTA.	Both
/SERVER	Reports information about the server, including details of the Stores and the accounts that hold permissions for various operations (such as log on locally).	Neither
/RG	Dumps information about routing groups. The WinRoute utility provides better information through a good GUI.	Neither

4. http://www.ecora.com/ecora/products/exchange/auditor.asp

11.10 ExchDump

Table 11.6 *ExchDump Command-Line Switches (continued)*

Switch	Meaning	Runs: IPCONFIG and/or NETSTAT
/RP	Dumps details of recipient policies, including the policies for default address generation.	Neither
/AL	Dumps the contents of the Address List Container to show all of the address lists (including the LDAP search criteria for each). Also dumps details of the Recipient Update Service (RUS) showing how many RUS run inside the organization and the servers that host each RUS.	Neither
/FH	Dumps details of the public folder hierarchies used inside the organization.	Neither
/CA	Dumps details of the Active Directory Connector agreements. Only present when the ADC synchronizes the Exchange 5.5 DS with the AD.	Neither
/ALL	Dumps all of the above information.	Both
/IM	Dumps information about the Exchange-specific version (if deployed) of Instant Messaging.	Neither
/HOSTING	Dumps a mixture of information that Microsoft has identified as typical of a hosted Exchange environment, including SMTP and HTTP data, address lists, and so on.	IPCONFIG
/USER	Dumps details of a single user object, which you identify with either its login name (e.g., /user:Redmond) or its UPN (e.g., /USER:Tony.Redmond@hp.com). If the user name is ambiguous, ExchDump reports the first match.	Neither
/GUID	Dumps a single AD object identified by its GUID, which can be expressed in either a binary string or GUID string format.	Neither
/DN	Dumps a single AD object identified by its distinguished name (e.g., /DN:"cn=Redmond,ou=Test,dc=hpqnet,dc=net). Uses the /V switch to report details of child objects.	Neither
/REMOTE	By default, ExchDump connects to the local server and queries the local metabase and the AD from that server. Uses the /REMOTE switch to connect to another Exchange 2003 server in the same organization and generates dumps for its data.	N/A
/NOACL	Disables reporting of ACL information. ExchDump sometimes is unable to report on an object because it cannot dump its ACL. You may be able to work around the problem by specifying this switch.	N/A
/APPEND	The default is to always overwrite existing output files. Use this switch to append instead.	N/A
/V	Generate verbose information.	—

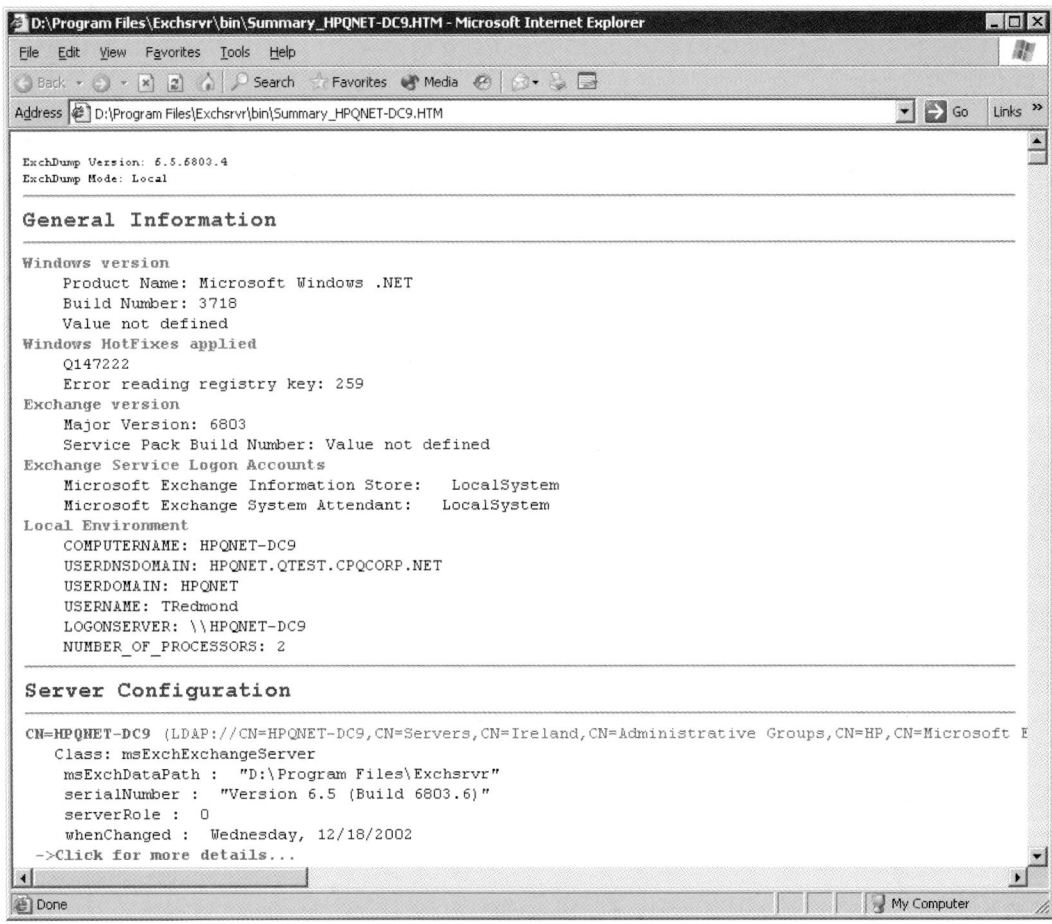

Figure 11.55   *HTML summary output from ExchDump.*

Note that if you run ExchDump on a cluster, the program will prompt you for the name of one of the virtual servers in the cluster from which to fetch configuration data.

During processing, ExchDump generates two files:

- Summary_server.htm (Figure 11.55). This file is useful because it contains a lot of information divided into sections that you can expand to see more information.

- Full_server.txt (Figure 11.56). This file contains more information, but it is not formatted as well and the information is harder to interpret. However, it is very useful to support engineers.

11.10 ExchDump

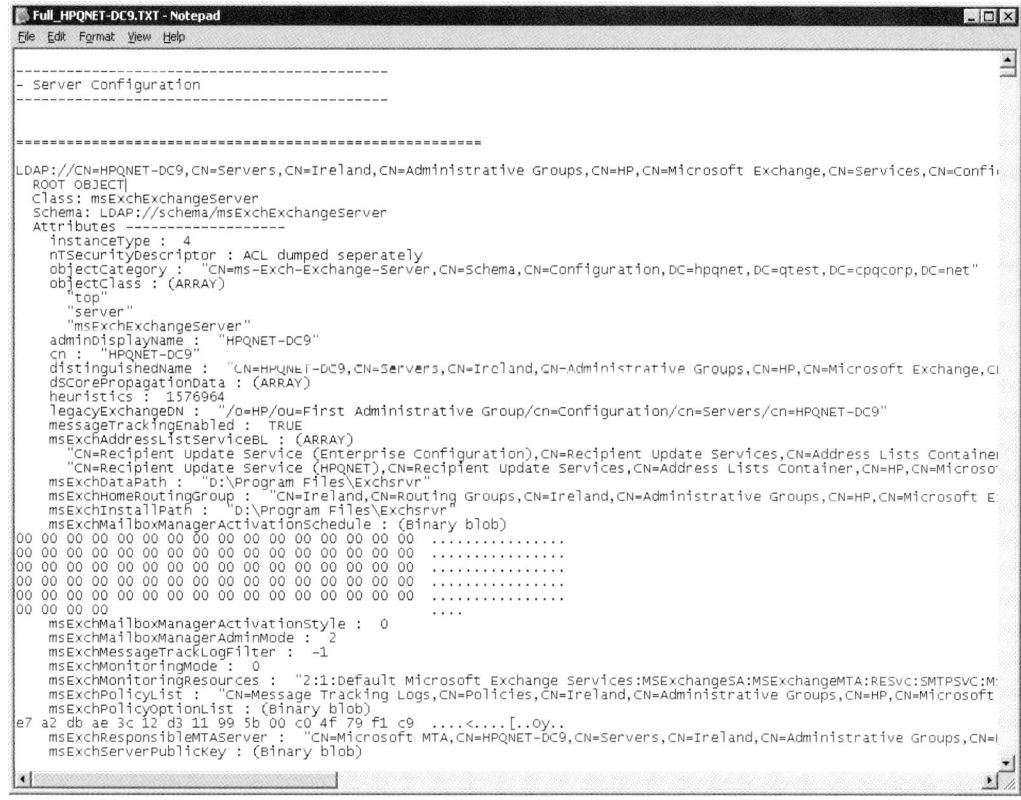

Figure 11.56 *Full-text report from ExchDump.*

The summary report describes information such as the version of Windows, the build level, the hot fixes applied to the server, the version of Exchange, and so on. Afterward, the data reported varies with the command-line switch that you specify. The reports generated with the /ALL switch are the most comprehensive—you will see details about policies; recipient update services; connectors; protocol settings such as SMTP, HTTP, and RPC; details about OWA configuration; TCP/IP settings (IPCONFIG) for the server; and current network connections (NETSTAT –AN).

On a server in a small organization, running a complete dump configuration (using the /ALL switch, illustrated in Figure 11.57), takes less than a minute. However, running the same command in a large organization, such as HP's, where the AD is huge and there are hundreds of servers in the organization, takes much longer, largely because it takes longer to resolve ACLs on all of the objects the program examines. ExchDump required six

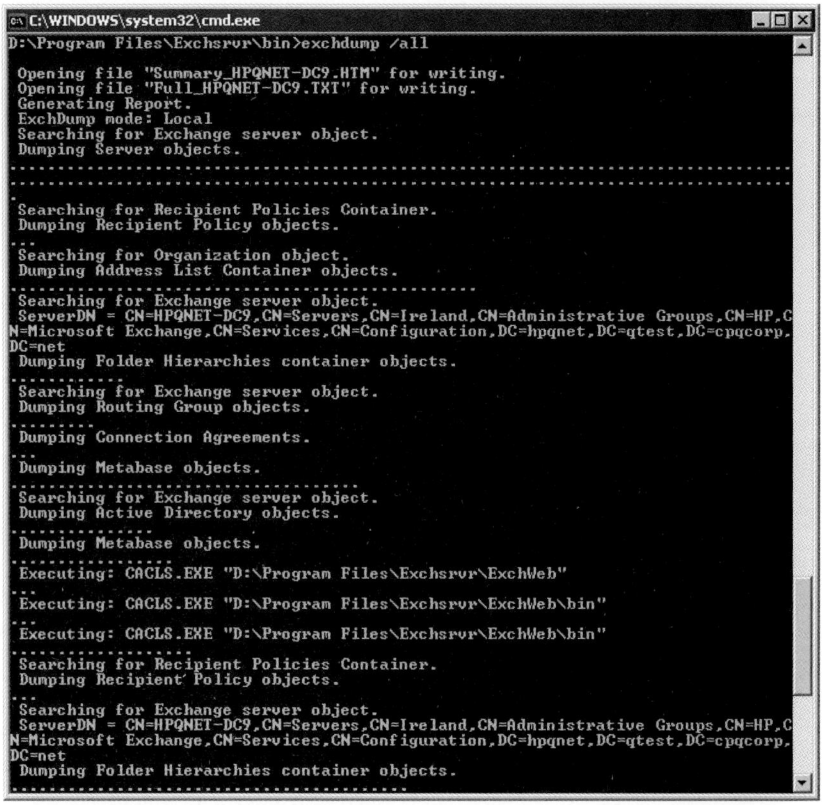

Figure 11.57
Running ExchDump.

```
C:\WINDOWS\system32\cmd.exe
D:\Program Files\Exchsrvr\bin>exchdump /all
Opening file "Summary_HPQNET-DC9.HTM" for writing.
Opening file "Full_HPQNET-DC9.TXT" for writing.
Generating Report.
ExchDump mode: Local
Searching for Exchange server object.
Dumping Server objects.
..............................................
..............................................
.
Searching for Recipient Policies Container.
Dumping Recipient Policy objects.
...
Searching for Organization object.
Dumping Address List Container objects.
.........................................
Searching for Exchange server object.
ServerDN = CN=HPQNET-DC9,CN=Servers,CN=Ireland,CN=Administrative Groups,CN=HP,C
N=Microsoft Exchange,CN=Services,CN=Configuration,DC=hpqnet,DC=qtest,DC=cpqcorp,
DC=net
Dumping Folder Hierarchies container objects.
............
Searching for Exchange server object.
Dumping Routing Group objects.
...............
Dumping Connection Agreements.
...
Dumping Metabase objects.
............................
Searching for Exchange server object.
Dumping Active Directory objects.
...............
Dumping Metabase objects.
.............
Executing: CACLS.EXE "D:\Program Files\Exchsrvr\ExchWeb"
...
Executing: CACLS.EXE "D:\Program Files\Exchsrvr\ExchWeb\bin"
...
Executing: CACLS.EXE "D:\Program Files\Exchsrvr\ExchWeb\bin"
...............................
Searching for Recipient Policies Container.
Dumping Recipient Policy objects.
...
Searching for Exchange server object.
ServerDN = CN=HPQNET-DC9,CN=Servers,CN=Ireland,CN=Administrative Groups,CN=HP,C
N=Microsoft Exchange,CN=Services,CN=Configuration,DC=hpqnet,DC=qtest,DC=cpqcorp,
DC=net
Dumping Folder Hierarchies container objects.
............
```

minutes to process a /ALL dump for an Exchange 2003 server in HP's production environment, while the equivalent in a smaller organization took less than a minute.

You can reduce the time required to run the program slightly by specifying the /NOACL switch. This also has the effect of reducing the size of the ExchDump reports. Table 11.7 compares the execution time and report sizes for both a large and small Exchange organization. With the /NOACL switch, the size of the summary report in the large organization dropped to 1,759 KB.

ExchDump does not produce pretty reports, and there is no doubt that you can find third-party products that will generate more information presented in a more readable fashion. Third-party products will probably offer more features, such as integration into a management framework, but you will have to pay for them. The big value of ExchDump is that it is available on every Exchange 2003 server, so there is no excuse for not docu-

Table 11.7 *Time Taken to Run ExchDump*

	Large Exchange Organization	Small Exchange Organization
Number of servers	147	8
Time required	6 minutes	>1 minute
Size of summary HTM file	2,991 KB	5,461 KB
Size of full TXT file	2,351 KB	5,024 KB

menting server configurations in the future. In addition, ExchDump is a superb support tool, which will help to improve communications between system administrators and Microsoft PSS.

11.11 Monitoring Exchange

You can take two approaches to monitoring Exchange. If you operate a small to medium organization, the standard tools included in the ESM "Monitoring and Status" node are enough to get the job done. On the other hand, if your organization spans more than 20 or so servers, you may find it more efficient to purchase and deploy specialized monitoring software, such as Microsoft Operations Manager, NetIQ AppManager, or HP OpenView. The situation becomes more complex when you need to manage multiple applications or multiple platforms, and these issues will be a major influence over your final choice. In this section, we discuss the standard tools built into ESM, and then move on to look at specialized monitoring software.

The "Monitoring and Status" node of ESM replaces the server and link monitors supported by Exchange 5.5. This subsystem allows administrators to:

- Set up email or script notifications for events that have occurred on monitored servers.

- Display the status of the servers and connectors within the organization.

Figure 11.58 illustrates the basic working environment. Notifications display the monitoring activity performed by this server, together with the notifications that the server executes when problems occur. The Status node reveals the information about the servers and connectors visible across the organization. You can think of the connector information as being roughly

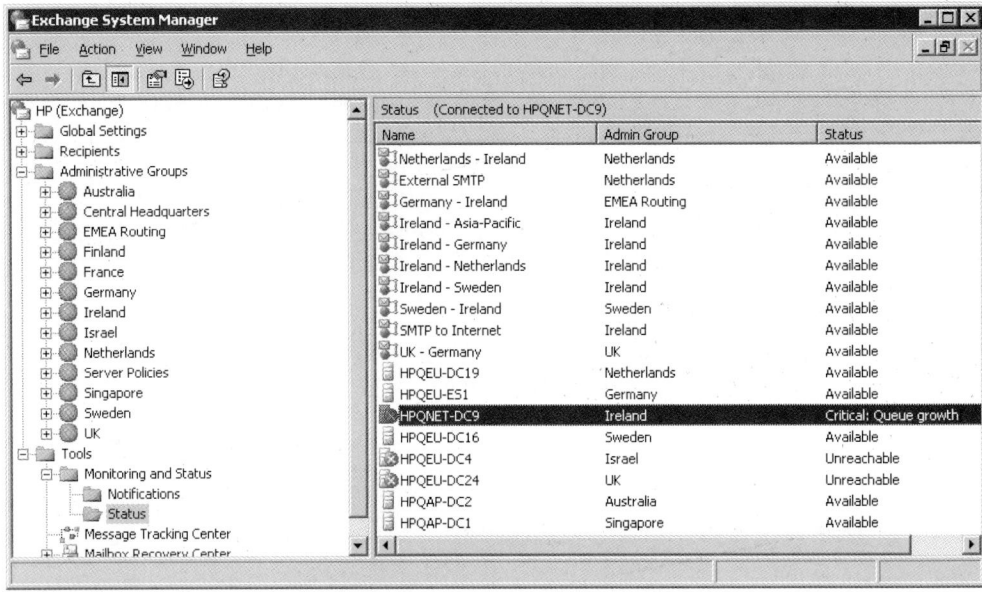

Figure 11.58 *Viewing the status of servers and connectors.*

equivalent to a basic snapshot of the routing table or the information you can see through the WinRoute utility.

You connect to a server to retrieve information, and ESM displays the name of the currently connected server at the top of the right-hand panel. If you run ESM on a server, it becomes the default connection for monitoring. If you have administrative permission on another server, you can use the "Connect to" option in the Status node to connect to that server and view the monitoring and status information available to it. Although refreshed at frequent intervals, status information is largely static. You can elect to refresh the information at any time by right-clicking on the Status node and selecting the refresh option. This forces ESM to rebuild its view from the routing table and the AD configuration information. Behind the scenes, ESM fetches the data using Exchange WMI providers. Connector information comes from the routing table via the ExchangeRoutingTableProvider, while server status comes via the ExchangeClusterProvider provider.

In Figure 11.58, you can see that several servers are marked as "Unreachable." This does not mean that the servers are down. Instead, this status indicates that the server we are connected to (HPQNET-DC9) is unable to contact the servers for some reason, perhaps a transient network condition

11.11 Monitoring Exchange

that prevents our server from contacting the target servers. Essentially, Exchange attempts to ping a server to discover if it is active and reports that its status is "unreachable" if the ping fails. We can also see that ESM reports a server to be in maintenance mode. This happens when an administrator changes the properties of a server through ESM to disable reporting.

Use the following checklist to help determine the source of the problem if you see a server in an "Unknown" or "Unreachable" state and you know that the network is available and the server is running:

- The System Attendant service is not running.
- The Routing Engine is not running.
- The WMI service is not running.

Figure 11.59 shows what you see if you select a server from the list and examine its properties. The default action is to list the resources currently monitored on the server. If you have Exchange Administrator permission for the server, you can disable monitoring on the server by setting the appropriate checkbox. In this case, we simply review what level of monitor-

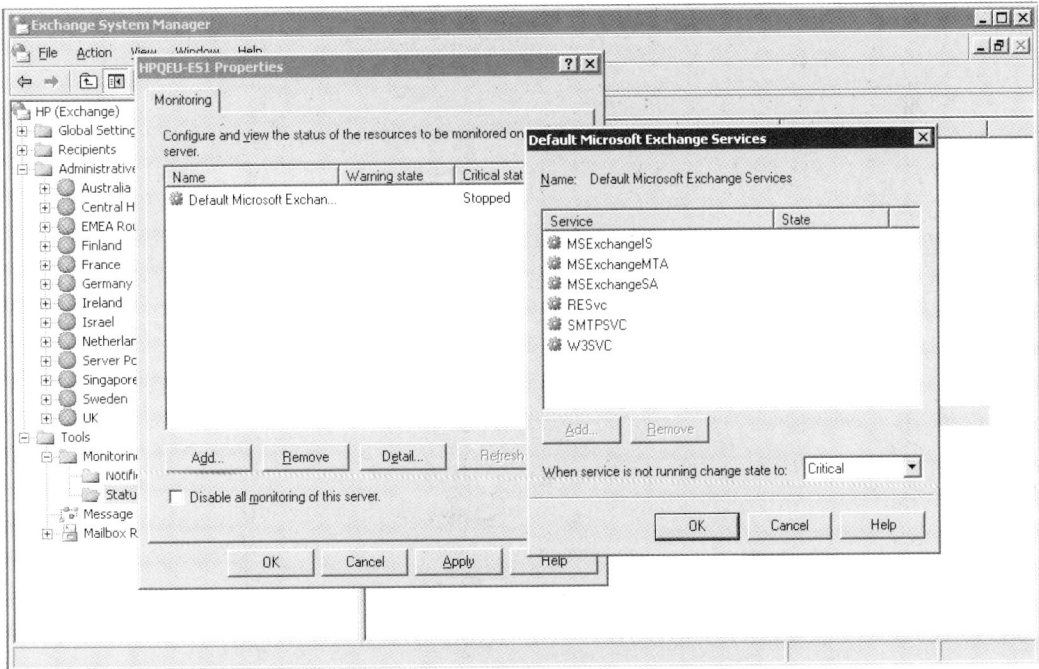

Figure 11.59   *Viewing the monitoring properties for a server.*

ing the server performs by clicking on the only item in the list of monitored resources, which happens to be a set of essential Exchange services that must run on a server. You can also select an item in the list and click on the Detail button to view the same information. As you can see, ESM defines the set of essential Exchange services as:

- The Information Store (MSExchangeIS)
- The MTA (MSExchangeMTA)
- The System Attendant (MSExchangeSA)
- The Routing Engine (RESvc)
- The Windows SMTP service (SMTPSVC)
- The World Wide Web (IIS) publishing service (W3SVC)

Apart from the set of essential services, we can add other resources for Exchange to monitor. Figure 11.60 shows the available resources (virtual memory, CPU, disk space, SMTP queues, another Windows service, and the X.400 queue). After you select the resource you want to monitor, you then set the monitoring criteria. Exchange stores monitoring settings along with the rest of its configuration data in the AD. Figure 11.61 illustrates how ESM flags problems. The HPQNET-DC9 server reports that a queue (either SMTP or X.400) has reached a critical limit.

ESM is not a purpose-designed monitoring utility and now it begins to display some flaws. We know that a problem exists on a server, but double-clicking on the problem server does not reveal any further information apart from the threshold that triggers the report. In this case, we know that SMTP messages have been queued for more than five minutes, but we do not know how many messages are on the queue or why the problem exists.

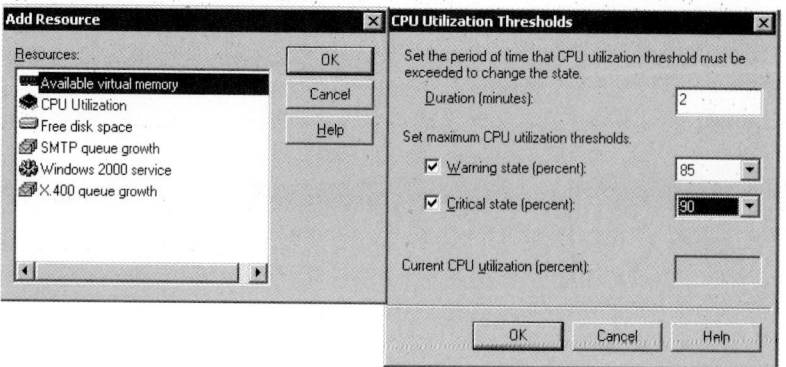

Figure 11.60
Adding a new resource to monitor.

11.11 Monitoring Exchange

Figure 11.61
Critical queue.

To take further action, we need to locate the server in its administrative group and examine its queues and then look at other information such as the application event log on the server to determine the root cause. ESM can reveal the queue information, but an ability to provide other pointers is lacking.

In addition, to display monitoring status, ESM must fetch data from multiple sources and this slows response. For example, it takes ESM nearly 90 seconds to retrieve and display information about HP's Exchange 2000/2003 organization (124 connectors and 234 servers listed). The number of connectors seems excessive, even for a company as large and distributed as HP, but routing group connectors usually have two entries, one for the routing group at each side of the partnership, so this inflates the number. In addition, large organizations tend to have multiple Internet connections and host gateways for different email systems, which drives the number up further. The sluggish responsiveness of ESM when faced with large numbers of servers and connectors is one reason why you should consider deploying specialized monitoring software if your organization spans more than 20 servers. In fact, even below this point, dedicated monitoring software delivers great value, because it can identify and report on outages faster than you can notice problems, unless you are connected to the affected server when the outage occurs.

To get a view of the connectors and servers in an organization, you can click on Status and take the "Export" option to have ESM export the information listed in the right-hand panel to a comma-separated value file. You can then load the file into Notepad or, better still, Excel, to examine and analyze the data, as shown in Figure 11.62.

11.11.1 Monitoring and notifications

Exchange 5.5 uses server monitors to check periodically that everything is running as expected on a server. Exchange 2000 and 2003 use much the same idea, but notifications now implement the same basic principles as server monitors:

- You establish a set of conditions that you wish to monitor on a server and assign a server to do the monitoring.

Figure 11.62
Examining monitoring data with Excel.

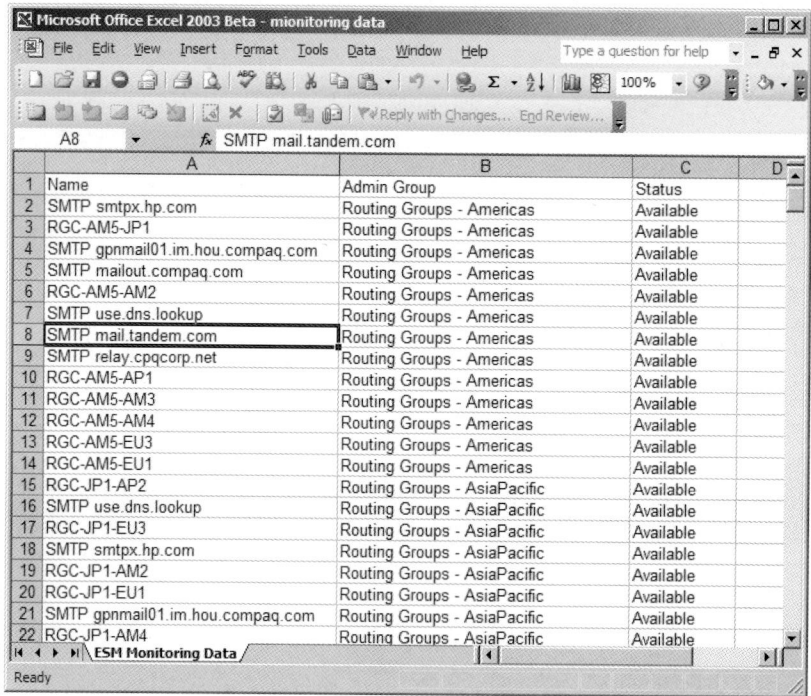

- The System Attendant process monitors servers with RPCs, so you cannot monitor a server unless the network connection between the two servers supports RPCs.

- If the System Attendant detects any problems on a server, it dispatches a notification via email or by executing a script that you define.

- Email notifications can go to any valid email address, including pagers or via SMS to cell phones, or you can use a Windows script to call an executable or perform any other processing available to scripts. Because they can execute a wider range of actions, scripts are the more functional option, but most administrators opt for email notification because of the difficulty of automating a suitable response to the wide range of problems that can afflict servers.

As you can see in Figure 11.63, the HPQNET-DC9 server is monitoring itself, all the other servers in the organization, and all the connectors in the organization. Except in small or highly centralized organizations, where all the servers connect over a reliable high speed network, it is not usually feasible for a single server to monitor every other server. It is more common

11.11 Monitoring Exchange

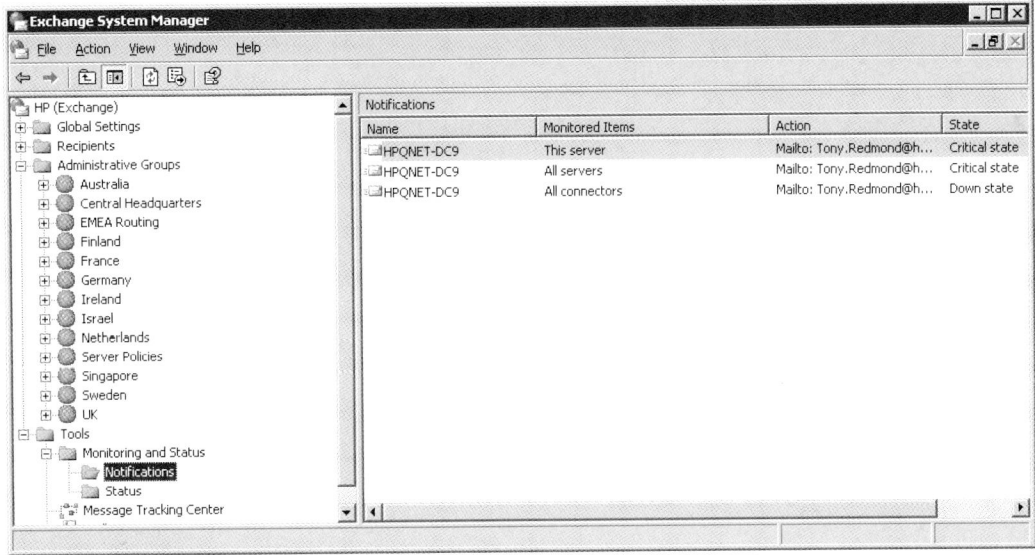

Figure 11.63 *Server monitoring.*

to have one or two servers per administrative group monitor the other servers in the group. When you create a new notification, you decide which objects you want to monitor. ESM provides the following options:

- This server (but if a server that monitors itself encounters a problem, it may not be able to report that a problem exists)

- All servers

- Any server in this routing group (that the connected server belongs to)

- All connectors

- Any connector in this routing group (that the connected server belongs to)

- Custom list of servers (selected from the set of Exchange servers in the organization)

- Custom list of connectors (selected from the set of connectors in the organization)

If a condition occurs on a monitored server, such as disk space going under a predefined threshold, the monitoring server detects the problem and executes the notification action. In the cases shown in Figure 11.63, we elect to send an email message.

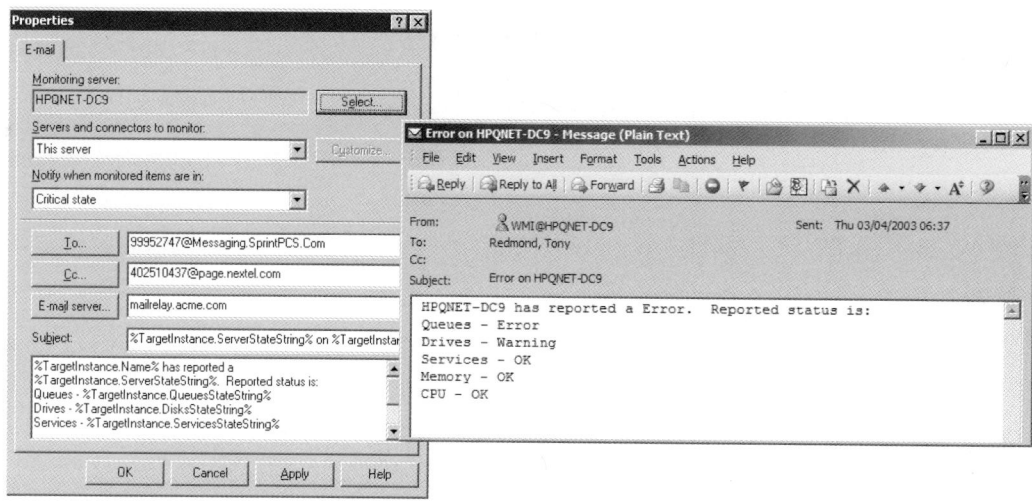

Figure 11.64 *Notification parameters and a notification message.*

You can click on a notification to see the instructions for the System Attendant when it detects a problem on a server that it monitors. Figure 11.64 shows the notification parameters and an example message. In this case, we determine that email should go to two addresses for pager devices. Because an Exchange outage may affect our ability to send messages outside the organization, we define a special email server for the System Attendant to send the messages through. It is quite common to use a special SMTP server, perhaps a relay server in the DMZ, for this purpose, because you never want to be in a situation where the messaging system is inoperative and you do not know about the problem.

You can edit the subject and the content of the notification message as long as you are careful not to change the predefined fields that Exchange fills with information about the problem. TargetInstance is used to reference the name of the server being monitored, and, as you can see in Figure 11.64, TargetInstance has a number of properties that are used for reporting, including QueuesStateString, which is used to insert the status of the message queues (both SMTP and X.400). The details of reported problems are limited, but certainly enough to alert system administrators that they need to take some action, if only to get some additional information about the problem.

You can define monitoring parameters for a server in two ways. First, you can select the server from its administrative group, and then set parameters through the "Monitoring" property page. Alternatively, you can click

11.11 Monitoring Exchange

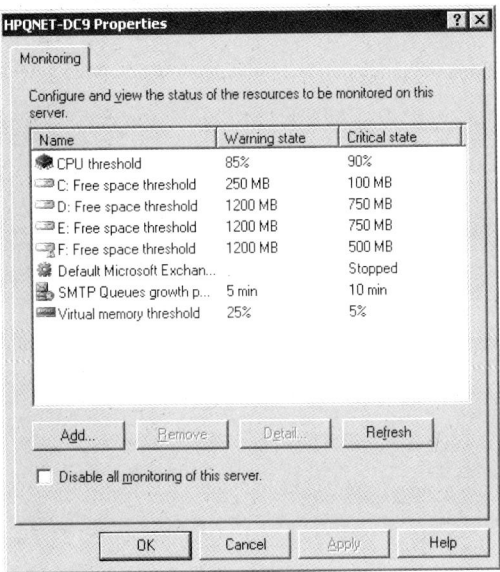

Figure 11.65
Defining conditions for monitoring.

on Status and select a server from the list ESM displays, and then look at its properties. In either case, you will see something similar to the screen shown in Figure 11.65, which details a common set of monitoring parameters. The "Disable all monitoring of this server" checkbox allows or prevents server monitoring. By default, Exchange clears the checkbox, meaning that servers automatically publish monitoring data via WMI. You should not set this checkbox unless you have a good reason not to monitor a server. Table 11.8 lists the monitoring conditions that you can define.

Table 11.8 *Monitoring Conditions*

Condition	Notes
Free space threshold	Set warning and critical levels for available space on a selected volume. You can set different conditions for every volume connected to the server. Typically, you monitor free space on the C: drive, as well as those used for the Exchange databases and transaction logs.
CPU threshold	Set warning and critical levels for CPU use over a sustained period. It is best practice not to exceed 80 percent CPU use over five minutes on an Exchange server.
Available virtual memory	Set warning and critical thresholds for available virtual memory. Do not let virtual memory fall below 25 percent (free) on an Exchange server.
Windows service available	You can monitor the availability of any Windows service. For example, you could check to ensure that the IIS Admin service is running or that a service used by a third-party backup utility is available.

Table 11.8 *Monitoring Conditions (continued)*

Condition	Notes
Exchange service available	Monitor that the standard set of Exchange services is available. You can add to this list of services if required.
SMTP queue growth	Set thresholds for continuous queue growth for the SMTP virtual server. Given the speed of the Routing Engine and SMTP transport, queues should not accumulate over a sustained period. If messages are on the queue for longer than five minutes, and you have a constant network link to other routing groups and servers, this is probable evidence of a problem with a connector.
X.400 queue growth	Similar to the SMTP queue growth, except that this pertains to MTA queues for connectors such as Lotus Notes or GroupWise.

11.12 Standard diagnostics

The application event log is a rich source of information for an Exchange administrator. Events logged include:

- Starting and stopping of services
- Mounting and dismounting of databases
- Results of background system maintenance, such as database defragmentation
- Security failures, such as attempts made to log on to a mailbox from an unauthorized account
- Failures in normal operation

Events in the last category are obviously the most important to be aware of and respond to quickly. Unfortunately, the application event log (the location where these events are written to) normally holds hundreds of events, and it can be difficult to isolate important instances in such a mass of data. Browsing through the event log with the Windows Event Viewer (Figure 11.66) can be very unproductive unless you use a filter (an option from the View menu) to isolate specific events. In this case, we apply a filter to find all instances of event 1207 (which reports how many items in a store are past their deleted retention period) and the filter isolates 507 events from 35,176. This is not surprising, because the application event log on this server extends over six months and there are two Stores (Mailbox and Public), each of which logs an event nightly. Even with an applied filter, we still have much data to understand.

11.12 Standard diagnostics

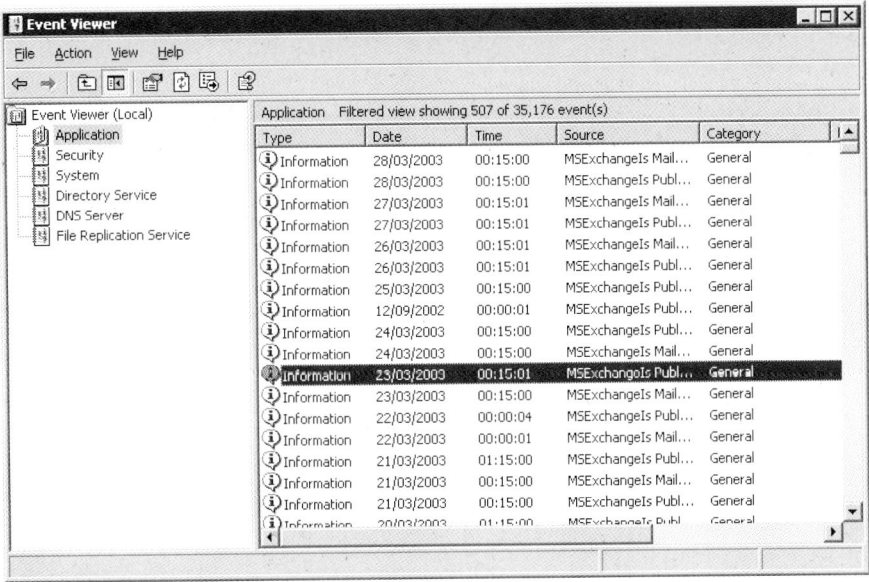

Figure 11.66 *Event Viewer.*

Products such as NetIQ or MOM are very useful to system administrators, because they can filter information from many different servers and flag critical errors in an effective manner. If you only have one or two servers to manage, investing in a specialized monitoring product may be a touch expensive, especially if it requires a SQL license, so in this situation you will just have to pay attention to the system event log and check its contents on a regular basis.

Every version of Exchange has added new events to the set that the server logs. Even if you are an experienced administrator, it is a good idea to look through the application event log for a live server and make a note of logged events. The set of events can then become a checklist for administrators to review regularly to ensure that everything is running as expected. It is also helpful if you can come up with a procedure to respond to particular events. As discussed previously, −1018 events are not welcome on any Exchange server, but administrators need to understand what these and other events mean and the steps they should take to address the problem.

11.12.1 Turning up logging

Inevitably, problems do occur during normal operation. When this happens, you can turn up the level of diagnostic logging on a server to force

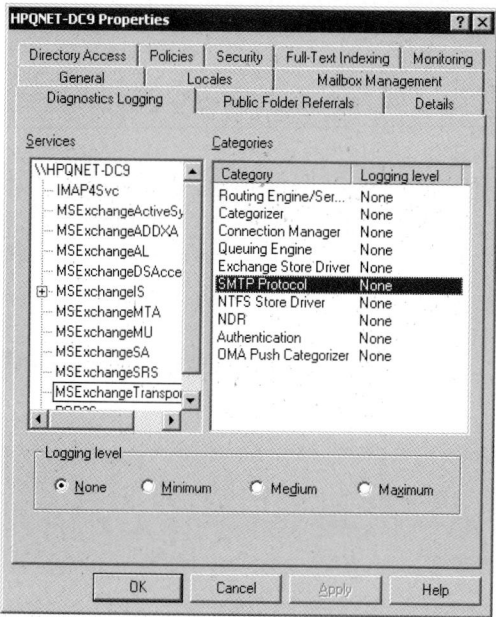

Figure 11.67
Setting diagnostic logging level for a server.

Exchange to capture additional information. Hopefully, a clue to the problem will then turn up in the information recorded in the application event log. Microsoft PSS often ask administrators to turn up logging before attempting to reproduce a problem.

Diagnostics logging is set as a property of a server. As you can see in Figure 11.67, a number of settings for each subsystem can be individually turned up—from "None," the normal level, to "Maximum," which will force the server to record a great deal of information. The default level is somewhat misleading, because it does not really mean that Exchange records no information in the event log. Instead, "None" means that Exchange records details of critical errors but ignores informational events. There are exceptions to this rule, since Exchange does report some informational events even when logging is set to "None." For example, event 701 from the Store reports when a background defragmentation pass has completed for a Mailbox Store; and event 9535 reports how many deleted mailboxes the System Attendant removes from the Store during its regular scan for mailboxes past their retention period.

It is great to be able to gather lots of information, but you have to be careful about generating too much data. Only turn up logging when you need to. Exchange records quite enough information in the event log with its default settings, and you do not want to miss something important just because you are not able to spot a significant event among a whole mass of informational messages.

11.13 Management frameworks

After your organization begins to grow, administrators will spend more and more time grappling with servers and event logs. The manual tools are good enough to monitor Exchange, but the amount of manual intervention required quickly becomes a problem. Without automation, you run the risk that you:

- Miss early warning signs for problems. For example, you miss a transient −1018 event, which may point to a storage problem, or you miss events flagged when virtual memory fragmentation occurs.

- Experience avoidable outages caused by disk space exhaustion on important volumes.

- Fail to notice signs of security breeches, such as users logging on to mailboxes without permission.

- Fail to notice gradual performance degradation of a server until it reaches a point that affects users.

- Fail to notice gradual or heavy accumulation of messages on email queues or network problems that cause mail flow to halt.

- Fail to collate reports from multiple servers that may point to common problems across the infrastructure.

- Fail to notice that a server is down or that a critical service (e.g., the Information Store) or component (an individual Store) is offline.

Management frameworks help system administrators by automating system monitoring to identify potential problems and then suggest solutions. Unless you are very paranoid and spend all your time monitoring servers or are just lucky enough to be looking when a problem happens, management frameworks are always faster than people at detecting and reporting problems. Generally, you have to install agent software that runs on the servers you want to monitor and management packs that interpret the data. The agents collect information from various sources and collate it in a database or other repository, which you can then query with management consoles.

Management packs are specific to each application and provide the frameworks with added intelligence over simple analysis by applying rules that search the collated data for warning signs and then compare problem symptoms against their knowledge base to arrive at a recommendation for the administrator to action. Management packs typically include rules to process the data, thresholds that help determine when problems exist, off-the-shelf reports, and scripts. For example, the Exchange 2003 management pack for MOM (which Microsoft provides as part of Exchange 2003) includes rules that look at over 1,700 different events that the various Exchange components (Store, Routing Engine, MTA, System Attendant, protocol stacks, etc.) log. The events are tagged with their severity level and pointers to possible solutions in the MOM knowledge base. Various notifications are supported, including messages to pagers and so on.

There are three major management frameworks suitable for Exchange 2000/2003:

- Microsoft Management Operations Manager (MOM)
- HP OpenView
- NetIQ AppManager

Many factors influence the choice of which framework is best for your organization, including:

- If you have already deployed a framework to manage other applications such as SQL/Server, it makes sense to extend that framework to cover Exchange. This is especially true if your company has invested in any customization, such as the development of knowledge scripts used by the monitoring agents.

- If you operate a heterogeneous computing environment spanning multiple operating systems, it is best to select a single framework that can span all platforms. For example, HP OpenView is especially powerful when you need to monitor UNIX and Windows systems and network components.

- One of MOM's major strengths is its use of Microsoft's own knowledge base and information gleaned from developers, and you might want to benefit from that experience. It is also good to be able to add to the knowledge base to reflect your own experience.

- You may be able to use the prepackaged tools to assist in storage, server, and network capacity planning and replace other utilities that you deploy for this purpose.

- Cost of deployment and maintenance. You have to purchase the central monitoring software plus the other components that you need, including agents and management packs tailored for the applications that you want to monitor, and then license them for your organization. You also need to pay for ongoing support, updates to the knowledge base, and so on. You probably need different versions of the software for each version of Exchange you operate.

In all cases, you should conduct a test to ensure that the chosen framework performs reliably and meets your needs. Of course, you can write your own management and monitoring tools using the Exchange WMI providers, other APIs such as ADSI, and a mass of code that gathers and interprets system data. Large Exchange organizations have existed since the earliest days of the product, so the need for automated monitoring of large numbers of servers is not new. It is reasonably common to find monitoring code, but few companies are willing to take on the development and maintenance when they realize that off-the-shelf packages are available. For this reason, while Exchange continues to provide better programmatic access to its data with each release, it is less common to attempt to write custom code to attack the monitoring problem. A curious symmetry indeed!

11.14 Exchange and WMI

WMI is Microsoft's implementation of WBEM, the Web-Based Enterprise Management architecture as defined by DMTF, the Desktop Management Task Force,[5] an industry body devoted to the definition of cross-platform management standards. DMTF also lobbies computer companies to adopt the defined standards. DMTF wants WBEM to be a uniform access method to management information gathered from different types of servers. The management information includes system state, memory use, a list of applications installed and running on the server, and connected clients.

Exchange 2000 supports WMI with a set of providers that you can exploit to manipulate Exchange objects programmatically. Exchange 2003 expands and improves the capabilities of the providers to support even more access. However, the details of the Exchange WMI providers, including how to leverage them through programs and scripts, are beyond the scope of this book. If you are interested, you can investigate the WMI and Exchange provider interface technical information available on Microsoft TechNet at www.microsoft.com/technet or buy one of the many books on the market. My favorite is Alain Lissoir's two-volume set, largely because the books contain so many practical examples (see Appendix A).

---

5. See http://www.dmtf.org for further information.

A
Recommended Books for Further Reading

Pierre Bijaoui, *Scaling Microsoft Exchange 2000,* 1555582397.

Understanding and assessing the performance of Exchange 2000, including how to conduct benchmarks.

Jerry Cochran, *Mission-Critical Microsoft Exchange 2000: Building Highly-Available Messaging Systems,* 1555582338.

How to approach building highly available and resilient Exchange servers.

Mike Daugherty, *Monitoring and Managing Exchange 2000,* 155558232X.

How to approach the management and administration of Exchange 2000 servers.

Jan De Clercq, *Windows Server 2003 Infrastructures,* 1555582834.

A solid treatment of the essential points of deploying a Windows 2003 infrastructure.

Kevin Laahs, Emer McKenna, and Don Vickers, *Microsoft SharePoint Portal Server 2001: Building Knowledge Sharing Applications,* 1555582443.

How to customize and deploy SharePoint Portal Server to improve your knowledge management capabilities.

Alain Lissoir, *Understanding Windows Management Instrumentation Scripting* and *Leveraging Windows Management Instrumentation Scripting,* 155582664 and 155582990.

A two-volume set that explores and interprets the power of WMI providers and Windows scripting. Lots of practical examples.

Kieran McCorry, *Microsoft Exchange Server 2003 Deployment and Migration,* 1555583164.

Detailed description of how to go about deploying Exchange 2003, including a comprehensive discussion on migration from Exchange 5.5.

Paul Robichaux, *Secure Messaging with Exchange 2003,* 0735619905.

Updated version of the best book on how to secure Exchange servers.

B

Message Tracking Log Codes

This appendix documents the event identifiers that the Routing Engine logs in the message tracking logs as messages make their way from submission to delivery.

Event Identifier	Meaning	Explanation
0	Message transfer in	The MTA completed transfer of responsibility for a message from a gateway or X.400 link into the local MTA.
1	Probe transfer in	The MTA completed transfer of responsibility for a probe from a gateway or X.400 link into the local MTA.
2	Report transfer in	The MTA completed transfer of responsibility for a report from a gateway or X.400 link into the local MTA.
4	Message submission	A message was submitted by a local email client (usually through the Store).
5	Probe submission	An X.400 probe was submitted by a local email client (usually through the Store).
6	Probe transfer out	The MTA completed transfer of responsibility for a probe from the local MTA to a gateway, X.400 link, or another MTA.
7	Message transfer out	The MTA completed transfer of responsibility for a message from the local MTA to a gateway, X.400 link, or another MTA.
8	Report transfer out	The MTA completed transfer of responsibility for a message from the local MTA to a gateway, X.400 link, or another MTA.
9	Message delivered	The MTA completed transfer of responsibility for a report from the local MTA to a gateway, X.400 link, or another MTA.
10	Report delivered	The MTA completed delivery of a receipt or NDR to local recipients (usually through the Store).

Event Identifier	Meaning	Explanation
29	Message rerouted	The MTA has rerouted a message, report, or probe because of a problem with the next route X.400 link or MTA.
31	Downgrading	The MTA has mapped a message, report, or probe into the 1984 X.400 protocol before transferring it to a remote 1984 MTA.
33	Report absorption	The MTA has scheduled a report for deletion because a user did not request it. In the X.400 protocols, NDRs are always rerouted back to the originating MTA, even if a user did not request the report.
34	Report generation	The MTA has created a delivery receipt or NDR.
43	Unroutable report discarded	The MTA has discarded a report because it cannot be sent to the apparent destination.
50	Gateway deleted message	The administrator deleted an X.400 message that was queued by the MTA for transfer to a gateway. No delivery report was generated.
51	Gateway deleted probe	The administrator deleted an X.400 probe that was queued by the MTA for transfer to a gateway. No delivery report was generated.
52	Gateway deleted report	The administrator deleted an X.400 report that was queued by the MTA for transfer to a gateway. No delivery report was generated.
1000	Local delivery	The sender and recipient are on the same server.
1001	Backbone transfer in	A message was received from another MAPI system across a connector or gateway.
1002	Backbone transfer out	A message was sent to another MAPI system across a connector or gateway.
1003	Gateway transfer out	A message was sent through a gateway.
1004	Gateway transfer in	A message was received from a gateway.
1005	Gateway report transfer in	A delivery receipt or NDR was received from a gateway.
1006	Gateway report transfer out	A delivery receipt or NDR was sent through a gateway.
1007	Gateway report generation	A gateway generated an NDR for a message.
1010	SMTP queued outbound	Outbound mail was queued for delivery by the SMTP service.
1011	SMTP transferred outbound	Outbound mail was transferred to an SMTP recipient.
1012	SMTP received inbound	Inbound mail was received from the SMTP service.
1013	SMTP transferred inbound	Mail received by the SMTP service was transferred to the Store.

Message Tracking Log Codes

Event Identifier	Meaning	Explanation
1014	SMTP message rerouted	An Internet message is being rerouted or forwarded to the proper location.
1015	SMTP report transferred in	A delivery receipt or NDR was received by the SMTP service.
1016	SMTP report transferred out	A delivery receipt or NDR was sent to the SMTP service.
1017	SMTP report generated	A delivery receipt or NDR was created.
1018	SMTP report absorbed	The delivery receipt or NDR could not be delivered.
1019	SMTP submit to AQ	A new message is submitted to Advanced Queuing.
1020	SMTP begin outbound transfer	A message is about to be sent over the network by the SMTP service.
1021	SMTP bad mail	The Routing Engine transferred a message to the badmail directory.
1022	SMTP AQ failure	A fatal error occurred in the Advanced Queuing engine. More information is available in the Application Event log.
1023	SMTP local delivery	A message was successfully delivered by the Store Driver.
1024	SMTP submit message to categorizer	Advanced Queuing submitted a message to the categorizer.
1025	SMTP begin to process message	A new message is processed by Advanced Queuing.
1026	SMTP AQ failed message	Advanced Queuing failed to process a message. The message will be NDR'd or moved into the badmail directory.
1027	SMTP submit message to SD	A message was submitted to the Store Driver.
1028	SMTP SD local delivery	The Store Driver successfully delivered a message to a local mailbox.
1029	SMTP SD gateway delivery	The Store Driver transferred a message to the MTA.
1030	SMTP NDR	Some recipients on the message will cause an NDR to be generated (invalid email address, etc.).
1031	SMTP end outbound transfer	The message was successfully transferred outbound.
1033	????	
1036	????	

Third-party extensions that log events use events numbered past 2000.

C

TCP/IP Ports Used by Exchange

It is common to encounter a requirement to allow access to mailboxes on Exchange servers through a firewall, perhaps to accommodate the needs of traveling users who wish to connect across the public Internet without a VPN. In this scenario, you have a front-end server placed in the DMZ to accept incoming requests from clients and relay them onward to the mailbox server. Firewalls are in place to control external traffic into the DMZ and from the DMZ to the internal network. To make this all work, you need to understand the ports used by Exchange and other associated components in order to define what ports to open on each firewall. In most cases, you use Outlook Web Access as the client, although you can take the same approach with Outlook 2003 when it connects to Exchange over HTTP.

The situation is simple enough on the external-facing firewall, since all you have to open are ports 80 and 443 to allow HTTP and HTTP-SSL traffic.

Many more ports are involved when communicating from the Exchange front-end server to the mailbox server through the firewall from the DMZ to the internal network, as shown in the following chart.

Source	Destination	Port/Protocol	Description
Exchange Front-End Server	Exchange Mailbox Server	80/TCP (HTTP-basic)	Relayed HTTP traffic. Note that even if the client connection is secured by the means of SSL, the front-end server communicates with the back-end server in clear mode (no use of SSL).
Exchange Front-End Server	Active Directory Domain Controller	389/TCP (LDAP)	Access required for the front-end server to access the DC (required to retrieve Exchange configuration information queries).

Source	Destination	Port/Protocol	Description
Exchange Front-End Server	Global Catalog	3268/TCP (LDAP)	Access required for the front-end server to access the GC (required to determine on which back-end server a user's mailbox is located).
Exchange Front-End Server	Global Catalog	88/TCP (Kerberos)	Access required for the front-end server for mailbox access authentication.
Exchange 2000 Front-End Server	Global Catalog	88/UDP (Kerberos)	Access required for the front-end server for mailbox access authentication.
Exchange Front-End Server	DNS Server	53/TCP (DNS Lookup)	Access required for the front-end server to resolve names for back-end server, DCs, GCs, etc.
Exchange Front-End Server	DNS Server	53/UDP (DNS Lookup)	Access required for the front-end server to resolve names for back-end server, DCs, GCs, etc.
Exchange Front-End Server	Global Catalog	135/TCP (RPC Port Mapper)	RPC end-point mapper for the front-end server to query the AD services. This connection will return the RPC service port used by the AD service upon startup of the DC or GC.
Exchange Front-End Server	Global Catalog	1127/TCP (Active Directory service)	This is a fixed IP port, which the AD uses to advertise its service for replication and logon. Windows normally assigns the port dynamically in the upper 1,024–65,365 range. In a DMZ environment, you can hardcode the port to force Windows to always use a fixed port.
Exchange Front-End Server	Global Catalog	445/TCP (SMB for NetLogon)	SMB traffic for the NetLogon service, required for communication and authentication of the services.
Exchange Front-End Server	Global Catalog	123/TCP (NTP)	Network Time Protocol required for synchronizing the time between the various machines. You can use the GC as the time source to synchronize all the servers.

To define a specific port for the AD to use for the logon service on DCs and GCs, set the following key in the registry on the DCs and GCs that serve the mailbox servers:

```
HKLM\System\CurrentControlSet\Services\NTDS\Parameters
Value name: TCP/IP Port
Value type: REG_DWORD
Value data: 1127 (or whatever port you elect to use)
```

Glossary

A: Address record. A DNS resource record that maps a Fully Qualified Domain Name (FQDN) to an IP address.

ACE: Access Control Entry, or the basic unit of Windows 2000 security. ACEs control access to NTFS files and AD objects. They consist of a security principal (SID) and an access mask, which define the access rights for the SID.

ACL: Access Control List, a set of ACEs that defines the rights to a file or AD object.

AD: Active Directory, the directory service used by Windows and associated applications, such as Exchange 2000/2003.

ADC: The Active Directory Connector, the component that controls synchronization between the AD and the Exchange 5.5 DS. The ADC manages one or more connection agreements that define how and when the two directories synchronize objects.

Administration group: A collection of Exchange 2000 and Exchange 2003 servers that share common administration policies.

ADO: Application Data Objects or Active Data Objects. A programming layer built on top of OLE/DB that allows high-level programming languages such as Visual BASIC to access a data store via a common query language.

ADSI: Active Directory Services Interface, the API used to programmatically manipulate AD objects. The interface is supported by COM-compatible programming languages, such as Visual BASIC, Vbscript, and C++.

API: Application Programming Interface.

ASN.1: A method of encoding X.400 messages.

ASP: Application Service Provider. A company acting as a service provider that focuses on delivery of a specific application rather than just facilitating access to the Internet.

Attribute: A characteristic of an Active Directory object—for example, a user's password. Attributes are also referred to as "properties."

Basic disk: The default logical disk partition configuration for Windows. Cluster resources are only able to use basic disks, which can contain primary partitions and extended partitions with logical drives. By default, all Windows disks are basic unless you convert them to dynamic disks.

BLOB: Binary Large Object.

CA: Certification Authority. A service that issues and manages X.509 certificates that can then be used to secure communications, such as browser to server Web transactions or encryption and signing of email messages.

CAL: Client Access License. Every client that connects to Exchange must have a CAL.

CDO: Collaboration Data Objects, a programmable interface designed to make it easier for programmers to manipulate complex objects such as a mailbox or collection of messages.

Child domain: A Windows domain whose DNS name is subordinate to another domain. For example, sales.hp.com is subordinate to the hp.com domain. A child domain is also called a subdomain.

Cluster: A set of individual computers connected together and capable of acting as a single server.

Connection agreement: The specifications for a synchronization link between the AD and the DS. A connection agreement determines exactly what objects are synchronized and when synchronization occurs. It may also determine how new objects are created in a directory and whether any organizational unit remapping occurs.

Container: An Active Directory object that holds groups of objects and other containers.

DCPROMO: The process that you use to promote a Windows member server or standalone server to become a DC by creating a replica of the AD and joining or creating a domain. You can also use the process to demote a DC.

DDNS: Dynamic DNS. The facility that allows DHCP and Windows clients to dynamically update DNS records (in the AD or a DNS database) instead of using the traditional method of manually or programmatically adding the data to static DNS files.

Delegation: The capability of an administrative authority to grant specific rights to groups and individuals.

DFS: Distributed File System.

DHCP: Dynamic Host Configuration Protocol, a protocol for assigning IP addresses on a dynamic basis within a network. DHCP is also able to assign network configuration details to clients, such as the addresses of default gateways, WINS servers, and DNS servers.

Digital certificate: An attachment on a data stream that can be used to confirm the sender's identity or that encrypts the data.

DN: Distinguished Name. A unique description of an object and its path within the AD. For example: CN=Tony Redmond, OU=Ireland, DC=QEMEA, DC=CPQCORP, DC=NET. Unlike the Exchange 5.5 DS, the AD does not use the DN as the primary key for directory objects.

DNS: Domain Name Service. A service that translates IP addresses to names and vice versa.

Domain tree: A Windows domain hierarchy, connected by transitive trusts to form a contiguous namespace.

Down-level trust: A trust explicitly established between a Windows 2000/2003 domain and a Windows NT 4.0 or 3.51 domain.

DS: The Exchange 5.5 Directory Store. The repository that holds information about users, servers, and other objects on Exchange 4.0, 5.0, and 5.5 servers.

DSA: Directory Services Agent, the process that manages physical storage for the AD.

Dynamic disk: A disk that supports volume sets. Dynamic disks cannot contain partitions or logical drive.

EDB: Exchange database, or MAPI property database. The database used to store messages generated by MAPI clients and the properties of messages generated by any client.

EML: Exchange Mail Link, the file extension allocated by ExIFS and OWA for Exchange mail messages.

EMO: Exchange Management Objects. A set of programmable objects that can be manipulated to perform management operations on an Exchange server.

Encryption: The process of taking readable data (plain text) and making it unreadable (cypertext) by applying an encryption algorithm.

Epoxy: A high-speed interprocess communication layer based on shared memory that is used to connect the Exchange Store process to IIS.

ESM: Exchange System Manager. The name of the MMC snap-in provided to manage Exchange servers and server-side configuration objects such as administration and routing groups.

ESMTP: Extended or Enhanced SMTP. The mechanism that allows developers to add new functionality to the basic SMTP protocol.

ExIFS (or IFS): The Exchange Installable File System, a kernel-level file system that maps Exchange objects as if they were files.

Explicit trust: A trust that you manually establish between two Windows domains, or between a Windows 2000/2003 domain and a down-level domain.

Forest: One or more domain trees that do not form a contiguous namespace but share a common schema and configuration data. A forest can only support a single Exchange organization.

FQDN: Fully Qualified Domain Name, a DNS term that describes a host name plus the full path to the host that contains all domain memberships from left to right—for example, Windows2000.Engineering.hp.com.

FSMO: Flexible Single Master Operations (otherwise known as Operations Masters). There are five FSMO roles, also called operations masters, in a Windows forest. Two of these are forest-wide, while three are domain-wide. FSMOs are authoritative masters for specific functions, such as the PDC emulator or schema master, and are consulted by other DCs as the need occurs.

GAL: Global Address List. A complete list of all of the mail-enabled objects—users, groups, contacts, and visible public folders found in an Exchange organization.

Global Catalog (GC): An index containing every AD object within the forest. A full set of attributes is maintained for objects from the domain where the GC is situated, together with a reduced set of attributes (to limit replication activity) for objects from other domains. Exchange uses the GC as the source of the GAL and to make decisions on how best to route messages.

GPO: Group Policy Object. Group policies allow administrators to define settings for groups of users and computers to simplify management.

GUID: Globally Unique Identifier. A very large (128-bit) number used to identify objects within the AD and for other purposes.

HTTP: Hypertext Transport Protocol. The basic protocol used to communicate between Web browsers and servers.

HTTP-DAV: Hypertext Transport Protocol with Distributed Authoring and Versioning extensions. Also known as WebDAV.

ICMP: Internet Control Message Protocol.

IETF: Internet Engineering Task Force, the body responsible for defining Internet protocols.

IIS: Internet Information Server.

IMAP: Internet Mail Access Protocol Version 4. An Internet client messaging protocol used by clients such as Outlook Express that Exchange supports.

IMC: Internet Mail Connector. The connector used to link Exchange 4.0 servers with other SMTP messaging systems.

IMS: Internet Mail Service. The connector used by Exchange 5.0 and 5.5 to connect to other SMTP messaging systems.

Inheritance: The ability of a child object to automatically acquire specific rights from a parent object.

IP address: A numbering method to uniquely identify a node and to specify routing information on a network using the TCP/IP protocol. Each node on the network must have a unique IP address, which consists of the network identifier and a unique host identifier assigned by the network administrator. IP addresses can also be assigned dynamically to clients by a DHCP server.

IPSec: IP security, a method to authenticate and encrypt data at the IP level.

ISP: Internet Service Provider. A company that offers consumers or organizations access to Internet services, including Web, email, and NNTP.

KCC: Knowledge Consistency Checker. An AD function that monitors and dynamically configures replication connection objects between DCs.

KDC: Key Distribution Center. A Kerberos function that runs on every DC to control the distribution of keys and tickets.

Kerberos: An authentication protocol defined by the IETF in RFC 1510. Kerberos is the standard authentication protocol used by Windows 2000/2003.

LDAP: Lightweight Directory Access Protocol, a standards-based protocol for directory access defined by the IETF.

LRA: LDAP Replication Agent. The process within the ADC that handles the replication of directory information between the DS and the AD.

LSA: Link State Algorithm. The mechanism used by Exchange 2000/2003 servers to update each other with information about the current state of the network.

MDB: Mail Database. A combination of an EDB database and a streaming file.

MIME: Multipurpose Internet Mail Extensions.

MMC: Microsoft Management Console. A framework that establishes a common user interface for management tasks. Applications provide MMC snap-ins to insert into the console to perform specific management tasks.

MTA: Message Transport Agent.

Namespace: A bounded area in which a name can be resolved. In the AD, the namespace is equal to the directory tree, and DNS is used to resolve names.

NC: Naming Context. The AD unit of replication. The AD supports three naming contexts, and all objects fall into one of these contexts. Objects are then replicated according to the boundaries established by the contexts.

NNTP: Network News Transport Protocol.

NSE: Namespace Extension. Commonly used to describe the technique of extending the common file namespace exposed by Windows Explorer to handle objects held in other repositories such as the Store.

NSPI: Name Service Provider Interface, the interface that MAPI clients use to access the GAL.

NTLM: The Windows NT LAN Manager challenge/response authentication mechanism. NTLM is the standard authentication mechanism used in Windows NT 4.0 and supported in Windows 2000 and 2003. If applications don't support Kerberos, a DC automatically downgrades and attempts to use NTLM to establish credentials.

Object: A collection of attributes that represents a self-contained entity—for example, a user or group.

OID: Object identifier. A globally unique identifier required by OSI international standards to identify an X.500 object.

OLE/DB: An API that allows low-level programming languages such as C and C++ to access data stores through a common query language. Exchange supports OLE/DB access to the Store.

OSI: Open Systems Interconnection.

OU: Organizational Unit, a named section of the AD that is used to collect objects in a convenient manner.

Parent domain: A Windows domain that has another domain subordinate to it in the DNS namespace.

PFH: Public Folder Hierarchy. Exchange 2000 and 2003 support multiple public folder hierarchies, whereas previous versions only supported the single default hierarchy.

PKI: Public Key Infrastructure. A system of digital certificates, certification authorities, and other registration authorities that verify and authenticate the validity of parties engaged in an electronic transaction.

POP3: Post Office Protocol Version 3. An Internet client messaging protocol that Exchange supports.

Private key: One half of a key pair that is kept private to a user and then used to decrypt data encrypted with a user's public key.

PTR: A DNS pointer record that maps an IP address to an FQDN. Often referred to as a reverse lookup record.

Replication topology: The configuration of the replication scheme between DCs in a forest.

RFC: Request For Comments, the basic definition of an Internet protocol as agreed upon by the IETF.

RID: Relative Identifier. A component of the SID.

Root domain: The top-level domain in a Windows domain tree. Also the top-level DNS domain in the Internet.

Routing group: A collection of Exchange 2000 and 2003 servers that share a common routing table. All of the servers within a routing group make automatic and consistent connections to each other to send messages.

RR: Resource record. A DNS zone file entry. DNS RRs include Start of Authority (SOA), Mail Exchange (MX), host, CNAME, and service (SRV). Each RR describes different types of information about hosts (computers) in the DNS domain. Windows 2000 uses DNS as the location service for network resources such as DCs and GCs, both of which are identified by service records.

SAS: Secure Attention Sequence. The CTRL/Alt/Del key sequence used to begin a login or authentication sequence.

Schema: The definition of all the object types and attributes that can be stored by the AD. Exchange extends the schema to add definitions of its own attributes, such as mailbox quotas.

SID: Security identifier. A unique number that identifies a user or group within a Windows domain.

Signed data: Data with a digital certificate attached as proof of origin or authenticity.

Site: A collection of DCs that share a high-speed (LAN quality) network and defined by one or more IP subnets. Sites also define locality for client workstations. Similar in concept and definition to the term used by previous versions of Exchange.

Site connector: The link over which replication between two sites occurs. You can use TCP/IP or SMTP links for this purpose.

Site link: A means of weighing the relative cost of replication between sites.

SMB: Simple Message Block.

SMP: Symmetric Multiprocessing.

SMS: Short Message Service, a method of sending messages between cell phones over the GSM/GPRS standard. An alternate definition is System Management Server, a Microsoft product designed to simplify management tasks such as software distribution and inventory.

SMTP: Simple Mail Transport Protocol.

Snap-in: A management object that can be added to the MMC to perform specific tasks, such as Exchange system management or AD user management.

SOA RR: A DNS Start of Authority Resource Record.

SRS: Site Replication Services. The ADC component that replicates site configuration data between Exchange 2000/2003 and downstream Exchange servers.

SSL: Secure Sockets Layer.

SSP: Security Support Provider. Windows supports plug-in security services. Windows NT only supports NTLM, but Windows 2000 supports Kerberos, PKI, and NTLM.

SSPI: Security Support Provider Interface. The API used by applications to access SSPs such as Kerberos.

STM: Streaming file or database. Exchange directs incoming Internet content to this repository, which holds messages generated by Internet (IMAP, POP3) clients.

TCP/IP: Transmission Control Protocol/Internet Protocol.

Ticket: A Kerberos object that contains user information, access rights, an expiration time, and some NT-specific security information.

Titanium: The internal Microsoft code name for Exchange 2003.

TLD: Top-Level Domain. A DNS term that describes the top of the DNS domain hierarchy—for example, .com.

Transitive trust: A trust between Windows domains that allows referrals from one domain to another.

Tree: A group of domains that form a contiguous namespace and share a common schema and configuration data. The name of the tree is always the same as the domain's DNS name.

UNC: Universal Naming Convention.

UPN: User Principal Name. A UPN consists of the user's logon name and the DNS name of the domain where the account resides in—for example, Tony.Redmond@test.hp.com.

URL: Unique Resource Locator. The format used to address Web objects.

USN: Update Sequence Number. A 64-bit number that Windows uses to track updates to objects and attributes. It is the basis of all AD replication activities.

VS: Virtual Server. A logical instance of a server that offers a particular service such as SMTP or HTTP to clients. A physical computer may host many virtual servers. Also sometimes referred to as a VSI (Virtual Server Instance).

WBEM: Web-Based Enterprise Management. Formerly known as WMI.

Web storage system: The term used by Microsoft when it first released Exchange 2000 to describe the ability of objects held in the Exchange Store to be addressed through standard URLs. Now referred to as the "Exchange Store" or simply just "Store."

WINS: Windows Internet Naming Service.

WLBS: Windows Load Balancing Services.

WMI: Windows Management Instrumentation. A specification for allowing management applications to share information across disparate environments.

WSH: Windows Script Host or Windows Scripting Host. A facility to run scripted procedures to execute management or administrative operations on a Windows server.

XML: Extensible Markup Language.

XSL: Extensible Stylesheet Language.

XSO: Exchange System Objects, an interface first provided by Exchange 2003 to allow programmatic access to Exchange objects.

X.400: The international standard for messaging interoperability that has now largely been surpassed by the combination of SMTP and MIME.

X.500: A comprehensive definition of a standard for enterprise directories. Many directories, including the DS and the AD, are derived from X.500. However, these directories are not fully X.500 compliant, because they do not support the X.500 access protocols.

X.509: A standard for digital certificates used by Kerberos and Exchange advanced security.

Index

64-bit windows, 542–43, 544
–1018 errors, 15, 456, 457
–1019 errors, 456, 458
–1022 errors, 456, 458

Access control, 136–45
   administrative delegation, 138–45
   example, 137–38
   models, 137
Access Control Entries (ACEs), 136, 502
Access Control Lists (ACLs)
   elements, 136
   public folder, 502, 518
   upgrade, 521
Accounts, 160–72
   administrative, removing, 154
   advanced options, 732
   creating, 161, 724–28
   deleting, 775–76
   display names, 725, 727
   maintaining accuracy, 730
   moving, between forests, 117
   naming, 724
   naming policies, 726–27
   naming schemes, 726
   policies, 725

   user, 160–72
   See also Users
Active/active clustering, 452
Active Directory (AD), 26, 35–132
   access configuration, 362
   components, 39–40
   contents illustration, 40
   database size, 66
   design, 98–99
   GUIDs, 50
   high watermark vector tables, 47
   ideal, 36
   implementation, 37
   membership processing, 176
   multimaster model, 151
   namespace, 40, 41
   naming contexts (NCs), 50–53
   object storage, 39
   populating, with organizational information, 729
   preparing, 45–46
   public folders in, 518
   replication, 46–67
   tools, 124–32
   Users and Computers, 163, 164, 172, 729

   user table in, 57, 58, 59
   USNs, 48
   write operations, 50
   See also Forests
Active Directory Connector (ADC), 17, 23, 67–82
   bidirectional synchronization support, 67, 68
   connection agreements (CAs), 70–75, 78–79
   connection agreements (CAs) scheduling, 77–78
   synchronization, 76–77
   unidirectional synchronization support, 67
   versions, 69
ActiveSync, 368, 371–73
   client-side, 376
   defined, 371
   server, 372
   synchronization conflict, 380
   synchronization modes, 372
   synchronization settings, 380
ADCUserCheck, 30
Address Book, 75

Administration Delegation
wizard, 141–43
  invoking, 141
  running, 142
Administrative delegation,
  138–45
Administrative flexibility,
  31–32
Administrative groups, 145–56
  adding, 150
  changing and, 152–53
  as containers, 148
  current, 150
  defined, 146
  defining, 146–48
  delegating control over, 141
  displaying, 151
  division of functions, 157
  icon, 149
  moving from sites to,
    148–52
  multiple, 153
  multiple routing groups
    within, 158
  renaming and, 152
  routing groups and, 156,
    157–58
  separating routing into, 159
  special, 146
Administrative permissions,
  144–45
Administrators, 151, 152
  deleted items cache and,
    775
  up-to-date on threats, 802
  user account information,
    728
AD schema
  attributes set in, 44
  changes, registry values
    allowing, 112
  changing, 109–12

Exchange and, 104–15
  extensibility, 104
  ForestPrep and, 26
  inconsistencies, 46
  loading, into memory, 112
  snap-in, 111
  update impact, 106
  updating, for ambiguous
    name resolution,
    112–13
  updating, with installation,
    106–9
  version, checking, 105
  viewing attributes in, 111
  See also Active Directory
    (AD)
ADSIEDIT utility, 53, 83,
  124–30, 736, 823,
  880
  adding, to console, 126
  benefits, 108
  connecting, to naming
    context, 127
  default, 125
  defined, 124
  as double-edged sword, 124
  editing database locations
    with, 882
  illustrated, 127
  for LegacyExchangeDN
    attribute discovery,
    238
  in removing references, 130
  in schema version report,
    105–6
  snap-in, loading, 125
  in updating server
    properties, 897
ADSI programming interface,
  131–32
  providers, 132
  support, 131–32

Advanced Queuing, 606
  defined, 599–600
  functions, 600
Advanced Security snap-in, 717
Advanced Spam Defense, 708
Affinity, 519
AirSync standard, 375
Ambiguous Name Resolution
  (ANR), 111
  attributes for, 113
  enabling, 114
  invocation, 112
  process, 112
  support, 111
  updating schema for,
    112–13
Antigen, 812, 813
Antispam software, 682, 683
  defined, 682
  running, 804
Antivirus protection policy, 806
Antivirus tools, 807–13
  agreement on, 805
  Antigen, 812, 813
  GroupShield, 812
  impact on multilingual
    clients, 810–11
  list of, 812
  MAPI and, 807–8
  MAPI logons, 810
  ScanMail, 812, 813
  selecting, 811–13
  vendors, 808
Antivirus Web sites, 805
Apple Macintosh
  connection options, 364
  Entourage, 365
  Outlook for, 365
  supporting, 364–65
Application development, 33
Application Event Log, 470
  browsing, 924

errors in, 862
events, 924
Application Solution Providers, 345
Archiving
  auto, 276–77
  enabling, at Mailbox Store, 759
  messages, 757–64
  Outlook folders, 276
  PSTs, 275–77
  SMTP, 671–75, 760
  standard mailbox, 760
  user-based, 760
ARPANET, 681
ASP.NET, 25
Atomicity, Consistency, Isolation, Durability (ACID), 401–3
  compliance, 402–3
  defined, 402
  transactions, 402
Attachments
  blocking configuration, 325
  EDB databases and, 417
  handling, 323–24
  large file, 787–89
  OWA expiration dates for, 350
  Pocket PC and, 383
  suspect, 801–2
  table, 408
  type identification, 324
Attribute-level replication, 175
Attributes
  accessing, for mail-enabled objects, 163–68
  for building queries, 189
  indexing, 111
  multivalued, 110
  name of, 110

  in query-based groups, 191–92
  single-valued, 110
  syntax type, 110
  viewing, 111
Authentication, 202–3
  forms-based, 316
  Kerberos, 202
  user, 741–44
Authentication Header Protocol, 348
Auto Accept Agent, 16
Auto-archiving, 276–77
AUTODL utility, 180
Automatic topology detection, 91
Auto-signature files, 783–85
  corporate information, 785
  graphically rich, 784
  HTML code added to, 797
  illustrated, 85
  netiquette, 783

Backfilling, 516–17
Background maintenance, 463–72
  backups and, 464
  common events, 471–72
  control of, 463
  deleted folders check, 466
  deleted mailbox check, 466–67
  deleted public folders check, 467
  message examination, 466
  recorded events, 472
  registry settings, 468–70
  scheduling, 464–65
  setting, through server policy, 465
  tasks, 465–68
  tasks, registry settings, 470

  tasks list, 464
  tombstone, 466
  tracking, 470–72
Backup agents, 837, 843, 844
Backups, 832–66
  checkpoint file and, 842–43
  concurrent processes, 848
  differential, 840
  to disk, 549
  full, 837–40
  hot, 52, 550, 550–52
  incremental, 840
  individual mailboxes, 852–53
  online, 832, 834
  operation flow, 848
  operations, 837–41
  patch files, 841–42
  in progress, 838
  as snapshots, 832
  storage groups and, 836–37
  strategy, creating, 833–36
  third-party utilities, 847–52
  times, 834–35
  timestamp, 841
  transaction logs and, 838, 839
  VSS-based, 554
  See also Restores
Backup Wizard, 836, 837
Bandwidth
  consumption reduction, 634
  optimization, 288–89
  "reply all" and, 786–87
  between routing groups, 663
BDAT, 586–88
Benchmarks, 547
Bidirectional connection agreements, 71, 73
Bidirectional synchronization, 74
  defined, 68

Bidirectional synchronization (cont'd.)
  gain, 74
  support, 67
  See also Synchronization
BlackBerries, 384–95
  filters, setting, 389
  keyboard, 390, 391
  PIN-to-PIN communications, 385
  Pocket PC vs., 392
  SMS messages on, 385
  solution, 386
  speed, 390
  synchronization, 392
  usage, 385
  using, 390–92
BlackBerry Enterprise Server (BES), 386–90
  Attachment Server, 391
  connectivity, 386
  filters, 389
  installing, 386
  issues, 387–88
  message transfer, 387
  registering devices with, 388
  service packs, 387, 391
  SRP, 387
  using, 390–92
Blackhole lists, 690–92
  providers, 690–91, 692
  support, 691
BLAT utility, 162, 397
Blocked Senders list, 243, 244, 245
  illustrated, 244
  setup with OWA, 306
Blocking
  clients for IP access, 236–37
  Outlook clients, 235–36
  selective, 237–39
  values required for, 238

Bluetooth connectivity, 377
Branding, OWA, 341–42
Brightmail Anti-Spam for Exchange, 708
Browsers, 292
  IE4, 302
  IE5, 302–3
  IE6, 303, 307, 311, 351, 375
  rich, feature support, 305–7
B+trees, 406
B-tree structure, 405
Build numbers, 718–19
  determining with ESM, 719
  viewing, 719

Cached Exchange mode, 211–13
  advantage, 214
  as default option, 206
  deploying, 220–24
  problems, 220–21
  setting up, 212
Cached-mode mailboxes, 169–70
Calendar
  interoperability, 118–20
  local, 283–85
  OWA functionality, 342
Categorized Message Queue, 602
Categorizer, 600
Certificate Server, 25
Change Number Sets (CNS), 512
Chat, 25
Chat Networks snap-in, 717
Checkpoint file, 414–16
  access, 414
  availability, 415
  backups and, 842–83
  checkpoint, advancing, 421

defined, 414
  header dump, 415
  removing, 416
  in soft recoveries, 842
CHKDSK, 477
Chunking, 586–88
Circular logging, 423, 435–36, 436, 441
  benefits, 435
  disabled, 431
  enabling, for storage group, 436
  use of, 436
Citrix terminal services, 364
Client access license (CAL), 398
Clients
  access, blocking, 232–35
  blocking, for Internet Protocol access, 236–37
  block registry setting, 234
  IMAP4, 353–61
  licenses, 398
  Linux, 366–67
  multilingual, 810–11
  new types, integrating, 196
  Outlook, blocking, 235–36
  Outlook 2003 as best, 228–30
  OWA, 195, 314
  Pocket PC, 375–84
  POP3, 195, 361
  publishing free/busy information, 262
  selective blocks, 237–39
  sending messages without, 395–98
  UNIX, 366–67
  Web-based, 291–93
Client-side rules, 239

Clones, 550–51
    defined, 550
    illustrated, 551
Cluster Administrator utility, 26
Clusters, 556–80
    active-active, 452, 568
    basics, 560–80
    complexity, 558–59
    decision, 575–77
    decision not to use, 576–77
    defined, 440
    dependencies, 567
    designs, 566
    Exchange 2003 and, 577–79
    ExchDump on, 912
    hardware, 558
    history, 556–57
    installing Exchange on, 565–66
    management services, 560
    memory fragmentation and, 567–71
    names, 562–63
    not supported, 566–67
    operation requirements, 558
    performance monitor, 571
    pros/cons, 576
    quality/robustness, 558
    registry, 563–64
    resource groups, 560–65
    resource models, 567
    resources, 560
    second-generation, 557–59
    service implementation, 559
    state transition, 568
    storage groups on, 440
    stretched, 574–75
    successful deployments (Exchange 2003), 579
    summary, 579–80
    terms, 563–64
    upgrading, with service packs, 574
Collaboration, 32–33
Command-line switches (Outlook), 289
Compression utilities, 788
Conferencing components, 25
Conferencing Services snap-in, 717
Configuration domain controllers, 88
Configuration NC
    defined, 50
    routing information in, 52
    See also Naming contexts (NCs)
Connection agreements (CAs), 70–75
    adding multiple sites to, 74
    bidirectional, 71, 73
    configuring, 70
    defined, 70
    interorganizational, configuring, 81
    nonprimary, 78–79
    primary, 78–79
    scheduling, 77–78
    support, 70
    type determination, 71
    unidirectional, 71
    See also Active Directory Connector (ADC)
Connection filters, 690–92
    applying, to SMTP VS, 696
    defining, 693
    policy configuration, 692–93
    spam and, 696
Connection Manager, 603–4
Connection object schedule, 64
Connectors
    foreign, 609, 621
    routing group, 645–50
    SMTP, 593, 594, 620, 638, 645–46, 654–56
    status, viewing, 916
    viewing, 919
    X.400, 230, 646, 661–63
Contacts
    in AD, 722
    defined, 722
    naming convention, 728
Containers, 133
    administrative groups as, 148
    contents, 134
    Offline Address Lists, 260
    routing groups, 627
Cpqcorp.net, 43
CPUs
    extra, adding, 537
    multiple, 537–38
    performance, 533, 535
CrossOver utility, 366

Databases
    background maintenance, 463–72
    dismounted, 448
    EDB, 403–16, 417
    errors, 456–63
    ESE, 399, 403, 405
    mounted, 448
    move warning, 455
    repairing, 460, 478–80
    restoring, 843–47, 879–81
    STM, 403
    tables, 406–8
    temporary, creating, 481
    temporary "dial-tone," 874–76
    utilities, 473–84
    zeroing, 436, 441
Database utilities, 473–84

DATA command, 588
Data Definition Language
     (DDL), 400
Data Manipulation Language
     (DML), 400
Davrex.dll, 297
DCdiag, 30
Defragmentation, 476
    offline, 475
    online, 475
    success, 478
    See also ESEUTIL utility
Delegate access, 738–41
Deleted items cache
    cleaning, 770
    data display, 773
    exploring, 764–75
    as help to administrators,
         775
    item recovery, 765–67
    item size and, 768
    items removed from, 770
    recovery, enabling, 767
    retention period, 767–69
    retention period, setting,
         768, 769
    retention size, 771
    size estimation, 775
    size influences, 771
    sizing, 770–75
    "soft" deletes, 767
    total size, 773
    two-phase deletes, 767
    viewing, by mailbox, 774
Deleted Items folder, 764
    controlling, 765
    default, 766
    emptying, 768–69
Deleted mailboxes
    identifying, 866
    list, viewing, 870
    marking, 866

    reconnecting, 867
    recovering, 866–70
    viewing, 867
    See also Mailboxes
Deleted Mailbox Recovery
     feature, 853
Delivery Status Notification
     (DSN), 585–86
    defined, 585
    display, 586
    error codes, 587–88
Deployments, 5, 7, 21
Deployment tools, 28–30
Diagnostic logging, 87
    level, setting, 926
    as property of servers, 926
    turning up, 925–27
Diagnostics, 924–27
Differential backups, 840
Dijkstra's algorithm, 601, 637
Disclaimers
    abusing, 790–91
    adding, 791
    appearance of, 790
    example, 790–91
Dismounted databases, 448
Distinguished names, 190
    defined, 82
    email addresses and, 83
    OAB, 256
    relative, 190
    routing groups, 627
    viewing, 83
Distributed Server Boycott List,
     682
Distribution groups, 172–85
    advanced properties, 907
    forming, 174–77
    General properties, 173
    hiding, from GAL, 831
    limiting, 182
    maintenance problems, 90

    membership, viewing, 174
    membership processing,
         176
    number of objects in,
         178–79
    for permissions, 185
    properties, 181
    protected, 182–83
    query-based, 185–94, 830
    types of, 172
Distribution lists
    adding new members,
         179–80
    expanding, 177–78
    large, 178, 231
    managing, 179–82
    members, 180
    obsolete members,
         removing, 181
    public folder repositories for,
         184–85
    setting up, 179
DMZ
    IMF deployment in, 702
    installing Exchange servers
         in, 597–98
    servers, 702
DNS, 40
    namespaces, 43
    as Windows namespace
         foundation, 41
Document retention
    legal actions and, 777
    mailboxes and, 776–77
Document retention policies,
     744–46
    compliance, 746
    components, 745
    concept, 744
    data management, 745
    defining, 744–46
    disaster recovery, 746

document management/
  publication, 746
litigation support, 746
Mailbox Manager and, 745
Domain controllers (DCs), 9,
  23, 724
  access purposes, 36
  allocation registry values, 90
  configuration, 88
  default schedule, 63
  Global Catalog property,
    setting, 54
  installation and, 28
  requirement, 12
  responsibilities, 47
  selection for DSAccess,
    88–91
  software versions and, 24
  transforming, to GCs,
    53–55
  upgrading, 13
Domain Mapping and
  Configuration Table,
  602
Domain NC
  defined, 50
  partial replicas of, 54
  See also Naming contexts
    (NCs)
DomainPrep
  functions, 45
  Public Folder Proxy
    Container creation,
    46
  running, 26, 45, 46
  SETUP, 107
Domains
  contiguous namespace, 42
  naming context, 50
  NT resource, removing,
    154
  renaming, 44

spam monitoring, 682
unreachable, 619–22
Domain Servers group, 45
  defined, 831
  membership in, 27
DOS
  DIR command, 528
  TYPE command, 529, 530
Drag-and-drop, 305
Drizzle-mode synchronization,
  213–14
DSAccess, 55, 84–96
  automatic topology
    detection, 91
  cache, 85, 86
  DC/GC selection for, 88–91
  defined, 84
  diagnostics, setting, 93
  DS list, building, 89
  in failover situations, 87
  functions, 84–85
  ICMP pings, 92
  messaging components and,
    87
  optimum servers for, 93
  performance, 86
  registry values affecting, 85
  server data, 94–95
  SRV records and, 95–96
  suitability report, 94
  suitability tests, 92–96
  tasks, 87–88
  test categories, 92–93
  timeout, 101
DSADIAG utility, 88
DSProxy, 97, 264
DSScopeScan, 30
DS Service Agent (DSA), 80
Dynamic Buffer Allocation
  (DBA), 538, 568
  monitoring, 540
  self-tuning capability, 539

EDB database
  attachments and, 417
  defined, 403
  fields, 406–8
  file size, 404
  header, 404
  matching STM database,
    403
  page structure, 404
  restoring, 845
  streaming file and, 417
  structure, 403–16
  tables, 406–8
  trees, 404–6
Eforms Registry folder, 266
Email
  archiving, 744
  enabling, 160
  good habits, 789
  junk, processing, 239–49
  new, notifications, 239, 342
  outbound, disabling, 613
  retention policies, 750
  storms, 786–87
  viruses and, 793–807
Email addresses
  deleting, 168
  enabling, 168
  proxies, default values, 820
  in recipient policy, 819
Email viruses, 271, 793–807
  authors, 800
  damage, 800–803
  detection, 803
  document-borne, 803
  executable-based, 793
  hidden, 793
  history, 794
  HTML dangers, 797–99
  Love Bug, 800–801
  luring users, 796–97
  Melissa, 794–95

Email viruses *(cont'd.)*
  mistakes, 807
  monitoring, 805–6
  multistage protection, 803–7
  Nimda, 795
  Papa, 796
  Prank macro, 794
  security policy, 805–7
  suspect attachments, 801–2
  threats, up-to-date with, 802
  Worm.ExploreZip, 795
Encapsulating Security Payload (ESP) protocol, 348
Encryption
  SMTP communications, 654
  VSAPI and, 809
Enterprise Servers group, 831
Entourage, 365
Epoxy layer, 484–85
  defined, 484
  remote links and, 484
Error Correcting Code (ECC), 483–84
Errors, database, 456–63
  –1018, 15, 456, 457
  –1019, 456, 458
  –1022, 456, 458
  list of, 456
  recoveries, 458–63
  soft recoveries, 459–62
  types of, 456
ESE databases
  B-tree structure, 405
  errors, 456–63
  model, 399, 403
  See also Extensible Storage Engine (ESE)
ESEFILE utility, 482
  location, 473
  processing speed, 482

  purpose, 473, 482
  replacement, 482
ESEUTIL utility, 275, 285, 439, 449, 774
  in database rebuilding, 463, 476–78
  in database repair, 460, 463
  /D, 476–78
  defined, 473
  defragmentation, 475, 476, 478
  hard repair, 478
  location, 473
  low disk space and, 480–81
  misapplication of, 474
  offline rebuild and, 476
  /P, 478–80
  purpose, 473
  rebuild steps, 477
  repair mode, 478–80
  running, 474–81, 872–73
  speed, 478
  STM file creation, 480
  temporary database creation, 481
  uses, 464
ESMTP, 591
ESX Server, 555
Events Root folder, 266
Event Viewer, 924, 925
Exadmin, 326
Exchange
  ACID, 401–3
  Active Directory (AD) and, 35–132
  AD schema and, 104–15
  antispam add-on products, 690
  basics, 133–94
  client licenses, 20
  clustering, 556–57
  cluster resource models, 567

  competition, 20–22
  design documents, 2–3
  development group, 21
  development of, 2
  essential services, 918
  first generation, 1–5
  history of, 1–34
  IIS applications, 326
  management snap-ins, 716–18
  managing, 711–813
  Mobile Services, 367–75
  monitoring, 915–24
  MX records and, 622–23
  performance, 533–49
  running, in multiple forests, 115–24
  second generation, 5–13
  SMTP extensions in, 585–92
  stretched clusters and, 574–75
  support matrix, 13
  third generation, 18–22
  URL namespace, 333–37
  version 4.0, 2
  version 5.0, 3–4
  Windows combinations, 12
  Windows timeline and, 11
  WMI and, 929
Exchange 5.5, 4
  data replication, 69
  directory, 6
  moving from, 16–18
  multiple organizations, synchronizing, 79–80
  permissions, 518
  public folder replication, 517–18
  routing calculation, 639
  server management, 82
  server migration, 22–23

sites, 148
Windows 2003 and, 24
Exchange 2000
   Advanced Properties, 165
   Chat, 25
   Conferencing components, 25
   deployments, 5, 7, 21
   ESM, 714–15
   Key Management Server (KMS), 25
   move to Exchange 2003 and, 22
   Outlook network activity connected to, 224
   OWA, 293
   upgrade schedule, 24
   Windows 2003 and, 24
   Windows and, 12
Exchange 2003, 8–9
   administrative flexibility, 31–32
   advantages, 7
   capabilities, 34
   clusters and, 577–79
   collaboration, 32–33
   deployment, 23–30
   ESM, 166
   Exchange Mobile Services, 367–75
   Features Property page, 165
   focus, 9
   IIS changes in, 296
   installation procedure, 27
   Mailbox Recovery Center, 853
   message compression, 225
   message tracking changes, 899
   move preparation steps, 22–23
   Outlook network activity connected to, 224
   queues, 615–16
   queue viewer, 613, 614
   running, 8
   server installation, 17
   SP1, 14–18
   VSS use with, 554–55
   Windows support, 12
Exchange Development Kit (EDK), 637
ExchangeDSAccessProvider, 95
Exchange Installable File System. *See* ExIFS
Exchange Server Objects (XSOs), 33
Exchange servers
   configuration evolutions, 534
   dependencies, 561
   installing, in DMZ, 597–98
   I/O, 535
   manageability, 535
   message tracking and, 893
   multi-CPU, 535, 538
   MX records and, 623
   properties, 896
   properties, updating, 897–99
   quantity, 535
   recoverability, 535
   resilience, 535
   restoring, 853–56
   status, 916
   viewing, 919
   virtual, 555–56
Exchange-specific property pages, 163–64
   Email Addresses, 163–64
   Exchange Advanced, 164
   Exchange Features, 164
   Exchange General, 163
Exchange Stress and Performance (ESP), 545
Exchange System Manager (ESM), 14, 36, 52, 53, 470, 711–16
   in build number determination, 719
   configuration DC use, 88
   default behavior, 433
   defined, 711
   essential Exchange services, 918
   Exchange 2000, 714–15
   Exchange 2003, 166
   functionality, 713
   Global Settings, 702
   Mailbox Manager integration, 747
   managing Exchange through, 712
   Message Delivery, 703
   monitoring and, 918–19
   mounting/dismounting databases with, 448
   new columns, 714
   OAB properties, 258
   public folder management, 716
   routing groups and, 157
   running, on workstations, 720–21
   server types shown by, 713
   snap-ins, 718
   storage group creation, 453
   upgrade, 713–14
ExchDump, 909–15
   on cluster, 912
   command-line switches, 910–11
   downloading, 910
   files, 912

ExchDump (cont'd.)
    full-text report from, 913
    HTML summary output, 912
    processing time, 913–14, 915
    run illustration, 914
    running, 910–15
    value, 914–15
ExchUtil, 910
Exchweb, 326
ExDeploy toolset, 22
    defined, 28
    illustrated, 29
    tools, 29–30
ExIFS, 522–31
    architecture, 525
    default letter, 526
    defined, 522
    design, 523
    drive, hiding, 527
    exposing, 527
    flaws, 531
    folder creation, 527
    functioning, 523–24
    hiding, 524
    HTTP-DAV and, 524
    as internal file system, 524
    letters, 526–27
    mailbox content, 526
    role, 525–31
    for Store access, 523
ExMerge utility, 763, 864, 865, 884–92
    in batch mode, 891
    defined, 884
    for detecting mailboxes, 891
    for exporting mailbox data, 865, 874
    export process, 888
    features, 890
    importing mailboxes, 889

import options, 886
item selection functionality, 890
log file, 888–89
mailbox data recovery, 881–83
mailbox selection, 887
Mailbox Stores display, 887
in moving mailboxes, 889
one-step process, 881
options, 885, 886
scripting runs, 891
two-step process, 881
for viewing mailbox information, 886
wizard-based format, 885
Extensible Storage Engine (ESE), 18
    balance tree technology, 404–5
    B+trees, 406
    checkpoint file, 414–16
    defined, 400
    evolution, 19
    inconsistencies and, 419
    indexes, 418
    LRCK algorithm, 434
    optimization, 401
    recovery instances, 843
    scalability, 401
    See also ESE databases

Failures, 833–34
    categories, 833
    decisions, 834
Fan-out, 907–8
Favorites, public folder, 498–99
File Replication Services (FRS), 67
Filters
    BlackBerry, 389
    connection, 690–92

LDAP, 51
    message, 687–90
    recipient, 697–99
    sender, 695–97
Firewalls, 344–50
Folders utility (Outlook), 495–96, 717
    defined, 495
    illustrated, 496
Foreign connectors, 609, 621
ForestPrep
    running, 26
    SETUP, 107
Forests
    creation of, 61
    moving accounts/mailboxes between, 117
    multiple, 37–39, 115–24
    trees, 42
    See also Active Directory (AD)
Forms-based authentication, 316
    defined, 316
    enabling, 317
Forwarding
    address, using, 779
    address specification, 778
Free/busy information, 262–66
    age limit, 264
    client publishing, 262
    MDBVU32 utility and, 265–66
    publication control, 264
    setting, 265–66
    system folders for, 263
FreeDocs, 336–37
    defined, 336
    supported values, 337
FrontPage, 798
Full backups
    completion, 840

Index

daily, 851
starting, 839
steps, 837–40
See also Backups

GALSync, 118
GC logon cache, 102–3
defined, 102
enabling, 103
implementing, 103
GET commands, 332
Global Address Lists (GALs), 36, 51, 727
default, 829, 830
hiding mailboxes/ distribution groups from, 831
name resolution with, 261
viewing query-based groups from, 193
well-organized, 728
Global Catalogs (GCs), 9, 23, 44–45
access purposes, 36
allocation registry values, 90
application load and, 99
client interaction, 96–103
contents, 44
defined, 44
hardware availability and, 99
importance, 45
number needed, 98–101
objects, 47
performance problems and, 101
requirement, 12
selection for DSAccess, 88–91
software versions and, 24
transforming DCs to, 53–55
upgrading, 13
See also GC logon cache

Global message delivery settings, 675, 680–81
default values, 680
defined, 680
properties, 680
uses, 681
Global messaging settings, 675–81
defined, 675
delivery, 675, 680–81
Internet message formats, 675, 676–80
Internet Messaging, 675
Mobile Access, 675
Good handheld software, 392–93
GoodLink server software, 393
GPRS mobile phone protocol, 385
Groups, 90, 172–85
in AD, 722
defined, 722
forming, 174–77
General properties, 173
limiting, 182
membership, hiding/ revealing, 167
membership, viewing, 174
membership processing, 176
naming convention, 728
number of objects in, 178–79
for permissions, 185
properties, 181
protected, 182–83
query-based, 185–94
resource, 560–65
types of, 172
universal, 172
GroupShield, 812
GUIDs, 50, 76

GWART, 626–27, 632
generation, 639
static, 637

Hard recoveries, 462–63
defined, 458
goal, 462
log file availability and, 463
requirements, 462
soft recoveries and, 463
See also Errors, database
Hardware Compatibility List (HCL), 557
High Speed Circuit Switched Data (HSCSD), 378
High watermark vector tables, 64–65
HomeMDB attribute, 622
Hot backups, 550
defined, 550
implementation, 552
HTML
code, creating with FrontPage, 798
code with command buttons, 799
dangers, 797–99
as Outlook default format, 210
viruses, detecting, 799
HTTP
disabling, 331
epoxy stub, 298
messages, 608
in OWA architecture, 296, 297, 298
RPC over, 207–8
HTTP-DAV, 365
ExIFS and, 524
extensions, 298–301
OWA use of, 298

HTTP-DAV, *(cont'd.)*
   PROPFIND/PROPPATCH
      commands, 299
HTTPS, 346
Hyperthreading, 542

IE
   behaviors, 304
   enhanced security, 349–50
   IE4, 302
   IE5, 302–3
   IE6, 303
      enhanced security, 351
      OWA and, 302, 303, 375
      runs reach interface, 311
      on Windows 2000/
         Windows XP
         workstations, 307
IHateSpam, 247–48
IIS
   application properties, 328
   application properties,
      viewing, 327
   changes in Exchange 2003,
      296
   Exchange applications, 326
   Exchange registration with,
      297
   "lockdown" tool for, 295
   logs, 332
IMAP
   clients, 335
   configuring access to
      Exchange, 356
   connected client details, 360
   defined, 353
   engine, 355
   features, 356
   secure logon, 744
   servers, 357, 358
   SSL, 357
   transmission cost, 354

   virtual server properties,
      359, 360
   virtual server settings,
      358–61
   IMAP4 clients, 353–64
Incremental backups, 840
Incremental Change
   Synchronization
   (ICS), 219–20
Incremental restores, 847
Incremental synchronization,
   219–20
Independent software vendors
   (ISVs), 198
Indexes, 406
Information Store. *See* Store
Installation
   on cluster, 565–66
   domain controller
      communication, 28
   Exchange servers in DMZ,
      597–98
   LocalSystem and, 156
   X.400 transport stack,
      659
Instant Messaging (IM), 25,
   167, 758
Intelligent Message Filter
   (IMF), 15, 34, 245,
   683, 699–709
   activation, 701
   applying, to SMTP virtual
      servers, 707–8
   archiving, 705
   competence, 709
   configuring, 703
   defined, 699
   deploying, 701–2
   design, 700
   installing, 702–5
   licensing, 708–9
   limit, 708

   message processing, 704
   release, 699
   spam detection, 700
IntelliSync server, 381
Internal snooping, 761–64
Internet Control Message
   Protocol (ICMP), 92
Internet Free/Busy Service, 119
Internet Key Exchange (IKE)
   protocol, 348
Internet Mail Access Protocol
   Revision 4.
   See IMAP4 clients
Internet Mail Service (IMS),
   593
Internet message formats, 675,
   676–80
   default, 677
   defined, 675
   granularity, 676
   illustrated, 676
   properties, 678
   selection used at HP, 679
   See also Global messaging
      settings
Internet Security and
   Acceleration (ISA)
   server, 9, 344, 347
   integration, 9
   uses, 347
InterOrg Replication Utility,
   119, 503
Intersite Topology Generator
   (ISTG), 62
   connection objects created
      by, 62
   defined, 61
IPSec, 347–49
   applying, 348
   defined, 347
   policies, 349
   protocols, 348

IP Security Policy wizard, 348–49
ISAPI, 327
ISINTEG utility, 285, 407, 463, 481–82
   defined, 473
   for fixing logical errors, 481
   hardware corruption problems and, 482
   location, 473
   purpose, 464, 473, 481
ISSCAN utility, 809

JetInit function, 458–59
JetStress, 545–46
   defined, 545
   understanding, 546
Joint Engine Technology (JET), 18, 400
   defined, 18
   top-down allocation, 570
Journal folder, 342
Junk mail, 239–49
   Blocked Senders list, 243, 244, 245
   detecting, 240
   detection accuracy, 242
   filter, 240, 241–48
   options, 241
   processing, 239–49
   processing technology, 247
   ranking, 242
   Safe Recipients list, 243–44
   Safe Senders list, 243, 245
   See also Mail; Outlook 2003
Junk Mail folder, 241, 242, 684

Kerberos authentication, 202
Kerberos V5, 741
Key Management Server (KMS), 25

Knowledge Consistency Checker (KCC), 61
   defined, 61
   replication connection setup, 62
KVS Enterprise Vault, 760

LDAP
   directory access, IMAP4/POP3, 361–64
   directory synchronization solutions, 117
   filters, 51
   mail-enabled directory entries, 364
   queries, 186, 821
   queries, executing, 190
   queries, in recipient policy, 819
   requests, 87
   search, 818
   search, executing, 363
   syntax, 131
LDAP Directory Synchronization Utility (LDSU), 38, 118
LDIFDE utility, 131
   defined, 131, 186
   output for query-based groups, 187
LDP utility, 130–31
   defined, 130
   illustrated, 131
   uses, 130
LegacyDN utility, 860–61
   defined, 860
   illustrated, 860
   running, 861
LegacyExchangeDN attribute, 82–84, 829
   for backward compatibility, 160

   defined, 83
   discovery with ADSIEDIT, 238
   indexing, 84, 237
   restores and, 859
   values, 84, 152, 861
   values, checking, 862
   values, not matching, 862
Link queues, 603–4, 621
Link state routing, 632–45
   information, viewing, 642–45
   methods, 632–33
   model, 159
   network outages and, 640
   retries and, 640–42
   update performance, 633
   updates and, 640–42
   See also Routing
Link state tables (LSTs), 625
   connection availability/cost, 635
   dynamic flux, 635
   example, 636
   last known, 626
   updating, 626, 635
Linux clients, 366–67
LoadSim, 545
Local cache, 215, 217, 285
   synchronization overhead, 215
   use philosophy, 218
Local calendar, 283–85
   access, 284
   Outlook 2000, 284
   updating, 283
LocalSystem
   benefits, 155–56
   installation and, 156
   mailbox access and, 155
   move to, 154–56
   passwords and, 155

Log Record Checksum (LRCH), 434
Love Bug, 800–801
LSA protocol, 633

Mail. *See* Email
Mailbox Cleanup Agent, 863, 866
   defined, 863
   running, 866
Mailboxes, 160–72
   administrator access and, 155
   backing up, 852–53
   cached-mode, 169–70
   creating, 161–62, 724–28
   decommissioning, 775–81
   delegate access, granting, 739–40
   deleted, recovering, 866–70
   deleting, 166
   details, maintaining, 728–31
   detecting, 891
   dividing within databases, 441
   document retention and, 776–77
   of former users, 781
   hiding, from GAL, 831
   increasing, 533
   migrating, 120–24
   moving, 166, 168–72
   moving, between forests, 117
   multiple, moving, 169
   number of, 99
   operations, 169–70
   permissions, 137
   quotas, 170
   recovering, with ExMerge, 883
   restricting, 731–33
   searching, 764
   selecting, for processing, 887
   surrogacy, 738–41
   transferred between servers, 444
   unassociated, after restore, 863
   viewing, in restored RSG, 880
Mailbox management policies, 750–52
   criteria, 751
   parts, 750–51
   server, 753
   settings, 751
Mailbox Manager, 746–57
   criteria, 751
   defined, 746
   diagnostics, 756–57
   document retention and, 745
   email and discovery, 747–49
   email retention policies, 750
   ESM integration, 747
   implementing, 737
   management policy definition, 750–52
   message classes and, 751
   notification messages, 754–56
   policy settings, 751
   processing, 754
   running, 752–54
   size criteria and, 752
   starting, 753
   summary message, 755, 756
   System Attendant process and, 756
Mailbox quotas, 733–38
   allocations by user type, 735
   applying, 736
   appropriate values, 734
   exceed actions, 734
   listing, 737
   restrictions, 731
   setting, 733–34
   small, 771
   updated, 736
Mailbox Recovery Center, 63, 853, 868–70
   centralized management, 866
   context, 870
   defined, 868
Mailbox Stores, 408–10
   enabling archiving on, 759
   ExMerge display, 887
   finding, 869
   moving, 455
   multiple, 444
   multiple, creating, 733
   properties, 454
   recovering, 858–64
   splitting, 449
   tables in, 408–10
   viewing list of, 869
Mail-enabled public folders, 496–98
   automatic, 497
   defined, 496
   illustrated, 497
   See also Public folders
MailNickname attribute, 160
Management frameworks, 927–29
   benefits, 927
   choice, 928–29
   types of, 928
Management packs, 927–28
MAPI, 123, 196–203
   components, 162
   defined, 196–97
   logons, 810
   messages, 608, 895

Index

as Outlook platform, 197
problems, 807–8
role, 196
RPCs, 203
RPCs compression
    parameters, 225
for Store access, 235
TLH, 491
MAPI clients
    authentication, 202–3
    demand estimation, 231
    OST use, 277
    pass-through proxy, 744
    RTF format, 410
    RTF support, 210
    supporting, 199–201
    types of, 96, 199
    versions, 234
    versions of connected users,
        viewing, 233
    workload, 569
MAPI profile, 97, 277
    creating, 199
    details, 200
    information, 199
    moving between
        administrative groups
        and, 201–2
    update, 170
MAPI providers
    defined, 232
    number of, 235
    version number, examining,
        233
MAPISEND utility, 396–97
    connections, 397
    defined, 396
MAPS
    defined, 691
    service providers, 693
    services, 691
Max Compression, 788

MBCONN utility, 864, 868
MDBVU32 utility, 265–66
Mean time between failures
    (MTBF), 834
Melissa virus, 794–95
Memory, 538–40
    fragmentation, 567–71
    management algorithm, 570
    monitoring with DBA, 540
    more than 1 GB, 540–42
    nonoptimal, 541
    used by Store, 539
    virtual, 571–73
Message filters
    applying, 689
    capability, 687
    defining, 687–90
    policy, 687–89
    sample, 690
Message journaling, 758
    custom recipient, 760
    location, 758
Messages
    archiving, 757–64
    average size, 735
    blackhole for, 777–78
    categorization, 610
    complex, 906
    disclaimer text, 790–91
    headers, examining, 644
    HTTP, 608
    incoming/outgoing,
        capturing, 759
    list server, processing, 781
    MAPI, 608
    moving off queues, 611–19
    multiple copies of, 907
    notification, 754–56
    notification text, 752
    processing, with Outlook
        rules, 779–81
    properties, viewing, 619

for protected groups,
    610–11
on queue, properties, 618
redirecting, 778–79
reducing number of, 789
size restrictions, 731
SMTP, 604–8
terminating, 685
waiting to go, 612
who can send messages to,
    732
X.400, 608–9
MessageStats, 495, 908
    analysis illustration, 909
    defined, 908
Message tracking, 893–909
    allowing, 893
    complex messages, 906
    enabling, 895
    Exchange 2003 changes,
        899
    process, 895–97
    request results, 900
    results, 901
    speed, 904
    starting, 899–903
    system policy, 897
    through multiple servers,
        902
Message Tracking Center, 513,
    717, 893–909
    accessing, 899
    destination bridgehead
        servers list, 902
    mail-enabled public folder
        deliveries list, 902–3
    searches, beginning,
        899–900
    user interface, 900
Message tracking logs
    data, analyzing, 908–9
    data, understanding, 904–8

Message tracking logs *(cont'd.)*
  directory, 898
  duration, 896
  format, 903–4
  illustrated, 894
  large, 904
  location, changing, 897–99
  MessageStats analysis, 909
  for replication messages, 904
  storage, 894
  tracking events in, 905–6
Message Tracking Logs WMI provider, 908
Message Transfer Agent (MTA), 581, 638
  connectors, 632
  in decline, 583
  defined, 5, 582
  as essential service, 918
  existence, 582
  fan-out, 907–8
  GWART, 626–27, 632, 637
  ongoing role, 598–99
  remote, 657, 660, 662
  role differences, 599
  Store integration, 602
  throughput, 583
  X.400 message handling, 608
Messaging Application Protocol. *See* MAPI
MetaDirectory Services (MMS), 38
MetaMessage for Wireless, 391
Microbrowsers, 292
Microsoft Baseline Security Analyzer (MBSA), 892–93
Microsoft Knowledge Base, 479, 572, 574
Microsoft Metadirectory Services (MMS), 117

Microsoft Mobile Information Server (MMIS), 376
Microsoft Operations Manager. *See* MOM
Microsoft support policy, 10–12
Migrations
  ADC connections during, 77
  information selection, 121
  successful, 123
Migration wizard, 120–24, 891
  email address preservation, 123
  illustrated, 122
  options, 121
MIME, 584
MimeSweeper, 791
Mixed-mode organizations, 149, 152
MMB2, 546
MMB3, 547
Mobile Services, 367–75
  defined, 367
  features, 370–71
  global settings, 368
  integration, 367
  using, 377
MOM, 6, 925
  knowledge base, 928
  management pack for, 928
  strengths, 928
Monitoring, 915–24
  conditions, 923–24
  conditions, defining, 923
  data examination, 920
  ESM and, 918–19
  notification parameters, 922
  notifications, 915, 919–24
  parameters, 922
  properties, viewing, 917
  resources, adding, 918

  reviewing, 917–18
  server, 921
  System Attendant, 920
Mounted databases, 448
Move Mailbox wizard, 17, 120, 891
  Exchange 2003 version, 169
  illustrated, 168
Move Server wizard, 135
MSExchangeDSAccess service, 93
MsExchDynamicDLFilter attribute, 186
MsExchExpansionServerName attribute, 829–30
MsExchMailboxSecurityDescriptor attribute, 160
MSN, notification services, 368
MTACHECK utility, 664
MTS-ID, 409
Multiple forests, 115–24
  calendar interoperability, 118–20
  common platforms, 120
  costs, 116–17
  deployment reasons, 115
  directory synchronization, 117–18
  running, 115–20
  See also Forests
MX records, 622–23
  Exchange servers and, 623
  locating, 623
  use, 622

Name resolution
  GAL, 261
  OAB, 261–62
Naming contexts (NCs), 50–53
  configuration, 50, 52
  connecting ADSIEDIT to, 127

defined, 51
domain, 50, 54
in editing property values, 129
in examining object properties, 128, 129
schema, 50
uses, 128–30
Native mode, moving to, 153–54
NetDiag, 30
NetIQ, 925, 928
.NET, 33, 263
Network Address Translation (NAT), 239
Network Attached Storage (NAS), 536, 537
Network Location Awareness (NLA), 213
Nimda virus, 795
    attack, 295, 296
    defined, 795
NNTP, 566–67
Notification messages, 754–56
    defined, 754
    illustrated, 755
    user reception, 756
    See also Mailbox Manager
NSLOOKUP utility, 619
NTBACKUP.EXE, 833, 879
    defined, 847
    servers list, 836
    user interface extension, 833
NTDSUTIL utility, 854
NTLM, 742

OAB, 249–62
    for address validation, 218
    age, 253
    data files, 256
    defined, 249
    distinguished names, 256
    downloading, 251, 252, 254, 259
    downloading changes to, 255
    download options, 250
    entries, 256
    fetching, 250
    files, 254
    files, updating, 252
    GAL entries, 219
    generation process, 257–60
    generation/replication problems, 260
    as information subset, 261
    name resolution, 261–62
    outdated, 253, 255
    as preferred address book provider, 218
    properties in ESM, 258
    public folder, 258
    replica synchronization, 260
    restrictions, 249
    server, 257
    size, 253
    user details, viewing, 250
OABGEN, 257
OAB Version 2 folder, 257
Offline Address Book. *See* OAB
Offline Address Book folder, 260, 266
Offline Address Lists container, 260
Offline defragmentation, 475
Offline store files (OSTs), 123, 211, 277–85
    access, 278
    bloat, reducing, 212
    errors, checking for, 287
    first aid for, 285–87
    mailbox size and, 213
    MAPI client use, 277
    new unicode format and, 221
    PSTs vs., 279
    recreating, 285
    scan results, 286
    size, 212
    size control, registry values, 268
    as slave replicas, 280–81
    synchronization, 278–82
    value of, 287
Offline working, 288–89
    downside, 288
    online working and, 288–89
ONDL utility, 180
Online backups
    capability, 834
    support, 832
Online defragmentation, 475
Online working, 288–89
OOFs, 791–92
    controlling, 792
    defined, 183, 791
    information usefulness, 792
    messages, 183, 184
    proper use of, 791
    suppressing, 183–84
    text, 791
Open Shortest Path First (OSPF), 637
Open Source Applications Foundation (OSAF), 366–67
Opera, 368
Operations Master, 835
Oracle, Collaboration Suite, 21
Organizational units (OUs), 187
    moving to, 723
    top-level, 723
Organizations, 133–36
    defined, 133

Organizations *(cont'd.)*
  mixed-mode, 149, 152
  naming, 136
  permissions, 139
  properties, 150
OrgPrepCheck, 29–30
Outlfltr.dat, 243
Outlook, 195–289
  authentication modes, 203
  clients, 234, 235–36
  command-line switches, 289
  connections to Exchange, 98
  database table access, 411
  default format, 210
  defined, 198
  folder sizes view, 736
  Folders utility, 495, 496, 717
  graphics compression, 209
  for Mac, 365
  MAPI platform, 197
  notification registration, 216
  offline working, 288–89
  persistent referrals, 97
  progress bar, 215
  registry settings, 200
  smart tags, 786
  use numbers, 198–99
Outlook 2000, 97
  local calendar, 284
  persistent referrals, 97
Outlook 2002, 100
  buffer sizes, 226
  Send and Receive groups, 251
Outlook 2003, 97
  bad item check, 210
  best body support, 210
  as best Exchange client, 228–30
  buffer sizes, 226

cached Exchange mode, 206, 211–13, 220–24
conflict resolution, 226–28
download activity, 214–19
drizzle-mode synchronization, 213–14
features, 230
graphics compression, 209
improvements, 204
incremental synchronization, 219–20
interface, 204
junk mail processing, 239–49
Local Failures folder, 227
mail logging, enabling, 229
networking improvements, 206–10
new mail notifications, 239
OAB download, 251
performance clusters updated by, 223
replication behavior, 207
replication semantics, 207
Server Failures folder, 227
success, 232
synchronization mechanism, 282–83
Outlook Express, 353–61
  account details, 743
  components, 355
  illustrated, 354
  rules processing, 357
Outlook Mobile Manager (OMM), 370, 373–75
  AirSync standard, 375
  defined, 373
Outlook Resource Kit (ORK), 201

Outlook Web Access (OWA), 4, 13, 17, 226, 291–352
  2003, 294
  access control, 369
  administration, 325–33
  administration tools, 329
  advantages, 351
  architecture, 296–301
  architecture illustration, 297
  attachment blocking configuration, 325
  Blocked Senders list setup, 306
  branding, 341–42
  browser support, 301
  calendar, 342
  client logs, 906
  clients, 314
  command-line qualifiers, 339
  compatibility problems, 301
  components, 340
  contacts, 342
  content expiration timeout, 329
  as core component, 298
  cross-client compatibility, 294
  CTRL/K keystroke support, 307
  customization changes, 340–41
  customizing, 337–44
  data display, 300, 301
  directories, 340
  Exchange 2000, 293
  expiration dates for attachments, 350
  external content handling, 324
  feature segmentation, 344

firewall access, 344–50
first-generation architecture, 6
first release, 293
functionality, 301–22
functionality, segmenting, 342–44
goal, 303–4
HTTP-DAV use, 298
IE6 and, 302, 375
IE behaviors and, 304
as IIS application, 327
journal, 342
language support, 340
logoff button, 306
messaging, 342
missing features, 319–21
new mail notifications, 342
operation performance counters, 333
Options dialog box, 315
password expiration check, 307
password updates, 321–22
performance, 294
providing credentials to, 743
public folders, 342
richness, limiting, 311–12
rules in, 320
scalability, 331–33
second-generation, 293–96
securing, 346–47
security, 294
segmentation bit values, 343
server-side processing support, 306
signed/encrypted email, 308
spell checking, 307, 312–14
as stateless client, 320
subscriptions, 314–15
tasks, 342
updating slowly, 310–11

user interface, 339
user requests, 294
Web administration, 330
Web application properties, 369
Web beacons and, 323
Outlook Web Access Web Administration. *See* OWAWA
OWALOGON.ASP, 317–18
    defined, 317
    properties, 318
OWAWA, 16
    change implementation, 331
    defined, 329
    flags, 331
    running, 330
    simplicity, 329–31

Page checksum, 416
Palm Pilots, 384
Papa virus, 796
Partitioning, 436–46
    advantages, 437–38
    defining, 438
    planning, 438–41
Passwords
    for Exchange 2000 logon, 742
    LocalSystem and, 155
    OWA, updates, 321–22
    Pocket PC, 378–79
    synchronizing, 156
Patch files, 841–42
    application, 842
    function, 841
    writing of, 842
Performance, 533–49
    advanced, 542–43
    aspects, 534–43
    balanced system, 543
    CPU, 533, 535

link state routing update, 633
measuring, 543–49
measuring tools, 544–46
memory and, 538–40
multiple CPUs and, 537–38
over time, 538
RPC Requests, 573
testing, 546–49
Performance counters, 333
SIS, 445
virtual memory, 572
Performance Monitor
    counters, 771
    counter updating, 772
    for tracking size of deleted items cache, 772
Permissions
    Administrator, 143, 144–45
    client, 499
    delegate, granting, 740
    examining, after delegation, 144
    on Exchange organization, 139
    Exchange-specific, 113–15
    extended-rights, 113
    Full Administrator, 142–43
    groups for, 185
    high, 140
    insufficient, 513
    mailbox, 137
    multiple, manipulating, 115
    public folder, 499–502
    relay, 686
    for tasks, 139–40
    from top to bottom, 138
    View Administrator, 143
    zombie, 519
Persistent referrals, 97
Personal folders (PSTs), 267–69
    ANSI-format, 267

Personal folders (PSTs) *(cont'd.)*
  archiving, 275–77
  backing up, 271
  configuring, 273–74
  defined, 267
  disconnection from, 271
  effective use of, 274
  ExMerge creation, 881–82
  first aid for, 285–87
  location, 267
  mail delivery to, 269–73
  multiple, configuring, 273
  OSTs vs., 279
  properties, 269
  properties, changing, 274
  pros/cons, 272–73
  restoring, 271
  scanning, for viruses, 271
  selecting, as mail delivery location, 270
  size control, registry values, 268
Personal Information Manager (PIM), 4
PFDAVADMIN utility, 495
PFINFO utility, 495
PFTREE utility
  defined, 494
  illustrated, 495
Phased recovery, 865
PING command, 619
Pipelining, 585
Pocket Explorer, 373
Pocket PC, 371, 372
  add-on devices, 377
  attachments and, 383
  best features, 383
  BlackBerry vs., 392
  clients, 375–84
  docking station, 376
  email access, 378
  handhelds vs., 394–95
  illustrated, 394
  infrared port, 376–77
  Office application compatibility, 383
  partnerships, 376
  security and passwords, 378–79
  synchronization, 379–81
  updating, 379
  using, 382–84
Point-and-click, 305
Policy Manager, 748
POLL command, 314
POP3 clients, 361
  access support, 361
  LDAP directory access for, 361–64
Powercontrols, 892
Primary connection agreements, 78–79
Private Store, 447
PROPFIND command, 299
PROPPPATCH command, 299
Protected groups, 182–83
Protocol dependency, 195
PST2GB utility, 268
PubFoldCheck utility, 519
Public Folder Proxy Container, 46
Public folder replication, 502–22
  design, 503
  diagnostics, adjusting, 514
  events, 515
  with Exchange 5.5, 517–18
  flow, monitoring, 513–15
  occurrence, 511
  problems with, 519–21
  process, 511–13
  pull model, 506
  push model, 505–6
  replica creation, 505–7
  scheduling, 509–11
  status, viewing, 504
Public Folder Replication Agent (PFRA), 502
  dispatching details, 512
  message size generated by, 510
  monitoring, 511
  responsibilities, 503
Public folders, 32, 485–522
  access control, 501
  ACLs, 502, 518
  in AD, 518
  adding, to offline store, 280
  administrative permissions, 500
  administrative rights, 502
  affinity, 519
  applying views to, 300
  auditing, 494–96
  backfilling, 516–17
  contents, viewing, 487
  dedicated servers, 492–94
  deleted, 467
  deleted items, recovering, 766
  design layout, 488–502
  Exchange-specific permissions, 518
  favorites, 498–99
  folder administration, 488
  folder naming convention, 488
  folder organization, 488
  goals, 485–88
  hierarchy illustration, 489
  large, OWA access, 300
  long-term options, 521–22
  mail-enabling, 496–98, 723
  managing, 488–89
  marking as "favorite," 279

permissions, 499–502
in Public Store, 446
referrals, 507–9
replication, 467, 502–22
repositories for distribution lists, 184–85
review, 520
roles, 500–501
root for browser access to, 326
top-level folder layout, 488, 489
top-level hierarchies (TLH), 490–92
uses, 485–86
Public Store, 447, 485–88
defined, 485
mailboxes and, 446
moving, 455
Purpose-built cluster aware, 563

QEMEA-ES1, 158
Query-based groups, 185–94
creating, 187–91
custom attributes, 191–92
defined, 186
LDIFDE output, 187
normal groups vs., 186
query parameters, setting, 190
query results, previewing, 191
success, 194
uses, 194
using, 192–94
viewing, from GAL, 193
Windows security principals and, 193
See also Groups
QueueAdmin API, 600

Queues
examining, 618
Exchange 2003, 615–16
freezing, 615
link, 603–4, 621
moving messages off, 611–19
OnSubmission, 605, 608
per-destination, 604
per-link, 603–4, 616
Pre-Categorizer, 609
properties, 617
search message, 614
states, 613
swamping, 617
viewing, 611, 613
Queue viewer, 613, 614
Queuing engine
processing management, 602
support, 600
Quorum resources, 564
Quota Service, 738

RAID 0+1, 536, 550
RAID 1, 536
RAID 5, 433, 536
Rapid online phased recovery (ROPR), 864–66
defined, 864
flaws, 865–66
Recipient containers, 75
Recipient filters, 697–99
addresses, 698
defined, 697
enabling, 698
illustrated, 698
See also Filters
Recipient policies, 817–25
application of, 819
defined, 817
editing, 819

email addresses in, 819
functions, 817–18
illustrated, 818
LDAP query in, 819
Recipient Update Service (RUS), 23, 161, 162, 818, 825–32
AD attributes, 830
attributes created by, 829
creation, 828
defined, 825
domain, 826
enterprise, 826
illustrated, 827
importance, 826
mail-enabled objects, 828–31
multiple threads, 828
processing, dividing, 828
properties, 827
responsibilities, 162
role, 828
running, 867
schedule, 826
types, 826
Recovery servers, 856–58
defined, 856
hardware allocation, 857
prerequisites, 857–58
uses, 857
Recovery Storage Group (RSG), 721, 856, 870–84
adding databases to, 877, 878
cleaning up, 883–84
creating, 876–78
database restore, 879–81
database support, 877
defined, 871
design, 871
effectiveness, 872

Recovery Storage Group (RSG) (cont'd.)
   file location, 875
   mailboxes, viewing, 880
   setting locations for, 877
   use example, 872–74
   uses, 871–72
Recovery utilities, 891–92
Redirecting messages, 778–79
Referrals, 507–9
   advantages, 507
   defined, 507
   persistent, 97
   planning, 519
   replication vs., 507
   routing groups and, 631–32
   selective, 508
   See also Public folders
Relative Distinguished Names (RDNs), 190
Relays
   blocking, 684–87
   permissions, setting, 686
   restrictions, setting, 685
   SMTP, 594–95
Remote Insight Lights-Out Edition (RILOE), 721
Replication (AD), 46–67
   attribute-level, 175
   basics, 46–49
   characteristics, 63
   defined, 424
   drizzle-mode, 213
   duplicate, 72
   Exchange 5.5 data, 69
   flow, monitoring, 513–15
   "forced," 59
   FRS, 67
   goal, 46
   intersite, 60–64
   intrasite, 60–64
   load, reducing, 177
   object creation, 49
   object deletion, 49
   object modification, 49
   occurrence, 49–50, 511
   operations, 49
   per-value, 66
   process, 511–13
   time-critical information, 66
   unidirectional, 72
   urgent, 59–60
   USNs and, 55–59
   Windows 2003 changes, 65–67
Replication latency, 666
Replication (public folders), 467, 502–22
   design, 503
   diagnostics, adjusting, 514
   events, 515
   with Exchange 5.5, 517–18
   problems, 519–21
   pull model, 506
   push model, 505–6
   replica creation, 505–7
   scheduling, 509–11
   status, viewing, 504
Reserved logs, 424–25
Resource groups, 560–65
   contents, 561
   defined, 560
   illustrated, 562
Resources, 560
   allocating, 569
   dependency, 561
   illustrated, 562
   logical, 561
   physical, 561
   quorum, 564
Restores, 843–47
   database, with RSG, 879–81
   database selection for, 844
   EDB, 845
   Exchange server, 853–56
   files used by, 846
   importance, 835
   incremental, 847
   LegacyExchangeDN attribute and, 859
   Mailbox Store, 858–64
   operations, 835
   parameters, 845
   in progress, 846
   steps, 843–46
   Store and, 843
   streaming files, 845
   system state, 854
   transaction logs and, 845, 846, 847
   unassociated mailboxes after, 863
   well-planned, 836
   See also Backups
Restricting mailboxes, 731–33
Return status codes, 693–95
Rich text editor, 305
Rich Text Format (RTF), 410
RID master, 638–39
Rights Management Service (RMS), 749
Risk management, 892–93
Roaming, 385
Roles, 145–46
   custom, 501
   public folder, 500–501
Routing, 609–23
   calculation, 639
   environment snapshot, 643
   for foreign connectors, 621
   improved naming convention, 643
   information, viewing, 642–45
   link state, 632–45
   topology, 625

transport core, 599–604
understanding, 664–67
Routing Engine, 85, 160, 177, 178, 582, 621
  defined, 600–601
  as essential service, 918
  flexibility, 624, 625
  queues, 603
  in recipient filtering, 699
  recipient identification, 611
  Store driver event, 605
  transferring messages to MTA, 902
Routing group connectors (RGCs), 645–50
  before creating, 647
  configuration, 649
  creating, 646–50
  default connection cost, 648
  defined, 645
  delivery options, 649
  general properties, 646
  illustrated, 650
  links, 646, 647
  remote bridgehead server for, 647
  setting up, 647
  SMTP connectors vs., 645–46
  SMTP use, 645
  unidirectional, 646
Routing groups, 156–60, 623–32
  administrative groups and, 156–57
  bandwidth between, 663
  connecting, 645–50
  connectors, deleting, 630
  container, 627
  creating, 627–31
  creation decision, 624
  decommissioning, 631

  defined, 156
  defunct, 631
  deployment recommendation, 160
  design, 157
  division of functions, 157
  dragging/dropping servers between, 629–30
  duplicate, 629
  ESM and, 157
  with geographical terms, 628
  hub, 158
  management, 157
  master, 625–27
  moving error, 631
  multiple, within administrative group, 158
  names, 627
  naming convention, 629
  properties, 630
  public folder referrals and, 631–32
  renaming, 631
  server move restrictions, 630
  uses, 156
  version number, 636
RPCs
  client requests, 573–74
  compression parameters, 225
  failures, 222
  hanging, 205
  latency, 204–6
  MAPI, 203
  transport with HTTP, 207–8
Rules, 248–49
  client-side, 239
  creating, from messages, 249

  in message processing, 779–81
  in OWA 2003, 320
  server-side, 239
Rules Wizard, 249

Safe Recipients list, 243–44
Safe Senders list, 243, 245
ScanMail, 812, 813
SCANPST, 285–87
  defined, 286
  errors, 286
  log file, 286
  running, 287
Scheduling, 424
  background maintenance, 464–65
  CA, 77–78
  connection object, 64
  replication, 509–11
Schema folder, 266
SEARCH commands, 332
Search folders, 410–14
  active, 411, 413
  control registry values, 413
  creating, 412
  default lifetime, 414
  defined, 410
  existence, 412
  illustrated, 414
  inactive, 413
  lifetime, 414
  query part, 412
  states, 413
Secure Mail, 748
Security, 34
  IE enhanced, 349–50
  OWA, 346–47
  Pocket PC, 378–79
  proactive policy, 295–96
  risk management and, 892–93

Security (cont'd.)
    settings, changing, 804
Security Identifiers (SIDs), 136, 742
Selective blocks, 237–39
Sender filters, 695–97
    creating, 696
    setting up, 697
    See also Filters
Sensitive files, 349
Server monitors, 919–20
Server Routing Protocol (SRP), 387
Servers
    back-end, 804
    build numbers, 718–19
    consolidation, 556
    dedicated, 548
    front-end, 804
    IMAP, 357, 358
    ISA, 9, 344, 347
    OAB, 257
    recovery, 856–58
    referral, 632
    remote bridgehead, 647
    RTF support, 210
    SMTP, 583, 595, 603
    virtual exchange, 555–56
    See also Exchange servers
Server-side rules, 239
Service-level agreements, 451
Service Pack 1 (SP1), 14–18
    benefits, 17–18
    biggest change, 17
    bug fixes, 14
    Error Correcting Code (ECC), 483–84
    functionality, 15
    launch, 14
    online backup processing, 484

Recovery Mailbox Data option, 14
    UI, 15
    updates, 14–15
SETUP, 106–7
    DomainPrep, 107
    ForestPrep, 107
SetupPrep, 30
SharePoint
    Store, 88
    technology, 33
SharePoint Portal Server (SPS), 34, 88, 245
    as catchall repository, 522
    deployment cost, 522
    hiding ExIFS drive, 527
    replication support and, 521
ShowInAddressBook attribute, 160, 830
Single-instance storage (SIS), 441–46, 468
    advantages, 442
    defined, 441
    disk I/O activity and, 442
    disk space and, 442
    maximum Store size, 442–43
    monitoring, 445
    multiple databases and, 452
    performance counter, 445
    sharing ratio, 443
    use of, 442
Site Replication Services (SRS), 23, 80–82, 146, 446, 855
    components, 81–82
    configuration, 81
    defined, 80
Sites
    Exchange 5.5, 148
    moving to administrative groups, 148–52

multiple, adding to CAs, 74
Smart change synchronization, 283
Smartphones, 372
    graphics, 394
    interface, 373
    for OMA, 373
Smart tags, 786
S/MIME, 307–8, 309, 584
    control, 309, 310
    messages, creating/reading/ signing, 307
    V2, 307–8
    V3, 307
SMTP, 581
    8-bit clean, 585
    banners, changing, 595–97
    chunking, 586–88
    commands, 395
    communications, tracing, 669
    conversations, 667
    defined, 582
    DSN, 585–86
    encrypted communications, 654
    engine, 582
    entry point, 612
    error in system event log, 620
    evolution, 583–99
    extended, commands, 590
    extensions, 585–92
    gateway, 606
    log file extract, 635
    message formatting, 396
    MX records, 622–23
    pipelining, 585
    as primary mail transport, 821
    proxy, 123
    relays, 594–95

replication, 63
servers, 583, 595, 603
service, 61, 62
service dependencies, 592
traffic, 592, 612, 669
SMTP addresses, 820
  changing, 825
  display names, changing, 822–25
  generating, 822
  generation, replacement strings, 823
  proxies, 820
  secondary, adding, 825
SMTP archiving, 671–75, 760
  as debug/analysis tool, 761
  default, 671
  defined, 671
  functioning of, 760
  implementation, 671
  messages, reading, 674
  registry entries, 672
  sink, disabling, 675
  sink code, 672
  sink registry settings, 673
  when to use, 671
SMTP connectors, 593, 594, 620, 638, 645–46
  address space specification, 652
  advanced properties, 653
  creating, 650–54
  defined, 650
  delivery restrictions, 654–56
  general properties, 651
  hosting, 701
  limiting users on, 655
  restriction registry values, 656
  routing techniques, 650
  scope, 652
  setting up, 651

shared organization-wide, 656
  working with, 653
SMTP logging, 667–71
  defined, 664
  enabling, 668
  extended properties, 668
  file, examining, 670
  space, 671
SMTP messages, 604–8
  badmail registry settings, 607
  cannot be processed, 607
  capturing content of, 671
SMTP virtual servers, 395, 588, 592–94
  applying connection filters to, 696
  applying IMF to, 707–8
  concurrent transactions, 670
  default, 671
  filtering, enabling, 689
  properties, changing, 685
  settings, 594
Snapshots, 550
  defined, 550
  illustrated, 551
  as point-in-time picture, 550
Snooping, 761–64
  internal, 761–64
  intrusive, 763
Soft recoveries, 459–62
  administrator intervention and, 459
  checkpoint file in, 842
  defined, 458
  hard recoveries and, 463
  requirements, 460
  See also Errors, database
Software Assurance program, 708

Spam
  checking messages for, 248
  combating, 681–99
  connection filters and, 696
  deleting, 241
  detection accuracy, 242
  detection software, 240
  as growing menace, 682
  IMF detection, 700
  monitoring, 682–83
  recognition ability, 244–45
  relays, blocking, 684–87
  See also Junk mail
Spam Confidence Level (SCL), 683–84
  concept, 701
  defined, 683, 701
  gateway threshold, 704
  higher value, 684
  as message property, 701
  message stores and, 706
  property, setting, 684
  rating removal, 705
  Store threshold and, 706
Spam Manager for Antigen, 683
Spammers, 681
  known, list of, 682, 683
  list of, 244
  tactics, 246
Spector Pro, 763
Spell checking, 312–14
  illustrated, 313
  as ISAPI extension, 312
  registry values, 313–14
  server performance and, 312
  support, 307
  See also Outlook Web Access (OWA)
Squirrel, 357–58
STARTTLS command, 590

STM database
  defined, 403
  file creation, 480
Storage, 535–37
  best practice, 536
  cost, 535, 735
  technology, 536
Storage Area Networks (SAN), 579
Storage groups
  advantages, 437–38
  backups and, 836–37
  circular logging, 436
  on clusters, 440
  control, 446
  creating, 452–55
  creating, from ESM, 453
  details, specifying, 453
  illustrated, 447
  as management entities, 441
  managing, 446–55
  naming conventions, 450, 451
  per-server limit, 440
  planning, 438–41, 449–52
  prefix, viewing, 421
  recovery, 847
  transaction logs and, 420
  transaction logs information, 452
Store, 399–531
  64-bit architecture and, 543
  access with ExIFS, 523
  adding, to system policy, 769
  architectural concepts, 446–47
  background maintenance, 463–72
  Change Number Sets (CNS), 512
  consistency, 419
  database locations, viewing, 455
  defined, 399
  dismount option, 448
  as essential service, 918
  maximum size, 442–43
  memory used by, 539
  mounting, at startup, 449
  moving, 455
  as multithreaded process, 538
  nested folders, 408
  online backup processing, 484
  page checksum, 416
  partitioning, 436–46
  rebuilding, 449
  restore operations, 843
  search folders, 410–14
  service, restarting, 423
  status, 448–49
  structure, 399–401
  structure illustration, 400
Store Events folder, 266
Store Kernel, 399
Streaming files, 417–18
  EDB differences, 418
  restoring, 845
  size, 417
Stretched clusters, 574–75
  defined, 575
  resilience, 575
  See also Clusters
SubmitRelaySD attribute, 686
Subscriptions, 314–15
  default, 315
  illustrated, 315
  use of, 314
  See also Outlook Web Access (OWA)
SUBST command, 527
Suitability tests, 92–96
Summary message, 755, 756
Super Knowledge Consistency Checker (SKCC), 82
Support policy, Microsoft, 10–12
Sybar Spam Manager, 708
Symmetric multiprocessing, 538
Synchronization, 76–77
  ActiveSync, 371–73, 380
  background, 284
  benefits, 67
  bidirectional, 67, 68, 74
  BlackBerry, 392
  conflict, 380
  defined, 210
  drizzle, 213–14
  explicit, 372
  implicit, 372
  incremental, 219–20
  multiple Exchange 5.5 organizations, 79–80
  multiple forests and, 117–18
  notification-driven, 372
  OAB replica, 260
  OST, 278–82
  Outlook 2003 mechanism, 282–83
  passwords, 156
  process, 76–77
  restricting, 281
  rules, 381
  server inbox, 382
  settings, 380, 382
  smart change, 283
  traffic, restricting, 282–83
  unidirectional, 67, 74
System Access Control List (SACL), 95
System Attendant, 567
  as essential service, 918

message filter policies and, 689
monitoring, 920
System Configuration folder, 266–67
System policies, 146–47, 815–17
  applied to multiple stores, 147
  before creating, 815
  classes, 815–16
  defined, 815
  message/folder, 408
  message tracking, 897
  server, displayed in ESM, 817
  for server objects, 816
  for storage limits, 816

Tables
  accuracy, 480
  attachments, 408
  as collection of trees, 407
  database, 406–8
  folders, 408
  header information, 409
  mailbox, 408
  in Mailbox Store, 408–10
  message, 408
  Outlook access, 411
Tablet PCs, 383
Tasks folder, 342
Task Wizard, 167
  actions, 168
  illustrated, 167
  log files, 171
  for protocol management, 236
  reports, viewing, 171
TaskWizardReport.xslt, 172
Technical Account Manager (TAM), 11

Testing
  benchmarks, 547
  vendor, 546–48
  your, 548–49
Third-party backup utilities, 847–52
  advantages, 849–51
  DLLs for, 847
  drawbacks, 851–52
  list of, 849
  mailbox backups, 852
  specialized package, 850
  See also Backups
Timestamps, 57
Titanium. *See* Exchange 2003
TLS command, 590
Tombstone maintenance, 466
Top-level hierarchies (TLH), 490–92
  default, 490
  defined, 490
  general-purpose, 491
  MAPI, 491
  multiple, 490–91
  multiple, dividing folders across, 492
  properties, 491
  See also Public folders
Transaction logs, 418–36
  in backup process, 838, 839
  checking, 459–60
  checkpoint position, 429
  checksum, 434
  checksum failure, 434
  creation date/time, 431
  database files and, 419
  data in, 427
  data records, 431–32
  dumping, 429–31
  editing, with Notepad, 428
  examining, 428–29
  file numbering, 420

  generation number, 429
  generations, creating, 421–24
  header, 429–31
  importance, 418
  internal contents, 428
  I/O, 432–33
  locating, 425–26
  location, 431
  managing, 419–21
  protecting, 433
  purging, 425
  recovery operations and, 461
  relocating, 426
  reserved, 424–25
  restores and, 845, 846, 847
  set of, 422
  size, 423
  storage group and, 420
  turnover, 423
Transactions, 426–28
  ESE management, 432
  number of, 420
  replaying, 428, 458
  in sequential order, 432
  tracking, 459
Transport core, 599–604
  Advanced Queuing, 599–600
  categorizer, 600
  defined, 599
  Exchange Store Driver, 600
  illustrated, 601
  Routing Engine, 600–601
Transport Neutral Encapsulated Format (TNEF), 608
Trees, 42, 404–6
  B+, 406
  B-tree structure, 405
  long value, 406

UDETAILS.OAB, 253
Unidirectional synchronization, 68
Universal Datagram Packet (UDP), 239
Universal distribution groups (UDGs), 499
Universal groups, 172–73
   availability, 172
   membership, 173
   See also Groups
Universal security groups (USGs), 499
UNIX clients, 366–67
Up-to-date vector tables, 64–65
URLs
   accessing items with, 334
   finalizing, 334
   generation, 333, 335
   namespace, 333–37
   passing, 336
   refining, 337
   suffixes, 338
   unique, creating, 335
   updating, 336
USENET, 493
Users
   access, 721–41
   access to protocols, disabling, 236–37
   in AD, 722
   authentication, 741–44
   bad habits, eliminating, 782–89
   death, 781
   good email habits, 789
   helping, 782–93
   luring (viruses), 796–97
   mailbox quota actions, 734
   mail-enabled, 722
   network load generation, 782

   tasks, 166–68
   See also Accounts
Users and Computers snap-in, 163, 164, 172, 729
UI, 735
user logon name, 729
USNs, 48
   defined, 48
   highest known, 64
   illustrated, 48
   incremented, 58
   for propagation dampening, 59
   replication and, 55–59
   server, 56, 57

VBScript, 811
Vector tables
   high watermark, 64–65
   up-to-date, 64–65
Virtual Exchange servers, 555–56
Virtual memory
   management, 571
   monitoring, 571–73
   monitoring illustration, 572
   performance counters, 572
   Store use of, 573
   See also Memory
Virtual Private Network (VPN), 377
Virtual servers. *See* SMTP virtual servers
Viruses (email), 271, 793–807
   authors, 800
   damage caused by, 800–803
   detection, 803
   document-borne, 803
   executable-based, 793
   hidden, 793
   history, 794
   HTML dangers, 797–99

   Love Bug, 800–801
   luring users, 796–97
   Melissa, 794–95
   mistakes, 807
   monitoring, 805–6
   multistage protection, 803–7
   Nimda, 795
   Papa, 796
   Prank macro, 794
   security policy, 805–7
   suspect attachments, 801–2
   threats, up-to-date with, 802
   Worm.ExploreZip, 795
Virus Scanning Application Programming Interface. *See* VSAPI
Volume ShadowCopy Services (VSS), 552–55, 578
   defined, 552
   elements, 552–53
   with Exchange 2003, 554–55
   requesters, 553, 554
   ShadowCopy processing, 553
   vendor use, 553
VSAPI, 808–10
   defined, 808
   encrypted messages and, 809
   support, 809
   updated versions, 809

Web beacons
   defined, 322
   OWA and, 323
   suppressing, 322–23
Web clients, 291–93
   benefits, 291–92
   importance, 292
Web release (WR04), 16

Windows
- 64-bit, 542–43, 544
- Backup Wizard, 836, 837
- default naming service, 40
- Event Viewer, 924, 925
- Exchange combinations, 12
- Exchange timeline and, 11
- supporting, 12–13
- support matrix, 13

Windows 2000
- Datacenter Edition, 577
- deployment, 21
- native mode, 12
- release, 5
- support, 12, 24

Windows 2003, 8
- AD replication changes, 65–67
- Certificate Server, 25
- Datacenter Edition, 542
- GC logon cache, 102–3
- servers, promoting, 65–66
- support, 12

Windows NT
- cluster services, 556
- domain designs, 55
- infrastructures, 43
- namespace, 40–41
- support for, 16–17

WINMAIL.DAT, 674
WinRoute utility, 642, 664–67, 916
- defined, 664–65
- details exposed by, 666
- functioning of, 665
- illustrated, 665
- launching, 665
- outdated information and, 666
- value of, 667

WinZIP, 788
Wireless Business Engine for Exchange, 377
WMI, 929
Wolfpack, 556
Worker Process Isolation Mode (WPIM), 296
Workstations, running ESM on, 720–21
Worm.ExploreZip virus, 795
Write-back caching, 416, 461

X.400, 11, 582–83
- addresses, 661
- backbones, 659, 663
- messages, 608–9
- MIXER, 664
- older systems, 663
- transport stack, 658
- transport stack, installation, 659
- *See also* Message Transfer Agent (MTA)

X.400 connectors, 230, 646
- address space definition, 661
- advanced properties, 662
- complexity, 656
- configuration, 663
- creating, 656–64
- defined, 656
- general properties, 657
- routing group links, 658
- stack properties, 660
- support, 658
- use decision, 663–64

XDR-Fixup utility, 44
XML-HTTP, 302
XrML, 749

Zeroing, 436, 441
Zombies
- erasing, 518–19
- problems, 519